PHILIP'S

STREET ATLAS

UNRIVALLED DETAIL FROM THE BEST-SELLING ATLAS RANGE*

NAVIGATOR®
NOTTINGHAMSHIRE

www.philips-maps.co.uk
Published Philip's, a division of
Octopus Publishing Group Ltd
www.octopusbooks.co.uk
Carmelite House
50 Victoria Embankment
London EC4Y 0DZ
www.hachette.co.uk

First edition 2023
First impression 2023
NOTFA

978-1-84907-641-8 (spiral)

© Philip's 2023

Ordnance Survey
Licensed Data

This product
includes
mapping data
licensed from
Ordnance
Survey® with the permission of the
Controller of His Majesty's Stationery
Office. © Crown copyright 2023. All rights
reserved. Licence number 100011710.

CONTENTS

III **Key to map symbols**

IV **Key to map pages**

VI **Route planning**

X Administrative and Postcode boundaries

1 **Street maps** at 3½ inches to 1 mile

221 **Approach map of Nottingham**

222 **Street map of Nottingham city centre**
at 7 inches to 1 mile

224 **Index** of towns and villages, streets, hospitals,
industrial estates, railway stations, schools,
shopping centres, universities and places of interest

Key to map symbols

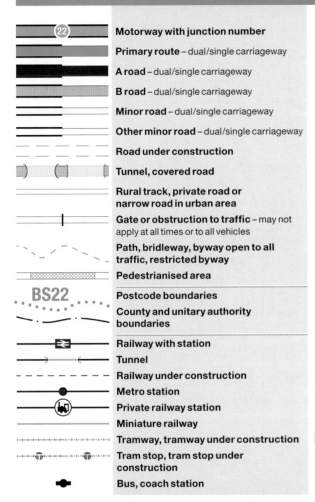

	Motorway with junction number (22)
	Primary route – dual/single carriageway
	A road – dual/single carriageway
	B road – dual/single carriageway
	Minor road – dual/single carriageway
	Other minor road – dual/single carriageway
	Road under construction
	Tunnel, covered road
	Rural track, private road or narrow road in urban area
	Gate or obstruction to traffic – may not apply at all times or to all vehicles
	Path, bridleway, byway open to all traffic, restricted byway
	Pedestrianised area
BS22	Postcode boundaries
	County and unitary authority boundaries
	Railway with station
	Tunnel
	Railway under construction
	Metro station
	Private railway station
	Miniature railway
	Tramway, tramway under construction
	Tram stop, tram stop under construction
	Bus, coach station

Ambulance station
Coastguard station
Fire station
Police station

Accident and Emergency entrance to hospital

H Hospital

+ Place of worship

i Information centre – open all year

Shopping centre, parking

P&R Park and Ride, Post Office

Camping site, caravan site

Golf course, picnic site

Church ROMAN FORT Non-Roman antiquity, Roman antiquity

Univ Important buildings, schools, colleges, universities and hospitals

Built-up area

Woods

River Medway Water name
River, weir
Stream
Canal, lock, tunnel

Water

Tidal water

58 87 Adjoining page indicators

112

Adjoining page indicators and overlap bands – the colour of the arrow and band indicates the scale of the adjoining or overlapping page (see scales below)

The dark grey border on the inside edge of some pages indicates that the mapping does not continue onto the adjacent page

The small numbers around the edges of the maps identify the 1-kilometre National Grid lines

Enlarged maps only

Railway or bus station building

Place of interest

Parkland

Abbreviations

Acad	Academy	Meml	Memorial
Allot Gdns	Allotments	Mon	Monument
Cemy	Cemetery	Mus	Museum
C Ctr	Civic centre	Obsy	Observatory
CH	Club house	Pal	Royal palace
Coll	College	PH	Public house
Crem	Crematorium	Recn Gd	Recreation ground
Ent	Enterprise		
Ex H	Exhibition hall	Resr	Reservoir
Ind Est	Industrial Estate	Ret Pk	Retail park
IRB Sta	Inshore rescue boat station	Sch	School
		Sh Ctr	Shopping centre
Inst	Institute	TH	Town hall / house
Ct	Law court	Trad Est	Trading estate
L Ctr	Leisure centre	Univ	University
LC	Level crossing	W Twr	Water tower
Liby	Library	Wks	Works
Mkt	Market	YH	Youth hostel

The map scale on the pages numbered in blue is 3½ inches to 1 mile
5.52 cm to 1 km • 1:18 103

0	¼ mile	½ mile	¾ mile	1 mile
0	250m	500m	750m	1km

The map scale on the pages numbered in red is 7 inches to 1 mile
11.04 cm to 1 km • 1:9051

0	220yds	440yds	660yds	½ mile
0	125m	250m	375m	500m

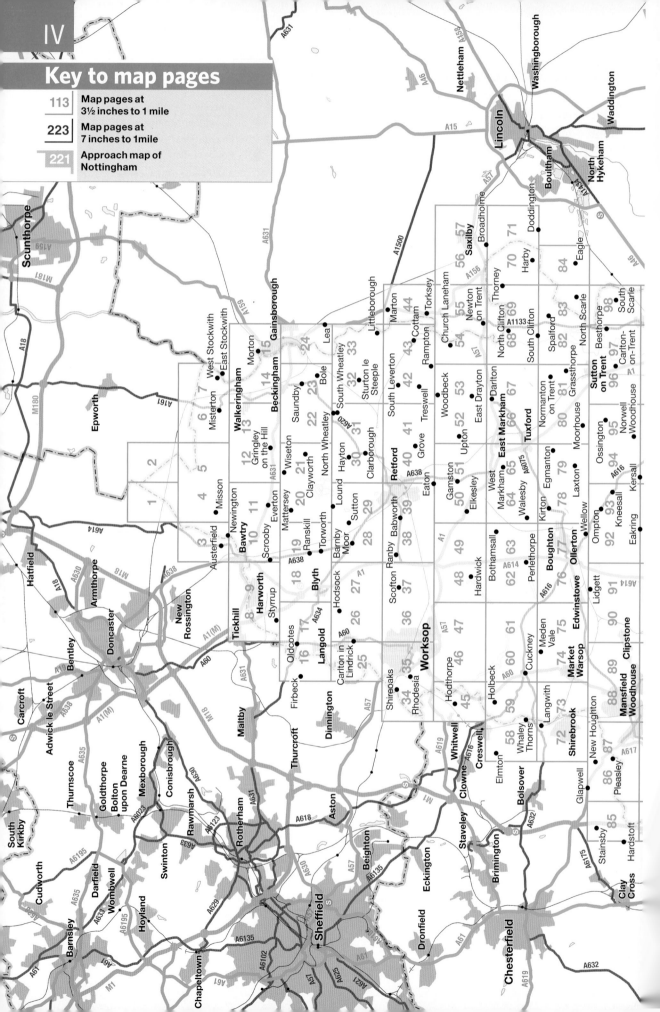

IV

Key to map pages

113	Map pages at 3½ inches to 1 mile
223	Map pages at 7 inches to 1mile
221	Approach map of Nottingham

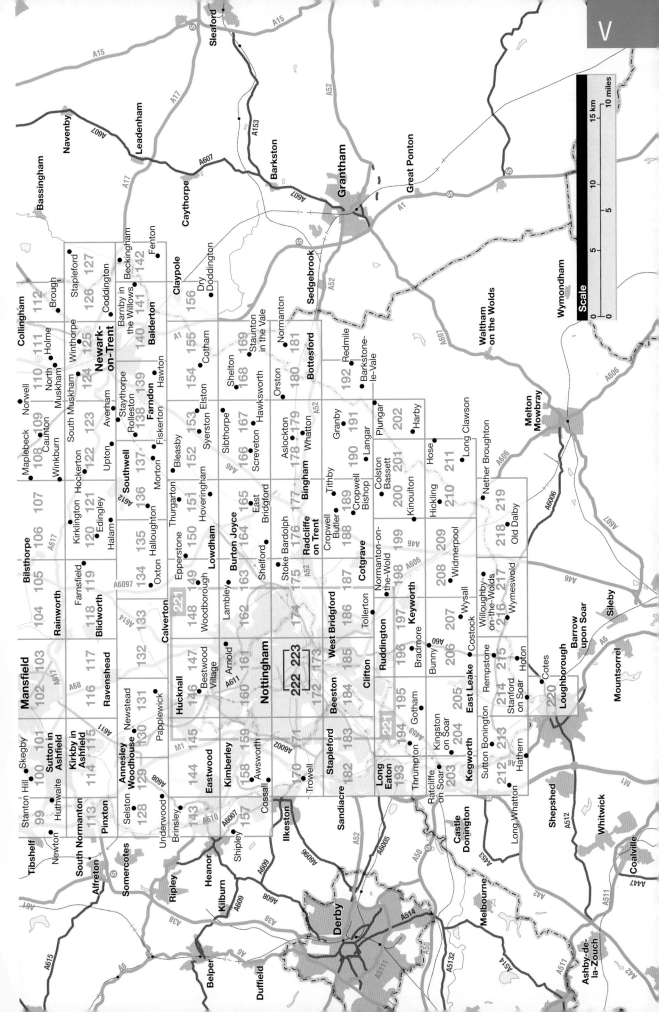

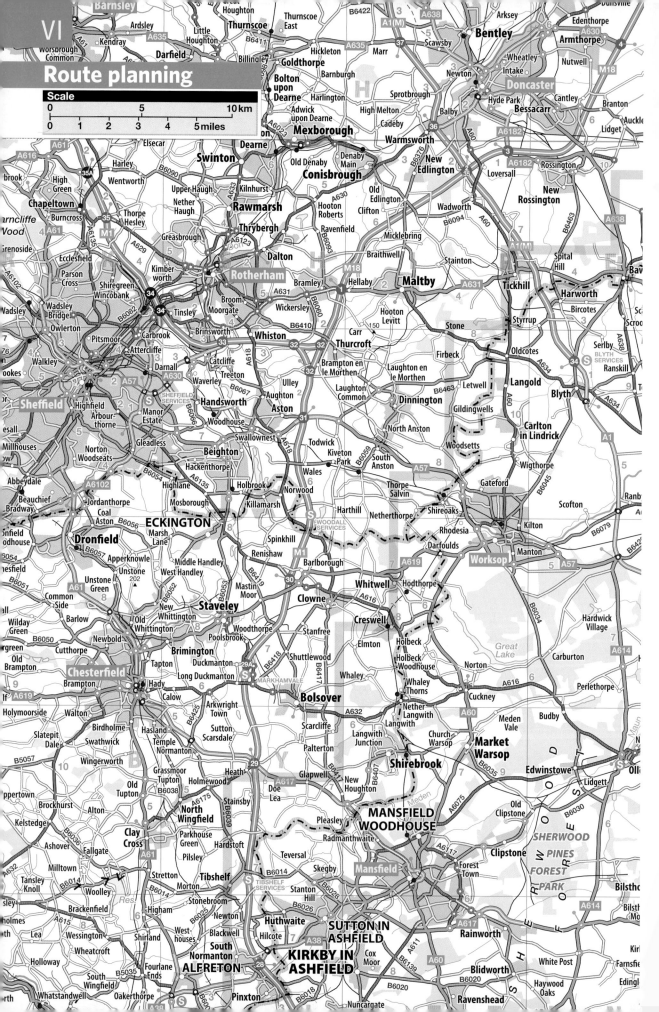

Route planning

Scale

0   5   10 km

0   1   2   3   4   5 miles

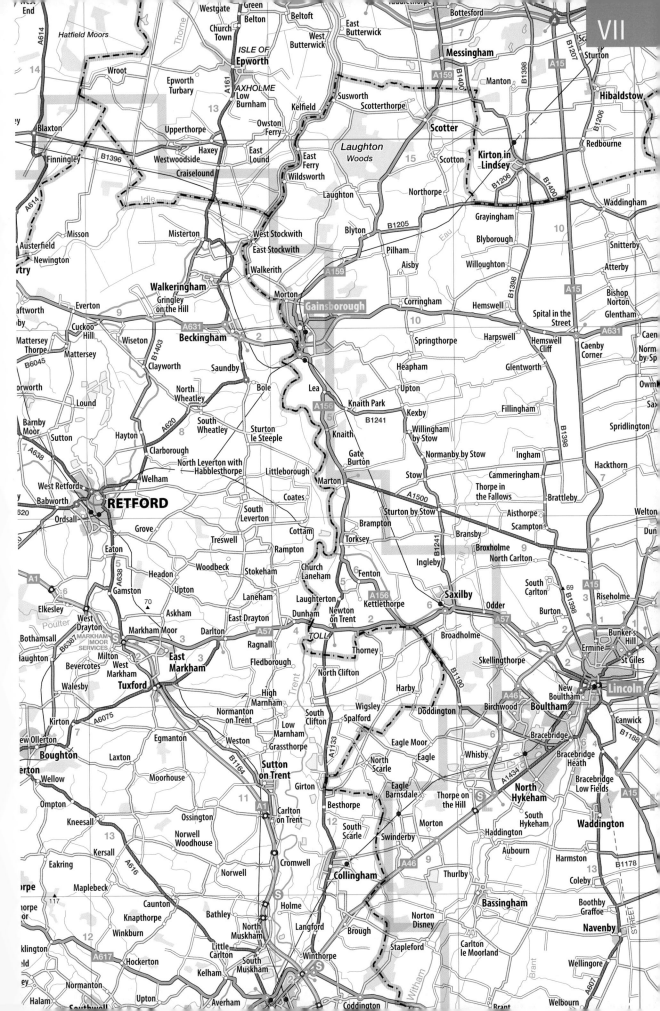

Thorne
Westgate
Green
Belton
Beltoft
Bottesford
A
7
B1207
Sturton
B1398
A15
Hatfield Moors
West End
Church Town
West Butterwick
East Butterwick
Messingham
Manton
B1400
ISLE OF
Epworth
AXHOLME
Low Burnham
Kelfield
Susworth
Scotterthorpe
A159
B1400
B1206
Hibaldstow
Wroot
Epworth Turbary
Owston Ferry
Scotter
Scotton
Kirton in Lindsey
Redbourne
13
14
A161
Upperthorpe
Haxey
East Lound
East Ferry
Laughton Woods
15
Northorpe
B1206
B1400
Waddingham
Blaxton
B1396
Westwoodside
Wildsworth
Scotton
Finningley
Craiselound
Idle
Laughton
Grayingham
A15
A614
Misson
Misterton
West Stockwith
Blyton
B1205
Eau
Blyborough
Snitterby
Austerfield
East Stockwith
Pilham
Willoughton
Atterby
Newington
Walkerith
Aisby
Bishop Norton
try
Walkeringham
Gringley on the Hill
Morton
A159
Corringham
Hemswell
B1398
Spital in the Street
Glentham
aftworth
Everton
9
Gainsborough
10
Harpswell
Hemswell Cliff
A631
Caen
by
Cuckoo Hill
Wiseton
B1403
Saundby
Lea
Springthorpe
Glentworth
Caenby Corner
Normanby-Sp
Mattersey Thorpe
Clayworth
Bole
Heapham
Owm
B6045
Mattersey
North Wheatley
Knaith Park
A156
Upton
Kexby
Fillingham
Ingham
Spridlington
Sax
orworth
Lound
A620
South Wheatley
Sturton le Steeple
Knaith
Willingham by Stow
Normanby by Stow
Hackthorn
Barnby Moor
Sutton
Hayton
Clarborough
North Leverton with Habblesthorpe
Gate Burton
Stow
Cammeringham
7
A638
Welham
Littleborough
Marton
A1500
Thorpe in the Fallows
Brattleby
Welton
West Retford
Babworth
RETFORD
Coates
Sturton by Stow
Aisthorpe
Scampton
Dun
620
Ordsall
Grove
South Leverton
Cottam
Brampton
Bransby
Broxholme
North Carlton
9
Treswell
Rampton
Torksey
B1241
Ingleby
A1
Eaton
Woodbeck
Stokeham
Church Laneham
Fenton
Saxilby
South Carlton
69
A15
Riseholme
Headon
Upton
6
Laneham
5
Kettlethorpe
A156
6
Odder
Burton
B1398
Elkesley
West Drayton
Gamston
70
Askham
East Drayton
Laughterton
Newton on Trent
2
A57
Broadholme
Ermine
Bunker's Hill
St Giles
Bothamsall
B6387
MARKHAM MOOR SERVICES
Markham Moor
Darlton
A57
Dunham
TOLL
Thorney
Skellingthorpe
2
Lincoln
haughton
Milton
West Markham
Ragnall
North Clifton
B1190
New Boultham
Bevercotes
East Markham
Fledborough
Harby
Doddington
Birchwood
Boultham
Walesby
Tuxford
High Marnham
Wigsley
Spalford
Eagle Moor
Whisby
Bracebridge
Canwick
Kirton
A6075
Normanton on Trent
Low Marnham
South Clifton
A1133
Eagle
Bracebridge Heath
B1188
ew Ollerton
7
Egmanton
Weston
Grassthorpe
North Scarle
Thorpe on the Hill
New Hykeham
Bracebridge Low Fields
A15
Boughton
Laxton
Moorhouse
Sutton on Trent
Girton
Eagle Barnsdale
Morton
South Hykeham
Waddington
erton
Wellow
Ompton
11
A1
Carlton on Trent
Besthorpe
12
Swinderby
Haddington
Kneesall
Ossington
South Scarle
Aubourn
Kersall
13
Norwell Woodhouse
Cromwell
Collingham
A46
9
Harmston
Eakring
Norwell
Bassingham
Coleby
B1178
orpe
Maplebeck
117
Caunton
Holme
Thurlby
Boothby Graffoe
Navenby
Knapthorpe
Bathley
Langford
Norton Disney
rpe or
Winkburn
North Muskham
Brough
Carlton le Moorland
klington
12
A617
Little Carlton
Stapleford
Wellingore
Hockerton
Kelham
South Muskham
Winthorpe
A607
Halam
A46
Coddington
Welbourn
Southwell
Averham
Coddington

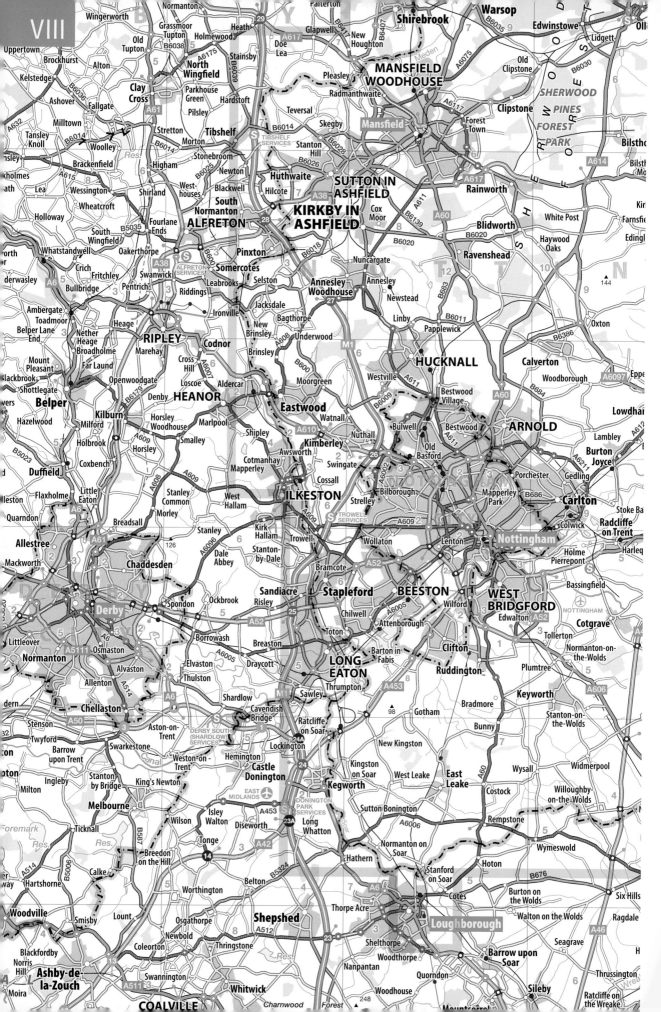

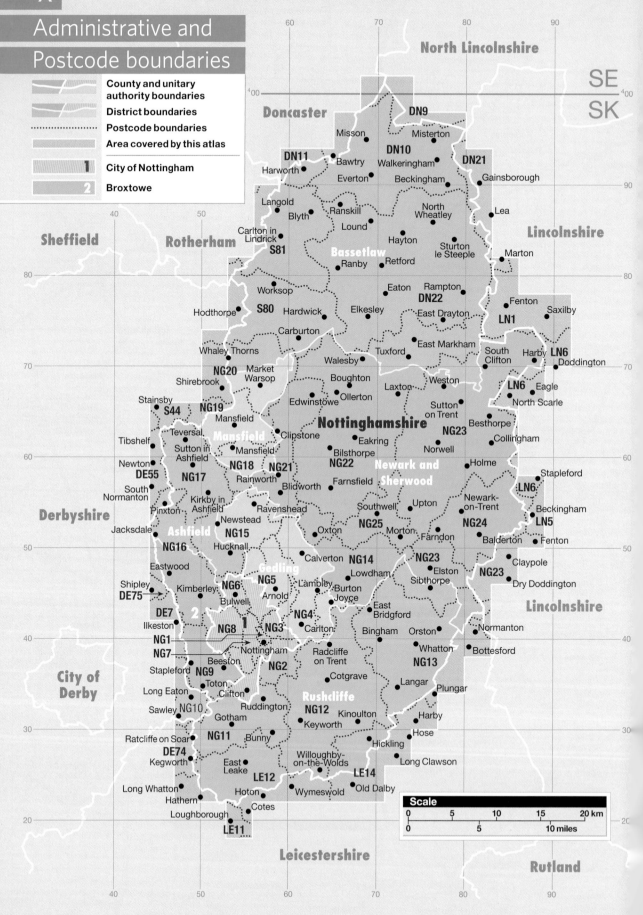

County and unitary
authority boundaries

District boundaries

Postcode boundaries

Area covered by this atlas

1 City of Nottingham

2 Broxtowe

North Lincolnshire

Doncaster

DN9

Misson
Misterton

DN11
DN10
DN21

Harworth
Bawtry
Walkeringham

Everton
Beckingham
Gainsborough

Langold
Lea

Blyth
Ranskill
North
Wheatley

Carlton in
Lindrick
Lound
Hayton

S81
Bassetlaw
Sturton
le Steeple
Marton

Ranby
Retford

Sheffield
Rotherham

Worksop
Eaton
Rampton
Fenton
Saxilby

Hodthorpe
S80
Hardwick
Elkesley
DN22
East Drayton
LN1

Carburton
East Markham
South
Clifton
Harby
LN6
Doddington

Whaley Thorns
Tuxford

Walesby
Weston
LN6
Eagle

NG20
Market
Warsop
Boughton
North Scarle

Shirebrook
Edwinstowe
Ollerton
Laxton

Stainsby
S44
NG19
Nottinghamshire
Sutton
on Trent
Besthorpe

Mansfield
Eakring
NG23
Collingham

Teversal
Mansfield
Clipstone
Bilsthorpe
Norwell
Holme

Tibshelf
Sutton in
Ashfield
Mansfield
NG22
Newark and
Sherwood

Newton
NG18
NG21

DE55
NG17
Rainworth
Blidworth
Farnsfield
Stapleford

South
Normanton
Kirkby in
Ashfield
Ravenshead
Southwell
Upton
Newark-
on-Trent
LN6

Pinxton
Newstead
NG25
NG24
Beckingham

Jacksdale
Ashfield
NG15
Oxton
Morton
Farndon
LN5

NG16
Hucknall
NG14
Balderton
Fenton

Eastwood
Calverton
NG23
Claypole

Shipley
Gedling
NG5
Lowdham
Elston
NG23
Dry Doddington

DE75
Kimberley
NG6
Lambley
Burton
Joyce
Sibthorpe

DE7
2
Bulwell
Arnold
East
Bridgford
Lincolnshire

Ilkeston
NG8
1
NG4
Bingham
Orston
Normanton

NG1
NG3
Carlton
Whatton
Bottesford

NG7
Nottingham
Radcliffe
on Trent
NG13

Beeston
NG2
Langar
Plungar

Stapleford
NG9
Cotgrave
Kinoulton
Harby

City of
Derby
Long Eaton
Toton
Clifton
Rushcliffe
NG12
Hose

Sawley
NG10
Ruddington
Keyworth
Hickling
Long Clawson

Ratcliffe on Soar
NG11
Gotham
Bunny
Willoughby-
on-the-Wolds
LE14

DE74
Kegworth
East
Leake
Old Dalby

Long Whatton
Hoton
Wymeswold

Hathern
LE12
Cotes

Loughborough

LE11

Leicestershire
Rutland

SE
SK

Scale				
0	5	10	15	20 km
0		5		10 miles

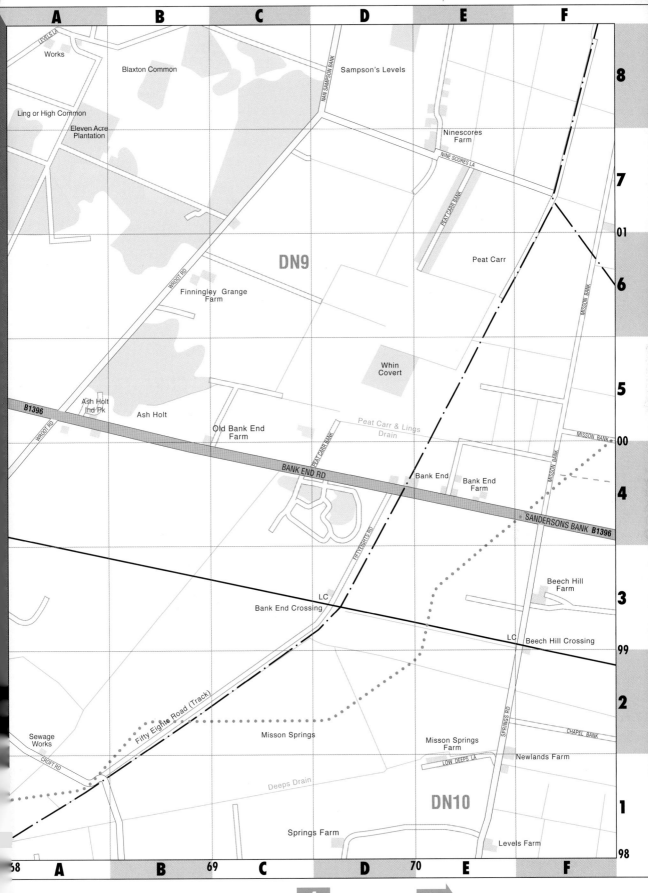

A B C D E F

8

7

01

6

5

00

4

3

99

2

1

98

LEVELS LA

Works

Blaxton Common

Sampson's Levels

NAN SAMPSON BANK

Ling or High Common

Eleven Acre
Plantation

Ninescores
Farm

NINE SCORES LA

PEAT CARR BANK

DN9

Peat Carr

WROOT RD

Finningley Grange
Farm

MISSON BANK

Whin
Covert

B1396

Ash Holt
Ind Pk

Ash Holt

Old Bank End
Farm

Peat Carr & Lings
Drain

MISSON BANK

WROOT RD

PEAT CARR BANK

BANK END RD

Bank End

Bank End
Farm

MISSON BANK

SANDERSONS BANK B1396

Beech Hill
Farm

FIFTY EIGHTS RD

LC

Bank End Crossing

LC

Beech Hill Crossing

Fifty Eights Road (Track)

Sewage
Works

Misson Springs

Misson Springs
Farm

SPRINGS RD

CHAPEL BANK

Newlands Farm

CROFT RD

LOW DEEPS LA

DN10

Deeps Drain

Springs Farm

Levels Farm

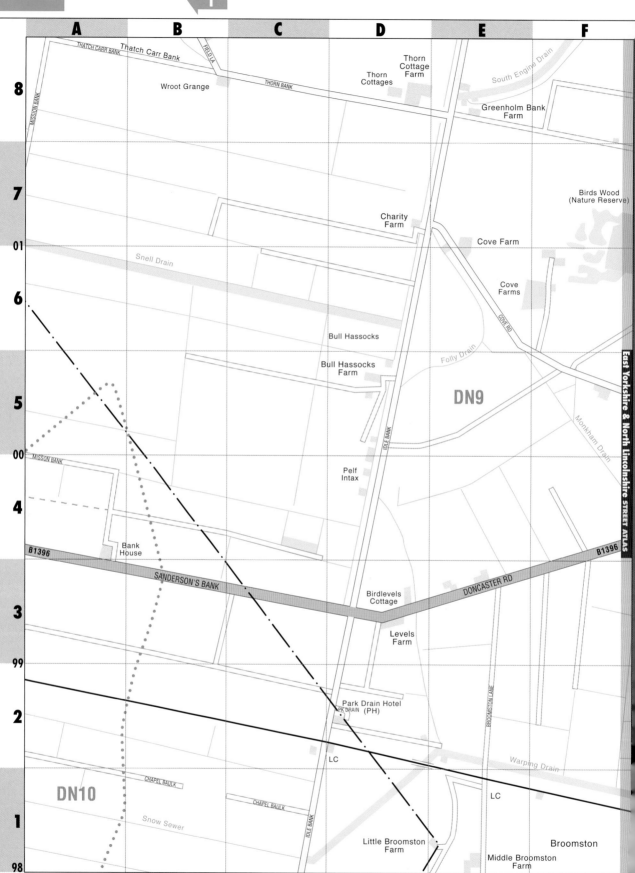

A **B** **C** **D** **E** **F**

8

THATCH CARR BANK

Thatch Carr Bank

Thatch Carr Bank

FIELD LA

THORN BANK

Wroot Grange

Thorn Cottages

Thorn Cottage Farm

Greenholm Bank Farm

South Engine Drain

MISSION BANK

7

Charity Farm

Cove Farm

Birds Wood (Nature Reserve)

01

Snell Drain

Cove Farms

6

Bull Hassocks

Bull Hassocks Farm

COVE RD

Folly Drain

Monkham Drain

DN9

5

IDLE BANK

00

MISSON BANK

Pelf Intax

4

B1396

Bank House

B1396

SANDERSON'S BANK

Birdlevels Cottage

DONCASTER RD

3

Levels Farm

99

BROOMSTON LANE

2

Park Drain Hotel (PH)

PK DRAIN

Warping Drain

LC

DN10

CHAPEL BAULK

LC

1

Snow Sewer

CHAPEL BAULK

IDLE BANK

Little Broomston Farm

Broomston

Middle Broomston Farm

98

71 **A** **B** 72 **C** **D** **E** 73 **F**

East Yorkshire & North Lincolnshire STREET ATLAS

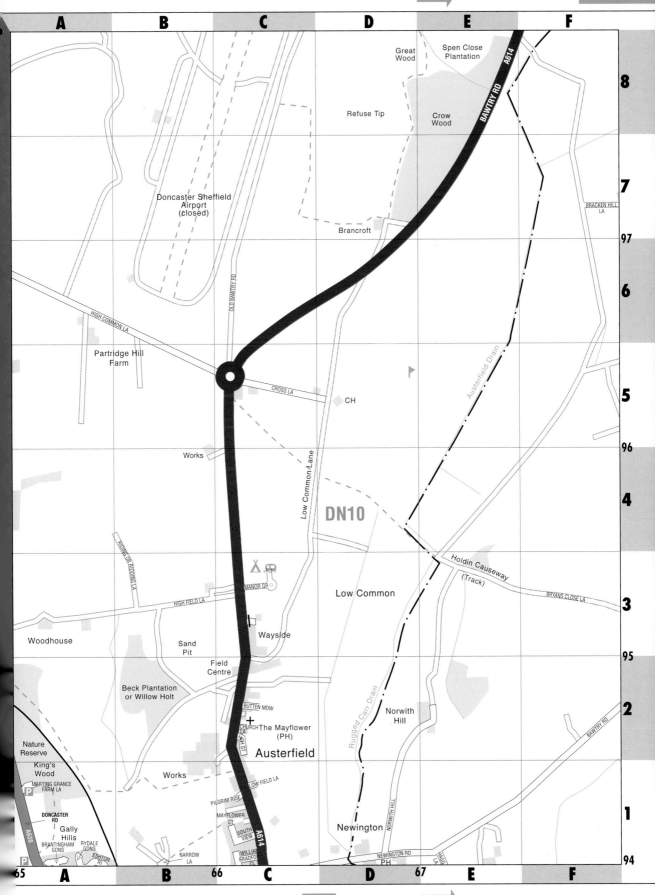

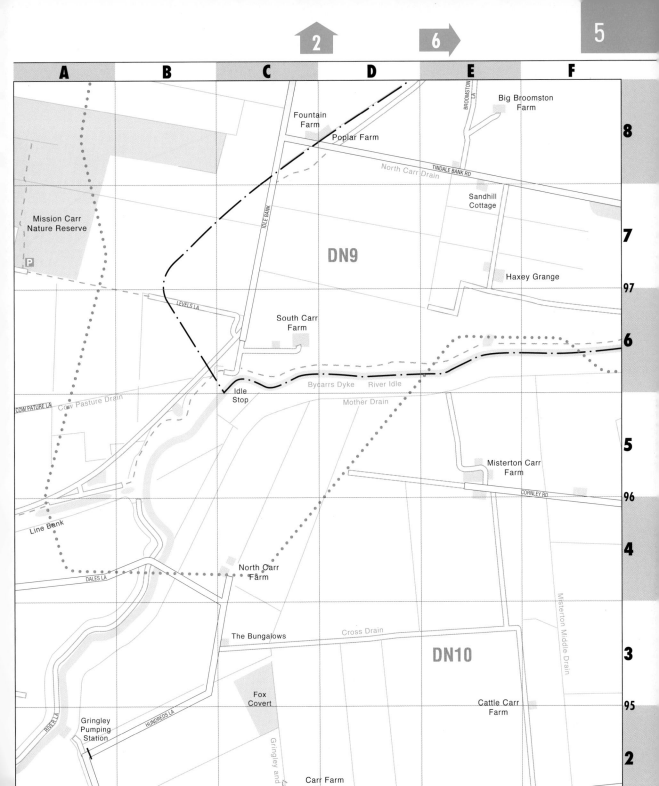

A   B   C   D   E   F

Big Broomston
Farm

Fountain
Farm

Poplar Farm

BROOMSTON LA

TINDALE BANK RD

North Carr Drain

8

Mission Carr
Nature Reserve

Sandhill
Cottage

IDLE BANK

DN9

7

Haxey Grange

97

LEVELS LA

South Carr
Farm

6

Idle
Stop

Bycarrs Dyke   River Idle

COW PATURE LA   Cow Pasture Drain

Mother Drain

Misterton Carr
Farm

5

Line Bank

CORNLEY RD

96

North Carr
Farm

DALES LA

4

Misterton Middle Drain

The Bungalows

Cross Drain

DN10

3

Fox
Covert

Cattle Carr
Farm

95

RIVER LA

Gringley
Pumping
Station

HUNDREDS LA

Gringley and Misterton Boundary Drain

2

Carr Farm

CATTLE RD

Misterton Carr

CARR RD

1

CROSS LA

94

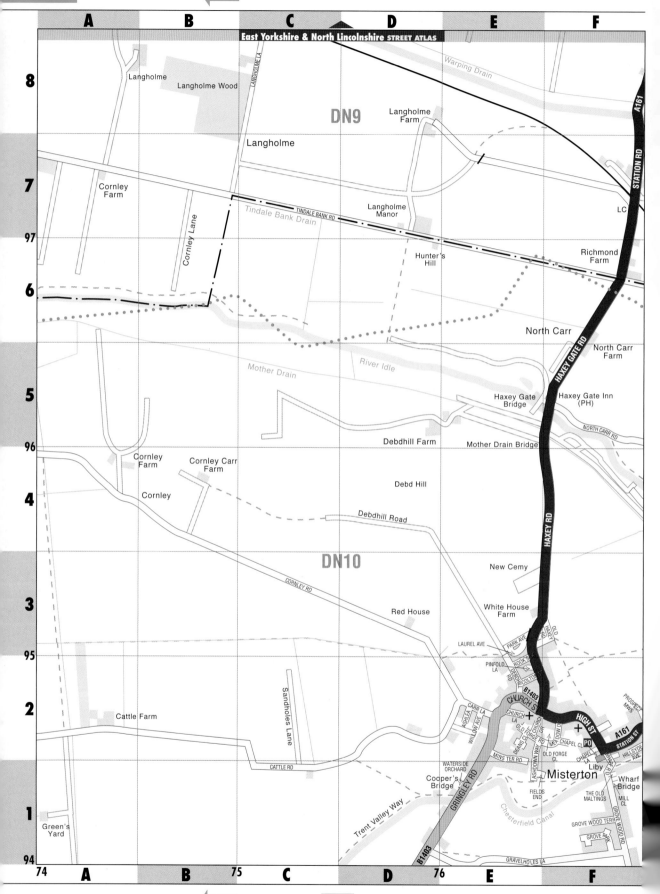

East Yorkshire & North Lincolnshire STREET ATLAS

A B C D E F

8

Langholme

Langholme Wood

DN9

Langholme Farm

Warping Drain

A161

STATION RD

Langholme

7

Cornley Farm

Cornley Lane

LANGHOLME LA

Tindale Bank Drain

TINDALE BANK RD

Langholme Manor

LC

97

Hunter's Hill

Richmond Farm

6

Mother Drain

River Idle

North Carr

HAXEY GATE RD

North Carr Farm

5

Haxey Gate Bridge

Haxey Gate Inn (PH)

NORTH CARR RD

96

Cornley Farm

Cornley Carr Farm

Debdhill Farm

Mother Drain Bridge

4

Cornley

Debd Hill

HAXEY RD

Debdhill Road

DN10

CORNLEY RD

New Cemy

3

Red House

White House Farm

95

Sandholes Lane

LAUREL AVE

PARK AVE

OLD HAXEY RD

ROOK'S CL

DEBD RD

COLTON CL

PROSPECT MWS

PINFOLD LA

2

Cattle Farm

CHURCH ST

B1403

HIGH ST

A161

STATION ST

CATTLE RD

CARR LA

ASHLEA

WILLOW AVE

CHURCH LA

OLD FORGE RD

DEAN'S LA

MINS TER RD

LASDOWN WAY

CHURCH DR

MKT

OLD DOW CL

CHAPEL CL

OLD FORGE CL

CHAPEL LA

WHARF RD

HILLYSIDE AVE

Liby

PO

WATERSIDE ORCHARD

Cooper's Bridge

GRINGLEY RD

Misterton

THE OLD MALTINGS

Wharf Bridge

MILL CL

1

Green's Yard

Trent Valley Way

FIELDS END

Chesterfield Canal

GROVE WOOD TERRE

GROVE WOOD RD

GROVE BK

94

B1403

GRAVELHO LES LA

A B C D E F

74 75 76

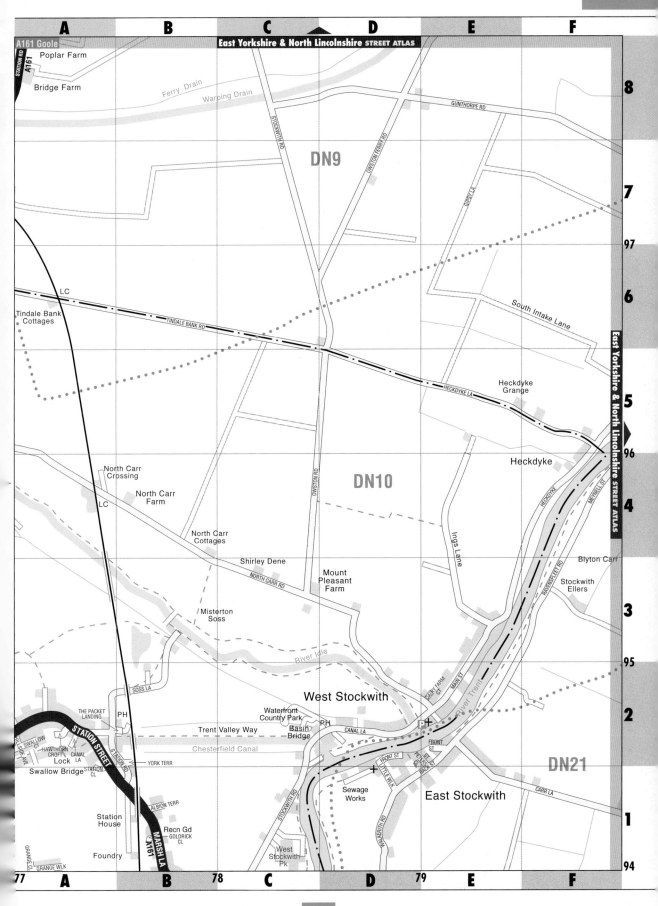

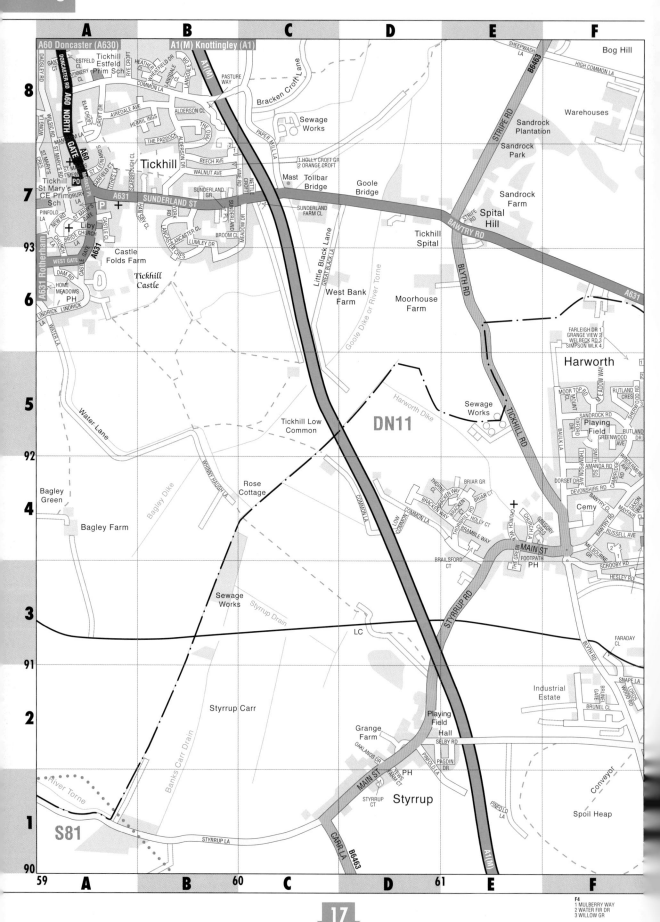

F4
1 MULBERRY WAY
2 WATER FIR DR
3 WILLOW GR

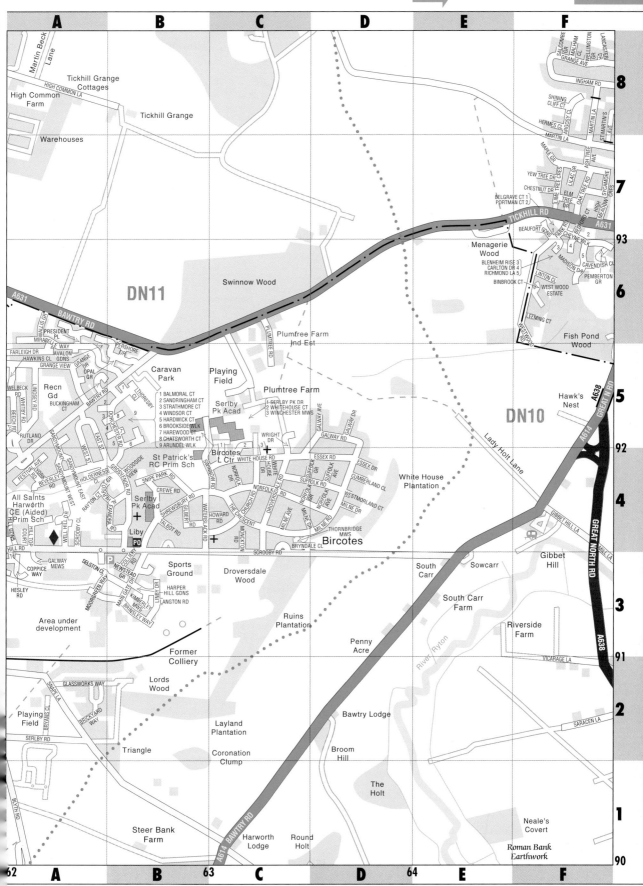

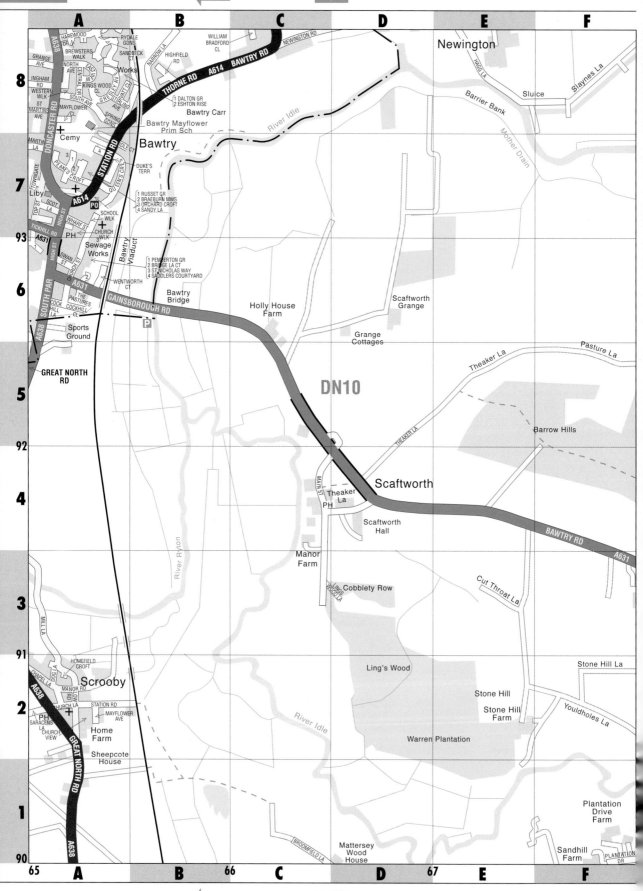

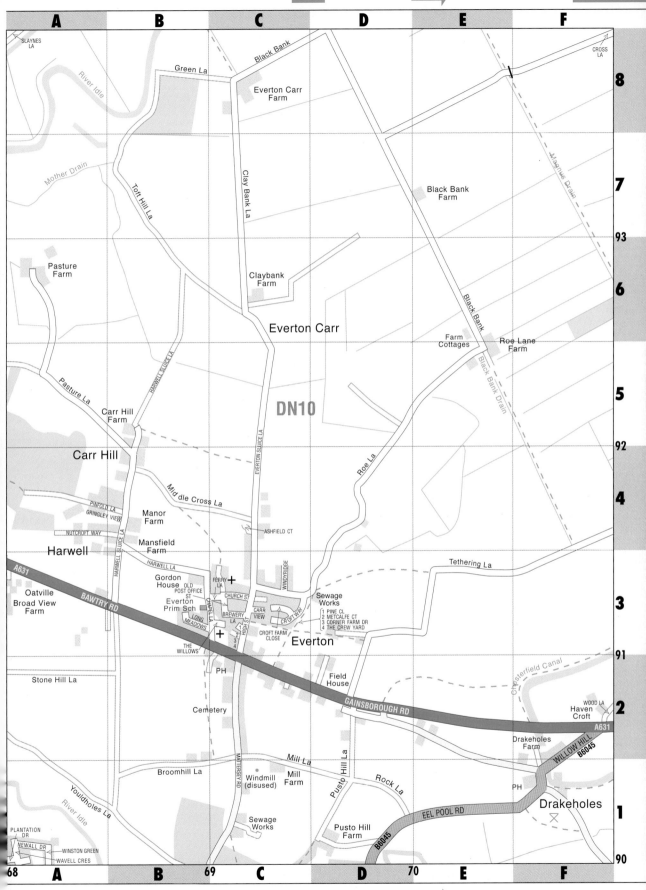

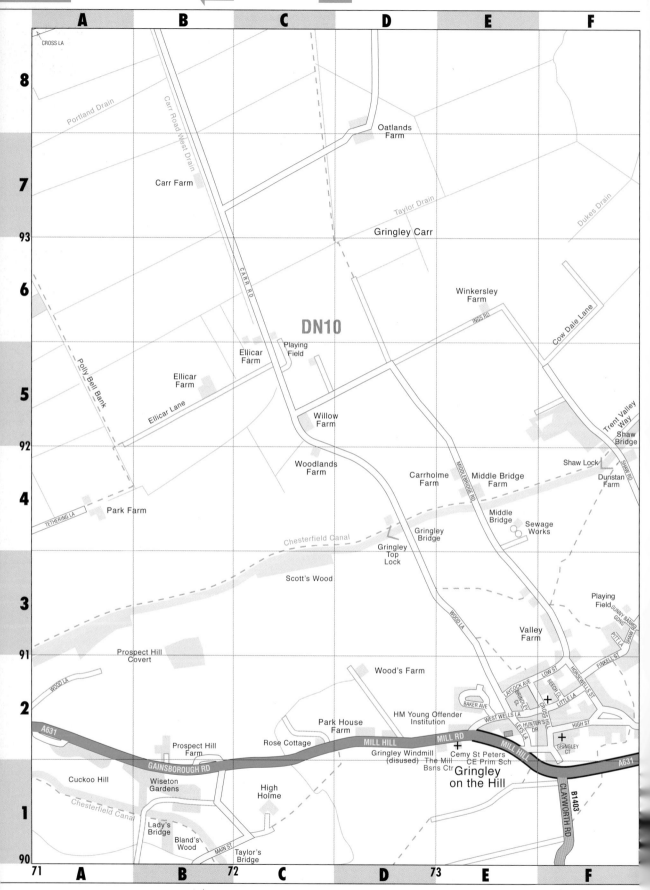

A B C D E F

CROSS LA

8

Portland Drain

Carr Road West Drain

Carr Farm

7

Taylor Drain

Dukes Drain

Gringley Carr

93

Winkersley Farm

INGS RD

6

Cow Dale Lane

CARR RD

Polly Bell Bank

DN10

Playing Field

Ellicar Farm

Trent Valley Way

Ellicar Farm

Shaw Bridge

5

Ellicar Lane

Willow Farm

92

Shaw Lock

SHAW RD

Dunstan Farm

Woodlands Farm

Carrholme Farm

Middle Bridge Farm

TETHERING LA

Park Farm

MIDDLE BRIDGE RD

Middle Bridge

Sewage Works

4

Chesterfield Canal

Gringley Bridge

Gringley Top Lock

Scott's Wood

Playing Field

SUNNY BANK GDNS

3

WOOD LA

Valley Farm

PITT LA

SHAW

FINKEL ST

Prospect Hill Covert

91

Wood's Farm

LOW ST

HORSWELLS ST

WOOD LA

LAYCOCK AVE

BRINDLEY CL

BECK CL

LITTLE LA

HIGH ST

2

BAKER AVE

WEST WELLS LA

CROSS HILL

HUNTERS DR

Park House Farm

HM Young Offender Institution

A631

Prospect Hill Farm

Rose Cottage

MILL HILL

MILL RD

Cemy St Peters

MILL HILL

Gringley CT

A631

GAINSBOROUGH RD

Gringley Windmill (disused)

The Mill Bsns Ctr

CE Prim Sch

Gringley on the Hill

Cuckoo Hill

Wiseton Gardens

High Holme

CLAYWORTH RD

B1403

Chesterfield Canal

1

Lady's Bridge

Bland's Wood

MAIN ST

Taylor's Bridge

90

71 A B 72 C D 73 E F

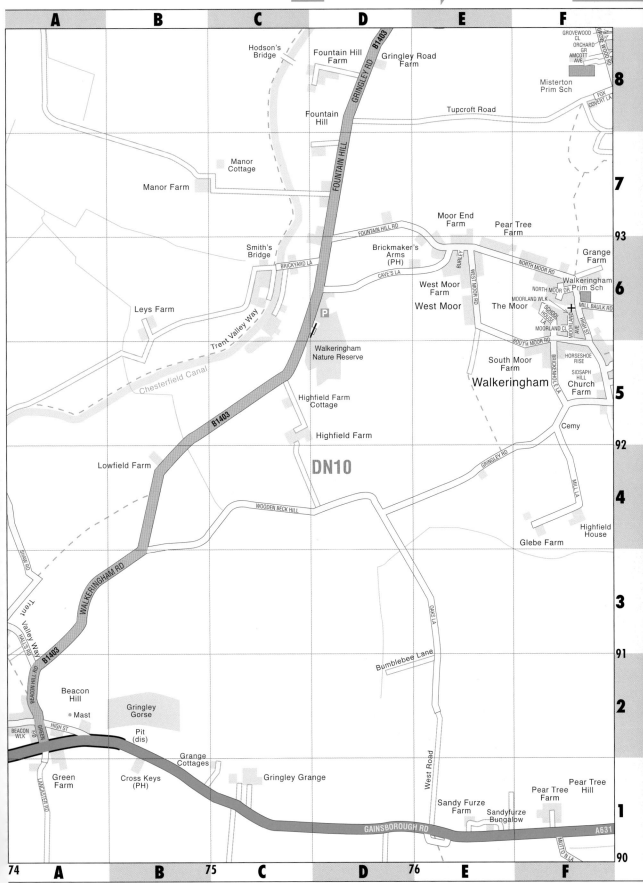

A B C D E F

8

GROVEWOOD
CL
ORCHARD
GR
AMCOTT
AVE

Hodson's
Bridge

Fountain Hill
Farm

Gringley Road
Farm

Misterton
Prim Sch

GRINGLEY RD

B1403

FOX COVERT LA

GROVE WOOD RD

Fountain
Hill

Tupcroft Road

7

Manor
Cottage

Manor Farm

93

Moor End
Farm

Pear Tree
Farm

Grange
Farm

FOUNTAIN HILL

FOUNTAIN HILL RD

Smith's
Bridge

Brickmaker's
Arms
(PH)

Walkeringham
Prim Sch

BURLEY

NORTH MOOR RD

WEST MOOR RD

NORTH MOOR DR

6

BRICKYARD LA

CAVE'S LA

West Moor
Farm

West Moor

The Moor

MOORLAND WLK

SCHOOL
HOUSE
LA

MILL BAULK RD

Leys Farm

MOORLAND CL

HIGH ST

MILL AVE

Trent Valley Way

P

Walkeringham
Nature Reserve

SOUTH MOOR RD

HORSESHOE
RISE

Chesterfield Canal

South Moor
Farm

SIDSAPH
HILL

Walkeringham

Church
Farm

5

Highfield Farm
Cottage

BRICKENHOLE LA

Highfield Farm

Cemy

92

B1403

DN10

Lowfield Farm

Gringley Rd

MILL LA

4

Highfield
House

WOODEN BECK HILL

Glebe Farm

SHAW RD

Trent Valley Way

3

HALL'S RD

BEACON HILL RD

OAKS LA

B1403

91

Bumblebee Lane

Beacon
Hill

Mast

Gringley
Gorse

2

BEACON
WLK

GREEN

HIGH ST

Pit
(dis)

West Road

Grange
Cottages

LANCASTER RD

Green
Farm

Cross Keys
(PH)

Gringley Grange

Sandy Furze
Farm

Sandyfurze
Bungalow

Pear Tree
Farm

Pear Tree
Hill

1

GAINSBOROUGH RD

A631

MAUTON LA

74 A 75 B 75 C 76 D 76 E F 90

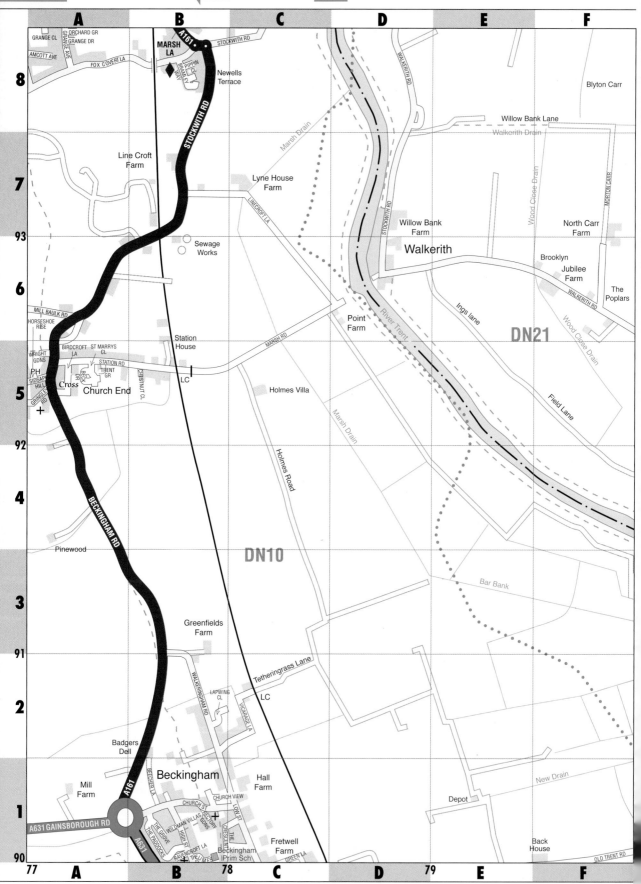

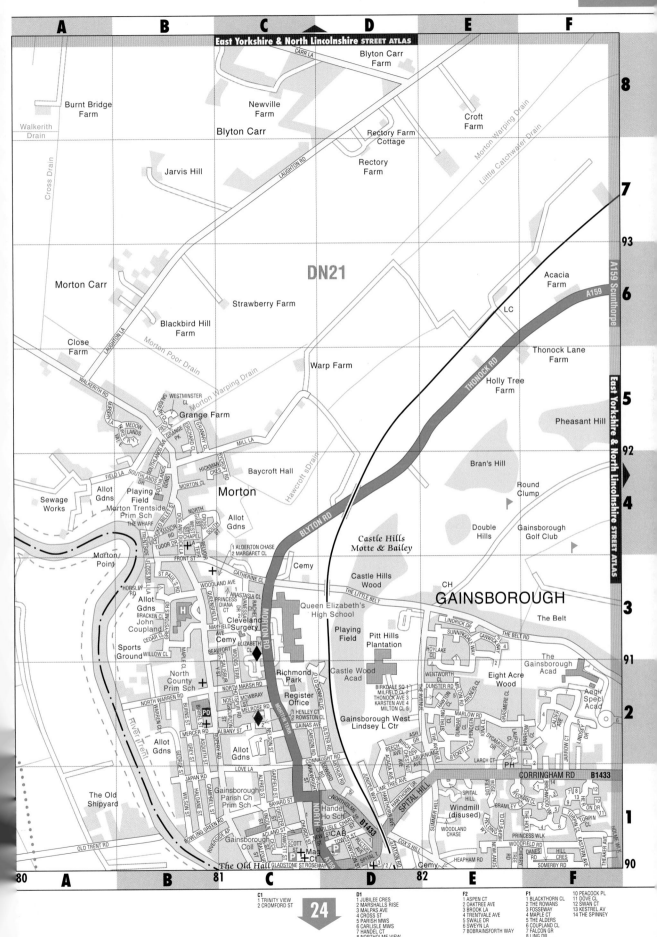

East Yorkshire & North Lincolnshire STREET ATLAS

Blyton Carr Farm

Burnt Bridge Farm

Walkerith Drain

Newville Farm

Blyton Carr

Croft Farm

Rectory Farm Cottage

Rectory Farm

Cross Drain

Morton Warping Drain

Little Catchwater Drain

Jarvis Hill

DN21

A159 Scunthorpe

Acacia Farm

Morton Carr

Strawberry Farm

LC

A159

Blackbird Hill Farm

Morton Poor Drain

Warp Farm

Thonock Lane Farm

Close Farm

Walkerith Rd

Morton Warping Drain

THONOCK RD

Holly Tree Farm

East Yorkshire & North Lincolnshire STREET ATLAS

WESTMINSTER CL

Grange Farm

MILL LA

Hawcroft Drain

Pheasant Hill

Bran's Hill

Round Clump

Baycroft Hall

Sewage Works

Allot Gdns

Playing Field

Morton Trentside Prim Sch

Morton

Allot Gdns

BLYTON RD

Castle Hills Motte & Bailey

Double Hills

Gainsborough Golf Club

THE WHARF

1 ALDERTON CHASE
2 MARGARET CL

Cemy

Castle Hills Wood

CH

GAINSBOROUGH

Morton Point

CATHERINE CL

THE LITTLE BELT

The Belt

ST PAUL'S RD

WOODLAND AVE

ANASTASIA CL

Queen Elizabeth's High School

LINDRICK DR

THE BELT RD

Allot Gdns
John Coupland

Cleveland Surgery

Cemy

MORTON RD

Playing Field

Pitt Hills Plantation

SUNNINGDALE WAY

CANWICK

HOYLAKE CL

The Gainsborough Acad

Sports Ground

WILLOW CL

ELIZABETH

Richmond Park

Castle Wood Acad

WENTWORTH CL

Eight Acre Wood

Aegir Specl Acad

North County Prim Sch

Register Office

BIRKDALE SQ 1
MILFIELD CL 2
THONOCK AVE 3
KARSTEN AVE 4
MILTON CL 5

MARLOW RD

STIRLING CL

GRASMERE CL

PO

MELROSE RD

1 HENLEY CT
2 ROWSTON CL

Gainsborough West Lindsey L Ctr

ASH GR

The AVENUE

LAUREL

WOODHILL AVE

JARROW CT

LINDSEY DR

Allot Gdns

NELSON ST

GAINAS AVE

BEECH AVE

BIRCH CL

CHESTNUT AVE

ACACIA AVE

LARCH CT

PH

CORRINGHAM RD   B1433

Allot Gdns

LOVE LA

LIME TREE AVE

SPITAL HILL

SPITAL FIELDS

ROSE FIELDS

REDMAN CL

BIRCHWOOD

The Old Shipyard

Gainsborough Parish Ch Prim Sch

Handel Ho Sch

NORTHOLME

Windmill (disused)

WOODLAND CHASE

SUMMER HILL

BRAMLEY CL

OLD THORN RD

PRINCESS WLK

TURPIN CL

TURPIN RD

River Trent

Gainsborough Coll

CAB

Mag CT

P

WOODFIELD RD

DANES RD

HILL CRES

HOME WLK

EASTERN AVE

THE Old Hall

Roseway

Cemy

HEAPHAM RD

SOMERBY RD

C1
1 TRINITY VIEW
2 CROMFORD ST

24

D1
1 JUBILEE CRES
2 MARSHALLS RISE
3 MALPAS AVE
4 CROSS ST
5 PARISH MWS
6 CARLISLE MWS
7 HANDEL CT
8 NORTHOLME VIEW

F2
1 ASPEN CT
2 OAKTREE AVE
3 BROOK LA
4 TRENTVALE AVE
5 SWALE DR
6 SWEYN LA
7 BOBRAINSFORTH WAY

F1
1 BLACKTHORN CL
2 THE ROWANS
3 FOSSEWAY
4 MAPLE CT
5 THE ALDERS
6 COUPLAND CL
7 FALCON GR
8 LING DR
9 HEATHER CL

10 PEACOCK PL
11 DOVE CL
12 SWAN CT
13 KESTREL AV
14 THE SPINNEY

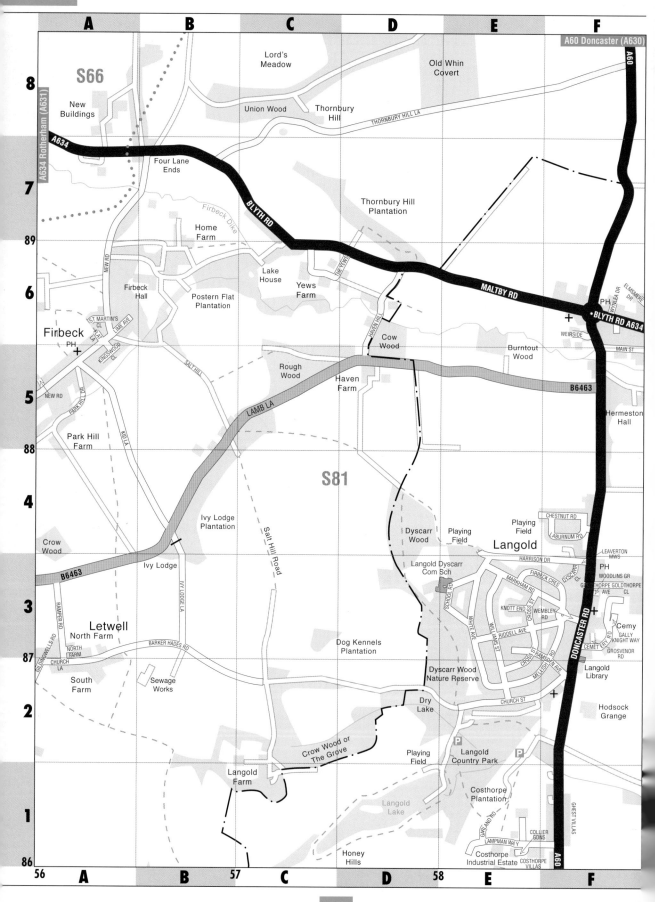

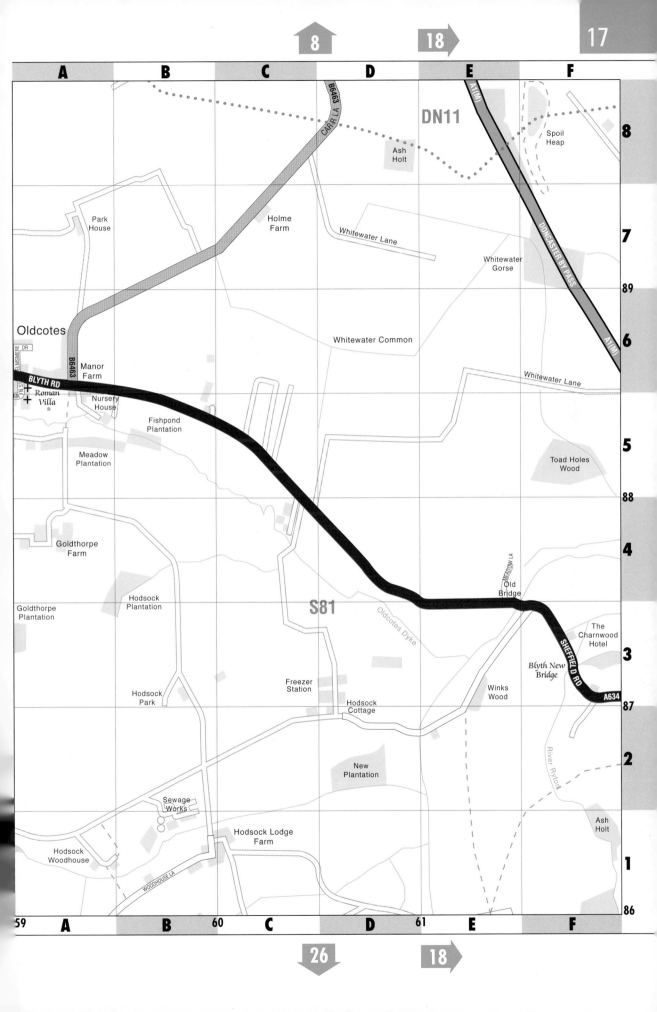

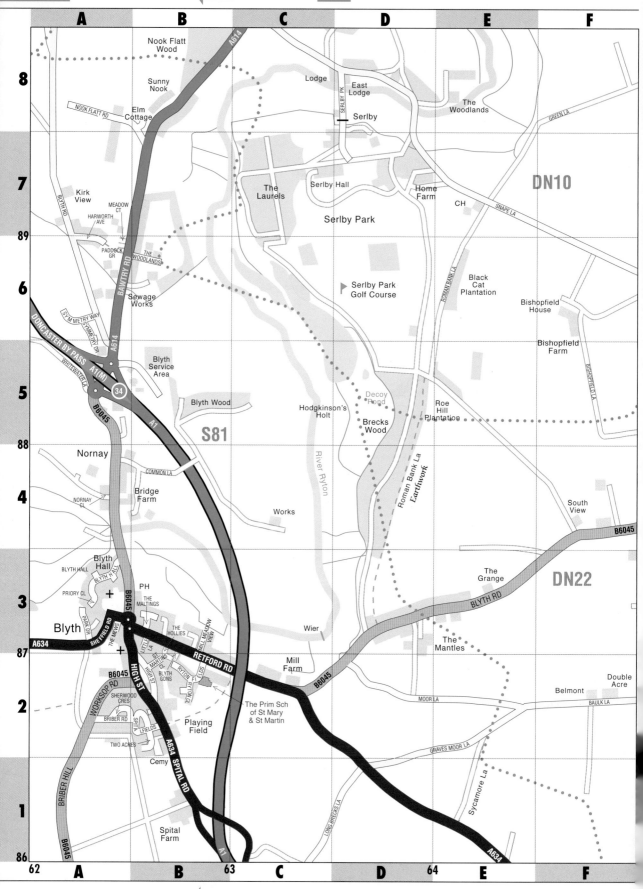

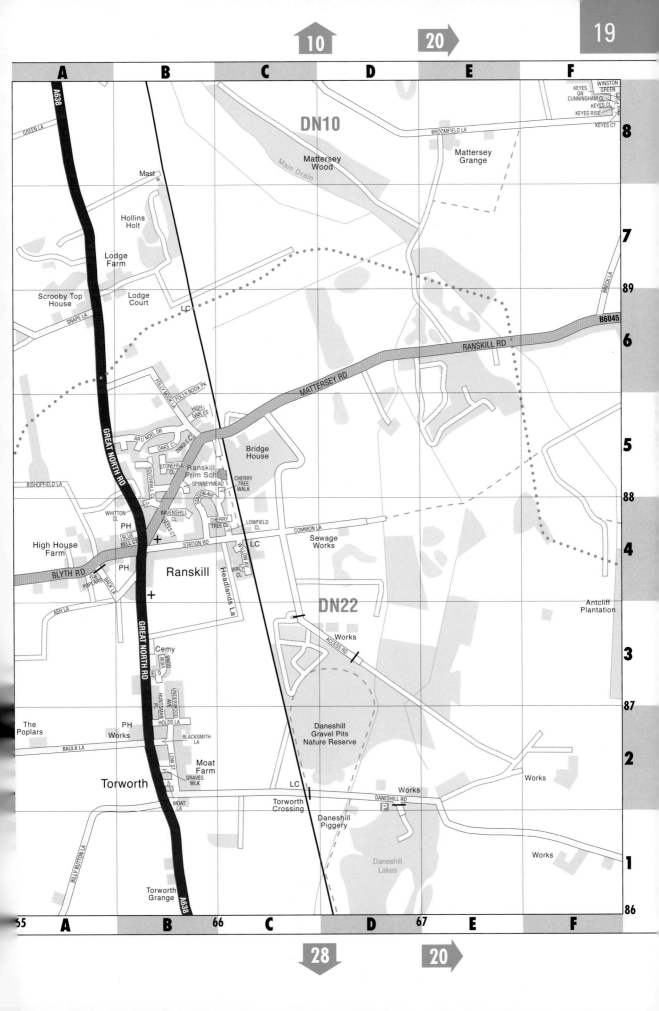

A B C D E F

DN10

Mattersey Wood

Main Drain

KEYES GN
CUNNINGHAM CL
KEYES CL
KEYES RISE
KEYES CT

WINSTON GREEN

Mattersey Grange

BROOMFIELD LA

8

Hollins Holt

Mast

7

Lodge Farm

BRECK LA

89

Scrooby Top House

Lodge Court

LC

B6045

RANSKILL RD

6

SNAPE LA

MATTERSEY RD

GREEN LA

A638

FOLLY NOOK PK
FOLLY NOOK LA

HIGH GABLES

5

ARUNDEL DR
OAKS CL
DINGLE CT
STONEHILL CL

Bridge House

BISHOPFIELD LA

Ranskill Prim Sch

SOUTHALL CL

SPINNEYMEAD

CHERRY TREE WALK

88

STATION AVE

WHITTON CL

RAVENSHILL CL

CHERRY TREE CL

LOWFIELD CL

COMMON LA

Sewage Works

4

PH

BLUE BELL CT

BATES CT

STATION RD

LC

BIRCH CL

WILLOW AV

GREAT NORTH RD

BLYTH RD

PH

Ranskill

HEADLANDS LA

Antcliff Plantation

High House Farm

ASH LA

DN22

3

Cemy

Works

ACCESS RD

87

The Poplars

PH

Works

UNDERWOOD AVE

HUNTSMAN PL

HOLDS LA

BLACKSMITH LA

VIEW PL

FIELD CL

BAULK LA

Daneshill Gravel Pits Nature Reserve

Works

2

Moat Farm

LOW ST

GRAVES WLK

LC

Works

DANESHILL RD

Torworth

MOAT LA

Torworth Crossing

Daneshill Piggery

P

1

BILLY BUTTON LA

Torworth Grange

A638

Daneshill Lakes

Works

86

65 A B 66 C D 67 E F

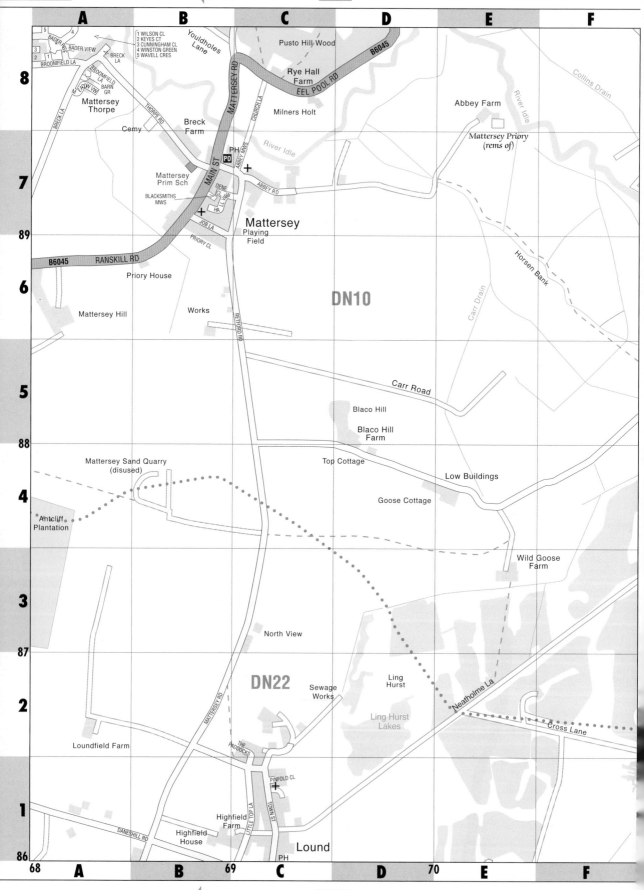

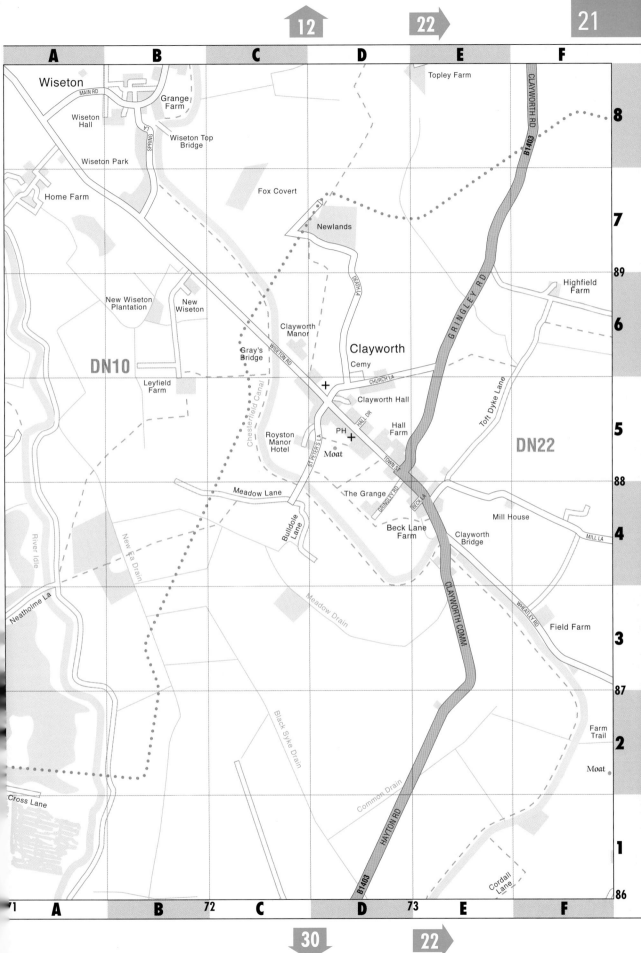

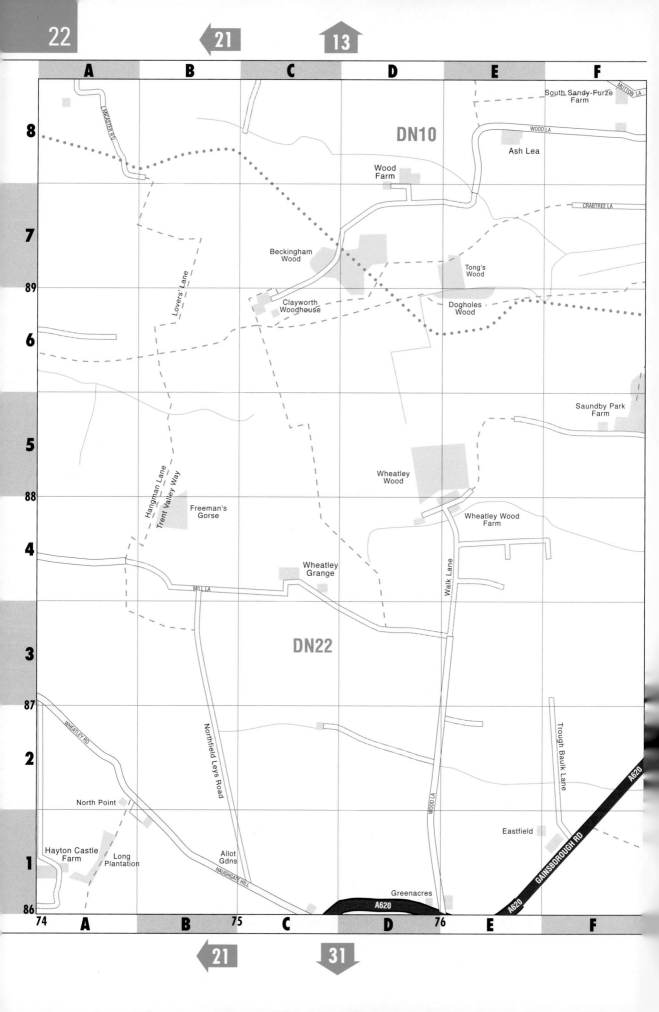

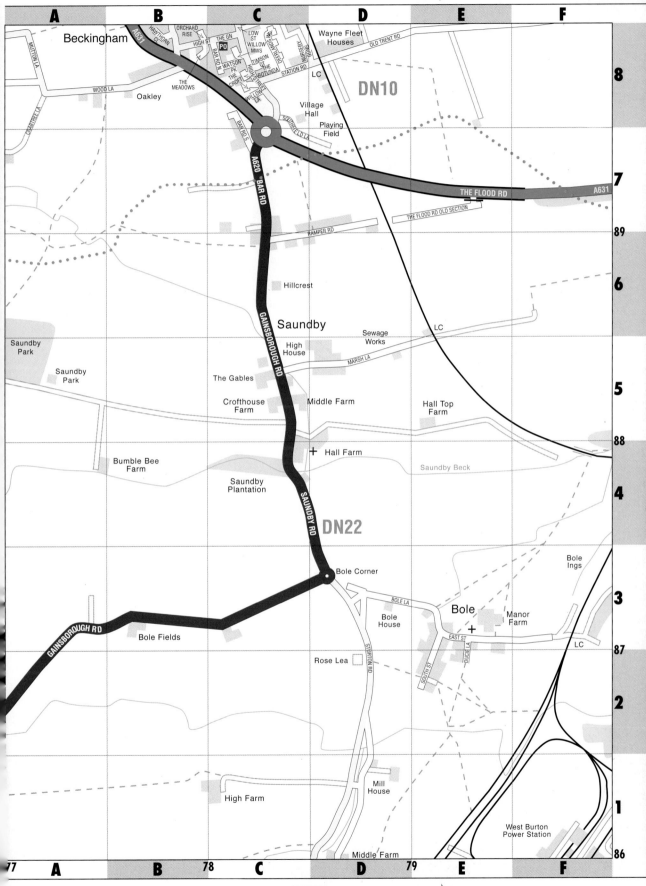

F8
1 NEWTON CL
2 HALTHAM GN
3 HEAPHAM CRES
4 DANES RD
5 WHITE'S WOOD LA

A B C D E F

8

The Guildhall
Cobden St
Liby
MORLEY ST 1
BRIGHT ST 2
PARNELL ST 3
CASKGATE ST
ROPERY RD
LORD ST
CHAPEL STAITH
Guildhall
Health Centre
Bend in the River Gallery
Moat
Dog Island
Wks
PILLARED HOUSE LA
CROSS ST
MKT PL
MKT ST
HEATON ST
LINDSEY CR
SPRING GDNS
MARSHALL'S STA
Sta Hill
A159
Albert Terr
Hawksworth St
Colville Terr
Wks
The Old Nick Theatre
STATION RD
Cemy
Gainsborough Central
HICKMAN
WHITE'S WOOD LA
White's Wood Acad
NEW LANDS
CHERRY TREE
CL
QUEENSWAY
PO
Charles Baines Com Prim Sch
RICHMOND RD
SPRINGTHORPE RD
THEAKER AVE
EASTERN
ELSHAM
PASTURE RD

HICKMAN ST
TORR ST
WEMBLEY ST
SOUTHOLME
TOOLEY ST
Superstore
Trinity Arts Centre
HEAPHAM RD
PINGLE CL
Sports Gd
Hillcrest Com Inf Sch
CONINGSBY

The Flood Rd
A631

7

A631
Flood Arches
Playing Field
PH
Gainsborough Bridge
The Maltings Craft Centre
FLORENCE TERR
LINDEN TERR
PRIMROSE ST
WILLOUGHBY
CLINTON ST
THORNTON
TRENT ST
TRINITY ST
QUEEN ST
KING ST
PRTLND TERR
MRLBRGH
WELLINGTON ST
ST JOHN'S ST
STRAFFORD RD
DUNHOLME CL
ROTHWELL CL
KINGERBY CL
HAINTON
RAVENDALE RD
LISSINGTON RD
RAVENDALE RD
LUDFORD CRES
BRADSHAW WAY
THE DRIVE
THE GREEN
JOHN JENKINSON CL
APLEY CL 1
CAENBY CL 2

Thorndike Way

89

Gainsborough Craft Centre
Gainsborough Waterfront Enterprise Centre
A156
ASHCROFT RD
WATERWORKS
BRIDGE RD
CARR LA
GORDON ST
STANLEY ST
CROMWELL
BACON ST
DUKE ST
SANDSFIELD LA
SHAKESPEARE
1 PROSPECT TERR
2 WHEELDON ST
3 DICKENSON TERR
4 BRITANNIA TERR
5 HIGH ST
6 CLEVELAND ST
Warren Wood Specialist Acad
Gainsborough Benjamin Adlard Com Sch
1 RUSKIN ST
2 DARWIN ST
3 WASHINGTON ST
FOXBY WARREN
FOXBY HILL
ST GEORGE'S
RICHARDSON RISE
AUSTIN DR
SIR THOMAS AVE
SCAMPTON WAY
SARACEN CL
KENWARE CL
PARK SPRINGS RD
AEGIR CL
CLAREMON
PILGRIMS APP
FAIRFAX CL
THE PINES
RISEHOLME RD
FRANCIS CHICHESTER CL
VICTORIA RD
BREWSTER CL
FOXBY LA
ADLINGTON MWS
PARKSIDE WAY
PINTER LA

6

Factory
Mill
River Trent
Playing Field
P
East Trent Junction
SUMMERGANGS LA
Humble Carr Lane
Humble Carr Drain
Gainsborough Lea Road
LEA RD W
LEA RD
MELDRUM DR
WILLOUGHBY
WINTERN CT
FOXBY MWS
HAROLD BRACE RD
MILLER WAY
GEOFF LA
THOMAS COOPER DR

GAINSBOROUGH

5

Long Bank
Saundby Beck
West Trent Junction
Playing Field
PH
DROVERS CT
TRAFALGAR CT
BETTYS LA
COPPER BEECH CL
MAYFLOWER CL
Brickyard Plantation
Warren Wood
Lea Wood Farm

88

Bole Ings Drain
Sewage Works
Causeway

4

Bole Ings

3

DN22
DN21
Lea Marsh
GREEN LA
CROW GARTH LA
CAVENDISH DR
CHURCHILL WAY
CROMWELL VIEW
GAINSBOROUGH RD
ANDERSON WAY
THE CRESCENT
RECTORY CL

87

Lea Marsh Drain

2

Lea
WILLINGHAM RD
B1241

1

Sewage Works
River Road
River Trent
Lea Park
Playing Field
Sherriff's Walk
A156

86

80 A 81 B C 82 D E F

Lincolnshire STREET ATLAS

A631 Market Rasen

F7
1 PINFOLD DR
2 GREENFIELD WAY
3 HARVEST CL
4 PLOUGH DR
5 COWSLIP DR
6 SNOWDROP GDNS
7 BLUEBELL CL
8 REDHOLME CL

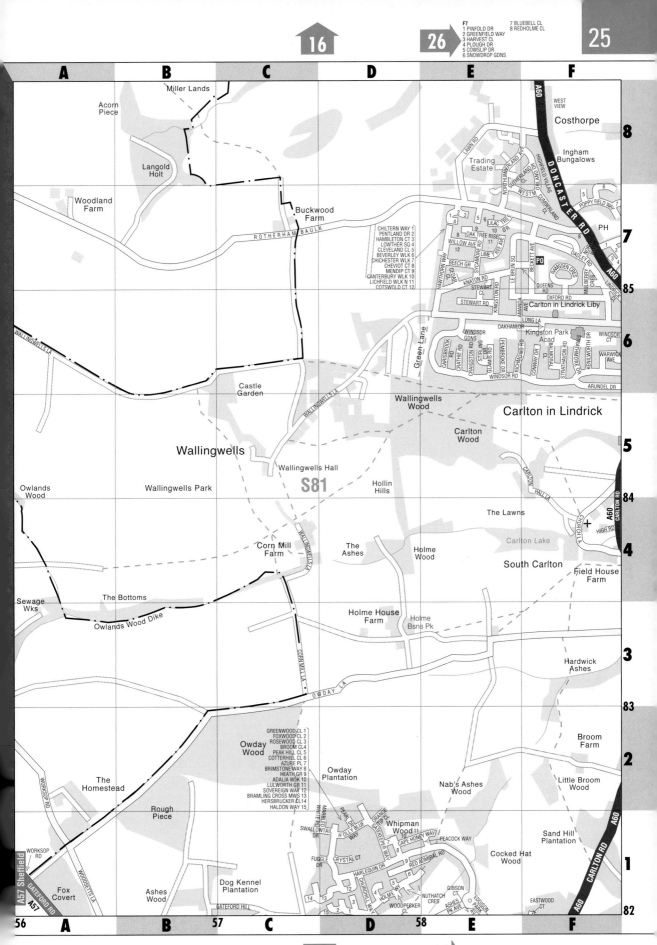

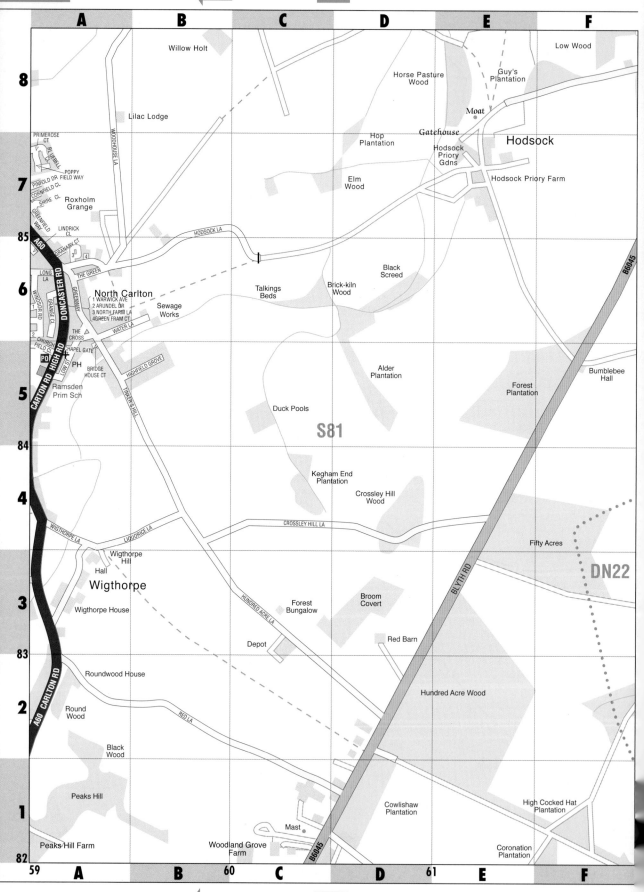

Willow Holt

Low Wood

Horse Pasture Wood

Guy's Plantation

Moat

Hodsock

Lilac Lodge

PRIMROSE CT
BLUEBELL CL
POPPY FIELD WAY
PINFOLD DR
CORNFIELD CL
SHIRE CL

WOODHOUSE LA

Hop Plantation

Gatehouse

Hodsock Priory Gdns

Hodsock Priory Farm

Roxholm Grange

Elm Wood

LINDRICK CL

HODSOCK LA

Black Screed

B6045

GRANARY CT
3 4

THE GREEN

GREENFIELD WAY
A60

North Carlton
1 WARWICK AVE
2 ARUNDEL DR
3 NORTH FARM LA
4 GREEN FRAM CT

Talkings Beds

Brick-kiln Wood

Sewage Works

LONG LA

DONCASTER RD

WATER LA

WINDSOR RD
GRANGE CL

GREENWAY

THE CROSS

HIGHFIELD GROVE

Alder Plantation

Forest Plantation

Bumblebee Hall

CHURCH FIELD CL
CHAPEL GATE

Duck Pools

Ramsden Prim Sch

CARTON RD
HIGH RD
PO
PH
BRIDGE HOUSE CT

TINKER'S HILL

S81

84

Kegham End Plantation

Crossley Hill Wood

Fifty Acres

WIGTHORPE LA

LIQUORICE LA

CROSSLEY HILL LA

DN22

Wigthorpe Hill

Hall

Wigthorpe

BLYTH RD

Wigthorpe House

HUNDRED ACRE LA

Forest Bungalow

Broom Covert

Red Barn

Depot

Roundwood House

RED LA

Round Wood

Hundred Acre Wood

A60 CARLTON RD

Black Wood

Peaks Hill

High Cocked Hat Plantation

Cowlishaw Plantation

Peaks Hill Farm

Mast

B6045

Woodland Grove Farm

Coronation Plantation

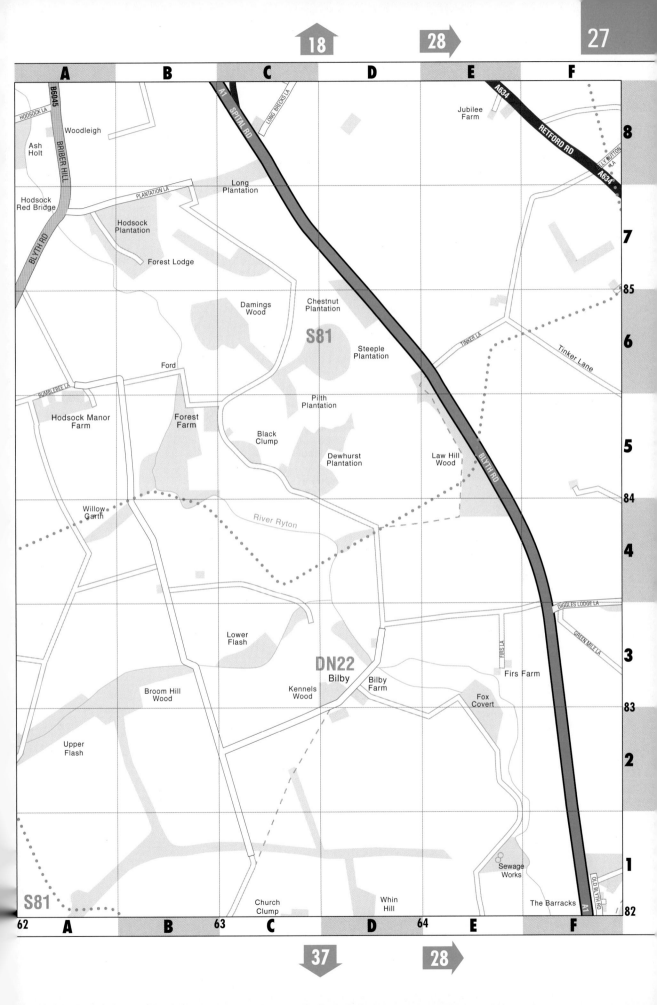

A   B   C   D   E   F

HODSOCK LA
B6045
BLYTH RD
BRIBER HILL

Ash
Holt

Woodleigh

Hodsock
Red Bridge

PLANTATION LA

Hodsock
Plantation

Forest Lodge

Damings
Wood

Ford

BUMBLEBEE LA

Hodsock Manor
Farm

Forest
Farm

Willow
Garth

Black
Clump

Dewhurst
Plantation

Lower
Flash

DN22
Bilby

Kennels
Wood

Bilby
Farm

Broom Hill
Wood

Upper
Flash

Church
Clump

Whin
Hill

A1
SPITAL RD
LONG BRECKS LA

Long
Plantation

Chestnut
Plantation

S81

Steeple
Plantation

Pilth
Plantation

River Ryton

A634
RETFORD RD
BLYTH/DUTTON LA
A634

Jubilee
Farm

TINKER LA
Tinker Lane

Law Hill
Wood

BLYTH RD

DIGGLES LODGE LA
GREEN MILE LA

FIRS LA
Firs Farm

Fox
Covert

Sewage
Works

The Barracks

OLD BLYTH RD
A1

8   85   7   6   85   5   84   4   3   83   2   1   82

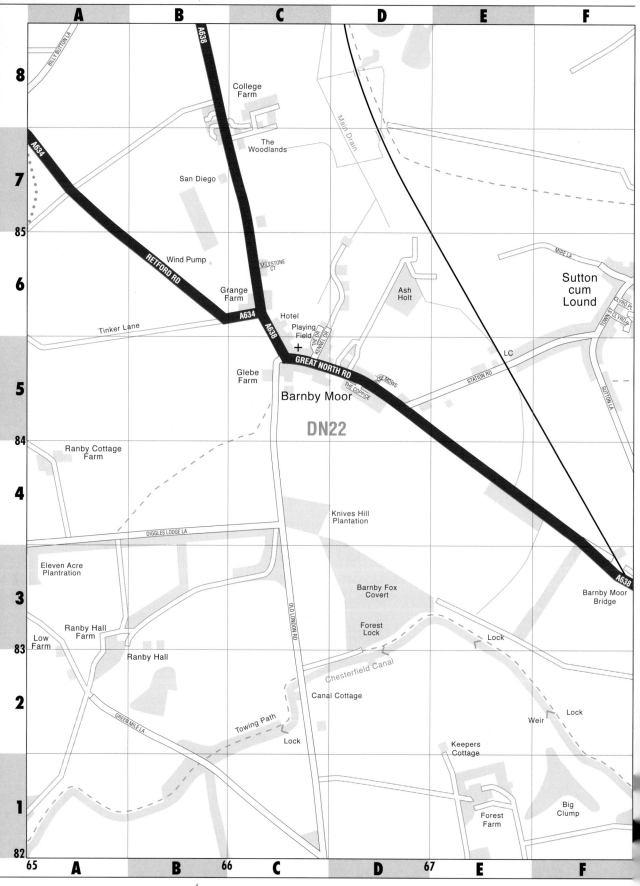

A B C D E F

8

7

85

6

5

84

4

3

83

2

1

82

BILLY BUTTON LA

A638

A634

College Farm

The Woodlands

San Diego

Main Drain

RETFORD RD

Wind Pump

MILESTONE CT

Grange Farm

A634

A638

Tinker Lane

Hotel

Playing Field

THE DR

KENNEL DR

Ash Holt

MIRE LA

Sutton cum Lound

CLYRO PL

TOWN ST CLYRO

GREAT NORTH RD

Glebe Farm

Barnby Moor

DN22

ROSE MDWS

THE COPPICE

STATION RD

LC

SUTTON LA

Ranby Cottage Farm

DIGGLES LODGE LA

Knives Hill Plantation

Eleven Acre Plantration

Barnby Fox Covert

Barnby Moor Bridge

A638

Ranby Hall Farm

OLD LONDON RD

Forest Lock

Lock

Low Farm

Ranby Hall

Chesterfield Canal

Canal Cottage

GREEN MILE LA

Towing Path

Lock

Weir

Lock

Keepers Cottage

Forest Farm

Big Clump

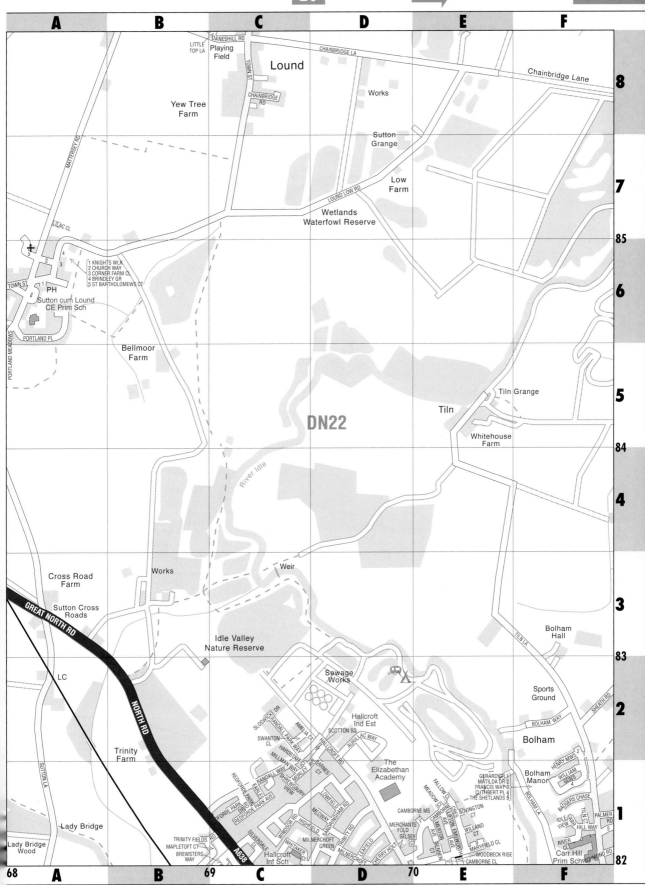

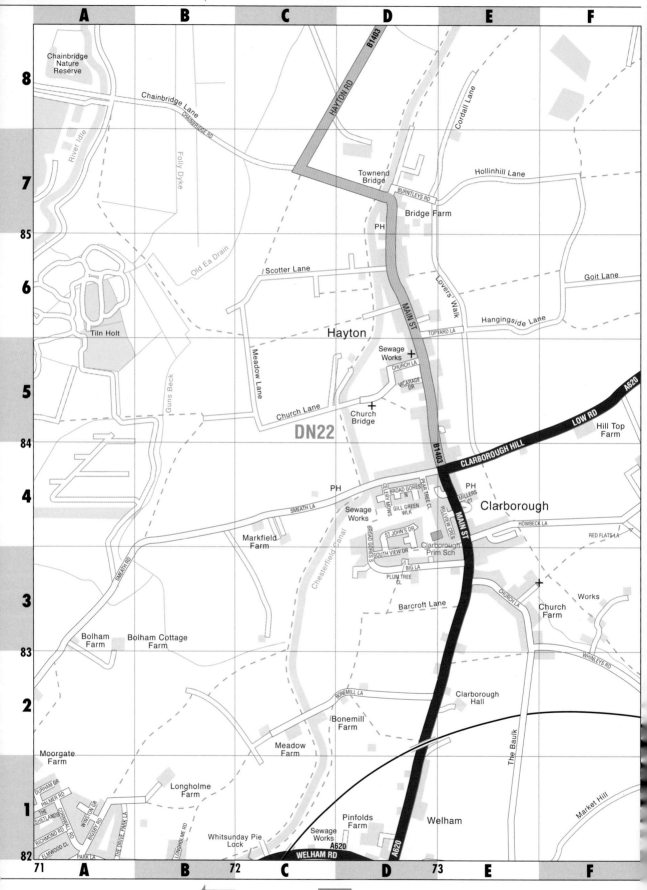

A B C D E F

8 Chainbridge Nature Reserve

Chainbridge Lane

CHAINBRIDGE RD

River Idle

Folly Dyke

B1403

HAYTON RD

7 Townend Bridge

BURNTLEYS RD

Bridge Farm

PH

Hollinhill Lane

Cordall Lane

85

Old Ea Drain

Scotter Lane

MAIN ST

Lovers' Walk

6 Hayton

Goit Lane

Hangingside Lane

TOPYARD LA

Tiln Holt

Meadow Lane

Sewage Works

CHURCH LA

Guns Beck

VICARAGE DR

Church Lane

5

Church Bridge

B1403

A620

LOW RD

Hill Top Farm

84 DN22

CLARBOROUGH HILL

PH

SMEATH LA

BROAD GORES N

PEAR TREE CT

PH

MILLERS CT

Clarborough

4 Markfield Farm

Sewage Works

CELERY MDWS

GILL GREEN WLK

HILLVIEW CRES

MAIN ST

HOWBECK LA

RED FLATS LA

SMEATH RD

Chesterfield Canal

ST JOHN'S DR

SOUTH VIEW DR

BROAD GORES S

Clarborough Prim Sch

BIG LA

PLUM TREE CL

CHURCH LA

Church Farm

Works

3 Bolham Farm

Bolham Cottage Farm

Barcroft Lane

WHINLEYS RD

83

BONEMILL LA

Clarborough Hall

2

Bonemill Farm

Meadow Farm

The Baulk

Moorgate Farm

DURHAM GR

PALMER RD

THE SHETLANDS

WINSTON GR

Longholme Farm

Market Hill

1

RICHMOND RD

CORNWALL RD

BIGSBY RD

THE DRIVE

PARK LA

LONGHOLME RD

Pinfolds Farm

Welham

ELMWOOD CL

PARK LA

Whitsunday Pie Lock

Sewage Works

A620

A620

82 **WELHAM RD**

71 A B 72 C D 73 E F

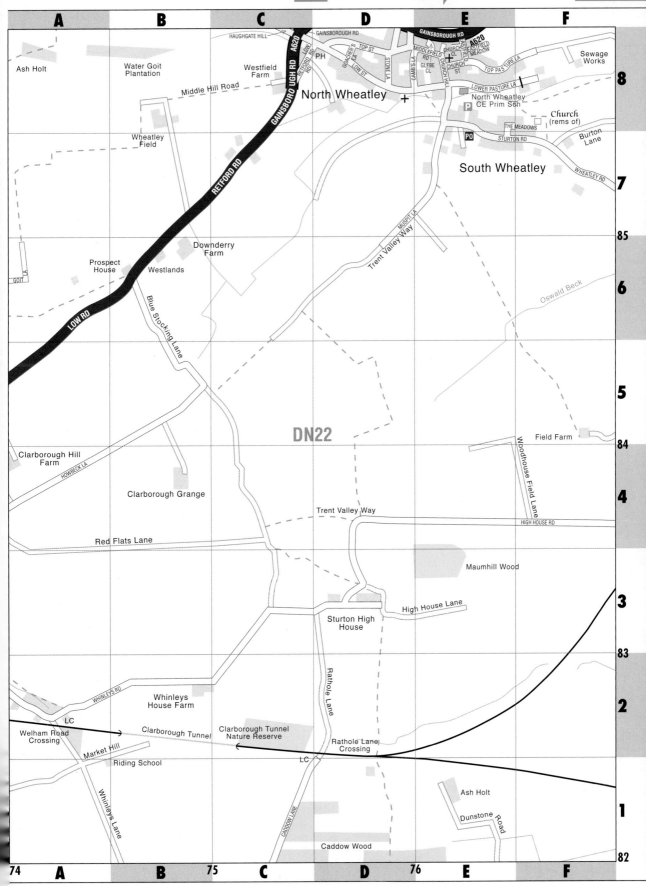

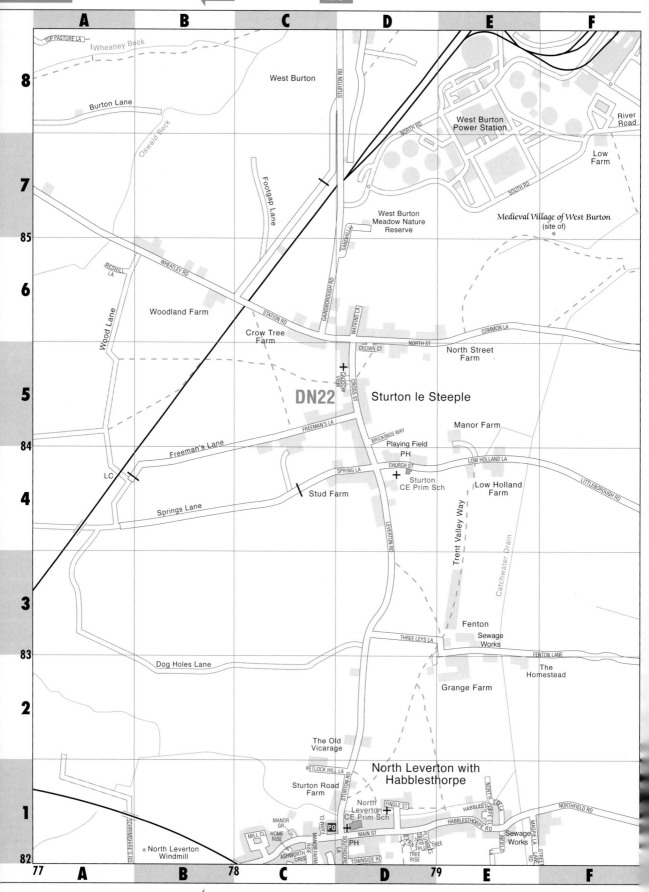

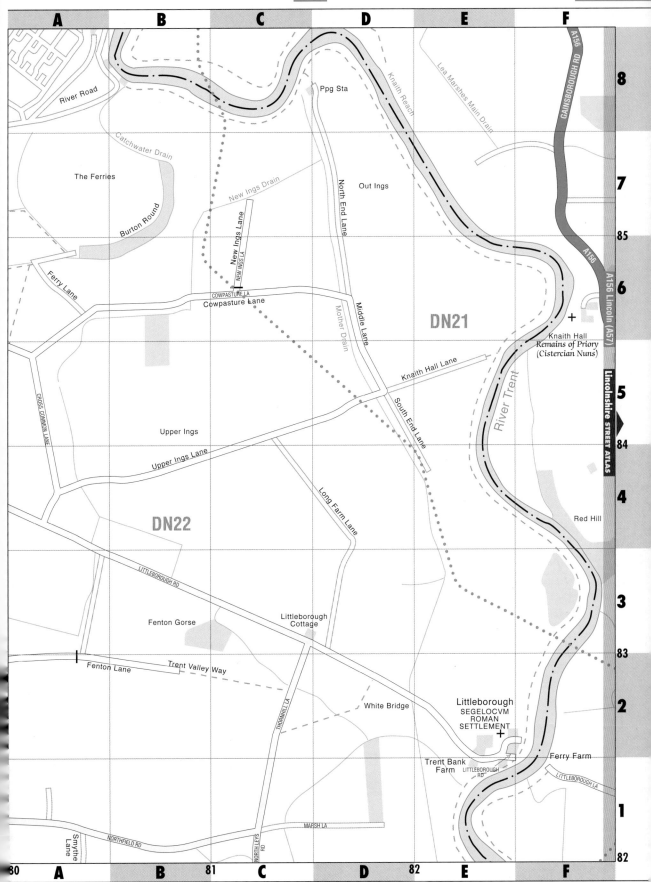

A156 GAINSBOROUGH RD

River Road

The Ferries

Catchwater Drain

Burton Round

Ferry Lane

New Ings Drain

New Ings Lane

NEW INGS LA

COWPASTURE LA

Cowpasture Lane

Ppg Sta

North End Lane

Out Ings

Knaith Reach

Lea Marshes Main Drain

A156

A156 Lincoln (A57)

CROSS COMMON LANE

Mother Drain

Middle Lane

DN21

Knaith Hall Lane

Knaith Hall
Remains of Priory
(Cistercian Nuns)

River Trent

Lincolnshire STREET ATLAS

South End Lane

Upper Ings

Upper Ings Lane

Long Farm Lane

DN22

Red Hill

LITTLEBOROUGH RD

Fenton Gorse

Littleborough
Cottage

Fenton Lane

Trent Valley Way

THORNHILL LA

White Bridge

Littleborough
SEGELOCVM
ROMAN
SETTLEMENT

Trent Bank
Farm

LITTLEBOROUGH RD

Ferry Farm

LITTLEBOROUGH LA

Smythe Lane

NORTHFIELD RD

NORTH LEYS RD

MARSH LA

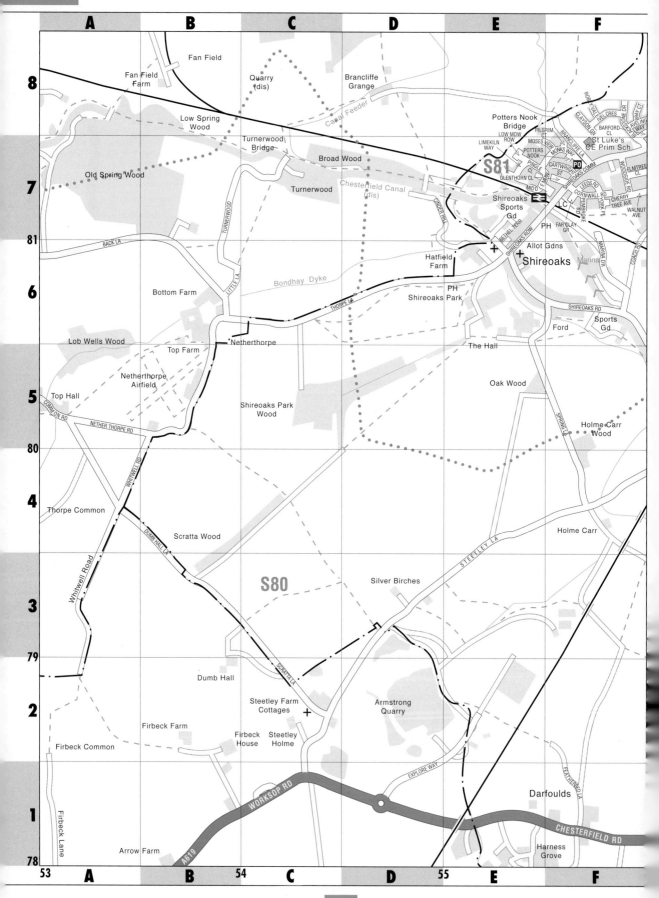

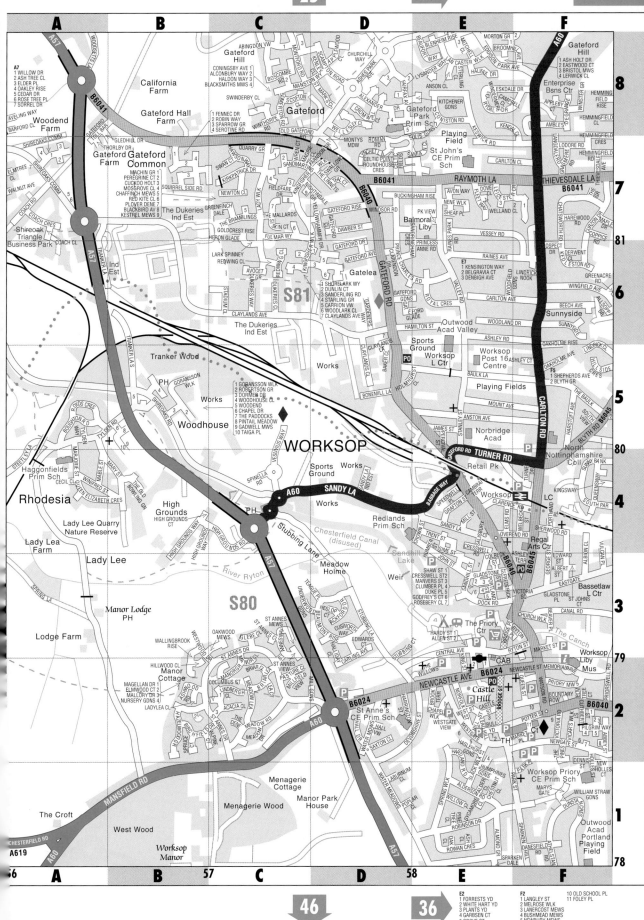

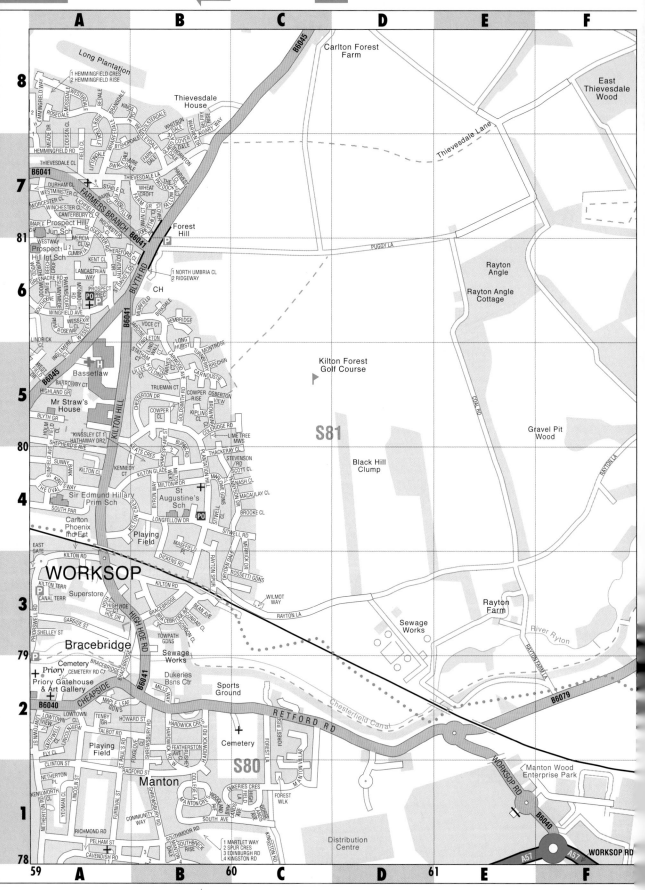

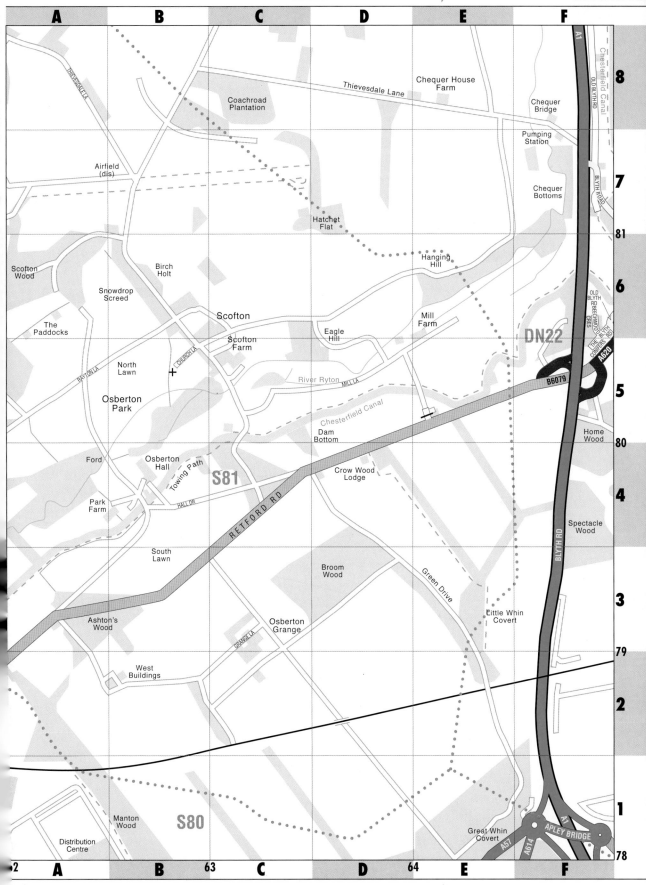

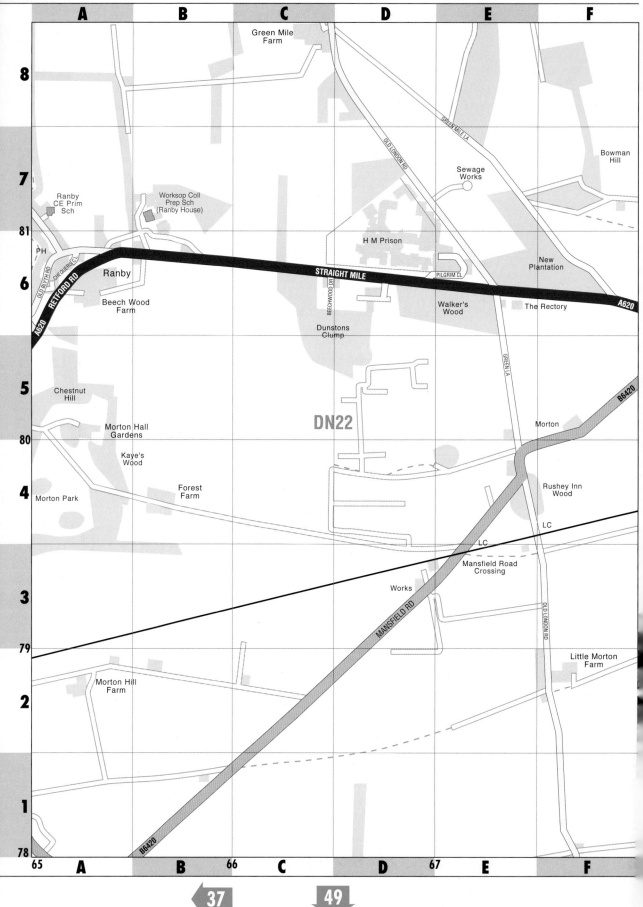

8

Green Mile
Farm

7

Bowman
Hill

81

Ranby
CE Prim
Sch

Worksop Coll
Prep Sch
(Ranby House)

GREEN MILE LA

OLD LONDON RD

Sewage
Works

H M Prison

New
Plantation

PH

6

OLD BLYTH RD

CHEQUERS CL

RETFORD RD

Ranby

STRAIGHT MILE

BEECHWOOD DR

PILGRIM CL

Walker's
Wood

The Rectory

A620

Beech Wood
Farm

Dunstons
Clump

A620

GREEN LA

5

Chestnut
Hill

DN22

Morton

B6420

80

Morton Hall
Gardens

Kaye's
Wood

Rushey Inn
Wood

4

Morton Park

Forest
Farm

LC

LC

Mansfield Road
Crossing

OLD LONDON RD

3

Works

MANSFIELD RD

79

Little Morton
Farm

2

Morton Hill
Farm

B6420

1

78

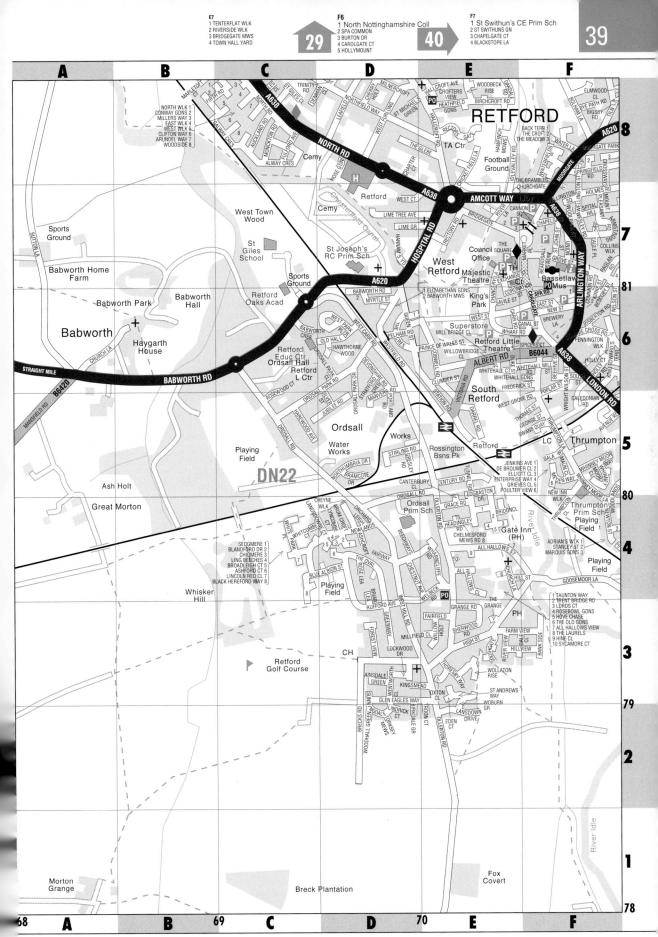

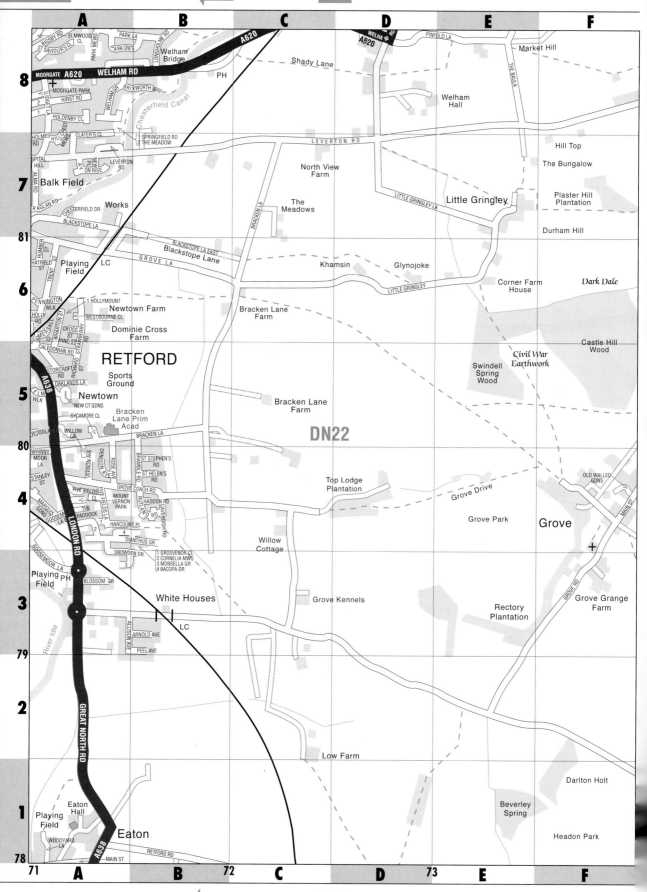

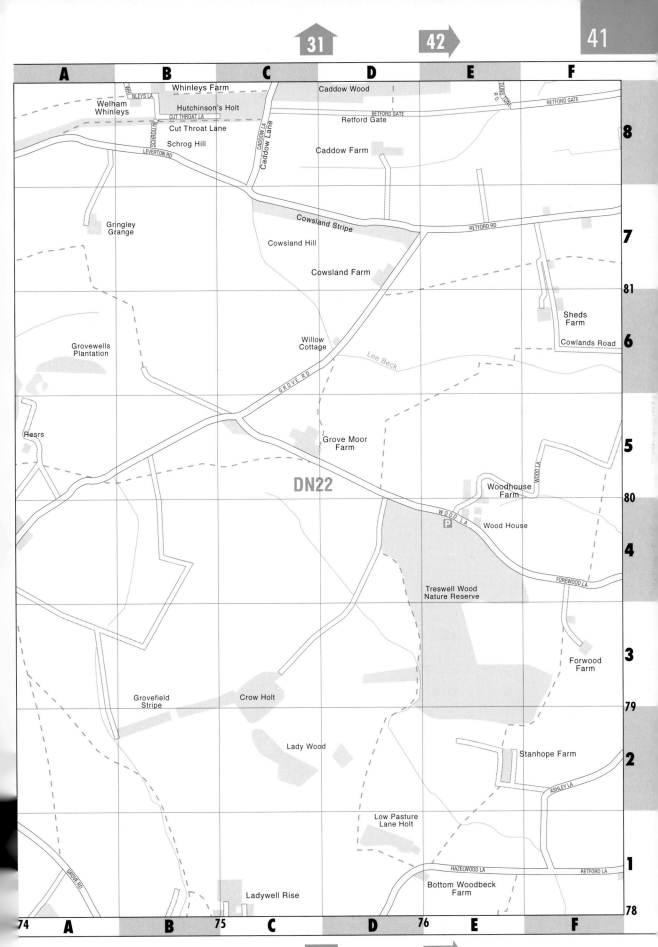

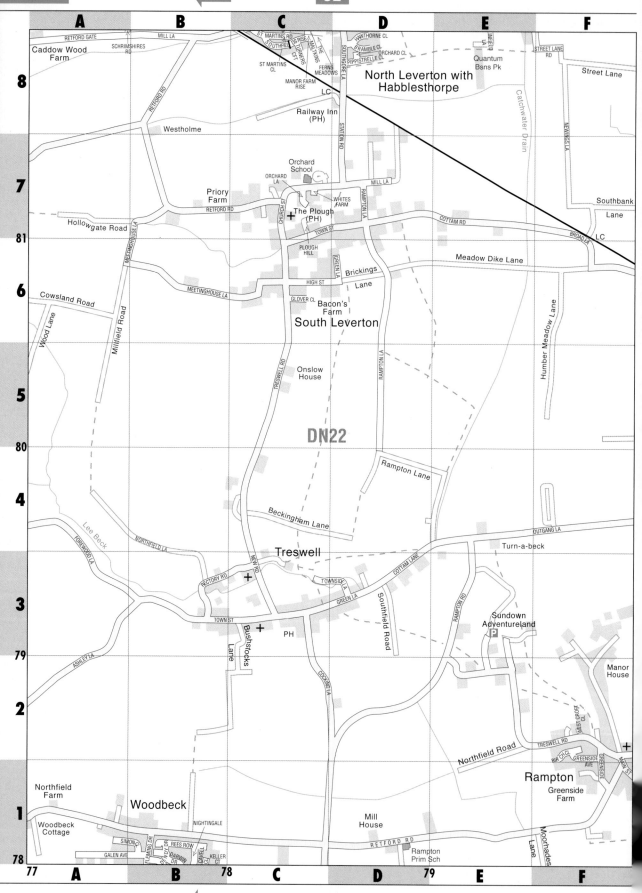

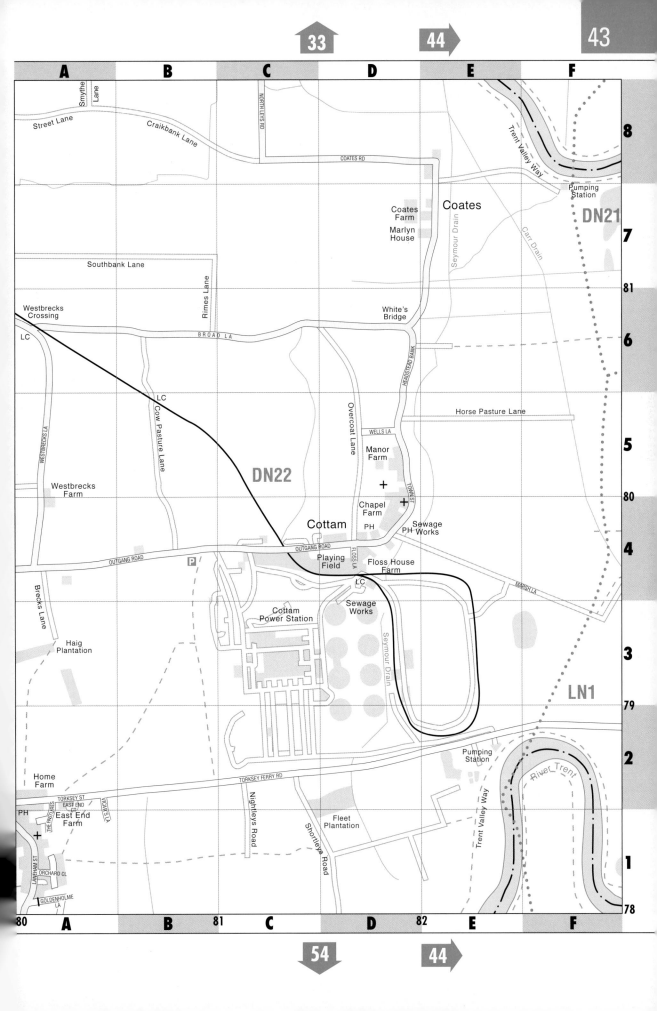

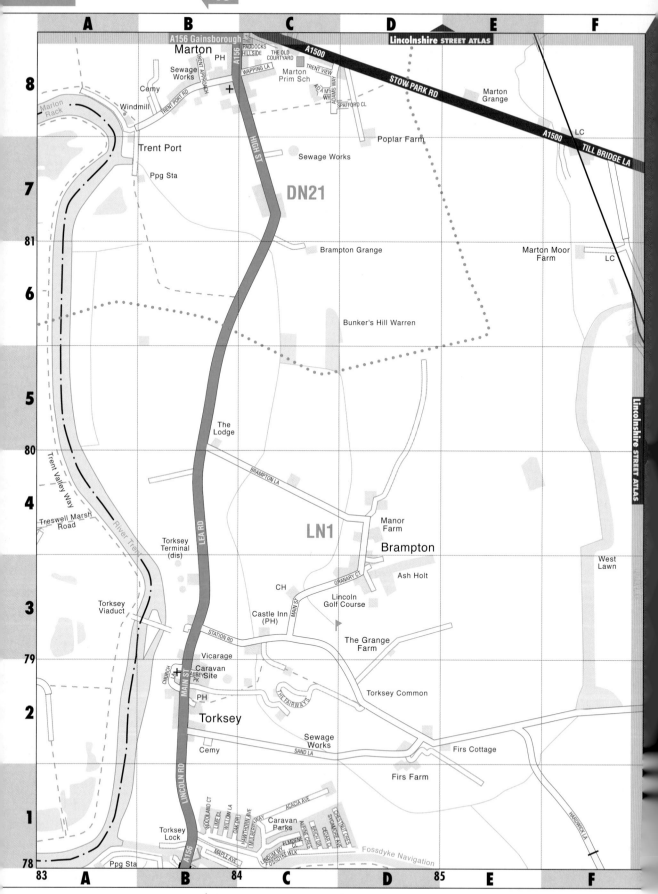

A156 Gainsborough

Marton

A1500

STOW PARK RD

A1500

TILL BRIDGE LA

THE PADDOCKS
HILLSIDE
THE OLD
COURTYARD

PH

Sewage
Works

TRENT APPROACH

WAPPING LA

TRENT VIEW

Marton
Prim Sch

ADA'S WY

SWAN WY

Marton
Grange

Cemy

TRENT PORT RD

SPAFFORD CL

LC

Windmill

Marton Rack

Trent Port

HIGH ST

DN21

Poplar Farm

Sewage Works

Ppg Sta

Marton Moor
Farm

Brampton Grange

LC

Bunker's Hill Warren

Lincolnshire STREET ATLAS

The
Lodge

Trent Valley Way

River Trent

BRAMPTON LA

LN1

Manor
Farm

Brampton

West
Lawn

Treswell Marsh
Road

LEA RD

Torksey
Terminal
(dis)

GRANARY CT

Ash Holt

CH

Lincoln
Golf Course

Torksey
Viaduct

MAIN ST

Castle Inn
(PH)

STATION RD

The Grange
Farm

Vicarage

Caravan
Site

Torksey Common

CHURCH LA

MAIN ST

ABBEY PK

PH

THE FAIRWAYS

Firs Cottage

Cemy

Torksey

Sewage
Works

SAND LA

Firs Farm

LINCOLN RD

WOODLAND CT
LIME CL
WILLOW LA
OAK CRT
HAWTHORN AVE
MULBERRY WAY

ACACIA AVE

CHESTNUT CRES
SYCAMORE AVE
CEDAR CL
BRICK LA

HARDWICK LA

Caravan
Parks

ALPINE CRES

Torksey
Lock

A156

MAPLE AVE

LINDUM WY
ELMDENE CL
FOSSDYKE WLK

Fossdyke Navigation

Ppg Sta

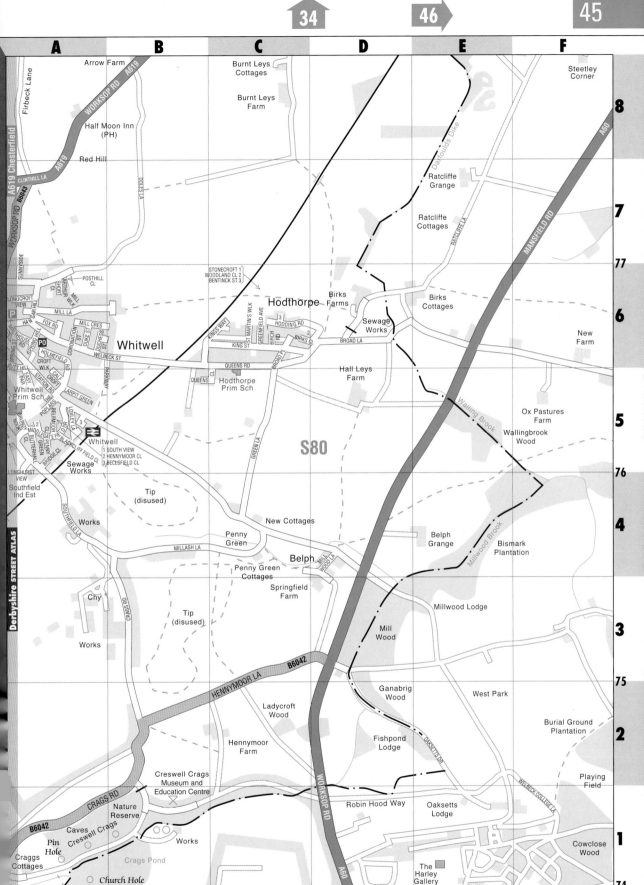

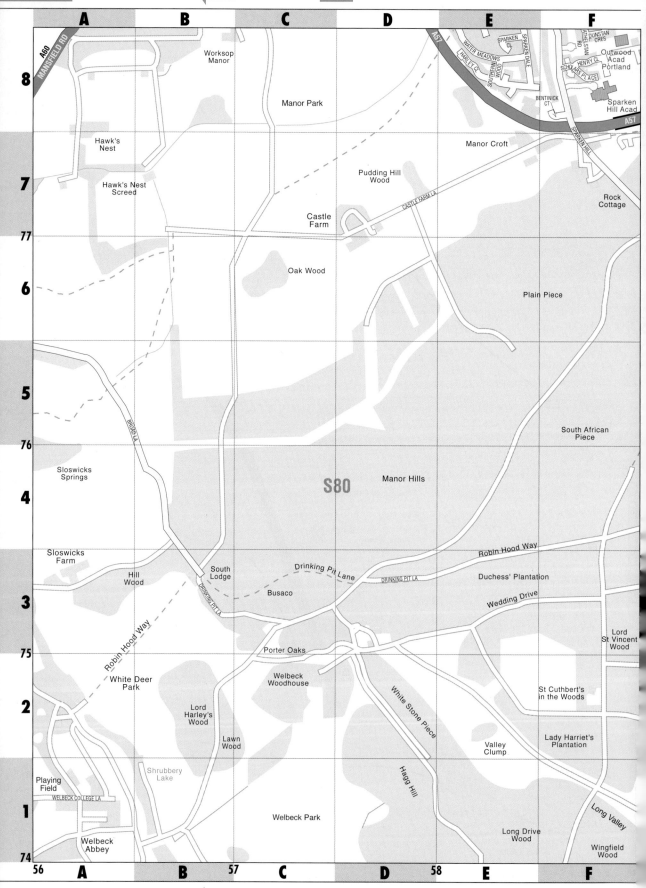

A   B   C   D   E   F

8

A60 MANSFIELD RD

Worksop Manor

Manor Park

A57

HARLEY CL

WATER MEADOWS

SPARKEN CL

SPARKEN DALE

SOUTHERN WOOD

DUNSTAN CRES

ATHELSTAN RD

SCHOLARS PLACE

HENRY CL

Outwood Acad Portland

BENTINICK CT

Sparken Hill Acad

A57

Hawk's Nest

Manor Croft

SPARKEN HILL

7

Hawk's Nest Screed

Pudding Hill Wood

CASTLE FARM LA

Rock Cottage

77

Castle Farm

Oak Wood

Plain Piece

6

BROAD LA

5

South African Piece

76

Sloswicks Springs

S80

Manor Hills

4

Sloswicks Farm

Robin Hood Way

Duchess' Plantation

Hill Wood

South Lodge

Drinking Pit Lane

DRINKING PIT LA

Wedding Drive

Busaco

3

DRINKING PIT LA

Robin Hood Way

Lord St Vincent Wood

75

Porter Oaks

White Deer Park

Welbeck Woodhouse

St Cuthbert's in the Woods

2

Lord Harley's Wood

White Stone Piece

Lady Harriet's Plantation

Lawn Wood

Valley Clump

Shrubbery Lake

Playing Field

Hagg Hill

WELBECK COLLEGE LA

Welbeck Park

Long Drive Wood

Long Valley

1

Welbeck Abbey

Wingfield Wood

74

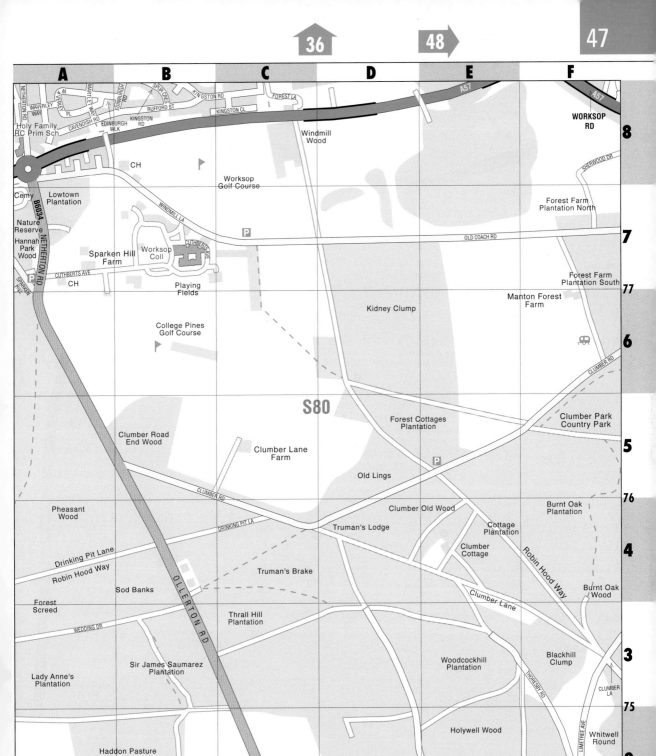

A57

WORKSOP RD

8

Holy Family RC Prim Sch

Waverley Way
Netherton Rd
Martle Way
Edinburgh Rd
Spur Cres
Kingston Rd
Forest La
Rufford St
Kingston Cl
Cavendish Rd
Edinburgh Wlk
Kingston Rd

Windmill Wood

CH

Cemy
Lowtown Plantation

Forest Farm Plantation North

B6034

Worksop Golf Course

Sherwood Dr

Nature Reserve
Hannah Park Wood

Windmill La

P

Old Coach Rd

7

Sparken Hill Farm

Worksop Coll

Cuthbert's Ave

Forest Farm Plantation South

77

Cuthberts Ave
CH

Playing Fields

Kidney Clump

Manton Forest Farm

Sparken Hill

P

College Pines Golf Course

Clumber Rd

6

Netherton Rd

S80

Forest Cottages Plantation

Clumber Park Country Park

Clumber Road End Wood

Clumber Lane Farm

5

Old Lings

P

Clumber Rd

76

Pheasant Wood

Clumber Old Wood

Burnt Oak Plantation

Drinking Pit La

Truman's Lodge

Cottage Plantation

Robin Hood Way

4

Drinking Pit Lane
Robin Hood Way

Truman's Brake

Clumber Cottage

Sod Banks

Ollerton Rd

Burnt Oak Wood

Forest Screed

Clumber Lane

Wedding Dr

Thrall Hill Plantation

Woodcockhill Plantation

Blackhill Clump

3

Lady Anne's Plantation

Sir James Saumarez Plantation

Thoresby Rd

CLUMBER LA

75

Haddon Pasture

Holywell Wood

Limetree Ave
Whitwell Round

2

Scotland Farm

New Road

Lord Howe's Plantation

Long Valley Screed

Westfield Wood

1

B6034

Long Valley Lodge

74

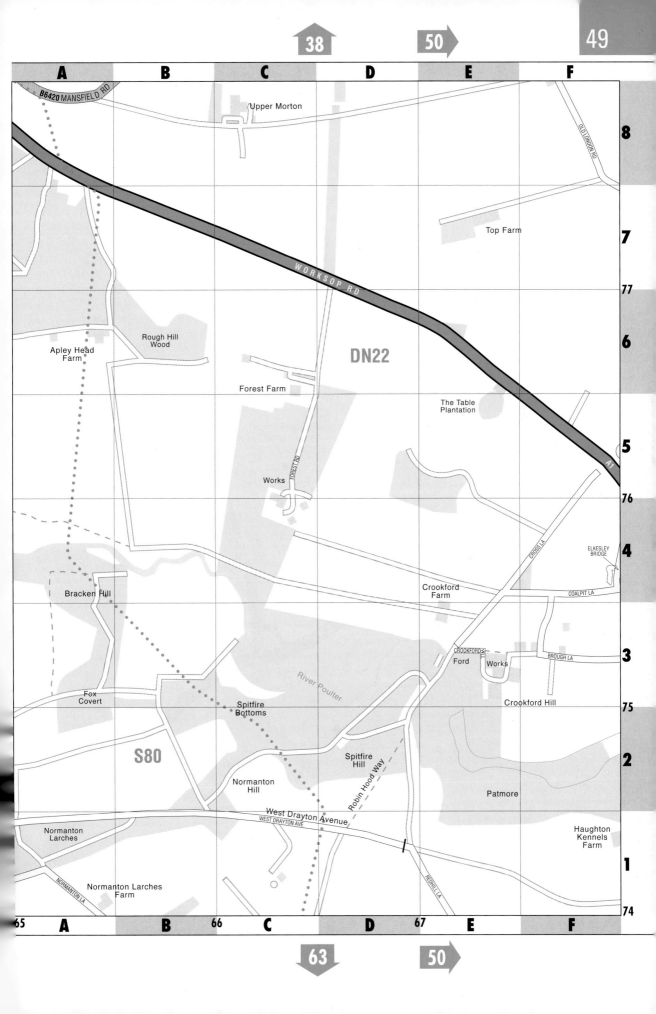

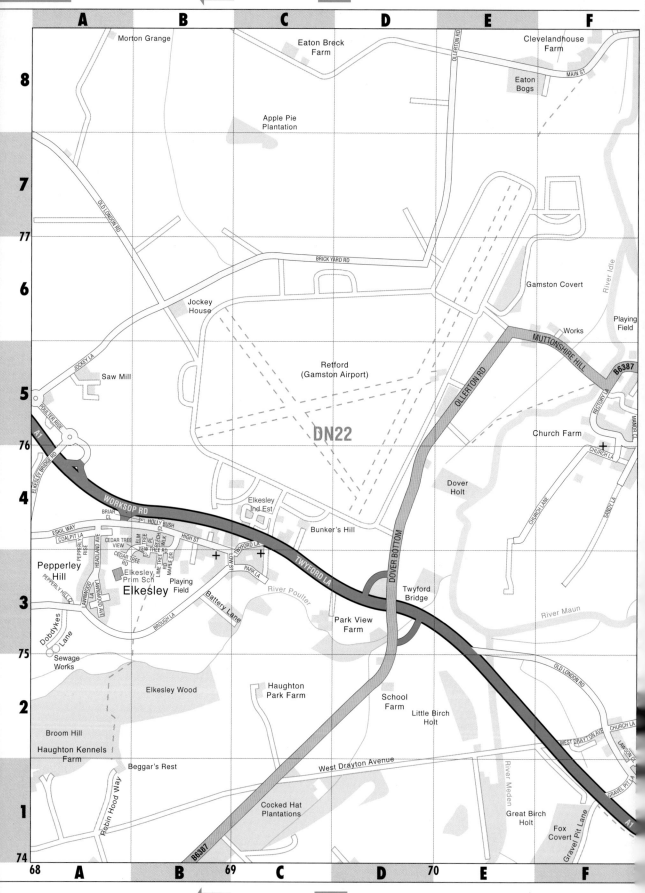

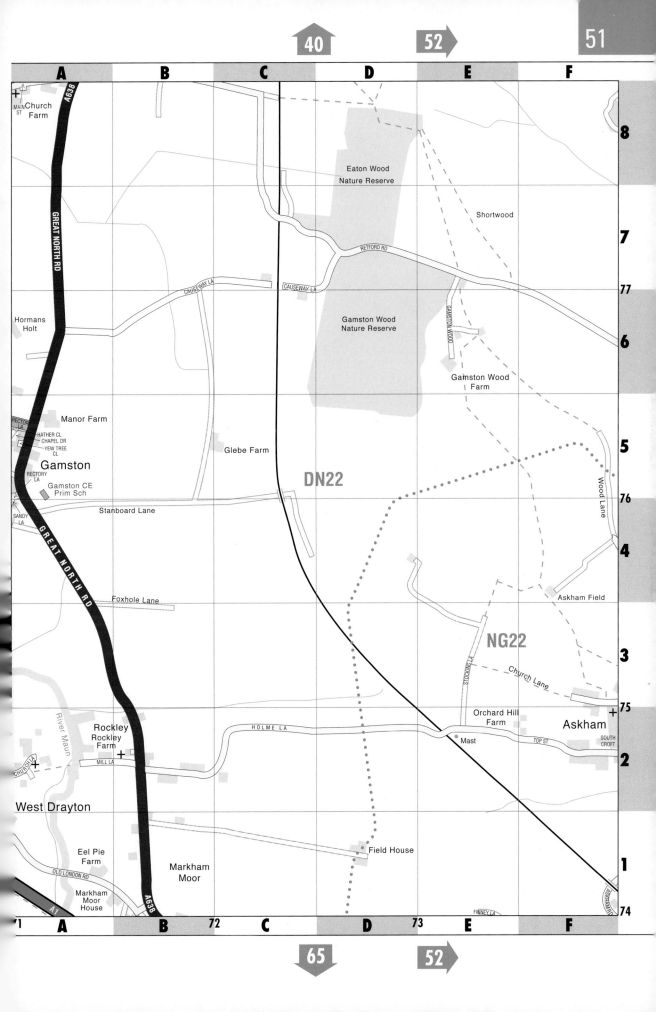

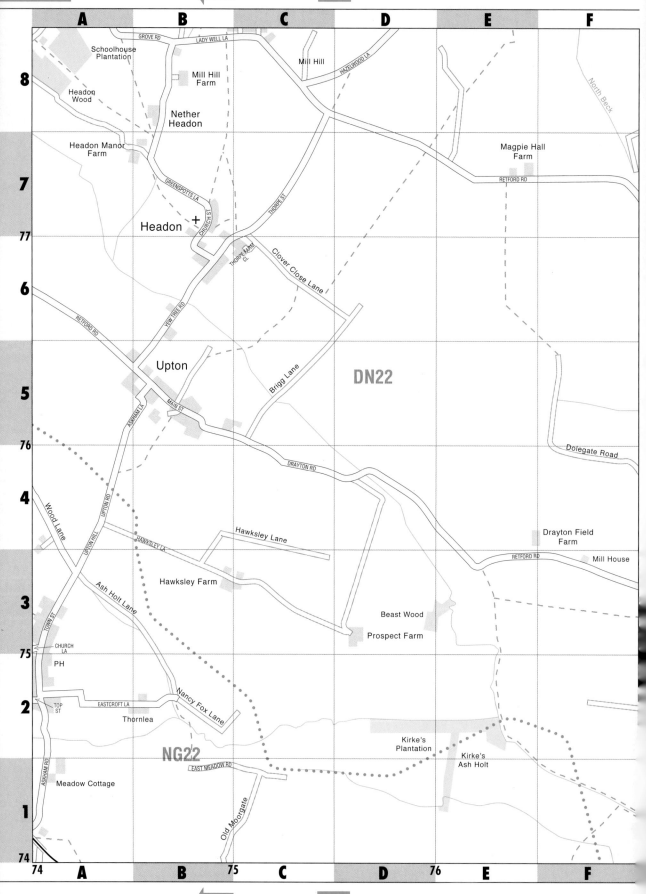

A B C D E F

8

7

77

6

5

76

4

3

75

2

1

74

Schoolhouse Plantation

GROVE RD

LADY WELL LA

Mill Hill

HAZELWOOD LA

Mill Hill Farm

Headon Wood

Nether Headon

Magpie Hall Farm

Headon Manor Farm

GREENSPOTTS LA

CHURCH ST

THORPE ST

RETFORD RD

Headon

THORPE FARM CL

Clover Close Lane

RETFORD RD

YEW TREE RD

Upton

Brigg Lane

DN22

ASKHAM LA

MAIN ST

Dolegate Road

DRAYTON RD

Wood Lane

UPTON HILL

UPTON RD

HAWKSLEY LA

Hawksley Lane

Drayton Field Farm

Ash Holt Lane

Hawksley Farm

RETFORD RD

Mill House

TOWN ST

Beast Wood

Prospect Farm

CHURCH LA

PH

Nancy Fox Lane

EASTCROFT LA

TOP ST

Thornlea

Kirke's Plantation

Kirke's Ash Holt

NG22

ASKHAM RD

EAST MEADOW RD

Meadow Cottage

Old Moorgate

North Beck

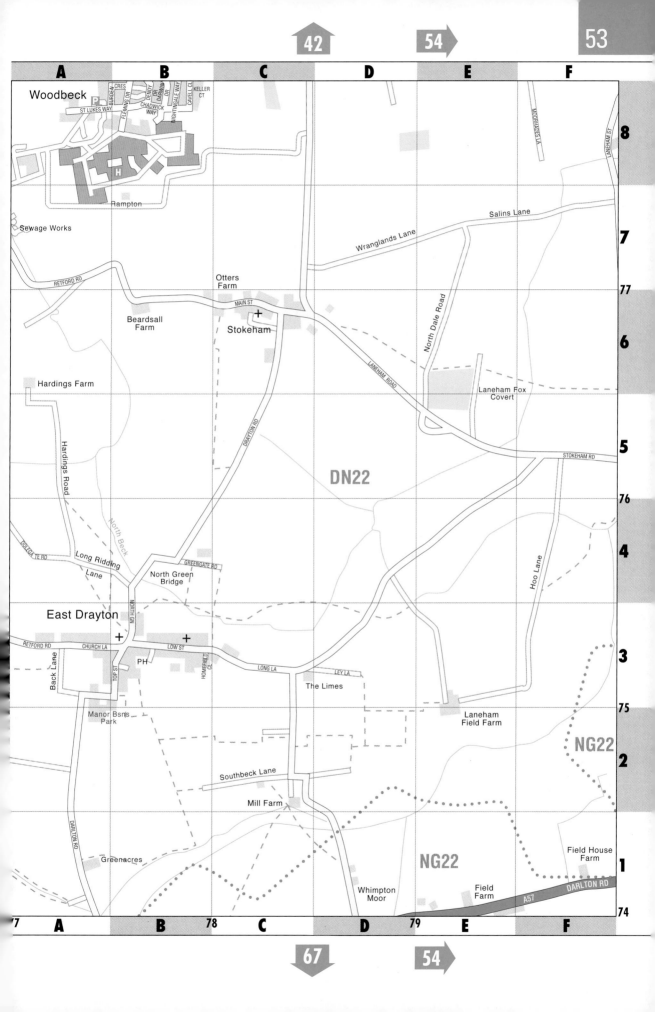

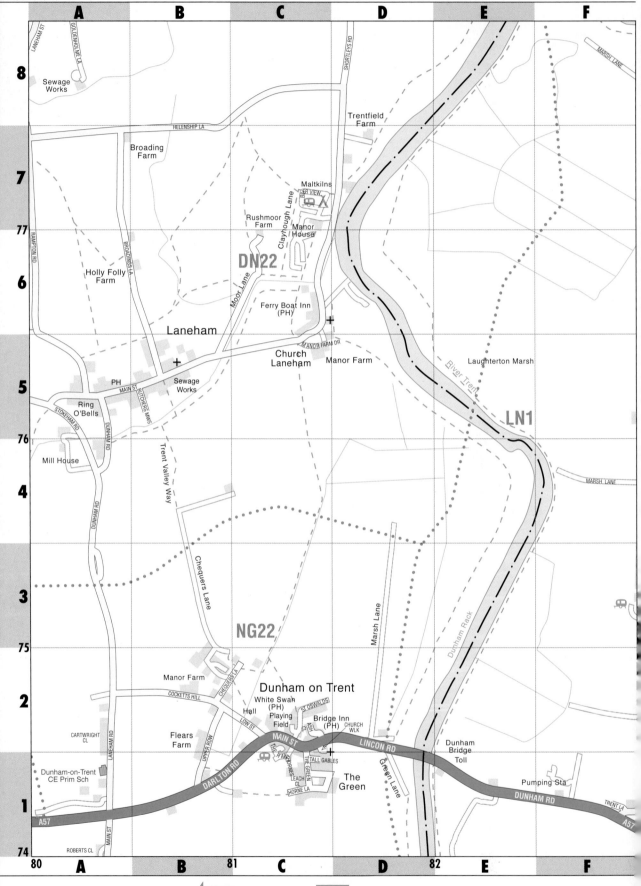

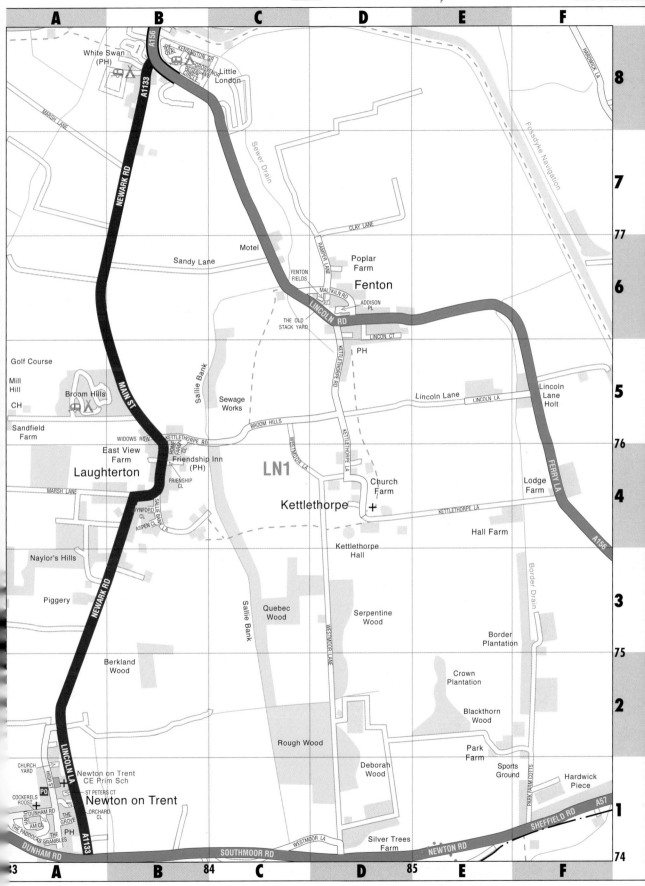

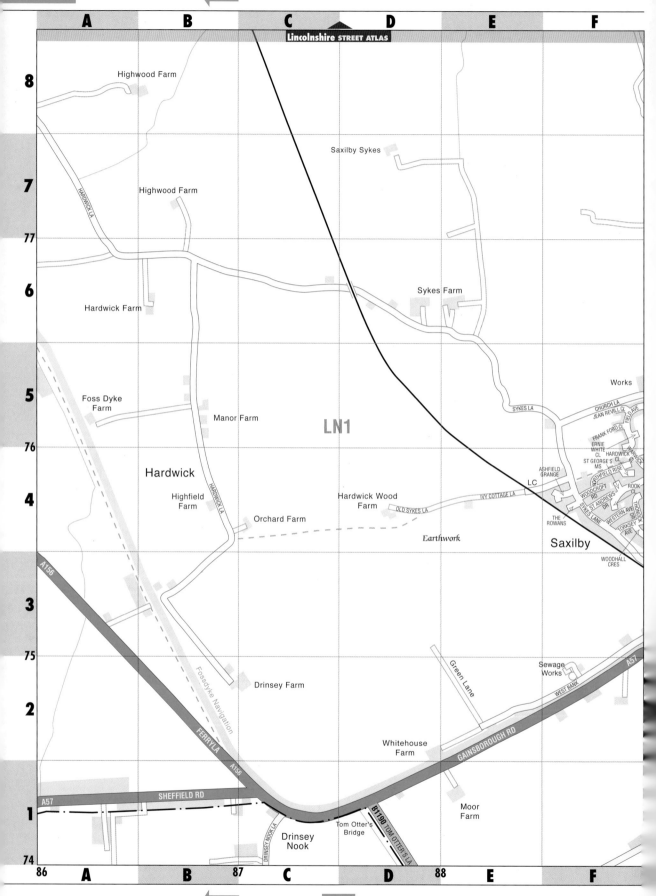

Lincolnshire STREET ATLAS

A **B** **C** **D** **E** **F**

8

Highwood Farm

Saxilby Sykes

7

Highwood Farm

77

Sykes Farm

6

Hardwick Farm

Works

5

Foss Dyke Farm

Manor Farm

LN1

SYKES LA

CHURCH LA
JEAN REVILL CL
FIELD AVE

76

FRANK FORD CL
ERNIE WHITE CL
ST GEORGE'S MS
HARDWICK CL

Hardwick

ASHFIELD GRANGE
ASHFIELD RISE
SHEFFIELD RISE
WOODCROFT RD

4

Highfield Farm

Hardwick Wood Farm

IVY COTTAGE LA

LC

ST ANDREWS DR
ROOK CL

Orchard Farm

OLD SYKES LA

THE ROWANS
SYKES LANE
WESTERN AVE
CHADWICK
TORKSEY AVE

Earthwork

Saxilby

WOODHALL CRES

3

A156

75

Green Lane

Sewage Works

WEST BANK

A57

2

Drinsey Farm

Fossdyke Navigation

Whitehouse Farm

GAINSBOROUGH RD

FERRYLA
A156

SHEFFIELD RD

A57

1

Moor Farm

B1190 TOM OTTER'S LA

DRINSEY NOOK LA

Drinsey Nook

Tom Otter's Bridge

74

86 **A** **B** 87 **C** **D** 88 **E** **F**

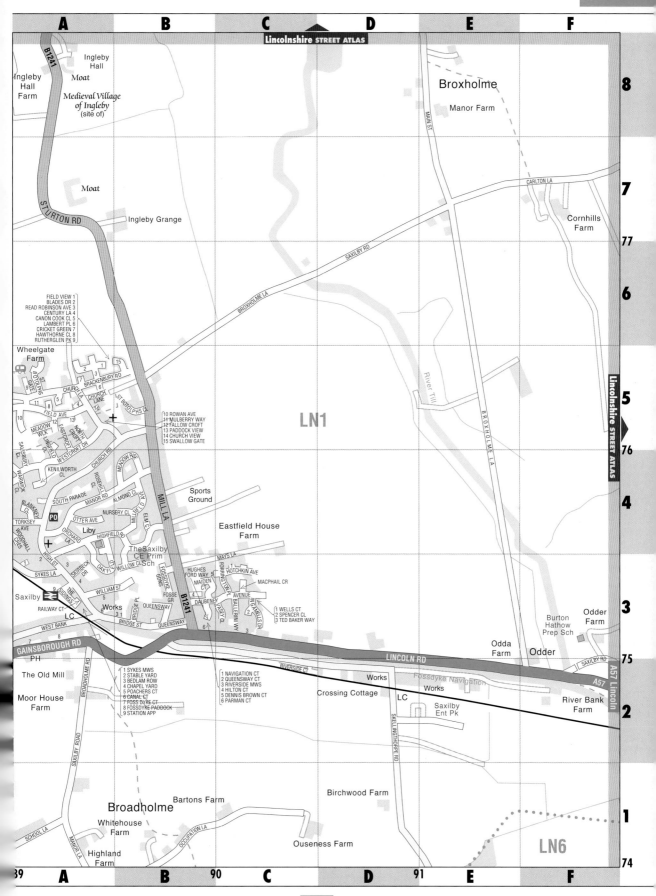

Broxholme

Manor Farm

Ingleby Hall

Ingleby Hall Farm

Moat

Medieval Village of Ingleby (site of)

Moat

Ingleby Grange

STURTON RD

B1241

CARLTON LA

Cornhills Farm

SAXILBY RD

BROXHOLME LA

FIELD VIEW 1
BLADES DR 2
READ ROBINSON AVE 3
CENTURY LA 4
CANON COOK CL 5
LAMBERT PL 6
CRICKET GREEN 7
HAWTHORNE CL 8
RUTHERGLEN PK 9

Wheelgate Farm

BRACKENBURY RD

CHURCH LANE

ST BOTOLPHS CL

10 ROWAN AVE
11 MULBERRY WAY
12 FALLOW CROFT
13 PADDOCK VIEW
14 CHURCH VIEW
15 SWALLOW GATE

LN1

River Till

BROXHOLME LA

Lincolnshire STREET ATLAS

MEADOW WLK
FIELD AVE
SALISBURY CL
WARWICK CL
BLANKNEY CL
TORKSEY AVE
WOODHALL CRES
KENILWORTH CL
SOUTH PARADE
ROSEHILL CT
MANOR RD
MEADOW RISE
ALMOND CL
NURSERY CL
ELM CL
ST EDE LA AVE
MILL LA

Sports Ground

Eastfield House Farm

Liby
ORCHARD LA
HIGHFIELD RD
OTTER AVE
PO

TheSaxilby CE Prim Sch

MAYS LA

HUGHES FORD WAY
FORRINGTON PL
HOTCHKIN AVE
MACPHAIL CR
MAIDEN CT
FOSSDYKE GDNS
FOSSE GR
DALIBENEY
VIXSEY CL
BALLERINI WY
INGRAMS DR
AVENUE

1 WELLS CT
2 SPENCER CL
3 TED BAKER WAY

HIGH ST
SYKES LA
SKIRBECK DR
OAK FI
WILLOW CL
WILLIAM ST
BRIDGE PL
QUEENSWAY
BRIDGE ST
QUEENSWAY
B1241

Saxilby
Railway CT
LC
WEST BANK

Works

1 SYKES MWS
2 STABLE YARD
3 BEDLAM ROW
4 CHAPEL YARD
5 POACHERS CT
6 CANAL CT
7 FOSS DYKE CT
8 FOSSDYKE PADDOCK
9 STATION APP

1 NAVIGATION CT
2 QUEENSWAY CT
3 RIVERSIDE MWS
4 HILTON CT
5 DENNIS BROWN CT
6 PARMAN CT

RIVERSIDE CT

Works

Fossdyke Navigation

Works

LC

Saxilby Ent Pk

Burton Hathow Prep Sch

Odda Farm

Odder

Odder Farm

SAXILBY RD

A57 Lincoln

LINCOLN RD

GAINSBOROUGH RD

PH

The Old Mill

Moor House Farm

BROADHOLME RD

SAXILBY ROAD

River Bank Farm

SKELLINGTHORPE RD

Crossing Cottage

Birchwood Farm

Broadholme

Bartons Farm

Whitehouse Farm

OCCUPATION LA

SCHOOL LA

MANOR LA

Highland Farm

Ouseness Farm

LN6

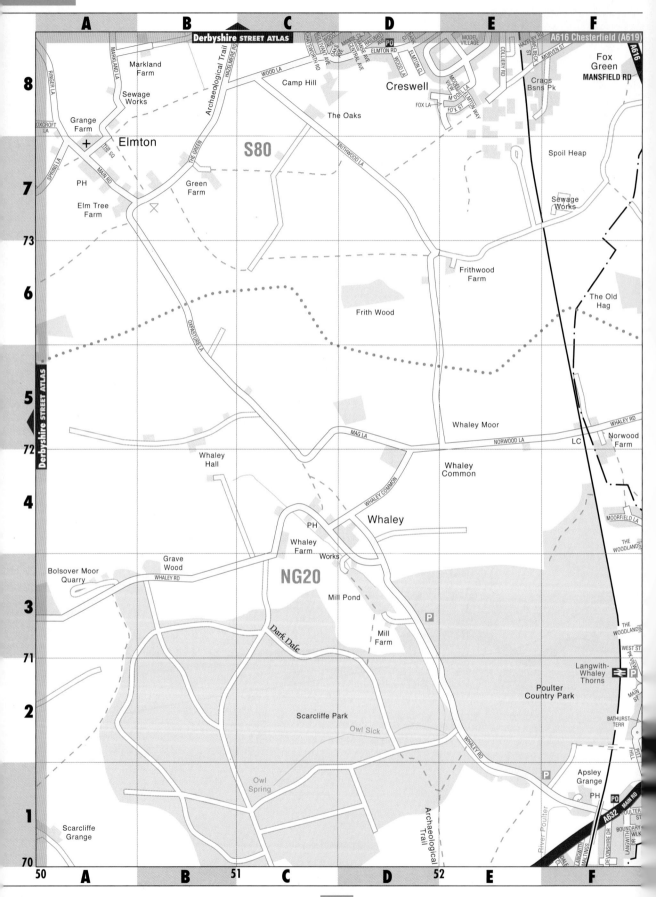

A616 Chesterfield (A619)

A B C D E F

8
Markland Farm
Sewage Works
Camp Hill
Creswell
Fox Green
MANSFIELD RD
Crags Bsns Pk
MODEL VILLAGE

Grange Farm
Elmton
S80
The Oaks
FOX LA
Spoil Heap

7
PH
Elm Tree Farm
Green Farm
Sewage Works

73
Frithwood Farm

6
Frith Wood
The Old Hag

5
Whaley Moor
WHALEY RD
Norwood Farm

72
MAG LA
NORWOOD LA
LC

Whaley Hall
Whaley Common

4
PH
Whaley
MOORFIELD LA
THE WOODLANDS

Grave Wood
Bolsover Moor Quarry
Whaley Farm
Works
NG20
WHALEY RD

3
Mill Pond
P
THE WOODLANDS

Dark Dale
Mill Farm
WEST ST

71
Langwith-Whaley Thorns
Poulter Country Park

2
Scarcliffe Park
Owl Sick
BATHURST TERR

Owl Spring
P
Apsley Grange
PH PO

1
A632

Scarcliffe Grange
Archaeological Trail
River Poulter

70
50 A 51 B C 52 D E F

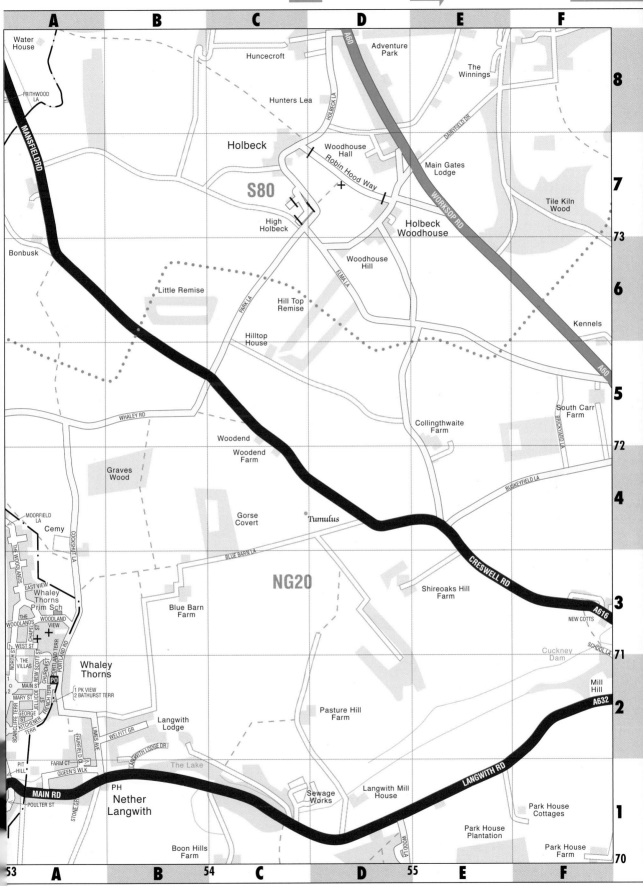

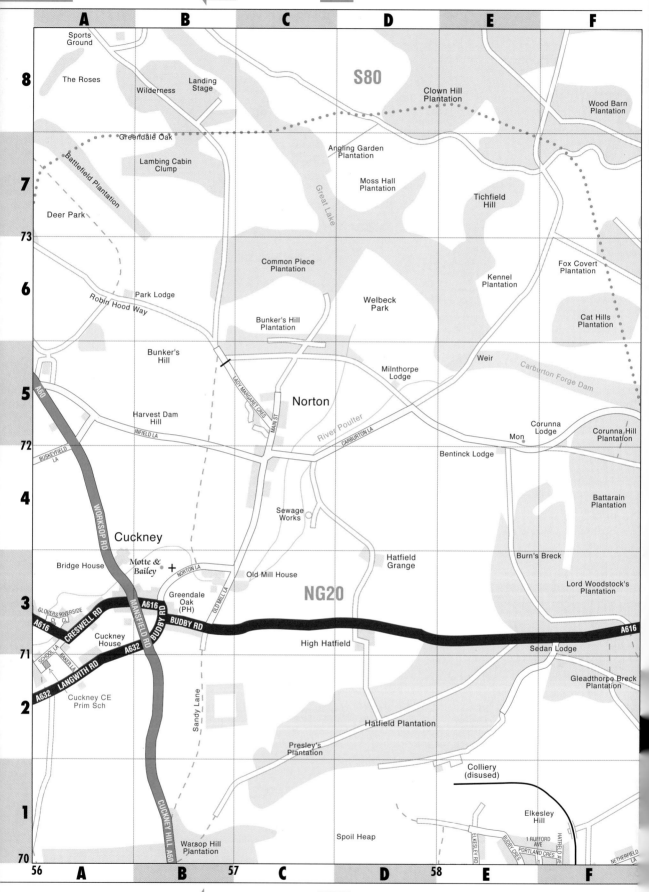

8

The Roses

Sports
Ground

Wilderness

Landing
Stage

S80

Clown Hill
Plantation

Wood Barn
Plantation

Greendale Oak

7

Battlefield Plantation

Lambing Cabin
Clump

Angling Garden
Plantation

Moss Hall
Plantation

Tichfield
Hill

73

Deer Park

6

Common Piece
Plantation

Kennel
Plantation

Fox Covert
Plantation

Park Lodge

Robin Hood Way

Welbeck
Park

Cat Hills
Plantation

Bunker's Hill
Plantation

5

Bunker's
Hill

Norton

Milnthorpe
Lodge

Weir

Carburton Forge Dam

LADY MARGARET CRES

MAIN ST

Harvest Dam
Hill

A60

72

INFIELD LA

River Poulter

CARBURTON LA

Corunna
Lodge

Corunna Hill
Plantation

BUSKEYFIELD
LA

Mon

Bentinck Lodge

4

WORKSOP RD

Battarain
Plantation

Cuckney

Sewage
Works

Hatfield
Grange

Burn's Breck

Bridge House

Motte &
Bailey

+

NORTON LA

OLD MILL LA

Old Mill House

NG20

Lord Woodstock's
Plantation

3

GLOVERS RIVERSIDE
CL   CL

A616

CRESWELL RD

MANSFIELD RD

BUDBY RD

Greendale
Oak
(PH)

BUDBY RD

A616

A616

SCHOOL LA

BAKER LA

A632

Cuckney
House

A632

High Hatfield

Sedan Lodge

71

LANGWITH RD

A632

Cuckney CE
Prim Sch

Sandy Lane

Gleadthorpe Breck
Plantation

2

Hatfield Plantation

Presley's
Plantation

Colliery
(disused)

Elkesley
Hill

1

CUCKNEY HILL A60

Warsop Hill
Plantation

Spoil Heap

ELKESLEY RD

BUDBY CRES

1 RUFFORD
AVE

PORTLAND CRES

HATFIELD AVE

NETHERFIELD LA

70

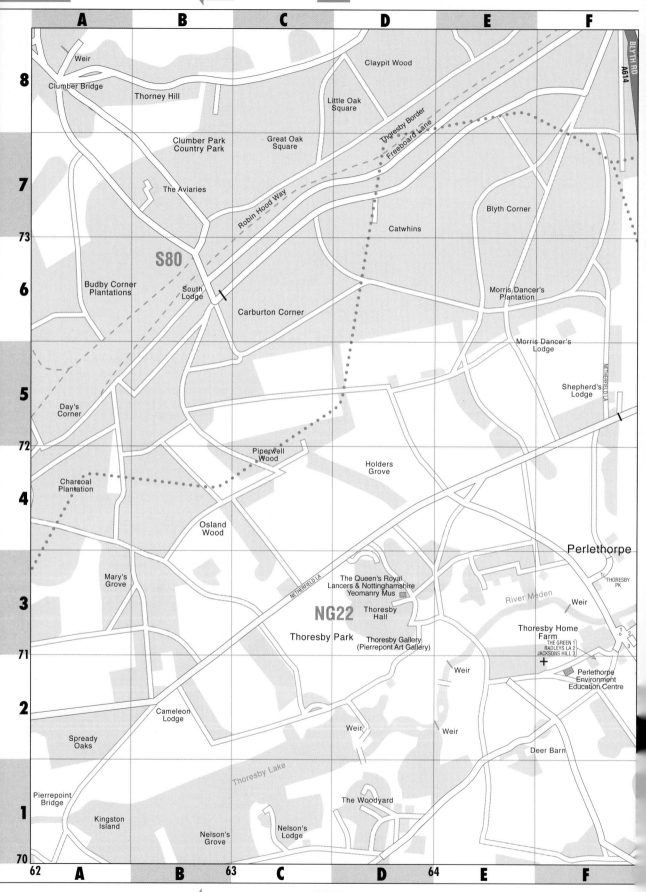

BLYTH RD

A614

8

Weir

Clumber Bridge

Thorney Hill

Claypit Wood

Little Oak
Square

Clumber Park
Country Park

Great Oak
Square

Thoresby Border

Freeboard Lane

7

The Aviaries

Robin Hood Way

Blyth Corner

73

Catwhins

S80

6

Budby Corner
Plantations

South
Lodge

Carburton Corner

Morris Dancer's
Plantation

Morris Dancer's
Lodge

NETHERFIELD LA

5

Day's
Corner

Shepherd's
Lodge

72

Piperwell
Wood

Holders
Grove

4

Charcoal
Plantation

Osland
Wood

Perlethorpe

THORESBY
PK

3

Mary's
Grove

River Meden

Weir

NG22

The Queen's Royal
Lancers & Nottinghamshire
Yeomanry Mus

Thoresby Home
Farm

THE GREEN 1
RADLEYS LA 2
JACKSONS HILL 3

Thoresby Park

Thoresby
Hall

Thoresby Gallery
(Pierrepont Art Gallery)

Perlethorpe
Environment
Education Centre

71

Weir

2

Cameleon
Lodge

Weir

Weir

Spready
Oaks

Deer Barn

Thoresby Lake

1

Pierrepoint
Bridge

Kingston
Island

The Woodyard

Nelson's
Grove

Nelson's
Lodge

70

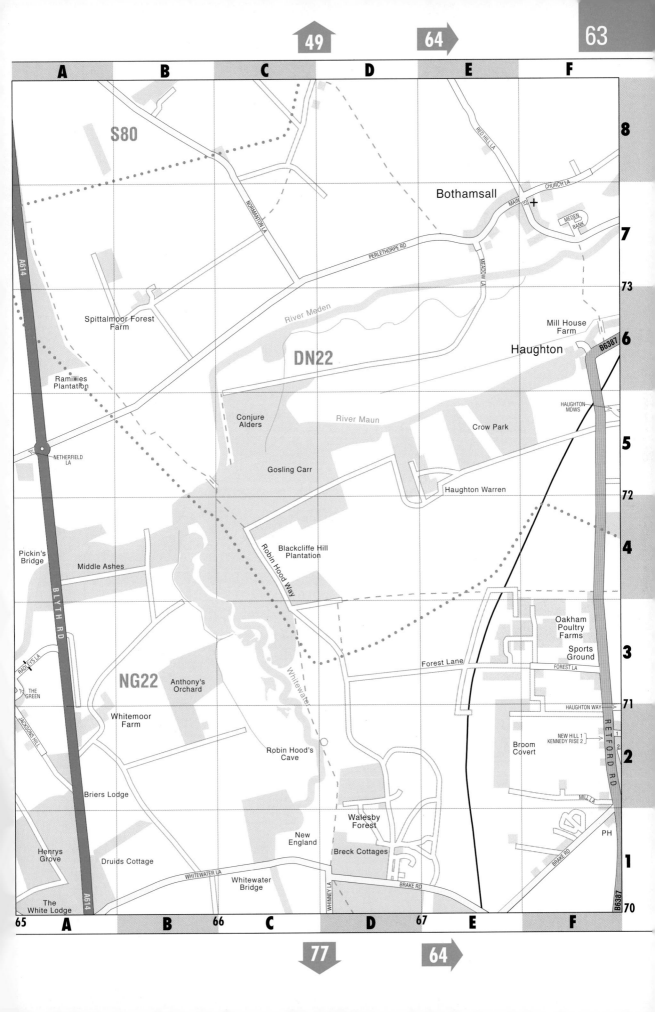

A B C D E F

8

S80

Bothamsall

RED HILL LA

CHURCH LA

MAIN ST

MEDEN BANK

7

73

NORMANTON LA

PERLETHORPE RD

River Meden

MEADOW LA

Spittalmoor Forest Farm

Mill House Farm

DN22

Haughton

B6387

6

Ramillies Plantation

Conjure Alders

River Maun

HAUGHTON MDWS

Crow Park

5

NETHERFIELD LA

Gosling Carr

Haughton Warren

72

73

Pickin's Bridge

Blackcliffe Hill Plantation

Robin Hood Way

4

Middle Ashes

BLYTH RD

Oakham Poultry Farms

3

RADLEYS LA

THE GREEN

NG22

Anthony's Orchard

Forest Lane

FOREST LA

Sports Ground

HAUGHTON WAY

71

JACKSONS HILL

Whitemoor Farm

Whitewater

Robin Hood's Cave

Broom Covert

NEW HILL 1
KENNEDY RISE 2

RETFORD RD

1
2

2

Briers Lodge

MILL LA

Henrys Grove

Druids Cottage

New England

Walesby Forest

Breck Cottages

BRAKE RD

PH

1

The White Lodge

A614

WHITEWATER LA

Whitewater Bridge

WHINNEY LA

BRAKE RD

B6387

70

65 A 66 B C 66 D 67 E F

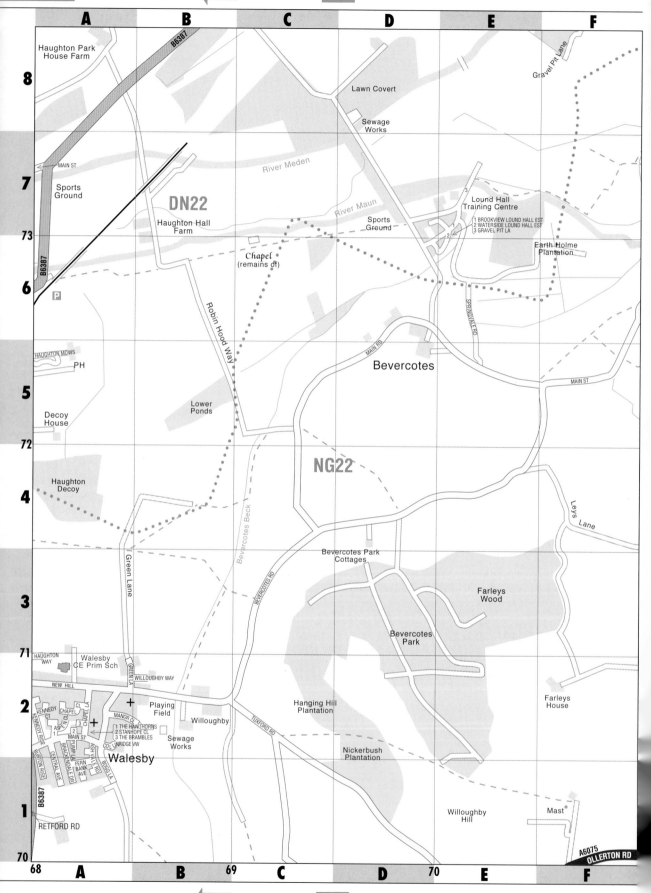

Haughton Park
House Farm

Sports
Ground

MAIN ST

DN22

Haughton Hall
Farm

B6387

P

Haughton MDWS

PH

Decoy
House

Haughton
Decoy

Green Lane

Robin Hood Way

Chapel
(remains of)

Lower
Ponds

River Meden

River Maun

Lawn Covert

Sewage
Works

Sports
Ground

Lound Hall
Training Centre

1 BROOKVIEW LOUND HALL EST
2 WATERSIDE LOUND HALL EST
3 GRAVEL PIT LA

Gravel Pit Lane

Earth Holme
Plantation

SPRINGVALE RD

Bevercotes

MAIN RD

MAIN ST

NG22

Bevercotes Beck

Bevercotes Park
Cottages

BEVERCOTES RD

Leys
Lane

Farleys
Wood

Bevercotes
Park

Farleys
House

HAUGHTON
WAY

Walesby
CE Prim Sch

GREEN LA

WILLOUGHBY WAY

NEW HILL

KENNEDY
CT

CHAPEL
CL

MANOR CL

Playing
Field

ASP CL

CHAPEL LA

MAIN ST

1 THE HAWTHORNS
2 STANHOPE CL
3 THE BRAMBLES

Willoughby

Sewage
Works

TUXFORD RD

Hanging Hill
Plantation

KENNEDY RISE

BRACKENDALE DR

PUMP LA

COLONRIDGE VW

FERN
BANK AVE

ASH VALE RD

BOGS LA

Walesby

BURTON RISE

CENTRAL AVE

B6387

RETFORD RD

Nickerbush
Plantation

Willoughby
Hill

Mast

A6075
OLLERTON RD

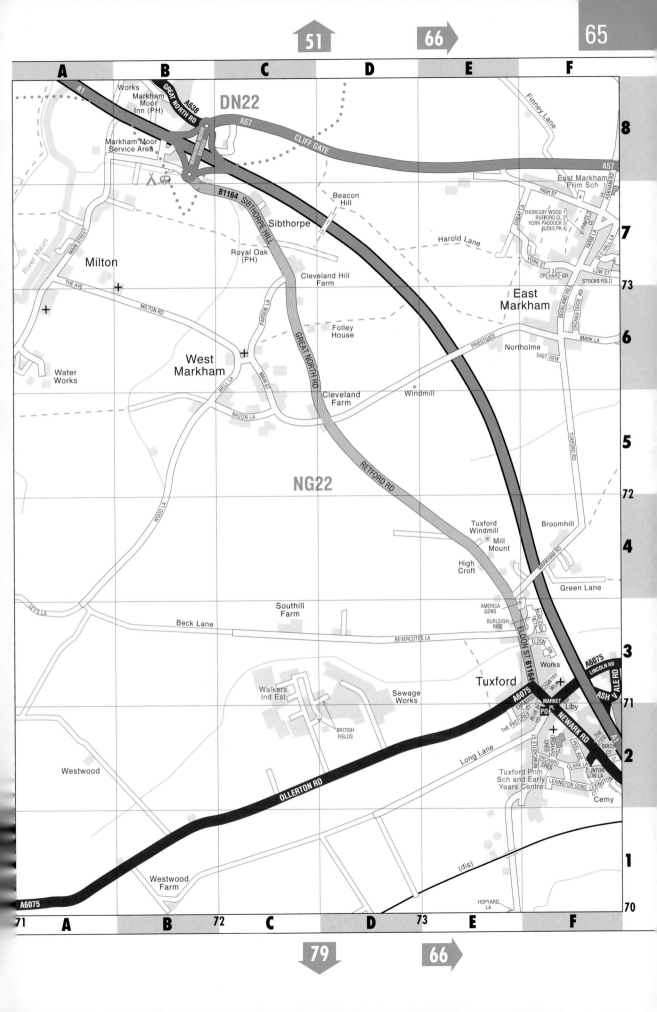

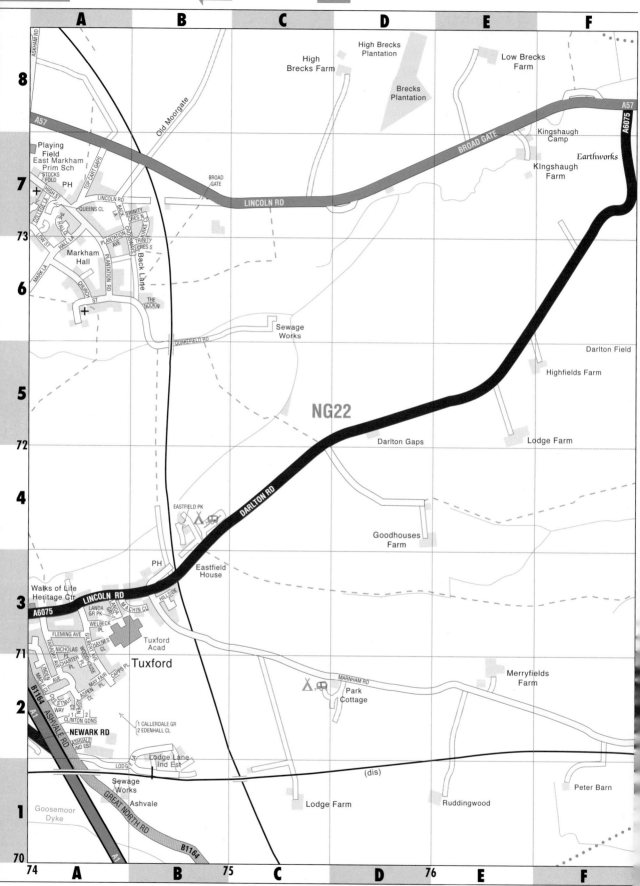

66

A B C D E F

8

ASKHAM RD

A57

High Brecks Farm

High Brecks Plantation

Brecks Plantation

Low Brecks Farm

Old Moorgate

Playing Field
East Markham Prim Sch

STOCKS FOLD

PH

HIGH ST

COLLEGE LA

THE HALL

LOW ST

HALL LA

MARK LA

BROAD GATE

A57

A6075

Kingshaugh Camp

Earthworks

Kingshaugh Farm

7

LINCOLN RD

BROAD GATE

BROAD GATE

Queens Cl

Lincoln Rd

TOP CART GAPS

BACK LA

TRINITY CRES N

TRINITY CRES S

PLANTATION AVE

PLANTATION RD

CROSSDALE

73

Markham Hall

CHURCH ST

THE NOOKIN

Back Lane

QUAKEFIELD RD

Sewage Works

Darlton Field

Highfields Farm

6

5

NG22

Darlton Gaps

Lodge Farm

72

DARLTON RD

EASTFIELD PK

Goodhouses Farm

4

PH

Eastfield House

HILLSIDE

3

Walks of Life Heritage Ctr

LINCOLN RD

A6075

LANDA GR PK

ANDA GR

MACHIN CL

WELBECK PL

FLEMING AVE

NICHOLAS PL

GILBERT AVE

HAYNES PL

WOODHOUSE

Tuxford Acad

Merryfields Farm

71

FARADAY AVE

CHARTER PL

LINDEN AVE

MARPLE CL

MAY FAIR PL

CAPPS PL

Tuxford

MARNHAM RD

Park Cottage

2

A1

ASHVALE RD

B1164

CHESTNUT WAY

ASPEN

ASPEN

CLINTON GDNS

1 CALLERDALE GR
2 EDENHALL CL

NEWARK RD

ASHVALE IND EST

LODG

Lodge Lane Ind Est

(dis)

1

Goosemoor Dyke

GREAT NORTH RD

Sewage Works

Ashvale

B1164

A1

Lodge Farm

Ruddingwood

Peter Barn

70

74 A B 75 C D 76 E F

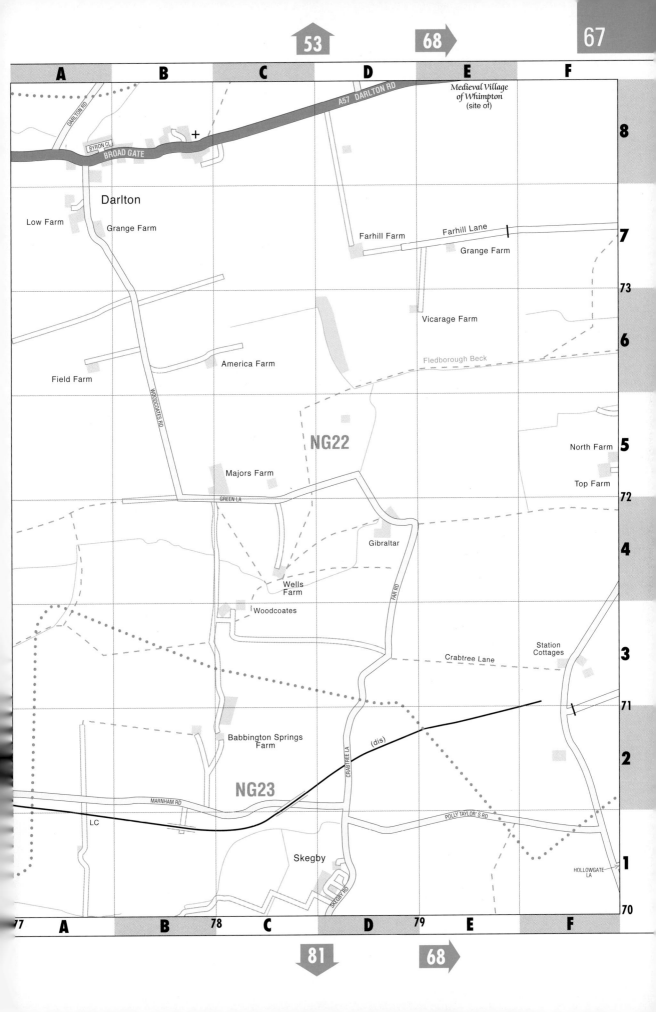

A B C D E F

8
7
73
6
5
72
4
3
71
2
1
70

A57 DARLTON RD

Medieval Village
of Whimpton
(site of)

BYRON CL
BROAD GATE

Darlton

Low Farm
Grange Farm

Farhill Farm
Farhill Lane
Grange Farm

Vicarage Farm

WOODCOATES RD

America Farm

Fledborough Beck

Field Farm

NG22

North Farm

Majors Farm
GREEN LA

Top Farm

Gibraltar

FAR RD

Wells
Farm

Woodcoates

Crabtree Lane
Station
Cottages

Babbington Springs
Farm

CRABTREE LA

(dis)

NG23

MARNHAM RD

LC

Skegby

SKEGBY RD

POLLY TAYLOR'S RD

HOLLOWGATE
LA

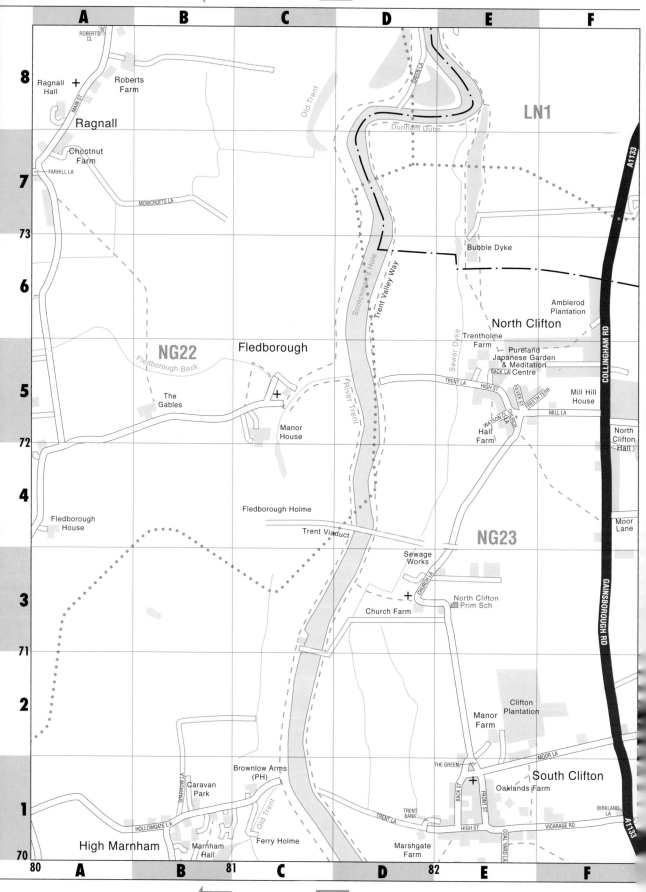

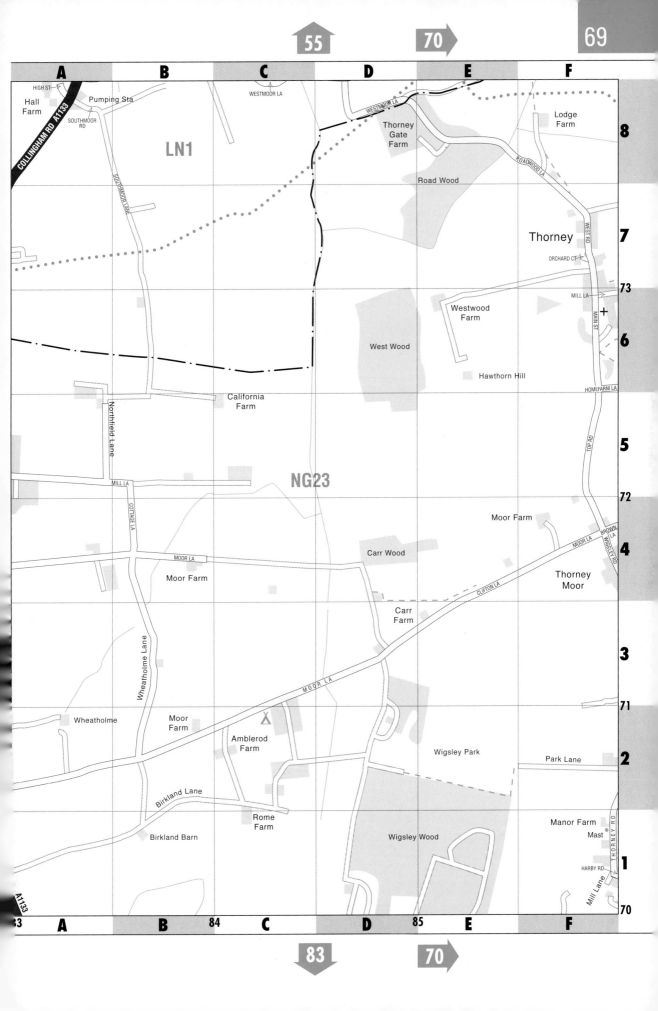

A B C D E F

69

84

8

Spring Wood

Springwood Farm

The Ring

Gibbelwood Farm

Gibbet Wood

LN1

Saxilby Moor

B1190

SAND LA

SCHOOL LA

TOM OTTER'S LA

HARBY LA

7

Glover's Wood

Gibbet Lane Cottages

DR NSEY NOOK LA

73

Crow Wood

Castle Farm

Five Lane Ends

Ox Pasture Drain

Saxilby Moor Farm

CARR LA

BROWN WOOD LA

6

Lee Nook Farm

HOMEFARM LA

Plot Farm

North Harby

B1190

Grange Farm

Half Moon Plantation

BROWN WOOD LA

5

Fir Tree Farm

Manor Farm

Wallrudding Farm

72

NG23

Thorney Brown

4

Lodge's Farm

WIGSLEY RD

Station Farm

LN6

Manterfield Farm

Clay Lane

3

STATION RD

Harby Queen Eleanor County Prim Sch

71

Plot Wood

THORNEY RD

Wigsley Drain

Ox Pasture Drain

Windmill

ENFIELD CT

Bottle and Glass (PH)

2

PK LA

MILL FIELD CL

LOW ST

HIGH ST

Harby

CROSS LA

Sewage Works

WIGSLEY RD

DARBYSHIRE CL

Moat

Wigsley

HARBY RD

Playing Field

CHURCH RD

1

NORTH SCARLE RD

HARBY LA.

Grange Farm

70

86 A B 87 C D 88 E F

OCCUPATION LA

MANOR LA

Manor Farm

Broadholme House

LN1

Broadholme Gorse

SKELLINGTHORPE RD

Lound Farm

SAXILBY RD

Western Plantation

Works

OLD WOOD

Magtree Hill

Skellingthorpe Big Wood

Old Wood

Carr Farm

B1190

Old Wood House

LN6

Woodbank Farm

Lincolnshire STREET ATLAS

LANCASTER WAY 1
BLENHEIM CL 2
STIRLING WAY 3

Old Wood Nursery

CARR LA

SAXILBY RD

Old Hag Wood

Old Hag Farm

Little Sale

Ash Lound

Skellingthorpe

OLD PITS PL

MOSSLEM RD

JERUSALEM RD

QUEENSWAY

Works

Jerusalem Farm

Birch Spring Farm

JERUSALEM

Strunch Hill

B1190 MAIN ST

Church Farm House

KENNEL LA

SMYTHSON GREEN

HALL YARD

Doddington Hall

Doddington

Top House Farm

BLACK LA

8 7 73 6 5 72 4 3 71 2 1 70

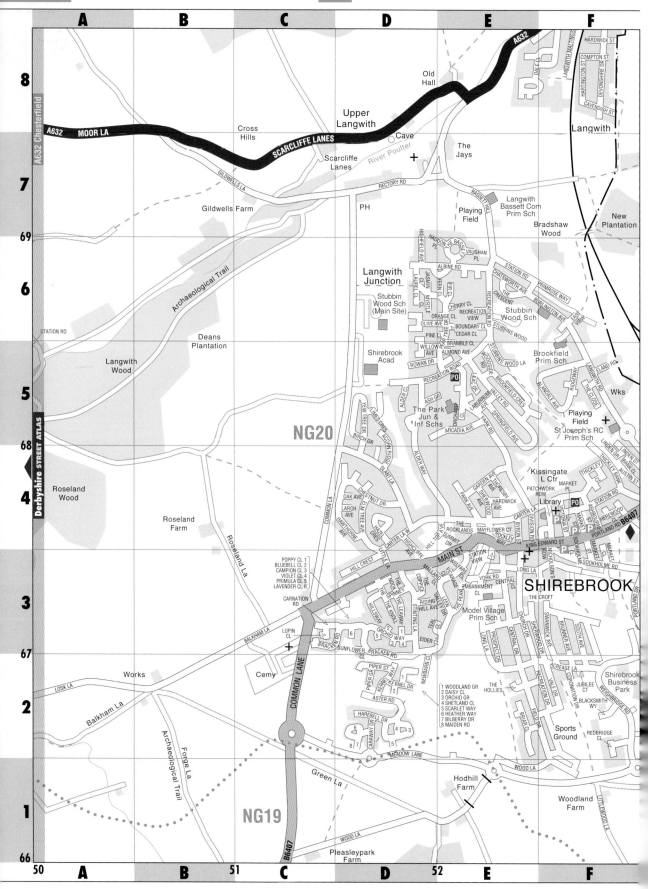

A   B   C   D   E   F

8

MOOR LA

A632

Old Hall

Upper Langwith

Cross Hills

SCARCLIFFE LANES

Scarcliffe Lanes

Cave

River Poulter

The Jays

Langwith

7

GILDWELLS LA

RECTORY RD

PH

BASSETT HILL

Playing Field

Langwith Bassett Com Prim Sch

Bradshaw Wood

New Plantation

Gildwells Farm

69

Archaeological Trail

STATION RD

Langwith Junction

Stubbin Wood Sch (Main Site)

Langwith Bassett Com Prim Sch

Stubbin Wood Sch

Brookfield Prim Sch

6

Deans Plantation

Langwith Wood

Shirebrook Acad

ROWAN DR

RECREATION ROAD

PO

Brookfield Prim Sch

Playing Field

St Joseph's RC Prim Sch

Wks

5

NG20

ASH GR

The Park Jun & Inf Schs

ORCHARD CL

Kissingate L Ctr

PATCHWORK ROW

Library

PO

P

68

Roseland Wood

COMMON LA

ALDER WAY

The Rocklands

MAYFLOWER CT

P

P

P

4

Roseland Farm

Roseland La

HAWTHORNE AVE

MAIN ST

STATION VIEW

KING EDWARD ST

SHIREBROOK

The Croft

POPPY CL 1
BLUEBELL CL 2
CAMPION CL 3
VIOLET CL 4
PRIMULA CL 5
LAVENDER CL 6

CARNATION RD

Model Village Prim Sch

3

BALKHAM LA

LUPIN CL

ORCHID WAY

BRACKEN RD

EIDER CL

Long La

Sports Ground

67

Works

COMMON LANE

Cemy

PIPER ST

KERNEL DR

ASTER RD

1 WOODLAND GR
2 DAISY CL
3 ORCHID GR
4 SHETLAND CL
5 SCARLET WAY
6 HEATHER WAY
7 BILBERRY DR
8 MAIDEN RD

The Hollies

Shirebrook Business Park

Blacksmith Wy

REDBRIDGE CL

2

LOSK LA

Balkham La

Forge La

Archaeological Trail

HAREBELL DR

CARAWAY DR

MEADOW LANE

Hodhill Farm

Woodland Farm

1

NG19

Green La

WOOD LA

B6407

66

50   A   B   51   C   D   52   E   F

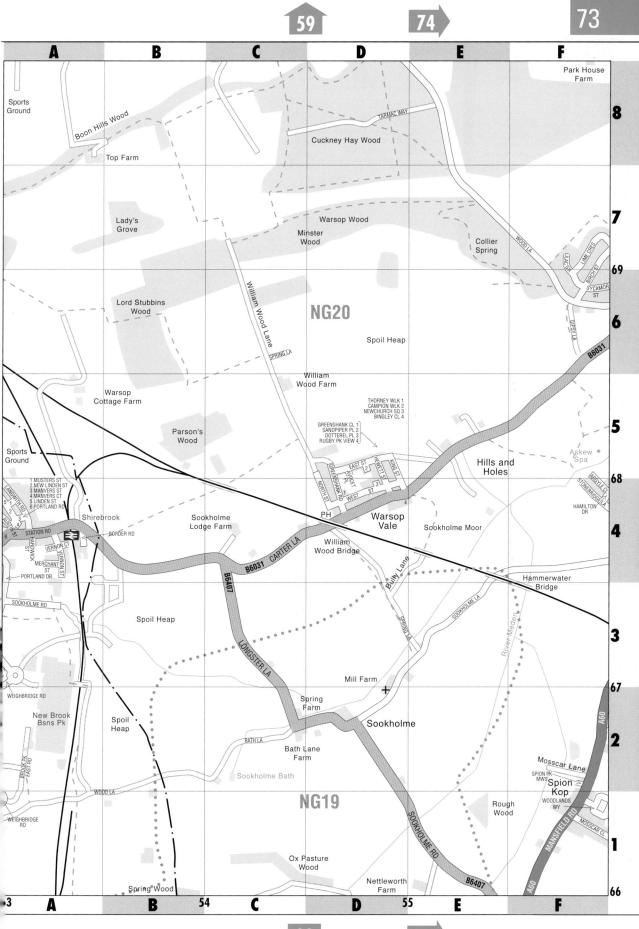

Sports Ground

Boon Hills Wood

Top Farm

Park House Farm

TARMAC WAY

Cuckney Hay Wood

Warsop Wood

Lady's Grove

Minster Wood

Collier Spring

WOOD LA

LILAC GR

LIME CRES

BIRCH ST

SYCAMOR ST

NG20

Lord Stubbins Wood

WILLIAM WOOD LANE

SPRING LA

Spoil Heap

GIPSY LA

B6031

William Wood Farm

Warsop Cottage Farm

THORNEY WLK 1
CAMPION WLK 2
NEWCHURCH SQ 3
BINGLEY CL 4

GREENSHANK CL 1
SANDPIPER PL 2
DOTTEREL PL 3
RUGBY PK VIEW 4

Parson's Wood

Sports Ground

Askew Spa

Hills and Holes

ARGYLE CL

STONEBRIDGE LA

HAMILTON DR

1 MUSTERS ST
2 NEW LINDEN ST
3 MANVERS ST
4 MANVERS CT
5 LINDEN ST
6 PORTLAND RD

LANGWITH RD

AUSTIN ST

EAST ST

AUDCET PL

HEWETT ST

KING ST

GREENSHANK RD

NORTH ST

WEST ST

Shirebrook

STATION RD

VERNON CT

VERNON ST

BORDER RD

Sookholme Lodge Farm

PH

Warsop Vale

Sookholme Moor

HARDWICK ST

MERCHANT ST

PORTLAND DR

SOOKHOLME RD

CARTER LA

B6031

William Wood Bridge

BUIN Lane

Hammerwater Bridge

River Meden

Spoil Heap

B6407

LONGSTER LA

SOOKHOLME LA

SPRING LA

WEIGHBRIDGE RD

New Brook Bsns Pk

Spoil Heap

Mill Farm

Spring Farm

Sookholme

Mosscar Lane

A60

BROOK PK EAST RD

BATH LA

Bath Lane Farm

SPION PK MWS

Spion Kop

WOODLANDS WY

MANSFIELD RD

MOSSCAR CL

WEIGHBRIDGE RD

WOOD LA

Sookholme Bath

NG19

Rough Wood

SOOKHOLME RD

Ox Pasture Wood

Spring Wood

Nettleworth Farm

B6407

A60

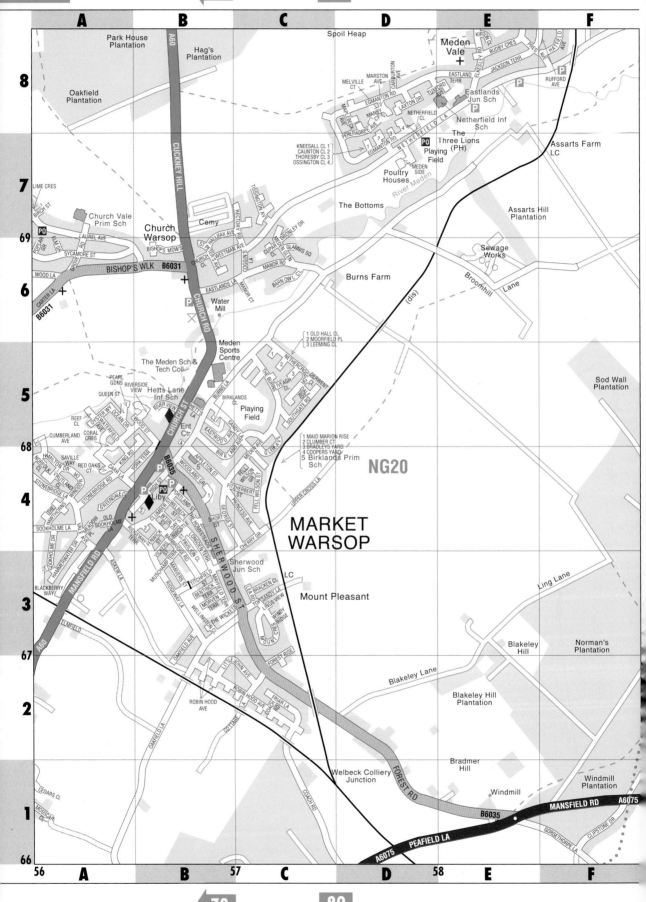

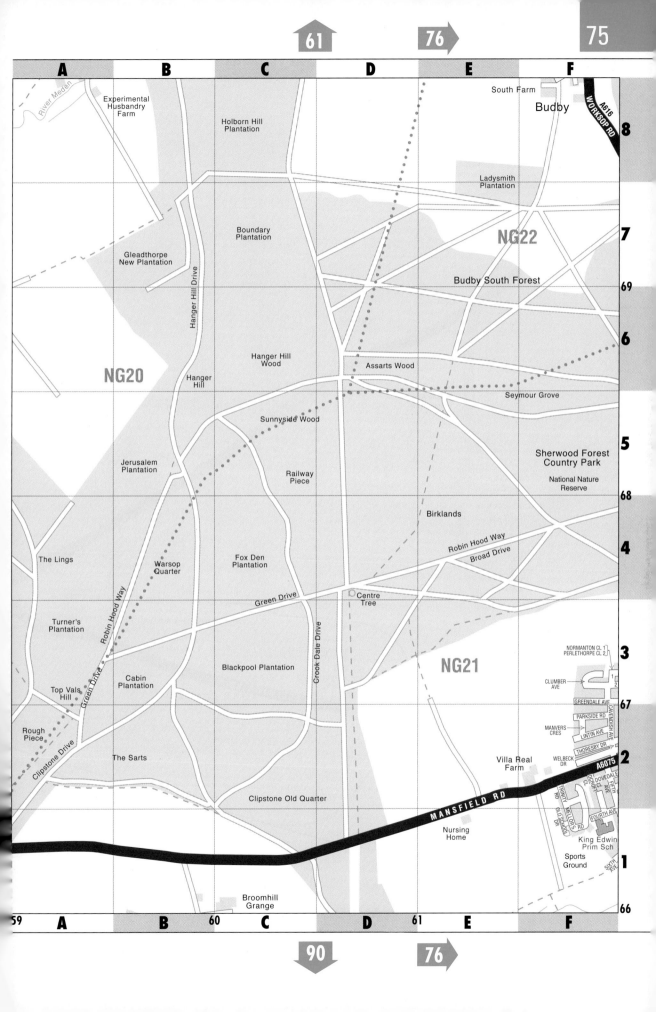

A B C D E F

River Meden

Experimental Husbandry Farm

South Farm

Budby

A616 WORKSOP RD

Holborn Hill Plantation

Ladysmith Plantation

Boundary Plantation

NG22

Gleadthorpe New Plantation

Hanger Hill Drive

Budby South Forest

Hanger Hill Wood

NG20

Assarts Wood

Hanger Hill

Seymour Grove

Sunnyside Wood

Sherwood Forest Country Park

Jerusalem Plantation

Railway Piece

National Nature Reserve

Birklands

The Lings

Fox Den Plantation

Robin Hood Way

Broad Drive

Warsop Quarter

Robin Hood Way

Green Drive

Centre Tree

Turner's Plantation

Crook Dale Drive

NG21

Top Vals Hill

Cabin Plantation

Blackpool Plantation

Green Drive

NORMANTON CL 1
PERLETHORPE CL 2

CLUMBER AVE

GREENDALE AVE

CAVENDISH AVE

PARKSIDE RD

Rough Piece

MANVERS CRES

LINTIN AVE

THORESBY DR

Clipstone Drive

The Sarts

Villa Real Farm

WELBECK DR

A6075

DOVEDALE CL

Clipstone Old Quarter

MANSFIELD RD

Nursing Home

TRINITY RD
MELLORS RD
OLD SCHOOL DR
FIFTH AVE
FOURTH AVE

King Edwin Prim Sch

Sports Ground

SIXTH AVE

Broomhill Grange

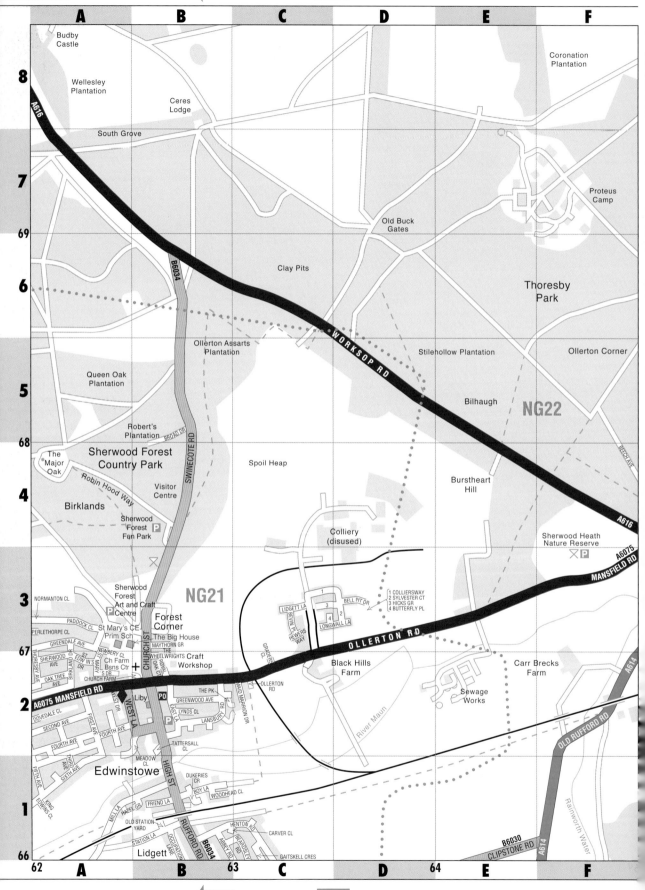

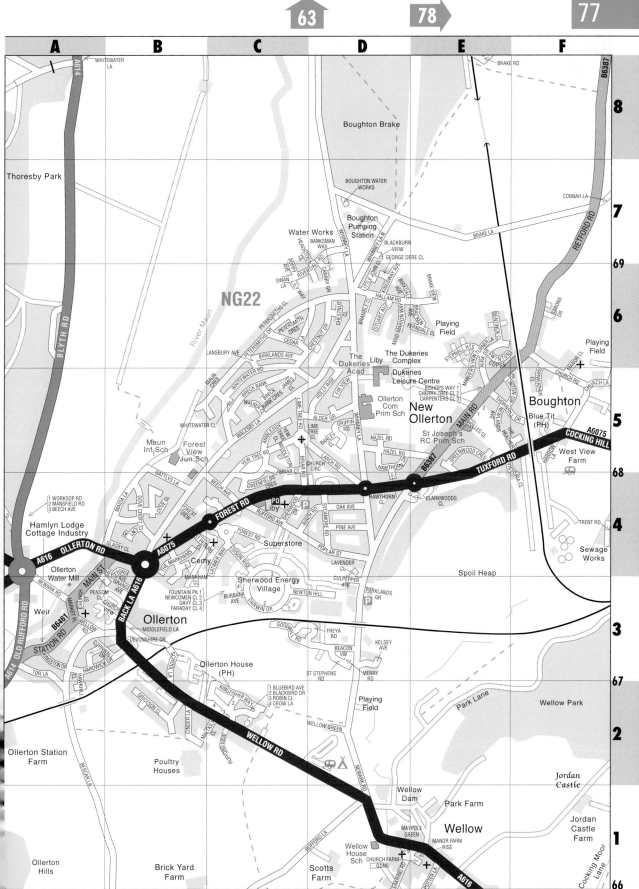

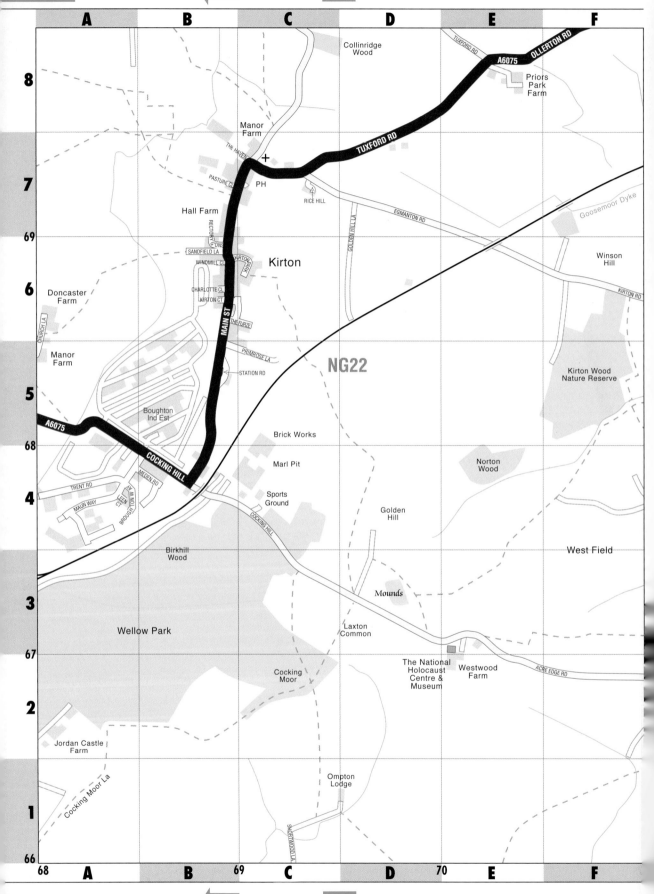

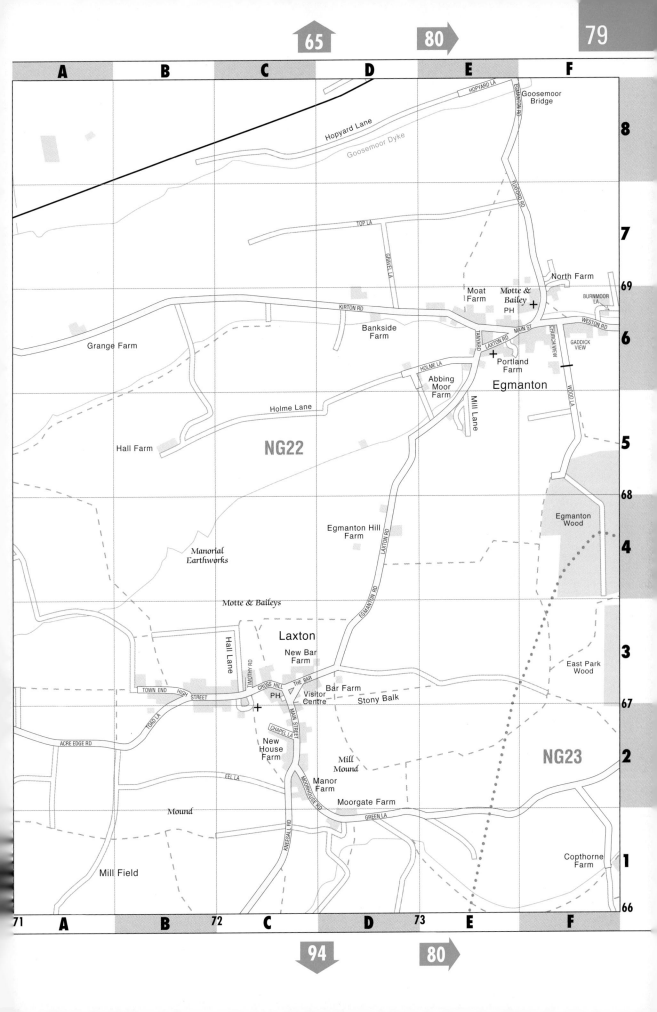

79
66

A B C D E F

8

7

69

6

NG22

5

68

4

3

67

2

NG23

1

66

74 A B 75 C D 76 E F

A1

BT164

BURNMOOR LA

Burnmoor La

Egmanton Crossing

Stone Rd End
LC

Ruddings
Cottage

NORMANTON RD

Stone Road
End Farm

Windmill
(dis)

Goosemoor Dyke

BURNMOOR LA

Scarthingmoor
Mill

GREAT NORTH RD

Scarthingmoor
House Farm

WESTON RD

Scarthingmoor
Farm

Scarthingmoor
Cottage Farm

Gipsy Lodge
Farm

Bell Farm

Lady Wood

BELL LA

HAGG LA

LADYWOOD LA

BT164

Egmanton Common
Farm

Ladywood
Farm

Egmanton
Wood

MOORHOUSE RD

WADNAL LA

A1

East
Park
Wood

Breck's
Farm

Moorhouse Beck

Aggrie House
Farm

Breck
Cottage

GREEN LA

MOORHOUSE RD
Church
Farm

Moorhouse

Thorpe
Farm

Wadnal
Plantation

Cocked Hat
Plantation

Copthorne
Farm

Brookdale
Farm

OSSINGTON RD

MOORHOUSE RD

Commonside
Plantation

North Park
Farm

A B C D E F

8

MARNHAM RD

Skegby Manor

Waterloo Farm

Hanginghill La

The Ruddings Farm

Thurber

Stonehill House

St Matthew's CE Prim Sch

GRACEFIELD LA

7

NORMANTON RD

Mount Pleasant

MILL LA

Square and Compass (Inn)

CAD LA

BELL CL

EASTGATE

Vic

CHESTNUT CT POOLES YARD

TUXFORD RD

69

HAWBUSH RD

Church Farm

HAWTHORNE LEYS

The Crown (P.H)

BROTTS LA

Trentman Lodge

6

Mount Pleasant Farm

Normanton on Trent

Vines House Farm

MANOR GR

SOUTH ST

BROTTS RD

Archway Farm

WESTON LA

SOUTH LA

NG23

Grassthorpe Beck

Border Farm

GRASSTHORPE RD

5

Manor Farm

Moor Farm

BELL LA

Moat

CHURCH WK

68

CHESTNUT CL

MAIN ST

MEADOW LA

WALNUT CL

COLLEY LA

HAYFIELD GR

Grassthorpe

Weston

Stud Farm

INGRAM LA

COPPER HILL

TOWN ST

SILVER ST

4

WADNAL LA

INGLE LA

GREAT NORTH RD

TOWN LA

Grassthorpe Lane Crossing

LC

GRASSTHORPE LA

Mill Farm

Grange Farm

3

Lodge Plantation

67

Dunstall Lodge

A1

2

Crow Park Farm

The Crest

GRASSTHORPE RD

Parry Bsns Pk

Cemy

1

BULHAM LA

Rod Holt

OLD GREAT NORTH RD

B1164

Poplar Farm

CROW PARK AVE

SNELL CL

THE MEERINGS

STERNTHORPE CL

STATION RD

OLDENGLAND GDNS

66

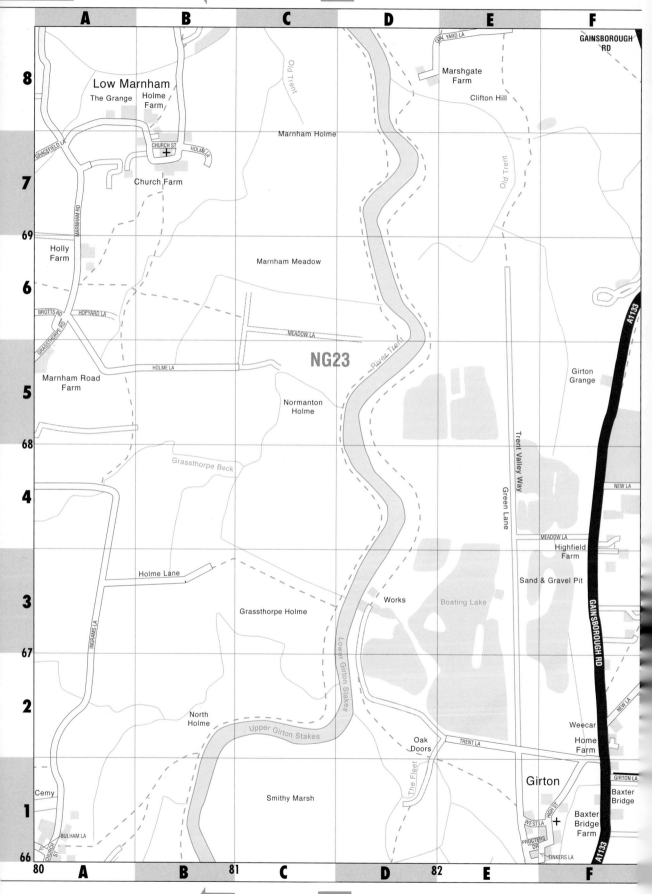

GAINSBOROUGH RD

Marshgate Farm

Clifton Hill

Low Marnham

The Grange

Holme Farm

CHURCH ST

Church Farm

Marnham Holme

Old Trent

Old Trent

GHACEFIELD LA

MARNHAM RD

HOLME LA

Holly Farm

Marnham Meadow

BROTTS RD

HOPYARD LA

GRASSTHORPE RD

MEADOW LA

NG23

River Trent

HOLME LA

Marnham Road Farm

Normanton Holme

Girton Grange

Grassthorpe Beck

Trent Valley Way

Green Lane

NEW LA

MEADOW LA

Highfield Farm

Holme Lane

Sand & Gravel Pit

Grassthorpe Holme

Works

Boating Lake

INGRAMS LA

Lower Girton Stakes

GAINSBOROUGH RD

A1133

North Holme

Upper Girton Stakes

Oak Doors

TRENT LA

NEW LA

Weecar Home Farm

GIRTON LA

The Fleet

Girton

Cemy

BULHAM LA

Smithy Marsh

WEST LA

HIGH ST

Baxter Bridge

Baxter Bridge Farm

CHURCH ST

PROCTERS DR

TINKERS LA

A1133

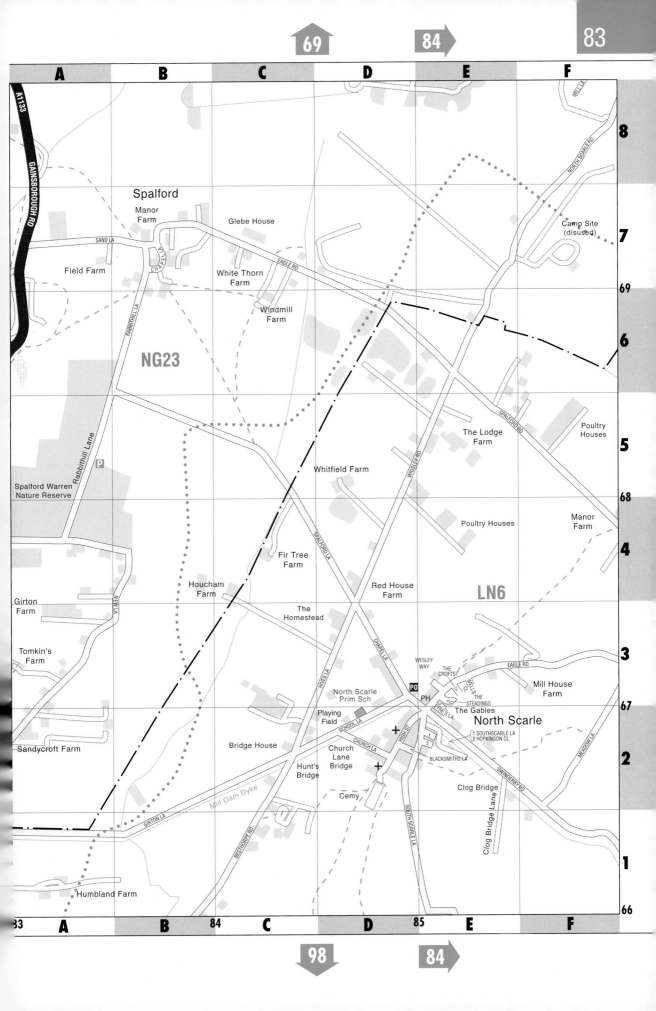

A   B   C   D   E   F

A1133

GAINSBOROUGH RD

Spalford

Manor Farm

Glebe House

SAND LA

CHAPEL LA

Field Farm

White Thorn Farm

EAGLE RD

Windmill Farm

RABBITHILL LA

NG23

Rabbithill Lane

P

Spalford Warren Nature Reserve

Camp Site (disused)

MILL LA

NORTH SCARLE RD

SPALFORD RD

The Lodge Farm

Poultry Houses

WHISBY RD

Whitfield Farm

Poultry Houses

Manor Farm

NEW LA

Girton Farm

Houcham Farm

SPALFORD LA

Fir Tree Farm

Red House Farm

LN6

Tomkin's Farm

The Homestead

CHAPEL LA

HIVES LA

WESLEY WAY

THE CROFTS

EAGLE RD

WELLS CL

THE STEADINGS

Mill House Farm

Sandycroft Farm

North Scarle Prim Sch

PO

PH

The Gables

North Scarle

EYRE'S LA

1 SOUTHSCARLE LA
2 HOPKINSON CL

SCHOOL LA

Playing Field

Bridge House

CHURCH LA

Church Lane Bridge

HIGH ST

1
2

BLACKSMITHS LA

MEADOW LA

Hunt's Bridge

SWINDERBY RD

Clog Bridge

Mill Dam Dyke

Cemy

SOUTH SCARLE LA

Clog Bridge Lane

GIRTON LA

BESTHORPE RD

Humbland Farm

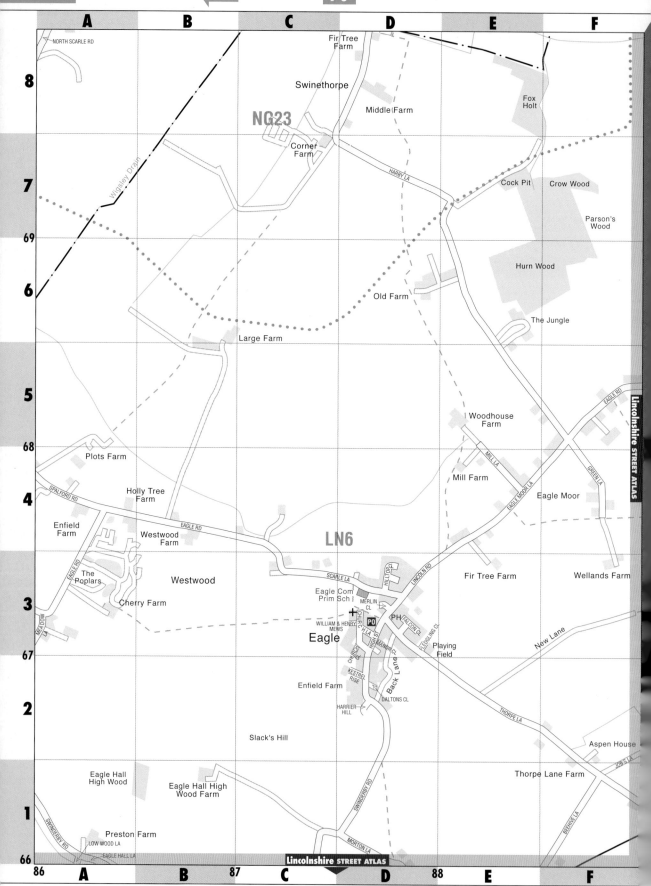

Lincolnshire STREET ATLAS

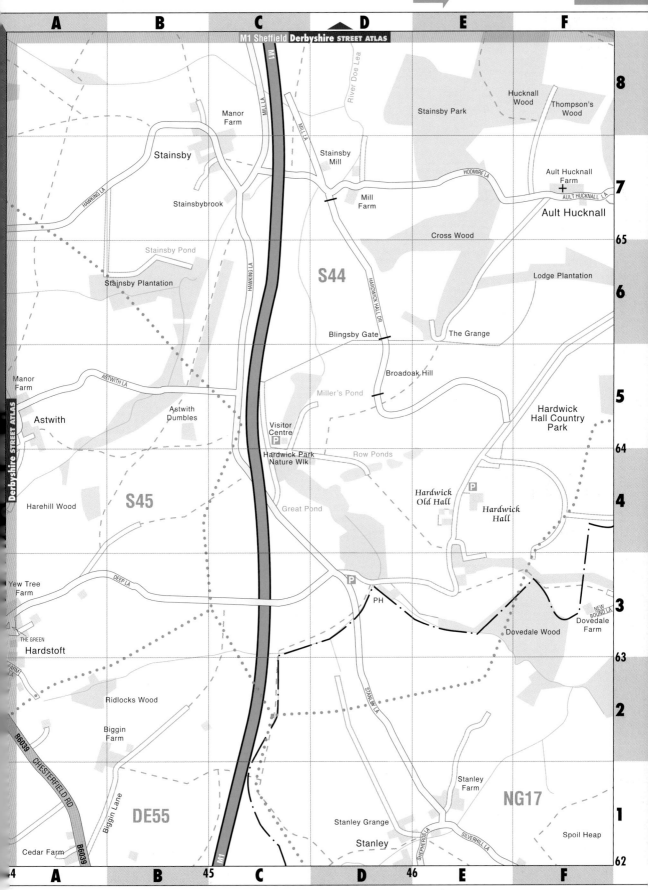

M1 Sheffield **Derbyshire** STREET ATLAS

A **B** **C** **D** **E** **F**

8

River Doe Lea

Manor
Farm

Stainsby Park

Hucknall
Wood

Thompson's
Wood

Stainsby

MILL LA

Stainsby
Mill

HODMIRE LA

Ault Hucknall
Farm

7

Stainsbybrook

HAWKING LA

Mill Farm

Mill
Farm

AULT HUCKNALL LA

Ault Hucknall

65

Stainsby Pond

Cross Wood

S44

HAWKING LA

Lodge Plantation

6

Stainsby Plantation

HARDWICK HALL DR

Blingsby Gate

The Grange

Manor
Farm

ASTWITH LA

Broadoak Hill

5

Astwith
Dumbles

Miller's Pond

Hardwick
Hall Country
Park

Astwith

64

Visitor
Centre
P

Hardwick Park
Nature Wlk

Row Ponds

Harehill Wood

S45

Hardwick
Old Hall

P

Hardwick
Hall

4

Great Pond

Yew Tree
Farm

DEEP LA

P
PH

Dovedale Wood

NEW
BOUND LA
Dovedale
Farm

3

THE GREEN

Hardstoft

63

FARM

STAINBY LA

Ridlocks Wood

2

B6039

Biggin
Farm

Stanley
Farm

NG17

CHESTERFIELD RD

Biggin Lane

DE55

Stanley Grange

SHEPHERDS LA

SILVERHILL LA

1

B6039

Cedar Farm

Stanley

Spoil Heap

62

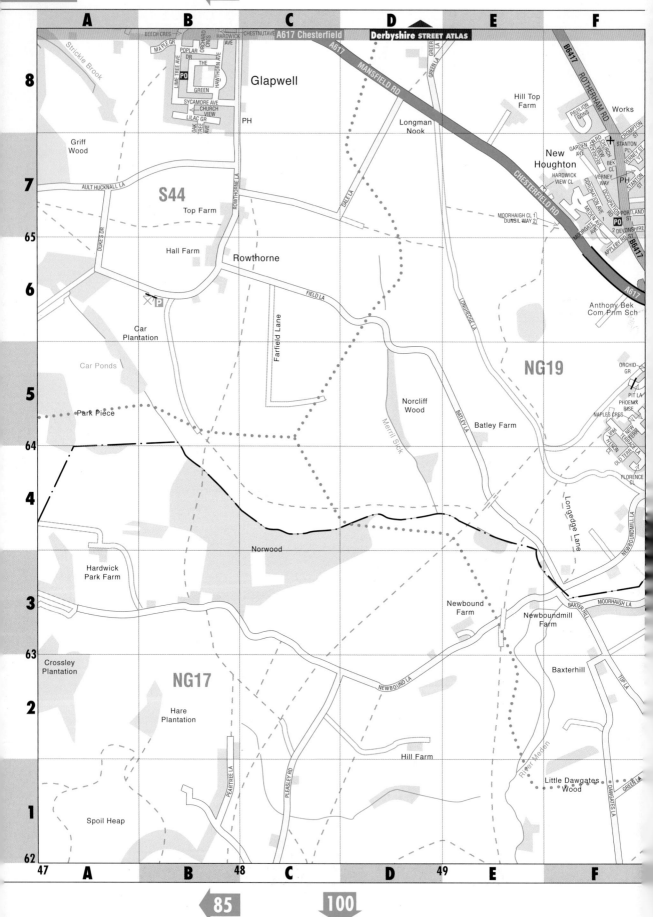

A617 Chesterfield

Derbyshire STREET ATLAS

Strickle Brook

Griff Wood

Glapwell

BEECH CRES
MAPLE GR
ORCHARD CRES
CHESTNUT AVE
POPLAR DR
LIME TREE AVE
THE GREEN
HAWTHORN AVE
HARDWICK AVE
PO
SYCAMORE AVE
CHURCH VIEW
OAK TREE LA
LILAC GR
PH

S44

AULT HUCKNALL LA

ROWTHORNE LA

Top Farm

Hall Farm

Rowthorne

DUKE'S DR

Car Plantation

Car Ponds

Park Piece

FIELD LA

Farfield Lane

DALE LA

MANSFIELD RD
A617

GREER LA
GREEN LA

Longman Nook

CHESTERFIELD RD

New Houghton

Hill Top Farm

PAVILION GDNS
GARDEN AVE
CHURCH VIEW
SNO RD
ROTHERHAM RD
B6417
Works
CROMPTON ST
STANTON PL
VERNEY ST
STANTON ST
BEK CL
VERNEY WAY
HARDWICK VIEW CL
OCCUPATION AVE
OCCUPATION RD
PH
MEDEN AVE
MOORHAIGH CL 1
DUNSIL WAY 2
NESTGATE AVE
PORTLAND ST
PO
1 2 DEVONSHIRE ST
APPLEBY RD
B6417

Anthony Bek Com Prim Sch

NG19

ORCHID GR
PIT LA
PHOENIX RISE
NAPLES CRES
NEW TERRACE LA
HENRY ST
OLD TERR LA
FLORENCE CL

Norcliff Wood

Merrit Sick

BATLEY LA

Batley Farm

LONGRIDGE LA

Norwood

Hardwick Park Farm

Crossley Plantation

NG17

Hare Plantation

PEARTREE LA

PLEASLEY RD

Newbound Farm

NEWBOUND LA

Hill Farm

Newboundmill Farm

Longedge Lane

NEWBOUNDMILL LA

BAXTER HILL

MOORHAIGH LA

Baxterhill

TOP LA

River Meden

Little Dawgates Wood

DAWGATES LA

GREEN LA

Spoil Heap

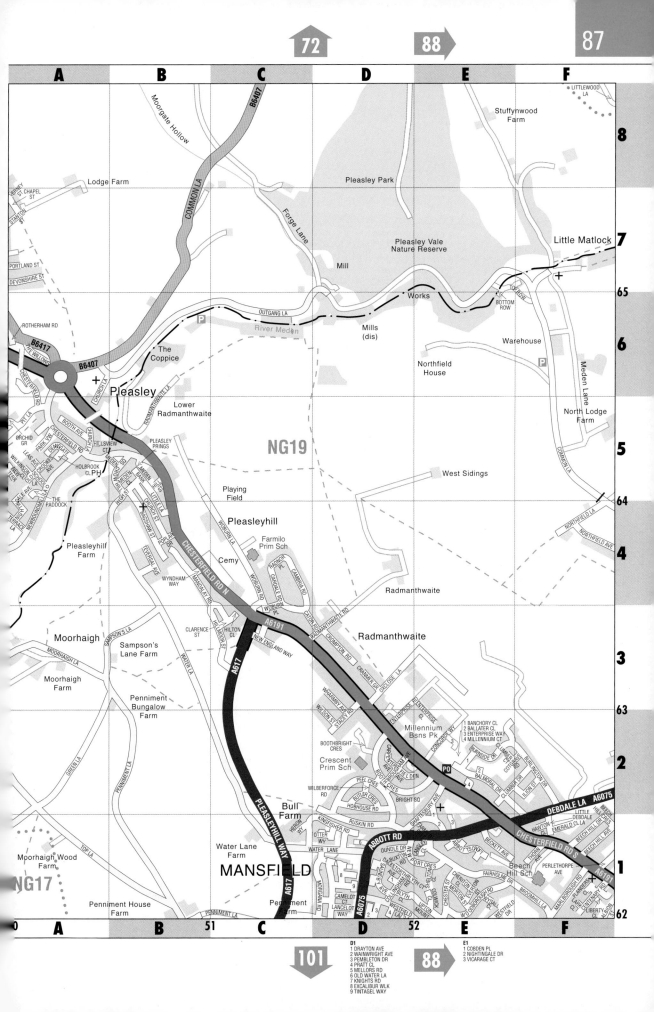

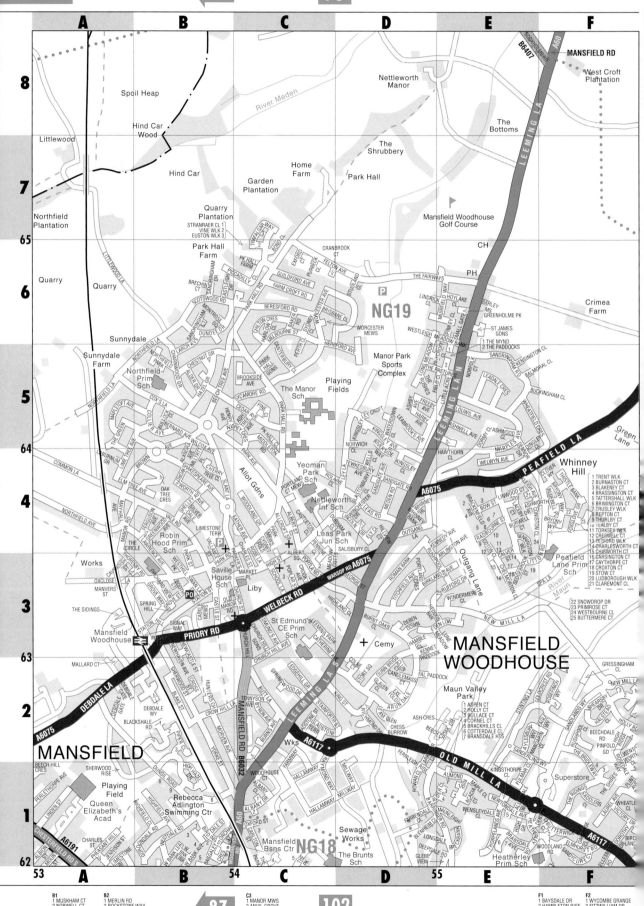

B1
1 MUSKHAM CT
2 NORWELL CT
3 MISTERTON CT
4 MATTERSEY CT
5 THE WOODLANDS
6 MAIN BRIGHT WALK
7 MAIN BRIGHT RD
8 DUNSIL CL
9 DUNSIL CT

B2
1 MERLIN RD
2 ROCKSTONE WAY
3 WATERLOO RD

C1
1 ALBANY PL
2 DOROTHY AVE
3 OLD BAKERY WAY
4 NEW PK LA
5 COLLEGE SIDE

C3
1 MANOR MWS
2 ANVIL GROVE
3 HAYMANS CORNER

F1
1 BAYSDALE DR
2 HAMBLETON RISE
3 SHET LAND CL
4 THE DOWNS
5 SAFFRON ST

F2
1 WYCOMBE GRANGE
2 FITZWILLIAM DR
3 LONGBOURNE CT
4 CASPIAN CL
5 POCHARD CL

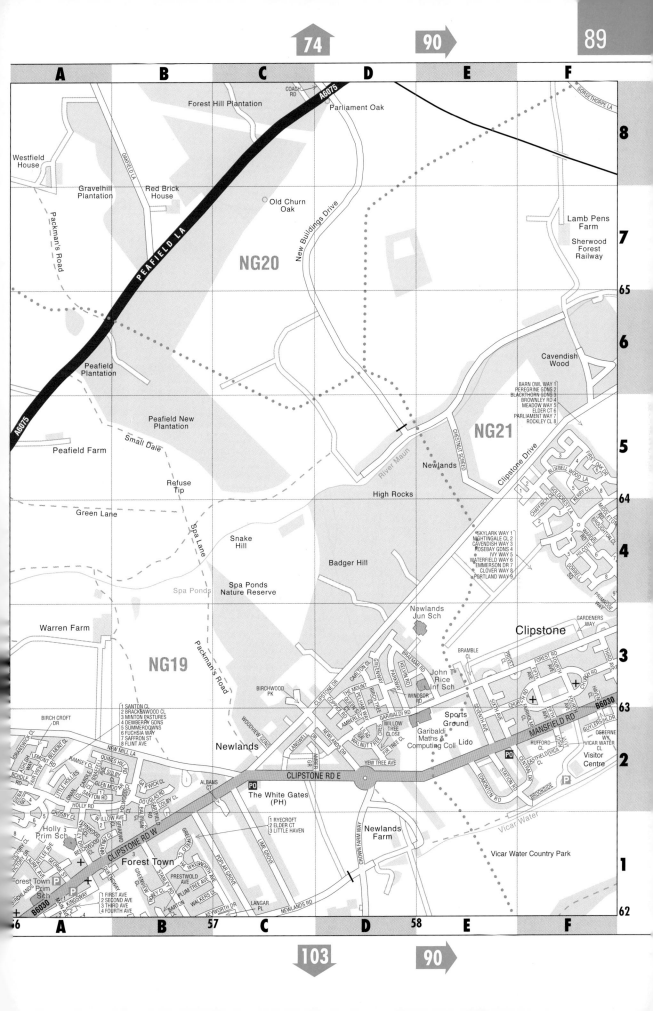

A | B | C | D | E | F

8

7

65

6

Westfield House

Gravelhill Plantation

Red Brick House

Forest Hill Plantation

COACH RD

A6075

Parliament Oak

Old Churn Oak

New Buildings Drive

NG20

PEAFIELD LA

Packman's Road

A6075

Peafield Plantation

Peafield New Plantation

Small Dale

Peafield Farm

Refuse Tip

Green Lane

Spa Lane

Snake Hill

Spa Ponds

Spa Ponds Nature Reserve

Warren Farm

NG19

Packman's Road

Birch Croft Dr

Lamb Pens Farm

Sherwood Forest Railway

Cavendish Wood

BARN OWL WAY 1
PEREGRINE GDNS 2
BLACKTHORN GDNS 3
BROWNLEY RD 4
MEADOW WAY 5
ELDER CT 6
PARLIAMENT WAY 7
ROCKLEY CL 8

NG21

Clipstone Drive

Newlands

High Rocks

Badger Hill

River Maun

CHESTNUT SPEED

Bluebell Wood La

SKYLARK WAY 1
NIGHTINGALE CL 2
CAVENDISH WAY 3
ROSEBAY GDNS 4
IVY WAY 5
WATERFIELD WAY 6
EMMERSON DR 7
CLOVER WAY 8
PORTLAND WAY 9

Newlands Jun Sch

Clipstone

GARDENERS WAY

5

64

4

3

63

2

62

Newlands

BIRCHWOOD PK

1 SANTON CL
2 BRACKENWOOD CL
3 MINTON PASTURES
4 DEWBERRY GDNS
5 SUMMERDOWNS
6 FUCHSIA WAY
7 SAFFRON ST
8 FLINT AVE

NEW MILL LA

WOODVIEW GDNS

CLIPSTONE DR

THE MOUNT
PELHAM WAY
BIRCH TREE
QUEENS WALK

BRACKHAM RD
KELVIN RD
GREENWAY

PARKWAY

WINDSOR RD

John T. Rice Inf Sch

BRAMBLE CL

PRIVET CL

FOREST RD

PRIVET AVE

Sports Ground

Garibaldi Maths & Computing Coll

Lido

CHURCH AVE

THIRD AVE

CHURCH CL

HAVEN CL

FOURTH AVE

MANSFIELD RD

B6030

GUYLERS HLL DR

OSBERNE WY
VICAR WATER CL

Vicar Water Visitor Centre

Holly Prim Sch

Forest Town

Forest Town Prim Sch

B6030

The White Gates (PH)

1 RYECROFT
2 ELDER CT
3 LITTLE HAVEN

CROWN FARM WAY

Newlands Farm

Vicar Water

Vicar Water Country Park

CLIPSTONE RD E

CLIPSTONE RD W

YEW TREE AVE

1 FIRST AVE
2 SECOND AVE
3 THIRD AVE
4 FOURTH AVE

LANGAR PL

NEWLANDS RD

56 | A | 57 | B | C | 58 | D | E | F

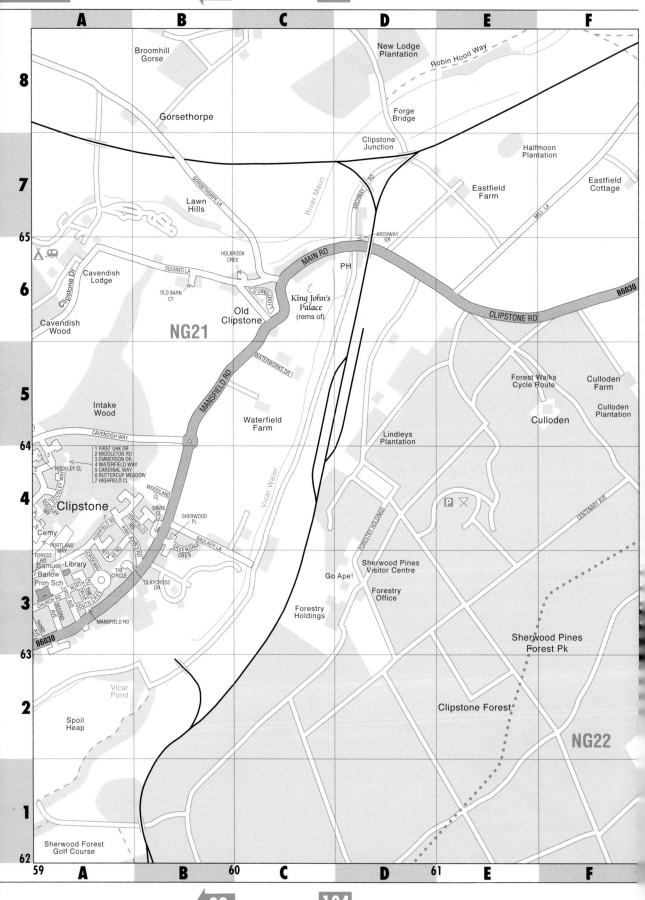

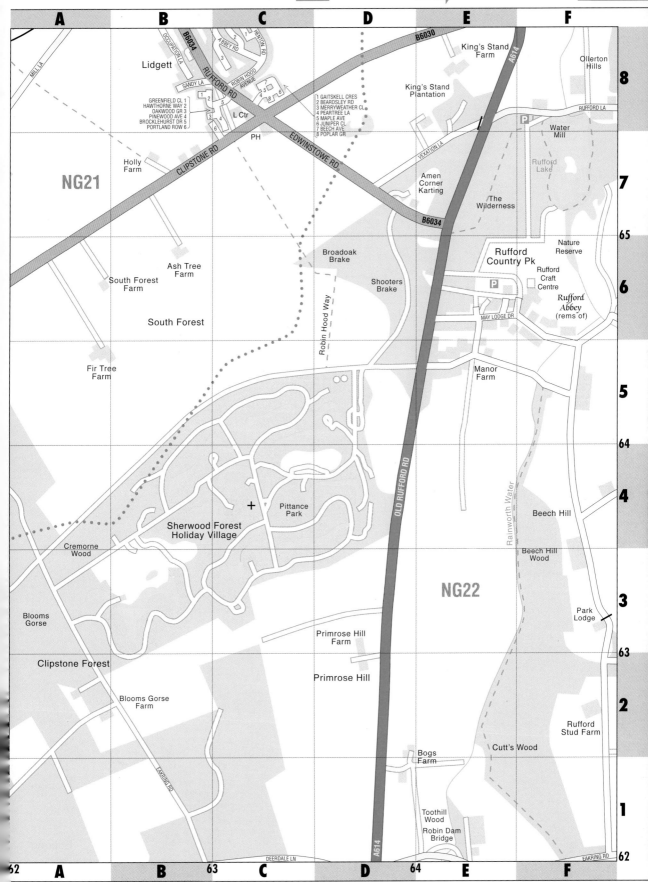

MILLLA

OCCUPATION LA
B6034
Lidgett
ABBEY RD
HENTON RD
ROBIN HOOD AVENUE
RUFFORD RD
SANDY LA

GREENFIELD CL 1
HAWTHORNE WAY 2
OAKWOOD GR 3
PINEWOOD AVE 4
BROCKLEHURST DR 5
PORTLAND ROW 6

L Ctr

PH

CLIPSTONE RD

EDWINSTOWE RD

1 GAITSKELL CRES
2 BEARDSLEY RD
3 MERRYWEATHER CL
4 PEARTREE LA
5 MAPLE AVE
6 JUNIPER CL
7 BEECH AVE
8 POPLAR GR

B6030

King's Stand
Farm

King's Stand
Plantation

Ollerton
Hills

A614

RUFFORD LA

P

Water
Mill

Rufford
Lake

VEXATION LA

Amen
Corner
Karting

NG21

Holly
Farm

The
Wilderness

B6034

Nature
Reserve

Broadoak
Brake

Rufford
Country Pk

Ash Tree
Farm

South Forest
Farm

Shooters
Brake

Rufford
Craft
Centre

Rufford
Abbey
(rems of)

Robin Hood Way

P

South Forest

MAY LODGE DR

Fir Tree
Farm

Manor
Farm

Sherwood Forest
Holiday Village

Pittance
Park

+

OLD RUFFORD RD

Beech Hill

Rainworth Water

Cremorne
Wood

NG22

Beech Hill
Wood

Park
Lodge

Blooms
Gorse

Primrose Hill
Farm

Clipstone Forest

Primrose Hill

Blooms Gorse
Farm

EAKRING RD

Rufford
Stud Farm

Cutt's Wood

Bogs
Farm

Toothill
Wood

Robin Dam
Bridge

A614

DEERDALE LN

EAKRING RD

91
77

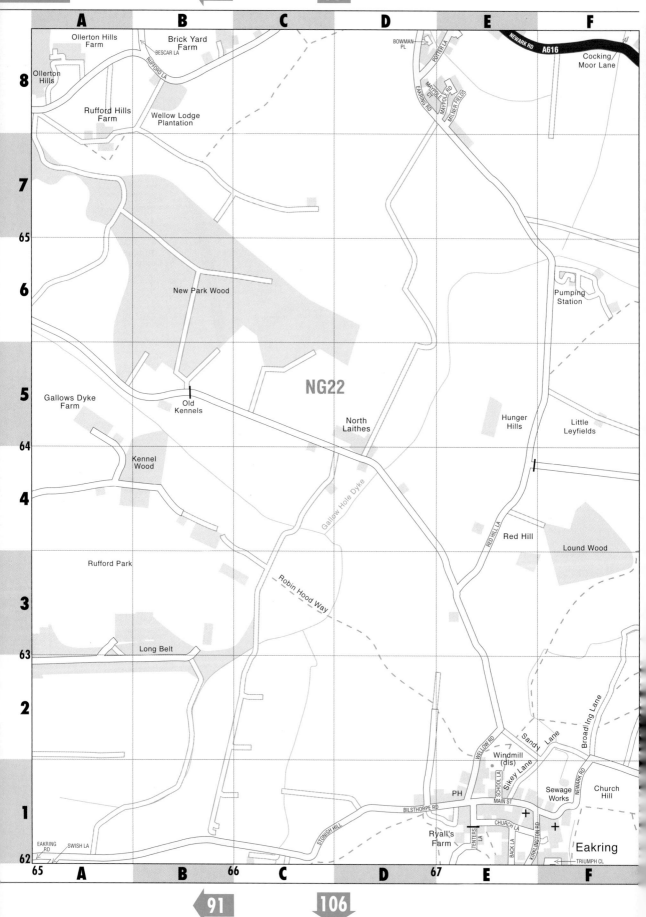

Ollerton Hills Farm

Brick Yard Farm

BESCAR LA

RUFFORD LA

BOWMAN PL

POTTER LA

NEWARK RD A616

Cocking Moor Lane

Ollerton Hills

Rufford Hills Farm

Wellow Lodge Plantation

EAKRING RD

MAYPOLE CT

MAYPOLE RD

MILNER FIELDS

New Park Wood

Pumping Station

NG22

Gallows Dyke Farm

Old Kennels

North Laithes

Hunger Hills

Little Leyfields

Kennel Wood

Gallow Hole Dyke

RED HILL LA

Red Hill

Lound Wood

Rufford Park

Robin Hood Way

Long Belt

Broadling Lane

WELLOW RD

Sandy Lane

Windmill (dis)

SCHOOL LA

Skey Lane

NEWARK RD

Sewage Works

Church Hill

PH

MAIN ST

BILSTHORPE RD

STONISH HILL

CHURCH LA

BACK LA

KIRKLINGTON RD

TENTERS LA

Ryall's Farm

EAKRING RD

SWISH LA

TRIUMPH CL

Eakring

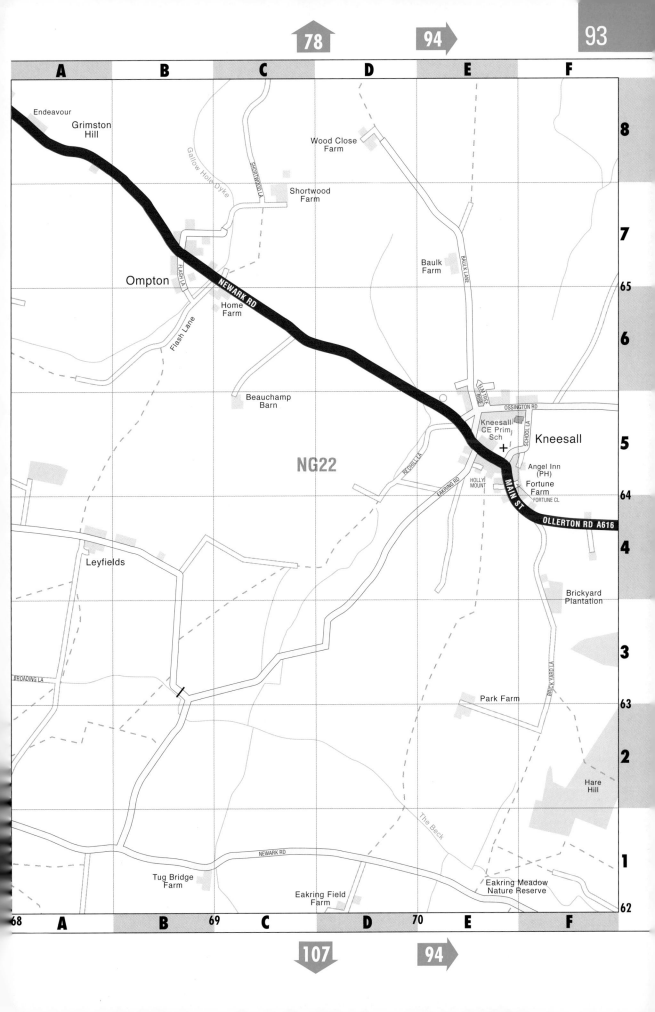

93 79

A B C D E F
8
7
65
6
5
64
4
3
63
2
1
62
71 72 73
South Field
Brockilow Farm
Knapeney Farm
Saywood
Kneesall Wood
Laxton Wood
Laxton Middle Wood
OSSINGTON RD
KNEESALL RD
Kneesall Green Farm
NG22
Mainwood Farm
Hartshorn Farm
Victoria Plantation
A616
High Wood
Laxton Lodge
KERSALL RD
Buckshaw Farm
OLLERTON RD
NG23
Kneesall Lodge
NORWELL WOODHOUSE RD
NORWELL RD
Kersall Lodge
Woodhouse Gorse
Woodhouse Common Farm
Mill Lane
Kersall
Cocked Hat Plantation
Manor Farm
WOOD LA
A616

93 108

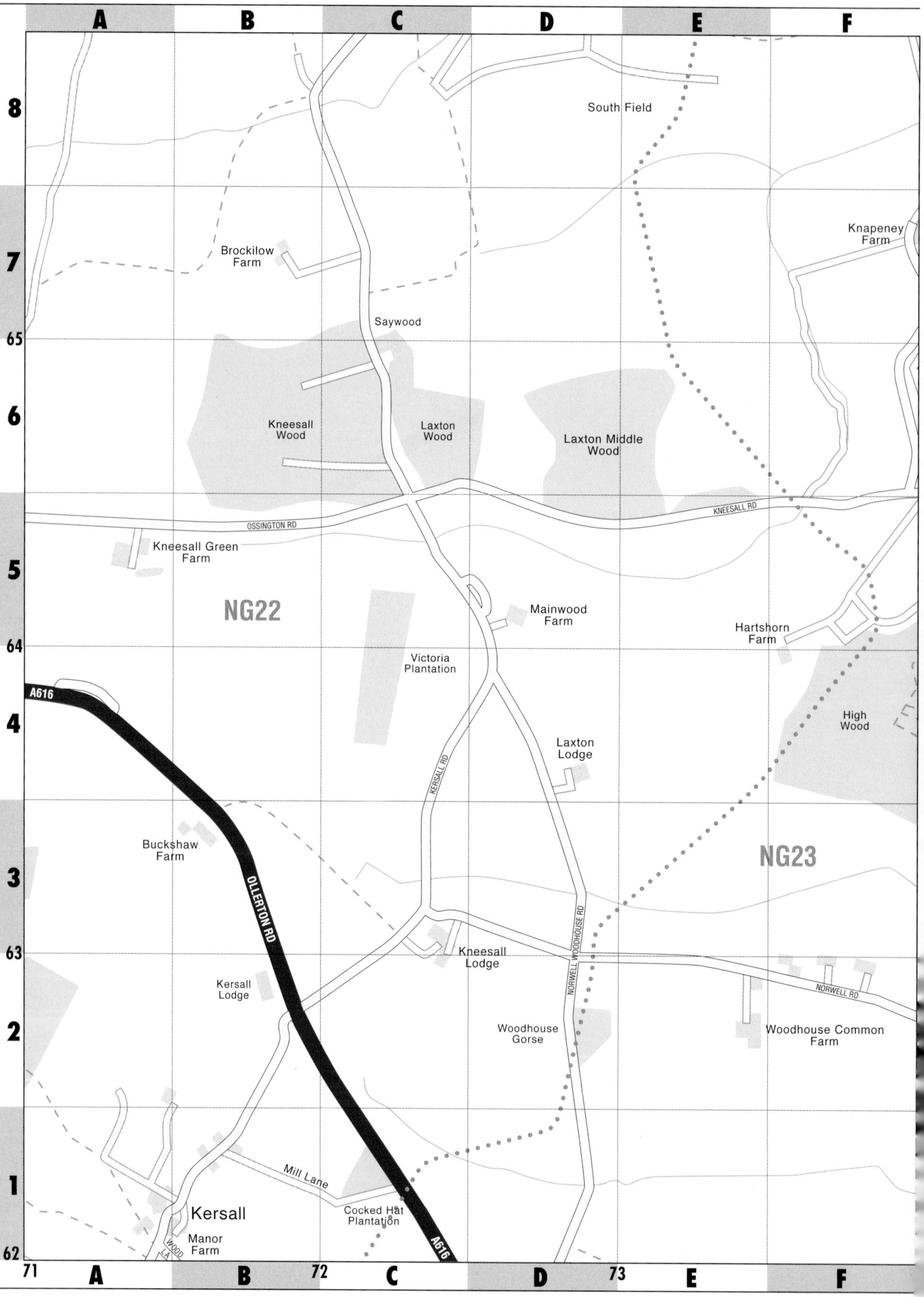

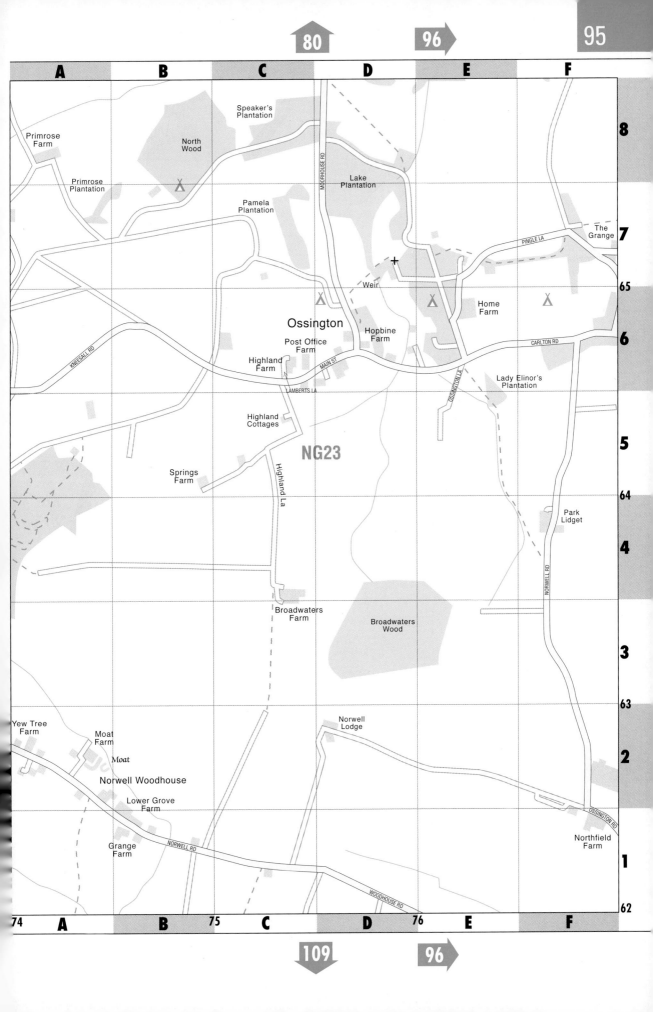

A B C D E F

8

Primrose
Farm

Speaker's
Plantation

North
Wood

Primrose
Plantation

MOORHOUSE RD

Lake
Plantation

Pamela
Plantation

7

PINGLE LA

The
Grange

65

Weir

Home
Farm

Ossington

Hopbine
Farm

CARLTON RD

6

Post Office
Farm

Highland
Farm

MAIN ST

Highland
Cottages

LAMBERTS LA

OSSINGTON LA

Lady Elinor's
Plantation

NG23

5

Springs
Farm

Highland La

64

Park
Lidget

4

NORWELL RD

Broadwaters
Farm

Broadwaters
Wood

3

63

Yew Tree
Farm

Norwell
Lodge

Moat
Farm

Moat

2

Norwell Woodhouse

Lower Grove
Farm

OSSINGTON RD

Northfield
Farm

Grange
Farm

NORWELL RD

1

WOODHOUSE RD

62

74 A B 75 C D 76 E F

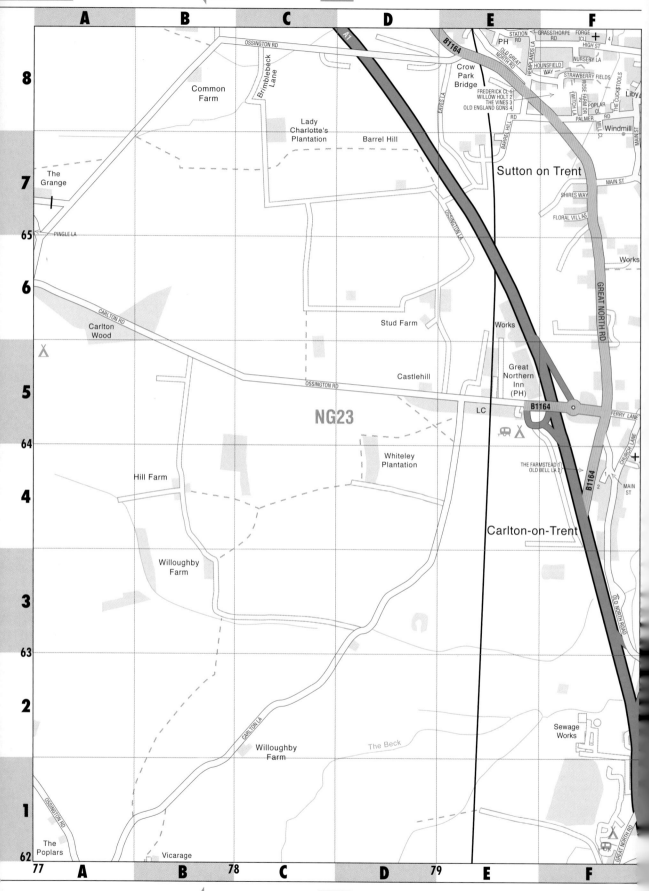

A B C D E F

8
7
65
6
5
64
4
3
63
2
1
62

The Grange
The Poplars
PINGLE LA
OSSINGTON RD
Common Farm
Brimblebeck Lane
Lady Charlotte's Plantation
Barrel Hill
OSSINGTON RD
Carlton Wood
CARLTON RD
Stud Farm
Castlehill
NG23
Hill Farm
Whiteley Plantation
Willoughby Farm
CARLTON LA
Willoughby Farm
The Beck
Vicarage
OSSINGTON RD

A1
B1164
OSSINGTON LA
EAVES LA
Crow Park Bridge
B1164
OLD GREAT NORTH RD
STATION RD
GRASSTHORPE RD
FORGE JCL
HIGH ST
HEMPLANDS LA
HOUNSFIELD WAY
NURSERY LA
STRAWBERRY FIELDS
FREDERICK CL 1
WILLOW HOLT 2
THE VINES 3
OLD ENGLAND GDNS 4
PH
ROSE RAW LA
WITCH LA
POPLAR CL
PALMER
THE DUCKACOOLS
Liby
Windmill
MAIN ST
BARREL HILL RD
Sutton on Trent
MAIN ST
SHIRES WAY
FLORAL VILLAS
Works
GREAT NORTH RD
Works
Great Northern Inn (PH)
LC
B1164
FERRY LANE
CHURCH LANE
THE FARMSTEAD 1
OLD BELL LA 2
B1164
MAIN ST
Carlton-on-Trent
OLD NORTH ROAD
Sewage Works
GREAT NORTH RD

77 78 79

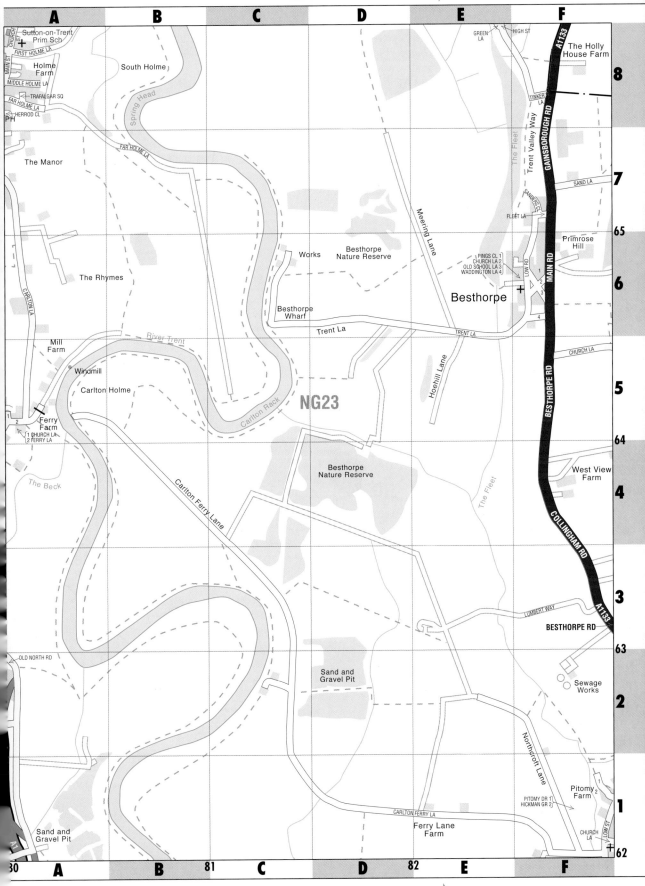

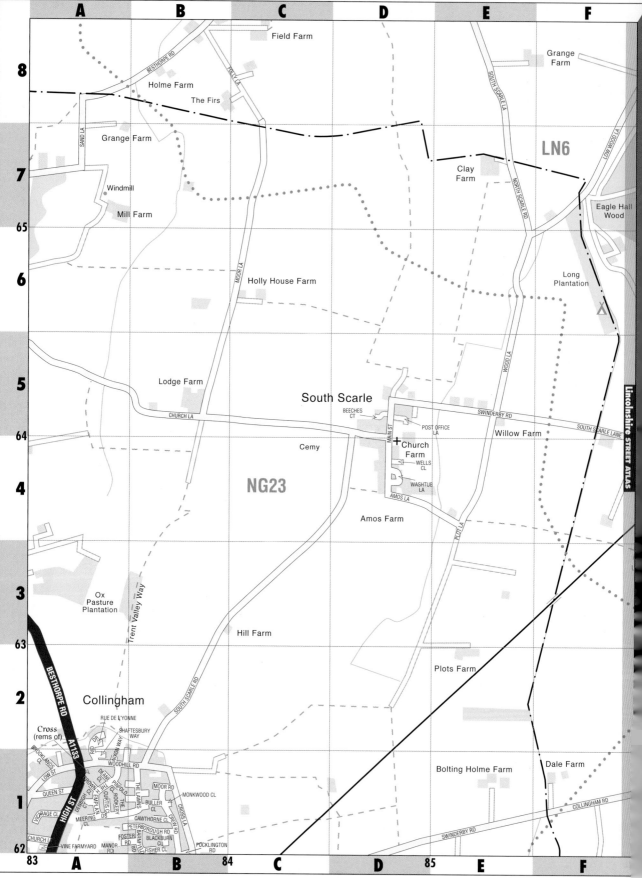

98

97 **83**

A B C D E F

8

Field Farm

Grange
Farm

BESTHORPE RD

Holme Farm

The Firs

FELL LA

LN6

Grange Farm

SAND LA

7

Clay
Farm

SOUTH SCARLE LA

LOW WOOD LA

Windmill

Eagle Hall
Wood

Mill Farm

65

NORTH SCARLE RD

6

MOOR LA

Holly House Farm

Long
Plantation

5

Lodge Farm

South Scarle

WOOD LA

SWINDERBY RD

CHURCH LA

BEECHES
CT

POST OFFICE
LA

Willow Farm

SOUTH SCARLE LANE

64

Cemy

MAIN ST

Church
Farm

WELLS
CL

Lincolnshire STREET ATLAS

NG23

WASHTUB
LA

4

AMOS LA

Amos Farm

PLOT LA

3

Ox
Pasture
Plantation

Trent Valley Way

Hill Farm

Plots Farm

63

SOUTH SCARLE RD

2

Collingham

RUE DE L'YONNE

SHAFTESBURY
WAY

BESTHORPE RD

Cross
(rems of)

A1133

Bolting Holme Farm

Dale Farm

WOODHILL RD

MOOR RD

MONKWOOD CL

COLLINGHAM RD

QUEEN ST

LOW ST

HIGH ST

THE LAWNS

BULLER
CL

CROSS RD

SWINDERBY RD

VICARAGE CL

MEERING
CL

CAWTHORNE CL

PETERBOROUGH RD

BLACKBURN
CL

1

CHURCH LA

Vine Farmyard

FOSTER
RD

MANOR
RD

FISHER CL

PUCKLINGTON
RD

62

83 A 84 B C 85 D E F

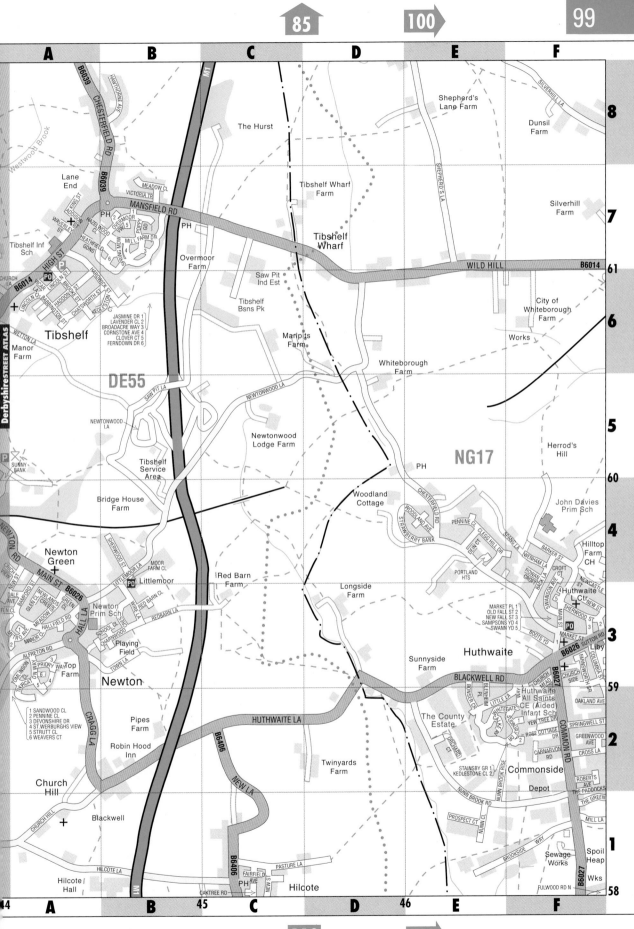

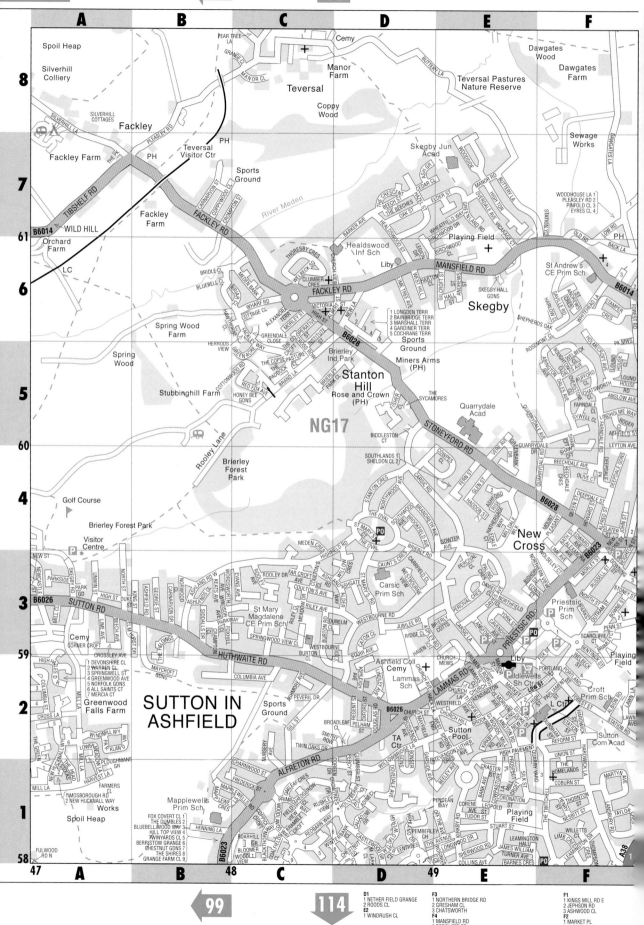

A   B   C   D   E   F

8
7
61
6
5
60
4
3
59
2
1
58

Spoil Heap

Silverhill
Colliery

SILVERHILL COTTAGES

Fackley

Fackley Farm

TIBSHELF RD

B6014 WILD HILL

Orchard
Farm

LC

PEAR TREE LA
GRANGE CL
MANOR CL

Teversal

PLEASLEY RD

PH

Teversal Visitor Ctr

PH

Fackley
Farm

FACKLEY RD

Sports
Ground

CARNATION ST
COPPYWOOD ST
CRAMPTON ST

River Meden

Spring Wood
Farm

Spring
Wood

MEDEN BANK
BELPAR CL
HAWTHORNE
FACKLEY WAY
GREEN ACRE RD

BRIDLE CL
BLUEBELL CL

WHARF RD
COTTAGE CL

Stubbinghill Farm

COTTONWOOD RD

HERRODS VIEW

THE COPSE
THE PADDOCK

RED FOX AVE
HONEY BEE GDNS

Rooley Lane

Brierley
Forest
Park

Golf Course

Brierley Forest Park

Visitor
Centre

P

NEW ST
NEWCASTLE
SKEGBY RD
Park Gd
UNWIN ST
HIGH ST
KING ST
DUKE ST

PARKSIDE
NORTH ST
ASHFIELD RD
CARNARVON GR

B6026
SUTTON RD
Cemy
CORNER CROFT
LIME AVE
BEECH LA
ELM WEST DR
THE HEDINGS
MAYCROFT
GDNS

CROSSLEY AVE
1 DEVONSHIRE CL
2 WARREN CL
3 SPRINGWELL ST
4 GREENWOOD AVE
5 NORFOLK GDNS
6 ALL SAINTS CT
7 MERCIA CT

Greenwood
Falls Farm

THE GREEN
MILL LA
LOWER
WHITEWELL LA
COLUMBIA ST
CROSS LA
HIGH HAZELS DR
PLOUGHMANS
HARVEST LA
FARMERS

WINDMILL WY
KLAN
MILLA

SUTTON IN
ASHFIELD

Sports
Ground

NURSERY RD

CHARNWOOD ST

FREDERICK ST

COLUMBIA AVE

PEVERIL DR

GILL ST

BROADLEAF CL

SMITHY ROW

TWIN OAKS DR

ALFRETON RD

Works

Spoil Heap

FULWOOD RD N

1 MOSBOROUGH RD
2 NEW HUCKNALL WAY

Mapplewells
Prim Sch

FOX COVERT CL 1
THE DUMBLES 2
BLUEBELL WOOD WAY 3
HILL TOP VIEW 4
TWINYARDS CL 5
BERRISTOW GRANGE 6
CHESTNUT GDNS 7
THE SHIRES 8
GRANGE FARM CL 9

HENNING LA

B6023

BOARHILL GR

BLUEBELL WOOD 1
VIEW

Manor
Farm

Coppy
Wood

CEMY

BUTTERY LA

Teversal Pastures
Nature Reserve

Dawgates
Wood

Dawgates
Farm

Sewage
Works

DAWGATES LA

Skegby Jun
Acad

WOODSIDE

WOODHOUSE LA 1
PLEASLEY RD 2
PINFOLD CL 3
EYRES CL 4

LOW RD
OLD RD
BACK LA
PH

B6014

THE CRESCENT
THE BEECHES
OAK ST
BEECH LA
ASH GR
CEDAR CL

HEALDSWOOD ST
LEIGH ST
BARKER AVE

Healdswood
Inf Sch

Liby

FACKLEY RD

CLUMBER
CRES

WELBECK RD

THORESBY CRES

MORLEY ST

VICTORIA TERR

GREENDALE
CLOSE

HIGH ST

ALEXANDRA TERR

THE CO-OPERATIVE
GREENDALE
CLOSE

THE CROFT
THE PASTURE
BRAND LA

Brierley
Ind Park

BRIERLEY
PARK CL

MEDEN RD
FISHER

CHURCH ST

ALBERT ST

LIME TREE AVE

WEST HILL
HARTON ST

GILCROFT ST
ST ANDREWS
HALL ST

1 LONGDEN TERR
2 BAINBRIDGE TERR
3 MARSHALL TERR
4 GARDINER TERR
5 COCHRANE TERR

Sports
Ground

Miners Arms
(PH)

Stanton
Hill

Rose and Crown
(PH)

NG17

BIDDLESTON
CT

SOUTHLANDS 1
SHELDON CL 2

B6028

STONEYFORD RD

THE
SYCAMORES

Quarrydale
Acad

MANOR RD
OVERDALE AVE
GREENLAND RD
BIRCHWOOD DR

WHEATFIELD DR

BIRCHWOOD

HIGH TOR

BUTTERY LA

Playing Field

St Andrew's
CE Prim Sch

PK MWS

VICARAGE CT

SHEPHERDS OAK

Skegby Hall
GDNS

Skegby

ROSEMONT CL

WHITEHEAD LA
SAVILLE RD
HARLOW CT

STAMPER
CRES

FOREST RD

ST ANDREWS LA

PRECKBROFT AVE

ABINGDON
DALE'S AVE

RUFFORD

FARNDALE
SYWELL CL

LOUND
HOUSE

ANSLOW AVE

CHATSWORTH

ROGER

LINDHOLME WAY

ASHFIELD
RD

LEYTON AVE

BEECHDALE AVE

OLIVE CL

DEEPDALE ST

B6028

STANTON WY
SOUTHWOOD
NORTHWOOD
AVE

CARSIC RD

CARSIC LA

FERN ST

GLEN ST

ASHFORD
RISE

HADDON ST

MILLDALE

THE OVAL
THE OVAL

ST MARY'S

BRANDRETH AVE

BROOKFIELD AVE

PO

BRIERLEY RD

SOWTER
AVE

MEDEN CRES

HIGHFIELD RD

Carsic
Prim Sch

ASHWORTH
ALDER
ALLER

RILEY AVE
MEADOW RD
BURTON CL
DUNELM
WESTBOURNE RD

STARR AVE
JUBILEE RD

PERCIVAL CRES

DAVIES ST

LANGFORD ST

BISHOPS DR
NORTHFIELD
VIEW

MOUNT
PLEASANT

New
Cross

B6023

ST EDWARD
ST ALEXANDRA
MORLEY ST

RUSSELL ST
DOWNING ST

STONEY ST

PENN ST

SCARCLIFFE

BENTINCK ST

Playing
Field

Croft
Prim Sch

NEWARK ST

Sutton
Pool

TA Ctr

LAMMAS RD

Ashfield Coll
Cemy

Lammas
Sch

CHURCH
MEWS

ABBEY DR

CHURCH
HILL

PELHAM ST

B6026

DOUGLAS RD

HUTHWAITE RD

BURTON

WESTBOURNE

WORDSWORTH
KEATS AVE

ASHLAND RD W

ROOLEY DR

FAR CROFT AVE

COULTON'S AVE

ASHGATE RD

CHAMPION

ASHGATE

RILEY CL

MAGNOLIA CL

CATON CL

WESTBOURNE RD

St Mary
Magdalene
CE Prim Sch

EVANS AVE
WINDSOR AVE

COLUTON'S AVE

SIDDALLS DR

BURTON RD

BROADLEAF CL

IDLEWELLS SH CTR

STEVENSON PL

KENSINGTON

Idlewells
Sh Ctr
P

L Ctr

Liby

HIGH PAVEMENT

PRIESTSIC RD

Priestsic
Prim Sch

P

PO

P

CHURCH ST

PORTLAND SQ

PORTLAND

QUARRY YARD

STATION RD

REFORM ST

Sutton
Com Acad

UNION ST

THE HOMELANDS

MARTYN
AVE

LANSBURY RD

A38

CHURCH
HILL

WESTFIELD LA

FOREST ST

Playing
Field

Leamington
Hall

JAMES WILLIAM
TURNER AVE

BARNES CRES

COLLINS AVE

SHERWOOD RD

WILLETTS CT

LIMB CT

THORNTON ST

NESBITT ST

TAYLOR

COBURN ST

LEAMINGTON DR

SILK ST

BANK AVE

LEOPOLD ST

CORENE
AVE
TUDOR ST

STUART ST

PENDEAN
WAY

CRASTER

HIGH PAVEMENT

MARKET

JEPSON
ST

RICHARD ST

KIRKBY RD

ALFRETON RD

CLUMBER ST

DOVEDALE AVE

CROWTREES DR

BEELEY ST

PERCY ST

LANGTON RD

KIRKBY RD

CORONATION

CHESTNUT AVE

THE AVENUE

PEMBERLEY
CH

WINTERBANK

REDRED WAY

RUSHLEY
VIEW

CASTLEWOOD DR

HOLLYBERRY
VIEW

PRIMROSE
DR

BRAMBLE
VIEW

DUROSE
VIEW

WILLOWBRIDGE
GDNS

BONSER
GDNS

GARTSIDE AVE

DEVONSHIRE

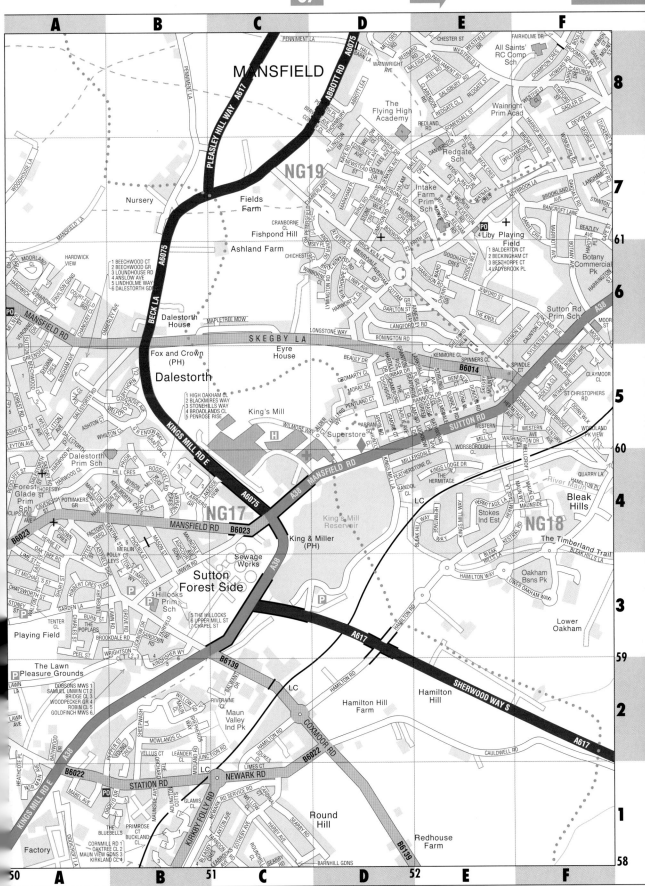

101
88

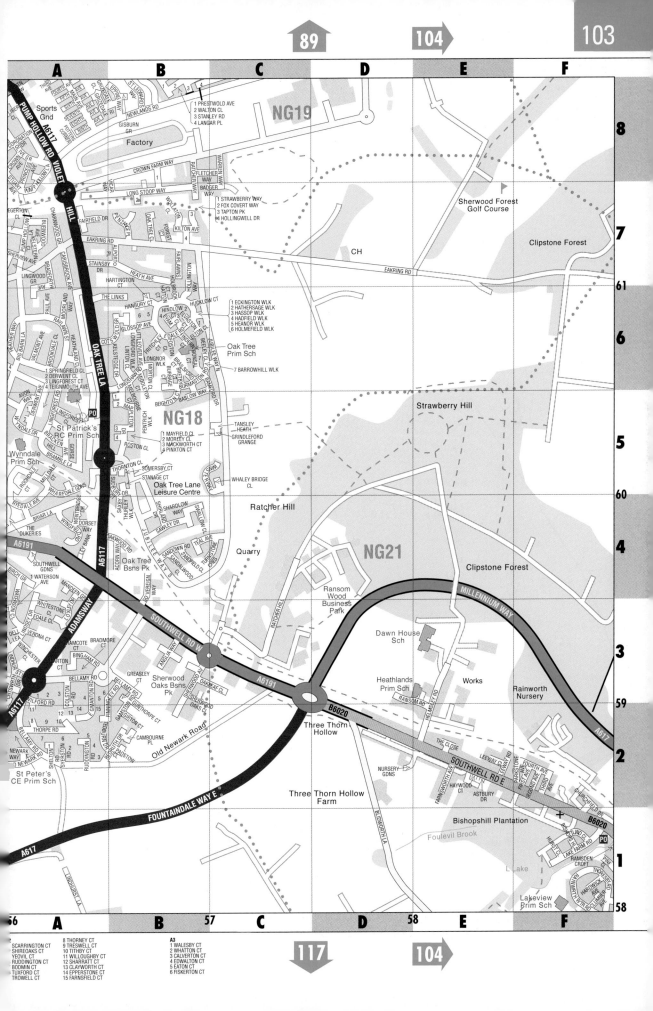

Map labels

A
- 89 (top)
- Sports Gnd
- Factory
- PUMP HOLLOW RD
- VIOLET HILL
- A6117
- CHARNWOOD GR
- EGERTON CL
- CORONATION DR
- THIRD AV
- FOURTH AV
- SIXTH AV
- EPPING WAY
- ST LEONARDS WAY
- NEWLANDS RD
- GISBURN GR
- CROWN FARM WAY
- VICAR WAY
- WOLLATON
- FAIRFIELD DR
- EAKRING RD
- ALPORTO
- STAINSBY DR
- HEATH AVE
- HARTINGTON
- LINGWOOD GR
- BRAIDWOOD AVE
- CARISBROOK AVE
- BURNWOOD AVE
- SHERVIEW AVE
- PAUL AVE
- AMBERGATE RD
- THE LINKS
- HANBURY CT
- GLOSSOP AVE
- BRACKEN HILL
- GORSE RD
- BRAMBLE LA
- OAK TREE LA
- A6117
- OAKWOOD DR
- THORNTON CL
- SOMERSBY CT
- STANAGE CT
- THIRLEY WLK
- SILVERBIRCH
- SAWLEY DR
- Wynndale Prim Sch
- St Patrick's RC Prim Sch
- 1 SPRINGFIELD CL
- 2 DERWENT CL
- 3 LINGFOREST CT
- 4 TEIGNMOUTH AVE
- LINGFOREST RD
- DERWENT DR
- AVON WAY
- HEATHLAND AVE
- TYNDALE DR
- ROCKDALE CT
- RYEDALE AVE
- WHARFEDALE GDNS
- BRIAR LA
- WINGFIELD WAY
- DORSET WAY
- LEY BANK
- The Dukeries
- A6191
- SOUTHWELL GDNS
- 1 WATERSON AVE
- BIRCH GR
- WHITESTONE CL
- EDALE CL
- VERONA CT
- DELL LEA
- WINCHESTER CL
- CHATSWORTH
- A6117
- WILFORD RD
- COLSTON RD
- BELLAMY RD
- THORPE RD
- NEWARK WAY
- NEW NEWARK RD
- St Peter's CE Prim Sch
- FOUNTAINDALE WAY E
- A617

B
- 1 PRESTWOLD AVE
- 2 WALTON CL
- 3 STANLEY RD
- 4 LANGAR PL
- FLETCHER WAY
- BADGER WAY
- RATCHER WAY
- WARREN WAY
- 1 STRAWBERRY WAY
- 2 FOX COVERT WAY
- 3 TAPTON PK
- 4 HOLLINGWELL DR
- PENZANCE PL
- OAK TREE CL
- KILTON AVE
- FORREST
- HOLBROOK
- HUCKLOW
- HINDLOW
- FAIRLAWNS
- 1 ECKINGTON WLK
- 2 HATHERSAGE WLK
- 3 HASSOP WLK
- 4 HADFIELD WLK
- 5 HEANOR WLK
- 6 HOLMEFIELD WLK
- LONGNOR WLK
- COTSWOLD
- KELSTEDGE DR
- LITTLEOVER AVE
- LONGFORD AVE
- MELBOURNE
- ROSTON CL
- UNION CT
- NG18
- Oak Tree Prim Sch
- 7 BARROWHILL WLK
- BEIGHTON
- MAPPLETON
- PENTRICH
- 1 MAYFIELD CL
- 2 MORLEY CL
- 3 MACKWORTH CT
- 4 PINXTON CT
- BASLOW WAY
- Oak Tree Lane Leisure Centre
- SHARDLOW WAY
- SWALLOW LA
- SANDWN RD
- TEAL AVE
- CAMPFIELD CL
- SANDALWOOD
- Oak Tree Bsns Pk
- ADAMSWAY
- SOUTHWELL RD W
- OAKLEAF CL
- SHERWOOD OAKS CL
- Sherwood Oaks Bsns Pk
- NAMCOTE CT
- BRADMORE CT
- BINGHAM RD
- ANGLIA WAY
- GREASLEY CT
- LANGHAM
- BELLAMY RD
- GUNTHORPE CT
- GADSBY
- THOROTON CT
- CAMBOURNE PL
- RUDDINGTON
- REDBOURNE
- GADSTON
- SHELTON
- Old Newark Road

C
- NG19
- 1 (top)
- Long Stoop Way
- EDALE
- BEELEY CL
- BARKER
- BURMASTON DR
- JUBILEE LA W
- JUBILEE LA E

D
- CH
- EAKRING RD
- TANSLEY HEATH
- GRINDLEFORD GRANGE
- WHALEY BRIDGE CL
- Ratcher Hill
- Quarry
- NG21
- Ransom Wood Business Park
- RATCHER HILL
- A6191
- B6020
- Three Thorn Hollow
- Three Thorn Hollow Farm
- BLIDWORTH LA
- NURSERY GDNS
- Foulevil Brook

E
- Sherwood Forest Golf Course
- Strawberry Hill
- Clipstone Forest
- MILLENNIUM WAY
- Dawn House Sch
- Heathlands Prim Sch
- Works
- RANSOM RD
- HELMSLEY RD
- THE CLOSE
- LEEWAY RD
- Rainworth Nursery
- SOUTHWELL RD E
- FARNSWORTH AVE
- HAYWOOD CT
- ASTBURY DR
- Bishopshill Plantation
- L Lake
- Lakeview Prim Sch

F
- Clipstone Forest
- A617
- A617
- B6020
- PARKSTONE AVE
- FOURTH AVE
- THIRD AVE
- SECOND AVE
- FIRST AVE
- CHURCHFIELD DR
- HURST CL
- LAKE FARM RD
- PINE
- RAMSDEN CROFT
- HARDWICK AVE
- THORESBY RD
- RAINWORTH
- PO
- +

Grid references (right side)
8, 7, 61, 6, 5, 60, 4, 3, 59, 2, 1, 58

Grid references (bottom)
56 A 57 B C D 58 E F

Index (bottom left)

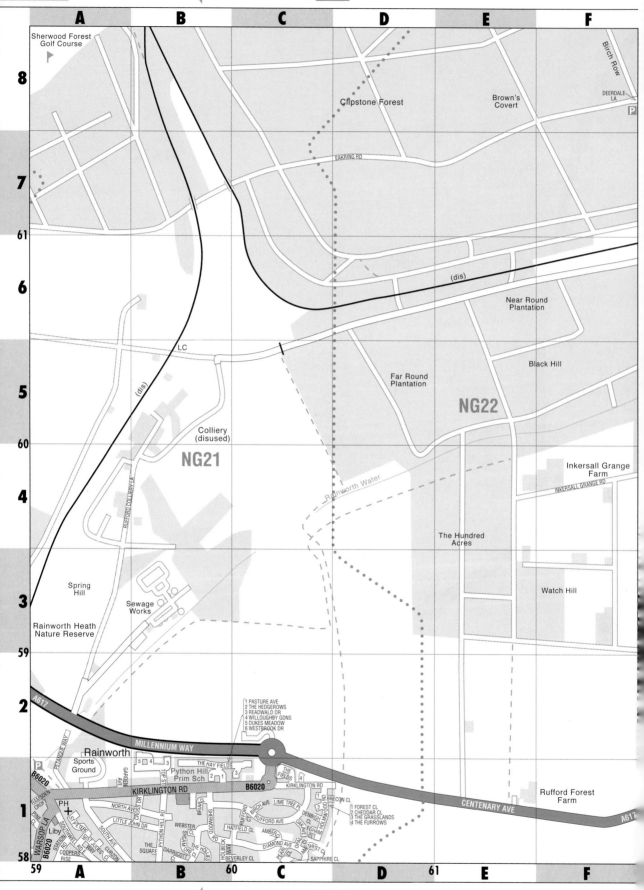

Sherwood Forest
Golf Course

8

Birch Row

Clipstone Forest

Brown's
Covert

DEERDALE LA

P

EAKRING RD

7

61

(dis)

6

Near Round
Plantation

LC

Black Hill

(dis)

5

Far Round
Plantation

NG22

60

Colliery
(disused)

NG21

Inkersall Grange
Farm

INKERSALL GRANGE RD

4

Rainworth Water

The Hundred
Acres

RUFFORD COLLIERY LA

Spring
Hill

Watch Hill

3

Sewage
Works

Rainworth Heath
Nature Reserve

59

A617

2

MILLENNIUM WAY

1 PASTURE AVE
2 THE HEDGEROWS
3 READWALD DR
4 WILLOUGHBY GDNS
5 DUKES MEADOW
6 WESTBROOK DR

Rainworth

P

Sports
Ground

PETANQUE WAY

B6020

5 3
4

THE HAY FIELDS

Python Hill
Prim Sch

3

THE
FIELDS

4

KIRKLINGTON RD

Rufford Forest
Farm

CENTENARY AVE

A617

GARDEN AVE

TOP ST

B6020

KIRKLINGTON RD

1

PH

Libv

WARSOP LA

B6020

NORTH AVE

LITTLE JOHN DR

ST PETERS

SOUTHWELL RD

WEBSTER
CL

BRIAR
CL

SHERWOOD
RD

RUFFORD
PYTHON HILL RD

BIRCH AVE

LIME TREE PL

RUFFORD AVE

DENBIGH
CL

BRECON CL

WILMWOOD RD

EGHAM
CL

1 FOREST CL
2 CHEDDAR CL
3 THE GRASSLANDS
4 THE FURROWS

HATFIELD CL

AMBERG

OAK TREE

PINE AVE

SOUTH AVE

CURZON

DARRICOTT CL

THE
SQUARE

THE
HOLMES

HOLBECK WAY

BEVERLEY CL

DIAMOND AVE

PEARL AVE

AMETHYST CL

SAPPHIRE CL

58

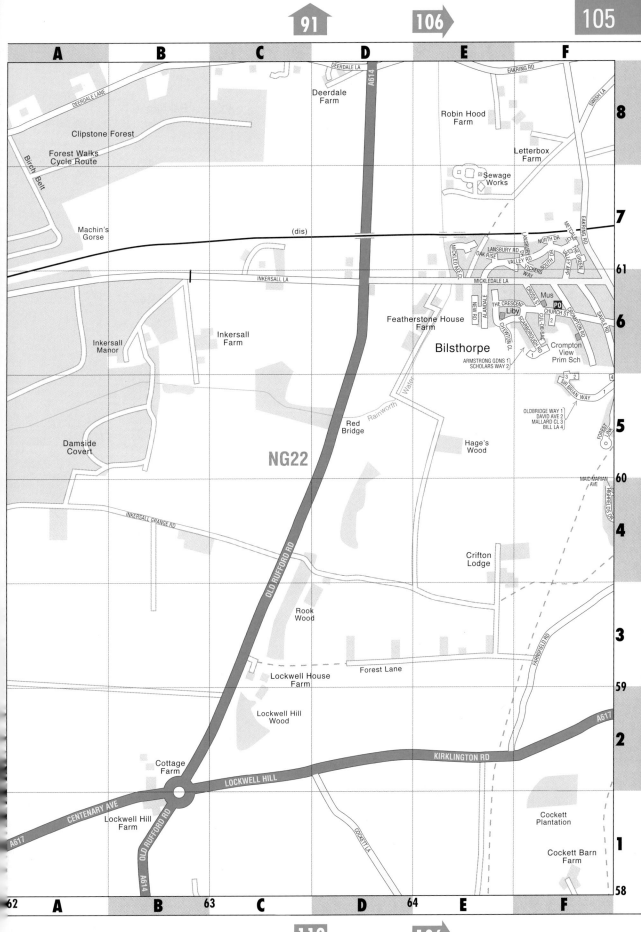

A   B   C   D   E   F

8

DEERDALE LA

Deerdale Farm

Clipstone Forest

Forest Walks Cycle Route

Birch Belt

DEERDALE LANE

Robin Hood Farm

EAKRING RD

SWISH LA

Letterbox Farm

Sewage Works

7

Machin's Gorse

(dis)

MICKLE AVE CL

NORTH DR

METCALFE CT

EAKRING RD

61

INKERSALL LA

Oak Rise

LANSBURY RD

LANSBURY DR

VALLEY RD

VICKERS WAY

THE GREEN

VALLEY APP

MICKLEDALE LA

6

Inkersall Farm

Inkersall Manor

Featherstone House Farm

NEW RD

ALANDALE

THE CRESCENT

CHERITON CL

Liby

CROSS ST

SCARBROUGH RD

CUL-DE-SAC

Mus

PO

CHURCH ST

CROMPTON RD

SAVILE RD

Bilsthorpe

Crompton View Prim Sch

ARMSTRONG GDNS 1
SCHOLARS WAY 2

SIR BRIAN WAY

OLDBRIDGE WAY 1
DAVID AVE 2
MALLARD CL 3
BILL LA 4

Red Bridge

Rainworth Water

Hage's Wood

FOREST LINK

5

NG22

Damside Covert

MAID MARIAN AVE

HIGHFIELDS DR

60

INKERSALL GRANGE RD

OLD RUFFORD RD

Crifton Lodge

4

Rook Wood

FARNSFIELD RD

3

Forest Lane

Lockwell House Farm

59

Lockwell Hill Wood

A617

2

KIRKLINGTON RD

LOCKWELL HILL

Cottage Farm

CENTENARY AVE

Lockwell Hill Farm

OLD RUFFORD RD

A614

A617

COCKETT LA

Cockett Plantation

1

Cockett Barn Farm

58

62   A   B   63   C   D   64   E   F

105
92

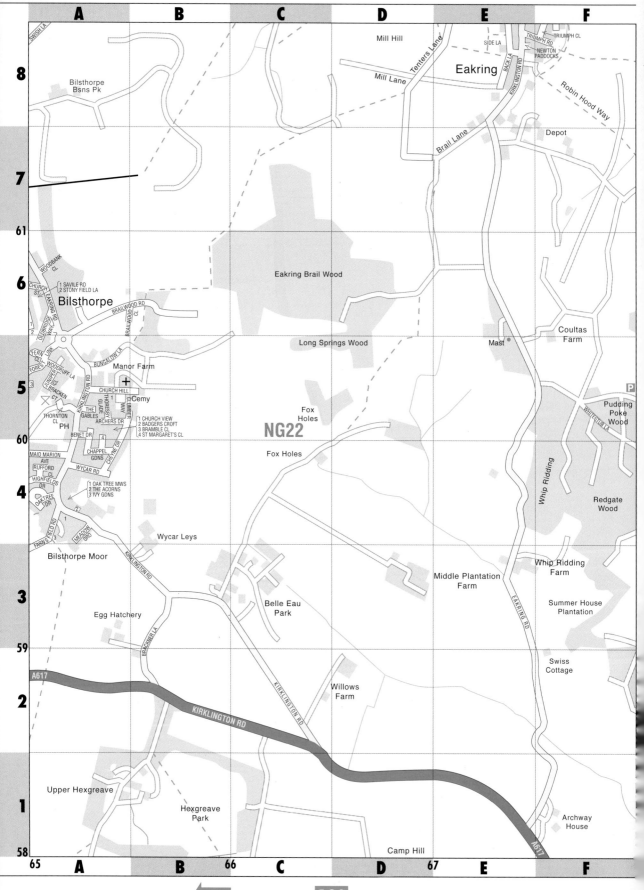

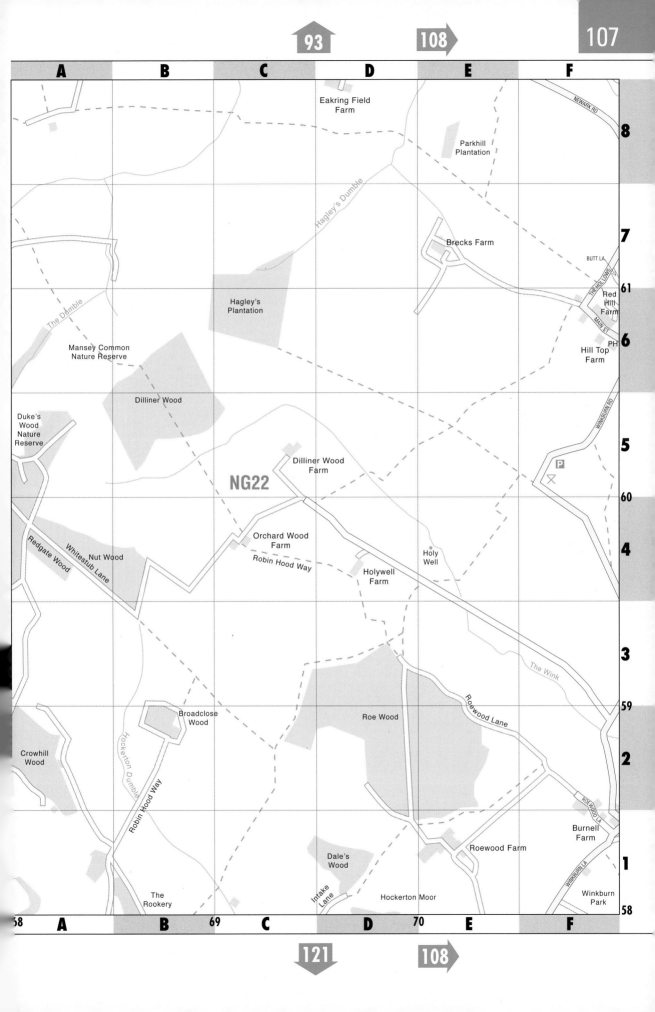

NEWARK RD

Eakring Field
Farm

Parkhill
Plantation

Hagley's Dumble

Brecks Farm

BUTT LA

THE HOLLOWS

Red
Hill
Farm

Hagley's
Plantation

The Dumble

MAIN ST

PH

Hill Top
Farm

Mansey Common
Nature Reserve

Dilliner Wood

Duke's
Wood
Nature
Reserve

WINKBURN RD

P

Dilliner Wood
Farm

NG22

Redgate Wood

Whitestub Lane

Nut Wood

Orchard Wood
Farm

Robin Hood Way

Holywell
Farm

Holy
Well

The Wink

Roewood Lane

Broadclose
Wood

Roe Wood

Hockerton Dumble

Crowhill
Wood

Robin Hood Way

ROEWOOD LA

Burnell
Farm

Roewood Farm

WINKBURN LA

Dale's
Wood

The
Rookery

Intake Lane

Hockerton Moor

Winkburn
Park

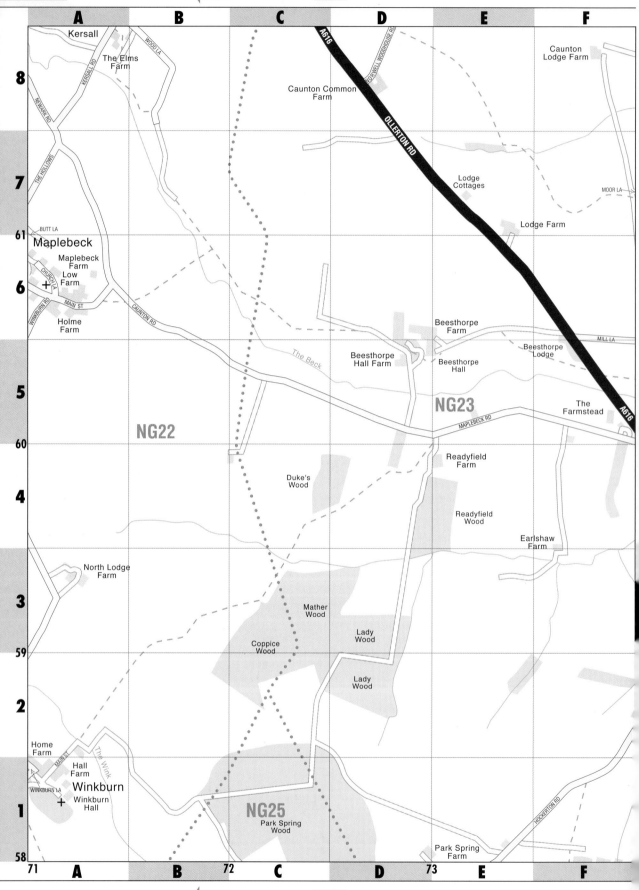

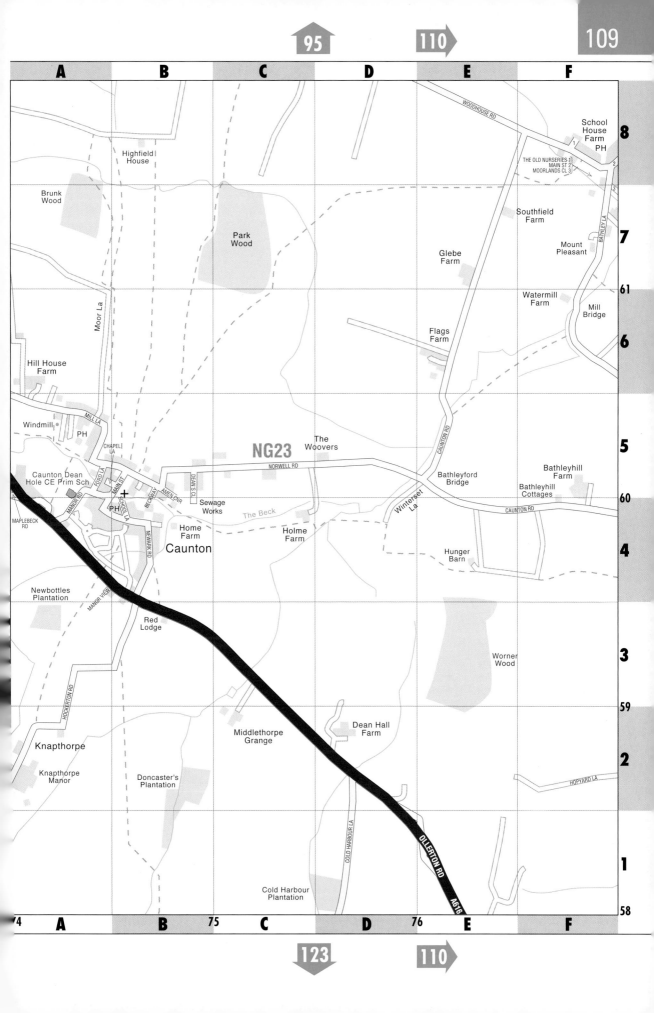

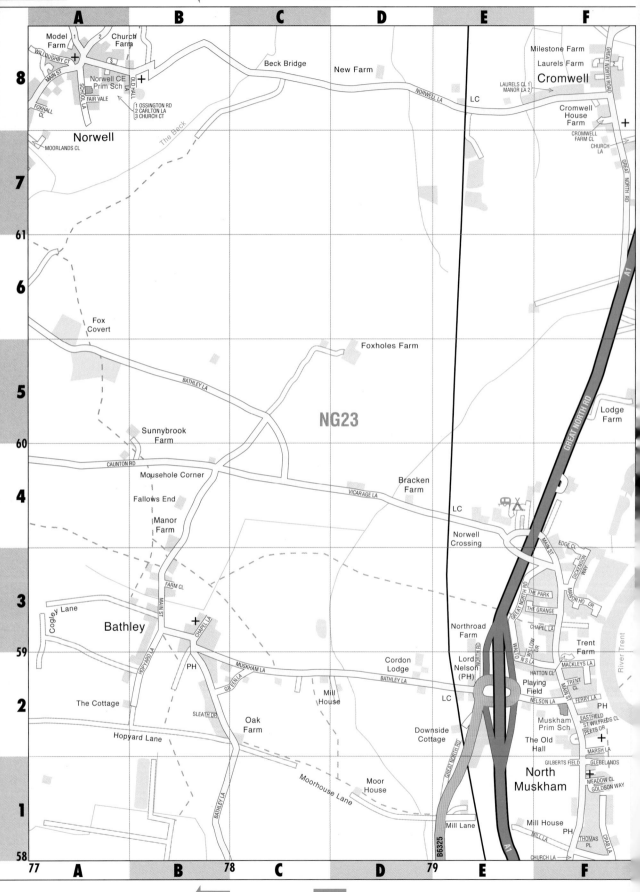

A B C D E F

8

7

61

6

5

60

4

3

59

2

1

58

Model Farm
Church Farm
WILLOUGHBY CT
MAIN ST
Norwell CE Prim Sch
OLD HALL
SCHOOL LA
FAIR VALE
FOXHALL CL
Norwell
MOORLANDS CL

1 OSSINGTON RD
2 CARLTON LA
3 CHURCH CT

Beck Bridge
New Farm
NORWELL LA
LC

The Beck

Milestone Farm
Laurels Farm
Cromwell
GREAT NORTH ROAD
LAURELS CL
MANOR LA 2
Cromwell House Farm
CROMWELL FARM CL
CHURCH LA
GREAT NORTH RD
A1

Fox Covert

Foxholes Farm

NG23

Lodge Farm

BATHLEY LA

Sunnybrook Farm

CAUNTON RD

Mousehole Corner

VICARAGE LA

Bracken Farm

LC

GREAT NORTH RD

Fallows End

Manor Farm

Norwell Crossing

MAIN ST

EDGE CL

DICKENSON WAY

FARM CL

Cogley Lane

Bathley

MAIN ST

CHAPEL LA

Northroad Farm

THE PARK

THE GRANGE

CHAPEL LA

MANOR HO. DR

Trent Farm

River Trent

HOPYARD LA

PH

GREEN LA

MUSKHAM LA

Cordon Lodge

BATHLEY LA

LC

Lord Nelson (PH)

WALTON'S LA

WILLOW DR

HATTON CL

TRENT CL

MACKLEYS LA

Playing Field

NELSON LA

MAIN ST

FERRY LA

PH

The Cottage

SLEATH DR

Oak Farm

Mill House

Downside Cottage

NORTH RD

Muskham Prim Sch

ST WILFREDS CL

EASTFIELD

PEETS DR

The Old Hall

MARSH LA

Hopyard Lane

BATHLEY LA

Moorhouse Lane

Moor House

GREAT NORTH RD

North Muskham

GILBERTS FIELD

GLEBELANDS

MEADOW CL

GOLDSON WAY

Mill Lane

B6325

Mill House

MILL LA

PH

THOMAS PL

CRAB LA

A1

CHURCH LA

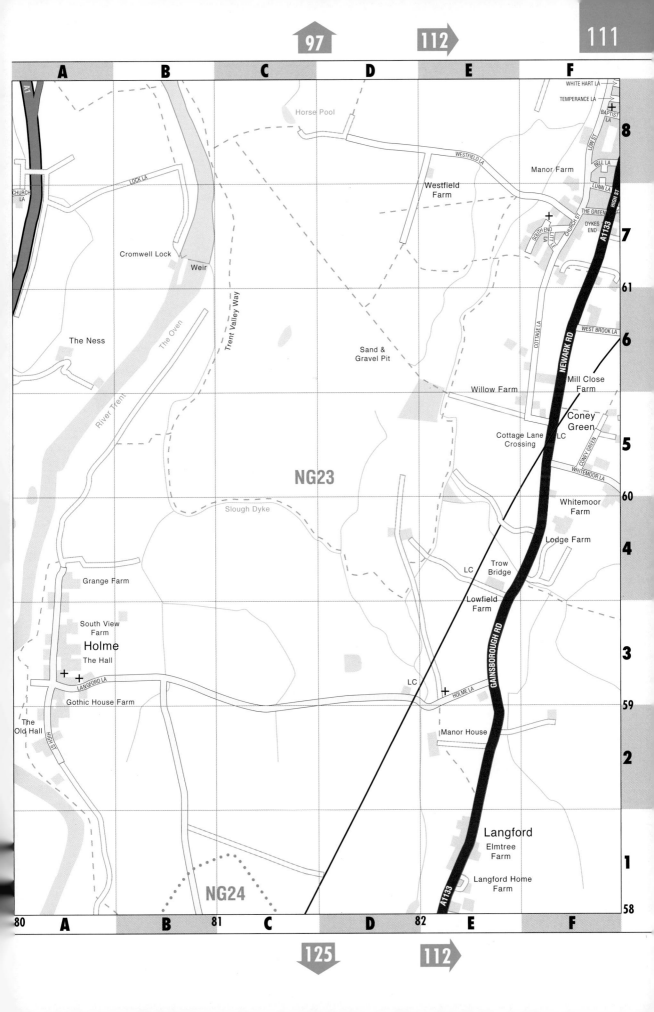

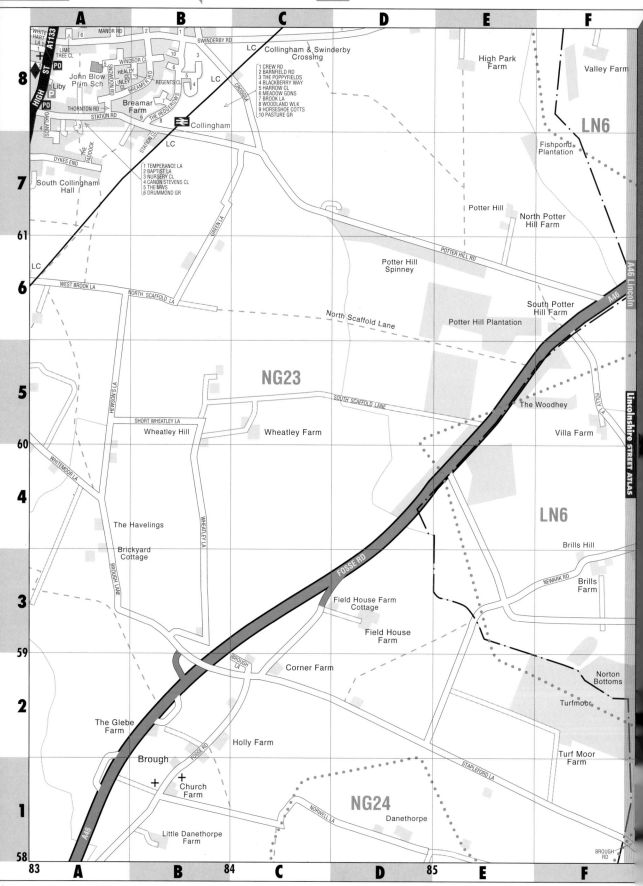

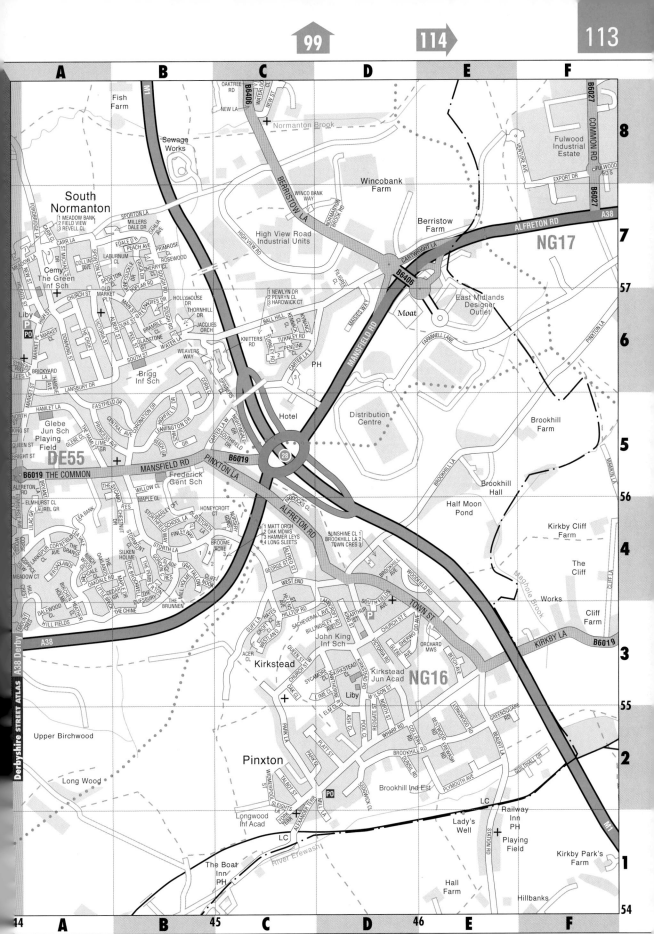

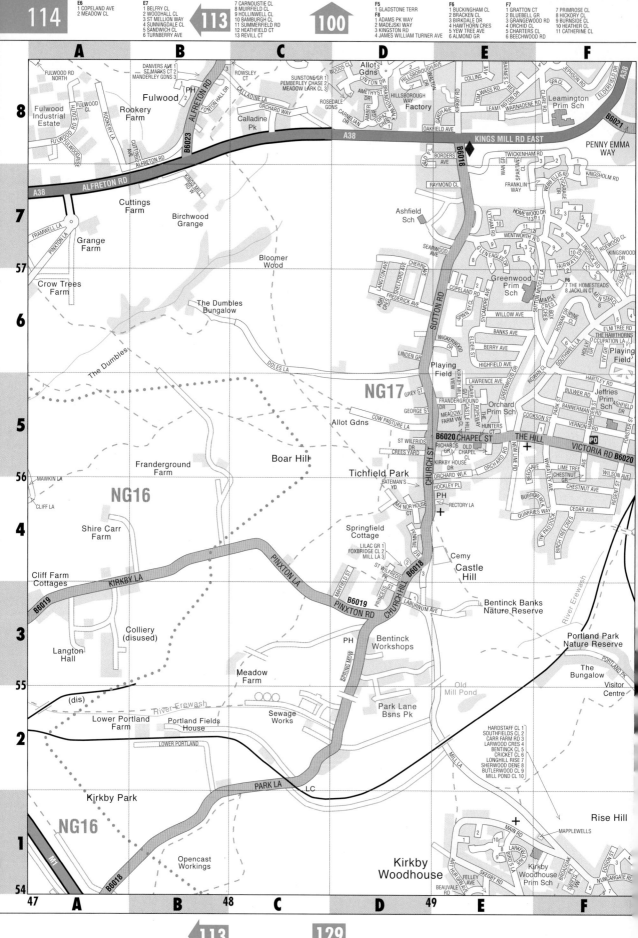

113
100
113
129

E6
1 COPELAND AVE
2 MEADOW CL

E7
1 BELFRY CL
2 WOODHALL CL
3 ST MELLION WAY
4 SUNNINGDALE CL
5 SANDWICH CL
6 TURNBERRY AVE

7 CARNOUSTIE CL
8 MUIRFIELD CL
9 HOLLINWELL CL
10 BAMBURGH CL
11 SUMMERFIELD RD
12 HEATHFIELD CT
13 REVILL CT

F5
1 GLADSTONE TERR
F8
1 ADAMS PK WAY
2 MADEJSKI WAY
3 KINGSTON RD
4 JAMES WILLIAM TURNER AVE

F6
1 BUCKINGHAM CL
2 BRACKEN CL
3 BIRKDALE DR
4 HAWTHORN CRES
5 YEW TREE AVE
6 ALMOND GR

F7
1 GRATTON CT
2 BLUEBELL GR
3 GRANGEWOOD RD
4 ORCHID CL
5 CHARTERS CL
6 BEECHWOOD RD

7 PRIMROSE CL
8 HICKORY CL
9 BURNSIDE CL
10 HEATHER CL
11 CATHERINE CL

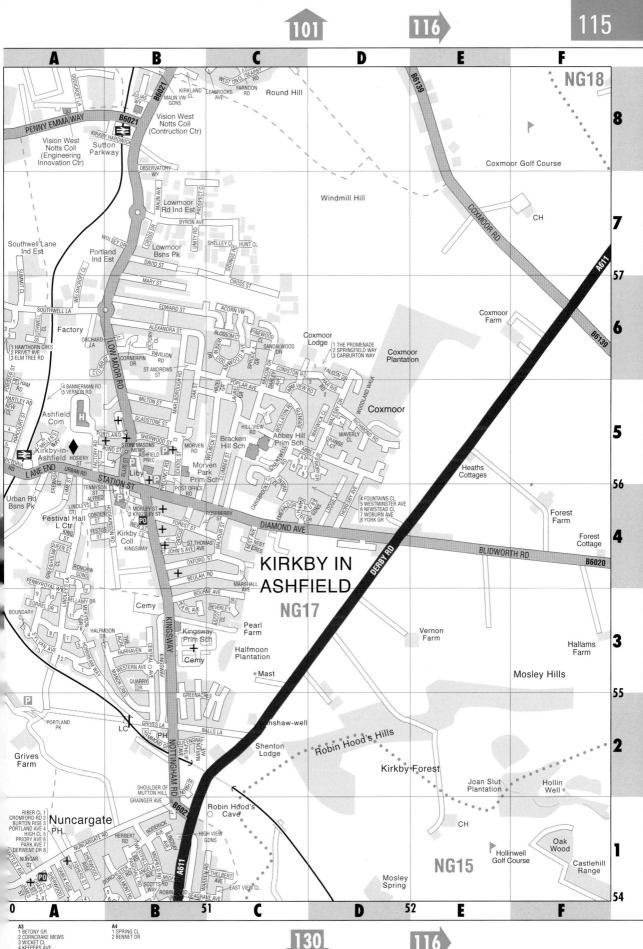

KIRKBY IN
ASHFIELD

NG17

Nuncargate

A3
1 BETONY GR
2 CORNCRAKE MEWS
3 WICKET CL
4 KEEPERS AVE
5 LINNET CL
6 CAMPION GDNS
7 ROBIN DOWN CT
8 HAREBELL CL
9 AMARELLA LA

A4
1 SPRING CL
2 BENNET DR

◁ 115
◇ 102

A B C D E F

8 Stonehills Farm

DERBY RD

A611

Works

THIEVES WOOD LA

THE SPINNEY

MAPLE DR

POPLARS WY

LIME TREE DR

7 Two Oaks Farm

A611

NG18
Thieves' Wood

OAK VIEW RISE

PINES WY

CHESTNUT CL

Harlow Wood

57

Greenwood Craft Centre

Forest Stone

BLACK SCOTCH LA

6 B6139

COXMOOR RD

Fountaindale Sch

P

Portland Coll

Forest Walks

Robin Hood Way

NG21

Sheppard's Stone

Woodlands Farm

5

Nomanshill Wood

SUTTON BACK LA

P

P

Forest Walks

RICKET LA

Holly Lodge

Twin Hill

4 NG17

Little Nomanshill Wood

B6139

Campfield Farm

LITTLE RICKET LA

MANSFIELD RD (NORTH)

The Larch Farm

BEECH AVE

B6020 BLIDWORTH RD

KIRKBY RD

PH

MAIN RD

B6020

ROSEDALE

3

HIGH LEYS DR

FAIRFIELD DR

COPSE CL

HAGGNOOK WOOD

Haggnook Wood

BYRON CRES

SHEEPWALK LA

WOODSIDE RD

HASLEMERE GDNS

SUMMERPORT RD

WESTBROOK

LINWOOD CRES

55

Gosford Plantation

NG15

Gunthorpe Hagg Wood

CAMBOURNE GDNS

DOVER BECK CL

2

Knightcross Dale

NOTTINGHAM RD

SHEEPWALK

SWINTON

CHURCH DR

MILTON CR

Liby

PILGRIM CL

THE HOLLIES

MILTON DR

VERNON CRES

Pilgrim Oak

Hotel

1 Monksbarn Farm

Reedwater

NEWSTEAD ABBEY PARK

Upper Lake

Knightcross

Newstead Park

Swinecotte Dale

Lady Wildman's Wood

A60

LONGDALE LA

MISTERTON CRES

REGINA CRES

54 Castle Wood

53 A 54 B C D 55 E F

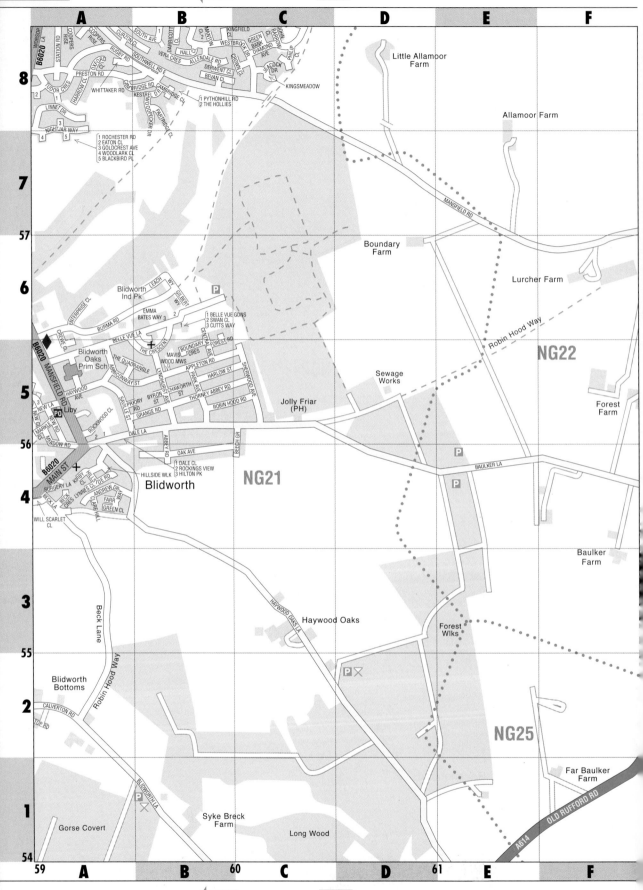

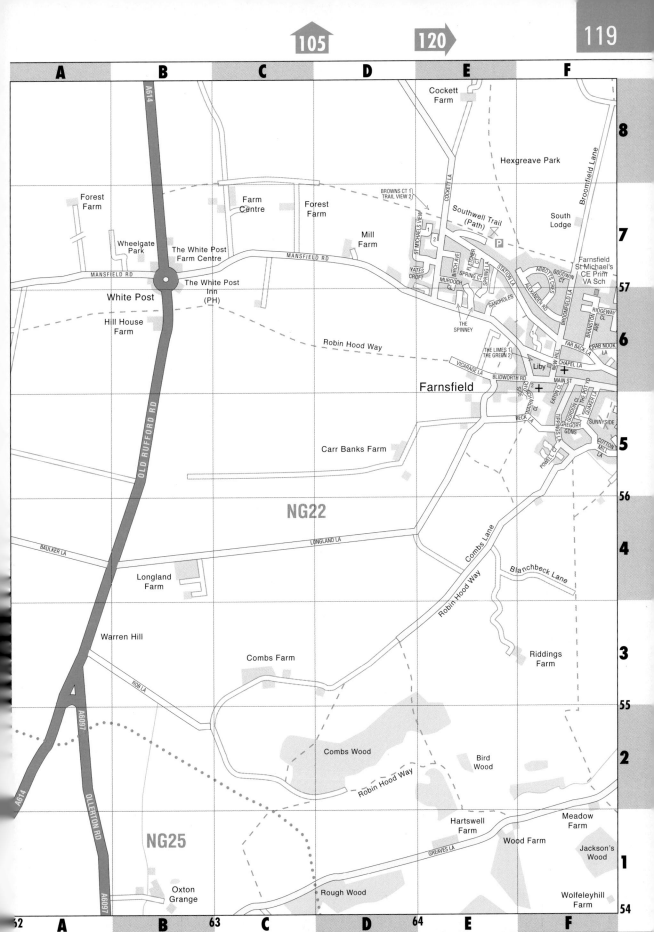

A B C D E F

8

Forest Farm

Cockett Farm

Hexgreave Park

Broomfield Lane

7

BROWNS CT 1
TRAIL VIEW 2

Southwell Trail (Path)

South Lodge

Forest Farm

Farm Centre

Forest Farm

Mill Farm

P

COCKETT LA

ST MICHAEL'S VIEW

Farnsfield St Michael's CE Prim VA Sch

57

Wheelgate Park

The White Post Farm Centre

MANSFIELD RD

BIRCH AVE

FLETCHER CT

SPRING CT

SPRING LA

GOODWIN CT

ABBOTS CL

STATION LA

ALEXANDER RD

RIDGEWAY CL

YATES CROFT

MURDOCH CL

BROOMFIELD LA

BRANSTON AVE

MANSFIELD RD

White Post

The White Post Inn (PH)

SANDHOLES

CRAB NOOK LA

6

Hill House Farm

THE SPINNEY

Robin Hood Way

VICARAGE LA

THE LIMES 1
THE GREEN 2

BLIDWORTH RD

Liby

NEW HILL

CHAPEL LA

FAR BACK LA

Farnsfield

MAIN ST

EATON CL

GORDON CL

QUAKER LA

SUNNYSIDE

BECK LA

GREGORY GDNS

COTTON MILL LA

5

Carr Banks Farm

POWELL CT

56

NG22

LONGLAND LA

Combs Lane

4

BAULKER LA

Blanchbeck Lane

Longland Farm

Robin Hood Way

Riddings Farm

3

Warren Hill

ROB LA

Combs Farm

55

A6097

A614

OLLERTON RD

NG25

Combs Wood

Bird Wood

2

Robin Hood Way

Hartswell Farm

Meadow Farm

1

Wood Farm

Jackson's Wood

GREAVES LA

Oxton Grange

Rough Wood

Wolfeleyhill Farm

54

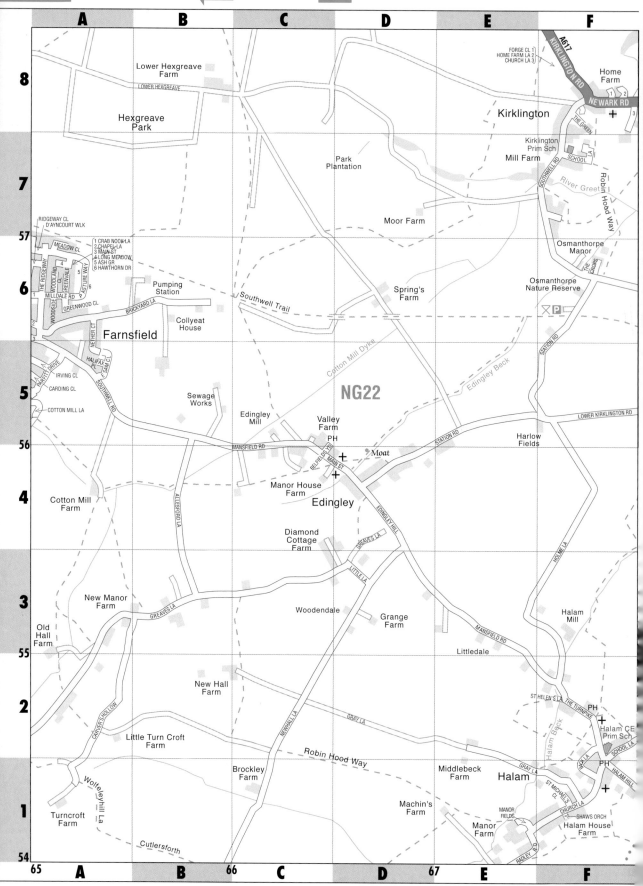

Lower Hexgreave
Farm

LOWER HEXGREAVE

Hexgreave
Park

Park
Plantation

Moor Farm

FORGE CL 1
HOME FARM LA 2
CHURCH LA 3

A617
KIRKLINGTON RD
NEWARK RD

Home
Farm

Kirklington

THE GREEN
SCHOOL LA

Kirklington
Prim Sch
Mill Farm

SOUTHWELL RD

River Greet

Robin Hood Way

Osmanthorpe
Manor

THE CROPS

Osmanthorpe
Nature Reserve

RIDGEWAY CL
D'AYNCOURT WLK

MEADOW CL

THE RIDGEWAY
WOODLAND CL
GREENVALE

MILLDALE RD
WOODSIDE
GREENWOOD CL
PASTURE WAY
NETHER CT

1 CRAB NOOK LA
2 CHAPEL LA
3 MAIN ST
4 LONG MEADOW
5 ASH GR
6 HAWTHORN DR

Pumping
Station

Collyeat
House

BRICKYARD LA

Southwell Trail

Spring's
Farm

STATION RD

P

Farnsfield

PARTITT DRIVE
IRVING CL
CARDING CL

COTTON MILL LA

HALIFAX PL
SAM CL
SOUTHWELL RD

Sewage
Works

Edingley
Mill

Cotton Mill Dyke

NG22

Edingley Beck

LOWER KIRKLINGTON RD

Cotton Mill
Farm

ALLESFORD LA

MANSFIELD RD

Valley
Farm
PH

BELFIELD CL
MAIN ST

Moat

STATION RD

Harlow
Fields

Manor House
Farm

Edingley

EDINGLEY HILL

HOLME LA

New Manor
Farm

GREAVES LA

Diamond
Cottage
Farm

GREAVES LA

LITTLE LA

Woodendale

Grange
Farm

MANSFIELD RD

Halam
Mill

Old
Hall
Farm

Littledale

CARVER'S HOLLOW

New Hall
Farm

NEWHALL LA

GRAY LA

ST HELEN'S LA
THE TURNPIKE

PH

Halam CE
Prim Sch

Halam Beck

SCHOOL LA

PH

Little Turn Croft
Farm

Robin Hood Way

Brockley
Farm

Middlebeck
Farm

Halam

GRAY LA

PARK LA
HALAM HILL

Wolfeleyhill La

Turncroft
Farm

Machin's
Farm

ST MICHAEL'S CL
CHURCH LA

MANOR
FIELDS

Manor
Farm

SHAWS ORCH

Halam House
Farm

RADLEY RD

Cutlersforth

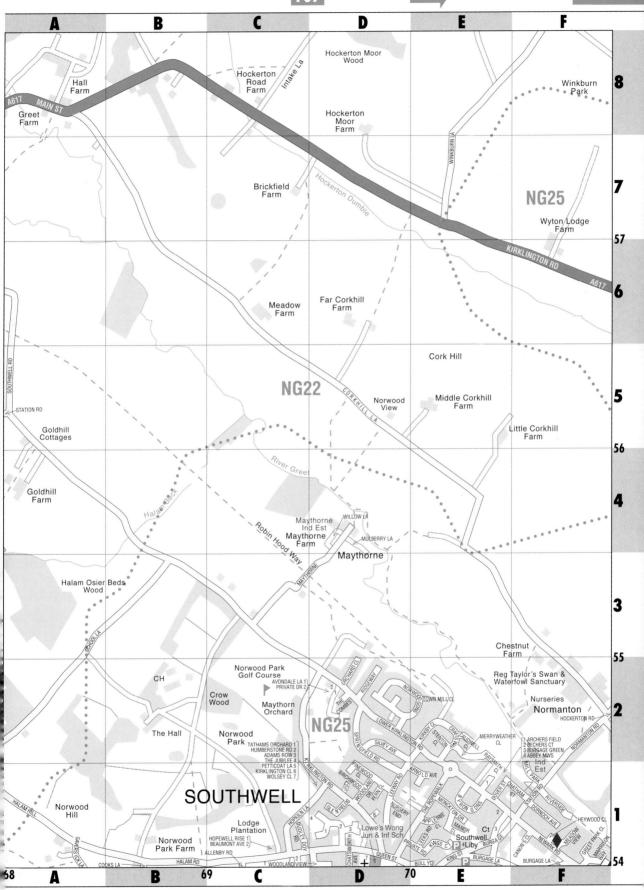

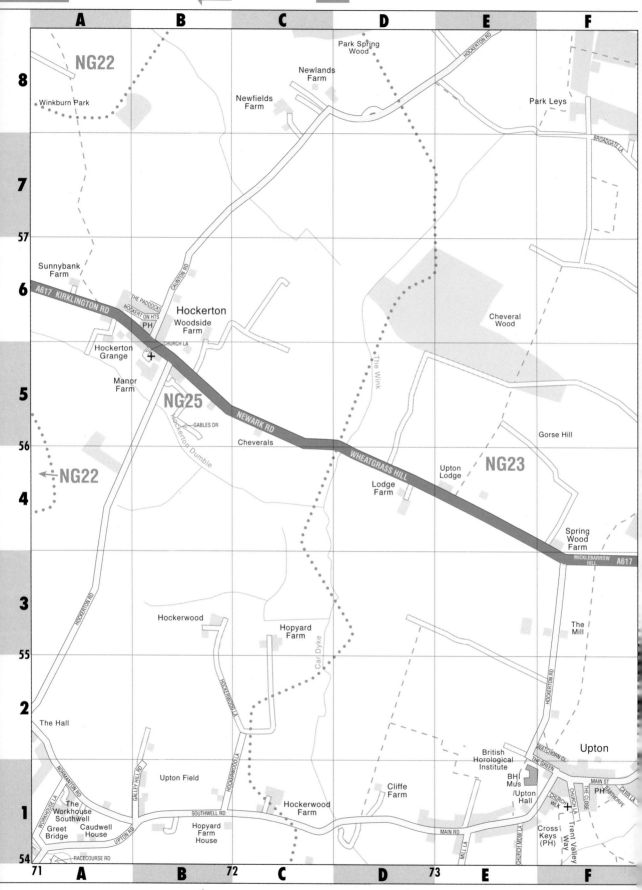

NG22

Winkburn Park

Sunnybank Farm

A617 KIRKLINGTON RD

THE PADDOCKS
HOCKERTON HTS
PH

Hockerton Grange

Manor Farm

NG25

Hockerton Dumble

GABLES DR

NEWARK RD

Cheverals

NG22

Hockerton

Woodside Farm

CHURCH LA

CAUNTON RD

Newfields Farm

Newlands Farm

Park Spring Wood

HOCKERTON RD

Park Leys

BROADGATE LA

Cheveral Wood

The Wink

NG23

Gorse Hill

Upton Lodge

WHEATGRASS HILL

Lodge Farm

Spring Wood Farm

MICKLEBARROW HILL A617

Hockerwood

Hopyard Farm

Car Dyke

HOCKERWOOD LA

The Mill

HOCKERTON RD

The Hall

NORMANTON RD

GALLEY HILL RD

Upton Field

Hockerwood Farm

Cliffe Farm

British Horological Institute

BHI Mus

Upton Hall

THE GREEN

WATCHORN CL

Upton

MAIN ST

CABELLA

EASTHORPE

The Workhouse Southwell

WORKHOUSE LA

Greet Bridge

Caudwell House

UPTON RD

SOUTHWELL RD

Hopyard Farm House

MAIN RD

MILL LA

CHURCH MOW LA

CHURCH LA

CHURCH WLK

Cross Keys (PH)

Trent Valley Way

THE CLOSE

RACECOURSE RD

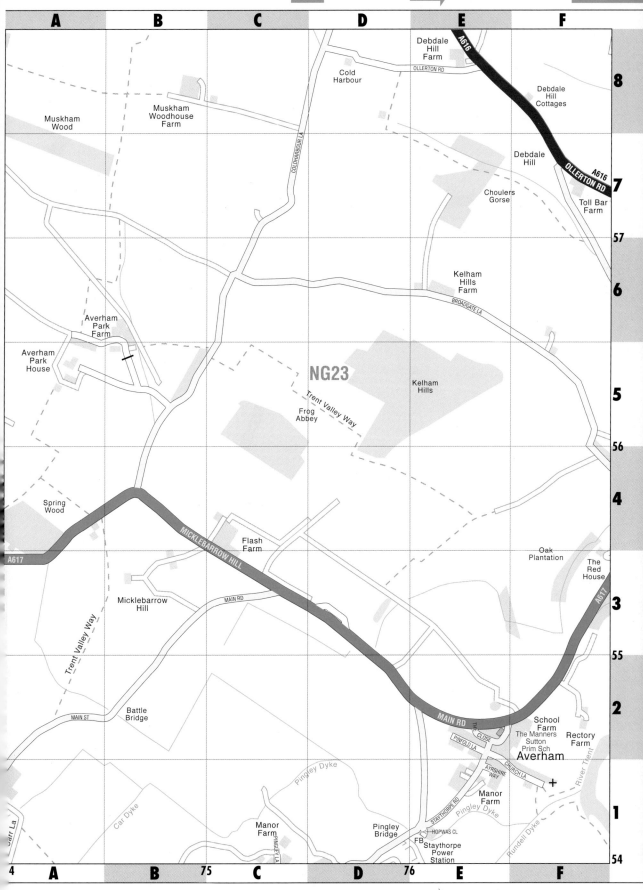

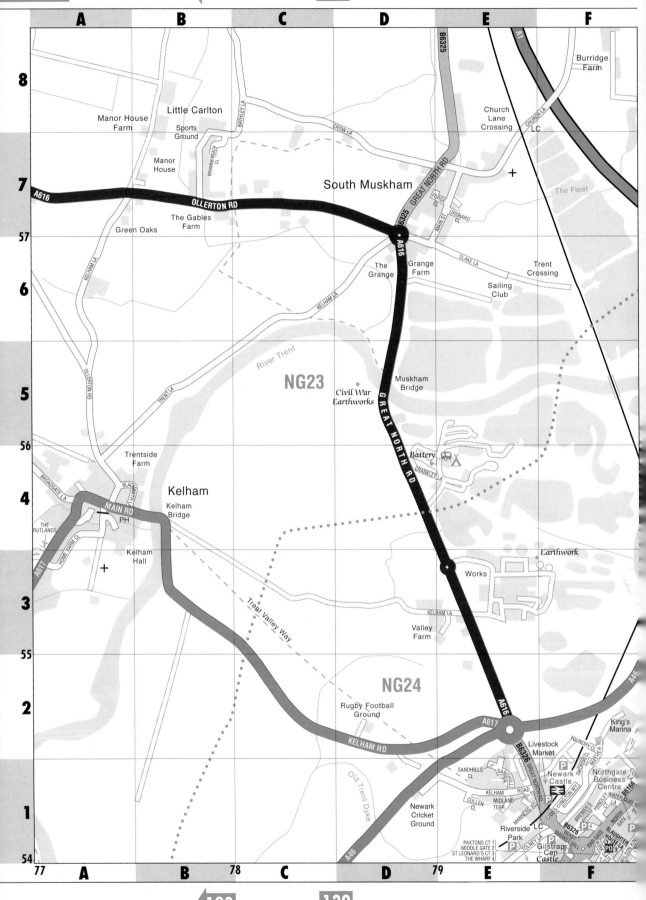

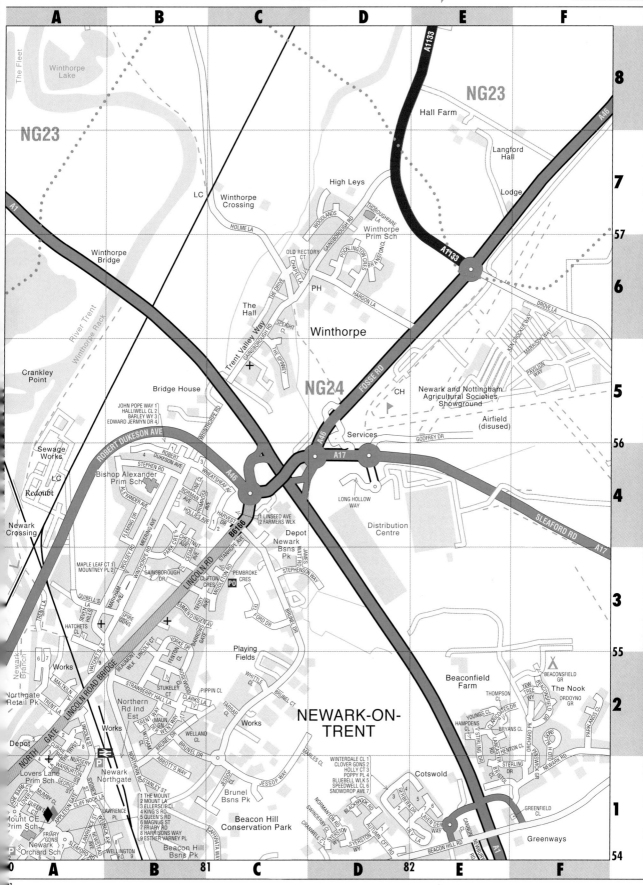

A2
ALLIANCE ST
SUMMER'S RD
NEWNHAM RD
MEYRICK RD
WARWICK BREWERY
WATERS EDGE
KINGS SCONCE AVE
HIGGINS CL
APPLE TREE CL

125
112

A **B** **C** **D** **E** **F**

NG23

NG23

8

NG23

Thorpe Field
Farm

Danethorpe Hill

High
Wood

Danethorpe Hill
Farm

7

Little Danethorpe
Farm

LN6

57

6

Langford Moor
Farm

Lingspot
Farm

Langford Moor

PALINGS RIDE

5

NG24

Stapleford Wood

CODDINGTON LA

Newark Air
Museum

HIGHFIELD DR

56

Northlea

4

Drove Cottage
Farm

DROVE LA

STAPLEFORD LA

The Bungalow

A17

3

Moor
Brats

The
Cottage

Moor
Plantation

55

Flawford
Farm

2

THE
GREEN

Sports
Ground

Coddington
Moor

The
Tinderbox

Hall
Farm

MORGANS CL

THORPE CL

ROSS CL

PARKES CL

SLEAFORD RD

A17

Coddington

BECKINGHAM RD

MAIN ST

CHAPEL LA

PH

NEWARK
RD

VALLEY VIEW

BROWNLOW'S HILL

OLD MANOR CT

Manor
Farm

Kelwick
Wood

LONG LA

Coddington
CE Prim Sch

BALDERTON LA

HOUGHS
YARD

1

Vale Farm

Newark Golf Course

CH

54

83 **A** **B** **84** **C** **D** **85** **E** **F**

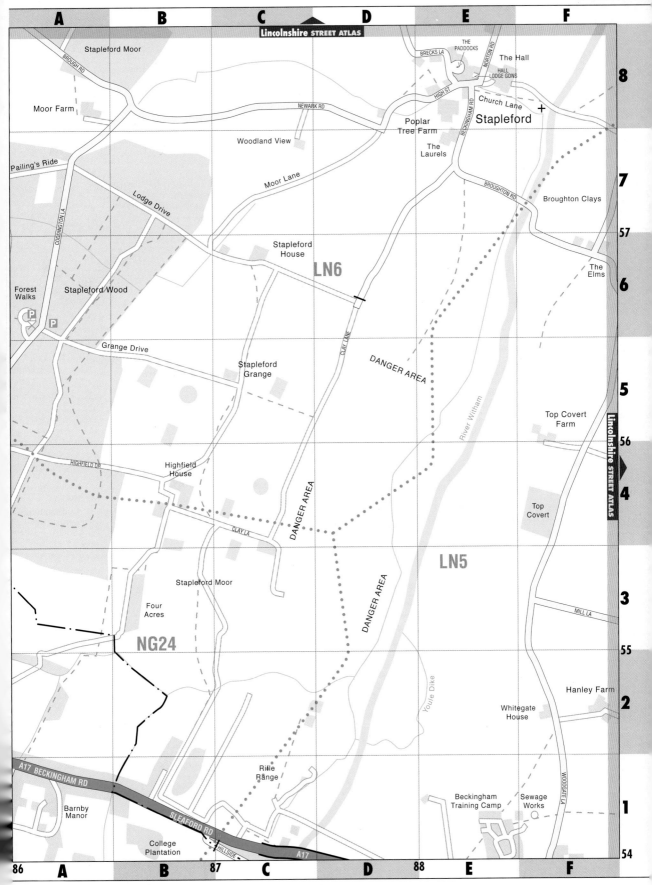

Stapleford Moor

Moor Farm

Pailing's Ride

BROUGH RD

CODDINGTON LA

Forest Walks

Stapleford Wood

Lodge Drive

Woodland View

NEWARK RD

Moor Lane

Stapleford House

LN6

Grange Drive

Stapleford Grange

HIGHFIELD DR

Highfield House

CLAY LA

Stapleford Moor

Four Acres

NG24

A17 BECKINGHAM RD

Barnby Manor

College Plantation

SLEAFORD RD

HILLSIDE

A17

Rifle Range

DANGER AREA

DANGER AREA

DANGER AREA

CLAY LANE

River Witham

Youle Dike

BRECKS LA

THE PADDOCKS

The Hall

NORTON RD

HALL LODGE GDNS

Church Lane

Stapleford

HIGH ST

BECKINGHAM RD

Poplar Tree Farm

The Laurels

BROUGHTON RD

Broughton Clays

The Elms

Top Covert Farm

Top Covert

LN5

MILL LA

Hanley Farm

Whitegate House

WOODGATE LA

Beckingham Training Camp

Sewage Works

8

7

57

6

5

56

4

55

3

2

1

54

86   A   B   87   C   D   88   E   F

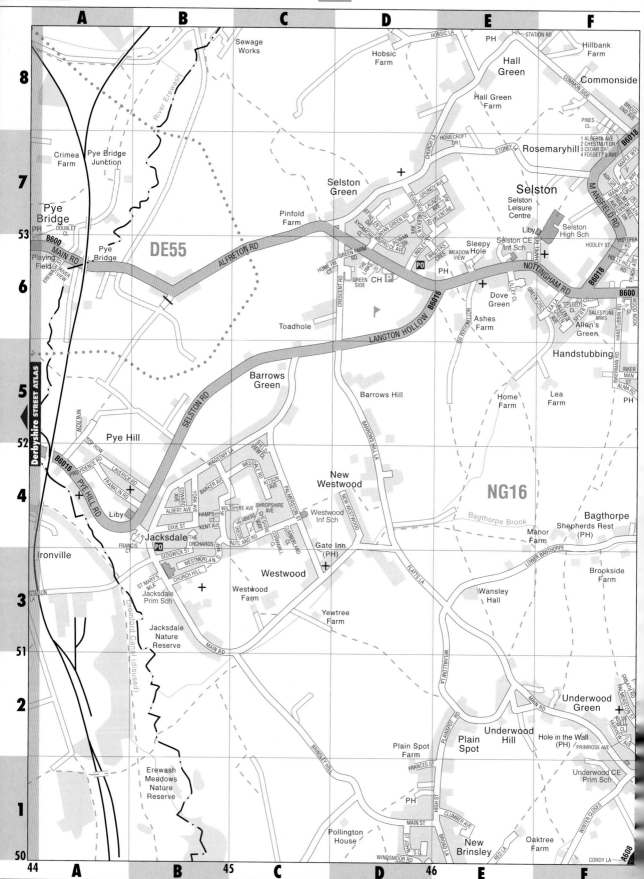

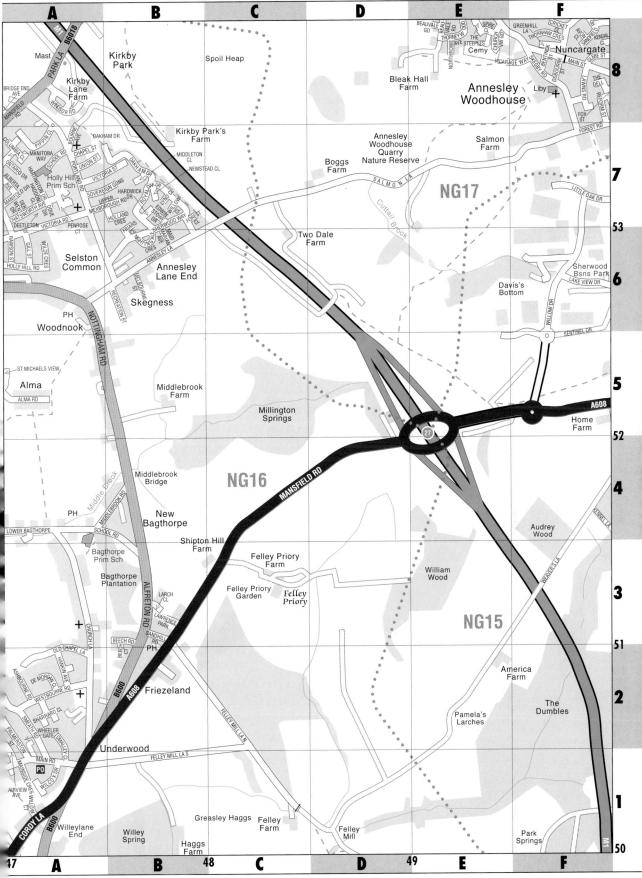

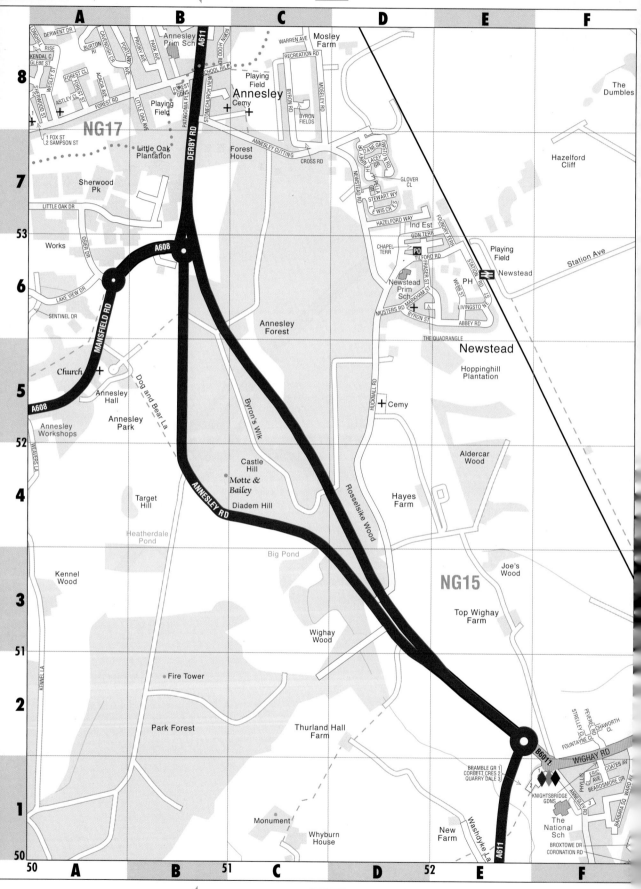

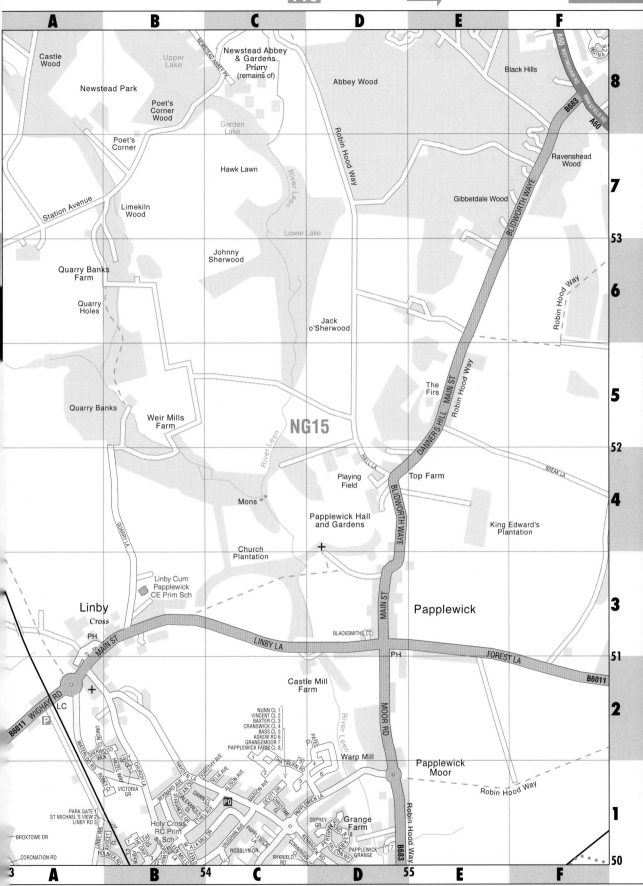

A B C D E F

8

7

53

6

5

52

4

3

51

2

1

50

Castle Wood

Newstead Park

Poet's Corner Wood

Poet's Corner

Station Avenue

Limekiln Wood

Quarry Banks Farm

Quarry Holes

Quarry Banks

Weir Mills Farm

Upper Lake

NEWSTEAD ABBEY PK

Newstead Abbey & Gardens Priory (remains of)

Garden Lake

Hawk Lawn

River Leen

Lower Lake

Johnny Sherwood

QUARRY LA

Abbey Wood

Robin Hood Way

Jack o'Sherwood

NG15

River Leen

Mons

Playing Field

Papplewick Hall and Gardens

Church Plantation

Linby Cum Papplewick CE Prim Sch

Linby

Cross

PH

MAIN ST

+

WIGHAY RD

LC

P

B6011

UNION CL

WATERLOO RD

SHERWOOD WLK

HAZEL WAY

ROBEY CL

DAVY CL

CHURCH LA

VICTORIA GR

BERNARD AVE

HADEN LA

ST FRANCES CT

SUS AN CL

ALEXANDER LA

ETHEL AVE

DAWN CL

DELIA AVE

ALISON AVE

DOROTHY AVE

MARION AVE

DEVITT DR

CHRISTINE AVE

PAPPLEWICK LA

CHA DBURN RD

PATES CL

The Firs

DANNERS HILL

MAIN ST

Robin Hood Way

Top Farm

HALL LA

BLIDWORTH WAYE

Black Hills

B683

A60

MANSFIELD RD

A60 NOTTINGHAM RD

REYNA CR

Ravenshead Wood

Gibbetdale Wood

Robin Hood Way

BREAK LA

King Edward's Plantation

Papplewick

BLACKSMITHS CT

MAIN ST

PH

FOREST LA

B6011

Castle Mill Farm

MOOR RD

River Leen

Papplewick Moor

Robin Hood Way

Warp Mill

NUNN CL 1
VINCENT CL 2
BAXTER CL 3
CRANSWICK CL 4
BASS CL 5
ASKEW RD 6
GRANGEMOOR 7
PAPPLEWICK FARM CL 8

PO

VAUGHAN AVE

WALK MILL DR

PAPPLEWICK LA

ROSSLYN DR

Holy Cross RC Prim Sch

PARK GATE 1
ST MICHAEL'S VIEW 2
LINBY RD 3

BROXTOWE DR

CORONATION RD

LINBY WLK

AVOCET CL

HOLBECK RD

The PEAK

BISHOPS DR

FEA MILLS

The DRIFT

The PIPER

OSPREY GR

KINGROOK

CORINTH DR

REDPART

OSPREY GR

RYKNIELD RD

VERD

Grange Farm

Papplewick Grange

FALCON WY

B683

Robin Hood Way

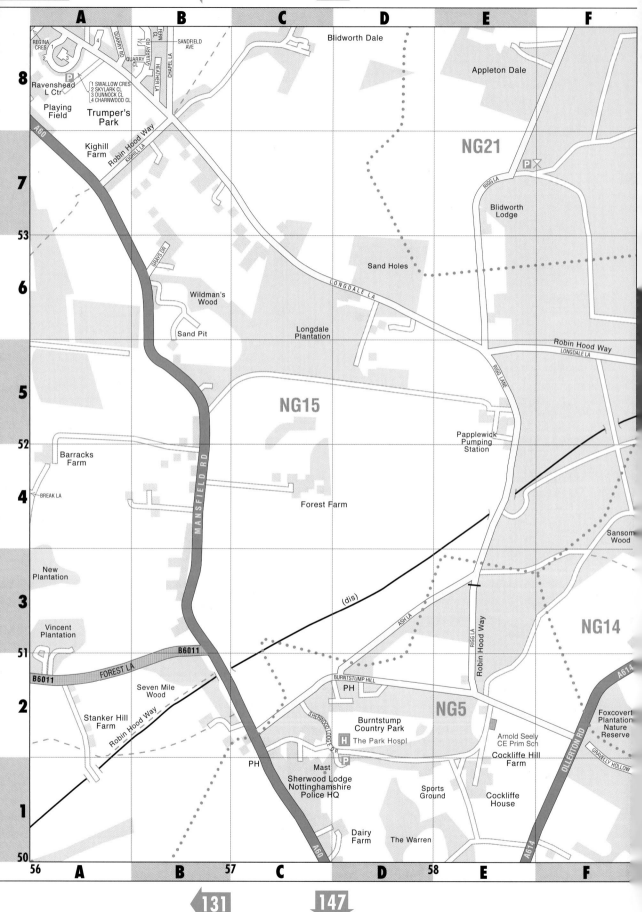

118   134

A   B   C   D   E   F

8

NG21

HAYWOOD OAKS LA

A614

OAKS LA

Far Tops

Archer's Water
Farm

7

Robin Hood Way

Oakmere Park
Golf Course

53

Little Tithe Farm

Forest
Walk

CH

6

OLD KENNEL DR

Darcliff Hill

NG25

NG15

OLD RUFFORD RD

P X

Big
Tithe
Farm

Salterford
Farm

Salterford
Dam

LONGDALE LA

SALTERFORD LA

Salterford
House
Sch

5

(dis)

52

WHINBUSH LA

Gorse
Covert

4

OLD RUFFORD RD

War
Memorial

Oxton
Bogs

Sansom Wood
Farm

Beanford
Farm

3

OLLERTON RD

Watchwood
Plantation

NG14

BEANFORD LA

Richmond
Farm

WHINBUSH LA

Bean
Ford

A614

51

NOTTINGHAM RD

B6386

2

Lodge
Farm

Thorndale
Plantation

GRAVELLY HOLLOW

OXTON RD

Whitehaven
Farm

MANSFIELD LA

1

HIND ST LA

JAMES DR

HOYLE RD

CARRINGTON LA

B6386

HOLLINWOOD
LA

NORTH
GREEN

PATON

WILLIAMS DR

50

9   A   B   60   C   D   61   E   F

148   134

NG22

NG25

NG14

Margaret's Spring
Horsepasture Wood
Loath Hill
Robin Hood Hill
Robin Hood Way
Fallows Farm
Far Leys Holt
Dairy Farm
Moorfields Farm
Oaks La
Godson Plantation
Honeyknab La
Oxton Dumble
Cockglode Plantation
Windmill Hill
Far Leys
Oxton Hill Farm
Oxton Hill
Forest Rd
Oxton Byepass
Hatfield Lane
Chapel La
Deer Leap
Middlehey Sch
Birkhouse Wood
The Orchards
Oxton
Southwell Rd
PO
Blind La
Manor Cl
Salterford House Sch
Elmcroft
Main St
New Rd
Sandy La
Holly Lodge
Rossellewood Farm
School Gdns
Water La
Nether Field
PH
Beanford La
Nottingham Rd
B6386
Southwell Rd
Park Farm
Thorndale Plantation
Oxton By-Pass
Mill Farm
Epperstone Rd
Dover Beck
Epperstone Park
A6097
Ollerton Rd
Oxton By-Pass
Greaves La

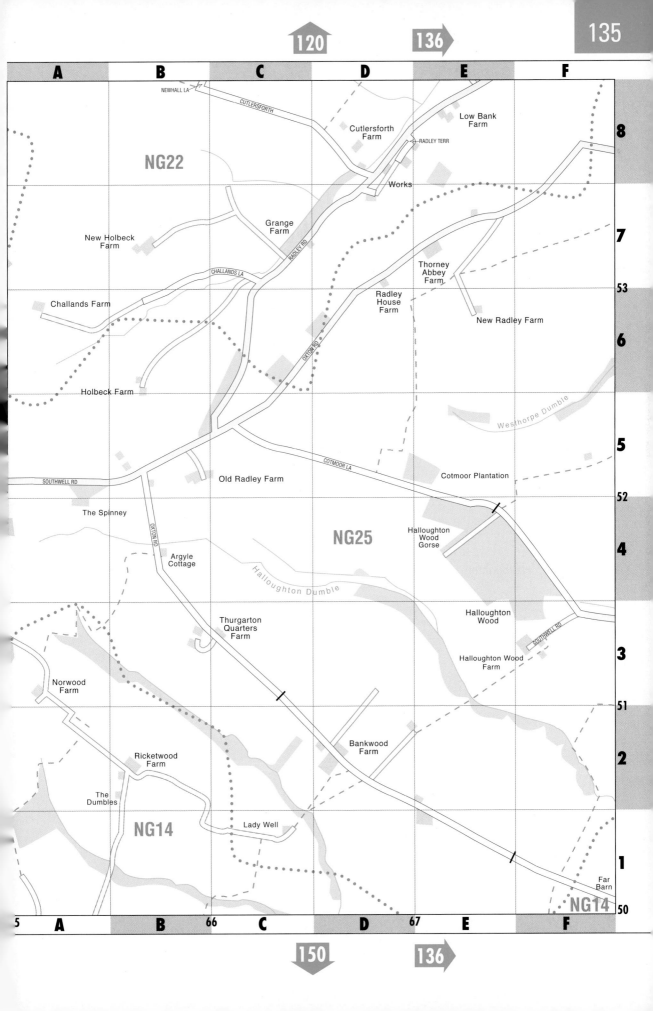

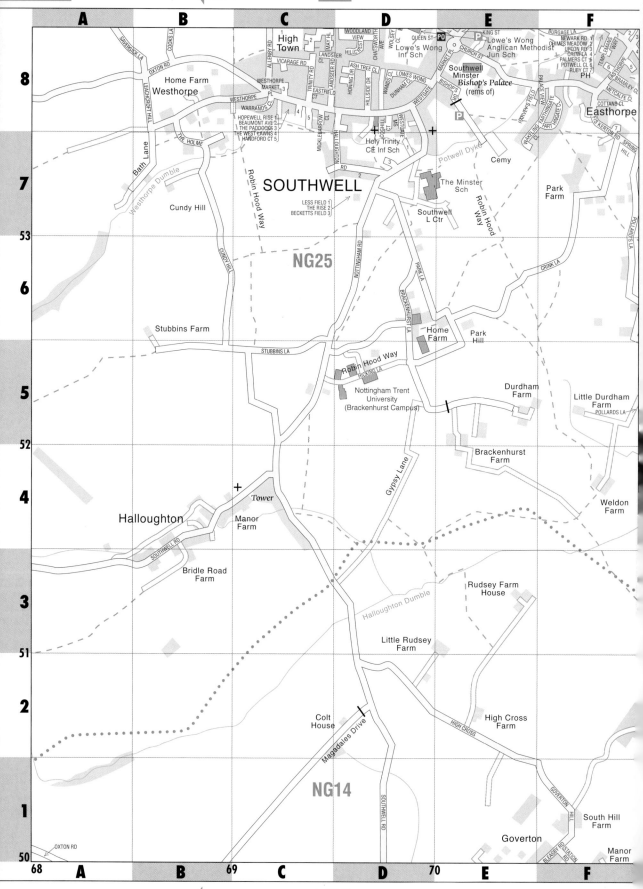

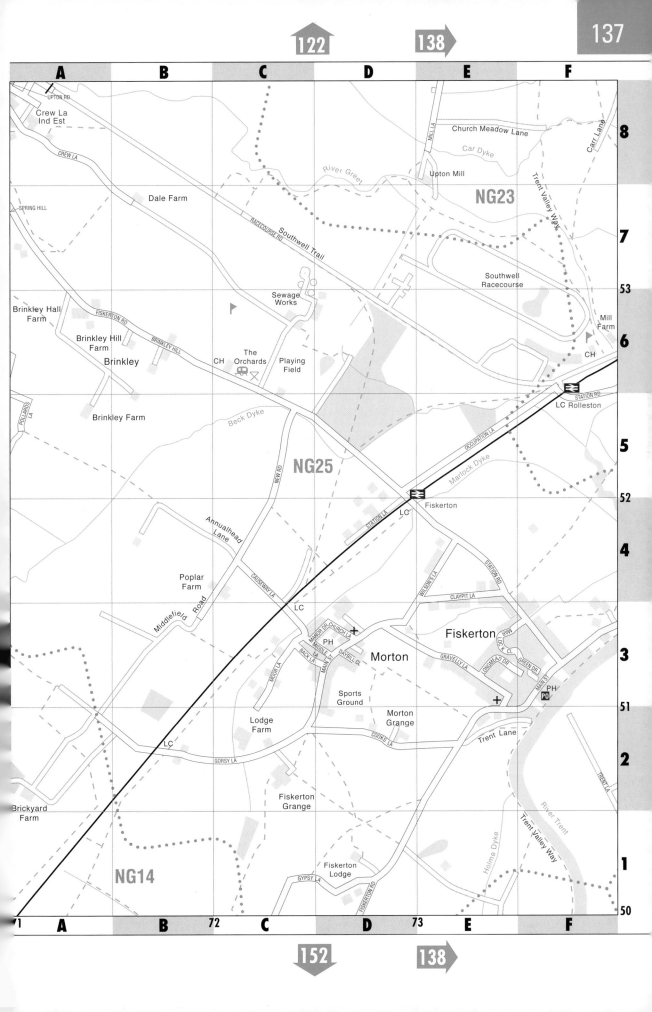

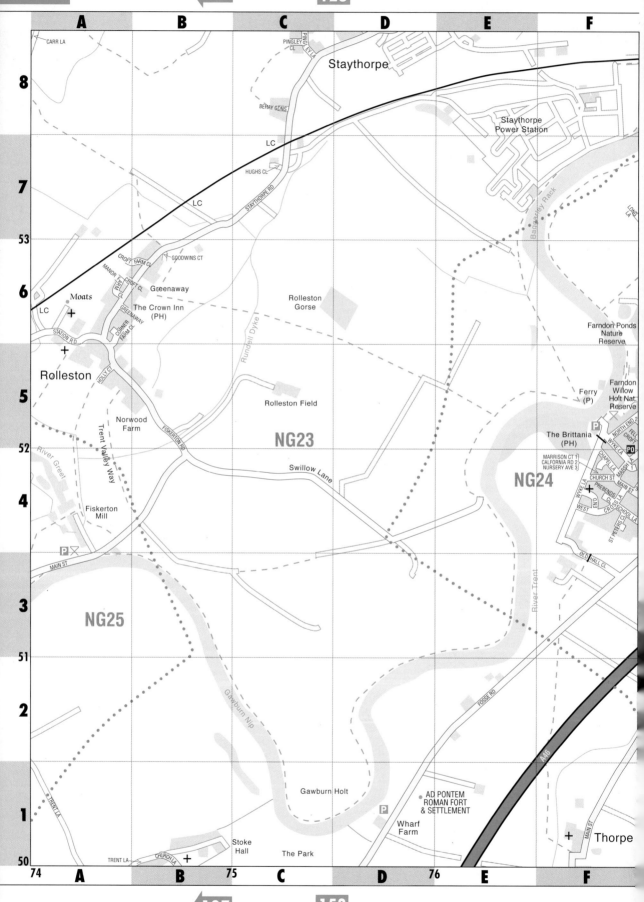

Staythorpe

Staythorpe
Power Station

PINGLEY CL
PINGLEY LA
BERAY GDNS
HUGHS CL
STAYTHORPE RD
LC
LC
LC

Baggarley Rack
LONG LA

CARR LA

CROFT FARM CL
GOODWINS CT
MANOR FARM CL
CROFT CL
Greenaway
Moats
GREENAWAY
The Crown Inn
(PH)
CORNER FARM CL
STATION RD
LC

Rolleston Gorse

Rolleston Ponds
Nature Reserve

Farndon Willow
Holt Nat.
Reserve

Ferry
(P)

Rolleston

HOLLY CT
Norwood
Farm
FISKERTON RD
Rolleston Field

Rundell Dyke

NG23

The Brittania
(PH)
NORTH END
FELD CROFT
WYKE LA
MARRISON CT 1
CALFORNIA RD 2
NURSERY AVE 3
CHAPEL LA
CHURCH ST
MAIN ST
NG24
WYKE LA
PREBENDS
CRO
SCHOOL LA
WEST
END
ST PETERS CL

Trent Valley Way

River Greet

Swillow Lane

Fiskerton
Mill

P

MAIN ST

OLD HALL CL

River Trent

NG25

Gawburn Nip

FOSSE RD

A46

Gawburn Holt

P

AD PONTEM
ROMAN FORT
& SETTLEMENT

Wharf
Farm

TRENT LA

Stoke
Hall
CHURCH LA
The Park

TRENT LA

Thorpe
MAIN ST

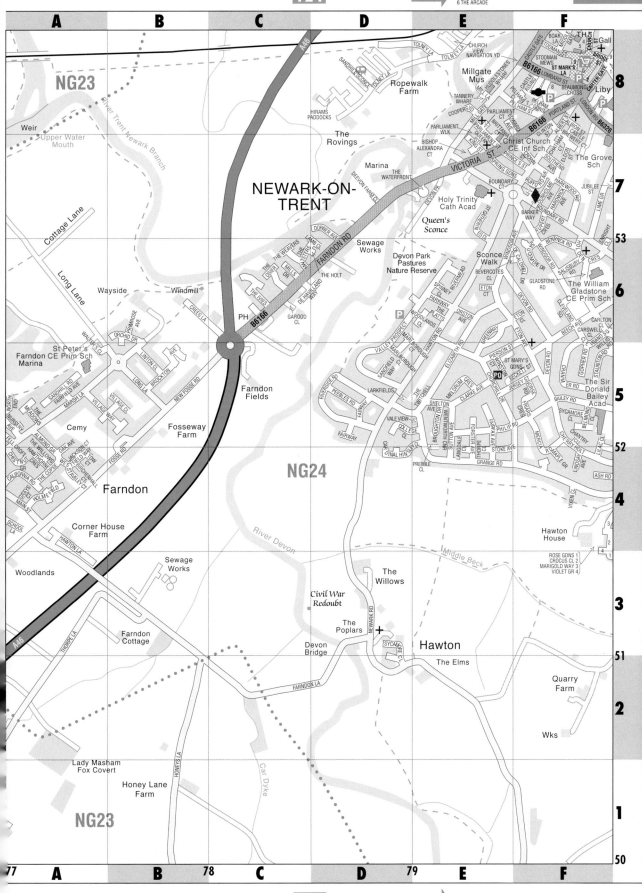

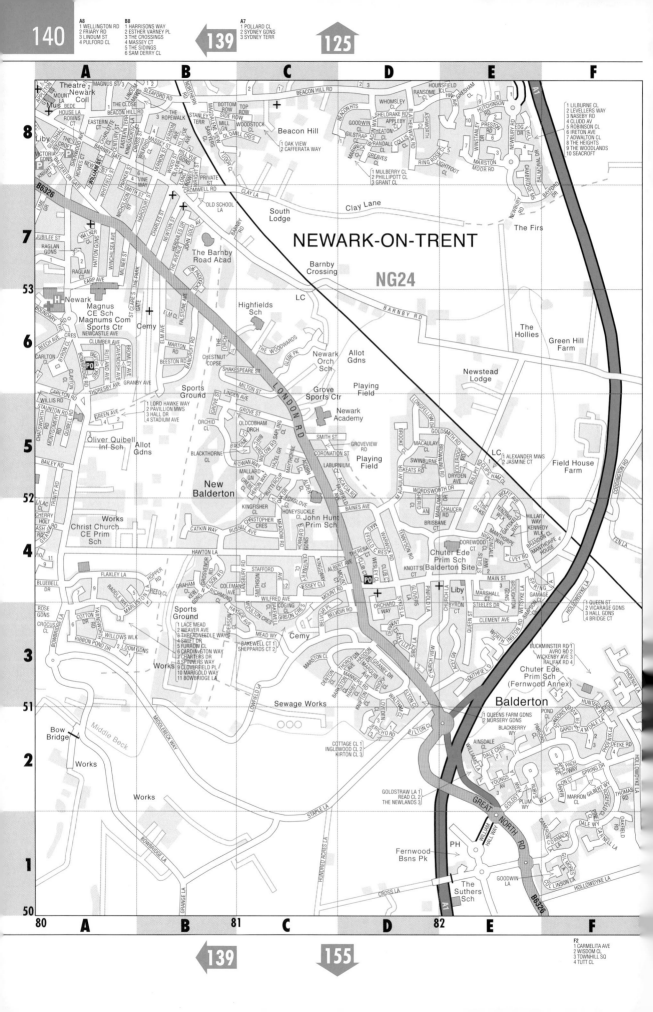

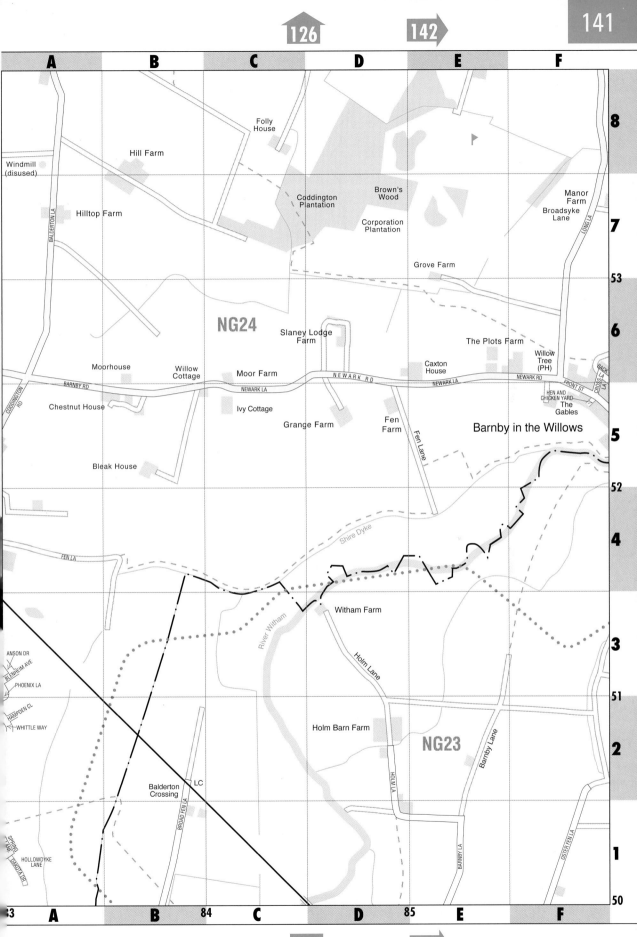

A   B   C   D   E   F

8

Folly
House

Windmill
(disused)

Hill Farm

7

Hilltop Farm

Coddington
Plantation

Brown's
Wood

Manor
Farm
Broadsyke
Lane

Corporation
Plantation

53

NG24

Grove Farm

6

Slaney Lodge
Farm

The Plots Farm

Willow
Tree
(PH)

Moorhouse

Willow
Cottage

Moor Farm

NEWARK RD

Caxton
House

NEWARK RD

BACK LA

BARNBY RD

NEWARK LA

NEWARK LA

CROSS LA

FRONT ST

HEN AND
CHICKEN YARD

The
Gables

Chestnut House

Ivy Cottage

Grange Farm

Fen
Farm

Fen Lane

Barnby in the Willows

5

Bleak House

52

Shire Dyke

4

FEN LA

River Witham

Witham Farm

3

ANSON DR

BLENHEIM AVE

PHOENIX LA

Holm Lane

51

HAMPDEN CL

WHITTLE WAY

Holm Barn Farm

NG23

Barnby Lane

2

Balderton
Crossing

LC

BROAD FEN LA

HOLM LA

BARNBY LA

OSIER FEN LA

1

SPRING LANE

HOLLOWDYKE
LANE

DAKOTA DR

50

83   A   B   84   C   D   85   E   F

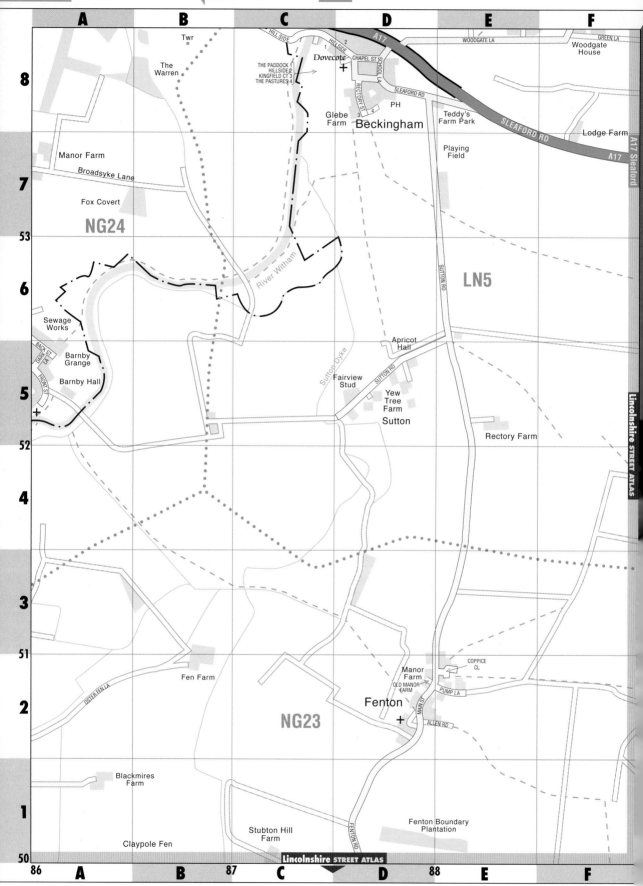

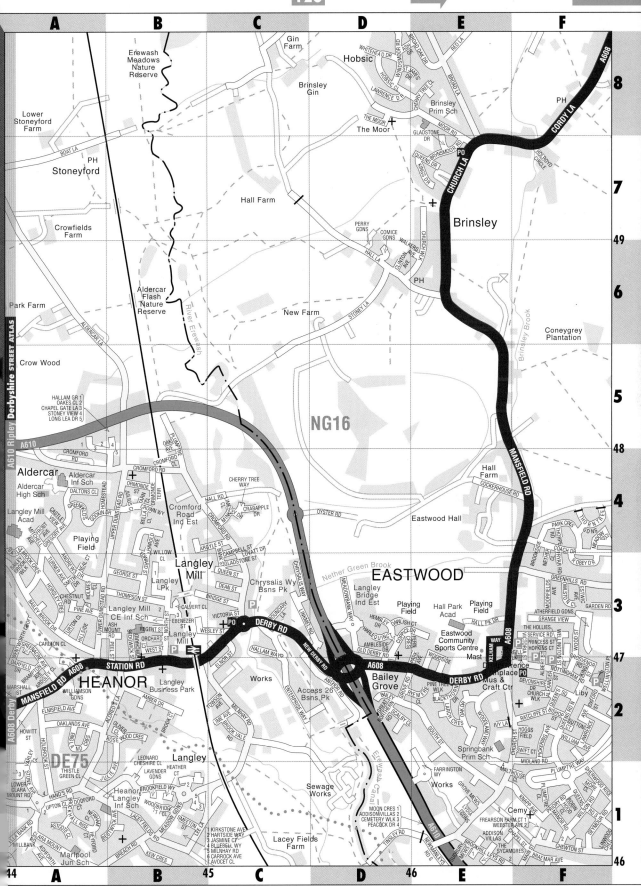

Lower Stoneyford Farm

Erewash Meadows Nature Reserve

Gin Farm

Hobsic

Brinsley Gin

PH Stoneyford

BOAT LA

Park Farm

Crowfields Farm

Aldercar Flash Nature Reserve

River Erewash

Hall Farm

The Moor

Brinsley Prim Sch

PH

Brinsley

Perry Gdns

New Farm

Coneygrey Plantation

Crow Wood

HALLAM GR 1
OAKES CL 2
CHAPEL GATE LA 3
STONEY VIEW 4
LONG LEA DR 5

NG16

Hall Farm

Eastwood Hall

A610 Ripley Derbyshire STREET ATLAS

A610

Aldercar

Aldercar High Sch

Aldercar Inf Sch

Cromford Road Ind Est

Cherry Tree Way

Langley Mill Acad

Langley Mill

Oyster Rd

Nether Green Brook

EASTWOOD

Playing Field

Chrysalis Wy Bsns Pk

Langley Bridge Ind Est

Hall Park Acad

Playing Field

Langley LPk

Langley Mill CE Inf Sch

Eastwood Community Sports Centre

Mast

Derby Rd

PO

Langley Mill

STATION RD

HEANOR

Williamson Gdns

Langley Business Park

Hallam Way

New Derby Rd

A608

Bailey Grove

DERBY RD

Liby

Works

Access 26 Bsns Pk

Springbank Prim Sch

DE75

Langley

Heanor Langley Inf Sch

Sewage Works

Erewash Canal

Works

Cemy

Marlpool Jun Sch

KIRKSTONE AVE 1
HARTSIDE WAY 2
JASMINE CT 3
BLUEBELL WY 4
MILNHAY RD 5
CARROCK AVE 6
AVOCET CL 7

Lacey Fields Farm

MOON CRES 1
ADDISON VILLAS 2
CEMETERY WLK 3
PEACOCK DR 4

The Sycamores

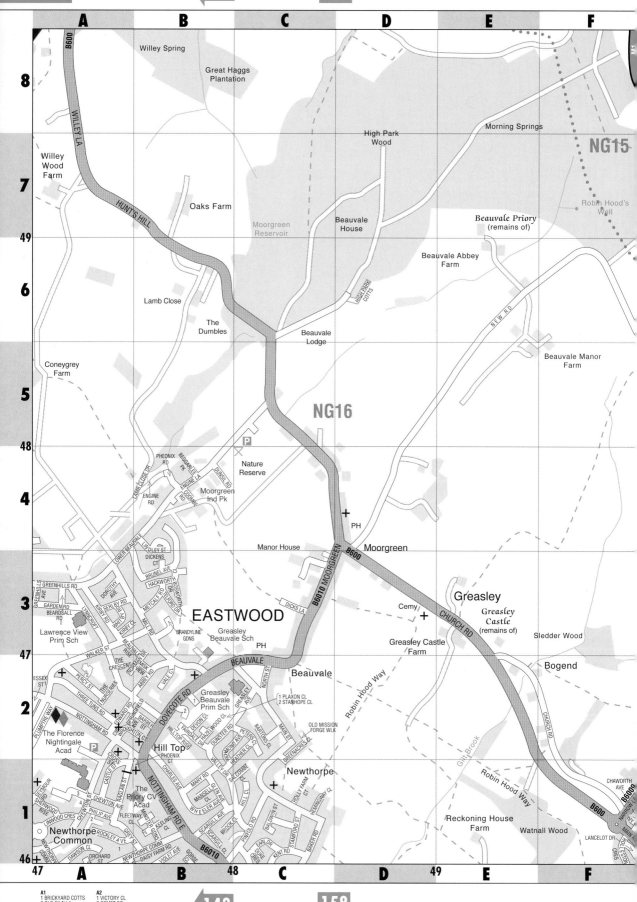

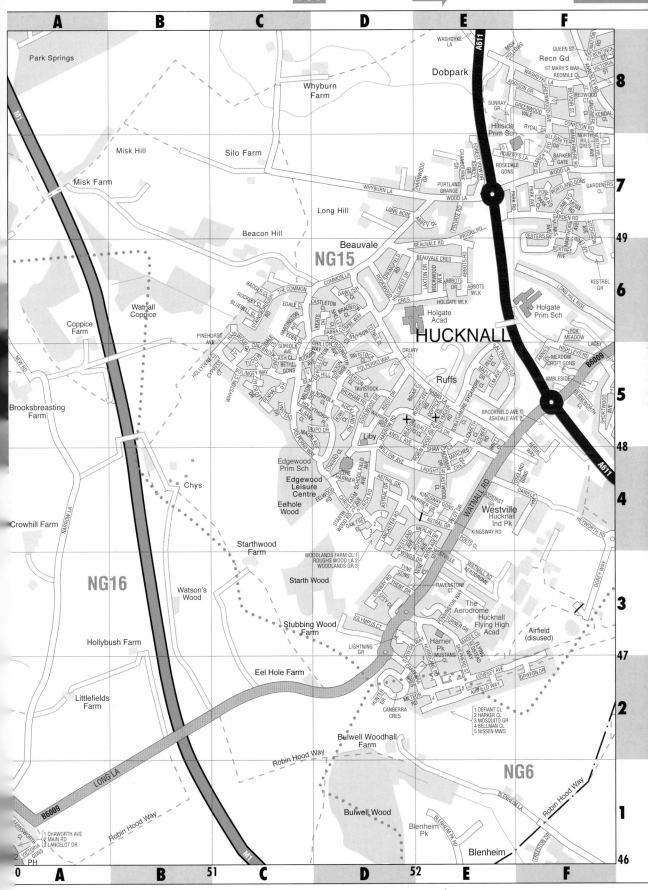

146

B7
3 Byron Bsns Ctr

B8
1 BOATSWAIN DR
2 LOVELACE WLK
3 BLATHERWICK CL

◁ 145

131 ⬡

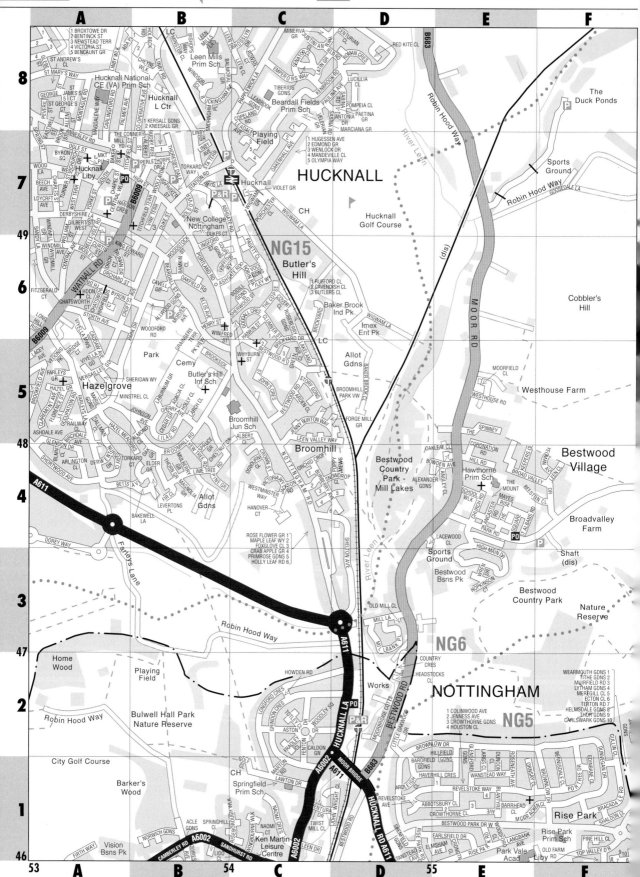

HUCKNALL

NG15

Butler's Hill

Hazelgrove

Broomhill

Bestwood Village

Broadvalley Farm

Cobbler's Hill

Westhouse Farm

The Duck Ponds

NOTTINGHAM

NG6

NG5

Rise Park

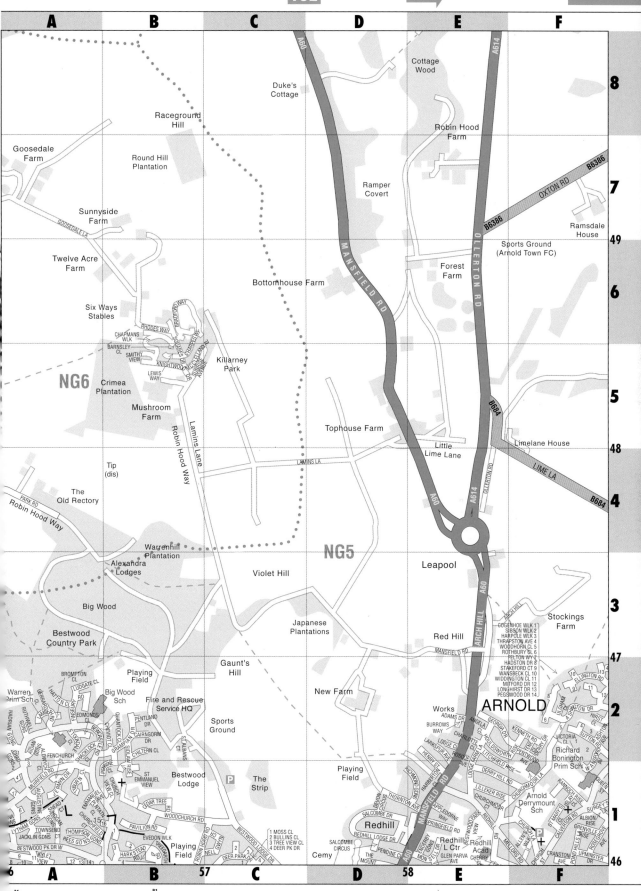

A1
1 HEXHAM GDNS
2 TITHE GDNS
3 BENEDICT CT
4 BONIFACE GDNS
5 WEARMOUTH GDNS
6 LINDISFARNE GDNS
7 MASSON CT
8 GOATCHURCH CT
9 HEATHRINGTON GDNS

10 TREVINO GDNS
11 WHITCOMBE GDNS
12 CHEVIN GDNS
13 CROSSFIELD DR
14 COXMOOR CT
15 Woodview Bsns Ctr
16 LOCKWOOD CL
17 BEDE CL

B1
1 PARKLANDS CL
2 SNOWDON CL
3 WHITTON CL
4 BESTWOOD PARK DR

147
133

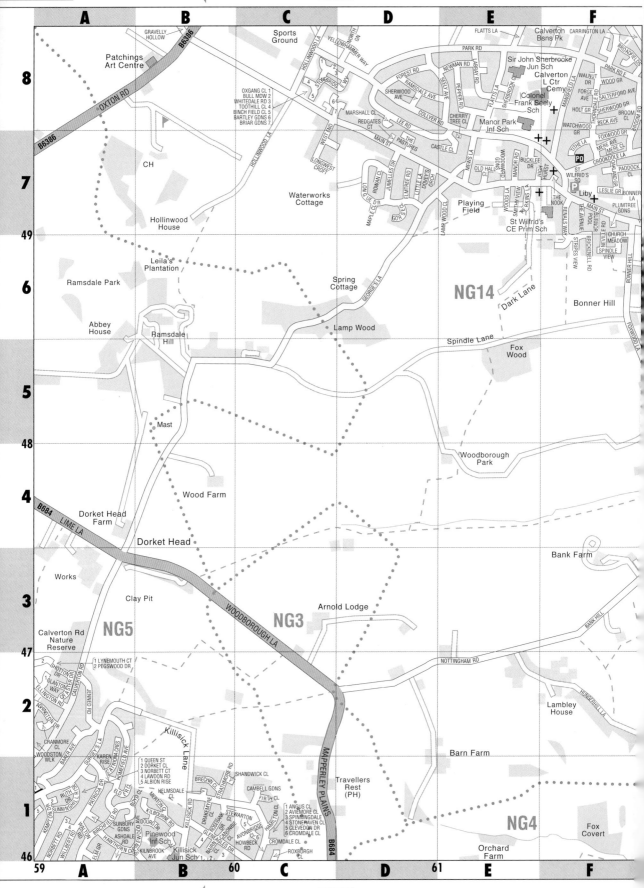

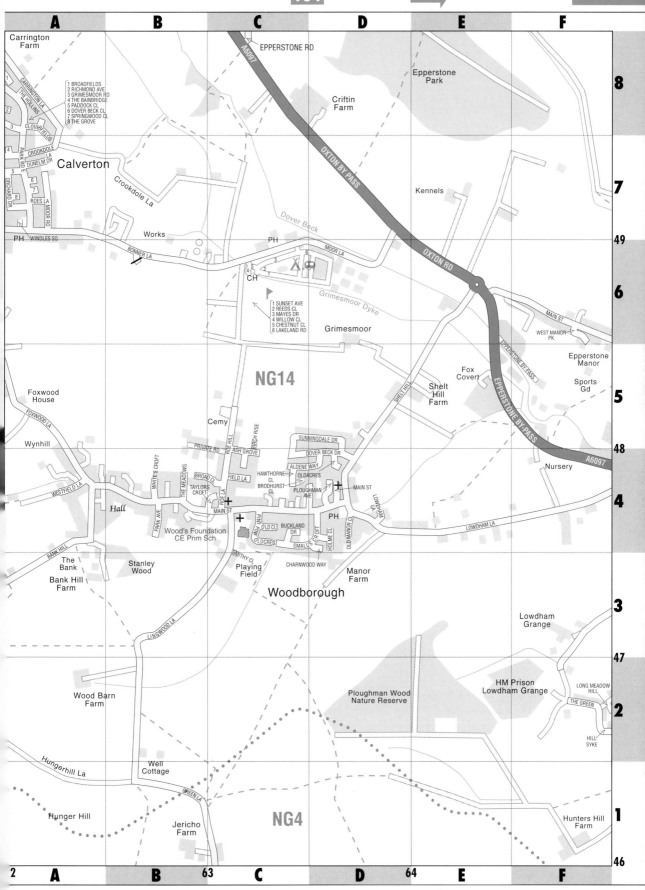

149
135

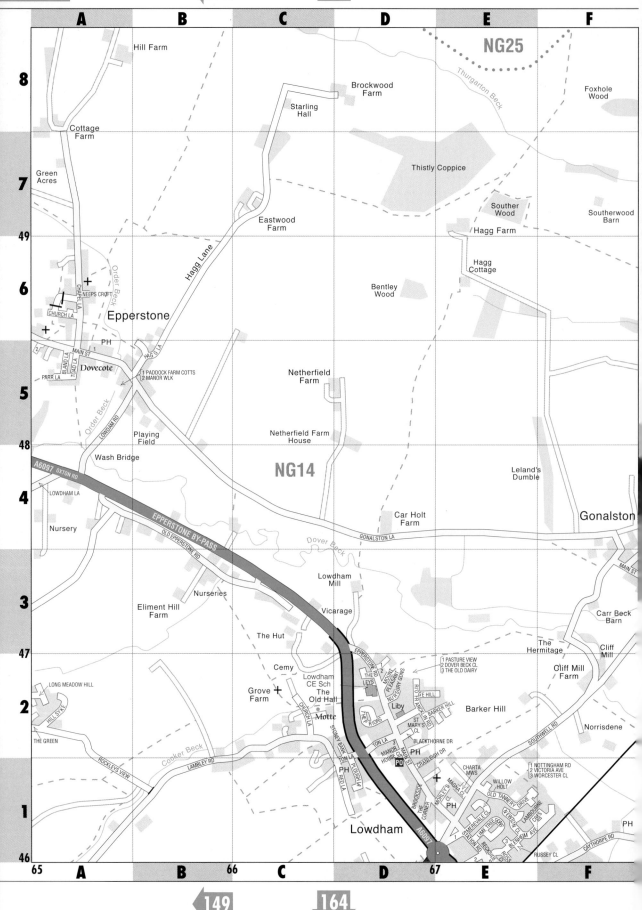

NG25

A B C D E F

8

Hill Farm

Brockwood
Farm

Foxhole
Wood

Cottage
Farm

Starling
Hall

Thistly Coppice

7

Green
Acres

Southerwood
Barn

Souther
Wood

Eastwood
Farm

Hagg Farm

49

Hagg Lane

Hagg
Cottage

6

NEEPS CROFT

Bentley
Wood

CHAPEL LA

Epperstone

CHURCH LA

PH

MAIN ST

HAG'S LA

1 PADDOCK FARM COTTS
2 MANOR WLK

Netherfield
Farm

BLAND LA
TOAD LA

Dovecote

2

PARR LA

5

Order Beck

LOWDHAM RD

Playing
Field

Netherfield Farm
House

Wash Bridge

48

NG14

Leland's
Dumble

A6097 OXTON RD

EPPERSTONE BY-PASS

4

LOWDHAM LA

Car Holt
Farm

Gonalston

Nursery

GONALSTON LA

OLD EPPERSTONE RD

Dover Beck

MAIN ST

Lowdham
Mill

Eliment Hill
Farm

Nurseries

Carr Beck
Barn

3

Vicarage

The Hermitage

Cliff
Mill

47

The Hut

EPPERSTONE RD

1 PASTURE VIEW
2 DOVER BECK CL
3 THE OLD DAIRY

Cemy

Cliff Mill
Farm

Long Meadow Hill

Grove
Farm

Lowdham
CE Sch
The
Old Hall

THE
LEYS

MOUNT
PLEASANT

NURSERY GDNS

RIDGE HILL

BARKER HILL

Barker Hill

Norrisdene

2

HILL SYKE

CHURCH LA

Motte

THE
PRIORS

ST
MARY'S
CL

Blackthorne Dr

SOUTHWELL RD

THE GREEN

STONEY BANK LA

TON LA

MANOR
HOUSE CL

MAIN ST

PH

1 NOTTINGHAM RD
2 VICTORIA AVE
3 WORCESTER CL

ROCKLEYS VIEW

LAMBLEY RD

Cooker Beck

RED LA

PLOUGH LA

PH

PO

CRANLEIGH DR

MAGNA CL

CHARTA
MWS

WILLOW
HOLT

OLD TANNER DRIVE

1

MORLEYS CL

BROOKSIDE

THE
CORNER

MAGRA CL

PH

SOMERDALE CL

LIME TREE GDNS

BECKSIDE

CRESS

TWIST CL

LAMBOURNE
CRES

BLENHEIM AVE

WILLOW
HOLT

PH

Lowdham

A6097

STATION RD

RUSSEY CL

CAYTHORPE RD

46

65 A 66 B C 67 D E F

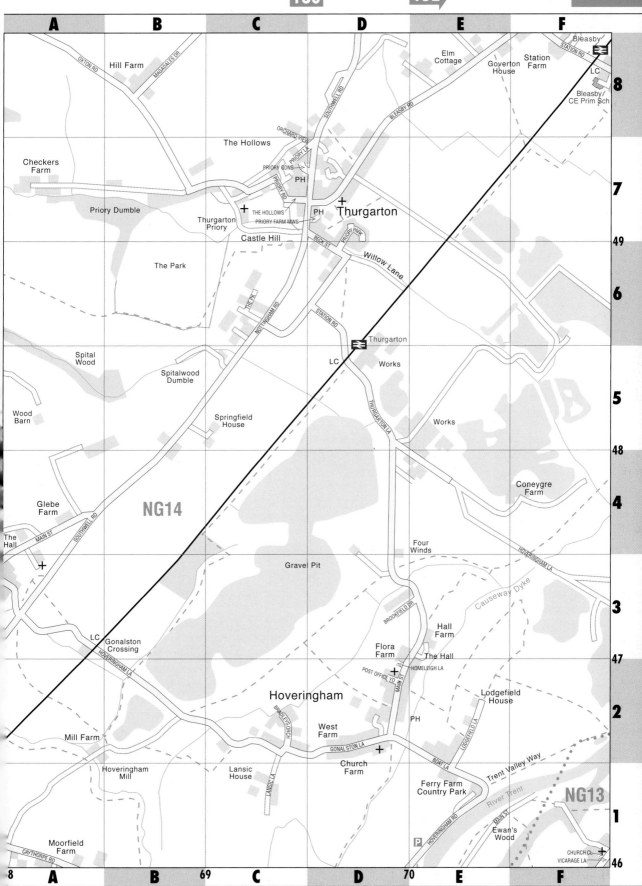

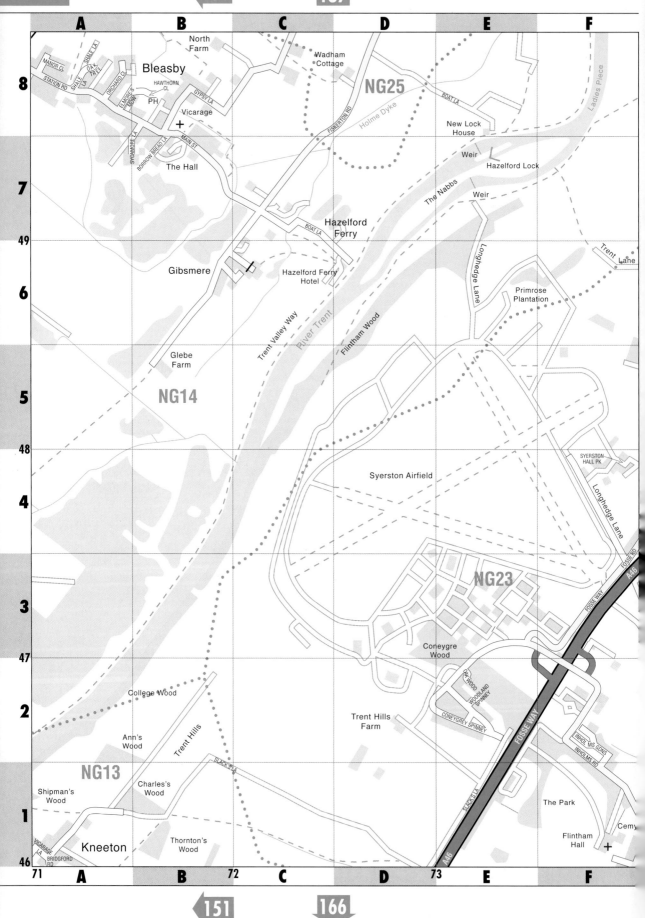

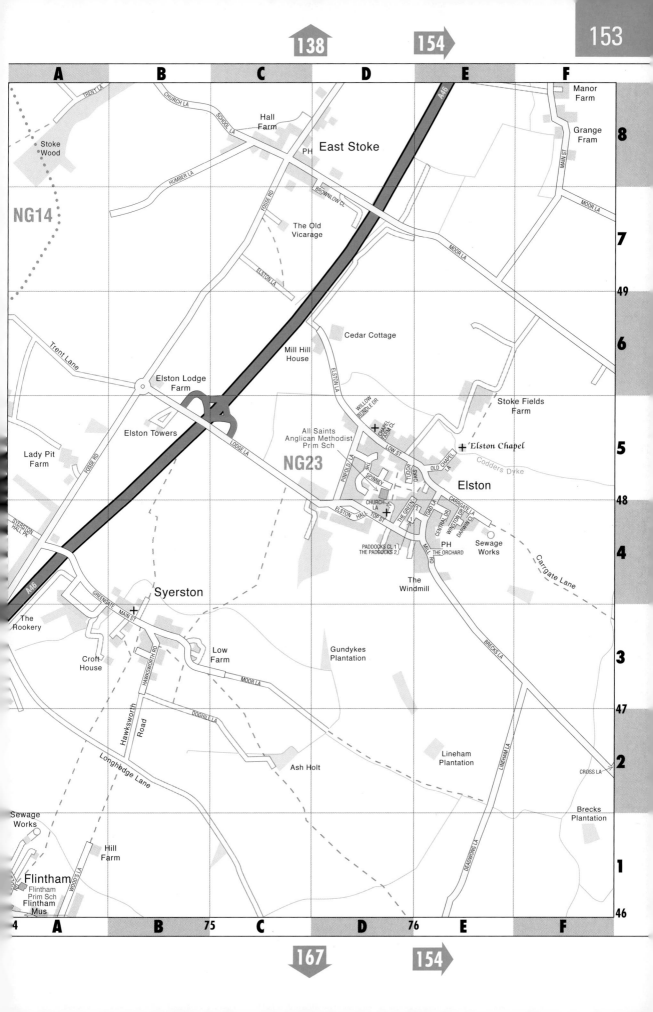

153
139

A B C D E F

8

7 Thorpe Lodge

49

6 Honies Farm

Car Dyke

MOOR LA

5

48

4 Fox Covert Manor Farm

Cotham

NG23 The Old Hall Farm

Meadow Farm

Carrgate Lane
CARRGATE LA TRACK

3 Devon Farm

47

River Devon

Back Dyke

NG24

The Grange

NEWARK RD

ELSTON LA

THE LANE

2

Grange Farm

1 Elston Grange Station House

BRECKS LA

BAXTER LA

STATION RD

MOOR LA

HONEYS LA

CROSS LA

46

77 A B 78 C D 79 E F

A · B · C · D · E · F

8

CLAYPOLE LA

Staple Farm

NG24

7

49

Balderton Grange

Cowtham House

6

Shire
Bridge

Holmes
Farm

Shire Dyke

Shirebridge
Farm

5

48

Bennington Fen

Fen Farm

4

Cotham
Thorns

Willow Tree
Farm

NEWARK RD

3

Fen Lane
Farms

NG23

47

FEN LA

Pasture Lodge
Farm

Red House
Farm

2

Cotham
Buildings

Askerton Hill

Bennington Lodge
Farm

STATION RD

STAUNTON RD

Valley Lane
Cottages

VALLEY LA

White House
Farm

Middle
Farm

1

Stonepit
Plantation

46

A · 81 · B · C · 82 · D · E · F

NEWARK RD
GRANGE LA
GREAT NORTH ROAD
GREAT NORTH RD
B6326
SYLVAN WAY
A1
HOLMES LA TRACK

155
141

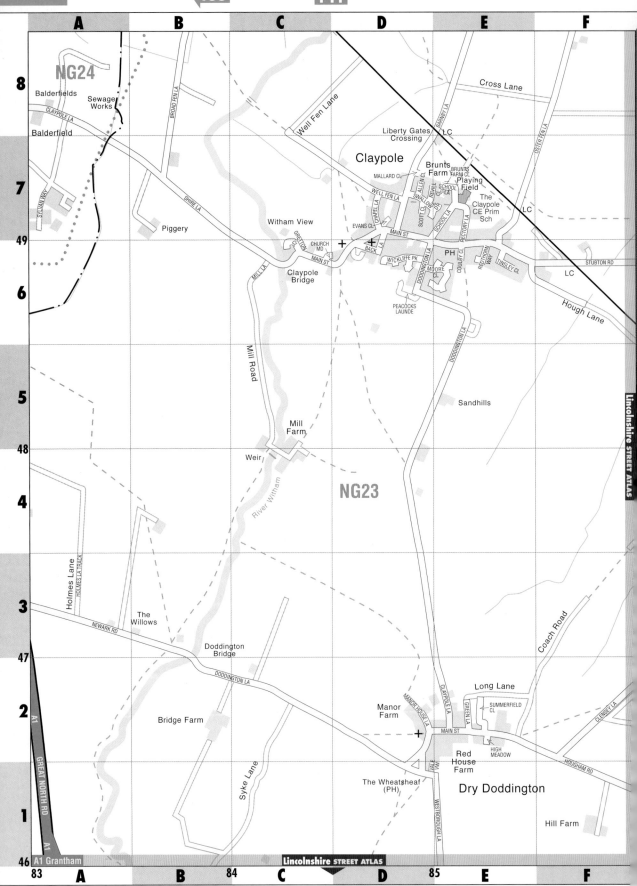

NG24

8

Balderfields Sewage Works

BROAD FEN LA

Cross Lane

Balderfield

CLAYPOLE LA

Well Fen Lane

Liberty Gates Crossing LC

BARNEY LA

Claypole

7

SHIRE LA

SYLVAN WAY

Piggery

Witham View

MALLARD CL

Brunts Farm

BRUNTS FARM CL

Playing Field

ALLEN CL

SCHOOL DR

REVIL

The Claypole CE Prim Sch

WELL FEN LA

CHAPEL LA

SCOTT CL

SCHOOL LA

LC

49

GRETTON CL

CHURCH MD

EVANS CL

Main St

BACK LA

SWALLOW CL

RECTORY LA

LC

MILL LA

Claypole Bridge

WICKLIFFE PK

DODDINGTON LA

MOORE

PH

COULBY CL

REDTHORN WAY

TINSLEY CL

STUBTON RD

LC

6

Mill Road

PEACOCKS LAUNDE

Hough Lane

DODDINGTON LA

5

Sandhills

Mill Farm

48

Weir

River Witham

NG23

4

Holmes Lane

HOLMES LA TRACK

Coach Road

3

NEWARK RD

The Willows

47

Doddington Bridge

DODDINGTON LA

Long Lane

A1

GREAT NORTH RD

2

Bridge Farm

Syke Lane

Manor Farm

MANOR HOUSE LA

CLAYPOLE LA

GREEN LA

SUMMERFIELD CL

CLENSEY LA

MAIN ST

Main St

HIGH MEADOW

HOUGHAM RD

The Wheatsheaf (PH)

VAT LA

Red House Farm

Dry Doddington

1

WESTBOROUGH LA

Hill Farm

46

155

Lincolnshire STREET ATLAS

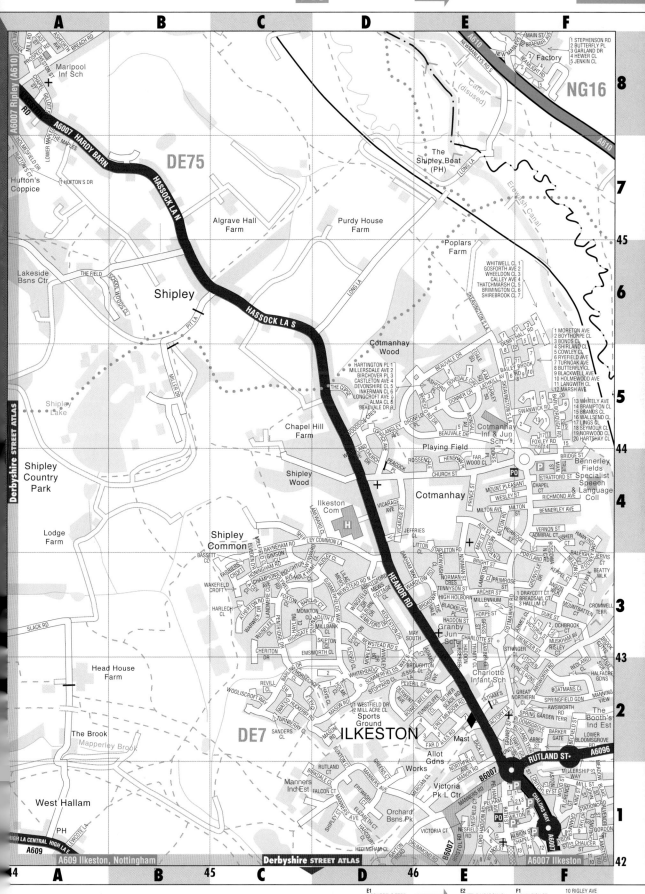

158>

E1
1 BRUSSELS TERR
2 STAMFORD ST
3 STATION CT
4 FULLWOOD AVE
5 PROVIDENCE PL
6 FULLWOOD ST
7 WHARNCLIFFE RD
8 JACKSON AVE
9 GREGORY ST

E2
1 LITTLE MEADOW CL
2 TARRAT ST
3 GREENHALGH CRES
4 SCOLLINS CT

F1
1 BURLEIGH ST
2 ESSEX ST
3 DURHAM ST
4 NORTHGATE ST
5 WILTON ST
6 WEST TERR
7 NORTH ST
8 CHAPEL ST
9 LOWER CHAPEL ST

10 RIGLEY AVE
11 GRESLEY RD
12 BURR LA
13 BAKER ST
14 ALBION ST

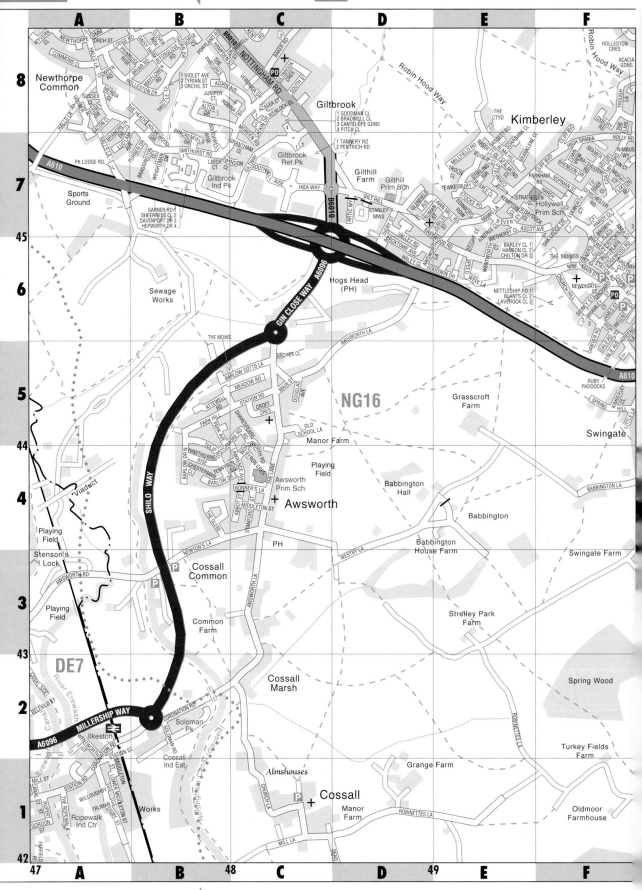

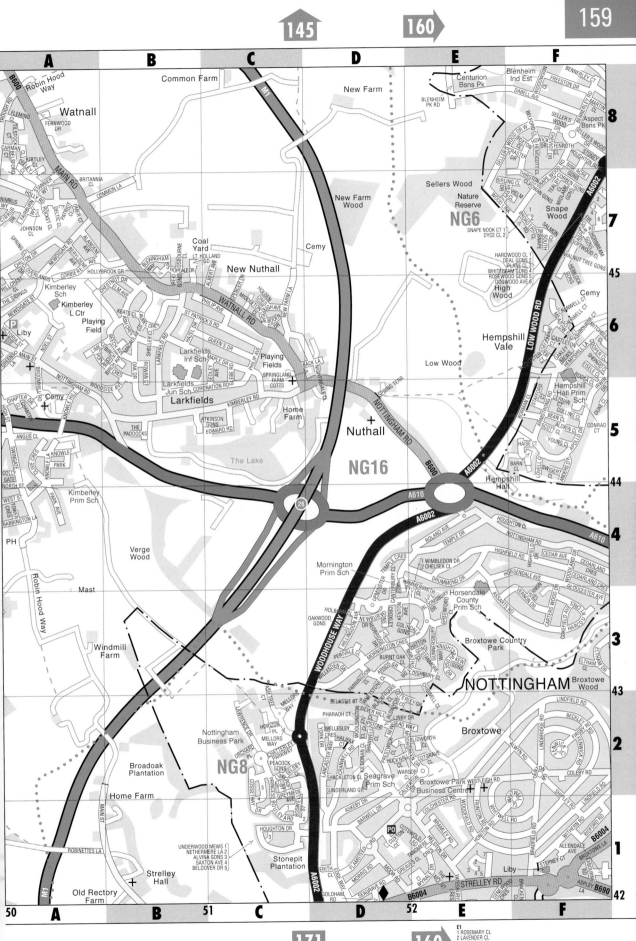

E1
1 ROSEMARY CL
2 LAVENDER CL
3 MAGNOLIA CL
4 HONEYSUCKLE CL
5 JASMINE CL
6 BRIDGE GREEN WALK
7 LILAC CL

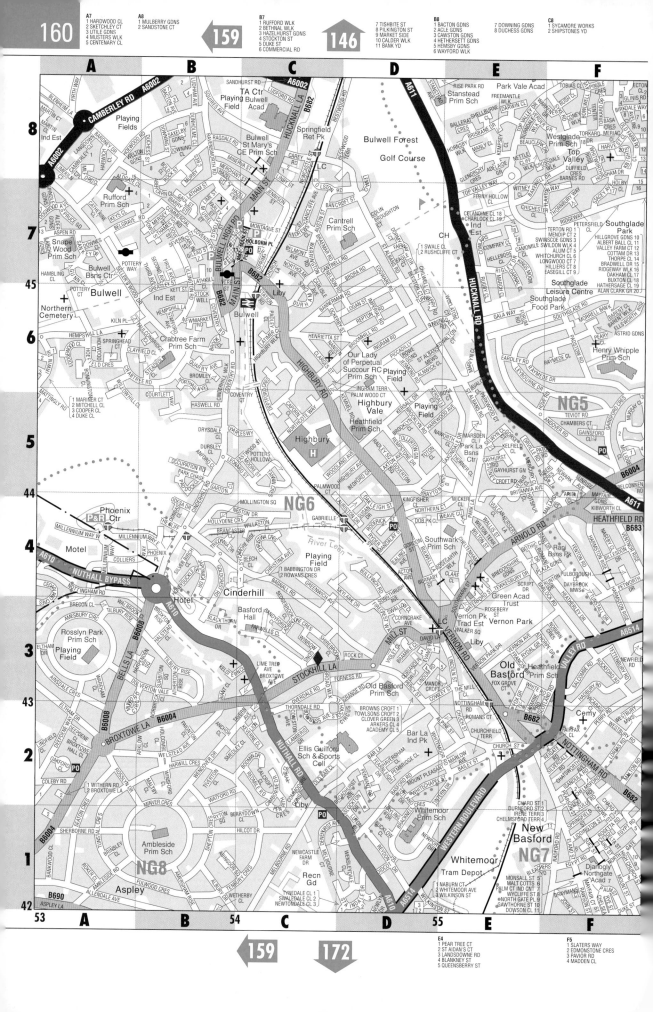

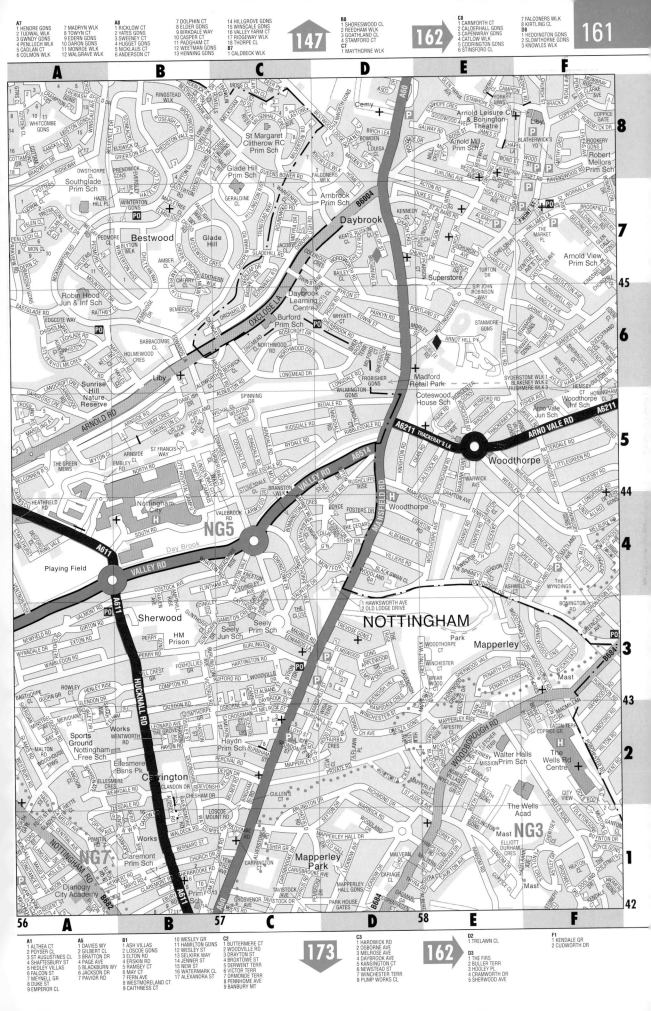

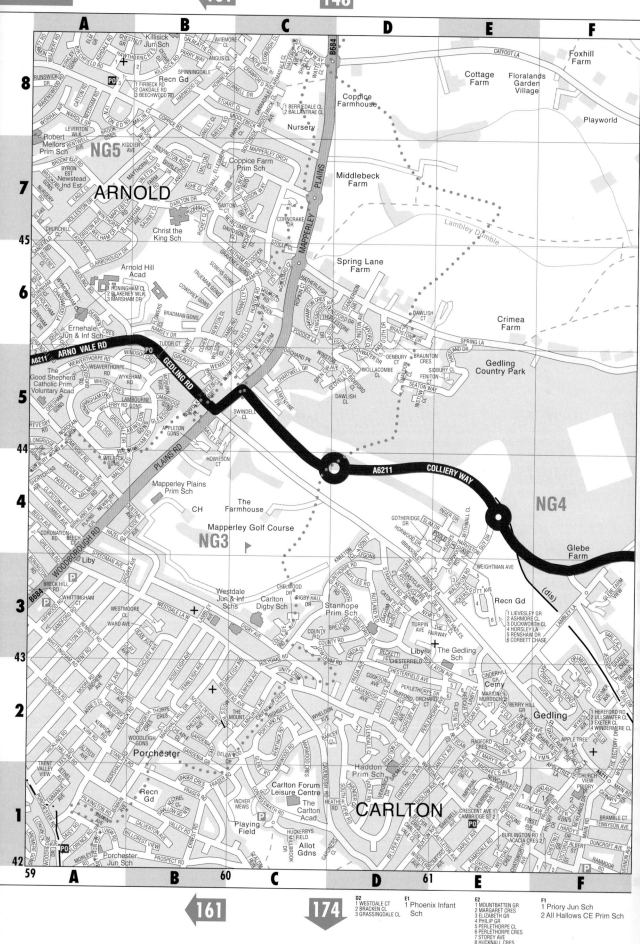

161 148

D2
1 WESTDALE CT
2 BRACKEN CL
3 GRASSINGDALE CL

E1
1 Phoenix Infant
  Sch

E2
1 MOUNTBATTEN GR
2 MARGARET CRES
3 ELIZABETH GR
4 PHILIP GR
5 PERLETHORPE CL
6 PERLETHORPE CRES
7 STOREY AVE
8 HUCKNALL CRES
9 BABBINGTON CRES

F1
1 Priory Jun Sch
2 All Hallows CE Prim Sch

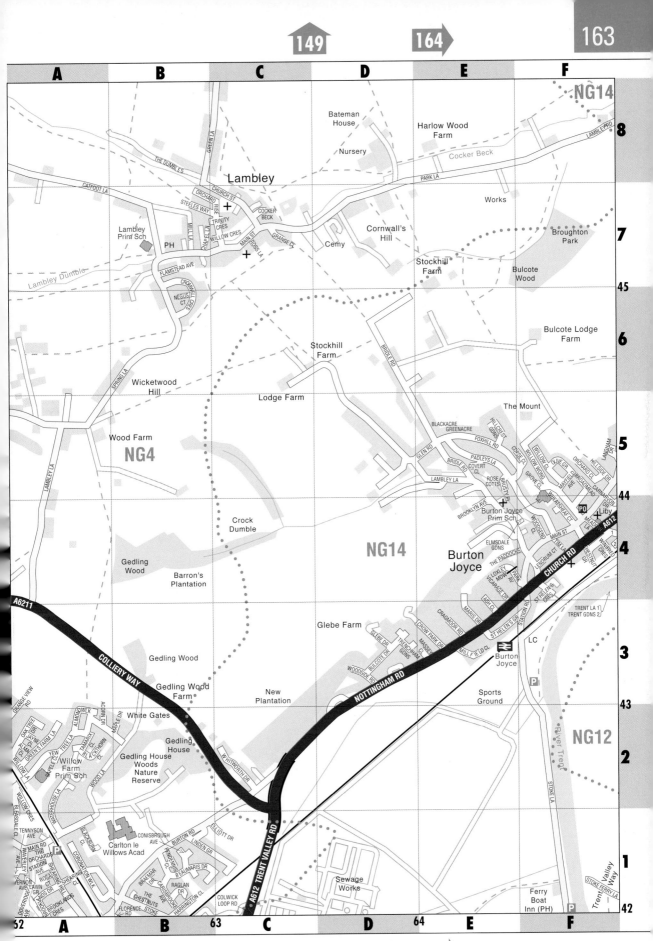

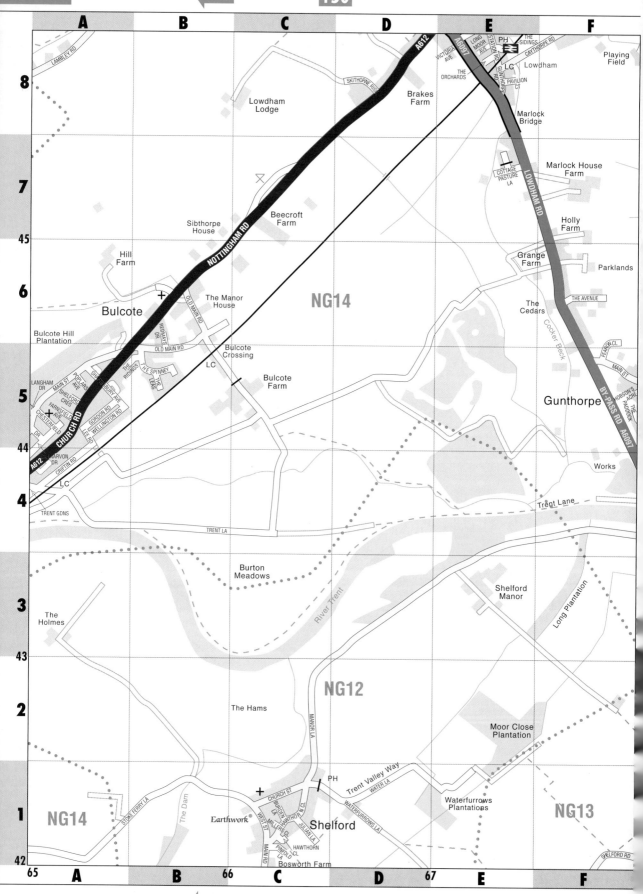

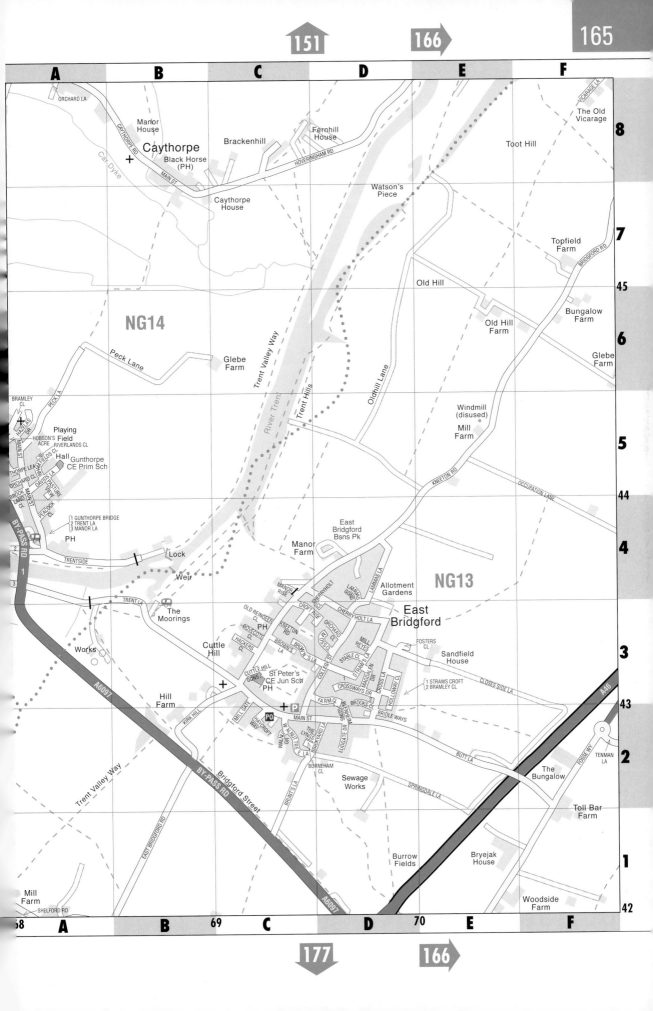

165 152

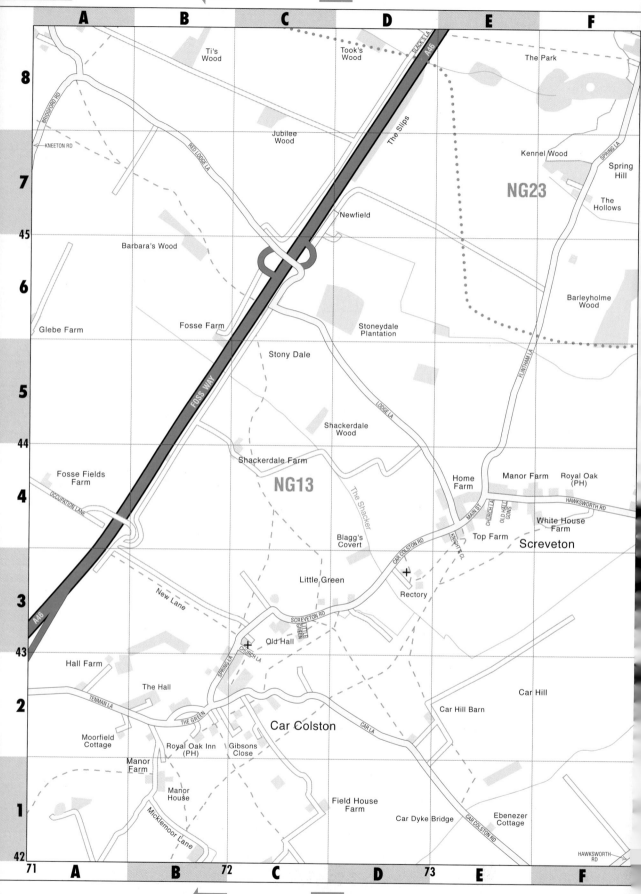

A B C D E F

165 178

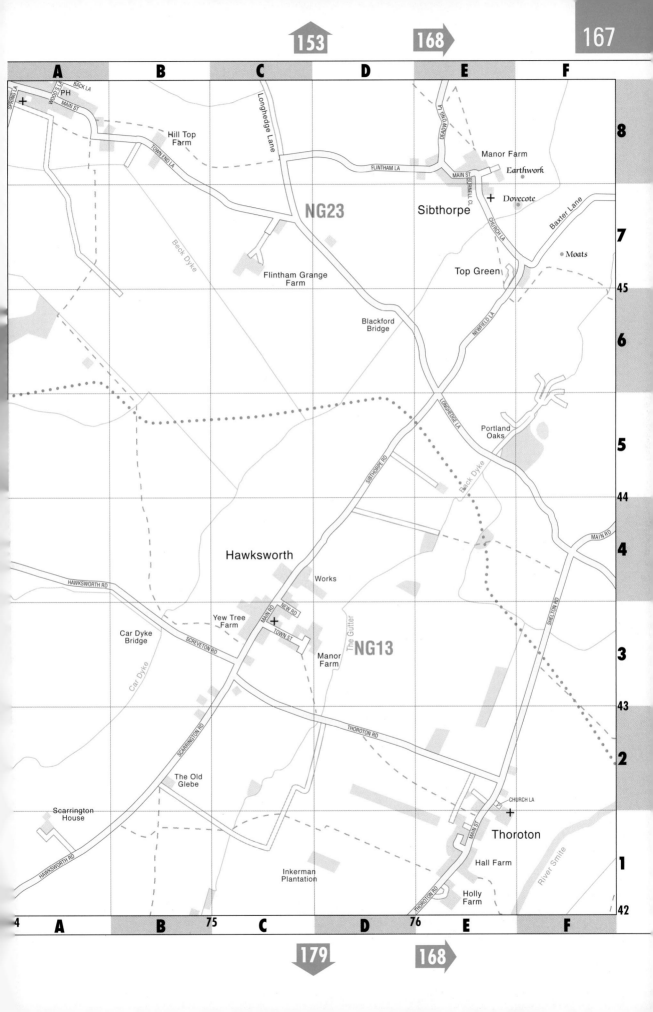

A B C D E F

8

SPRING LA
WOOD'S LA
BACK LA
PH
MAIN ST
Hill Top Farm
TOWN END LA
Longhedge Lane

MEADOW LA
Manor Farm
Earthwork
MAIN ST
BURNELL CL
Dovecote
Sibthorpe
CHURCH LA
Baxter Lane

NG23

7

FLINTHAM LA

Beck Dyke

Flintham Grange Farm

Top Green
Moats

45

Blackford Bridge

NEWFIELD LA

6

Longhedge La

Portland Oaks

5

SIBTHORPE RD

Back Dyke

44

Hawksworth

MAIN RD

4

HAWKSWORTH RD

Works

The Gutter

SHELTON RD

Yew Tree Farm

Car Dyke Bridge

SCREVETON RD

MAIN RD
NEW RD
TOWN ST

Manor Farm

NG13

3

Car Dyke

SCARRINGTON RD

THOROTON RD

43

2

The Old Glebe

Scarrington House

CHURCH LA
Thoroton

MAIN ST
Hall Farm

River Smite

1

HAWKSWORTH RD

Inkerman Plantation

THOROTON RD

Holly Farm

42

A B 75 C D 76 E F
4

167
154

A   B   C   D   E   F

Firs Farm

BAXTER LA

BRECKS LA

Wensor Bridge

ELSTON LA

Booth's Farm

Back Dyke

ELSTON RD

Fox Covert

Limekiln Covert

Staunton Grange

NG23

Shelton

Shelton House Farm

Hall Farm

The Hall

ST ANN'S WAY

Manor Farm

Little Orchard

Fishpond Plantation

River Smite

Fourteen Acre Covert

Staunton Works

Top Farm

MAIN RD

Fairfields

River Devon

SHELTON LA

Brickyard Plantation

Works

Greenacres

Shelton Lodge Farm

Lane Side

NG13

LONGHEDGE LA

Flawborough

Flawborough Hall

Manor Farm

Oscar Bridge

Manor Farm

MANOR FARM CL

Stonehouse Farm

MAIN ST

Sunnymede

NEWARK RD

ORSTON LA

FLAWBOROUGH RD

Chestnut Farm

Grange Farm

Alverton

MILL LA

77   A   B   78   C   D   79   E   F

167
180

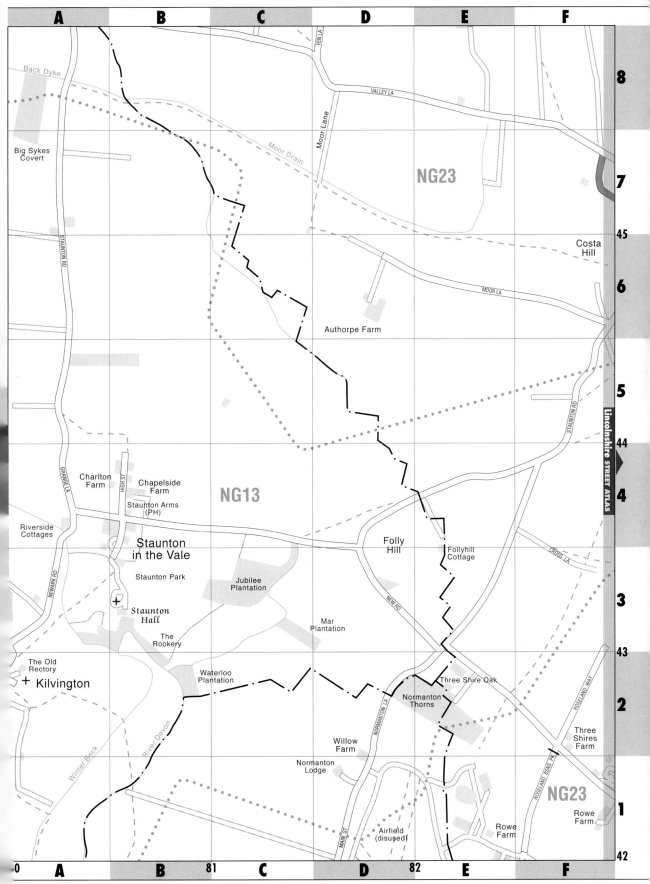

A B C D E F

8
7
45
6
5
44
4
43
3
2
1
42

Back Dyke

Big Sykes
Covert

STAUNTON RD

GRANGE LA

NEWARK RD

Charlton
Farm

HIGH ST

Chapelside
Farm

Staunton Arms
(PH)

Riverside
Cottages

NG13

Staunton
in the Vale

Staunton Park

Staunton
Hall

The
Rookery

The Old
Rectory

+ Kilvington

Winter Beck

River Devon

Waterloo
Plantation

Jubilee
Plantation

Mar
Plantation

MAIN ST

Willow
Farm

Normanton
Lodge

Airfield
(disused)

NORMANTON LA

Normanton
Thorns

Three Shire Oak

NEW RD

Folly
Hill

Follyhill
Cottage

Authorpe Farm

Moor Drain

Moor Lane

FEN LA

VALLEY LA

NG23

MOOR LA

Costa
Hill

STAUNTON RD

CROSS LA

Lincolnshire STREET ATLAS

ROSELAND WAY

ROSELAND BSNS PK

Three
Shires
Farm

Rowe
Farm

Rowe
Farm

NG23

80

A B 81 C D 82 E F

170

A7
1 BROMLEY CT
2 REDBRIDGE CL
3 KENSINGTON GDNS
4 ST JOHNS RD
5 CONCORDE CL
6 Kensington Jun Acad

158

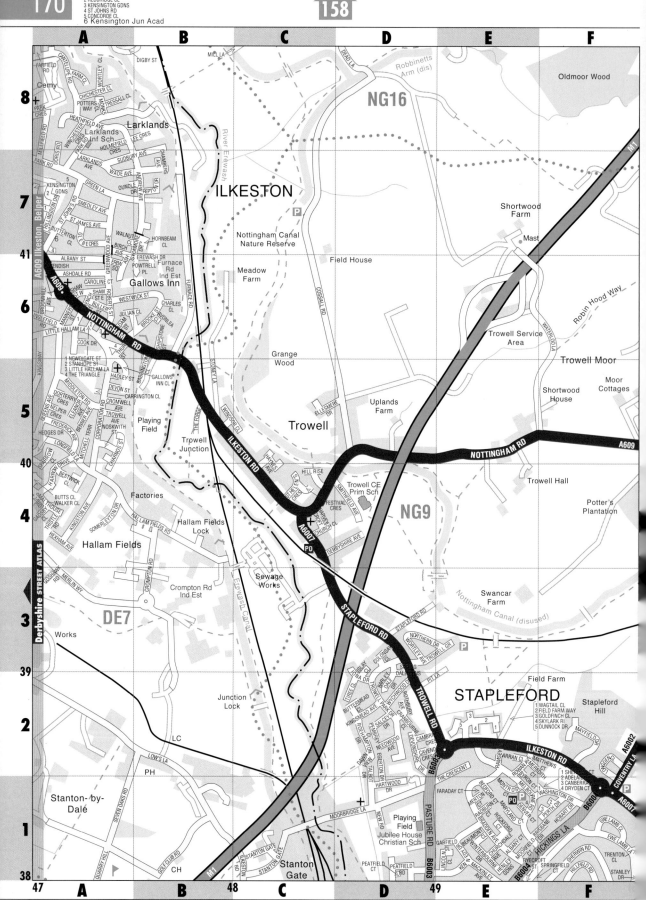

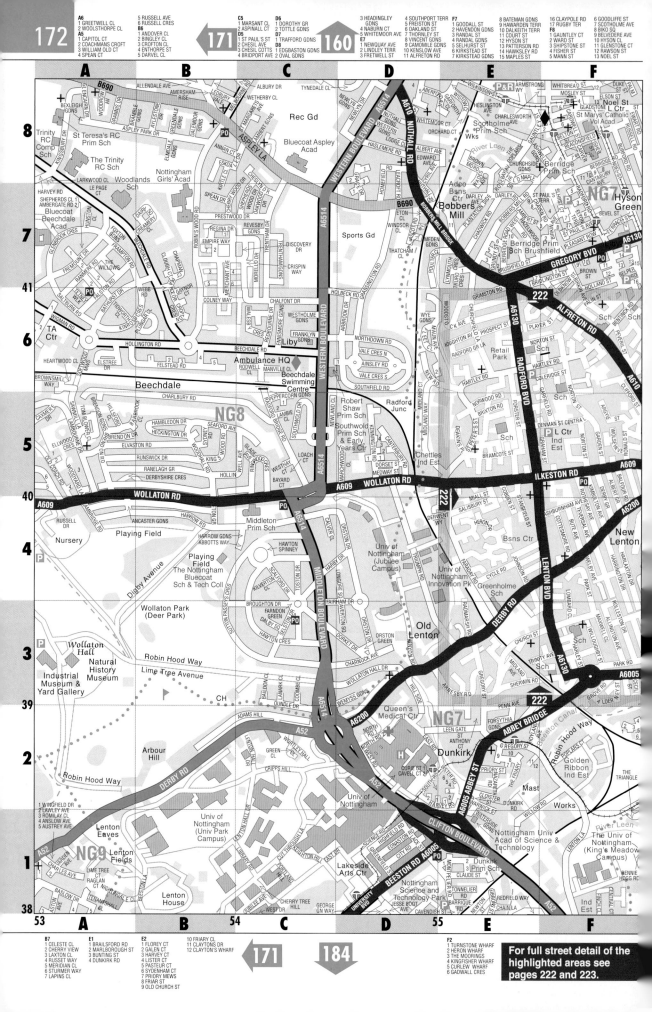

161   174   185   222   223

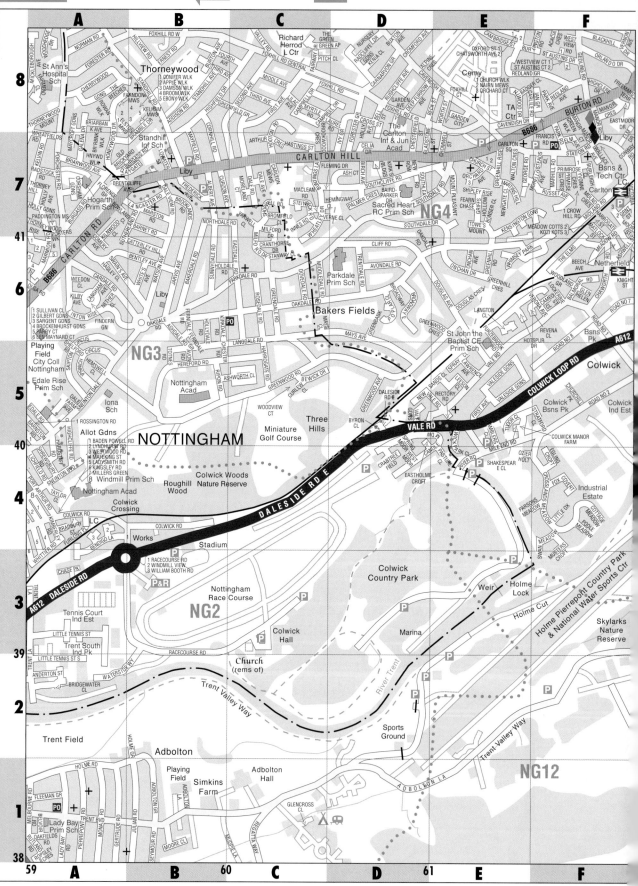

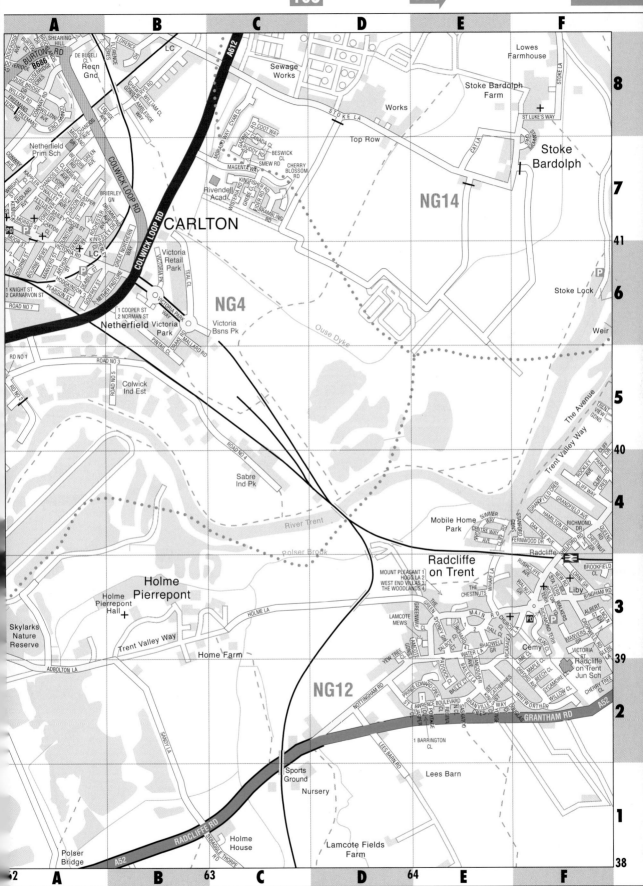

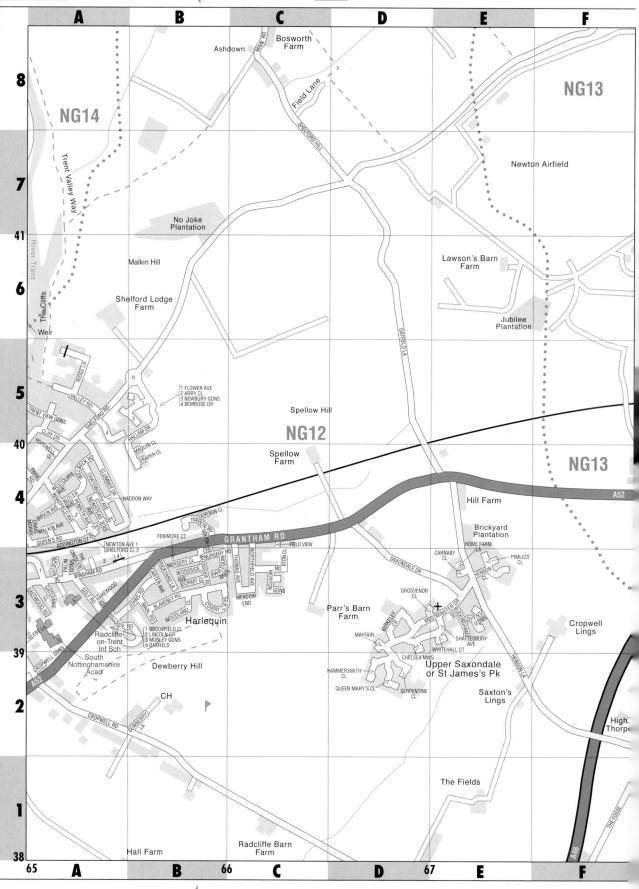

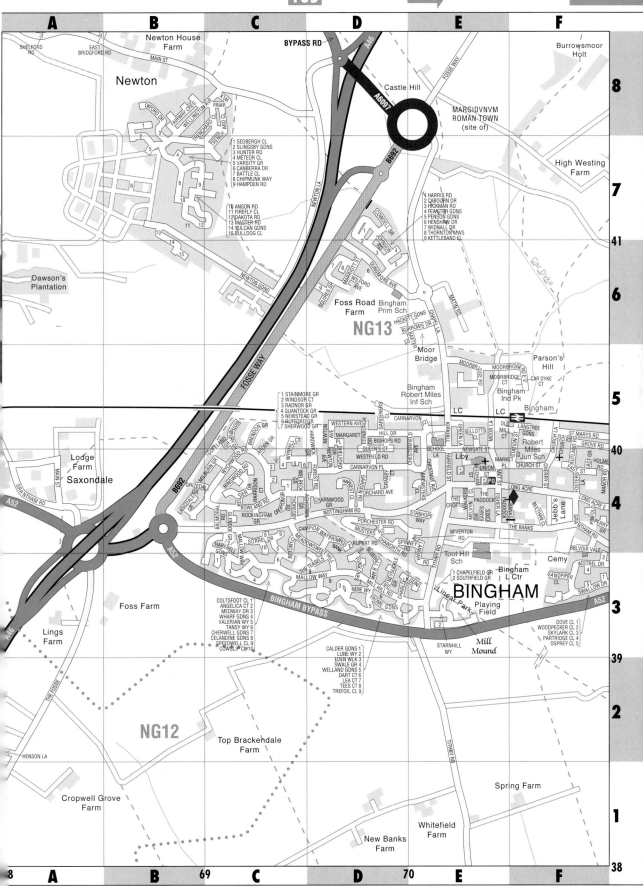

A   B   C   D   E   F

8

Thoroughfare Holt

MICKLEMORE LA

Hall

The Old Vicarage

CAR COLSTON RD
LONGMOOR LA
HAWKSWORTH RD

Scarrington

CHAPEL LA

MAIN ST
THE SAUCERS

Manor Farm

ASLOCKTON RD
MILL LA

Bottom Plantation

7

41

Holme Farm

6

NEW LA

Sewage Works

MOOR LA

5

NG13

Archbishop Cranmer CE Prim Sch

CRAWFORDS MDW
THORNFIELD WAY
ABBEY LA
BUCKTHORN DR
BIRCH CL

Abbey Farm

FIELDS DR
WALNUT LA
ABBEY CL
THE CAPES

LC

40

St MARYS RD
PRIORS CL
GROVE RD
BUTT RD
HOLME RD
COGLEY LA
ABBEY RD
BROWNES RD
VICTORIA
NURSERY RD
CARR RD
DOUGLAS RD
CARR ST
BANES RD

LC

Aslockton Hall

BEVERLEYS AVE
GREEN WLK
SMITE CL
COTTAGE AVE

CROW CT
Carnarvon Prim Sch

Brocker Farm

4

LONG ACRE E
DARK LA
RAYMOND DR
ROMAN CL
LARCH CL
POPLAR CL
ASPEN CL
OAK AVE
JUNIPER CL
BLACKTHORN CL
HOLLY RD
WILLOW RD
ASH CL
MAPLE
HAZEL CL
BEECH AVE
DERBY LA
CEDAR CL
ELM AV

HM Prison Whatton

Sewage Works

OLD GRANTHAM RD

SWALLOW DR
NIGHTINGALE WY
GRANTHAM RD
BINGHAM BYPASS

BELVOIR CL
CROMWELL RD
CRANMER AVE

A52

GRANTHAM RD

A52

3

1 AVOCET CL
2 MALLARD CL
3 SYCAMORE CL
4 GOLDCREST CL

Aslockton Grange

39

River Smite

2

Thorough Bridge

GRANBY LA

CONERY LA

Starnhill Farm

Starnhill Plantation

1

Vicars Croft

38

71   A   72   B   C   73   D   E   F

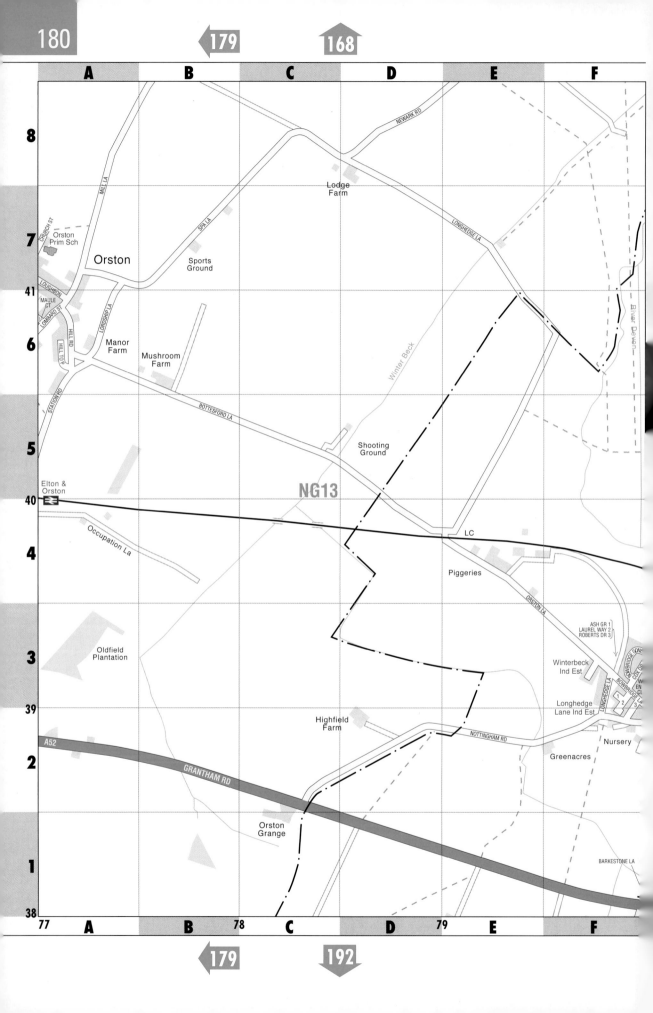

A **B** **C** **D** **E** **F**

8

NEWARK RD

MILL LA

Lodge
Farm

SPA LA

LONGHEDGE LA

7

CHURCH ST

Orston
Prim Sch

Orston

Sports
Ground

River Devon

41

LOUGHBRON

MAULE
CT

LOMBARD ST

LORDSHIP LA

Manor
Farm

Mushroom
Farm

Winter Beck

6

HILL RD

HILL TOP

BOTTESFORD LA

STATION RD

5

Shooting
Ground

NG13

Elton &
Orston

40

Occupation La

LC

4

Piggeries

ORSTON LA

ASH GR 1
LAUREL WAY 2
ROBERTS DR 3

3

Oldfield
Plantation

Winterbeck
Ind Est

BOWBRIDGE GDNS

BOWBRIDGE LA

LONGHEDGE LA

39

Longhedge
Lane Ind Est

A52

Highfield
Farm

Nottingham RD

Nursery

2

GRANTHAM RD

Greenacres

Orston
Grange

BARKESTONE LA

1

38

A B C D E F

8

Roseland Bsns Pk

River Devon

Piggery

Airfield (disused)

Ease Drain

7

NG23

41

6

Normanton Hall

Normanton House

Peacock Farm

Normanton

Little Covert Farm

Elm Farm

NORMANTON CT

Home Farm

5

Lincolnshire STREET ATLAS

NG13

40

4

Sewage Works

Beacon Hill

CHALLANDS DR

PALMER AVE

3

LC

Rectory Farm

The Nook
COX DR

Beckingthorpe

Bsns Pk

HARDYS VIEW

STARE VIEW

BEACON VIEW

LC

Bottesford

1 MARSH CT
2 SUTTON CL
3 STROUD CL

Bottesford

Bottesford

WINTERBECK CL

PINFOLD CL

CHURCH LA

STATION RD

OLD STATION YD

39

DEVON LA

RECTORY LA

Ford

CHURCH ST

WYGGESTON AVE

DAYBELL'S DR

RINGTHORPE RD

CROWN CL

FLEMING AVE

VAUGHAN AVE

WALKERS CL

ALBERT ST

QUEEN ST

MARKET ST

ST MARY'S LA

RUTLAND LA

EASTHORPE RD

EASTHORPE VIEW

CASTLE CL

GRANTHAM RD

2

1 WEST END CL
2 NOTTINGHAM RD
3 BOWBRIDGE LA

PO

PH

HAND'S WLK

ST MARY'S LA

1 GRANARY CL
2 BEECH DR
3 DAYBELLS BARNS

FREDA LA 1
CALCRAFT DR 2

South View

WALNUT RD

GRANBY DR

NORTH CREST RD

DOCKS

The Elms

Manor Farm

River Devon

Bottesford CE Prim Sch

SILVERWOOD CL

SCHOOL VIEW

SOUTH CREST

KEEL CL

BELVOIR RD

MANOR RD

GREEN LA

CASTLE VIEW RD

Easthorpe

Bottesford Liby

The Priory Belvoir Acad

BARKESTONE LA

HOWITTS RD

JAY'S CL
VINE CL

BELVOIR AVE

THE WICKETS

COVER DR

THE SANDS

Castleview Farm

MUSTON LA

GRANTHAM RD

A52

Corner Farm

1

A52

Winterbeck Bridge

A52

BOTTESFORD BYPASS

CASTLE VIEW RD

EASTHORPE LA

Hospital Farm

MAIN ST

SKERRY LA

A52 Grantham

Muston

38

182

A5
1 FRIESLAND DR
2 PAIGE GDNS
C6
1 BROOKFIELD MWS
2 BRAMBLE CT

170

E8
1 MACKINLEY AVE
2 SHERWIN RD
F8
1 PLACKETT CL
2 PARKER GDNS

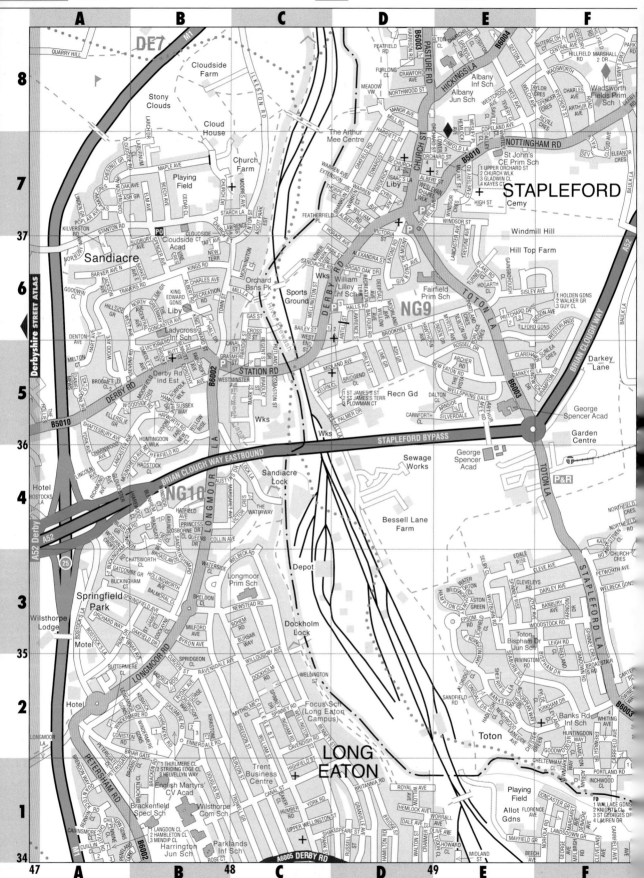

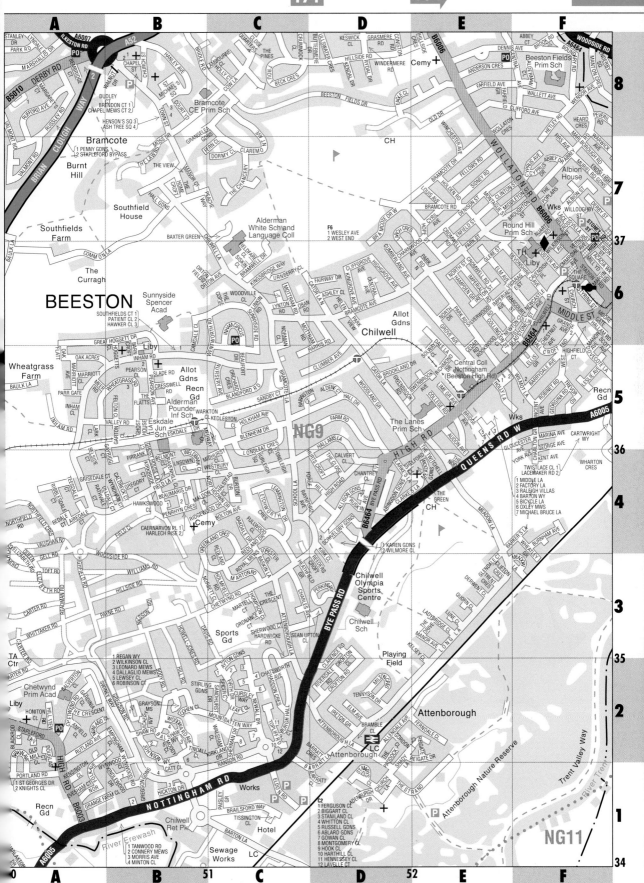

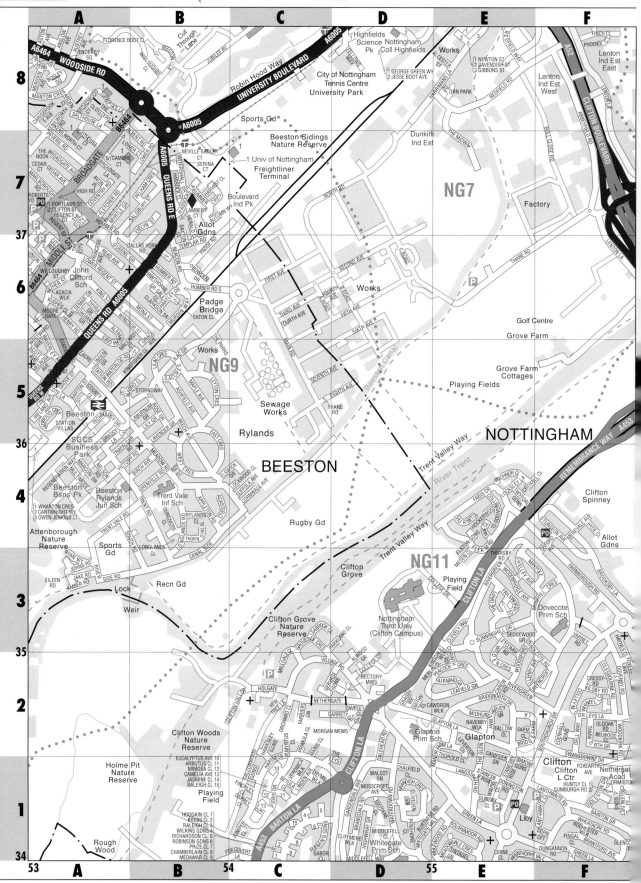

A   B   C   D   E   F

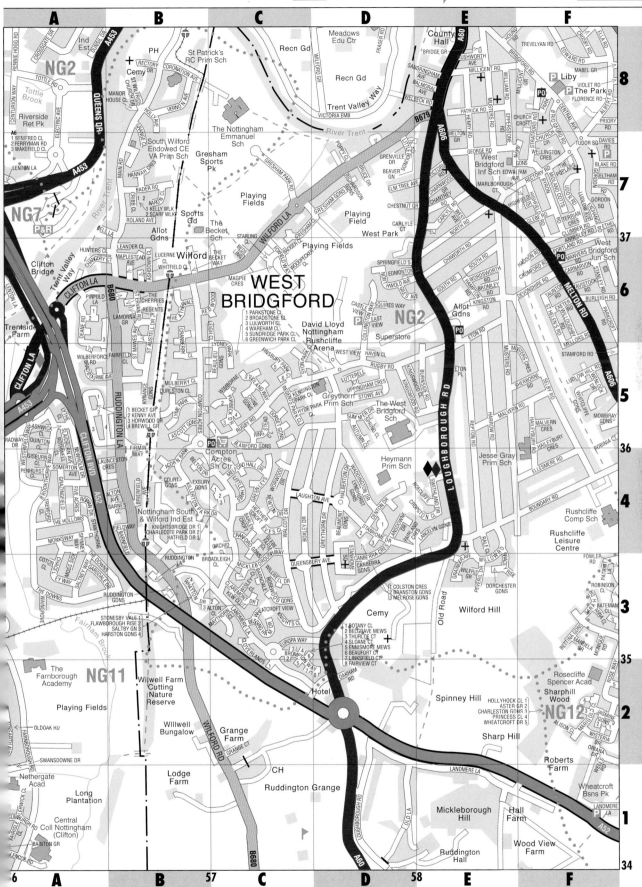

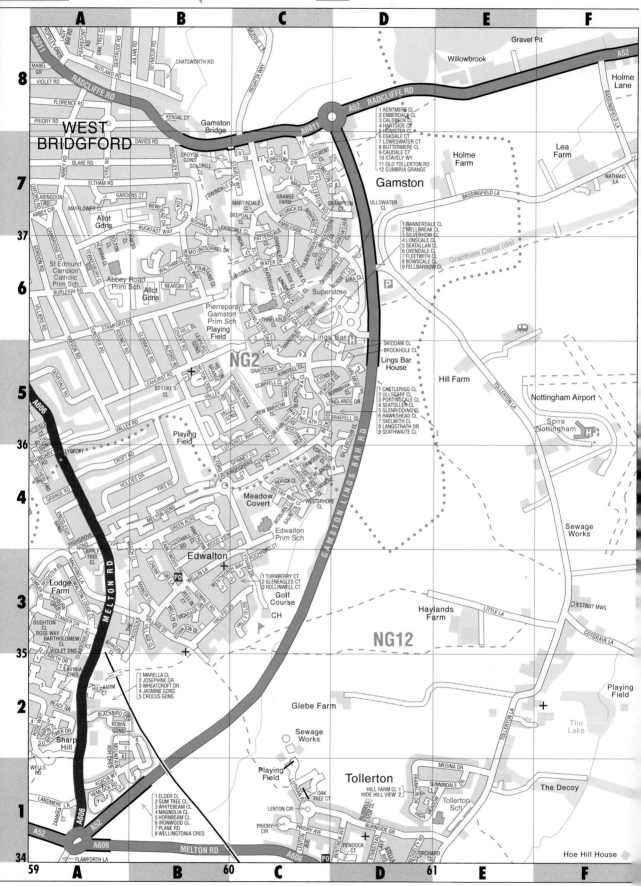

A   B   C   D   E   F

RADCLIFFE RD   A52

NATHANS LA

Bassingfield

Polser Brook

Shepherd's
(PH)

Cotgrave
Place
CH

Thornton's Holt
Farm

STRAGGLETHORPE RD

Sewage
Works

North Farm

Nursery

Grantham Canal (dis)

P

Cotgrave
Bridge

MAIN RD

HERON CRES

PEASHILL LA

NG12

Peashill Farm

Thurlbeck Dyke

Windmill Hill

FIELDS
VIEW

MAIN RD

MILL

CHICHESTER DR

MORKINSHIRE CRES

THE OLD
PARK

THE PARK

PINFOLD CL

Sewage
Works

WOODGATE LA

Cotgrave
CE Prim
Sch

MORKINSHIRE

VINE FARM CL

BLACKSMITH

CHURCH LA

THE
CROSS

PO

PH

THURMAN DR

EAST ACRES

LOW PENCE CL

BINGHAM RD

CANDLEBY
CT

SCOTLAND
BANK

HOLLYGATE CL

COLSTON
PASTURES

GATE

MILLER HIVES CL

HALES CL

RECTORY RD

Cemy

PLUMTREE RD

WALNUT
GR

CHERRY DR

ROSEGATE

ROSEGATE
GDNS

CANDLEBY LA

THE
PRECINCT

EAG

SCOTLAND
Liby

P

AVONDALE

BACKERS CL 1
WOODGATE CL 2
COTGRAVE RD 3

BAKER'S HOLLOW

1
2
3

GOOSE
GATE

MEETING AVE

FOREST CL

BROAD MEER

CANDLEBY LA

CANDLEBY
GDNS

Cotgrave
Candleby
Lane Sch

PLUMTREE RD

Cotgrave

LAMPLANDS

WHITE FURROWS

FERN LEA
AVE

GREENFIELDS DR

Ash Lea
Sch

ASH LEA CL

HAWTHORN
AVE

WOODLAND
CL

GARTHRIDGE

MANNS LEYS

CORN
CL

TOFT CL

SPINNEY
CL

SAMUEL

RING LEAS

MILLERS BRIDGE 1
INGLEBY CL 2

WESTWAY

THE DALE

MANORWOOD
RD

FLAGHOLME

OXTHORPE RD

RUNCIE
CL

EAST
MOOR

BONNY MEAD

THE WARREN

GRIPPS COMM
FIELD

SAXON WAY

WARWICK GDNS

Brickyard
Plantation

Scotton's
Hill

Tollerton
Wood

COTGRAVE LA

COTGRAVE RD

Hoehill Farm

GILLIVER LA

CHURCH GATE

Clipston

Manor
Farm

Blackberry
Farm

WOLDS LA

Mill Lane

GREEN LA

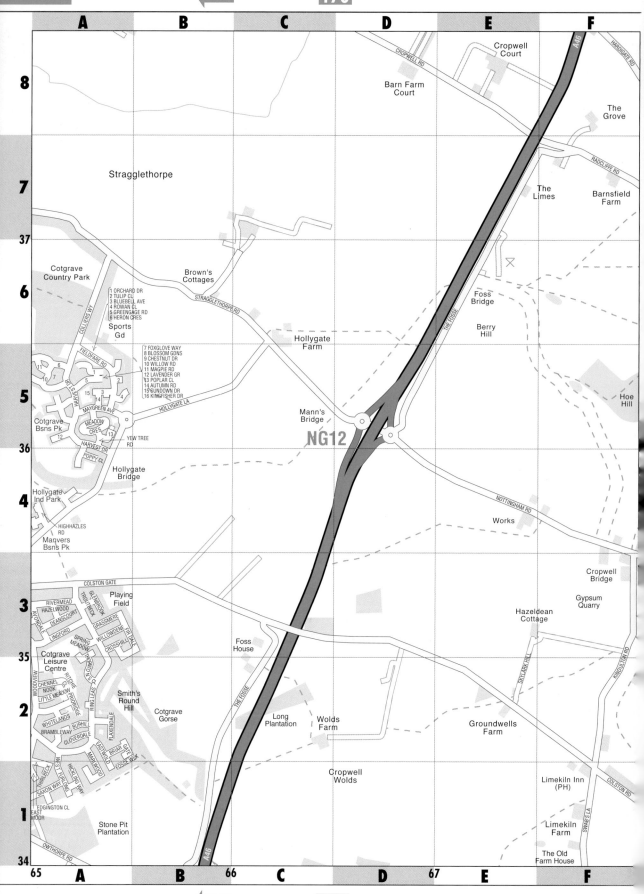

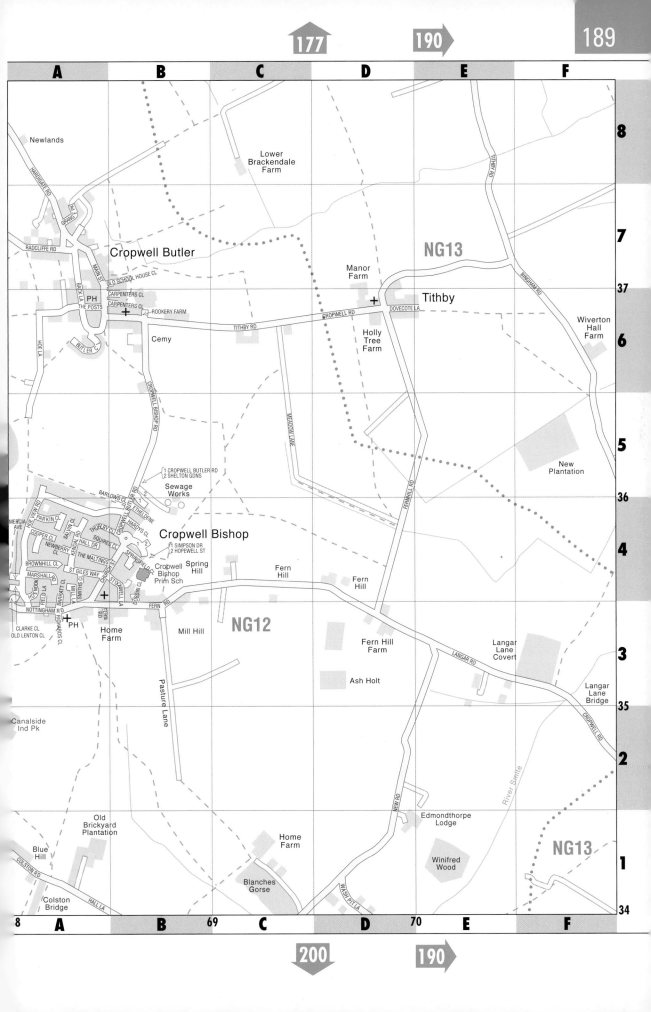

8

Newlands

Lower
Brackendale
Farm

HARDIGATE RD
GRANGE
McVAY
RADCLIFFE RD
Cropwell Butler

7

NG13

MAIN ST
BACK LA
OLD SCHOOL HOUSE CL
Manor
Farm
Tithby

37

PH
THE POSTS
CARPENTERS CL
CARPENTERS CL
Rookery Farm
CROPWELL RD
DOVECOTE LA
BINGHAM RD
Wiverton
Hall
Farm

HOE LA
BUTLER CL
TITHBY RD
Cemy
Holly
Tree
Farm

6

CROPWELL BISHOP RD
MEADOW LANE

5

1 CROPWELL BUTLER RD
2 SHELTON GDNS
Sewage
Works
New
Plantation

36

BARLOWS CL
ETHELDENE
CROPWELL BUTLER RD
HARDYS CL
MERCIA AVE
HOE VIEW RD
PARKIN CL
SALVIN CL
KENDAL RD
HALL DR
THURLBY CL
SQUIRES CL
Cropwell Bishop
1 SIMPSON DR
2 HOPEWELL ST
FERNHILL RD

4

COOPER CL
NEWBERRY CL
THE MALTINGS
ST GILES WAY
SPRINGFIELD CL
STOCKWELL
Cropwell Bishop
Prim Sch
Spring
Hill
Fern
Hill
Fern
Hill
New
Plantation

BROWNHILL CL
MARSHALL CL
HOLYOAK
FIELD LA
BARRATT CL
SMITHS CL
MILL CL
DOBBIN CL
FERN RD
Fern
Hill
Farm
Langar
Lane
Covert

NOTTINGHAM RD
RICHARDS CL
PH
Home
Farm
Mill Hill
NG12
Ash Holt
LANGAR RD

3

CLARKE CL
OLD LENTON CL
Pasture Lane

35

Langar
Lane
Bridge
CROPWELL RD

Canalside
Ind Pk

2

River Smite

COLSTON RD
Old
Brickyard
Plantation
Home
Farm
NEW RD
Edmondthorpe
Lodge
NG13

Blue
Hill
Blanches
Gorse
Winifred
Wood

1

COLSTON RD
Colston
Bridge
HALL LA
WASH PIT LA

34

189
178

A
B
C
D
E
F
8
7
37
6
5
36
4
3
35
2
1
34
71
72
73
Tythby Grange
Crane's Covert
Whatton Fields
CONERY LA
Manor Lodge
GRANBY LA
MANOR LA
Smite Hill Covert
Moat Covert
River Smite
Wiverton Hall
Smite Hill Farm
NG13
Northfield Farm
Wiverton Smite Bridge
BINGHAM RD
Walnuts Farm
MAIN RD
ORCHARD CL
Church Farm
Roadside Farm
Barnstone
PARK RD
WORKS LA
NG12
Stroom Dyke
LANGAR RD
Works
Works
BUTLERS FIELD
Langar CE Prim Sch
TONE RD
MUSTERS RD
Langar
Hall
CHURCH LA
BARNS
BELVOIR CRES
EARL HOWE CRES
MAIN ST
WILLOW LA
P
PH
Works Farm
Stroom Dyke
CROPWELL RD
Langar Ind Est
HARBY RD
Ragnal Farm
COACH GAP LA
Naturescape Wild Flower Farm
Sewage Works
Stroomfields
LANGAR LA

189
201

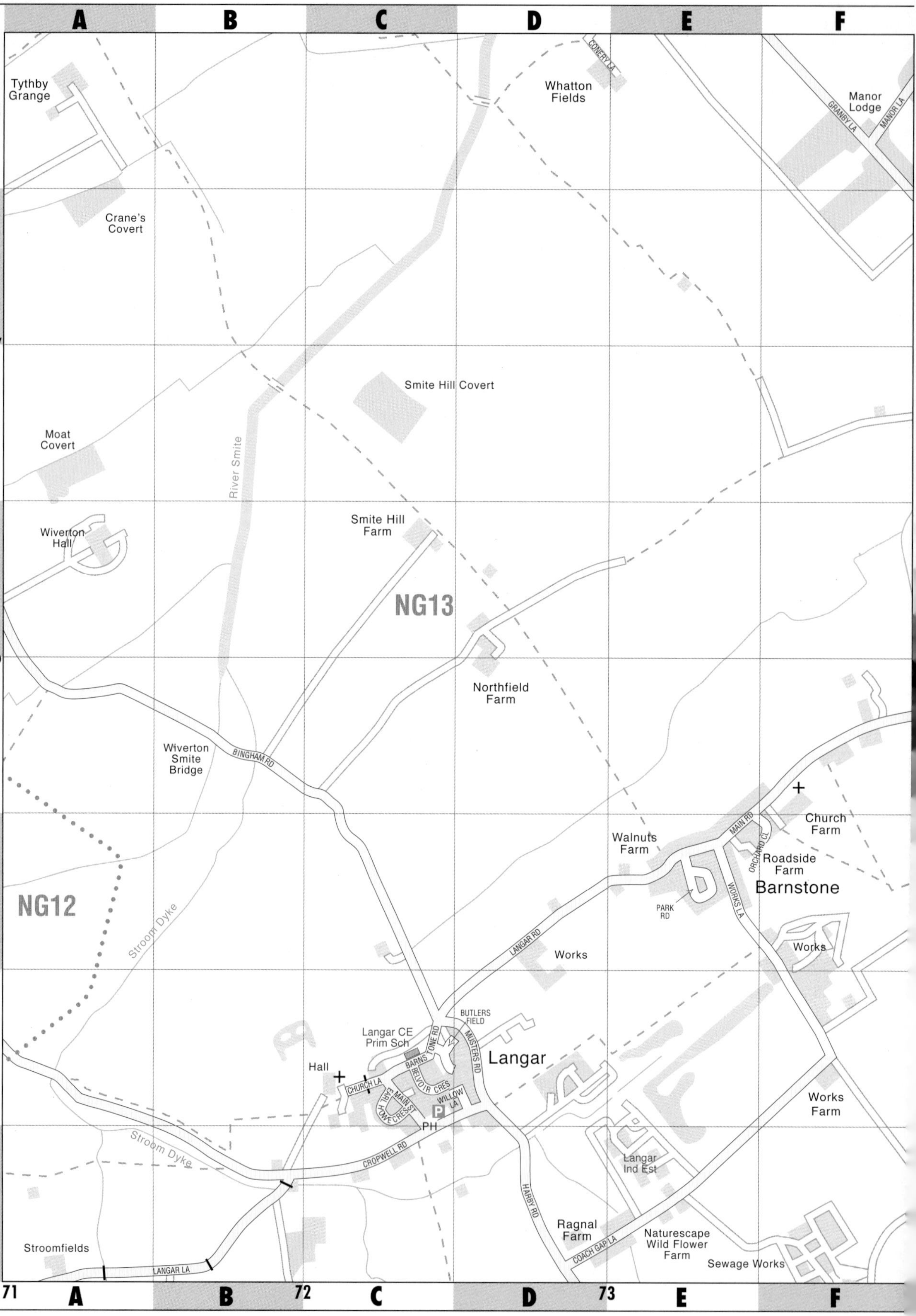

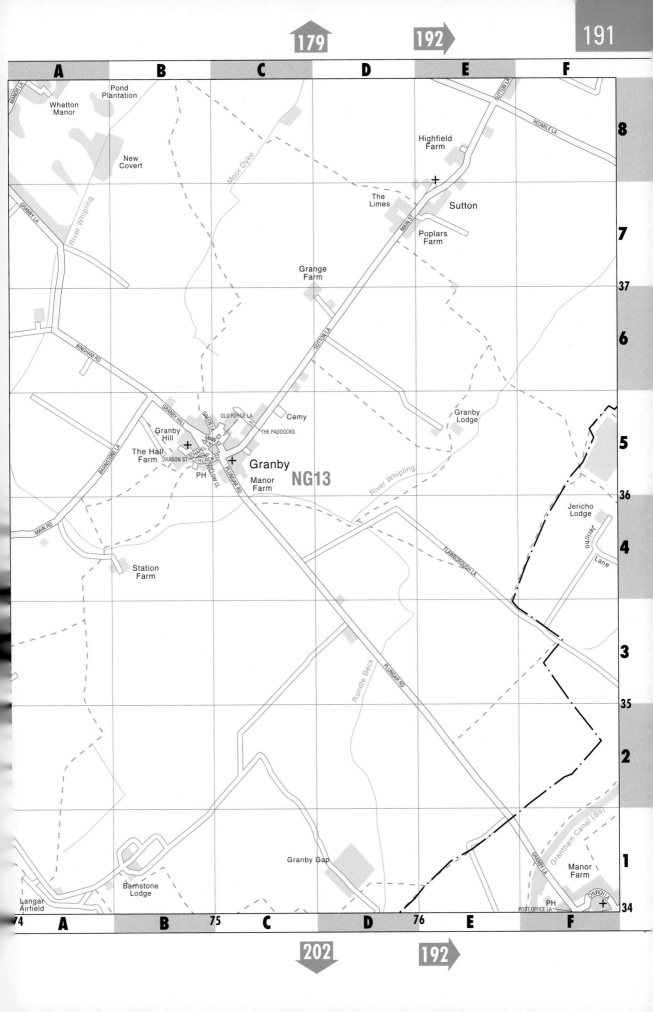

A B C D E F

8

7

37

6

5

36

4

3

35

2

1

34

The Becks
Plantation

REDMILE LA

River Whipling

Old Hill Farm

Glebe
Farm

SUTTON RD

Jericho
Covert

NG13

The Lodge

Grantham Canal (disused)

JERICHO LA

Hill Farm

Barkestone Bridge

Ivy House
Farm

THE GREEN
MARSHALL
FARM CL
NEW CAUSEWAY

Wilders Farm

PH

PLUNGAR LA

ORCHARD CL

THE OLD LA

Barkestone-le-Vale

MIDDLE ST

Home
Farm

Playing
Field

WOOD LA

Vale House

BARKESTONE LA

CHERRY TREE DR

REDMILE LA

The Grimmer

Eady Farm

New Vale
Farm

BARKESTONE LA

Lodge Farm

Peacock Farm

MAIN RD

Peacock Inn
(PH)

Sewage Works

House
Farm

CHURCH LA

CHURCH CNR

MAIN ST

Redmile
CE Prim Sch

Drift
Hill

EASTHORPE
LA

BAKER'S LA

POST OFFICE LA

BELVOIR RD

Redmile

Lincolnshire STREET ATLAS

LONG LA

193
183

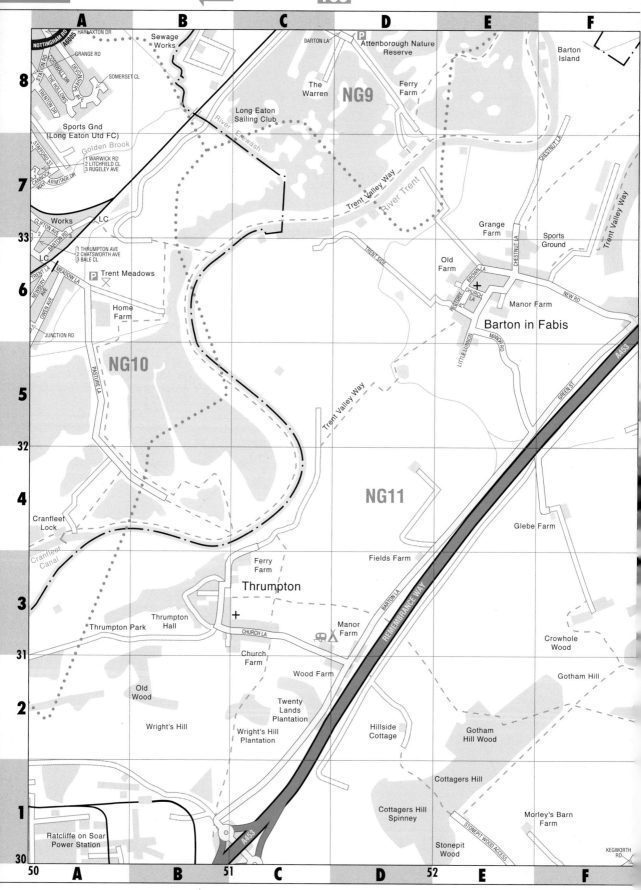

8

Nottingham Rd
A6005
HARLAXTON DR
STATION RD
CORNWALL DR
DEVONSHIRE AVE
TRENTON DR
THE HOLLOWS
GRANGE RD
SOMERSET CL

Sewage
Works

BARTON LA

Attenborough Nature
Reserve

Barton
Island

The Warren

NG9

Ferry
Farm

7

Sports Gnd
(Long Eaton Utd FC)
STAFFORD ST
Golden Brook
CANNOCK WAY
ARMITAGE DR
1 WARWICK RD
2 LITCHFIELD CL
3 RUGELEY AVE

Long Eaton
Sailing Club

River Erewash

Trent Valley Way

River Trent

CHESTNUT LA

Trent Valley Way

33

Works
LC
CLIFTON AVE
BARTON RD
1 THRUMPTON AVE
2 CHATSWORTH AVE
3 BALE CL

Trent Side

Grange
Farm

Sports
Ground

6

LC
TRENT LA
NEWBERY AVE
MEADOW LA
OWEN AVE
P Trent Meadows

Home
Farm

Old
Farm

CHESTNUT LA

BROWN LA

CHURCH LA

RECTORY PL

NEW RD

Manor Farm

Barton in Fabis

JUNCTION RD

LITTLE LUNNON

MANOR RD

GREEN ST

A453

5

NG10

PASTURE LA

Trent Valley Way

32

4

NG11

Cranfleet
Lock

Glebe Farm

Cranfleet
Canal

REMEMBRANCE WAY

BARTON LA

Fields Farm

Crowhole
Wood

3

Ferry
Farm

Thrumpton

Thrumpton
Hall

Thrumpton Park

CHURCH LA

Manor
Farm

Gotham Hill

31

Church
Farm

Wood Farm

2

Old
Wood

Twenty
Lands
Plantation

Hillside
Cottage

Gotham
Hill Wood

Wright's Hill

Wright's Hill
Plantation

Cottagers Hill

Cottagers Hill
Spinney

Morley's Barn
Farm

1

Ratcliffe on Soar
Power Station

A453

Stonepit
Wood

STONEPIT WOOD ACCESS

KEGWORTH
RD

30

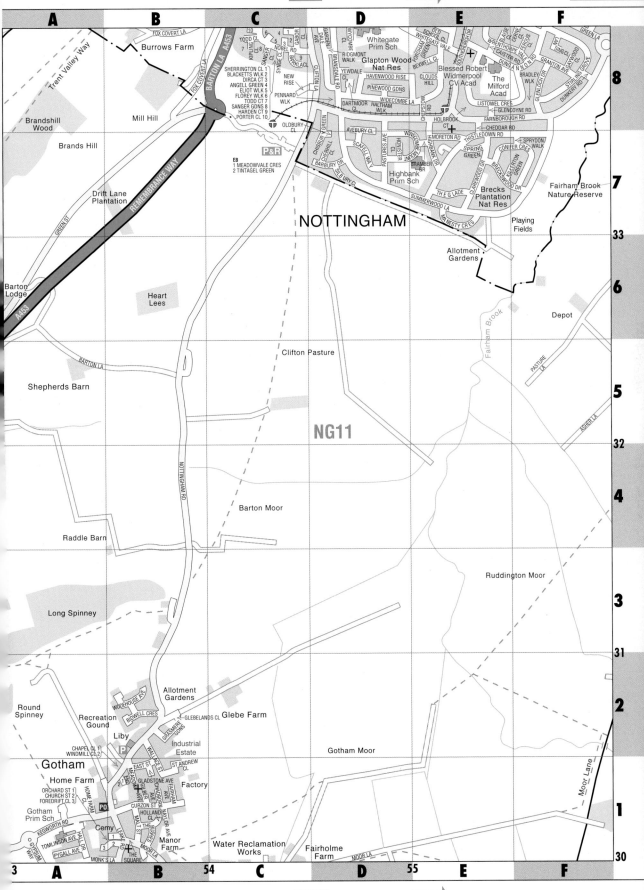

A | B | C | D | E | F

Trent Valley Way

Burrows Farm

Fox Covert La

Barton La A453

Brandshill Wood

Brands Hill

Mill Hill

Drift Lane Plantation

REMEMBRANCE WAY

Barton Lodge

A453

Heart Lees

Shepherds Barn

Clifton Pasture

NOTTINGHAM

NG11

Barton Moor

Raddle Barn

Ruddington Moor

Long Spinney

Round Spinney

Recreation Gound

Allotment Gardens

Glebe Farm

Industrial Estate

Gotham

Home Farm

Gotham Prim Sch

Gotham Moor

Manor Farm

Water Reclamation Works

Fairholme Farm

Moor Lane

Depot

Pasture La

Asher La

Fairham Brook Nature Reserve

Playing Fields

Allotment Gardens

Brecks Plantation Nat Res

Glapton Wood Nat Res

Whitegate Prim Sch

Highbank Prim Sch

Blessed Robert Widmerpool CV Acad

The Milford Acad

Fairham Brook

SHERRINGTON CL 1
BLACKETTS WLK 2
DIRCA CT 3
ANGELL GREEN 4
ELIOT WLK 5
FLOREY WLK 6
TODD CT 7
SANGER GDNS 8
HARDEN CT 9
PORTER CL 10

E8
1 MEADOWVALE CRES
2 TINTAGEL GREEN

P&R

33

32

31

30

8

7

6

5

4

3

2

1

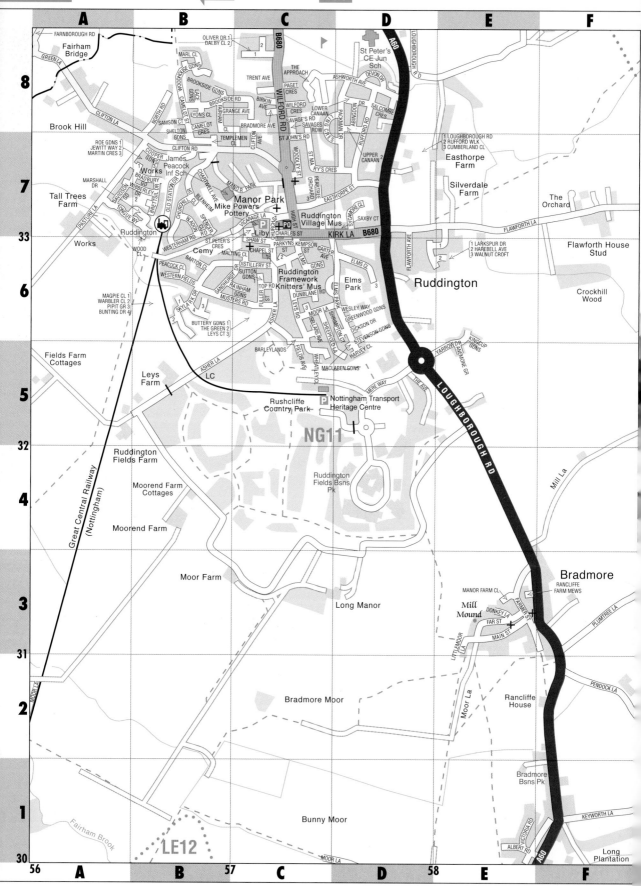

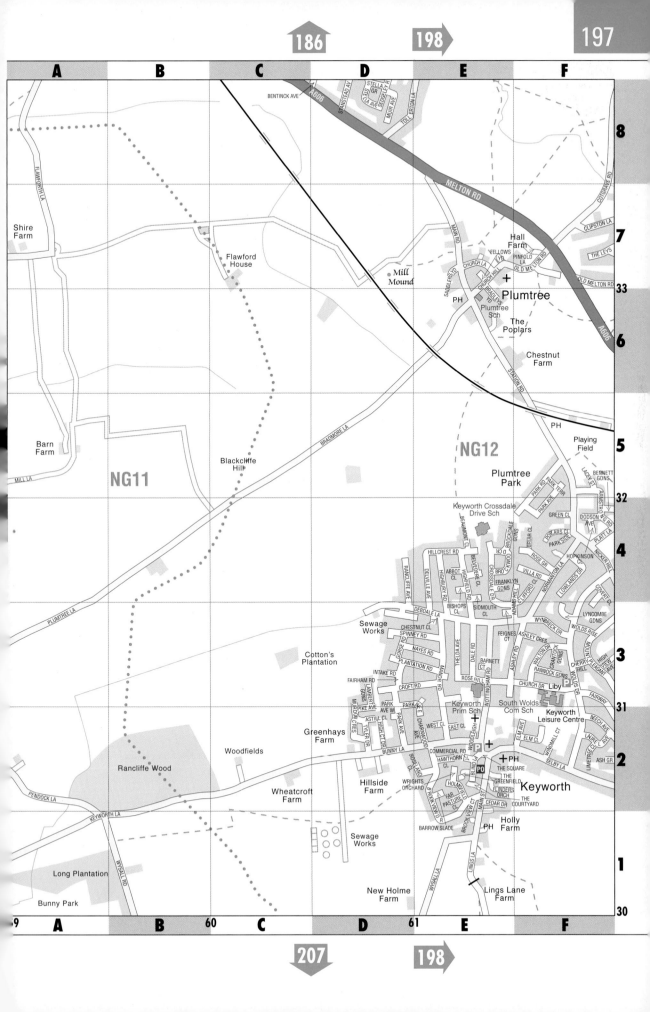

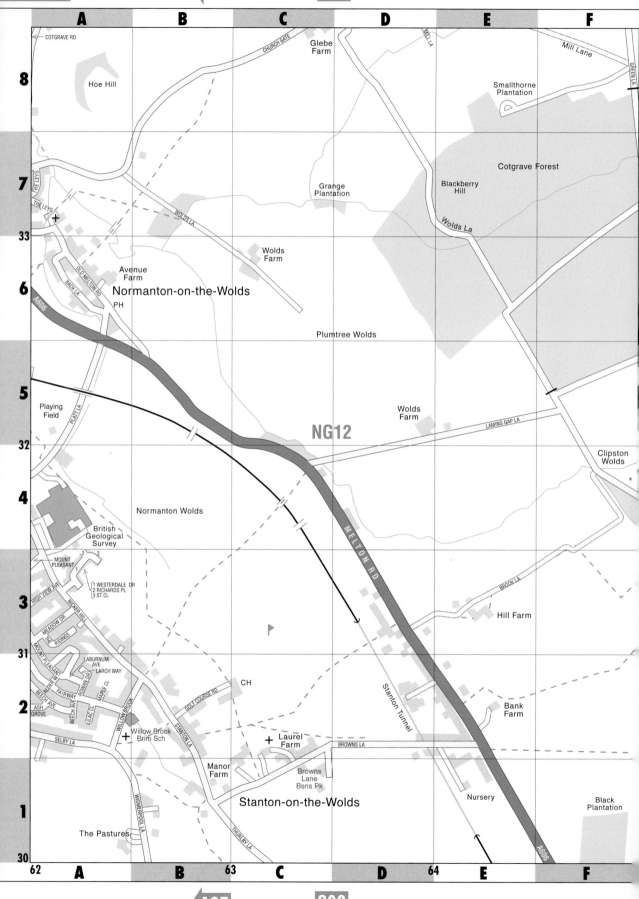

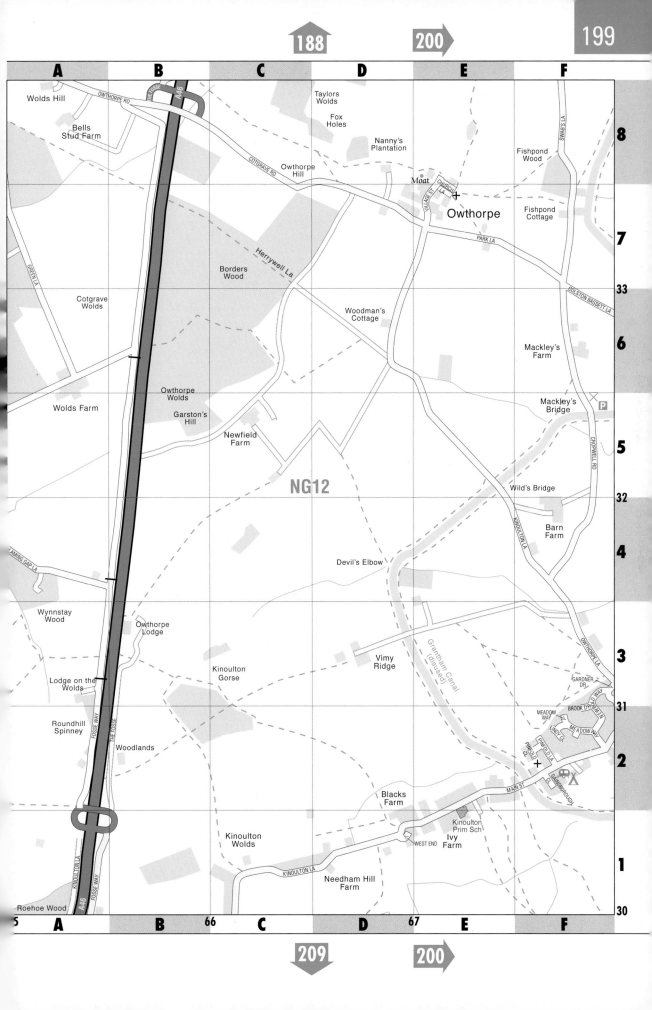

199
189

A   B   C   D   E   F

8

NG13

COLSTON ROAD

NEW RD

St Mary's Church
(remains of)

China
Bridge

WASH PIT LA

Old
Gorse

HALL GROUNDS DR

Sandpit
Hollow

HALL GROUNDS

Home
Farm

LANGAR LA

The Lodge

Colston Hall

HALL LA

Smite
Bridge

Church
Farm

CHURCH GATE

7

Colston
Bassett

Cross

Martin's Arms
(PH)

BAKER'S LA

Manor
House
Farm

OWTHORPE RD

SCHOOL LA

Colston Basset
Sch

BUNNISON LA

33

Oddhouse Farm

Bunnison
Lane Farm

COLSTON BASSETT LA

HARBY LA

6

Spencer's Bridge

Grantham Canal (disused)

Kaye Wood

5

Kaye Wood
Farm

Hills
Farm

32

NG12

4

Barges
Spinney

River Smite

Dalby Brook

Home Farm

Hall Farm

3

Manor
Farm

HALL LA

GARDNER
DR

BAILEY'S
ROW

Water Reclamation
Works

HALL LA

HIND CL

31

OWTHORPE
LA

PH

BRADSHAW CL

NEVILL DR

MAIN ST

BUSWELL CL

2

Kinoulton

Sausethorpe
Farm

HICKLING RD

LE14

1

Grove Farm

Kinoulton Grange

30

68   A   B   69   C   D   70   E   F

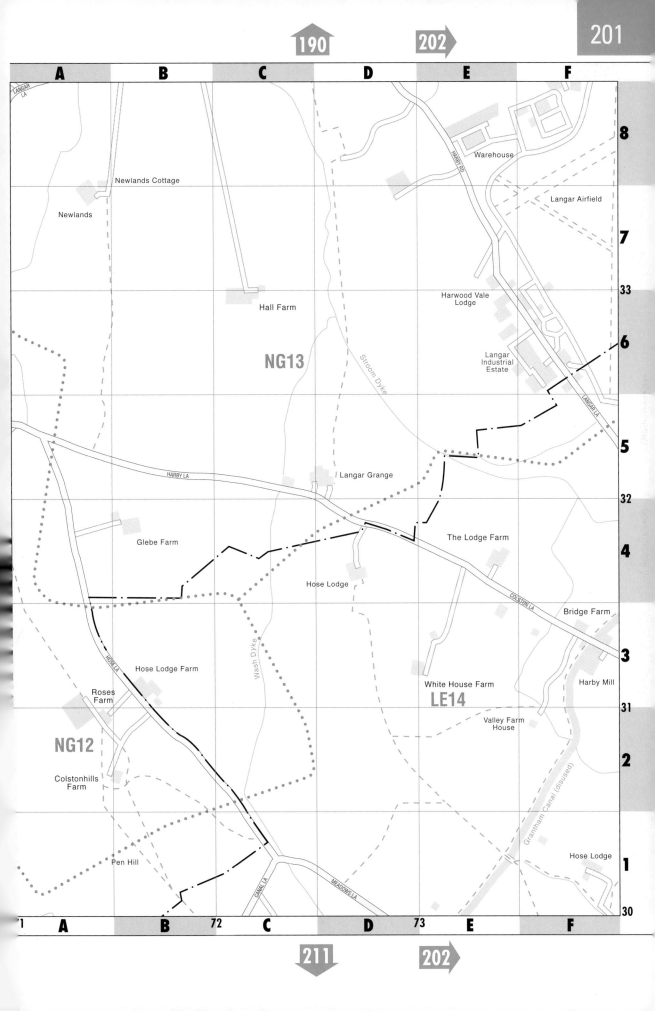

A B C D E F

8

7

33

6

NG13

Post Office La
Anchor Inn (PH)
Home Farm
Highgate Cl
Plungar
Grantham La
Barkestone La
Highgate La
Frog La

Small Farm Ctr

Lodge Farm

Harby La

Woodland Farm

5

32

4

Stathern Lodge

Stathern Bridge

P

Rundle Beck

White House

Long La

Lodge Farm

LE14

Grantham Canal (disused)

Glebe Farm

Langar Bridge

Canal La

Washdyke Farm

Penn La

Stathern

Harby La

Eyesley Gdns

City Rd

Valebrook Rd

Swallows Dr

3

31

2

1

30

Langar La

Dairy Gdns

Harby CE Prim Sch

P

Kimberley Farm

Harby Rd

Stathern Rd

Pinfold Pl

Pinfold

Whitakers Farm

Colston La

Nether St

School La

Button Cl

Coys La

Main St

Burden La

Walnut Paddock

Dickman St

Gas Walk

Harefield Cl

Boyer's Orchard

PH

White Hart Inn (PH)

Stathern La

THE RED CAUSEWAY

Green La

Sewage Works

Harby

Hose La

Waltham La

Lodge Farm

Willow Farm

Pasture Lane

Leicestershire STREET ATLAS

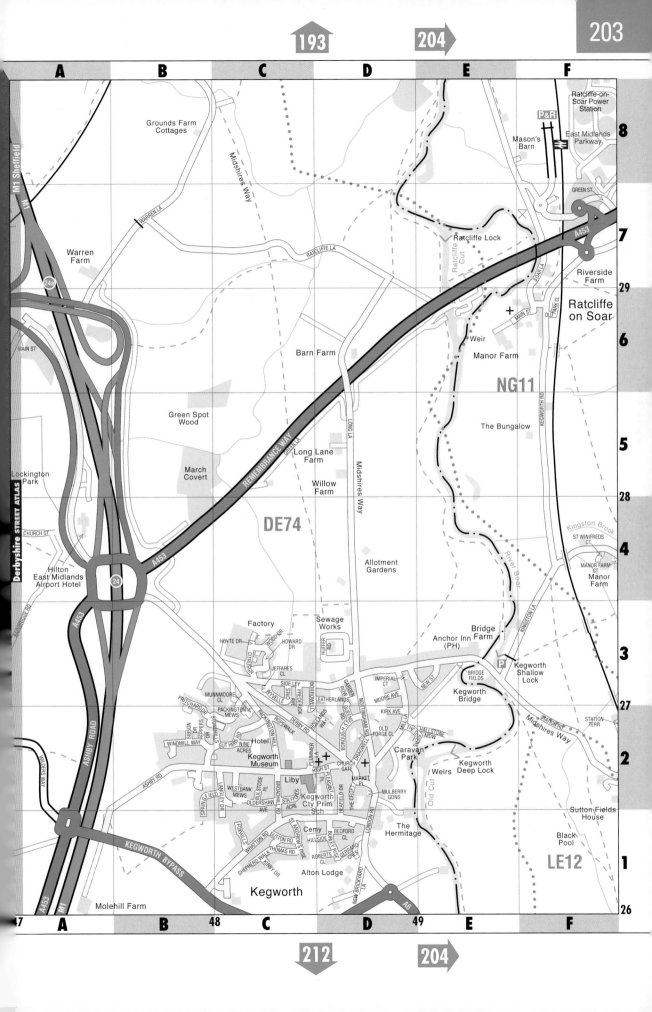

A B C D E F

Ratcliffe-on-Soar Power Station

P&R

Mason's Barn

East Midlands Parkway

8

Grounds Farm Cottages

GREEN ST

Midshires Way

WARREN LA

7

A453

RATCLIFFE LA

Ratcliffe Lock

Ratcliffe Cut

SOAR LA

Riverside Farm

29

Warren Farm

MAIN ST

Barn Farm

Weir

Manor Farm

MAIN ST

OLD PARK CL

Ratcliffe on Soar

6

NG11

KEGWORTH RD

The Bungalow

Green Spot Wood

GREEN LA

Long Lane Farm

LONG LA

5

28

Lockington Park

REMEMBRANCE WAY

March Covert

Willow Farm

Midshires Way

Kingston Brook

ST WINIFREDS CT

4

DE74

Allotment Gardens

River Soar

MANOR FARM CT

Manor Farm

A453

Hilton East Midlands Airport Hotel

SAUNDERS RD

CHURCH ST

KINGSTON LA

Bridge Farm

Anchor Inn (PH)

P

Kegworth Shallow Lock

3

27

Factory

Sewage Works

HUFFEN RD

BRIDGE FIELDS

Kegworth Bridge

HOYTE DR

WOOD QR

HOWARD DR

JEFFARES CL

SIDE LEY

FREDERICK

BORROWELL

GARDEN

IMPERIAL CT

MOORE AVE

NEW ST

Kegworth Deep Lock

Midshires Way

STATION RD

STATION TERR

BAINBRIDGE RD

CITRUS DR

WYVELLE

DERBY AVE

ROLANDS WAY

LEATHERLANDS

NOTTINGHAM RD

QUEENS RD

KIRK AVE

OLD FORGE CL

MILL LA

THE DODDERS

HALLSTONE MDW

Caravan Park

2

ASHBY ROAD

PRITCHARD DR

MUNNMOORE CL

PACKINGTON MEWS

STENHILLS

PACKINGTON HILL

ROSEWALK

SUTHERS RD

NINE ACRES

Hotel

BOROUGH ST

BRADWELL

THE CROFT

Weirs

OLD CUT

Kegworth Museum

Kegworth Cty Prim Sch

MARKET PL

MULBERRY GDNS

Sutton Fields House

SIBSON DR

WINDMILL WAY

PEPPERS DR

Liby

BROADHILL RD

BULL STONE PL

STA FLDS ACRE

HIGH ST

THE PLEASANT

HEAFIELD DR

Black Pool

LE12

SPRINGFIELD

WESTBANK MEWS

LANGLEY DR

OLDERSHAW AVE

ST ANDREWS RISE

Cemy

BEDFORD CL

HILLSIDE

LONDON RD

The Hermitage

ASHBY RD

FOXHILLS

WHATTON RD

SUTTON RD

THOMAS RD

BURLEY RISE

ROBERTS CL

GERARD CRES

1

SHEPHERD WALK

KIRBY DR

Alton Lodge

NEW BRICKYARD LA

A6

KEGWORTH BYPASS

Molehill Farm

Kegworth

A453 M1

26

47 A B 48 C D 49 E F

203
194

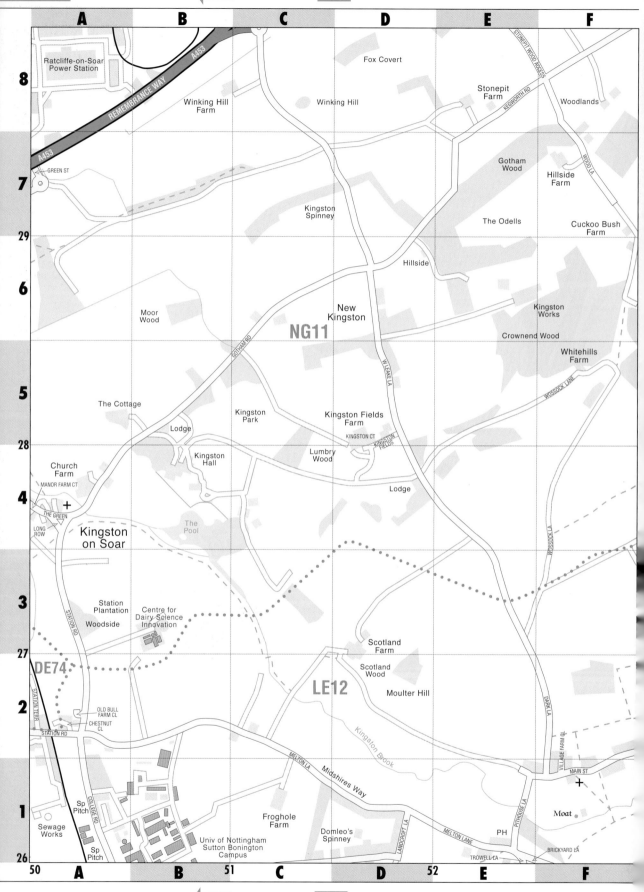

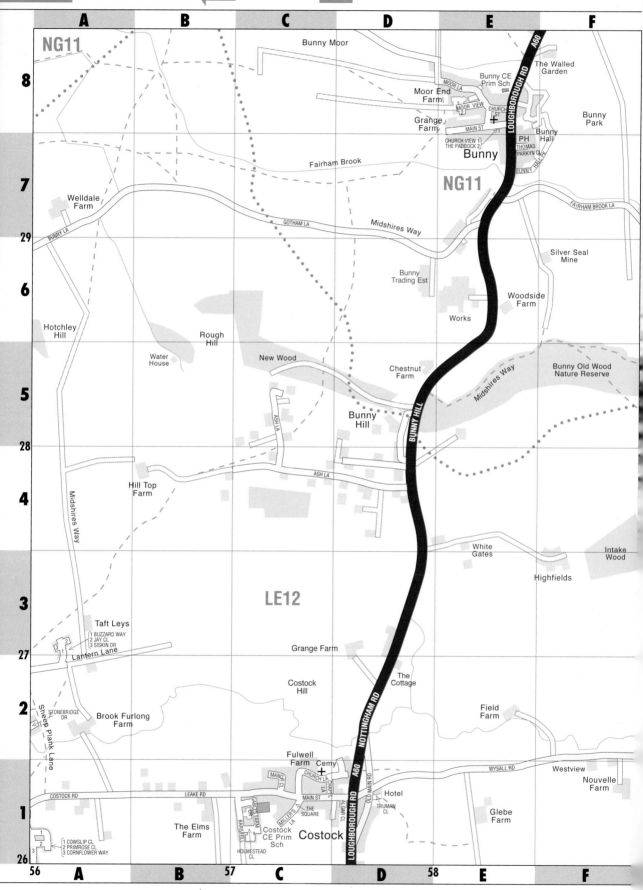

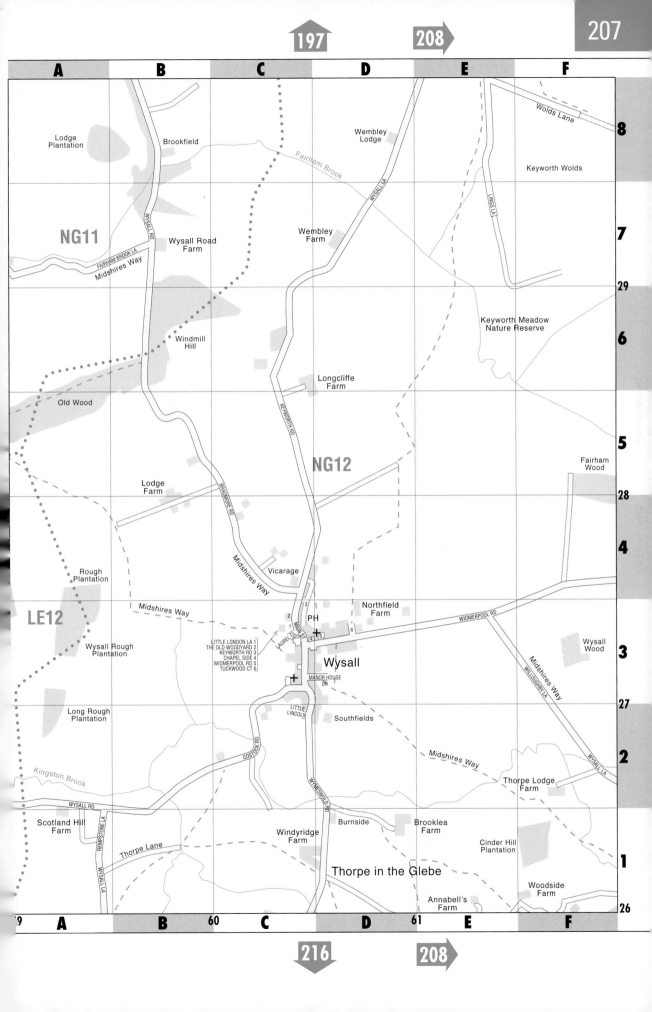

207
198

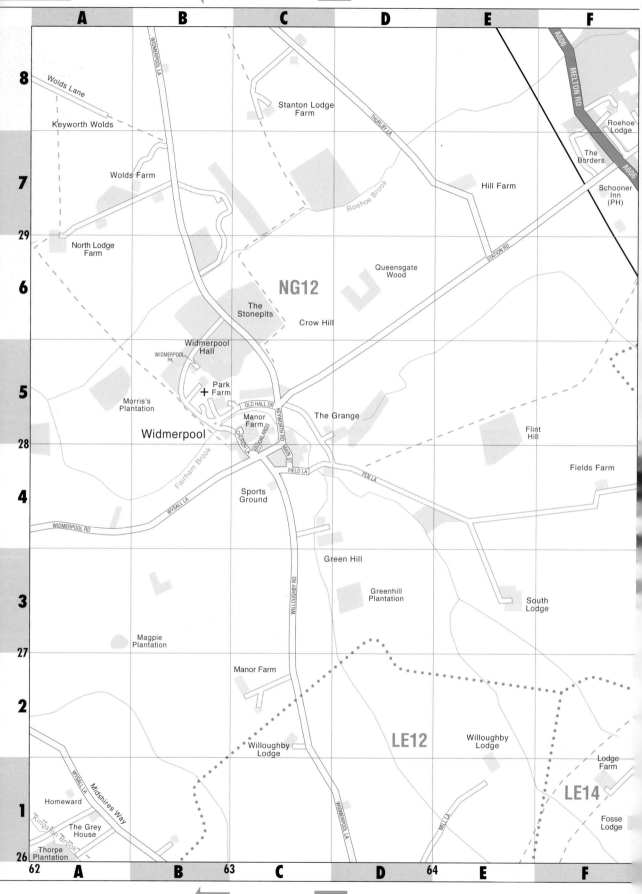

207
217

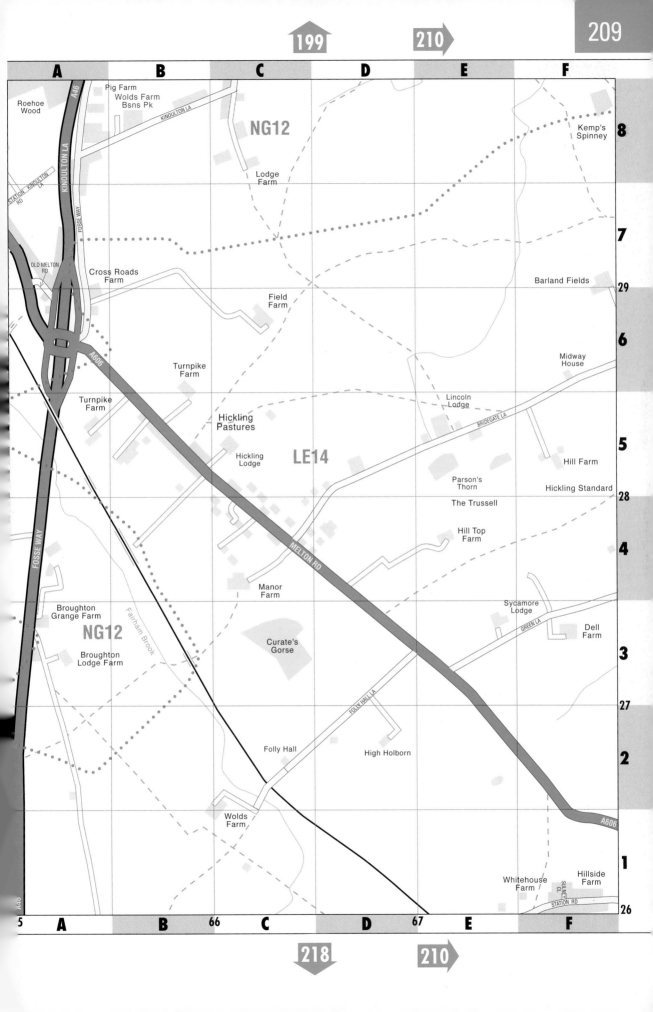

NG12

Hickling La

Bridge
Farm

Bridge
Farm

Grantham Canal (disused)

Clarke's
Bridge

Canal
Farm

The Plough Inn
(PH)

MILL LA

Church
Farm

Waterlane
Farm

Elms Farm

Hickling

MARSH'S
PADDOCK

Burial
Ground

CLAWSON LA

Cricket
Ground

BRIDEGATE LA

Manor
House

Canal
Farm

THE GREEN

The Green

HICKLING LA

LONG LA

MAIN ST

HARLES ACRES

PUDDING
LA

Oak
Farm

WASH PIT
LA

LE14

Castle
View

Hickling Standard

Dalby Brook

GREEN LA

Sherbrooke Fox
Covert

River Smite

HICKLING LA

HICKLING RD

Muxlow
Hill

27

Bridge
Farm

BROUGHTON LA

A606

MELTON RD

COLONEL'S LA

Sulney
Fields

CHURCH LA

Upper
Broughton

CLAWSON LA

The Golden Fleece
(PH)

MAIN RD

CHAPEL LA

STA
RD

TOP GREEN

WELL LA

BOTTOM GREEN

NOTTINGHAM RD

Corner Farm

MAIN
RD

A606

CHURCH END

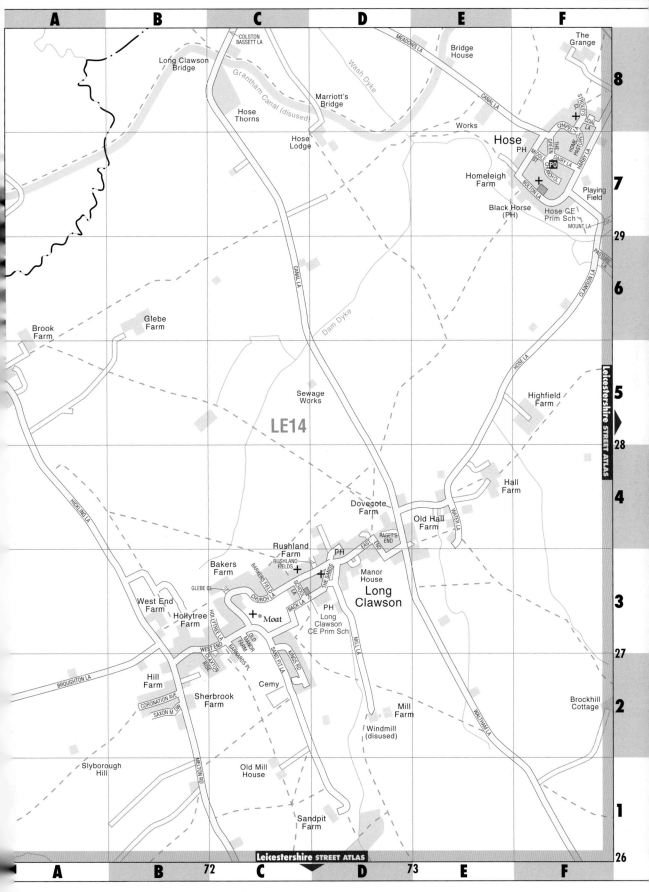

A   B   C   D   E   F

Long Clawson Bridge

COLSTON BASSETT LA

Grantham Canal (disused)

Hose Thorns

Hose Lodge

Marriott's Bridge

Wash Dyke

MEADOWS LA

Bridge House

Works

CANAL LA

The Grange

Hose

PH

STROUD'S CL

CHAPEL LA

COAL LA

HOME PASTURES

THE GREEN

MIDDLE ST

DAIRY LA

PO

DARBY LA

BOLTON LA

CHURCH CL

Homeleigh Farm

Black Horse (PH)

Playing Field

Hose CE Prim Sch

MOUNT LA

Brook Farm

Glebe Farm

CANAL LA

Dam Dyke

Sewage Works

LE14

PASTURE LA

CLAWSON LA

Highfield Farm

HOSE LA

Hall Farm

HICKLING LA

Dovecote Farm

Old Hall Farm

WATER LA

Rushland Farm

RUSHLAND FIELDS

PH

EAST END

PAGET'S END

Manor House

Bakers Farm

BARKERSTREET LA

THE SANDS

Long Clawson

West End Farm

Hollytree Farm

GLEBE CL

HOLLYTREE LA

CHURCH LA

SCHOOL LA

BACK LA

Moat

PH

Long Clawson CE Prim Sch

MILL LA

Hill Farm

BROUGHTON LA

WEST END

CLAXTON RISE

OLD MANOR

BARNARDS PL

SANDPIT LA

KINGS RD

Cemy

Sherbrook Farm

CORONATION AVE

SAXON M DW

MELTON RD

Old Mill House

Windmill (disused)

Mill Farm

WALTHAM LA

Brockhill Cottage

Slyborough Hill

Sandpit Farm

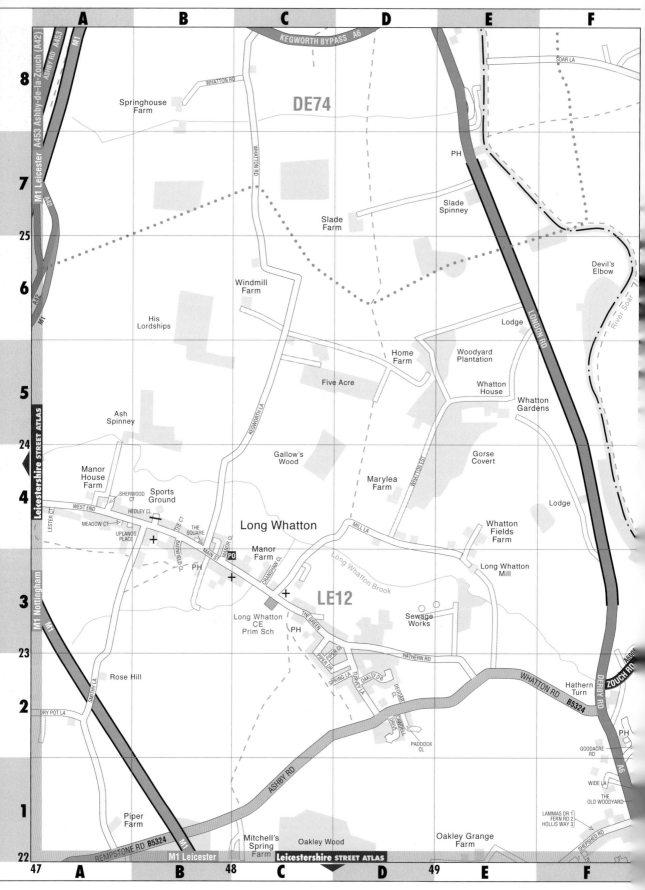

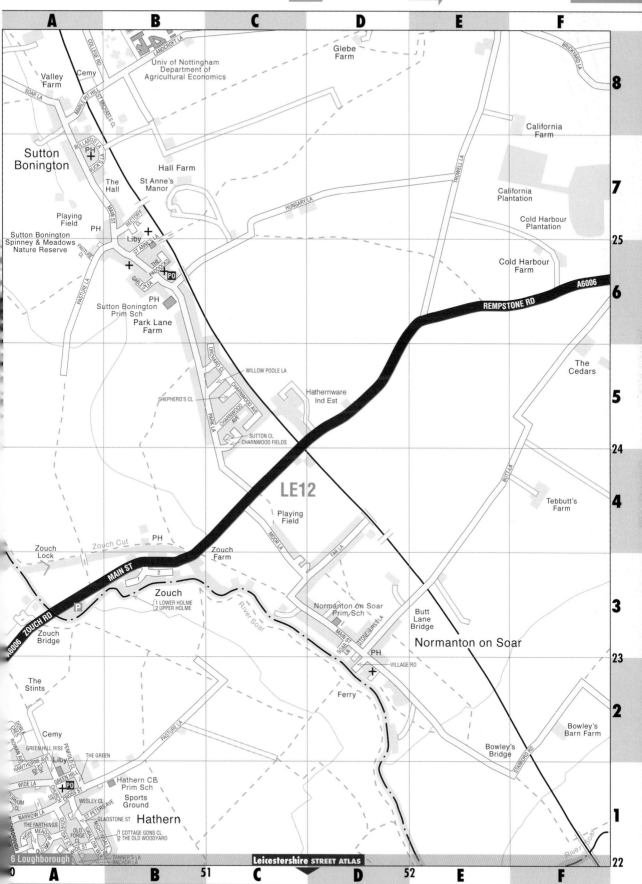

A B C D E F

8

California
Farm

Valley
Farm

Cemy

Univ of Nottingham
Department of
Agricultural Economics

Glebe
Farm

California
Plantation

7

Sutton
Bonington

Hall Farm

Cold Harbour
Plantation

St Anne's
Manor

HUNGARY LA

25

The
Hall

Playing
Field

Liby

Cold Harbour
Farm

Sutton Bonington
Spinney & Meadows
Nature Reserve

PH

PO

REMPSTONE RD   A6006

6

PH

Sutton Bonington
Prim Sch

Park Lane
Farm

The
Cedars

WILLOW POOLE LA

Hathernware
Ind Est

5

SHEPHERD'S CL

ORCHARD CL

CHARNWOOD AVE

PARK LA

SUTTON CL
CHARNWOOD FIELDS

24

BUTT LA

LE12

Tebbutt's
Farm

4

Playing
Field

MOOR LA

FAR LA

Zouch
Lock

Zouch Cut

PH

Zouch
Farm

Zouch

1 LOWER HOLME
2 UPPER HOLME

River Soar

Normanton on Soar
Prim Sch

MAIN ST

Butt
Lane
Bridge

3

A6006   ZOUCH RD

MAIN ST

P

Normanton on Soar

Zouch
Bridge

STONEHURST LA

SOAR LA

PH

23

The
Stints

Village RD

Cemy

PASTURE LA

Ferry

2

DOBIE
CRES

Green Hill Rise

THE GREEN

Bowley's
Barn Farm

Liby

Hathern CE
Prim Sch

GREEN HILL

Bowley's
Bridge

STANFORD RD

1

PO

Sports
Ground

WIDE LA

Hathern

GLADSTONE ST

NARROW LA

THE FARTHINGS

1 COTTAGE GDNS CL
2 THE OLD WOODYARD

River Soar

22

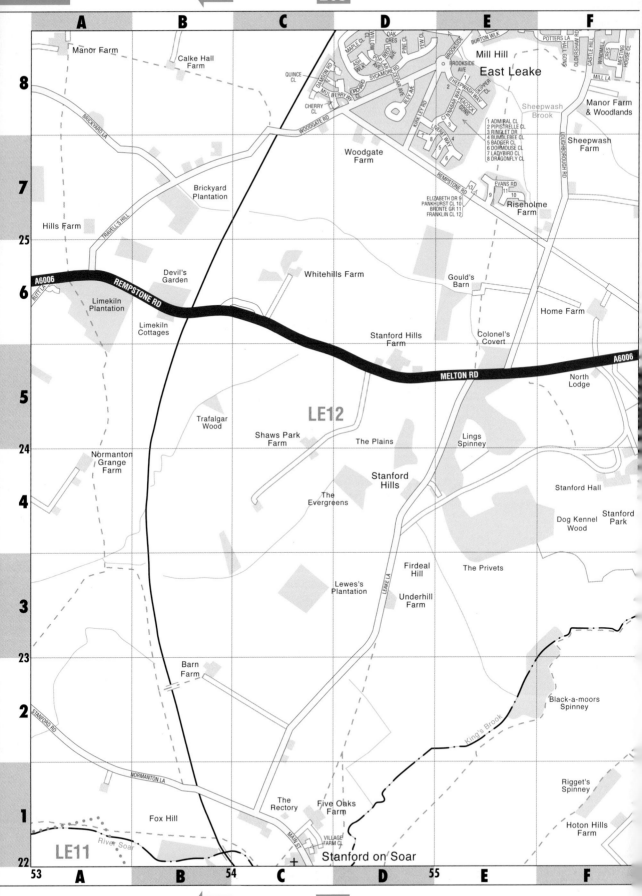

A B C D E F

8

Manor Farm

Calke Hall Farm

QUINCE CL

DAMSON RD

MULBERRY WAY

ORCHARD CL

CHERRY CL

SYCAMORE RD

MAPLE CL

ASH WLK

MOTTRAM

POPLAR AVE

PINE CL

OAK CRES

CEDAR AVE

YEW CL

BURTON WLK

BROOKSIDE

POTTERS LA

HALL GDNS

OLDERSHAW RD

CASTLE HILL

WINDMILL CRES

MEETING HOUSE CL

MILL LA

Mill Hill

East Leake

Brookside Ave

Sheepwash Way

Kirk Ley Rd

Beley Ave

Liverpool Way

Dunbar Way

Peacock Gdns

Skipper Cl

1 ADMIRAL CL
2 PIPISTRELLE CL
3 RINGLET DR
4 BUMBLEBEE CL
5 BADGER CL
6 DORMOUSE CL
7 LADYBIRD CL
8 DRAGONFLY CL

Sheepwash Brook

Manor Farm & Woodlands

LOUGHBOROUGH RD

Sheepwash Farm

WOODGATE RD

Woodgate Farm

REMPSTONE RD

EVANS RD

ELIZABETH DR 9
PANKHURST CL 10
BRONTE GR 11
FRANKLIN CL 12

Riseholme Farm

BRICKYARD LA

7

Brickyard Plantation

Hills Farm

TRAVELL'S HILL

25

A6006

Devil's Garden

Whitehills Farm

Gould's Barn

Home Farm

6

BUTT LA

REMPSTONE RD

Limekiln Plantation

Limekiln Cottages

Stanford Hills Farm

Colonel's Covert

A6006

MELTON RD

North Lodge

5

Trafalgar Wood

LE12

Shaws Park Farm

The Plains

Lings Spinney

Stanford Hall

24

Normanton Grange Farm

The Evergreens

Stanford Hills

Stanford Park

Dog Kennel Wood

4

LEAKE LA

Firdeal Hill

The Privets

Stanford Hills

Lewes's Plantation

Underhill Farm

3

STANFORD RD

Barn Farm

King's Brook

Black-a-moors Spinney

23

2

NORMANTON LA

Rigget's Spinney

The Rectory

Five Oaks Farm

Hoton Hills Farm

1

LE11

Fox Hill

River Soar

MAIN ST

VILLAGE FARM CL

Stanford on Soar

22

53 A 54 B C 55 D E F

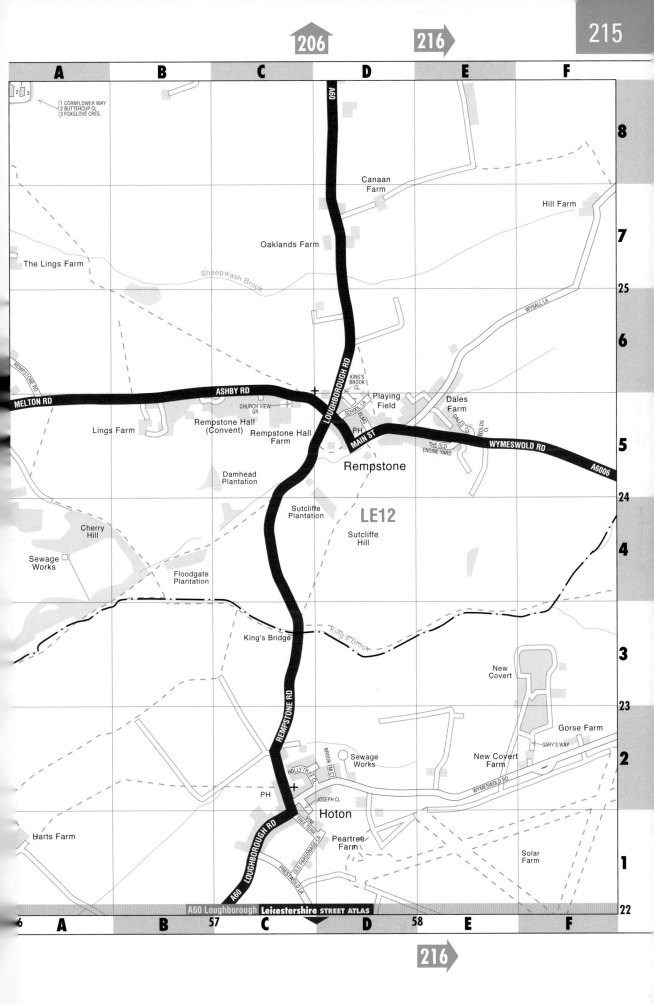

A B C D E F

8

7

25

6

1 CORNFLOWER WAY
2 BUTTERCUP CL
3 FOXGLOVE CRES

A60

Canaan
Farm

Hill Farm

Oaklands Farm

The Lings Farm

Sheepwash Brook

WYSALL LA

ASHBY RD

LOUGHBOROUGH RD

KING'S
BROOK
CL

Playing
Field

Dales
Farm

MELTON RD

CHURCH VIEW
GR

SCHOOL LA

THE
ELMS

DALES CL

COTSWOLDS CL

5

Lings Farm

Rempstone Hall
(Convent)

Rempstone Hall
Farm

MAIN ST

PH

THE OLD
ENGINE YARD

WYMESWOLD RD

A6006

Rempstone

24

Damhead
Plantation

Sutcliffe
Plantation

LE12

Cherry
Hill

Sutcliffe
Hill

4

Sewage
Works

Floodgate
Plantation

REMPSTONE RD

3

King's Bridge

King's Brook

New
Covert

23

Gorse Farm

GARY'S WAY

Harts Farm

BROOK FM CL

Sewage
Works

New Covert
Farm

WYMESWOLD RD

2

HOLLY TR FC CL

PH

JOSEPH CL

Hoton

VINE
TREE TERR

OLD PARSONAGE LA

Peartree
Farm

Solar
Farm

1

LOUGHBOROUGH RD

A60

PRESTWOLD LA

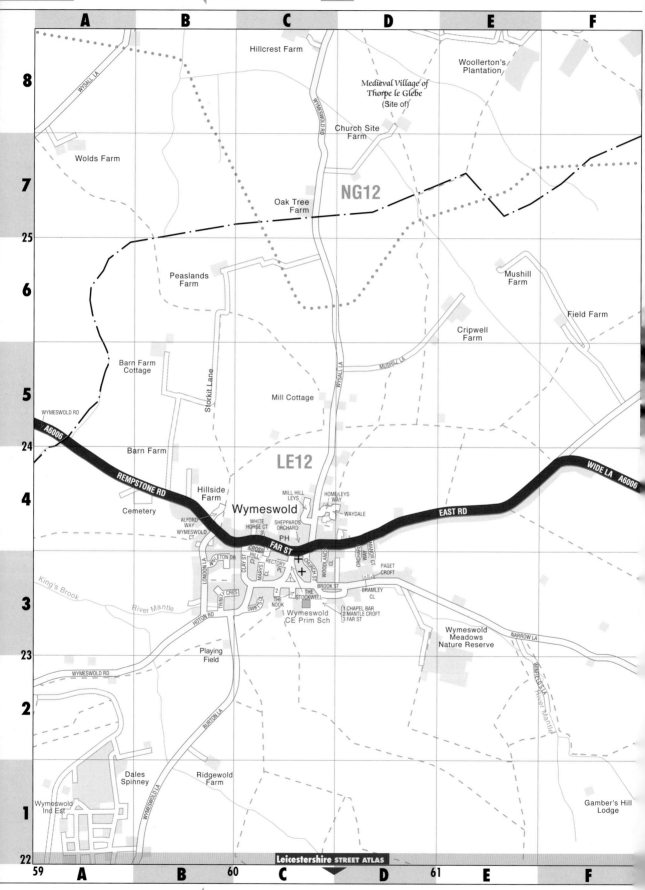

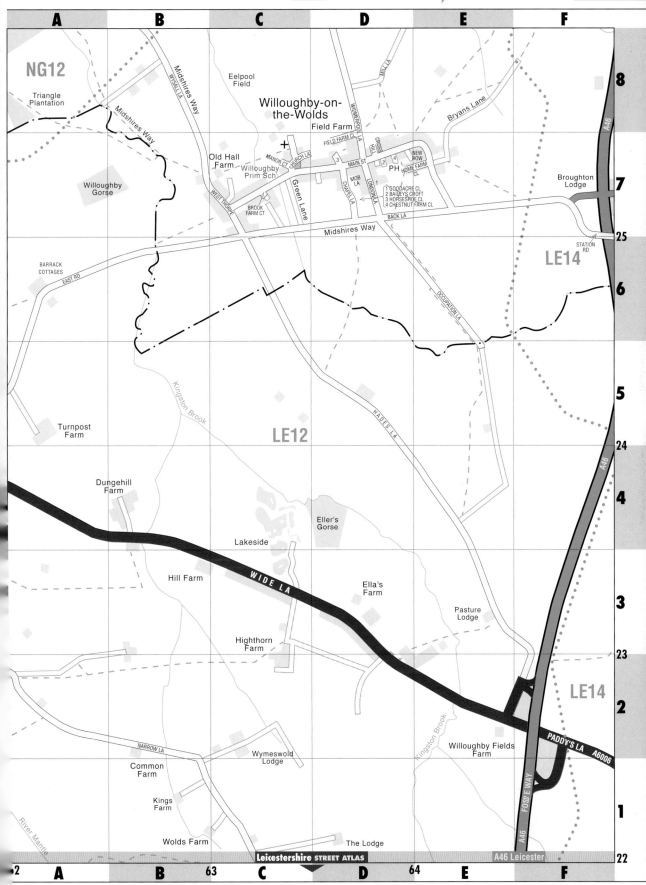

NG12

Triangle
Plantation

Midshires Way

Willoughby
Gorse

Old Hall
Farm

Eelpool
Field

Willoughby-on-
the-Wolds

Field Farm

Field Farm Cl

Willoughby
Prim Sch

Bryans Lane

Broughton
Lodge

MANOR CT

CHURCH LA

Green Lane

WEST THORPE

BROOK
FARM CT

MAIN ST

CROSS HILL

PH

NEW
ROW

HOME
FARM
CL

MOB
LA

CHAPEL LA

LONDON LA

WIDMERPOOL LA

MILL LA

1 GOODACRE CL
2 BAILEYS CROFT
3 HORSESHOE CL
4 CHESTNUT FARM CL

BACK LA

Midshires Way

STATION
RD

LE14

BARRACK
COTTAGES

EAST RD

OCCUPATION LA

25

LE14

Turnpost
Farm

LE12

HADES LA

Kingston Brook

24

Dungehill
Farm

Eller's
Gorse

Lakeside

Hill Farm

WIDE LA

Ella's
Farm

Pasture
Lodge

Highthorn
Farm

NARROW LA

Wymeswold
Lodge

Common
Farm

Kings
Farm

Wolds Farm

The Lodge

Kingston Brook

Willoughby Fields
Farm

PADDY'S LA

A6006

FOSSE WAY

A46

LE14

River Mantle

A46 Leicester

A B C D E F

8

Manor Barn Farm

Manor Farm

Brookside Cottage

STATION RD

Midshires Way

Top Cottage

7

Nottingham Raceway

Motel

Fairham Brook

Longcliff Hill

25

6

Wad House

Spruce Haven

Dalby Lodges

Beazley's Farm

Midshires Way

Longcliffe Hill

North Lodge

LE14

North Lodge Farm

1 NORTH LODGE RD
2 HEDGEROW CL
3 THE PADDOCK

Old Dalby CE Prim Sch

LONGCLIFF CL

STATION RD

Old Dalby

5

NOTTINGHAM LA

24

LONGCLIFF HILL

HAWTHORN CL

CROFT GDNS

PH

DEBDALE HILL

CHAPEL LA

THE GREEN

LAWN LA

MAIN RD

CHURCH LA

PARADISE LA

4

Wood's Hill

Vale View Farm

WOOD HILL

Woodhill Farm

Old Dalby Hall

Hall Plantation

Fishpond Plantation

3

Hill Top Farm

Thorney Hollow

Old Dalby Wood

23

Yard Farm

Upper Grange Farm

Grange Cottages

GIBSON'S LA

Wavendon Grange

MIDSHIRES WAY

LAWN LA

Old Dalby Wood House

2

Old Dalby Grange

Home Lodge Farm

PERKINS LA

A6006

PADDY'S LA

Lower Grange Farm

Bridgets Covert

SIX HILLS LA

1

A6006

Dalby Wolds

Lodge Farm

22

65 A B 66 C D 67 E F

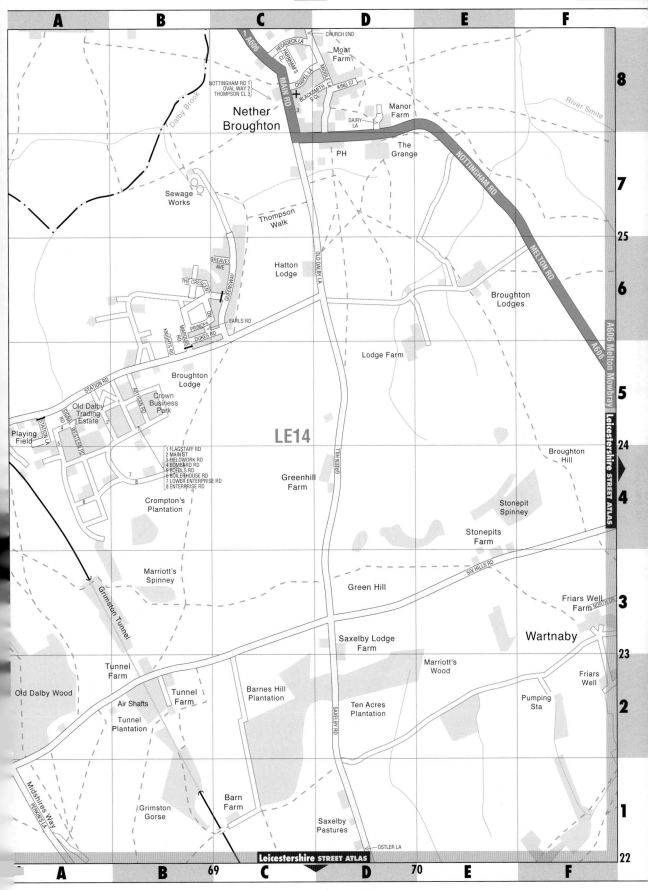

214

Loughborough Meadows

Moat Hill
Spinney

Moat Hill

Fishpond
Spinney

LE12

Park
Farm

Sewage
Works

Allot Gdns

Engineering
Works

Cotes

Cotes Mill
(PH)

Cotes
Bridge

Belton Rd

Nottingham Rd

Barrow Rd

Weirs

Bandalls
Farm

LOUGHBOROUGH

LE11

Little
Moorlane
Bridge

Moor
Farm

Moor Lane

Moors
Farm

Woodthorpe
Bridge

Moor Lane
Farm

Loughborough
Moors

Charnwood
Leisure
Centre

Southfields
Park

Fairfield
Prep Sch

Loughborough
High Sch

Miller's
Bridge

Advance
Business
Centre

Loughborough
Amherst Sch

Loughborough
Grammar
Sch

Quorn Fields
Farm

Sports
Ground

TA
Ctr

Charnwood
Water

LE12

Ashmount
Sch

Epinal Way

Sacred
Heart Roman
Catholic
Prim Sch

Ling Road

Shelthorpe
Com Sch

Shelthorpe

Cemy

Sports
Gd

Crem

A6 Leicester Leicestershire STREET ATLAS

Superstore

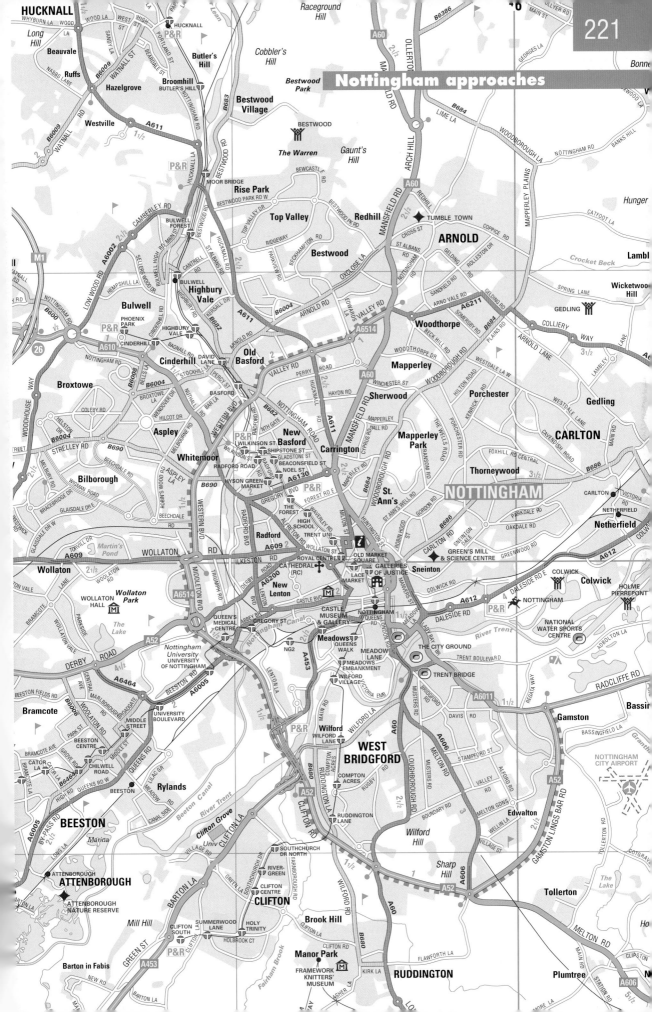

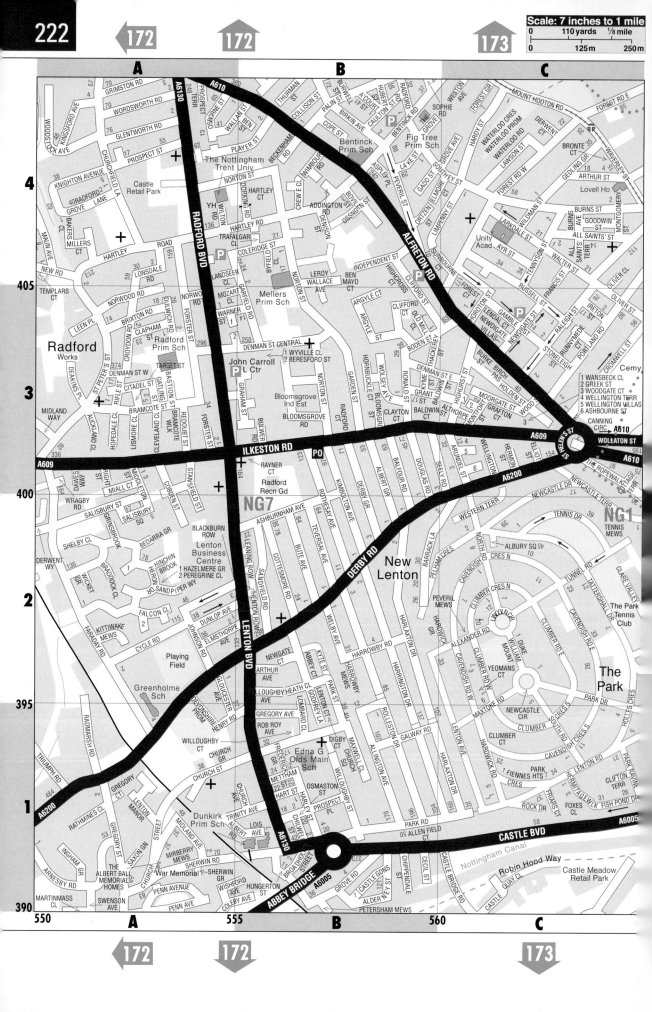

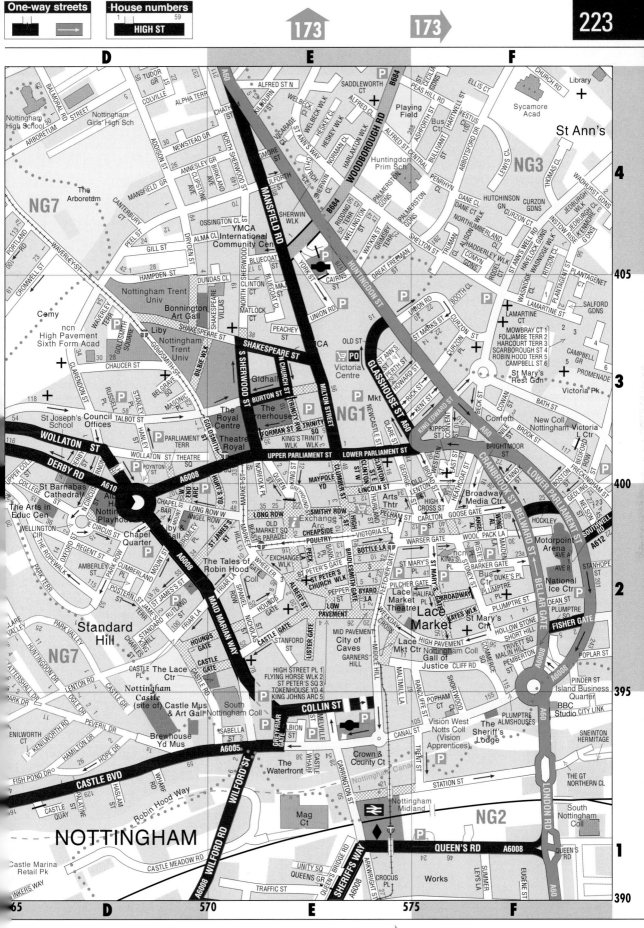

Index

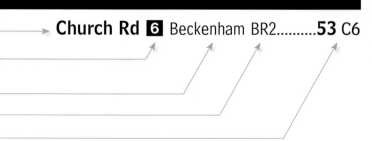

Place name May be abbreviated on the map

Location number Present when a number indicates the place's position in a crowded area of mapping

Locality, town or village Shown when more than one place has the same name

Postcode district District for the indexed place

Page and grid square Page number and grid reference for the standard mapping

Church Rd ⑥ Beckenham BR2.........53 C6

Cities, towns and villages are listed in CAPITAL LETTERS

Public and commercial buildings are highlighted in magenta   **Places of interest** are highlighted in blue with a star ⋆

Abbreviations used in the index

Acad	**Academy**	Comm	**Common**	Gd	**Ground**	L	**Leisure**	Prom	**Promenade**
App	**Approach**	Cott	**Cottage**	Gdn	**Garden**	La	**Lane**	Rd	**Road**
Arc	**Arcade**	Cres	**Crescent**	Gn	**Green**	Liby	**Library**	Recn	**Recreation**
Ave	**Avenue**	Cswy	**Causeway**	Gr	**Grove**	Mdw	**Meadow**	Ret	**Retail**
Bglw	**Bungalow**	Ct	**Court**	H	**Hall**	Meml	**Memorial**	Sh	**Shopping**
Bldg	**Building**	Ctr	**Centre**	Ho	**House**	Mkt	**Market**	Sq	**Square**
Bsns, Bus	**Business**	Ctry	**Country**	Hospl	**Hospital**	Mus	**Museum**	St	**Street**
Bvd	**Boulevard**	Cty	**County**	HQ	**Headquarters**	Orch	**Orchard**	Sta	**Station**
Cath	**Cathedral**	Dr	**Drive**	Hts	**Heights**	Pal	**Palace**	Terr	**Terrace**
Cir	**Circus**	Dro	**Drove**	Ind	**Industrial**	Par	**Parade**	TH	**Town Hall**
Cl	**Close**	Ed	**Education**	Inst	**Institute**	Pas	**Passage**	Univ	**University**
Cnr	**Corner**	Emb	**Embankment**	Int	**International**	Pk	**Park**	Wk, Wlk	**Walk**
Coll	**College**	Est	**Estate**	Intc	**Interchange**	Pl	**Place**	Wr	**Water**
Com	**Community**	Ex	**Exhibition**	Junc	**Junction**	Prec	**Precinct**	Yd	**Yard**

Index of towns, villages, streets, hospitals, industrial estates, railway stations, schools, shopping centres, universities and places of interest

1st–Ald

1st Ave NG7 . . . . 173 B8
2nd Ave NG7 . . . . 173 B8
3rd Ave NG7 . . . . 173 B8
4th Ave NG7 . . . . 173 B8

A

Aaron Cl NG11 . . . . . . 185 B7
Abba Cl NG16 . . . . 158 F7
Abbey Bridge NG7 . . 172 E2
Abbey Cir NG2 . . . . 186 A7
Abbey Cl
Aslockton NG13 . . . . . . 178 F5
Hucknall NG15 . . . . 145 E2
Abbey Ct
Beeston NG9 . . . . 183 F8
Mansfield NG18 . . . . . . 102 F7
Nottingham NG7 . . . . . . 222 B2
Abbeydale Dr NG18 . . 102 D3
Abbey Dr NG9 . . . . 183 F7
Abbeyfield Rd NG7 . . . 184 F8
Abbey Gates Prim Sch
NG15 . . . . 117 A1
Abbey Gr NG3 . . . . 173 F7
Abbey Hill Prim Sch
NG17 . . . . 115 C5
Abbey La NG13 . . . . . . 178 F5
Abbey Mws NG25 . . . . 121 E1
Abbey Prim Sch NG19 . 102 F8
Abbey Rd
Beeston NG9 . . . . 183 F7
Bingham NG13 . . . . 178 A4
Blidworth NG21 . . . . . . 118 B5
Eastwood NG16 . . . . . . 144 B2
Edwinstowe NG21 . . . . . 91 C8
Kirkby-in-Ashfield NG17 115 D5
Mansfield NG18 . . . . . . 102 E7
Mattersey DN10 . . . . 20 C7
Newstead NG15 . . . . . . 130 E6
West Bridgford NG2 . . 186 A7
Abbey Road Prim Sch
NG2 . . . . 186 A6
Abbey St
Ilkeston DE7 . . . . 157 F2
Nottingham NG7 . . . . . . 172 E2
Worksop S80 . . . . 35 F2
Abbot Cl NG12 . . . . . . 197 E4
Abbotsbury Cl NG5 . . . 146 E1
Abbots Cl NG5 . . . . 161 D6

Abbots Dr NG15 . . . . . . 145 E6
Abbotsford Dr NG3 . . . 223 F4
Abbotsford Mews DE7 . 157 D3
Abbots Rd NG15 . . . . . . 145 E6
Abbot St NG16 . . . . . . 158 C4
Abbots Wlk NG15 . . . . . 145 E6
Abbott Lea NG11 . . . . . 101 D8
Abbotts Cres NG22 . . . . 119 F7
Abbotts Croft NG19 . . . . 87 E1
Abbott St NG10 . . . . . . 193 D6
Abbotts Way NG8 . . . . . 172 C4
Abbott's Way NG24 . . . 125 B1
Abel Collin's Homes
NG8 . . . . 171 E1
Abercarn Cl NG6 . . . . . . 160 B7
Aberconway St NG21 . . 118 A5
Aberdeen St ③ NG3 . . 173 E5
Aberford Ave NG8 . . . . 172 D8
Abingdon Dr NG11 . . . 196 D8
Abingdon Gdns
Arnold NG5 . . . . 162 B5
Beeston NG9 . . . . 183 D4
Abingdon Rd NG2 . . . . 186 A7
Abingdon Sq NG8 . . . . 160 B1
Abingdon View S81 . . . . 35 C8
Abington Ave NG17 . . . 100 F5
Ablard Gdns ⑥ NG9 . . 183 C2
Acacia Ave
Annesley Woodhouse
NG17 . . . . 130 A8
Gainsborough DN21 . . . . 15 C1
Torksey Lock LN1 . . . . . . 44 C1
Acacia Cl
Hucknall NG15 . . . . 146 B5
Worksop S80 . . . . 35 C2
Acacia Cres NG4 . . . . . 162 F1
Acacia Ct NG19 . . . . 88 E1
Acacia Gdns NG16 . . . . 158 F8
Acacia Rd NG24 . . . . . . 140 D5
Acacia Wlk NG9 . . . . . . 183 F6
Acacia Wy NG12 . . . . . 186 A1
Academy Cl NG6 . . . . . 160 D2
Acaster Cl NG9 . . . . . . 184 B4
Access 26 Bsns Pk
NG16 . . . . 143 D2
Acer Cl NG16 . . . . 113 C3
Ackford Dr S80 . . . . 35 D3
Acland St DN21 . . . . 15 C1
Acle Gdns NG6 . . . . 146 B1
Acorn Ave NG16 . . . . . . 158 B8
Acorn Bank NG2 . . . . . . 185 B4
Acorn Bsns Pk ⑪
NG18 . . . . 102 B6
Acorn Cl NG24 . . . . 140 C5

Acorn Dr NG4 . . . . 163 A2
Acorn Pk NG7 . . . . 184 E8
Acorn Ridge NG20 . . . . . 72 D5
Acorns The NG22 . . . . . 106 A4
Acorn Vw NG17 . . . . . . 115 C6
Acorn Way NG18 . . . . . 103 B4
Acourt St NG7 . . . . 222 B4
Acreage La NG20 . . . . . . 72 F2
Acre Edge Rd NG22 . . . . 78 F2
Acre The NG17 . . . . 115 B3
Acton Ave
Long Eaton NG10 . . . . . 193 E6
Nottingham NG6 . . . . . . 160 D4
Acton Cl NG10 . . . . 193 E6
Acton Gr NG10 . . . . 193 E6
Acton Rd
Arnold NG5 . . . . 161 E7
Long Eaton NG10 . . . . . 193 E6
Acton Rd Ind Est NG10 193 E6
Acton St NG10 . . . . 193 E6
Adalia Wlk S81 . . . . 25 D1
Adam Dale LE11 . . . . . . 220 A3
Adams Ct DE7 . . . . 157 E3
Adams Dr NG5 . . . . 147 E2
Adams Hill
Keyworth NG12 . . . . . . 197 F3
Nottingham NG7 . . . . . . 172 C2
Adams Pk Way ❶
NG17 . . . . 114 F8
Adams Row NG25 . . . . . 121 D1
Adam St DE7 . . . . 170 A6
Adamsway
Mansfield NG18 . . . . . . 102 F2
Mansfield NG18 . . . . . . 103 A3
Adams Way DN21 . . . . . 44 C8
Ada Pl NG15 . . . . 146 B8
ADBOLTON 174 B2
Adbolton Ave NG4 . . . . 162 F1
Adbolton Gr NG2 . . . . . 174 B1
Adbolton La
West Bridgford NG12 . . 174 D1
West Bridgford NG4 . . . 174 B1
Adco Bsns Ctr NG7 . . . 172 E7
Adcocks Cl LE11 . . . . . 220 B5
Adderley Cl NG5 . . . . . . 161 A6
Addington Ct NG12 . . . 176 A4
Addington Rd NG7 . . . . 222 B4
Addison Dr NG15 . . . . . 145 F8
Addison Pl LN1 . . . . 55 D6
Addison Rd NG4 . . . . . . 174 B8
Addison St
Nottingham NG1 . . . . . . 223 D4
Tibshelf DE55 . . . . 99 A7
Addison Villas NG16 . . 143 E1

Adelaide Cl
Gainsborough DN21 . . . 24 F6
Stapleford NG9 . . . . 170 F1
Adelaide Gr NG5 . . . . . 160 E8
Adel Dr NG4 . . . . 162 E1
Adenburgh Dr NG9 . . . 183 D1
Adlington Cotts NG17 . 101 B1
Adlington Mws DN21 . . . 24 F6
Admiral Cl LE12 . . . . . . 214 E8
Admiral Ct DE7 . . . . . . 157 F4
Admirals Ct NG18 . . . . 102 D5
Adrian Cl NG9 . . . . 182 F1
Adrians Cl NG18 . . . . . 102 E5
Adrian's Wlk DN22 . . . . 39 F4
Advance Bsns Ctr LE12 220 A2
Adwalton Cl ⑦ NG24 . . 140 E8
Aegir Cl DN21 . . . . 24 F6
Aegir Specl Acad DN21 . 15 F2
Aeneas Ct ⑥ NG5 . . . . 173 B8
Aerial Way NG15 . . . . . 145 F5
Aerodrome The NG15 . 145 E3
Agnes Villas NG3 . . . . . 161 E2
Aidan Gdns NG5 . . . . . 147 A2
Ainsdale Cl NG24 . . . . 140 E2
Ainsdale Cres NG8 . . . 160 A3
Ainsdale Gn DN22 . . . . . 39 C3
Ainsley Rd NG8 . . . . . . 172 D6
Ainsworth Dr NG2 . . . . 173 B1
Aintree Cl NG16 . . . . . . 158 E7
Aira Cl NG2 . . . . 186 D6
Airedale S81 . . . . 36 A7
Airedale Ave DN11 . . . . . 8 A8
Airedale Cl NG10 . . . . . 193 A6
Airedale Ct NG9 . . . . . . 183 A4
Airedale Wlk NG8 . . . . 171 C3
Airfield Way NG6 . . . . . 145 E2
Aisby Wlk DN21 . . . . . . 24 F7
Aitchison Ave NG15 . . . 145 F7
Alan Clark Gr ㉒ NG5 . 160 F8
Alandale NG22 . . . . 105 E6
Alandale Ave NG20 . . . . 72 F5
Alandene Ave NG16 . . . 159 A7
Albans Ct NG21 . . . . 89 C2
Albany Cl
Arnold NG5 . . . . 161 E7
Hucknall NG15 . . . . 145 C5
Mansfield Woodhouse
NG19 . . . . 88 C1
Albany Ct NG9 . . . . 170 E1
Albany Dr NG19 . . . . 88 C1
Albany Inf Sch NG9 . . . 182 E8
Albany Jun Sch NG9 . . 182 E8
Albany Pl NG19 . . . . 88 C1
Albany Rd NG7 . . . . 173 A8

Albany St
Gainsborough DN21 . . . 15 C2
Ilkeston DE7 . . . . 170 A6
Albemarle Rd NG5 . . . . 161 D4
Alberta Ave NG16 . . . . 129 A7
Alberta Terr NG7 . . . . . 173 A8
Albert Ave
Balderton NG24 . . . . . . 140 C4
Carlton NG4 . . . . 174 B7
Nottingham NG8 . . . . . . 172 D8
Nuthall NG16 . . . . 159 C6
Stapleford NG9 . . . . 182 D7
Westwood NG16 . . . . . . 128 B4
Albert Ball Cl NG5 . . . . 160 F8
Albert Dr NG7 . . . . 222 B3
Albert Pl LE11 . . . . 220 B3
Albert Prom LE11 . . . . 220 C3
Albert Rd
Beeston NG9 . . . . 184 B7
Bunny NG11 . . . . 196 E1
Long Eaton NG10 . . . . . 193 D8
Nottingham NG7 . . . . . . 222 A1
Nottingham, Alexander Park
NG3 . . . . 173 D8
Retford DN22 . . . . 39 E6
Sandiacre NG10 . . . . . . 182 B6
West Bridgford NG2 . . 185 F8
Albert Sq NG17 . . . . . . 100 E2
Albert St
Bottesford NG13 . . . . . 181 A3
Carlton NG4 . . . . 162 F1
Eastwood NG16 . . . . . . 143 F3
Hucknall NG15 . . . . 146 B7
Loughborough LE11 . . . 220 B3
Mansfield NG18 . . . . . . 102 B6
Mansfield Woodhouse
NG19 . . . . 88 C1
Newark-on-Trent NG24 139 F8
Nottingham NG1 . . . . . . 223 E2
Radcliffe on Trent NG12 175 F3
South Normanton DE55 113 B6
Stanton Hill NG17 . . . . 100 C6
Stapleford NG9 . . . . 182 D7
Worksop S80 . . . . 35 F3
Albert Terr DN21 . . . . . 24 D8
Albine Rd NG20 . . . . . . 72 E6
Albion Cl S80 . . . . 35 F3
Albion House NG9 . . . . 183 F7
Albion Rd
Long Eaton NG10 . . . . . 193 F8
Sutton in Ashfield NG17 100 F1
Albion Rise NG5 . . . . . . 147 F2

Albion St
Beeston NG9 . . . . 183 F7
Ilkeston DE7 . . . . 157 F1
Mansfield NG19 . . . . 87 F1
Newark-on-Trent NG24 . 139 F8
Nottingham NG1 . . . . . . 223 E1
Albion Terr DN10 . . . . 7 B1
Albury Dr NG8 . . . . 160 B1
Albury Sq NG7 . . . . 222 C2
Alcester St NG7 . . . . . . 184 E8
Alcock Ave NG18 . . . . . 102 E7
Alconbury Way S81 . . . . 35 C8
Aldene Rd NG9 . . . . 183 D5
Aldene Way NG14 . . . . 149 C4
ALDERCAR 143 A4
Aldercar Flash Nature
Reserve ⋆ NG16 . . . . . 143 B6
Aldercar High Sch
NG16 . . . . 143 A4
Aldercar Inf Sch NG16 . 143 A4
Aldercar La NG16 . . . . 143 A6
Alder Cl
Mansfield NG19 . . . . 88 D1
New Balderton NG24 . . 140 C5
Shirebrook NG20 . . . . . . 72 D5
Worksop S80 . . . . 35 E1
Alder Ct NG19 . . . . 101 D5
Alder Gdns NG6 . . . . . . 160 A4
Alder Gr
Mansfield Woodhouse
NG19 . . . . 88 B6
New Ollerton NG22 . . . . 77 D5
Alderman Cl NG9 . . . . . 183 F8
Alderman Pounder Inf Sch
NG9 . . . . 183 A4
Alderman White Sch and
Language Coll NG9 . . 183 C7
Aldermens Cl NG2 . . . . 173 C2
Alderney St NG7 . . . . . 222 B1
Alderson Cl DN11 . . . . 8 B8
Alderson Dr DN11 . . . . . . 8 B8
Alderson Rd S80 . . . . . . 35 E1
Alders The ⑤ DN21 . . . 15 F1
Alderton Chase DN21 . . 15 F2
Alderton Rd NG5 . . . . . 161 C6
Alder Way
Keyworth NG12 . . . . . . 198 A2
Shirebrook NG20 . . . . . . 72 D5
Sutton in Ashfield NG17 100 D3
Aldgate Cl NG6 . . . . . . 160 A8
Aldred's La DE75 . . . . . 143 B2
Aldridge Cl NG9 . . . . . . 182 E2
Aldrin Cl NG6 . . . . 159 F5

Aldworth Cl NG5 ... 161 C6
Aldwych Cl
Nottingham NG5 ... 147 A1
Nuthall NG16 ... 159 D2
Alec Rose Gr DN21 ... 24 F7
Alexander Ave
Newark-on-Trent NG24 ... 125 B4
Selston NG16 ... 128 D7
Alexander Cl NG15 ... 131 B1
Alexander Gdns NG15 ... 146 E4
Alexander Mws NG24 ... 140 E5
Alexander Rd
Farnsfield NG22 ... 119 F6
Nottingham NG7 ... 222 C2
Alexander St NG16 ... 143 F2
Alexander Terr NG16 ... 113 C1
Alexandra Ave
Mansfield NG18 ... 102 B4
Mansfield Woodhouse
NG19 ... 88 B5
Sutton in Ashfield NG17 ... 100 F4
Alexandra Cres NG9 ... 184 A6
Alexandra Rd
Bircotes DN11 ... 9 B4
Long Eaton NG10 ... 193 D8
Alexandra St
Kirkby-in-Ashfield
NG17 ... 115 B6
Nottingham NG5 ... 161 B1
Nottingham NG5 ... 173 B8
Stapleford NG9 ... 182 D6
Alexandra Terr NG17 ... 100 C6
Alford Cl NG9 ... 184 B5
Alford Rd NG2 ... 186 B5
Alford Way LE12 ... 216 B4
Alfred Ave NG3 ... 162 A4
Alfred Cl NG3 ... 223 E4
Alfred Ct 4 NG18 ... 102 B7
Alfred St Central NG3 ... 223 E4
Alfred St N NG3 ... 223 E4
Alfred St S NG3 ... 173 E5
Alfred St
Gainsborough DN21 ... 15 C1
Kirkby-in-Ashfield NG17 ... 115 A4
Loughborough LE11 ... 220 B5
Pinxton NG16 ... 113 C4
Sutton in Ashfield NG17 ... 100 F4
Alfreton Rd
Huthwaite NG17 ... 113 F7
Newton DE55 ... 99 A3
Nottingham NG7 ... 222 B4
11 Nottingham NG8 ... 172 E7
Pinxton NG16 ... 113 C4
Selston, Selston Green DE55,
NG16 ... 128 C6
Selston, Underwood
NG16 ... 129 B3
South Normanton DE55 ... 113 A5
South Normanton DE55 ... 113 D6
Sutton in Ashfield NG17 ... 100 C1
Algar Cl LE12 ... 206 D1
Alison Ave NG15 ... 131 C1
Alison Cl NG12 ... 185 F2
Alison Wlk NG3 ... 223 F4
Allcroft St NG19 ... 88 C4
Allenby Rd NG25 ... 136 C8
Allen Cl NG23 ... 156 D7
Allendale Ave
Beeston NG9 ... 183 D2
Nottingham NG16 ... 159 F1
Nottingham NG8 ... 160 A1
Allendale Rd NG21 ... 118 B8
Allendale Way NG19 ... 88 E1
Allen Dr NG18 ... 102 F5
Allen Field Ct NG7 ... 222 B1
Allen Rd NG23 ... 142 D2
Allen's Gn Ave NG16 ... 128 F6
Allen St
Hucknall NG15 ... 146 A8
Worksop S80 ... 35 E3
Allen's Wlk NG5 ... 147 F1
Allesford La NG22 ... 120 B4
All Hallows CE Prim Sch 2
NG4 ... 162 F1
All Hallows Cl DN22 ... 39 E4
All Hallows Dr NG4 ... 162 F2
All Hallows St DN22 ... 39 E4
All Hallows View DN22 ... 39 E4
Alliance St NG24 ... 125 A2
Allington Ave NG7 ... 222 B1
Allington Dr NG19 ... 101 D7
Allison Ave DN22 ... 40 B3
Allison Gdns NG9 ... 183 D4
All Saints Anglican
Methodist Prim Sch
NG23 ... 153 D5
All Saints' CE Inf Sch
NG17 ... 99 F2
All Saints Ct NG17 ... 100 A2
All Saints Harworth CE
(Aided) Prim Sch
Harworth DN11 ... 8 F3
Harworth DN11 ... 9 A4
All Saints' RC Comp Sch
NG19 ... 101 F8
All Saints' St NG7 ... 222 C4
All Saints' Terr NG7 ... 222 C4
Allsopp Dr S81 ... 35 F6
Allsopp's La LE11 ... 220 D5
Allwood Cl NG18 ... 102 E8
Allwood Dr NG4 ... 174 E8
Allwood Gdns NG15 ... 146 B6
Alma Cl
Carlton NG4 ... 163 A2
Ilkeston DE7 ... 157 E5
Nottingham NG1 ... 223 E4
Alma Hill NG16 ... 158 E7
Alma Rd
Nottingham NG3 ... 173 F6
Retford DN22 ... 40 A7
Selston NG16 ... 129 A5
Alma St NG7 ... 173 A8
Almond Ave NG20 ... 72 E5
Almond Cl
Hucknall NG15 ... 146 B5
Kimberley NG16 ... 158 E7
Saxilby LN1 ... 57 B4
Almond Gr
Farndon NG24 ... 139 A5
6 Kirkby-in-Ashfield
NG17 ... 114 F6
Worksop S80 ... 35 E1
Almond Rise NG19 ... 88 E1
Almond Way NG8 ... 171 C7
Almond Wlk NG4 ... 163 A2
Alnwick Cl NG6 ... 160 D6
Alpha Terr NG1 ... 223 D4
Alpine Cres
Carlton NG4 ... 174 D8
Torksey Lock LN1 ... 44 C1
Alpine Ct S80 ... 35 C2
Alpine St NG6 ... 160 E2
Alport Pl NG18 ... 103 B7
Althea Ct 1 NG7 ... 161 A1
Althorpe St NG7 ... 222 C3
Alton Ave NG11 ... 185 B4
Alton Cl NG11 ... 185 C3
Alton Dr NG16 ... 158 B8
Alum Ct NG5 ... 160 F8
Alvenor St DE7 ... 157 F1
Alverstone Rd NG3 ... 161 C1
Alvey Rd NG24 ... 140 E4
Alvina Gdns NG8 ... 159 C1
Alway Cres DN22 ... 39 C8
Alwood Gr NG11 ... 184 D2
Alwyn Rd NG8 ... 159 F2
Amanda Ave S81 ... 25 E6
Amanda Rd DN11 ... 8 F4
Amarella La 9 NG17 ... 115 A3
Amber Cl
Nottingham NG5 ... 161 B7
Rainworth NG21 ... 104 C1
Amber Dr NG16 ... 143 B2
Ambergate Rd NG8 ... 172 A7
Amber Gr
Kirkby-in-Ashfield
NG17 ... 114 D8
Newlands NG19 ... 89 D2
Amber Hill NG5 ... 161 B7
Amberley NG19 ... 89 D2
Amberley St NG1 ... 223 D2
Amber Rd NG9 ... 184 A3
Amber St NG18 ... 102 C5
Ambleside
Hucknall NG15 ... 145 F5
New Ollerton NG22 ... 77 C5
West Bridgford NG2 ... 186 C7
Ambleside Dr NG16 ... 143 D3
Ambleside Grange S81 ... 35 F8
Ambleside Prim Sch
NG8 ... 160 B1
Ambleside Rd NG8 ... 160 A1
Ambleside Way NG4 ... 175 B8
Amcott Ave
Misterton DN10 ... 14 A8
Walkeringham DN10 ... 13 F8
Amcott Way DN22 ... 39 E7
Amelia Ct DN22 ... 29 C2
Amen Cnr NG23 ... 109 B5
Amen Cnr Karting★
NG22 ... 91 E7
America Gdns NG22 ... 65 F3
Amersham Rise NG8 ... 160 B1
Amesbury Circ NG8 ... 160 A3
Amethy St Gdns NG18 ... 102 D4
Amherst Rise 4 S81 ... 35 D8
Amos La NG23 ... 98 D4
Ampthill Rise NG5 ... 161 B4
Amrthyst Dr NG17 ... 114 D8
Anastasia Cl DN21 ... 15 C3
Ancaster Gdns NG8 ... 172 A4
Anchor Cl NG8 ... 160 B2
Anchor Rd NG16 ... 143 D2
Anders Dr NG6 ... 159 F5
Anderson Cl NG24 ... 140 B3
Anderson Cres NG9 ... 183 E8
Anderson Ct 6 NG5 ... 161 A8
Anderson Rd DN21 ... 24 F2
Anderson Way NG21 ... 75 F1
Anderton St NG4 ... 174 A2
Andover Cl 1 NG8 ... 172 B6
Andover Rd
Mansfield NG19 ... 101 D7
Nottingham NG5 ... 160 E5
Andrew Ave
Ilkeston DE7 ... 170 B7
Nottingham NG3 ... 162 A2
Andrew Dr NG21 ... 118 A4
Andrews Dr NG16 ... 143 A3
Anemone Gr NG11 ... 196 E5
Anfield Cl NG9 ... 183 A2
Anford Cl NG6 ... 160 B5
Angela Ave NG17 ... 115 B1
Angela Cl NG5 ... 147 E2
Angel Alley NG1 ... 223 F2
Angelica Ct NG13 ... 177 C3
Angell Gn NG11 ... 195 C8
Angel Row NG1 ... 223 E2
Angel Row Gall★ NG1 ... 223 D2
Angel Yd LE11 ... 220 B4
Anglia Way NG18 ... 103 B3
Angrave Cl NG3 ... 173 E7
Angus Cl
Arnold NG5 ... 148 B1
Arnold NG5 ... 162 B8
Kimberley NG16 ... 159 A5
Anmer Cl 9 NG2 ... 173 B1
Anna Cl NG12 ... 185 F3
Annan Ct NG8 ... 172 B8
Anne's Cl NG3 ... 162 A2
ANNESLEY ... 130 C8
Annesley Cutting
NG15 ... 130 C7
Annesley Gr
Nottingham NG1 ... 223 D4
Nottingham NG14 ... 173 B6
Annesley La NG16 ... 129 B6
Annesley Prim Sch
NG17 ... 130 B8
Annesley Rd
Hucknall NG15 ... 145 F8
West Bridgford NG2 ... 185 F7
Annesley Way NG19 ... 101 D6
ANNESLEY
WOODHOUSE ... 129 E8
Annesley Woodhouse
Quarry Nature Reserve★
NG17 ... 129 D7
Annesley Workshops
NG15 ... 130 A5
Annies Cl NG15 ... 145 F5
Annies Wharf LE11 ... 220 B5
Anslow Ave
Beeston NG9 ... 184 A8
Dalestorth NG17 ... 101 A5
Sutton in Ashfield NG17 ... 100 F5
Anson Dr NG24 ... 141 A3
Anson Rd NG13 ... 177 B7
Anson Wlk DE7 ... 157 F3
Anstee Rd NG10 ... 193 C4
Anstey Rise NG3 ... 173 F5
Anston Ave S81 ... 35 E5
Anthony Bek Com Prim Sch
NG19 ... 86 F6
Antill St NG9 ... 182 D6
Antonia Dr NG15 ... 146 D8
Anvil Ct NG18 ... 102 B4
Anvil Grove 2 NG19 ... 88 C3
Apley Cl DN21 ... 24 F7
Apollo Dr NG6 ... 159 F5
Appin Rd NG19 ... 101 D5
Apple Ave NG24 ... 140 F2
Appleby Cl NG24 ... 140 D8
Appleby Ct S81 ... 35 F8
Appleby Rd NG19 ... 86 F6
Appledore Ave NG8 ... 171 E2
Appledorne Way NG5 ... 147 E1
Appleton Dr LE12 ... 216 B3
Appleton Gate
Newark-on-Trent NG24 ... 125 A1
9 Newark-on-Trent
NG24 ... 139 F8
Appleton Gdns NG3 ... 162 B5
Appleton Rd
Beeston NG9 ... 184 B4
Blidworth NG21 ... 118 B5
Appleton St NG20 ... 74 B4
Appletree Cl NG25 ... 121 E1
Apple Tree Cl
9 Newark-on-Trent
NG24 ... 125 A2
West Bridgford NG12 ... 186 A4
Appletree La NG4 ... 162 F1
Apple Tree La NG4 ... 162 F2
Apple Wlk NG4 ... 174 A8
Applewood Cl S81 ... 35 D8
Applewood Gr NG5 ... 161 D3
Approach The NG11 ... 196 C8
Arboretum St NG1 ... 223 D4
Arbrook Dr NG8 ... 172 D6
Arbutus Cl NG11 ... 184 C1
Arcade The NG24 ... 139 F8
Arcadia Ave NG20 ... 72 E5
Archbishop Cranmer CE
Prim Sch
NG13 ... 179 A5
Aslockton NG13 ... 178 F5
Archdale Rd NG5 ... 161 C6
Archer Cres NG8 ... 171 F5
Archer Rd NG9 ... 182 E5
Archers Dr NG22 ... 106 A5
Archers Field NG25 ... 121 E1
Archer St DE7 ... 157 E3
Arches Cl NG16 ... 158 C5
Arches Rd NG19 ... 102 D5
Arches The LE12 ... 205 E2
Arch Hill
Arnold NG5 ... 147 E3
Arnold NG5 ... 147 F3
Archway Gr NG21 ... 90 D6
Archway Rd NG21 ... 90 D7
Arden Cl
Beeston NG9 ... 184 A8
Hucknall NG15 ... 146 C5
Arden Gr NG13 ... 177 C5
Ardleigh Cl NG5 ... 146 D1
Ardmore Cl NG2 ... 173 F3
Ardsley Cl DE75 ... 143 A2
Argosy Cl DN10 ... 9 F8
Argyle Cl NG20 ... 73 F4
Argyle Ct NG7 ... 222 B3
Argyle St
Langley Mill NG16 ... 143 C4
Mansfield NG18 ... 102 E6
Nottingham NG7 ... 222 B3
Ariel Cl NG6 ... 160 F5
Arkers Cl NG6 ... 160 D3
Arklow Cl NG8 ... 160 B2
Arkwright St
Gainsborough DN21 ... 15 C1
Nottingham NG2 ... 173 C3
Arkwright Wlk
Nottingham NG14 ... 173 D2
Nottingham NG2 ... 173 C2
Arleston Dr NG8 ... 171 D4
Arley Gdns LE12 ... 205 D1
Arlington Ave NG19 ... 88 E4
Arlington Cl NG15 ... 146 A4
Arlington Dr NG3 ... 161 C2
Arlington Way DN22 ... 39 F7
Armadale Cl NG5 ... 162 C8
Armes Cl DE7 ... 157 F3
Armfield Rd NG5 ... 162 C6
Armitage Cl 3 LE11 ... 220 A4
Armitage Dr NG10 ... 194 A7
Armstrong Gdns NG22 ... 105 F6
Armstrong Rd
Keyworth NG12 ... 197 F4
Mansfield NG19 ... 101 D7
Nottingham NG6 ... 159 F5
Retford DN22 ... 39 F7
Arnbrook Prim Sch
NG5 ... 161 D7
Arncliff Cl NG8 ... 171 C4
Arndale Rd NG5 ... 161 C5
Arne Ct 5 NG2 ... 173 C1
Arnesby Rd NG7 ... 222 A1
Arno Ave 2 NG7 ... 173 B8
ARNOLD ... 162 A7
Arnold Ave
Long Eaton NG10 ... 193 A4
Retford DN22 ... 40 B3
Southwell NG25 ... 121 E1
Arnold Cres NG10 ... 193 A4
Arnold Derrymount Sch
NG5 ... 147 F1
Arnold Hill Acad NG5 ... 162 A6
Arnold La NG3 ... 162 D4
Arnold L Ctr NG5 ... 161 E8
Arnold Mill Prim Sch
NG5 ... 161 E8
Arnold Rd NG5 ... 161 A5
Arnold Seely CE Prim Sch
NG5 ... 132 E2
Arnold View Prim Sch
NG5 ... 161 F7
Arnos Gr NG8 ... 159 D3
Arnot Hill Pk NG5 ... 161 E6
Arnot Hill Rd NG5 ... 161 E6
Arno Vale Gdns NG5 ... 161 E5
Arno Vale Jun Sch
NG5 ... 161 F5
Arno Vale Rd NG5 ... 161 F5
Arnside NG9 ... 182 E5
Arnside Cl NG5 ... 161 B5
Arnside Rd NG5 ... 161 B5
Arran Cl NG9 ... 170 E2
Arran Sq NG19 ... 101 D5
Arry Cl NG12 ... 176 B5
Arthur Ave
Nottingham NG7 ... 222 B2
Stapleford NG9 ... 182 F8
Arthur Cres NG4 ... 174 C7
Arthur Gn Ave NG17 ... 114 E1
Arthur Lee Centre The
NG9 ... 182 D7
Arthur Mee Rd NG9 ... 182 E5
Arthur Rd DN21 ... 15 D2
Arthur Short Cl S80 ... 45 A6
Arthur St
Carlton NG4 ... 175 A6
Mansfield NG18 ... 102 C6
Nottingham NG7 ... 222 C4
Pinxton NG16 ... 113 D3
Artic Way NG16 ... 158 D7
Artisan Rd LE14 ... 219 B5
Arum Croft DN22 ... 39 D4
Arun Dale NG19 ... 88 D2
Arundel Cl
Gainsborough DN21 ... 15 E2
Sandiacre NG10 ... 182 B4
Arundel Dr
Beeston NG9 ... 171 B1
Carlton in Lindrick S81 ... 25 F6
Carlton in Lindrick S81 ... 26 A6
Mansfield NG19 ... 101 F8
Ranskill DN22 ... 19 B5
Arundel St NG7 ... 222 C3
Arundel Way DN22 ... 39 C8
Arundel Wlk DN11 ... 9 B5
Ascot Ave NG16 ... 158 E7
Ascot Cl NG17 ... 115 C3
Ascot Dr
Arnold NG5 ... 161 D8
Hucknall NG15 ... 145 D5
Mansfield NG18 ... 102 F7
Ascot Pk Est NG10 ... 182 B4
Ascot Rd NG8 ... 172 D7
Ascott Gdns NG2 ... 185 A5
Ashbourne Cl NG9 ... 171 A1
Ashbourne Ct NG6 ... 159 F6
Ashbourne Rd NG16 ... 129 A2
Ashbourne St
Nottingham NG7 ... 222 C3
Shirebrook NG20 ... 72 F4
Ashburnham Ave
Nottingham NG7 ... 222 B2
Nottingham NG8 ... 172 F4
Ashby Ave NG19 ... 88 D5
Ashby Rd
Kegworth DE74 ... 203 A2
Kegworth DE74 ... 203 B2
Long Whatton LE12 ... 212 C1
Loughborough LE11 ... 220 A4
Rempstone LE12 ... 215 C6
Ashby Sq LE11 ... 220 A4
Ashchurch Dr NG8 ... 171 D2
Ash Cl
Bingham NG13 ... 178 A4
Burton Joyce NG14 ... 163 E4
Dunham-on-Trent NG22 ... 54 C2
Hucknall NG15 ... 145 C5
Pinxton NG16 ... 113 D2
Worksop S80 ... 35 E1
Ashcourt Gdns NG17 ... 101 B4
Ash Cres
Kirkby-in-Ashfield
NG17 ... 114 D6
Mansfield Woodhouse
NG19 ... 88 E2
Nuthall NG16 ... 159 B6
Ashcroft DN22 ... 39 D4
Ashcroft Rd DN21 ... 24 D6
Ash Ct NG4 ... 174 D7
Ashdale Ave
Hucknall NG15 ... 145 F5
Hucknall NG15 ... 146 A5
Ashdale Rd
Arnold NG5 ... 162 A8
Ilkeston DE7 ... 170 A6
Nottingham NG3 ... 174 B6
Ashdown Cl NG11 ... 185 B6
Ashdown Gr NG13 ... 177 D4
Ashdown Way DN10 ... 6 E1
Ashe Cl NG5 ... 162 B7
Asher La
Ruddington NG11 ... 195 F5
Ruddington NG11 ... 196 B5
Ruddington NG11 ... 196 C6
Ashes Pk Ave
Worksop S81 ... 25 D1
Worksop S81 ... 35 D8
Ashfield Ave
Beeston NG9 ... 184 B5
Mansfield NG18 ... 102 B7
Ashfield Coll NG17 ... 100 D2
Ashfield Com Hospl
NG17 ... 115 A5
Ashfield Ct DN10 ... 11 C4
Ashfield Dr NG17 ... 114 F5
Ashfield Grange LN1 ... 56 F4
Ashfield Prec NG17 ... 115 B5
Ashfield Rd
Huthwaite NG17 ... 100 B3
Nottingham NG2 ... 173 F4
Ashfield Sch NG17 ... 114 D7
Ashfield St NG17 ... 101 A5
Ashford Ct DN22 ... 39 D4
Ashford Dr NG15 ... 117 B3
Ashford Pl DE7 ... 157 E5
Ashford Rise
Nottingham NG8 ... 171 D2
Sutton in Ashfield NG17 ... 100 E4
Ashforth Ave DE75 ... 143 A1
Ashforth St NG3 ... 223 F4
Ashgate NG17 ... 100 D3
Ashgate Rd
Hucknall NG15 ... 146 B6
HUCKNALL NG15 ... 146 B7
Ash Gr
Brinsley NG16 ... 143 D8
Farnsfield NG22 ... 120 A6
Gainsborough DN21 ... 15 D2
Hathern LE12 ... 213 A1
Keyworth NG12 ... 198 A2
Long Eaton NG10 ... 193 C6
Sandiacre NG10 ... 182 A7
Selston NG16 ... 128 F7
Shirebrook NG20 ... 72 D5
Stapleford NG9 ... 182 D5
Sutton in Ashfield NG17 ... 100 D7
Woodborough NG14 ... 149 C4
Ash Holt Dr S81 ... 35 F8
Ash Holt Ind Pk DN9 ... 1 A5
Ashington Dr
Arnold NG5 ... 147 F2
Arnold NG5 ... 148 A2
Ash La
Costock LE12 ... 206 C4
Papplewick NG15 ... 132 D3
Ranskill DN22 ... 19 A3
Ashland Rd NG17 ... 100 C3
Ashland Rd W NG17 ... 100 B3
Ashlands Cl NG17 ... 100 B3
Ashlea DN10 ... 6 E2
Ash Lea Cl NG12 ... 187 F2
Ash Lea Sch NG12 ... 187 F2
Ashleigh Dr NG17 ... 100 D2
Ashleigh Way NG19 ... 89 A2
Ashley Cl NG9 ... 183 D6
Ashley Cres NG12 ... 197 F3
Ashley Ct S81 ... 35 F5
Ashley Gr NG15 ... 145 E7
Ashley La DN22 ... 41 F2
Ashley Rd
Keyworth NG12 ... 197 E3
Worksop S81 ... 35 E6
Ashley St 7 NG3 ... 173 E5
Ashley Terr S80 ... 35 F3
Ashling St NG2 ... 173 D2
Ashmore Ave NG17 ... 100 C2
Ashmore Cl
2 Carlton NG4 ... 162 E3
Carlton NG5 ... 162 E3
Ashmount Cl LE11 ... 220 A1
Ash Mount Rd NG16 ... 143 B3
Ashmount Sch LE11 ... 220 A1
Ashness Cl NG2 ... 186 C6
Ashover Cl
Nottingham NG3 ... 173 E8
Ravenshead NG15 ... 117 B3
Ash Rd NG24 ... 139 F4
Ashridge Way NG2 ... 186 C4
Ash St DE7 ... 157 E4
Ashton Ave NG5 ... 147 F2
Ashton Ct
Nottingham NG8 ... 171 D7
Sutton in Ashfield NG17 ... 101 A5
Ash Tree Ave
Bawtry DN10 ... 9 F7
Mansfield Woodhouse
NG19 ... 88 C5
Ash Tree Cl
2 Shireoaks S81 ... 35 A7
Southwell NG25 ... 136 D8
Ash Tree Ct NG8 ... 159 C2
Ash Tree Sq NG9 ... 183 B8
Ashurst Gr NG15 ... 145 E4
Ashvale Ind Est NG22 ... 66 A2
Ashvale Rd NG22 ... 66 A2
Ash Vale Rd NG22 ... 64 A2
Ashview Cl NG10 ... 193 A8
Ash Villas 1 NG7 ... 161 B1
Ashville Cl NG2 ... 173 A1
Ashwater Dr NG3 ... 162 D5
Ashwell Ave NG19 ... 88 E5
Ashwell Ct NG5 ... 161 E3
Ashwell Gdns NG7 ... 172 E8
Ashwell St NG4 ... 174 F6
Ashwick Cl NG11 ... 185 A5
Ash Wlk LE12 ... 214 D8
Ashwood Ave NG17 ... 115 C6
Ashwood Cl
Mansfield Woodhouse
NG19 ... 88 E5
3 Sutton in Ashfield
NG17 ... 100 F1
Ashwood Rd S80 ... 35 B2
Ashworth Ave NG11 ... 196 C8
Ashworth Bsns Ctr
NG1 ... 223 F4
Ashworth Cl
Newark-on-Trent NG24 ... 140 D8
Nottingham NG3 ... 174 C5
Ashworth Cres
North Leverton with
Habblesthorpe DN22 ... 32 C1
Nottingham NG3 ... 162 B2
Ashworth Dr NG19 ... 88 E4
Askeby Dr NG8 ... 159 D1
Askew La NG20 ... 74 A3
Askew Rd NG15 ... 131 D1
ASKHAM ... 51 F2
Askham La DN22 ... 52 B5
Askham Rd NG22 ... 51 F1
ASLOCKTON ... 179 A5
Aslockton Dr NG8 ... 160 D2
Aslockton Rd NG13 ... 178 F7
Aslockton Sta NG13 ... 179 A4
Aspect Bsns Pk NG6 ... 159 F8
Aspen Cl
Bingham NG13 ... 178 A4
Laughterton LN1 ... 55 B4
Tuxford NG22 ... 66 A2
Walesby NG22 ... 64 A2
Aspen Ct
Gainsborough DN21 ... 15 F2
Mansfield NG19 ... 88 E1
Tuxford NG22 ... 66 A2
Aspen Rd NG6 ... 159 F7
Asper St NG4 ... 175 A7
Aspinall Ct 2 NG8 ... 172 C5
Aspley La NG8 ... 172 C8
Aspley Pk Dr NG8 ... 172 B8
Aspley Pl NG7 ... 222 B4
Aspley Rd NG17 ... 100 D3
Asquith Mews NG18 ... 102 E6
Asquith Prim Sch
NG18 ... 102 E6
Asquith St
Gainsborough DN21 ... 15 B2
Mansfield NG18 ... 102 E6
Assarts Rd NG16 ... 159 E3
Astbury Dr NG21 ... 103 E2
Astcote Cl DE75 ... 143 A1
Aster Gr 2 NG12 ... 185 F2
Aster Rd
Nottingham NG3 ... 173 E7
Shirebrook NG20 ... 72 D2
Astill Cl NG12 ... 197 D2
Astle Ct NG5 ... 162 C6
Astley Cl NG17 ... 130 A8
Astley Dr NG3 ... 161 F1
Aston Ave NG9 ... 172 A1
Aston Ct DE7 ... 157 F1
Aston Dr NG6 ... 146 C2
Aston Gn NG9 ... 182 E3
Astral Gr NG15 ... 145 E4
Astrid Gdns NG5 ... 160 F6
ASTWITH ... 85 A5
Astwith La S44, S45 ... 85 B5
Astwood Cl NG8 ... 171 E8
Athelstan Rd S80 ... 35 F1
Atherfield Gdns NG16 ... 143 F3
Atherton Rd DE7 ... 157 C3
Atherton Rise NG8 ... 160 B3
Athorpe Gr NG6 ... 160 E3
Atkin La NG18 ... 102 B3
Atkinson Gdns NG16 ... 159 C5
ATTENBOROUGH ... 183 E2
Attenborough La NG9 ... 183 C3
Attenborough Nature
Reserve★ NG9 ... 183 E1
Attenborough Sta NG9 183 D2
Attercliffe Terr 8
NG2 ... 173 C1
Attewell Rd NG16 ... 158 B5
Attlee Ave NG19 ... 89 A1
Aubrey Ave 15 NG2 ... 173 E4
Aubrey Rd NG5 ... 161 B2
Auckland Cl NG7 ... 222 A3
Auckland Rd
Hucknall NG15 ... 145 D5
Retford DN22 ... 39 C8
Audley Cl DE7 ... 157 D3
Audley Dr NG9 ... 171 F1
Audon Ave NG9 ... 183 E5
Audrey Cres NG19 ... 88 C5
Augustine Gdns NG5 ... 147 A1
AULT HUCKNALL ... 85 F7
Ault Hucknall La
Ault Hucknall S44 ... 85 F7
Ault Hucknall S44 ... 86 A7
Aumberry Gap LE11 ... 220 B4
Aurillac Way DN22 ... 29 D2
Austen Ave
Long Eaton NG10 ... 193 C5
Nottingham NG7 ... 173 A7
AUSTERFIELD ... 3 C2
Austin Cl NG18 ... 102 E8
Austin Dr DN21 ... 24 E6
Austin Gr 12 NG17 ... 115 A3

Austins Dr NG10 ... 182 B4
Austin St
Nottingham NG6 ... 160 C7
Shirebrook NG20 ... 73 A4
Austrey Ave NG9 ... 184 A8
Autumn Cft Rd NG24 ... 125 D1
Autumn Cl NG12 ... 185 D5
Autumn Rd NG12 ... 188 A5
Autumn Way NG9 ... 184 B7
Avalon Cl NG6 ... 160 E6
Avalon Gdns DN11 ... 9 A5
Avebury Cl NG11 ... 195 D8
Aveling Way
Shireoaks S81 ... 34 F8
Shireoaks S81 ... 35 A8
Avenue A NG1 ... 223 F2
Avenue B NG1 ... 223 F2
Avenue C NG1 ... 223 F2
Avenue Cl NG5 ... 160 F8
Avenue D NG1 ... 173 E4
Avenue E 4 NG1 ... 173 E5
Avenue Rd DN22 ... 39 F5
Avenue The
Calverton NG14 ... 148 F7
Gainsborough DN21 ... 15 E2
Gunthorpe NG14 ... 164 F6
Mansfield NG18 ... 102 E3
Newark-on-Trent NG24 ... 140 B7
Sutton in Ashfield NG17 ... 100 E1
AVERHAM ... 123 F2
Averham Cl NG19 ... 101 D6
Averton Sq NG8 ... 172 D3
Ave The
Milton NG22 ... 65 A7
Ruddington NG11 ... 196 D5
Aviary Way S81 ... 36 B8
Aviemore Cl NG5 ... 162 B8
Avocet Cl
Bingham NG13 ... 178 A3
Heanor DE75 ... 143 B1
Hucknall NG15 ... 131 B1
Avocet Gr S81 ... 35 C6
Avocet Pl NG20 ... 73 E4
Avon Ave NG15 ... 145 E4
Avonbridge Cl NG5 ... 148 C1
Avon Cl NG17 ... 129 F8
Avondale
Cotgrave NG12 ... 188 A3
Mansfield NG18 ... 102 E7
Avondale Cl NG10 ... 193 A6
Avondale La NG25 ... 121 D2
Avondale Rd NG4 ... 174 D6
Avon Gdns NG2 ... 185 F7
Avonlea Cl DE7 ... 170 B6
Avon Pl NG9 ... 184 A7
Avon Rd
Carlton NG4 ... 162 F2
Nottingham NG3 ... 174 B5
Avon Rise DN22 ... 40 A7
Avon Vale Rd LE11 ... 220 C1
Avon Way
Mansfield NG18 ... 103 A5
Worksop S81 ... 35 E7
Avro Rd NG24 ... 140 F3
AWSWORTH ... 158 C4
Awsworth La NG16 ... 158 D6
Awsworth Prim Sch
NG16 ... 158 C4
Awsworth Rd DE7 ... 157 F2
Axford Cl NG4 ... 162 F2
Axmouth Dr NG5 ... 162 D6
Aylesbury Way NG19 ... 88 E2
Aylesham Ave NG5 ... 161 F6
Aylestone Dr NG8 ... 172 B8
Ayrshire Way NG23 ... 123 E1
Ayr St NG7 ... 222 C4
Ayscough Ave NG16 ... 159 C6
Ayton Cl NG2 ... 173 B2
Ayton Gdns NG9 ... 183 C2
Azalea Ct NG16 ... 158 C8
Azimghur Rd NG13 ... 179 A4
Azure Pl S81 ... 25 D1

B

Babbacombe Cl NG5 ... 161 B6
Babbacombe Way
NG15 ... 145 D6
Babbage Way S80 ... 35 E4
Babbington Cl DE7 ... 170 B5
Babbington Cres NG4 ... 162 E2
Babbington Dr NG6 ... 160 C4
Babbington La NG16 ... 158 F4
Babbington St DE55 ... 99 A6
Babington Ct NG9 ... 183 C5
Babthorpe NG23 ... 122 F1
BABWORTH ... 39 A6
Babworth Cres DN22 ... 39 C6
Babworth Ct NG18 ... 102 D7
Babworth Mws DN22 ... 39 D6
Babworth Rd DN22 ... 39 B6
Backers Cl NG12 ... 187 E3
Back La
Claypole NG23 ... 156 D6
Cotes LE12 ... 220 F6
Cropwell Butler NG12 ... 189 A6
Eakring NG22 ... 106 E8
East Markham NG22 ... 66 A7
Flintham NG23 ... 167 A8
Halam NG22 ... 120 F2
Huthwaite NG17 ... 99 F3
Ilkeston DE7 ... 157 E2
Keyworth NG12 ... 198 A6
Long Clawson LE14 ... 211 C3
Misson DN10 ... 4 B2
Morton NG25 ... 137 C3
North Clifton NG23 ... 68 E5
Back La *continued*
Nuthall NG16 ... 159 D6
Ollerton NG22 ... 77 B3
Ranskill DN22 ... 19 A4
Sutton in Ashfield NG17 ... 100 F6
Thorpe Salvin S80 ... 34 A6
Willoughby-on-t-W LE12 ... 217 D7
Back St
Barnby in the Willows
NG24 ... 142 A5
East Stockwith DN21 ... 7 D1
South Clifton NG23 ... 68 E1
Back Terr DN22 ... 39 F8
Bacon Cl NG16 ... 158 A8
Bacon La NG22 ... 65 C5
Bacon St DN21 ... 24 D6
Bacopa Dr DN22 ... 40 A4
Bacton Ave NG6 ... 160 B8
Bacton Gdns 1 NG6 ... 160 B8
Baden Powell Rd NG2 ... 174 A4
Bader NG11 ... 185 B7
Bader Rise DN10 ... 20 A8
Bader View DN10 ... 20 A8
Badger Cl
East Leake LE12 ... 214 E7
Hucknall NG15 ... 145 C6
Nottingham NG4 ... 174 E8
West Bridgford NG12 ... 185 C6
Badgers Chase DN22 ... 29 F1
Badgers Croft NG22 ... 106 A5
Badger Vale NG9 ... 171 E5
Badger Way NG19 ... 103 B7
Baggaley Cres NG19 ... 88 B1
Bagnall Ave NG5 ... 161 C7
Bagnall Rd NG6 ... 160 C4
Bagshaw St NG19 ... 87 B4
Bagthorpe Cl NG5 ... 161 A3
Bagthorpe Prim Sch
NG16 ... 129 A4
Baildon Cl NG8 ... 172 C3
Bailey Brook Cres
NG16 ... 143 A4
Bailey Brook Dr NG16 ... 143 A3
Bailey Brook Rd DE7 ... 157 F5
Bailey Brook Wlk
NG16 ... 143 A3
Bailey Cl NG5 ... 161 D7
Bailey Cres NG19 ... 101 E7
Bailey Ct NG12 ... 175 E2
Bailey Dr NG3 ... 162 B5
Bailey Gr Rd NG16 ... 143 D2
Bailey La NG12 ... 175 E2
Bailey Rd NG24 ... 139 F5
Baileys Croft LE12 ... 217 D7
Baileys Row NG12 ... 200 A2
Bailey St
Carlton NG4 ... 175 A7
Nottingham NG6 ... 160 E2
Stapleford NG9 ... 182 C6
Bainbridge Ct 7 NG24 ... 139 F8
Bainbridge Rd
Loughborough LE11 ... 220 C1
Market Warsop NG20 ... 74 B4
Bainbridge Terr NG17 ... 100 D6
Bainbridge The NG14 ... 149 A7
Bainbrigge Rd DE74 ... 203 A3
Baines Ave NG24 ... 140 D4
Baines Rd DN21 ... 24 F8
Bainton Gr NG7 ... 184 F1
Baird-Parker Dr NG4 ... 174 D7
Baker Ave
Arnold NG5 ... 148 A2
Gringley on the Hill DN10 ... 12 E2
Baker Brook Cl NG15 ... 146 D5
Baker Brook Ind Pk
NG15 ... 146 C6
Baker Cl
Long Eaton NG10 ... 182 C1
Worksop S81 ... 35 D5
Bakerdale Rd NG3 ... 174 B6
Baker La NG20 ... 60 A2
Baker Rd
Eastwood NG16 ... 144 C1
Mansfield Woodhouse
NG19 ... 88 C6
Bakers Cl NG7 ... 222 A4
BAKERS FIELDS ... 174 C6
Baker's Hollow NG12 ... 187 E3
Baker's La
Colston Bassett NG12 ... 200 E7
Redmile NG13 ... 192 F3
Baker St
Hucknall NG15 ... 146 A7
13 Ilkeston DE7 ... 157 F1
Nottingham NG1 ... 173 B7
Bakewell Ave NG4 ... 162 E1
Bakewell Cl NG24 ... 140 C4
Bakewell Dr NG5 ... 160 E7
Bakewell La NG15 ... 146 B4
Bakewell Rd NG10 ... 193 E5
Bala Dr NG5 ... 161 A7
BALDERTON ... 140 E3
Balderton Ct NG19 ... 101 E7
Balderton Gate NG24 ... 140 A8
Balderton La NG24 ... 141 A7
Baldwin Cl NG19 ... 89 B2
Baldwin Ct NG7 ... 222 B3
Baldwin St
Eastwood NG16 ... 144 C1
Nottingham NG7 ... 222 C3
Balfour Rd
Nottingham NG7 ... 222 B3
Stapleford NG9 ... 182 D6
Balfour St
Gainsborough DN21 ... 15 C1
Kirkby-in-Ashfield NG17 ... 115 C4
Balfron Gdns 7 NG2 ... 173 B2
Balkham La NG20 ... 72 C3
Ballantrae Cl NG5 ... 162 B8
Ballater Cl NG19 ... 87 E2
Ballerat Cres NG5 ... 160 E8
Ballerini Way LN1 ... 57 C3
Ball Hill DE55 ... 113 C6
Balloon Houses NG9 ... 171 B4
Balloon Wood Ind Est
NG8 ... 171 A4
Balls La NG17 ... 115 C2
Ball St NG3 ... 173 F7
Balmoral Ave NG2 ... 185 E8
Balmoral Cl
Carlton in Lindrick S81 ... 25 F6
Mansfield Woodhouse
NG19 ... 88 E5
Sandiacre NG10 ... 182 B3
Balmoral Cres NG8 ... 171 C5
Balmoral Ct DN11 ... 9 B5
Balmoral Dr
Beeston NG9 ... 171 C2
Mansfield NG19 ... 87 E2
Newark-on-Trent NG24 ... 140 E8
Balmoral Gr NG15 ... 146 B8
Balmoral Rd
Bingham NG13 ... 177 C4
Carlton NG4 ... 174 F6
Nottingham NG1 ... 223 D4
Balshaw Way NG9 ... 183 B2
Balwant Dr NG17 ... 101 C2
Bamburgh Cl 10 NG17 ... 114 E7
Bamford Dr NG18 ... 103 B6
Bamford St DE55 ... 99 A3
Bamkin Cl NG15 ... 146 B6
Bampton St 8 LE11 ... 220 B3
Banbury Ave NG9 ... 182 F3
Banbury Mount 9
NG5 ... 161 C2
Banchory Cl NG19 ... 87 E2
Bancroft La NG18 ... 101 F7
Bancroft Rd NG24 ... 140 B6
Bancroft St NG6 ... 160 C7
Banes Rd NG13 ... 178 B4
Bangor Wlk 3 NG3 ... 173 C7
Bank Ave NG17 ... 100 E1
Bank Cl
Creswell S80 ... 58 D8
Shirebrook NG20 ... 72 F4
Bank End Cl NG18 ... 102 D4
Bank End Rd DN10 ... 1 C4
Bankfield Dr NG9 ... 171 C1
Bank Hill NG14 ... 149 A4
Bank Pl NG1 ... 223 E2
Banks Ave NG17 ... 114 E6
Banks Cl NG5 ... 162 B6
Banks Cres NG13 ... 177 E4
Bank Side DN22 ... 39 F3
Banksman Cl NG14 ... 173 F7
Banksman Way NG22 ... 77 D7
Banks Paddock
NG13 ... 177 F4
Banks Rd NG9 ... 182 E2
Banks Road Inf Sch
NG9 ... 182 F2
Bank St
Langley Mill NG16 ... 143 C3
Long Eaton NG10 ... 193 E7
Banks The NG13 ... 177 F4
Bankwood Cl NG8 ... 160 A1
Bank Yd 11 NG6 ... 160 B7
Bannerman Rd
Kirkby-in-Ashfield NG17 ... 114 F5
Nottingham NG6 ... 160 C6
Baptist La
Collingham NG23 ... 111 F8
Collingham NG23 ... 112 A7
Barbara Sq NG15 ... 130 F1
Barber Cl DE7 ... 157 F3
Barber St NG16 ... 144 B2
Barbers Wood Cl
NG15 ... 117 A1
Barbrook Cl NG8 ... 172 A5
Barbury Dr NG11 ... 195 D7
Barclay Ct DE7 ... 157 C3
Barden Rd NG3 ... 162 A4
Bardfield Gdns NG5 ... 146 D1
Bardney Dr NG6 ... 160 A8
Bardsey Gdns NG5 ... 161 A7
Barent Cl NG5 ... 160 F6
Barent Wlk NG5 ... 160 F6
Barford Cl
Shireoaks S81 ... 34 F8
Shireoaks S81 ... 35 A8
Bar Gate NG24 ... 124 F1
Barker Ave
Sutton in Ashfield
NG17 ... 100 D7
Westwood NG16 ... 128 B4
Barker Ave E NG10 ... 182 A6
Barker Ave N NG10 ... 182 A6
Barker Gate
Hucknall NG15 ... 145 F7
Ilkeston DE7 ... 157 F2
Nottingham NG1 ... 223 F2
Barker Hades Rd S81 ... 16 B3
Barker Hill NG14 ... 150 E2
Barkers Field LE14 ... 211 C3
Barker's La NG9 ... 183 E4
Barker St NG17 ... 99 F4
Barker Way NG24 ... 139 F7
Barkestone La
Bottesford NG13 ... 181 A1
Plungar NG13 ... 192 A1
Plungar NG13 ... 202 F8
BARKESTONE-LE-
VALE ... 192 C2
Barkla Cl NG11 ... 195 C8
Barkston Cl NG24 ... 140 D3
Bar La NG6 ... 160 D2
Bar La Ind Pk NG6 ... 160 D2
Barlborough Rd DE7 ... 157 F5
Barley Cl
Carlton NG5 ... 162 D2
Kimberley NG16 ... 158 F7
New Ollerton NG22 ... 77 D5
Barley Croft
South Normanton DE55 ... 113 B4
West Bridgford NG2 ... 185 C4
Barley Dale Dr NG9 ... 170 D2
Barleylands NG11 ... 196 C6
Barley Ms NG19 ... 88 E6
Barley Wy 4 NG24 ... 125 B4
Barling Dr DE7 ... 157 C2
Barlock Rd NG6 ... 160 E4
Barlow Cotts La NG16 ... 158 B5
Barlow Dr N NG16 ... 158 B4
Barlow Dr S NG16 ... 158 B4
Barlows Cl NG12 ... 189 B4
Barnards Pl LE14 ... 211 C3
Barnby Gate NG24 ... 140 A8
BARNBY IN THE
WILLOWS ... 141 F5
Barnby La NG23 ... 156 E8
BARNBY MOOR ... 28 C5
Barnby Rd
Newark-on-Trent NG24 ... 140 B7
Newark-on-Trent NG24 ... 140 D6
Barnby Road Acad The
NG24 ... 140 B7
Barnby Wlk NG5 ... 161 C4
Barn Cl
Cotgrave NG12 ... 187 E2
Mansfield NG18 ... 102 F5
Nottingham NG16 ... 159 F5
Worksop S81 ... 36 A7
Barn Croft
Beeston NG9 ... 183 B5
Mansfield NG18 ... 102 F6
Barndale Cl NG2 ... 185 C3
Barnes Cl NG11 ... 185 B4
Barnes Cres NG17 ... 114 E8
Barnes Ct DN22 ... 29 D2
Barnes Rd NG5 ... 160 E8
Barnet Rd NG3 ... 174 B7
Barnett Ct NG12 ... 197 E3
Barnfield NG11 ... 185 B4
Barnfield Cl LE12 ... 212 B4
Barnfield Rd
Collingham NG23 ... 98 B1
Collingham NG23 ... 112 B8
Barnhill Gdns NG17 ... 101 C1
Barn La DN22 ... 32 D1
Barn Owl Cl NG20 ... 74 C6
Barn Owl Way NG21 ... 89 F5
Barnsdale Cl LE11 ... 220 A5
Barnsley Cl NG6 ... 147 B5
Barnsley Terr 9 NG2 ... 173 C1
BARNSTONE ... 190 F3
Barnstone La NG13 ... 191 A5
Barnstone Rd NG13 ... 190 C2
Barnston Rd NG2 ... 174 A5
Barnum Cl NG8 ... 171 E5
Barn Vw DN10 ... 20 A8
Barons Cl NG4 ... 162 E1
Barons Dr NG22 ... 77 F6
Barrack Cotts LE12 ... 217 A6
Barrack La NG7 ... 222 B2
Barrack Row 4 LE11 ... 220 B4
Barra Mews 10 NG2 ... 173 B2
Barratt Cl
Beeston NG9 ... 183 D1
Cropwell Bishop NG12 ... 189 A4
Barratt Cres NG9 ... 183 D2
Barratt La NG9 ... 183 D1
Bar Rd DN10 ... 23 C7
Bar Rd N DN10 ... 23 C8
Bar Rd S DN10 ... 23 C8
Barrel Hill Rd NG23 ... 96 E7
Barrhead Cl NG5 ... 146 E1
Barringer Rd NG19 ... 88 D1
Barrington Cl NG12 ... 175 E2
Barrique Rd NG7 ... 172 E1
Barrowby Ct S81 ... 36 A5
Barrowhill Wlk NG18 ... 103 B6
Barrow Rd LE12 ... 220 F6
Barrows Gate NG24 ... 125 B3
Barrows Hill La NG16 ... 128 D5
Barrow Slade NG12 ... 197 E2
Barrow St LE11 ... 220 B3
Barrydale Ave NG9 ... 183 F5
Barry St NG6 ... 160 B7
Bars Hill LE12 ... 206 C1
Bar The NG22 ... 79 C3
Bartholomew Cl NG12 ... 186 A3
Bartley Gdns NG14 ... 148 C8
Bartlow Rd NG8 ... 171 D7
Barton Cl
Mansfield Woodhouse
NG19 ... 89 B1
Ruddington NG11 ... 196 B6
BARTON IN FABIS ... 194 E6
Barton La
Barton in Fabis NG11 ... 195 A3
Beeston NG9 ... 183 C1
Beeston NG9 ... 194 D8
Long Eaton NG11 ... 194 D3
Nottingham NG11 ... 184 C1
Barton Rd NG10 ... 194 A6
Bartons Cl NG16 ... 144 C2
Barton St NG9 ... 184 A5
Barton Wy NG9 ... 183 E5
Barwell Dr NG8 ... 159 D1
Basa Cres NG5 ... 160 F8
Basford Hall NG6 ... 160 C3
Basford Rd NG6 ... 160 D2
Baskin La NG9 ... 183 C3
Baslow Ave NG4 ... 162 D1
Baslow Cl NG10 ... 193 A5
Baslow Dr NG9 ... 172 A1
Baslow Way NG18 ... 103 B5
Bass Cl NG15 ... 131 C1
Bassetlaw District General
Hospl S81 ... 36 A5
Bassetlaw Leisure
Centre S80 ... 35 F3
Bassetlaw Mus* DN22 ... 39 F7
Bassett Cl
Ilkeston DE7 ... 157 C3
Kimberley NG16 ... 158 E7
Bassett Hill NG20 ... 72 E7
Bassett Rd NG16 ... 158 E7
Bassett The NG20 ... 72 E6
Bassingfield La NG12 ... 186 F8
Bastion St NG7 ... 222 A3
Bateman Cl NG12 ... 185 F3
Bateman Gdns 8 NG7 ... 172 F7
Bateman Rd LE12 ... 205 E1
Bateman's Yd NG17 ... 114 D4
Bath La
Mansfield NG18 ... 102 C8
Market Warsop NG19 ... 73 C2
BATHLEY ... 110 A3
Bathley La
Bathley NG23 ... 110 B5
Little Carlton NG23 ... 124 C7
Norwell NG23 ... 109 F7
South Muskham NG23 ... 110 B1
Bathley St NG2 ... 173 D1
Baths La NG15 ... 146 B7
Bath St
Ilkeston DE7 ... 157 E1
Mansfield NG18 ... 102 B6
Nottingham NG1 ... 223 F3
Nottingham NG14 ... 173 D5
Sutton in Ashfield NG17 ... 100 F4
Bathurst Dr NG8 ... 172 A6
Bathurst Terr
Creswell NG20 ... 58 F2
Whaley Thorns NG20 ... 58 F2
Whaley Thorns NG20 ... 59 A2
Bathwood Dr
Mansfield NG17, NG18 ... 101 E5
Sutton in Ashfield NG17,
NG18 ... 101 A2
Batley La NG19 ... 86 E4
Battle Cl NG13 ... 177 B7
Baulker La
Blidworth NG21 ... 118 E4
Clipstone NG21 ... 90 B4
Farnsfield NG22 ... 119 A4
Baulk La
Beeston NG9 ... 183 A6
Harworth DN11 ... 8 F5
Kneesall NG22 ... 93 E7
Stapleford NG9 ... 183 A5
Torworth DN22 ... 19 A2
Worksop S81 ... 35 E5
Baulk The
Clarborough DN22 ... 40 E8
Worksop S81 ... 35 F5
Baum's La NG18 ... 102 C5
BAWTRY ... 10 B7
Bawtry Cl DN11 ... 8 F4
Bawtry Mayflower
Prim Sch DN10 ... 10 A8
Bawtry Rd
Bawtry DN10 ... 10 C8
Bircotes DN10 ... 9 C1
Blyth S81 ... 18 A6
Everton DN10 ... 11 A3
Finningley DN10 ... 3 E8
Harworth DN11 ... 9 A5
Misson DN10 ... 4 A3
Tickhill DN11 ... 8 E7
Bawtry Wlk NG3 ... 173 F6
Baxter Cl
Bingham NG13 ... 177 E6
Hucknall NG15 ... 131 C1
Baxter Green NG9 ... 183 B7
Baxter Hill NG19 ... 86 F3
Baxter La
Sibthorpe NG23 ... 154 B1
Sibthorpe NG23 ... 168 A8
Baxter St LE11 ... 220 B4
Bayard Ct NG8 ... 172 C5
Bayard St DN21 ... 15 C1
Bayford Dr NG24 ... 140 F7
Bayliss Rd NG4 ... 162 D3
Baysdale Dr 1 NG19 ... 88 F1
Bayswater Rd NG16 ... 158 F7
Baythorn Rd NG8 ... 171 D6
Beacon Dr
Kirkby-in-Ashfield
NG17 ... 115 C6
Loughborough LE11 ... 220 A1
Beacon Hill Bsns Pk
NG24 ... 125 B1
Beacon Hill Conservation
Park* NG24 ... 125 C1
Beacon Hill Dr NG15 ... 145 D5
Beacon Hill Rd
Gringley on the Hill
DN10 ... 13 A2
Newark-on-Trent NG24 ... 140 C8
Beacon Hill Rise NG3 ... 173 E6
Beacon Hts NG24 ... 140 B8
Beacon Rd
Beeston NG9 ... 184 B6
Loughborough LE11 ... 220 A2
Beaconsfield Dr NG24 ... 125 F2
Beaconsfield Green
NG24 ... 125 F2
Beaconsfield St
Long Eaton NG10 ... 193 E7
Nottingham NG7 ... 172 F8
Beacon View NG13 ... 181 B3
Beacon Vw NG22 ... 77 D3
Beacon Way NG24 ... 140 D8
Beacon Wlk DN10 ... 13 F2
Beamlight Rd DE7 ... 157 F8
Bean Ave S80 ... 36 B3
Bean Cl NG6 ... 159 F5
Beanford La
Calverton NG14 ... 133 F3
Oxton NG25 ... 134 A3
Beardall Fields
Prim Sch NG15 ... 146 C8
Beardall St
Hucknall NG15 ... 146 B6
7 Mansfield NG18 ... 102 A7
Beardsall Rd NG16 ... 144 A3
Beardsall's Row DN22 ... 39 F7
Beardsley Gdns NG2 ... 173 B2
Beardsley Rd NG21 ... 76 C1
Beardsmore Gr NG15 ... 130 F1
Beast Mkt Hill
Newark-on-Trent NG24 ... 124 F1
Nottingham NG1 ... 223 E2
Beatty Wlk DE7 ... 157 F3
Beauclerk Dr NG5 ... 160 E8
Beaufit La NG16 ... 113 E2
Beaufort Ct NG11 ... 185 C3
Beaufort Dr NG9 ... 183 C5
Beaufort Gdns DN10 ... 9 F7
Beaufort St DN21 ... 15 C3
Beaufort Way S81 ... 35 E8
Beaulieu Gdns NG2 ... 185 C5
Beauly Dr NG19 ... 101 D5
Beaumaris Dr
Beeston NG9 ... 183 B4
Carlton NG4 ... 163 B1
Beaumond Cross NG24 ... 139 F8
Beaumont Ave
Mansfield NG18 ... 102 F5
Southwell NG25 ... 121 C1
Southwell NG25 ... 136 C8
Beaumont Cl
Keyworth NG12 ... 197 E4
Stapleford NG9 ... 170 E1
Beaumont Ct LE11 ... 220 A6
Beaumont Gdns NG2 ... 185 D4
Beaumont Rd LE11 ... 220 B1
Beaumont Rise S80 ... 35 D3
Beaumont Sq NG9 ... 171 C5
Beaumont St
Gainsborough DN21 ... 24 D8
Nottingham NG2 ... 173 E4
Beaumont Wlk NG24 ... 125 B2
Beauvale NG16 ... 144 C2
Beauvale Cres NG15 ... 145 E6
Beauvale Dr DE7 ... 157 E5
Beauvale Rd
Annesley Woodhouse
NG17 ... 129 E8
Hucknall NG15 ... 145 E6
Nottingham NG2 ... 173 C1
Beauvale Rise NG16 ... 144 A3
Beaver Gn 5 NG12 ... 185 D7
Beaver Pl S80 ... 35 F3
Beazley Ave NG18 ... 101 F7
Bechers Ct NG25 ... 121 E1
Beck Ave NG14 ... 148 F8
Beck Cres
Blidworth NG21 ... 118 A4
Mansfield NG19 ... 101 E7
Beck Dr DN21 ... 14 A5
Beckenham Rd NG7 ... 222 B4
Becket Gr NG11 ... 185 A5
Becket Sch The NG2 ... 185 B7
Beckett Ave
Carlton in Lindrick S81 ... 25 F7
Gainsborough DN21 ... 15 E2
Mansfield NG19 ... 87 E1
Beckett Ct NG4 ... 162 D3
Becketts Field NG25 ... 136 D7
Beckett St NG24 ... 139 F5
Beckett Way The NG12 ... 185 B6
Beckford Rd 8 NG2 ... 173 F3
Beckhampton Rd NG5 ... 161 A7
BECKINGHAM
Lincs ... 142 D8
Notts ... 14 B1
Beckingham Ct NG19 ... 101 E7
Beckingham Prim Sch
DN10 ... 14 B1
Beckingham Rd
Beckingham NG24 ... 127 A1
Coddington NG24 ... 126 C2
Stapleford LN6 ... 127 E8
Walkeringham DN10 ... 14 A4
Beckingthorpe Dr
NG13 ... 181 B3
Beck La
Blidworth NG21 ... 118 A4
Clayworth DN22 ... 21 E4
Farnsfield NG22 ... 119 F5
Sutton in Ashfield NG17,
NG19 ... 101 B6
West Markham NG22 ... 65 B3
Beckland Hill NG22 ... 65 F6
Beckley Rd NG8 ... 159 F2
Beckon Mdw DN10 ... 23 C8
Beckside
Lowdham NG14 ... 150 E1
West Bridgford NG2 ... 186 C5
Beck St
Carlton NG4 ... 174 E8
Nottingham NG1 ... 223 F3
Thurgarton NG14 ... 151 D7
Beckway NG23 ... 109 B5
Bedale S81 ... 36 A8
Bedale Ct NG9 ... 183 A4
Bedale Rd NG5 ... 161 D5
Bedarra Gr NG7 ... 222 A2
Bede Cl NG5 ... 147 A1
Bede House La NG24 ... 140 A8
Bede Ling NG2 ... 185 C6
Bedford Ave NG18 ... 102 E7
Bedford Cl DE74 ... 203 D1
Bedford Ct
Bawtry DN10 ... 9 F7
Stapleford NG9 ... 170 E1
Bedford Gr NG6 ... 160 D5
Bedford Row NG1 ... 223 F3
Bedford Sq 3 LE11 ... 220 B3
Bedford St LE11 ... 220 B3
Bedlam Row LN1 ... 57 A3
Bedlington Gdns NG3 ... 161 E1

Beecham Ave NG3 . . . . . 173 F7
Beech Ave
  Beeston NG9 . . . . .184 B5
  Bingham NG13. . . . . .178 A4
  Carlton NG4. . . . . .174 F6
  East Leake LE12 . . . . . . .214 D8
  Edwinstowe NG22 . . . . . . .76 F4
  Gainsborough DN21 . . . . . .15 D2
  Hucknall NG15. . . . . .146 A7
  Huthwaite NG17 . . . . . . .100 A3
  Keyworth NG12 . . . . .198 A2
  Kirkby-in-Ashfield NG17 . .114 F5
  Lidgett NG21. . . . . .91 C8
  Long Eaton NG10. . . . . . .182 F1
  12 Mansfield NG18. . . .102 B6
  New Ollerton NG22 . . . . . .77 C4
  Nottingham, Hyson Green
  NG7 . . . . .173 A8
  Nottingham, Mapperley
  NG3. . . . . .162 A4
  Nuthall NG16. . . . . .159 B6
  Ollerton NG22 . . . . .77 A4
  Pinxton NG16. . . . . .113 E3
  Ravenshead NG15. . . . . . .116 F3
  Sandiacre NG10. . . . . . . .182 B7
  Tickhill DN11. . . . . .8 B7
  Worksop S81 . . . . .35 F6
Beech Cl
  Gringley on the Hill DN10 . .12 F2
  Nottingham NG6 . . . . . . .160 C4
  Radcliffe on Trent NG12 . .175 F2
  West Bridgford NG12 . . . .186 A4
Beech Cres
  Glapwell S44 . . . . .86 B8
  Mansfield Woodhouse
  NG19. . . . . .88 D2
Beechcroft S81. . . . . .36 B6
Beech Ct
  Nottingham NG3 . . . . . . .162 A4
  Selston NG16. . . . . .129 B3
BEECHDALE 172 B6
Beechdale Ave NG17. . . . .100 F4
Beechdale Cres NG17. . . . .100 F4
Beechdale Rd
  Mansfield Woodhouse
  NG19. . . . . .89 A2
  Nottingham NG8 . . . . . . .172 B7
Beechdale Swimming Ctr
  NG8. . . . . .172 C6
Beech Dr NG3 . . . . .181 B2
Beecher La DN10 . . . . .14 B1
Beeches Ct NG23 . . . . .98 D5
Beeches Rd LE11 . . . . .220 C2
Beeches The
  Carlton NG3. . . . . .174 A8
  Sutton in Ashfield NG17 . .100 D7
  Tuxford NG22 . . . . .65 F2
Beech Gr
  Blidworth NG21. . . . . . . .118 C5
  Carlton in Lindrick S81 . . . .25 E7
  South Normanton DE55. . .113 B5
Beech Hill Ave NG19 . . . . . .87 F1
Beech Hill Cres NG19 . . . . . .87 F1
Beech Hill Dr NG19 . . . . . . .87 F1
Beech Hill Sch NG19 . . . . . .87 F1
Beech Rd
  Harworth DN11. . . . . .9 A5
  Selston NG16. . . . . .129 B3
Beech St NG17. . . . . .100 D7
Beech Tree Ave NG19 . . . . .88 B5
Beechways DN22 . . . . .39 D4
Beech Wlk DN20. . . . . .50 B4
Beechwood Cl
  Mansfield Woodhouse
  NG19. . . . . .89 A4
  Sutton in Ashfield NG17 . .101 A5
Beechwood Cres DN22. . . . .37 F6
Beechwood Ct NG17. . . . . .101 A5
Beechwood Dr DN22. . . . . . .38 E6
Beechwood Gr NG17. . . . . .101 A5
Beechwood Rd
  Arnold NG5 . . . . .162 A4
  6 Kirkby-in-Ashfield
  NG17. . . . . .114 F7
Beedham Way NG5. . . . . . .162 C8
Beehive La LN6. . . . . .84 F1
Bee Hive La **4** LE11. . . . .220 B3
Beehive St DN22. . . . . .39 F6
Beeley Ave NG17 . . . . .100 E1
Beeley Cl NG18 . . . . .103 B6
BEESTON 183 A6
Beeston Bsns Pk NG9 . .184 A4
Beeston Cl NG6. . . . . .146 F4
Beeston Ct NG6. . . . . .160 D6
Beeston Fields Dr NG9 183 D8
Beeston Fields Prim Sch
  NG9 . . . . .183 F8
Beeston La NG9 . . . . .184 B8
Beeston Rd
  Newark-on-Trent NG24. . .140 B5
  Nottingham NG7 . . . . . . .172 D1
Beeston Rylands Jun Sch
  NG9 . . . . .184 A4
Beeston Sidings Nature
  Reserve* NG11 . . . . . . .184 C7
Beeston Sta NG9. . . . . . . .184 A5
Beethan Cl NG13 . . . . .177 F4
Beggarlee Pk NG16 . . . . . .144 B4
Behay Gdns NG23. . . . . . . .138 C8
Beighton Cl NG18. . . . . . . .103 B5
Beighton St NG17. . . . . . . .100 F3
Bek Cl NG19. . . . . .86 F7
Belconnen Rd NG5. . . . . . .161 A5
Beldover Dr **5** NG16. . . .159 C2
Belfield Gdns NG10 . . . . . .193 E7
Belfields Yd NG22 . . . . . . .120 C4
Belfmoor Cl NG23. . . . . .45 A5
Belford Cl NG6 . . . . .159 F8
Belfry Cl **1** NG4 . . . . . . .114 E7
Belfry Rise S81. . . . . .36 B8
Belfry Way NG2. . . . . .186 C4

Belgrave Ct DN10 . . . . .9 F7
Belgrave Mews NG11 . . . .185 C3
Belgrave Rd NG6 . . . . .160 A4
Belgrave Sq NG1 . . . . .223 D3
Belgravia Ct **2** S81. . . . . .35 E7
Bella Cl NG16. . . . . .143 B4
Bellamy Dr NG17 . . . . .115 A3
Bellamy Rd NG18 . . . . .103 A2
Bellar Gate NG1 . . . . .223 F2
Bell Cl NG23 . . . . .81 E7
Belle-Isle Rd NG15 . . . . . .146 A7
Belleville Dr NG5 . . . . .161 B8
Bellevue Ct NG3 . . . . .173 E6
Belle Vue Gdns NG3 . . . . .173 E6
Belle Vue La NG21. . . . . . .118 A6
Bell Foundry Mus*
  LE11. . . . . .220 C4
Bell La
  Collingham NG23. . . . . . .111 F8
  Nottingham NG11 . . . . . .185 A7
  Weston NG23. . . . . .80 F5
  Weston NG23. . . . . .81 A5
Bellmore Gdns NG8. . . . . .171 D5
Bell Pit Dr NG21. . . . . .76 D3
Bellsfield Cl S80. . . . . .45 A5
Bells La NG8. . . . . .160 A3
Bell St NG4. . . . . .174 D8
Bell View NG18 . . . . .102 C7
Belmond Cl NG24. . . . . . . .139 F5
Belmont Ave NG6. . . . . . . .160 C7
Belmont Cl
  Beeston NG9 . . . . .183 B4
  Hucknall NG15. . . . . .146 A4
  Mansfield Woodhouse
  NG19. . . . . .89 A2
Belmont Rd NG17. . . . . . . .115 B1
Belper Ave NG4. . . . . .162 D1
Belper Cres NG4. . . . . .162 D1
Belper Rd NG7. . . . . .172 F7
Belper St NG18 . . . . .102 D7
Belper Way NG18 . . . . . . .102 D7
Belsay Rd NG5. . . . . .161 A7
Belsford Ct NG16 . . . . .159 A8
Belton Cl NG10. . . . . .182 B4
Belton Dr NG2 . . . . .185 B4
Belton Rd LE11 . . . . .220 A5
Belton Rd W Extension
  LE11 . . . . .220 A6
Belton St NG7 . . . . .172 F8
Belt Rd The DN11. . . . . .15 E3
Belvedere Ave **9** NG7 . .172 F8
Belvedere St NG18. . . . . . .102 B6
Belvoir Ave NG13 . . . . .181 A1
Belvoir Cl
  Aslockton NG13 . . . . .178 E3
  Long Eaton NG10. . . . . . .193 E5
Belvoir Cres
  Langar NG13 . . . . .190 C2
  Newark-on-Trent NG24 . .140 A6
Belvoir Hill NG2 . . . . .173 F4
Belvoir Pl NG24. . . . . .140 D4
Belvoir Rd
  Balderton NG24. . . . . . . .140 D3
  Bottesford NG13 . . . . . . .181 A3
  Carlton NG4. . . . . .175 A4
  Redmile NG13 . . . . .192 F3
  West Bridgford NG2 . . . . .174 A1
Belvoir St
  Hucknall NG15. . . . . .145 F8
  Nottingham NG3 . . . . . . .161 F2
Belvoir Terr DN21 . . . . .15 B4
Belvoir Vale Gr NG13. . . . .177 F4
Belward St NG1. . . . . .223 F2
Belwood Cl NG7 . . . . .184 F2
Bembridge S81. . . . . .36 B6
Bembridge Ct NG9. . . . . . .183 A8
Bembridge Dr NG5 . . . . . . .161 B6
Bemrose Dr NG12. . . . . . . .176 A5
Bencaunt Grove NG15 . . . .146 A8
Bendigo La NG2 . . . . .174 A4
Benedict Ct **3** NG5. . . . . .147 A1
Benet Dr NG22. . . . . .106 A5
Benington Dr NG8. . . . . . . .171 C3
Ben Mayo Ct NG7. . . . . . . .222 B4
Benner Ave DE7 . . . . .170 A5
Bennerley Ave DE7 . . . . . .157 F4
Bennerley Ct NG6. . . . . . . .159 F8
Bennerley Fields Specialist
  Speech & Language Coll
  DE7. . . . . .157 F4
Bennerley Rd NG6. . . . . . . .159 F8
Bennet Dr **2** NG17. . . . . .115 A4
Bennett Ave NG18 . . . . . . .102 F6
Bennett Gdns NG16. . . . . . .197 F4
Bennett Rd NG3 . . . . .162 A3
Bennett St
  Long Eaton NG10. . . . . . .182 C2
  Nottingham NG3 . . . . . . .161 F2
Benneworth Cl NG15. . . . . .145 F5
Bennington Wlk NG19 . . . . .88 E4
Ben St NG7. . . . . .222 B4
Bentick St NG18 . . . . .102 D7
Bentinck Ave NG22 . . . . . .186 D1
Bentinck Banks Nature
  Reserve* NG17 . . . . . . .114 E3
Bentinck Cl
  Annesley Woodhouse
  NG17. . . . . .114 F1
  Boughton NG22 . . . . .77 F4
Bentinck Ct **8** NG2 . . . . . .173 E4
Bentinck Prim Sch
  NG7 . . . . .222 B4
Bentinck Rd
  Carlton NG4. . . . . .162 C2
  Newark-on-Trent NG24 . .139 F6
  Nottingham NG7 . . . . . . .222 B4
Bentinck St
  Annesley Woodhouse
  NG17. . . . . .129 F8
  Hodthorpe S80. . . . . .45 C6

Bentinck St continued
  Hucknall NG15. . . . . .145 F8
  Sutton in Ashfield NG17 . .100 F3
Bentinck Terr NG20. . . . . . .74 B3
Bentinck Workshops
  NG17. . . . . .114 D3
Bentinck S80. . . . . .46 F8
Bentley Ave NG3. . . . . .174 B6
Bentley Cl LE11. . . . . .220 C4
Bentwell Ave NG17. . . . . . .162 A7
Beresford Dr DE7. . . . . . . .157 E5
Beresford Rd
  Long Eaton NG10. . . . . . .193 A5
  Mansfield Woodhouse
  NG19. . . . . .88 C6
Beresford St
  Mansfield NG18. . . . . . . .102 D6
  Nottingham NG7 . . . . . . .222 A3
Berkeley Ave
  Long Eaton NG10. . . . . . .193 C6
  Nottingham NG3 . . . . . . .173 C8
Berkeley Cres NG12. . . . . .176 D3
Berkeley Rd NG18 . . . . . . .102 C5
Bernard Ave
  Hucknall NG15. . . . . .131 B1
  Mansfield Woodhouse
  NG19. . . . . .88 B5
Bernard Rd NG19 . . . . .101 E8
Bernard St NG5. . . . . .161 B1
Bernisdale Cl NG5. . . . . . . .146 F1
Berridge Adult Ctr The
  NG7 . . . . .173 A8
Berridge Jun Sch NG7 .172 E7
Berridge Prim Sch
  NG7 . . . . .172 F8
Berridge Prim Sch
  Brushfield NG7. . . . . .172 E7
Berridge Rd E NG7. . . . . . .173 A8
Berridge Rd W NG7. . . . . . .172 F7
Berriedale Cl NG5 . . . . . . .162 C8
Berristow Grange
  NG17. . . . . .100 D1
Berristow La DE55 . . . . . . .113 C7
Berry Ave NG17. . . . . .114 E6
Berrydown Cl NG8. . . . . . . .160 C1
Berry Hill Cl NG18 . . . . . . .102 C4
Berry Hill Gdns NG18 . . . .102 F4
Berry Hill Gr NG4 . . . . .162 E2
Berry Hill La
  Mansfield NG18. . . . . . . .102 C4
  Mansfield NG18. . . . . . . .102 D4
Berry Hill Mews NG18. . . .102 D4
Berry Hill Prim Sch
  NG18 . . . . .102 C4
Berry Hill Rd NG18. . . . . . .102 C4
Berry Pk Lea NG18. . . . . . .102 D3
Berwick Ave NG19 . . . . . . .101 D8
Berwick Cl NG5. . . . . .161 C6
Berwin Cl NG10. . . . . .182 A1
Beryldene Ave NG16 . . . . .159 A7
Bescar La
  Ollerton NG22 . . . . .77 A2
  Rufford NG22 . . . . .92 B8
Bescoby St DN22 . . . . .39 F6
Besecar Ave NG4 . . . . .162 E2
Besecar Cl NG4. . . . . .162 E2
Bessemer Dr NG18. . . . . . .102 B4
Bessingham Dr NG11 . . . . .185 C3
BESTHORPE 97 E6
Besthorpe Ct NG19 . . . . . .101 E7
Besthorpe Nature Reserve
  (North)* NG23. . . . . . . .97 C6
Besthorpe Nature Reserve
  (South)* NG23. . . . . . . .97 C4
Besthorpe Rd
  Besthorpe NG23 . . . . .97 F3
  Collingham NG23. . . . . . . .98 A2
  North Scarle LN6. . . . . . . .83 C1
Bestwick Ave DE75 . . . . . .143 B1
Bestwick Cl DE7 . . . . .170 A4
Bestwood Ave NG5. . . . . . .161 E8
Bestwood Bsns Pk
  NG6 . . . . .146 E3
Bestwood Cl NG5. . . . . . . .161 E8
Bestwood Country Park -
  Mill Lakes* NG6 . . . . . .146 B2
Bestwood Ctry Pk*
  NG6 . . . . .146 F3
Bestwood Lodge Dr
  NG5. . . . . .161 D8
Bestwood Park Drive **4**
  NG5. . . . . .147 B1
Bestwood Pk Dr NG5. . . . .161 B8
Bestwood Pk Dr W
  NG5. . . . . .146 E1
Bestwood Pk View
  NG5. . . . . .147 E1
Bestwood Rd
  Hucknall NG15. . . . . .146 C5
  Nottingham NG6 . . . . . . .146 D2
  Pinxton NG16. . . . . .113 E2
Bestwood Terr NG6. . . . . . .160 C8
BESTWOOD VILLAGE . .146 F4
Beswick Cl NG4. . . . . .175 C7
Betford Gate DN22. . . . . . . .41 D8
Bethel Gdns NG15 . . . . . . .145 C5
Bethel Terr S80. . . . . .34 E7
Bethnal Wlk **2** NG6. . . . . .160 B7
Betony Cl NG13 . . . . .177 C4
Betony Gr **1** NG17. . . . . .115 A3
Bettina Gdns NG12. . . . . . .185 F3
Betts Ave NG15. . . . . .146 A4
Bettys La DN11. . . . . .24 E4
Betula Cl NG11. . . . . .184 C1
Beulah Rd NG17. . . . . .115 B4
Bevan Cl NG21. . . . . .118 B8
Bevel St NG7. . . . . .172 F7
Bevercotes Cl NG24. . . . . .139 F6
Bevercotes La NG22 . . . . . .65 D3

Bevercotes Rd NG22 . . . . .64 C3
Beverley Cl
  Nottingham NG8 . . . . . . .171 B4
  Rainworth NG21 . . . . . . .104 B1
Beverley Dr
  Kimberley NG16. . . . . . . .158 E7
  Kirkby-in-Ashfield NG17 . .115 C3
  Mansfield NG18. . . . . . . .102 D2
Beverley Gdns NG4 . . . . . .162 F1
Beverley Rd DN11. . . . . .9 A4
Beverleys Ave NG13. . . . . .178 F4
Beverley Wlk S81. . . . . .25 E7
Bevin Pl NG21 . . . . .76 C3
Bewcastle Rd NG5 . . . . . . .147 A2
Bewick Dr NG3 . . . . .174 C5
Bexhill Cl NG8. . . . . .171 E1
Bexwell Cl NG11 . . . . .195 E5
Biant Cl NG8. . . . . .160 B3
Bicycle La NG9 . . . . .183 E5
Biddlestone Ct NG17. . . . . .100 D5
Bideford Cl NG3 . . . . .162 D5
Bidford Rd NG8. . . . . .159 F1
Bidwell Cres NG11. . . . . . . .195 B2
Big Barn La NG18 . . . . .102 F5
Biggart Cl **2** NG9. . . . . . .183 C2
Biggin St LE11. . . . . .220 B4
Big House The NG7 . . . . . . .76 B3
Big La DN22 . . . . .30 D3
Bigsby Rd
  Retford DN22. . . . . .30 A1
  Retford DN22. . . . . .39 F8
Big Wood Sch NG5. . . . . . .147 B2
Biko Sq **8** NG7 . . . . .172 F8
Bilberry Dr NG20 . . . . .72 D2
Bilberry Wlk NG3 . . . . .173 E7
Bilbie Wlk NG1 . . . . .223 D3
BILBOROUGH 171 E4
Bilborough Coll NG16. . . . .171 C7
Bilborough Rd NG8. . . . . . .171 C6
Bilby Gdns **3** NG3. . . . . . .173 F5
Billesdon Dr NG5 . . . . .160 F4
Billingsley Ave NG16. . . . . .113 D3
Bill La NG17. . . . . .105 F5
Billy Button La
  Torworth DN22 . . . . .19 A1
  Torworth S81. . . . . .27 F8
BILSTHORPE 105 E6
Bilsthorpe Bsns Pk
  NG22 . . . . .106 A8
Bilsthorpe Heritage
  Museum* NG22. . . . . . .105 F6
Bilsthorpe Dr NG22. . . . . . . .92 D1
Bilton Cl NG24. . . . . .140 D2
Binbrook Ct DN10 . . . . .9 F6
Binch Field Cl NG14. . . . . .148 C8
Birch Ave
  Beeston NG9 . . . . .184 A1
  Carlton NG4. . . . . .174 D7
  Farnsfield NG22. . . . . . . .119 E7
  Ilkeston DE7 . . . . .170 A4
  Nuthall NG16. . . . . .159 B6
  Rainworth NG21 . . . . . . .104 C1
Birch Cl
  Aslockton NG13 . . . . .178 F5
  Nuthall NG16. . . . . .159 B6
  Rampton DN22. . . . . .42 F2
  Ranskill DN22 . . . . .19 C4
  Ravenshead NG15. . . . . . .117 A1
Birch Croft Dr NG19. . . . . . .89 A2
Birchcroft DN22 . . . . .39 E8
Birch Ct NG22 . . . . .65 F2
Birchdale Ave NG15. . . . . .146 A5
Birchenhall Ct NG24 . . . . .139 A4
Birchen Holme DE55. . . . . .113 A4
Birches The NG15. . . . . . . .117 A3
Birchfield Dr S80 . . . . .35 B2
Birchfield Rd NG5. . . . . . . .148 A1
Birch Gr
  Gainsborough DN21 . . . . . .15 D2
  Mansfield NG18. . . . . . . .103 A4
  Shirebrook NG20. . . . . . . .72 D5
Birchlands NG19. . . . . .88 F1
Birch Lea
  Arnold NG5 . . . . .161 D8
  East Leake LE12 . . . . . . .205 D1
Birchover Pl DE7. . . . . .157 E5
Birchover Rd NG8 . . . . .171 C6
Birch Pas NG7. . . . . .222 C3
Birch Rd
  Hodthorpe S80. . . . . .45 C6
  New Balderton NG24. . . . .140 C5
  New Ollerton NG22 . . . . . .77 D4
Birch Rise NG14 . . . . .149 C5
Birch St NG20. . . . . .73 F6
Birch Tree Cl NG19 . . . . . . .89 D3
Birch Tree Cres NG17 . . . .114 F4
Birchwood Ave
  Breaston NG10 . . . . .193 A7

Birchwood Ave continued
  Long Eaton NG10. . . . . . .193 C5
Birchwood Cl
  Ravenshead NG15. . . . . . .117 B1
  South Normanton DE55. . .113 A4
  Southwell NG25. . . . . . . .121 D1
  Sutton in Ashfield NG17 . .100 E6
Birchwood Dr
  Ravenshead NG15. . . . . . .117 A1
  Sutton in Ashfield NG17 . .100 D7
Birchwood Pk NG19 . . . . . . .89 C3
Birchwood Rd NG8 . . . . . . .171 C4
Birchwood View DN21 . . . . .15 F1
BIRCOTES 9 D4
Bircotes L Ctr DN11. . . . . . . .9 C5
Bird Cl NG18. . . . . .102 C3
Birdcroft La DN10 . . . . .14 A5
Birding St NG19 . . . . .88 B1
Birdsall Ave NG8. . . . . .171 E4
Bird's La NG17. . . . . .114 E1
Birkdale Ave NG22 . . . . .77 D6
Birkdale Cl
  Ilkeston DE7 . . . . .157 D1
  West Bridgford NG2. . . . . .186 A3
Birkdale Dr **3** NG17 . . . . .114 F6
Birkdale Gr NG22 . . . . .39 D2
Birkdale Sq DN21 . . . . .15 E3
Birkdale Way
  Nottingham NG5 . . . . . . .160 F8
  9 Nottingham NG5. . . .161 A8
Birkin Ave
  Beeston NG9 . . . . .183 A6
  Nottingham NG7 . . . . . . .172 F7
  Radcliffe on Trent NG12 . .176 A4
  Ruddington NG11. . . . . . .196 C8
Birkland Ave
  Mansfield Woodhouse
  NG19. . . . . .88 D3
  Market Warsop NG20 . . . . .74 B4
  Nottingham, Mapperley
  NG3. . . . . .162 A4
  Nottingham, St Ann's
  NG1. . . . . .223 E4
Birkland Dr NG22. . . . . .76 A2
Birkland La NG23 . . . . .68 F1
Birklands Ave
  New Ollerton NG22 . . . . . .77 C6
  Worksop S80 . . . . .36 C1
Birklands Cl NG20 . . . . .74 B5
Birklands Prim Sch
  NG20 . . . . .74 B5
Birkland St NG18 . . . . .102 C7
Birks Cl S80 . . . . .45 C6
Birks Rd NG19 . . . . .101 D7
Birley St NG9 . . . . .182 D5
Birling Cl NG6 . . . . .159 F7
Birrell Rd NG7 . . . . .173 A8
Birrel St DN21. . . . . .15 B2
Bisham Dr NG2 . . . . .186 B7
Bishop Alexander Prim Sch
  NG24 . . . . .125 A4
Bishop Alexandra Ct
  NG24. . . . . .139 F5
Bishopdale S81. . . . . .36 A7
Bishopdale Cl NG10 . . . . . .193 A6
Bishopdale Dr NG16 . . . . . .159 B7
Bishopfield La DN22 . . . . . . .19 A5
Bishops Cl NG12. . . . . .197 E4
Bishop's Dr NG25. . . . . .136 E8
Bishops Hill NG21. . . . . . . .103 F1
Bishops Mdws NG20 . . . . . .74 B6
Bishops Rd NG13 . . . . .177 D5
Bishop St
  Eastwood NG16. . . . . . . .143 F2
  Loughborough LE11. . . . .220 C4
  Sutton in Ashfield NG17 . .100 E3
Bishops Way
  Boughton NG22 . . . . .77 E5
  Hucknall NG15. . . . . .146 B8
Bishop's Wlk NG20 . . . . .74 A4
Bispham Dr NG9. . . . . .182 F2
Blackacre NG14 . . . . .163 E5
Black Beny DN10 . . . . .4 D1
Blackberry Way
  Collingham NG23. . . . . . .112 B8
  Market Warsop NG20 . . . . .74 A3
  Newark-on-Trent NG24 . .140 C2
Blackbird Cl **6** S81 . . . . . .35 C7
Blackbird Cres NG22. . . . . .186 A2
Blackbird Dr NG22. . . . . .77 C2
Blackbird Pl NG21 . . . . .118 A8
Blackbrook Rd NG24 . . . . .125 D1
Blackburn Cl
  Carlton NG4. . . . . .163 A1
  Collingham NG23. . . . . . . .98 B1
Blackburn Pl DE7 . . . . .157 E3
Blackburn Row NG2 . . . . . .222 B2
Blackburn View NG22. . . . . .77 F4
Blackburn Wy **5** NG5. . . .161 A5
Blackcliff Field Cl S80 . . . . .45 A5
Blacketts Wlk NG11. . . . . . .195 C5
Blackfriars Cl NG8. . . . . . . .159 D3
Blackham Rd LE11. . . . . . . .220 A1
Black Hereford Way
  DN22. . . . . .39 C4
Blackhill Dr NG4. . . . . .174 F8
Black La LN6. . . . . .71 F4
Blackmires Way NG17 . . . .101 A4
Black Rock Wy NG16. . . . . .102 D5
Blackrod Cl NG9 . . . . .183 A2
Black Scotch Cl
  Mansfield NG18. . . . . . . .102 E4
  Mansfield NG18. . . . . . . .102 E4
Black Scotch La
  Harlow Wood NG18. . . . . .117 A4
  Mansfield NG18. . . . . . . .116 F8
Blackshale Rd NG19 . . . . . . .88 B2
Blacksmith Ct NG12. . . . . .187 C2

Birchwood Ave continued
  Long Eaton NG10. . . . . . .193 C5

Blacksmith La
  Kelham NG23. . . . . .124 A4
  Torworth DN22 . . . . .19 B2
Blacksmiths Cl LE14 . . . . . .219 D8
Blacksmiths La NG15. . . . . .131 D5
Blacksmiths La LN6. . . . . . .83 D2
Blacksmiths Mws NG25 . . . .35 C8
Blacksmith Wy NG20. . . . . . .72 F2
Blackstone Dr S81. . . . . .34 B4
Blackstone Wlk NG2 . . . . . .173 C2
Blackstope La
  4 Retford DN22. . . . . . . .39 F7
  Retford DN22. . . . . .40 A7
Blackstope La East
  DN22. . . . . .40 B6
Black Swan Cl NG5 . . . . . . .161 D4
Blackthorn Cl
  Bingham NG13. . . . . .178 A4
  Carlton NG4. . . . . .163 A2
  1 Gainsborough DN21. . .15 F1
Blackthorn Dr
  5 Mansfield NG18. . . . .102 C5
  Nottingham NG6 . . . . . . .160 B4
Blackthorne Cl NG24 . . . . . .140 B5
Blackthorne Dr NG14 . . . . .150 D2
Blackthorn Gdns
  NG21. . . . . .89 F5
Blackthorn Way NG17. . . . .100 C1
Blackwell Rd NG17 . . . . .99 E3
Blackwith Ave DE7. . . . . . . .157 F5
Blades Dr LN1 . . . . .57 A5
Bladon Cl NG3. . . . . .161 E2
Bladon Rd NG11. . . . . .196 B7
Blair Ct **4** NG2 . . . . .173 C1
Blair Gr NG10. . . . . .182 A4
Blaise Cl NG11 . . . . .195 E8
Blake Cl
  Arnold NG5 . . . . .162 A7
  Nottingham NG14 . . . . . .173 E5
Blake Cres NG18. . . . . .102 E7
Blake Ct NG10. . . . . .193 B5
Blakeney Cl NG19 . . . . .88 E4
Blakeney Dr NG18 . . . . .102 C4
Blakeney Rd NG12 . . . . . . .176 B3
Blakeney Wlk NG5 . . . . . . .161 F5
Blake Rd
  Stapleford NG9 . . . . .182 E6
  West Bridgford NG2 . . . . .186 A7
Blake St
  Ilkeston DE7 . . . . .157 F1
  Mansfield Woodhouse
  NG19. . . . . .88 B2
Blandford Ave NG10 . . . . . .193 B5
Blandford Dr DN22 . . . . .39 D4
Blandford Gdns NG2. . . . . .185 C5
Blandford Rd NG9 . . . . .183 C5
Bland La NG14. . . . . .150 A5
Blankney St **4** NG5. . . . . .160 E4
Blants Cl NG16. . . . . .158 F6
Blantyre Ave NG5. . . . . . . .146 E1
Blatherwick Cl **3**
  NG15. . . . . .146 B8
Blatherwick Rd NG24 . . . . .140 D8
Blatherwick's Yd NG5. . . . .161 F8
Bleaberry Cl NG2 . . . . .186 C5
Bleachers Yd NG7 . . . . .160 F1
Bleak Hills La NG18. . . . . . .101 E4
Bleak Hills Lane NG18. . . . .102 A4
Bleak Hill Way NG18. . . . . .101 E4
BLEASBY 152 B8
Bleasby CE Prim Sch
  NG14 . . . . .151 F8
Bleasby Cres NG17. . . . . . .101 B1
Bleasby Rd NG14 . . . . .151 D8
Bleasby Sta NG14. . . . . . . .151 F8
Bleasdale Cl NG4 . . . . .163 A2
Bleinheim Pk NG6. . . . . . . .145 E1
Blencathra Cl NG2. . . . . . . .186 C5
Blenheim Ave
  Fernwood NG24. . . . . . . .141 A3
  Lowdham NG14 . . . . .150 E1
  Nottingham NG3 . . . . . . .162 C2
Blenheim Cl
  Mansfield NG19. . . . . .88 D1
  Ruddington NG11. . . . . . .196 B7
  Skellingthorpe LN6 . . . . . .71 F4
Blenheim Gdns NG13 . . . . .165 D2
Blenheim Ind Est NG6 . . . .159 E7
Blenheim La NG6, NG15 145 E1
Blenheim Pk Rd
  Nottingham NG16 . . . . . .159 E8
  Nottingham NG15 . . . . . .145 E1
Blenheim Pl NG17. . . . . .99 E3
Blenheim Rise
  Bawtry DN10 . . . . .9 F6
  Worksop S81. . . . . .35 E8
Blenheim Terr NG10 . . . . . .182 B4
Blessed Robert
  Widmerpool CV Acad
  NG11. . . . . .195 E8
Bletchley Cl NG9 . . . . .171 E1
Bley Ave LE12 . . . . .214 D8
BLIDWORTH 118 B4
Blidworth Ind Pk NG21. . . .118 B6
Blidworth Rd
  Blidworth NG21. . . . . . . .133 C8
  Mansfield NG21. . . . . . . .103 D1
  Rainworth NG21 . . . . . . .104 A1
Blidworth Oaks Primary
  Sch NG21 . . . . .118 A5
Blidworth Rd
  Farnsfield NG22. . . . . . . .119 D6
  Kirkby-in-Ashfield NG15. .115 E4
Blidworth Waye NG15. . . . .131 F7

Bee–Bli 227

Blind La
Keyworth NG12 . . . .**197** E2
Oxton NG25 . . . .**134** C4
Bloomgrove Dr DE7 . . . .**157** F2
Bloomsbury Dr NG16 . . .**159** E3
Bloomsbury Gdns
NG18 . . . .**102** E4
Bloomsgrove Ind Est
NG7 . . . .**222** B3
Bloomsgrove Rd NG7 . . .**222** B3
Bloomsgrove St NG7 . . .**222** B3
Blossom Ct NG17 . . . . . .**115** C6
Blossom Gdns NG12 . . . .**188** A5
Blossom Gr DN22 . . . .**40** A3
Blue Albion St NG20 . . . . .**39** D4
Blue Barn La **59** C3
Bluebell Ave NG12 . . . . . .**188** A5
Bluebell Bank NG13 . . . .**177** D3
Bluebell Cl
Carlton in Lindrick S81 . . .**26** A7
Hucknall NG15 . . . .**145** C6
Selston NG16 . . . .**128** F2
Shirebrook NG20 . . . .**72** D3
Stanton Hill NG17 . . . . . .**100** B6
Blue Bell Ct DN22 . . . .**19** B4
Bluebell Dr NG24 . . . . . .**140** A4
Bluebell Gr 2 NG17 . . . .**114** F7
Blue Bell Hill Prim Sch
NG3 . . . .**173** F6
Blue Bell Hill Rd NG3 . . .**173** E6
Bluebell Pl NG19 . . . .**88** F4
Bluebells The NG17 . . . .**101** B1
Bluebell Wlk NG4 . . . . . .**125** E1
Bluebell Wood La
Clipstone NG21 . . . .**89** F4
Mansfield NG19 . . . .**89** F5
Bluebell Wood Way
NG17 . . . .**100** C1
Bluebell Wy NG16 . . . . . .**143** B1
Blue Bell Yd NG22 . . . .**66** F5
Bluebird Ave NG22 . . . . . .**77** C2
Bluecoat Aspley Acad
NG8 . . . .**172** C8
Bluecoat Beechdale Acad
. . . .**172** A7
Bluecoat Beechdale Acad
The NG8 . . . .**171** F7
Bluecoat Cl NG1 . . . .**223** E3
Bluecoat Prim Acad
NG9 . . . .**171** F4
Bluecoat St NG1 . . . .**223** E4
Blundell Cl NG3 . . . .**173** F8
BLYTH **18** A3
Blyth Cl NG19 . . . .**87** D1
Blyth Ct NG19 . . . .**87** D1
Blyth Gdns
Blyth S81 . . . .**18** B2
Nottingham NG3 . . . .**161** E2
Blyth Gr
Worksop S81 . . . .**35** F5
Worksop S81 . . . .**36** A5
Blyth Hall S81 . . . .**18** A3
Blyth Rd
Blyth, Bilby S81, DN22. . . .**27** E5
Blyth, Nornay S81 . . . .**18** A7
Carlton in Lindrick DN22 . .**26** E3
Elkseley S80 . . . .**48** F4
Firbeck S81 . . . .**16** C7
Harworth DN11 . . . .**8** F3
Hodsock S81 . . . .**27** A7
New Ollerton NG22 . . . .**77** A6
Oldcotes S81 . . . .**16** F6
Ranskill DN22 . . . .**19** A4
Walesby DN22 . . . .**63** A3
Worksop, Kilton S81 . . . . . .**36** B6
Blyth St NG3 . . . .**161** E2
Blyton Rd DN21 . . . .**15** C4
Blyton Wlk NG5 . . . .**161** B7
Boar La NG24 . . . .**139** F8
Boat La
Aldercar NG16 . . . .**143** A7
Bleasby NG14 . . . .**152** C7
Bleasby NG14 . . . .**152** E8
Hoveringham NG14 . . . . . .**151** E2
Boatmans Cl DE7 . . . .**157** F2
Boatswain Dr 1 NG15 . .**146** B8
BOBBERS MILL **172** E7
Bobbers Mill Bridge
DN21 . . . .**15** F2
Bobbinsforth Way 7
. . . .**15** F2
Boden Dr NG16 . . . .**159** C6
Boden St NG7 . . . .**222** B3
Bodill Gdns NG15 . . . . . .**146** C6
Bodmin Ave NG15 . . . . . .**145** C5
Bodmin Ct 5 NG18 . . . . .**103** C4
Bodmin Dr NG8 . . . .**160** C2
Body Rd NG9 . . . .**183** B2
Bofors Rd LE14 . . . .**219** A5
Bogg La NG22 . . . .**64** A1
Bohem Rd NG10 . . . .**182** C3
Boilerhouse Rd LE14. . . .**219** A4
Bold Cl NG6 . . . .**160** B8
BOLE **23** E3
Bole La DN22 . . . .**23** D3
Bolero Cl NG8 . . . .**171** E5
Bolham La DN22 . . . .**29** F1
Bolingey Way NG15 . . . .**145** C5
Bollard's La LE12 . . . .**213** A3
Bolsover St
Hucknall NG15 . . . .**146** B7
Mansfield NG18 . . . .**102** D6
Bolton Ave NG9 . . . .**183** C4
Bolton Cl NG2 . . . .**186** A7
Bolton La LE14 . . . .**211** F7
Bolton Terr NG12 . . . .**175** F3

Bombard Rd LE14 . . . . . .**219** A5
Bond Cl
Loughborough LE11 . . . . . .**220** C1
Mansfield Woodhouse
NG19 . . . .**88** C6
Bond St
Arnold NG5 . . . .**161** E8
Nottingham NG2 . . . .**173** E4
Bonemill La
Clarborough DN22 . . . .**30** D2
Worksop S81 . . . .**35** D5
Bonetti Cl NG5 . . . .**162** C5
Boniface Gdns 4 NG5 . .**147** A1
Bonington Art Gall★
NG1 . . . .**223** D3
Bonington Dr NG5 . . . . . .**161** F7
Bonington Rd
Arnold NG5 . . . .**161** F4
Mansfield NG19 . . . .**101** E6
Nottingham NG3 . . . .**162** A3
Bonington Theatre★
NG5 . . . .**161** E8
Bonner Hill NG14 . . . . . .**148** F6
Bonner La NG14 . . . .**149** B6
Bonner'S La LE12 . . . . . .**158** C4
Bonnington Cl NG6 . . . . .**160** A6
Bonnington Cres NG5 . .**161** C4
Bonny Mead NG12 . . . . .**187** E2
Bonsal Cl NG18 . . . .**103** B6
Bonsall St NG10 . . . .**193** E8
Bonser Cl NG4 . . . .**174** E7
Bonser Cres NG17 . . . .**99** E2
Bonser Gdns NG17 . . . . .**100** C2
Bonser Hedge Ct NG10 .**193** B4
Booth Cl NG3 . . . .**223** F3
Booth Cres NG19 . . . .**87** D2
Booth's Ind Est The
DE7 . . . .**157** F2
Booth St NG19 . . . .**88** B3
Boots Yd NG17 . . . .**99** F3
Border Rd NG20 . . . .**73** A4
Borders Ave NG17 . . . . . .**114** E8
Borlace Cres NG9 . . . . . .**182** E6
Borman Cl NG6 . . . .**159** F5
Borough St DE74 . . . .**203** D2
Borrow Bread La NG14 .**152** B7
Borrowdale Cl NG2 . . . . .**186** D6
Borrowdale Dr NG10 . . .**193** A6
Borrowell DE74 . . . .**203** C3
Boscombe Rd S81 . . . .**35** C8
Boscowan Ct DE7 . . . . . .**157** F4
Bosden Ct NG8 . . . .**171** C6
Bosley Sq NG9 . . . .**184** A8
Bostocks La NG10 . . . . . .**182** A4
Bostock's La NG10 . . . . . .**182** A4
Boston St NG1 . . . .**223** F3
Boswell Cl
Kinoulton NG12 . . . .**200** A2
Mansfield NG18 . . . .**102** C3
Boswell St NG15 . . . .**159** C1
Bosworth Dr NG16 . . . . .**144** B3
Bosworth St NG19 . . . . . .**101** D7
Bosworth Way NG10 . . .**193** C6
Bosworth Wlk 10 NG2. .**173** B1
Botany Ave
Mansfield NG18 . . . .**101** F6
Nottingham NG3 . . . .**173** F7
Botany Cl NG11 . . . .**185** C2
Botany Mews NG14 . . . .**173** F7
BOTHAMSALL **63** D7
Bothe Cl NG10 . . . .**193** C6
BOTTESFORD **181** C3
Bottesford Bypass
NG13 . . . .**181** D1
Bottesford CE Prim Sch
NG13 . . . .**181** A3
Bottesford La NG13 . . . .**180** B5
Bottesford Sta NG13 . . . .**181** C2
Bottleacre La LE11 . . . . .**220** B6
Bottle La NG1 . . . .**223** E2
Bottom Gn LE14 . . . .**210** A1
Bottom Row
Mansfield NG19 . . . .**87** E6
Newark-on-Trent NG24 . .**140** B8
BOUGHTON **77** F5
Boughton Cl NG17 . . . . .**100** F5
Boughton Ind Est NG22 .**78** B5
Boughton Ppg Sta★
NG22 . . . .**77** D7
Boughton Rd S80 . . . .**35** A5
Boughton Water Works
NG22 . . . .**77** D7
Boulevard Ind Pk NG7. .**184** C7
Boundary Cres
Beeston NG9 . . . .**171** F1
Blidworth NG21 . . . .**118** A4
Boundary Ct NG24 . . . . .**139** F7
Boundary La NG16 . . . . .**143** C3
Boundary Rd
Beeston NG9 . . . .**183** B8
Newark-on-Trent NG24 . .**139** F7
West Bridgford NG2 . . . . .**185** F4
Boundary Row S80 . . . . . .**35** F2
Boundary Wlk NG20 . . . . .**58** F1
Bourne Ave
Kirkby-in-Ashfield
NG17 . . . .**115** B3
Selston NG16 . . . .**129** A7
Bourne Cl NG9 . . . .**171** D1
Bourne Dr NG15 . . . .**117** A2
Bourne Mews NG4 . . . . .**175** A6
Bourne St NG4 . . . .**175** A6
Bournmoor Ave NG7 . . .**184** B1
Bovill St NG7 . . . .**222** B4
Bovington Ct DN22 . . . . .**29** E1
Bowbridge Gdns NG13 .**181** A3

Bowbridge La
Balderton NG24 . . . .**140** B1
Bottesford NG13 . . . .**180** F3
Newark-on-Trent NG24 . .**140** A4
New Balderton NG24 . . . .**140** A3
Bowbridge Rd NG24 . . . .**140** A6
Bowden Ave NG6 . . . . . .**146** L4
Bowden Cl NG5 . . . .**161** D8
Bowden Dr NG9 . . . .**184** B6
Bowers Ave 6 NG3 . . . .**173** D7
Bowes Well Rd DE7 . . . .**157** E2
Bowland Cl NG3 . . . .**174** A7
Bowland Rd NG13 . . . . . .**177** C4
Bowler Ct 3 LE11 . . . . . .**220** C4
Bowling Gn Rd DN21 . . . .**15** B1
Bowling St NG18 . . . .**102** D6
Bowlwell Ave NG5 . . . . .**160** F8
Bowman Pl NG22 . . . .**92** D1
Bowness Ave NG6 . . . . . .**160** C2
Bowness Cl NG2 . . . .**186** C7
Bowne St NG17 . . . .**100** F3
Bowscale Cl NG2 . . . .**186** C5
Bow St NG19 . . . .**88** E4
Box Cres NG17 . . . .**114** F6
Boxley Dr NG2 . . . .**185** C4
Boxtree Ave NG15 . . . . . .**145** F6
Boyce Gdns NG3 . . . .**161** F1
Boycroft Ave NG3 . . . . . .**173** F8
Boyd Cl NG5 . . . .**148** A1
Boyer's Orch LE14 . . . . .**202** B3
Boyer St LE11 . . . .**220** C4
Boy La NG21 . . . .**76** B1
Boynton Dr NG3 . . . .**161** F1
Boythorpe Cl DE7 . . . . . .**157** F5
Bracadale Rd NG5 . . . . .**146** F1
BRACEBRIDGE **36** A3
Bracebridge S80 . . . .**36** B3
Bracebridge Ave S80 . . . .**36** B3
Bracebridge Ct S80 . . . . . .**36** A2
Bracebridge Dr NG8 . . . .**171** D7
Bracey Rise NG2 . . . .**185** E3
Bracken Ave NG22 . . . .**77** E6
Brackenbury Rd LN1 . . . . .**57** A5
Bracken Cl
2 Carlton NG4 . . . .**162** D2
Gainsborough DN21 . . . . . .**15** B3
2 Kirkby-in-Ashfield
NG17 . . . .**114** F6
Long Eaton NG10 . . . .**182** B1
Market Warsop NG20 . . . . .**74** C3
Nottingham NG8 . . . .**159** F1
Bracken Ct
Bilsthorpe NG22 . . . .**106** A5
Harworth DN11 . . . .**8** E4
Brackendale Ave NG5 . .**161** F8
Brackendale Dr NG22 . . . .**64** A2
Brackenfield Ave NG19 . .**88** E4
Brackenfield Dr NG16 . .**158** B7
Brackenfield Rise
NG15 . . . .**117** A3
Brackenfield Specl Sch
NG10 . . . .**182** B1
Bracken Hill NG18 . . . . .**103** A5
Bracken Hill La
Austerfield DN10 . . . .**3** F7
Misson DN10 . . . .**4** A5
Misson DN10 . . . .**4** A7
Bracken Hill Sch NG17 .**115** C5
Bracken La
Retford DN22 . . . .**40** B5
Retford DN22 . . . .**40** C7
Bracken Lane Prim Sch
DN22 . . . .**40** A5
Bracken Rd
Long Eaton NG10 . . . .**182** B1
Shirebrook NG20 . . . .**72** D3
Bracken Way
Harworth DN11 . . . .**8** D4
Harworth DN11 . . . .**8** E4
Brackenwood Cl NG19 . .**89** A1
Brackhills LE11 . . . .**88** E1
Bracknell Cres NG8. . . . .**160** D1
Brackner La NG22 . . . . . .**106** B3
Bracton Dr NG3 . . . .**173** F6
Bradbourne Ave NG11 .**185** A5
Bradbury Gd NG3 . . . . . .**196** F2
Bradbury St NG2 . . . .**174** A4
Bradden Ave NG9 . . . .**170** E1
Bradder Way NG18 . . . . .**102** A5
Braddock Cl NG7 . . . .**222** A2
Bradfield Rd NG8 . . . .**159** F1
Bradford Way NG6 . . . . .**147** B6
Bradforth Ave NG18. . . . .**103** A7
Bradgate Cl NG10 . . . . . .**182** B4
Bradgate Rd 2 NG7 . . . .**173** A8
Bradleys Orch NG14 . . . .**151** C2
Bradley St NG10 . . . .**182** C5
Bradleys Yard 3
NG20 . . . .**74** B4
Bradman Gdns NG5. . . . .**162** B6
BRADMORE **196** F3
Bradmore Ave NG11 . . . .**196** C8
Bradmore Bsns Pk
NG11 . . . .**196** F1
Bradmore Ct NG18. . . . . .**103** A3
Bradmore La NG12. . . . . .**197** D5
Bradmore Rd NG12 . . . . .**207** C4
Bradmore Rise NG5 . . . .**161** C4
Bradshaw Ct NG12 . . . . .**200** A2
Bradshaw St NG10 . . . . .**193** B5
Bradshaw Way DN21. . . . .**24** E7
Bradstone Dr NG5 . . . . . .**162** D6
Bradwell Cl NG16 . . . .**158** C8
Bradwell Dr NG5. . . . .**161** A8
Braeburn Mws DN10 . . . . .**10** A7
Braefell Cl NG2 . . . .**186** D5
Braemar Ave NG16 . . . . .**143** F1
Braemar Dr NG4 . . . .**163** B1
Braemar Rd
Clipstone NG19 . . . .**89** E3
Nottingham NG6 . . . .**160** C7

Brailsford Ct
Harworth DN11 . . . .**8** E4
Mansfield NG18 . . . .**103** B6
Brailsford Rd 1 NG7 . . .**172** E1
Brailsford Way NG9. . . . .**183** C1
Brailwood Cl NG22. . . . . .**106** A6
Brailwood Rd NG22 . . . . .**106** A6
Brake La
Boughton NG22 . . . .**77** E8
Walesby NG22 . . . .**63** D1
Brake View NG22 . . . .**77** E6
Bramber Gr NG11 . . . . . .**195** E7
Bramble Cl
Beeston NG9 . . . .**183** D2
Bilsthorpe NG22 . . . .**106** A5
Clipstone NG21 . . . .**89** E3
Long Eaton NG10. . . . .**182** B1
New Ollerton NG22 . . . .**77** D6
North Leverton with
Habblesthorpe DN22. . . . .**42** D8
Nottingham NG6 . . . .**160** D3
Shirebrook NG20 . . . .**72** E6
South Normanton DE55 . . .**113** B6
Bramble Croft NG17 . . . .**100** C1
Bramble Ct
Carlton NG4 . . . .**162** F1
2 Sandiacre NG10 . . . . .**182** C6
Stapleford NG10 . . . .**182** C6
Bramble Dr NG3 . . . .**174** B8
Bramble Gdns NG8 . . . . .**172** A8
Bramble Gr NG15 . . . .**130** F1
Bramble La NG18 . . . .**103** A5
Bramble Rd DN22 . . . .**40** B4
Brambles The
Newton on Trent LN1. . . . . .**55** A1
Retford DN22 . . . .**39** F7
Walesby NG22 . . . .**64** A2
Brambleway NG12 . . . . .**188** A2
Bramble Way DN11 . . . .**8** E4
Brambling Cl NG18 . . . . .**102** E7
Brambling Rd NG4 . . . . . .**175** C7
Bramblings The S81 . . . . .**35** C7
BRAMCOTE **183** A7
Bramcote Ave NG9 . . . . .**183** D6
Bramcote CE Prim Sch
NG9 . . . .**183** B8
Bramcote Ct NG18 . . . . .**103** A3
Bramcote Dr
Beeston NG9 . . . .**183** E7
Nottingham NG8 . . . .**171** B8
Retford DN22 . . . .**39** D5
Bramcote Dr W NG9 . . . .**183** D7
BRAMCOTE HILLS **171** C2
Bramcote Hills Coll
NG9 . . . .**171** B2
Bramcote Hills Prim Sch
NG9 . . . .**171** B1
Bramcote La
Beeston NG9 . . . .**183** C5
Nottingham NG8 . . . .**171** D3
Bramcote L Ctr NG9. . . . .**171** A1
Bramcote Park Bus & Ent
Sch The NG9 . . . .**171** A1
Bramcote Rd NG9 . . . . . .**183** E7
Bramcote St NG7 . . . .**222** A3
Bramcote Wlk NG7 . . . . .**222** A3
Bramerton Rd NG8. . . . . .**171** D6
Bramhall Rd NG8 . . . .**171** C6
Bramley Cl
East Bridgford NG13 . . . .**165** D3
East Leake LE12 . . . .**205** E1
Gunthorpe NG14 . . . .**165** A5
Southwell NG25 . . . .**136** F8
Wymeswold LE12 . . . .**216** D3
Bramley Ct
Gainsborough DN21 . . . . . .**15** C1
Kimberley NG16 . . . .**158** F6
Sutton in Ashfield NG17 . .**100** F3
Bramley Rd
Long Eaton NG10 . . . .**193** B5
Nottingham NG8 . . . .**159** E1
Bramley Way DN10 . . . . . .**14** B8
Bramley Wlk NG19 . . . . .**101** D7
Bramling Cross Mws
S81 . . . .**25** C1
Brammersack Cl NG23 .**124** B7
Brampton Ave DE75. . . . .**143** A2
Brampton Cl NG22 . . . . . .**106** C7
Brampton Ct 14 DE7 . . . .**157** F5
Brampton Dr NG9 . . . . . .**182** F5
Brampton La LN1 . . . .**44** C4
Bramwell Dr NG9 . . . .**183** C6
Brancaster Cl NG6 . . . . . .**160** B4
Brancliffe La S81 . . . .**34** F7
Brand La NG17 . . . .**100** C5
Brandon Cl NG24 . . . .**140** E4
Brandon Walk NG17 . . . .**114** D8
Brandreth Ave
Nottingham NG3 . . . .**173** F8
Sutton in Ashfield NG17 . .**100** D4
Brandreth Dr NG16 . . . . .**158** A8
Brands Cl 15 DE7 . . . . . .**157** F5
Brand St NG2 . . . .**173** F2
Brandyline Gdns NG16 .**144** B3
Branklene Cl NG16. . . . . .**158** E7
Branksome Wlk 3
NG2 . . . .**173** C2
Bransdale S81 . . . .**36** A8
Bransdale Ave NG19 . . . . .**88** E3
Bransdale Cl NG10 . . . . .**193** B6
Bransdale Hts NG19. . . . . .**88** E1
Bransdale Rd NG11. . . . . .**184** D1
Branston Ave NG22 . . . . .**119** F6
Branston Cl NG24 . . . . . .**125** D4
Branston Gdns NG2. . . . .**185** D4
Branston Wlk NG5 . . . . . .**161** C4
Brantford Ave NG7 . . . . .**184** D2
Brantingham Gdns DN10 .**3** A4
Brassington Cl NG16 . . . .**158** B7

Brassington Ct NG19. . . .**88** E4
Bratton Dr 3 NG5 . . . . .**161** A5
Braunton Cl NG15 . . . . . .**145** D6
Braunton Cres NG5 . . . . .**162** D6
Bray Ct S81 . . . .**34** F8
Brayton Cres NG6. . . . . . .**160** D5
B Rd NG9 . . . .**184** D6
Breach Rd DE75 . . . .**157** A8
Breadsall Ct DE7 . . . .**157** F3
Break La
Papplewick NG15 . . . .**131** F4
Papplewick NG15 . . . .**132** A4
Breamer Rd NG23 . . . . . .**112** B8
BREASTON **193** A8
Brechin S81 . . . .**36** B5
Brechin Cl NG5 . . . .**148** B1
Brechin Ct NG19 . . . .**88** B6
Brechbank NG19 . . . .**88** E1
Breck Bank NG22 . . . .**77** C5
Breck Bank Cres NG22 . .**77** C5
Breck Hill Rd NG3 . . . . . .**161** F4
Breck La DN10 . . . .**20** A8
Brecknock Dr NG10. . . . .**193** A7
Brecks La
Elston NG23 . . . .**154** B1
Shelton NG23 . . . .**168** C8
Stapleford LN6 . . . .**127** E8
Brecks Plantation Nature
Reserve★ NG11 . . . .**195** D8
Brecks Rd DN22 . . . .**39** D3
Breckswood Dr NG11 . . .**195** E7
Brecon Cl
4 Long Eaton NG10. . . . .**193** A8
Nottingham NG8 . . . .**160** A3
Rainworth NG21 . . . .**104** C1
Breconshire Gdns NG6 .**160** E5
Bredon St NG10 . . . .**182** C6
Brendon Cl NG9 . . . .**183** B8
Brendon Dr
Kimberley NG16. . . . .**158** F7
Nottingham NG8 . . . .**172** A5
Brendon Gdns NG8 . . . . .**172** A5
Brendon Gr NG13 . . . .**177** C5
Brendon Rd NG8 . . . .**172** A5
Brendon Way NG10. . . . .**182** A1
Sandiacre NG10 . . . .**182** C6
Saxilby LN1 . . . .**57** B3
Worksop S80 . . . .**35** E2
Brentcliffe Ave NG3. . . . .**174** A7
Brentnall Cl NG10 . . . . . .**193** B7
Bretby Ct NG18 . . . .**103** B6
Brett Cl NG15 . . . .**145** E5
Bretton Rd NG15. . . . .**117** B3
Brettsil Dr NG11 . . . .**196** B7
Brewers Way NG18 . . . . .**102** F5
Brewer's Wharf NG24. . .**124** F1
Brewery La
Everton DN10 . . . .**11** C3
Retford DN22 . . . .**39** F4
Brewery St NG16 . . . .**158** F6
Brewhouse Yd Mus-The
Mus of Nottingham Life★
NG7 . . . .**223** D1
Brewill Gr NG11 . . . .**185** A5
Brewster Rd DN22 . . . .**24** F6
Brewsters Cl NG13. . . . . .**177** E4
Brewsters Rd NG3 . . . . . .**173** F8
Brewsters Way DN22 . . . .**29** C1
Brewsters Wlk DN10 . . . . .**10** A8
Brian Clough Way
Stapleford NG9 . . . .**182** D5
Stapleford NG9 . . . .**182** F5
Brian Clough Way
Eastbound NG10 . . . .**182** B4
Briar Ave NG10 . . . .**182** B3
Briarbank Ave NG3 . . . . .**174** A8
Briarbank Wlk NG3 . . . . .**174** A7
Briar Cl
Beeston NG9 . . . .**171** E1
Elkseley DN22 . . . .**50** B4
Hucknall NG15 . . . .**145** E5
Keyworth NG12 . . . .**197** F4
Rainworth NG21 . . . .**104** B1
Stanton Hill NG17 . . . . . .**100** C6
Worksop S80 . . . .**35** C2
Briar Ct
Harworth DN11 . . . .**8** E4
New Ollerton NG22 . . . .**77** C5
Nottingham NG2 . . . .**173** B1
Briar Gate
Cotgrave NG12 . . . .**188** A2
Long Eaton NG10 . . . .**182** B2
Briar Gdns NG14 . . . .**148** C8
Briar Gn DN11 . . . .**8** E4
Briar La NG18 . . . .**103** A4
Briar Lea
Retford DN22 . . . .**39** D4
Worksop S80 . . . .**35** C2
Briar Rd
Eastwood NG16 . . . .**158** B8
New Ollerton NG22 . . . .**77** C5
Briars The DN10 . . . .**4** B3
Briarwood Ave NG3 . . . . .**174** A7
Briarwood Ct NG19 . . . . . .**89** B1
Briarwood Ct NG3 . . . . . .**161** E3
Briber Hill
Blyth S81 . . . .**18** A1
Blyth S81 . . . .**27** A8
Briber Rd S81 . . . .**18** A2
Brich Gr LN1 . . . .**44** C1
Brickcliffe Rd LE12 . . . . .**205** F2
Brickenell Rd NG14 . . . . .**148** F8
Brickenhole La DN10 . . . .**13** F5
Brickley Cres LE12 . . . . .**205** F1
Brickyard NG15 . . . .**146** C6
Brickyard La
East Bridgford NG13 . . . . .**165** C4
East Leake LE12 . . . .**214** A3

Brickyard La *continued*
Farnsfield NG22 . . . .**120** B6
Misson DN10 . . . .**4** A2
Norton and Cuckney NG20 .**59** F5
Radcliffe on Trent NG12 . .**176** B3
South Normanton DE55. . .**113** A6
Sutton Bonington LE12 . . .**213** F8
Walkeringham DN10 . . . . . .**13** C6
Brick Yard La NG22 . . . . . .**93** F3
Brickyard Way DN11 . . . . .**9** A2
Brick Yd Rd DN22 . . . .**50** C6
Bride Church La DN11 . . .**8** A7
Bridegate La LE14 . . . . . .**209** E5
Bridge Ave NG9 . . . .**183** E5
Bridge Cl
Sutton Forest Side
NG17 . . . .**101** B3
Whitwell S80 . . . .**45** A5
Bridge Ct
Balderton NG24 . . . .**140** E4
Hucknall NG15 . . . .**146** A5
Bridge End Ave NG16 . . .**128** F8
Bridge Farm La NG7 . . . .**184** E1
Bridge Fields DE74. . . . . .**203** E3
Bridgegate DN22 . . . .**39** F7
Bridge Gn Wlk 6 NG8 . .**159** E1
Bridge Gr NG2 . . . .**185** E8
Bridge House Ct S81. . . . .**26** A5
Bridge La Ct DN10 . . . .**10** A6
Bridgeland Rd 10 LE11 .**220** B4
Bridgend Cl NG9 . . . .**182** D5
Brecon Cl
4 Long Eaton NG10. . . . .**193** A8
Nottingham NG8 . . . .**160** A3
Saxilby LN1 . . . .**57** B3
Worksop S80 . . . .**35** E3
Bridge Rd
Gainsborough DN21 . . . . . .**24** D7
Nottingham NG8 . . . .**171** D5
Bridge St
Gainsborough DN21 . . . . . .**24** C7
Ilkeston DE7 . . . .**157** F4
Langley Mill NG16 . . . . . .**143** C3
Long Eaton NG10 . . . .**182** D1
Loughborough LE11. . . . . .**220** A4
Mansfield NG18 . . . .**102** C4
Newark-on-Trent NG24 . .**139** F8
Sandiacre NG10 . . . .**182** C6
Saxilby LN1 . . . .**57** B3
Worksop S80 . . . .**35** E2
Bridgeway Ct NG2 . . . . . .**173** D2
Bridgeway Ctr NG2 . . . . .**173** C2
Bridgford Rd
Kneeton NG13 . . . .**165** F7
Kneeton NG13 . . . .**166** A8
West Bridgford NG2 . . . . .**185** F8
Bridgford St NG18 . . . . . .**102** F5
Bridgnorth Dr NG7 . . . . .**184** E2
Bridgnorth Way NG9. . . .**182** E3
Bridle Cl NG17 . . . .**100** B6
Bridle Rd
Beeston NG9 . . . .**183** B8
Burton Joyce NG14 . . . . . .**163** D6
Burton Joyce NG14 . . . . . .**163** E5
Bridlesmith Gate
Nottingham NG1 . . . .**223** E2
Newark-on-Trent NG24 . .**173** C4
Bridle Ways NG13. . . . . . .**165** D2
Bridleway The NG19 . . . . .**88** F1
Bridlington St NG7 . . . . .**172** F7
Bridon Cl DN22 . . . .**39** E4
Bridport Ave 4 NG8 . . . .**172** D5
Brielen Rd NG12 . . . .**176** A3
Brierfield Ave NG11 . . . .**185** B4
Brierley Forest Pk★
NG17 . . . .**100** D3
Brierley Gn NG4 . . . .**175** A7
Brierley Ind Est NG17 . .**100** D5
Brierley Pk Ck NG17 . . . .**100** E5
Brierly Cotts NG17. . . . . .**100** E3
Brierly Rd NG17 . . . .**100** D3
Brigg Inf Sch DE55. . . . . .**113** B6
Brightmoor St NG1 . . . . .**223** F3
Bright Sq NG19 . . . .**87** D2
Bright St
Gainsborough DN21 . . . . . .**24** C8
Ilkeston DE7 . . . .**157** E3
Kimberley NG16. . . . .**158** E6
Nottingham NG7 . . . .**222** A3
South Normanton DE55. . .**113** A5
Brimington Cl DE7 . . . . . .**157** F5
Brimington Ct NG19 . . . . .**88** E4
Brimstone Way S81. . . . . .**25** D1
Brindley Gr DN22 . . . .**29** A6
Brindley Rd NG8 . . . .**171** C5
Brinkhill Cres NG11 . . . .**184** F3
Brinkley Hill NG25 . . . . .**137** B6
BRINSLEY **143** E7
Brinsley Cl NG8 . . . .**160** A1
Brinsley Hill NG16 . . . . .**128** C2
Brinsley Prim Sch
NG16 . . . .**143** E8
Brinsley Way DN11 . . . . . .**9** B3
Brisbane Ct NG19 . . . .**88** C6
Brisbane Ct NG24 . . . . . .**140** E4
Brisbane Dr
Nottingham NG5 . . . .**160** E8
Stapleford NG9 . . . .**170** E1
Bristol Cl NG24 . . . .**125** E1
Bristol Rd DE7 . . . .**157** E1
Britannia Ave NG6 . . . . . .**160** E5
Britannia Cl NG16 . . . . . .**159** A7
Britannia Rd NG10 . . . . . .**182** D1
Britannia Terr DN21 . . . . .**24** C8
British Fields NG22 . . . . . .**65** D3
British Horological Inst★
NG23 . . . .**122** C2
Brittania Ct NG24 . . . . . .**139** E8
Britten Gdns NG3 . . . . . .**173** F6
Brixham Rd NG15 . . . .**145** D5
Brixton Rd NG7 . . . .**222** A3

Brixworth Way DN22 . . . . 40 B8
Broadacre Way **3** DE55. 99 B7
Broad Cl NG14 . . . . .149 C4
Broad Dr NG21 . . . . .76 B5
Broad Eadow Rd NG6 . .159 F7
Broad Fen La NG23 . . . . .156 B8
Broadfields NG18 . . . . . .148 F8
Broadgate NG9 . . . . .184 A4
Broad Gate NG22 . . . . . . .66 E7
Broadgate Ave NG9 . . . .184 A7
Broadgate La
    Beeston NG9 . . . . .184 A7
    Kelham NG23 . . . . .123 E6
    Kelham NG25 . . . . .122 F7
Broad Gores DN22 . . . . . .30 D3
Broadhill Rd DE74 . . . . .203 C2
BROADHOLME 57 B1
Broadholme Rd LN1 . . . .57 A2
Broadholme St NG7 . . . .222 B1
Broadhurst Ave NG6 . . .160 D2
Broading La NG22 . . . . . .93 A3
Broadings La DN22 . . . . .54 A6
Broad La
    Brinsley NG16 . . . . .143 E8
    Hodthorpe S80 . . . . .45 D6
    South Leverton DN22 . . .43 B6
Broadlands
    Sandiacre NG10 . . . . . .182 B3
    South Normanton DE55. .113 A4
Broadlands Cl NG17 . . . .101 B4
Broadleaf Cl NG11 . . . . .100 D2
Broadleigh Cl NG11 . . . .113 C5
Broadleigh Ct DN22 . . . .39 D4
Broad Marsh Sh Ctr
    NG1 . . . . .223 E2
Broadmead NG14 . . . . . .163 F5
Broad Meer NG12 . . . . . .187 E3
Broad Oak Cl NG3 . . . . .173 E7
Broad Oak Dr
    Brinsley NG16 . . . . .143 E8
    Stapleford NG9 . . . . . . .182 D6
Broadoak Pk NG17. . . . .114 F1
Broad Pl S80 . . . . .45 C6
Broad St
    Long Eaton NG10 . . . . .193 D7
    Loughborough LE11. . . .220 A4
    Nottingham NG1 . . . . . .223 F3
Broadstairs Rd NG9. . . .182 F2
Broadstone Cl NG2 . . . .185 C5
Broad Valley Dr NG6 . . .146 E4
Broadway
    Carlton NG4 . . . . .174 D6
    Ilkeston DE7 . . . . .157 E3
    Nottingham NG1 . . . . . .223 F2
Broadway E NG4 . . . . . .174 D6
Broadway Ind Est
    NG18 . . . . .102 C6
Broadway Media Ctr★
    NG1 . . . . .223 F2
Broadway The NG18 . . . .102 C6
Broad Wlk NG6 . . . . . . .160 C3
Broadwood Ct NG9 . . . .184 A8
Broadwood Rd NG5 . . . .161 B8
Brockdale Gdns NG12. . .197 E4
Brockenhurst Gdns
    NG3. . . . . .174 A6
Brockenhurst Rd
    NG19 . . . . .101 D6
Brockhall Rise DE75 . . .143 A1
Brockhole Cl NG2. . . . . .186 B6
Brockhurst Gdns NG3. . .173 F6
Brocklehurst Dr NG21. . .91 C8
Brocklesby Cl DN21. . . . .24 F7
Brocklewood Prim
    NG8 . . . . .171 F8
Brockley Rd NG2 . . . . . .186 B7
Brockton Ave NG24 . . . .139 B5
Brockwell The DE55 . . . .113 B4
Brockwood Cres NG12 . .197 E4
Brodhurst Cl NG14. . . . .149 C4
Brodwell Grove NG3 . . .161 F1
Bromfield Cl NG3. . . . . .174 C7
Bromhead St LE11 . . . . .220 C5
Bromley Ave NG24 . . . . .140 A4
Bromley Cl NG6 . . . . . . .160 B6
Bromley Pl NG1 . . . . . . .223 D2
Bromley Rd NG2 . . . . . .185 E6
Brompton Cl NG5. . . . . .147 A2
Brompton Way NG11. . . .185 C3
Bronte Cl NG10 . . . . . . .193 A4
Bronte Ct NG7 . . . . .222 C4
Bronte Gr LE12 . . . . . . .214 E7
Brook Ave NG5 . . . . . . .162 B8
Brook Cl
    Eastwood NG16 . . . . . .144 B1
    Long Eaton NG10 . . . . .193 E5
    Nottingham NG6 . . . . . .160 B6
Brook Cotts DE7 . . . . . .157 F3
Brook Ct NG16. . . . . . . .143 B2
Brookdale Cl NG5 . . . . .161 D5
Brookdale Rd NG17 . . . .101 B4
Brook Dr NG12 . . . . . . .199 F2
Brooke Cl
    Balderton NG24 . . . . . .140 D5
    Worksop S81 . . . . .36 C4
Brooke St
    Ilkeston DE7 . . . . .170 B6
    Sandiacre NG10. . . . . . .182 B5
Brook Farm Ct LE12 . . . .217 C7
Brookfield Ave
    Hucknall NG15 . . . . . . .145 F5
    Hucknall NG15 . . . . . . .146 A5
    Sutton in Ashfield NG17 .100 D4
Brookfield Cl
    Radcliffe on Trent
        NG12 . . . . .175 F3
    Radcliffe on Trent NG12 .175 F3
Brookfield Cres NG20. . . .72 E5
Brookfield Ct **8** NG2 . .173 C2

Brookfield Dr NG14 . . . .151 D3
Brookfield Gdns NG5 . . .162 A7
Brookfield Mws **1**
    NG10. . . . . .182 C6
Brookfield Rd NG5. . . . .162 A7
Brookfields Way LE12. . .205 E2
Brookfield Way DE75 . . .143 B1
Brook Gdns NG5. . . . . . .162 A8
Brookhill Ave NG15 . . . .113 D4
Brookhill Cres NG8 . . . .171 E3
Brookhill Dr NG8 . . . . . .171 E3
Brookhill Ind Est NG16 .113 D2
Brookhill La
    Pinxton NG16. . . . . . . .113 D4
    Pinxton NG16. . . . . . . .113 E5
Brookhill Leys Prim Sch
    NG16 . . . . .144 A2
Brookhill Leys Rd
    NG16 . . . . .143 E1
Brookhill Rd NG16 . . . . .113 D2
Brookhill St NG9. . . . . . .182 D6
Brook La
    Collingham NG23. . . . . .112 B8
    3 Gainsborough DN21. .15 F2
    Stanton-on-the-Wolds
        NG12. . . . . .198 E3
Brookland Ave NG18 . . .101 F7
Brookland Cl NG14 . . . .165 A5
Brookland Dr NG9 . . . . .183 D5
Brooklands NG12 . . . . . .208 C4
Brooklands Cl NG23 . . . .98 A1
Brooklands Cres NG4 . . .163 A1
Brooklands Dr NG4 . . . .163 A1
Brooklands Prim Sch
    NG10 . . . . .193 D7
Brooklands Rd NG3 . . . .174 B7
Brooklyn Ave NG14 . . . .163 E5
Brooklyn Cl NG6 . . . . . .160 D5
Brooklyn Rd NG6 . . . . . .160 D5
Brookside
    Clipstone NG19 . . . . . . .89 F2
    East Leake LE12 . . . . . .214 E8
    Eastwood NG16 . . . . . .143 F4
    Hucknall NG15. . . . . . .146 B5
    Lowdham NG14 . . . . . .150 D1
Brook Side **8** LE11 . . .220 A4
Brookside Ave
    East Leake LE12 . . . . . .205 D1
    Mansfield Woodhouse
        NG19 . . . . .88 C5
    Nottingham NG8 . . . . . .171 D2
Brookside Cl NG10. . . . .193 D7
Brookside Gdns NG11. . .196 B8
Brookside Rd NG11. . . . .196 B8
Brookside Way NG17 . . .99 F1
Brookside Wlk DN11. . . . .9 B4
Brook St
    Hucknall NG15. . . . . . .146 A7
    Nottingham NG1 . . . . . .223 F3
    Sutton in Ashfield NG17 .100 E2
    Tibshelf DE55. . . . . .99 A6
    Wymeswold LE12. . . . . .216 C3
Brook Terr S80 . . . . .35 E1
Brookthorpe Way
    NG11. . . . . .185 A4
Brookvale Cl NG16 . . . . .144 B3
Brook Vale Rd NG16 . . .143 C2
Brook View Dr NG12 . . .197 E1
Brook View Dr NG12 . . .197 E2
Brookview Lound Hall Sch
    DN22. . . . . .64 E7
Brookwood Cres NG4 . . .174 C7
Broom Cl
    Calverton NG14 . . . . . .148 F8
    Carlton in Lindrick S81 . .25 D1
    Tickhill DN11 . . . . .8 B7
    Worksop S81. . . . . .36 C8
Broome Acre DE55. . . . .113 C4
Broome Cl NG24 . . . . . .140 B5
Broomfield Cl NG10. . . .182 A5
Broomfield La
    Farnsfield NG22. . . . . . .119 F6
    Mattersey DN10 . . . . . . .19 E7
    Mattersey Thorpe DN10 . .20 A8
Broomhill Ave
    Ilkeston DE7 . . . . .170 A6
    Worksop S81 . . . . .35 B4
Broomhill Jun Sch
    NG15 . . . . .146 B5
Broomhill La
    Mansfield NG19 . . . . . . .87 F1
    Mansfield NG19 . . . . . . .101 F8
Broomhill Pk View
    NG15. . . . . .146 C5
Broomhill Rd
    Hucknall NG15. . . . . . .146 B4
    Kimberley NG16 . . . . . .159 A6
    Nottingham NG6 . . . . . .160 D6
Broom Hills LN1 . . . . . . .55 C5
Broom Rd NG14 . . . . . . .148 F8
Broomston La DN9 . . . . . .2 E2
Broom Wlk NG4 . . . . . . .174 B8
Brotts La NG23 . . . . .81 E6
Brotts Rd NG23 . . . . . . .81 F6
BROUGH. 112 B1
Brougham Ave NG19. . . .87 D2
Brough La
    Brough NG23. . . . . .112 B3
    Brough NG23. . . . . .112 C2
    Elkesley DN22. . . . . .50 B3
Brough Rd LN6 . . . . . . .127 A8
Broughton Cl
    Clipstone NG21 . . . . . . .89 F4
    Ilkeston DE7 . . . . .157 D2
Broughton Dr
    Newark-on-Trent NG24 . .139 E5

Broughton Dr continued
    Nottingham NG8 . . . . . .172 C3
Broughton Gdns NG24. . .140 E4
Broughton La LE14 . . . . .211 A2
Broughton Rd NG16 . . . .127 E2
Broughton St NG9 . . . . .183 F7
Broughton Way NG22 . . .78 A4
Brown Ave NG19. . . . . . .88 B4
Brown Cres NG17 . . . . . .101 A4
Brownes Rd NG13 . . . . .178 A5
Brownhill Cl NG12 . . . . .189 A4
Browning Cl
    Arnold NG5 . . . . .161 D7
    Worksop S81 . . . . .36 B5
Browning Rd NG24 . . . . .140 E5
Browning St **5** NG18 . .102 A7
Brown La
    Barton in Fabis NG11 . . .194 E6
    Thorney NG23 . . . . .70 B5
Brownley Rd NG21. . . . . .89 F5
Brownlow Cl NG23. . . . .153 D7
Brownlow Dr NG5 . . . . .146 F1
Brownlow's Hill NG24. . .126 A1
Brown Md NG8 . . . . . . .172 E8
Browns Croft NG6 . . . . .160 D3
Brown's Flats NG16 . . . .158 F7
Browns La
    Loughborough LE11. . . .220 A3
    Stanton-on-the-Wolds
        NG12. . . . . .198 D5
Brown's La NG13 . . . . . .165 C3
Browns Lane Bsns Pk
    NG12. . . . . .198 C1
Brownsmill Way NG8 . . .172 A6
Brown's Wood NG8 . . . .193 B8
Brown St
    Mansfield NG19 . . . . . . .101 F7
    Nottingham NG7 . . . . . .172 F7
Brown Wood La NG20 . . .70 B6
BROXHOLME 57 E8
Broxholme La LN1 . . . . . .57 C6
Broxton Rise NG8. . . . . .160 B3
Broxtowe Ave
    Kimberley NG16. . . . . . .158 D6
    Nottingham NG8 . . . . . .160 C2
Broxtowe Ctry Pk★
    NG8 . . . . .159 E3
Broxtowe Dr
    Hucknall NG15. . . . . . . .131 A1
    Mansfield NG18. . . . . . .102 C6
Broxtowe Hall Cl NG8 . .160 A2
Broxtowe La NG8 . . . . . .160 A2
Broxtowe Pk Bsns Ctr
    NG8 . . . . .159 E2
Broxtowe St **4** NG5 . .161 C2
Bruce Cl NG2 . . . . .173 D2
Bruce Dr NG2 . . . . .185 D7
Brunel Ave NG16 . . . . . .144 B3
Brunel Bsns Pk NG24. . .125 C1
Brunel Cl DN11 . . . . .8 F2
Brunel Dr NG24 . . . . . . .125 C2
Brunel Gate DN11 . . . . . .8 F2
Brunnen The DE55. . . . .113 B4
Brunner Ave NG20 . . . . .72 F3
Brunswick Dr NG9 . . . . .182 E5
Bruntings The NG18 . . . .102 F7
Brunts Bsns Ctr NG18 . .102 C8
Brunts Farm Ct NG23. . .156 F2
Brunts Sch The NG18. . . .88 D1
Brunts St NG18 . . . . . . .102 C6
Brush Dr LE11 . . . . .220 B6
Brushfield St NG7 . . . . .172 E7
Brussels Terr **1** DE7. .157 E1
Brusty Pl NG14 . . . . . . .163 E5
Bryans Cl
    Coddington NG24. . . . . .125 E2
    Styrrup DN11 . . . . .9 A2
Bryans Cl La DN10 . . . . . .3 F3
Bryant La DE55 . . . . . . .113 A5
Bryndale Cl DN11 . . . . . .9 C4
Brynsmoor Rd NG16 . . .143 E7
Bryony Way NG19. . . . . .88 F4
Buckfast Way NG2 . . . . .186 B7
Buckingham Ave NG15 . .146 B8
Buckingham Cl
    1 Kirkby-in-Ashfield
        NG17 . . . . .114 F6
    Mansfield Woodhouse
        NG19 . . . . .88 C5
Buckingham Ct
    Harworth DN11 . . . . .9 A5
    Sandiacre NG10. . . . . . .182 A3
Buckingham Dr NG12 . . .176 E3
Buckingham Rd
    Arnold NG5 . . . . .161 B5
    Sandiacre NG10. . . . . . .182 A3
Buckingham Rise S81. . . .35 E7
Buckingham Way
    NG16. . . . . .159 B7
Buckland Cl NG17 . . . . .101 B1
Buckland Dr NG14 . . . . .149 C4
Bucklee Dr NG14 . . . . . .148 E8
Bucklow Cl NG8 . . . . . . .160 D1
Buckminster Rd NG24. . .140 F3
Buck's La LE12 . . . . .213 A7
Buckthorn Dr NG13 . . . .178 F5
BUDBY 75 F8
Budby Ave NG18 . . . . . .102 F6
Budby Cres NG20 . . . . . .74 E8
Budby Rd
    Cuckney NG20 . . . . .60 B3
    Norton and Cuckney NG20 .61 A3
Budby Rise NG15 . . . . . .146 B7
BULCOTE 164 A6
Bulcote Dr NG14. . . . . . .163 D3
Bulcote Rd NG11 . . . . . .184 E3
Bulgrave Mews NG2 . . . .185 C3
Bulham La
    Sutton on Trent NG23 . . .81 A1
    Sutton-on-Trent NG23 . . .82 A1

Bullace Ct NG19 . . . . . . .88 E1
Bullace Rd NG3. . . . . . . .173 E7
Bull Cl Rd NG7 . . . . .184 F7
Bulldog La NG12 . . . . . .177 B6
Buller Cl NG23. . . . . .98 B1
Buller St DE7 . . . . .170 A6
Buller Terr **2** NG5 . . . .161 D3
Bullfinch Cl LE12 . . . . . .205 D5
Bullfinch Rd NG6 . . . . . .160 D4
Bullins Cl NG5 . . . . .147 C1
Bullivant Ave NG19 . . . .88 C5
Bullivant St NG3. . . . . . .223 F4
Bull Meadow NG14 . . . .148 C8
Bullock Cl NG19 . . . . . . .88 B5
Bullpit Rd NG24. . . . . . .140 D5
Bull Yd
    Southwell NG25 . . . . . . .121 E1
    Worksop S80 . . . . .35 E2
Bulstode Pl DE74 . . . . . .203 C2
BULWELL. 160 A6
Bulwell Acad NG16 . . . .160 C8
Bulwell Bsns Ctr NG6 . .160 A7
Bulwell Hall Pk Nature
    Reserve★ NG6 . . . . . . .146 B2
Bulwell High Rd NG6. . .160 B7
Bulwell La NG6 . . . . . . .160 D4
Bulwell St Mary's CE Prim
    Sch NG6 . . . . .160 C8
Bulwell Sta NG6 . . . . . .160 C6
Bulwer Rd
    Kirkby-in-Ashfield NG17 .114 F5
    Nottingham NG7 . . . . . .222 B3
Bumblebee Cl LE12 . . . .214 E7
Bumblebee La S81. . . . . .27 A6
Bunbury St NG2 . . . . . . .173 D1
Bungalow La NG2. . . . . .106 A5
Bunnison La NG12 . . . . .200 E7
BUNNY 206 E7
Bunny CE Prim Sch
    NG11. . . . . .206 E7
Bunny Hall Pk NG11. . . .206 E7
Bunny Hill LE12, NG11 . .206 D5
Bunny La
    East Leake NG11 . . . . . .205 E6
    Keyworth NG12. . . . . . .197 D2
Bunny Trad Est NG11 . . .206 D6
Bunting Dr NG11. . . . . . .196 B6
Buntings La NG4. . . . . . .174 C7
Bunting St **3** NG7 . . . .172 E1
Bunyan Gn Rd NG16 . . .128 D7
Burbage Ct NG18 . . . . . .103 B6
Burbank Ave NG17 . . . . .77 C3
Burberry Ave NG15 . . . .146 C4
Burden Cres DN22 . . . . . .53 B8
Burden La
    Harby LE14 . . . . .202 B3
    Shelford NG12 . . . . .164 C1
Burder St LE11 . . . . .220 C5
Burfield Ave LE11 . . . . .220 A3
Burford Prim Sch
    NG5. . . . . .161 C6
Burford Rd NG7 . . . . . . .172 F8
Burford St NG5. . . . . . . .161 E8
Burgage NG25 . . . . .121 E1
Burgage Green NG25 . . .121 E1
Burgage La NG25 . . . . . .121 E1
Burgass Rd
    Carlton NG4 . . . . .174 B7
    Nottingham NG4 . . . . . .174 A7
Burge Cl NG2. . . . . .173 C2
Burgh Cl DN21 . . . . .24 F7
Burgh Hall Cl NG9 . . . . .183 C2
Burhill NG12. . . . . .188 A2
Burke St NG7 . . . . .222 C3
Burleigh Cl NG4 . . . . . . .174 F7
Burleigh Ct NG22 . . . . . .65 F3
Burleigh Rd
    Loughborough LE11. . . .220 A4
    West Bridgford NG2 . . . .186 A6
Burleigh Rise NG22 . . . . .65 F3
Burleigh Sq NG9 . . . . . .183 C4
Burleigh St **1** DE7. . . .157 F1
Burley DN10. . . . . .13 E6
Burley Rise DE74 . . . . . .203 D1
Burlington Ave
    Nottingham NG5 . . . . . .161 B3
    Shirebrook NG20. . . . . . .72 F6
Burlington Dr NG19. . . . .87 F2
Burlington Rd
    Carlton NG4 . . . . .174 F8
    Nottingham NG5 . . . . . .161 C3
Burma Rd NG21. . . . . . .118 A6
Burmaston Rd NG18 . . . .103 B6
Burnaby St NG6 . . . . . . .160 D4
Burnaston Ct NG19 . . . . .88 E4
Burnbank Cl NG2 . . . . . .186 D5
Burnbreck Gdns NG8 . . .171 E4
Burndale Wlk NG5 . . . . .160 E8
Burneham Cl NG13 . . . . .165 C2
Burnell Cl NG23 . . . . . . .167 E7
Burnham Ave NG9 . . . . .183 F4
Burnham Ct NG18 . . . . .102 C4
Burnham St NG5 . . . . . .161 C2
Burnham Way NG1 . . . . .173 C3
Burnmoor La
    Egmanton NG22. . . . . . .79 F6
    Egmanton NG22. . . . . . .80 A7
    Egmanton NG22. . . . . . .80 B8
Burnor Pool NG14 . . . . .148 F7
Burns Ave
    Mansfield Woodhouse
        NG19 . . . . .88 C2
    Nottingham NG7 . . . . . .222 B1
Burnside Cl **9** NG17 . .114 F7
Burnside Dr
    Beeston NG9 . . . . .171 C4
    Nottingham NG8 . . . . . .171 B7
Burnside Green NG8. . . .171 D6
Burnside Grove NG12 . .186 D1

Burnside Rd
    Nottingham NG8 . . . . . .171 D6
    West Bridgford NG2 . . . .185 E5
Burns Rd S81. . . . . .36 B4
Burns St
    Gainsborough DN21 . . . .15 B2
    Mansfield NG18. . . . . . .102 A7
    Nottingham NG7 . . . . . .222 C4
Burns The NG20 . . . . . . .74 C5
Burntleys Rd DN22. . . . . .30 D7
Burnt Oak Cl NG16 . . . .159 D3
Burnt Oaks Cl LE12. . . . .85 D5
Burntstump Ctry Pk★
    NG5 . . . . .132 D1
Burntstump Hill NG5. . . .132 D2
Burnwood Ave NG18 . . .103 A3
Burnwood Dr NG8 . . . . .171 D5
Burr La **12** DE7. . . . . . .157 F1
Burrows Ave NG9 . . . . . .171 F1
Burrows Cres NG9 . . . . .171 F1
Burrows Ct NG3 . . . . . . .173 F5
Burrows Dr NG13 . . . . . .177 E6
Burrows The LE12 . . . . .205 E2
Burrows Way NG5 . . . . .147 C2
Burrow Wlk NG17 . . . . .114 E4
Bursar Way NG10 . . . . . .182 C3
Burtness Rd NG7 . . . . . .184 D1
Burton Ave NG4 . . . . . . .174 A7
Burton Cl
    Carlton NG4 . . . . .175 A8
    Harby LE14 . . . . .202 A3
Burton Dr
    Beeston NG9 . . . . .183 C6
    3 Retford DN22 . . . . .39 F6
BURTON JOYCE 163 E4
Burton Joyce Prim Sch
    NG14 . . . . .163 F4
Burton Joyce Sta
    NG14 . . . . .163 E3
Burton La
    Whatton NG13 . . . . . . .179 B4
    Wymeswold LE12. . . . . .216 B2
Burton Manderfield Ct **4**
    NG2. . . . . .173 C2
Burton Rd
    Carlton NG4 . . . . .175 A8
    Sutton in Ashfield NG17 .100 C3
Burton Rise
    Annesley NG17 . . . . . . .130 A8
    Annesley Woodhouse
        NG17 . . . . .115 A4
    Walesby NG22 . . . . .64 A1
Burton St
    Gainsborough DN21 . . . .24 D7
    Loughborough LE11. . . .220 B6
    Nottingham NG1 . . . . . .223 E3
Burton Wlk LE12 . . . . . .214 E8
Burton Wlks LE11. . . . . .220 B2
Burwell Cl NG19 . . . . . . .88 E4
Burwell St NG7 . . . . . . .222 B4
Bush Cl NG5. . . . . .161 C6
Bushmead Mews **4** S80 .35 F2
Bushy Cl NG10. . . . . . . .193 A6
Buskeyfield La NG20 . . . .59 F4
Butchers Wk NG22 . . . . .54 B5
Butchers Way **4** DE75 .143 A1
Bute Ave NG7 . . . . .222 B2
Butler Ave NG12 . . . . . .176 A4
Butler Cl NG12 . . . . .189 A6
Butler Cres NG19 . . . . . .87 D2
Butler Dr NG21 . . . . . . .117 F4
Butlers Cl NG15. . . . . . .146 C5
Butlers Field NG13 . . . . .190 C2
Butler's Hill Infant Sch
    NG15 . . . . .146 B5
Butterwood Cl **9**
    NG17. . . . . .114 E1
Buttercup Cl
    East Leake LE12 . . . . . .215 A8
    New Balderton NG24 . . .140 C5
Buttercup Meadow
    NG21 . . . . .90 A4
Butterfly Cl DE7 . . . . . . .157 F5
Butterfly Pl
    2 Eastwood DE7 . . . .157 F8
    Edwinstowe NG21 . . . . .76 C3
Butterhall Cl S80 . . . . . . .45 A5
Buttermarket Sh Ctr
    NG24 . . . . .139 F8
Buttermead Cl NG9 . . . .170 D2
Buttermere Cl
    Long Eaton NG10 . . . . .182 A2
    West Bridgford NG2 . . . .186 D7
Buttermere Ct
    Mansfield Woodhouse
        NG19 . . . . .88 E3
    1 Nottingham NG5. . .161 C2
Butterton Cl DE7 . . . . . .170 A7
Butterwick Cl NG19 . . . .88 F1
Buttery Gdns NG11 . . . .196 C6
Buttery La NG17 . . . . . . .100 F2
Butt Hill S80. . . . . .45 A8
Butt La
    East Bridgford NG13 . . .165 E2
    Mansfield Woodhouse
        NG19 . . . . .88 C2
    Maplebeck NG22 . . . . . .107 F7
    Normanton on S LE12 . .213 B4
Butt Rd NG13 . . . . .178 A4
Butts Cl DE7 . . . . .170 A4
Butt St NG10. . . . . .182 B5
Buxton Ave NG4 . . . . . . .162 D1
Buxton Cl NG5. . . . . . . .160 F8
Buxton Rd DN19 . . . . . . .87 D1
Buzzard Way LE12 . . . . .206 A3

Byard La NG1 . . . . .223 E2
Bycroft Rd DN21. . . . . . .15 C4
Bye Pass Rd
    Beeston NG9 . . . . .183 D3
    Gunthorpe NG14 . . . . . .164 F5
Bye Path Rd NG22 . . . . . .39 E8
Byfield Cl NG7 . . . . .222 B4
Byford Cl NG3 . . . . .161 E2
Byley Rd NG8 . . . . .171 B5
Bypass Rd NG13 . . . . . .177 D8
Byrne Ct NG5. . . . . .162 B5
Byron Ave
    Kirkby-in-Ashfield
        NG17 . . . . .115 B7
    Long Eaton NG10 . . . . .182 B3
    Mansfield Woodhouse
        NG19 . . . . .88 C2
    Sutton in Ashfield NG17 .101 B4
Byron Bsns Ctr **3**
    NG15 . . . . .146 B7
Byron Cl
    Darlton NG22 . . . . .67 A8
    Newark-on-Trent NG24 . .140 A6
    Newark-on-Trent NG4 . . .174 D5
Byron Cres
    Awsworth NG16 . . . . . .158 C4
    Ravenshead NG15 . . . . .116 E3
Byron Ct
    Balderton NG24 . . . . . .140 E3
    7 Nottingham NG2. . .173 E4
    Stapleford NG9 . . . . . . .170 E2
Byron Est NG5 . . . . .162 A7
Byron Fields NG15 . . . . .130 E6
Byron Gdns NG25 . . . . . .121 E1
Byron Gr NG5. . . . . .161 C3
Byron Rd
    Annesley NG15 . . . . . . .130 C8
    West Bridgford NG2 . . . .185 F7
Byron Square
    NG15. . . . . .146 B7
Byron St
    Arnold NG5 . . . . .161 E2
    Blidworth NG21 . . . . . . .118 B5
    Hucknall NG15. . . . . . .146 A6
    Ilkeston DE7 . . . . .157 F1
    Mansfield NG18. . . . . . .102 A7
    Newstead NG15. . . . . . .130 D6
    Shirebrook NG20. . . . . . .72 E4
Byron Way S81 . . . . .36 B4
Bythorn Cl NG17 . . . . . .101 B3

C

Cabin Leas **4** LE11 . . . .220 B5
Cabourn Dr NG13 . . . . . .177 D6
Caddaw Ave NG15 . . . . .146 A5
Caddow La
    Clarborough and Welham
        DN22 . . . . .41 C8
    Retford DN22 . . . . .31 C1
Caddow View DN22. . . . .32 D5
Cad La S81 . . . . .81 E7
Cadlan Cl NG5 . . . . .161 A7
Cadlan Ct **5** NG5 . . . .161 A7
Caenby Cl DN21 . . . . . . .24 F7
Caernarvon Pl NG9 . . . .183 B4
Cafferata Way
    Newark-on-Trent NG24 . .125 C1
    Newark-on-Trent NG24 . .140 C8
Caincross Rd NG8 . . . . .171 D7
Cairngorm Dr
    Mansfield NG19. . . . . . .102 D5
    Nottingham NG5 . . . . . .147 B2
Cairns Cl NG5 . . . . .161 A5
Cairnsmore Cl NG10 . . .182 A1
Cairns St NG7 . . . . .160 F1
Caister Rd NG11 . . . . . .195 E8
Caithness Ct **9** NG5 . .161 A5
Calcraft Dr NG13 . . . . . .181 D2
Calcroft Cl NG8 . . . . . . .160 C2
Caldbeck Cl NG2 . . . . . .186 C7
Caldbeck Ct NG9 . . . . . .183 B4
Caldbeck Wlk **1** NG5 . .161 C2
Calder Ave DN21 . . . . . . .15 F2
Calderdale NG8 . . . . . . .171 B3
Calderdale Dr NG10. . . .193 A6
Calder Gdns NG13 . . . . .177 D3
Calderhall Gdns **2**
    NG5. . . . . .161 C8
Calder Wlk **10** NG6 . . .160 B7
Caldon Gn NG6 . . . . . . .146 C2
Caldwell St **1** LE11 . . .220 A4
Caledonian Rd
    Retford DN22 . . . . .39 F5
    Retford DN22 . . . . .40 A5
Caledon Rd NG5 . . . . . .161 B3
California Rd NG24 . . . . .124 A4
California Rd NG24 . . . . .139 A4
Calke Ave NG17 . . . . . . .99 C2
Calladine Cl NG17 . . . . .100 D1
Calladine Gr NG17 . . . . .100 D1
Calladine La NG17 . . . . .114 C8
Calladine Pk NG17 . . . . .114 C8
Callaway Cl NG6 . . . . . .171 E5
Callerdale Gr NG22 . . . . .66 A2
Calley Ave DE7 . . . . .157 F6
Calstock Rd NG5 . . . . . .161 E5
Calveley Rd NG8 . . . . . .171 E8
Calver Cl NG8 . . . . .172 C4
Calver St NG19 . . . . .88 E4
Calvert Cl
    Beeston NG9 . . . . .183 D4
    Heanor NG16 . . . . .143 B3
CALVERTON 149 A7
Calverton Ave NG4. . . . .162 B1

Calverton Bsns Park
NG14 . . . . 148 F8
Calverton Cl NG9 . . . . .183 A2
Calverton Ct 3 NG18 . .103 A3
Calverton Dr NG8 . . . . .159 D2
Calverton Forum
Leisure Ctr NG4 . . . . 162 C1
Calverton Rd
Arnold NG5 . . . . .148 A2
Blidworth NG21 . . . . . .117 E2
Blidworth NG21 . . . . . .118 A2
Calverton Road Nature
Reserve★ NG5 . . . . .148 A3
Cambell Gdns NG5 . . . .148 C1
Camberley Cl NG6 . . . .160 A8
Camberley Rd NG6 . . . .160 A8
Camborne Cl DN22 . . . .29 E1
Camborne Cres DN22 . . .29 E1
Camborne Dr NG8 . . . .160 C2
Camborne Ms DN22 . . . .29 E1
Cambourne Gdns
NG15 . . . . .116 F2
Cambourne Pl NG18 . . .103 B2
Cambrai Terr S80 . . . . . .35 E4
Cambria Mews NG3 . . . .173 C7
Cambria Rd NG9 . . . . . .87 C4
Cambridge Cl NG21 . . . .118 B8
Cambridge Cres NG9 . . .170 D2
Cambridge Gdns NG5 . .162 B5
Cambridge Ms NG24 . . .140 E8
Cambridge Rd
Harworth DN11 . . . . 8 F4
Nottingham NG8 . . . . .172 A4
Rainworth NG21 . . . . . .118 A8
West Bridgford NG2 . . .186 A6
Cambridge St
Carlton NG4 . . . . .174 E8
Loughborough LE11 . . .220 B8
Mansfield NG18 . . . . . .102 A5
Camb's La DN22 . . . . . .31 D8
Camdale Cl NG9 . . . . . .183 B6
Camdale La NG4 . . . . . .140 F2
Camden Cl NG2 . . . . . .173 E4
Camelia Ave NG11 . . . .184 C1
Camelot Ave NG5 . . . . .161 A1
Camelot Cres NG11 . . . .196 B8
Camelot St NG11 . . . . . .87 D1
Camelot St NG11 . . . . . .196 B8
Cameo Cl NG4 . . . . . . .174 F6
Cameron La NG24 . . . . .140 E1
Cameron St NG5 . . . . . .161 C2
Camerons The NG11 . . . .101 D5
Camomile Cl NG5 . . . . .160 E7
Camomile Gdns 9
NG7 . . . . .172 E7
Campbell Cl
Nottingham NG6 . . . . .160 A1
Worksop S81 . . . . .35 F8
Campbell Dr NG4 . . . . .174 C8
Campbell Gr NG2 . . . . .223 F3
Campbell St
Gainsborough DN21 . . . .15 B1
Langley Mill NG16 . . . .143 C4
Nottingham NG3 . . . . .223 F3
Campden Gn NG7 . . . . .184 E2
Campion Cl NG20 . . . . .72 D3
Campion Gdns 6
NG17 . . . . .115 A3
Campion St NG5 . . . . . .161 E8
Campion Way NG13 . . . .177 D4
Camrose Cl NG8 . . . . . .171 F8
Canada Cl NG4 . . . . . . .175 C8
Canalbridge Cl LE11 . . .220 A5
Canal Ct LN1 . . . . .57 A3
Canal La
Harby NG13 . . . . .202 D5
Hose LE14 . . . . .211 C6
West Stockwith DN10 . . .7 D2
Canal Rd S80 . . . . .35 F3
Canal Side
Beeston NG9 . . . . .184 B3
Ilkeston DE7 . . . . .157 F1
Ilkeston DE7 . . . . .158 A2
Canalside Industrial
Park NG12 . . . . .189 A2
Canal St
Ilkeston DE7 . . . . .158 A1
Long Eaton NG10 . . . . .182 C1
Nottingham NG1 . . . . .223 E1
Retford DN22 . . . . .39 F6
Sandiacre NG10 . . . . . .182 C5
Canal Terr S80 . . . . .36 A3
Canary Dr NG22 . . . . . . .77 D6
Canberra Cl NG9 . . . . . .170 F1
Canberra Cres
Hucknall NG15 . . . . . .145 F5
Hucknall NG6 . . . . . . .145 D2
West Bridgford NG2 . . .185 D3
Canberra Dr NG13 . . . . .177 B7
Canberra Gdns NG2 . . .185 D3
Candleby Cl NG12 . . . . .187 F3
Candleby Ct NG12 . . . . .187 F3
Candleby La NG12 . . . . .187 F3
Candlemass Ct NG19 . . . .88 D2
Candle Mdw NG2 . . . . .174 D5
Canning Circ NG7 . . . . .222 C3
Cannock Way NG10 . . . .194 A7
Cannon Cl NG24 . . . . . .125 C1
Cannon Sq DN22 . . . . . .39 F8
Cannon St NG5 . . . . . . .161 C3
Canonbie Cl NG5 . . . . .161 D4
Canon Cook Cl LN1 . . . .57 A5
Canon's Cl NG25 . . . . . .121 F1
Canon Stevens Cl
NG23 . . . . .112 A7
Cantabury Ave NG7 . . . .172 E6
Cantelupe Gdns NG16 . .158 C8
Cantelupe Rd DE7 . . . .170 A8

Canterbury Cl
Mansfield Woodhouse
NG19 . . . . .88 C5
Nuthall NG16 . . . . . . .159 D3
Retford DN22 . . . . .39 E5
Worksop S81 . . . . .36 A7
Canterbury Ct NG1 . . . .223 D4
Canterbury Rd NG8 . . . .172 D5
Canterbury Wlk S81 . . . .25 E7
Cantley Ave NG4 . . . . . .162 E2
Cantrell Prim Sch NG6 .160 C7
Cantrell Rd NG6 . . . . . .160 C7
Canver Cl NG8 . . . . . . .171 C6
Canwick Cl NG8 . . . . . .171 C5
Canwick Way DN21 . . . . .15 E3
Cape Honey Way S81 . . .25 D1
Capenwray Gdns 3
Cape St NG18 . . . . .101 F7
Capes The NG13 . . . . . .178 F4
Capitol Ct 1 NG8 . . . . .172 A5
Caporn Cl NG6 . . . . . . .160 C5
Capps Pl NG22 . . . . .66 A2
Capt Ball Meml Homes
NG7 . . . . .222 A1
Caraway Dr NG20 . . . . . .72 D3
Carburton Ave NG20 . . . .74 D8
Carburton La NG20 . . . . .60 D5
Carburton Way NG17 . . .115 D2
CAR COLSTON 166 C2
Car Colston Rd
Car Colston NG13 . . . .166 E1
Scarrington NG13 . . . .178 F8
Screveton NG13 . . . . .166 D4
Cardale Rd
Nottingham NG3 . . . . .174 A6
Radmanthwaite NG19 . . .87 C4
Cardiff St 2 NG3 . . . . .173 F5
Cardigan Cl 5 NG3 . . . .173 C7
Cardinal Cl NG3 . . . . . .173 C7
Cardinal Hinsley Cl
NG24 . . . . .139 D4
Cardinal Way NG21 . . . . .90 D4
Carding Cl NG22 . . . . . .120 A5
Cardington Cl NG5 . . . .146 E1
Cardington Way NG24 . .140 A4
Cardle Cl NG19 . . . . .89 A2
Cardwell St NG7 . . . . . .172 F8
Car Dyke Ct NG13 . . . . .177 F5
Carew Rd NG7 . . . . . . .184 E2
Carey Rd NG6 . . . . .160 C8
Cariage Cl NG5 . . . . . . .161 D1
Carisbrook Ave NG18 . .103 A7
Carisbrooke Ave
Beeston NG9 . . . . .184 A8
Carlton NG4 . . . . .163 B1
Nottingham NG3 . . . . .161 C1
Carisbrooke Cl NG17 . . .115 C5
Carisbrooke Dr NG3 . . .161 C1
Car La NG13 . . . . .166 D2
Carlile Rd NG4 . . . . . . .174 E8
Carling Ave S80 . . . . . . .35 D3
Carlingford Rd NG15 . . .146 A8
Carlin St NG6 . . . . .160 B7
Carlisle Ave NG6 . . . . . .160 C7
Carlisle Mws 6 DN21 . . .15 D1
Carlisle St DN21 . . . . . .15 D1
Carlswark Gdns NG5 . .146 F1
CARLTON 162 D1
Carlton Acad The NG4 .162 C1
Carlton Bsns & Tech Ctr
NG4 . . . . .174 F7
Carlton Central Jun Sch
NG4 . . . . .174 D8
Carlton Cl
Clipstone NG19 . . . . . . .89 D3
Heanor DE75 . . . . .143 A3
Newark-on-Trent NG24 . .139 F6
Worksop S81 . . . . .35 E7
Carlton Cres LE12 . . . . .205 F2
Carlton Digby Sch
NG3 . . . . .162 C3
Carlton Dr NG10 . . . . . . .9 F6
Carlton Ferry La NG23 . . .97 C1
Carlton Fold 6 NG2 . . .173 F3
Carlton Forum L Ctr
NG4 . . . . .162 C1
Carlton Hall La S81 . . . .24 C5
Carlton Hill NG4 . . . . . .174 C7
Carlton Inf & Jun Acad The
NG4 174
CARLTON IN LINDRICK . .25 F5
Carlton La
Broxholme LN1 . . . . . . .57 F7
Norwell NG23 . . . . .96 C3
Norwell NG23 . . . . . . .110 A8
Sutton on Trent NG23 . . .97 A6
Carlton le Willows Acad
NG4 . . . . .163 A1
Carlton Mews NG4 . . . .174 C7
CARLTON-ON-TRENT . . .96 E4
Carlton Phoenix Ind Est
S80 . . . . .36 A4
Carlton Rd
Long Eaton NG10 . . . . .193 B5
Newark-on-Trent NG24 . .140 A5
Nottingham NG3 . . . . .173 C5
Ossington NG23 . . . . . .95 F6
Ossington NG23 . . . . . .96 A6
South Carlton S80 . . . . .25 F4
Worksop S80, S81 . . . . .35 F5
Carlton Sq NG4 . . . . . . .174 E7
Carlton St
Mansfield Woodhouse
NG19 . . . . .88 C1
Nottingham NG1 . . . . .223 F2
Carlton Vale Cl NG4 . . .162 D1
Carlyle Ct NG12 . . . . . .185 E7

Carlyle Rd NG2 . . . . . . .185 E7
Carman Cl NG16 . . . . . .159 A8
Carmel Gdns NG5 . . . . .161 F6
Carmelita Ave 1 NG24 .140 F2
Canaby Cl NG1 . . . . . . .223 D4
Carnarvon Cl NG13 . . . .177 E5
Carnarvon Dr NG14 . . . .164 A5
Carnarvon Gr
Carlton, Gedling NG4 . . .162 F1
Carlton, Thorneywood
NG4 . . . . .174 D8
Sutton in Ashfield NG17 . .100 B3
Carnarvon Pl NG2 . . . . .177 D4
Carnarvon Prim Sch
NG13 . . . . .178 B4
Carnarvon St
Carlton NG4 . . . . .175 A6
Teversal NG17 . . . . . . .100 B7
Carnation Rd NG20 . . . . .72 C3
Carnelian Dr NG17 . . . .114 D8
Carnell La NG24 . . . . . .140 F1
Carnforth Cl NG21 . . . . .182 D5
Carnforth Ct 1 NG5 . . .161 C8
Carnoustie S81 . . . . .36 B5
Carnoustie Cl 7 NG17 . .114 E7
Carnwood Rd NG5 . . . . .161 A5
Carolgate DN22 . . . . . . .39 F6
Carolgate Ct 4 DN22 . . .39 F6
Caroline Cl NG5 . . . . . .117 B3
Caroline Ct DE7 . . . . . .170 A6
Caroline Wlk NG3 . . . . .173 D6
Carpenter Ave NG19 . . . .87 D2
Carpenters Cl
Cropwell Butler NG12 . . .189 B6
Kirton NG22 . . . . .77 F5
Carradale Cl NG5 . . . . .162 C8
Carr Farm Rd NG17 . . . .114 F1
Carrfield Ave NG10 . . . .182 F1
Carrfield Cl NG17 . . . . . .100 D3
Carrgate La NG23 . . . . .153 E5
Carrgate La Track
NG23 . . . . .154 A3
Carr Gr NG17 . . . . .114 E5
CARR HILL 11 A4
Carr Hill Prim Sch
DN22 . . . . .29 F1
Carr Hill Way DN22 . . . .29 F1
Carr La
Blyton DN21 . . . . .15 C8
Doddington LN6 . . . . . .71 B3
East Stockwith DN21 . . . .7 E1
Gainsborough DN21 . . . .24 C6
Market Warsop NG20 . . .74 A4
Misterton DN10 . . . . . . .6 E2
South Normanton DE55 . .113 A7
Styrrup DN11 . . . . .8 D1
Styrrup DN11 . . . . .17 D8
Upton NG23 . . . . .122 F1
Upton NG23 . . . . .138 A8
Carrock Ave DE75 . . . . .143 B1
Carroll Gdns NG2 . . . . .173 C1
Carr Rd
Bingham NG13 . . . . . . .178 B5
Gringley on the Hill DN10 .12 C6
Retford DN22 . . . . .39 E6
Carr View DN10 . . . . . . .11 C3
Carsic La NG17 . . . . . . .100 E3
Carsic Rd NG17 . . . . . . .100 D4
Carsington Ct NG19 . . . .88 E3
Carson Rd DN21 . . . . . . .15 C2
Carswell Cl NG24 . . . . .139 F6
Cartbridge NG12 . . . . . .187 F2
Carter Ave
Radcliffe on Trent
NG12 . . . . .176 B3
Ruddington NG11 . . . . .196 C6
Carter Gate NG24 . . . . .139 F8
Carter La
Mansfield NG18 . . . . . .102 A6
Shirebrook NG20 . . . . . .72 E4
Warsop Vale NG19 . . . . .73 C4
Carter La E DE55 . . . . . .113 C6
Carter La W
Shirebrook NG20 . . . . . .72 D4
South Normanton DE55 . .113 C5
Carter Rd NG9 . . . . .183 A3
Carters Wood Dr NG16 . .159 F3
Carton Rd S81 . . . . .26 A5
Cartwright Cl NG22 . . . . .54 A2
Cartwright La DE55 . . . .113 D7
Cartwright St
Loughborough LE11 . . . .220 C5
Shireoaks S81 . . . . . . .34 F7
Cartwright Way
Beeston NG9 . . . . .183 F5
Beeston NG9 . . . . .184 A5
Carver Cl NG21 . . . . .76 B1
Carver's Hollow NG22 . .120 A2
Carver St NG7 . . . . .172 F8
Carwood Rd NG9 . . . . . .171 D1
Caskgate St DN21 . . . . . .24 C8
Casper Ct 10 NG5 . . . . .161 A8
Caspian Cl 4 NG19 . . . . .88 F2
Castellan Rise NG5 . . . .161 C8
Casterton Rd NG5 . . . . .161 B7
Castle Brewery Ct
NG24 . . . . .139 F7
Castlebridge NG2 . . . . .173 A2

Castlebridge Office Village
NG2 . . . . .173 A2
Castle Bridge Rd NG2 . .173 A2
Castle Cl
Bottesford NG13 . . . . .181 D2
Calverton NG14 . . . . . .148 E7
Castle Ct 1 DE75 . . . . .143 A1
Castledine St Extension
LE11 . . . . .220 B2
Castledine St LE11 . . . .220 B2
Castle Farm La S80 . . . . .46 D7
Castlefields NG2 . . . . . .173 C2
Castle Gate
Newark-on-Trent NG24 . .139 F8
Nottingham NG1 . . . . .223 E2
Castle Gdns NG7 . . . . . .222 B1
Castle Gr NG7 . . . . .223 D1
Castle Hill LE12 . . . . . .205 F1
Castle Hill Cl NG15 . . . .114 E5
Castle Marina Pk NG2 . .173 A2
Castle Marina Rd NG2 . .173 A2
Castle Mdw Rd NG2 . . . .223 D1
Castle Mdw Ret Pk
NG7 . . . . .222 C1
Castle Mews NG15 . . . . .88 B3
Castle Mus & Art Gall★
NG7 . . . . .223 D1
Castle Pk NG2 . . . . .173 B2
Castle Pl NG1 . . . . .223 D2
Castle Quay NG7 . . . . . .223 D1
Castle Quay Cl NG7 . . . .222 C1
Castle Rd NG1 . . . . .223 D2
Castlerigg Cl NG2 . . . . .186 C5
Castle Rising NG24 . . . .139 F8
Castle St
Eastwood NG16 . . . . . .144 A1
12 Mansfield NG18 . . . . .102 A7
Mansfield Woodhouse
NG19 . . . . .88 B3
Nottingham NG2 . . . . .173 F4
Worksop S80 . . . . .35 E2
Castleton Ave
Arnold NG5 . . . . .161 F6
Carlton NG4 . . . . .162 E1
Ilkeston DE7 . . . . .157 E5
Castleton Cl
Hucknall NG15 . . . . . .145 D6
Mansfield Woodhouse
NG19 . . . . .88 C4
8 Nottingham NG2 . . . .173 B1
Ravenshead NG15 . . . . .117 A3
Castleton Ct NG6 . . . . .159 F6
Castle View
Aldercar NG16 . . . . . . .143 A4
West Bridgford NG2 . . .185 D6
Castle View Rd NG13 . . .181 C1
Castle Wood Acad
DN10 . . . . .10 A8
Caterham Cl NG8 . . . . . .171 D7
Catfoot La NG4 . . . . . . .162 E8
Catherine Ave NG19 . . . .88 C3
Catherine Cl
11 Kirkby-in-Ashfield
NG17 . . . . .114 F7
Morton DN21 . . . . .15 C3
Nottingham NG6 . . . . .160 A4
Nuthall NG16 . . . . . . .159 F4
Catkin Dr NG16 . . . . . . .158 C8
Catkin Way NG24 . . . . .140 B4
Cat La NG14 . . . . .175 D8
Catlow Wlk 4 NG5 . . . .161 C8
Caton Cl NG17 . . . . .100 D3
Cator Cl NG4 . . . . .162 D3
Cator La NG9 . . . . .183 D5
Cator La N NG9 . . . . . .183 D6
Cator Rd NG19 . . . . .87 C3
Catriona Cres NG5 . . . .148 A1
Catt Cl NG9 . . . . .183 B1
Catterley Hill Rd NG3 . .174 B6
Cattle Mkt 1 LE11 . . . .220 B3
Cattle Mkt NG2 . . . . . . .173 D2
Cattle Rd NG5 . . . . .162 A8
Caudale Ct NG2 . . . . . .186 C7
Caudwell Cl NG25 . . . . .121 E2
Caudwell Dr NG18 . . . . .102 C3
Cauldwell Rd
Mansfield NG18 . . . . . .102 A1
Mansfield NG18 . . . . . .102 B1
Sutton in Ashfield NG17 . .101 E2
Caulton St NG7 . . . . . . .222 B4
CAUNTON 109 B4
Caunton Ave NG3 . . . . .161 E1
Caunton Cl
Mansfield NG18 . . . . . .101 F6
Meden Vale NG20 . . . . .74 D7
Caunton Dean CE Hole
Prim Sch NG23 . . . . . .109 A5
Caunton Rd
Bathley NG23 . . . . .109 E4
Caunton NG23 . . . . . . .109 C5
Hockerton NG25 . . . . .122 B6
Maplebeck NG22 . . . . .108 B6
Caunt's Cres NG17 . . . . .100 D3
Causeway DN21 . . . . . . .24 E3
Causeway La
Gamston DN22 . . . . . . .51 B7
Gamston DN22 . . . . . . .51 C7
Morton NG25 . . . . . . .137 C4
Causeway Mews 4
NG2 . . . . .173 B1
Cavan Ct 3 NG2 . . . . . .173 C1
Cavell Cl
Nottingham NG11 . . . . .184 D2
Woodbeck DN22 . . . . . .53 B8
Cavell Ct NG7 . . . . .172 D2
Cavell Gr NG15 . . . . . . .146 B6
Cavendish Ave
Carlton NG4 . . . . .162 D2
Edwinstowe NG21 . . . . .75 F2

Cavendish Ave continued
Newark-on-Trent NG24 . .140 A6
Nottingham NG4 . . . . .162 C2
Sutton in Ashfield NG17 . .100 E3
Cavendish Cl
Bawtry DN10 . . . . .9 F6
Hucknall NG15 . . . . . .146 C5
Cavendish Cres
Annesley Woodhouse
NG17 . . . . .130 A8
Carlton NG4 . . . . .162 C2
Kirkby-in-Ashfield NG17 . .115 A4
Stapleford NG9 . . . . . .170 D2
Cavendish Cres N NG7 .222 C2
Cavendish Cres S NG7 .222 C1
Cavendish Dr
Carlton NG4 . . . . .174 E8
Lea DN21 . . . . .24 F2
Cavendish Pl NG9 . . . . .183 F6
Cavendish Rd
Carlton NG4 . . . . .162 C1
Ilkeston DE7 . . . . .170 A6
Long Eaton NG10 . . . . .182 C2
Retford DN22 . . . . .40 B4
Worksop S80 . . . . .47 A8
Cavendish Rd E NG7 . . .222 C2
Cavendish Rd W
Nottingham NG4 . . . . .173 A4
Nottingham NG7 . . . . .222 C2
Cavendish St
Arnold NG5 . . . . .161 E8
Langwith NG20 . . . . . . .72 F8
Mansfield NG18 . . . . . .102 C5
Cavendish Vale NG5 . . .161 D3
Cavendish Way
Clipstone NG21 . . . . . . .89 F4
Clipstone NG21 . . . . . . .90 A5
Cave's La DN10 . . . . .13 D6
Cawdell Dr LE12 . . . . . .212 D2
Cawdron Wlk NG7 . . . . .184 E2
Cawston Gdns 3 NG6 . .168 B8
Cawthorne Cl NG23 . . . . .98 B1
Cawthorne Way NG18 . .102 F7
Caxmere Dr NG8 . . . . . .171 F5
Caxton Cl NG4 . . . . . . .175 A7
Caxton Rd NG5 . . . . . . .161 B1
CAYTHORPE 165 B8
Caythorpe Cres NG5 . . .161 C3
Caythorpe Ct NG19 . . . . .88 E3
Caythorpe Rd NG14 . . . .150 F1
Caythorpe Rise NG5 . . .161 C3
Cecil Cl S80 . . . . .35 A4
Cecil St
Gainsborough DN21 . . . .15 C1
Nottingham NG7 . . . . .222 B1
Cedar Ave
Beeston NG9 . . . . .184 A7
East Leake LE12 . . . . . .214 D8
Kirkby-in-Ashfield NG17 . .114 F4
Long Eaton NG10 . . . . .193 C5
Cedar Cl
Carlton in Lindrick S81 . . .25 E7
Gainsborough DN21 . . . .15 B3
Shirebrook NG20 . . . . . .72 C6
Sutton in Ashfield NG17 . .100 D7
Torksey Lock LN1 . . . . .44 C1
Cedar Ct NG9 . . . . .184 A7
Cedar Dr
Keyworth NG12 . . . . . .197 E2
Selston NG16 . . . . .128 F7
5 Shireoaks S81 . . . . . . .35 A7
Cedar Gr
Arnold NG5 . . . . .162 B8
Hucknall NG15 . . . . . .146 B5
Nottingham NG8 . . . . .171 F4
South Normanton DE55 . .113 B4
Cedar La NG22 . . . . .77 C3
Cedarland Cres NG16 . .159 F4
Cedar Rd
Beeston NG9 . . . . .183 E5
Loughborough LE11 . . .220 C1
Nottingham NG7 . . . . .173 A8
Cedars Cl NG20 . . . . . . .74 A1
Cedar St NG18 . . . . . . .102 C5
Cedars The NG15 . . . . .161 D4
Cedar Tree Rd
Elkesley DN22 . . . . .50 A3
Nottingham NG5 . . . . .147 B1
Cedar Tree View DN22 . .50 B3
Celandine Cl NG5 . . . . .160 E7
Celandine Gdns NG13 . .177 C4
Celery Mdws DN22 . . . . .30 D4
Celeste Ct 1 NG8 . . . . .172 B7
Celia Dr NG4 . . . . .174 D7
Celtic Fields S81 . . . . . . .35 D7
Celtic Point S81 . . . . . . .35 D7
Cemetery Rd
Langold S81 . . . . .16 F3
Stapleford NG9 . . . . . .182 E7
Worksop S80 . . . . .36 A2
Cemetery Wlk NG16 . . .143 E1
Centenary Ave
Bilsthorpe NG22 . . . . . .105 A1
Kings Clipstone NG21 . . . .90 F4
Rainworth NG22 . . . . . .104 E1
Centenary Cl
New Balderton NG24 . . .140 C4
5 Nottingham NG6 . . . .160 A8
Centenary Rd NG19 . . . . .87 F1
Central Ave
Arnold NG5 . . . . .161 E7
Beeston NG9 . . . . .183 F5

Central Ave continued
Beeston, Chilwell NG9 . .183 D6
Blidworth NG21 . . . . . .118 B5
Creswell S80 . . . . .58 D8
Hucknall NG15 . . . . . .146 A6
Kirkby-in-Ashfield NG17 . .115 C3
Mansfield NG18 . . . . . .103 A4
Nottingham, Mapperley
NG3 . . . . .162 A4
Nottingham, New Basford NG7,
NG5 . . . . .161 A1
Sandiacre NG10 . . . . . .182 B6
South Normanton DE55 . .113 B5
Stapleford NG9 . . . . . .182 F8
Walesby NG22 . . . . .64 A1
West Bridgford NG2 . . .185 F8
Worksop S80 . . . . .35 E3
Central Ave S NG5 . . . . .161 F7
Central Cl NG20 . . . . . . .72 E3
Central Coll Nottingham
(Beeston High Rd)
NG9 . . . . .183 E5
Central Coll Nottingham
(Clifton) NG11 . . . . . .185 A1
Central Coll Notts (Wheeler
Gate) NG1 . . . . .223 E2
Central Ct NG7 . . . . . . .172 F1
Central Dr
Bawtry DN10 . . . . .10 A8
Clipstone NG21 . . . . . . .89 F2
Elston NG23 . . . . .153 E4
Shirebrook NG20 . . . . . .72 E3
Central St
3 Nottingham NG3 . . . .173 E6
Sutton in Ashfield NG17 . .101 B4
Central Wlk NG15 . . . . .146 A7
Centre Way NG12 . . . . .175 E4
Centurian Cl NG15 . . . .146 D8
Centurion Bsns Pk
NG6 . . . . .159 E8
Centurion Way NG11 . . .185 A8
Century Ave NG18 . . . . .101 F5
Century La LN1 . . . . .57 A5
Century Rd DN22 . . . . . .39 E5
Century St NG24 . . . . . .140 A8
Cernan Ct NG6 . . . . . . .159 F5
Cerne Ct NG7 . . . . .184 E1
Chaceley Way NG11 . . . .185 A3
Chadborn Ave NG11 . . . .195 B6
Chadburn Rd
Hucknall NG15 . . . . . .131 C2
Mansfield NG18 . . . . . .102 E8
Chaddesden The NG3 . .173 C7
Chad Gdns NG5 . . . . . . .147 A2
Chadwick Rd NG7 . . . . .172 E7
Chadwick Way DN22 . . . .53 B8
Chaffinch Cl
Clipstone NG21 . . . . . . .89 F4
Mansfield NG18 . . . . . .102 F7
Chaffinch Mews S81 . . . .35 C7
Chainbridge Cl LE11 . . .220 A5
Chainbridge La DN22 . . .29 D8
Chainbridge Nature
Reserve★ DN22 . . . . . .30 A8
Chainbridge Rd DN22 . . .30 B8
Chain La
5 Newark-on-Trent
NG24 . . . . .139 F7
Nottingham NG7 . . . . .172 E1
Chalfield Cl NG11 . . . . .184 D1
Chalfont Dr NG8 . . . . . .172 C6
Challands Dr NG13 . . . .181 B4
Challands La NG22 . . . . .135 C2
Chalons Cl DE7 . . . . . . .157 F1
Chamberlain Cl NG11 . .184 C1
Chambers Ave DE7 . . . .170 B7
Chambers Ct NG5 . . . . .160 F5
Champion Ave DE7 . . . .157 C3
Champion Cres NG19 . .101 F8
Chancery Cl NG17 . . . . .101 A6
Chancery Ct NG11 . . . . .185 A6
Chancery La DN22 . . . . .39 E6
Chancery The NG9 . . . . .183 C7
Chandos Ave NG4 . . . . .175 A8
Chandos Ct NG22 . . . . . .65 F3
Chandos St
Carlton NG4 . . . . .175 A7
Nottingham NG3 . . . . .173 E7
Chantrey Cl NG9 . . . . . .183 D4
Chantrey Rd NG2 . . . . .185 E7
Chantry Cl
Kimberley NG16 . . . . . .159 A5
Long Eaton NG10 . . . . .193 A4
Newark-on-Trent NG24 . .139 F5
Chantry The NG18 . . . . .102 F5
Chantry Wlk NG22 . . . . .65 F3
Chapel Bank DN10 . . . . . .1 F2
Chapel Bar
Nottingham NG1 . . . . .223 D2
Wymeswold LE12 . . . . .216 C3
Chapel Baulk DN9 . . . . . .2 B1
Chapel Cl
Gotham NG11 . . . . . . .195 B1
Misterton DN10 . . . . . . .6 F2
Walesby NG22 . . . . .64 A2
Chapel Ct DE7 . . . . .157 F4
Chapel Dr
Gamston DN22 . . . . . . .51 A3
Worksop S80 . . . . .35 B5
Chapel Farm Cl NG23 . .153 D5
Chapelfield Gr NG13 . . .177 E3
Chapel Fields NG15 . . . .117 B3
Chapel Garth NG13 . . . .179 F6
Chapel Gate S81 . . . . . . .26 A5
Chapel Gate NG3 . . . . . .39 F7
Chapelgate Ct 3 DN22 . .39 F7
Chapel Gate La NG16 . .143 E4
Chapel La
Arnold NG5 . . . . .161 E8
Aslockton NG13 . . . . . .179 A5

Chapel La continued
Bathley NG23.........110 B3
Bingham NG13........177 E6
Bingham NG13........178 E8
Caunton NG23.........109 A5
Claypole NG23........156 D7
Coddington NG24......126 B1
Costock LE12.........206 C1
Cotgrave NG12........187 F3
Epperstone NG14......150 A6
Everton DN10...........11 C3
Farndon NG24.........138 F4
Farnsfield NG22.......119 F5
Granby NG13..........191 B5
Hose LE14............211 B3
Lambley NG4..........163 B7
Laxton NG22...........79 C2
Misterton DN10.........6 F2
Morton DN21...........15 B4
Nether Broughton LE14..219 C8
North Scarle LN6......83 D3
Old Dalby LE14.......218 E4
Oxton NG25...........134 C4
Ravenshead NG15......117 B2
Scrooby DN10..........10 A2
Spalford NG23.........83 B7
Upper Broughton LE14 .210 A1
Walesby NG22..........64 A2
Willoughby-on-t-W LE12 .217 D7
Winthorpe NG24.......125 C6
Chapel Mews Ct NG9 .183 B8
Chapel Pl NG16.......158 F6
Chapel Quarter Bsns
 Development NG1....223 D2
Chapel Rd NG16.......128 E6
Chapel Side NG12.....207 C3
Chapel St
 Annesley Woodhouse
  NG17.............115 A1
 Barkestone-le-Vale
  NG13.............192 B2
 Beckingham LN5 .....142 D8
 Beeston NG9.........183 B8
 Bottesford NG13.....181 A3
 Eastwood NG16.......143 F1
 Heanor DE75.........157 A8
 Hucknall NG15.......146 A7
 8 Ilkeston DE7......157 F1
 Kimberley NG16......158 F6
 Kirkby-in-Ashfield NG17 .114 E5
 Long Eaton NG10.....193 E7
 New Houghton NG19....87 A7
 Orston NG13.........179 F7
 Ruddington NG11.....196 C6
 Selston NG16........129 A4
 Sutton Forest Side NG17 .101 B3
 Whaley Thorns NG20...59 A3
Chapel Staith DN21.....24 B4
Chapel Terr NG15.......130 D6
Chapel Wlk
 Whatton-in-the-Vale
  NG13.............179 B4
 Worksop S80..........35 E2
Chapel Yard LN1........57 A3
Chapman Ct NG8 ....172 B7
Chapman St LE11.......220 C4
Chapmans Wlk NG6......145 C5
Chappel Gdns NG22......106 A4
Chapter Dr NG16.......159 A5
Chard St NG7...........160 F2
Charlbury Ct NG9.......171 B4
Charlbury Rd NG8.......172 B5
Charlecote Dr NG8......171 D3
Charlecote Pk Dr NG2 .185 C4
Charles Ave
 Beeston NG9.........172 A1
 Beeston, Chilwell NG9..183 C4
 Eastwood NG16.......144 B1
 Sandiacre NG10......182 B6
 Stapleford NG9......182 F8
Charles Baines Com Prim
 Sch DN21...........24 F8
Charles Cl
 Carlton NG4.........162 F2
 Ilkeston DE7........170 B6
Charles St
 Arnold NG5..........161 E7
 Gainsborough DN21 ....15 D1
 Hucknall NG15.......146 A7
 Long Eaton NG10.....193 D6
 Loughborough LE11....220 B5
 Mansfield NG19.......88 A1
 Mansfield Woodhouse
  NG19..............88 C3
 Newark-on-Trent NG24 .140 A4
 Ruddington NG11.....196 C7
 Sutton in Ashfield NG17 .101 A3
Charleston Gdns **3**
 NG12.............185 F2
Charles Way NG6.......160 B5
Charlesworth Ave NG7 .172 E8
Charlesworth Ct NG19 ..88 E3
Charlock Cl NG5.......160 E7
Charlock Gdns NG13....177 D3
Charlotte Cl
 Arnold NG5..........147 E2
 Kirton NG22..........78 B6
 Newark-on-Trent NG24 .140 A8
Charlotte Gr NG9.......171 D1
Charlton Ave NG10......182 F1
Charlton Gr NG9.......183 F5
Charlton Rd S81........26 A2
Charnock Ave NG8......172 D3
Charnos St DE7........170 A5
Charnwood Ave
 Beeston NG9.........183 E6
 Keyworth NG12.......197 E2
 Long Eaton NG10.....193 B4
 Sandiacre NG10......182 B5
 Sutton Bonington LE12 .213 C5
Charnwood Cl NG15.....132 A8

Charnwood Cres DE55 ..99 B3
Charnwood Fields
 LE12.............213 C5
Charnwood Gr
 Bingham NG13........177 D4
 Hucknall NG15.......145 E7
 Mansfield NG18......103 A4
 Mansfield Woodhouse
  NG19..............88 B5
 West Bridgford NG2 ..185 E7
Charnwood La NG5......162 A6
Charnwood L Ctr LE11 .220 A3
Charnwood Mus★
 LE11.............220 A3
Charnwood Rd LE11.....220 B2
Charnwood St NG17.....100 C1
Charnwood Way NG14 ..149 D4
Charta Mws NG14.......150 E1
Charter Ct DN22.........39 D8
Charter Pl NG22.........66 A2
Charters Cl **5** NG17....114 F7
Charters Dr NG24.......140 A4
Chartwell Ave NG11.....196 B7
Chartwell Gr NG3.......162 C5
Chartwell Rd NG17.....115 C5
Chase Pk NG2...........174 A3
Chatham Ct NG24.......139 F7
Chatham St
 Nottingham NG1......223 E4
 Southwell NG25......121 F1
Chatsworth NG17.......100 F3
Chatsworth Ave
 Beeston NG9.........183 C2
 Carlton NG4.........162 E1
 Long Eaton NG10.....194 A6
 Nottingham NG7......160 F5
 Radcliffe on Trent NG12 .176 A4
 Selston NG16........129 A7
 Shirebrook NG20......72 E6
 Southwell NG25......121 D1
Chatsworth Cl
 Mansfield NG18......102 E2
 Ravenshead NG15....117 A3
 Sandiacre NG10......182 B4
 Sutton in Ashfield NG17 .100 F5
Chatsworth Ct
 Harworth DN11........9 B5
 Hucknall NG15.......146 A6
Chatsworth Dr
 Hucknall NG15.......146 A6
 Mansfield NG18......102 E2
Chatsworth Rd
 Creswell S80.........58 C8
 Newark-on-Trent NG24 .140 A5
 West Bridgford NG2 ..186 B8
 Worksop S81..........35 F7
Chatsworth St
 Sutton in Ashfield
  NG17.............101 A3
 Tibshelf DE55.........99 A6
Chatterley Parkway
 NG16.............159 C2
Chaucer Cres NG17.....101 B4
Chaucer Rd NG24.......140 E4
Chaucer St
 Ilkeston DE7........157 F1
 Mansfield NG18......102 A7
 Nottingham NG1......223 D3
Chaworth Ave NG16.....145 A1
Chaworth Cl NG15......130 F2
Chaworth Rd
 Bingham NG13........177 D4
 Carlton NG4.........174 F6
 West Bridgford NG2 ..185 E6
Chaworth St NG21......118 B5
Cheadle Cl
 Nottingham, Bilborough
  NG8.............171 D8
 Nottingham, Portchester
  NG3.............162 B2
Cheapside
 Nottingham NG1......223 E2
 Worksop S80..........36 A2
Cheddar Cl NG21......104 C1
Cheddar Rd NG16......195 E8
Chedington Ave NG3....162 D6
Chediston Vale NG5....161 B8
Chedworth Cl **1** NG3 .173 F5
Chelmsford Mews Rd
 DN22.............39 E4
Chelmorton Cl NG19.....88 E3
Chelmsford Rd NG7.....160 F2
Chelmsford Terr NG7...160 F2
Chelsea Cl NG16.......159 E3
Chelsea St NG7.......160 F1
Cheltenham Cl NG9.....182 F1
Cheltenham Ct NG18....102 F7
Cheltenham St NG6.....160 E4
Chelwood Dr NG6......162 C3
Chennel Nook NG12....188 A2
Chepstow Rd NG11.....195 E8
Chepstow Wlk NG18....102 F7
Chequers Cl DN22........38 A6
Chequers La NG22........54 B2
Cherhill Cl NG11......195 D7
Cheriton Cl NG19......87 E1
Cheriton Dr
 Ravenshead NG15....117 B2
 Shipley DE7.........157 C3
Chermside Cl NG15....117 B3
Chernside NG15.......117 A3
Cherries The NG12....185 B6
Cherry Ave
 Hucknall NG15......146 B5
 Kirkby-in-Ashfield NG17 .114 D7
Cherry Cl
 Arnold NG5..........161 E8
 East Leake LE12......214 C8
 Nottingham NG5......161 B7
 Shirebrook NG20......72 E6
 South Normanton DE55 .113 B7

Cherry Gr
 Mansfield NG18......101 E6
 Market Warsop NG20...74 C4
Cherry Hill NG12......197 F3
Cherry Holt
 Newark-on-Trent NG24 .139 F5
 Retford DN22.........29 D1
Cherryholt Cl NG13....165 D4
Cherryholt La NG13....165 D3
Cherry La NG18.......102 B3
Cherry Orch NG12.....187 E3
Cherry Orch Mount
 NG5.............161 B7
Cherry St NG13.......177 F4
Cherry Tree Ave S81...34 F7
Cherry Tree Cl
 Boughton NG22........77 C5
 Brinsley NG16.......143 E8
 Calverton NG5.......148 E8
 Mansfield Woodhouse
  NG19..............88 B4
 Radcliffe on Trent NG12 .175 F2
 Ranskill DN22.........19 C4
Cherry Tree Dr NG13...192 A1
Cherry Tree Hill NG12..172 C1
Cherry Tree La NG12....186 B3
Cherry Tree Rd DN21....15 E1
Cherry Tree Way NG16 .143 E4
Cherry Tree Wlk DN22 ..19 C5
Cherry View **2** NG8....172 B7
Cherry Wood Dr NG8....172 B7
Cherrywood Gdns NG3 .174 A8
Chertsey Cl NG3.......161 F1
Cherwell Ct NG6.......159 F6
Cherwell Gdns NG13....177 C3
Chesham Dr
 Beeston NG9.........171 B2
 Nottingham NG5......161 B1
Cheshire Way NG16....128 C6
Chesil Ave **2** NG8....172 D5
Chesil Cotts **3** NG8....172 D5
Cheslyn Dr NG8.......172 C8
Chesnut Cl NG23.......81 A4
Chesnut Gdn NG17.....100 D1
Chess Burrow NG19......88 D2
Chester Cl **3** LE11....220 A3
Chesterfield Ave
 Bingham NG13........177 E5
 Carlton NG4.........162 D2
 Long Eaton NG10.....193 F7
Chesterfield Ct NG4 ..162 D3
Chesterfield Dr
 Burton Joyce NG14....164 A5
 Retford DN22.........40 A7
Chesterfield Rd
 Darfoulds S80.........34 F1
 Darfoulds S80.........35 A1
 Hardstoft DE55........85 A1
 Huthwaite NG17.......99 E4
 New Houghton NG19....86 E7
 Pleasley NG19........87 A5
Chesterfield Rd N NG19..87 C4
Chesterfield Rd S
 Mansfield NG18......102 A8
 Mansfield NG18......102 B8
Chesterfield St NG4....174 D7
Chester Gn NG9.......182 E2
Chesterman Cl NG16....158 B4
Chester Rd NG3.......174 B5
Chester St
 Mansfield NG19.......87 E1
 Mansfield NG19......101 E8
Chesterton Dr S81......36 B5
Chestnut Ave
 Beeston NG9.........183 F6
 Bingham NG13........177 E4
 Gainsborough DN21 ....15 D2
 Glapwell S44..........86 B8
 Kirkby-in-Ashfield NG17 .114 F6
 Newark-on-Trent NG24 .125 B4
 Nottingham NG3......162 B2
 Ravenshead NG15....117 B1
 Retford DN22.........39 D4
Chestnut Cl
 Bottesford NG13.....181 C3
 Calverton NG14......149 C6
 Church End DN21.......14 A5
 Keyworth NG12.......197 E3
 New Ollerton NG22....77 D6
 Ravenshead NG15....116 E7
 Sutton Bonington LE12 .204 A2
 Worksop S80..........35 E1
Chestnut Copse NG24 .140 B6
Chestnut Cres LN1......44 C1
Chestnut Ct NG23.......81 E7
Chestnut Dr
 Bawtry DN10...........9 F7
 Cotgrave NG12.......188 A5
 Mansfield NG18......102 C2
 New Ollerton NG22....77 D6
 Nuthall NG16........159 B6
 Selston NG16........128 F7
 Shirebrook NG20......72 D4
 South Normanton DE55 .113 B4
Chestnut Farm Cl
 LE12.............217 D7
Chestnut Gdns NG17....100 D1
Chestnut Gr
 Arnold NG5..........162 A8
 Burton Joyce NG14....163 F4
 Carlton NG4.........162 F1
 Farndon NG24.......139 A4
 Hucknall NG15......146 B4
 Kirkby-in-Ashfield NG17 .114 F5
 Mansfield Woodhouse
  NG19..............88 B5
 Nottingham NG3......173 C7
 Radcliffe on Trent NG12 .175 F4
 Sandiacre NG10......182 A4
 West Bridgford NG2 ..185 D4
Chestnut Hill NG18.....102 E2

Chestnut La NG11......194 E6
Chestnut Mews NG18....102 E2
Chestnut Mws NG12....186 F3
Chestnut Rd
 Langley Mill NG16....143 A3
 Langold S81...........16 F4
Chestnut Screed NG21..89 E5
Chestnut St LE11......220 A4
Chestnuts The
 Carlton NG4.........163 B1
 Long Eaton NG10.....193 A8
 Nottingham NG3......161 F1
 Radcliffe on Trent NG12 .175 E3
Chestnut Walk NG5.....161 B3
Chestnut Way NG22......66 A2
Chettles Ind Est NG8 ..172 D5
Chetwin Rd NG8.......171 D5
Chetwynd Prim Acad
 NG9.............183 A2
Chetwynd Rd
 Beeston, Chilwell NG9..183 C3
 Beeston, Toton NG9....183 A2
Cheverton Ct **7** NG3...173 C7
Cheviot Cl NG5........147 B2
Cheviot Cl S81.........25 E7
Cheviot Dr NG6........159 F8
Cheviot Rd NG10.......182 A1
Chewton Ave NG16......144 A1
Chewton Cl NG22......105 E6
Chewton St NG16......144 A1
Cheyne Dr NG22.......106 A4
Cheyne Wlk
 Bawtry DN10...........9 F7
 HUCKNALL NG15......146 B8
 Retford DN22.........39 D4
Cheyny Cl NG2.........173 C1
Chichester Cl
 Ilkeston DE7........170 A8
 Mansfield NG19......101 D6
 Sutton in Ashfield NG17 .100 E2
Chichester Dr NG12....187 E4
Chichester Wlk S81.....27 E7
Chidlow Rd NG8.......171 D7
Chigwell Cl NG16......159 E3
Chillon Way NG15......145 D6
Chiltern Cl NG5.......147 B2
Chiltern Gdns NG10....182 A1
Chiltern Way
 Carlton in Lindrick S81..25 E7
 Nottingham NG5......161 B7
Chilton Cres NG19......88 C6
Chilton Dr
 Kimberley NG16......158 F7
 Watnall NG16........159 A7
Chilvers Cl NG5.......161 A7
CHILWELL............183 D6
Chilwell Cl NG6.......160 D7
Chilwell La NG9.......183 C6
Chilwell Olympia NG9 .183 D3
Chilwell Rd NG9......183 F6
Chilwell Ret Pk NG9...183 A2
Chilwell Sch NG9......183 D3
Chilwell St NG7.......222 B1
Chimes Mdw NG25.....136 F8
Chine Gdns NG5.......185 C5
Chine The DE55........113 B3
Chingford Rd NG8......171 E8
Chiomere DN22.........39 D4
Chipmunk Way NG13....177 B7
Chippendale St NG7....222 B1
Chippenham Rd NG5....161 C7
Chirnside NG19........101 D5
Chisbury Gn NG11......195 D7
Chisholm Way NG5....161 A6
Chisworth Ct NG19......88 E3
Christ Church CE Inf Sch
 NG24.............139 E7
Christ Church CE Prim Sch
 NG24.............140 A4
Christchurch Rd NG15 .145 D4
Christina Ave NG6.....160 C4
Christina Cres NG6....160 C4
Christine Cl NG15.....131 C1
Christopher Cl NG8....171 F6
Christopher Cres
 NG24.............140 C4
Christ the King Sch
 NG5.............162 B7
Chrysalis Way NG16....143 C3
Chrysalis Way Bsns Pk
 DE75.............143 C3
Church Ave
 Arnold NG5..........161 E7
 Long Eaton NG10.....193 A4
 Nottingham NG7......222 B1
 Sutton in Ashfield NG17 .100 D2
Church Circ NG22.......77 C5
Church Cl
 Arnold NG5..........161 E7
 Bingham NG13........177 F5
 Church Warsop NG20...74 B6
 Eagle LN6............84 D3
 East Leake LE12......205 E1
 Hose LE14............211 F7
 Kneeton NG13........151 F1
 North Wheatley DN22...31 E8
 Nottingham NG5......223 E4
 Radcliffe on Trent NG12 .175 D3
 Trowell NG9..........170 C4
Church Cnr NG13.......192 F4
Church Cres
 Arnold NG5..........161 D7
 Beeston NG10........182 F3
 Beeston NG9.........183 A3
Church Croft NG2.....185 F8
Church Ct NG23.......110 A8
Churchdale Ave NG9....170 C6
Church Dr
 Arnold NG5..........161 E7
 Hucknall NG15......146 A7

Church Dr continued
 Ilkeston DE7........157 D4
 Keyworth NG12.......197 E3
 Misterton DN10........6 E2
 Nottingham NG5......161 B1
 Ravenshead NG15....117 A2
 Sandiacre NG10......182 B7
 Shirebrook NG20......72 C3
 West Bridgford NG2 ..185 F7
Church Dr E NG5.......161 E7
Church End LE14......210 C1
Church Farm NG21......76 A2
Church Farm Bsns Ctr
 NG21..............76 A2
Church Farm Gdns
 NG22..............77 E1
Church Field Cl S81.....26 A5
Churchfield Ct NG5....147 A1
Churchfield Dr NG21...103 F2
Churchfield La NG7.....160 E3
Churchfield Terr NG7...160 E3
Churchgate DN22.......39 F7
Church Gate
 Colston Bassett NG12 ..200 C3
 Cotgrave NG12.......198 C8
 Kegworth DE74......203 D2
 Loughborough LE11....220 A4
 Loughborough LE11....220 B4
Church Gr NG7.........222 A1
Church Hill
 Bilsthorpe NG22.....106 A5
 Jacksdale NG16......128 B3
 Keyworth NG12.......197 E7
 Kimberley NG16......158 F6
 Kirkby-in-Ashfield NG17 .114 D3
 Mansfield Woodhouse
  NG19..............88 C3
 Newton DE55..........99 A1
 North Wheatley DN22...31 E8
 Sutton in Ashfield NG17 .100 E2
Church Hill Ave NG19...88 C3
Church Hill Gdns NG19..88 C3
Churchill Cl NG5.......161 F6
Churchill Dr
 Newark-on-Trent NG24 .139 E5
 Ruddington NG11.....196 B7
 Stapleford NG9......182 E8
Churchill Pk NG4......174 C3
Churchill Way
 Lea DN21.............24 F3
 Worksop S81..........25 D1
 Worksop S81..........35 D8
Church La
 Arnold NG5..........147 F1
 Askham NG22..........52 A3
 Austerfield DN10.......3 C2
 Averham NG23........123 F1
 Babworth DN22........39 A6
 Balderton NG24......140 E4
 Barton in Fabis NG11 .194 E6
 Beeston NG9.........183 D1
 Besthorpe NG23.......97 E6
 Besthorpe NG23.......98 B5
 Bingham NG13........177 F5
 Bothamsall DN22......63 F7
 Bottesford NG13.....181 B3
 Boughton NG22........77 F5
 Brinsley NG16.......143 E7
 Car Colston NG13.....166 B5
 Carlton in Lindrick S81 .25 F4
 Carlton-on-Trent NG23...96 A4
 Carlton-on-Trent NG23...97 B5
 Clarborough DN22......30 E3
 Clayworth DN22.......21 D5
 Collingham NG23......98 A1
 Cossall NG16........158 C1
 Costock LE12........206 C1
 Cotgrave NG12.......187 E3
 Cromwell NG23......110 F7
 Eagle LN6............84 D3
 Eakring NG22..........92 E1
 East Drayton DN22....53 A3
 East Stoke NG23.....138 B1
 East Stoke NG23.....153 B8
 Elston NG23.........153 D4
 Epperstone NG14.....150 A6
 Gamston DN22.........50 F4
 Halam NG22..........120 F1
 Harworth DN11.........8 E4
 Hayton DN22..........30 C5
 Hockerton NG25......122 B5
 Kirklington NG22.....120 E8
 Langar NG13........190 C2
 Letwell S81..........16 A2
 Long Clawson LE14....211 C3
 Lowdham NG14.......150 C2
 Mansfield NG18......102 C6
 Maplebeck NG22.....108 A6
 Misterton DN10........6 E2
 Morton NG25........137 D3
 North Clifton NG23....68 D3
 North Scarle LN6......83 D2
 Nottingham NG6......160 C7
 Old Dalby LE14......218 E4
 Owthorpe NG12......199 E8
 Pleasley NG19........87 A6
 Plumtree NG12......197 E2
 Plungar NG13.......191 F1
 Redmile NG13.......192 F3
 Retford DN22.........39 E4
 Saxilby LN1...........56 F5
 Screveton NG13......166 E4
 Scrooby DN10.........10 A2
 Selston, Selston Green
  NG16.............128 C2
 Selston, Underwood
  NG16.............129 A3
 Sibthorpe NG23......167 C5
 South Muskham NG23...124 E7
 Stapleford NG9......182 D1

Church La continued
 Sutton in Ashfield NG17 .100 E2
 Thoroton NG23.......167 E3
 Thrumpton NG11......194 C3
 Tibshelf DE55.........99 A6
 Tickhill DN11.........44 B2
 Torksey LN1..........44 B2
 Upper Broughton LE14 .210 A1
 Upton NG23..........122 F1
 West Drayton DN22....50 F2
 Widmerpool LE12.....208 C5
 Willoughby-on-t-W LE12 .217 C7
Church Lands **2** LE11 .220 B6
Church Mdw
 Calverton NG14......148 E7
 Claypole NG23.......156 C6
Church Mdw La NG23...122 E1
Church Mead NG17......99 F3
Church Mews
 1 Nottingham NG2....173 D1
 Sutton in Ashfield NG17 .100 E2
Churchmoor Ct NG5.....147 E1
Churchmoor La NG5....147 F1
Church Rd
 Bestwood Village NG6..146 E4
 Bircotes DN11........9 C4
 Burton Joyce NG14...163 F4
 Church Warsop NG20...74 B6
 Clipstone NG21.......89 F3
 Eastwood NG16......144 F2
 Greasley NG16.......144 E3
 Harby NG23...........70 D1
 Nottingham NG3......223 F4
 Saxilby LN1...........57 A4
Church St E NG16......113 D4
Church St W NG16......113 D4
Church Side
 Farnsfield NG22.....119 F6
 Huthwaite NG17.......99 F3
 Mansfield NG18......102 C6
Churchside Gdns NG7 .172 E8
Church Sq NG7.........222 B1
Church St
 Arnold NG5..........161 F8
 Bawtry DN10..........10 A6
 Beckingham DN10......14 B1
 Beeston NG9.........183 F6
 Beeston, Bramcote NG9 .183 B8
 Bilsthorpe NG22.....105 F6
 Bingham NG13........177 F4
 Bottesford NG13.....181 B2
 Bunny NG11..........206 E8
 Carlton NG4.........174 E7
 Collingham NG23......111 F7
 Cropwell Bishop NG12 .189 A4
 East Markham NG22....66 A6
 Eastwood NG16......143 F2
 Edwinstowe NG21......76 B2
 Everton DN10.........11 C3
 Farndon NG24.......138 F4
 Gainsborough DN21 ....15 C1
 Gotham NG11........195 B1
 Granby NG13........191 B5
 Hathern LE12.......213 A1
 Headon DN22.........52 B7
 Ilkeston DE7........157 E4
 Kegworth DE74......203 A4
 Kirkby-in-Ashfield NG17 .114 D4
 Lambley NG4.........163 C7
 Langold S81..........16 E2
 Low Marnham NG23....82 B7
 Mansfield NG18......102 C6
 Mansfield Woodhouse
  NG19..............88 C3
 Market Warsop NG20...74 B5
 Misson DN10..........4 C2
 Misterton DN10........6 E2
 Newark-on-Trent NG24 .139 F8
 North Wheatley DN22...31 E8
 Nottingham NG7......222 A1
 Nottingham, Old Basford
  NG6.............160 C2
 Ollerton NG22........77 A3
 Orston NG13........179 F7
 Orston NG13........180 A7
 Pleasleyhill NG19.....87 B4
 Ruddington NG11.....196 C7
 Sandiacre NG10......182 B7
 Shelford NG12.......164 B4
 South Leverton DN22...42 C7
 South Normanton DE55 .113 B4
 Southwell NG25......136 E8
 Stapleford NG9......182 F7
 Sturton le Steeple DN22..32 D4
 Sutton in Ashfield NG17 .100 E2
 Sutton on Trent NG23...97 A8
 Whaley Thorns NG20...59 A2
 Whatton NG13........179 A3
 Wymeswold LE12.....216 C3
Church Vale Prim Sch
 NG20..............74 A7
Church View
 Balderton NG24......140 D3
 Beckingham DN10......14 B1
 Bilsthorpe NG22.....106 A5
 Bottesford NG13.....181 A3
 Bunny NG11.........206 E8
 Carlton NG4.........162 F1
 Egmanton NG22........79 F6
 Glapwell S44..........86 B8
 Newark-on-Trent NG24 .125 A1
 New Houghton NG19....86 F7
 Ollerton NG22........77 B3
 Saxilby LN1...........57 A5
 Scrooby DN10.........10 A2
 Stanton Hill NG17....100 D6
Church View Cl NG5....147 B1
Church View Gd NG17 .129 E8

Church View Gr LE12 . . **215** F6
Church Walk
Bawtry DN10 . . . . **10** A7
Brinsley NG16 . . . . **143** E7
Carlton NG4 . . . . **174** E7
Eastwood NG16 . . . . . . **143** F2
Harworth DN11 . . . . **8** E4
Stapleford NG9 . . . . . . **182** E7
Upton NG23 . . . . **122** F1
Weston NG23 . . . . **81** A5
Whatton NG13 . . . . **179** B4
Worksop NG80 . . . . **35** F3
CHURCH WARSOP **74** A7
Church Way
Sutton NG20 . . . . **29** A6
Sutton cum Lound DN22 . . **29** A6
Church Way LN1 . . . . . . **55** A1
Churnet Cl NG11 . . . . . **184** E4
Chuter Ede Prim Sch
NG24 . . . . **140** E4
Chuter Ede Prim Sch
(Fernwood Annex) . . . **140** F3
CINDERHILL **160** B4
Cinderhill Gr NG4 . . . . . **162** E2
Cinderhill Rd NG6 . . . . **160** B5
Cinderhill Wlk NG6 . . . **160** B6
Cinder La NG22 . . . . **77** B2
Cinnabar Way LE12 . . **214** E8
Circle The NG19 . . . . . . **88** B4
Circuit Dr NG10 . . . . . . **193** F8
Cirrus Dr NG16 . . . . . . **159** A7
Citadel St NG7 . . . . **222** A3
Citrus Gr DE74 . . . . **203** C3
City Coll Nottingham
NG4 . . . . **174** E6
City Gd (Nottingham Forest
FC) The NG2 . . . . **173** E1
City Gnd (Nottingham
Forest FC) The NG2 . . **173** E1
City Hospital Campus NG5
161 . . . . **B5**
City Link NG1, NG2 . . . . **173** F3
City of Caves ★ NG1 . . **223** E2
City of Nottingham Tennis
Ctr NG7 . . . . **184** C8
City Rd
Beeston NG9 . . . . **184** A6
Nottingham NG7 . . . . . **172** D1
Stathern LE14 . . . . **202** F3
City The NG9 . . . . **184** A6
City View NG5 . . . . **161** F1
Clandon Dr NG5 . . . . . . **161** B2
Clanfield Rd NG8 . . . . . **171** E7
Clapham St NG7 . . . . . . **222** A3
Clara Mount Rd DE75 . . **143** A1
CLARBOROUGH **30** E4
Clarborough Dr NG5 . . **162** A6
Clarborough Hill DN22 . . **30** E3
Clarborough Prim Sch
DN22 . . . . **30** E3
Clarborough Tunnel Nature
Reserve ★ DN22 . . . . . **31** C2
Clare Cl NG6 . . . . **160** E4
Clarehaven NG9 . . . . . . **182** E5
Clare Hill NG21 . . . . . . **118** A4
Claremont Ave
Beeston NG9 . . . . **183** C7
Hucknall NG15 . . . . . . **146** A5
Claremont Dr NG11 . . . **185** C3
Claremont Prim Sch
NG5 . . . . **161** B1
Claremont Rd
Gainsborough DN21 . . . **24** F6
Nottingham NG5 . . . . . **161** B1
Claremount Cl NG19 . . . **88** C4
Clarence Rd
Beeston NG9 . . . . **183** D3
Long Eaton NG10 . . . . . **193** C6
Worksop NG80 . . . . **35** E4
Clarence St
Loughborough LE11 . . . **220** C4
Mansfield NG18 . . . . . . **102** A4
Nottingham NG3 . . . . . **173** E5
Pleasleyhill NG19 . . . . . **87** B3
Clarendon Ct NG5 . . . . **173** B8
Clarendon Dr S81 . . . . . **35** D6
Clarendon Pk NG5 . . . . **173** B8
Clarendon Rd NG19 . . . **101** E8
Clarendon St NG1 . . . . **223** D3
Clare Rd NG17 . . . . **114** F8
Clare St
Nottingham NG1 . . . . . **223** E3
Nottingham NG14 . . . . **173** E5
Clare Valley
Nottingham NG7 . . . . . **222** C2
Nottingham NG7 . . . . . **223** D2
Clarewood Gr NG11 . . . **195** E7
Clarges St NG6 . . . . **160** E4
Claricoates Dr NG24 . . **125** E2
Clarke Ave
Arnold NG5 . . . . **161** F8
Newark-on-Trent NG24 . . **139** E5
Clarke Cl NG12 . . . . **189** A4
Clarke Dr NG10 . . . . . . **193** A4
Clarke Rd NG2 . . . . **173** E2
Clarke's La NG9 . . . . . . **183** D4
Clark La NG22 . . . . **65** F2
Clarks La NG24 . . . . . . **125** B2
Clarkson Dr NG9 . . . . . **184** B6
Clarkwoods Cl NG22 . . . **77** E4
Clater's Cl DN22 . . . . . . **40** A8
Claude St NG7 . . . . **172** E1
Clawson La
- Hickling LE14 . . . . **210** D6
Hose LE14 . . . . **211** F6
Nether Broughton LE14 . **210** E1
Claxton Rise LE14 . . . . **211** C2
Clay Ave NG3 . . . . **162** A3

Claycross Dr NG21 . . . . . **90** A3
Claye St NG10 . . . . **193** E7
Clayfield Cl NG6 . . . . . **160** A6
Claygate NG3 . . . . **174** A7
Clay La
Fenton LN1 . . . . **55** D7
Newark-on-Trent NG24 . **140** C7
Stapleford NG24 . . . . . **127** C4
Claylands Ave
Worksop S81 . . . . **35** C6
Worksop S81 . . . . **35** D6
Claylands Cl S81 . . . . . . **35** D5
Claylands La S81 . . . . . . **35** D6
Claymoor Cl NG19 . . . . **101** F5
Claypit La NG25 . . . . . . **137** E3
CLAYPOLE **156** E7
Claypole CE Prim Sch The
NG23 . . . . **156** E7
Claypole La
Dry Doddington NG23 . . **156** E2
Fernwood NG23 . . . . . . **156** A8
Fernwood NG24 . . . . . . **155** F8
Claypole Rd NG7 . . . . . **172** F7
Clay St LE12 . . . . **216** C3
Claythorne Dr DN21 . . . **24** E8
Clayton Cl NG24 . . . . . . **140** A6
Clayton Ct NG7 . . . . . . **222** B3
Claytons Dr NG7 . . . . . **172** E2
Clayton's Wharf
NG7 . . . . **172** E2
CLAYWORTH **21** D6
Clayworth Comm DN22 . **21** E3
Clayworth Ct NG18 . . . **103** A2
Clayworth Rd DN10 . . . . **12** F1
Clegg Hill Dr NG17 . . . . **99** E4
Clement Ave NG24 . . . . **140** E3
Clementine Dr NG3 . . . **162** C5
Clensey La NG23 . . . . . **156** F2
Clerkson's Alley
NG18 . . . . **102** B7
Clerkson St NG18 . . . . . **102** B6
Clether Rd NG8 . . . . . . **171** D6
Cleve Ave NG9 . . . . **182** E3
Clevedon Dr NG5 . . . . **148** C1
Cleveland Ave NG10 . . . **182** F1
Cleveland Cl
Carlton in Lindrick S81 . . **25** E7
Nottingham NG7 . . . . . **222** A4
Cleveland Sq NG24 . . . **139** F6
Cleveland St DN21 . . . . . **24** D7
Cleveleys Rd NG9 . . . . **182** E3
Clevely Way NG11 . . . . **184** E3
Cliff Bvd NG9 . . . . **158** F7
Cliff Cres NG12 . . . . . . **175** F4
Cliff Dr NG12 . . . . **176** A5
Cliffe Hill Ave NG9 . . . **182** D7
Cliff Gate **65** C8
Cliffgrove Ave NG9 . . . **183** D6
Cliffhill La NG13 . . . . . **179** C6
Cliff La NG16 . . . . **113** F4
Cliffmere Wlk NG11 . . . **184** D1
Cliff Nook DE55 . . . . . . **113** B4
Cliff Nook La NG24 . . . **125** A1
Clifford Ave NG9 . . . . . **183** F8
Clifford Cl
Keyworth NG12 . . . . . . **197** F4
Long Eaton NG10 . . . . . **193** A4
Nottingham NG7 . . . . . **222** B3
Clifford Ct NG7 . . . . . . **222** B3
Clifford St
Long Eaton NG10 . . . . . **193** E7
Mansfield NG18 . . . . . . **102** B4
Nottingham NG7 . . . . . **222** B3
Cliff Rd
Carlton NG4 . . . . **174** D6
Nottingham NG1 . . . . . **223** F2
Radcliffe on Trent NG12 . **175** E4
Cliff St NG18 . . . . **102** C7
Cliff The NG6 . . . . **160** B4
Cliff Way NG12 . . . . . . **175** F4
CLIFTON **184** F1
Clifton Ave
Long Eaton NG10 . . . . . **194** A4
Ruddington NG11 . . . . **196** C2
Clifton Bvd NG7 . . . . . **184** F8
Clifton Cres
Beeston NG9 . . . . **183** E3
Newark-on-Trent NG24 . **125** B3
Clifton Gdns NG18 . . . . **102** F4
Clifton Gr
Carlton NG4 . . . . **162** E2
Mansfield NG18 . . . . . . **102** F4
Clifton Grove Nature
Reserve ★ NG11 . . . . **184** C3
Clifton La
Nottingham NG11 . . . . **184** E3
Ruddington NG11 . . . . **196** A8
Thorney NG23 . . . . **69** E4
Clifton L Ctr NG11 . . . . **184** F1
Clifton Pl NG18 . . . . . . **102** B7
Clifton Rd NG11 . . . . . . **196** B7
Clifton St NG9 . . . . **184** A6
Clifton Terr
Nottingham NG14 . . . . **173** A3
Nottingham NG7 . . . . . **222** C1
Clifton Way DN22 . . . . . **39** C8
Clifton Woods Nature
Reserve ★ NG11 . . . . **184** C3
Clinthill La S80 . . . . **45** A7
Clinton Ave
Brinsley NG16 . . . . **143** D6
Nottingham NG5 . . . . . **173** B8
Clinton Ct NG1 . . . . . . **223** E4
Clinton Gdn La NG22 . . **65** F2
Clinton Gdns NG22 . . . . **66** A2
Clinton St E NG1 . . . . . **223** E3
Clinton St W NG1 . . . . **223** E3
Clinton Terr
Arnold NG5 . . . . **161** E7
Newark-on-Trent NG24 . **139** F8
Worksop S80 . . . . **36** A1

Clinton Terr DN21 . . . . **24** D7
Clipsham Cl NG24 . . . . **140** E5
CLIPSTON **187** C1
CLIPSTONE **89** F3
Clipstone Ave
Mansfield NG18 . . . . . . **102** C8
Nottingham NG1 . . . . . **223** D4
Nottingham, Mapperley
NG3 . . . . **162** A4
Sutton in Ashfield NG17 . **101** A4
Clipstone Cl NG8 . . . . . **159** D2
Clipstone Dr
Clipstone NG19 . . . . **89** D3
Kings Clipstone NG20 . . . **74** F1
Clipstone Rd
Edwinstowe NG22 . . . . . **76** E1
Kings Clipstone NG21 . . . **90** E6
Lidgett NG21 . . . . **90** E7
Clipstone Rd E NG19 . . . **89** C2
Clipstone Rd W NG19 . . **89** B1
Clipston La NG12 . . . . . **197** F7
Clive Cres NG16 . . . . . . **159** A5
Cliveden Gn NG11 . . . . **184** D1
Cloister St NG7 . . . . . . **172** E2
Cloisters The NG9 . . . . **184** A8
Close Quarters NG9 . . . **183** C8
Closes Side La NG13 . . . **165** E3
Close The
Averham NG23 . . . . **123** E2
Beeston NG9 . . . . **183** D4
Mansfield NG21 . . . . . . **103** F2
Newark-on-Trent NG24 . **140** A8
Nottingham NG5 . . . . . **161** C3
Shirebrook NG20 . . . . . . **72** F5
Upton NG23 . . . . **122** F1
Cloud Ave NG9 . . . . **182** F7
Clouds Hill NG11 . . . . . **195** E8
Cloudside Acad NG10 . . **182** B6
Cloudside Ct NG10 . . . . **182** C7
Cloudside Rd NG10 . . . **182** B7
Clough Ct NG8 . . . . **172** B7
Clovelly Dr NG3 . . . . . . **162** D5
Clover Cl NG12 . . . . **189** A3
Clover Ct NG5 . . . . **99** B7
Cloverdale NG12 . . . . . **188** A2
Cloverfield Pl NG24 . . . **140** A4
Cloverfields NG14 . . . . **149** A8
Clover Gdns NG24 . . . . **125** D1
Clover Gn NG6 . . . . **160** D3
Cloverlands NG11 . . . . **185** C3
Cloverlands Dr NG16 . . **159** A7
Clover Rise NG16 . . . . . **158** B8
Clover St NG17 . . . . **115** A6
Clover Way
Clipstone NG21 . . . . **89** F4
Mansfield Woodhouse
NG19 . . . . **88** F4
Club Ct NG24 . . . . **140** D4
Cludd Ave NG24 . . . . . . **140** E8
Clumber Ave
Beeston NG9 . . . . **183** D5
Brinsley NG16 . . . . **128** E1
Carlton NG4 . . . . **175** A7
Edwinstowe NG21 . . . . . **75** F3
Mansfield NG21 . . . . . . **103** F1
Nottingham NG5 . . . . . **161** C3
Nottingham, Mapperley
NG3 . . . . **162** A4
Clumber Cres NG17 . . . **100** C6
Clumber Cres N NG7 . . **222** C2
Clumber Cres S NG7 . . **222** C1
Clumber Ct
Mansfield NG19 . . . . **87** E2
Market Warsop NG20 . . . **74** B4
Nottingham NG7 . . . . . **222** C1
Clumber Dr
Mansfield NG19 . . . . **87** E2
Radcliffe on Trent NG12 . **176** A4
Clumber La S80 . . . . **47** F3
Clumber Pk Ctry Pk ★
S80 . . . . **48** B3
Worksop S80 . . . . **36** B1
Clumber Pl S80 . . . . **35** E3
Clumber Rd
Clumber and Hardwick
S80 . . . . **47** F6
Clumber and Hardwick
S80 . . . . **48** A6
West Bridgford NG2 . . . **185** F7
Worksop S80 . . . . **47** B5
Clumber Rd E NG7 . . . . **222** C2
Clumber Rd W NG7 . . . **222** C2
Clumber St
Hucknall NG15 . . . . **146** C6
Kirkby-in-Ashfield NG17 . **115** C5
Long Eaton NG10 . . . . . **193** D7
Mansfield NG18 . . . . . . **102** B7
Market Warsop NG20 . . . **74** B4
Nottingham NG1 . . . . . **223** E3
Retford DN22 . . . . **39** E6
Sutton in Ashfield NG17 . **100** D2
Clumber Way NG22 . . . **106** A5
Clun Ct NG19 . . . . **88** D2
Clyro Pl
Sutton DN22 . . . . **28** F6
Sutton cum Lound DN22 . **28** F6
Coach Cl S81 . . . . **35** A7
Coach Cres S81 . . . . **35** A7
Coach Dr NG16 . . . . **143** F4
Coach Gap La NG13 . . . **190** D1
Coachmans Croft
NG8 . . . . **172** A5
Coach Rd
Market Warsop NG20 . . . **74** C1
Shireoaks S81 . . . . **34** F6
Worksop S81 . . . . **35** A7
Coalfields Cl NG17 . . . . **100** C1
Coal La LE14 . . . . **211** F8
Coalpit La
Elkesley DN22 . . . . **49** F4

Coalpit La *continued*
Elkesley DN22 . . . . **50** A4
Coal Rd S81 . . . . **36** E5
Coal Yd La NG23 . . . . . . **82** E8
COATES **43** E7
Coates Ave NG15 . . . . . **130** F1
Coates Rd DN22 . . . . **43** D8
Coatsby Rd NG16 . . . . . **158** F7
Cobblestone Dr NG18 . . **102** D5
Cobden Pl
Mansfield NG19 . . . . **87** E1
Mansfield NG19 . . . . **87** E2
Cobden Prim Sch & Com
Ctr LE11 . . . . **220** B4
Cobden St
Gainsborough DN21 . . . **24** C8
Kirkby-in-Ashfield NG17 . **115** A4
Long Eaton NG10 . . . . . **193** E7
Nottingham NG7 . . . . . **222** A3
Nottingham NG8 . . . . . **172** E4
Coburn St NG17 . . . . . . **100** F1
Cobwell Rd DN22 . . . . . . **39** E6
Cochrane Terr NG17 . . . **100** D6
Cockayne Cl NG10 . . . . **182** B3
Cocker Beck NG4 . . . . . **163** C7
Cockerels Roost LN1 . . . **55** A1
Cockerhouse Rd NG16 . **143** E4
Cockett La NG22 . . . . . . **119** E2
Cockhill Cl DN10 . . . . . . **10** A6
Cock Hill La DN10 . . . . . **10** A6
Cocking Hill
Boughton NG22 . . . . **77** F5
Kirton NG22 . . . . **78** B4
Kirton NG22 . . . . **78** C4
Cocking La DN22 . . . . . . **42** C2
Cockington Rd NG8 . . . **171** C5
Cockle Cl NG18 . . . . **102** E5
Cockleys NG10 . . . . **193** C6
Cockshut La NG20 . . . . . **59** A4
CODDINGTON **126** A2
Coddington CE Prim Sch
NG24 . . . . **126** A1
Coddington La NG16 . . . **127** A6
Coddington Rd NG24 . . **140** F5
Codrington Gdns
NG5 . . . . **161** C8
Cogenhoe Wlk NG5 . . . **147** F2
Coggin's La NG20 . . . . . **74** C6
Coghill Ct NG25 . . . . . . **136** D8
Coging Cl NG24 . . . . . . **140** C3
Cogley La NG13 . . . . . . **178** A4
Cohen Cl
Arnold NG5 . . . . **162** B6
Beeston NG9 . . . . **183** B2
Cokefield Ave NG16 . . . **159** F3
Colbeck St S80 . . . . **35** E3
Colborn St NG3 . . . . . . **173** F7
Colby Cl NG19 . . . . **89** B2
Coldharbour La NG23 . . **123** C7
Cold Harbour La NG23 . **109** D1
Coleby Ave NG7 . . . . . . **222** A1
Coleby Rd NG8 . . . . **159** F2
Coledale NG2 . . . . **186** C6
Coleman Ave NG24 . . . **140** B4
Coleridge Cres NG5 . . . **161** D7
Coleridge Rd
Balderton NG24 . . . . . . **140** E5
Worksop S80 . . . . **36** B5
Coleridge St NG7 . . . . . **222** B4
Colesbourne Rd NG7 . . **184** F2
Colgrove Rd LE11 . . . . . **220** A2
Colin Broughton Ct
NG6 . . . . **160** D7
Colindale Gdns NG16 . . **159** E3
Colinwood Ave NG5 . . . **146** E1
College Cl NG24 . . . . . . **139** D5
College Dr
Nottingham NG11 . . . . **184** D2
Nottingham NG11 . . . . **184** E3
College La
East Markham NG22 . . . . **66** A7
Worksop S80 . . . . **36** B1
College Rd
Beeston NG9 . . . . **183** E5
Carlton NG3 . . . . **162** C3
Sutton Bonington LE12 . **204** A1
College Side NG18 . . . . . **88** C1
College St
East Bridgford NG13 . . . **165** D3
Long Eaton NG10 . . . . . **182** C2
Nottingham NG1 . . . . . **223** D3
College Way NG8 . . . . . **171** C7
Colley La NG23 . . . . **81** B4
Colleymoor Leys La
NG7 . . . . **184** F2
Collier Ave NG19 . . . . . . **88** B5
Collier Gdns S81 . . . . . . **16** E1
Colliersway NG21 . . . . . **76** C3
Colliers Way NG6 . . . . . **160** A4
Colliers Wy NG12 . . . . . **188** A5
Colliery Cl NG2 . . . . **173** B1
Colliery Rd
Bircotes DN11 . . . . **9** B3
Creswell S80 . . . . **58** E8
Pinxton NG16 . . . . **113** D2
Colliery Way
Carlton NG4 . . . . **163** B3
Carlton NG4 . . . . **163** B4
Collin Ave NG10 . . . . . . **182** B4
COLLINGHAM **98** A2
Collingham Rd
Besthorpe NG23 . . . . **97** F4
Collingham LN6 . . . . **98** F1
Mansfield NG19 . . . . **87** D1
Newton on Trent LN1 . . . **69** A8
North Clifton NG23 . . . . . **68** F5
Collingham Sta NG23 . . **112** B8
Collin Gn NG5 . . . . **161** D4
Collington St NG9 . . . . **183** E6

Collington Way NG2 . . . **185** D6
Collingwood Cl NG11 . . **184** E2
Collingwood Rd NG10 . . **193** E6
Collinridge View NG22 . . **64** A2
Collins Ave
South Normanton DE55 . **113** A7
Sutton in Ashfield NG17 . **114** E7
Collins Cl NG6 . . . . **159** F5
Collinson La NG24 . . . . **140** F1
Collin St
Beeston NG9 . . . . **183** F6
Nottingham NG1 . . . . . **223** E1
Collins Wlk DN22 . . . . . . **39** F7
Collis Cl NG24 . . . . **140** D8
Collison St NG7 . . . . . . **222** B4
Collyer Rd NG14 . . . . . . **148** D8
Colly Gate NG16 . . . . . . **159** A5
Collygate Rd NG2 . . . . . **173** D1
Colmon Cl NG5 . . . . **161** A7
Colmon Wlk NG5 . . . . . **161** A7
Colne Ct NG19 . . . . **88** D2
Colney Way NG8 . . . . . **172** B6
Colonel Frank Seely Sch
NG14 . . . . **148** E8
Colonel's La LE14 . . . . . **210** A1
Colonsay Cl NG9 . . . . . **170** D3
Colsterdale S81 . . . . **36** B8
COLSTON BASSETT **200** C7
Colston Bassett La
Hose LE14 . . . . **211** C8
Owthorpe NG12 . . . . . . **199** F6
Owthorpe NG12 . . . . . . **200** A6
Colston Bassett Sch
NG12 . . . . **200** D7
Colston Cres NG2 . . . . . **185** D6
Colston Gate NG12 . . . . **188** A3
Colston La LE14 . . . . . . **201** E4
Colston Pastures NG12 **187** E3
Colston Rd
Colston Bassett NG12 . . **200** B8
Cropwell Bishop NG12 . . **189** A1
Mansfield NG18 . . . . . . **103** A3
Nottingham NG6 . . . . . **160** C7
Coltman Dr LE11 . . . . . **220** D3
Colton St DN10 . . . . **6** E2
Coltsfoot Cl NG13 . . . . . **177** C3
Columbia Ave
Mansfield NG18 . . . . . . **102** F5
Sutton in Ashfield NG17 . **100** C2
Columbia Cl NG16 . . . . **129** A7
Columbia St NG17 . . . . **100** A2
Columbus Ct S80 . . . . . . **35** C2
Colville St NG1 . . . . **173** B7
Colville Terr
Gainsborough DN21 . . . **24** D8
Nottingham NG1 . . . . . **173** B7
Colville Villas NG1 . . . . **173** B7
COLWICK **174** F5
Colwick Bsns Pk NG4 . . **174** F5
Colwick Cl NG19 . . . . . . **87** E1
Colwick Ctry Pk ★ NG2 **174** D3
Colwick Hall ★ NG2 . . . **174** C3
Colwick Ind Est NG4 . . **174** F5
Colwick Loop Rd
Carlton NG4 . . . . **163** C1
Carlton NG4 . . . . **175** A6
Carlton NG4 . . . . **175** B6
Colwick Manor Farm
NG4 . . . . **174** E5
Colwick Pk Cl NG4 . . . . **174** E5
Colwick Rd
Nottingham NG2 . . . . . **174** B4
West Bridgford NG2 . . . **173** C1
Colwick Woods Nature
Reserve ★ **174** B4
Combes The NG25 . . . . **121** D2
Comery Ave NG3 . . . . . . **174** A6
Comet Dr NG16 . . . . . . **144** A2
Comfrey Cl NG5 . . . . . . **160** E7
Comice Gdns NG16 . . . **143** D6
Commerce Sq NG1 . . . . **223** F2
Commercial Ave NG9 . . **183** F6
Commercial Gate
NG18 . . . . **102** B6
Commercial Rd
Keyworth NG12 . . . . . . **197** D3
Nottingham NG6 . . . . . **160** D7
Commercial St
NG18 . . . . **102** B6
Commodore Gdns
NG8 . . . . **160** C2
Common La
Beeston NG9 . . . . **183** A8
Blyth S81 . . . . **18** B4
Harworth DN11 . . . . **8** C3
Hucknall NG15 . . . . **145** D6
Mansfield Woodhouse
NG19 . . . . **88** A4
Ranskill DN22 . . . . **19** C4
Shirebrook NG20 . . . . . . **72** C2
Sturton le Steeple DN22 . **32** E6
Watnall NG16 . . . . **159** B7
Common Rd
Huthwaite NG17 . . . . **99** F2
Retford DN22 . . . . **39** F7
Thorpe Salvin S80 . . . . . **34** A5
Commons Cl NG16 . . . . **158** A8
Common Side NG16 . . . **128** F8
Common The
Hucknall NG15 . . . . **145** C6
South Normanton DE55 . **113** B6
Community Way S80 . . . **36** B1
Compton Acres NG2 . . . **185** B5
Compton Acres Sh Ctr
NG2 . . . . **185** C5
Compton Rd NG5 . . . . . **161** B3
Compton St NG20 . . . . . **72** F8
Comyn Gdns NG3 . . . . . **223** F4
Concorde Cl DE7 . . . . . **170** A7
Concorde Wy NG19 . . . . **87** E2
Conduit Cl NG2 . . . . **173** C2

Coneries The LE11 . . . . **220** B4
Conery Gdns NG13 . . . . **179** A3
Conery La
Whatton NG13 . . . . **178** F2
Whatton-in-the-Vale
NG13 . . . . **190** D8
Coney Green NG23 . . . . **111** F5
Coneygrey Spinney
NG23 . . . . **152** E2
Confetti NG7 . . . . **222** F3
Conifer Cres NG11 . . . . **195** E7
Conifer Wlk NG3 . . . . . **174** A8
Coningsby Ave S81 . . . . **35** C8
Coningsby Gdns East
NG5 . . . . **161** F4
Coningsby Rd NG5 . . . . **161** F5
Coningswath Rd NG4 . . **162** C1
Conisborough Terr
NG2 . . . . **173** C1
Conisbrough Ave NG4 . **163** B1
Coniston Ave NG6 . . . . **160** C2
Coniston Cl
Mansfield Woodhouse
NG19 . . . . **88** E4
West Bridgford NG2 . . . **186** C7
Coniston Rd
Beeston NG9 . . . . **183** D8
Hucknall NG15 . . . . **145** F8
Kirkby-in-Ashfield NG17 . **115** C6
Long Eaton NG10 . . . . . **182** A2
Worksop S81 . . . . **35** E8
Connah La NG22 . . . . . . **77** F7
Connaught Rd DN21 . . . **15** D2
Connelly Cl NG5 . . . . . . **162** C6
Connery Mews NG9 . . . **183** B1
Connery The NG15 . . . . **146** A7
Conrad Cl S80 . . . . **36** B3
Conrad Cl NG16 . . . . . . **159** F5
Constance St NG7 . . . . **161** A1
Continuation NG18 . . . . **102** B6
Convent St NG1 . . . . . . **223** F3
Conway Ave NG4 . . . . . **175** A7
Conway Cl
Mansfield NG19 . . . . . . **101** D8
Nottingham NG3 . . . . . **173** C7
Conway Cres NG4 . . . . **175** A8
Conway Dr S81 . . . . **25** F6
Conway Gdns
Arnold NG5 . . . . **161** F6
Retford DN22 . . . . **39** B8
Conway Rd
Carlton NG4 . . . . **175** A7
Hucknall NG15 . . . . **145** D3
Conway St NG10 . . . . . **193** F8
Conway Wlk NG3 . . . . . **173** C7
Cook Dr DE7 . . . . **170** A6
Cooke Cl NG10 . . . . **193** B7
Cooks La
Fiskerton NG25 . . . . **137** D2
Southwell NG25 . . . . . . **136** B8
Cookson Ave NG4 . . . . . **162** D2
Cookson St NG17 . . . . . **114** E5
Coombe Cl NG8 . . . . . . **172** C3
Coombe Rd NG16 . . . . . **144** B4
Co-Operative Ave
NG15 . . . . **146** B8
Co-Operative St
Long Eaton NG10 . . . . . **193** E6
Stanton Hill NG17 . . . . . **100** C6
Cooper Cl
Arnold NG5 . . . . **162** C6
Cropwell Bishop NG12 . . **189** A4
Nottingham NG6 . . . . . **159** F6
Cooper Ct LE11 . . . . . . **220** D2
Cooper Gdns NG11 . . . . **196** B7
Coopers Gn NG8 . . . . . **171** E2
Cooper Rise NG21 . . . . **104** A1
Cooper St NG4 . . . . **175** A6
Coopers Yard NG20 . . . . **74** B4
Coopers Yd NG24 . . . . . **139** E8
Coot Way NG4 . . . . **175** C3
Copeland Ave
Kirkby-in-Ashfield
NG17 . . . . **114** E6
Stapleford NG9 . . . . . . **182** E8
Copeland Gr NG13 . . . . **177** C3
Copeland Rd
Hucknall NG15 . . . . **146** C6
Kirkby-in-Ashfield NG17 . **114** E6
Copenhagen Ct NG3 . . . **161** D1
Cope St NG7 . . . . **222** B4
Copestake Cl NG10 . . . . **193** A7
Copper Beech Cl DN21 . **24** E4
Copper Hill NG23 . . . . . . **81** E4
Coppice Ave DE7 . . . . . **157** D5
Coppice Cl
Fenton NG23 . . . . **142** E2
Hucknall NG15 . . . . **145** E5
Nottingham NG5 . . . . . **161** E1
Coppice Croft NG17 . . . **100** C1
Coppice Dr NG16 . . . . . **143** D3
Coppice Form Prim Sch
NG5 . . . . **162** B7
Coppicegate NG5 . . . . . **161** F8
Coppice Gr NG3 . . . . . . **161** E1
Coppice Rd
Arnold NG5 . . . . **162** B8
Clipstone NG19 . . . . **89** D3
Worksop S81 . . . . **35** F7
Coppice The
Barnby Moor DN22 . . . . **28** D5
Shirebrook NG20 . . . . . . **72** D3
Coppice View DE55 . . . **113** A4
Coppice Way DN11 . . . . . **9** A3
Coppywood Dr NG3 . . . **162** C5
Coppywood Ct NG17 . . . **100** B7
Copse Cl
Burton Joyce NG14 . . . . **163** F5
Ravenshead NG15 . . . . . **116** C3
Copseside Cl NG10 . . . . **193** A8

Copse The
Beeston NG9 ... 183 C6
Farndon NG24 ... 139 A4
Hucknall NG15 ... 146 C6
Ilkeston DE7 ... 157 D5
Mansfield NG18 ... 102 C2
Stanton Hill NG17 ... 100 C5
Copsewood DE55 ... 113 A4
Coral Cres NG20 ... 74 A5
Corben Gdns NG6 ... 159 F7
Corbett Chase 6 NG4 ... 162 E3
Corbett Cres NG15 ... 130 F1
Corbiere Ave NG16 ... 159 A7
Corby Rd NG3 ... 161 E1
Cordy La
Brinsley NG16 ... 143 F8
Underwood NG16 ... 128 F1
Corene Ave NG17 ... 100 E1
Coriander Dr NG6 ... 160 D3
Corinthian Cl NG15 ... 131 C1
Corinth Rd NG7 ... 184 E2
Corkhill La NG22 ... 121 D5
Cormack La NG24 ... 140 F1
Corn Cft NG11 ... 184 F1
Corn Cl
Cotgrave NG12 ... 187 E2
South Normanton DE55 ... 113 A5
Corncrake Ave NG6 ... 160 D3
Corncrake Dr NG5 ... 162 C7
Corncrake Mews 2
NG17 ... 115 A3
Cornelia Mws DN22 ... 40 A4
Cornell Dr NG5 ... 162 C8
Corner Croft NG17 ... 100 A3
Corner Farm Cl
Rolleston NG23 ... 138 A6
Sutton cum Lound DN22 ... 29 A6
Corner Farm Dr DN10 ... 11 C3
CornerhouseThe★
NG1 ... 223 E3
Cornerpin Dr NG17 ... 115 B6
Corner The NG14 ... 150 D1
Cornfield Ave DE55 ... 113 A4
Cornfield Cl S81 ... 26 A7
Cornfield Rd NG16 ... 158 E7
Cornflower Way
East Leake LE12 ... 205 F1
East Leake LE12 ... 215 A8
Cornhill Rd NG4 ... 174 B7
Cornley Rd DN10 ... 6 C3
Corn Mill La S81 ... 25 C3
Cornmill Rd
Sutton Forest Side
NG17 ... 101 B1
Sutton in Ashfield NG17 ... 101 B1
Cornstone Ave 4 DE55 ... 99 B7
Cornwall Ave
Beeston NG9 ... 184 C4
Mansfield NG18 ... 102 F6
Cornwall Cl NG16 ... 128 C4
Cornwall Dr
Barton in Fabis NG10 ... 194 A8
Ollerton NG22 ... 77 A3
Cornwallis Cl NG10 ... 193 D6
Cornwall Rd
Arnold NG5 ... 161 C7
Retford DN22 ... 30 A1
Shireoaks S81 ... 34 F7
Coronation Ave
Long Clawson LE14 ... 211 B2
Misson DN10 ... 4 B3
New Houghton NG19 ... 86 F7
Nottingham NG11 ... 185 B8
Sandiacre NG10 ... 182 A7
Coronation Dr
Mansfield NG19 ... 103 A8
Shirebrook NG20 ... 72 F2
South Normanton DE55 ... 113 B6
Coronation Rd
Arnold NG3 ... 161 F3
Awsworth DE7 ... 158 A1
Bestwood Village NG6 ... 146 E4
Cossall NG16 ... 158 B2
Hucknall NG15 ... 145 F8
Nuthall NG16 ... 159 C5
Coronation St
Mansfield NG18 ... 102 D6
New Balderton NG24 ... 140 C5
Retford DN22 ... 39 E6
Sutton in Ashfield NG17 ... 100 E1
Whitwell S80 ... 45 A6
Coronation Wlk NG4 ... 163 A1
Corporation Oaks
NG3 ... 173 C7
Corporation Rd DE7 ... 170 A5
Corporation St 8
NG18 ... 102 A7
Corringham Rd DN21 ... 15 F1
Corsham Gdns NG3 ... 174 A7
Cosby Dr LE12 ... 205 E3
Cosby Rd 4 NG2 ... 173 F3
Cosgrove Ave NG17 ... 101 B5
COSSALL ... 158 C1
Cossall Ind Est NG16 ... 158 B2
Cossall Rd NG9 ... 170 D5
Cossethay Dr NG8 ... 159 C2
Costhorpe Ind Est S81 ... 16 E1
Costhorpe Villas S81 ... 16 E1
COSTOCK ... 206 C1
Costock Ave NG5 ... 161 B4
Costock Rd
East Leake LE12 ... 206 A1
Wysall NG12 ... 207 C2
COTES ... 220 F6
Cotes Dr LE11 ... 220 B6
Cotes La LE11 ... 220 C8
Cotes Rd LE12 ... 220 F5
Coteswood House Sch
NG5 ... 161 E5
COTGRAVE ... 187 E2
Cotgrave Ave NG4 ... 162 F2
Cotgrave Bsns Pk
NG12 ... 188 A4
Cotgrave Candleby Lane
School NG12 ... 187 F3
Cotgrave CE Prim Sch
NG12 ... 187 E3
Cotgrave Cl NG8 ... 159 E2
Cotgrave Ctry Pk★
NG12 ... 188 A6
Cotgrave La NG12 ... 187 A2
Cotgrave L Ctr NG12 ... 188 A3
Cotgrave Rd
Cotgrave NG12 ... 187 A1
Cotgrave NG12 ... 187 E3
Mansfield NG19 ... 87 F2
Owthorpe NG12 ... 199 C8
COTHAM ... 154 F4
COTMANHAY ... 157 E4
Cotmanhay Rd DE7 ... 157 E3
Cotmoor La NG25 ... 135 D5
Coton Cl
Mansfield Woodhouse
NG19 ... 88 E4
Nottingham NG11 ... 185 A3
Cotswold Cl 2 NG10 ... 193 B8
Cotswold Ct
Beeston NG9 ... 171 D1
Carlton in Lindrick S81 ... 25 E7
Cotswold Gr NG18 ... 103 B6
Cotswold Rd NG8 ... 159 E1
Cottage Ave NG13 ... 178 F4
Cottage Cl
Balderton NG24 ... 140 D2
Blidworth NG21 ... 117 F4
East Leake LE12 ... 205 E3
Ilkeston DE7 ... 157 D3
Stanton Hill NG17 ... 100 C6
Cottage Gdns Cl LE12 ... 213 A1
Cottage La
Collingham NG23 ... 111 F6
Market Warsop NG20 ... 74 C2
North Clifton NG23 ... 69 B4
Cottage Mdw NG4 ... 174 F4
Cottage Pasture La
NG14 ... 164 E7
Cottage Terr NG1 ... 222 C3
COTTAM ... 43 D4
Cottam Dr NG5 ... 161 A8
Cottam Gdns NG5 ... 161 A8
Cottam Gr NG19 ... 101 D6
Cottam La DN22 ... 42 D6
Cottam Rd
Cottam DN22 ... 43 C4
South Leverton DN22 ... 42 E7
Cottans Cl NG25 ... 136 F8
Cotterdale Cl NG19 ... 88 E1
Cotterhill Cl S81 ... 25 D1
Cottesmore Rd NG7 ... 222 B2
Cotton Dr NG24 ... 140 A4
Cotton Mill La NG22 ... 120 A5
Cottonwood Rd NG17 ... 100 C5
Coulby Cl NG23 ... 156 E6
Coulton's Ave NG17 ... 100 C3
Coulton's Cl NG17 ... 100 C3
Country Cres NG15 ... 146 D2
County Bsns Pk NG2 ... 173 E2
County Cl NG9 ... 184 A5
County Estate The NG17 ... 99 E2
County Rd
Carlton NG4 ... 162 C3
Nottingham NG2 ... 173 E2
Coupe Gdns NG15 ... 146 B6
Coupland Cl 6 DN21 ... 15 F1
Court Cres NG8 ... 171 F4
Courtenay Gdns NG3 ... 173 D7
Court-Field Rd NG17 ... 101 A6
Court Gdns NG11 ... 185 B4
Courtlett Way NG6 ... 160 B5
Courtney Cl NG8 ... 171 E5
Court St 11 NG7 ... 172 F7
Court The LE12 ... 212 B4
Courtyard The NG12 ... 197 E2
Court Yd NG9 ... 183 B8
Covedale Rd NG5 ... 161 C5
Covent Gdns NG12 ... 176 E3
Coventry Ct NG6 ... 160 C5
Coventry Dr S81 ... 36 A6
Coventry La NG9 ... 171 A3
Coventry Rd
Beeston NG9 ... 184 A7
Nottingham NG6 ... 160 B6
Cove Rd DN9 ... 2 E6
Coverdale S81 ... 36 B7
Cover Dr NG13 ... 181 B1
Covert Cl
Burton Joyce NG14 ... 163 E5
Hucknall NG15 ... 146 C6
Keyworth NG12 ... 197 F4
Covert Rd NG2 ... 186 B6
Cowan St NG1 ... 223 F3
Cowdell Gr NG13 ... 177 D7
Cowdray Cl LE11 ... 220 A1
Cowdrey Gdns NG5 ... 162 B6
Cow La
Beeston NG9 ... 183 C8
Newark-on-Trent NG24 ... 124 F1
Cowlairs NG5 ... 160 E7
Cowley Cl DE7 ... 157 F5
Cowley St NG6 ... 160 D3
Cowpasture La
Sturton le Steeple DN21 ... 33 C6
Sutton in Ashfield NG17 ... 100 E1
Cow Pasture La
Kirkby-in-Ashfield
NG17 ... 114 D5
Misson DN10 ... 4 F5
Cow Pature La DN9 ... 5 A5
Cowper Cl S81 ... 36 B5
Cowper Rd
Arnold NG5 ... 161 E4
Eastwood NG16 ... 158 A8
Cowper Rise S81 ... 36 B5
Cowpes Cl NG17 ... 100 E4
Cowslip Cl
Bingham NG13 ... 177 C3
East Leake LE12 ... 206 A1
Cowslip Dr S81 ... 25 F7
Cox Dr NG13 ... 180 F3
Coxmoor Cl NG2 ... 186 C4
Coxmoor Ct 14 NG5 ... 147 A1
Coxmoor Rd NG17,
NG15 ... 115 E7
Cox's Hill DN21 ... 15 D1
Cox's La NG19 ... 88 B5
Crabapple Dr NG16 ... 143 C4
Crab Apple Gr NG15 ... 146 C4
Crab La NG23 ... 110 F1
Crab Nook La NG22 ... 119 F6
Crabtree Farm Prim Sch
NG6 ... 160 B6
Crabtree Field NG2 ... 174 D4
Crabtree La
Beckingham DN10 ... 22 F7
Beckingham DN10 ... 23 A8
High Marnham NG23 ... 67 D2
Crabtree Rd NG6 ... 160 A6
Craddock St LE11 ... 220 B4
Crafts Way NG25 ... 121 E1
Cragdale Rd NG5 ... 161 C5
Cragg La DE55 ... 99 A2
Cragmoor Rd NG14 ... 163 E3
Crags Bsns Pk S80 ... 58 E8
Crags Rd
Belph S80 ... 45 B3
Creswell S80 ... 45 A1
Craig Moray NG12 ... 176 A4
Craigs Gn NG19 ... 101 E5
Craig St NG10 ... 193 E7
Craigston Rd S81 ... 25 E6
Crammond Cl 3 NG2 ... 173 B2
Crampton Cl NG17 ... 100 B3
Crampton Ct NG5 ... 161 A8
Crampton Rd NG18 ... 102 E8
Cramworth Gr 4 NG5 ... 161 D3
Cranberry Cl NG2 ... 185 B5
Cranborne Cl NG19 ... 101 D7
Cranbourne Cl NG9 ... 170 D2
Cranbourne Gr NG15 ... 145 E7
Cranbrook Ct NG19 ... 88 C6
Cranbrook St NG1 ... 223 F3
Craneworks Cl LE11 ... 220 B6
Cranfleet Way NG10 ... 193 B7
Cranford Gdns NG2 ... 185 C4
Crankley La NG23 ... 124 D4
Cranleigh Dr NG14 ... 150 D1
Cranmer Ave NG13 ... 178 E3
Cranmer Gr
8 Nottingham NG3 ... 173 C7
Radmanthwaite NG19 ... 87 D3
Cranmer Rd NG24 ... 139 F5
Cranmer St
Ilkeston DE7 ... 157 F1
Long Eaton NG10 ... 182 D1
Nottingham NG3 ... 173 C7
Cranmore Cl NG5 ... 148 A2
Cranshaw Cl LE12 ... 212 C3
Cransley Ave NG8 ... 171 D2
Cranston Ave NG5 ... 147 F1
Cranston Rd NG9 ... 171 C1
Cranswick Cl
Hucknall NG15 ... 131 D1
Mansfield Woodhouse
NG19 ... 89 A2
Cranthorne Dr NG3 ... 174 C6
Crantock Gdns NG12 ... 197 F3
Cranwell Cl NG24 ... 125 D1
Cranwell Ct NG6 ... 159 F6
Cranwell Rd NG8 ... 159 D2
Craster Dr
Arnold NG5 ... 148 A2
Nottingham NG6 ... 159 F8
Craster St NG17 ... 100 E1
Crathie Rd S81 ... 25 E6
Craven Rd NG7 ... 172 E7
Crawford Ave NG9 ... 182 D8
Crawford Cl NG8 ... 171 E5
Crawford Rise NG5 ... 162 C8
Crawfords Mdw NG13 ... 178 F5
C Rd NG9 ... 184 D6
Creamery Cl NG8 ... 172 B7
Crees La NG24 ... 139 B6
Crees Yard NG17 ... 114 A4
Crescent Ave NG4 ... 162 E1
Crescent Prim Sch
NG19 ... 87 D2
Crescent Rd NG16 ... 128 D6
Crescent The
Arnold NG5 ... 161 E4
Beckingham DN10 ... 14 B1
Beeston, Chilwell NG9 ... 183 C3
Beeston, Toton NG9 ... 183 A2
Bilsthorpe NG22 ... 105 E6
Bircotes DN11 ... 9 C4
Blidworth NG21 ... 118 B5
East Leake LE12 ... 205 F2
Eastwood NG16 ... 144 A2
Lea DN21 ... 24 F2
Mansfield NG18 ... 102 C3
Newark-on-Trent NG24 ... 140 A6
Nottingham NG3 ... 173 D8
Old Dalby LE14 ... 219 B6
Radcliffe on Trent NG12 ... 176 A3
Retford DN22 ... 39 D6
Shirebrook NG20 ... 72 E6
Stapleford NG9 ... 170 E2
Sutton in Ashfield NG17 ... 100 D7
Cresswell Rd
Beeston NG9 ... 183 B5
Worksop S80 ... 35 E4
Cresswell St S80 ... 35 E3
Cressy Rd NG7 ... 184 F2
Cresta Gdns NG3 ... 161 D2
CRESWELL ... 58 D8
Creswell Crags Mus & Ed
Ctr★ S80 ... 45 B1
Creswell Ct NG19 ... 88 E4
Creswell Rd
Cuckney NG20 ... 59 E3
Cuckney NG20 ... 60 A3
Crewe Cl
Blidworth NG21 ... 118 A6
Nottingham NG7 ... 222 B4
Crewe Rd DN11 ... 9 B4
Crew La NG25 ... 137 A8
Crew La Ind Est NG25 ... 137 A8
Crew Rd
Collingham NG23 ... 98 B1
Collingham NG23 ... 112 B8
Crew Yard The DN10 ... 11 C3
Cribb Cl NG11 ... 185 B7
Crich View
Newton DE55 ... 99 A4
Nottingham NG5 ... 161 C2
Cricket Cl NG17 ... 129 F8
Cricketers Ct NG2 ... 173 F1
Cricketers Dr LE11 ... 220 A6
Cricket Field La DN22 ... 39 E8
Cricket Green LN1 ... 57 A5
Criftin Rd NG14 ... 164 A4
Crink La NG25 ... 136 F6
Cripps Hill NG7 ... 172 C2
Crispin Way NG8 ... 172 C7
Critchley St DE7 ... 157 F1
Critch's Flats NG16 ... 158 F6
Crocus Close
Newark-on-Trent NG24 ... 139 F4
Newark-on-Trent NG24 ... 140 A4
Crocus Gardens 5
NG12 ... 186 A2
Crocus St
Kirkby-in-Ashfield
NG17 ... 115 B4
Nottingham NG2 ... 173 D2
Croft Ave
Hucknall NG15 ... 146 A6
Mansfield NG18 ... 102 C2
Croft Cl
Pinxton NG16 ... 113 C3
Rolleston NG23 ... 138 A6
Croft Cres NG16 ... 158 C5
Croft Ct NG17 ... 99 F4
Croft Dr DN11 ... 8 A8
Crofters View DN22 ... 39 E8
Croft Farm Cl
Everton DN10 ... 11 C3
Rolleston NG23 ... 138 B6
Croft Gdns LE14 ... 218 E4
Crofton Cl
Beeston NG9 ... 183 D3
3 Nottingham NG8 ... 172 B6
Crofton Rd NG9 ... 183 D2
Croft Prim Sch NG17 ... 100 F2
Croft Rd
Arnold NG5 ... 161 F8
Finningley DN10 ... 1 A1
Keyworth NG12 ... 197 D3
West Bridgford NG12 ... 186 A4
Croft Rise NG13 ... 165 C3
Crofts The
Bingham NG13 ... 177 E4
North Scarle LN6 ... 83 E3
Croft The
Beckingham DN10 ... 23 C8
Kegworth DE74 ... 203 D2
Newark-on-Trent NG24 ... 140 A8
Retford DN22 ... 39 F8
Shirebrook NG20 ... 72 E3
South Normanton DE55 ... 113 B6
Stanton Hill NG17 ... 100 C5
Croft Way DN10 ... 11 C3
Croft Wlk S80 ... 45 A6
Cromarty Cl NG19 ... 101 D5
Cromarty Ct 2 NG2 ... 173 B2
Cromdale Cl NG5 ... 148 C1
Cromer Cl NG18 ... 102 C4
Cromer Rd NG3 ... 173 E7
Cromford Ave
Carlton NG4 ... 174 D8
Mansfield NG18 ... 102 A4
Cromford Cl
Aldercar NG16 ... 143 B4
Long Eaton NG10 ... 193 A5
Cromford Rd
Annesley Woodhouse
NG17 ... 115 A1
Langley Mill NG16 ... 143 B4
West Bridgford NG2 ... 185 F6
Cromford Road Ind Est
DE75 ... 143 B4
Cromford St
Gainsborough DN21 ... 15 C1
2 Gainsborough DN21 ... 15 D1
Crompton Rd
Bilsthorpe NG22 ... 105 F6
Ilkeston DE7 ... 170 B3
Radmanthwaite NG19 ... 87 D3
Crompton St
New Houghton NG19 ... 86 F8
Teversal NG17 ... 100 B7
Crompton View Prim Sch
NG22 ... 105 F6
CROMWELL ... 110 E7
Cromwell Ave
Ilkeston DE7 ... 170 A5
Lea DN21 ... 24 F3
Cromwell Cres NG4 ... 163 B7
Cromwell Dr LE12 ... 205 E1
Cromwell Farm Cl
NG23 ... 110 F8
Cromwell Rd
Aslockton NG13 ... 178 E3
Beeston NG9 ... 183 E6
Newark-on-Trent NG24 ... 140 B7
Cromwell St
Carlton NG4 ... 174 E7
Eastwood NG16 ... 158 C8
Gainsborough DN21 ... 24 D6
Mansfield NG18 ... 102 C6
Nottingham NG7 ... 222 C3
Cromwell Terr DE7 ... 157 F3
Crookdole La NG14 ... 148 F7
Crooked Billet St DN21 ... 15 B4
Crookes Ave NG19 ... 87 A5
Crookford Hill
Clumber and Hardwick
DN22 ... 48 E3
Elkesley DN22 ... 49 E3
Crook's Ave NG19 ... 88 C3
Croome Cl LE11 ... 220 C1
Crops The NG22 ... 120 F6
Cropston Cl NG2 ... 185 E4
Cropton Cres NG8 ... 172 B6
Cropton Gr NG13 ... 177 C4
CROPWELL BISHOP ... 189 B4
Cropwell Bishop Prim Sch
NG12 ... 189 B4
Cropwell Bishop Rd
NG12 ... 189 B6
CROPWELL BUTLER ... 189 B7
Cropwell Butler Rd
Cropwell Bishop NG12 ... 189 B4
Cropwell Bishop NG12 ... 189 B5
Cropwell Ct NG18 ... 102 D7
Cropwell Gdns NG12 ... 176 A2
Cropwell Gn NG3 ... 173 F6
Cropwell Rd
Colston Bassett NG12 ... 189 F2
Cropwell Butler NG12 ... 188 D8
Langar NG13 ... 190 C1
Owthorpe NG12 ... 199 F5
Radcliffe on Trent NG12 ... 176 A2
Tithby NG13 ... 189 D6
Crosby Cl NG19 ... 89 A1
Crosby Rd NG2 ... 185 F8
Cross Comm La DN22 ... 33 A5
Crossdale Dr NG12 ... 197 E4
Crossdale Wlk NG5 ... 160 E8
Cross Dr
Kirkby-in-Ashfield
NG17 ... 115 B7
Rainworth NG21 ... 104 B1
Crossfield Dr
13 Nottingham NG5 ... 147 A1
Nottingham NG5 ... 161 A8
Crossgate Dr NG2 ... 173 A1
Crosshill NG12 ... 188 A3
Cross Hill
Gringley on the Hill DN10 ... 12 F2
Laxton NG22 ... 79 C3
Cross Hill Cl LE12 ... 216 C3
Crossings The 3
NG24 ... 140 B8
Cross La
Austerfield DN10 ... 3 C5
Balderton NG24 ... 140 D1
Blidworth NG21 ... 117 D6
Collingham NG23 ... 112 C8
East Bridgford NG13 ... 165 D3
Elkesley DN22 ... 49 F4
Elston NG23 ... 153 F2
Elston NG23 ... 154 A3
Farndon NG24 ... 138 F4
Gringley on the Hill DN10 ... 5 A1
Harby NG23 ... 70 D2
Long Bennington NG13 ... 169 F3
Staunton in the Vale
NG23 ... 169 F2
Crossland Rd NG5 ... 161 A5
Crosslands Mdw NG4 ... 174 F4
Crossley Ave NG17 ... 100 A3
Crossley Hill La S81 ... 26 C4
Crossley St NG5 ... 161 B2
Crossman St NG5 ... 161 C2
Cross Rd NG15 ... 130 C7
Cross Row
Huthwaite NG17 ... 100 A2
Stanton Hill NG17 ... 100 C5
Cross St
Arnold NG5 ... 161 E8
Barnby in the Willows
NG24 ... 141 F5
Beeston NG9 ... 183 F7
Bilsthorpe NG22 ... 105 F6
Carlton, Netherfield NG4 ... 175 A7
Carlton, Thorneywood
NG4 ... 174 D8
Eastwood NG16 ... 144 A2
4 Gainsborough DN21 ... 15 D1
Gainsborough DN21 ... 24 D8
Hathern LE12 ... 213 A1
Kirkby-in-Ashfield NG17 ... 115 C6
Langold S81 ... 16 E3
Long Eaton NG10 ... 193 E8
Loughborough LE11 ... 220 C5
Mansfield Woodhouse
NG19 ... 88 B2
Morton DN21 ... 15 B4
Newark-on-Trent NG24 ... 140 B8
Retford DN22 ... 40 A6
Sandiacre NG10 ... 182 C6
Sturton le Steeple DN22 ... 32 D5
Cross The
Carlton in Lindrick S81 ... 26 A6
Cotgrave NG12 ... 187 E3
Crossways
East Markham NG22 ... 66 A7
Retford DN22 ... 39 F8
Crossways Dr NG13 ... 165 D3
Crowborough Ave NG8 ... 171 E2
Crowcroft Way NG10 ... 182 B2
Crow Ct NG13 ... 178 A4
Crow Hill NG19 ... 87 B5
Crow Hill Ct NG18 ... 102 B8
Crow Hill Dr NG18 ... 102 B8
Crow Hill La NG19 ... 88 B2
Crow Hill Rd NG4 ... 174 F7
Crow Hl Ri NG18 ... 102 B8
Crow La
Ollerton NG22 ... 77 C2
South Muskham
NG23, NG24 ... 124 D7
Crowley Cl NG8 ... 171 C6
Crown Ave NG19 ... 103 A8
Crown Cl
Collingham NG23 ... 98 A1
Long Eaton NG10 ... 193 A7
Rainworth NG21 ... 118 C8
Crown Ct DN22 ... 32 D5
Crown Farm Way
Forest Town NG19 ... 89 D1
Mansfield NG19 ... 103 B8
Crown St
Mansfield NG18 ... 102 F6
Newark-on-Trent NG24 ... 139 F7
Nottingham NG15 ... 146 C4
Worksop S80 ... 35 E4
Crown Wy NG16 ... 143 B4
Crow Pk Ave NG23 ... 81 E1
Crow Pk Dr NG14 ... 163 E3
Crowthorne Cl NG5 ... 146 E1
Crowthorne Gardens
NG5 ... 146 E1
Crowtrees Dr NG17 ... 100 D1
Croxall Cl NG11 ... 184 E4
Croxley Gdns NG16 ... 159 D3
Croxton Ct NG19 ... 88 E3
Croyde Gdns NG12 ... 186 B7
Croydon Rd NG7 ... 222 A3
Crummock Cl NG9 ... 183 C8
Crystal Ct S81 ... 25 D1
CUCKNEY ... 60 A4
Cuckney CE Prim Sch
NG20 ... 60 A2
Cuckney Hill
Church Warsop NG20 ... 74 B7
Cuckney NG20 ... 60 B1
Cuckney Rd NG20 ... 61 D3
Cuckoo Holt S81 ... 35 C7
Cuckstool The NG23 ... 96 F8
Cudworth Dr NG3 ... 161 F2
Cuillin Cl NG10 ... 182 A1
Cul-de-sac NG22 ... 105 F6
Cullen Cl NG24 ... 124 E1
Cullen's Ct NG5 ... 161 C2
Cullin Cl NG5 ... 146 F2
Culpepper Ave NG22 ... 77 D3
Cultivation Rd 4
NG16 ... 144 A1
Culvert Rise NG14 ... 173 E2
Cumberland Ave
Beeston NG9 ... 183 D6
Market Warsop NG20 ... 74 A5
Cumberland Cl
Bircotes DN11 ... 9 D4
Carlton in Lindrick S81 ... 25 F7
Ruddington NG11 ... 196 D7
Westwood NG16 ... 128 C4
Cumberland
Drive NG19 ... 101 D7
Cumberland
Place NG1 ... 223 D2
Cumbria Grange 12
NG12 ... 186 C7
Cumbria Rd S81 ... 36 A6
Cundy Hill NG25 ... 136 B6
Cunningham Close
DN10 ... 19 F8
Cupar Cl NG20 ... 74 C6
Curbar Cl NG19 ... 102 D5
Curie Ct NG7 ... 172 D2
Curlew Cl NG3 ... 174 C5
Curlew Wharf 5 NG7 ... 172 F2
Currie Rd NG24 ... 125 A2
Cursley Way NG9 ... 183 C2
Curtis Cl NG23 ... 98 A1
Curtis St NG15 ... 146 A6
Curzon Ave NG4 ... 174 B7
Curzon Cl NG21 ... 118 A8
Curzon Ct NG3 ... 223 F4
Curzon Dr S81 ... 35 F7
Curzon Gdns NG3 ... 223 F4
Curzon Pl NG3 ... 223 F3
Curzon St
Carlton NG4 ... 175 A7
Gainsborough DN21 ... 15 C2
Gotham NG11 ... 195 B1
Long Eaton NG10 ... 182 B2
Loughborough LE11 ... 220 A3
Nottingham NG3 ... 223 F3
Cusworth Way S80 ... 35 D3
Cuthbert Pl DN22 ... 29 F1
Cuthberts Ave
Worksop S80 ... 47 A7
Worksop S80 ... 47 B7
Cutlersforth NG22 ... 135 C8
Cut Throat La DN22 ... 41 B8
Cut Through La NG8 ... 172 C1
Cuttings Ave NG17 ... 114 B8
Cutts Way NG21 ... 118 B6
Cuxton Cl NG8 ... 159 D1
Cyan Close NG4 ... 175 C8
Cycle Rd NG7 ... 222 A2
Cygnet Fold NG19 ... 88 C4
Cypress Ct NG15 ... 145 C5
Cyprus Ave NG9 ... 183 F7
Cyprus Dr NG9 ... 183 F7
Cyprus Rd NG3 ... 161 C1
Cyril Ave
Beeston NG9 ... 183 E7
Nottingham NG8 ... 172 D8
Stapleford NG9 ... 182 D7
Cyril Rd NG2 ... 186 A7

D

Dabek Rise NG17 . . . . . .115 A1
Dabell Ave NG6. . . . . . .159 F8
Dadley Rd S81. . . . . . . .25 F7
Dadsley Rd DN11 . . . . . . 8 A8
Dagmar Gr
　Beeston NG9 . . . . .184 A6
　Nottingham NG3 . . . . . .161 D1
Dahlia Ave DE55 . . . . . .113 B7
Dairy Farm Ct DN21. . . . .7 E2
Dairyfield Dr S80 . . . . . .59 E8
Dairy Gdns LE14 . . . . . .202 A3
Dairy La
　Hose LE14 . . . . .211 F7
　Nether Broughton LE14. .219 D8
Dairy Square NG8 . . . . .172 B7
Daisy Cl
　Cotgrave NG12 . . . . . . .187 E2
　Shirebrook NG20. . . . . . .72 D2
Daisy Farm Rd NG16 . . .158 B8
Daisy Rd NG3. . . . . . . .162 A1
Dakeyne Mws NG14. . . .173 E4
Dakeyne St NG3 . . . . . .173 E5
Dakota Dr NG24 . . . . . .141 A1
Dakota Rd NG13 . . . . . .177 B7
Dalbeattie Cl NG5 . . . . .162 B8
Dalby Cl NG11 . . . . . . .196 B8
Dalby Sq NG8. . . . . . . .172 C3
Dale Ave
　Carlton NG4. . . . . .174 C7
　Long Eaton NG10. . . . . .182 D1
　Newton DE55. . . . . .99 A3
　Nottingham NG3 . . . . . .162 A2
Dalebrook Cres NG15. . .145 C5
Dale Cl
　Blidworth NG21. . . . . . .118 A5
　Hucknall NG15. . . . . . . .145 C5
　Langwith NG20. . . . . . . .72 B8
　Retford DN22. . . . . .39 D6
　Sutton in Ashfield NG17 .101 A5
　West Bridgford NG2 . . . .186 B7
　Whaley Thorns NG20. . . . .58 F1
Dale Cres NG24 . . . . . .140 E2
Dale Farm Ave NG3 . . . .174 A5
Dale Gr NG2. . . . . .173 F4
Dalehead Rd NG11. . . . .184 D2
Dale La
　Ault Hucknall S44. . . . . .86 D7
　Beeston NG9 . . . . .183 E5
　Blidworth NG21. . . . . . .118 B5
Dalemoor Gdns NG8 . . .172 B8
Dale Rd
　Carlton NG4. . . . . .174 C7
　Keyworth NG12. . . . . . .197 E3
　Kimberley NG16. . . . . . .158 F5
　Market Warsop NG20 . . . .74 C5
Dales Ave NG17. . . . . . .100 F5
Dales Cl LE12. . . . . . . .215 E5
Daleside NG12 . . . . . . .187 E2
Daleside Rd NG2 . . . . . .174 A3
Daleside Rd E
　Nottingham NG2, NG3. .174 C4
　Nottingham NG4. . . . . . .174 D5
Dales La DN10. . . . . .4 F4
Dale St
　Mansfield NG19. . . . . . . .88 B1
　Nottingham NG2 . . . . . .173 E4
Dalestorth Ave NG19. . . .87 D1
Dalestorth Cl NG17 . . . .101 A5
Dalestorth Gdns NG17 . .101 A5
Dalestorth Prim Sch
　NG17 . . . . .101 A4
Dalestorth Rd NG17. . . .101 A4
Dalestorth St NG17 . . . .101 A4
Dales Way NG9 . . . . . . .171 B4
DALESWORTH 101 B5
Dale View Rd NG3 . . . . .174 B7
Dalewood Cl DE55. . . . .113 A3
Dale Wy NG24 . . . . . . .140 F1
Dalkeith Terr [10] NG17 . .172 F7
Dallaglio Mews NG9 . . .183 B2
Dallas St NG18. . . . . . . .102 A6
Dallas York Rd NG9 . . . .184 B6
Dalley Cl NG9. . . . . . . .182 F7
Dallington St NG9 . . . . .171 F8
Dallman Cl NG15 . . . . . .146 A5
Dalton Cl NG9 . . . . .182 E5
Dalton Dr DN10. . . . . . . .10 A8
Daltons Cl
　Aldercar NG16. . . . . . . .143 A4
　Eagle LN6. . . . . .84 D2
Dame Flogan St NG18. . .102 B6
Dame La DN10. . . . . .4 B2
Dam Rd DN11. . . . . .8 A6
Damson Rd LE12. . . . . .214 C8
Damson Wlk NG3. . . . . .174 B8
Dane Cl NG3. . . . . .223 F4
Dane Ct NG3 . . . . .223 F4
Dane Gr NG15 . . . . .130 D7
Danes Cl NG5. . . . . . . .161 D8
Danesfield Rd S80 . . . . .35 F1
Daneshill Gravel Pits Nature Reserve*
　DN22 . . . . .19 D1
Daneshill Rd
　Lound DN22. . . . . .20 A1
　Lound DN22. . . . . .29 C8
Danes Rd DN21. . . . . . . .15 F1
Danethorpe La NG24. . . .126 B8
Danethorpe Vale NG5. . .161 C4
Daniel Cres NG18 . . . . .101 F7
Daniel Mews NG10. . . . .182 A5
Daniels Way NG15 . . . . .145 E4
Danners Hill NG15. . . . .131 E5
Danvers Ave NG17 . . . . .114 B8

Danvers Dr NG19 . . . . . .101 E7
Darbyshire Cl NG23 . . . . .70 D2
Darfield Ct DN11. . . . . . . .8 A7
Darfield Dr DE75. . . . . . .143 A2
Darkey La NG9 . . . . . . .182 E5
Dark La
　Aslockton NG13. . . . . . .179 A4
　Barnby in the Willows
　　NG24. . . . . .142 A5
　Bingham NG13. . . . . . . .178 A4
　West Leake LE12. . . . . .204 F2
Darley Ave
　Beeston NG9 . . . . .182 F3
　Carlton NG4. . . . . .174 D1
　Kirkby-in-Ashfield NG17 .115 C5
　Nottingham NG7 . . . . . .172 E7
Darleydale Cl NG18 . . . .102 D3
Darley Dr NG10 . . . . . . .193 A5
Darley Rd NG7. . . . . . . .172 E7
Darley Sq DE7 . . . . . . .157 E5
DARLTON. 67 B7
Darlton Dr NG5 . . . . . . .162 B7
Darlton Rd
　Darlton NG22. . . . . .67 A8
　Dunham-on-Trent NG22. . .54 B1
　East Drayton DN22 . . . . .53 A1
　Ragnall NG22. . . . . .53 F1
　Tuxford NG22. . . . . .66 C4
Darlton St NG19 . . . . . .101 D6
Darnal Cl NG5 . . . . .160 E7
Darnhall Cres NG8 . . . . .171 D7
Daron Gdns [10] NG5. . . . .161 A7
Darrel Rd NG2 . . . . .39 E5
Darricott Cl NG21. . . . . .118 B8
Dart Ct NG13 . . . . .177 D3
Dartmoor Cl NG11 . . . . .195 D8
Darvel Cl [5] NG8. . . . . . .172 B6
Darwin Cl
　Elston NG23. . . . . .153 E4
　Mansfield NG18. . . . . . .102 C3
　Nottingham NG5 . . . . . .160 E8
Darwin Dr
　New Ollerton NG22. . . . . .77 C3
　Woodbeck DN22 . . . . . . .42 B1
Darwin St NG10 . . . . . . .193 B5
Daubeney Ave LN1. . . . . .57 B3
Davenport Dr NG16 . . . .158 B7
Davey Rd NG18 . . . . . . .102 A7
David Ave NG22. . . . . . .105 F5
David Gr NG9. . . . . .171 E1
David La NG6. . . . . .160 D1
Davids La NG14. . . . . . .165 A5
Davidson Cl NG5. . . . . . .162 C7
Davidson Gd NG11. . . . .196 A7
Davidson St [5] NG2. . . . .173 F3
David St NG17 . . . . .115 B7
Davies Ave NG17. . . . . .100 E3
Davies Cl NG17. . . . . . .100 E3
Davies Rd NG2. . . . . . . .186 A7
Davies Way [1] NG5 . . . . .161 A5
Davis Cl NG21 . . . . .90 B4
Davis Rd NG9. . . . . .183 B3
Davy Cl
　Hucknall NG15. . . . . . . .131 B2
　New Ollerton NG22 . . . . .77 C3
Dawber St S81. . . . . . . .35 D7
Dawes Way NG7. . . . . . .222 A3
Dawgates La NG19. . . . . .86 F1
Dawlish Cl
　Carlton NG3. . . . . .162 D5
　Hucknall NG15. . . . . . . .145 D6
Dawlish Ct
　Arnold NG5. . . . . .162 D6
　Eastwood NG16. . . . . . .143 D3
Dawlish Dr NG5. . . . . . .161 B5
Dawn Cl NG15 . . . . .131 C1
Dawn House School
　NG21 . . . . .103 E3
Dawn's La LE12. . . . . . .179 A5
Dawn View NG9 . . . . . .170 D2
Dawson Cl NG16. . . . . . .144 A1
Dawver Rd NG16. . . . . .158 F6
Daybell Cl NG13 . . . . . .181 B3
Daybells Barns NG13. . . .181 B2
Daybill Cl NG25. . . . . . .137 D3
DAYBROOK. 161 D7
Daybrook Ave [4] NG5. . . .161 C6
Daybrook Learning Centre
　NG5. . . . . .161 C6
Daybrook Mws NG5. . . . .160 F4
Daybrook St NG5. . . . . .161 C3
D'Ayncourt Wlk NG22. . .120 A6
Day St NG20 . . . . .74 B4
Deabill St NG4. . . . . . . .175 A6
Dead La
　Cossall NG16. . . . . . . .158 D1
　[1] Loughborough LE11. . .220 B4
Deadwong La NG23. . . . .153 E1
Deakins Cl NG18. . . . . .102 C6
Deakins Pl NG7. . . . . . .222 A3
Deal Gdns NG6 . . . . . . .159 F7
Dean Ave NG3. . . . . . . .162 A3
Dean Cl
　Mansfield NG18. . . . . . .102 C4
　Nottingham NG8. . . . . . .171 D5
Deane Cl NG23 . . . . .98 A1
Deane Rd NG2. . . . . . . .185 A6
Deans Cl NG15 . . . . . . .161 E5
Deans Cl DN10. . . . . .6 E2
Dean's Cl NG23 . . . . . . .109 B5
Deanscourt NG12. . . . . .188 A3
Deans Croft NG9. . . . . . .171 B1
Deansgate NG19 . . . . . . .87 A5
Dean St
　Langley Mill NG16. . . . .143 C4
　Nottingham NG1. . . . . . .223 F2
Death La DN22. . . . . . . .21 D6
Debdale Gate NG19. . . . .88 A2
Debdale Hill LE14. . . . . .218 E4

Debdale La
　Keyworth NG12. . . . . . .197 E3
　Mansfield NG19. . . . . . . .88 A2
Debdale Wy NG19 . . . . . .88 B2
Debdhill Rd DN10. . . . . . .6 E2
Deben Down NG19. . . . . .88 D3
De Brouwer Cl DN22 . . . .39 F5
De Buseli Cl NG4 . . . . . .175 A8
De Caldwell Dr NG24. . .139 F6
Deddington La NG9. . . . .171 C2
Deeley Cl NG16. . . . . . .159 A7
Deepdale Ave NG9. . . . .182 D6
Deepdale Cl NG2 . . . . . .186 C7
Deepdale Gdns NG17 . . .100 F4
Deepdale Pk NG17 . . . . .100 F4
Deepdale Rd
　Long Eaton NG10. . . . . .193 A5
　Mansfield NG19. . . . . . . .88 E1
　Nottingham NG8. . . . . . .171 D4
Deepdale St NG17. . . . . .100 F4
Deepdene Cl NG8. . . . . .160 A2
Deepdene Way NG8 . . . .160 A2
Deep Furrow Ave NG4 . .174 D8
Deeps La NG20. . . . . .4 B7
Deerdale La
　Bilsthorpe NG22. . . . . . .105 A8
　Edwinstowe NG21. . . . . .91 C1
　Rainworth NG21 . . . . . .104 F8
Deerlands Way NG10 . . . .23 C8
Deerleap Dr NG5 . . . . . .161 C7
Deer Pk Dr
　Arnold NG5 . . . . .147 C1
　[4] Nottingham NG5. . . . .147 C1
　Nottingham NG5 . . . . . .161 B8
　Nottingham NG5 . . . . . .161 C8
Deers Acre LE11. . . . . . .220 B6
Dees La DN10. . . . . .4 B7
Deetleton Cl NG16. . . . .129 A7
Deevon Farm Cl NG24. .139 D7
De Ferrers Cl LE12. . . . .205 C1
De Havilland Way
　NG24. . . . . .139 C6
Dein Ct DE55. . . . . .99 E4
De Lacy Ct NG22. . . . . . .77 B4
Delamere Cl NG18 . . . . .102 C4
Delamere Dr NG18 . . . . .102 C4
Delia Ave NG15 . . . . . . .131 C1
Dell Lea NG18 . . . . .103 A3
Dell The NG7 . . . . .129 F8
Dell Way NG7. . . . . .184 F2
Dellwood Cl NG4 . . . . . .162 C2
Delta St NG7 . . . . .160 F1
Delville Ave NG12. . . . . .197 E4
De Morgan Cl NG16. . . .129 A2
Denacre Ave NG10. . . . .182 F1
Denbigh Ave [3] S81 . . . . .35 E7
Denbigh Cl NG21. . . . . .104 C1
Denbigh Ct NG23 . . . . . .98 A1
Denbury Ct NG5. . . . . . .162 D6
Denbury Rd NG15. . . . . .117 A2
Denby Dr NG18 . . . . . . .102 D2
Denby Hall Rd DE7. . . . .157 F6
Dendy Dr DN22 . . . . . . .53 B8
Dene Cl DN10. . . . . .20 B7
Denehurst Ave NG8. . . . .160 C1
Dene The S80 . . . . .35 C2
Denewood Ave NG6. . . . .171 C2
Denewood Cres NG8. . . .171 E8
Denholme Rd NG8. . . . . .171 D5
Denison Ave DN22. . . . . .40 A4
Denison St
　Beeston NG9 . . . . .183 E7
　Nottingham NG7 . . . . . .222 B4
Denman Cl DN22 . . . . . .39 D8
Denman St Central
　NG7. . . . . .222 B3
Denman St E NG7. . . . . .222 B3
Denman St W NG7. . . . . .222 A3
Denmark Grove [1]
　NG3. . . . . .173 D8
Dennett Cl NG3. . . . . . . .173 E6
Dennis Ave NG9 . . . . . . .183 E8
Dennis Brown Ct LN1. . . .57 B3
Dennis St
　Carlton NG4. . . . . .175 A7
　Worksop S80 . . . . .35 F2
Dennor Dr NG19 . . . . . . .88 E5
Denstone Rd NG3. . . . . .173 E5
Dentdale Dr NG8 . . . . . .171 B4
Denton Ave NG10. . . . . .182 A6
Denton Cl
　Balderton NG24. . . . . . .140 C3
　Mansfield NG19. . . . . . . .88 C1
Denton Dr NG2 . . . . . . .185 D4
Denton Gn NG8. . . . . . . .159 F2
Denver Ct NG9. . . . . . . .170 E1
Deodar Cl LE12. . . . . . .212 D2
Deptford Cres NG6 . . . . .160 C5
Derby Gr NG7 . . . . .222 B3
Derby Rd
　Annesley Woodhouse NG15,
　　NG17. . . . . .130 B7
　Beeston NG9 . . . . .171 D1
　Eastwood NG16. . . . . . .143 E2
　Hathern LE12. . . . . .212 F2
　Kegworth DE74. . . . . . .203 C2
　Kirkby-in-Ashfield NG17 .115 C4
　Langley Mill NG16. . . . .143 C1
　Long Eaton NG10 . . . . .193 B8
　Loughborough LE11. . . .220 A5
　Mansfield NG17, NG18 . .116 B8
　Nottingham NG7 . . . . . .222 B2
　Sandiacre NG10. . . . . . .182 A5
Derbyshire Ave NG10 . . .182 D4
Derbyshire Cres NG8 . . .172 A5
Derbyshire Dr NG16. . . .128 A6
Derbyshire La NG15. . . .146 A7
Derby Sq LE11. . . . . . . .220 A4

Derby St
　Arnold NG5 . . . . .161 F7
　Beeston NG9 . . . . .183 F7
　Mansfield NG18. . . . . . .102 C6
　Nottingham NG1 . . . . . .223 D3
Dereham Dr NG5 . . . . . .162 A6
Derry Dr NG5. . . . . .147 F2
Derry Hill Rd NG5. . . . . .147 E1
Derry La NG13 . . . . .178 B3
Derwent Ave
　Ilkeston DE7. . . . . .157 D2
　Mansfield NG18. . . . . . .103 A5
Derwent Cl
　Beeston NG9 . . . . .183 E3
　Mansfield NG18. . . . . . .103 A5
　Market Warsop NG20 . . . .74 C5
　Rainworth NG21 . . . . . .118 B8
　West Bridgford NG2 . . . .186 C7
　Worksop S81 . . . . .35 F6
Derwent Cres NG5. . . . .162 A6
Derwent Ct
　Balderton NG24. . . . . . .140 D3
　Nottingham NG7 . . . . . .222 C4
Derwent Dr
　Annesley Woodhouse
　　NG17. . . . . .130 A8
　Hucknall NG15. . . . . . . .146 A4
　Nuncargate NG17 . . . . .115 A1
　Selston NG16. . . . . .129 A7
Derwent St Ind Est
　NG10. . . . . .193 D6
Derwent St NG10 . . . . . .193 C6
Derwent Terr [5] NG5 . . . .161 C2
Derwent Way
　Newark-on-Trent NG24. .125 B2
　Nottingham NG7 . . . . . .172 D4
　Nottingham NG7 . . . . . .222 A2
Desborough Rd NG16. . .128 D7
Desford Rd NG5. . . . . . .161 A4
De Vere Gdns NG5. . . . .162 A4
Devitt Dr NG15 . . . . . . .131 C1
Devon Cir NG5 . . . . . . .147 D1
Devon Cl
　Eastwood NG16. . . . . . .144 B2
　Sandiacre NG10. . . . . . .182 B5
Devon Dr
　Mansfield NG18. . . . . . .101 F8
　Nottingham NG5 . . . . . .161 C2
　Ruddington NG11. . . . . .196 D8
Devon La NG13 . . . . . . .181 B3
Devon Pk NG24 . . . . . . .139 F7
Devon Rd NG24 . . . . . . .139 F6
Devonshire Ave
　Beeston NG9 . . . . .183 F6
　Long Eaton NG10. . . . . .194 A8
Devonshire Cl
　Ilkeston DE7. . . . . .157 E5
　[1] Sutton in Ashfield
　　NG17. . . . . .100 A2
Devonshire Cres NG5. . .161 B2
Devonshire Dr
　Eastwood NG16. . . . . . .143 F2
　Langwith NG20. . . . . . . .72 F8
　[3] Newton DE55. . . . . . .99 A3
　Ollerton NG22. . . . . .77 A3
　Stapleford NG9 . . . . . . .170 D2
Devonshire La LE11. . . . .220 B3
Devonshire Promenade
　NG7. . . . . .222 A1
Devonshire Rd
　Harworth DN11. . . . . .8 F4
　Nottingham NG5 . . . . . .161 B2
　Retford DN22. . . . . .39 D6
　West Bridgford NG2 . . . .185 F6
Devonshire Sq [2] LE11 . .220 B3
Devonshire St
　New Houghton NG19. . . . .87 A7
　Worksop S80 . . . . .35 E2
Devon St
　Ilkeston DE7. . . . . .170 A5
　Nottingham NG3 . . . . . .173 F5
Dewberry Gdns NG19 . . . .89 A2
Dewberry La NG12. . . . .176 B2
Dexters Gr NG15. . . . . . .145 F7
DH Lawrence Birthplace
　Mus* NG16. . . . . .143 F3
Dial The NG12 . . . . .187 E1
Diamond Ave
　Kirkby-in-Ashfield
　　NG17. . . . . .115 C4
　Rainworth NG21 . . . . . .104 C1
Dianthus Gr DN22. . . . . .40 B4
Dickens Cl NG16. . . . . . .144 B3
Dickenson Terr DN21 . . . .24 D7
Dickenson Way NG23 . . .110 F3
Dickens Rd S81. . . . . . . .36 B3
Dickinson St NG3. . . . . .173 E7
Dickman's La LE14. . . . .202 B3
Dicks La NG16. . . . . . . .144 C3
Dickson Dr NG11 . . . . . .196 D6
Didcot Dr NG8 . . . . .160 D1
Digby Ave NG3 . . . . . . .162 C3
Digby Ct NG7. . . . . .222 B1
Digby Hall Dr NG4 . . . . .162 C3
Digby St
　Cossall DE7 . . . . .158 A1
　Ilkeston DE7. . . . . .170 A8
　Kimberley NG16. . . . . . .158 D7
Diggles Lodge La
　Barnby Moor DN22 . . . . .28 B4
　Barnby Moor S81. . . . . . .27 F3
Dingle Ct DN22 . . . . . . .19 B5
Dingley Cl NG19 . . . . . . .88 E5
Dirca Ct NG11 . . . . .195 C8
Discovery Dr NG8. . . . . .172 C7
Diseworth Gr [3] NG2 . . .173 D1
Distillery St NG11. . . . . .196 C6
Division Rd NG20 . . . . . .72 E4
Dixie St NG16. . . . . .128 B4

Djanogly City Acad
　Nottingham NG7 . . . . . .161 A1
Djanogly Northgate Acad
　NG7 . . . . .160 F1
Dobbin Cl NG12. . . . . . .189 B4
Doble Cres LE12 . . . . . .213 A2
Dob Pk Cl NG6. . . . . . . .160 D4
Dobsons Mws NG11. . . .101 B3
Dockholm Rd NG10. . . . .182 C2
Dock Rd S80 . . . . .35 E3
DODDINGTON. 71 C1
Doddington Hall* LN6. . .71 B1
Doddington La
　Claypole NG23. . . . . . . .156 B2
　Dry Doddington NG23. . .156 C5
Dodford Ct DE75. . . . . . .143 A1
Dodsley Way NG21. . . . . .90 A4
Dodson Ave NG12. . . . . .197 F4
Dog & Duck La DN21. . . .15 B4
Doghill La NG23 . . . . . . .153 B2
Dog La DN10. . . . . .10 A2
Dogwood Ave
　Nottingham NG16 . . . . .159 F7
　Nottingham NG6 . . . . . .160 A7
Dolegate Rd DN22 . . . . . .53 A4
Doles La
　Kirkby-in-Ashfield
　　NG17. . . . . .114 C6
　Whitwell S80 . . . . .45 B7
Dolphin Ct [7] NG5 . . . . .161 A8
Dominie Cross Rd
　DN22. . . . . .39 F6
Donbas Cl NG6 . . . . . . .160 B4
Doncaster Ave NG10. . . .182 B6
Doncaster By Pass
　Blyth DN11. . . . . .17 F7
　Blyth S81. . . . . .18 A6
Doncaster Gr NG10 . . . .182 F1
Doncaster Rd
　Austerfield DN10. . . . . . . .3 A1
　Bawtry DN10. . . . . .10 A8
　Carlton in Lindrick S81 . . .25 F7
　Carlton in Lindrick S81 . . .26 A8
　Langold S81. . . . . .16 F3
　Tickhill DN11. . . . . .8 A8
　Westwoodside DN9 . . . . . .2 D7
Doncaster Sheffield Airport
　DN10. . . . . .3 B7
Doncaster Terr [11]
　NG2. . . . . .173 C1
Donington Rd NG7. . . . .184 E1
Donkey La NG11. . . . . . .196 E3
Donner Cres DE7 . . . . . .157 E5
Dooland Dr NG3. . . . . . .161 F1
Dorchester Cl NG18. . . .102 D2
Dorchester Dr NG18 . . . .102 D2
Dorchester Gdns NG2. . .185 E3
Dorchester Rd
　Annesley Woodhouse
　　NG17. . . . . .115 B1
　Harworth DN11. . . . . .9 B5
　Kimberley NG16. . . . . . .158 F7
Doreen Dr NG17. . . . . . .100 D2
Dorewood Ct NG24 . . . .140 E4
Dorey Way NG5. . . . . . .146 A4
Doris Rd DE7 . . . . .170 A7
Dorket Cl NG5. . . . . . . .148 A1
Dorket Dr NG8. . . . . . . .172 D3
Dorking Rd NG7. . . . . . .222 B4
Dormer Dr S80 . . . . .35 B5
Dormouse Cl LE12 . . . . .214 E7
Dormy Cl
　Beeston NG9 . . . . .183 C7
　Mansfield Woodhouse
　　NG19. . . . . .88 C5
　Radcliffe on Trent NG12 .176 B3
Dormy Ct NG6. . . . . . . .160 D7
Dorner Ave NG24 . . . . . .139 D7
Dornoch Ave
　Nottingham NG5 . . . . . .161 D2
　Southwell NG25. . . . . . .121 F1
Dorothy Ave
　Eastwood NG16. . . . . . .144 A3
　Hucknall NG15. . . . . . . .131 B1
　Mansfield Woodhouse
　　NG19. . . . . .88 C1
　Sandiacre NG10. . . . . . .182 B5
Dorothy Dr NG19 . . . . . . .88 F1
Dorothy Gr [1] NG8. . . . .172 D6
Dorset Cl NG17 . . . . .8 F4
Dorset Gdns NG2 . . . . . .185 C5
Dorset St NG8 . . . . .172 D5
Dorset Way NG18. . . . . .103 A4
Dorterry Cres DE7 . . . . .170 A5
Dorton Ave DN21 . . . . . .24 F8
Dotterel Pl NG20. . . . . . .73 E4
Doublet Cl NG16 . . . . . .128 A6
Douglas Ave
　Awsworth NG16. . . . . . .158 C5
　Carlton NG4. . . . . .174 E6
Douglas Cl NG12 . . . . . .175 E2
Douglas Cres NG4 . . . . .174 E6
Douglas Ct NG9 . . . . . . .183 A2
Douglas Rd
　Bingham NG13. . . . . . . .178 B4
　Long Eaton NG10. . . . . .182 B1
　Long Eaton NG10 . . . . .193 C8
　Mansfield Woodhouse
　　NG19. . . . . .89 B2
　Nottingham NG7 . . . . . .222 B3
　Sutton in Ashfield NG17 .100 D2
Douro Dr NG5. . . . . . . .148 B1
Dove Cl
　Bingham NG13. . . . . . . .177 F3
　[11] Gainsborough DN21. .15 F1
　Ollerton NG22. . . . . .77 B4
　Worksop S81 . . . . .35 E7
Dovecoat Cl NG13. . . . .213 A1
Dovecote Cl NG13 . . . . .165 C3
Dovecote Dr NG8. . . . . .171 E4

Dovecote La
　Beeston NG9 . . . . .184 A5
　Tithby NG13. . . . . .189 D6
Dovecote Prim Sch
　NG9 . . . . .184 F3
Dovecote Rd NG16. . . . .144 B2
Dove Croft NG22. . . . . . .77 B4
Dovedale Ave
　Long Eaton NG10. . . . . .193 A6
　Sutton in Ashfield NG17 .100 D1
Dovedale Cir DE7. . . . . .157 E5
Dovedale Ct
　Edwinstowe NG21. . . . . .76 A2
　Mansfield NG18. . . . . . .102 D3
Dovedale Ct NG10 . . . . .193 B6
Dovedale Prim Sch
　NG10. . . . . .193 A6
Dovedale Rd
　Nottingham NG3 . . . . . .174 C6
　West Bridgford NG2 . . . .186 A5
Dove Dr NG16 . . . . .129 A7
Dove La NG10 . . . . .193 C8
Dovenby Rd NG7. . . . . . .184 F2
Dover Beck Cl
　Calverton NG14. . . . . . .149 A7
　Lowdham NG14 . . . . . . .150 D2
　Ravenshead NG15. . . . . .116 F2
Dover Beck Dr NG14 . . . .149 D4
Dover Bottom DN22. . . . .50 D3
Doveridge Ave NG4 . . . .175 A8
Doveridge Ct NG15 . . . .117 A3
Doveridge Rd NG4 . . . . .175 A8
Dover St NG25. . . . . . . .121 E1
Dove St NG6. . . . . .160 B7
Dovey's Orch NG14. . . . .148 D7
Downes Cl NG6. . . . . . .160 A7
Downham Cl NG5 . . . . . .162 A6
Downham Gdns NG15. . .117 B2
Downing Cl NG6. . . . . . .160 B8
Downing Gdns [7]
　NG6. . . . . .160 B8
Downing St
　Nottingham NG6 . . . . . .160 B8
　South Normanton DE55. .113 A6
　Sutton in Ashfield NG17 .100 F3
Downs The
　[4] Mansfield Woodhouse
　　NG19. . . . . .88 E1
　Nottingham NG11. . . . . .185 A3
Dowson Cl
　[11] Nottingham NG7 . . .160 F1
　Radcliffe on Trent NG12 .176 B4
Dowson Ct NG3. . . . . . .173 C1
Doyne Ct [2] NG2. . . . . .173 C1
Dozen Dr NG19 . . . . . . .101 D7
Dragonfly Cl LE12. . . . . .214 D7
Dragon St NG13 . . . . . .191 B5
Dragwell DE74. . . . . . . .203 D2
DRAKEHOLES 11 F1
Drakemyre Cl NG5. . . . .148 B1
Drake Rd NG4 . . . . .175 B6
Drake St DN21. . . . . .24 D6
Draper Cl NG12. . . . . . .176 B4
Draycott Ct DE7 . . . . . . .157 F3
Draycott Rd NG10 . . . . .193 A4
Draymans Ct NG7. . . . . .160 F1
Drayton Ave NG19 . . . . . .87 D2
Drayton St
　Stokeham DN22 . . . . . . .53 C5
　Upton DN22. . . . . .52 C4
Drayton St [3] NG5 . . . . .161 C2
Drift Hill NG13 . . . . .192 F4
Drift The
　Hucknall NG15. . . . . . . .131 B1
　Nottingham NG11. . . . . .184 E1
Drinking Pit La
　Welbeck S80 . . . . .46 D3
　Welbeck S80 . . . . .47 C4
　Whitwell S80 . . . . .47 C4
Drinsey Nook La NG23 . . .70 C7
Drive The
　Beeston NG9 . . . . .183 E6
　Clipstone NG21 . . . . . . .90 A3
　Gainsborough DN21 . . . .24 F7
　Winthorpe NG24 . . . . . .125 C6
Drive The Pk La DN22. . . .30 A1
Drmonde Terr [7] NG3. . .161 C2
Dronfield Pl DE7. . . . . . .157 D5
Dronley Dr NG20. . . . . . .74 C7
Drove La NG24. . . . . . . .126 A4
Drovers Ct DN21. . . . . . .24 E5
Droversdale Rd DN11. . . .9 C4
Drummond Ave NG4 . . . .175 B7
Drummond Dr NG16 . . . .159 E4
Drummond Gr NG23 . . . .112 A7
Drummond Rd DE7 . . . . .157 E1
Drury Cl NG15 . . . . .145 D5
Drury La DN11. . . . . .8 A7
Dryden Ave NG24 . . . . . .140 E5
Dryden Ct NG9 . . . . . . .170 E1
Dryden Dale S81. . . . . . .36 B3
Dryden St
　Nottingham NG1 . . . . . .223 D4
　Nottingham NG14. . . . . .173 B5
DRY DODDINGTON 156 E1
Dry Pot La LE12. . . . . . .212 A2
Drysdale Cl NG6. . . . . . .160 E5
Duchess Gdns [8] NG6. .160 B8
Duchess St
　Nottingham NG6 . . . . . .160 B8
　Whitwell S80 . . . . .45 A6
Ducie La DN22 . . . . .23 E3
Duckworth Cl [3] NG4. . .162 E3
Dudley Cl NG9. . . . . . . .183 A8
Dudley Doy Rd NG7. . . .121 C1
Duesbury The DE55. . . .113 B4
Duffield Cl NG10 . . . . . .193 A5
Duffield Cres NG5. . . . . .160 F8
Duke Cl NG6. . . . . .144 C4
Duke Cres NG16 . . . . . .144 C1
Duke Pl S80 . . . . .35 E3

Dukeries Acad The NG22 . . . . 77 D5
Dukeries Bsns Ctr S80 . . 36 B2
Dukeries Cl S81 . . . . . . 35 C6
Dukeries Complex The★ NG22 . . . . 77 D5
Dukeries Cres
  Edwinstowe NG21 . . . . 76 B1
  Worksop S80 . . . . 36 C1
Dukeries Industrial Estate The S81 . . . . . . 35 C6
Dukeries L Ctr NG22 . . . 77 D6
Dukeries The
  Mansfield NG18 . . . . . 102 F5
  Mansfield NG18 . . . . . 103 A4
Dukeries Way S81 . . . . . 35 C6
Dukes Cl NG17 . . . . . . 101 C2
Dukes Ct NG15 . . . . . . 146 B7
Duke's Dr S44 . . . . 86 A7
Dukes Meadow NG21 . . 104 B1
Dukes Pl DE7 . . . . 157 F4
Duke's Pl NG1 . . . . 223 F2
Dukes Rd LE14 . . . . . . 219 B6
Duke St
  Arnold NG5 . . . . 161 E7
  Hucknall NG15 . . . . . 146 B7
  Huthwaite NG17 . . . . 100 A3
  Ilkeston DE7 . . . . 157 F3
  Loughborough LE11 . . 220 B5
  🖪 Nottingham NG5 . . . 161 A1
  🖪 Nottingham NG7 . . . 160 B7
  Retford DN22 . . . . 39 E6
  South Normanton DE55 . 113 B6
  Sutton in Ashfield NG17 . 100 E2
  Whitwell S80 . . . . 45 A6
Duke's Terr DN10 . . . . . 10 A7
Duke's Wood Nature Reserve★ NG22 . . . . 107 A5
Duke William Mount NG7 . . . . 222 C2
Dulverton Vale NG8 . . . 160 B3
Dulwich Rd NG7 . . . . . 222 A3
Dumb Hall La S80 . . . . . 34 B4
Dumbles The
  Lambley NG4 . . . . 163 B8
  Sutton in Ashfield NG17 . 100 C1
Dunbar Cl
  Gainsborough DN21 . . . 15 E2
  Long Eaton NG10 . . . . 193 E4
Dunbar Dr NG19 . . . . . 101 D5
Dunblane Rd NG11 . . . 196 C6
Duncan Ave NG15 . . . . 117 A1
Duncombe Cl NG3 . . . . 173 E7
Duncroft Ave NG4 . . . . 162 F1
Dundas Cl
  Nottingham NG1 . . . . 223 E3
  Nottingham NG14 . . . 173 C5
Dundee Dr NG19 . . . . . . 88 B6
Dunelm Cl NG17 . . . . . 100 C3
Dunelm Dr NG14 . . . . . 149 A7
Dungannon Rd NG11 . . 195 E8
Dunham Cl
  Newton on Trent LN1 . . 55 A1
  Southwell NG25 . . . . 136 D8
DUNHAM-ON-TRENT . . 54 C2
Dunham-on-Trent CE Prim Sch NG22 . . . . . 54 A1
Dunham Rd
  Laneham DN22 . . . . . . 54 A4
  Laneham DN22 . . . . . . 54 A5
  Newton on Trent DN22, LN1 . . . . 54 E1
  Newton on Trent LN1 . . 55 A1
Dunholme Ave NG24 . . 139 F7
Dunholme Cl
  Gainsborough DN21 . . . 24 E8
  Nottingham NG6 . . . . 160 B8
Dunholme Rd DN21 . . . 24 E7
Dunkery Rd NG11 . . . . 195 E8
DUNKIRK 172 E2
Dunkirk Ind Est NG7 . . 184 D7
Dunkirk Prim School (Abbey Campus) NG7 . 222 B1
Dunkirk Prim Sch (Highfield Campus) NG7 . . . . 172 E1
Dunkirk Rd 🖪 NG7 . . . 172 E1
Dunlin Wharf 🖪 NG2 . . 173 A2
Dunlop Ave NG7 . . . . . 222 A2
Dunn Brigg NG19 . . . . . 88 D2
Dunn Dr NG10 . . . . . . 193 B7
Dunnett Rd NG19 . . . . 101 E5
Dunnock Cl NG15 . . . . 132 A8
Dunnock Dr NG9 . . . . . 170 E2
Dunoon Cl NG5 . . . . . . 146 E1
Dunoon Rd NG19 . . . . 101 E5
Dunsby Cl NG7 . . . . . . 184 E1
Dunsford Dr NG3 . . . . 162 C6
Dunsil Cl NG19 . . . . 88 B1
Dunsil Ct NG19 . . . . 88 B1
Dunsil Dr NG11 . . . . . 185 A8
Dunsil Rd
  Eastwood NG16 . . . . . 144 B4
  Mansfield NG19 . . . . . . 88 B1
  Pinxton NG16 . . . . . . 113 D2
Dunsil Way NG19 . . . . . 86 F2
Dunsmore Avenue NG19 . . . . 177 D6
Dunsmore Cl NG9 . . . . 184 B4
Dunstall Wlk DN21 . . . . 24 F7
Dunstan Cres S80 . . . . . 35 F1
Dunstan St NG4 . . . . . 175 A7
Dunster Rd
  Eastwood NG16 . . . . . 144 B1
  Gainsborough DN21 . . . 15 E2
  West Bridgford NG2 . . 186 A6
Dunston Cl NG10 . . . . 193 F7
Dunstone Rd DN22 . . . . 41 E8
Dunvegan Dr NG5 . . . . 146 F2
Dunwoody Cl NG18 . . . 102 F7
Durham Ave NG2 . . . . 173 F4

Durham Cl
  Mansfield Woodhouse NG19 . . . . 88 C4
  🖪 Nottingham NG2 . . 173 F4
  Worksop S81 . . . . 36 A7
Durham Cres NG6 . . . . 160 C6
Durham Gr DN22 . . . . . 30 A1
Durham St 🖪 DE7 . . . 157 F1
Durlston Cl NG2 . . . . . 185 B5
Durnford St NG7 . . . . . 160 F2
Dursley Cl NG6 . . . . . . 160 B5
Dyce Cl NG6 . . . . 159 F7
Dykes End NG23 . . . . . 112 A8
Dylan Thomas Rd NG5 . 161 C8
Dyscarr Cl S81 . . . . 16 F3
Dyscarr Wood Nature Reserve★ S81 . . . . . . 16 E3

E

EAGLE 84 C3
Eagle Cl
  Arnold NG5 . . . . 162 A5
  Beeston NG9 . . . . . . 183 D8
Eagle Com Prim Sch LN6 . . . . 84 D3
Eagle Ct NG6 . . . . 160 D7
Eagle Moor La LN6 . . . . 84 F4
Eagle Pl DN22 . . . . 39 F7
Eagle Rd LN6 . . . . 84 B4
Eagle Way NG19 . . . . . 88 F2
EAKRING 92 F1
Eakring Cl NG18 . . . . . 103 C7
Eakring Meadow Nature Reserve★ NG22 . . . . 93 E1
Eakring Rd
  Bilsthorpe NG22 . . . . 105 E8
  Kirklington NG22 . . . . 106 E3
  Kneesall NG22 . . . . . . 93 E5
  Mansfield NG18, NG21, NG22 . . . . 103 D7
  Rufford NG22 . . . . 91 B1
  Rufford NG22 . . . . 91 F1
  Rufford NG22 . . . . 92 A8
  Wellow NG22 . . . . 92 D8
Ealing Ave NG6 . . . . . . 160 D4
Eardley Rd NG5 . . . . . . 160 E6
Earl Cres NG4 . . . . . . 162 F3
Earl Dr NG16 . . . . 144 C1
Earles Ct DN22 . . . . . . 29 C1
Earl Howe Cres NG13 . . 190 C2
Earls Cl NG8 . . . . 171 C4
Earlsfield Dr NG5 . . . . 146 E1
Earls Rd LE14 . . . . . . 219 B6
Earlswood Dr
  Mansfield NG18 . . . . 102 F5
  West Bridgford NG12 . 186 B4
Earp Ave NG24 . . . . . . 140 A7
Easedale Cl NG2 . . . . 186 C7
Easegill Ct NG5 . . . . . 160 F8
East Acres NG12 . . . . 187 F3
EAST BRIDGFORD . . . 165 D3
East Bridgford Bsns Pk NG13 . . . . 165 D4
East Bridgford Rd
  East Bridgford NG13 . . 165 B1
  Newton NG13 . . . . . . 177 A8
East Cir St NG1 . . . . . 223 D2
East Cl NG12 . . . . 197 E2
Eastcliffe Ave NG4 . . . 162 D3
Eastcote Ave NG9 . . . . 171 B2
East Cres NG9 . . . . . . 184 B5
Eastcroft LN1 . . . . 57 A5
Eastcroft La NG22 . . . . 52 A2
Eastdale Rd NG3 . . . . 174 C6
East Dr NG7 . . . . 172 C1
EAST DRAYTON 53 A3
East End LE14 . . . . . . 211 D4
Eastern Ave DN21 . . . . 15 F1
Eastern Ct NG24 . . . . 140 A8
Eastern Terr La NG24 . 140 A8
Eastfield
  North Muskham NG23 . 110 F2
  North Wheatley DN22 . . 31 E8
Eastfield Cl NG21 . . . . 89 F2
Eastfield Ct NG25 . . . . 136 C8
Eastfield Dr DE55 . . . . 113 A5
Eastfield Meadow DN22 . 31 E8
Eastfield Pk NG22 . . . . 66 B4
Eastfield Side NG17 . . 101 A4
Eastgate
  Normanton on Trent NG23 . 81 D7
  Worksop S80 . . . . 35 F3
East Gate S81 . . . . 36 A3
Eastglade Rd NG5 . . . . 161 A6
East Gr
  Bingham NG13 . . . . . 177 F4
  Nottingham NG7 . . . . 173 A8
Eastham Cl NG3 . . . . . 173 E6
Eastham Rd NG5 . . . . . 162 C6
Eastholme Croft NG2 . . 174 D5
Easthorpe LE12 . . . . . 220 C7
Easthorpe La NG13 . . . 192 F4
Easthorpe Rd NG13 . . . 181 C2
Easthorpe St NG11 . . . 196 C7
Easthorpe View NG13 . 181 C2
East La NG21 . . . . 76 B2
Eastlands Jun Sch NG20 . . . . 74 E8
Eastlands La NG20 . . . . 74 E8
Eastland Terr NG20 . . . 74 E8
EAST LEAKE 205 D2
East Leake Acad LE12 . 205 C3
East Leake L Ctr LE12 . 205 F2
Eastleigh Dr NG19 . . . . 88 B6
EAST MARKHAM 65 F7

East Markham Prim Sch
  East Markham NG22 . . . 65 F8
  East Markham NG22 . . . 66 A7
East Meadow Rd NG22 . 52 B1
East Midlands Designer Outlet NG17 . . . . . . 113 E6
East Midlands Parkway NG11 . . . . 203 F8
East Moor
  Cotgrave NG12 . . . . . 187 F2
  Cotgrave NG12 . . . . . 188 A1
Eastmoor Dr NG4 . . . . 174 F8
East Rd
  Nottingham NG8 . . . . 172 D2
  Willoughby-on-the-Wolds LE12 . . . . 217 A6
  Wymeswold LE12 . . . 216 E4
East St
  Bingham NG13 . . . . . 177 F4
  Bole DN22 . . . . 23 E3
  Gotham NG11 . . . . . . 195 B1
  Harworth DN11 . . . . . . 9 A5
  Heanor DE75 . . . . . . 157 A8
  Long Eaton NG10 . . . 193 F8
  Market Warsop NG20 . . 73 D5
  Nottingham NG1 . . . . 223 F3
  Retford DN22 . . . . . . 39 F6
  Sutton in Ashfield NG17 . 101 A3
EAST STOCKWITH 7 C1
EAST STOKE 153 D8
East View
  Bawtry DN10 . . . . 10 A8
  East Markham NG22 . . . 65 F6
  Shirebrook NG20 . . . . . 72 F6
  West Bridgford NG2 . . 185 D6
  Whaley Thornes NG20 . 59 A3
East View Cl NG17 . . . 115 C1
Eastwell St NG15 . . . . 146 A8
East Wlk DN22 . . . . . . 39 C8
Eastwold NG12 . . . . . 188 A2
EASTWOOD 143 E3
Eastwood Ave NG20 . . . 74 B5
Eastwood Cl NG15 . . . 145 E4
Eastwood Com Sports Ctr NG16 . . . . 143 E3
Eastwood Ct
  Worksop S81 . . . . 25 F1
  Worksop S81 . . . . 35 F8
Eastwood La DN10 . . . . 4 D3
Eastwood Rd
  Kimberley NG16 . . . . 158 E6
  Radcliffe on Trent NG12 . 176 A3
Eastwood St NG6 . . . . 160 C5
Easy Par S80 . . . . 45 A5
Eather Ave NG19 . . . . . 88 C4
EATON 40 A1
Eaton Ave NG5 . . . . . 162 A7
Eaton Cl
  Beeston NG9 . . . . . . 184 B6
  Farnsfield NG22 . . . . 119 F6
  Rainworth NG21 . . . . 118 A8
Eaton Ct 🖪 NG18 . . . 103 A3
Eaton Grange Dr NG10 . 193 A8
Eaton Hall DN22 . . . . . 40 A1
Eatons Rd NG9 . . . . . 182 D6
Eaton St NG3 . . . . . . 161 E1
Eaton Terr NG3 . . . . . 161 E1
Ebenezer St
  Ilkeston DE7 . . . . . . 157 F3
  Langley Mill NG16 . . . 143 B3
Ebers Gr NG3 . . . . . . 173 C8
Ebers Rd NG3 . . . . . . 173 C8
Ebony Wlk NG3 . . . . . 174 B8
Ebury Rd NG5 . . . . . . 161 B1
Eckington Terr 🖪 NG2 . 173 C1
Eckington Wlk NG18 . . 103 B6
Eclipse Yd 🖪 NG18 . . 102 B7
Ecton Cl NG5 . . . . . . 146 F1
Edale Cl
  Hucknall NG15 . . . . . 145 C6
  Long Eaton NG10 . . . 193 B6
  Mansfield NG18 . . . . 103 A3
Edale Ct NG17 . . . . . . 100 E4
Edale Dr DE55 . . . . . . 113 B7
Edale Rd
  Mansfield NG18 . . . . 103 B6
  Nottingham NG2 . . . . 174 A5
Edale Rise NG9 . . . . . 182 E3
Edale Rise Prim Sch NG2 . . . . 174 A5
Edale Sq DE7 . . . . . . 157 E5
Eddery View NG18 . . . 102 F7
Eddison Cl S81 . . . . . . 36 A7
Eddison Pk Ave S81 . . . 35 E8
Eddleston Dr NG7 . . . 184 F1
Edelin Rd LE11 . . . . . 220 B1
Edenbridge Ct NG8 . . . 171 D2
Eden Cl
  Arnold NG5 . . . . 162 A6
  Hucknall NG15 . . . . . 145 C6
Eden Ct DN22 . . . . 39 E3
Edenhall Cl NG22 . . . . 66 A7
Edenhall Gdns NG7 . . . 184 F2
Eden Low NG19 . . . . . . 88 D3
Eden Wlk NG13 . . . . . 177 D3
Edern Cl NG5 . . . . . . 161 A7
Edern Gdns 🖪 NG5 . . 161 A7
Edgar Ave NG18 . . . . 102 C8
Edgbaston Dr DN22 . . . 39 E5
Edgbaston Gdns 🖪 NG8 . . . . 172 D8
Edgcote Way NG5 . . . . 161 A6
Edge Cl NG23 . . . . . . 110 F4
Edge Hill Ct NG10 . . . 193 D4
Edgehill Dr NG24 . . . . 140 E8
Edgehill Gr NG18 . . . . . 88 C2
Edge Way NG8 . . . . . . 159 D1
Edgewood Dr NG15 . . . 145 D5

Edgewood Leisure Centre NG15 . . . . 145 D4
Edgewood Prim Sch NG15 . . . . 145 C4
Edgewood Rd NG16 . . 158 F6
Edgington Cl NG12 . . . 188 A1
Edginton St NG3 . . . . 173 F7
Edgware Rd NG6 . . . . 160 D7
Edinbane Cl NG5 . . . . 146 F1
Edinboro Row NG16 . . 158 F7
Edinburgh Dr NG13 . . . 177 D5
Edinburgh Rd
  Worksop S80 . . . . 36 B1
  Worksop S80 . . . . 47 A8
Edinburgh Wlk S80 . . . 47 A8
EDINGLEY 120 C4
Edingley Ave
  Mansfield NG19 . . . . 101 D7
  Nottingham NG5 . . . . 161 C4
Edingley Hill NG22 . . . 120 D4
Edingley Sq NG5 . . . . 161 B3
Edison Rise NG22 . . . . 77 C4
Edison St NG17 . . . . . 114 F1
Edison Way NG5 . . . . 162 C7
Edlington Dr NG8 . . . . 171 C3
Edmond Gr NG15 . . . . 146 C7
Edmonds Cl NG5 . . . . 147 A2
Edmonstone Cres 🖪 NG5 . . . . 160 F5
Edmonton Ct NG2 . . . 185 D6
Edmonton Rd NG21 . . . 89 C2
Edna G Olds Main Sch NG7 . . . . 222 B1
Ednaston Rd NG7 . . . 172 D1
Edwald Rd NG12 . . . . 186 B3
Edwaltham Ave NG18 . 185 E7
EDWALTON 186 B3
Edwalton Cl NG12 . . . 186 B3
Edwalton Ct
  🖪 Mansfield NG18 . . 103 A3
  Nottingham NG6 . . . . 160 E6
Edwalton Lodge Cl NG12 . . . . 186 A3
Edwalton Prim Sch NG12 . . . . 186 C4
Edward Ave
  Newark-on-Trent NG24 . 139 E8
  Nottingham NG8 . . . . 172 D8
  Sutton in Ashfield NG17 . 100 E4
  Westwood NG16 . . . . 128 B4
Edward Cl NG15 . . . . 145 D4
Edward Jermyn Dr NG24 . . . . 125 B4
Edward Rd
  Eastwood NG16 . . . . 144 A2
  Gainsborough DN21 . . . 15 D1
  Long Eaton NG10 . . . 193 D8
  Nuthall NG16 . . . . . . 159 C5
  West Bridgford NG2 . . 185 F8
Edwards La NG5 . . . . 161 C5
Edward St
  Aldercar NG16 . . . . . 143 B3
  Kirkby-in-Ashfield NG17 . 115 B6
  Stapleford NG9 . . . . . 182 D7
  Worksop S80 . . . . 35 F4
Edwin St
  Arnold NG5 . . . . 161 E7
  Sutton in Ashfield NG17 . 100 E3
EDWINSTOWE 76 A1
Edwinstowe Dr
  Nottingham NG5 . . . . 161 C4
  Selston NG16 . . . . . . 129 B7
Edwinstowe Rd NG21 . . 91 C7
Eel Hole La NG22 . . . . 79 C2
Eel Pool Rd DN10 . . . . 11 E1
Eelwood Rd NG15 . . . . 145 D4
Egerton Cl NG18 . . . . 103 A7
Egerton Dr NG9 . . . . . 170 D2
Egerton Rd NG5 . . . . . 161 E4
Egerton St NG3 . . . . . 173 C7
Egerton Wlk 🖪 NG3 . . 173 C7
Egham Cl NG21 . . . . . 104 C1
Egling Croft NG4 . . . . 174 F4
EGMANTON 79 E6
Egmanton Rd
  Egmanton NG22 . . . . . 79 E8
  Kirton NG22 . . . . 78 D7
  Laxton NG22 . . . . 79 D3
  Mansfield NG18 . . . . 103 A3
  Meden Vale NG20 . . . . 74 F7
  Tuxford NG22 . . . . . . 65 E1
Egmont Ct 🖪 NG2 . . . 173 C1
Egypt Rd NG7 . . . . . . 160 F1
Eider Cl NG20 . . . . 72 D3
Eider Rd NG4 . . . . . . 175 C7
Eighth Ave
  Beeston NG9 . . . . . . 184 C5
  Mansfield NG19 . . . . 103 A8
Eileen Rd NG6 . . . . . . 184 A3
Eisele Cl NG6 . . . . . . 159 F6
Ekowe St NG7 . . . . . . 160 F2
Eland Rd NG20 . . . . . . 72 F5
Eland St NG7 . . . . . . 160 F1
Elder Cl
  Arnold NG5 . . . . 148 A1
  🖪 Edwalton NG12 . . 186 A1
Elder Ct
  Clipstone NG21 . . . . . 89 F5
  Forest Town NG19 . . . . 89 B1
Elderfield Dr NG11 . . . 114 F8
Elder Gdns 🖪 NG5 . . . 161 A8
Elder Pl 🖪 S81 . . . . . . 35 A7
Elder St
  Kirkby-in-Ashfield NG17 . 114 F6
  Sutton in Ashfield NG17 . 100 E7
Eldon Gn NG22 . . . . . . 65 F3
Eldon Rd NG9 . . . . . . 183 C1

Eldon St
  Newark-on-Trent NG24 . 139 F7
  Tuxford NG22 . . . . . . 65 F3
Eleanor Ave DE7 . . . . 170 A5
Eleanor Cres NG9 . . . 182 F7
Electric Ave NG11 . . . 185 A8
Eley Cl DE7 . . . . 157 C2
Elford Rise NG3 . . . . . 173 F5
Elgar Dr NG10 . . . . . . 193 B5
Elgar Gdns NG3 . . . . . 173 F7
Eliot Cl
  Gainsborough DN21 . . . 24 C1
  Long Eaton NG10 . . . 193 B5
Eliot Wlk NG11 . . . . . 195 C8
Elizabethan Academy The DN22 . . . . 29 D1
Elizabethan Gdns DN22 . 39 D6
Elizabeth Cl
  Gainsborough DN21 . . . 15 C3
  Hucknall NG15 . . . . . 145 E5
Elizabeth Ct DE7 . . . . 157 D1
Elizabeth Dr
  East Leake LE12 . . . . 214 F1
  Edwalton NG12 . . . . 186 A2
Elizabeth Gr NG4 . . . . 162 E2
Elizabeth Rd
  Beeston NG9 . . . . . . 183 A3
  Newark-on-Trent NG24 . 139 E5
ELKESLEY 50 B3
Elkesley Bridge DN22 . . 48 F4
Elkesley Bridge Rd DN22 . . . . 50 A4
Elkesley Ind Est DN22 . 50 C4
Elkesley Prim Sch DN22 . . . . 50 A3
Elkesley Rd NG20 . . . . 74 E8
Ella Bank Rd DE75 . . . 143 A1
Ella Rd NG2 . . . . 173 F1
Ellastone Ave NG5 . . . 161 C8
Ellerby Ave NG7 . . . . 184 E2
Ellerslie Cl NG24 . . . . 125 A1
Ellerslie Gr NG10 . . . . 182 A5
Ellesmere Bsns Pk NG5 . . . . 161 B2
Ellesmere Cl NG5 . . . 162 B7
Ellesmere Dr NG9 . . . 170 C5
Ellesmere Rd
  Mansfield NG18 . . . . 102 F8
  West Bridgford NG2 . . 185 F4
Ellington Rd
  Arnold NG5 . . . . 147 F2
  Arnold NG5 . . . . 148 A2
Elliott Cl DN22 . . . . . . 39 F5
Elliott Dr NG4 . . . . . . 163 C1
Elliott Durhamcres NG5 . . . . 161 E1
Elliott St NG7 . . . . . . 222 C3
Ellis Ave NG15 . . . . . 146 B6
Ellis Cl NG10 . . . . . . 193 C6
Ellis Ct NG3 . . . . 223 F4
Ellis Gr NG9 . . . . 183 F5
Ellis Guilford Sch & Sports Coll NG6 . . . . 160 C2
Ellis St NG17 . . . . . . 115 B5
Ellsworth Rise NG5 . . . 160 F6
Ellwood Cres NG8 . . . 172 A5
Elma La NG20 . . . . 59 D6
Elm Ave
  Beeston, Attenborough NG9 . . . . 183 D2
  Beeston, Chilwell NG9 . 183 E6
  Bingham NG13 . . . . . 178 A4
  Carlton NG4 . . . . 174 F7
  East Leake LE12 . . . . 205 F3
  Hucknall NG15 . . . . . 145 E5
  Keyworth NG12 . . . . 197 F2
  Long Eaton NG10 . . . 193 D8
  Newark-on-Trent NG24 . 140 B6
  Nottingham NG3 . . . . 173 C5
  Nuthall NG16 . . . . . . 159 B6
  Sandiacre NG10 . . . . 182 B7
Elm Bank NG3 . . . . . . 173 C8
Elm Bank Dr NG3 . . . . 173 C8
Elmbridge NG5 . . . . . 161 B7
Elm Cl
  Keyworth NG12 . . . . 197 F2
  Newark-on-Trent NG24 . 140 B6
  Nottingham NG3 . . . . 173 C7
  Pinxton NG16 . . . . . 113 D2
  Saxilby LN1 . . . . 57 B4
Elmcroft NG25 . . . . . 134 B3
Elm Croft NG11 . . . . . . 8 A8
Elmdale Gdns NG8 . . . 172 B8
Elm Dr NG4 . . . . 174 F7
Elmfield NG20 . . . . . . 74 A3
Elm Gr
  Arnold NG5 . . . . 148 A1
  Church Warsop NG20 . . 74 A6
Elmhurst Ave
  Nottingham NG3 . . . . 162 C2
  South Normanton DE55 . 113 A4
Elmhurst Cl DE55 . . . . 113 A4
Elmhurst Dr NG17 . . . 100 A3
Elmhurst Rd NG19 . . . . 88 F1
Elmore Cl NG2 . . . . . 173 B2
Elmore's Mdw NG14 . . 152 A8
Elms Cl
  Rempstone LE12 . . . 215 D5
  Ruddington NG11 . . . 196 C6

Elms The
  Carlton NG4 . . . . . . 174 F6
  Watnall NG16 . . . . . 158 F8
Elmsthorpe Ave NG7 . . 222 A2
Elmswood Gdns NG5 . . 161 D3
ELMTON 58 A7
Elmton Cl S80 . . . . 58 D8
Elmton Rd S80 . . . . . . 58 D8
Elmton Way S80 . . . . . 58 E8
Elmtree Ave NG16 . . . 128 F7
Elm Tree Ave
  Mansfield Woodhouse NG19 . . . . 88 D4
  Shirebrook NG20 . . . . . 72 D4
  West Bridgford NG2 . . 185 D7
Elmtree Cl S81 . . . . . . 34 F7
Elm Tree Ct S80 . . . . . 35 F2
Elm Tree Dr DN10 . . . . . 9 F7
Elm Tree Pl DN22 . . . . 50 B4
Elmtree Rd NG14 . . . . 148 D7
Elm Tree Rise NG22 . . . 93 E5
Elm Tree St NG18 . . . 102 C7
Elm Wlk DN22 . . . . . . 40 A5
Elmwood Cl DN22 . . . . 30 A1
Elmwood Ct S80 . . . . . 35 B2
Elnor St NG16 . . . . . . 143 C3
Elsham Wlk DN21 . . . . 24 F8
Elson St NG7 . . . . . . 172 F8
ELSTON 153 E5
Elston Gdns NG11 . . . 184 E4
Elston Hall NG23 . . . . 153 D4
Elston La
  Cotham NG23 . . . . . 154 A3
  Cotham NG23 . . . . . 168 E8
  East Stoke NG23 . . . 153 C4
  Elston NG23 . . . . . . 153 D6
Elston Mws NG4 . . . . 174 A8
Elston Rd NG23 . . . . . 168 D7
Elswick Cl NG5 . . . . . 161 B8
Elswick Dr NG9 . . . . . 184 C4
Elterwater Dr NG2 . . . 186 C6
Eltham Cl NG8 . . . . . . 159 F3
Eltham Dr NG8 . . . . . 160 A2
Eltham Rd NG2 . . . . . 186 A7
Elton Cl
  Balderton NG24 . . . . 140 D3
  Mansfield NG18 . . . . 103 B6
  Stapleford NG9 . . . . 182 D8
Elton & Orston Sta NG13 . . . . 180 A5
Elton Rd
  Mansfield NG18 . . . . 102 F6
  🖪 Nottingham NG5 . . 161 B1
Elton Rd N NG5 . . . . . 161 A1
Elton Terr NG7 . . . . . 172 F7
Elvaston Ct NG18 . . . . 103 B6
Elvaston Dr NG10 . . . 193 A4
Elvaston Rd NG8 . . . . 172 B5
Eleveden Dr DE7 . . . . 157 C3
Elwin Dr NG8 . . . . . . 171 C1
Ely Cl
  Mansfield Woodhouse NG19 . . . . 88 D4
  Worksop S80 . . . . 36 A2
Embankment Cl NG20 . 72 E3
Embley Rd NG5 . . . . . 161 A5
Emerald Cl NG19 . . . . 87 F1
Emerald Gr NG17 . . . . 115 C4
Emerys Rd NG4 . . . . . 175 B8
Emma Bates Way NG21 . . . . 118 B6
Emmanuel Ave
  Nottingham, Portchester NG3 . . . . 162 A1
  Nottingham, Rise Park NG5 . . . . 147 A1
Emmendingen Av NG24 . . . . 125 B3
Emmerson Dr
  Clipstone NG21 . . . . . 89 F4
  Clipstone NG21 . . . . . 90 A4
  Clipstone NG21 . . . . . 90 A5
Emneth Cl NG3 . . . . . 173 F8
Emperor Cl 🖪 NG5 . . . 161 A1
Empingham Cl NG9 . . . 183 B2
Empire St NG18 . . . . 102 D6
Empire Way NG8 . . . . 172 B7
Empress Rd LE11 . . . . 220 D4
Emsworth Ave DN22 . . . 29 E1
Emsworth Cl DE7 . . . . 157 D3
Ena Ave NG2 . . . . . . 173 F5
Enderby Cres
  Gainsborough DN21 . . . 24 E7
  Mansfield NG18 . . . . 102 F6
Enderby Gdns NG5 . . . 147 E1
Enderby Sq NG9 . . . . 183 F8
Endor Rd NG18 . . . . . 102 F1
Endsleigh Gdns
  Beeston NG9 . . . . . . 183 F7
  West Bridgford NG12 . 186 A4
Enfield Cl NG23 . . . . . 70 D2
Enfield St NG9 . . . . . 183 F1
Engineers Ct LE11 . . . 220 B6
Engine La NG16 . . . . . 144 B4
Engine Rd NG16 . . . . 144 B4
England Cres DE75 . . . 143 A2
English Martyrs' CV Acad NG10 . . . . 182 B1
Ennerdale Cl NG2 . . . 186 C7
Ennerdale Rd
  Long Eaton NG10 . . . 182 B2
  Nottingham NG5 . . . . 161 D5
Ennismore Mews NG11 . . . . 185 C2
Enright Cl NG24 . . . . 139 F6
Enterprise Bsns Ctr S81 . 35 F8
Enterprise Cl NG21 . . . 118 A6

Enterprise Rd
Old Dalby LE14.........**219** B4
Pleasley NG19.........**87** D2

Enterprise Way
Heanor NG16.........**143** C2
3 Mansfield NG19.....**87** E2
Nottingham NG2.........**173** A2
Retford DN22.........**39** F5
Enterprise Wy NG21....**118** A6
Enthorpe St 4 NG8...**172** B6
Epinal Way LE11.........**220** A1
EPPERSTONE.........**150** A6
Epperstone By-pass
Epperstone NG14.......**150** B4
Woodborough NG14....**149** E5
Epperstone Ct 14
NG18.................**103** A2
Epperstone Rd
Lowdham NG14.........**150** D2
Oxton NG25.........**134** C1
West Bridgford NG2....**185** E8
Epping Way NG19......**103** B8
Epsom Rd NG9.........**182** E3
Epsom St NG18.........**102** F6
Erdington Way NG9....**182** E3
Erewash Ct DE7.........**157** D1
Erewash Dr DE7.......**170** B6
Erewash Gdns NG5....**161** A8
Erewash Gr NG9........**182** F2
*Erewash Meadows Nature
Reserve*.
Aldercar NG16.........**143** B8
Jacksdale NG16.........**128** B1
Erewash Rd NG16......**113** E2
Erewash Sq DE7.......**170** A6
Erewash St
Kirkby-in-Ashfield
NG17.................**115** A4
Long Eaton NG10.....**193** B8
Pye Bridge DE55.......**128** A6
Erica Dr DE55.........**113** B7
Eric Ave NG15.........**130** F1
Erith Cl NG8.........**159** D1
Ernehale Jun & Inf Sch
NG5.................**162** A6
Ernest Rd NG4.........**162** B1
Ernie White Cl LN1...**56** F5
Erskine Rd 4 NG5.....**161** B1
Esam Cl NG22.........**120** A5
Esher Gr NG3.........**161** C1
Eshton Rise
Austerfield DN10.........**3** A1
Bawtry DN10.........**10** A8
Eskdale Cl
Long Eaton NG10.....**193** B5
Mansfield NG18.......**102** F5
Eskdale Ct NG2.......**186** C7
Eskdale Dr
Beeston NG9.........**183** B5
Nottingham NG8.......**172** B8
Worksop S81.........**35** E8
Eskdale Jun Sch NG9..**183** B5
Eskhouse Cl NG2.....**186** C4
Eskil Way DN22.........**50** A4
Essex Dr DN11.........**9** D4
Essex Rd DN11.........**9** D4
Essex St
2 Eastwood NG16...**143** F2
2 Ilkeston DE7.......**157** F1
Estfeld Cl DN11.........**8** A8
Esther Varney Pl
Newark-on-Trent NG24..**125** B1
2 Newark-on-Trent
NG24.................**140** B8
Estwic Ave NG16......**143** F3
Ethel Ave
Hucknall NG15.........**131** C1
Nottingham NG3.......**162** A1
Ethelbert Ave NG17...**115** C1
Etheldene NG12.......**189** B4
Ethel Rd NG2.........**185** F7
Etherington St DN21...**24** D8
Eton Cl
Newark-on-Trent NG24..**139** F6
Nottingham NG8.......**172** D7
Eton Ct NG2.........**139** E6
Eton Gr NG8.........**172** B4
Eton Pl NG12.........**185** E5
Eton Rd NG2.........**185** E6
Eucalyptus Ave NG11..**184** C1
Eugene Gdns NG2.....**173** D2
Eugene St NG2.........**223** F1
Europa Way NG2......**185** C3
Euston Wlk NG19......**88** C6
Evans Ave NG17.......**100** C3
Evans Cl NG23.......**156** D7
Evans Rd
East Leake LE12.......**214** E7
Nottingham NG6.......**160** D3
Evedon Wlk NG5.......**147** B1
Evelyn St
Beeston NG9.........**184** B7
11 Nottingham NG2..**173** E4
Eversley Wlk NG5.....**161** B8
EVERTON.........**11** C3
Everton Prim Sch DN10..**11** B3
Everton Sluice La DN10..**11** C4
Everton St NG19......**87** E1
Evesham Cl NG3.......**183** A1
Evesham Mews 7 S80..**35** F2
Ewart Rd NG7.........**173** A8
Ewe Lamb Cl NG9......**170** F1
Ewe Lamb La NG9.....**170** F1
Ewell Rd NG8.........**171** E5
Exbourne Rd NG8......**159** F1
Exbury Gdns NG2......**185** B4
Excalibur Wlk 8 NG19..**87** D1
Exchange Arc NG1.....**223** E2

Exchange Rd NG2......**185** F7
Exchange Row 13
NG18.................**102** B7
Exchange St DN22......**39** E7
Exchange Wlk NG1.....**223** E2
Exe Fold NG19.........**88** D2
Exeter Cl
Carlton NG4.........**162** F2
East Leake LE12.......**205** D1
Exeter Rd
Nottingham NG7.......**173** A8
West Bridgford NG2...**185** F6
Exford Cl NG19.........**88** C6
Experian Wy NG2......**173** A1
Explore Way S80.......**34** D1
Export Dr NG17.......**113** F8
Exton Rd NG5.........**161** A3
Eyam Cl
Beeston NG9.........**171** C2
Mansfield NG18.......**103** B6
Eyres Cl NG17.........**100** F6
Eyre's Gdns DE7......**157** F2
Eyres La NG11.......**205** A8
Eyre's La LN6.........**83** E3
Eyre St NG2.........**173** E4

F

Fabis Dr NG11.......**184** A1
Fackley Rd NG17.....**100** C6
Fackley Way NG17....**100** C6
Factory La
Beeston NG9.........**183** E5
Ilkeston DE7.........**157** E2
Factory Rd NG17.....**115** A5
Factory St 2 LE11....**220** C3
Factory Yd NG17.....**101** A4
Failsworth Cl NG11...**184** B3
Fairbank Cres NG5....**161** D2
Fairburn Cl NG8.......**171** C4
Fairburn Cres NG12...**186** A3
Fairburn Wy NG16....**159** A7
Faircroft Ave NG10...**182** B5
Fairdale Dr NG16.....**144** B2
Fairfax Cl
Gainsborough DN21.....**24** F6
Nottingham NG7.......**160** F2
Fairfield DN22.........**39** E3
Fairfield Ave
Farndon NG24.........**139** A5
Hilcote DE55.........**99** C1
New Balderton NG24...**140** C5
Fairfield Cl
Nether Langwith NG20..**59** A2
Nottingham NG11......**185** B5
Fairfield Cres NG10...**193** A4
Fairfield Dr
Mansfield NG18.......**103** A7
Ravenshead NG15......**116** C3
Fairfield Prep Sch
LE11.................**220** B3
Fairfield Prim Sch
NG9.................**182** D6
Fairfield Rd NG17.....**101** B3
Fairfield St NG13.....**177** E4
Fairham Ave NG11.....**195** B1
Fairham Brook La
Bunny NG11.........**206** F7
Bunny NG11.........**207** A7
Fairham Cl NG11......**196** B8
Fairham Dr NG8.......**172** D4
Fairham Rd NG12.....**197** D3
Fairham Sch NG17....**115** B3
Fairholme Cl NG21....**89** F2
Fairholme Dr
Mansfield NG19.......**87** E1
Nottingham NG19.....**101** F8
Fairisle Cl NG11.......**185** A1
Fairland Cres NG2....**185** D4
Fairlawn Pl NG5.......**161** D2
Fairlawns NG18.......**103** B7
Fairlie Ave NG19.....**101** D5
Fairlight Way NG5.....**161** B7
Fairmaid Gr NG7......**184** E2
Fairmead Cl NG3......**174** A8
Fairnley Rd NG8......**171** D8
Fair Vale NG23.......**110** A8
Fair View NG19.......**89** A4
Fairview Ave
Selston NG16.........**128** F2
Underwood NG16......**129** A1
Fairview Ct NG11.....**185** D2
Fairview Rd NG5......**161** E4
Fairway
Keyworth NG12.......**198** A2
Newark-on-Trent NG24..**139** D5
Retford DN22.........**39** D3
Fairway Cres NG13....**177** B8
Fairways The
Mansfield Woodhouse
NG19.................**88** D6
Torksey LN1.........**44** C2
Fairway The NG4.....**162** E3
Fairweather Cl NG22...**77** F5
Falcon Cl
Eagle LN6.........**84** D3
Nottingham NG7.......**222** A2
Falcon Ct DE7.......**157** D1
Falcon Dr NG17.....**115** D6
Falcon Gr
7 Gainsborough DN21...**15** F1

Falcon Gr *continued*
Nottingham NG7.......**161** A1
Falcon St
Loughborough LE11....**220** C5
6 Nottingham NG7...**161** A1
Falcon Way
East Leake LE12.......**205** F3
Papplewick NG15......**131** D1
Falconwood Gdns
NG11.................**184** C1
Fallow Cl
Nottingham NG7.......**184** E2
Retford DN22.........**29** E1
Fallow Croft LN1......**57** A5
Fallow St S81.........**36** B7
Fallow Way NG18.....**102** E1
Fal Paddock NG19....**88** D2
Falstone Ave NG24...**140** B6
Falston Rd NG8.......**172** A1
Faraday Ave NG22....**66** A3
Faraday Cl
Harworth DN11.........**8** F3
New Ollerton NG22....**77** C3
Faraday Ct NG9.......**170** E1
Faraday Rd
Mansfield NG18.......**102** E5
Nottingham NG7.......**222** A2
Far Back La NG22.....**119** F6
Far Clay Gr S81.......**34** F7
Far Croft Ave NG17...**100** C3
Far Dales Rd DE7.....**157** E2
Farfield Ave NG9.....**183** E8
Farfield Gr NG9.......**183** E8
Farfield Rd DE7.......**170** A8
Farhill La NG22.........**68** A7
Far Holme La
Sutton on Trent NG23...**97** A8
Sutton-on-Trent NG23..**97** B7
Far La LE12.........**213** D3
Farleigh Dr
1 Harworth DN11.....**8** F5
Harworth DN11.........**9** A5
Farleys Gr NG15......**146** A5
Farleys La NG15......**146** A5
Farley St NG6.......**160** B7
Farm Ave NG15.......**145** D4
Farm Cl
Bathley NG23.........**110** B3
East Bridgford NG13...**165** D3
Ilkeston DE7.........**170** A8
Long Eaton NG10.....**193** C6
North Leverton with
Habblesthorpe DN22...**32** C1
Farm Croft Rd NG19...**88** C6
Farm Ct NG20.........**59** A1
Farmers Branch S81...**36** A7
Farmers Cl NG17.....**100** A1
Farmer St NG11......**196** E3
Farmers Wlk NG24....**125** C4
Farm Gr S81.........**36** B7
Farmhouse Cl NG13...**181** A3
Farmilo Cres NG19....**87** C4
Farmilo Prim Sch NG19..**87** C4
Farm La
East Markham NG22....**65** F7
Hardstoft S45.........**85** A2
Farm Rd
Arnold NG5.........**162** B7
Beeston NG9.........**183** D5
Farmstead The NG23..**96** F4
Farm View DN22.......**39** F4
Farm View Rd NG17...**115** C5
Farmway NG19.......**88** C2
Farnborough Acad The
NG11.................**185** A2
Farnborough Rd NG11..**185** A2
Farndale S81.........**36** B7
Farndale Cl
Long Eaton NG10.....**193** A4
Sutton in Ashfield NG17..**100** F5
Farndale Dr NG8.......**171** B4
Farndale Rd NG17....**100** F5
FARNDON.........**139** B4
Farndon Dr NG9.......**182** F3
Farndon Gn NG8......**172** C3
Farndon Gr S81.......**35** D7
Farndon La NG24.....**139** C2
Farndon Mws NG24....**74** B8
*Farndon Ponds Nature
Reserve*. NG24.......**138** F6
Farndon Rd
Newark-on-Trent NG24,
NG23.................**139** D6
Sutton in Ashfield NG17..**101** D1
*Farndon Willow Holt
Nature Reserve*.
NG24.................**138** F5
Farnes Ct S81.........**36** B5
Far New Cl NG21......**103** E2
Farnham Rd 1 LE11...**220** B1
FARNSFIELD.........**119** E6
Farnsfield Ave NG14..**164** A5
Farnsfield Ct 15 NG18..**103** A2
Farnsfield Rd
Bilsthorpe NG22.......**105** F3
Blidworth NG22.......**106** A4
**Farnsfield St Michael's CE
Prim VA Sch** NG22...**119** F7
Farnsworth Ave NG21..**103** E2
Farnsworth Cl NG16...**143** E2
Farnsworth Gr NG17...**99** F3
Far Pasture Cl NG12...**197** F2
Farrar Cl NG24.......**125** C2
Far Rd NG22.........**67** D4
Farrendale Cl NG16...**88** D1
Farriers Croft DE7....**157** D5
Farriers Gn NG11.....**184** C2
Farringdon Cl NG8....**159** D3
Farrington Wy NG16...**143** E1

Farr Way NG21.......**118** A4
Far Rye NG8.........**171** F6
Far St
Bradmore NG11.......**196** E3
Wymeswold LE12.....**216** C4
Farthingate NG25.....**136** F8
Farthingate Cl NG25...**136** F8
Farthings The LE12...**213** A1
Farthing Way 1 NG18..**102** E1
Farwells Cl NG6......**160** C3
Far Wood Cl DE7.....**157** E4
Faulconbridge Cl NG6..**160** B6
Fawcett St DN21......**15** C1
Fay Dr 8 LE11.......**220** C3
Fearn Chase NG4.....**174** E7
Fearn Cl DE72.......**193** A7
Fearnleigh Dr NG6....**160** D2
Fearon Cl NG14.....**164** F5
Featherbed La S80....**34** F1
Featherfield Pl NG9...**182** D7
Feathers Ave NG18...**36** B2
Featherstone Cl
Carlton NG4.........**162** D3
Mansfield NG18.......**101** D4
Feignes Ct NG12......**197** E3
Feilding Way DN21....**15** E1
Felen Cl NG5.........**161** A7
Fellbarrow Cl NG12...**186** C5
Fell Croft NG24.......**139** A5
Felley Ave NG17......**114** E1
Felley Mill La N NG16..**129** C2
Felley Mill La S NG16..**129** B1
Felley Priory Gdn.
NG16.................**129** C3
Fellows Rd NG9......**183** E7
Fellows Way NG9......**184** D8
Fellows Yd NG12......**197** E2
Fell Side NG5.........**162** A5
Fellside Cl NG2......**186** C6
Fell Wilson St NG20...**74** C4
Felly Cl NG15.......**145** E5
Felly Mill La S NG16...**129** B1
Felstead Ct NG9......**171** C1
Felton Ave NG19.....**88** C6
Felton Cl NG9.......**183** B5
Felton Rd NG2.......**173** D1
Felton Way NG5......**147** F2
Fenchurch Cl NG5.....**147** A1
Fen Cl DE55.........**99** A3
Fenimore Ct NG12....**176** B3
Feniton Ct NG5......**162** E5
Fen La
Balderton NG23.......**155** D3
Balderton NG24.......**141** A4
Fennec Dr S81.......**35** B7
Fennel St LE11.......**220** B4
Fenroth Cl NG6......**159** F8
FENTON
Balderton.........**142** D2
Saxilby.........**55** D6
Fenton Cl NG24.....**125** B2
Fenton Dr NG6......**146** C2
Fenton Fields LN1....**55** D5
Fenton Rd
Fenton NG23.........**142** D1
Nottingham NG5.......**160** F4
Edwinstowe NG21.....**75** F2
Mansfield NG19.......**103** A8
Fenwick Cl NG8......**159** F2
Fenwick Rd NG8......**159** F2
Fenwick St NG20.....**74** B4
Ferguson Ave NG19...**88** B4
Ferguson Cl 1 NG9...**183** C2
Fern Ave 7 NG5......**161** B1
Fern Bank Ave NG22..**64** A1
Fern Cl
Beeston NG9.........**183** C7
Bilsthorpe NG22.......**106** A5
Ravenshead NG15......**117** B1
Ravenshead NG15......**132** B8
Shirebrook NG20.......**72** E6
Southwell NG25.......**121** D1
Fern Cres NG16......**143** D3
Ferndale 6 NG16.....**102** C5
Ferndale Cl
Beeston NG9.........**183** E2
New Ollerton NG22....**77** E6
Ferndale Gr NG3.....**174** B6
Ferndale Rd NG3.....**174** B6
Ferndene Dr NG10....**193** A7
Ferndown Dr 6 DE55..**99** B7
Ferngill Cl 2 NG2.....**173** B1
Fernhill Rd NG12......**189** D4
Fern Lea Ave NG12...**187** E2
Fernleigh Ave NG3....**162** B2
Fernleigh Rise NG19...**88** D1
Fern Rd
Cropwell Bishop NG12..**189** A3
Cropwell Bishop NG12..**189** B3
Hathern LE12.........**212** F1
Ferns Meadows DN22..**42** C8
Fern St NG17.........**100** E4
Ferous Cl NG15......**195** F8
Ferrers Wlk NG3......**173** E5
Ferriby Terr 13 NG2...**173** C1
Ferry Farm Ctry Pk*.
NG14.................**151** C1
Ferry La
Carlton-on-Trent NG23..**96** F5
Carlton-on-Trent NG23..**97** A5
Everton DN10.........**11** C3

Ferry La *continued*
Kettlethorpe LN1......**55** F4
North Muskham NG23...**110** F2
Ferryman Rd
Loughborough LE11....**220** C5
2 West Bridgford NG2..**185** A6
Festival Ave DN11.....**9** A4
Festival Cres NG9.....**170** C4
Festival Dr LE11......**220** A6
Festival Hall L Ctr
NG17.................**115** A4
Festus Cl NG3.......**223** F4
Festus St
Carlton NG4.........**175** A7
Kirkby-in-Ashfield NG17..**115** A4
Fewster Gdns NG13...**177** D6
Field Ave
Beeston NG9.........**183** B4
Carlton NG4.........**162** C2
Mansfield Woodhouse
NG19.................**88** D5
Worksop S81.........**36** A7
Field Dr NG20.........**72** C2
Fielden Ave NG19.....**87** D2
Field End Cl LE12....**205** C1
Fieldfare Cl
Beeston NG9.........**183** D6
East Leake LE12.......**205** F3
Fieldfare Dr S81......**35** C7
Field Farm Way NG9..**170** E2
Field House Cl NG8...**171** D5
Fieldings The NG17...**100** B2
Field La
Ault Hucknall NG19, S44..**86** C6
Beeston NG9.........**183** B4
Blidworth NG21.......**117** F3
Cropwell Bishop NG12..**189** A4
Morton DN21.........**15** A4
Widmerpool NG11.....**208** C4
Woodborough NG14....**149** C4
Wroot DN9.........**2** B8
Field Maple Dr NG7...**172** E8
Field Pl NG17.......**114** D8
Fields Ave NG11.....**196** C5
Fields Dr NG13......**178** F5
Fields End DN10.......**6** E1
Fields Farm Rd NG10..**193** E5
Fields The NG21.....**104** C1
Fields View NG12....**187** E4
Field The DE75......**157** A6
Field View
Radcliffe on Trent
NG12.................**176** C4
Saxilby LN1.........**57** A5
South Normanton DE55..**113** A7
Sutton in Ashfield NG17..**100** C1
Field View Cl NG16...**128** C4
Fieldway NG11.......**185** B3
Fieldwork Rd LE14....**219** A5
Fiennes Cres NG7.....**222** C1
Fifth Ave
Beeston NG9.........**184** D6
Clipstone NG21.......**89** F3
Edwinstowe NG21.....**75** F2
Mansfield NG19.......**103** A8
Fiftyeights Rd DN10...**1** D3
Fig Tree Prim Sch
NG7.................**222** B4
Filigree Cl DE55.....**113** D7
Finch Cl NG7.......**184** F8
Finchley Cl NG11.....**184** C1
Findern Ct NG18......**103** B6
Findern Gn NG3......**174** A6
Fingal Cl NG7.......**184** E2
Fingle St DN22.......**32** D1
Fingleton S81.......**36** B6
Finkell St DN10......**12** F3
Finley Way DE55.....**113** B4
Finney La DN22.......**51** E1
Finningley Rd NG18...**103** A3
Finsbury Ave
4 Loughborough LE11..**220** C3
Nottingham NG2.......**173** C1
Finsbury Pk Cl NG2...**185** C5
Finsbury Rd
Beeston NG9.........**171** C3
Nottingham NG5.......**147** A2
Firbank Ct NG9......**183** B4
FIRBECK.........**16** A6
Firbeck Acad NG8.....**171** B4
Firbeck Ave NG18....**102** F5
Firbeck Cres S81.....**16** F3
Firbeck Rd
Arnold NG5.........**162** A8
Nottingham NG8.......**171** C4
Fir Cl
HUCKNALL NG15.....**146** B4
Nottingham NG6.......**159** F7
Shirebrook NG20.......**72** E6
Fircroft Ave NG8.....**171** F8
Fircroft Dr NG15.....**145** C5
Fir Dale NG12.......**188** A3
Firecrest Way NG6....**160** D3
Firefly Cl NG13......**177** B7
Firemen's Row NG17..**100** E4
Firmin Way NG12.....**185** B4
Firs Ave NG9.......**183** F7
Firs Cl S81.........**27** E3
Firs Rd NG12.......**186** B4
Firs St NG10.......**193** A4
First Ave
Beeston NG9.........**184** C6
Carlton, Colwick NG4..**174** C5
Carlton, Gedling NG4..**162** F1
Carlton, Thorneywood
NG4.................**174** C8
Clipstone NG21.......**90** A3

First Ave *continued*
Edwinstowe NG21.......**76** A2
Mansfield NG21.......**103** F2
Mansfield Woodhouse
NG19.................**89** A1
Nottingham NG6.......**160** B7
Firs The 1 NG5.......**147** F6
First Holme La NG23...**97** A8
First Oak Dr
Clipstone NG21.......**90** A4
Mansfield NG21.......**89** F5
Firth Cl
Arnold NG5.........**148** C1
East Leake LE12.......**205** E3
Firth Dr NG9.........**183** C2
Firth Rd DN22.........**39** C8
Firth Way NG6.......**146** A1
Fir Tree Cl NG19......**89** D2
Fir View NG22.........**77** D5
Fisher Ave NG5.......**161** C1
Fisher Cl
Collingham NG23.......**98** B1
East Leake LE12.......**205** E3
Sutton in Ashfield NG17..**100** D5
Fisher Ct DE7.......**157** F4
Fisher Gate NG1......**223** F2
Fisher La
Bingham NG13.......**177** E4
Mansfield NG18.......**102** C5
Fishers St NG17.....**115** A1
Fisher St 4 NG7......**172** F8
Fish Pond Dr NG7....**223** D1
Fishpool Rd NG13....**117** D3
FISKERTON.........**137** E3
Fiskerton Ct 6 NG18..**103** A3
Fiskerton Rd
Bleasby NG25.......**152** D8
Fiskerton NG25.......**137** D1
Rolleston NG23.......**138** B5
Southwell NG25.......**137** A6
Fiskerton Sta NG25...**137** E4
Fitzgerald Ct NG15...**146** A6
Fitzherbert St NG20...**74** C4
Fitzwilliam Dr 2 NG19..**88** F2
Five Acres NG11.....**185** A4
Five Fields La DN22...**40** A4
Five Fields La DN22...**40** A4
Flagholme NG12......**187** F2
Flagstaff Rd LE14....**219** A5
Flamingo Ct 5 NG2...**173** A2
Flamstead Ave NG4...**163** B7
Flamstead Rd DE7....**157** F1
Flamsteed Rd NG8....**159** D1
Flanders Cl NG19......**87** F1
Flash La NG22.......**93** B7
Flat La S81.........**16** A6
Flatts La
Calverton NG14.......**133** C1
Westwood NG16......**128** D3
Flatts The NG9......**183** B5
FLAWBOROUGH.....**168** C2
Flawborough La NG13..**191** E4
Flawborough Rd NG13..**168** B3
Flawborough Rise
NG2.................**185** B3
Flawforth Ave NG11...**196** D6
Flawforth La NG11....**196** E7
Flaxendale NG12......**188** A2
Flaxley La NG24......**140** A4
Flaxton Way NG5......**160** F7
Fleam Rd NG11.......**184** E4
FLEDBOROUGH.....**68** C5
Fledgling Cl LN6.....**84** D3
Fleeman Gr NG2......**174** A1
Fleet Cl NG7.........**172** D6
Fleet La NG23.........**97** F7
Fleetway S81.........**35** E7
Fleetwith Cl NG16....**144** B1
Fleetwith Cl NG2.....**186** C5
Fleming Ave
Bottesford NG13.......**181** D3
Tuxford NG22.........**66** A3
Fleming Cl NG16.....**159** A8
Fleming Dr
Carlton NG4.........**174** C7
Newark-on-Trent NG24..**125** B4
Woodbeck DN22.......**53** B8
Fleming Gdns NG11...**184** C1
Fletcher Cl NG22.....**119** E7
Fletcher Gate NG1....**223** E2
Fletcher Rd NG9......**184** A7
Fletcher St NG10.....**193** D8
Fletcher Terr NG3.....**161** E2
Fletcher Way NG19...**103** B8
Flewitt Gdns NG3.....**173** E6
Flinders Orch NG12...**197** E2
Flint Ave
Mansfield Woodhouse
NG19.................**88** B7
FLINTHAM.........**153** A1
Flintham Dr NG5......**161** C4
Flintham La
Screveton NG13.......**166** E5
Sibthorpe NG23.......**167** B8
Flintham Mus. NG23...**153** A1
Flintham Prim Sch
NG23.................**153** A1
Flixton Rd NG16......**158** F7
Flood Rd Old Section The
DN10.................**23** E7
Flood Rd The
Gainsborough DN21.....**24** B7
Saundby DN10.........**23** F5
Floralands Gdn Village.
NG4.................**162** B8
Floral Villas NG23......**96** F7
Florence Ave NG10...**193** C7
Florence Boot Cl NG9..**184** B8
Florence Cl NG19.....**86** F4
Florence Cres NG4...**175** B8

Florence Ct DE7 . . . . .157 F1
Florence Gr NG3. . . . . .174 A7
Florence Rd
 Carlton NG4 . . . . .175 B8
 Nottingham NG3 . . . . .162 A1
 West Bridgford NG2 . . . . . .186 A8
Florence St NG15 . . . . .146 A5
Florence Terr DN21 . . . . . . .24 D7
Florey Ct NG15 . . . . .172 E2
Florey Wlk NG11 . . . . .195 C8
Florin Gdns NG10 . . . . .193 A7
Florin Way NG18 . . . . .102 E1
Floss La DN22 . . . . .43 D4
Floss Mill La DN21 . . . . .15 B3
Flower Ave NG12 . . . . .176 B5
Flowers Cl NG5 . . . . .162 B6
Flying Bedstead Way
 NG6 . . . . .145 E2
Flying High Acad The
 NG19 . . . . .101 D8
Flying Horse Wlk NG1. .223 E2
Focus Sch (Long Eaton
 Campus) NG10 . . . . .182 C2
Foley Pl [1] S80 . . . . .35 F1
Foljambe Terr NG3 . . . . . . .223 F3
Folkton Gdns NG3 . . . . . . .161 F1
Folly Hall La LE12. . . . . . . .209 D3
Folly La
 Besthorpe NG23 . . . . .98 B8
 Stapleford LN6. . . . . .112 F5
Folly Nook La DN22 . . . . . . .19 A6
Folly Nook Pk DN22. . . . . . .19 B5
Fonton Hall Dr NG17. . . . . .114 B8
Forbes Cl NG10 . . . . .193 E5
Fordbridge La DE55. . . . . . .113 A7
Ford Cl NG24 . . . . .140 F3
Fordham Gn NG11 . . . . . . .195 E8
Ford La NG23 . . . . .109 A5
Ford St N NG7 . . . . .161 A1
Ford St NG7 . . . . .161 A1
Foredrift Cl NG11 . . . . .195 A1
Forest Ave NG18 . . . . .102 C5
Forest Cl
 Annesley Woodhouse
  NG17 . . . . .130 A8
 Cotgrave NG12 . . . . .187 E3
 Rainworth NG21 . . . . .104 C1
 Selston NG16 . . . . .129 B7
Forest Ct
 Mansfield NG18 . . . . .103 B7
 Nottingham NG7 . . . . .222 C3
Forester Cl NG9 . . . . .183 C4
Forester Gr NG4 . . . . .174 D8
Forester Rd NG3 . . . . .174 A8
Forester St NG4 . . . . .175 A7
Forest Fields Prim Sch
 NG7 . . . . .173 A8
Forest Folk Dr NG17 . . . . .117 F5
Forest Gdns NG15 . . . . . . .130 B8
Forest Glade Prim Sch
 NG17 . . . . .101 A4
Forest Gr NG7 . . . . .222 C4
Forest Hill NG18 . . . . .102 C2
Forest Hill Pk S81 . . . . .36 B7
Forest Hill Rd S81 . . . . .36 A7
Forest La
 Papplewick NG15. . . . . . . .131 E3
 Walesby NG22 . . . . .63 E3
 Worksop S80 . . . . .36 C2
 Worksop S80 . . . . .47 C8
Forest Link NG22 . . . . .105 F5
Forest Rd
 Annesley Woodhouse
  NG17 . . . . .130 A8
 Bingham NG13 . . . . .177 D4
 Blidworth NG21 . . . . .118 B5
 Calverton NG14 . . . . .148 D8
 Clipstone NG21 . . . . .89 F3
 Clipstone NG21 . . . . .90 A3
 Clumber and Hardwick
  DN22 . . . . .48 C5
 Elkesley DN22 . . . . .49 C5
 Loughborough LE11. . . . . .220 A3
 Mansfield NG18 . . . . .102 C5
 Market Warsop NG20 . . . . .74 D1
 New Ollerton NG22 . . . . . .77 C4
 Oxton NG25 . . . . .134 B5
 Sutton in Ashfield NG17 .101 A5
Forest Rd E NG1 . . . . .173 B7
Forest Rd W NG7 . . . . .222 C4
Forest Rise
 Market Warsop NG20 . . . . .74 C2
 Worksop S80 . . . . .36 C2
Forestry Holdings NG21. .90 D4
Forest St
 Annesley Woodhouse
  NG17 . . . . .130 A8
 Kirkby-in-Ashfield NG17 .115 B4
 Sutton in Ashfield NG17 .100 F3
FOREST TOWN 89 B1
Forest Town Prim Sch
 NG19 . . . . .89 A1
Forest View
 Blidworth NG21 . . . . .117 E3
 New Ollerton NG22 . . . . . .77 B4
 Retford DN22. . . . . .39 D3
Forest View Dr NG15. .145 E7
Forest View Jun Sch
 Boughton/Ollerton NG22 .77 D5
 New Ollerton NG22 . . . . . .77 B5
Forest Wlk S80 . . . . .36 C1
Forewood La
 Treswell DN22 . . . . .41 F4
 Treswell DN22 . . . . .42 A4
Forge Ave NG14 . . . . .148 F8
Forge Cl
 Kirklington NG22 . . . . . . .120 E8
 South Muskham NG23 . . . .124 E7
 Sutton on Trent NG23 . . . .96 F8
Forge Hill NG9 . . . . .183 D4
Forge Mill Gr NG15 . . . . . .146 C5

Forge The NG9 . . . . .170 B5
Forman St NG1 . . . . .223 E3
Forrests Yd S80 . . . . .35 E2
Forrington Pl LN1 . . . . .57 C3
Forster Ave NG24 . . . . . . .139 E5
Forster St
 Gainsborough DN21 . . . . . .15 C1
 Kirkby-in-Ashfield NG17 .114 F5
 Nottingham NG7 . . . . .222 A3
Forsythia Gdns NG7. . . . .172 E2
Fortune Cl NG22 . . . . .93 F5
Forum Rd NG5 . . . . .160 E6
Fosbrooke Dr NG10 . . . . . .193 D5
Foss Dyke Ct LN1 . . . . .57 A3
Fossdyke Gdns LN1 . . . . . .57 B3
Fossdyke Paddock LN1 . .57 A3
Fossdyke Wlk LN1 . . . . . . .44 C1
Fosse Gr LN1 . . . . .57 B3
Fosse Rd
 Brough NG23 . . . . .112 B2
 Brough NG23 . . . . .112 D3
 Brough NG23 . . . . .126 A8
 East Stoke NG23 . . . . .153 C7
 Elston NG23 . . . . .153 A5
 Farndon NG24, NG23. . . . .139 A4
 Syerston NG23 . . . . .152 F3
 Winthorpe NG24 . . . . .125 D5
Fosse The
 Bingham NG13 . . . . .177 A2
 Cotgrave NG12 . . . . .188 C2
 Cotgrave NG12 . . . . .199 B8
 Cropwell Butler NG12 . . . .176 F1
 Cropwell Butler NG12 . . . .188 E6
Fosse Way
 Bingham NG13. . . . . .177 D3
 East Bridgford NG13 . . . . .165 F2
 Flintham NG23 . . . . .152 E2
 Flintham NG23 . . . . .152 F3
 Kinoulton NG12 . . . . .199 A1
 Newton NG13 . . . . .177 E8
 Stanton-on-the-Wolds
  NG12 . . . . .199 A2
 Widmerpool LE14 . . . . . . .209 A7
 Widmerpool LE14 . . . . . . .209 A4
 Willoughby-on-the-Wolds
  LE12. . . . . .217 F1
Fosse Wlk NG12 . . . . .188 A1
Fossil Cl NG14. . . . . .173 B1
Foss Way NG13 . . . . .166 B5
Foster Ave NG9 . . . . .183 F6
Foster Rd NG23 . . . . .98 A1
Fosters Cl NG13 . . . . .165 A5
Fosters Dr NG5 . . . . .161 D4
Fosters La NG13 . . . . .177 F4
Foster St NG18 . . . . .102 C6
Foston Cl NG18 . . . . .103 B6
Fothergill Ct [1] NG3 . . . . .173 C7
Foundry Cl NG4. . . . . .124 F2
Foundry Terr NG15 . . . . . .130 D6
Fountain Dale Ct [2]
 NG3. . . . . .173 D7
Fountaindale Sch
 NG18 . . . . .116 D6
Fountaindale Way E
 Mansfield NG18 . . . . .102 F1
 Mansfield NG18 . . . . .103 A1
Fountaindale Way West
 NG18 . . . . .102 F1
Fountain Hill DN10. . . . . .13 D7
Fountain Hill Rd DN10 . .13 D7
Fountain Pk NG22 . . . . . . .77 C3
Fountains Cl
 Kirkby-in-Ashfield
  NG17 . . . . .115 C5
 West Bridgford NG2 . . . . .186 B6
Fountayne Cl NG15 . . . . . .130 F2
Four Seasons Sh Ctr
 NG18 . . . . .102 B7
Fourth Ave
 Beeston NG9 . . . . .184 C6
 Beeston NG9 . . . . .184 D6
 Carlton NG4 . . . . .174 B8
 Clipstone NG21 . . . . .89 F3
 Edwinstowe NG21 . . . . . . .76 A2
 Mansfield NG19 . . . . .103 A8
 Rainworth NG21 . . . . .103 F2
Fowler Rd
 Edwalton NG12 . . . . .185 F3
 Edwalton NG12 . . . . .186 A3
Fowler St NG3 . . . . .173 D8
Foxbridge Cl NG17 . . . . . .114 D4
Foxby Hill DN21 . . . . .24 E6
Foxby La DN21. . . . . .24 F6
Foxby Mws DN21 . . . . .24 E5
Foxby Warren DN21. . . . . .24 E6
Fox Cl NG10 . . . . .193 D5
Fox Covert
 Carlton NG4 . . . . .174 F4
 [3] Loughborough LE11. .220 B6
Fox Covert Cl NG17 . . . . .100 C1
Fox Covert La
 Misterton DN10 . . . . .14 A8
 Nottingham NG11 . . . . . . .184 C1
 Nottingham NG11 . . . . . . .195 C8
 Walkeringham DN10. . . . . .13 F8
Foxcovert Plantation
 Nature Reserve★
 NG14 . . . . .132 F2
Fox Covert Way NG19 . .103 B7
Foxearth Ave NG11 . . . . . .185 A2
Foxes Cl NG7 . . . . .222 C1
Foxfield Way NG12. . . . . .185 C6
Foxglove Cl
 New Balderton NG24. . . . .140 C5
 Nottingham NG15 . . . . . . .146 C4
 Worksop S80 . . . . .36 B2
Foxglove Cres LE12 . . . . .215 A8
Foxglove Gr NG19 . . . . . . .88 F4
Foxglove Rd NG16 . . . . . .158 B8

Foxgloves The NG13 . . . .177 D3
Foxglove Way NG12. . . . .188 A5
Fox Gr NG5. . . . . .160 E3
Fox Gr Ct NG6 . . . . .160 E3
Foxhall Bsns Ctr NG7. . .173 B7
Foxhall Rd NG7. . . . . .173 B8
Fox Hill NG12 . . . . .187 E2
Foxhill Cl NG17 . . . . .100 B3
Foxhill Ct NG4 . . . . .174 E8
Foxhill Rd
 Burton Joyce NG14 . . . . . .163 E5
 Carlton NG4 . . . . .174 C8
Foxhill Rd Central
 NG4. . . . . .174 C8
Foxhill Rd E NG4. . . . . . . .174 D8
Foxhill Rd W NG4 . . . . . . .174 B8
Foxhills DE74. . . . . .203 C1
Foxhollies Gr NG5 . . . . . .161 B3
Fox La S80 . . . . .58 E8
Foxley Rd DE7. . . . . .157 F5
Fox Mdw NG15 . . . . .145 F6
Fox Rd
 Nottingham NG2 . . . . .173 E1
 Whitwell S80 . . . . .45 A6
Fox St
 Annesley Woodhouse
  NG16 . . . . .129 F8
 Annesley Woodhouse
  NG17 . . . . .130 A8
 Creswell S80 . . . . .58 E8
 Sutton in Ashfield NG17 .100 F3
Foxton Cl NG6 . . . . .159 F8
Foxwood Acad NG9 . . . . .171 B1
Foxwood Cl
 Carlton in Lindrick S81 . . .25 D1
 Worksop S81 . . . . .25 D1
Foxwood Gr NG14 . . . . . . .148 F7
Foxwood La NG14 . . . . . . .149 A5
Fradley Cl NG6 . . . . .146 C2
Frampton Rd NG8 . . . . . . .172 A7
Frances Ct NG15 . . . . .131 B1
Frances Gr NG15 . . . . .131 B1
Frances Chichester Wlk
 DN21 . . . . .24 F7
Francis Ct NG16 . . . . .128 B4
Francis Gr NG6 . . . . .160 E3
Francis Rd NG4. . . . . .174 F8
Francis St
 Mansfield NG18 . . . . .102 E7
 Nottingham NG7 . . . . .222 C4
Francis Way DN22 . . . . . . .29 F1
Franckin Rd NG14. . . . . . .150 D2
Franderground Dr
 NG17. . . . . .114 E5
Frank Ave NG18 . . . . .101 F5
Frank Ford Cl LN1 . . . . . . .56 F5
Franklin Cl
 East Leake LE12 . . . . .214 E7
 Nottingham NG5 . . . . .161 C8
Franklin Dr NG12 . . . . . . .186 D1
Franklin Rd NG16 . . . . . . .128 A4
Franklin Way NG17 . . . . .114 E7
Franklyn Gdns
 Keyworth NG12 . . . . .197 E4
 Nottingham NG8 . . . . .172 C6
Fraser Cres NG4 . . . . .162 B1
Fraser Rd
 Carlton NG4. . . . . .162 B1
 Nottingham NG2 . . . . .173 D1
Fraser Sq NG4 . . . . .162 B1
Fraser St NG15 . . . . .130 D6
Frearson Farm Ct
 NG16 . . . . .143 F1
Freckingham St NG1. . . .223 F2
Freda Ave NG4 . . . . .162 D2
Freda Cl NG4 . . . . .162 D2
Freda La NG23 . . . . .181 D2
Frederick Ave
 Carlton NG4 . . . . .174 B7
 Ilkeston DE7 . . . . .170 A5
 Kegworth DE74 . . . . .203 C3
 Kirkby-in-Ashfield
  NG17 . . . . .114 D6
Frederick Cl NG23 . . . . . . .96 F8
Frederick Gent Sch
 DE55. . . . . .113 B5
Frederick Rd NG9. . . . . . .182 D7
Frederick St
 Long Eaton NG10 . . . . . . .193 F7
 Loughborough LE11. . . . . .220 A3
 Mansfield NG18 . . . . .102 C6
 Retford DN22. . . . . .39 F6
 Sutton in Ashfield NG17 .100 D3
 Worksop S80 . . . . .35 E3
Freeby Ave NG19 . . . . .88 D5
Freehold St LE11 . . . . . . .220 C4
Freeland Cl NG9 . . . . .182 F3
Freeman's La DN22 . . . . . .32 C5
Freemans Rd NG4 . . . . . .175 A8
Freemans Terr NG4 . . . . .175 A8
Freemantle Wlk NG5. . . .160 E8
Freeston Dr
 Nottingham NG6 . . . . .145 A4
 Nottingham NG6 . . . . .159 F8
Freeth St NG2 . . . . .173 F2
Freeth Terr NG23 . . . . .68 C5
Freiston St [5] NG7 . . . . . .172 E7
Fremount Dr NG8. . . . . . .172 A7
French Ave DN8 . . . . .170 A6
French Terr NG20. . . . . . . .59 A2
Fretwell St [3] NG7 . . . . . .172 E7
Freya Rd NG22 . . . . .77 D3
Friar La
 Market Warsop NG20 . . . . .74 C2
 Nottingham NG1 . . . . .223 D2

Friar St
 Long Eaton NG10. . . . . . . .193 D7
 [8] Nottingham NG7. . . . .172 E2
Friar Wlk NG13 . . . . .177 C8
Friary Cl [10] NG7 . . . . . . .172 E2
Friary Gdns NG24. . . . . . .125 A1
Friary Rd [2] NG24 . . . . . .140 A8
Friary The NG7 . . . . .172 E2
Friday La NG4 . . . . .162 F1
Frienship Cl LN1. . . . . .55 B4
Friesland Dr [1] NG10 . . . .182 A6
Frinton Rd NG8. . . . . .159 E1
Frisby Ave NG10 . . . . .193 E6
Fritchley Ct NG18. . . . . . .103 B6
Frith Gr NG15 . . . . .101 E7
Frithwood La
 Creswell S80 . . . . .58 D7
 Creswell S80 . . . . .59 A8
Frobisher Gdns NG5 . . . . .161 D6
Frog La NG13. . . . . .202 F3
Frogmore St NG1. . . . . . .223 E4
Frome Gdns NG13 . . . . . . .177 D3
Front St
 Arnold NG5 . . . . .161 F7
 Barnby in the Willows
  NG24 . . . . .141 F5
 East Stockwith DN21. . . . . .7 D2
 South Clifton NG23 . . . . . .68 E1
Frost Ave NG16 . . . . .143 A4
Fryar Rd NG16 . . . . .143 F3
Fuchsia Way NG16 . . . . . . .89 A1
Fuggle Dr S81. . . . . .25 D1
Fulford Ave DN22 . . . . .39 C8
Fulforth St NG1. . . . . .223 E4
Fuller Cl NG18 . . . . .102 B4
Fuller St NG11. . . . . .196 C6
Fullwood Ave [4] DE7. . . .157 E1
Fullwood Cl [6] DE7 . . . . .157 E1
Fulmar Cl NG11 . . . . .88 E1
Fulmar Way S81. . . . . .35 C7
Fulwood Cl NG17 . . . . . . .114 A8
Fulwood Cres NG8. . . . . . .160 B1
Fulwood Dr NG10 . . . . . . .193 A7
Fulwood Ind Est DE55. . .113 F8
Fulwood Rd N
 Huthwaite NG17 . . . . .99 F1
 Huthwaite NG17 . . . . .99 A1
 Sutton in Ashfield NG17 .114 A8
Fulwood Rd S NG17. . . . . .114 A8
Fulwood Rise NG17 . . . . .114 A8
Furlong Ave NG5 . . . . .161 E8
Furlong Cl NG9 . . . . .182 D8
Furlong Pl NG4 . . . . .174 A4
Furlong St NG5 . . . . .161 E8
Furnace Rd DE7 . . . . .170 B6
Furnace Road Ind Est
 DE7. . . . . .170 B6
Furness Cl NG2 . . . . .186 A7
Furness Rd NG6 . . . . .160 C3
Furnival St S80 . . . . .36 A1
Furrow Cl NG24. . . . . .140 A4
Furrows The NG21. . . . . . .104 C1
Furzebrook Rd NG4. . . . . .174 E6
Furze Gdns NG3 . . . . .173 D7
Furze The NG22 . . . . .78 C6
Fylde Cl NG9 . . . . .182 F2
Fylingdale Way NG8 . . . . .171 C4

G

Gables Dr NG25. . . . . .122 B5
Gables Farm Dr LE12. . . .206 C1
Gable's Lea LE12 . . . . .213 B6
Gables The NG22 . . . . .106 A5
Gabor Cl NG11. . . . . .195 C8
Gabrielle Cl NG6. . . . . . . .160 D4
Gaddick View NG22. . . . . .79 F6
Gadd St NG7 . . . . .222 B4
Gadsby Cl DE7. . . . . .170 A4
Gadwall Cres
 Nottingham NG14 . . . . . . .173 A2
 [6] Nottingham NG7. . . . .172 F2
Gadwall Mws S80. . . . . . . .35 B5
Gadwall Rd NG4 . . . . .175 C8
Gainas Ave DN21 . . . . .15 C2
GAINSBOROUGH 24 E5
Gainsborough Acad The
 DN21 . . . . .15 F2
Gainsborough Benjamin
 Adlard Com Sch DN21. .24 E6
Gainsborough Central Sta
 DN21 . . . . .24 D8
Gainsborough Cl
 Kinoulton NG12 . . . . .199 F2
 Long Eaton NG10 . . . . . . .193 E6
 Stapleford NG9 . . . . .182 E6
Gainsborough Coll
 DN21 . . . . .15 C1
Gainsborough Dr
 NG24. . . . . .125 B3
Gainsborough Lea Rd Sta
 DN21 . . . . .24 E4
Gainsborough Parish
 Church CE Prim Sch The
 DN21. . . . . .15 C1
Gainsborough Rd
 Bawtry DN10 . . . . .10 A6
 Beckingham DN10 . . . . . . .13 D1
 Besthorpe NG23 . . . . .97 F7
 Bole DN22 . . . . .23 A3
 Everton DN10 . . . . .11 D2
 Girton NG23 . . . . .82 F3
 Gringley on the Hill DN10 .11 B2
 Langford NG23. . . . . .111 B3
 Lea DN21. . . . . .24 F2
 North Wheatley DN22 . . . . .22 F1
 North Wheatley DN22 . . . . .31 C8
 Saundby DN22 . . . . .23 C5

Gainsborough Rd continued
 Saxilby LN1 . . . . .56 E2
 South Clifton NG23 . . . . . .68 F3
 South Clifton NG23 . . . . . .82 F8
 Spalford NG23 . . . . .83 A8
 Sturton le Steeple DN22 . .32 C6
 Winthorpe NG24. . . . . . . .125 C6
Gainsborough Waterfront
 Enterprise Ctr DN21 . . .24 C6
Gainsborough W Lindsey L
 Ctr DN21. . . . . .15 C2
Gainsford Cl NG5 . . . . . . .160 F5
Gainsford Cres NG5. . . . . .160 F5
Gaitskell Cres NG21. . . . . .76 C1
Gaitskell Way NG24 . . . . .140 E4
Gala Way
 Nottingham NG5 . . . . .160 E6
 Retford DN22. . . . . .39 F5
Gale Cl NG9 . . . . .184 B6
Galena Dr NG3 . . . . .174 A7
Galen Ave DN22 . . . . .42 A1
Galen Ct [2] NG7 . . . . .172 E2
Gallery of Justice★
 NG1 . . . . .223 F2
Galley Hill Rd NG25 . . . . .122 B1
Gallows Inn Cl DE7 . . . . . .170 A5
Gally Knight Way S81 . . . . .16 F3
Galway Ave DN11. . . . . .9 D5
Galway Cres DN22 . . . . . . .39 C8
Galway Dr DN11. . . . . .9 D5
Galway Mews DN11. . . . . . .9 A3
Galway Rd
 Arnold NG5 . . . . .161 E8
 Bircotes DN11 . . . . .9 D5
 Nottingham NG7 . . . . .222 B1
Gamage Cl NG24. . . . . . . .140 F4
Gamble St NG7 . . . . .222 C3
GAMSTON
 Retford 51 A5
 West Bridgford 186 D7
Gamston CE Prim Sch
 DN22 . . . . .50 F5
Gamston Cres NG5 . . . . . .161 C3
Gamston Lings Bar Rd
 NG12 . . . . .186 C3
Gamston Rd NG18 . . . . . .103 B3
Gamston Wood Nature
 Reserve★ DN22 . . . . . . .51 D6
Gant Ct DN11. . . . . .8 A8
Ganton Cl NG3 . . . . .161 F1
Garbsen Ct [4] S80 . . . . . .35 E2
Garden Ave
 Carlton NG4 . . . . .174 D8
 New Houghton NG19. . . . . .86 F7
 Rainworth NG21 . . . . .104 A1
 Shirebrook NG20 . . . . .72 E4
Garden City NG4. . . . . . . .174 E8
Gardendale Ave NG11. . . .184 D1
Gardeners Cl
 Hucknall NG15. . . . . .145 F7
 Newton NG13 . . . . .177 D5
Gardeners Way
 Clipstone NG21 . . . . .89 F3
 Worksop S81 . . . . .35 D6
Gardenia Cres NG3 . . . . . .162 B2
Gardenia Gr NG3 . . . . .162 B2
Garden La NG17 . . . . .101 A3
Garden Rd
 Bingham NG13. . . . . .177 D4
 Eastwood NG16 . . . . .144 A3
 Hucknall NG15. . . . . .145 F7
 [3] Mansfield NG18 . . . . .102 B6
Garden Row DE74 . . . . . . .203 D3
Gardens Ct NG2 . . . . .186 A7
Garden St NG7 . . . . .222 B3
Gardiner Ave NG24 . . . . . .140 F2
Gardiner Terr NG17. . . . . .100 D6
Gardinia Cl NG9 . . . . .183 A2
Gardner Dr NG12 . . . . . . .199 F3
Gardners Cl NG5. . . . . . . .162 D1
Garfield Cl NG9. . . . . .170 E1
Garfield Rd NG7 . . . . .222 B3
Garfield St DN21 . . . . .15 C1
Garforth Cl NG8 . . . . .172 E8
Garibaldi Maths and
 Computing Coll NG19. .89 E2
Garibaldi Rd NG19 . . . . . . .89 D2
Garland Dr [3] DE7. . . . . .157 F8
Garland Rd S81 . . . . .16 E1
Garner Rd NG16 . . . . .158 B7
Garners Hill NG1 . . . . . . .223 E2
Garnet Cl NG18 . . . . .102 C5
Garnet Ct NG3 . . . . .173 E5
Garnet St NG4 . . . . .174 F7
Garnon St NG18 . . . . .101 E6
Garood Cl NG24. . . . . .139 C6
Garratt Ave NG18 . . . . . . .102 C7
Garrett Gr NG11. . . . . .184 D2
Garsdale Cl NG2. . . . . .186 C6
Garsdale Dr NG11. . . . . . . .185 A3
Garside Ave NG17 . . . . . . .100 D1
Garside St S80. . . . . .36 A3
Garth Ave NG17 . . . . .114 E8
Garth Rd NG18 . . . . .102 A4
Garton Cl
 Beeston NG9 . . . . .183 B5
 Nottingham NG6 . . . . .160 B5
Garton Rd LE11. . . . . .220 A3
Garwick Cl NG19. . . . . .89 B2
Gary's Way LE12 . . . . .215 F2
Gas St NG10 . . . . .182 C6
Gas Wlk LE14 . . . . .202 B3
Gatcombe Cl NG12. . . . . . .176 A3
Gatcombe Gr NG10 . . . . . .182 A3
Gateford Ave S81. . . . . . . .35 D6
Gateford Cl
 Beeston NG9 . . . . .171 C2
 Worksop S81 . . . . .35 D7
Gateford Dr S81 . . . . .35 D6
Gateford Gdns S81 . . . . . . .35 D6
Gateford Glade S81. . . . . . .35 D6

Gateford Hill S81. . . . . . . .25 C1
Gateford Park Prim Sch
 S81. . . . . .35 D8
Gateford Rd
 Worksop S81 . . . . .35 E4
 Worksop S81 . . . . .35 D6
Gateford Rise S81 . . . . . . .35 E4
Gateford Toll Bar S81. . . . .35 A8
Gatekeeper Way S81 . . . . .25 D1
Gateside Rd NG2 . . . . .173 A1
Gatling St NG7. . . . . .222 A3
Gattlys La NG22. . . . . .77 B4
Gaul St NG6 . . . . .160 B7
Gauntley Ct [1] NG7 . . . . .172 E5
Gauntley St NG7 . . . . .172 E8
Gautries Cl NG5 . . . . .161 A8
Gawthorne St NG7. . . . . . .161 A1
Gayhurst Gn NG6 . . . . . . .160 E5
Gayhurst Rd NG6 . . . . . . .160 E5
Gaynor Ct NG8. . . . . .172 B6
Gayrigg Ct NG9 . . . . .183 E6
Gayton Cl NG8. . . . . .171 D8
Gayton Rd DE7 . . . . .157 D1
Gaywood Cl NG11. . . . . . . .195 E8
Gdn Terr NG15 . . . . .130 D6
GEDLING 162 F2
Gedling Country Pk★
 NG4 . . . . .162 E5
Gedling Gr NG7. . . . . .222 C4
Gedling Rd
 Arnold NG5 . . . . .162 B5
 Carlton NG4 . . . . .174 D8
Gedling Sch The NG4. . . .162 E3
Gedling St
 Mansfield NG18 . . . . .102 B6
 Nottingham NG1 . . . . .223 F2
Gedney Ave NG3. . . . . .173 F8
Gelding Gr NG5. . . . . .161 F7
Gelding House Woods
 Nature Reserve★
 NG4 . . . . .163 B2
Gell Rd NG9 . . . . .183 A3
Geoff La DN21. . . . . .24 E5
George Ave
 Beeston NG9 . . . . .183 F5
 Long Eaton NG10. . . . . . . .182 F1
George Dere Cl NG22 . . . . .77 D6
George Gn Way NG8 . . . . .172 D1
George Green Way
 NG7. . . . . .184 D8
George Rd
 Carlton NG4 . . . . .174 E7
 West Bridgford NG2 . . . . .185 E7
George's La NG14. . . . . . . .148 D6
George Spencer Acad
 Stapleford NG9 . . . . .182 A4
 Stapleford NG9 . . . . .182 E5
George St
 Arnold NG5 . . . . .161 E6
 Gainsborough DN21 . . . . . .15 B2
 Hucknall NG15. . . . . .146 A8
 Langley Mill NG16 . . . . . .143 B3
 Mansfield NG19 . . . . .101 F8
 Mansfield Woodhouse
  NG19. . . . . .88 D3
 Mansfield Woodhouse, Forest
  Town NG19 . . . . .89 A1
 Market Warsop NG20 . . . . .74 B4
 Newark-on-Trent NG24 . . .125 A1
 Nottingham NG1 . . . . .223 E3
 Pinxton NG16 . . . . .113 C4
 Retford DN22. . . . . .39 E5
 Sutton in Ashfield NG17 .100 B3
 Whaley Thorns NG20. . . . . .59 A2
 Worksop S80 . . . . .35 F3
George Yd [7] LE11. . . . . .220 B4
Georgia Dr NG5 . . . . .147 E2
Georgina Rd NG9 . . . . . . .183 F5
Geraldine Cl NG5 . . . . . . .161 C8
Gerard Gr DN22 . . . . .29 F2
Gerbera Dr NG24 . . . . .125 D1
Gerrard Cl NG5 . . . . .147 A2
Gerrard Cres DE74. . . . . . .203 D1
Gertrude Rd NG2 . . . . . . .174 A1
Gervase Gdns NG11. . . . . .184 D2
Ghest Villas S81 . . . . .16 F1
Ghost House La NG9. . . . .183 B4
Gibbet Hill La DN10. . . . . . .9 F4
Gibbons Ave NG9 . . . . . . .182 D6
Gibbons St NG7. . . . . .172 E1
Gibb St NG10. . . . . .193 E7
Gibdyke DN10 . . . . .4 C3
Gibson Cres NG24 . . . . . . .140 C3
Gibson Cl S81 . . . . .25 C1
Gibson Rd NG7 . . . . .173 A8
Gibson's La LE14. . . . . . . .218 C2
Gifford Gdns NG2. . . . . . . .173 B2
Gilbert Ave
 Gotham NG11 . . . . .195 B1
 Tuxford NG22. . . . . .66 A3
Gilbert Bvd NG5 . . . . .162 C2
Gilbert Cl [2] NG5. . . . . . .161 A5
Gilbert Gdns NG3 . . . . . . .174 A6
Gilbert Rd DN11. . . . . .9 B4
Gilbert St West NG15 . . . .146 A7
Gilberts Field NG21 . . . . . .110 F1
Gilbert Way NG24 . . . . . . .140 C2
Gilbert Wy NG21. . . . . .118 B6
Gilcroft St
 Mansfield NG18 . . . . .102 C6
 Sutton in Ashfield NG17 .100 E6
Gildingwells Rd S81 . . . . . .16 A2
Gildwells Ct NG20 . . . . . . .72 B7
Gilead St NG6 . . . . .160 B7
Giles Ave NG2 . . . . .185 D6
Gillercomb Cl NG2. . . . . . .186 D5
Gill Gn Wlk DN22 . . . . .30 D4
Gillies The NG19. . . . . . . .101 E5

Gilliver La NG12 . . . .**187** C1
Gillot St DE75. . . . .**157** A8
Gillotts Cl NG13. . . . .**177** E5
Gill St
 Nottingham NG1 . . . . . .**223** D4
 Selston NG16. . . . .**129** A6
 Sutton in Ashfield NG17 .**100** C2
Gilmores La NG24 . . . . . .**140** F1
Gilpet Ave NG3 . . . .**173** F8
Gilstrap Cl NG24 . . . .**140** D8
Gilstrap Ctr ★ NG24 . . . . .**124** E1
GILTBROOK **158** C8
Giltbrook Cres NG16 . . . .**158** C8
Giltbrook Ind Pk NG16 . . .**158** B7
Giltbrook Ret Pk NG16 . . .**158** C7
Gilt Hill NG16. . . . .**158** C8
Gilthill Prim Sch NG16 .**158** C8
Giltway NG16. . . . .**158** C6
Gimson Cl DE7 . . . .**157** C3
Gin Cl Way NG16. . . . .**158** C6
Gipsy La
 Gunthorpe DN9 . . . .**7** E7
 Warsop Vale NG20 . . . . . .**73** F6
GIRTON. **82** E1
Girton Ct NG18 . . . .**103** B2
Girton La
 Girton NG23. . . . .**82** F1
 North Scarle LN6. . . . .**83** B1
Girton Rd NG5. . . . .**161** A3
Gisburn Cl NG11. . . . .**185** A4
Gisburn Gr NG19. . . . .**103** B8
Glade Ave NG8 . . . .**172** C5
Glade Hill Prim Sch
 NG5. . . . .**161** C8
Gladehill Rd NG5 . . . . . .**161** C7
Glade The NG11 . . . .**195** E2
Gladstone Ave
 Gotham NG11 . . . .**195** B1
 Loughborough LE11. . . . .**220** B5
Gladstone Dr NG16 . . . . .**143** E7
Gladstone Rd NG24 . . . . .**139** F6
Gladstone St
 Beeston NG9 . . . .**183** F6
 Carlton NG4 . . . .**174** D7
 Gainsborough DN21 . . . . .**15** C1
 Hathern LE12. . . . .**213** A1
 Kirkby-in-Ashfield NG17 .**115** B5
 Langley Mill NG16. . . . . .**143** C4
 Long Eaton NG10. . . . . . .**193** D6
 Loughborough LE11. . . . .**220** B5
 Mansfield NG18. . . . .**102** D7
 Mansfield Woodhouse
  NG19 . . . .**88** C2
 Nottingham NG7 . . . .**173** A8
 South Normanton DE55. .**113** B6
 Worksop S80 . . . .**35** E3
Gladstone Terr
 1 Kirkby-in-Ashfield
  NG17 . . . .**114** F5
 Mansfield Woodhouse
  NG19 . . . .**88** C2
Gladwin Cl NG9. . . . .**182** E7
Gladys St NG7 . . . .**161** A1
Glaisdale S81. . . . .**36** B7
Glaisdale Dr E NG8 . . . . .**171** E6
Glaisdale Drive Ind Est
 NG8 . . . .**171** D6
Glaisdale Dr W NG8. . . . .**171** D5
Glaisdale Parkway
 NG8. . . . .**171** D5
Glamis Cl NG17 . . . .**101** B1
Glamis Rd
 Carlton in Lindrick S81 . .**25** E6
 Nottingham NG5 . . . .**161** A2
Glannis Sq NG20. . . . .**74** C6
Glanton Way NG5. . . . . . .**148** A2
Glapton La NG7 . . . .**184** C2
Glapton Prim Sch
 NG11 . . . .**184** D2
Glapton Rd NG2 . . . .**173** C1
Glapton Wood Nature
 Reserve ★ NG11 . . . . . .**195** D8
GLAPWELL **86** C8
Glaramara Cl **1** NG2. . .**173** B1
Glasby Cl NG22. . . . .**77** B4
Glasshouse St NG1 . . . . .**223** B3
Glastonbury Cl
 Edwalton NG12 . . . .**186** A3
 Mansfield Woodhouse
  NG19 . . . .**88** D4
Glaven Cl NG19 . . . .**88** D2
Glebe Ave
 Market Warsop NG20 . . . .**74** C4
 Pinxton NG16. . . . .**113** D3
Glebe Cl
 Long Clawson LE14 . . . . .**211** C3
 North Wheatley DN22 . . . .**31** E8
 South Normanton DE55. .**113** A5
 Worksop S80 . . . .**35** C3
Glebe Cres DE7. . . . .**170** A4
Glebe Dr NG14. . . . .**163** D3
Glebe Farm Cl NG2 . . . . .**185** C4
Glebe Farm View NG4 .**162** F3
Glebe Jun Sch DE55 . . . .**113** A5
Glebelands NG23 . . . .**110** F1
Glebelands Rd NG11. . . . .**195** B2
Glebe Pk NG24 . . . .**140** C6
Glebe Rd
 Carlton NG4. . . . .**162** C2
 Nuthall NG16. . . . .**159** C6
 West Bridgford NG2 . . . .**185** F2
Glebe St
 Annesley Woodhouse
  NG17 . . . .**129** F8
 Beeston NG9 . . . .**183** F6
 Hucknall NG15. . . . .**146** A8
 Loughborough LE11. . . . .**220** C5

Glebe The
 Awsworth NG16 . . . .**158** B4
 Retford DN22. . . . .**39** D8
Glebe View NG18 . . . . . .**102** E8
Gledhill Dr S81 . . . .**35** B7
Glenbrook NG12. . . . .**188** A3
Glenbrook Cres NG8 . .**172** A7
Glenbrook Prim Sch
 NG8. . . . .**171** F7
Glencairn Dr NG8 . . . . . .**172** A8
Glen Cl DE55 . . . .**99** A3
Glencoe Rd NG11. . . . . . .**185** A1
Glencoyne Rd NG11 . . . . .**195** E8
Glencross Cl NG4 . . . . . .**174** C1
Glendale Cl NG4 . . . .**162** D2
Glendale Ct NG9. . . . .**183** E3
Glendale Gdns NG5 . . . . .**161** F7
Glendon Dr
 Hucknall NG15. . . . .**146** A5
 Nottingham NG5 . . . .**161** A3
Gleneagles Ct NG12. . . . .**186** C3
Gleneagles Dr
 Arnold NG5 . . . .**148** B1
 Kirkby-in-Ashfield NG17 .**114** E7
Glen Eagles Way DN22 . .**39** D3
Glenfield Ave NG16 . . . . .**158** D7
Glenfield Rd NG10 . . . . . .**193** D5
Glen Helen NG4 . . . .**174** F6
Glenlivet Gdns NG7 . . . . .**184** F1
Glenloch Dr NG11 . . . . . .**195** F8
Glen Mooar Cl NG19 . . . . .**89** A2
Glenmore Rd NG2 . . . . . .**186** B6
Glen Parva Ave NG5 . . .**147** E1
Glenridding Cl NG2. . . . .**186** D5
Glensford Gdns NG5 . . . .**146** E2
Glenside
 Arnold NG5 . . . .**162** B5
 Kirkby-in-Ashfield NG17 .**115** C5
Glenside Rd NG9 . . . .**171** C1
Glen St NG17 . . . .**100** E4
Glenstone Ct **1** NG7 . . .**172** F8
Glen The NG7 . . . .**184** F2
Glenthorn Cl S81. . . . .**34** F7
Glentworth Rd NG7 . . . . .**222** A4
Glenwood Ave NG8 . . . . .**171** D3
Glinis Rd NG5 . . . .**160** F8
Glossop Ave NG18 . . . . . .**103** B6
Gloucester Ave
 Beeston NG9 . . . .**183** F5
 Nottingham NG7 . . . .**222** A2
 Nuthall NG16. . . . .**159** F4
 Sandiacre NG10. . . . .**182** A4
Gloucester Rd S81. . . . . . .**36** A7
Glover Ave NG8. . . . . . .**171** D4
Glover Cl
 Newstead NG15. . . . .**130** D7
 South Leverton DN22 . . . .**42** C6
Glovers Cl NG20. . . . .**60** A3
Glovers La NG24 . . . .**140** D4
Goacher's La DN22 . . . . . .**31** D8
Go Ape! ★ NG11 . . . .**90** D4
Goatchurch Ct **3** NG5 .**147** A1
Goathland Cl **3** NG5. . .**161** B8
Godber Rd
 East Leake LE12 . . . .**205** E3
 Hucknall NG15. . . . .**145** E5
Goddard Ct NG5 . . . .**162** C6
Godfrey Dr NG24 . . . .**125** E5
Godfrey La NG7. . . . .**222** B2
Godfrey's Ct S80. . . . .**35** E3
Godkin Dr NG16 . . . .**143** A4
Goit La DN33 . . . .**31** A6
Goldcrest Ave NG21. . . . .**118** A8
Goldcrest Cl NG13 . . . . . .**178** A3
Goldcrest La NG21. . . . . . .**89** F4
Goldcrest Rd
 Mansfield NG19. . . . .**88** F2
 Nottingham NG6 . . . .**160** B4
Golden Hill La NG22 . . . . .**78** D7
Goldenholme La DN22 . .**43** A1
Golden Ribbon Ind Est
 NG2 . . . .**172** F2
Goldfinch Cl
 Mansfield NG18. . . . .**102** E7
 Stapleford NG9 . . . .**170** E2
Goldfinch Mws NG17. . . .**101** B2
Goldham Rd NG8 . . . .**171** D8
Goldrick Cl DN10. . . . .**7** B1
Goldrill Cl NG2 . . . .**186** B7
Goldsmith Rd
 Balderton NG24. . . . .**140** D5
 Worksop S81 . . . .**36** B5
Goldsmith Sq NG1 . . . . . .**223** D3
Goldsmith St
 Mansfield NG18. . . . .**102** A7
 Nottingham NG1 . . . .**223** D3
Goldson Way NG23 . . . . .**110** F1
Goldstraw La
 Balderton NG24. . . . .**140** E2
 Newark-on-Trent NG24 . .**140** E2
Goldswong Terr NG3 . . . .**173** C7
Goldthorpe Ave S81 . . . . .**16** F3
Goldthorpe Cl S81. . . . . . .**16** F3
Golf Cl NG15. . . . .**146** C1
Golf Club Rd DE7 . . . .**170** E8
Golf Course Rd NG12 . . . .**198** B2
Golf Rd NG12. . . . .**176** A3
Gomersall Cl DN22. . . . . .**40** A6
Gonalston La
 Epperstone NG14 . . . . . .**150** D4
 Hoveringham NG14 . . . . .**151** D2
Goodacre Cl LE12. . . . . . .**217** D7
Goodacre Rd LE12 . . . . . .**212** F2
Goodacre St NG18 . . . . . .**102** C7

Goodall Cres NG15. . . . . .**146** C5
Goodall St **1** NG7 . . . . . .**172** F7
Goodhand Cres NG18 . . . .**101** E6
Goodliffe St **6** NG7. . . . .**172** F8
Goodman Cl NG16 . . . . . .**158** C8
Good Shepherd Catholic
 Prim Voluntary Acad
 The NG5 . . . .**62** A5
Goodwill Rd NG22 . . . .**77** C3
Goodwin Cl
 Newark-on-Trent NG24 . .**140** D8
 Sandiacre NG10. . . . .**182** A6
Goodwin Ct NG22. . . . . . .**119** F7
Goodwin Dr NG16. . . . . . .**158** E6
Goodwins St NG7 . . . .**222** C4
Goodwin La NG24. . . . . . .**140** F1
Goodwood Ave NG5 . . . . .**161** E8
Goodwood Dr NG9. . . . . .**182** F2
Goodwood Rd NG8 . . . . . .**171** D4
Goodwood Way NG18 . . .**102** F7
Goosedale La NG6 . . . . . .**147** A7
Goose Gate
 Cotgrave NG12 . . . .**187** E3
 Nottingham NG1 . . . .**223** F2
Goosemoor La
 Retford DN22. . . . .**39** F4
 Retford DN22. . . . .**40** A4
Goosemoor La E DN22 . .**40** A4
Gopher Rd NG24. . . . .**139** F5
Goransson Walk
 S80 . . . .**35** B5
Gordon Ave NG18 . . . . .**102** E6
Gordonbrae NG18 . . . . . .**102** C3
Gordon Cl
 Beeston NG9 . . . .**183** D2
 Farnsfield NG22. . . . .**119** F5
 Worksop S80 . . . .**36** B3
Gordon Cres DE55 . . . . . .**113** B4
Gordondale Rd NG19 . . . . .**88** B1
Gordon Rd
 Burton Joyce NG14 . . . . .**164** A5
 5 Loughborough LE11. .**220** B6
 Nottingham NG3 . . . .**173** F6
 West Bridgford NG2 . . . .**185** F7
Gordon Rise NG3 . . . .**161** E2
Gordon Sq NG2 . . . .**185** F7
Gordon St
 Gainsborough DN21 . . . . .**24** D6
 Ilkeston DE7 . . . .**158** A1
 Nottingham NG6 . . . .**160** D4
Gorman Ct NG5. . . . . . .**162** B7
Gorse Ave NG18 . . . . . .**103** A5
Gorse Cl
 Calverton NG14 . . . .**148** D7
 Eastwood NG16. . . . .**158** B8
 Long Eaton NG10. . . . . . .**182** B2
Gorse Ct NG6. . . . .**160** E5
Gorse Hill NG15 . . . .**117** A1
Gorselands Ave S80 . . . . .**36** C1
Gorse Rd
 Keyworth NG12 . . . .**197** D3
 Newark-on-Trent NG24 . .**139** F5
Gorsethorpe La
 Kings Clipstone NG20 . . . .**74** F1
 Kings Clipstone NG21 . . . .**89** F8
 Nottingham NG21. . . . . . .**90** A3
Gorsey Rd NG3 . . . .**173** D8
Gorsy La NG25. . . . .**137** C2
Gosforth Ave DE7 . . . . .**157** F6
Gosforth Ct NG2 . . . .**173** D1
Goshawk Rd DE7 . . . .**170** A3
GOTHAM **195** A1
Gotham La NG11. . . . .**206** C7
Gotham Prim Sch
 NG11 . . . .**195** A1
Gotham Rd
 East Leake LE12 . . . .**205** E3
 Kingston on Soar NG11. .**204** C5
Gotheridge Dr NG4 . . . . .**162** D4
Gothic Cl NG6. . . . .**160** E4
Gough Rd NG10 . . . .**193** C6
Goverton Hill NG14 . . . . .**136** F1
Goverton Sq NG6. . . . . . .**160** D5
Gowan Cl **7** NG9 . . . . . .**183** C2
Goyden Cl NG5. . . . .**161** A8
Grace Ave NG9 . . . .**184** B6
Grace Dr NG6. . . . .**172** D8
Gracefield La NG23 . . . . . .**81** F7
Grace Rd DN22 . . . .**39** E4
Graders Ct NG21. . . . .**76** C2
Grafton Ave NG5. . . . .**161** E5
Grafton Cl NG17 . . . .**101** B5
Grafton Ct NG7. . . . .**222** C3
Grafton St S80. . . . .**35** E4
Graham Cl NG24 . . . .**140** B4
Graham St NG7 . . . .**222** B3
Grainger Ave
 Annesley Woodhouse
  NG17. . . . .**115** B1
 West Bridgford NG2 . . . .**185** E3
Grainger St NG2. . . . .**173** F4
Graingers Terr NG15. . . . .**146** B6
Grampian Dr NG5. . . . . . .**147** B2
Grampian Way NG10 . . . .**193** A8
Granary Cl
 Bottesford NG13 . . . .**181** B2
 Morton DN21. . . . .**15** B5
Granary Ct
 Brampton LN1. . . . .**44** C4
 Carlton in Lindrick S81 . . .**26** A6
GRANBY. **191** C5
Granby Ave
 Mansfield NG18. . . . .**102** B8
 Newark-on-Trent NG24 . .**140** B6
Granby Ct NG13. . . . .**177** D4
Granby Dr
 Balderton NG24. . . . .**140** D3
 Bottesford NG13 . . . .**181** A2
Granby Hill NG13 . . . .**191** B5

Granby La
 Plungar NG13 . . . .**191** F1
 Whatton NG13 . . . .**178** D2
Granby St
 Ilkeston DE7 . . . .**157** F2
 Loughborough LE11. . . . .**220** A4
Grandfield Ave NG12. . . .**175** F4
Grandfield Cres NG12. . . .**175** F4
Grange Ave
 Bawtry DN10 . . . .**9** F8
 Beeston NG9 . . . .**183** F6
 Mansfield NG18. . . . .**101** F5
 Misterton DN10. . . . .**14** A8
 Newark-on-Trent NG24 . .**139** E4
 Ollerton NG22 . . . .**77** B3
 Ruddington NG11. . . . . . .**196** C8
Grange Cl
 Carlton in Lindrick S81 . . .**26** A6
 Lambley NG4 . . . .**163** C7
 Misterton DN10. . . . .**14** A8
 Nottingham NG11 . . . . . .**185** B8
 Teversal NG17 . . . .**100** C8
Grange Cres NG4 . . . .**162** F3
Grange Ct
 Kirkby-in-Ashfield
  NG17. . . . .**115** D5
 West Bridgford NG2 . . . .**185** C2
Grange Dr
 Harworth DN11 . . . .**9** A5
 Long Eaton NG10. . . . . . .**193** F8
 Misterton DN10. . . . .**14** A8
Grange Farm NG12 . . . .**186** C7
Grange Farm Cl
 Beeston NG9 . . . .**183** A1
 Sutton in Ashfield NG17 .**100** C1
Grange La
 Balderton NG24. . . . .**155** A4
 Staunton in the Vale
  NG13. . . . .**169** A4
 Worksop S80 . . . .**37** C3
Grangelea Gdns NG9. . . .**183** B8
Grangemoor NG15. . . . . .**131** D1
Grange Pk
 Cropwell Butler NG12 . . .**189** A7
 Gainsborough DN21 . . . . .**15** B5
 West Bridgford NG2 . . . .**186** C5
Grange Prim Sch NG10 . .**193** F8
Granger Ct 4 LE11 . . . .**220** A4
Grange Rd
 Arnold NG5 . . . .**161** E4
 Barton in Fabis NG10 . . .**194** A8
 Blidworth NG21. . . . .**118** B5
 Long Eaton NG10. . . . . . .**193** F8
 Nottingham NG6 . . . .**160** D3
 Retford DN22. . . . .**39** E3
 West Bridgford NG2 . . . .**186** A4
Grange The
 North Muskham NG23. . .**110** F3
 Retford DN22. . . . .**39** E3
 South Normanton DE55. .**113** A4
Grange View
 Eastwood NG16 . . . .**143** F3
 2 Harworth DN11 . . . . . .**8** F5
 Harworth NG11 . . . .**9** A5
Grange View Rd NG4. . . .**163** A2
Grange Wlk DN10. . . . .**7** A1
Grangewood Ct NG8. . . . .**171** C3
Grangewood Rd
 3 Kirkby-in-Ashfield
  NG17. . . . .**114** F7
 Nottingham NG8 . . . .**171** C3
Grannis Dr NG8. . . . .**172** A8
Grant Cl NG24 . . . .**140** D8
Grantham Cl NG16. . . . . .**158** C7
Grantham Rd
 Bingham NG13. . . . .**178** C3
 Bottesford NG13 . . . .**181** D2
 Muston NG13 . . . .**181** E7
 Orston NG13 . . . .**180** B2
 Radcliffe on Trent NG4 . .**175** F2
 Saxondale NG13 . . . .**177** A4
 Whatton-in-the-Vale
  NG13. . . . .**179** A3
Grantleigh Cl NG8 . . . . . .**171** F5
Granton Ave NG11 . . . . . .**195** F8
Granton Rise NG19 . . . . .**101** D5
Grant St NG7 . . . .**222** B3
Granville Ave NG10 . . . . .**182** D1
Granville Cres NG12 . . . .**175** E2
Granville Ct **4** NG3. . . . .**173** F6
Granville Gr **4** NG3. . . . .**173** F5
Granville St LE11 . . . .**220** A4
Grasby Walk NG9 . . . .**184** D2
Grasmere Cl
 Gainsborough DN21 . . . . .**15** E2
 Hucknall NG15. . . . .**145** F8
Grasmere Rd
 Beeston NG9 . . . .**183** C8
 Long Eaton NG10. . . . . . .**182** B2
 Worksop S81 . . . .**35** F7
Grasmere St NG10 . . . . . .**182** C5
Grasmoor Cl NG14. . . . . .**173** F8
Grassingdale Cl
 Carlton NG4. . . . .**162** D2
 3 Carlton NG5. . . . .**162** D2
Grassington Rd NG8 . . . .**172** D7
Grasslands The
 Rainworth NG21 . . . .**104** B1
 Rainworth NG21 . . . .**104** C1
Grassmere NG12 . . . .**188** A3
Grass St DE7 . . . .**157** E3
GRASSTHORPE. **81** E4
Grassthorpe La NG23 . . . .**81** D3
Grassthorpe Rd
 Grassthorpe NG23. . . . . . .**81** F5
 Low Marnham NG23 . . . . .**82** A5
 Sutton on Trent NG23 . . . .**81** E2
 Sutton on Trent NG23 . . . .**96** E8
Grassy La NG9 . . . .**184** A5
Gratton Ct **1** NG17 . . . . .**114** F7
Gravelholes La DN10. . . . . . .**6** E1

Gravel La NG22 . . . .**79** D7
Gravelly Hollow NG14. . . .**133** A1
Gravelly La NG25 . . . .**137** E3
Gravel Pit La
 Newark DN22. . . . .**64** E7
 West Drayton DN22. . . . . .**50** F1
Graveney Gdns NG5 . . . .**162** C6
Graves Moor La S81 . . . . .**18** C3
Graves Wlk DN22 . . . .**19** B2
Gray Fallow DE55 . . . . . .**113** B4
Gray La
 Halam NG22. . . . .**120** D2
 Halam NG22. . . . .**120** E1
Graylands Rd NG8 . . . . . .**171** E6
Grays Dr NG15. . . . .**132** B6
Grayson Ms NG9. . . . .**183** B2
Gray St LE11. . . . .**220** B2
Graystones Cl NG2. . . . . .**186** C5
Grazingfield NG11 . . . . . .**185** A4
GREASLEY **144** E3
Greasley Ave NG16 . . . . .**144** C4
Greasley Beauvale Prim
 Sch NG16 . . . .**144** B2
Greasley Beauvale Sch
 NG16 . . . .**144** B3
Greasley Ct NG18 . . . . . .**103** B3
Greasley St NG6 . . . .**160** B7
Greasley Street Ind Est
 NG6 . . . .**160** B6
Great Central Rd
 Loughborough LE11. . . . .**220** C3
 Mansfield NG18. . . . .**102** C6
Great Central Rly ★
 LE11 . . . .**220** C2
Great Central Sta LE11 .**220** C3
Great Freeman St NG3 .**223** E4
Great Hoggett Dr NG9 .**183** B6
Great La NG22 . . . .**65** F7
Great Northern Cl DE7 .**157** F2
Great Northern Cl The
 NG2 . . . .**223** F1
Great Northern Rd
 NG16 . . . .**143** D2
Great Northern Way
 NG4 . . . .**175** D4
Great North Rd
 Balderton NG23, NG24 . .**155** F5
 Barnby Moor DN22 . . . . . .**28** C5
 Bawtry DN10 . . . .**10** A5
 Bircotes DN10 . . . .**9** F5
 Claypole NG24 . . . .**155** F4
 Cromwell NG23 . . . .**110** F8
 Eaton DN22 . . . .**40** A2
 Gamston DN22. . . . .**51** A4
 Gamston DN22. . . . .**51** A4
 Newark-on-Trent NG24 . .**124** E1
 North Muskham NG23. . .**110** F3
 North Muskham NG23. . .**110** F3
 North Muskham NG23. . .**110** F5
 Ranskill DN22 . . . .**19** B3
 Scrooby DN10 . . . .**10** A2
 South Muskham NG23,
  NG24. . . . .**124** D5
 West Markham NG22 . . . .**65** C7
 Weston NG23. . . . .**81** C3
Greaves Ave LE14. . . . . . .**219** C6
Greaves Cl
 Arnold NG5 . . . .**162** B5
 Newark-on-Trent NG24 . .**140** D8
 Nottingham NG8 . . . .**159** D1
Greaves La NG22 . . . .**120** B3
Grebe Cl
 Carlton NG4. . . . .**175** C7
 New Balderton NG24. . . .**140** C5
Greek St NG7 . . . .**222** C3
Green Acad Trust NG6. . .**160** E4
Greenacre
 Burton Joyce NG14 . . . . .**163** D5
 Mansfield NG18. . . . .**102** F5
 Stanton Hill NG17 . . . . . .**100** C5
Green Acre
 Nottingham NG8 . . . .**171** B5
 West Bridgford NG12 . . .**186** B4
Greenacre Ave DE75 . . . .**143** A3
Greenacre Rd
 Worksop S80 . . . .**35** F6
 Worksop S81 . . . .**36** A6
Greenacres Cl NG17. . . . .**115** B2
Greenacres Cl NG16 . . . .**144** C2
Greenacres Dr DE55 . . . .**113** B6
Green App NG4 . . . .**174** C8
Green Ave NG4 . . . .**175** A7
Greenaway NG23 . . . .**138** A6
Greenbank NG4 . . . .**174** D6
Green Bank NG11 . . . . . .**118** C8
Greenbank Dr NG17 . . . .**100** C5
Greenburn Cl NG2. . . . . .**186** D6
Green Cl
 Blidworth NG21. . . . .**118** A4
 Hucknall NG15. . . . .**146** C5
 Keyworth NG12 . . . .**197** F4
 Newton DE55 . . . .**99** A3
 Stapleford NG7 . . . .**172** C2
Greenclose La **9** LE11. .**220** A4
Green Cres NG16 . . . .**128** C6
Greencroft NG11 . . . .**184** F2
Greendale Ave NG21. . . . .**76** A3
Greendale Cl
 Market Warsop NG20 . . . .**74** A4
 Stanton Hill NG17 . . . . . .**100** C6
Greendale Cres NG21 . . . .**90** B4
Greendale Gdns NG8 . . . .**172** B8
Greendale Rd
 Arnold NG5 . . . .**161** F6
 Nottingham NG3 . . . .**174** C6
Green Dr NG25 . . . .**137** F3
Green Farm Rd NG16 . . . .**128** D6
Greenfield Ave S80 . . . . . .**45** C6
Greenfield Cl
 Coddington NG24 . . . . . .**125** F1

Greenfield Cl continued
 Edwinstowe NG21 . . . . . .**91** B8
 Mansfield Woodhouse
  NG19 . . . .**89** B1
Greenfield Gr NG4 . . . . . .**174** C8
Greenfields NG16. . . . . . .**143** A4
Greenfields Com Sch
 . . . .**173** D1
Greenfields Cres NG22. . .**77** C4
Greenfields Dr NG12 . . . .**187** F2
Greenfield St NG7 . . . . . .**172** D1
Greenfield The NG12. . . .**197** E2
Greenfield Way S81 . . . . .**25** C7
Greenfinch Dale S81. . . . .**35** C7
Greenford Cl NG16. . . . . .**159** E3
Green Fram Ct S81 . . . . . .**26** A6
Greengage Rd NG2 . . . . .**188** A5
Greengate NG23 . . . .**153** A4
Greengate Rd DN22. . . . . .**53** B4
Greengates Ave S43. . . . .**161** F3
Greenhalgh Cres **3**
 DE7 . . . .**157** C7
Green Hill
 Hathern LE12. . . . .**213** A1
 Wartnaby LE14 . . . .**219** D4
Greenhill Cres NG4 . . . . .**174** E6
Greenhill La NG17 . . . . . .**129** F8
Greenhill Rd NG4 . . . .**174** E6
Greenhill Rise LE12 . . . . .**213** A1
Greenhills Rd NG16 . . . . .**143** F3
Greenholme Cl NG17 . . . .**115** A4
Greenholme Pk NG19 . . . .**26** A6
Greenholme Sch NG7. . .**222** A2
Green Inf Sch The
 DE55. . . . .**113** A7
Green La
 Babworth DN22 . . . .**38** E5
 Bathley NG23 . . . .**110** B3
 Beckingham LN5 . . . .**142** F8
 Bingham NG13 . . . .**177** E4
 Bottesford NG13 . . . .**181** C1
 Clifton NG6 . . . .**184** D1
 Clumber and Hardwick
  S80. . . . .**48** D5
 Collingham NG23 . . . . . .**112** A7
 Cotgrave NG12 . . . .**187** F1
 Cotgrave NG12 . . . .**198** F8
 Cotgrave NG12 . . . .**199** A7
 Darlton NG22. . . . .**67** C4
 Dry Doddington NG23 . .**156** E2
 Dunham-on-Trent LN1 . .**68** B7
 Eagle LN6. . . . .**84** F4
 Girton NG23 . . . .**97** E8
 Granby NG13 . . . .**191** B5
 Harby LE14 . . . .**202** C2
 Hodthorpe S80. . . . .**45** C5
 Ilkeston DE7 . . . .**170** A7
 Kegworth DE74 . . . .**203** C5
 Lambley NG4 . . . .**149** B1
 Laxton NG22 . . . .**79** D1
 Lea DN21. . . . .**24** F3
 Mansfield NG18. . . . .**102** C3
 Mansfield, Moorhaigh
  NG19. . . . .**87** A2
 Nottingham NG7 . . . .**184** E1
 Pleasley S44 . . . .**86** D8
 Ranskill DN10 . . . .**18** F3
 Treswell DN22 . . . .**42** D4
 Upper Broughton LE14 . .**210** A4
 Walesby NG22. . . . .**64** A2
Greenland Cres NG9 . . . .**183** C4
Greenland Rd NG17. . . . .**100** E7
Green Leys NG2. . . . .**185** C4
Green Mews The NG5. . . .**161** A5
Green Mile La DN22 . . . . .**38** E8
Green Platt NG12 . . . .**187** E3
Green Rd DN10 . . . .**13** A2
Greens Ct DE7 . . . .**157** D1
Green's Farm La NG4 . .**163** A2
Greenshank Cl NG20 . . . .**73** A4
Greenshank Rd NG20 . . . .**73** D4
Greenside DN22 . . . .**42** F2
Green Side NG16 . . . .**128** D6
Greenside Ave DN22. . . . .**42** F2
Greenside Cl NG10. . . . . .**193** E7
Greens La NG16 . . . .**159** A6
Greenspotts La DN22 . . . .**52** B7
Greensquare Rd NG16 .**113** E2
Green St
 Barton in Fabis NG11 . . .**195** A7
 Nottingham NG2 . . . .**173** D1
 Ratcliffe on Soar NG11 . .**203** F7
 Ratcliffe on Soar NG11 . .**204** A7
Green The
 Barkestone-le-Vale
  NG13. . . . .**192** B2
 Beckingham DN10 . . . . . .**23** C8
 Beeston NG9 . . . .**183** B4
 Bilsthorpe NG22 . . . .**105** F7
 Car Colston NG13 . . . . . .**166** B2
 Carlton in Lindrick S81 . . .**26** A6
 Coddington NG24. . . . . . .**126** B2
 Collingham NG23 . . . . . .**111** F7
 Dunham-on-Trent NG23 . .**54** C1
 East Leake LE12 . . . .**205** A1
 Elmton S80. . . . .**58** B7
 Elston NG23. . . . .**153** D4
 Farnsfield NG22. . . . .**119** F6
 Gainsborough DN21 . . . . .**24** F7
 Glapwell S44 . . . .**86** B8
 Hardstoft S45 . . . .**85** A3
 Harworth DN11 . . . .**8** E4
 Hathern LE12. . . . .**213** A1
 Hickling LE14 . . . .**210** C6
 Hose LE14. . . . .**211** F7
 Huthwaite NG17 . . . .**99** F1
 Kingston on Soar LE12 . .**204** A4

Green The continued
Kirklington NG22 . . . . 120 F8
Long Whatton LE12 . . . . . 212 C3
Lowdham NG14 . . . . 149 F2
Lowdham NG14 . . . . 150 A2
Mansfield Woodhouse
NG19 . . . . .88 A5
Nottingham NG4 . . . . 174 C8
Orston NG13 . . . . 179 F7
Perlethorpe NG22 . . . . 62 F3
Perlethorpe NG22 . . . . 63 A3
Radcliffe on Trent NG12 . . 175 D3
Ruddington NG11 . . . . . . 196 C6
South Clifton NG23 . . . . . . 68 L1
Upton NG23 . . . . 122 F1
Greentrees Ct NG17 . . . 100 D1
Greenvale NG22 . . . . . . 120 A6
Greenview Cl NG19 . . . . . 89 B1
Greenway
Carlton in Lindrick S81 . . . 26 A6
Clipstone NG19 . . . . 89 D3
Newark-on-Trent NG24 . . 139 E6
Retford DN22 . . . . 39 D3
Greenway Cl NG12 . . . . 175 E3
Greenway The NG10 . . . 182 B6
Greenwich Ave NG6 . . . 160 C4
Greenwich Pk Cl NG2 . . 185 C5
Green Wlk NG13 . . . . . 178 F4
Greenwood Ave
Edwinstowe NG21 . . . . . . 76 B2
Harworth DN11 . . . . 8 F5
Hucknall NG15 . . . . 145 F8
Huthwaite NG17 . . . . 99 F2
Huthwaite NG17 . . . . 100 A2
Ilkeston DE7 . . . . 170 A4
Mansfield Woodhouse
NG19 . . . . .88 B4
Nottingham NG3 . . . . 174 D5
Greenwood Cl
Carlton in Lindrick S81 . . . 25 D1
Farnsfield NG22 . . . . 120 A6
Worksop S81 . . . . 25 D1
Greenwood Cotts
NG18 . . . . 102 F8
Greenwood Craft Ctr★
NG18 . . . . 116 E6
Greenwood Cres
Boughton NG22 . . . . 77 E5
Carlton NG4 . . . . 174 E6
Greenwood Dr NG17 . . . 114 F5
Greenwood Gdns
Nottingham NG8 . . . . 171 C7
Ruddington NG11 . . . . . . 196 D6
Greenwood Prim Sch
NG17 . . . . 114 E6
Greenwood Rd NG3 . . . 174 C5
Greenwood Vale NG15 . . 145 F8
Greer La S44 . . . . 86 D8
Greet Park Cl NG25 . . . 121 F1
Greetwell Cl 1 NG8 . . . 172 A6
Gregory Ave
Aldercar NG16 . . . . 143 A4
Nottingham, New Lenton
NG7 . . . . 222 B1
Nottingham, Portchester
NG3 . . . . 162 A2
Gregory Bvd NG7 . . . . . 173 A7
Gregory Cl NG7 . . . . . . 182 F8
Gregory Cres DN11 . . . . .8 E4
Gregory Ct
Beeston NG9 . . . . 183 B4
Nottingham NG7 . . . . 222 A1
Gregory Gdns NG22 . . . 119 F5
Gregory St
9 Ilkeston DE7 . . . . . . 157 F1
6 Loughborough LE11 . . 220 B3
Nottingham NG7 . . . . 172 E2
Gregson Gdns NG9 . . . . 183 B1
Gregson Rd NG9 . . . . . . 183 B2
Grendon Way NG17 . . . . 101 B5
Grenville
Ilkeston DE7 . . . . 157 F3
Stapleford NG9 . . . . 182 E8
West Bridgford NG12 . . . . 185 D7
Grenville Rd NG9 . . . . . 184 B4
Grenville Rise NG5 . . . . 147 F1
Gresham Cl
Newark-on-Trent NG24 . . 140 E4
Sutton in Ashfield NG17 . . 100 F3
West Bridgford NG2 . . . . . 185 C7
Gresham Gdns
Arnold NG5 . . . . 162 A5
West Bridgford NG2 . . . . . 185 D7
Gresham Park Rd NG2 . . 185 C7
Gresley Ave DN10 . . . . . 10 A8
Gresley Dr NG2 . . . . 173 F3
Gresley Rd
11 Ilkeston DE7 . . . . . . 157 F1
Retford DN22 . . . . 39 D5
Gressingham Cl NG19 . . . 88 F3
Greta N Rd NG13 . . . . . . 96 F3
Gretton Cl NG23 . . . . . . 156 C6
Gretton Rd NG3 . . . . . . 162 A4
Greyfriar Gate NG1 . . . . 223 E1
Greyhound St NG1 . . . . 223 E2
Grey Meadow Rd DE7 . . 157 E2
Greymede Ave NG8 . . . . 159 C2
Greys Rd NG5 . . . . 161 F4
Grey St
Eastwood NG16 . . . . 144 A1
Gainsborough DN21 . . . . . 15 B2
Kirkby-in-Ashfield NG17 . . 114 D5
Greystoke Dr NG8 . . . . . 171 C7
Greystones Rd DN21 . . . 15 B3
Greythorn Dr NG2 . . . . . 185 D4
Greythorn Prim Sch
NG2 . . . . 185 D4
Griceson Cl NG22 . . . . . . 77 B2
Grierson Ave NG5 . . . . . 161 B8
Grieves Cl DN22 . . . . 39 F5
Griffin Rd NG22 . . . . 77 D5

Griffins End NG13 . . . . . 179 B3
Griffiths Way NG15 . . . . 146 B6
Griffon Dr NG6 . . . . 145 F2
Grimesmoor Rd NG14 . . 149 A8
Grimsby Terr NG3 . . . . . 223 E4
Grimston Rd NG7 . . . . . 222 A4
Grindleford Grange
NG18 . . . . 103 C5
Grindon Cres NG6 . . . . . 146 C2
Gringley Ct DN10 . . . . . . 12 F2
GRINGLEY ON THE
HILL 12 E1
Gringley Rd
Clayworth DN22 . . . . 21 D4
Clayworth DN22 . . . . 21 E6
Misterton DN10 . . . . 6 E1
Walkeringham DN10 . . . . . 13 E4
Gringley View DN10 . . . . 11 B4
Grinsbrook NG7 . . . . . . 222 A2
Gripps Comm NG12 . . . . 187 F1
Grisedale Ct NG9 . . . . . 183 A4
Gritley Mews NG2 . . . . . 173 B2
Grives La NG17 . . . . 115 B2
Grizedale Cl NG19 . . . . . 103 A8
Grizedale Gr NG13 . . . . . 177 B4
Grizedale Ri NG19 . . . . . 103 A8
Grosvenor Ave
Long Eaton NG10 . . . . . . 193 A4
Nottingham NG3 . . . . 161 C1
Sutton in Ashfield NG17 . . 100 D2
Torksey Lock LN1 . . . . 55 B8
Grosvenor Cl
Radcliffe on Trent
NG12 . . . . 176 D3
Retford DN22 . . . . 40 A4
Grosvenor Rd
Bircotes DN11 . . . . 9 B4
Eastwood NG16 . . . . 143 F2
Langold S81 . . . . 16 F3
New Balderton NG24 . . . . 140 B4
Grouville Dr NG5 . . . . . . 162 A5
GROVE 40 F4
Grove Ave
Beeston NG9 . . . . 183 B6
Nottingham NG7 . . . . 222 C4
Grove Cl NG14 . . . . 149 B7
Grove Coach Rd DN22 . . . 40 B4
Grove Ct 5 S80 . . . . 35 E2
Grove La DN22 . . . . 40 B6
Grove Mews NG16 . . . . . 143 E1
Grove Pk DN10 . . . . 6 F1
Grover Ave NG3 . . . . 162 A3
Grove Rd
Church Warsop NG20 . . . . 74 A6
Grove DN22 . . . . 40 F3
Grove DN22 . . . . 41 C6
Headon DN22 . . . . 52 B8
Headon cum Upton
DN22 . . . . 41 A1
Nottingham NG7 . . . . 222 B1
Retford DN22 . . . . 40 C3
Sutton in Ashfield NG17 . . 101 B3
Grove Sch The NG24 . . . 139 F7
Groveside Cres
NG11 . . . . 184 C3
Grove Sports Ctr
NG24 . . . . 140 C5
Grove St
Beeston NG9 . . . . 184 A5
6 Mansfield NG18 . . . . 102 B6
Mansfield Woodhouse
NG19 . . . . .88 B3
New Balderton NG24 . . . . 140 B5
Retford DN22 . . . . 39 F7
Grove The
Beckingham DN10 . . . . . . 14 B1
Calverton NG14 . . . . 149 A7
Newton on Trent LN1 . . . . 55 A4
Nottingham NG7 . . . . 222 B4
Nottingham, Carrington
NG5 . . . . 161 B2
Groveview Rd NG4 . . . . . 140 C5
Grove Way NG19 . . . . . . 88 B3
Grovewood Cl DN10 . . . . 13 F8
Grove Wood Rd DN10 . . . . 6 F1
Grove Wood Terr
DN10 . . . . 6 F1
Grundy Ave NG16 . . . . . 128 D7
Grundy Nook S80 . . . . . . 45 A5
Grundy St NG7 . . . . 172 E7
Guildford Ave NG19 . . . . 88 C6
Guildford Dr NG16 . . . . . 113 E2
Guildhall St NG24 . . . . . 140 A8
Guinea Cl NG16 . . . . 193 A7
Gum Tree Cl 2 NG12 . . . 186 A1
Gunn Cl NG6 . . . . 160 A7
Gunnersbury Way NG8 . . 159 E3
GUNTHORPE 164 F5
Gunthorpe Bridge 164 F4
Gunthorpe CE Prim Sch
NG14 . . . . 165 A4
Gunthorpe Cl NG5 . . . . . 161 B3
Gunthorpe Cl NG18 . . . . 103 B3
Gunthorpe Dr NG5 . . . . . 161 B3
Gunthorpe Rd
Carlton NG4 . . . . 162 D3
Lowdham NG14 . . . . 164 E8
West Stockwith DN9 . . . . . . 7 E8
Gutersloh Ct NG9 . . . . . 182 F8
Guy Close NG9 . . . . 182 E6
Guy Drive NG4 . . . . 162 E4
Guy Gibson Ct DN21 . . . 24 F7
Guylers Hill Dr NG21 . . . 89 F2
Gwenbrook Ave
NG9 . . . . 183 E5
Gwenbrook Rd NG9 . . . . 183 E5
Gwndy Gdns 3 NG5 . . . 161 A7
Gypsum Way NG11 . . . . 205 A7
Gypsy La NG14 . . . . 152 B8

H

Habblesthorpe Cl DN22 . 32 E1
Habblesthorpe Rd DN22 . 32 E1
Hackers Cl NG13 . . . . . . 165 C3
Hackett Gdns NG13 . . . . 177 E6
Hackworth Cl NG16 . . . . 144 B3
Hadbury Rd NG5 . . . . . . 160 F3
Hadden Ct NG8 . . . . 171 D5
Hadderley Wlk NG3 . . . . 223 F4
Haddon Cl
Carlton NG4 . . . . 162 D2
Hucknall NG15 . . . . 146 A6
Selston NG16 . . . . 129 B7
Haddon Cres NG9 . . . . . 183 C2
Haddon Dr NG24 . . . . . . 140 D3
Haddon Nurseries DE7 . . 157 F3
Haddon Pl NG20 . . . . 72 D7
Haddon Prim Sch NG4 . . 162 D1
Haddon Rd
Mansfield NG18 . . . . 102 B8
Ravenshead NG15 . . . . . . 117 A3
Retford DN22 . . . . 40 B4
West Bridgford NG2 . . . . . 185 F6
Haddon St
Ilkeston DE7 . . . . 157 E3
Nottingham NG5 . . . . 161 B2
Sutton in Ashfield NG17 . . 100 E4
Tibshelf DE55 . . . . 99 A6
Haddon Way NG12 . . . . . 176 A4
Hades La LE12 . . . . 217 D5
Hadfield Wlk NG18 . . . . 103 B6
Hadleigh Cl NG9 . . . . . . 182 E2
Hadley St DE7 . . . . 170 A5
Hadrian Gdns NG5 . . . . . 147 A2
Hadstock Cl NG10 . . . . . 182 B4
Hadston Dr NG5 . . . . 147 F2
Hagg La
Bawtry DN10 . . . . 10 E8
Egmanton NG22 . . . . 80 A5
Epperstone NG14 . . . . . . 150 B5
Haggnook Wood NG16 . . 116 D3
Haggonfields Prim Sch
S80 . . . . 35 A4
Hagley Cl NG3 . . . . 174 A6
Haileybury Cres NG2 . . . 185 F5
Haileybury Rd NG2 . . . . 185 F5
Hainton Cl DN21 . . . . 24 E7
Haise Ct NG6 . . . . 159 F5
HALAM 120 E1
Halam CE Prim Sch
NG22 . . . . 120 F2
Halam Cl NG19 . . . . 101 D7
Halam Hill NG22 . . . . . . 121 A1
Halberton Dr NG2 . . . . . 185 D4
Haldane St DN21 . . . . 15 B1
Haldon Way
Worksop S81 . . . . 25 D1
Worksop S81 . . . . 35 C8
Hales Cl NG12 . . . . 187 E3
Haley Cl NG16 . . . . 158 D6
Halfacre Gdns DE7 . . . . . 157 F2
Halfmoon Dr NG17 . . . . 115 B3
Halford Ave NG5 . . . . . . 162 C8
Halifax Ct NG8 . . . . 159 D2
Halifax Dr S81 . . . . 35 E8
Halifax Pl
Farnsfield NG22 . . . . 120 A5
Nottingham NG1 . . . . 223 E2
Halifax Rd NG24 . . . . . . 140 F3
Hallam Dr NG12 . . . . . . 176 B5
Hallam Fields Rd DE7 . . 170 B4
Hallam Gr NG16 . . . . . . 143 A5
Hallam Rd
Beeston NG9 . . . . 183 F6
New Ollerton NG22 . . . . . . 77 D6
Nottingham NG3 . . . . 162 A2
Hallams La NG9 . . . . 183 D5
Hallam's La NG5 . . . . . . 161 F7
Hallamway NG18 . . . . 88 C1
Hallam Way NG16 . . . . . 143 C3
Hall Barn La NG19 . . . . . 101 D8
Hall Cl
Nottingham NG5 . . . . 161 A2
Radcliffe on Trent NG12 . . 175 E3
Rainworth NG21 . . . . 118 B8
Hall Cl The NG22 . . . . . . 66 A7
Hall Croft NG9 . . . . 183 F5
Hallcroft Ave DN22 . . . . . 39 E8
Hallcroft Ind Est DN22 . . 29 C2
Hallcroft Inf Sch DN22 . . 29 C1
Hall Dr
Beeston NG9 . . . . 183 D5
Clayworth DN22 . . . . 21 B5
Cropwell Bishop NG12 . . 189 A4
Gotham NG11 . . . . 195 E4
Newark-on-Trent NG24 . . 140 A5
Nottingham NG8 . . . . 172 B6
Sandiacre NG10 . . . . 182 B6
Worksop S80 . . . . 35 D2
Hallfield Rd DE55 . . . . . . 99 A3
Hallfields NG12 . . . . 186 B3
Hall Gdns
Balderton NG24 . . . . 140 E4
Beeston NG9 . . . . 183 B7
East Leake LE12 . . . . 214 F8
Hall Grounds NG12 . . . . 200 C7
Hall Grounds Dr NG12 . . 200 C8
Halliday St S80 . . . . 35 D3
Hallifax Ave NG20 . . . . . . 74 B7
Halliwell Cl NG24 . . . . . . 125 B4
Hall La
Brinsley NG16 . . . . 143 D6
Colston Bassett NG12 . . . 189 A1
Colston Bassett NG12 . . . 200 A1
East Markham NG22 . . . . . 66 A7
Kinoulton NG12 . . . . 200 A3
Newton DN55 . . . . 99 A3

Hall La continued
Papplewick NG15 . . . . . . 131 D4
Hall Lodge Gdns NG6 . . 127 E8
HALLOUGHTON 136 B4
Halloughton Rd NG25 . . 136 D7
Hallowell Dr NG8 . . . . . . 171 F5
Hall Park Acad NG16 . . . 143 E4
Hall Pk NG16 . . . . 143 E3
Hall Rd NG16 . . . . 143 C4
Halls Brook LE12 . . . . . . 205 E2
Halls La
Eastwood NG16 . . . . 158 A7
Newthorpe Common
NG16 . . . . 158 A8
Halls Rd NG9 . . . . 182 D6
Hall's Rd DN10 . . . . 13 A3
Hall St
Mansfield NG18 . . . . 102 E6
Nottingham NG5 . . . . 161 D3
Sutton in Ashfield NG17 . . 100 E4
Hallstone Mdw DE74 . . . 203 D2
Hallum Ct DE7 . . . . 157 F3
Hall View
Mattersey DN10 . . . . 20 B7
Worksop S80 . . . . 35 D2
Hall View Dr NG8 . . . . . . 171 D6
Hall Yard NG16 . . . . 71 C1
Halstead Cl
Beeston NG9 . . . . 183 C4
Mansfield Woodhouse
NG19 . . . . .88 F2
Nottingham NG8 . . . . 160 B3
Haltham Gn 2 DN21 . . . . 24 F8
Haltham Wlk NG11 . . . . 195 D8
Hamble Cl NG19 . . . . 88 D3
Hambledon Dr NG8 . . . . 172 B5
Hambleton Cl NG10 . . . . 182 A1
Hambleton Ct S81 . . . . . . 25 E7
Hambleton Rise 2
NG19 . . . . 88 F2
Hambling Cl NG6 . . . . . . 160 A7
Hamilton Cl
Arnold NG5 . . . . 148 C1
Beeston NG9 . . . . 182 F2
Hamilton Dr
Market Warsop NG20 . . . . 73 F4
Market Warsop NG20 . . . . 74 A4
Nottingham NG14 . . . . . . 173 B3
Nottingham NG7 . . . . 223 D1
Radcliffe on Trent NG12 . . 175 F4
Hamilton Gdns 11 NG5 . 161 B1
Hamilton Pl NG17 . . . . . 101 F4
Hamilton Rd
Long Eaton NG10 . . . . . . 182 D1
11 Nottingham NG5 . . . 161 B1
Nottingham NG5 . . . . 173 B3
Sutton in Ashfield NG17 . . 101 C2
Hamilton St
Mansfield NG18 . . . . 102 E6
Worksop S81 . . . . 35 E6
Hamilton Way NG18 . . . 101 E3
Hamlet La DE55 . . . . 113 A5
Hamlet The DE55 . . . . . . 113 A5
Hammer Leys DE55 . . . . 113 B4
Hammersmith Cl
Nuthall NG16 . . . . 159 E4
Radcliffe on Trent NG12 . 176 D2
Hammerwater Dr
NG20 . . . . 74 A3
Hammond Gr NG17 . . . . 115 B2
Hampden Cl NG24 . . . . . 141 A2
Hampden Gr NG9 . . . . . . 183 E6
Hampden Rd NG13 . . . . . 177 B7
Hampdens Cl NG24 . . . . 125 E2
Hampden St
Eastwood NG16 . . . . 158 B8
Kirkby-in-Ashfield NG17 . . 114 F5
Nottingham NG1 . . . . 223 D3
Hampshire Ct NG16 . . . . 128 B4
Hampshire Dr NG10 . . . . 182 B5
Hampstead Rd NG3 . . . . 161 C1
Hampton Cl NG9 . . . . . . 182 E3
Hampton Rd NG2 . . . . . . 185 E6
Hampton View NG18 . . . 102 A4
Hanbury Ct NG18 . . . . . . 103 B6
Handel Ct 7 DN21 . . . . . 15 D1
Handel House Sch
DN21 . . . . 15 D1
Handel St NG3 . . . . 173 E5
Handford St NG25 . . . . . 136 C8
Handley Arc 5 NG18 . . . 102 B7
Handley Ct NG24 . . . . . . 124 F1
Hand's Rd DE75 . . . . 143 A1
Hand's Wlk NG13 . . . . . . 181 A2
Hanford Way LE11 . . . . . 220 B5
Hangar Hill S80 . . . . 45 A6
Hankin Ave NG16 . . . . . . 129 A2
Hankin St NG15 . . . . 146 C6
Hanley Ave NG9 . . . . 183 B8
Hanley St NG1 . . . . 223 D3
Hannah Cres NG11 . . . . 185 B7
Hannam's Yd DN22 . . . . . 39 D7
Hanover Ct
HUCKNALL NG15 . . . . . . 146 C4
Nottingham NG8 . . . . 171 D6
Hansby Cl DN11 . . . . 8 B7
Hanslope Cres NG8 . . . . 171 D7
Hanson Cl NG16 . . . . 158 F7
Hanson Cres NG15 . . . . 146 A7
Hanstubbin Rd NG16 . . . 128 F6
Hanworth Gdns NG5 . . . 161 D8
Harberton Cl NG5 . . . . . 147 E1
HARBY
Leics 202 B2
Notts 70 E2
Harby Ave
Mansfield Woodhouse
NG19 . . . . .88 D5
Sutton in Ashfield NG17 . . 101 C1
Harby Cl NG24 . . . . 140 D3
Harby Dr NG8 . . . . 172 C4

Harby La
Colston Bassett NG12 . . . 200 F6
Hose LE14 . . . . 211 F2
Plungar LE14 . . . . 202 F3
Saxilby NG23 . . . . 70 F7
Swinethorpe NG23 . . . . . . 70 D1
Swinethorpe NG23 . . . . . . 84 D7
Harby Queen Eleanor
County Prim Sch NG23 . 70 E3
Harby Rd
Langar NG13 . . . . 190 D1
Langar NG13 . . . . 201 E8
Stathern LE14 . . . . 202 D3
Wigsley NG23 . . . . 69 F1
Wigsley NG23 . . . . 70 A1
Harcourt Cl DE7 . . . . . . 157 D1
Harcourt Cres NG16 . . . 159 F3
Harcourt Pl DN22 . . . . . . 40 A4
Harcourt Rd NG7 . . . . . . 173 A8
Harcourt St
Beeston NG9 . . . . 183 E6
Kirkby-in-Ashfield NG17 . . 115 A5
Mansfield NG18 . . . . 102 D6
Newark-on-Trent NG24 . . 140 B7
Harcourt Terr NG3 . . . . . 223 F3
Harden Ct NG11 . . . . 195 C8
Hardie Ave DE55 . . . . . . 113 A6
Hardigate Rd NG12 . . . . 189 A8
Hardstaff Cl
Annesley Woodhouse
NG17 . . . . 114 E1
Retford DN22 . . . . 29 C1
Hardstaff Rd NG2 . . . . . 174 A4
HARDSTOFT 85 A3
Hardwick Ave
Mansfield NG21 . . . . 103 F1
Newark-on-Trent NG24 . . 139 F7
Shirebrook NG20 . . . . 72 E4
Sutton in Ashfield NG17 . . 101 A6
Hardwick Cl
Saxilby LN1 . . . . 56 F4
Sutton in Ashfield NG17 . . 101 A6
Hardwick Cres S80 . . . . . 36 B2
Hardwick Ct
Harworth DN11 . . . . 9 B5
South Normanton DE55 . . 113 C6
Hardwick Dr
Ollerton NG22 . . . . 77 A3
Selston NG16 . . . . 129 B7
Hardwicke Rd NG9 . . . . 183 C3
Hardwick Gr
Nottingham NG7 . . . . 222 B2
West Bridgford NG2 . . . . . 173 F1
Hardwick Hall★ S44 . . . . 85 E4
Hardwick Hall Ctry Pk★
S44 . . . . 85 F5
Hardwick Hall Dr S44 . . . 85 D6
Hardwick La
Hardwick LN1 . . . . 56 B4
Sutton in Ashfield NG17 . . 100 F2
Torksey LN1 . . . . 44 F1
Torksey LN1 . . . . 55 F8
Torksey LN1 . . . . 56 A7
Hardwick Old Hall★
S44 . . . . 85 E4
Hardwick Pk Nature Wlk★
S44 . . . . 85 C4
Hardwick Rd
1 Nottingham, Carrington
NG5 . . . . 161 C3
Nottingham, The Park
NG7 . . . . 222 C1
Hardwick Rd E S80 . . . . . 36 B2
Hardwick Rd W S80 . . . . . 36 B2
Hardwick St
Langwith NG20 . . . . 72 F8
Mansfield NG18 . . . . 102 D7
Shirebrook NG20 . . . . 73 A4
Sutton in Ashfield NG17 . . 100 F3
Tibshelf DE55 . . . . 99 A7
Hardwick Terr S80 . . . . . 48 D4
Hardwick Top Rd S80 . . . 48 C5
Hardwick View NG17 . . . 101 A6
Hardwick View NG19 . . . . 86 F7
Hardwood Cl
1 Nottingham NG6 . . . 159 F7
1 Nottingham NG6 . . . 160 A7
Hardy Barn DE75 . . . . . . 157 A7
Hardy Cl
Bottesford NG13 . . . . 181 B3
Kimberley NG16 . . . . 158 F7
Long Eaton NG10 . . . . . . 193 D6
Hardy Pl NG18 . . . . 101 F6
Hardys Cl NG12 . . . . 189 B4
Hardy's Dr NG4 . . . . 162 F1
Hardy St
Kimberley NG16 . . . . 158 F7
Nottingham NG7 . . . . 222 C4
Worksop S80 . . . . 35 E3
Hardy Way LE12 . . . . . . 205 E3
Harebell Cl 8 NG17 . . . . 115 A3
Harebell Dr NG20 . . . . . . 72 D2
Harebell Gdns NG13 . . . 177 C3
Harefield Cl LE12 . . . . . . 205 E3
Harefield Cl LE14 . . . . . . 202 B3
Hareholme St NG18 . . . . 102 A8
Harewood Ave
Newark-on-Trent NG24 . . 139 F7
Nottingham NG6 . . . . 160 D5
Retford DN22 . . . . 39 C5
Harewood Cl
Radcliffe on Trent
NG12 . . . . 176 A3
Sandiacre NG10 . . . . 182 B4
Harewood Ct DN11 . . . . . .9 B5
Harewood Dr DN10 . . . . . 10 A8
Harewood Rd S81 . . . . . . 35 F7
Hargon La
Newark-on-Trent NG24 . . 125 D6
Winthorpe NG24 . . . . 125 A8

Harlaxton Dr continued
Nottingham NG14 . . . . . . 173 A3
Nottingham NG7 . . . . 222 B2
Harlaxton Wlk NG3 . . . . 223 E4
Harlech Cl DE7 . . . . 157 C3
Harlech Rise NG9 . . . . . 183 B4
Harlequin Cl NG12 . . . . . 176 B3
Harlequin Ct NG16 . . . . . 143 D3
Harlequin Dr S81 . . . . . . 25 D1
Harles Acres LE14 . . . . . 210 C6
Harley Cl S80 . . . . 46 E8
Harley Gall The★ S80 . . . 45 E1
Harley St NG7 . . . . 222 B1
Harlow Ave NG18 . . . . . . 102 C3
Harlow Cl
Mansfield Woodhouse
NG19 . . . . .88 C6
Sutton in Ashfield NG17 . . 100 F6
Harlow Gr NG4 . . . . 162 E2
Harlow St NG21 . . . . 118 B5
Harmston Rise NG5 . . . . 160 F4
Harold Ave NG16 . . . . . . 143 B4
Harold Brace Rd DN21 . . 24 E5
Harold St NG2 . . . . 173 E4
Harpenden Sq NG8 . . . . 160 B3
Harper Hill Gdns DN11 . . .9 B2
Harpham Rd DN21 . . . . . . 44 B8
Harpole Wlk NG5 . . . . . . 147 F2
Harrier Gr NG15 . . . . 145 E4
Harrier Hill LN6 . . . . 84 D2
Harrier Pk NG15 . . . . 145 D2
Harriers Gr NG17 . . . . . . 101 B4
Harrier The NG15 . . . . . . 145 D4
Harriett St NG9 . . . . 182 D7
Harrimans La NG2 . . . . . 184 E8
Harrington Cl NG4 . . . . . 163 B1
Harrington Dr NG7 . . . . . 222 B2
Harrington Jun Sch
NG10 . . . . 182 B2
Harrington St
Long Eaton NG10 . . . . . . 193 B5
Mansfield NG18 . . . . 102 A4
Worksop S80 . . . . 35 D2
Harris Cl NG8 . . . . 171 F5
Harrison Ct NG13 . . . . . . 177 C4
Harrison Dr S81 . . . . 16 E3
Harrison Rd
Mansfield NG18 . . . . 101 E6
Stapleford NG9 . . . . 182 D8
Harrison's Plantation
Nature Reserve★
NG8 . . . . 171 F5
Harrisons Way
Newark-on-Trent NG24 . . 125 B1
1 Newark-on-Trent
NG24 . . . . 140 B8
Harris Rd
Beeston NG9 . . . . 183 D6
Bingham NG13 . . . . 177 D7
Kirkby-in-Ashfield NG17 . . 115 D6
Harrogate Rd NG3 . . . . . 174 C5
Harrogate St NG4 . . . . . 175 A5
Harrop White Rd NG19 . . 101 F8
Harrowby Mews NG7 . . . 222 B2
Harrowby Rd NG7 . . . . . 222 B2
Harrow Cl
Collingham NG23 . . . . . . 112 B8
Gainsborough DN21 . . . . . 15 F2
Rainworth NG21 . . . . 118 A8
Harrow Dr DE7 . . . . 170 A4
Harrow Gdns NG8 . . . . . 172 C4
Harrow La NG22 . . . . 77 F5
Harrow Rd
Hucknall NG15 . . . . 145 D5
Nottingham NG8 . . . . 172 B4
West Bridgford NG2 . . . . . 185 E5
Harstoft Ave S81 . . . . 35 F5
Harston Gdns NG2 . . . . . 185 B3
Hart Ave NG10 . . . . 182 A5
Hartcroft Rd NG5 . . . . . . 161 B6
Hartford Cl 2 NG2 . . . . . 173 D2
Harthill 10 DE7 . . . . 183 C2
Hartill Dr NG19 . . . . 101 D5
Hartland Ave
Carlton NG4 . . . . 162 D1
Hucknall NG15 . . . . 145 C6
Hartington Ct NG18 . . . . 103 B6
Hartington Dr
Selston NG16 . . . . 129 A7
Sutton in Ashfield NG17 . . 101 B4
Hartington Pl DE7 . . . . . 157 C5
Hartington Rd NG5 . . . . 161 C3
Hartington St
Langwith NG20 . . . . 72 F8
11 Loughborough LE11 . 220 B4
Hartland Dr S80 . . . . 162 E5
Hartland Rd S80 . . . . 35 E2
Hartley Ct NG7 . . . . 222 B4
Hartley Dr NG9 . . . . 184 B6
Hartley Rd
Kirkby-in-Ashfield NG17 . . 114 F5
Nottingham NG7 . . . . 222 B4
Hartness Rd NG11 . . . . . 184 C1
Harton Cl NG17 . . . . 100 D6
Hartshay Cl 20 DE7 . . . . 157 F5
Hartside Cl NG2 . . . . 186 C7
Hartside Gdns 1
NG10 . . . . 193 A8
Hartside Wy NG16 . . . . . 143 B3
Hart St NG7 . . . . 222 B1
Hartwell St NG3 . . . . . . 223 F4
Hartwood Dr NG9 . . . . . 170 D1
Harvest Cl
Beeston NG9 . . . . 184 B7
Bingham NG13 . . . . 177 B8
Carlton in Lindrick S81 . . . 25 C7
Nottingham NG5 . . . . 160 D4
Worksop S81 . . . . 36 B7

Harvest Cres NG9.....171 E5
Harvest Dr
　Cotgrave NG12......188 A5
　Newark-on-Trent NG24...125 C4
Harvester Way NG18...102 D1
Harvest La NG17......100 A1
Harvest Rd 3 NG16...144 A1
Harvey Cl NG11......196 D5
Harvey Croft NG9...170 C4
Harvey Ct 3 NG7...172 E2
Harvey Hadden Sports Ctr
　NG8......171 F7
Harvey Rd
　Mansfield NG18......102 A4
　Nottingham, Bilborough
　　NG8......171 F7
　Nottingham, Dunkirk
　　NG7......172 E2
Harvey's Field NG25...136 E8
Harviston Ave NG4...162 E4
HARWELL......11 A4
Harwell Sluice La DN10..11 D3
Harwich Cl NG6......160 A8
Harwill Cres NG8...160 B2
Harwood Cl
　Arnold NG5......162 B8
　Sutton in Ashfield NG17...101 A4
Harwood Pl NG17...101 A4
HARWORTH......8 F5
Harworth Ave S81......18 A6
Harworth Cl NG19...101 D6
Haslam St NG7...223 D1
Haslehurst Gdns S80...35 E2
Haslemere Gdns NG15...116 F2
Haslemere Rd
　Long Eaton NG10......193 B8
　Nottingham NG8......172 D8
Hassock Cl NG9...184 D6
Hassock La N DE75...157 B7
Hassock La S DE75...157 C6
Hassocks La NG9...184 B7
Hassop Wlk NG18...103 B6
Hastings St
　Carlton NG4......174 C7
　6 Loughborough LE11...220 A4
Haswell Rd NG6...160 B5
Hatchets Cl NG24...125 A3
Hatchet's La NG24...125 A3
Hatfield Ave
　Meden Vale NG20......74 F8
　Sandiacre NG10......182 B4
Hatfield Cl NG21...104 B1
Hatfield Dr NG2...185 C4
Hatfield Rd NG3...161 C1
Hatfield St DN22......40 A6
Hathaway Dr S81......36 B4
Hather Cl DN22......51 A5
Hatherleigh Cl NG3...162 C6
HATHERN......213 B1
Hathern Cl NG10...193 D5
Hathern Gn NG9...184 A8
Hathern Rd LE12...212 D2
Hathern Turn LE12...212 F2
Hathernware Ind Est
　LE12......213 D5
Hathersage Ave NG10...193 A5
Hathersage Cl NG5...160 F8
Hathersage Rise NG15...117 A3
Hathersage Way NG17...100 A4
Hathersage Wlk NG18...103 B6
Hatley Cl 7 NG2...173 B1
Hatton Cl
　North Muskham NG23...110 F2
　Nottingham NG5......147 A4
Hatton Crofts NG10...193 C6
Hatton Ct NG18...103 B6
Hatton Gdns
　Newark-on-Trent NG24...140 B4
　Nuthall NG8......159 E3
Haughage Hill DN22...22 B1
HAUGHTON......63 F6
Haughton Mdws
　Haughton DN22......63 F5
　Haughton DN22......64 A5
Haughton Way
　Walesby DN22......63 F2
　Walesby DN22......64 A2
Havelock Gdns NG3...223 F4
Haven Cl
　Clipstone NG21......89 F3
　Sutton in Ashfield NG17...100 D3
　West Bridgford NG2...185 D5
Havenden Gdns 2
　NG7......172 E7
Haven St S81......16 D6
Haven The NG22......78 C7
Havenwood Rise NG11...195 D8
Haverhill Cres NG5...146 D1
Haversham Cl NG6...160 D2
Hawarden Terr 9 NG7...172 F7
Hawbush Rd NG23...81 A4
Hawfinch Mdws DN22...39 E8
Hawker Cl DE7......157 F4
Hawkesworth Ave NG19...89 B1
Hawkhill NG22......77 A3
Hawkhurst Dr NG8...171 D2
Hawking La
　Stainsby S44......85 A7
　Stainsby S44......85 C6
Hawkins Cl DN11......9 A5
Hawkins Ct DE7......157 F4
Hawk Ridge Gdns 1
　NG3......173 E5
Hawkshead Cl NG2...186 D5
Hawksley Gdns NG11...184 C2
Hawksley La DN22......52 B4
Hawksley Rd 14 NG7...172 F7
Hawkswood Cl NG9...183 B4

HAWKSWORTH......167 C4
Hawksworth Ave NG5...161 D4
Hawksworth Rd
　Hawksworth NG13......167 B3
　Scarrington NG13......166 F1
　Scarrington NG13......167 A1
　Scrooby NG13......178 F8
　Screveton NG13......166 F4
　Syerston NG13......153 B3
　West Bridgford NG2...173 F1
Hawksworth St
　Gainsborough DN21......24 D8
　10 Nottingham NG3...173 E5
Hawley Cl LE12...205 F1
Hawson Way S81......35 C7
Hawthorn Ave
　Gainsborough DN21......15 D1
　Glapwell S44......86 B8
　Hucknall NG15......145 F7
　Stapleford NG9......182 D6
　Torksey Lock LN1......44 C1
Hawthorn Cl
　Beckingham DN10......23 B8
　Bleasby NG14......152 B8
　Keyworth NG12......197 E2
　Mansfield Woodhouse
　　NG19......88 E5
　New Ollerton NG22......77 D5
　5 Nottingham NG2...173 B1
　Old Dalby LE14......218 E4
　Shelford NG12......164 C1
　Shelford NG13......164 C1
　West Bridgford NG12...186 B4
Hawthorn Cres
　Arnold NG5......148 A1
　4 Kirkby-in-Ashfield
　　NG17......114 F6
　Kirkby-in-Ashfield NG17...115 A6
Hawthorn Ct 6 NG2...173 B1
Hawthorn Dr
　Farnsfield NG22......120 A6
　New Ollerton NG22......77 D5
Hawthorne Ave
　Hathern LE12......213 A1
　Long Eaton NG10......193 C6
　Shirebrook NG20......72 D4
　Tibshelf DE55......99 B8
Hawthorne Cl
　North Leverton with
　　Habblesthorpe DN22...42 D8
　Saxilby LN1......57 A5
　Stanton Hill NG17......100 B6
　Woodborough NG14...149 C4
Hawthorne Gr NG9...184 B6
Hawthorne Leys NG3...81 E6
Hawthorne Prim Sch
　NG6......146 E4
Hawthorne Rd NG16...113 D3
Hawthorne Rise NG16...158 B4
Hawthornes The NG22...54 C2
Hawthorne Way NG21...91 B8
Hawthorn Wood DN22...39 D6
Hawthorn Gr DN11......15 D1
Hawthorns The
　Kirkby-in-Ashfield NG17...114 F6
　Market Warsop NG20...74 A4
　Walesby DN22......64 A2
　Hawthorn Way S81......25 E7
HAWTON......139 E3
Hawton Cl
　Gainsborough DN21......15 E2
　Mansfield NG19......87 F1
Hawton Cres NG8...172 C3
Hawton La
　Farndon NG24......139 A4
　New Balderton NG24...140 B4
Hawton Rd NG24...139 E5
Hawton Spinney NG8...172 C4
Haxey Gate Rd DN10......6 F5
Haxey Rd DN10......6 F4
Haycroft Cl NG19...88 E5
Haycroft Way NG13...165 C2
Hayden La NG15...131 B1
Haydn Ave NG5...161 C2
Haydn Prim Sch NG5...161 C2
Haydn Rd NG5...161 B2
Haydock Cl NG16...158 E7
Hayes Cl NG16...113 C3
Hayes Ct DN22......19 B4
Hayes Rd NG12...197 E3
Hayfield Gr NG23...81 A4
Hay Fields The NG21...104 B1
Hayles Cl NG5...161 B6
Hayling Cl DE7...157 C3
Hayling Dr NG8...160 D1
Haymans Corner 3
　NG19......88 C3
Haynes Ave NG9...170 C5
Haynes Cl
　Nottingham NG11...184 F3
　Tuxford NG22......66 A3
Hays Cl DE7...157 D2
Hayside Ave NG24...140 B3
HAYTON......30 D6
Hayton Rd
　Hayton DN22......21 D1
　Hayton DN22......30 C8
Hayward Ave LE11...220 C2
Haywood Ave NG21...118 A5
Haywood Ct
　Mansfield NG21......103 E2
　2 Nottingham NG2...173 E4
Haywood Oaks La
　NG21......118 C3
Haywood Rd NG3...162 A3
Haywood St NG2...173 E4
Hazelas Dr NG15...165 A5
Hazel Bank NG18...102 E8
Hazelby Rd S80......58 E8

Hazel Cl NG13......178 A4
Hazel Cres NG20......72 D4
Hazel Dr NG16......159 B6
Hazelford Way NG15...130 D7
Hazel Gr
　Edwinstowe NG21......76 B1
　Hucknall NG15......146 A5
　Kirkby-in-Ashfield NG17...115 C5
　Nottingham NG3......162 A4
　South Normanton DE55...113 B5
Hazel Hill Cres NG5...161 B8
Hazel Hill Pl NG5...161 B7
Hazelhurst Gdns 3
　NG6......160 B7
Hazel Mdws NG15......146 A5
Hazelmere Gr NG7...222 A2
Hazelmere Rd S80......58 B8
Hazel Rd NG22......77 D5
Hazel St
　Nottingham NG6......160 B8
　Sutton in Ashfield NG17...100 D7
Hazel Way NG15......131 B2
Hazelwood NG12......188 A3
Hazelwood Cl
　Eastwood NG16......144 B2
　Mansfield Woodhouse
　　NG19......89 B2
　Tibshelf DE55......99 B7
Hazelwood Dr NG15...145 C6
Hazelwood Gr S80......35 C2
Hazelwood La DN22......41 E1
Hazelwood Rd NG7...172 E7
Headingley Gdns 3
　NG8......172 D8
Headingley Rd DN22...39 E4
Headland Ave NG22...50 A3
HEADON......52 B7
Headstead Bank DN22...43 D6
Headstock Cl NG22...77 C7
Headstocks Cl NG15...146 D2
Head Stocks The NG17...100 A1
Heafield Dr DE74...203 D2
Healdswood Inf Sch
　NG17......100 D6
Healdswood St NG17...100 D7
Healey Cl
　Collingham NG23......112 A8
　Nottingham NG2...173 C2
HEANOR......143 B2
Heanor Langley Inf Sch
　DE75......143 B1
Heanor Rd DE7......157 D3
Heanor Wlk NG18...102 A6
Heapham Cres DN21...24 F8
Heapham Rd
　Gainsborough DN21......15 E1
　3 Gainsborough DN21...24 F8
Heard Cres NG9...183 F8
Heartwood Cl NG8...172 A6
Heath Ave NG18...103 B7
Heath Cl NG7...222 B7
Heathcoat St
　12 Loughborough LE11...220 A4
　Nottingham NG1...223 F3
Heathcote Pl NG17...101 A4
Heather Cl
　Eastwood NG16......144 C2
　3 Gainsborough DN21...15 F1
　10 Kirkby-in-Ashfield
　　NG17......114 F7
　Mansfield NG3......173 D7
　South Normanton DE55...113 A3
　Tickhill DN11......8 B8
Heather Croft NG2...185 C4
Heather Ct DE75...143 B1
Heather La NG15...132 B8
Heatherley Dr
　Mansfield NG19......88 E1
　Nottingham NG6......160 F4
Heatherley Prim Sch
　NG19......88 E1
Heather Rd NG4...162 D1
Heather Rise NG9...171 E1
Heathers The NG22...77 F5
Heathervale NG2...185 B6
Heather Way
　Mansfield NG18......103 A6
　Shirebrook NG20......72 D2
Heathfield Ave DE7...170 A4
Heathfield Ct 12 NG17...114 E7
Heathfield Gdns
　Retford DN22......39 E8
　Tibshelf DE55......99 A7
Heathfield Gr NG9...183 C3
Heathfield Prim Sch
　NG6......160 D5
Heathfield Rd
　(Kersall Rd) NG5...160 D5
Heathfield Prim Sch
　(Scotland Rd) NG5...160 F3
Heathfield Rd
　Nottingham NG5......160 F4
　Nottingham NG5......161 A4
Heathfield Wy NG18...102 D5
Heath Gdns DE72...193 A8
Heath Gr S81......25 D1
Heathland Cl NG18...103 A6
Heathlands Prim Sch
　NG21......103 D3
Heathrington Gdns 9
　NG5......147 A1
Heath The NG16...188 B8
Heaton Cl
　Newark-on-Trent NG24...140 D8
　Nottingham NG3...161 F1
Heaton St DN21......24 D8
Heavenside LE12...205 E3

Heavytrees Ave NG15...117 A1
Hecadeck La LE14...219 C8
HECKDYKE DN10......7 F4
Heckdyke DN10......7 F4
Heckdyke La DN10......7 E5
Heckington Dr NG8...172 B5
Heddington Gdns 1
　NG5......161 D8
Heddon Bar NG8......88 E3
Hedgerow Cl
　Old Dalby LE14......218 E5
　Sutton in Ashfield NG17...100 C1
Hedgerows The
　Collingham NG23......112 B8
　Rainworth NG21......104 B3
Hedges Dr DE7......170 A5
Hedingham Cl DE7...157 D1
Hedley Cl LE12......212 A4
Hedley St NG7......173 A8
Hedley Villas 5 NG7...161 A1
Heights The NG24...140 E8
Helen Cl NG9......183 D6
Helenship La DN22...54 B7
Hellebore Cl NG5...160 E7
Helm Cl NG6......159 F7
Helmsdale Cl
　Arnold NG5......148 B1
　Mansfield NG19......101 E5
Helmsdale Gdns NG5...146 F1
Helmsley Rd NG21...103 E3
Helston Dr NG8...159 E1
Helvellyn Cl 7 NG2...173 C2
Helvellyn Way NG10...182 B2
Hemingway Cl
　Carlton NG4......174 C7
　Eastwood NG16......144 C1
Hemlock Ave
　Long Eaton NG10......182 D1
　Stapleford NG9......182 E8
Hemlock Gdns NG6...159 F6
Hemlock Rd NG12...186 A1
Hemmingfield Cl S81...35 F8
Hemmingfield Cres
　Worksop S81......35 F7
　Worksop S81......36 A8
Hemmingfield Rd S81...36 A7
Hemmingfield Rise S81...36 A8
Hemmingfield Way S81...36 A8
Hemplands La NG23...96 E8
Hemplands The NG23...98 A1
Hempshill Hall Prim Sch
　NG6......159 F5
Hempshill La NG6...160 A6
HEMPSHILL VALE......159 E6
Hemsby Cl NG5...161 F6
Hemsby Gdns 5 NG6...160 B8
Hemscott Cl NG9...159 F8
Hemsley Dr NG16...143 D3
Hemswell Cl NG3...174 A5
Hen And Chicken Yard
　NG24......141 F5
Henderson Way 7
　LE11......220 C3
Hendon Rise NG3...173 F8
Hendre Gdns 1 NG5...161 A7
Henfrey Dr NG5...130 D7
Henley Cl NG4...175 A6
Henley Ct DN21......15 C2
Henley Gdns NG5...170 E1
Henley Rise NG5...161 A3
Hennessey Cl 11 NG9...183 C2
Henning Gdns 13 NG5...161 A8
Henning La NG17...100 B1
Hennymoor Cl S80......45 A5
Hennymoor La S80......45 C2
Henrietta St NG6...160 C6
Henry Ave NG19......88 B5
Henry Cl S80......46 F8
Henry Ct NG2...173 C2
Henry Mws DN22......29 F1
Henry Rd
　Beeston NG9......184 A6
　Nottingham NG7......222 A2
　West Bridgford NG2...185 E8
Henry St
　Arnold NG5......147 E2
　Hucknall NG15......146 B6
　6 Nottingham NG2...173 E4
　Sutton in Ashfield NG17...100 F1
Henry Whipple Prim Sch
　NG5......160 F6
Henshaw Dr NG13...177 D6
Henshaw Pl DE7...157 E4
Henson La NG12...176 E3
Henson La
　Bingham NG13......177 A2
　Cropwell Butler NG12...176 E2
Henson's Sq NG17...183 B8
Henton Cl NG24...125 E2
Henton Rd NG21......76 C1
Henton Row NG7...222 B2
Hepple Dr NG6...159 F7
Hepworth Dr NG16...158 B7
Herald Cl NG9...184 B7
Herbert Rd
　Annesley Woodhouse
　　NG17......115 B1
　Nottingham NG5......161 B1
Herbert St
　Loughborough LE11...220 B5
　Mansfield NG18......102 A6
Hercules Dr NG24...140 B7
Hereford Ave
　Mansfield Woodhouse
　　NG19......88 C6
　Ollerton NG22......77 B4
Hereford Cl S81......36 A6
Hereford Rd
　Arnold NG5......161 E5
　Carlton NG4......162 F2
　Nottingham NG3...174 B5

Hereford Rd continued
　Ravenshead NG15...117 A3
Herewood Cl NG20......72 F4
Hermes Cl DN10......9 F8
Hermitage Ave NG18...101 F5
Hermitage La NG18...101 E4
Hermitage Sq 1 NG2...173 F3
Hermitage The NG18...101 E4
Hermitage Way
　NG18......101 E4
Hermitage Wlk NG7...222 C1
Hermon St NG7...222 C3
Herne St NG17......101 A4
Heron Cres
　Cotgrave NG12......187 D5
　Cotgrave NG12......188 A5
Heron Dr
　Gainsborough DN21......15 F1
　Nottingham NG7...222 A2
Heron Glade S81......35 C7
Herons Ct NG2...186 C4
Heron Way
　Mansfield NG19......87 C1
　New Balderton NG24...140 C5
Herrick Rd LE11...220 A2
Herril Ings DN11......8 B8
Herriot Gr DN11......9 A4
Herrod Cl NG23......97 A8
Herrods View NG17...100 C6
Hervey Gr NG7...184 E2
Heskey Cl NG3...223 E4
Heskey Wlk NG3...223 E4
Hesley Rd
　Harworth DN11......8 F3
　Harworth DN11......9 A3
Heslington Ave NG8...172 E8
Heslop Ct S80......35 D3
Hethbeth Ct 5 NG2...173 C2
Hethersett Gdns 4
　NG6......160 B8
Hetley Rd NG9...183 F8
Hett's La NG20......74 B5
Hetts Lane Inf Sch
　NG20......74 B5
Hewer Cl 4 DE7...157 F8
Hewers Way NG21...76 C3
Hewett St NG20......73 D5
Hewson's La NG23...112 A5
Hexham Ave DE7...170 A4
Hexham Cl
　Mansfield NG18......102 F5
　West Bridgford NG2...186 A6
Heyes The NG15...117 A1
Heyford Ct DN22......143 A1
Heymann Prim Sch
　NG2......185 D4
Hey St NG10...193 C4
Heyward St NG18...102 D7
Heywood Cl NG25...121 F1
Heywood St NG18...102 D7
Heyworth Rd NG15...145 F4
Hibbert Cres NG17...101 A3
Hibbert Rd NG18...102 D7
Hicking La
　Southwell NG25......136 D5
　Southwell NG25......136 D6
Hickings La NG9...182 E8
HICKLING......210 B7
Hickling Cl NG10...193 B5
Hickling Ct NG18...102 D7
Hickling La
　Hickling NG12......210 B8
　Long Clawson LE14...211 A4
　Upper Broughton LE14...210 B3
Hickling Rd
　Hickling LE14......210 C3
　Kinoulton NG12......200 B2
　Nottingham NG3...162 A2
Hickling Way NG12...188 A1
Hickman Cres DN21...15 C4
Hickman Ct DN21......24 E8
Hickman Gr NG23......97 F1
Hickman Rd NG13...177 D6
Hickman St DN21......24 D8
Hickory Cl 8 NG17...114 F7
Hickton Dr NG9...183 B1
Hide Hill View NG11...186 D1
Higgins Cl 8 NG24...125 A2
Highbank Dr NG11...195 E7
Highbank Prim Sch
　NG11......195 D7
Highbury Ave NG6...160 D5
Highbury Cl NG8...159 E3
Highbury Hospl NG6...160 C5
Highbury Rd
　Keyworth NG12......197 E4
　Nottingham NG6...160 C6
Highbury Wlk NG6...160 C6
High Church St NG7...161 A1
High Church Street 1
　NG7......173 A8
High Cl NG17......115 B1
Highclere Dr NG4...174 F8
Highcliffe Ave NG20...72 C4
Highcliffe Rd NG3...174 A5
High Common La
　Austerfield DN10......3 A6
　Tickhill DN11......9 A8
Highcroft NG3...161 F4
Highcroft Cl NG10...193 E5
Highcroft Dr NG8...171 B5
High Cross NG14...136 E2
High Cross St NG1...223 E3
Highcross Hill NG25,
　NG14......136 D3
High Cross St NG1...223 F3
High Ct NG12...197 D2
Highfield DN22......29 C1

Highfield Ave
　Kirkby-in-Ashfield
　　NG17......114 E6
　Mansfield NG19......88 B1
　Shirebrook NG20......72 D6
Highfield Cl
　Clipstone NG21......90 A4
　Gainsborough DN21......15 E1
　Mansfield NG19......88 B1
　Ravenshead NG15...117 A2
Highfield Ct NG9...183 F6
Highfield Dr
　Bilsthorpe NG22......105 F4
　Carlton NG4......174 B8
　Nuthall NG16......159 F4
　South Normanton DE55...113 B5
　Stapleford LN6......127 A4
Highfield Gr
　Carlton in Lindrick S81...26 B5
　West Bridgford NG2...185 F7
Highfield La S80......36 C1
High Field La DN10......3 B3
Highfield Rd
　Bawtry DN10......10 B8
　Beeston NG9......183 A3
　Clipstone NG21......90 A4
　Keyworth NG12......197 E4
　Nottingham NG7...172 D1
　Nuthall NG16......159 E4
　Saxilby LN1......57 A4
　Sutton in Ashfield NG17...100 C3
　West Bridgford NG2...185 F7
Highfields Ct NG15...146 A6
Highfields Dr NG22...106 A4
Highfields Sch NG24...140 C6
Highfield Terr 8 NG18...102 B6
Highfield Villas S81...25 F8
Highfield Way NG18...102 A5
High Gables DN22...19 B5
Highgate Cl
　Carlton NG4......162 C2
　Plungar NG13......202 F8
Highgate Dr DE7...157 C3
Highgate La NG13...202 F8
High Gr NG19...88 E1
High Grounds Cts S80...35 B4
High Grounds Rd S80...35 B4
High Grounds Way S80...35 B4
Highgrove Ave NG9...183 D6
Highgrove Gdns NG12...186 A4
High Hazel Dr NG18...88 B1
Highhazels Rd NG12...188 A4
High Hazles Cl NG4...162 E3
High Hazles Dr NG17...100 A2
High Hoe Ct S80......36 A3
High Hoe Dr S80......36 A3
High Hoe Rd S80......36 B3
High Holborn DE7...157 E3
High House Rd DN22...31 F4
High Hurst NG14...148 E7
High La Central DE7...157 A1
High La E DE7...157 A1
Highland Cl NG19...88 D3
Highland Dr NG17...100 D1
Highlanders Hill NG18...102 F5
Highland Gr S81......36 A5
Highland Rd NG18...102 E2
High Leys Dr NG15...116 C3
High Leys Rd NG15...145 F5
High Main Dr NG6...146 E3
HIGH MARNHAM......68 B1
High Mdw
　Bawtry DN10......9 F7
　Hathern LE12......213 A1
　Tollerton NG12......186 D1
High Meadow NG23...156 E2
High Oakham Ct NG17...101 B4
High Oakham Dr NG18...102 B3
High Oakham Grange
　NG18......102 B3
High Oakham Hill
　NG18......102 A4
High Oakham Pk NG18...102 B3
High Oakham Prim Sch
　NG18......102 B3
High Oakham Rd NG18...102 B4
High Pavement
　Nottingham NG1......223 F2
　Sutton in Ashfield NG17...100 C2
High Pk Cotts NG16...144 D6
High Rd
　Beeston NG9......184 A7
　Beeston, Chilwell NG9...183 D4
　Beeston, Toton NG9...183 A1
　Carlton in Lindrick S81...26 A5
　South Carlton S81......25 F4
High Ridge NG19......88 F2
High St Ave NG5...161 E7
High St Pl NG1...223 E2
High Spania NG16...158 F7
High St
　Arnold NG5......161 E7
　Austerfield DN10......3 C2
　Bawtry DN10......10 A7
　Beckingham DN10......23 B8
　Blyth S81......18 B2
　Bottesford NG13...181 A2
　Brinsley NG16......128 C3
　Collingham NG23......112 A8
　Eagle LN6......84 D3
　East Markham NG22......65 F7
　Edwinstowe NG21......76 B1
　Elkesley DN22......50 B4
　Everton DN10......11 C3
　Gainsborough DN21......24 D7
　Girton NG23......82 F1
　Girton NG23......97 E8
　Gringley on the Hill DN10...12 F2
　Harby NG23......70 D2
　Holme NG23......111 A2

High St continued
Hucknall NG15 . . . .**146** B7
Huthwaite NG17 . . . .**100** A3
Kegworth DE74 . . . .**203** C2
Kimberley NG16 . . . .**158** F6
Laxton NG22 . . . .**79** B3
Long Eaton NG10 . . . .**193** E8
Loughborough LE11 . . . . .**220** B4
Mansfield Woodhouse
NG19 . . . .**88** C3
Market Warsop NG20 . . . .**74** B4
Marton DN21 . . . .**44** C7
Misson DN10 . . . .**4** B2
Misterton DN10 . . . .**6** F2
Newton on Trent LN1 . . . . .**55** A1
Newton on Trent LN1 . . . . .**69** A8
North Scarle LN6 . . . .**83** D2
Nottingham NG1 . . . .**223** E2
Orston NG13 . . . .**179** F7
Pleasleyhill NG19 . . . .**87** B5
Retford DN22 . . . .**39** E3
Ruddington NG11 . . . .**196** C2
Saxilby LN1 . . . .**57** A3
South Clifton NG23 . . . . . .**68** E1
South Leverton DN22 . . . . .**42** C6
South Normanton DE55 . .**113** A6
Stanton Hill NG17 . . . . . .**100** C6
Stapleford LN6 . . . .**127** E8
Stapleford NG9 . . . .**182** E7
Staunton in the Vale
NG13 . . . .**169** B4
Sutton in Ashfield NG17 . .**100** C3
Sutton on Trent NG23 . . . .**96** F8
Tibshelf DE55 . . . .**99** A7
Walkeringham DN10 . . . . .**13** F6

High Tor
Mansfield NG18 . . . .**102** C2
Sutton in Ashfield NG17 . .**100** E7
Highurst St NG7 . . . .**222** C3
High View Ave NG3 . . . . .**198** A3
High View Gdns NG17 . .**115** B1
High View Rd DE55 . . . .**113** C7
High View Rd Ind Units
DE55 . . . .**113** C7
Highwood Ave NG8 . . . .**171** F8
Highwood Player Jun Sch
NG8 . . . .**171** E8
Highwray Gr NG11 . . . . .**184** D1
Hilary Cl NG8 . . . .**171** D3
Hilcot Dr NG8 . . . .**160** C1
HILCOTE **99** C1
Hilcote Dr NG19 . . . .**89** F4
Hilcote La DE55 . . . .**99** A1
Hilcote St DE55 . . . .**113** A6
Hillary Way NG24 . . . . . .**140** E4
Hillbeck Cres NG8 . . . . .**171** C4
Hill Cl
Eastwood NG16 . . . .**144** C1
West Bridgford NG2 . . . . .**186** B6
Hill Cres
Gainsborough DN21 . . . . .**15** F1
Sutton in Ashfield NG17 .**101** B4
Hillcrest NG25 . . . .**136** D8
Hill Crest NG20 . . . .**72** D3
Hillcrest Ave DE55 . . . . .**113** A4
Hillcrest Cl NG16 . . . . . .**159** A6
Hillcrest Dr NG15 . . . . . .**145** D6
Hillcrest Gdns NG14 . . . .**163** E5
Hill Crest Gr NG5 . . . . . .**161** B3
Hillcrest Mews DN22 . . . .**40** A7
Hillcrest Rd NG12 . . . . . .**197** E4
Hillcrest View NG4 . . . . .**162** B1
Hill Dr NG13 . . . .**177** D5
Hill Farm Cl NG12 . . . . . .**186** D1
Hill Farm Ct NG12 . . . . .**186** A2
Hillfield Gdns NG5 . . . . .**146** E1
Hillfield Rd NG9 . . . .**170** F1
Hill Fields DE55 . . . .**113** A3
Hill Gdns DN11 . . . .**9** A4
Hillgrove Gdns [14] NG5 .**161** A8
Hilliers Ct NG5 . . . .**160** F8
Hillingdon Ave NG16 . . .**159** D3
Hillingdon Dr DE7 . . . . .**170** A7
Hillington Rise NG5 . . . .**161** C7
Hillmoor St NG19 . . . .**87** C3
Hillocks Prim Sch
NG17 . . . .**101** B3
Hillocks The NG17 . . . . .**101** B3
Hill Rd
Beeston NG9 . . . .**183** B2
Bestwood Village NG6 . . .**146** E4
Gotham NG11 . . . .**205** B7
Harworth DN11 . . . .**9** A4
Orston NG13 . . . .**180** A6
Tuxford NG22 . . . .**66** B3
Hill Rise NG9 . . . .**170** C4
Hillsborough Ave
NG17 . . . .**114** D8
Hillsborough Way
NG17 . . . .**114** D8
Hillsford Cl NG8 . . . .**172** A5
Hillside
Beckingham LN5 . . . .**142** C8
Beckingham LN5 . . . .**142** D8
Beckingham NG24 . . . . . .**127** C1
Kegworth DE74 . . . .**203** D1
Langley Mill NG16 . . . . . .**143** A3
Marton DN21 . . . .**44** C8
Tuxford NG22 . . . .**66** B3
Hill Side
Beckingham LN5 . . . .**142** D8
Nottingham NG7 . . . .**172** D3
Hillside Ave
Misterton DN10 . . . .**7** A2
Nottingham NG3 . . . .**162** A4
Hillside Cres
Beeston NG9 . . . .**183** E8
Worksop S81 . . . .**35** F5
Hillside Dr
Burton Joyce NG14 . . . . .**163** F5
Long Eaton NG10 . . . . . .**193** B8
Southwell NG25 . . . .**136** D8

Hillside Gr NG10 . . . . . .**182** A6
Hillside Prim Sch
NG15 . . . .**145** E8
Hillside Rd
Beeston, Bramcote
NG9 . . . .**183** D8
Beeston, Chilwell NG9 . . .**183** B3
Blidworth NG21 . . . .**118** A4
Radcliffe on Trent NG12 . .**176** A3
Hillside Wlk NG21 . . . . . .**118** A4
Hills Rd NG5 . . . .**161** F4
Hill St
Pleasleyhill NG19 . . . .**87** B5
Retford DN22 . . . .**39** E4
Worksop S80 . . . .**35** E2
Hillsview Ct NG19 . . . . . .**87** A5
Hillsway NG20 . . . .**72** D3
Hillsway Cres NG18 . . . .**102** A4
Hill Syke
Lowdham NG14 . . . .**150** A2
Woodborough NG14 . . . .**149** F2
Hill The NG17 . . . .**114** C5
Hill Top NG13 . . . .**180** A6
Hill Top Ave NG20 . . . . . .**72** E4
Hilltop Cl DN6 . . . .**84** D3
Hill Top Ct DN11 . . . .**9** A4
Hilltop Rd NG16 . . . .**113** C3
Hilltop Rise NG16 . . . . . .**144** B2
Hill Top View NG17 . . . .**100** C1
Hillview Ave NG3 . . . . . .**161** D2
Hillview Cres DN22 . . . . .**30** E4
Hillview Ct NG19 . . . .**88** D4
Hillview Rd
Carlton NG4 . . . .**162** A1
Retford DN22 . . . .**39** E3
Hill View Rd
Beeston NG9 . . . .**183** A8
Kirkby-in-Ashfield NG17 .**115** C5
Hill Vue Ave NG24 . . . . .**140** B8
Hill Vue Gdns NG24 . . . .**140** B8
Hillwood Cl S80 . . . .**35** B2
Hilton Cl NG19 . . . .**87** C3
Hilton Cres NG2 . . . .**186** B5
Hilton Ct LN1 . . . .**57** B3
Hilton Grange NG2 . . . . .**186** B5
Hilton Pk
Blidworth NG21 . . . .**117** F5
Blidworth NG21 . . . .**118** A5
Hilton Rd NG3 . . . .**162** A3
Hinchin Brook NG7 . . . . .**222** A2
Hind Cl NG12 . . . .**200** A2
Hindlow Ct NG18 . . . . . .**103** B6
Hind St
Calverton NG14 . . . .**133** E1
Retford DN22 . . . .**40** A4
Hine Ave NG24 . . . .**140** E8
Hine Ct DN22 . . . .**39** E4
Hinsley Cl NG5 . . . .**162** B8
Hirams Paddocks
NG24 . . . .**139** D8
Hirst Cl NG5 . . . .**147** F2
Hirst Cres NG8 . . . .**171** E4
Hirst Rd DN22 . . . .**40** A8
Hitchen Rd NG10 . . . . . .**193** B7
Hives La LN6 . . . .**83** D3
Hobart Cl NG2 . . . .**173** C1
Hobart Dr NG9 . . . .**170** F1
Hobben Cres NG15 . . . . .**131** D1
Hobhouse Rd NG19 . . . . .**87** D2
Hobsic Cl NG16 . . . .**143** D8
Hobsic La NG16 . . . .**128** E8
Hobson's Acre NG14 . . . .**165** A5
HOCKERTON **122** B6
Hockerton Hts NG23 . . . .**122** B6
Hockerton Rd
Caunton NG23 . . . .**108** F1
Knapthorpe NG23 . . . . . .**109** A2
Knapthorpe NG23 . . . . . .**122** E8
Southwell NG25 . . . .**121** F2
Southwell NG25, NG23 . .**122** F2
Hockerwood NG11 . . . . .**184** E4
Hockerwood La
Southwell NG23 . . . .**122** C2
Southwell NG25 . . . .**122** B2
Hockey Cl LE11 . . . .**220** A7
Hockley
Nottingham NG1 . . . .**223** F2
Nottingham NG7 . . . .**222** F2
Hockley Pl NG17 . . . .**114** E4
Hodding Rd S80 . . . .**45** C6
Hodgkin Cl NG11 . . . . . .**184** C1
Hodgkinson Rd NG17 . . .**115** B4
Hodgkinson St NG4 . . . .**175** A6
Hodmire La S44 . . . .**85** E7
HODSOCK **26** E7
Hodsock La
Blyth S81 . . . .**27** A8
Carlton in Lindrick S81 . .**26** B7
Hodsock Priory Gdns ★
S81 . . . .**26** E7
Hodson Ct LE11 . . . .**220** B2
HODTHORPE **45** C6
Hodthorpe Prim Sch
S80 . . . .**45** C5
Hoefield Cres NG6 . . . . .**160** A6
Hoe La NG12 . . . .**189** A6
Hoe Nook NG12 . . . .**189** A4
Hoe View Rd NG12 . . . . .**189** A4
Hoewood Rd NG6 . . . . . .**160** A8
Hogan Gdns NG5 . . . . . .**147** A1
Hogarth Prim Sch
NG3 . . . .**174** A7
Hogarth St NG3 . . . .**173** F6
Hoggetts Cl NG9 . . . .**183** B5
Hogg La NG12 . . . .**175** E3
Hoggs Field NG16 . . . . . .**143** F2
HOLBECK **59** C7
Holbeck La S80 . . . .**59** D8
Holbeck Rd
Hucknall NG15 . . . .**131** B1

Holbeck Rd continued
Nottingham NG8 . . . .**172** D6
Holbeck Way NG21 . . . . .**104** B3
Holbein Cl LE11 . . . .**220** C4
Holborn Ave NG2 . . . . . .**173** F4
Holborn Cl NG16 . . . .**159** D3
Holborn Pl NG6 . . . .**160** C7
Holbrook Cl NG19 . . . . . .**87** A5
Holbrook Cres NG21 . . . .**90** C6
Holbrook Ct
Mansfield NG18 . . . .**103** B6
Nottingham NG11 . . . . . .**195** E8
Holbrook St DE75 . . . . . .**143** A2
Holby Cl NG5 . . . .**160** F8
Holcombe Cl NG8 . . . . . .**160** B2
Holdale Rd NG3 . . . .**174** B6
Holdenby Cl DN22 . . . . . .**40** A8
Holden Cres
Newark-on-Trent NG24 . .**139** F6
Nuthall NG16 . . . .**159** C6
Holden Gdns NG9 . . . . . .**182** E6
Holden Rd NG9 . . . .**183** E7
Holden St
Mansfield NG18 . . . .**102** A4
Nottingham NG7 . . . .**222** C3
Holderness Cl DN11 . . . . . .**9** A4
Holding S81 . . . .**36** B5
Holds La DN22 . . . .**19** B2
Holgate Acad NG15 . . . .**145** E6
Holgate Prim Sch
NG15 . . . .**145** F6
Holgate Rd NG2 . . . .**173** C1
Holgate Wlk NG15 . . . . .**145** E6
Holkham Ave NG9 . . . . .**183** C5
Holkham Cl
Arnold NG5 . . . .**162** A6
Shipley DE7 . . . .**157** C3
Holland Cl NG11 . . . .**195** B1
Holland Cres NG16 . . . . .**129** B7
Holland Mdw NG10 . . . .**193** D5
Holland St NG7 . . . .**172** F7
Hollands Way DE74 . . . .**203** D2
Holles Cl NG22 . . . .**77** E5
Holles Cres NG7 . . . .**222** C1
Holles St S80 . . . .**35** F2
Hollies Ave NG24 . . . . . .**125** B4
Hollies Dr NG12 . . . .**186** A4
Hollies The
Blyth S81 . . . .**18** B2
Eastwood NG16 . . . .**143** F2
Rainworth NG21 . . . .**104** B1
Rainworth NG21 . . . .**118** B8
Ravenshead NG15 . . . . . .**116** F1
Sandiacre NG10 . . . .**182** A5
Shirebrook NG20 . . . .**72** E2
Hollington Rd NG8 . . . . .**172** B6
Hollington Way NG18 . . .**103** B7
Hollingwell Dr [4]
NG18 . . . .**103** B7
Hollingworth Ave
NG10 . . . .**182** B3
Hollins The NG14 . . . . . .**149** A8
Hollinwell Ave NG8 . . . .**172** C5
Hollinwell Cl [9] NG17 . .**114** E7
Hollinwell Ct NG12 . . . . .**186** B3
Hollinwood La NG14 . . . .**133** C1
Hollinwood Lane NG14 .**148** C8
Hollis Mdw LE12 . . . .**205** E3
Hollis St NG7 . . . .**161** A1
Hollis Way LE12 . . . .**212** F1
Holloway Cl NG13 . . . . . .**165** D3
Hollowdyke La
Balderton NG24 . . . .**140** F2
Balderton NG24 . . . .**140** F3
Hollowgate La
High Marnham NG23 . . . .**67** F1
South Clifton NG23 . . . . .**68** B1
Hollows The
Long Eaton NG10 . . . . . .**194** A8
Maplebeck NG22 . . . . . .**108** A7
Nottingham NG11 . . . . . .**185** A4
Thurgarton NG14 . . . . . .**151** C7
Hollow Stone NG1 . . . . .**223** F2
Holly Ave
Carlton NG4 . . . .**174** D8
Nottingham, Wilford
NG11 . . . .**185** B8
Hollyberry Croft NG17 .**100** D1
Holly Blue Way S81 . . . . .**25** D1
Hollybrook Gr NG16 . . . .**159** B7
Holly Bush Cl DN22 . . . . .**50** B4
Holly Cl
Bingham NG13 . . . .**178** A4
Hucknall NG15 . . . .**146** B5
Hollycroft NG2 . . . .**186** A4
Holly Croft Gr DN11 . . . . .**8** B7
Holly Ct
Beeston NG9 . . . .**183** C8
Harworth DN11 . . . .**8** E4
Mansfield NG19 . . . .**88** E1
Newark-on-Trent NG24 . .**125** D1
Retford DN22 . . . .**39** F6
Rolleston NG23 . . . .**138** A5
Hollydale Rd NG3 . . . . . .**174** B6
Hollydene Cl NG15 . . . . .**145** C5
Hollydene Cres NG6 . . . .**160** B4
Holly Dr NG19 . . . .**89** A1
Holly Farm Ct NG6 . . . . .**146** E4
Hollygate Ind Pk NG12 .**188** A4
Hollygate La NG12 . . . . .**188** B5
Hollygirt Sch NG3 . . . . . .**173** C7
Homewood Dr NG17 . . . .**114** F6
Holly Hill Prim Sch
NG16 . . . .**129** A7
Holly Hill Rd NG16 . . . . .**129** A6
Hollyhock Cl [1] NG17 . .**114** F6
Hollyhock Dr DE55 . . . . .**113** B6
Holly La NG9 . . . .**183** E5
Holly Leaf Rd NG15 . . . .**146** C4

Hollymount
[5] Retford DN22 . . . .**39** F6
[7] Retford DN22 . . . .**40** A6
Holly Mount NG22 . . . . . .**93** E5
Holly Prim Sch NG19 . . . .**89** A1
Holly Rd
Mansfield Woodhouse
NG19 . . . .**89** A2
Retford DN22 . . . .**39** F6
Watnall NG16 . . . .**159** A7
Holly Rise NG22 . . . .**77** D5
Hollythorpe Pl NG15 . . .**145** C5
Hollytree Cl LE12 . . . . . .**215** C2
Hollytree La LE14 . . . . . .**211** C3
Hollywell Prim Sch
NG16 . . . .**158** F7
HOLME **111** A3
Holme Ave LE12 . . . .**205** E3
Holme Bsns Pk S81 . . . . .**25** D3
Holme Cl
Ilkeston DE7 . . . .**157** D2
Woodborough NG14 . . . .**149** A4
Holmecroft Ave NG17 . .**100** F5
Holmefield NG24 . . . . . .**139** A4
Holmefield Cres DE7 . . .**157** A8
Holmefield Rd S80 . . . . . .**45** A6
Holmefield Wlk NG18 . . .**103** B6
Holme Gr NG2 . . . .**174** B2
Holme La
Egmanton NG22 . . . .**79** E6
Halam NG22 . . . .**120** F3
Langford NG23 . . . .**111** E3
Normanton on T NG23 . . .**82** B5
Radcliffe on Trent NG12 .**175** C3
Rockley DN22 . . . .**51** C2
Winthorpe NG24 . . . .**125** F5
HOLME PIERREPONT . .**175** B3
Holme Pierrepont Ctry Pk ★
NG12 . . . .**174** F3
Holme Pierrepont Hall ★
NG12 . . . .**175** B3
Holme Pit Nature Reserve ★
NG11 . . . .**184** C3
Holme Rd
Bingham NG13 . . . .**178** A4
West Bridgford NG2 . . . .**174** A1
Holmes Cl NG16 . . . .**143** A3
Holmesfield Dr DE75 . . .**157** A7
Holme La Track
Dry Doddington NG23 . . .**156** A3
Long Bennington NG23 . .**156** F5
Holmes Rd DN22 . . . .**39** F7
Holme St NG2 . . . .**173** E2
Holmestead Cl LE12 . . . .**206** C1
Holme The NG25 . . . . . .**136** B7
Holme Way S81 . . . .**25** D1
Holme Wlk DN21 . . . .**15** F1
Holmewood Ave DE7 . . .**157** D2
Holmewood Cres NG5 . .**161** B6
Holmewood Dr NG16 . . .**158** B8
Holmfield Cl S81 . . . .**36** A5
Holmfield Rd NG9 . . . . . .**183** C3
Holmhurst Cl S81 . . . .**35** E5
Holmsfield NG12 . . . . . .**197** E2
Holmwood Rd NG21 . . . .**104** C1
Holroyd Ave NG2 . . . . . .**173** F4
Holroyd Circle NG16 . . . .**143** F7
Holt Dr [1] LE11 . . . .**220** A1
Holt Gn NG14 . . . .**148** F7
Holt The
Gainsborough DN21 . . . . .**15** F1
Newark-on-Trent NG24 . .**139** D6
Holwood Ct NG6 . . . .**160** A6
Holy Cross RC Prim Sch
NG15 . . . .**131** B1
Holy Family RC Prim Sch
S80 . . . .**47** A8
Holyoake Rd NG3 . . . . . .**162** C3
Holyrood Ct NG9 . . . . . .**171** C1
Holy Trinity Cath Acad
NG24 . . . .**139** E7
Holy Trinity CE Inf Sch
NG25 . . . .**136** D7
Holywell Rd DE7 . . . .**157** C3
Home Cl NG5 . . . .**161** F8
Homecroft Dr NG16 . . . .**128** C7
Home Croft The NG9 . . .**183** B7
Home Farm Cl
Gotham NG11 . . . .**195** A1
Kelham NG24 . . . .**124** A3
Laughterton LN1 . . . .**55** B4
Newark-on-Trent NG24 . .**124** A4
Willoughby-on-the-Wolds
LE12 . . . .**217** E7
Homefarm La NG23 . . . . .**70** A6
Home Farm La
Kirklington NG22 . . . . . .**120** E8
Upper Saxondale NG12 . .**177** C5
Homefield Ave NG5 . . . .**148** A1
Homefield Cl NG22 . . . . . .**53** B3
Homefield Croft DN10 . . .**10** A2
Homefield Rd NG8 . . . . .**172** D7
Home Fm Ct NG16 . . . . .**128** D6
Homelands The NG17 . . .**100** F1
Homeleigh La NG14 . . . . .**82** A6
Home Leys Way LE12 . . .**216** C4
Home Mdws DN11 . . . .**8** A6
Home Pastures LE14 . . . .**211** F7
Home Rise DN22 . . . .**32** C1
Homestead NG16 . . . . . .**143** A4
Homesteads The
Kirkby-in-Ashfield NG17 .**114** F6
Market Warsop NG20 . . . .**74** B4
Homewood Dr NG17 . . . .**114** F6
Honey Bee Gdns NG17 .**100** C5
Honeycroft Ct DE55 . . . .**113** B4
Honeyknab La NG25 . . . .**134** D5
Honey Pot Cl NG10 . . . . .**193** E8
Honeys La NG23 . . . .**139** B1
Honeysuckle Cl
New Balderton NG24 . . . .**140** C4

Honeysuckle Cl continued
[4] Retford DN22 . . . .**39** F6
Honeysuckle Dr DE55 . .**113** B7
Honeysuckle Gr
Bingham NG13 . . . .**177** D3
Nottingham NG6 . . . .**160** B4
Honeywood Dr NG3 . . . .**174** A7
Honeywood Wlk NG3 . . .**174** A7
Honing Dr NG25 . . . .**136** D8
Honingham Cl NG5 . . . . .**162** A6
Honingham Rd DE7 . . . .**157** C3
Honister Cl
Mansfield NG18 . . . .**102** C4
Nottingham NG11 . . . . . .**195** D7
West Bridgford NG2 . . . .**186** C7
Honister Ct NG18 . . . . . .**102** C4
Honiton Cl NG9 . . . .**183** A2
Honiton Rd NG8 . . . .**159** E1
Hood St NG5 . . . .**161** D2
Hook Cl [9] NG9 . . . .**183** C2
Hooley Cl NG10 . . . .**193** B6
Hooley Pl [3] NG5 . . . . . .**161** D3
Hooley St NG16 . . . .**128** F6
Hoopers Cl NG13 . . . . . .**181** A2
Hoopers Wlk [6] NG2 . . .**173** C2
Hooton Rd NG4 . . . .**174** C7
Hooton St NG3 . . . .**173** F5
Hope Cl NG2 . . . .**173** B2
Hopedale Cl NG7 . . . . . .**222** A3
Hope Dr NG7 . . . .**223** D1
Hope St
Beeston NG9 . . . .**183** E7
Mansfield NG18 . . . .**102** D6
Hopewell Cl NG12 . . . . .**176** A4
Hopewell Rise
Southwell NG25 . . . .**121** C1
Southwell NG25 . . . .**136** C8
Hopewell St NG5 . . . . . .**189** B4
Hopkin La NG25 . . . .**121** C1
Hopkin Ct NG5 . . . .**162** C6
Hopkins Ct NG16 . . . . . .**143** F3
Hopkinson Cl
Keyworth NG12 . . . .**197** F4
North Scarle LN6 . . . .**83** E2
Hopkinson Ct NG6 . . . . .**146** E3
Hopper Rd NG24 . . . .**140** A4
Hopwas Cl NG23 . . . .**123** E1
Hopwood Rd NG5 . . . . . .**162** E3
Hopyard La
Bathley NG25 . . . .**109** F2
Cromwell NG23 . . . .**110** B2
Egmanton NG22 . . . .**79** E6
Normanton on T NG23 . . .**82** A6
Tuxford NG22 . . . .**65** E1
Horace Ave NG9 . . . .**182** D6
Horizon Pl NG8 . . . .**159** C2
Hornbeam Cl
[5] Edwalton NG12 . . . . .**186** B1
Ilkeston DE7 . . . .**170** B1
Hornbeam Gdns NG6 . . .**159** F7
Hornbeam Way NG17 . . .**115** A3
Hornbuckle Ct NG7 . . . . .**222** B3
Hornchurch Rd NG8 . . . .**171** D8
Horne La NG22 . . . .**54** C1
Hornsby Wlk NG5 . . . . . .**160** E8
Horridge St DE7 . . . .**157** F4
Horsecroft Cl DE7 . . . . . .**157** C2
Horsendale Ave NG16 . . .**159** F4
Horsendale County Prim
Sch NG16 . . . .**159** E3
Horseshoe Cl LE12 . . . . .**217** D7
Horseshoe Cotts NG23 . .**112** B8
Horseshoe Rise DN10 . . .**13** F5
Horsewells St DN10 . . . . .**12** F2
Horsham Dr NG5 . . . .**160** F8
Horsley Cres NG16 . . . . .**143** A3
Horsley Rd [4] NG4 . . . . .**162** E3
Horsley Rd DN21 . . . .**15** B3
Horwood Dr
Carlton NG4 . . . .**162** D4
West Bridgford NG11 . . .**185** A5
HOSE **211** F7
Hose CE Prim Sch
LE14 . . . .**211** F7
Hose La
Colston Bassett LE14 . . . .**201** A3
Harby LE14 . . . .**202** A1
Hose LE14 . . . .**211** F5
Hoselett Field Rd
NG10 . . . .**193** E5
Hosiery St NG17 . . . .**115** A5
Hospital Rd DN22 . . . . . .**39** E7
Hotchkin Ave LN1 . . . . . .**57** C3
Hoten Rd [7] NG2 . . . . . .**173** F3
HOTON **215** D1
Hoton Rd LE12 . . . .**216** B3
Hotspur Cl NG6 . . . .**160** E5
Hotspur Rd DN21 . . . .**15** C2
Houfton Rd NG18 . . . . . .**102** E8
Hougham Rd NG23 . . . . .**156** F1
Houghs Yard NG24 . . . . .**126** A1
Houghton Cl NG16 . . . . .**159** E4
Houghton St NG16 . . . . .**128** D6
Houldsworth Rise NG5 . .**147** E2
Hound Rd NG2 . . . .**185** E8
Hounds Gate NG1 . . . . . .**223** D2
Hounsfield Cl NG24 . . . .**140** E8
Hounsfield Way NG23 . . .**96** F8
Houseman Gdns NG2 . . .**173** C2
Houston Cl NG5 . . . .**146** E1
Hove Chase DN22 . . . . . .**39** E4
Hove Rd NG5 . . . .**160** E5
HOVERINGHAM **151** D2
Hoveringham La
Hoveringham NG14 . . . .**151** B2
Kneeton NG13 . . . .**151** F3
Hoveringham Rd NG14 . .**165** C8
Howard Cl NG10 . . . .**182** E1
Howard Dr DE74 . . . .**203** C3
Howard Rd
Bircotes DN11 . . . .**9** C4

Howard Rd continued
Mansfield NG19 . . . .**101** F8
Howard's Gdns NG24 . . .**140** C4
Howard St
Loughborough LE11 . . . .**220** B5
Nottingham NG1 . . . .**223** E3
Sutton in Ashfield NG17 .**100** A3
Worksop S80 . . . .**36** B2
Howarth Cl NG10 . . . . . .**193** A7
Howbeck La
Clarborough DN22 . . . . . .**30** E4
Clarborough DN22 . . . . . .**31** A4
Howbeck Rd NG5 . . . . . .**162** B8
Howden Rd NG6 . . . .**146** C1
Howell-Jones Rd NG9 . .**183** B3
Howells Cl NG15 . . . .**161** C8
Howe Rd LE11 . . . .**220** B1
Howes Ct NG24 . . . .**140** A8
Howick Dr NG6 . . . .**159** F8
Howieson Ct NG3 . . . . . .**162** B5
Howitts Rd NG13 . . . . . .**181** A1
Howitt St
Heanor DE75 . . . .**143** A2
Long Eaton NG10 . . . . . .**193** E7
Hoylake Cl
Gainsborough DN21 . . . . .**15** E3
Mansfield Woodhouse
NG19 . . . .**88** E6
Hoylake Cres NG8 . . . . .**171** D7
Hoyland Ave NG7 . . . . . .**172** E2
Hoyle Rd NG14 . . . .**133** F1
Hoyte Dr DE74 . . . .**203** C3
Hubert St NG7 . . . .**222** B4
Huckerby Rd DE7 . . . . . .**157** C2
Huckerbys Field NG4 . . .**162** C1
Hucklow Ct NG18 . . . . . .**103** B6
HUCKNALL **145** E6
Hucknall Cl NG8 . . . .**159** D2
Hucknall Cres NG4 . . . . .**162** E2
Hucknall Flying High Acad
NG15 . . . .**145** E3
Hucknall Ind Pk NG15 . .**145** E4
Hucknall La NG6 . . . .**146** D2
Hucknall L Ctr NG15 . . . .**146** A8
Hucknall National CE (VA)
Prim Sch NG15 . . . . . .**146** A8
Hucknall Rd
Newstead NG15 . . . .**130** D5
Nottingham NG6 . . . .**160** D6
Hucknall Sta NG15 . . . . .**146** C7
Huddlestones Wharf
NG24 . . . .**139** E8
Hudson St
Loughborough LE11 . . . .**220** C4
Nottingham NG3 . . . .**173** F6
Hudson Wy NG12 . . . . . .**176** B4
Huffer Rd NG4 . . . .**203** D3
Hufton's Ct DE75 . . . . . .**157** A7
Hufton's Dr DE75 . . . . . .**157** A7
Hugessen Ave NG15 . . . .**146** C8
Hugget Gdns [4] NG5 . . .**161** A8
Hughes Ford Way LN1 . . .**57** B3
Hughes La NG4 . . . .**162** E4
Hughs Cl NG23 . . . .**138** C7
Humber Cl NG2 . . . .**173** C2
Humber La NG23 . . . . . .**153** B8
Humber Rd
Beeston NG9 . . . .**184** A7
Long Eaton NG10 . . . . . .**182** C1
Humber Rd S NG9 . . . . .**184** B6
Humber St
Retford DN22 . . . .**40** A6
Worksop S80 . . . .**35** E4
Humberstone Rd
NG25 . . . .**121** C1
Humberston Rd NG8 . . . .**171** C3
Hume St LE11 . . . .**220** C4
Humphrey Cl LE11 . . . . .**220** B2
Humphries Gdns S80 . . . .**35** E1
Hundred Acre La S81 . . . .**26** C3
Hundred Acres La
NG24 . . . .**140** D1
Hundreds La DN10 . . . .**5** B2
Hungary La LE12 . . . . . .**213** C2
Hungerhill La NG5 . . . . .**148** E2
Hungerhill Rd NG3 . . . . .**173** D7
Hungerton St NG7 . . . . .**222** B1
Hunston Cl NG8 . . . .**172** A7
Hunt Cl
Kirkby-in-Ashfield
NG17 . . . .**115** C7
Radcliffe on Trent NG12 .**175** F3
Hunter Dr NG6 . . . .**145** D2
Hunter Rd
Arnold NG5 . . . .**162** C6
Newton NG13 . . . .**177** B8
Hunters Chase NG19 . . . .**88** B2
Hunters Cl NG11 . . . .**185** A6
Hunters Ct NG17 . . . . . .**114** E5
Hunter's Dr DN10 . . . . . .**12** E2
Hunters Rd NG24 . . . . . .**140** F3
Huntingdon Dr NG7 . . . .**223** D2
Huntingdon Prim Sch
NG3 . . . .**223** E4
Huntingdon St NG1 . . . .**223** E3
Huntingdon Way NG9 . .**182** F2
Huntingdon Wlk NG10 . .**182** B5
Huntly Cl
Mansfield NG19 . . . .**101** F8
Nottingham NG7 . . . .**184** F1
Hunt's Hill NG16 . . . .**144** A7
Huntsman Pl DN22 . . . . .**19** B2
Hurcomb St NG3 . . . . . .**173** F7
Hurricane Rd NG15 . . . . .**145** E2
Hurst Cl NG21 . . . .**103** F1
Hurst Gr NG7 . . . .**222** B4
Hurt's Croft NG9 . . . . . .**183** D4
Hurt's Yd NG1 . . . .**223** E2
Huss's La NG10 . . . .**193** F7

Hutchinson Gn NG3 223 F4
Hutchinson Rd NG24 140 E8
HUTHWAITE 99 E3
Huthwaite All Saints CE (Aided) Infant Sch NG17 99 F4
Huthwaite La DE55 99 C2
Huthwaite L Ctr NG17 99 F3
Huthwaite Rd NG17 100 C2
Hutton Cl NG9 171 D1
Hutton St NG2 173 F3
Huxley Cl NG8 171 D7
Hyde Cl NG11 184 F4
Hyde Pk Cl NG2 185 C5
Hyson Cl 10 NG7 172 F8
HYSON GREEN 172 F7
Hyson St 12 NG7 172 F7

I

Ian Gr NG4 174 F8
Ibbinson Ct NG4 162 D4
IBTE Mus of Telecommunications★ S81 35 F2
Idle Bank DN9 2 D5
Idle Ct DN10 10 A7
Idle Valley Nature Reserve★ DN22 29 B3
Idlevalley Rd DN22 39 E8
Idle View DN22 29 F1
Idlewells Sh Ctr NG17 100 E2
Ikea Way NG16 158 C7
Ilam Sq DE7 157 E5
Ilford Cl DE7 157 D3
Ilion St NG19 87 F2
ILKESTON
157 D2
170 B7
Ilkeston Com Hospl DE7 157 D4
Ilkeston Rd
Sandiacre NG10 182 C8
Stapleford NG9 170 F2
Trowell NG9 170 C5
Ilkeston Sta DE7 158 A2
Imex Ent Pk NG15 146 D6
Imperial Ave
Beeston NG9 183 E6
Carlton NG4 162 E1
Imperial Ct DE74 203 D3
Imperial Rd
Beeston NG9 183 E6
Nottingham NG6 160 D6
Incher Mews NG5 162 C1
Inchwood Cl NG9 182 F2
Incinerator Rd NG2 173 E2
Independent St NG7 222 B4
Industrial Mus & Yd Gall★ NG8 172 A3
Infield La
Cuckney NG20 60 B5
North Leverton with Habblesthorpe DN22 32 E1
Weston NG23 81 B3
Ingamells Dr LN1 57 C3
Inger Dr NG4 162 E4
Ingham Gr NG7 222 A1
Ingham Rd
Bawtry DN10 9 F8
Long Eaton NG10 182 C2
Ingleborough Gdns 6 NG10 193 A8
Ingleby Cl
Cotgrave NG12 187 E2
Nottingham NG8 171 B4
Ingleby Medieval Village of★ LN1 57 A8
Inglefield Rd DE7 170 A6
Inglemere Cl S81 36 A5
Ingle Pingle LE11 220 A3
Inglewood Cl NG24 140 D2
Inglewood Rd NG7 184 E1
Ingram Rd NG6 160 D6
Ingrams La NG23 82 A3
Ingram Terr NG6 160 C6
Ings Rd DN10 12 E6
Inham Cir NG9 183 C6
Inham Cl NG9 183 A5
Inham Fields Cl NG14 165 A5
Inham Rd
Beeston NG9 183 A5
Beeston NG9 183 B5
Inholms Gdns NG23 152 F2
Inholms Rd NG23 152 F2
Inkerman Cl DE7 157 E5
Inkerman Rd NG16 128 F5
Inkerman St NG16 128 F5
Inkersall Grange Rd
Bilsthorpe NG22 105 B4
Rainworth NG21 104 F4
Inkersall La NG22 105 C6
Innes Rd NG4 174 C7
Institute St NG17 100 C6
Instow Cl NG5 162 D5
Instow Rise NG3 223 F4
Intake Ave NG18 101 F5
Intake Farm Prim Sch NG19 101 E7
Intake Rd
Clipstone NG21 90 A3
Keyworth NG12 197 D3
intu Victoria Ctr NG1 223 E3
Iona Cl DN21 15 E2
Iona Dr NG9 170 D2
Iona Gdns NG5 147 A1
Iona Sch NG3 174 A5
Ipswich Cir NG3 174 A5
Ireland Ave NG9 184 A5
Ireland Cl NG9 184 A5
Iremonger Rd NG2 173 D2
Irene Terr NG7 160 F2
Ireton Ave 6 NG24 140 E8
Ireton Gr NG9 183 D2
Ireton St
Beeston NG9 183 E6
Nottingham NG7 222 C3
Ironwood Cl 6 NG12 186 A2
Irving Cl NG22 120 A5
Irwin Dr NG6 160 A6
Isaac's La NG9 182 D7
Isabella St NG7 223 E1
Isandula Rd NG7 160 F2
Island Bsns Quarter NG1 223 F1
Islay Cl
Arnold NG5 147 F1
Stapleford NG9 170 D3
Ivatt Cl DN10 10 A8
Ivatt Dr NG2 173 F3
Iveagh Cl NG20 74 C5
Ivel Cres S81 34 F8
Ives Cl NG2 185 C4
Ivies The NG24 139 C6
Ivy Cl NG16 144 F1
Ivy Cottage La LN1 56 E4
Ivy Gdns NG22 106 A4
Ivy Gr
Carlton NG4 174 D7
Kirkby-in-Ashfield NG17 114 F6
Nottingham NG7 173 A8
Ivy La NG16 143 E2
Ivy Lodge La S81 16 B3
Ivy Way NG21 89 F4

J

Jacklin Ct NG17 114 F6
Jacklin Gdns NG5 147 A1
Jacksdale Nature Reserve★ NG16 128 B3
Jacksdale Prim Sch NG16 128 B3
Jackson Ave
8 Ilkeston DE7 157 E1
Sandiacre NG10 182 A6
Jackson Cres LE12 205 E3
Jackson Dr 6 NG5 161 A5
Jackson Rd NG15 146 C4
Jacksons Hill
Perlethorpe NG22 62 F3
Perlethorpe NG22 63 A2
Jackson Terr NG20 74 E8
Jacoby Cl NG5 161 C7
Jacques Orch DE55 113 B6
Jade Ct NG18 102 D4
Jadella Cl NG19 101 F5
Jake Rd NG9 184 A3
James Cl NG22 77 C5
James Dr NG14 133 F1
James' Murray Mews NG18 102 C7
James Peacock Inf Sch NG11 196 B7
James St
Annesley Woodhouse NG17 115 A1
Arnold NG5 161 E8
Kimberley NG16 158 F6
Worksop S81 35 E5
James Watt Rd NG24 125 C3
James William Turner Ave
Sutton in Ashfield NG17 100 E1
4 Sutton in Ashfield NG17 114 F8
Jamia Al-Hudaa Ind NG3 173 C8
Japan Rd DN21 15 B1
Japonica Dr NG6 160 B4
Jardine S81 36 B6
Jardines The NG9 171 C1
Jarrow Ct DN21 15 F2
Jarrow Gdns NG5 146 F2
Jarvis Ave NG3 174 B6
Jasmin Cl NG20 72 D6
Jasmine Cl
Beeston NG9 171 D1
5 Nottingham, Broxtowe NG8 159 E1
Nottingham, Glapton NG11 184 C1
Jasmine Ct
Balderton NG24 140 E5
Nottingham NG16 143 B1
Jasmine Dr DE55 99 B7
Jasmine Gdns
Edwalton NG12 185 F2
4 Edwalton NG12 186 A2
Jasmine Rd NG5 160 E3
Jasper Cl NG12 175 E2
Jay Cl LE12 206 A3
Jayne Cl
Carlton NG4 163 A2
Nottingham NG8 171 E5
Jay's Cl NG13 181 A1
Jeacock Dr NG21 118 C8
Jean Revill Cl LN1 56 F5
Jedburgh Cl NG3 223 F4
Jedburgh Wlk NG3 223 F4
Jeffares Cl DE74 203 C3
Jeffries Cl DE7 157 D4
Jeffries Prim Sch NG17 114 F5
Jellicoe St NG20 59 A2
Jenford St NG18 101 E6
Jenkin Close 5 DE7 157 F8
Jenkins Ave
Mansfield NG19 101 D7
Retford DN22 39 F5
Jenned Rd NG5 148 A2
Jenner St 14 NG5 161 B1
Jenness Ave NG5 146 E1
Jennison St
Mansfield NG19 88 A1
Nottingham NG6 160 C7
Jenny Beckett's La NG18 102 F4
Jenny Burton Way NG15 146 C5
Jensen Way NG5 161 B1
Jephson Rd
2 Sutton in Ashfield NG17 100 F1
Sutton in Ashfield NG17 114 F8
Jericho La NG13 192 A3
Jericho Rd NG24 140 D2
Jermyn Dr NG5 147 A1
Jersey Gdns NG3 173 E6
Jersey St NG24 139 F5
Jerusalem LN6 71 F2
Jerusalem Rd LN6 71 F3
Jervis Ct DE7 157 F3
Jesmond Rd NG6 160 D6
Jesse Boot Ave
Nottingham NG7 184 D8
Nottingham NG8 172 D1
Jesse Gray Prim Sch NG2 185 E4
Jessie La DE7 157 D2
Jessop Cl NG24 125 C1
Jessop's La NG4 162 F2
Jessop Way NG24 125 C1
Jewitt Way NG11 196 B7
Job La DN10 20 B7
Job's La LN6 84 F2
Jockey La DN22 50 A5
John Barrow Cl NG21 118 C8
John Blow Prim Sch NG23 112 A8
John Carroll Ct 2 NG3 173 F6
John Carroll L Ctr NG7 222 B3
John Clifford Sch NG9 184 A6
John Coupland Hospl DN21 15 B3
John Gold Av NG24 140 B7
John Hunt Prim Sch NG24 140 C4
John Jenkinson Cl DN21 24 F7
John King Inf Sch NG16 113 D3
John King Workshop Mus★ NG16 113 D3
John Pope Way NG24 125 B4
Johnson Ave NG15 146 B5
Johnson Cl NG16 159 A7
Johnson Dr NG18 102 C3
Johnson Rd NG7 222 A2
Johnsons Rd NG24 140 F2
Johnson Way NG9 183 B2
Johns Rd
Beeston NG9 184 A3
Radcliffe on Trent NG12 176 B3
John St
Ilkeston DE7 157 F1
Nottingham NG7 160 F1
Sutton in Ashfield NG17 100 F4
Worksop S80 35 E3
John T Rice Inf Sch NG19 89 E3
John Wright Cl NG5 146 D1
Josephine Gr 2 NG12 186 A2
Joseph Whitaker Sch NG21 117 F8
Joyce Ave
Beeston NG9 182 E3
Nottingham NG5 161 D5
Joyce Cl NG5 161 D4
Jubilee Acad NG8 171 F8
Jubilee Ave
Beeston NG9 184 B8
Nottingham NG8 172 C1
Jubilee Cl DN10 4 B3
Jubilee Cres 1 DN21 15 D1
Jubilee Ct NG20 72 F2
Jubilee Dr LE11 220 A6
Jubilee House Christian Sch NG9 170 D1
Jubilee Rd
Arnold NG5 161 E6
Retford DN22 39 D5
Sutton in Ashfield NG17 100 D3
Jubilee St
Kimberley NG16 158 E7
Newark-on-Trent NG24 140 A7
3 Nottingham NG2 173 F4
Jubilee The NG25 121 D1
Jubilee Way LE11 220 B4
Jubilee Way N NG18 103 C6
Jubilee Way S NG18 103 B4
Judes Pk NG22 65 F7
Judges St LE11 220 C3
Judson Ave NG9 182 F6
Julian Cl DE7 170 A6
Julian La NG12 164 C1
Julian Rd NG2 174 B1
Julias Wy NG17 115 B8
Julie Ave DE75 143 A1
Julius Cl NG16 143 A4
Jumelles Dr NG14 148 D7
Junction Rd
Long Eaton NG10 194 A6
Sutton in Ashfield NG17 101 B2
Juniper Cl
Bilsthorpe NG22 106 A5
Lidgett NG21 91 C8
Juniper Cl *continued*
Nottingham NG11 184 C1
Juniper Ct NG16 158 C8
Juniper Gdns NG13 178 A4
Juniper Way DN21 15 D1
Jupiter Mws 1 NG18 102 E2
Justinian Cl NG15 146 C8

K

Kansington Ct 5 NG5 161 C3
Kappler Cl NG4 175 A7
Karen Gdns NG9 183 D4
Karen Rise NG5 148 A1
Karsten Ave DN21 15 E3
Katherine Dr NG9 182 F4
Kaye Rd NG19 101 D7
Kayes Ct NG9 182 E7
Kayes Wlk NG1 223 F2
Keane Cl NG21 117 F5
Keats Ave NG17 100 B3
Keats Cl
Arnold NG5 161 D7
Long Eaton NG10 193 B5
Nuthall NG16 159 B6
Keats Cres S81 36 B4
Keats Dr NG15 145 D6
Keats Rd NG24 140 D5
Kedleston Cl
Beeston NG9 183 C5
Long Eaton NG10 193 A5
Kedleston Ct DE55 99 B6
Kedleston Dr DE7 157 D3
Kedlestone Cl NG17 99 F2
Kedleston Rd S81 35 F6
Keel Dr NG13 181 A2
Keeling Cl NG16 144 B1
Keepers Ave 4 NG17 115 A3
Keepers Cl NG6 146 E4
Keep The LE12 205 F1
KEGWORTH 203 C1
Kegworth Bypass
Kegworth DE74 203 B1
Kegworth DE74 212 C8
Kegworth La DE74 212 C5
Kegworth Mus★ DE74 203 C2
Kegworth Rd
Gotham NG11 194 F1
Gotham NG11 195 A1
Ratcliffe on Soar NG11 203 F5
Keighton Hill NG7 172 C1
Keilder Dr NG13 177 C4
Kelfield Cl NG6 160 E5
KELHAM 124 B4
Kelham Dr NG5 161 A2
Kelham Gn NG3 173 F6
Kelham La
Kelham NG23 124 A6
Newark-on-Trent NG24 124 D3
Kelham Mws NG4 174 B8
Kelham Rd
Mansfield NG19 101 E7
Newark-on-Trent NG24 124 E1
Kelham Way NG16 143 E3
Keller Ct DN22 53 B8
Kelling Cl NG5 161 A6
Kelly Wlk NG2 185 B7
Kelsey Ave NG22 77 D3
Kelsey Cl NG9 183 E3
Kelso Gdns NG2 173 B2
Kelstedge Dr NG18 103 B6
Kelstern Cl
Mansfield NG18 103 A7
Nottingham NG8 160 C3
Kelvedon Gdns NG3 173 E6
Kelvin Cl NG9 182 C5
Kelvin Rd
Clipstone NG19 89 D3
Nottingham NG3 174 A7
Kemmel Rd NG6 160 D5
Kempsey Cl NG5 160 E8
Kempson St NG11 196 C6
Kempton Cl NG16 158 E7
Kempton Dr NG5 148 A1
Kempton Rd NG18 102 F7
Kenbrook Rd
Hucknall NG15 146 C8
Papplewick NG15 131 D1
Ken Crocker Way NG24 125 E5
Kendal Cl
Annesley Woodhouse NG16 129 F8
Annesley Woodhouse NG17 130 A8
Hucknall NG15 145 F8
Worksop S81 35 E8
Kendal Ct NG2 186 B8
Kendal Dr NG9 183 D8
Kendale Ct NG3 161 F1
Kendale Gr 1 NG5 161 F1
Kendal Rd NG12 189 A4
Kenia Cl NG4 174 D8
Kenilworth Ave NG17 101 B4
Kenilworth Cl
Saxilby LN1 57 A4
Worksop S80 36 A1
Kenilworth Ct
Beeston NG9 184 A7
Nottingham NG7 223 D1
Kenilworth Dr S81 25 F6
Kenilworth Rd
Beeston NG9 184 A8
Nottingham NG14 173 B3
Nottingham NG7 223 D1
Kenley Cl S81 35 D8
Kenmare Cres DN21 24 F6
Ken Martin Leisure Ctr NG6 146 C1
Kenmore Cl NG19 101 E5
Kenmore Gdns NG3 223 F4
Kennack Cl DE55 113 C6
Kennedy Ave
Long Eaton NG10 193 C5
Mansfield Woodhouse NG19 88 D4
Kennedy Cl NG5 161 E7
Kennedy Ct
Walesby NG22 64 A2
Worksop S81 36 A4
Kennedy Dr NG9 170 E1
Kennedy Rise NG22 64 A2
Kennedy Wlk NG24 140 E4
Kennel Dr DN22 28 C5
Kennel La LN6 71 C1
Kenneth Rd NG5 147 F2
Kennet Paddock NG19 88 D3
Kennington Rd NG8 172 D5
Kenny Ave NG11 185 A5
Kenrick Rd NG3 162 A2
Kenrick St NG4 175 A7
Kensington Cl
Beeston NG9 183 A1
Mansfield Woodhouse NG19 88 E5
Sutton in Ashfield NG17 100 E2
Kensington Gdns
Carlton NG4 174 E7
Ilkeston DE7 170 A7
Kensington Gr LN1 55 B8
Kensington Jun Acad (6) DE7 170 A7
Kensington Pk Cl NG2 185 C5
Kensington Rd NG10 182 A4
Kensington Way 1 S81 35 E7
Kenslow Ave 10 NG7 172 E7
Kent Ave
Beeston NG9 183 F4
Westwood NG16 128 B4
Kent Cl S81 36 A6
Kentmere Cl NG2 186 C7
Kenton Ave NG16 159 D3
Kenton Ct 6 NG2 173 D1
Kent Rd
Eastwood NG16 158 C8
Nottingham NG3 162 A3
Kent St NG1 223 F3
Kentwood Rd NG2 173 F4
Kenyon Rd
Nottingham NG7 172 D3
Nottingham NG8 172 D3
Keppel Ct DE7 157 F3
Kernel Dr NG20 72 D2
Kernel Way NG20 72 D2
Kerry Cl NG21 89 F5
KERSALL 94 B1
Kersall Ct NG6 160 D5
Kersall Dr NG6 160 D5
Kersall Gdns NG15 146 B7
Kersall Rd
Kersall NG22 94 C3
Kersall NG22 108 A8
Kestral Dr NG13 177 F3
Kestral Rd NG18 101 E4
Kestrel Av 13 DN21 15 F1
Kestrel Cl NG4 162 B1
Kestrel Dr NG21 118 B8
Kestrel Gr NG15 145 F7
Kestrel Mws S81 35 C7
Kestrel Rise LN6 84 D2
Keswick Cl
Beeston NG9 183 D8
West Bridgford NG2 186 C7
Keswick Ct
Long Eaton NG10 182 B2
3 Nottingham NG2 173 E4
Keswick Rd S81 35 E7
Keswick St NG2 173 E4
Ketlock Hill La DN22 32 C1
Kettleband Cl NG13 177 D6
KETTLETHORPE 55 C4
Kettlethorpe La LN1 55 E4
Kettlethorpe Rd
Fenton LN1 55 D5
Laughterton LN1 55 B5
Ketton Cl NG5 161 B8
Kett St NG6 160 B6
Keverne Cl NG8 160 C2
Kevin Rd NG8 171 D2
Kew Cl NG11 185 C3
Kew Cres DE75 143 B1
Kew Gdns
New Balderton NG24 140 B4
Nuthall NG8 159 E3
Kexby Wlk DN21 24 F7
Keyes Cl DN10 19 F8
Keyes Ct DN10 19 F8
Keyes Gn DN22 19 F8
Keyes Rise DN10 19 F8
Keys Cl NG6 160 A7
Key St NG3 173 F5
KEYWORTH 197 F2
Keyworth Cl NG19 101 E7
Keyworth Crossdale Drive Sch NG12 197 E4
Keyworth Dr NG19 89 C1
Keyworth L Ctr NG12 197 F2
Keyworth Mdw Nature Reserve★ NG12 207 E6
Keyworth Prim Sch NG12 197 E3
Keyworth Rd
Carlton NG4 162 D3
Widmerpool NG12 208 C5
Wysall NG12 207 C3
Wysall NG12 207 C5
Kibworth Cl NG5 160 F4
Kiddier Ave NG5 162 B7
Kid La S81 16 A5
Kighill La NG15 132 B7
Kilbourne Rd NG5 148 B1
Kilbourn St NG3 223 E4
Kilburn Cl NG9 171 B2
Kilby Ave NG3 174 A6
Kildare Rd NG3 173 F8
Kildonan Cl NG8 159 D2
Killerton Gn NG11 195 E7
Killerton Pk Dr NG11 185 B4
Killisick Jun Sch NG5 162 B8
Killisick Rd NG5 162 B8
Kilnbrook Ave NG5 148 B1
Kiln Pl NG6 160 A6
Kilnwood Cl NG3 174 A7
Kilsby Rd NG7 184 F2
Kilton Ave NG18 103 B7
Kilton Cl S81 36 A4
Kilton Cres S81 36 B4
Kilton Glade S81 36 B4
Kilton Hill S81 36 A5
Kilton Rd S80 36 A3
Kilton Terr S80 36 A3
Kilverston Rd NG10 182 A6
Kilverton Cl NG8 172 C4
Kilvington Rd NG5 162 B7
Kimber Cl NG8 171 D6
KIMBERLEY 158 E8
Kimberley Cl NG16 158 F5
Kimberley L Ctr NG16 159 A6
Kimberley Mws DN11 9 B3
Kimberley Prim Sch
Kimberley NG16 158 F6
Kimberley NG16 159 A6
Kimberley Rd
Nottingham NG2 174 A4
Nuthall NG16 159 C5
Kimberley Sch NG16 159 A6
Kimbolton Ave NG7 222 B2
Kindlewood Dr NG9 183 B1
King Charles St NG1 223 D2
Kingcup Gdns NG11 196 E5
King Edward Ave NG18 102 B4
King Edward Gdns NG10 182 B6
King Edward Prim Sch NG18 102 C6
King Edward Rd LE11 220 C3
King Edward St
Hucknall NG15 146 A6
Nottingham NG1 223 F3
Sandiacre NG10 182 B6
Shirebrook NG20 72 F4
King Edward's Terr DN22 39 F6
King Edwin Prim Sch NG21 75 F1
King Edwins Cl NG21 76 A1
Kingerby Cl DN21 24 E7
Kingfield Cl NG21 118 B8
Kingfield Ct LN5 142 D8
Kingfisher Cl
New Balderton NG24 140 C5
Nottingham NG6 160 D4
Kingfisher Ct
Beeston NG9 184 B5
2 Loughborough LE11 220 A2
Kingfisher Dr NG12 188 A4
Kingfisher Rd
Carlton NG4 175 C7
Mansfield NG19 87 D1
Kingfishers Ct NG2 186 C4
Kingfisher Way
1 Loughborough LE11 220 A2
Sutton in Ashfield NG17 101 B3
Kingfisher Wharf
4 Nottingham NG7 172 F2
1 Nottingham NG7 173 A2
Kingfisher Wlk S81 35 C7
Kingfisher Wy NG22 77 C4
King George Ave LE11 220 D2
King George Rd LE11 220 D2
King George V Ave NG18 102 E5
King Johns Arc NG1 223 E2
King John's Rd NG21 90 A4
Kinglake Pl NG2 173 C2
King Rd NG20 74 A4
Kingrove Ave NG9 183 D6
King St E DN21 24 D7
Kings Ave NG4 162 E2
Kingsbridge Ave NG3 162 C6
Kingsbridge Way NG9 183 C6
Kingsbury Dr NG8 172 A8
Kings Ct NG25 121 E1
Kingsdale S81 36 B8
Kingsdale Cl NG10 193 A5
Kingsdown Mount NG8 171 E2
Kings Dr NG16 143 E7
Kingsford Ave NG7 222 A4
Kingshaugh Camp (Ancient Mon)★ NG22 66 F8
Kingsholm Rd NG17 114 F7
Kingsley Ave NG19 88 D5
Kingsley Cl NG19 88 D4
Kingsley Cres NG10 193 B4
Kingsley Ct
Mansfield Woodhouse NG19 88 D5
Worksop S81 36 B4
Kingsley Dr NG4 175 A7
Kingsley Rd NG2 174 A3
Kingsley St NG17 115 B4
Kings Lodge Dr NG18 101 E4
King's Marina★ NG24 124 F2
Kingsmead DN22 39 D3
Kingsmead Ave NG9 170 D2
Kingsmeadow NG21 118 C8
King's Mill★ NG17 101 C5
King's Mill Ctr Hospl NG17 101 C5
Kings Mill La NG18 101 D4

Kings Mill Rd E
1 Sutton in Ashfield
  NG17 . . . .**100** F1
Sutton in Ashfield NG17,
  NG19 . . . .**114** E8
Kings Mill Rd W NG17. .**114** B7
Kings Mill Way NG18. . .**101** E4
Kings Moor NG5 . . . .**160** E7
Kingsnorth Cl NG24 . . . .**140** A8
King's Pl NG1. . . . .**223** F2
Kings Rd
Long Clawson LE14 . . . . .**211** C2
Sandiacre NG10. . . . .**182** B6
King's Rd NG24 . . . .**124** F1
Kings Sconce Ave 7
  NG24 . . . .**125** A2
Kings Stand NG18 . . . . .**102** E4
King St
Beeston NG9 . . . .**184** A6
Eastwood NG16 . . . .**143** F2
Gainsborough DN21 . . . . . .**24** D7
Hodthorpe S80 . . . .**45** C6
Huthwaite NG17 . . . .**100** B3
Ilkeston DE7 . . . .**157** F1
Kirkby-in-Ashfield NG17 .**115** A4
Long Eaton NG10 . . . .**193** D8
Loughborough LE11. . . . . .**220** C3
Mansfield NG18 . . . .**102** D7
Mansfield Woodhouse
  NG19 . . . .**88** D2
Nether Broughton LE14. .**219** D8
Newark-on-Trent NG24 . . .**139** E7
Nottingham NG1 . . . .**223** E3
Pinxton NG16 . . . .**113** D4
South Normanton DE55. .**113** A5
Southwell NG25 . . . .**121** E1
Southwell NG25 . . . .**136** E8
Sutton in Ashfield NG17 .**100** E2
Tibshelf DE55. . . . .**99** A7
Warsop Vale NG20 . . . .**73** D5
Worksop S80 . . . .**35** E2
Kingsthorpe Cl NG19. . . .**88** E1
Kingston DE7. . . . .**170** A4
Kingston Cl S80 . . . .**47** C8
Kingston Ct
Kingston on Soar NG11. . .**204** D5
14 Nottingham NG2. . . . .**173** E4
Kingston Dr
Cotgrave NG12 . . . .**187** F1
Ollerton NG22 . . . .**77** A3
Kingston Fields NG11. . .**204** D5
Kingston La DE74. . . . . .**203** F3
KINGSTON ON SOAR. . .**204** A4
Kingston Park Acad S81 .**25** F6
Kingston Rd
Carlton in Lindrick S81 . . .**25** E6
3 Kirkby-in-Ashfield
  NG17 . . . .**114** F8
Mansfield NG18 . . . .**102** D7
West Bridgford NG2 . . . . .**185** E6
Worksop S80 . . . .**36** B1
Worksop S80 . . . .**47** B8
Kings Walk NG19 . . . . . .**102** D4
Kingsway
Ilkeston DE7 . . . .**170** A6
Kirkby-in-Ashfield NG17 .**115** B3
Kirkby-in-Ashfield NG17 .**115** B4
Mansfield Woodhouse
  NG19 . . . .**89** A4
New Balderton NG24. . . . .**140** C3
Radcliffe on Trent NG12 .**175** E2
Worksop S80 . . . .**36** A4
Kings Way S80 . . . .**45** C6
Kingsway Ave NG16 . . . . .**77** D6
Kingsway Gdns NG15 . . .**145** E4
Kingsway Prim Sch
  NG17 . . . .**115** B3
Kingsway Rd NG15. . . . .**145** E4
Kingswell Rd NG5 . . . . . .**161** F7
Kingswell Rd NG5 . . . . . .**161** F6
Kings Wlk NG18 . . . .**102** E4
King's Wlk NG1. . . . .**223** E3
Kingswood Cl S81. . . . . . .**16** A5
Kings Wood DN10. . . . . . .**10** A8
Kingswood Dr NG17 . . . .**114** F6
Kingswood Rd
Nottingham NG8 . . . .**172** B5
West Bridgford NG2 . . . . .**185** D5
Kinlet Rd NG5 . . . .**161** A6
KINOULTON. **200** A2
Kinoulton La
Kinoulton NG12 . . . .**209** B8
Kinoulton, Owthorpe
  NG12 . . . .**199** F4
Stanton-on-the-Wolds
  NG12 . . . .**199** A1
Widmerpool NG12 . . . . . .**209** A8
Kinoulton Prim Sch
  NG12 . . . .**199** E1
Kinoulton Rd NG12 . . . . .**188** F2
Kinsdale Wlk NG11 . . . . .**184** E3
Kipling Cl
Nottingham NG11 . . . .**195** C8
Worksop S81 . . . .**36** B5
Kipling St 6 NG18. . . . .**102** A7
Kipps St NG1 . . . .**223** F3
Kirby Cl
Blidworth NG21. . . . .**118** A4
Eastwood NG16. . . . .**144** A3
Kirby Dr DE74 . . . .**203** C1
Kirby Rd NG16. . . . .**144** A3
Kirk Ave DE74 . . . .**203** D2
Kirkbride Ct NG9 . . . . . .**183** B4
Kirkby Cl NG25 . . . .**121** E2
Kirkby Coll NG17. . . . . . .**115** B4
Kirkby Folly Rd NG17. . .**101** B1
Kirkby Gdns NG3 . . . . . .**173** E5
Kirkby Hardwick NG17 .**115** B8
Kirkby House Dr NG17. .**114** E5
KIRKBY-IN-
  ASHFIELD. **115** C4

Kirkby-in-Ashfield Sta
  NG17 . . . .**115** A5
Kirkby La
Pinxton NG16 . . . .**113** F3
Pinxton NG16 . . . .**114** B4
Kirkby Mill View NG17 .**114** E5
Kirkby Rd
Ravenshead NG15 . . . . . .**116** C3
Sutton in Ashfield NG17 .**100** C1
KIRKBY
  WOODHOUSE **114** D1
Kirkby Woodhouse Prim
  Sch NG17 . . . .**114** E1
Kirk Cl NG9. . . . .**183** D4
Kirkdale Cl NG8 . . . .**171** B4
Kirkdale Gdns NG10 . . . .**193** B6
Kirkdale Rd
Long Eaton NG10. . . . . . .**193** B6
Nottingham NG3 . . . .**174** B6
Kirk Dr NG22 . . . .**77** E6
Kirke Cl NG22 . . . .**66** B7
Kirke St DN22 . . . .**39** F7
Kirkewhite Ave NG10 . . .**193** D7
Kirkfell Cl NG2 . . . .**186** C5
Kirk Gate NG24 . . . .**124** F1
Kirkham Dr NG9 . . . .**182** F2
Kirkhill NG13 . . . .**177** E5
Kirk Hill NG13 . . . .**165** B2
Kirk La NG11 . . . .**196** C2
Kirkland Ave NG18. . . . .**101** F6
Kirkland Cl
Sutton Forest Side
  NG17 . . . .**101** B1
Sutton in Ashfield NG17 .**115** B8
Kirkland Dr NG9 . . . .**183** C2
Kirkley Gdns NG5. . . . . .**162** A8
Kirk Ley Rd LE12. . . . . . .**214** D8
KIRKLINGTON. **120** E8
Kirklington Cl NG25. . . .**121** D1
Kirklington Prim Sch
  NG22 . . . .**120** E7
Kirklington Rd
Bilsthorpe NG22 . . . .**105** D2
Bilsthorpe NG22 . . . .**106** A3
Bilsthorpe NG22 . . . .**106** B2
Eakring NG22. . . . .**106** E8
Hockerton NG25 . . . .**121** F6
Hockerton NG25 . . . .**122** A6
Rainworth NG21, NG22 . .**104** C1
Southwell NG25. . . . .**121** D1
Kirkpatrick Dr S81. . . . . .**35** C7
Kirk Rd NG3 . . . .**162** A2
Kirk's Bldgs NG4 . . . . . .**174** D7
Kirks Croft NG21. . . . . . .**117** F4
KIRKSTEAD. **113** D3
Kirkstead Gdns 7 NG7. .**172** F7
Kirkstead Jun Acad
  NG16 . . . .**113** D3
Kirkstead Rd NG16. . . . .**113** D3
Kirkstead St 6 NG7 . . . .**172** F7
Kirkstone Ave NG16. . . .**143** B1
Kirkstone Ct NG10 . . . . .**182** B2
Kirkstone Dr NG2. . . . . .**186** C7
Kirk White Ct NG2 . . . . .**173** D2
Kirtle Cl NG8 . . . .**172** B8
Kirtley Cl NG16 . . . .**159** A8
Kirtley Dr NG2 . . . .**173** A2
Kirtling Cl NG5 . . . .**161** C8
KIRTON. **78** C6
Kirton Ave NG10 . . . .**193** D7
Kirton Cl
Balderton NG24. . . . .**140** C2
Mansfield NG19. . . . .**101** D7
Meden Vale NG20 . . . .**74** E8
Kirton Ct NG22 . . . .**78** B6
Kirton Pk NG22 . . . .**78** C6
Kirton Rd
Egmanton NG22. . . . .**79** D6
Kirton NG22. . . . .**78** F6
Kitchener Wood Nature
  Reserve★ NG22 . . . . . .**78** F5
Kitchener Dr NG18. . . . .**102** C6
Kitchener Gdns S81 . . . . .**35** E8
Kitchener Terr NG20 . . . .**59** A2
Kitson Ave NG16. . . . . . .**128** C4
Kittiwake Mews NG7. . . .**222** A2
Kiwi Cl NG15 . . . .**145** D5
Knapp Ave NG16. . . . . . .**143** F1
Knaton Rd S81 . . . .**25** E7
KNEESALL. **93** F5
Kneesall Cl NG20 . . . .**74** D7
Kneesall Gr NG15 . . . . . .**146** B7
Kneesall Rd
Laxton NG22 . . . .**79** C1
Ossington NG22 . . . .**94** E5
Ossington NG23 . . . .**95** A6
KNEETON. **152** A1
Kneeton Cl
Carlton NG4 . . . .**162** D4
Nottingham NG5 . . . .**161** C4
Kneeton Rd
East Bridgford NG13 . . . .**165** C3
East Bridgford NG13 . . . .**165** E5
Kneeton NG13 . . . .**166** A7
Kneeton Vale NG5 . . . . .**161** C4
Knighton Av NG7 . . . . . .**172** E6
Knighton Ave NG7 . . . . .**222** A4
Knighton Rd NG5 . . . . . .**161** D5
Knightsbridge Dr
Nuthall NG8 . . . .**159** B3
West Bridgford NG2 . . . . .**185** C4
Knightsbridge Gdns
  NG15 . . . .**130** F1
Knights Cl
Beeston NG9 . . . .**182** F2
Beeston NG9 . . . .**183** A2
Nottingham NG5 . . . .**160** F8
West Bridgford NG2 . . . . .**185** C3
Knight's Cl NG13. . . . . . .**166** E4
Knight's Ct NG24 . . . . . .**140** A8

Knights Rd
7 Mansfield NG19 . . . . .**87** D1
Knight St NG4 . . . .**175** A6
Knights Wlk NG22 . . . . . .**29** A6
Knipton Cl NG24 . . . .**140** D3
Knitters Rd DE55 . . . . . .**113** C6
Knole Rd NG8 . . . .**171** E5
Knoll Ave NG15 . . . .**145** D5
Knoll The
Mansfield NG18 . . . .**101** E6
Shirebrook NG20 . . . .**72** D3
Knott End S81 . . . .**16** E3
Knott's Ct NG24 . . . .**140** D4
Knowle Hill NG16 . . . . . .**159** A5
Knowle La NG16 . . . .**159** A5
Knowle Pk NG16 . . . .**159** A5
Knowles Wlk NG5. . . . . .**161** D8
Kozi Kots NG4 . . . .**174** F7
Krebs Cl NG11 . . . .**184** C1
KS4 Support Centre
  NG10 . . . .**193** B4
Kyle View NG5. . . . .**147** A1
Kyme St NG7 . . . .**222** B3
Kynance Cl DE55. . . . . . .**113** C6
Kynance Gdns NG15 . . . .**185** B5
Kyte St NG7 . . . .**222** B2

L

Labray Rd NG14 . . . .**148** E8
Laburnium Cl NG24 . . . .**140** C5
Laburnum Ave
Gainsborough DN21 . . . . .**15** D2
Keyworth NG12 . . . .**198** A2
Kirkby-in-Ashfield NG17 .**114** D3
Shirebrook NG20 . . . .**72** E5
Laburnum Cl
Hathern LE12. . . . .**213** A1
Sandiacre NG10. . . . .**182** B7
South Normanton DE55. .**113** B7
Worksop S80 . . . .**35** D1
Laburnum Gr
Beeston NG9 . . . .**184** B5
Hucknall NG15 . . . .**146** B5
Mansfield Woodhouse
  NG19 . . . .**88** A4
Laburnum Rd S81 . . . .**16** F4
Laburnum St NG3. . . . . .**173** D7
Laceby Ct NG19. . . . .**88** E4
Lace Ctr The★ NG1 . . . .**223** D2
Lace Gdns NG11 . . . .**196** B8
Lacemaker Rd NG24 . . . .**183** F4
Lace Market Theatre The★
  NG1 . . . .**223** E2
Lace Mead NG24. . . . . . .**140** A4
Lace Mkt Ctr The★
  NG1 . . . .**223** E2
Lace Rd NG9 . . . .**183** F7
Lace St NG7 . . . .**172** C1
Lace Way NG14 . . . .**173** E4
Lacewood Cl NG15. . . . . .**146** E4
Lace Wy NG1 . . . .**173** E3
Lacey Ave NG15 . . . .**146** A5
Lacey Cl DE7 . . . .**157** C3
Lacey Fields Rd DE75 . . .**143** B1
Lacey Gn NG24 . . . .**140** E3
Lacey Gr NG15 . . . .**130** D7
Lacey St NG12 . . . .**197** F5
Ladbrooke Cres NG6. . . .**160** C3
Ladybank Rise NG5 . . . .**162** C8
Lady Bay Ave NG2 . . . . .**173** F1
Lady Bay Bridge NG2 . . .**173** E2
Lady Bay Prim Sch
  NG2 . . . .**174** A1
Lady Bay Rd NG2 . . . . . .**174** A1
Lady Bay Ret Pk NG2. . .**173** E3
Ladybird Cl
East Leake LE12 . . . .**214** D7
Loughborough LE11. . . . .**220** C4
Ladybridge Cl NG9. . . . .**183** E3
Ladybrook La NG18 . . . .**101** F7
Ladybrook Pl NG19 . . . .**101** E7
Ladybrook Primary Sch
  NG19 . . . .**101** D8
Ladycroft Ave NG15. . . .**146** A7
Ladycross Inf Sch
  NG10 . . . .**182** B6
Ladylea Cl S80. . . . .**35** B2
Ladylea Rd NG10 . . . .**193** A4
Lady Margaret Cres
  NG20. . . . .**60** C5
Ladysmith Rd NG2. . . . .**174** A4
Ladysmock Gdns NG2. . .**173** D2
Lady Well La DN22. . . . . .**52** B8
Lady Wlk S81. . . . .**35** C7
Ladywood La NG23 . . . . . .**80** E5
Lake Ave NG19 . . . .**101** E7
Lake Farm Rd NG21 . . . .**103** F1
Lakeland Ave NG15 . . . .**146** C5
Lakeland Rd NG14. . . . . .**149** C6
Lakeside Arts Ctr★
  NG7 . . . .**172** D1
Lakeside Ave NG10 . . . . .**193** C4
Lakeside Bsns Ctr
  DE75. . . . .**157** A6
Lakeside Cres NG10. . . . .**193** C5
Lakeside View NG17. . . .**101** B4
Lake St NG7 . . . .**222** B4
Lake View S80 . . . .**61** C6
Lake View Dr NG17 . . . . .**129** F6
Lakeview Prim Sch
  NG21 . . . .**103** F1
Lamartine Cl NG3. . . . . .**223** F4
Lamartine St NG3. . . . . .**223** F3
Lamb Cl NG24 . . . .**139** C2
Lamb Cl Dr NG16 . . . . . .**144** B4
Lambcroft Rd NG16. . . . .**113** D4

Lambert Ct NG9 . . . .**184** B7
Lambert Gdns
Keyworth NG12 . . . .**197** D3
Nottingham NG8 . . . .**172** C8
Lambert Pl LN1. . . . .**57** A5
Lambert St NG7 . . . .**222** C7
Lambeth Rd NG5 . . . .**147** A2
Lambie Cl NG8 . . . .**172** C5
Lamb La S81 . . . .**16** C5
LAMBLEY. **163** C8
Lambley Ave
Mansfield NG18 . . . .**102** F5
Nottingham NG3 . . . .**162** B3
Lambley La
Burton Joyce NG14 . . . . .**163** F5
Carlton NG4 . . . .**162** F3
Lambley Prim Sch
  NG4 . . . .**163** B7
Lambley Rd NG14. . . . . .**150** B1
Lamborne Cl NG9 . . . . . .**183** C8
Lambourne Cres NG14. .**150** F1
Lambourne Dr NG8 . . . . .**172** A5
Lambourne Gdns NG5 . .**162** A5
Lambton Cl DE7 . . . .**157** F2
Lamcote Gdns NG12 . . . .**175** E3
Lamcote Gr NG2. . . . . . .**173** D1
Lamcote Mews NG4 . . . .**175** E3
Lamcote St NG2 . . . .**173** D1
Laming Gap La NG12. . . .**198** E5
Lamins La NG5. . . . .**147** D4
Lammas Cl NG17 . . . .**100** E2
Lammas Dr LE12. . . . . . .**212** F1
Lammas Gdns
East Bridgford NG13 . . . .**165** D4
Nottingham NG2 . . . .**173** D2
Lammas La NG13 . . . .**165** D4
Lammas Rd NG17 . . . . . .**100** E2
Lammas Sch The NG17. .**100** E3
Lamond Cl NG19 . . . .**101** E5
Lamorna Gr NG11. . . . . .**185** B6
Lamplands NG12 . . . . . .**187** F3
Lampman Way S81 . . . . . .**16** A1
Lamp Wood Cl NG14 . . . .**148** E7
Lanark Cl NG8 . . . .**172** C3
Lancaster Ave
Sandiacre NG10. . . . .**182** A4
Stapleford NG9 . . . .**182** E7
Lancaster Cl DN11 . . . .**8** B7
Lancaster Dr DN10 . . . .**9** F8
Lancaster Rd
Bestwood Village NG6. . . .**146** E4
Gringley on the Hill DN10 .**22** A8
Hucknall NG15. . . . .**145** E4
Newark-on-Trent NG24 . . .**125** C4
Nottingham NG3 . . . .**174** B7
Lancaster Way
Nottingham NG8 . . . .**159** D2
Skellingthorpe LN6 . . . . . .**71** F4
Lancaster Wlk S81. . . . . . .**35** E8
Lancastrian Way S81 . . . .**36** A4
Lancelot Dr NG16 . . . . . .**145** A1
Lancelot Way NG19 . . . . .**87** D1
Lancelyn Gdns NG2 . . . .**185** E4
Lancster Cres DN11. . . . . .**8** B7
Landa Gr NG22 . . . .**66** A3
Landa Gr Pk NG22 . . . . . .**66** A3
Landcroft Cres NG5. . . . .**161** A6
Landcroft La LE12 . . . . . .**204** D1
Landmere Cl DE7 . . . . . .**157** C3
Landmere Gdns NG3 . . . .**161** F1
Landmere La
West Bridgford NG11 . . . .**185** C3
West Bridgford NG11,
  NG12 . . . .**185** E1
Landsdowne Ct NG2 . . . . .**39** D4
Landsdowne Rd 9
  NG5 . . . .**160** E4
Landsdown Gr NG10 . . . .**182** F1
Landseer Cl
Nottingham NG7 . . . .**222** A4
Southwell NG25 . . . .**136** C8
Landseer Rd NG25 . . . . . .**136** C8
Lane End NG17 . . . .**115** A5
LANEHAM. **54** B6
Laneham Ave NG5. . . . . .**162** A7
Laneham Rd
Dunham-on-Trent NG22. . .**54** A2
Stokeham DN22. . . . .**53** D6
Laneham St DN22. . . . . . .**43** A1
Lanercost Mews 3 S80. . .**35** F2
Lanesborough Ct LE11 .**220** B2
Laneside Ave NG9 . . . . . .**182** E2
Lanes Prim Sch The
  NG9 . . . .**183** D5
Lane The
Awsworth NG16. . . . .**158** C4
Cotham NG23. . . . .**154** F3
Laneward Cl DE7 . . . .**157** C4
LANGAR. **190** D2
Langar CE Prim Sch
  NG13 . . . .**190** C2
Langar Cl NG5 . . . .**161** C8
Langar Industrial Estate
  NG13 . . . .**201** E6
Langar La
Colston Bassett NG12 . . . .**200** F8
Harby LE14 . . . .**202** A4
Langar Pl NG19 . . . .**103** B8
Langar Rd
Bingham NG13. . . . .**177** E4
Langar NG13 . . . .**190** D3
Tithby NG12. . . . .**189** D3
Langdale Cl NG24. . . . . .**139** E4
Langdale Dr
Long Eaton NG10 . . . .**193** A6
Tickhill DN11 . . . .**8** B7
Langdale Gr NG13 . . . . . .**177** B4
Langdale Rd
Nottingham NG3 . . . .**174** C5
Worksop S81 . . . .**35** F7

Langdon Cl
Long Eaton NG10. . . . . . .**182** A1
Nottingham NG5 . . . .**161** A2
Langdown Cl NG6 . . . . . .**160** A8
Langer Ind Est NG13 . . .**190** E1
LANGFORD. **111** E1
Langford La NG23. . . . . .**111** A3
Langford Moor La
  NG24. . . . .**126** B5
Langford Rd
Arnold NG5 . . . .**162** B7
Mansfield NG18 . . . .**101** D6
Langford St NG17. . . . . .**100** E3
Langham Ave NG3 . . . . .**174** A6
Langham Dr
Burton Joyce NG14 . . . . .**163** F5
Burton Joyce NG14 . . . . .**164** A5
Langham Pl NG18. . . . . .**101** F7
Langholme La DN9 . . . . . .**6** C8
Langland Cl NG5 . . . .**161** A3
Langley Ave
Arnold NG5 . . . .**161** F6
Ilkeston DE7 . . . .**157** D5
Langley Bridge Ind Est
  DE75. . . . .**143** D3
Langley Cl
Mansfield NG19 . . . .**87** E1
Nottingham NG8 . . . .**146** E4
Langley Dr DE74 . . . .**203** C2
LANGLEY MILL. **143** B3
Langley Mill Business Park
  NG16 . . . .**143** B2
Langley Mill CE Inf Sch
  NG16 . . . .**143** B3
Langley Mill Jun Sch
  NG16 . . . .**143** A4
Langley Mill Sta NG16. .**143** B2
Langley Pk NG16 . . . .**143** B3
Langley St 1 S80. . . . .**35** F2
LANGOLD. **16** E4
Langold Ctry Pk★ S81 . . .**16** E2
Langold Dyscarr Com Sch
  S81. . . . .**16** D3
Langstrath Dr NG2 . . . . .**186** C4
Langstrath Rd NG7 . . . . .**184** C1
Langton Ave NG17 . . . . .**114** D6
Langton Cl NG4 . . . .**174** E6
Langton Hollow NG16. . .**128** D6
Langton Rd
Bircotes DN11 . . . .**9** B3
Sutton in Ashfield
  NG17 . . . .**100** E2
Langtree Gdns NG13. . . .**177** F5
Langtry Gr NG7 . . . .**161** A1
Langwell Dr NG19 . . . . . .**89** C2
LANGWITH. **72** F3
Langwith Bassett Com Prim
  Sch NG20 . . . .**72** E2
Langwith Cl DE7 . . . .**157** F5
Langwith Dr NG20 . . . . . .**58** F1
Langwith Lodge Dr
  NG20. . . . .**59** B1
Langwith Maltings
  NG20. . . . .**72** F8
Langwith Rd
Cuckney NG20 . . . .**60** A2
Nether Langwith NG20. . . .**59** E1
Shirebrook NG20 . . . .**72** F5
Langwith-Whaley Thorns
  Sta NG20. . . . .**58** F2
Lansbury Ave NG20 . . . . .**77** C6
Lansbury Dr
Bilsthorpe NG22 . . . .**105** F2
South Normanton DE55. .**113** A6
Lansbury Gdns NG18 . . . .**102** E8
Lansbury Rd
Bilsthorpe NG22 . . . .**105** E2
Edwinstowe NG21 . . . .**76** B2
New Balderton NG24 . . . .**140** C4
Sutton in Ashfield NG17 .**100** F1
Lansdale Ave DN21. . . . . .**24** E3
Lansdown Cl NG9 . . . . . .**183** B4
Lansdowne Ave NG18 . . .**102** D2
Lansdowne Dr
Loughborough LE11. . . . .**220** A1
West Bridgford NG2 . . . . .**185** D4
Lansic La NG14 . . . .**151** C1
Lansing Cl NG11 . . . .**195** F8
Lantern La LE12 . . . .**205** F2
Lantern La Prim Sch
  Annex LE12 . . . .**205** F2
Lanthwaite Cl NG7. . . . .**184** F1
Lanthwaite Rd NG7 . . . .**184** F1
Lapford Cl NG3 . . . .**162** D6
Lapwing Cl DN21 . . . .**14** B2
Larch Ave
Mansfield Woodhouse
  NG19 . . . .**88** B4
Shirebrook NG20 . . . .**72** D4
Larch Cl
Bingham NG13. . . . .**178** A4
Friezeland NG16 . . . .**129** B3
Hucknall NG15. . . . .**146** B5
Nottingham NG5 . . . .**161** C8
Larch Cres
Beeston NG9 . . . .**183** D7
Eastwood NG16 . . . .**143** E4
Larch Ct DN21 . . . .**15** E2
Larchdale Cl DE55 . . . . . .**113** A4
Larchdene Ave NG8. . . . .**171** D3
Larch Dr NG10 . . . .**182** B7
Larch Rd NG22 . . . .**77** D5
Larch Way NG12 . . . .**198** A2
Largs Cl NG5 . . . .**146** E1
Lark Cl
Beeston NG9 . . . .**183** A5
Mansfield NG19. . . . .**87** F1
Larkdale St NG7 . . . .**222** C4
Larkfield Ave NG17 . . . . .**114** E1
Larkfield Rd NG16 . . . . . .**159** B6
Larkfields NG24 . . . .**139** D5

Larkfields Inf Sch
  NG16 . . . .**159** B6
Larkfields Jun Sch
  NG16 . . . .**159** B5
Larkhall Pl NG19 . . . . . .**101** E5
Larklands Ave DE7. . . . .**170** A7
Lark Spinney S81. . . . . . .**35** C3
Larkspur Ave NG5 . . . . .**147** C5
Larkspur Cl
Mansfield NG19 . . . .**88** D2
South Normanton DE55. .**113** A4
Larkwood Cl NG8 . . . . . .**172** A8
Larpit Gn S80. . . . .**45** A5
Larwood Ave S81 . . . .**36** B5
Larwood Cres NG17. . . . .**114** F1
Larwood Gr NG5. . . . . . .**161** C4
Lascelles Ave NG4 . . . . . .**162** D2
Latham St NG6 . . . .**160** B1
Lathkill Ave DE7 . . . .**157** E5
Lathkill Cl NG6. . . . .**146** E1
Lathkilldale Cres NG10 .**193** A5
Lathkill Dr NG16 . . . .**128** F7
Latimer Cl NG6 . . . .**160** C6
Latimer Dr NG9. . . . .**171** B3
Latimer Way NG22 . . . . . .**77** C4
Latin Gr NG15 . . . .**146** C8
LAUGHTERTON. **55** A4
Laughton Ave NG2. . . . .**185** C4
Laughton Cres NG15 . . . .**145** E4
Laughton La DN21 . . . . . .**15** A5
Laughton Rd DN21 . . . . . .**15** C7
Launceston Cres NG11 . .**185** C4
Launder St
Nottingham NG2 . . . .**173** C2
Orston NG13 . . . .**179** F7
Launds Ave NG16 . . . . . .**128** D7
Laurel Ave
Church Warsop NG20 . . . . .**74** A7
Keyworth NG12 . . . .**197** F2
Mansfield NG18 . . . .**102** C5
Mansfield Woodhouse
  NG19 . . . .**89** A1
Misterton DN10. . . . .**6** E3
Laurel Cl
Gainsborough DN21 . . . . .**15** E2
Shirebrook NG20 . . . .**72** D6
Wysall NG12 . . . .**207** C3
Laurel Cres
Long Eaton NG10 . . . .**193** C6
Nuthall NG16 . . . .**159** B6
Laurel Gr
Kirkby-in-Ashfield
  NG17 . . . .**115** C5
South Normanton DE55. .**113** A4
Laurel Rd NG4 . . . .**174** C8
Laurels Cl NG23 . . . .**110** F8
Laurels The DN22. . . . . . .**39** E4
Laurence View Prim Sch
  NG16 . . . .**144** A3
Lauren Gr NG9 . . . .**182** F2
Laurie Ave NG7 . . . .**173** A4
Laurie Cl 4 NG7 . . . .**173** A4
Lauriston Dr NG6 . . . . . .**160** D4
Lavelle Cl NG9. . . . .**183** D1
Lavender Cl
New Ollerton NG22 . . . . . .**77** D4
2 Nottingham NG8. . . . .**159** E1
Shirebrook NG20 . . . .**72** D3
Tibshelf DE55. . . . .**99** B7
Lavender Cres NG4. . . . .**162** D2
Lavender Gdns DE75 . . . .**143** B1
Lavender Gr
Beeston NG9 . . . .**184** B5
Cotgrave NG12 . . . .**188** A5
Lavender Way NG24 . . . .**125** C1
Lavender Wlk NG3 . . . . .**173** D7
Lavenham Mews 8 S80. .**35** F2
Laver Cl NG5 . . . .**162** B7
Laverick Rd NG16. . . . . .**128** A4
Laverock Cl NG16. . . . . .**158** F6
Lavinia Cres NG12 . . . . .**186** A3
Lawdon Rd NG5 . . . .**148** A1
Lawley Ave NG9 . . . .**172** A1
Lawn Ave NG17 . . . .**100** F2
Lawn Gr NG24 . . . .**163** A1
Lawn La
Old Dalby LE14. . . . .**218** F4
Sutton in Ashfield NG17 .**100** F2
Lawn Mill Rd NG16. . . . .**158** F5
Lawn Rd
Carlton in Lindrick S81 . . .**25** E8
Sutton in Ashfield NG17 .**101** B3
Lawns Ave NG17 . . . .**129** F8
Lawns The
Beeston NG9 . . . .**183** B7
Collingham NG23 . . . .**98** B1
Whatton NG13. . . . .**179** A3
Lawnswood Dr NG22 . . . . .**50** A3
Lawnwood La DN22. . . . . .**50** A3
Lawrence Ave
Awsworth NG16. . . . .**158** C4
Carlton NG4 . . . .**174** C5
Eastwood NG16. . . . .**143** F4
Kirkby-in-Ashfield NG17 .**114** E5
Mansfield Woodhouse
  NG19 . . . .**88** B4
Lawrence Cl NG12 . . . . . .**187** F3
Lawrence Cres NG17. . . .**101** B4
Lawrence Dr
Brinsley NG16 . . . .**143** D8
Nottingham NG8 . . . .**159** C2
Lawrence Pk NG16. . . . . .**129** B3
Lawrence Pl NG24 . . . . . .**125** A1
Lawrence St
Long Eaton NG10 . . . .**193** D8
Newark-on-Trent NG24 . . .**125** A1
Sandiacre NG10. . . . .**182** B7
Stapleford NG9 . . . .**182** D6

Lawrence Way **6** NG2 .173 A2
Lawson Ave NG10 . . . . .193 E7
Lawson Cl DN22 . . . . . . .50 F2
Lawson Sq S81 . . . . .18 B2
Lawson St NG2 . . . . . . .222 C4
Lawton Dr NG6 . . . . . . .146 C1
LAXTON 79 C3
Laxton Ave
　Nottingham NG6 . . . . . .160 D5
　Sutton in Ashfield NG17 .101 C1
Laxton Cl **3** NG8 . . . .172 B7
Laxton Dr
　Hucknall NG15 . . . . . . .145 E6
　Meden Vale NG20 . . . . .74 D8
Laxton Rd NG2 . . . . .79 D4
Laxton Visitors Ctr ★
　NG22 . . . . .79 C3
Laycock Ave DN10 . . . . .12 E2
Layton Ave NG18 . . . . .102 A7
Layton Burroughs **11**
　NG18 . . . . .102 A7
LEA 24 F2
Lea Bank DE55 . . . . . . .113 A4
Leabrook Cl NG11 . . . . .184 C3
Leabrook Gdns NG15 .146 C8
Leabrooks Ave
　Mansfield Woodhouse
　NG19 . . . . .88 D5
　Sutton in Ashfield NG17 .101 C1
Leach Cl NG22 . . . . .54 C1
Leachcroft Hill NG25 . . .136 B8
Leach Wy NG11 . . . . . .118 B6
Lea Cl NG15 . . . . .117 B2
Leacroft Rd NG8 . . . . . .172 D8
Lea Ct
　Bingham NG13 . . . . . . .177 D3
　Worksop S80 . . . . .35 C2
Leadale Ave NG15 . . . .146 C8
Leadale Cres NG19 . . . .88 E5
Lead Hill S80 . . . . .35 E2
Leaf Cl NG15 . . . . .131 B1
Leafe Cl NG9 . . . . .183 C2
Leafield DN22 . . . . .39 D8
Leafield Gn NG7 . . . . . .184 E2
Leahurst Gdns NG2 . . . .186 B6
Leahurst Rd NG2 . . . . . .186 B5
Leake La LE12 . . . . . . .214 D3
Leake Rd
　Costock LE12 . . . . .206 B1
　Gotham NG11 . . . . . . .205 C6
Lea La NG16 . . . . .128 F6
Leam Glen NG19 . . . . . .88 D2
Leamington Dr
　Beeston NG9 . . . . .183 C4
　South Normanton DE55 . .113 A5
　Sutton in Ashfield NG17 .114 D8
Leamington Hall NG17 .100 E1
Leamington Prim Sch
　NG17 . . . . .114 F8
Leander Cl
　Nottingham NG11 . . . . .185 B6
　Sutton Forest Side NG17 101 B2
Leaning Row NG7 . . . . .222 B2
Lea Rd
　Gainsborough DN21 . . . .24 E5
　Market Warsop NG20 . . .74 C3
　Ravenshead NG15 . . . .117 B2
　Torksey LN1 . . . . .44 B4
Lea Rd W DN21 . . . . . . .24 D5
Leas Ave NG19 . . . . . . .87 A5
Leas Park Jun Sch
　NG19 . . . . .88 C4
Leas Rd NG19 . . . . .88 D4
Leas The NG14 . . . . . . .164 B5
Leatherlands DE74 . . . . .203 D3
Lea Vale DE55 . . . . . . .113 A4
Leaverton Mws S81 . . . .16 F3
Leaway The NG20 . . . . .72 D3
Le Brun Sq S81 . . . . . . .25 E7
Lechlade Rd NG5 . . . . . .161 A6
Ledbury Vale NG8 . . . . .172 B8
Leech Cl NG16 . . . . . . .158 B7
Leeds Rd S81 . . . . .34 F7
Leeks Rd NG25 . . . . . . .121 E1
Lee La DE75 . . . . .143 B1
Leeming Cl NG22 . . . . . .74 C5
Leeming Ct DN11 . . . . . .9 F6
Leeming La NG19, NG20 .88 E7
Leeming La N NG19 . . . .88 E5
Leeming La S NG17 . . . .88 C2
Leeming Pk NG19 . . . . .88 C3
Leeming St NG18 . . . . .102 B7
Leen Cl
　Bestwood Village NG6 . .146 F4
　Hucknall NG15 . . . . . . .146 C8
Leen Ct NG22 . . . . .78 C4
Leen Dr
　Hucknall NG15 . . . . . . .131 B1
　Nottingham NG6 . . . . . .146 C1
Leen Gate NG7 . . . . . . .172 E2
Leen Mills La NG15 . . . .131 A1
Leen Mills Prim Sch
　NG15 . . . . .146 B8
Leen Pl NG7 . . . . .222 A4
Leen Valley Dr NG20 . . .72 E3
Leen Valley Way
　NG15 . . . . .146 C5
Lee Rd
　Burton Joyce NG14 . . . .164 A5
　Calverton NG14 . . . . . .148 D8
Lees Ave NG19 . . . . . . .101 D7
Lees Barn Rd NG12 . . . .175 D2
Lees Hill St NG2 . . . . . .173 E4
Lees La DE55 . . . . .113 A6
Leeson Cl NG4 . . . . . . .174 E5
Lees Rd NG3 . . . . .162 A2
Leeway Cl NG21 . . . . . .103 E2

Leeway Rd
　Mansfield NG21 . . . . . .103 E2
　Mansfield NG25 . . . . . .121 D1
Legion Dr NG17 . . . . . .100 D6
Leicester Cres S81 . . . . .35 E7
Leicester Rd LE11 . . . . .220 C2
Leicester St NG10 . . . . .193 E6
Leigh Cl NG2 . . . . .185 C6
Leigh Rd NG9 . . . . .182 F3
Leighton St NG3 . . . . . .173 F6
Leiston Gdns NG5 . . . . .161 A8
Leivers Ave NG5 . . . . . .161 F8
Leivers Ct LE12 . . . . . . .205 E1
Lema Cl NG6 . . . . .160 D7
Lemont Rd NG19 . . . . . .89 A2
Lemynton St LE11 . . . . .220 B4
Lendrum Ct NG14 . . . . .163 F4
Len Maynard Ct NG4 . . .174 A6
Lennox St NG1 . . . . . . .223 F3
Lenton Ave
　Nottingham NG7 . . . . . .222 C1
　Tollerton NG12 . . . . . . .186 C1
Lenton Bvd NG7 . . . . . .222 B2
Lenton Cir NG12 . . . . . .186 C1
Lenton Ct NG7 . . . . . . .222 B2
Lenton Hall Dr NG7 . . . .172 C1
Lenton Ind Est E NG7 . .184 F8
Lenton Ind Est W NG7 . .184 F8
Lenton La NG7 . . . . .184 F8
Lenton Manor NG7 . . . .222 A1
Lenton Prim Sch NG7 . . .222 B1
Lenton Rd NG7 . . . . . . .223 D2
Lenton St NG10 . . . . . .182 C7
Leonard Ave NG5 . . . . .161 B2
Leonard Cheshire Cl
　DE75 . . . . .143 B1
Leonard Mews NG9 . . . .183 B1
Leonard St NG6 . . . . . .160 B5
Leopold St
　Long Eaton NG10 . . . . .193 D8
　Loughborough LE11 . . . .220 A5
　Sutton in Ashfield NG17 .100 E1
Le Page Ct NG8 . . . . . .172 A7
Leroy Wallace Ave
　NG7 . . . . .222 B4
Lerwick Cl
　Nottingham NG11 . . . . .185 A1
　Worksop S81 . . . . .35 E8
Leslie Ave
　Beeston NG9 . . . . .183 F5
　Kimberley NG16 . . . . . .158 F5
Leslie Gr NG14 . . . . . . .148 F7
Leslie Rd NG7 . . . . .173 A8
Less Field NG25 . . . . . .136 D7
Letchworth Cres NG3 . . .183 C4
LETWELL 16 A3
Levellers Way NG24 . . . .140 E8
Levels La
　Blaxton DN9 . . . . .1 A8
　Misson DN10 . . . . .4 B6
Leverton Gn NG7 . . . . . .184 E2
Leverton Rd
　Mansfield NG19 . . . . . .101 E7
　Retford DN22 . . . . .40 A8
　Retford DN22 . . . . .40 C7
　Sturton le Steeple DN22 . .32 D4
Levertons Pl NG15 . . . . .146 B4
Leverton Wlk NG5 . . . . .162 A8
Levesley Gdns LE14 . . . .202 F3
Levick Ct **2** NG2 . . . . .173 C2
Lewcote La DE7 . . . . . . .157 A1
Lewindon Ct NG5 . . . . .161 E4
Lewis Cl NG3 . . . . .223 F4
Lewis Cres NG15 . . . . . .130 D7
Lewis St DN21 . . . . .24 D8
Lewis Way NG16 . . . . . .147 B5
Lewsey Cl NG9 . . . . . . .183 B2
Lexington Ct NG22 . . . . .65 F2
Lexington Gdns
　Nottingham NG5 . . . . . .161 D4
　Tuxford NG22 . . . . .65 F2
Ley Bank NG18 . . . . . . .103 A4
Leybourne Dr NG5 . . . . .160 E6
Ley Croft NG19 . . . . . . .88 D5
Ley La
　East Drayton DN22 . . . .53 D3
　Mansfield Woodhouse
　NG19 . . . . .88 D4
Leyland Cl NG9 . . . . . . .182 F2
Leys Ct NG11 . . . . .196 C6
Leys La
　Gringley on the Hill DN10 .12 B2
　Tuxford NG22 . . . . .65 A3
Leys Rd NG11 . . . . .196 C6
Ley St NG4 . . . . .175 A7
Leys The
　Lowdham NG14 . . . . . .150 D2
　Normanton-on-the-Wolds
　NG12 . . . . .197 F7
Leyton Ave NG17 . . . . .101 A5
Leyton Cres NG9 . . . . . .184 B5
Liber Cl NG18 . . . . .102 F8
Liberty Cl NG19 . . . . . . .87 F1
Library Rd NG7 . . . . . . .172 C1
Lichfield Ave NG18 . . . .102 C2
Lichfield Cl
　Beeston NG9 . . . . .182 E3
　Mansfield NG18 . . . . . .102 C2
　Worksop S81 . . . . .36 A7
Lichfield La NG18 . . . . .102 D3
Lichfield Rd NG2 . . . . . .174 A4
Lichfield Wlk S81 . . . . . .25 E7
Liddell Gr NG8 . . . . . . .171 F4
Liddington St NG7 . . . . .160 F1
LIDGETT 91 B8
Lidgett La NG21 . . . . . . .76 C3

Lido Cl NG6 . . . . .145 C1
Lievesley Gr **1** NG4 . . .162 E3
Lifton Ave DN22 . . . . . . .29 E1
Lightfoot Cl NG24 . . . . .140 E8
Lightning Gr NG15 . . . . .145 D3
Lilac Ave NG4 . . . . .174 C8
Lilac Cl
　Keyworth NG12 . . . . . . .198 A2
　Newark-on-Trent NG24 . .139 F4
　7 Nottingham NG8 . . . .159 E1
　Sutton cum Lound DN22 . .29 A7
Lilac Cres NG9 . . . . .184 B5
Lilac Gr
　Bawtry DN10 . . . . .9 F7
　Beeston NG9 . . . . .184 B5
　Clipstone NG19 . . . . . . .89 D2
　Glapwell S44 . . . . .86 B8
　Kirkby-in-Ashfield NG17 .114 D4
　Market Warsop NG20 . . .73 F7
　Shirebrook NG20 . . . . . .72 E5
　South Normanton DE55 . .113 A4
Lilac Mews DE7 . . . . . . .157 D3
Lilac Rd NG15 . . . . .146 B8
Lilac Tree Gr S81 . . . . . .25 E7
Lilburne Cl NG24 . . . . . .140 E8
Lillee Ct S81 . . . . .36 B5
Lilley Cl NG18 . . . . .128 E6
Lillington Rd NG6 . . . . . .160 B7
Lily Ave NG4 . . . . .175 A7
Lily Gr NG9 . . . . .184 B5
Lily La NG24 . . . . .125 D1
Lily Way NG22 . . . . .77 C6
Limb Cres NG17 . . . . . .100 F1
Lime Ave
　Firbeck S81 . . . . .16 A6
　Huthwaite NG17 . . . . . .100 A3
　Langley Mill NG16 . . . . .143 C2
　Loughborough LE11 . . . .220 C3
　Sutton in Ashfield NG17 .100 F4
Lime Cl
　Nuthall NG16 . . . . .159 A6
　Pinxton NG16 . . . . .113 D4
　Radcliffe on Trent NG12 .175 F3
　Torksey Lock LN1 . . . . .44 B1
　Lime Cres NG20 . . . . . .73 F7
Lime Gr
　Bottesford NG13 . . . . . .181 A2
　Long Eaton NG10 . . . . .193 D8
　Mansfield Woodhouse
　NG19 . . . . .89 C1
　Newark-on-Trent NG24 . .139 F4
　Retford DN22 . . . . .39 D7
　Sandiacre NG10 . . . . . .182 B6
　South Normanton DE55 . .113 A5
　Stapleford NG9 . . . . . .182 D5
Lime Gr Ave NG9 . . . . . .183 E5
Limehurst Ave LE11 . . . .220 A5
Limehurst High Sch
　LE11 . . . . .220 A5
Limekiln Ct NG6 . . . . . .160 A8
Lime Kiln Pl NG18 . . . . .102 B6
Limekiln Way S81 . . . . .34 F7
Lime La NG5 . . . . .147 F4
Limes Ave NG20 . . . . . .59 A2
Limes Cl NG16 . . . . . . .143 C4
Limes Cres NG20 . . . . . .72 D5
Limes Ct NG17 . . . . . . .101 C1
Lime St
　Kirkby-in-Ashfield
　NG17 . . . . .115 A5
　Nottingham NG6 . . . . . .160 B7
　Sutton in Ashfield NG17 .101 A3
Limes The
　Beckingham DN10 . . . . .14 B1
　Farnsfield NG22 . . . . . .119 F6
Limestone Ri NG19 . . . .102 A3
Limestone Rise NG19 . . .88 A1
Limestone Terr NG18 . . .88 B4
Lime Terr NG10 . . . . . . .193 D8
Limetree Ave
　Carlton in Lindrick S81 . .25 E7
　Gainsborough DN21 . . . .15 D1
　Glapwell S44 . . . . .86 B8
　Kirkby-in-Ashfield NG17 .114 D3
　Mansfield Woodhouse
　NG19 . . . . .88 A5
　Nottingham NG8 . . . . . .160 C3
　Retford DN22 . . . . .39 D7
　Sutton in Ashfield NG17 .100 D6
Limetree Cl NG12 . . . . .197 F2
Lime Tree Ave
　Carlton in Lindrick S81 . .25 E7
　Gainsborough DN21 . . . .15 D1
　Glapwell S44 . . . . .86 B8
　Kirkby-in-Ashfield NG17 .114 F5
　Mansfield Woodhouse
　NG19 . . . . .88 A5
　Nottingham NG8 . . . . . .160 C3
　Retford DN22 . . . . .39 D7
　Sutton in Ashfield NG17 .100 D6
Lime Tree Cl
　Collingham NG23 . . . . . .112 A8
　New Ollerton NG22 . . . .77 D5
Lime Tree Cres DN10 . . .9 F7
Lime Tree Ct NG9 . . . . .172 A1
Lime Tree Dr NG18 . . . .116 E7
Lime Tree Gdns NG16 . .150 E1
Lime Tree Mws S81 . . . .36 B5
Lime Tree Pl
　Mansfield NG18 . . . . . .102 C6
　Rainworth NG21 . . . . . .104 C1
Lime Tree Rd
　Elkesley DN22 . . . . . . .50 B3
　Hucknall NG15 . . . . . . .146 B4
　New Ollerton NG22 . . . .77 C5

Linby Dr
　Bircotes DN11 . . . . .9 B3
　Nottingham NG8 . . . . . .159 D2
Linby Gr NG15 . . . . . . .146 B7
Linby La NG15 . . . . . . .131 C3
Linby Rd
　Hucknall NG15 . . . . . . .131 B1
　Hucknall NG15 . . . . . . .146 B8
Linby St NG6 . . . . .160 C8
Linby Wk NG15 . . . . . . .131 A1
Linby Wlk NG15 . . . . . .146 A8
Lincoln Ave NG10 . . . . .182 A4
Lincoln Cir NG7 . . . . . . .222 C2
Lincoln Cl
　Stapleford NG9 . . . . . . .170 E1
　Tibshelf DE55 . . . . .99 A6
Lincoln Ct
　Newark-on-Trent NG24 . .125 B2
　Nottingham NG8 . . . . . .171 E7
Lincoln Dr NG19 . . . . . .88 D4
Lincoln Gr
　Radcliffe on Trent
　NG12 . . . . .175 F3
　Radcliffe on Trent NG12 .176 A3
Lincoln La LN1 . . . . .55 E5
Lincoln Rd
　Eagle LN6 . . . . .84 D3
　East Markham NG22 . . . .66 A7
　East Markham NG22 . . . .66 C7
　Fenton LN1 . . . . .55 D6
　Newark-on-Trent NG24 . .125 B3
　Saxilby LN1 . . . . .57 D3
　Torksey LN1 . . . . .44 B1
　Tuxford NG22 . . . . .66 A3
Lincoln Rd Bridge
　NG24 . . . . .125 A2
Lincoln Red Cl DN22 . . .39 C4
Lincoln St
　Gainsborough DN21 . . . .15 C1
　Newark-on-Trent NG24 . .125 A2
　Nottingham NG1 . . . . . .223 E2
　Nottingham, Old Basford
　NG6 . . . . .160 E3
　Tibshelf DE55 . . . . .99 A6
　Worksop S80 . . . . .36 A1
Lincoln View S80 . . . . . .36 A2
Lindale Cl NG2 . . . . . . .186 C6
Lindbergh Cl S80 . . . . . .35 C2
Lindbridge Rd NG8 . . . .159 F2
Lind Cl NG21 . . . . .103 F1
Linden Ave
　New Balderton NG24 . . .140 B5
　Nottingham NG11 . . . . .184 C1
　Tuxford NG22 . . . . .66 A2
Linden Gr
　Beeston NG9 . . . . .184 A5
　Carlton NG4 . . . . .163 B1
　Kirkby-in-Ashfield NG17 .114 D6
　Sandiacre NG10 . . . . . .182 A7
　Shirebrook NG20 . . . . . .72 F4
　Stapleford NG9 . . . . . .182 E6
Linden Pl NG5 . . . . .162 C6
Linden St
　Mansfield NG18 . . . . . .102 F8
　Nottingham NG3 . . . . . .173 D7
　Shirebrook NG20 . . . . . .72 F4
　Shirebrook NG20 . . . . . .73 A4
Linden Terr DN21 . . . . . .24 D7
Linden Way City Hospital
　Campus NG5 161 . . . . . .B5
Lindfield Cl NG8 . . . . . .160 A2
Lindfield Rd NG8 . . . . . .159 F2
Lindholme Way
　Dalestorth NG17 . . . . . .101 A5
　Sutton in Ashfield NG17 .100 F5
Lindhurst La NG18 . . . . .102 F4
Lindhurst Way W
　NG18 . . . . .102 E1
Lindisfarne Gdns **6**
　NG5 . . . . .147 A1
Lindley Ave NG17 . . . . .100 D2
Lindley's La NG17 . . . . .115 A3
Lindley St
　Eastwood NG16 . . . . . .144 B4
　Mansfield NG18 . . . . . .102 A7
　Selston NG16 . . . . .128 D6
Lindley Terr **2** NG7 . . .172 E7
Lindrick DN11 . . . . .8 A6
Lindrick Cl
　Carlton in Lindrick S81 . .25 F7
　Mansfield Woodhouse
　NG19 . . . . .88 D6
　West Bridgford NG2 . . .186 C4
　Worksop S81 . . . . .35 F5
Lindrick Ct DN22 . . . . . .39 D2
Lindrick Dr DN21 . . . . . .15 E3
Lindrick La DN11 . . . . . .8 A6
Lindrick Nook S81 . . . . .35 F6
Lindrick Rd NG17 . . . . .114 F7
Lindsay Ave
　Annesley Woodhouse
　NG17 . . . . .115 A1
　Newark-on-Trent NG24 . .139 F4
　Tollerton NG12 . . . . . . .186 E3
Lindsay Cl NG18 . . . . . .102 A6
Lindsey Cl DN21 . . . . . .24 F6
Lindsey Dr
　Gainsborough DN21 . . . .15 F2
　Mansfield NG18 . . . . . .103 A3
Lindsey Rd DN11 . . . . . .9 A5
Lindum Gr **3** NG2 . . . . .173 F5
Lindum Mews NG24 . . . .140 A8
Lindum St NG18 . . . . . .102 C6
Lindum St NG24 . . . . . .140 A8
Lindum Wy LN1 . . . . . . .44 C1
Lindy Cl NG12 . . . . .199 F2
Linecroft La DN10 . . . . .14 C7
Linette Cl NG5 . . . . .161 A2

Linford Ct NG9 . . . . .171 B3
Ling Beeches DN22 . . . .39 D4
Ling Cres NG11 . . . . . . .196 C6
Lingdale Cl LE11 . . . . . .220 B1
Ling Dr **8** DN21 . . . . . . .15 F1
Lingfield Cl
　Mansfield NG18 . . . . . .102 F5
　Saxilby LN1 . . . . .57 A4
Lingfield Ct NG8 . . . . . .171 D3
Lingford NG12 . . . . .188 A3
Lingford St NG15 . . . . . .146 B6
Lingforest Cl NG18 . . . .103 A5
Lingforest **3** NG18 . . .103 A5
Lingforest Rd NG18 . . . .103 A5
Lingmell Cl NG2 . . . . . .186 C6
Ling Rd LE11 . . . . .220 B1
Lings Bar Hospl NG2 . . .186 B6
Lings **11** DE7 . . . . .157 F5
Lings La NG12 . . . . .207 F2
Lings View NG20 . . . . . .74 C3
Lings Wood Rd DN10 . . .10 D3
Lingwood Gr
　Mansfield NG18 . . . . . .102 F7
　Mansfield NG18 . . . . . .103 A4
Lingwood La NG14 . . . . .149 B3
Linkin Rd NG9 . . . . .183 C6
Linkmel Cl NG2 . . . . . . .173 A1
Linkmel Rd NG16 . . . . . .143 C3
Linklands Ct NG11 . . . . .185 C2
Links The
　Mansfield NG18 . . . . . .103 B6
　Selston NG16 . . . . .128 D6
Linley Cl NG23 . . . . .112 A8
Linnell St NG3 . . . . .173 F6
Linnet Cl **5** NG17 . . . . .115 A3
Linnet Dr NG18 . . . . . . .102 E7
Linnets The S81 . . . . . . .35 D7
Linnet Wy NG15 . . . . . .145 F6
Linsdale Cl NG8 . . . . . .171 B5
Linsdale Gdns NG4 . . . .162 D4
Linseed Ave NG24 . . . . .125 C4
Linseed Gr NG18 . . . . . .102 D1
Lintin Ave NG21 . . . . . .75 F2
Linton Cl
　Bawtry DN11 . . . . .9 F6
　Farndon NG24 . . . . . . .139 B5
　Mansfield NG18 . . . . . .103 B6
Linton Dr NG8 . . . . .77 F5
Linton Rise NG3 . . . . . .174 A6
Linwood Cl DN21 . . . . . .24 F7
Linwood Cres
　Eastwood NG16 . . . . . .144 A1
　Ravenshead NG15 . . . .116 F3
Linwood Ct NG19 . . . . . .88 E4
Lion Cl NG8 . . . . .160 C2
Liquorice La S81 . . . . . .26 A4
Lisle St **1** LE11 . . . . . . .220 A5
Lismore Cl NG7 . . . . . . .222 A3
Lismore Ct NG19 . . . . . .101 D5
Lissington Rd DN21 . . . .24 E7
Lister Ct **4** NG7 . . . . . .172 E2
Lister Gate NG1 . . . . . . .223 E2
Lister Rd NG7 . . . . .172 E2
Listowel Cres NG11 . . . .195 E8
Litchen Cl DE7 . . . . . . .157 F2
Litchfield Cl NG10 . . . . .194 A7
Litchfield Rise NG5 . . . .147 E2
Little Acre NG19 . . . . . . .88 E5
Little Barn Cl NG18 . . . .102 F6
Little Barn Gdns NG18 . .102 F5
Little Barn La NG18 . . . .102 F6
Little Belt The DN21 . . . .15 D3
Littleborough Rd
　Littleborough DN22 . . . .33 E1
　Sturton le Steeple DN22 . .33 B3
Little Bounds NG11 . . . .185 D1
Little Breck DE55 . . . . . .113 A4
LITTLE CARLTON 124 B8
Little Carter La NG18 . . .102 E7
Little Debdale La NG19 . .87 F1
Little Green NG13 . . . . .166 C3
Littlegreen Rd NG5 . . . .161 F5
LITTLE GRINGLEY 40 E7
Little Gringley La DN22 . .40 D7
Little Hallam La DE7 . . . .170 A6
Little Haven NG19 . . . . .89 B1
Little Hayes NG2 . . . . . .185 C4
Little Holland Gd NG16 . .159 B7
Little Hollies NG19 . . . . .89 A2
Little John Ave NG20 . . .74 C2
Little John Cl NG22 . . . .77 D6
Little John Dr NG21 . . . .104 A1
Little John Wlk **1**
　NG3 . . . . .173 D7
Little La
　Blyth S81 . . . . .18 B3
　Calverton NG14 . . . . . .148 D7
　Collingham NG23 . . . . . .111 F7
　Edingley NG22 . . . . . . .120 D3
　Gringley on the Hill DN10 .12 B2
　Huthwaite NG17 . . . . . .99 E2
　Kimberley NG16 . . . . . .158 F5
　Pleasleyhill NG19 . . . . . .87 B5
　Shirebrook NG20 . . . . . .72 D3
　Thorpe Salvin S80 . . . . .34 B6
　Tollerton NG12 . . . . . . .186 E3
Little Lincoln NG12 . . . .207 C2
Little London La NG12 . .207 C3
Little Lunnon NG11 . . . .194 E6
Little Mdw NG12 . . . . . .188 A2
Little Meadow Cl **1**
　DE7 . . . . .157 E2
Littlemoor La NG11 . . . .196 E3
Little Moor La LE11 . . . .220 C4
Little Oak Ave NG17 . . . .130 A7
Little Oak Dr NG17 . . . .129 F7
Little Ox NG4 . . . . .174 F4

Little Ricket La NG15 . . .116 D3
Little Tennis St S NG2 . .174 A2
Little Tennis St NG2 . . . .174 A3
Little Top La
　Lound DN22 . . . . .20 C1
　Lound DN22 . . . . .29 C8
Little Wlk DN21 . . . . .7 D1
Littlewood Gdns NG8 . . .171 C5
Littlewood La
　Mansfield Woodhouse
　NG19 . . . . .88 A6
　Shirebrook NG19 . . . . . .87 F8
　Shirebrook NG20 . . . . . .72 F1
Littleworth NG18 . . . . . .102 C5
Litton Ave NG17 . . . . . .101 A5
Litton Cl
　Arnold NG5 . . . . .161 E4
　Ilkeston DE7 . . . . .157 E4
　Ravenshead NG15 . . . .117 A3
Littondale S81 . . . . .36 A7
Litton Rd NG19 . . . . . . .88 E3
Liveret Way LE12 . . . . . .214 E8
Liverpool St NG3 . . . . . .173 E5
Livingstone St NG15 . . .130 E6
Llanberis Gr NG8 . . . . . .160 C2
Lloyd St NG5 . . . . .161 C2
Loach Ct NG8 . . . . .172 C5
Lobelia Cl NG3 . . . . . . .173 D7
Lockerbie St NG4 . . . . . .174 F6
Lock La
　Collingham NG23 . . . . . .111 B8
　Long Eaton NG10 . . . . .193 C4
　Sandiacre NG10 . . . . . .182 C4
Locksley La NG11 . . . . . .184 E4
Lockwell Hill NG2 . . . . .105 C2
Lockwood Cl
　Beeston NG9 . . . . .184 C4
　6 Nottingham NG5 . . . .147 A1
Lockwood Dr DN22 . . . .39 D3
Lodge Cl
　Arnold NG5 . . . . .147 E2
　Nottingham NG8 . . . . . .172 D8
Lodge Farm La NG5 . . . .147 E1
Lodgefield La NG14 . . . .151 E2
Lodge La
　Elston NG23 . . . . .153 C5
　Kirkby-in-Ashfield NG17 .115 D4
　Screveton NG13 . . . . . .166 D5
　Tuxford NG22 . . . . .66 A1
Lodge Lane Ind Est
　NG22 . . . . .66 B1
Lodge Rd
　Eastwood NG16 . . . . . .158 A6
　Long Eaton NG10 . . . . .193 D5
Lodgewood Cl NG6 . . . .160 A4
Lodore Cl NG2 . . . . .186 C6
Lodore Rd S81 . . . . .35 F7
Logan St NG6 . . . . .160 D6
Lois Ave NG7 . . . . .222 B1
Lombard Cl NG7 . . . . . .222 B2
Lombard St
　Newark-on-Trent NG24 . .139 F8
　Orston NG13 . . . . .180 A6
Lonan Cl NG19 . . . . . . .89 A2
London La
　Willoughby-on-t-W
　LE12 . . . . .217 D7
　Wymeswold LE12 . . . . .216 B3
London Rd
　Kegworth DE74 . . . . . . .203 D1
　Newark-on-Trent NG24 . .140 C5
　Nottingham NG2 . . . . . .173 D2
　Retford DN22 . . . . .40 A3
Longacre NG5 . . . . .161 F4
Long Acre NG15 . . . . . .145 D7
Longbeck Ave NG3 . . . .162 A1
Longbourne Ct **3** NG19 .88 F2
Long Brecks La S81 . . . .18 C1
LONG CLAWSON 211 D3
Long Clawson CE Prim Sch
　LE14 . . . . .211 D3
Longcliff Cl LE14 . . . . . .218 E4
Longcliff Hill LE14 . . . . .218 E4
Longcroft Ave DE7 . . . . .157 E5
Longcroft View S80 . . . .45 A6
Longdale NG19 . . . . .88 E1
Longdale Ave NG15 . . . .117 A1
Longdale La
　Arnold NG15 . . . . .132 F5
　Calverton NG21 . . . . . .133 B5
　Ravenshead NG15 . . . .132 C6
Longdale Rd NG5 . . . . . .161 D6
Longden Cl NG9 . . . . . . .170 F2
Longden St **5** NG3 . . . .173 E5
Longden Terr
　Market Warsop NG20 . . .74 B4
　Stanton Hill NG17 . . . . .100 D6
LONG EATON 193 C6
Long Eaton Sch The
　NG10 . . . . .193 C6
Long Eaton Sta NG10 . . .193 C5
Longfellow Dr
　Balderton NG24 . . . . . .140 D5
　Worksop S81 . . . . .36 B4
Longfellows NG15 . . . . .161 B8
Longfield Ave NG8 . . . . .171 C7
Longfield La DE7 . . . . . .170 A5
Longford Cres NG6 . . . .146 C2
Longford Wlk NG18 . . . .103 B6
Longhedge La
　Bottesford NG13 . . . . . .180 F3
　Flawborough NG13,
　NG23 . . . . .168 A2
　Orston NG13 . . . . .180 E7
　Pleasley NG19 . . . . . . .86 D6
　Sibthorpe NG13 . . . . . .167 E5
Longhill Rise NG17 . . . .114 F1
Long Hill Rise NG15 . . . .145 F6
Longhirst Dr NG5 . . . . . .147 F2
Long Hollow Way
　NG24 . . . . .125 D4

Longholme Rd DN22 . . . 40 B8
Longhurst S81 . . . . 36 B5
Longhurst View S80 . . . 45 A5
Long La
 Barkestone-le-Vale
  NG13 . . . . 192 F1
 Barnby in the Willows
  NG24 . . . . 141 F7
 Beeston NG9 . . . . . . 183 E3
 Carlton in Lindrick S81 . 25 F6
 East Drayton DN22 . . . 53 C3
 Farndon NG24 . . . . . 138 F7
 Farndon NG24 . . . . . 139 B5
 Hickling LE14 . . . . . 210 C6
 Kegworth DE74 . . . . 203 D5
 Shipley DE75 . . . . . . 157 D6
 Shirebrook NG20 . . . . 72 E3
 Stathern LE14 . . . . . 202 F4
 Watnall NG16 . . . . . . 145 A1
Longland La NG22 . . . . 119 D4
Longlands Cl NG9 . . . . 184 B4
Longlands Dr NG2 . . . . 186 D5
Longlands Rd NG9 . . . . 184 B4
Long Lea Dr NG16 . . . . 143 A5
Longleat Cres NG9 . . . . 183 C5
Long Mdw
 Farnsfield NG22 . . . . 120 A6
 Mansfield Woodhouse
  NG19 . . . . 88 D5
Long Mdw Hill NG14 . . . 150 A2
Long Mdws DN10 . . . . . 11 B3
Longmead Cl NG5 . . . . 161 C6
Longmead Dr
 Fiskerton NG25 . . . . 137 E3
 Nottingham NG5 . . . . 161 C6
Long Meadow NG22 . . . 120 A6
Longmoor Ave NG14 . . . 164 E8
Longmoor Gdns NG10 . . 182 B2
Longmoor La
 Long Eaton NG10 . . . 182 A2
 Scarrington NG13 . . . 179 B8
Longmoor Prim Sch
  NG10 . . . . 182 C3
Longmoor Rd NG10 . . . 182 B2
Longnor Wlk NG18 . . . . 103 B6
Longridge Rd NG5 . . . . 161 F4
Long Row
 Kingston on Soar LE12 . 204 A4
 Newark-on-Trent NG24 . 140 B8
 Nottingham NG1 . . . . 223 E2
Long Row W NG1 . . . . 223 E2
Longshaw Rd NG18 . . . 103 B6
Long Sleets DE55 . . . . 113 C4
Longster La NG20 . . . . 73 C3
Longstone Way NG19 . . 101 D6
Long Stoop Way NG19 . . 103 B7
Longue Dr NG14 . . . . . 148 D7
Longwall Ave NG2 . . . . 173 A1
Longwall La NG21 . . . . 76 D3
Longwest Croft NG14 . . 148 C7
LONG WHATTON 212 C4
Long Whatton CE Prim Sch
  LE12 . . . . 212 C3
Longwood Ct NG5 . . . . 160 F8
Longwood Dr NG17 . . . 100 E1
Longwood Inf Acad
  NG16 . . . . 113 C2
Longwood Rd NG16 . . . 113 C2
Lonscale Cl NG2 . . . . . 186 C5
Lonsdale Dr NG9 . . . . 182 E1
Lonsdale Rd NG7 . . . . 222 A4
Loom Gdns NG24 . . . . 140 A4
Lord Haddon Rd DE7 . . 157 E1
Lord Hawke Way
  NG24 . . . . 140 A5
Lord Nelson St NG2 . . . 173 E4
Lords Ct DN22 . . . . . . 39 E4
Lordship La NG13 . . . . 180 A6
Lord St
 Gainsborough DN21 . . 24 C8
 Mansfield NG18 . . . . 102 B5
 Nottingham NG2 . . . . 173 E4
Lords Wood Rd DN11 . . .8 F2
Lorimer Ave NG4 . . . . 162 F2
Lorne Gr NG12 . . . . . . 175 F3
Lorne Wlk 6 NG3 . . . . 173 C7
Lortas Rd NG5 . . . . . . 160 F2
Loscoe Gdns 2 NG5 . . . 161 B1
Loscoe Mount Rd NG5 . 161 C2
Loscoe Rd NG5 . . . . . 161 C1
Losk La NG20 . . . . . . 72 A2
Lothian Rd NG12 . . . . 186 C1
Lothmore Ct 1 NG2 . . . 173 B2
Lotus Cl NG3 . . . . 173 E7
Loughbon NG13 . . . . . 180 A7
LOUGHBOROUGH 220 C4
Loughborough Amherst
 Sch LE11 . . . . 220 B2
Loughborough Ave
  NG2 . . . . 173 F4
Loughborough Carillon
 Tower & War
 Memorial★ LE11 . . . 220 B3
Loughborough Gram Sch
  LE11 . . . . 220 B2
Loughborough High Sch
  LE11 . . . . 220 B3
Loughborough Rd
 Bradmore NG11 . . . . 196 E5
 Bunny NG11 . . . . . . 206 E8
 East Leake LE12 . . . 214 F7
 Hathern LE12 . . . . . 213 A1
 Hoton LE12 . . . . . . 215 C1
 Loughborough LE11 . . 220 D1
 Rempstone LE12 . . . 215 D5
 Ruddington NG11 . . . 196 D7
 Ruddington NG11 . . . 196 D8
 West Bridgford NG2 . . 185 E5
Loughborough Sta
  LE11 . . . . 220 C5

Loughborough Univ Sch of
 Art & Design (14)
  LE11 . . . . 220 A4
Loughborough Rd LE12 . 220 F6
Loughrigg Cl 3 NG2 . . . 173 B1
Louis Ave NG9 . . . . . . 183 E7
Louise Ave NG4 . . . . . 175 A8
LOUND 29 C8
Lound House Cl NG17 . . 100 F5
Loundhouse Rd NG17 . . 101 A5
Lound House Rd NG16 . . 100 F5
Lound Low Rd DN22 . . . 29 D7
Louwil Ave NG19 . . . . 88 E5
Lovatt St NG16 . . . . . 143 C3
Loveden Cl NG24 . . . . 140 D3
Love La DN21 . . . . . . 15 C1
Lovelace Wk 2 NG15 . . 146 B8
Lovell Cl NG16 . . . . . . 159 F5
Lovell House Inf Sch
  NG7 . . . . 222 C4
Lover's La NG24 . . . . . 125 A1
Lovers Lane Prim Sch
  NG24 . . . . 125 A1
Lovesey Ave NG6 . . . . 145 E2
Lowater St NG4 . . . . . 174 B7
Low Common DN11 . . . .8 D4
Lowcroft NG5 . . . . . . 161 F4
Lowdam Rd NG14 . . . . 150 A5
Low Deeps La DN10 . . . .1 E1
LOWDHAM 150 D1
Lowdham CE Prim Sch
  NG14 . . . . 150 D2
Lowdham La
 Woodborough NG14 . . 149 D4
 Woodborough NG14 . . 149 E4
Lowdham Rd
 Carlton NG4 . . . . . . 162 C3
 Gunthorpe NG14 . . . 164 E7
Lowdham St 8 NG3 . . . 173 E5
Lowdham Sta NG14 . . . 164 E8
Lower Bagthorpe
 Bagthorpe NG16 . . . 129 A4
 Selston NG16 . . . . . 128 F3
Lower Beauvale NG16 . . 144 A3
Lower Bloomsgrove Rd
  DE7 . . . . 157 F2
Lower Brook St NG10 . . 193 E7
Lower Cambridge St
  LE11 . . . . 220 B5
Lower Canaan NG11 . . . 196 D8
Lower Chapel St 9
  DE7 . . . . 157 F1
Lower Clara Mount Rd
  DE75 . . . . 143 A1
Lower Ct NG9 . . . . . . 184 B7
Lower Dunstead Rd
  NG16 . . . . 143 A3
Lower Eldon St 12
  NG2 . . . . 173 E4
Lower Enterprise Rd
  LE14 . . . . 219 B4
Lower Gladstone St 3
  LE11 . . . . 220 B5
Lower Granby St DE7 . . 157 F2
Lower Hexgreave
  NG22 . . . . 120 B8
Lower Kirklington Rd
 Edingley NG22 . . . . 120 F5
 Southwell NG25 . . . . 121 D2
Lower Maples DE75 . . . 157 A7
Lower Meadow La
  NG17 . . . . 100 A2
Lower Middleton St
  DE7 . . . . 158 A1
Lower Oakham Way
  NG18 . . . . 101 F3
Lower Orch St NG9 . . . 182 D7
Lower Parliament St
 Nottingham NG1 . . . 223 E3
 Nottingham NG14 . . . 173 C5
Lower Pasture La DN22 . 31 B8
Lower Pk St NG9 . . . . 182 C5
Lower Portland NG17 . . 114 B2
Lower Rd NG9 . . . . . . 184 B7
Lower Regent St NG9 . . 184 A6
Loweswater Ct NG2 . . . 186 C2
Lowes Wong NG25 . . . 136 D8
Lowe's Wong Anglican
 Methodist Jun Sch
  NG25 . . . . 136 D8
Lowe's Wong Inf Sch
  NG25 . . . . 136 D8
Lowe's Wong Jun & Inf Sch
  NG25 . . . . 121 D1
Lowfield DN22 . . . . . . 29 D1
Lowfield Cl DE22 . . . . 19 C4
Lowfield La NG24 . . . . 140 C2
Low Field La DN10 . . . .3 C1
Low Holland La DN22 . . 32 E4
Lowlands Dr NG12 . . . 197 F4
LOW MARNHAM 82 A8
Low Mdw Row S81 . . . 34 E7
Lowmoor Bsns Pk
  NG17 . . . . 115 B7
Low Moor Rd NG17 . . . 115 B6
Lowmoor Rd Ind Est
  NG17 . . . . 115 B7
Low Pavement NG1 . . . 223 E2
Low Rd
 Besthorpe NG23 . . . 97 F6
 Clarborough DN22 . . . 30 F5
 Hayton DN22 . . . . . 31 A6
 North Wheatley DN22 . 31 C8
 Scrooby DN10 . . . . . 10 A2
 Sutton in Ashfield NG17 100 F7
Low's La DE7 . . . . . . 170 B2
Low St
 Beckingham DN10 . . . 14 C1
 Beckingham DN10 . . . 23 C8
 Carlton in Lindrick S81 . 26 A5
 Collingham NG23 . . . 98 A1

Low St continued
 Collingham NG23 . . . 111 F8
 Dunham-on-Trent NG22 . 54 C2
 East Drayton DN22 . . . 53 B3
 East Markham NG22 . . 66 A6
 Elkesley DN22 . . . . . 50 B3
 Elston DN23 . . . . . . 153 D5
 Gringley on the Hill DN10 . 12 F1
 Harby NG23 . . . . . . 70 D2
 North Wheatley DN22 . 31 D8
 Sutton in Ashfield NG17 100 E2
 Torworth DN22 . . . . . 19 B2
Lowther Sq S81 . . . . . 25 E7
Lowther Way LE11 . . . 220 B1
Lowtown Cl S80 . . . . . 36 A2
Lowtown St S80 . . . . . 36 A2
Lowtown View S80 . . . 36 A2
Low Wood La
 Eagle LN6 . . . . 84 A1
 South Scarle LN6 . . . 98 F7
Low Wood Rd NG6 . . . 159 F6
Loxley Cl NG15 . . . . . 145 E5
Loxley Dr NG18 . . . . . 103 A3
Loxley La S80 . . . . . . 45 A5
Loxley Rd NG14 . . . . . 163 E4
LRONVILLE 128 A3
Lucerne Cl NG11 . . . . 185 B6
Lucillia Cl NG15 . . . . . 146 D8
Lucknow Ave NG3 . . . . 161 D1
Lucknow Cl NG3 . . . . . 173 D8
Lucknow Dr
 Mansfield NG17, NG18 . 101 E5
 Nottingham NG3 . . . . 161 D1
 Sutton in Ashfield NG17,
  NG18 . . . . 101 B3
Lucknow Rd NG3 . . . . 161 D1
Ludborough Wlk NG19 . . 88 E4
Ludford Cres DN21 . . . 24 E7
Ludford Rd NG6 . . . . . 160 C8
Ludgate Cl NG5 . . . . . 147 A2
Ludgate Dr NG13 . . . . 165 D2
Ludham Ave NG6 . . . . 160 B8
Ludlam Ave NG16 . . . . 158 A7
Ludlow Ave NG2 . . . . 185 F7
Ludlow Cl NG9 . . . . . 171 D1
Ludlow Hill Rd NG2 . . . 185 F5
Lulworth Cl NG2 . . . . . 185 C5
Lulworth Ct NG16 . . . . 158 F7
Lutterell Ct S81 . . . . . 25 D1
Lumber Way NG3 . . . . 97 F3
Lumley Dr DN11 . . . . . .8 B7
Lune Cl NG9 . . . . 183 E3
Lune Mdw NG19 . . . . . 88 E3
Lune Wy NG13 . . . . . 177 D3
Lunness Ct NG18 . . . . 102 D6
Lunn La NG23 . . . . . . 111 F7
Lupin Cl
 Edwalton NG12 . . . . 186 A2
 Nottingham NG3 . . . 173 D7
 Shirebrook NG20 . . . 72 C3
Luther Ave NG17 . . . . 100 E2
Luther Cl NG3 . . . . . . 173 E7
Luton Cl NG8 . . . . . . 160 D1
Lutterell Ct NG2 . . . . 185 E5
Lutterell Way NG2 . . . 186 C5
Lybster Mews 6 NG2 . . 173 B2
Lydia Gdns NG16 . . . . 143 E1
Lydney Pk NG2 . . . . . 185 C5
Lyle Cl NG16 . . . . . . 158 E7
Lyme Pk NG2 . . . . . . 185 B5
Lymington Rd NG19 . . . 101 D6
Lymn Ave NG4 . . . . . 162 F2
Lynch Cl NG16 . . . . . 158 E7
Lyncombe Ct DN22 . . . 39 F4
Lyncombe Gdns NG12 . 197 F3
Lyndale Rd NG9 . . . . . 183 A8
Lynden Ave NG10 . . . . 193 D6
Lyndhurst Ave NG21 . . 118 B5
Lyndhurst Gdns NG2 . . 185 D4
Lyndhurst Rd NG2 . . . 173 F4
Lynds Cl NG21 . . . . . . 76 B2
Lynemouth Ct NG5 . . . 148 A2
Lyngs The NG13 . . . . 165 D2
Lynmouth Cres NG7 . . 172 E7
Lynmouth Dr DE7 . . . 157 D3
Lynncroft NG16 . . . . . 144 A3
Lynncroft St NG8 . . . . 159 C2
Lynnes Cl NG21 . . . . . 118 A4
Lynstead Dr NG15 . . . 145 C5
Lynton Gdns NG5 . . . . 162 A8
Lynton Rd NG9 . . . . . 183 C6
Lyons Cl NG11 . . . . . 196 B8
Lysander Way S81 . . . 35 E8
Lytham Dr NG12 . . . . 186 C3
Lytham Gdns NG5 . . . 147 A1
Lytham Rd NG17 . . . . 114 E7
Lythe Cl NG11 . . . . . 185 A5
Lytton Cl NG3 . . . . . . 173 E5

M

Mabel Ave NG17 . . . . . 101 A1
Mabel Gr NG2 . . . . . . 186 A8
Mabel St NG2 . . . . . . 173 D2
Mable St S80 . . . . 35 A4
Macaulay Cl
 Balderton NG24 . . . . 140 D5
 Worksop S81 . . . . . . 36 C4
Macaulay Dr NG24 . . . 140 D5
Macaulay Gr NG16 . . . 159 B6
Machin Cl NG22 . . . . . 66 B3
Machin St NG3 . . . . . . 35 C7
Machins La NG21 . . . . 186 A3
Mackinley Ave
 Stapleford NG9 . . . . 170 E1
 Stapleford NG9 . . . . 182 E8
Mackleys La NG23 . . . 156 D7
Mackworth Ct NG18 . . . 103 B5
Maclaren Gdns NG11 . . 196 D5

Maclean Rd NG4 . . . . 174 C7
Macmillan Cl NG3 . . . . 161 F2
Macphail Cres LN1 . . . 57 C3
Madden Cl 4 NG5 . . . . 160 F5
Madejski Way 2 NG17 . 114 F8
Madford Ret Pk NG5 . . 161 D6
Madison Dr NG10 . . . . .9 F6
Madryn Wlk 7 NG5 . . . 161 A7
Mafeking St NG2 . . . . 174 A4
Magdales Dr NG14 . . . 151 B8
Magdala Rd NG3 . . . . 173 C8
Magdalen Dr NG13 . . . 165 D3
Magdalene View NG24 . 140 B8
Magdalene Way NG15 . . 146 A7
Magee Cl NG6 . . . . . . 145 E2
Magellan Dr NG8 . . . . 35 B2
Magenta Way NG4 . . . 175 C7
Mag La NG20 . . . . . . 58 D5
Magna Cl NG14 . . . . . 150 E1
Magnolia Cl
 4 Edwalton NG12 . . . 186 A1
 3 Nottingham NG8 . . 159 E1
Magnolia Ct NG2 . . . . 173 C2
Magnolia Gr NG15 . . . 146 B4
Magnums Com Sports Ctr
  NG24 . . . . 140 A4
Magnus CE Sch NG24 . 140 A6
Magnus Rd NG5 . . . . . 161 C3
Magnus St NG24 . . . . 140 A8
Magpie Cl
 Ruddington NG11 . . . 196 B6
 Worksop S81 . . . . . . 35 C7
Magpie Cres NG12 . . . 185 C6
Magpie La DN22 . . . . . 32 E1
Magpie Rd NG22 . . . . 188 A5
Magson St NG3 . . . . . 173 E5
Maida La NG22 . . . . . 77 B4
Maiden Ct LN1 . . . . . 57 B3
Maiden La NG1 . . . . . 223 F4
Maiden Rd NG20 . . . . 72 D2
Maidens Dale NG5 . . . 161 D8
Maid Marian Ave
 Bilsthorpe NG22 . . . . 105 F4
 Selston NG16 . . . . . 129 B6
Maid Marian Way NG1 . 223 E2
Maid Marion Ave
  NG22 . . . . 106 A4
Maid Marion Rise 1
  NG20 . . . . 74 B4
Maid Marion Way NG22 . 77 D6
Maid Marrion Dr NG21 . 76 C2
Maidstone Dr NG8 . . . 171 D2
Main Ave NG19 . . . . . 103 A8
Main Bright Rd NG19 . . 88 B1
Main Bright Walk 6
  NG19 . . . . 88 B1
Main Gate Dr DN11 . . . .9 B3
Main La NG12 . . . . . . 164 C1
Main Rd
 Annesley Woodhouse
  NG17 . . . . 114 E1
 Averham NG23 . . . . 123 C3
 Averham NG23 . . . . 123 C2
 Barnstone NG13 . . . . 190 E3
 Barnstone NG13 . . . . 191 A4
 Beeston NG9 . . . . . 184 C5
 Besthorpe NG23 . . . . 97 F6
 Bevercotes NG22 . . . 64 D5
 Boughton NG22 . . . . 77 E5
 Carlton NG4 . . . . . . 163 A1
 Cotgrave NG12 . . . . 187 E4
 Elmton NG20 . . . . . 58 A7
 Hawksworth NG13 . . . 167 C3
 Kelham NG23 . . . . . 124 A4
 Kings Clipstone NG21 . 90 C6
 Nether Langwith NG20 . 59 A1
 Nottingham NG11 . . . 185 B3
 Old Dalby LE14 . . . . 218 E4
 Plumtree NG12 . . . . 197 E7
 Pye Bridge DE55 . . . 128 A6
 Radcliffe on Trent NG12 175 E3
 Radcliffe on T, Shelford
  NG12 . . . . 176 C8
 Ravenshead NG15 . . . 117 B3
 Redmile NG13 . . . . . 192 F4
 Selston NG16 . . . . . 128 F2
 Shelford NG13 . . . . . 164 C1
 Shelton NG23 . . . . . 167 F4
 Shelton NG23 . . . . . 168 A5
 Upton NG23 . . . . . . 122 E2
 Watnall NG16 . . . . . 159 A7
 Westwood NG16 . . . . 128 B3
 Wiseton DN10 . . . . . 21 A8
Mainside Cres NG16 . . 129 A1
Main St
 Annesley Woodhouse
  NG17 . . . . 129 F8
 Aslockton NG13 . . . . 179 A5
 Awsworth NG16 . . . . 158 C5
 Balderton NG24 . . . . 140 E4
 Bevercotes NG22 . . . 64 F5
 Bleasby NG14 . . . . . 152 B7
 Blidworth NG21 . . . . 117 F4
 Bothamsall DN22 . . . 63 F7
 Bothamsall DN22 . . . 64 A7
 Bottesford NG13 . . . 169 D1
 Bradmore NG11 . . . . 196 E3
 Brampton LN1 . . . . . 44 C3
 Brinsley NG16 . . . . . 128 D1
 Broxholme LN1 . . . . 57 E8
 Bunny NG11 . . . . . . 206 E8
 Burton Joyce NG14 . . 163 F4
 Calverton NG14 . . . . 148 F7
 Carlton-on-Trent NG23 . 96 F4
 Caunton NG23 . . . . 109 A3
 Caythorpe NG14 . . . 165 A4
 Clarborough DN22 . . . 30 D6
 Clarborough DN22 . . . 30 E4
 Claypole NG23 . . . . 156 C6
 Claypole NG23 . . . . 156 D7
 Coddington NG24 . . . 126 B2

Main St continued
 Collingham NG23 . . . 98 D5
 Costock LE12 . . . . . 206 C1
 Cropwell Butler NG12 . 189 A7
 Doddington LN6 . . . . 71 C1
 Dry Doddington NG23 . 156 E2
 Dunham-on-Trent NG22 . 54 C2
 Eakring NG22 . . . . . 92 E1
 East Bridgford NG13 . 165 C2
 East Leake LE12 . . . 205 E1
 Eastwood NG16 . . . . 143 F1
 Eastwood, Beauvale
  NG16 . . . . 144 C2
 Eaton DN22 . . . . . . 40 A1
 Eaton DN22 . . . . . . 50 F8
 Eaton DN22 . . . . . . 51 A8
 Edingley NG22 . . . . 120 C4
 Egmanton NG22 . . . . 79 F6
 Farndon NG24 . . . . . 139 A4
 Farnsfield NG22 . . . . 119 F6
 Fenton NG23 . . . . . 142 D2
 Fiskerton NG25 . . . . 137 F3
 Flawborough NG13 . . 168 D2
 Flintham NG13 . . . . 167 A8
 Flintham NG23 . . . . 153 A1
 Gonalston NG14 . . . . 150 F3
 Gonalston NG14 . . . . 151 A4
 Granby NG13 . . . . . 191 B5
 Grove DN22 . . . . . . 40 F4
 Gunthorpe NG14 . . . 165 A5
 Harby LE14 . . . . . . 202 A3
 Harworth DN11 . . . . .8 E4
 Hickling LE14 . . . . . 210 C6
 Hoveringham NG14 . . 151 D2
 Huthwaite NG17 . . . . 99 F3
 Keyworth NG12 . . . . 197 E2
 Kimberley NG16 . . . . 158 F6
 Kinoulton NG12 . . . . 199 E2
 Kirklington NG25 . . . 121 A8
 Kirton NG22 . . . . . . 78 B6
 Kneesall NG22 . . . . 93 E5
 Kneeton NG14 . . . . . 151 E1
 Lambley NG4 . . . . . 163 C7
 Laneham DN22 . . . . 54 A5
 Langar NG13 . . . . . 190 C2
 Laughterton LN1 . . . 55 B5
 Laxton NG22 . . . . . . 79 C2
 Linby NG15 . . . . . . 131 B3
 Lockington DE74 . . . 203 A6
 Long Eaton NG10 . . . 193 E7
 Long Whatton LE12 . . 212 B3
 Lowdham NG14 . . . . 150 D1
 Maplebeck NG22 . . . 107 F6
 Maplebeck NG22 . . . 108 A6
 Mattersey DN10 . . . . 20 B7
 Morton DN21 . . . . . 15 D3
 Morton DE55 . . . . . 137 D3
 Muston NG13 . . . . . 181 F1
 Newton DE55 . . . . . 99 A4
 Newton NG13 . . . . . 177 B8
 Normanton NG13 . . . 181 C7
 Normanton on S LE12 . 213 D3
 North Leverton with
  Habblesthorpe DN22 . 32 C1
 North Muskham NG23 . 110 F4
 Norton NG20 . . . . . 60 C5
 Norwell NG23 . . . . . 109 F8
 Norwell NG23 . . . . . 110 A8
 Nottingham NG6 . . . 160 C7
 Oldcotes S81 . . . . . 16 F5
 Old Dalby LE14 . . . . 219 A5
 Ollerton NG22 . . . . . 77 A3
 Ossington NG23 . . . . 95 D6
 Oxton NG25 . . . . . . 134 B3
 Papplewick NG15 . . . 131 E5
 Ragnall NG22 . . . . . 68 A8
 Rampton DN22 . . . . 42 F2
 Ratcliffe on Soar NG11 203 F6
 Redmile NG13 . . . . . 192 F3
 Saxondale NG13 . . . . 177 A4
 Scaftworth DN10 . . . 10 C4
 Scarrington NG13 . . . 178 E8
 Screveton NG13 . . . . 166 E4
 Sibthorpe NG23 . . . . 167 E8
 South Muskham NG23 . 124 D7
 South Normanton DE55 113 B6
 Stanford on Soar LE12 . 214 C1
 Stokeham DN22 . . . . 53 C7
 Strelley NG16 . . . . . 159 A1
 Sutton NG13 . . . . . . 191 E8
 Sutton Bonington LE12 . 213 B7
 Sutton on Trent NG23 . 96 F7
 Syerston NG23 . . . . 153 B4
 Thorney NG23 . . . . . 69 F7
 Thoroton NG13 . . . . 167 E1
 Thorpe NG23 . . . . . 153 F8
 Thorpe NG23 . . . . . 138 F1
 Torksey LN1 . . . . . . 44 B2
 Upton DN22 . . . . . . 52 B5
 Upton NG23 . . . . . . 122 F1
 Walesby NG22 . . . . 64 A2
 West Bridgford NG2 . . 186 C2
 West Markham NG22 . . 65 A7
 West Markham NG22 . . 65 C6
 Weston NG23 . . . . . 81 A4
 West Stockwith DN10 . .7 E2
 Whaley Thorns NG20 . . 58 F2
 Whaley Thorns S44 . . 59 A2
 Whatton NG13 . . . . . 179 B3
 Widmerpool NG11 . . . 208 C4
 Willoughby-on-t-W LE12 217 D7
 Winkburn NG22 . . . . 108 A1
 Wiseton DN10 . . . . . 12 B1
 Woodborough NG14 . . 149 C4
 Woodborough NG14 . . 149 D4
 Wysall NG12 . . . . . . 207 C3
 Zouch LE12 . . . . . . 213 B3
Maisies Way DE55 . . . 113 D6
Maitland Ave NG5 . . . 161 F4
Maitland Rd NG5 . . . . 161 F4
Maize Gr NG18 . . . . . 102 E1

Majestic Theatre★
  DN22 . . . . 39 E7
Major St NG1 . . . . . . 223 E3
Making It!★ NG18 . . . 102 C6
Malbon Cl NG3 . . . . . 173 F8
Malcolm Cl NG3 . . . . . 173 C7
Maldon Cl
 Beeston NG9 . . . . . 183 B4
 Long Eaton NG10 . . . 193 E5
Malham Cl DN10 . . . . .9 F8
Malin Cl NG5 . . . . . . 162 B8
Malin Hill NG1 . . . . . 223 F2
Malkin Ave NG12 . . . . 176 A4
Mallard Cl
 Bilsthorpe NG22 . . . . 105 F5
 Bingham NG13 . . . . 178 A3
 Claypole NG23 . . . . 156 D7
 Nottingham NG6 . . . 160 F4
 Shirebrook NG20 . . . 72 D3
Mallard Ct
 Beeston NG9 . . . . . 184 A5
 Mansfield NG19 . . . . 88 A2
Mallard Gn NG24 . . . . 140 C5
Mallard Rd NG4 . . . . . 175 B6
Mallards The S81 . . . . 35 C7
Mallatratt Pl NG19 . . . 88 B4
Mallory Dr S80 . . . . . 35 B2
Mallow Way NG13 . . . 177 C4
Malmesbury Rd NG3 . . 162 A4
Malpas Ave DN21 . . . . 15 D1
Maltby Cl NG8 . . . . . 160 B2
Maltby Rd
 Mansfield NG18 . . . . 102 E6
 Nottingham NG3 . . . 162 A4
 Oldcotes S81 . . . . . 16 E6
Malt Cotts NG7 . . . . . 160 F1
Malthouse Cl NG16 . . . 143 F1
Malthouse Rd
 Ilkeston DE7 . . . . . . 170 A4
 Whitwell S80 . . . . . 45 A6
Malting Cl NG11 . . . . 196 C6
Maltings The
 Blyth S81 . . . . 18 B3
 Cropwell Bishop NG12 . 189 A4
Maltkiln La NG24 . . . . 125 A2
Maltkiln Rd LN1 . . . . . 55 D6
Maltkins The DN22 . . . 42 C8
Maltmill La NG1 . . . . 223 E2
Malton Rd
 Nottingham NG5 . . . 160 F2
 Nottingham NG5 . . . 161 A2
Malt St NG11 . . . . . . 195 B1
Maltsters The NG24 . . . 139 C6
Malvern Cl NG3 . . . . . 161 E1
Malvern Cres NG2 . . . 185 F5
Malvern Gdns 3 NG10 193 A8
Malvern Rd
 Nottingham NG3 . . . 161 E1
 West Bridgford NG2 . . 185 E5
Manby Cl NG20 . . . . . 74 D8
Manchester St NG10 . . 193 D6
Mandalay Rd NG19 . . . 87 B4
Mandalay St NG6 . . . . 160 D4
Mandarin Cl NG19 . . . 88 E2
Mandeen Gr NG18 . . . 103 A4
Manderley Gdns NG17 . 114 B8
Mandeville Cl NG15 . . . 146 C8
Manesty Cres NG11 . . . 195 E7
Mangham La DN11 . . . .8 A3
Manifold Dr NG16 . . . 129 A7
Manifold Gdns NG2 . . . 173 C2
Manitoba Way NG16 . . 128 F7
Manly Cl NG5 . . . . . . 160 E8
Manners Ave DE7 . . . 157 D1
Manners Ind Est DE7 . . 157 F2
Manners Rd
 Balderton NG24 . . . . 140 D3
 Ilkeston DE7 . . . . . . 157 E1
 Newark-on-Trent NG24 . 124 E1
Manners St DE7 . . . . 170 A6
Manners Sutton Prim Sch
 The NG23 . . . . 123 F2
Manning St NG3 . . . . 173 D7
Manning View DE7 . . . 157 F2
Mannion Cres NG10 . . 193 B5
Manns Leys NG12 . . . 187 E2
Mann St 5 NG7 . . . . . 172 F2
Manor Arms Pl NG13 . . 179 F2
Manor Ave
 Beeston NG9 . . . . . 183 F5
 17 Nottingham NG2 . . 173 E4
 Stapleford NG9 . . . . 182 D8
Manor Bsns Pk DN22 . . 53 A2
Manor Cl
 Bleasby NG14 . . . . . 152 A8
 Boughton NG22 . . . . 77 F6
 Costock LE12 . . . . . 206 C1
 Eagle LN6 . . . . 84 D3
 Gamston DN22 . . . . 50 F5
 Long Whatton LE12 . . 212 B3
 Misson DN10 . . . . . .4 C3
 Newton DE55 . . . . . 99 A3
 Oxton NG25 . . . . . . 134 B3
 Southwell NG25 . . . . 121 D1
 Teversall NG17 . . . . 100 C8
 Walesby NG22 . . . . 64 A2
 West Bridgford NG12 . 186 B3
 Worksop S80 . . . . . 35 C2
Manor Cres
 Carlton NG4 . . . . . . 174 F8
 Kirkby-in-Ashfield NG17 115 B3
Manor Croft NG6 . . . . 160 E3
Manor Ct
 Beeston NG9 . . . . . 183 B7
 Carlton NG4 . . . . . . 174 F7
 Church Warsop NG20 . 74 C6
 Wymeswold LE12 . . . 216 D4

Manor Dr NG25 . . . . 137 D3
Manor Farm Cl
Bradmore NG11 . . . . . . **196** E3
Kilvington NG13 . . . . 168 F2
Rolleston NG23 . . . . 138 A6
Manor Farm Ct
Kingston on Soar NG11 . . **203** F4
Kingston on Soar NG11 . . **204** E8
Manor Farm Dr DN22 . . . **54** C5
Manor Farm La NG7 . . . **184** E2
Manor Farm Mdw
LE12 . . . . **205** E1
Manor Farm Rise
North Leverton with
  Habblesthorpe DN22 . . . **32** C1
North Leverton with
  Habblesthorpe DN22 . . . **42** C8
Wellow NG22 . . . . **77** E1
Manor Farm &
Woodlands★
LE12 . . . . **214** F8
Manor Fields NG22 . . . . 120 E1
Manor Gn Wlk NG4 . . . . 174 F8
Manor Gr
Austerfield DN10 . . . . **3** C3
Normanton on Trent NG23. **81** E6
North Leverton with
  Habblesthorpe DN22 . . . **32** C1
Worksop S80 . . . . **35** C2
Manor House Cl
Lowdham NG14 . . . . .150 D2
West Bridgford NG2 . . . . .**185** B8
Manor House Ct NG17 .114 D4
Manor House Dr
North Muskham NG23 . . . .110 F3
Wysall NG12 . . . .**207** F3
Manor House La NG23 .156 D2
Manor House Rd NG10 .193 F6
Manor La
Broadholme LN6 . . . . **71** A8
Cromwell NG23 . . . . .110 F8
Gunthorpe NG13 . . . . . . .165 A4
Shelford NG12 . . . . .164 C2
Whatton NG13 . . . . .179 A1
Manor Mws ⏹1 NG19 . . . .**88** C3
Manor Pk NG11 . . . . . . .196 C7
Manor Pk Inf Sch
NG14 . . . . 148 E8
Manor Rd
Barton in Fabis NG11 . . . .**194** E6
Bingham NG13 . . . .**177** F4
Bottesford NG13 . . . . . . .181 C2
Calverton NG14 . . . . .148 E7
Carlton NG4 . . . . .174 F8
Caunton NG23 . . . . .109 A4
Church Warsop NG20 . . . .**74** C6
Collingham NG23 . . . . . . .112 A8
East Leake LE12 . . . .**205** F3
Eastwood NG16 . . . . .143 F1
Ilkeston DE7 . . . . .157 E1
Keyworth NG12 . . . . .197 E3
Mansfield Woodhouse
  NG19 . . . .**88** A4
Morton DN21 . . . . **15** B4
Saxilby LN1 . . . . **57** A4
Scrooby DN10 . . . . **10** A2
Sutton in Ashfield NG17 . .100 E7
Manor Rise NG13 . . . . . .165 C4
Manor Sch The NG19. . . **88** C5
Manor St
Nottingham NG2 . . . . . . .173 E4
Sutton in Ashfield NG17 . .100 E2
Manor View NG5 . . . . . .109 A4
Manor Wlk NG14 . . . . . .150 A5
Manorwood Rd NG12 . .187 F2
Manse Ave S80 . . . . .58 D8
Manse Cl S80 . . . . .58 D8
Mansell Cl NG16 . . . . . .144 B1
Mansey Common Nature
Reserve★ NG22 . . . . . .107 A6
MANSFIELD 102 C6
Mansfield Bsns Ctr
NG19 . . . . **88** B1
Mansfield Coll of Art and
Design / VisionStudio Sch
⏹16 NG18 . . . . .102 B7
Mansfield Com Hospl
NG18 . . . . .102 A6
Mansfield Ct ⏹7 NG5 . .173 B8
Mansfield Gr
Nottingham NG1 . . . .**223** D4
Nottingham NG14 . . . . . .173 B6
Mansfield La
Calverton NG14 . . . . .148 F7
Sutton in Ashfield NG17 . .101 A7
Mansfield L Ctr NG19 . .102 A8
Mansfield L Pk★ NG18 .102 B5
Mansfield Mus★ NG18 .102 C7
Mansfield Rd
Annesley NG15 . . . . .130 A6
Arnold NG5 . . . . .147 E3
Arnold NG5, NG15 . . . . . .147 D6
Babworth DN22 . . . . .38 D3
Blidworth NG21 . . . . .118 A5
Brinsley NG16 . . . . .143 F4
Clipstone NG21 . . . . 90 A3
Clipstone NG21 . . . . 90 B5
Creswell S80 . . . . 58 F8
Creswell S80 . . . . 59 A8
Cuckney NG20 . . . . 60 B3
Dalesnorth NG17 . . . . . . .101 D4
Edingley NG22 . . . . .120 C5
Edwinstowe NG21 . . . . . . 75 E2
Mansfield Rd
Farnsfield NG22 . . . . .119 B7
Farnsfield NG22 . . . . .119 C7
Glapwell S44 . . . . 86 D8
Halam NG22 . . . . .120 D3
Heanor DE75 . . . . .143 A2

Mansfield Rd *continued*
Kings Clipstone NG20 . . . . **74** F1
Mansfield Woodhouse
  NG19 . . . .**88** C2
Mansfield Woodhouse
  NG19 . . . .**88** F1
Ollerton NG22 . . . . **76** D3
Ollerton NG22 . . . . **77** A4
Ravenshead NG15 . . . . . .131 F8
Selston NG16 . . . . .128 F7
Selston, Friezeland
  NG16 . . . . .129 C4
South Normanton DE55. . .113 D6
Sutton in A, Skegby
  NG17 . . . . .100 E6
Sutton in A, Sutton Forest Side
  NG17 . . . . .101 B4
Tibshelf DE55 . . . . 99 B7
Worksop DN22 . . . . 48 A8
Worksop S80 . . . . 46 A8
Mansfield Rd (North)
NG15 . . . . .116 B3
Mansfield St NG5 . . . . . .161 C2
Mansfield Town Sta
NG18 . . . . .102 B6
MANSFIELD
WOODHOUSE **88** E3
Mansfield Woodhouse Sta
NG19 . . . . **88** B3
Manston Way S81 . . . . . **35** C8
Manthorpe Cres NG5 . .116 F3
Manthorpe House
NG24 . . . . .140 E4
Manthorpe Way NG24. .140 E4
Mantle Croft LE12 . . . . .216 C3
MANTON **36** B1
Manton Cl NG21 . . . . . . .118 B8
Manton Cres
Beeston NG9 . . . . .184 A8
Worksop S80 . . . . **36** B1
Manton Dale S80 . . . . . . **36** B1
Manton Villas S80 . . . . **36** C1
Manton Wood Enterprise
Zone S81 . . . . **36** F1
Manuela Gr NG12 . . . . . .185 F3
Manvers Bsns Pk
NG12 . . . .**188** A4
Manvers Cres NG21 . . . . **75** F2
Manvers Ct
Market Warsop NG20 . . . . **73** A4
⏹9 Nottingham NG2 . . . . .173 E4
Manvers Gr NG12 . . . . . .175 F3
Manvers Rd
Retford DN22 . . . . .39 D5
West Bridgford NG2 . . . . .**185** F6
Manvers St
Carlton NG4 . . . . .175 A6
Mansfield NG18 . . . . .102 A7
Mansfield Woodhouse
  NG19 . . . . **88** A3
Market Warsop NG20 . . . . **74** B3
Nottingham NG2 . . . . . . .173 E4
Shirebrook NG20 . . . . **73** A4
Worksop S80 . . . . **35** E3
Manvers View NG22 . . . . **77** E6
Manville Cl
Beeston NG9 . . . . .171 B3
Nottingham NG8 . . . . . . .172 C6
Maori Ave NG15 . . . . . . .145 D5
Maple Ave
Beeston NG9 . . . . .184 B5
Lidgett NG21 . . . . 91 C8
Sandiacre NG10 . . . . .182 B7
Torksey Lock LN1 . . . . 44 B1
MAPLEBECK 108 A6
Maplebeck Ave NG20 . . . **74** D8
Maplebeck Rd
Arnold NG5 . . . . .162 A7
Caunton NG23 . . . . .108 E6
Caunton NG23 . . . . .109 A4
Maple Cl
Calverton NG14 . . . . .148 D7
East Leake LE12 . . . . . . .214 D8
Gainsborough DN21 . . . . . 15 B3
Keyworth NG12 . . . . .198 A2
Mansfield NG19 . . . . **88** E1
Radcliffe on Trent NG12 . .177 B8
South Normanton DE55 . . .113 B4
Tuxford NG22 . . . . .66 A2
Maple Cres NG17 . . . . . .114 F6
Maple Croft NG18 . . . . .102 F5
Maple Ct ⏹4 DN21 . . . . . 15 F1
Mapledene Cres NG8 . . .171 C3
Maple Dr
Carlton NG4 . . . . .163 B2
Elkesley DN22 . . . . 50 B3
Hucknall NG15 . . . . .145 E5
Nuthall NG16 . . . . .159 C6
Ravenshead NG18 . . . . . .116 D7
South Normanton DE55. . .113 B4
Worksop S81 . . . . 36 A7
Maple Gr
Bawtry DN10 . . . . 9 F7
Glapwell S44 . . . . 86 D8
Newark-on-Trent NG24 . . .139 F4
Maple Leaf Cl NG24 . . . .125 A3
Maple Leaf Gdns S80 . . . 36 A2
Maple Leaf Way NG15 . .146 C4
Maples St ⏹15 NG7 . . . . .172 F7
Maplestead Ave NG11. .185 B6
Maples The DE7 . . . . . . .157 E1
Mapletoft Ave NG19 . . . . 88 A5
Mapletoft Ct
Retford DN22 . . . . 29 B1
RETFORD DN22 . . . . 39 C8
Mapleton Way NG17 . . . .161 B7
Mapletree Cl NG5. . . . . .161 B7
Mapletree Mdw NG17. .101 C6

Maple Wy NG16. . . . . . .128 F7
MAPPERLEY 161 E3
Mapperley Cres NG3 . . .161 E2
Mapperley Hall Dr
NG3. . . . . .161 D2
Mapperley Hall Gdns
NG5. . . . . .161 D2
⏹1 New Cross NG17 . . . . .100 F4
Nottingham NG5 . . . . .161 D4
Mapperley Orch NG5 . . .162 C7
MAPPERLEY PARK 161 E3
Mapperley Pk Dr ⏹1
NG3. . . . . .161 D3
Mapperley Plains NG3 .162 C6
Mapperley Plains Prim Sch
NG3 . . . . .162 B4
Mapperley Rd NG3 . . . . .173 C7
Mapperley Rise NG3 . . .161 E2
Mapperley St NG5 . . . . .161 C2
Mappleton Dr NG18. . . .118 B5
Mapplewells NG17 . . . . .114 F1
Mapplewells Cres
NG17 . . . . .100 B1
Mapplewells Prim Sch
NG17 . . . . .100 B1
Mapplewells Rd NG17. .100 C1
Maquin Cl NG12 . . . . . . .176 B4
Marbled White Pl S81. . . 25 D1
March Cl NG5 . . . . .160 E7
Marches Cl NG15 . . . . . .145 E4
Marchwood Cl NG8 . . . .172 D5
Marciana Gr NG15 . . . . .146 C8
Marconi Dr NG9 . . . . . . .184 A4
Mardale Cl NG2 . . . . . . .186 C6
Mardling Av NG5 . . . . . .161 A5
Marella Cl ⏹1 NG12 . . . .186 A2
Margaret Ave
Long Eaton NG10 . . . . . . .182 F1
Sandiacre NG10 . . . . .182 B4
Margaret Cl DN22. . . . . . 15 C3
Margaret Cres ⏹2 NG4 .162 E2
Margaret Pl NG13. . . . . .177 D5
Margaret's Ct NG9 . . . . .183 A8
Marham Cl NG2 . . . . . . .173 E3
Marhill Rd NG4 . . . . .174 F7
Marie Gdns NG15 . . . . . .146 A5
Marigold Cl NG12 . . . . . .185 F2
Marigold Way
Newark-on-Trent NG24 . .139 F4
Newark-on-Trent NG24 . .140 A4
Marina Ave NG9 . . . . . . .183 F5
Marina Dr S81 . . . . 34 F6
Mariner Ct NG6 . . . . .160 A6
Marion Ave
Hucknall NG15 . . . . .131 C1
Kirkby-in-Ashfield NG17 . .115 B2
Marion Murdoch Ct
NG4 . . . . .162 E2
Maris Cl NG11 . . . . .184 C2
Maris Dr NG14 . . . . .163 E3
Marjorie St S80 . . . . 35 A4
Market Cl
Shirebrook NG20 . . . . 72 F3
South Normanton DE55. . .113 A6
Market House Pl ⏹12
NG18 . . . . .102 B7
Market Pl
Bingham NG13 . . . . .177 E4
Gainsborough DN21 . . . . . 24 C8
Hucknall NG15 . . . . .146 A4
Huthwaite NG17 . . . . 99 F3
Kegworth DE74 . . . . .203 D2
Long Eaton NG10 . . . . . . .193 E8
Loughborough LE11 . . . . .220 B4
⏹9 Mansfield NG18 . . . . .102 B7
Mansfield Woodhouse
  NG19 . . . . **88** C3
Nottingham NG6 . . . . . . .160 B7
Ollerton NG22 . . . . 77 A3
Retford DN22 . . . . 39 F7
Shirebrook NG20 . . . . 72 F4
South Normanton DE55. . .113 A6
Southwell NG25 . . . . .136 E8
Stanton Hill NG17 . . . . . .100 E2
Tickhill DN11 . . . . 8 A7
Tuxford NG22 . . . . 65 F3
Worksop S80 . . . . 35 F3
Market Pl The NG5 . . . . .161 F7
Market Side ⏹9 NG6. . . .160 B7
Market St
Bingham NG13 . . . . .177 E4
Bottesford NG13 . . . . . . .181 B2
Gainsborough DN21 . . . . . 24 C8
Huthwaite NG17 . . . . 99 F3
Loughborough LE11 . . . . .220 A4
⏹15 Mansfield NG18 . . . . .102 B7
Nottingham NG1 . . . .**223** E2
Shirebrook NG20 . . . . 72 F4
South Normanton DE55. . .113 A5
Sutton in Ashfield
  NG17 . . . . .100 E2
Worksop S80 . . . . 35 F3
MARKET WARSOP 74 C4
Markham Ave NG24 . . . .125 B3
Markham Cl NG22 . . . . . . 77 C4
Markham Cres NG5 . . . .161 C4
Markham Moor Bridge
DN22 . . . . 65 B8
Markham Pl NG19 . . . . . .101 D7
Markham Rd
Beeston NG9 . . . . .171 D1
Langold S81 . . . . 16 E3
Tuxford NG22 . . . . 65 F4
Markham St NG15 . . . . . .130 D6
Markhams The NG22. . . . 77 B4
Mark La NG22 . . . . 65 F4
Markland La NG20 . . . . . . 58 A8
Marklew Cl NG21 . . . . . . .118 A5
Mark St NG10 . . . . .182 C5
Markwick Cl NG24 . . . . .140 D8
Marlborough Cl
Newark-on-Trent NG24 . .139 D5
⏹3 Worksop S81 . . . . 35 D8

Marlborough Ct
Newark-on-Trent NG24 . .139 D6
West Bridgford NG12 . . . .**185** F7
Marlborough Rd
Arnold NG5 . . . . .161 E4
Beeston NG9 . . . . .183 F7
Kirkby-in-Ashfield NG17 . .115 B5
Long Eaton NG10 . . . . . . .182 F1
Mansfield NG18 . . . . 87 F1
Marlborough St
Gainsborough DN21 . . . . . 24 D7
⏹2 Nottingham NG7 . . . . .172 E1
Marl Cl NG11 . . . . .196 B8
Marldon Cl NG8 . . . . . . .171 C5
Marle Pit Hill LE12 . . . . .213 A8
Marles Cl NG24 . . . . .125 C2
Marleston La NG24 . . . . .140 A4
Marlock Cl NG25. . . . . . .137 E3
Marlow Ave NG6 . . . . . . .160 E2
Marlowe Dr NG24. . . . . .140 D4
Marlowe Gdns S81 . . . . . 36 A4
Marlow Rd DN21 . . . . 15 E2
Marl Rd NG2 . . . . .176 B3
Marlwood NG12 . . . . . . .188 A2
Marly Bank NG18 . . . . . .102 E5
Marmion Rd NG3 . . . . . .174 A6
Marnham Dr NG3. . . . . . .161 E1
Marnham Rd
Low Marnham NG23 . . . . .82 A7
Marnham NG23 . . . . .81 F8
Skegby NG23 . . . . 67 B2
Tuxford NG22 . . . . 66 D2
Marples Ave NG19 . . . . . 88 E5
Marple Sq NG3 . . . . .173 C7
Marquis Ave NG24 . . . . .140 D3
Marquis Gdns
Retford DN22 . . . . 39 F4
Retford DN22 . . . . 40 A4
Marquis Rd LE14 . . . . . .219 B6
Marriots La NG21 . . . . . .117 F4
Marriott Ave
Beeston NG9 . . . . .183 A5
Mansfield NG18 . . . . .101 F7
Marriott Cl NG9 . . . . . . .183 A5
Marriott Rd NG18 . . . . . .177 D6
Marrison Ct NG24 . . . . . .138 F5
Marrison Way
Southwell NG25 . . . . .121 F4
Winthorpe NG24 . . . . . . .125 F5
Marron Cl NG24 . . . . . . .140 F2
Marron Ct NG24 . . . . . . .140 F2
Marsant Cl ⏹1 NG8 . . . . .172 C5
Marsden Cl ⏹6 NG6 . . . .160 E5
Marshall Ave NG17 . . . . .115 C4
Marshall Cl NG5 . . . . . . .148 D8
Marshall Ct NG24 . . . . . .140 E4
Marshall Dr
Beeston NG9 . . . . .183 A8
Ruddington NG11 . . . . . .196 B7
Marshall Farm Cl
NG13 . . . . .192 B2
Marshall Hill Dr NG3 . . .162 B2
Marshall Rd
Cropwell Bishop NG12. . . .189 A4
Nottingham NG3 . . . . . . .162 A1
Marshalls Rise
⏹2 Gainsborough DN21. . . 15 C3
Gainsborough DN21 . . . . . 24 D8
Marshall St
Heanor DE75 . . . . .143 A2
Nottingham NG5 . . . . . . .161 C2
Marshall Terr NG17 . . . .100 D6
Marsham Dr NG5 . . . . . . .162 A6
Marsh Ave DE7 . . . . .157 F5
Marsh Ct NG13 . . . . .181 B3
Marsh La
Cottam DN22 . . . . 43 F4
Farndon NG24 . . . . .139 A5
Laughterton LN1 . . . . 55 A4
Misterton DN10 . . . . 7 B1
Misterton DN10 . . . . 14 B8
North Leverton with
  Habblesthorpe DN22 . . . 33 D1
North Muskham NG23 . . . .110 F2
Saundby DN22 . . . . 23 D5
Marsh Rd DN10 . . . . 14 C5
Marsh's Paddock LE14 .210 C6
Marston Ave NG20 . . . . . 74 D8
Marston Cl NG24 . . . . . .140 C3
Marston Moor Rd
NG24 . . . . .140 E8
Marston Rd NG3 . . . . . . .162 A1
Martin Cl NG6 . . . . .160 A8
Martin Cres NG11 . . . . . .196 B7
Martin Ct NG6 . . . . .160 A8
Martindale ⏹8 NG24 . . . .139 F8
Martindale Cl NG2 . . . . .186 C7
Marting Grange Farm La
DN10 . . . . 3 A1
Martin La DN10 . . . . 9 F8
Martinmass Cl NG7 . . . .222 A1
Martins Hill NG4 . . . . . . .174 E7
Martin's Pond Nature
Reserve★ NG8 . . . . . . .171 E5
Martlet Way
Worksop S80 . . . . 36 A1
Worksop S80 . . . . 47 A8
MARTON 44 B8
Marton Prim Sch DN21. . 44 C8
Marton Rd
Beeston NG9 . . . . .183 C3
Newark-on-Trent NG24 . .140 B6
Nottingham NG6 . . . . . . .146 C1
Martyn Ave NG17 . . . . . .100 F1
Marvin Rd NG9 . . . . .183 F6
Marvyn Cl NG6 . . . . .160 E6
Marwood Cres NG4. . . . .162 C2
Marwood Rd NG4. . . . . . .162 C2
Maryfield Cl NG24 . . . . . . 29 E1
Maryland Ct NG9 . . . . . . .170 E1
Mary Rd NG16 . . . . .144 B1

Marys Cl LE12 . . . . .216 C3
Marys Gate S80 . . . . 35 F1
Mary St
Kirkby-in-Ashfield
  NG17 . . . . .115 B6
Rhodesia S80 . . . . 35 B4
Whaley Thorns NG20 . . . . 59 A2
Masefield Cres NG24 . . .140 D4
Masefield Pl S81 . . . . 36 A4
Masonic Pl NG1 . . . .**223** D4
Mason Rd DE7 . . . . .157 D2
Mason St NG17 . . . . .101 B4
Massey Cl NG14 . . . . . . .163 E3
Massey Ct ⏹4 NG4 . . . . .140 B8
Massey Gdns ⏹1 NG3 . .173 E6
Massey St NG24 . . . . . . .140 B8
Masson Ct ⏹7 NG5 . . . . .147 A1
Master Rd NG13 . . . . . . .177 B7
Mather Rd NG24 . . . . . . .124 F1
Matilda Dr DN22. . . . . . . 29 F1
Matin Rd NG13 . . . . .177 B6
Matlock Ave NG18 . . . . . .102 A5
Matlock Cl NG1 . . . .**223** E3
Matlock St NG4 . . . . . . .174 F7
MATTERSEY 20 C7
Mattersey Ct ⏹4 NG19 . . 88 B1
Mattersey Prim Sch
DN10 . . . . 20 B7
Mattersey Rd
Everton DN10 . . . . .11 C1
Lound DN22 . . . . 20 B2
Ranskill DN22 . . . . .19 D6
Matthews Ct NG9 . . . . . .170 F2
Mattingly Rd NG6 . . . . . .160 A5
Mattley Ave NG17 . . . . . .115 A5
Matt Orch DE55. . . . . . . .113 B4
Maud St NG7 . . . . .161 A1
Maule Ct NG13 . . . . .180 A6
Maun Ave
Kirkby-in-Ashfield
  NG17 . . . . .115 B7
Nottingham NG7 . . . . . . .172 D6
Maun Cl
Mansfield NG18 . . . . .101 F4
Nottingham NG7 . . . . . . .172 D6
Maun Cres NG22 . . . . 77 C5
Maundale Ave NG17 . . . .101 B4
Maun Gn NG24 . . . . .125 B2
Maun Inf Sch NG22 . . . . 77 B5
Maunleigh NG19 . . . . 88 E1
Maunside NG18 . . . . .101 F4
Maunside Ave NG17 . . . .101 B1
Maun Valley Ind Pk
NG17 . . . . .101 C2
Maun View NG18 . . . . . . .102 C7
Maun View Gdns
Kirkby-in-Ashfield
  NG17 . . . . .115 B8
Sutton Forest Side NG17 .101 B1
Maun Way
Mansfield NG18 . . . . .101 F4
Wellow NG22 . . . . 78 A4
Maurice Dr NG3 . . . . . . .161 E2
Mavis Ave NG15 . . . . . . .117 A2
Mavis Wood Mws
NG21 . . . . .118 B5
Mawkin La
Kirkby-in-Ashfield
  NG17 . . . . .114 A4
Maws La NG16. . . . . .158 E7
Maxtoke Rd NG7. . . . . . .222 C1
Maxwell Cl NG7. . . . . . . .222 B1
May Ave NG8 . . . . .171 E4
Maycroft Gdns
Carlton NG3 . . . . .174 A7
Sutton In Ashfield NG17 . .100 B2
May Ct ⏹6 NG5 . . . . .161 B1
Maydene Cl NG11. . . . . . .184 D1
Mayes Dr NG14 . . . . .149 C6
Mayes Rise NG6 . . . . . . .146 E4
Mayfair NG12 . . . . .176 D3
Mayfair Ave NG18 . . . . . .102 D5
Mayfair Cl DN11 . . . . 8 A7
Mayfair Ct NG7 . . . . .160 F1
Mayfair Gdns NG5 . . . . .160 F5
May Fair Pl NG22 . . . . . . 66 A2
Mayfair Row ⏹6 S80 . . . . 35 E2
Mayfield Ave
Burton Joyce NG14 . . . . .163 F5
Gainsborough DN21 . . . . . 15 B3
Loughborough LE11 . . . . .220 B6
Mayfield Cl NG18 . . . . . .103 B5
Mayfield Ct NG2 . . . . . . .173 C2
Mayfield Dr
Loughborough LE11 . . . . .220 A4
Stapleford NG9 . . . . .170 F2
Mayfield Gr NG10. . . . . . .182 F1
Mayfield Pl NG17 . . . . . .100 D2
Mayfield Rd NG4. . . . . . .174 B7
Mayfield St NG17 . . . . . .114 D3
Mayfield Terr NG20 . . . . 74 B3
Mayflower Ave DN10. . . . 10 A2
Mayflower Cl
Bawtry DN10 . . . . 10 A8
Gainsborough DN21 . . . . . 24 E4
West Bridgford NG2 . . . . .186 A7
Mayflower Ct
Austerfield DN10 . . . . 3 C1
Mansfield NG18 . . . . .102 B3
Shirebrook NG20 . . . . 72 E4
Mayflower Jun & Inf Sch
DN10 . . . . 10 B8
Mayflower Rd NG16 . . . .158 B8
Mayhall Ave NG19 . . . . . . 88 A4
Mayland Cl NG8 . . . . . . .171 C6
May Lodge Dr NG22 . . . . 91 E6
Mayo Rd NG5. . . . . .161 B1
Maypole NG11 . . . . .184 E3
Maypole Cl NG22 . . . . . . 92 E8
Maypole Green NG22 . . . 77 E2

Maypole Rd NG22 . . . . . . 92 E8
Maypole Yd NG1. . . . . . .**223** E3
May S DE7 . . . . .157 D3
Mays Ave NG4 . . . . .174 D6
Mays Cl NG4. . . . . .174 C6
Mays La LN1. . . . . 57 C3
May St DE7. . . . . .157 E4
Maythorn Cl NG11 . . . . .185 C3
Maythorne NG25. . . . . . .121 C3
Maythorne Cl
Arnold NG5 . . . . .162 B7
New Balderton NG24. . . . .140 C5
Maythorne Ind Est
NG25 . . . . .121 D4
Maythorne Wlk ⏹1
NG5. . . . . .161 C7
Maythorn Gr NG21. . . . . 76 B3
Mccabe Ct NG8. . . . . . . .171 C6
Mcclelland Av NG6 . . . . .147 B5
Mccracken Cl NG15. . . . .146 E1
Mcintosh Rd NG4 . . . . . .162 D3
Meade Dr S81 . . . . 36 A7
Meadow Ave
Loughborough LE11 . . . . .220 B6
Mansfield NG18 . . . . .102 C6
Meadow Bank
Mansfield Woodhouse
  NG19 . . . .**88** E6
South Normanton DE55. . .113 A7
Meadowbank Day Hospl
NG2 . . . . .173 B1
Meadowbank Way
NG16. . . . . .143 D3
Meadow Cl
Aslockton NG13 . . . . .179 A5
Eastwood NG16 . . . . .143 F4
Edwinstowe NG22 . . . . . . 76 A2
Farnsfield NG22 . . . . .120 A6
Hucknall NG15 . . . . .145 D5
⏹2 Kirkby-in-Ashfield
  NG17 . . . . .114 E6
North Muskham NG23 . . . .110 F1
Nottingham NG2 . . . . . . .173 C1
Retford DN22 . . . . 29 E1
Tibshelf DE55. . . . . 99 B7
Meadow Cotts
Carlton NG4 . . . . .174 F7
Mansfield Woodhouse
  NG19 . . . .**88** C3
Meadow Cres NG12 . . . .188 A5
Meadow Croft Gdns
NG15 . . . . .145 F5
Meadow Ct
Blyth S81 . . . . 18 A6
Long Whatton LE12 . . . . .212 A4
Nottingham NG2 . . . . . . .173 C1
South Normanton DE55. . .113 A4
Meadow Dr
Keyworth NG12 . . . . .198 A3
Misterton DN10 . . . . 6 F2
Sutton in Ashfield NG17 . .100 C3
Tickhill DN11 . . . . 8 C7
Worksop S80 . . . . 35 C2
Meadow End
Gotham NG11 . . . . .195 B1
Radcliffe on Trent NG12 . .176 C3
Meadow Farm View
NG17 . . . . .114 F4
Meadow Gdns
Beeston NG9 . . . . .183 E4
Collingham NG23 . . . . . . .112 B8
Heanor DE75 . . . . .143 B1
Meadow Gr
Bilsthorpe NG22 . . . . . . .106 A4
Newton DE55 . . . . 99 A3
Nottingham NG2 . . . . . . .173 E2
Meadow La
Beeston NG9 . . . . .183 E4
Bothamsall DN22. . . . . . . 63 E7
Burton Joyce NG14 . . . . .163 F4
Girton NG23. . . . . 82 F4
Hodsock S81 . . . . 17 E4
Long Eaton NG10 . . . . . . .193 F7
Loughborough LE11 . . . . .220 B7
Low Marnham NG23 . . . . .82 C6
North Scarle LN6. . . . . . . 83 F7
⏹2 Nottingham NG2 . . . . .173 F3
Shirebrook NG20. . . . . . . 72 D2
South Normanton DE55. . .113 A7
Weston NG23. . . . . 81 B4
Meadow La Ind Est
LE11 . . . . .220 B6
Meadow Lands DN21 . . . 15 B5
Meadow Lane Inf Sch
NG9 . . . . .183 E4
Meadow La (Notts County
FC) NG2. . . . . .173 E2
Meadow Lark Cl NG17 . .114 D2
Meadow Pl NG20 . . . . 74 A4
Meadow Rd
Awsworth NG16. . . . . . . .158 C5
Beeston NG9 . . . . .184 B4
Blidworth NG21. . . . . . . .118 A5
Carlton NG4. . . . . .174 F7
New Balderton NG24. . . . .140 C4
Worksop S80 . . . . 35 C2
Meadow Rise
Nottingham NG6 . . . . . . .159 F6
Saxilby LN1 . . . . 57 B4
MEADOWS 173 C2
Meadows La LE14. . . . . . .201 D1
Meadow St DE7. . . . . . . .157 F1
Meadows The
Awsworth NG16. . . . . . . .158 B5
Beckingham DN10 . . . . . . 23 B8
Farndon NG24 . . . . .139 A5
South Wheatley DN22 . . . 31 E8
Woodborough NG14 . . . . .149 B4
Meadows Way NG2 . . . . .173 C2
Meadowsweet Hill
NG13. . . . . .177 C4

Meadow The
Retford DN22 . . . . .39 F8
Retford DN22 . . . . .40 A8
Meadowvale Cres
Nottingham NG11 . . . . . .195 E8
Nottingham NG7 . . . . . . .184 E1
Meadow View
Selston NG16 . . . . .128 E6
Southwell NG25 . . . . . . .121 F1
Stapleford NG9 . . . . .182 D8
Meadow Vw DN10 . . . .20 A8
Meadow Way
Clipstone NG21 . . . . .89 F5
Harworth DN11 . . . . .8 F5
Kinoulton NG12 . . . . . . .199 F2
Meadow Wlk LN1 . . . . . . .57 C5
Mead Way NG24 . . . . . .140 C3
Measham Cl NG14 . . . . .173 D1
Medawar Cl NG11 . . . . .184 C1
Meden Ave
Market Warsop NG20 . . . .74 C5
New Houghton NG19 . . . .86 F7
Meden Bank
Bothamsall DN22 . . . . . . .63 F7
Pleasleyhill NG19 . . . . . . .87 B5
Stanton Hill NG17 . . . . . .100 C6
Meden Cl
Nottingham NG11 . . . . . .184 C1
Pleasleyhill NG19 . . . . . . .87 B5
Meden Cres NG17 . . . .100 C4
Meden Gdns NG7 . . . . .172 D7
Meden Glen NG20 . . . . .74 C6
Meden Rd
Mansfield Woodhouse
  NG19 . . . . .88 D4
Wellow NG22 . . . . .78 B4
Meden Sch & Tech Coll The
  NG20 . . . . .74 B5
Meden Side NG20 . . . . .74 D7
Meden Sports Ctr NG20 . .74 B5
Meden Sq NG19 . . . . . . .87 B5
MEDEN VALE 74 E8
Meden Way DN22 . . . . . .39 F5
Medina Dr NG12 . . . . .186 E1
Medway DN22 . . . . .29 D1
Medway Cl NG9 . . . . . .183 C5
Medway Dr NG13 . . . . .177 C3
Meeks Rd NG5 . . . . . . .162 B8
Meering Ave NG24 . . . .125 B4
Meering Cl NG23 . . . . . .98 A1
Meerings The NG23 . . . .81 E1
Meer Rd NG9 . . . . .183 A5
Meeting House Cl
East Leake LE12 . . . . . . .205 F1
East Leake LE12 . . . . . . .214 F8
Meetinghouse La
South Leverton DN22 . . . .42 A6
South Leverton DN22 . . . .42 B6
Melbourne Ct
Mansfield NG18 . . . . . . .103 B6
Nottingham NG8 . . . . . .160 C1
Melbourne Gr DN11 . . . . .8 F4
Melbourne Rd
Nottingham NG8 . . . . . .160 C1
Stapleford NG9 . . . . .170 E1
West Bridgford NG2 . . . .174 A1
Melbourne St
Mansfield Woodhouse
  NG19 . . . . .88 C6
Selston NG16 . . . . .129 B6
Melbury Prim Sch
  NG8 . . . . .171 D8
Melbury Rd
Nottingham, Bilborough
  NG8 . . . . .171 D8
Nottingham, Woodthorpe
  NG3 . . . . .162 A4
Meldreth Rd NG8 . . . . .171 E6
Meldrum Cres NG24 . . .139 E5
Meldrum Dr DN21 . . . . .24 E5
Melford Hall Dr NG2 . . .185 C4
Melford Rd NG8 . . . . . .171 D8
Melksham Rd NG5 . . . .161 C8
Mellish Rd S81 . . . . .16 E2
Mellors Rd
Arnold NG5 . . . . .147 F1
Edwinstowe NG22 . . . . . .75 F1
  Mansfield NG19 . . . . . . .87 D1
Mansfield NG19 . . . . . . .101 D8
West Bridgford NG2 . . . .185 F6
Mellors Way
Nottingham NG16 . . . . . .159 C2
Nottingham NG8 . . . . . .159 C2
Melrose Ave
Beeston NG9 . . . . .184 A5
Mansfield NG18 . . . . . . .102 D5
  Mansfield NG19 . . . . . . .161 C3
Melrose Gdns NG2 . . . .185 C4
Melrose Rd DN21 . . . . . .15 C2
Melrose St NG5 . . . . . .161 C2
Melrose Wlk S80 . . . . . .35 F2
Melton Cl NG10 . . . . . .182 A5
Melton Gdns NG12 . . . .186 B4
Melton Gr NG2 . . . . . . .185 E2
Melton La LE12 . . . . . .204 C2
Melton Rd
East Leake LE12 . . . . . . .214 E5
Long Clawson LE14 . . . . .211 B1
Nether Broughton LE14 . .219 F6
Plumtree NG12 . . . . .197 E8
Rempstone LE12 . . . . . . .215 A5
Rempstone LE12 . . . . . . .215 C6
Stanton-on-the-Wolds
  NG12 . . . . .198 D4
Upper Broughton LE14 . .210 A1
West Bridgford NG12 . . . .186 A3
Widmerpool NG12, LE12 .209 C4
Melville Ct
Meden Vale NG20 . . . . . .74 D8

Melville Ct continued
3 Nottingham NG3 . . .173 C8
Melville Gdns NG3 . . . .173 E6
Melville St NG1 . . . . . .223 E1
Melvyn Dr NG13 . . . . . .177 E4
Memorial Ave S80 . . . . .35 F2
Mendip Cl
Long Eaton NG10 . . . . . .182 A1
Mansfield NG18 . . . . . . .102 E4
Mendip Ct
Carlton in Lindrick S81 . . .25 C7
Nottingham NG5 . . . . . . .160 F8
Mensing Ave NG12 . . . .187 E3
Mercer Rd DN21 . . . . . .15 B2
Merchant Ave NG8 . . . .172 B7
Merchants Fold DN22 . . .29 D1
Merchant St
Nottingham NG6 . . . . . .160 B8
Shirebrook NG20 . . . . . . .73 A4
Mercia Ave NG12 . . . . .189 A4
Mercia Cl
Giltbrook NG16 . . . . . . .158 A4
Worksop S81 . . . . .36 A7
Mercia Ct NG17 . . . . . .100 A2
Mercian Cl DE7 . . . . . .157 E1
Mercia Rd NG24 . . . . . .139 F5
Mercury Cl NG6 . . . . . .160 E5
Mercury Way 2 NG18 . .102 E1
Mere Ave NG14 . . . . . .148 F7
Mere Cl NG14 . . . . . . .148 F7
Meredith Cl NG2 . . . . . .173 B1
Meredith Ct NG9 . . . . . .170 E2
Meregill Cl NG5 . . . . . .146 F1
Merevale Ave NG11 . . . .184 F4
Merevale Cl NG14 . . . . .150 E1
Mere Way NG11 . . . . . .196 D5
Meriac St NG5 . . . . . . .160 F8
Meriden Ave NG9 . . . . .184 A8
Meridian Cl
Ilkeston DE7 . . . . .157 E4
5 Nottingham NG8 . . . .172 B7
Meridian Ct NG1 . . . . . .161 A2
Merlin Cl
Eagle LN6 . . . . .84 D3
Nottingham NG7 . . . . . . .184 E2
Merlin Ct NG17 . . . . . . .101 B3
Merlin Dr NG15 . . . . . . .145 E4
Merlin Rd 1 NG19 . . . . .88 B2
Merlin Way NG7 . . . . . .170 A3
Merrick Dr S81 . . . . . . .36 C3
Merrivale Ct NG3 . . . . .173 C8
Merry Rd NG22 . . . . . . .77 D3
Merryvale Dr NG19 . . . .101 D6
Merryweather Cl
Edwinstowe NG22 . . . . . .91 C8
Southwell NG25 . . . . . . .121 C2
Mersey St NG6 . . . . . . .160 B7
Merton Ave DN22 . . . . . .29 E1
Merton Cl NG5 . . . . . . .148 B1
Merton Ct NG9 . . . . . . .170 E1
Meryton Gr NG17 . . . . . .115 A3
Metcalf Ct NG22 . . . . . .105 F7
Metcalfe Cl NG25 . . . . .136 F8
Metcalfe St NG17 . . . . . .115 A4
Metcalf Rd NG16 . . . . . .144 B3
Meteor Ct NG13 . . . . . .177 B7
Meteor Rd NG6 . . . . . . .145 E2
Methuen Ave NG18 . . . .102 E6
Metro Ave DE55 . . . . . . .99 A3
Mettham St NG7 . . . . . .222 B1
Mews La NG14 . . . . . . .148 E8
Mews The
Blyth S81 . . . . .18 A3
Collingham NG23 . . . . . .112 A7
Meynell Gr 7 NG7 . . . .161 A1
Meynell Rd NG10 . . . . .193 D5
Meynell St DN10 . . . . . . .7 F4
Meyrick Rd NG24 . . . . .125 A1
Miall Cl NG7 . . . . .222 A3
Miall St NG8 . . . . .172 E5
Michael Bruce La NG9 .183 E5
Micklebarrow Cl NG25 .136 C8
Micklebarrow Hill
Averham NG23 . . . . .123 B4
Upton NG23 . . . . .122 F3
Mickleborough Ave
  NG3 . . . . .174 A8
Mickleborough Way
  NG2 . . . . .185 C3
Mickledale Cl NG22 . . . .105 E7
Mickledale La NG22 . . . .105 E6
Mickleden Cl 9 NG2 . . .173 B2
Mickledon Cl 1 NG10 . .193 B8
Micklemore La NG13 . . .178 B8
Middle Ave NG4 . . . . . .174 C8
Middlebeck Ave NG5 . . .162 C8
Middlebeck Dr NG5 . . . .162 C8
Middlebeck Way NG24 .140 B2
Middlebridge Rd DN10 . .12 E4
Middlebrook Rd NG16 . .129 B4
Middledale Rd NG4 . . . .174 C6
Middlefell Ct NG9 . . . . .184 D1
Middlefell Way NG11 . . .184 D1
Middlefield La
Gainsborough DN21 . . . . .24 E7
Ollerton NG22 . . . . .77 B3
Middlefield Rd DN22 . . . .31 E8
Middle Furlong Gdns 5
  NG2 . . . . .173 B2
Middle Furlong Mews 4
  NG2 . . . . .173 B2
Middle Furlong Mws 5
  NG14 . . . . .173 B2
Middle Gate NG24 . . . .139 F8
Middlegate Field Dr
  S80 . . . . .45 A5
Middleley Sch NG25 . . .134 E4
Middle Hill NG1 . . . . . .223 E2
Middle Holme La NG23 . .97 A8
Middle La
Beeston NG9 . . . . .183 E5

Middle La continued
Morton NG25 . . . . .137 D3
Nether Broughton LE14 . .219 D8
Middle Meadow S81 . . . .34 E7
Middle Pavement NG1 .223 E2
Middle St
Barkestone-le-Vale
  NG13 . . . . .192 C2
Beeston NG9 . . . . .184 A6
Hose LE14 . . . . .211 F7
Misson DN10 . . . . .4 C2
Middleton Bvd NG8 . . . .172 C3
Middleton Cl
Nuthall NG16 . . . . .159 C6
Selston NG16 . . . . .129 B7
Middleton Cres NG9 . . . .171 E1
Middleton Ct
Mansfield NG18 . . . . . . .103 B6
New Ollerton NG22 . . . . . .77 C5
Middleton Pl LE11 . . . . .220 A2
Middleton Prim Sch
  NG8 . . . . .172 C4
Middleton Rd
Clipstone NG21 . . . . .89 F4
Clipstone NG21 . . . . .90 A4
Ilkeston DE7 . . . . .170 A5
Mansfield Woodhouse
  NG19 . . . . .88 C5
Newark-on-Trent NG24 . .125 C3
Middleton St
Awsworth NG16 . . . . . . .158 C4
Beeston NG9 . . . . .183 F7
Cossall DE7 . . . . .158 A1
Nottingham NG7 . . . . . . .222 C1
Middle Wood La DN10 . . .4 C6
Midfield Rd NG17 . . . . . .115 B1
Midhurst Cl NG9 . . . . . .183 C4
Midhurst Way NG7 . . . .184 E2
Midland Ave
Carlton NG4 . . . . .175 A4
Nottingham NG7 . . . . . . .222 A1
Stapleford NG9 . . . . .182 C5
Midland Cotts NG12 . . . .185 F7
Midland Cres NG4 . . . . .174 F7
Midland Ct NG7 . . . . . . .172 C5
Midland Gr NG4 . . . . . .175 A8
Midland Rd
Carlton NG4 . . . . .174 F7
Eastwood NG16 . . . . . . .143 F2
Sutton in Ashfield NG17 . .101 B2
Midland St NG10 . . . . . .193 E8
Midland Terr NG24 . . . .124 E1
Midland Way NG7 . . . . .222 A3
Midland Wy
Mansfield NG18 . . . . . . .102 B5
Nottingham NG7 . . . . . . .172 C5
Midway The NG7 . . . . .184 E7
Midworth St NG18 . . . .102 B6
Mikado Rd NG10 . . . . . .193 C5
Mike Powers Pottery ★
  NG11 . . . . .196 C7
Milburn Gr NG13 . . . . . .177 C4
Mildenhall Cres NG5 . . .161 C8
Mile End Rd NG4 . . . . . .174 E5
Milestone Ct DN22 . . . . .28 C6
Miles Yd LE11 . . . . .220 B3
Milfield Cl DN21 . . . . . . .15 E3
Milford Acad The
  NG11 . . . . .195 E8
Milford Ave NG10 . . . . .182 B3
Milford Cl NG6 . . . . . . .160 A8
Milford Cres NG19 . . . .101 D7
Milford Ct NG5 . . . . . . .161 D6
Milford Dr
Ilkeston DE7 . . . . .157 D3
Nottingham NG3 . . . . . . .174 C7
Mill Acre Cl DE7 . . . . . .157 D2
Millash La S80 . . . . .45 B4
Millbank DE75 . . . . .157 A8
Millbank Cl DE7 . . . . . .157 D3
Millbank Pl NG6 . . . . . .146 D3
Mill Baulk Rd DN10 . . . . .14 A6
Millbeck Ave NG8 . . . . .171 C3
Millbeck Cl NG2 . . . . . .186 C6
Mill Bridge Cl DN22 . . . .39 E6
Millbrook Dr NG4 . . . . . .162 C1
Mill Bsns Ctr The DN10 . .12 E2
Mill Cl
Huthwaite NG17 . . . . . . .100 A3
Misterton DN10 . . . . .6 F1
North Leverton with
  Habblesthorpe DN22 . .32 C1
Sutton on Trent NG23 . . . .96 F8
Mill Cl The NG8 . . . . . .160 E3
Mill Cres
Arnold NG5 . . . . .161 E8
Whitwell S80 . . . . .45 A6
Mill Croft NG17 . . . . . . .100 E1
Mill Ct NG18 . . . . .101 E5
Milldale Cl NG11 . . . . . .184 C2
Milldale Ct NG18 . . . . . .103 A5
Milldale Rd
Farnsfield NG22 . . . . . . .120 A6
Long Eaton NG10 . . . . . .193 B6
Milldale Wlk NG17 . . . .100 E1
Millennium Bsns Pk
  NG19 . . . . .87 E2
Millennium Cl DE7 . . . .157 E3
Millennium Ct 4 NG19 . .87 E2
Millennium Way
Mansfield NG18 . . . . . . .103 B3
Rainworth NG21 . . . . . . .104 B1
Millennium Way E
  NG6 . . . . .160 A4
Millennium Way W
Nottingham NG6 . . . . . . .160 A4
Nuthall NG6 . . . . .160 A4
Miller Dr DE7 . . . . .157 B5
Miller Hives Cl NG12 . . .187 E3
Millers Bridge NG12 . . .187 E2

Millers Cl NG12 . . . . . .164 C1
Millers Ct
Clarborough DN22 . . . . . .30 E4
Nottingham NG7 . . . . . . .222 A4
Millersdale Ave
Ilkeston DE7 . . . . .157 E5
Mansfield NG18 . . . . . . .101 E4
Millers Dale Dr DE55 . . .113 B7
Millers Gn 7 NG2 . . . . .174 A4
Millership Way
Cossall DE7 . . . . .158 A2
Ilkeston DE7 . . . . .157 F2
Miller's La LE12 . . . . . .206 C1
Millers Way
Kirkby-in-Ashfield
  NG17 . . . . .115 A5
Retford DN22 . . . . .39 C8
Millers Wy NG17 . . . . . .101 D5
Miller Way DN21 . . . . . .24 E5
Mill Farm Dr NG17 . . . . .99 B7
Millfield Ave LN1 . . . . . .57 B4
Millfield Cl
Ilkeston DE7 . . . . .157 C3
Retford DN22 . . . . .39 E3
Mill Field Cl
Burton Joyce NG14 . . . . .163 E3
Harby NG23 . . . . .70 D2
Millfield Rd
Ilkeston DE7 . . . . .170 A8
Kimberley NG16 . . . . . . .158 E2
Millfield View S80 . . . . .35 C2
Mill Gate
East Bridgford NG13 . . . .165 C3
Newark-on-Trent NG24 . .139 E8
Millgate Mus ★ NG24 . .139 E8
Mill Gdns S80 . . . . .35 D2
Mill Gn NG24 . . . . .140 B8
Mill Heyes NG13 . . . . . .165 D3
Mill Hill
Gringley on the Hill
  DN10 . . . . .12 D2
Gringley on the Hill DN10 . .12 E2
Mill Hill Leys LE12 . . . . .216 C4
Mill Hill Rd NG13 . . . . . .177 D3
Mill Holme DE55 . . . . . .113 B4
Millicent Gr NG2 . . . . . .185 F8
Millicent Rd NG2 . . . . . .185 E8
Millidge Cl NG5 . . . . . . .160 F5
Mill La
Annesley Woodhouse
  NG17 . . . . .114 E2
Arnold NG5 . . . . .161 E8
Aslockton NG13 . . . . . . .179 A5
Beckingham NG24 . . . . . .127 F3
Bradmore NG12 . . . . . . .197 A5
Caunton NG23 . . . . .109 A5
Claypole NG23 . . . . .156 C6
Clayworth DN22 . . . . .21 F4
Clayworth DN22 . . . . .22 B4
Clipston NG12 . . . . .198 D8
Cossall DE7 . . . . .170 B8
Cossall NG16 . . . . .158 C1
Cotgrave NG12 . . . . .187 E4
Eagle LN6 . . . . .84 E4
East Leake LE12 . . . . . . .214 F8
Edwinstowe NG21 . . . . . .76 A1
Hickling LE14 . . . . .210 C7
Huthwaite NG17 . . . . . . .100 A1
Huthwaite NG17 . . . . . . .100 A2
Kegworth DE74 . . . . .203 D2
Kings Clipstone NG21 . . . .90 E6
Lambley NG4 . . . . .163 B7
Lidgett NG21 . . . . .91 A8
Long Clawson LE14 . . . . .211 D3
Long Whatton LE12 . . . . .212 D4
Loughborough LE11 . . . .220 C5
Morton DN21 . . . . .15 C5
Newark-on-Trent NG24 . .139 E8
Normanton on T NG23 . . .81 D7
North Clifton NG23 . . . . . .68 F5
North Leverton with
  Habblesthorpe DN22 . .42 B8
North Muskham NG23 . . .110 F1
Nottingham NG6 . . . . . .146 D3
Orston NG13 . . . . .180 A7
Pinxton NG16 . . . . .113 D2
Rockley DN22 . . . . .51 A2
Sandiacre NG10 . . . . . . .182 C6
Saxilby LN1 . . . . .57 B4
Scarrington NG13 . . . . . .178 F7
Scrooby DN10 . . . . .10 A3
South Leverton DN22 . . . .42 D7
Stainsby S44 . . . . .85 C8
Tichfield Park NG17 . . . .114 D4
Upton NG23 . . . . .137 E8
Walesby NG22 . . . . .63 F2
Walkeringham DN10 . . . . .13 F4
Whitwell S80 . . . . .45 A6
Wigsley NG23 . . . . .83 F8
Willoughby-on-t-W LE12 .217 D8
Worksop S80 . . . . .37 D5
Millman Way DN22 . . . .29 C1
Mill Mdw View S81 . . . . .18 B3
Mill Pk NG25 . . . . .121 F1
Mill Pond Cl NG17 . . . . .114 E1
Mill Rd
Eastwood NG16 . . . . . . .144 B3
Elston NG23 . . . . .153 D5
Gringley on the Hill DN10 . .12 E2
Heanor DE75 . . . . .157 A8
Stapleford NG9 . . . . .182 D8
Millrise Rd NG19 . . . . . .102 D5
Mills Dr NG24 . . . . .139 C6
Mill St
Ilkeston DE7 . . . . .157 E2
Mansfield NG18 . . . . . . .102 D6
Nottingham NG6 . . . . . . .160 B8
Retford DN22 . . . . .39 F6
Sutton in Ashfield NG17 . .100 F2
Worksop S80 . . . . .35 E4
Millstone Cl NG18 . . . . .102 E4

Mills Way S80 . . . . .36 B2
Millview Cl 6 NG2 . . . .173 F4
Millview Ct 13 NG2 . . .173 E4
Millway NG19 . . . . .88 D1
Mill Wlk S80 . . . . .45 A6
Mill Wood La S80 . . . . . .45 D4
Mill Yd
Beeston NG9 . . . . .183 F6
Hucknall NG15 . . . . .146 A4
Milne Ave DN11 . . . . .9 C4
Milne Dr DN11 . . . . .9 D4
Milne Gr DN11 . . . . .9 C4
Milnercroft DN22 . . . . . .29 D1
Milnercroft Gn DN22 . . . .29 D1
Milne Rd DN11 . . . . .9 D4
Milner Fields NG22 . . . . .92 E8
Milner Rd
Long Eaton NG10 . . . . . .193 D8
Nottingham NG5 . . . . . . .161 C2
Milner St
Newark-on-Trent NG24 . .140 A7
Sutton in Ashfield NG17 . .101 A6
Milnhay Rd
Heanor DE75 . . . . .143 C2
Nottingham NG16 . . . . . .143 B1
Milton Ave DE7 . . . . . . .157 E4
Milton Cl NG17 . . . . . . .101 D4
Milton Cres
Beeston NG9 . . . . .183 C2
Ravenshead NG15 . . . . . .117 A2
Milton Ct
Arnold NG5 . . . . .162 B7
Ravenshead NG15 . . . . . .117 A2
Milton Dr
Ravenshead NG15 . . . . . .117 A2
Worksop S81 . . . . .36 B4
Milton Rd
Gainsborough DN21 . . . . .15 E2
Ilkeston DE7 . . . . .157 E4
West Markham NG22 . . . .65 B6
Milton Rise NG15 . . . . . .145 C5
Milton St
Ilkeston DE7 . . . . .157 E2
Kirkby-in-Ashfield NG17 . .115 B5
Long Eaton NG10 . . . . . .193 D7
Mansfield NG18 . . . . . . .102 A7
New Balderton NG24 . . . .140 C6
Nottingham NG1 . . . . . . .223 E3
Milton Wlk S81 . . . . . . .36 B4
Milverton Rd NG5 . . . . .161 C8
Mimosa Cl NG11 . . . . . .184 C1
Minerva Gr NG15 . . . . . .146 C8
Minerva St NG6 . . . . . .160 B8
Minkley Dr NG16 . . . . . .143 C4
Minster Cl
Hucknall NG15 . . . . .146 B8
Kirkby-in-Ashfield NG17 . .114 F6
Minster Gdns NG16 . . . .144 B1
Minster Rd NG16 . . . . . . .6 E2
Minster Sch The NG25 . .136 E2
Minstral Av NG5 . . . . . .161 A2
Minstrel Cl NG15 . . . . . .146 A5
Mint Cl NG10 . . . . .193 A7
Minton Cl NG9 . . . . . . .183 B2
Minton Pastures 3
  NG19 . . . . .89 A1
Minver Cres NG8 . . . . . .160 B2
Mirabelle Way NG11 . . . .9 A6
Mirberry Mews NG7 . . . .222 A1
Mire La DN22 . . . . .28 F6
Misk Hollows NG15 . . . .145 E8
Misk View NG16 . . . . . .144 B2
Mission Bank DN9 . . . . . .2 A8
Mission Carr Nature
Reserve ★ DN9 . . . . . . .5 A7
Mission St NG5 . . . . . . .161 E2
MISSON 4 B2
Misson Bank
Blaxton DN9 . . . . .1 F4
Misson DN9 . . . . .1 F5
Misson Prim Sch DN10 . . .4 B3
MISTERTON 6 F1
Misterton Cres
Ravenshead NG15 . . . . . .116 F1
Ravenshead NG15 . . . . . .117 A1
Misterton Ct 3 NG19 . . .88 B1
Misterton Prim Sch
  DN10 . . . . .13 F8
Mitchell Ave NG16 . . . . .143 A4
Mitchell Cl
Nottingham NG6 . . . . . .160 A6
Worksop S81 . . . . .35 E8
Mitchell St NG10 . . . . . .193 E7
Mitchell Terr DE7 . . . . . .170 A5
Mitford Dr NG5 . . . . . . .147 F2
M Lark Cl NG17 . . . . . . .100 D1
Moat La NG17 . . . . .19 B2
Mob La LE12 . . . . .217 D7
Model La S80 . . . . .58 E8
Model View S80 . . . . . . .58 E8
Model Village S80 . . . . . .58 E8
Model Village Prim Sch
  NG20 . . . . .72 E3
Moffat Cl NG3 . . . . .173 F7
Moira St LE11 . . . . .220 B3
Mollington Sq NG6 . . . .160 B3
Mona Rd NG2 . . . . .174 A1
Mona St NG9 . . . . .184 B6
Monckton Dr NG25 . . . .121 C1
Monckton Rd
Bircotes DN11 . . . . .9 C4
Retford DN22 . . . . .39 C8
Monique Rd NG12 . . . . .185 F3
Monks Cl DE7 . . . . .170 A8
Monk's La NG11 . . . . . . .195 A1
Monks Mdw LE12 . . . . .205 F2
Monksway NG11 . . . . . . .185 A4
Monks Way S81 . . . . .34 F7
Monkton Cl DE7 . . . . . .157 C3
Monkton Dr NG8 . . . . . .171 E7

Monkwood Cl NG23 . . . .98 B1
Monmouth Cl NG8 . . . . .171 B4
Monmouth Rd S81 . . . . . .36 A6
Monroe Wlk 11 NG6 . . .161 A7
Monsaldale Cl NG10 . . . .193 B6
Monsall Ave DE7 . . . . . .157 E5
Monsall St NG7 . . . . . . .160 F1
Monsella Gr DN22 . . . . . .40 A3
Monsell Dr NG5 . . . . . . .147 E1
Montague Rd NG15 . . . .146 A8
Montague St
Beeston NG9 . . . . .183 E4
Mansfield NG18 . . . . . . .102 A6
Nottingham NG6 . . . . . . .160 C7
Montford Rd S81 . . . . . . .35 C8
Montfort Cres NG5 . . . . .161 D4
Montfort St NG7 . . . . . .222 C3
Montgomery Cl 8
  NG9 . . . . .183 C2
Montgomery Rd NG24 . .140 A5
Montgomery St NG7 . . . .222 C4
Montpelier Rd NG7 . . . .172 E1
Montrose S81 . . . . .36 B5
Montrose Ct NG9 . . . . . .170 E1
Montrose Sq NG19 . . . . .88 B6
Montys Mdw S81 . . . . . .35 D8
Monyash Cl DE7 . . . . . .157 E3
Moody Cl NG9 . . . . .183 B2
Moonbeam Way 2
  NG18 . . . . .102 E2
Moor Bridge NG6 . . . . . .146 D1
Moorbridge Cotts
  NG6 . . . . .146 D2
Moorbridge Ct NG13 . . .177 E5
Moorbridge La NG9 . . . .170 D1
Moorbridge Rd NG13 . . .177 E5
Moorbridge Rd E
  NG13 . . . . .177 E5
Moore Ave DE74 . . . . . .203 D3
Moore Cl
Claypole NG23 . . . . .156 D6
East Leake LE12 . . . . . . .205 F2
West Bridgford NG2 . . . .174 B1
Moore Gate NG9 . . . . . .184 A6
Moore Rd NG3 . . . . .162 A2
Moores Ave NG10 . . . . .182 C7
Moore St NG6 . . . . .160 C5
Moor Farm Cl DE55 . . . . .99 B4
Moor Farm Inn La
  NG9 . . . . .171 A2
Moorfield Cl NG15 . . . . .146 E5
Moorfield Cres NG10 . . .182 B5
Moorfield Ct NG9 . . . . . .170 E1
Moorfield La
Creswell NG20 . . . . .58 F4
Whaley Thorns NG20 . . . .59 A4
Moorfield Pl NG20 . . . . . .74 C5
Moorfields Ave NG16 . . .143 F3
Moorgate Pk DN22 . . . . .39 F8
Moorgate St NG7 . . . . . .222 C3
Moorgreen NG16 . . . . . .144 C3
Moorgreen Dr NG8 . . . .159 D2
Moorgreen Ind Pk
  NG16 . . . . .144 B4
Moorgreen Way DN11 . . . .9 A3
Moorhades La NG22 . . . .53 F8
Moorhaigh Cl NG19 . . . . .86 F7
Moorhaigh La NG19 . . . . .87 A3
MOORHOUSE 80 C2
Moorhouse Rd
Egmanton NG22 . . . . .80 C4
Laxton NG22 . . . . .79 C2
Moorhouse NG23 . . . . . . .80 C2
Nottingham NG8 . . . . . . .171 B6
Ossington NG23 . . . . .95 D3
Moorings The 3 NG7 . . .172 F2
Moor La
Aslockton NG13 . . . . . . .178 C5
Beeston NG9 . . . . .171 B2
Besthorpe NG23 . . . . .98 C6
Bingham NG13 . . . . .177 E5
Blyth S81 . . . . .18 D2
Bradmore NG11 . . . . . . .196 E2
Bunny NG11 . . . . .206 E8
Calverton NG14 . . . . . . .149 D6
Caunton NG23 . . . . .108 F7
Dry Doddington DN23 . . .169 E6
East Stoke NG23 . . . . . . .153 E7
Elston NG23 . . . . .154 B5
Gotham NG11 . . . . .205 C8
Loughborough LE11 . . . .220 C3
Mansfield NG18 . . . . . . .101 F6
Morton NG25 . . . . .137 C3
Normanton on S LE12 . . .213 C4
North Clifton NG23 . . . . . .69 B4
Ruddington NG11 . . . . . .196 C6
South Clifton NG23 . . . . . .69 D3
Stathern NG13 . . . . .202 F5
Syerston NG23 . . . . .153 C3
Thorney NG23 . . . . .69 F4
Thorpe NG23 . . . . .153 F7
Thorpe NG23 . . . . .154 A7
Upper Langwith S44 . . . . .72 A8
Moorland Ave
Stapleford NG9 . . . . .182 D6
Walkeringham DN10 . . . . .13 F6
Moorland Cl
Sutton in Ashfield
  NG17 . . . . .101 A6
Walkeringham DN10 . . . . .13 F6
Moorlands Cl
Long Eaton NG10 . . . . . .182 B2
Norwell NG23 . . . . .109 F8
Norwell NG23 . . . . .110 A7
Moorland Way NG18 . . .103 A6
Moorland Wlk DN10 . . . .13 F6

Moor Rd
Bestwood Village NG6 . . .146 E6
Brinsley NG16 . . . . .143 E8
Calverton NG14 . . . . . . .149 A7
Collingham NG23 . . . . . . .98 B1
Nottingham NG8 . . . . . . .159 D1
Moorsholm Dr NG8 . . .171 D4
Moor St
Carlton NG4 . . . . .175 A4
Mansfield NG18 . . . . . . .101 F5
Mansfield NG18 . . . . . . .102 A6
Moor The NG16 . . . . . .143 D8
Moor Top Rd DN11 . . . . .8 F5
Moor View NG11 . . . . .206 E8
Morado Way NG4 . . . .175 C2
Moray Ct NG16 . . . . . .158 F7
Moray Sq NG19 . . . . . .101 D5
Morden Cl NG8 . . . . . .171 D8
Morden Rd NG16 . . . . .158 C8
Moreland Ct
Carlton NG4 . . . . .174 C7
[10] Nottingham NG3 . . . .173 F3
Moreland Pl [11] NG2 . .173 F3
Moreland St NG2 . . . . .173 F3
Morel Cl NG16 . . . . . . .143 F1
Morello Ave NG4 . . . . .174 F7
Morello Dr NG8 . . . . . .172 C7
Moreton Ave DE7 . . . . .157 F5
Moreton Rd NG11 . . . .195 E7
Morgana Rd NG19 . . . . .87 D1
Morgan Mews NG7 . . . .184 D2
Morgans Cl NG24 . . . . .126 B2
Morkinshire Cres
NG12 . . . . .187 F4
Morkinshire La NG12 . .187 E4
Morley Ave
Nottingham NG3 . . . . . .161 E2
Retford DN22 . . . . .29 C1
Morley Cl NG18 . . . . . .103 B5
Morley Ct [5] NG2 . . . .173 E4
Morley Dr DE7 . . . . . . .157 D3
Morley Gdns NG14 . . . .176 A3
Morley Pl NG14 . . . . . .173 F8
Morley Rd NG3 . . . . . .162 A1
Morley's Cl NG14 . . . . .150 E1
Morley St
Arnold NG5 . . . . .161 D6
Gainsborough DN21 . . . . .24 C8
Kirkby-in-Ashfield NG17 .115 B4
Loughborough LE11 . . . .220 C5
Stanton Hill NG17 . . . . .100 C6
Sutton in Ashfield NG17 .100 F3
Mornington Cl NG18 . . .182 C6
Mornington Cres NG8 . .159 D3
Mornington Prim Sch
NG16 . . . . .159 D4
Morrell Bank NG5 . . . .160 F6
Morris Ave NG9 . . . . . .183 B1
Morris Cl LE11 . . . . . . .220 C4
Morris Rd NG8 . . . . . . .159 D1
Morris St NG4 . . . . . . .175 A7
MORTON
Lincs 15 C4
Notts 137 D3
Morton Carr DN21 . . . . .14 F7
Morton Cl
Mansfield NG18 . . . . . . .103 B6
Morton DN21 . . . . .15 B4
Radcliffe on Trent NG12 .176 C3
Morton Gdns NG22 . . . .176 C3
Morton Gr S81 . . . . . . .35 E8
Morton Hall Gdns *
DN22 . . . . .38 A5
Morton La LN6 . . . . . . .84 D1
Morton Rd DN21 . . . . . .15 C3
Morton St NG17 . . . . . .87 E1
Morton Terr DN21 . . . . .15 C2
Morton Trentside Prim Sch
DN21 . . . . .15 A4
Morval Rd NG8 . . . . . .171 E6
Morven Ave
Hucknall NG15 . . . . . . .146 B6
Mansfield Woodhouse
NG19 . . . . .88 B2
Sutton in Ashfield NG17 .100 E2
Morven Park Prim Sch
NG17 . . . . .115 B5
Morven Rd NG17 . . . . .115 B5
Morven St S80 . . . . . . .58 F8
Morven Terr NG20 . . . . .74 B3
Mosborough Rd NG17 . .100 A1
Moseley Rd NG15 . . . . .130 C8
Moses View S81 . . . . . .34 F7
Mosgrove Cl S81 . . . . . .35 C7
Mosley St
Hucknall NG15 . . . . . . .146 A6
Nottingham NG7 . . . . . .172 F8
Mosscar Cl NG20 . . . . . .73 F1
Moss Cl
Arnold NG5 . . . . .147 C1
East Bridgford NG13 . . . .165 D3
Mosscroft Ave NG11 . . .184 D1
Mossdale S81 . . . . .36 A8
Mossdale Rd
Mansfield NG18 . . . . . . .102 A8
Nottingham NG5 . . . . . .161 C5
Moss Dr NG9 . . . . .183 B7
Moss La LN6 . . . . .71 F3
Moss Rd NG15 . . . . . . .145 F7
Moss Rise NG3 . . . . . . .162 B2
Moss Side NG11 . . . . . .185 A3
Mosswood Cres NG5 . . .161 B7
Motorpoint Arena *
NG1 . . . . .223 F2
Mottram Rd NG9 . . . . .183 C6
Moulton Cres NG24 . . . .140 C3
Mountain Ash Cres
NG12 . . . . .186 A2

Mount Ave S81 . . . . . . .35 E5
Mountbatten Ct DE7 . . .157 F3
Mountbatten Gr NG4 . . .162 E2
Mountbatten Way NG9 .183 C2
Mount CE Prim Sch
NG24 . . . . .125 A1
Mount Cl DN11 . . . . .8 F5
Mount Cres
Market Warsop NG20 . . . .74 C3
South Normanton DE55 . .113 A3
Mount Ct NG24 . . . . . . .140 D4
Mountfield Ave NG10 . .182 B4
Mountfield Dr NG5 . . . .161 A7
Mount Hooton Rd NG7 .222 C4
Mount Hooton St NG7 . .173 D4
Mount La
Hose LE14 . . . . .211 F7
Newark-on-Trent NG24 . .140 A8
Mount Milner NG18 . . . .102 D6
Mountney Pl NG24 . . . .125 A3
Mount Pleasant
Carlton NG4 . . . . .174 E7
Ilkeston DE7 . . . . .157 E4
Keyworth NG12 . . . . . . .198 A3
[2] Mansfield NG18 . . . . .102 A7
Nottingham NG6 . . . . . .160 C4
Radcliffe on Trent NG12 .175 E3
Retford DN22 . . . . .39 F7
Sutton in Ashfield NG17 .100 F4
Mount Rd NG24 . . . . . .140 C4
Mountsorrel Dr NG2 . . .186 B6
Mount St
Mansfield NG18 . . . . . . .101 F8
Nottingham NG1 . . . . . .223 D3
Nottingham, New Basford
NG7 . . . . .160 F1
Stapleford NG9 . . . . . . .182 E7
Mount The
Arnold NG5 . . . . .147 D1
Bestwood Village NG6 . . .146 E4
Clipstone NG19 . . . . .89 D3
Nottingham, Broxtowe
NG8 . . . . .159 E1
Nottingham, Portchester
NG3 . . . . .162 C2
Stapleford NG9 . . . . . . .182 D6
Mount Vernon Pk DN22 . .40 A4
Mount View Cl NG18 . . .102 D6
Mowbray Ct NG3 . . . . .223 F3
Mowbray Gdns NG2 . . .185 C5
Mowbray Rise NG5 . . . .161 F8
Mowbray Str DN21 . . . . .15 C2
Mowcrofts La NG22 . . . .68 B7
Mowlands Cl NG17 . . . .101 B2
Moyra Dr NG5 . . . . . . .161 C7
Mozart Cl NG7 . . . . . . .222 A3
Muir Ave NG12 . . . . . .197 D8
Muirfield S81 . . . . .36 B6
Muirfield Cl [8] NG17 . .114 E7
Muirfield Rd NG5 . . . . .147 A1
Muirfield Way NG19 . . . .88 E6
Mulberry Cl
[4] Mansfield NG18 . . . .102 D5
Newark-on-Trent NG24 . .140 D8
West Bridgford NG2 . . . .185 B5
Mulberry Cres S81 . . . . .25 F7
Mulberry Ct DN10 . . . . . .4 B3
Mulberry Gdns
Kegworth DE74 . . . . . . .203 D2
[1] Nottingham NG6 . . . .160 A8
Mulberry Gr NG15 . . . .146 B4
Mulberry La NG25 . . . .121 D4
Mulberry Way
East Leake LE12 . . . . . .214 C8
[1] Harworth DN11 . . . . . .8 F4
Saxilby LN1 . . . . .57 A5
Torksey Lock LN1 . . . . . .44 C1
Multimode St NG19 . . .184 A4
Mumby Cl NG24 . . . . . .125 A1
Mundella Rd NG2 . . . . .173 D1
Mundy St DE7 . . . . . . .157 E2
Munks Ave NG15 . . . . .145 F7
Munnmoore Cl DE74 . . .203 C3
Murden Way NG6 . . . . .184 B6
Murdoch Cl NG22 . . . . .119 E7
Murdon Cres NG12 . . . .197 D2
Muriel Rd NG9 . . . . . . .183 F7
Muriel St NG6 . . . . . . .160 B7
Murray Cl NG5 . . . . . . .160 F5
Murray St NG18 . . . . . .102 B5
Muschamp Terr NG20 . . .74 B3
Mushill La LE12 . . . . . .216 D5
Muskham Ave DE7 . . . .157 E1
Muskham Ct [1] NG19 . . .88 B1
Muskham La NG23 . . . .110 C2
Muskham Prim Sch
NG23 . . . . .110 F2
Muskham St NG2 . . . . .173 D1
Mustang Cl NG18 . . . . .145 E2
Musters Cres NG2 . . . . .185 E5
Musters Croft NG4 . . . .174 F4
Musters Rd
Bingham NG13 . . . . . . .177 D4
Langar NG13 . . . . .190 D2
Newstead NG15 . . . . . . .130 D6
Ruddington NG11 . . . . . .196 C6
West Bridgford NG2 . . . .185 E5
Musters St NG20 . . . . . .74 C5
Musters Wlk [4] NG6 . . .160 A7
MUSTON 181 F1
Muston Cl NG3 . . . . . . .161 F1
Muston La NG13 . . . . . .181 D1
Mutton La DN10 . . . . . . .2 A8
Muttonshire Hill DN22 . .50 F5
Mynd The NG8 . . . . .88 C2
Myrtle Ave
Long Eaton NG10 . . . . . .193 C6

Myrtle Ave *continued*
[1] Nottingham NG7 . . . .173 B8
Stapleford NG9 . . . . . . .182 E6
Myrtle Cl NG20 . . . . . . .72 D6
Myrtle Gr NG9 . . . . . . .184 A7
Myrtle Rd NG4 . . . . . . .174 C8
Myrtle St DN22 . . . . . . .39 D6
Myrtus Cl NG11 . . . . . .184 C2
Mytholme Cl NG10 . . . .182 C2

N

Nabbs La NG15 . . . . . . .145 E5
Naburn Ct [4] NG8 . . . .172 D8
Nairn Cl
Arnold NG5 . . . . .148 B1
Farnsfield NG22 . . . . . . .119 F5
Nairn Mews NG4 . . . . .174 E7
Nan Sampson Bank DN9 . .1 D8
Nansen St NG6 . . . . . . .160 C6
Naomi Cres NG6 . . . . . .146 C1
Naomi Ct NG6 . . . . . . .146 C1
Naples Cres NG19 . . . . .86 F5
Narrow La
Austerfield DN10 . . . . .3 B1
Bawtry DN10 . . . . .10 B8
Greasley NG16 . . . . .145 A4
Hathern LE12 . . . . .213 A1
Wymeswold LE12 . . . . . .217 B2
Naseby Cl NG5 . . . . . . .160 F4
Naseby Dr NG10 . . . . . .193 E4
Naseby Rd NG24 . . . . . .140 E8
Nash Cl S81 . . . . .36 C4
Nathaniel Rd NG10 . . . .193 F7
Nathans La
Bassingfield NG12 . . . . .186 F7
Radcliffe on Trent NG12 .187 A7
National Holocaust Ctr &
Mus The * NG22 . . . . . .78 E3
National Ice Centre *
NG1 . . . . .223 F2
National Sch The
NG15 . . . . .130 F1
National Water Sports Ctr
NG12 . . . . .174 F3
Naturescape Wild Flower
Farm * NG13 . . . . . . .190 E1
Navenby Wlk NG7 . . . . .184 E2
Navigation Ct LN1 . . . . .57 B3
Navigation St NG2 . . . .173 F2
Navigation Way LE11 . . .220 A3
Navigation Yd NG24 . . .139 F8
Naworth Cl NG6 . . . . . .160 E5
Naylor Ave
Gotham NG11 . . . . .195 B1
Loughborough LE11 . . . .220 D2
Nazareth Rd NG7 . . . . .172 E2
ncn City (Adams) NG1 . .223 F2
ncn High Pavement Sixth
Form Acad NG1 . . . . . . .223 D3
Neal Cl NG16 . . . . .143 A3
Neale St NG10 . . . . . . .193 E7
Near Mdw NG10 . . . . . .193 E5
Nearsby Dr NG2 . . . . . .186 B6
Nebula Way NG18 . . . . .102 F1
Needham Rd NG5 . . . . .162 A8
Needham St NG5 . . . . . .147 B1
Needwood Ave NG9 . . . .170 D2
Neeps Croft NG14 . . . . .150 A6
Negus Ct NG4 . . . . .163 B6
Neighwood Cl NG9 . . . .182 E2
Nell Gwyn Cres NG5 . . .147 C1
Nelper Cres DE7 . . . . . .170 A5
Nelson Cl NG19 . . . . . . .101 E7
Nelson La NG23 . . . . . . .110 F2
Nelson Rd
Arnold NG5 . . . . .161 E7
Beeston NG9 . . . . .184 A4
New Balderton NG24 . . . .140 B4
Nottingham NG6 . . . . . .160 C7
Nelson St
Gainsborough DN21 . . . . .15 C2
Ilkeston DE7 . . . . .157 F1
Long Eaton NG10 . . . . . .193 D6
Nottingham NG1 . . . . . .223 F2
Retford DN22 . . . . .39 F6
Nene Cl NG15 . . . . .145 E3
Nene Wlk S81 . . . . .35 E7
Nene Way NG13 . . . . . .177 D3
Nesbitt St NG17 . . . . . .100 F1
Nesfield Ct DE7 . . . . . . .157 E1
Nesfield Rd DE7 . . . . . .157 E1
Nest Ave NG17 . . . . . . .115 C4
Nest Cres NG17 . . . . . . .115 C4
Neston Dr NG6 . . . . . . .160 C4
NETHER
BROUGHTON 219 C8
Nether Cl
Eastwood NG16 . . . . . . .143 F4
Nottingham NG3 . . . . . .174 A6
Nethercross Dr NG20 . . .74 C5
Nether Ct NG20 . . . . . . .74 A6
NETHERFIELD 175 B6
Netherfield Cl NG20 . . . .74 D8
Netherfield Inf Sch
NG20 . . . . .74 D8
Netherfield La
Budby NG22 . . . . .61 F2
Church Warsop NG20 . . . .74 D7
Market Warsop NG20 . . . .61 C1
Perlethorpe NG22 . . . . . .62 C3
Perlethorpe NG22 . . . . . .62 F5
Perlethorpe NG22 . . . . . .63 A5
Netherfield Prim Sch
NG4 . . . . .174 F6
Netherfield Rd
Long Eaton NG10 . . . . . .193 C4
Sandiacre NG10 . . . . . . .182 B4
Netherfield Sta NG4 . . .174 F6

Nethergate NG11 . . . . .184 C2
Nethergate Acad
Clifton NG11 . . . . .185 A1
Nottingham NG9 . . . . . .184 F1
NETHER LANGWITH 59 B1
Nethermere La NG8 . . . .159 C1
Nether Pasture NG4 . . .175 B6
Nether Slade Rd DE7 . . .157 E2
Nether St
Beeston NG9 . . . . .184 A6
Harby LE14 . . . . .202 A3
Nether Thorpe Rd S80 . .34 A5
Netherton Pl S80 . . . . . .36 A1
Netherton Rd S80 . . . . . .47 A7
Nettlecliff Wlk NG5 . . . .160 E8
Nettle Croft DN11 . . . . . .8 C7
Nettleship Rd NG16 . . . .158 F6
Nettleworth Inf Sch
NG19 . . . . .88 C4
Neville Dr NG12 . . . . . .200 A2
Neville Rd NG14 . . . . . .148 F6
Neville Sadler Ct NG9 . .184 B7
Newall Dr
Beeston NG9 . . . . .183 C2
Everton DN10 . . . . .11 A1
Newark Air Mus *
NG24 . . . . .126 A5
Newark Ave [16] NG2 . . .173 E4
Newark Bsns Pk NG24 . .125 C3
Newark Castle * NG24 . .139 F8
Newark Castle Sta
NG24 . . . . .124 F1
Newark Cl NG18 . . . . . .102 F2
Newark Coll NG24 . . . . .140 A8
Newark Cres NG2 . . . . .173 E4
Newark Ct NG5 . . . . . . .160 F5
Newark Dr NG18 . . . . . .102 F2
Newark High Acad
NG24 . . . . .139 F7
Newark Hospl NG24 . . . .140 A6
Newark La
Barnby in the Willows
NG24 . . . . .141 C3
Barnby in the Willows
NG24 . . . . .141 E5
Bingham NG13 . . . . . . .177 E5
Worksop S80 . . . . .35 F2
Newark Mus & Tudor Hall *
NG24 . . . . .140 A8
Newark North Gate Sta
NG24 . . . . .125 B1
NEWARK-ON-TRENT . . .140 C7
Newark Orchard Sch
NG24 . . . . .140 C6
Newark Rd
Alverton NG13 . . . . . . .180 D8
Barnby in the Willows
NG24 . . . . .141 D6
Caunton NG23 . . . . .109 B4
Coddington NG24 . . . . . .125 F1
Collingham LN6 . . . . . . .112 F3
Collingham NG23 . . . . . .111 F6
Cotham NG23 . . . . .154 F3
Cotham NG23 . . . . .155 A2
Dry Doddington NG23 . . .156 A3
Eakring NG22 . . . . .92 F1
Eakring NG22 . . . . .93 C1
Hawton NG24 . . . . .139 D3
Hockerton NG25 . . . . . . .122 C5
Kersall NG22 . . . . .108 A8
Kilvington NG13 . . . . . . .168 F2
Kilvington NG13 . . . . . . .169 A3
Kirklington NG22 . . . . . .120 F8
Laughterton LN1 . . . . . . .55 B7
Long Bennington NG23 . .155 F3
Maplebeck NG22 . . . . . .107 F8
Ollerton NG22 . . . . .77 A3
Ompton NG22 . . . . .93 C6
Southwell NG25 . . . . . . .121 F1
Stapleford LN6 . . . . . . .127 C8
Sutton in Ashfield NG17 .101 C1
Tuxford NG22 . . . . .65 F2
Tuxford NG22 . . . . .66 A2
Wellow NG22 . . . . .77 D2
Newark Rd Service Rd
NG17 . . . . .101 B1
Newark St NG2 . . . . . . .173 E4
Newark Way NG18 . . . .103 A2
NEW BALDERTON 140 B5
Newbarn Cl NG20 . . . . . .72 D2
Newberry Cl NG12 . . . . .189 A4
Newbery Ave NG10 . . . .193 F6
Newbery Cl NG21 . . . . . .76 A3
Newbold St NG9 . . . . . .171 E8
Newbold Way NG15 . . . .199 F2
Newbound La NG17 . . . . .86 C2
New Bound La NG17 . . . . .86 D2
Newboundmill La NG19 . .87 A4
New Brickyard La
DE74 . . . . .203 D1
New Brook Bsns Pk
NG20 . . . . .73 A2
Newbury Cl NG3 . . . . . .162 A4
Newbury Ct [3] NG5 . . .173 B8
Newbury Dr NG16 . . . . .159 D3
Newbury Gdns NG12 . . .198 A1
Newbury Mews [5] S80 . .35 F2
Newbury Rd
Balderton NG24 . . . . . . .140 E8
Newark-on-Trent NG24 . .125 E1
Newcastle Ave
Beeston NG9 . . . . .183 F6
Carlton NG4 . . . . .162 E1
Newark-on-Trent NG24 . .140 A6
Worksop S80 . . . . .35 E1
Newcastle Cir NG7 . . . . .222 C2
Newcastle Dr NG7 . . . . .222 C3
Newcastle Farm Dr
NG8 . . . . .160 C1
Newcastle St
Huthwaite NG17 . . . . . .100 A3

Newcastle St *continued*
[4] Mansfield NG18 . . . .102 A7
Mansfield Woodhouse
NG19 . . . . .88 B3
Market Warsop NG20 . . . .74 B4
Nottingham NG1 . . . . . .223 E3
Nottingham, Bulwell NG6 .160 C8
Tuxford NG22 . . . . .65 F2
Worksop S80 . . . . .35 F2
Newcastle Terr NG7 . . . .222 C3
New Cl
Blidworth NG21 . . . . . . .117 F5
Blidworth NG21 . . . . . . .118 A5
Kirkby-in-Ashfield NG17 .115 A5
New Coll Nottingham
Hucknall NG15 . . . . . . .146 B7
Nottingham NG3 . . . . . .223 F3
Newcombe Dr NG5 . . . .162 C7
Newcomen Ct NG22 . . . .77 C3
New Cotts NG20 . . . . . . .59 F3
NEW CROSS 100 E4
New Cross St NG17 . . . .100 F4
New Cswy NG13 . . . . . .192 C2
New Ct Gdns DN22 . . . . .40 A5
New Derby Rd NG16 . . . .143 C3
Newdigate Rd NG16 . . . .159 A7
Newdigate St
Ilkeston DE7 . . . . .170 A6
Kimberley NG16 . . . . . . .159 A6
Nottingham NG7 . . . . . .222 C3
Newdigate Villas NG7 . .222 C3
New Eaton Rd NG9 . . . .182 E5
New England Way NG19 . .87 C3
New Fall St NG17 . . . . . .99 F3
New Farm La NG16 . . . .159 C6
Newfield La NG23 . . . . . .167 C6
Newfield Rd NG5 . . . . . .161 A3
New Fosse Rd NG24 . . . .139 B5
Newgate Cl NG4 . . . . . .174 E7
Newgate Ct NG7 . . . . . .222 B2
Newgate La NG18 . . . . .102 D7
Newgate Lane Prim Sch
NG18 . . . . .102 C7
Newgate St
Bingham NG13 . . . . . . .177 E5
Worksop S80 . . . . .35 F2
Newhall Gr NG2 . . . . . .173 F1
Newhall La
Edingley NG22 . . . . .120 C2
Edingley NG22 . . . . .135 B8
Newham Cl DE75 . . . . . .143 A1
Newhaven Ave NG19 . . . .88 B3
New Hill
Farnsfield NG22 . . . . . . .119 F6
Walesby NG22 . . . . .64 A2
New Holles Ct S80 . . . . . .35 F2
Newholm Dr NG11 . . . . .185 A4
NEW HOUGHTON 86 F7
New Hucknall Way [2]
NG17 . . . . .100 A1
Newings La NG22 . . . . . .42 F8
New Ings La DN21 . . . . . .33 C6
NEWINGTON 10 E8
Newington Rd
Austerfield DN10 . . . . .3 D1
Austerfield DN10 . . . . . . .10 C8
New Inn Wlk DN22 . . . . .39 F5
New King St LE11 . . . . . .220 C3
New La
Aslockton NG13 . . . . . . .178 E6
Blidworth NG21 . . . . . . .117 C5
Girton NG23 . . . . .83 B4
Hilcote DE55 . . . . .99 C2
Hilcote DE55 . . . . .113 C8
Stanton Hill NG17 . . . . .100 D6
Newland Cl
Beeston NG9 . . . . .183 A2
Nottingham NG8 . . . . . .172 C5
Newlands
Gainsborough DN21 . . . . .15 C1
Retford DN22 . . . . .39 D4
Newlands Ave NG22 . . . . .77 C5
Newlands Cl NG12 . . . . .186 C4
Newlands Cres DE55 . . . .99 A3
Newlands Dr
Carlton NG4 . . . . .162 F1
Clipstone NG19 . . . . .89 C3
Newlands Jun Sch
NG19 . . . . .89 E3
Newlands Rd
Clipstone NG19 . . . . .89 C1
Mansfield NG18 . . . . . . .103 B8
Newlands The NG24 . . . .140 E2
NEW LENTON 172 F4
New Linden St NG20 . . . .73 A4
New Line Rd NG17 . . . . .114 C5
Newlyn Dr
Nottingham NG8 . . . . . .172 D8
South Normanton DE55 . .113 C6
Newlyn Gdns NG8 . . . . .172 D8
Newmanleys Rd NG16 . .157 E8
Newmanleys Rd S
NG16 . . . . .157 E8
Newman Rd NG14 . . . . .148 E8
Newmarket Rd NG6 . . . .160 D6
Newmarket St NG18 . . . .102 C6
Newmarket Way NG9 . . .182 F1
New Mill La
Mansfield Woodhouse
NG19 . . . . .88 E3
Mansfield Woodhouse
NG19 . . . . .88 F2
Newnham Rd NG24 . . . .125 C2
NEW OLLERTON 77 E5
New Pk La NG18 . . . . . . .88 C1
New Pl DN22 . . . . .40 A7
Newport Cres NG19 . . . . .87 E1
Newport Dr NG8 . . . . . .160 D1
Newquay Ave [1] NG7 . .172 E7
New Rd
Barton in Fabis NG11 . . .194 F6

New Rd *continued*
Bilsthorpe NG22 . . . . . . .105 E6
Blidworth NG21 . . . . . . .118 A5
Colston Bassett NG12 . . .189 D2
Firbeck S81 . . . . .16 A5
Firbeck S81 . . . . .16 A6
Greasley NG16 . . . . .144 E6
Hawksworth NG13 . . . . .167 C3
Morton NG25 . . . . .137 C5
Nottingham NG7 . . . . . .172 D6
Oxton NG25 . . . . .134 B3
Radcliffe on Trent NG12 .175 F4
Stapleford NG9 . . . . . . .170 D1
Staunton in the Vale
NG13 . . . . .169 D3
Tickhill DN11 . . . . .8 A7
Treswell DN22 . . . . .42 C3
New Rise NG11 . . . . . . .195 C8
New Row
Carlton NG4 . . . . .174 D7
Westwood NG16 . . . . . . .128 A5
New Scott St NG20 . . . . .59 A2
New St
Gainsborough DN21 . . . . .15 C1
Hilcote DE55 . . . . .113 C8
Huthwaite NG17 . . . . . .99 F3
Huthwaite NG17 . . . . . .100 A3
Kegworth DE74 . . . . . . .203 E3
Kirkby-in-Ashfield NG17 .115 B4
Long Eaton NG10 . . . . . .193 E8
Loughborough LE11 . . . .220 A3
Newark-on-Trent NG24 . .140 A8
Newton DE55 . . . . .99 A4
[15] Nottingham NG5 . . .161 B1
Retford DN22 . . . . .39 F6
South Normanton DE55 . .113 A4
Sutton in Ashfield NG17 .100 E2
NEWSTEAD 130 E5
Newstead Abbey & Gdns *
NG15 . . . . .131 C8
Newstead Abbey Pk
Newstead NG15 . . . . . . .116 B1
Newstead NG15 . . . . . . .131 B8
Newstead Ave
Newark-on-Trent NG24 . .125 A1
Nottingham NG3 . . . . . .162 C2
Radcliffe on Trent NG12 .176 A4
Newstead Cl
Kirkby-in-Ashfield
NG17 . . . . .115 C5
Selston NG16 . . . . .129 B7
Newstead Dr NG2 . . . . .186 B7
Newstead Gr
Bingham NG13 . . . . . . .177 C4
Nottingham NG1 . . . . . .223 D4
Newstead Ind Est NG5 . .162 A7
Newstead Prim Sch
NG15 . . . . .130 D6
Newstead Rd
Long Eaton NG10 . . . . . .182 C3
Newstead NG15 . . . . . . .130 D7
Newstead Rd S DE7 . . . .157 D3
Newstead St
Mansfield NG19 . . . . . . .101 D7
[6] Nottingham NG5 . . . .161 C3
Newstead Sta NG15 . . . .130 E6
Newstead Terr NG15 . . .146 A8
Newstead Way NG8 . . . .159 D2
New Terr
Pleasley NG19 . . . . .86 F5
Sandiacre NG10 . . . . . . .182 B6
Newthorpe Comm
Eastwood NG16 . . . . . . .144 A1
Newthorpe Common
NG16 . . . . .158 A8
NEWTHORPE 99 B3
Newthorpe St NG2 . . . . .173 D2
NEWTON 99 B3
Newton Ave
Bingham NG13 . . . . . . .177 D4
Radcliffe on Trent NG12 .176 A4
Newton Cl
Arnold NG5 . . . . .162 B6
[1] Gainsborough DN21 . . .24 F8
Lowdham NG14 . . . . . . .150 E1
Worksop S81 . . . . .35 C7
Newtondale Ave NG19 . . .88 E1
Newtondale Cl NG8 . . . .160 C1
Newton Dr
[3] Heanor DE75 . . . . . .143 A1
Stapleford NG9 . . . . . . .182 E6
West Bridgford NG2 . . . .185 C4
Newton Gdns NG13 . . . .177 C6
Newton Hill NG22 . . . . . .77 C3
Newton La NG13 . . . . . .177 D7
NEWTON ON TRENT 55 A1
Newton Paddocks
NG22 . . . . .106 E8
Newton Prim Sch DE55 . .99 A3
Newton Rd
Carlton NG4 . . . . .162 E3
Kettlethorpe LN1 . . . . . . .55 E1
Newton DE55 . . . . .99 A4
Newton's La NG16 . . . . .158 B4
Newton St
Beeston NG9 . . . . .183 E4
Mansfield NG18 . . . . . . .102 C6
Newark-on-Trent NG24 . .140 A7
Nottingham NG7 . . . . . .172 E1
Retford DN22 . . . . .39 F4
Newtonwood La
Tibshelf DE55 . . . . .99 B5
Tibshelf DE55 . . . . .99 C5
New Tythe St NG10 . . . .193 F7
New Vale Rd NG4 . . . . . .174 C5
New Westwood NG16 . . .128 D6
ng2 Bsns Pk NG2 . . . . .173 A1
Nicholas Cl NG22 . . . . . .66 A3
Nicholas Rd NG9 . . . . . .171 D1
Nicholson's Row NG20 . .72 F3
Nicholson St NG24 . . . . .140 A7
Nicker Hill NG12 . . . . . .198 A3

Nicklaus Ct **5** NG5 ....161 A8
Nidderdale NG8 ....171 C4
Nidderdale Cl NG8...171 C3
Nightingale DN22...... 42 B1
Nightingale Ave
  Hathern LE12........213 A1
  Pleasley NG19.........87 A4
Nightingale Cl
  Balderton NG24.......140 E4
  Clipstone NG21........89 F4
  Mansfield NG21.........89 F4
  Nottingham NG8 .....172 A1
  Nuthall NG16.........159 D6
Nightingale Cres NG16 129 B6
Nightingale Dr NG19....87 E1
Nightingale Gr
  South Normanton DE55..113 C5
  Worksop S81.........35 D7
Nightingale Way
  Bingham NG13.......178 A3
  Woodbeck DN22 ......53 B8
Nightjar Way
  Rainworth NG21 .....117 F8
  Rainworth NG21 .....118 A8
Nile St NG1..........223 F3
Nilsson Rd NG9........183 B3
Nimbus Wy NG16.......159 A7
Nine Acre Gdns NG6 ...159 F8
Nine Acres DE74......203 C4
Nine Corners NG16 ....158 F6
Nine Scores La DN9......1 E7
Ninth Ave NG19.......103 A8
Nixon Rise NG15.......145 D5
Nixon Walk LE12......205 E2
Nixon Way NG23........98 A1
Noble La NG13........179 A5
Noburn Cres NG6......160 F3
Noel St
  Gainsborough DN21 ....15 C2
  Kimberley NG16......159 A6
  Mansfield NG18.......102 A7
  Nottingham NG7 .....172 F8
Nook Flatt Rd DN10....18 A8
Nookin The NG22......66 B6
Nook The
  Beeston NG9........184 A7
  Beeston, Chilwell NG9..183 E4
  Calverton NG14.......148 F7
  East Leake LE12......205 E1
  Nottingham NG8 .....171 E4
  Shirebrook NG20......72 D3
Norbett Cl NG9.......183 C3
Norbett Ct NG5.......148 A1
Norbett Rd NG5.......148 A1
Norbreck Cl NG8......160 B3
Norbridge Acad S81.....35 E5
Norbury Dr NG18......102 E4
Norbury Way NG10.....182 A6
Nordean Rd NG5.......162 A5
Norfolk Ave
  Beeston NG9.........183 A1
  Bircotes DN11.........9 D4
Norfolk Cl
  Hucknall NG15.......145 D5
  Market Warsop NG20...74 A4
Norfolk Ct NG19........88 E5
Norfolk Dr
  Bircotes DN11.........9 C4
  Mansfield NG18.......102 B8
Norfolk Gdns NG17....100 A2
Norfolk Gr DN11.........9 C4
Norfolk Pl
  Arnold NG5..........162 B5
  Nottingham NG1 .....223 E3
Norfolk Rd
  Bircotes DN11.........9 C4
  Long Eaton NG10.....182 F1
Norfolk St S80.........35 E2
Norfolk Wlk NG10 ....182 B5
Norland Cl NG3.......173 E7
Norman Ave
  Newark-on-Trent NG24..125 B4
  Sutton in Ashfield NG17..101 A1
Normanby Rd NG8.....171 C3
Norman Cl
  Beeston NG9.........183 C6
  Nottingham NG3 .....173 C6
  Nottingham NG3 .....223 E4
Norman Cres DE7.....157 E3
Norman Dr
  Eastwood NG16......144 B2
  Hucknall NG15.......145 E4
  Norman Rd NG3 .....174 A8
Norman St
  Carlton NG4.........175 A6
  Ilkeston DE7........157 E3
  Kimberley NG16......158 F7
Normanton Brook Rd
  DE55 ....113 D7
Normanton Cl NG21....75 F3
Normanton Ct NG13 ...181 C5
Normanton Dr
  Loughborough LE11...220 B6
  Mansfield NG18.......102 E4
Normanton La
  Bothamsall NG22.......63 C7
  Bothamsall S80.......49 A1
  Bottesford NG13.....181 B5
  Bottesford NG23......169 D2
  Keyworth NG12......197 F4
  Stanford on Soar LE12..214 B1
NORMANTON ON
  SOAR 213 D2
Normanton on Soar Prim
  Sch LE12...........213 D3
NORMANTON-ON-THE-
  WOLDS 198 A6
NORMANTON ON
  TRENT 81 D6
Normanton Rd
  Newark-on-Trent NG24..125 D1

Normanton Rd continued
  Southwell NG25.......121 F2
  Weston NG23..........80 F7
  Weston NG23..........81 A7
Nornay Cl S81..........18 A4
Northall Ave NG6......160 B6
Northampton St **2**
  NG3 ....173 E6
North Ave
  Bawtry DN10..........10 A8
  Rainworth NG21 .....104 A1
  Sandiacre NG10......182 B6
North Carr Rd DN10.....7 C3
North Church St NG1 ..223 E3
North Cir St NG1......223 D2
Northcliffe Ave NG3 ..162 B2
NORTH CLIFTON.......68 E6
North Clifton Prim Sch
  NG23 ....68 E3
Northcote St NG10....193 E7
Northcote Way NG6...160 C5
North County Prim Sch
  DN21 ....15 B2
North Cres
  Bottesford NG13.....181 A2
  Clipstone NG21........90 A3
Northcroft LN1.........57 A5
Northdale Rd NG3 ....174 B7
Northdown Dr NG9 ...183 C4
Northdown Rd NG8 ...172 D6
North Dr
  Beeston NG9.........183 E6
  Bilsthorpe NG22......105 F7
  Wartnaby LE14 ......219 F3
North End NG24......138 F5
Northern Bridge Rd
  NG17...............100 F3
Northern Ct NG6.......160 F4
Northern Dr NG9 .....170 D3
Northern Rd NG24 ...125 B1
  NG24 ....125 B1
Northern View NG17...100 F3
North Farm La
  Budby NG22..........61 F1
  Carlton in Lindrick S81 ...26 A6
Northfield Ave
  Ilkeston DE7.........157 E2
  Long Eaton NG10.....193 A4
  Mansfield Woodhouse
    NG19..............88 A4
  Radcliffe on Trent NG12..176 C3
Northfield Cl NG18....102 E6
Northfield Cres NG9...183 A4
Northfield Dr NG18 ...102 E6
Northfield La
  Mansfield Woodhouse
    NG19..............88 A5
  Treswell DN22........42 B4
Northfield Pk NG19.....88 B5
Northfield Prim Sch
  NG19 ....88 B5
Northfield Rise
  Beeston NG9.........183 A4
  North Leverton with
    Habblesthorpe DN22...33 B1
Northfield Rise LN1.....56 F4
Northfields NG10.....193 B4
Northfields Cl NG17...100 E3
Northfields Way LE12..205 E3
Northfield Way DN22...39 D8
North Gate
  Newark-on-Trent NG24..125 A2
  Nottingham NG5 .....161 A2
  Nottingham NG7 .....160 F1
  Tickhill DN11..........8 A8
Northgate Bsns Ctr
  NG24 ....124 F1
North Gate Pk NG17...160 F1
Northgate Ret Pk
  NG24 ....125 A2
Northgate St **4** DE7...157 F1
North Gn
  Calverton NG14......133 D1
  Calverton NG5.......148 D8
  East Drayton DN22....53 B3
North Hill Ave NG15...145 F7
North Hill Cres NG15...145 F7
North Leverton CE Prim
  Sch DN22 ....32 D1
North Leverton Windmill★
  DN22 ....32 B1
NORTH LEVERTON WITH
  HABBLESTHORPE 42 D8
North Leys Rd DN22....43 C8
North Lodge Rd LE14 ..218 E5
North Marsh Rd DN21..15 C2
North Moor Dr DN10...13 F4
North Moor Rd DN10...13 F6
NORTH MUSKHAM....110 E1
North Nottinghamshire Coll
  1 East Retford DN22...39 F6
  Worksop S81.........35 F5
Northolme DN21.......15 D1
Northolme Ave NG6...160 C7
Northolme View **8**
  DN21...............15 D1
Northolt Dr NG8......159 D3
North Par DN21........24 F7
North Pk NG18........102 E3
North Rd
  Long Eaton NG10.....193 C6
  Loughborough LE11...220 B6
  North Muskham NG23..110 E2
  Nottingham NG5 .....161 B5
  Nottingham NG7 .....222 C2
  Nottingham NG9 .....184 D7
  Retford DN22.........29 B2
  Ruddington NG11.....196 B8
  West Bridgford NG2...185 B4
  West Burton DN22.....32 B8

North Rd 1 NG8........172 D2
North Rd 2 NG8........172 D2
Northrowe NG17......129 E8
North Scaffold La
  NG23 ....112 B2
NORTH SCARLE........83 E2
North Scarle Prim Sch
  LN6.................83 D2
North Scarle Rd
  South Scarle NG23 .....98 E7
  Wigsley NG23..........70 A1
  Wigsley NG23..........83 F8
  Wigsley NG23..........84 A8
North Sherwood St
  NG1................223 E4
Northside La DN22......32 F1
Northside Wlk NG5 ....147 F2
North St
  Beeston NG9........183 E6
  Eastwood NG16......144 C2
  Gainsborough NG21 ...15 C1
  Huthwaite NG17 .....100 A3
  7 Ilkeston DE7.......157 F1
  Kimberley NG16......159 A5
  Kirkby-in-Ashfield NG17..115 B2
  Langley Mill NG16 ...143 B3
  Morton DN21.........15 B4
  4 Nottingham NG2...173 E4
  Pinxton NG16........113 D3
  South Normanton DE55..113 A5
  Sturton le Steeple DN22..32 D6
  Sutton in Ashfield NG17..100 F3
  Warsop Vale NG20.....73 D4
  Whaley Thorns NG16...59 A2
Northumberland Ave
  S81.................25 E8
Northumberland Cl
  NG3................223 F4
Northumbria Cl S81.....36 B6
Northumbria Dr DN22...39 D5
North Warren Rd DN21..15 B2
North Way S81.........25 F7
NORTH WHEATLEY.....31 D8
North Wheatley CE Prim
  Sch DN22 ....31 E8
North Wlk DN22........39 C8
Northwold Ave NG2...185 D6
Northwood S81.........36 A6
Northwood Ave NG17..100 C4
Northwood Cres NG5 ..161 C6
Northwood Rd NG5....161 C6
Northwood St NG9....182 D8
Norton La NG20.........60 B3
Norton Rd LN6.......127 E8
Norton St NG7.......222 B3
NORWELL............110 A7
Norwell CE Prim Sch
  NG23 ....110 A8
Norwell Ct **2** NG19....88 B1
Norwell La
  Brough NG23.........112 C1
  Cromwell NG23......110 D8
Norwell Rd
  Caunton NG23.......109 C5
  Norwell NG22.........94 F2
  Norwell Woodhouse NG23 95 B1
  Ossington NG23........95 F4
Norwell Woodhouse Rd
  Caunton NG23.......108 D8
  Norwell NG22.........94 D2
Norwich Cl NG19.......88 D5
Norwich Gdns NG6....146 B1
Norwith Hill DN10......3 D1
Norwood Cl
  19 Ilkeston DE7 ......157 F5
  Sutton in Ashfield NG17..100 B3
Norwood Gdns NG5...121 C2
Norwood La NG20......58 E5
Norwood Rd NG7......222 A3
Noskwith St DE7......170 A5
Nostell Mews **6** S80...35 F2
Notintone St NG3.....173 E4
NOTTINGHAM..........173 B3
Nottingham Acad NG2..174 A4
Nottingham Acad The
  NG3................174 B5
Nottingham Airport
  NG12...............186 F5
Nottingham Arts Theatre★
  NG1................223 D3
Nottingham Bluecoat Sch &
  Tech Coll The NG8...172 B4
Nottingham Bsns Pk
  NG8................159 C2
Nottingham Canal Nature
  Reserve★ NG9 ......170 C2
Nottingham Castle (site
  of)★ NG7 ....223 D2
Nottingham Cath★
  NG1................223 D2
Nottingham City Hospl
  NG5................161 A4
Nottingham Coll NG7 .222 F2
Nottingham Coll Highfields
  NG7................184 D8
Nottingham Emmanuel Sch
  The NG11...........185 C8
Nottingham Free Sch
  NG5................161 A2
Nottingham Girls' Acad
  NG8................172 B8
Nottingham Girls' High Sch
  NG1................223 D4
Nottingham High Sch
  NG7................223 D4
Nottingham High Sch
  (Lovell House Inf Sch)
  NG7................222 C4
Nottingham Ice Ctr & Arena
  NG1................223 F2
Nottingham La LE14 ..218 C5

Nottingham Playhouse★
  NG1................223 D2
Nottingham Racecourse★
  NG2................174 B3
Nottingham Rd
  Arnold NG5.........161 E6
  Beeston NG9........183 B1
  Bingham NG13......177 D4
  Bottesford NG13....180 E2
  Burton Joyce NG14...163 D3
  Costock LE12.......206 D2
  Cropwell Bishop NG12...188 F4
  Eastwood NG16.....144 A2
  Eastwood, Giltbrook
    NG16.............158 C8
  Gotham NG11.......195 B4
  Gunthorpe NG14....164 B6
  Hucknall NG15......146 C4
  Ilkeston DE7........170 A6
  Kegworth DE74......203 D2
  Keyworth NG12......197 E3
  Kimberley NG16......159 A5
  Kirkby-in-Ashfield NG17..115 B2
  Long Eaton NG10.....193 E8
  Loughborough LE11...220 D6
  Mansfield NG18......102 C3
  Nether Broughton LE14..219 C8
  Nether Broughton LE14..219 E7
  Nottingham, New Basford
    NG7..............160 C1
  Nuthall NG16.......159 F4
  Oxton NG25.........134 A2
  Radcliffe on Trent NG12..175 D2
  Ravenshead NG15....116 B3
  Ravenshead NG15....131 F8
  Selston NG16.......128 E6
  Selston NG16.......129 A6
  Southwell NG25.....136 D6
  Stapleford NG9 .....182 E7
  Thurgarton NG14....151 C6
  Trowell NG9.........170 E5
  Upper Broughton LE14..210 B3
  Woodborough NG14 ..148 E2
Nottingham Rd E NG16 144 B1
Nottingham Science &
  Tech Pk NG2 ....172 D1
Nottingham Sta NG2..223 F1
Nottingham South &
  Wilford Ind Est NG2..185 B4
Nottingham Transport
  Heritage Ctr★ NG11..196 C5
Nottingham Trent Univ
  (Brackenhurst Campus)
  NG25..............136 D5
Nottingham Trent Univ
  (Clifton Campus)
  NG11..............184 D3
Nottingham Trent Univ The
  NG7................222 A4
Nottingham Univ NG1..223 D3
Nottingham Univ Acad of
  Science & Technology
  NG7................172 E1
Nottingham Univ
  Samworth Acad NG8 .171 C7
Nuart Rd NG9.........183 F7
Nugent Gdn NG3......173 E6
Nugent Gdns **4** NG3...173 E6
Nuncar Ct NG9.......115 A1
NUNCARGATE........115 A1
Nunn Brook Rd NG17...99 E1
Nunn Brook Rise NG17..99 E2
Nunn Cl
  Hucknall NG15......131 C1
  Huthwaite NG17 .....99 E1
Nurseries The NG16 ..144 A2
Nursery Ave
  Beeston NG9........183 C5
  Farndon NG24......138 F4
  Nottingham NG17....100 C2
  Sutton in Ashfield NG17..100 C2
Nursery Cl
  Collingham NG23....112 A7
  Hucknall NG15......146 A4
  Radcliffe on Trent NG12..176 B3
  Saxilby LN1..........57 B4
Nursery Ct
  Mansfield NG18......102 C8
  Newark-on-Trent NG24..125 A1
Nursery Dr NG4.......174 D8
Nursery End NG25....121 D1
Nursery Gdns
  Balderton NG24......140 E2
  Beckingham DN10.....23 C8
  Mansfield NG21......103 D2
  South Normanton DE55..113 C4
  Worksop S80.........35 B2
Nursery La
  Morton DN21.........15 A5
  Nottingham NG6.....160 E4
  Sutton on Trent NG23...96 F8
Nursery Rd
  Arnold NG5.........162 A7
  Bingham NG13......178 B4
  Radcliffe on Trent NG12..176 B3
Nursery St NG18......102 C8
Nursery Vale DN21....15 B5
Nursury Gdns NG14...150 D2
Nutcroft Way DN10....11 A4
NUTHALL............159 D5
Nuthall Bypass NG6...160 A4
Nuthall Gardens NG8..172 D8
Nuthall Rd NG8.......160 C2
Nuthatch Cres S81......25 D1
Nutkin Close **4**
  LE11 ....220 A2

Oak Acres NG9........183 A5
Oak Ave
  Aldercar NG16.......143 B5
  Bingham NG13......178 A4
  Blidworth NG21......118 B4
  Farndon NG24......139 A4
  Mansfield NG18......102 C8
  New Ollerton NG22....77 D4
  Radcliffe on Trent NG12..175 E4
  Rainworth NG21 .....104 C1
  Sandiacre NG10......182 A7
  Shirebrook NG20......72 D4
Oak Bank Cl NG18 ....102 B8
Oak Cl
  Pinxton NG16.......113 C3
  Worksop S80.........35 E1
Oak Cres LE12........214 D8
Oakdale Dr NG9......183 C4
Oakdale Rd
  Arnold NG5.........162 B8
  Carlton NG3.........174 C6
  Carlton NG4.........174 D7
  Mansfield NG18......101 F7
  Nottingham NG4.....174 B6
  South Normanton DE55..113 A4
Oak Dr
  Eastwood NG16.....143 C6
  Mansfield Woodhouse
    NG19.............88 E2
  New Balderton NG24...140 C4
  Nuthall NG16.......159 B6
  Torksey Lock LN1.....44 B1
Oakenhall Ave NG15...146 C7
Oakes Cl NG16.......143 A5
Oakfield
  Radcliffe on Trent
    NG12.............176 A3
  Saxilby LN1..........57 A3
Oakfield Ave
  Market Warsop NG20...74 B3
  Sutton in Ashfield NG17..114 E8
Oakfield Cl
  Mansfield NG18......102 F2
  Nottingham NG8 .....171 C3
Oakfield Dr NG10.....182 B3
Oakfield La NG20......74 B2
Oakfield Rd
  Hucknall NG15......146 B6
  Newark-on-Trent NG24..140 F1
  Nottingham NG8 .....171 C3
  Stapleford NG9 .....182 D7
Oak Field School and
  Sports Coll NG8.....171 F7
Oakfields Rd NG2.....174 A1
Oak Flatt NG9.........183 A5
Oakford Cl NG8.......160 A2
Oak Gr NG15.........146 A5
Oakham Bsns Pk NG18..101 F3
Oakham Cl
  Mansfield NG18......102 B4
  Nottingham NG5 .....160 F7
Oakham Ct NG5.......162 D3
Oakham Dr
  Carlton in Lindrick S81 ...25 F6
  Selston NG16.......129 B7
Oakhampton Cres NG3 162 C6
Oakham Rd NG11.....185 D2
Oakham Way DE7.....157 D3
Oakholme Ave S81......35 F5
Oakholme Rise S81.....35 F6
Oakington Cl NG5.....161 B5
Oakland Ave
  Huthwaite NG17 .....99 F2
  Long Eaton NG10.....193 C5
Oakland Ct NG9......171 A1
Oakland Gr NG14.....148 F7
Oakland Rd NG18.....102 F8
Oaklands NG23.......112 A8
Oaklands Ave DE75...143 A2
Oaklands Dr DN11......8 D2
Oaklands La DN22.....40 A5
Oakland St **6** NG7...172 E7
Oaklands The DE55...113 A4
Oakland Terr NG10 ...193 C5
Oakland Way NG18....171 D8
Oakleaf Cl
  Bestwood Village NG15..146 E4
  Mansfield NG18......103 B3
Oakleaf Cres NG17....100 C1
Oakleigh Ave
  Mansfield Woodhouse
    NG19.............88 E4
  Nottingham NG3 .....162 C2
Oakleigh St NG6......160 D4
Oakley Dr LE12.......212 D2
Oakley Mews NG6....159 F6
Oakley Rise **4** S81....35 A7
Oakley's Rd NG10....193 E7
Oakley's Rd W NG10 ..193 D6
Oak Lodge Dr NG15...158 F7
Oakmead Ave NG8....171 F8
Oakmere Cl NG2......186 C4
Oakridge Cl NG19......88 E1
Oak Rise NG22.......105 F2
Oaks Ave S80..........58 C8
Oaks Cl DN22.........19 B5
Oaksetts Dr S80.......45 E2
Oaks Ind Est LE11....220 A6
Oaks La
  Oxton NG25.........133 F7
  Walkeringham DN10...13 E3
Oak St
  Kirkby-in-Ashfield
    NG17.............115 B5
  Nottingham NG5 .....161 B1
  Sutton in Ashfield NG17..100 D7

Oaks The
  Mansfield NG18......102 C3
  Newark-on-Trent NG24..140 E4
Oak Tree NG14.......152 A8
Oaktree Ave **2** DN21...15 F2
Oak Tree Ave
  Edwinstowe NG21.....76 A2
  Glapwell S44........86 B8
  Radcliffe on Trent NG4..175 F4
Oak Tree Bsns Pk
  NG18 ....103 B4
Oaktree Cl NG17......101 B1
Oak Tree Cl
  Hucknall NG15......145 D4
  Mansfield NG18......103 B7
  West Bridgford NG2...186 A8
Oak Tree Cres NG19....88 B4
Oak Tree Ct LE12......186 C1
Oaktree Dr NG22.....106 A4
Oak Tree Dr NG4......163 A2
Oak Tree La NG18....103 A6
Oak Tree La L Ctr
  NG18 ....103 B5
Oak Tree Mws NG22...106 A4
OakTree Prim Sch
  NG18 ....103 C6
Oaktree Rd
  Hilcote DE55.........99 C1
  Hilcote DE55........113 C8
Oak Tree Rd
  Bawtry DN10..........9 F7
  Sutton in Ashfield NG17..101 A4
Oak Tree Rise S81......25 E7
Oak View NG24.......140 C8
Oak View Rise NG18 ..116 D7
Oakwood NG23.......152 E2
Oakwood Dr
  Nottingham NG8 .....172 C7
  Ravenshead NG15....117 A1
Oakwood Gdns NG16 .159 D3
Oakwood Gr NG21.....91 B8
Oakwood Mews S80....35 C3
Oakwood Rd NG18....103 B4
Oatfield La NG12......176 D6
Oban Rd NG19.......183 C6
Observatory Way NG17 115 B8
Occupation La
  Broadholme LN1......57 B1
  Broadholme NG23.....71 B8
  Edwinstowe NG21.....76 B1
  Kirkby-in-Ashfield NG17..114 F6
  Orston NG13.........179 A4
  Rolleston NG25......137 C5
  Willoughby-on-t-W LE12..217 D4
Occupation Rd
  Hucknall NG15......146 A5
  New Houghton NG19...86 F7
  Nottingham NG6 .....160 B5
Ocean Dr NG20.........74 A5
Ochbrook Ct DE7......157 F3
Ockbrook Dr **2** NG3...161 F1
Ockerby St NG6.......160 C6
Oddicroft La NG17....101 A1
Odesa Dr NG6........160 B4
Odins Wlk NG18......101 F5
Off The Ave NG17.....100 E1
Ogdon Ct NG3.......173 F6
Ogle Dr
  Nottingham NG7 .....173 B3
  Nottingham NG1 .....223 D1
Ogle St NG15........146 A7
Oldacres NG14.......149 D4
Old Bakery Way **3**
  NG18 ....88 C1
Old Bar Cl NG6.......160 C2
Old Barn Ct NG21.....90 B6
Old Basford Prim Sch
  NG6................160 D3
Old Bawtry Rd DN10....3 C4
Old Bell La NG25......96 F4
Old Blyth Rd
  Barnby Moor S81.....27 F1
  Ranby DN22.........38 A6
  Ranby S81............37 F8
  Scofton DN22........37 F7
Old Bowling Gn The
  S81................35 B4
Old Brickyard NG3....174 A7
Oldbridge Way
  Bilsthorpe NG22.....105 F5
  Bilsthorpe NG22.....106 A6
Old Bull Farm Cl LE12..204 D3
Oldbury Cl NG11......195 D7
Old Chapel Cl NG17...114 C6
Old Chapel La
  Elston NG23.........153 E5
  Selston NG16.......129 A3
Old Church St **9** NG7..172 E2
OLD CLIPSTONE........90 C6
Old Coach Rd
  Nottingham NG8 .....171 F5
  Nottingham NG8 .....171 F6
  Worksop S80.........47 E7
Oldcobham Orch
  NG24..............140 C5
Oldcotes NG14........17 A6
Old Ctyd The DN21.....44 C8
Old Dairy The NG14...150 D2
OLD DALBY..........218 F4
Old Dalby CE Prim Sch
  LE14 ....218 E4
Old Dalby CE Sch LE14 218 E5
Old Dalby La LE14....219 D6
Old Derby Rd NG16 ..143 D3
Old Dr NG9..........183 E6
Old Engine Yd The
  LE12 ....215 E5
Old England Gdns NG23 81 F1

Old England Gdns NG23. **96** F8
Old Epperstone Rd
NG14..............**150** B4
Oldershaw Ave DE74...**203** C2
Oldershaw Rd LE12....**205** F1
Old Farm Rd NG5....**160** F8
Old Forge Cl
Hathern LE12.......**213** A1
Kegworth DE74......**203** C2
Misterton DN10........ **6** F2
Old Forge La NG13...**191** C5
Old Forge Rd DN10.....**6** E2
Old Gateford Rd S81...**35** C8
Old Gdns The DN22...**39** E4
Old Grantham Rd
Aslockton NG13......**178** F3
Whatton NG13.......**179** A3
Old Great North Rd
NG23..............**96** E8
Old Hall Cl
Calverton NG14......**148** E7
Farndon NG24......**139** B6
Market Warsop NG20...**74** C5
Old Hall Dr
Nottingham NG3.....**161** D2
Retford DN22........**39** D6
Widmerpool NG12....**208** C3
Old Hall Gdns
Coddington NG24.....**125** F2
Screveton NG13......**166** B4
Old Hall La
East Markham NG22....**65** F7
Norwell NG23.......**110** B8
Old Hall The ★ DN21...**15** C1
Old Haxey Rd DN10......**6** F3
Old Kennel Dr NG14...**133** D6
Old Kiln La 🄿 NG16...**144** A1
Oldknow St NG7.......**172** F7
Old La NG12..........**185** D1
Old La The NG13......**192** B2
OLD LENTON...........**172** D3
Old Lenton Cl NG12...**189** A4
Old Lenton St NG1...**223** E4
Old Liby Arts Ctr The ★
NG18..............**102** B7
Old Lodge Dr NG5....**161** D4
Old London Rd
Babworth DN22........**49** F8
Barnby Moor DN22....**28** C3
West Drayton DN22....**50** F2
Old Main Rd
Bulcote NG14.......**164** B5
Costock LE12........**206** D1
Old Maltings The DN10...**6** F1
Old Manor Cl NG14...**149** D4
Old Manor Ct NG14...**126** B1
Old Manor Farm NG23.**142** D2
Old Manor Rd NG19....**88** B3
Old Meeting House Yard
NG18..............**102** B7
Old Melton Rd
Normanton-on-the-Wolds
NG12..............**197** D2
Normanton-on-the-Wolds
NG12..............**198** A6
Plumtree NG12......**197** F7
Widmerpool NG12....**209** A7
Old Mill Cl
Beeston NG9.......**183** A2
Bestwood Village NG6..**146** D3
Nottingham NG7.....**222** B3
Old Mill Cres NG24...**140** B8
Old Mill Cl NG13....**177** F5
Old Mill La
Cuckney NG20........**60** B3
Mansfield NG19........**88** E1
Old Mission Forge Wlk
NG16..............**144** C2
Old Mkt Pl
Mansfield NG18......**102** B7
South Normanton DE55..**113** A6
Old Mkt Sq NG1......**223** E2
Old Newark Rd NG18..**102** E2
Old North Rd NG23.....**97** A2
Old North Road NG23...**96** F6
Old Nurseries The
NG23..............**109** F8
Oldoak Rd NG11......**185** A2
Old Park Cl NG4......**171** E6
Old Parsonage La
LE12..............**215** C1
Old Pits Cl LN6.......**71** F3
Old Pk Cl NG11......**203** F6
Old Pk The NG12....**187** F4
Old Post Office St DN10..**11** C3
Old Rd NG17.........**100** F7
Old Rectory Cl LE12...**205** E1
Old Rectory Ct NG25..**125** C6
Old Rectory Mus & Wildlife
Gdn ★ LE11........**220** B4
Old Reindeer Cl NG13..**165** C3
Old Rufford Rd
Bilsthorpe NG22.....**105** C4
Calverton NG14......**133** C6
Edwinstowe NG22.....**91** D4
Farnsfield NG22......**119** B5
Ollerton NG22........**77** A3
Old Sch Cl NG11......**195** E8
Old Sch House Cl
NG12..............**189** B7
Old Sch La NG19......**87** A5
Old School Dr NG7.....**75** F1
Old School La
Awsworth NG16......**158** C5
Besthorpe NG23......**97** E6
Newark-on-Trent NG24..**140** B7
Old School Pl 🄰 S80....**35** F2
Old Showfields DN21...**15** D2

Old Sookholme La
NG20..............**74** A4
Old St NG1...........**223** E3
Old Stack Yard The LN1.**55** D6
Old Station Dr NG11....**196** B7
Old Station Yard NG21...**76** B1
Old Sta Yd NG13......**181** C3
Old Storth La DE55....**113** B4
Old Sykes La LN1......**56** D4
Old Tannery Dr NG14..**150** E1
Old Terr NG19.........**86** F4
Old Tollerton Rd
🄰 Gamston NG12.....**186** C7
West Bridgford NG2..**186** C7
Old Trent Rd DN10......**14** F1
Old Walled Gdns DN22..**40** F4
Old Water La 🄰 NG19...**87** D1
Old Way LE12........**213** A1
Old Wood LN6.........**71** E6
Old Woodyard The
Hathern LE12.......**212** F1
Hathern LE12.......**213** A1
Wysall NG12........**207** C3
Olga Ct NG3.........**173** F6
Olga Rd NG3.........**173** F6
Olive Ave
Long Eaton NG10....**182** E1
Shirebrook NG20......**72** D6
Olive Ct NG17.......**100** F4
Olive Gr
Burton Joyce NG14...**163** F5
Mansfield NG19......**103** A8
Oliver Cl
Heanor DE75........**143** B2
Nottingham NG7.....**222** C4
Oliver Ct NG24......**140** B8
Oliver Dr NG11......**196** B8
Oliver Quibell Inf Sch
NG24..............**140** A5
Oliver Rd LE11......**220** B2
Oliver St NG7.......**222** C3
OLLERTON............**77** B3
Ollerton Com Prim Sch
NG22..............**77** D5
Ollerton Rd
Arnold NG5.........**147** E6
Averham NG23.......**123** E8
Calverton NG14......**132** F2
Carburton NG22......**61** D6
Caunton NG23......**108** D8
Eaton DN22..........**50** E8
Edwinstowe NG21.....**76** C2
Edwinstowe NG21.....**76** D3
Farnsfield NG22......**119** A1
Gamston NG22........**50** E5
Kelham NG23........**124** A5
Kersall NG22.........**94** B3
Kirton NG22.........**78** F8
Kneesall NG22........**93** F4
Ollerton NG22........**77** A4
Retford DN22........**39** E2
Retford DN22........**39** E4
South Muskham NG23...**124** B7
Tuxford NG22........**65** C2
Worksop S80.........**47** B4
Ollerton Water Mill ★
NG22..............**77** A3
Olton Ave NG5......**171** F1
Olympia Way 🄰 NG15.**146** C7
Olympus Ct NG15....**145** D3
Omberley Ave NG17...**101** B6
Omer Ct NG16.......**159** A4
Onchan Ave NG4.....**174** E6
One Call Stadium
(Mansfield Town FC)
NG18..............**102** B5
Ontario Dr NG16.....**129** A7
Opal Cl
Mansfield NG18......**102** E4
Rainworth NG21.....**104** C1
Opal Gr DN11..........**9** B5
Orange Cl NG20.......**72** E6
Orange Croft
Tickhill DN11.........**8** B7
Tickhill DN11.........**8** B8
Orange Gdns NG2....**173** D2
Orange Tip Cl S81.....**25** D1
Orby Cl NG3........**173** F6
Orby Wlk NG3.......**173** F6
Orchard Ave
Bingham NG13......**177** D4
Carlton NG4.........**174** E7
Orchard Bsns Pk
Ilkeston DE7.......**157** D1
Sandiacre NG10.....**182** C6
Orchard Cl
Barkestone-le-Vale
NG13..............**192** B2
Barnstone NG13.....**190** F3
Bleasby NG14.......**152** A8
Burton Joyce NG14...**163** F5
East Bridgford NG13..**165** D3
East Leake LE12.....**214** D8
Gunthorpe NG14.....**165** A5
Mansfield NG18......**102** C2
Morton DN21.........**15** B5
Newton on Trent LN1...**55** A1
North Leverton with
Habblesthorpe DN22..**42** D8
Radcliffe on Trent NG12.**175** E3
Shirebrook NG20......**72** E2
South Muskham NG23..**124** E7
Southwell NG25.....**121** D2
Sutton Bonington LE12.**213** C5
Tollerton NG12......**186** D1

Orchard Cres
Beeston NG9.......**183** C5
Glapwell S44........**86** B8
Tuxford NG22........**65** F2
Orchard Croft DN10....**10** A7

Orchard Ct
Carlton NG4.......**174** E7
Gelding NG4........**162** D2
Hucknall NG15......**146** A6
Huthwaite NG17......**99** E2
Langley Mill NG16...**143** B3
Nottingham NG8....**172** E8
Thorney NG23........**69** F7
Orchard Dr
Calverton NG14.....**149** A7
Cotgrave NG12......**188** A5
Orchard Gr
Arnold NG5.........**161** C6
Misterton DN10.......**14** A8
Walkeringham DN10...**13** F8
Orchard La
Caythorpe NG14.....**165** A8
Kirkby-in-Ashfield NG17..**115** B6
Saxilby LN1..........**57** A4
South Leverton DN22..**42** C7
Orchard Leigh NG12...**189** D4
Orchard Mws NG16...**113** E3
Orchard Pk
Arnold NG5.........**162** C5
Newark-on-Trent NG24.**125** F2
Orchard Pl NG8......**159** C2
Orchard Prim Sch
NG17..............**114** E5
Orchard Rd NG17....**114** E5
Orchard Rise
Beckingham DN10.....**23** C8
Lambley NG4.......**163** C7
Orchardside Rd NG22...**65** F6
Orchard St
Eastwood NG16.....**144** A1
Gotham NG11.......**195** B1
Hucknall NG15......**146** A6
Kimberley NG16.....**158** F6
Langley Mill NG16...**143** B3
Long Eaton NG10....**193** E8
Stapleford NG9......**182** D7
Orchards The
Carlton NG4.........**163** A1
Lowdham NG14.....**164** E8
Oxton NG25.........**134** C4
Westwood NG16.....**128** B4
Orchard The
Elston NG23.........**153** E4
Newark-on-Trent NG24.**125** F2
Sutton in Ashfield NG17..**101** B1
Orchard View
Mansfield Woodhouse
NG19..............**88** B3
Thurgarton NG14....**151** C8
Orchard Way
Balderton NG24.....**140** D3
Sandiacre NG10.....**182** A3
Sutton in Ashfield NG17..**114** C8
Wymeswold LE12....**216** D3
Orchard Wlk NG17....**114** E5
Orchid Cl
🄰 Kirkby-in-Ashfield
NG17..............**114** F7
New Balderton NG24..**140** B5
West Bridgford NG11..**185** C4
Orchid Croft NG15....**146** C4
Orchid Dr
Farndon NG24......**139** B6
Sutton in Ashfield NG17..**101** B1
Orchid Gr
Pleasley NG19.......**86** F5
Pleasley NG19.......**87** A5
Shirebrook NG20......**72** D2
Orchid Way NG20.....**72** D2
Orchil St NG16......**158** B8
Orch St NG16.......**158** A8
Ordoyno Gr NG24....**125** F2
Ordsall Cl NG18.....**102** E6
Ordsall Pk Cl DN22....**39** D6
Ordsall Pk Dr DN22....**39** D6
Ordsall Pk Rd DN22....**39** D6
Ordsall Prim Sch DN22..**39** D4
Ordsall Rd DN22......**39** C5
Orford Ave
Nottingham NG11....**184** F4
Radcliffe on Trent NG12.**175** F2
Oriana Dr NG12......**185** F2
Orion Cl NG8.......**171** E7
Orion Dr NG8.......**171** E7
Orion Gr 🄰 NG18....**102** E1
Orlando Dr NG4......**174** F8
Orlock Wlk NG5......**161** B5
Ormiston Cl NG11....**184** F1
Ormonde St NG16....**143** B4
Ormonde Terr
Aldercar NG16......**143** B4
Nottingham NG5.....**161** C2
Ornsay Cl NG5......**146** E1
Orpean Way NG9....**182** E2
ORSTON.............**180** A7
Orston Ave
Arnold NG5.........**162** A7
Newark-on-Trent NG24..**139** E6
Orston Dr NG8.......**172** D4
Orston Gn NG8......**172** D3
Orston La
Bottesford NG13....**180** F3
Flawborough NG13..**168** B1
Orston Prim Sch NG13..**180** A7
Orston Rd E NG2.....**173** F1
Orston Rd W NG2....**173** E1
Orton Ave NG9......**183** C6
Orton Fields NG9....**183** B6
Orville Rd NG5......**160** E5
Osberne Wy NG19.....**89** F2
Osberton Rd DN22.....**39** F6
Osberton View S81.....**36** B5

Osborne Ave 🄰 NG5...**161** C3
Osborne Cl NG10.....**182** B4
Osborne Gr NG5.....**161** C3
Osborne St NG7.....**222** A4
Osbourne Cl
Nottingham NG15....**146** C4
Watnall NG16.......**159** B7
Osbourne St NG17....**129** F8
Osgood Rd NG5......**162** C5
Osier Dr NG15......**130** A6
Osier Fields LE12....**205** F2
Osier Rd NG2.......**173** C2
Osiers The
Kegworth DE74.....**203** D2
Newark-on-Trent NG24.**139** C6
Osman Cl NG2.......**173** B1
Osmanthorpe Nature
Reserve ★ NG22.....**120** F6
Osmaston St
Nottingham NG7.....**222** B1
Sandiacre NG10.....**182** C5
Osprey Cl
Bingham NG13......**177** F3
Nottingham NG11....**184** C1
Osprey Gr NG15.....**131** D1
OSSINGTON...........**95** D6
Ossington Cl
Meden Vale NG20.....**74** D8
Nottingham NG1.....**223** E4
Ossington La
Ossington NG23......**95** C6
Sutton on Trent NG23..**96** F3
Ossington Rd
Carlton-on-Trent NG23..**96** C5
Kneesall NG22.......**93** E5
Kneesall NG22.......**94** B5
Moorhouse NG23.....**80** C1
Norwell NG23........**95** F1
Norwell NG23.......**110** A8
Sutton on Trent NG23..**96** C8
Ossington St NG7....**222** B4
Ossington Way NG24..**124** F1
Oster Fen La
Claypole NG23......**142** A2
Claypole NG23......**156** F7
Osterley Gr NG8.....**159** D2
Ostler La LE14......**219** D1
Otter Ave LN1.........**57** A4
Otter Way NG19......**87** D1
Oughton Cl NG12....**186** A3
Oulton Cl NG5......**161** F6
Oundle Dr
Ilkeston DE7.......**170** A7
Mansfield NG19......**87** D1
Nottingham NG8.....**172** C3
Our Lady of Perpetual
Succour RC Prim Sch
NG6..............**160** D6
Our Lady & St Edward's
Cath Prim Sch NG3..**173** F7
Oursham St NG17....**100** F7
Ousebridge Cres NG4.**175** A8
Ouse Bridge Dr NG4..**175** A8
Outgang La
Mansfield Woodhouse
NG19..............**88** D4
Pleasley NG19.......**87** C6
Treswell DN22........**42** F4
Out Gang Road
Cottam DN22........**43** B4
Cottam DN22........**43** C4
Outram St NG17....**100** F3
Outwood Acad Portland
S80..............**35** F1
Worksop S80.........**46** F8
Outwood Acad Valley
S81..............**35** E6
Oval Gdns 🄰 NG8....**172** D8
Oval The
Retford DN22........**39** D4
Sutton in Ashfield NG17..**100** D4
Tickhill DN11.........**8** B8
Torksey Lock LN1.....**55** B8
Oval Way LE14......**219** C8
Overdale Ave NG17..**100** E7
Overdale Rd NG6....**160** C3
Overend Rd S80.......**35** F4
Overmoor View DE55...**99** B7
Overstone Cl NG17....**100** F5
Overstrand Cl NG5....**161** F6
Owday La S81........**25** D3
Owen Ave NG10......**194** A6
Owen Jenkins Cl 🄰
NG9..............**184** A5
Owlston Cl NG16....**143** F3
Owsthorpe Cl NG5....**161** A8
Owston Ferry Rd DN9....**7** D7
Owston Rd
Newstead NG15.....**130** D7
West Stockwith DN10....**7** C4
OWTHORPE...........**199** E7
Owthorpe Gr NG5....**161** B2
Owthorpe La
Kinoulton NG12.....**199** F3
Kinoulton NG12.....**200** A2
Owthorpe Rd
Colston Bassett NG12.**200** B7
Cotgrave NG12......**187** F2
Oxborough Rd NG5...**161** C7
Oxbow Cl NG2.......**173** C1
Oxbury Rd NG16....**158** F8
Oxclose La
Mansfield Woodhouse
NG19..............**88** A3
Nottingham NG5....**161** C6
Radmanthwaite NG19...**87** D3
Oxcroft La NG20......**58** A8
Oxengate NG5......**161** C6

Oxford Cl NG21......**118** A8
Oxford Dr
Harworth DN11.........**8** F5
Newton NG13.......**177** B8
Oxford Rd
Carlton in Lindrick S81..**25** F6
West Bridgford NG2..**186** A7
Oxford St
Carlton NG4.......**174** E8
Eastwood NG16.....**143** F2
Kirkby-in-Ashfield NG17.**115** B4
Long Eaton NG10....**193** D8
Loughborough LE11..**220** A4
Mansfield Woodhouse
NG19..............**88** C1
Nottingham NG1.....**223** D2
Sutton in Ashfield NG17..**100** D2
Oxgang Cl NG14.....**148** C8
Oxley Mws NG9.....**183** E5
Oxpasture La NG20....**58** B6
OXTON..............**134** C4
Oxton Ave NG5......**161** C4
Oxton Bypass
Epperstone NG14.....**149** D7
Oxton NG25.........**134** A4
Oxton NG25.........**134** B2
Oxton Cl
Mansfield NG19......**101** E7
Retford DN22........**39** E3
Oxton Hill NG25.....**134** F5
Oxton Rd
Calverton NG14.....**133** D1
Caythorpe NG14.....**151** A1
Epperstone NG14.....**149** E6
Epperstone NG14.....**150** A4
Oxton NG25.........**135** B4
Southwell NG25.....**135** C6
Thurgarton NG25....**136** A1
Oyster Rd NG16......**143** F3
Oyster Way NG20....**74** A5
Ozier Holt
Carlton NG4.......**174** E4
Long Eaton NG10....**193** C6

P
Pach Way NG24.....**140** F2
Packe St LE11......**220** A4
Packet Landing The
DN21..............**7** A2
Pack Horse La 🄰
LE11..............**220** B3
Packington Hill DE74.**203** C2
Packman Dr NG11...**196** D8
Paddington Ms NG3..**174** A7
Paddock Cl
Calverton NG14.....**148** C8
Edwinstowe NG21.....**76** A3
Long Eaton NG10....**193** D8
Mansfield NG18......**102** B3
Nottingham NG6....**160** B5
Radcliffe on Trent NG12.**175** E2
Paddock Farm Cotts
NG14..............**150** A5
Paddock Cl S81.......**18** A6
Paddocks Cl
Elston NG23.........**153** D4
Pinxton NG16.......**113** C4
Paddocks The
Beckingham DN10.....**14** B1
Bottesford NG13....**181** A2
Burton Joyce NG14...**163** D4
Elston NG23.........**153** E4
Granby NG13........**191** C5
Hockerton NG25.....**122** B6
Huthwaite DE55......**99** F1
Lound DN22..........**20** C2
Mansfield Woodhouse
NG19..............**88** C4
Marton DN21.........**44** C8
Newark-on-Trent NG24.**140** B7
Newton on Trent LN1...**55** A1
Sandiacre NG10.....**182** A5
Southwell NG25.....**136** C4
Stapleford NG9......**127** E8
Sutton Bonington LE12.**213** B6
West Bridgford NG12.**186** B3
Worksop S80.........**35** D5
Worksop S80.........**36** B7
Paddocks View
NG10..............**193** A8
Paddock The
Beckingham LN5.....**142** D8
Beeston NG9.......**183** D2
Bingham NG13......**177** E4
Bunny NG11........**206** E8
Collingham NG23....**112** A7
Gunthorpe NG14, NG14..**164** F2
Kirkby-in-Ashfield NG17.**114** D4
Old Dalby LE14.....**218** E4
Pleasley NG19.......**87** A5
Retford DN22........**40** A4
Stanton Hill NG17...**100** C5
Tickhill DN11.........**8** B8
Paddock View NG17....**57** A5
Paddy's La LE14.....**218** A1
Padge Rd NG9......**184** B6
Padgham Ct 🄰 NG5..**161** B8
Padley Cl NG6......**160** C6
Padley Hill NG18....**102** A6
Padleys La NG14....**163** C5
Padstow Cl NG18....**103** B2
Padstow Rd NG5....**160** F6
Paetina Gr NG15....**146** D8
Pagdin Dr DN11........**8** E1
Page Ave 🄰 NG5....**161** A5
Paget Cres NG11....**196** C6
Paget Croft LE12....**216** D3
Paget St 🄰 LE11....**220** A3
Pagett Cl NG15.....**146** C6

Paige Gdns
🄰 Sandiacre NG10....**182** A6
Sandiacre NG10.....**182** A6
Paignton Cl NG8.....**160** B2
Pailings Ride NG24...**126** C6
Paisley Gr NG9......**183** C1
Palace Theatre ★
NG24..............**140** A8
Palace View NG25...**136** F8
Palatine St
Nottingham NG1.....**173** B3
Nottingham NG7.....**223** D1
Paling Cres NG17....**100** E3
Palin Gdns NG12....**176** A3
Palin St NG7.......**222** B4
Palm Ct Ind Ctr NG7..**160** F1
Palmer Ave
Bottesford NG13....**181** B4
Hucknall NG15......**146** A8
Palmer Cres NG4....**174** D7
Palmer Dr NG9......**182** D5
Palmer Rd
Retford DN22........**30** A1
Sutton on Trent NG23..**96** F8
Palmers Ct 🄰 NG25...**136** F8
Palmerston Gdns NG3.**223** E4
Palmerston St
Selston NG16.......**128** F2
Underwood NG16....**129** A2
Westwood NG16.....**128** C4
Palm St NG7........**160** F1
Palmwood Ct NG6....**160** C5
Palm Wood Ct NG6...**160** C6
Pankhurst Cl LE12...**214** E7
Paper Mill La DN11.....**8** C8
PAPPLEWICK..........**131** D3
Papplewick Farm Cl
NG15..............**131** D1
Papplewick Grange
NG15..............**131** D1
Papplewick Hall & Gdns ★
NG15..............**131** D4
Papplewick La
Hucknall NG15......**131** C2
Hucknall NG15......**146** C8
Papplewick Ppg Sta ★
NG15..............**132** E5
Paradise La LE14....**218** F4
Parfitt Dr NG22.....**120** A5
Parish Mws 🄰 DN21...**15** D1
Park Ave
Annesley Woodhouse
NG17..............**130** B8
Arnold NG5.........**161** E5
Awsworth NG16.....**158** B5
Blidworth NG21.....**118** B5
Burton Joyce NG14...**163** E4
Carlton NG4.........**174** F8
Eastwood NG16.....**143** E3
Hucknall NG15......**145** F7
Keyworth NG12.....**197** F4
Kimberley NG16.....**159** A4
Loughborough LE11..**220** B1
Mansfield NG18......**102** C8
Mansfield Woodhouse
NG19..............**88** C4
Misterton DN10.......**6** E3
Nottingham NG3....**173** C2
Shirebrook NG20......**72** E4
West Bridgford NG2..**185** F8
Woodborough NG14..**149** B4
Park Ave E NG12....**197** D3
Park Ave W NG12....**197** D3
Park Chase NG6.....**160** B5
Park Cl
Lea DN21...........**24** F1
Nottingham NG3....**161** E2
Pinxton NG16.......**113** C2
Park Cres
Eastwood NG16.....**143** F4
Ilkeston DE7.......**170** A8
Newark-on-Trent NG24.**125** B4
Nottingham NG8....**171** C4
Retford DN22........**40** A8
Parkcroft Rd NG2....**185** F6
Park Ct
Loughborough LE11..**220** B2
Mansfield NG18......**102** C8
Parkdale Prim Sch
NG4..............**174** D6
Parkdale Rd NG3....**174** C6
Park Dr
Blyth S81...........**18** A3
Hucknall NG15......**146** B6
Nottingham NG7.....**222** C2
Sandiacre NG10.....**182** A3
Park Drain DN10........**2** D2
Parker Cl NG5......**162** C8
Parker Gdns NG9....**182** F8
Parker's La NG19.....**88** C3
Parker St
Hucknall NG15......**146** B7
Newark-on-Trent NG24.**140** A8
Parkes Cl NG24.....**125** B3
Park Farm Cotts LN1...**55** F1
Park Gate NG15.....**131** B1
Park Gdn NG17......**100** A3
Park Hall Cl NG19.....**88** C4
Park Hall Farm NG19...**88** C4
Park Hall Gdns NG19...**88** C5
Park Hall Rd NG19.....**88** C5
Parkham Rd NG16....**158** F7
Park Hill NG16......**158** B5
Park Hill Dr S81......**16** A5
Park Hospl The NG5..**222** C1
Park House Gates NG3.**161** D1
Park Hts NG7.......**222** C1
Parkin Cl NG12......**189** A4
Park La
Elkesley DN22.......**50** C3
Holbeck NG20........**59** C6

Park La continued
Kirkby-in-Ashfield NG17 .114 C2
Lambley NG4 . . . . .163 E8
Mansfield NG18. . . . . . . .102 B5
Nottingham NG6 . . . . . . .160 E4
Owthorpe NG12 . . . . . . .199 E7
Pinxton NG16 . . . . .113 C2
Retford DN22. . . . . .40 A8
Southwell NG25 . . . . . . .136 D6
Sutton Bonington LE12 . .213 C5
Wigsley NG23 . . . . .70 A2
Parkland Cl
Mansfield NG18. . . . . . . .102 E2
Nottingham NG11 . . . . . .184 D3
Parklands Cl
Coddington NG24. . . . . . .125 F2
1 Nottingham NG5. . . . .147 B1
Parklands Dr 2 LE11 . . .220 A1
Parklands Gr NG2 . . . . . .77 D3
Parklands Inf Sch
NG10 . . . . .182 B1
Parkland View NG17 . . . .100 A2
Park Lane Bsns Ctr
NG6 . . . . .160 E5
Park Lane Bsns Pk
NG17. . . . . .114 D2
Park Lodge Rd NG16 . . . .158 A7
Park Mews
Mansfield Woodhouse
NG19 . . . . .88 C4
Retford DN22. . . . . .40 A8
Park Mws NG17. . . . . . . .100 F6
Park Pl S80. . . . . .35 F1
Park Ravine
Nottingham NG14 . . . . . .173 A3
Nottingham NG7 . . . . . . .222 C1
Park Rd
Arnold NG5 . . . . .161 E5
Barnstone NG13 . . . . . . .190 E3
Bawtry DN10 . . . . .9 F7
Beeston, Bramcote
NG9 . . . . .183 A8
Beeston, Chilwell NG9. . .183 E6
Bestwood Village NG6. . .146 E4
Calverton NG14 . . . . .148 E2
Carlton NG4 . . . . .174 F7
Hucknall NG15 . . . . .145 F7
Ilkeston DE7 . . . . .170 A7
Keyworth NG12 . . . . .197 F5
Loughborough LE11. . . . .220 B2
Mansfield Woodhouse
NG19 . . . . .88 B3
Nottingham NG7 . . . . . . .222 B1
Radcliffe on Trent NG12 .175 F4
Shirebrook NG20 . . . . . . .72 C5
Park Rd E NG14 . . . . .149 A7
Park Rd N NG9 . . . . .183 E6
Park Row NG1 . . . . .223 D2
Parkside
Huthwaite NG17 . . . . . . .100 A3
Keyworth NG12 . . . . .197 F4
Nottingham NG8 . . . . . . .171 E2
Parkside Ave NG10 . . . . .193 B8
Parkside Dr NG10 . . . . . .193 B8
Parkside Gdns NG8 . . . . .171 E2
Parkside Rd NG21 . . . . . . .75 F2
Parkside Rise NG8 . . . . . .171 E2
Parkside Way DN21. . . . . .24 F5
Park Springs Rd DN21 . . .24 F6
Park St
Beeston NG9 . . . . .183 E6
Kirkby-in-Ashfield NG17 .114 F5
Long Eaton NG10. . . . . . .182 C1
Loughborough LE11. . . . .220 B3
Mansfield Woodhouse
NG19 . . . . .88 B3
Nottingham NG7 . . . . . . .222 C4
Stapleford NG9 . . . . .182 C5
Sutton in Ashfield NG17 .100 F3
Parkstone Ave NG21 . . . .103 F2
Parkstone Cl NG2 . . . . . .185 C5
Park Terr
Keyworth NG12 . . . . .197 F5
Nottingham NG1 . . . . . . .223 D2
PARK THE 173 A4
Park The
Cotgrave NG12 . . . . .187 F4
Edwinstowe NG21. . . . . . .76 B2
Fackley NG17 . . . . .100 A7
Mansfield NG18. . . . . . . .102 C8
Newark-on-Trent NG24 . .140 A7
North Muskham NG23 . . .110 F3
Thurgarton NG14. . . . . . .151 C6
Park Vale Acad
Nottingham NG15 . . . . . .146 E1
Nottingham NG6 . . . . . . .160 E8
Park Valley NG7 . . . . .223 D2
Park View
Beeston NG9 . . . . .183 D6
HUCKNALL NG15 . . . . . . .146 B5
Nottingham NG3 . . . . . . .161 E2
Pleasley NG19 . . . . .87 A5
Whaley Thorns NG20 . . . .58 F2
Whaley Thorns NG20 . . . .59 A2
Worksop S81 . . . . .35 E7
Parkview Rd NG5 . . . . . . .161 A4
Park View Way NG18. . . .102 C5
Parkway
Clipstone NG19 . . . . .89 D3
Newark-on-Trent NG24 . .139 E6
Sutton in Ashfield NG17 .100 B3
Whitwell S80 . . . . .45 A6
Parkway Ct NG8 . . . . . . .171 D5
Parkwood Cres NG5 . . . .161 E3
Parkwood Ct NG6. . . . . .160 E5
Parkyn Rd NG5 . . . . .161 D6
Parkyns Piece LE12. . . . .205 F2
Parkyns St NG11 . . . . . . .196 C6
Parliament Ct NG24. . . . .139 E8
Parliament Rd NG19 . . . .101 E8

Parliament St
Newark-on-Trent NG24 . .139 E7
Sutton in Ashfield NG17 .100 F2
Parliament Terr NG1. . . .223 D3
Parliament Way NG21. . . .89 F5
Parliament Wlk NG24 . . .139 E8
Parman Ct LN1 . . . . .57 C3
Parnell St DN21. . . . . .24 C8
Parnham's Cl LE14. . . . .219 C8
Parr Gate NG8 . . . . .183 A5
Parr La NG14 . . . . .150 A5
Parrs The NG9 . . . . .184 B6
Parry Bsns Pk NG23. . . . . .81 E1
Parry Cl 5 NG3 . . . . .174 A6
Parry Way NG5 . . . . .162 B8
Parson La NG2 . . . . .65 C6
Parsons Ct NG24. . . . . . .140 E2
Parsons Mdw NG4 . . . . . .174 F4
Parthenon Dr NG19 . . . . . .86 F5
Partridge Cl
Bingham NG13 . . . . .177 F3
Blidworth NG21. . . . . . . .118 B8
Paschall Rd NG17. . . . . . .115 B1
Pasteur Ct 5 NG7 . . . . . .172 E2
Pasture Ave NG21 . . . . . .104 B1
Pasture Cl
Carlton NG2 . . . . .174 E4
Kirton NG22 . . . . .78 B7
Stanton Hill NG17 . . . . . .100 C5
Sutton Bonington LE12 . .213 A6
Worksop S80 . . . . .35 C3
Pasture Gr NG23. . . . . . . .112 B8
Pasture La
Hathern LE12. . . . . .213 B2
Hilcote DE55 . . . . .99 C1
Hose LE14 . . . . .211 F6
Long Eaton NG10. . . . . . .194 A5
Ruddington NG11 . . . . . .196 A4
Sutton Bonington LE12 . .213 A6
Pasture Rd
Gainsborough DN21 . . . . .24 F8
Stapleford NG9 . . . . .170 D1
Pastures Ave NG11 . . . . .195 D7
Pastures The
Bawtry DN10 . . . . .10 A6
Beckingham LN5 . . . . . . .142 D8
Calverton NG14 . . . . .148 D7
Eastwood NG16 . . . . .158 B8
Mansfield Woodhouse
NG19 . . . . .88 E5
Rampton DN22. . . . . .43 A1
Tuxford NG22. . . . . .65 E2
Pasture View
Gunthorpe NG14 . . . . . . .165 A5
Lowdham NG14 . . . . .150 D2
Pasture Way
Farnsfield NG22. . . . . . . .120 A6
Tickhill DN11 . . . . .8 B8
Patagonia Pl NG15. . . . . .130 B8
Patchills The NG18 . . . . .102 F7
Patchings Art Ctr *
NG14 . . . . .148 A8
Patchwork Row
Shirebrook NG20 . . . . . . .72 E3
Shirebrook NG20 . . . . . . .72 F4
Pateley Rd NG3. . . . . . . .162 A4
Pates Cl NG15 . . . . .131 D2
Patient Cl NG9. . . . . .183 B5
Paton Ct NG14. . . . . .133 F1
Paton Rd NG5 . . . . .160 E5
Patricia Dr NG5 . . . . .148 A1
Patrick Rd NG2 . . . . .185 E8
Patriot Cl NG16 . . . . .159 A7
Patriot La NG12 . . . . .185 F3
Patterdale Cl NG2 . . . . . .186 C6
Patterdale Rd NG5. . . . . .161 F5
Patterson Pl NG18. . . . . .102 D7
Patterson Rd 18 NG7. . . .172 F7
Paul Ave NG18. . . . . .103 A6
Paulina Ave NG15. . . . . .146 C8
Paulson's Dr NG18. . . . . .102 B7
Pavilion Cl
Market Warsop NG20 . . . .74 B4
2 Nottingham NG5. . . . .173 D1
Pavilion Ct NG14. . . . . . .164 E8
Pavilion Gdns
New Houghton NG19. . . . .86 F8
Sutton in Ashfield NG17 .101 A6
Pavilion Rd
Kirkby-in-Ashfield
NG17. . . . . .115 B6
Nottingham NG5 . . . . . . .147 B1
West Bridgford NG2 . . . .173 C4
Pavilion Way NG24. . . . . .125 F5
Pavillion Mws NG24. . . . .140 E8
Pavillion Way LE11. . . . . .220 A7
Pavior Rd 8 NG5. . . . . . .160 F5
Paviour Rd NG5 . . . . .160 F5
Paxton Gdns NG3 . . . . . .173 E5
Paxtons Ct NG24. . . . . . .124 F1
Payne Rd NG9 . . . . .183 B3
Peace Gr NG12 . . . . .186 A2
Peach Ave
Selston NG16. . . . . .128 F6
South Normanton DE55. .113 B7
Peache Way NG9 . . . . . . .183 C7
Peachey St NG1 . . . . .223 E3
Peacock Cl
Gunthorpe NG14. . . . . . .165 A4
Ruddington NG11. . . . . . .196 B6
Peacock Cres NG7. . . . . .184 C2
Peacock Dr NG16 . . . . . . .143 F2
Peacock Gdns
East Leake LE12 . . . . . . .214 E8
Nottingham NG8 . . . . . . .159 C2
Peacock Launde
NG23. . . . . .156 D6
Peacock St 2 NG18 . . . .102 B6

Peacock Way S81. . . . . . . .25 E1
Peafield La NG19 . . . . .88 E4
Peafield Lane Prim Sch
NG19 . . . . .88 F4
Peakdale Cl NG10. . . . . . .193 A6
Peake's Croft DN10 . . . . .10 A7
Peak Hill Cl
Carlton in Lindrick S81 . . .25 D1
Worksop S81 . . . . .25 D1
Peak The NG20 . . . . .72 E3
Pearce Dr NG8 . . . . .172 B7
Pearl Ave NG17 . . . . .115 B3
Pearl Cl NG21 . . . . .104 C1
Pearl Dr S81. . . . . .25 D1
Pearl Gdns NG20 . . . . .74 A5
Pearmain Dr NG3 . . . . . . .173 F7
Pearson Ave NG9 . . . . . . .183 B5
Pearson Cl NG9. . . . . .183 B5
Pearson Ct NG5. . . . . .161 E7
Pearson St
Carlton NG4 . . . . .175 A6
Nottingham NG7 . . . . . . .160 F2
Pear Tree Cl NG20 . . . . . . .30 D4
Pear Tree Cl 1 NG6 . . . .160 E4
Pear Tree Dr NG20. . . . . . .72 E6
Peartree La
Lidgett NG21 . . . . .91 C8
Teversal NG17 . . . . .86 B2
Pear Tree La NG17. . . . . .100 C8
Peartree Orch NG11 . . . .196 C7
Peary Cl NG5 . . . . .160 F6
Peashill La NG12. . . . . . . .187 C5
Peas Hill Rd NG3 . . . . . . .223 F4
Peat Carr Bank
Finningley DN9. . . . . .1 D4
Finningley DN9. . . . . .1 E7
Peatfield Ct NG9. . . . . . . .170 A5
Peatfield Rd NG9 . . . . . . .170 D1
Peck La
Gunthorpe NG14. . . . . . .165 A5
Nottingham NG1 . . . . . . .223 E2
Pecks Hill NG18 . . . . .102 E7
Pedmore Cl NG5. . . . . . . .161 B7
Pedmore Valley NG5. . . .161 A7
Peebles Rd NG24 . . . . . . .139 D5
Peel Ave
Retford DN22. . . . . .40 B3
Tuxford NG22. . . . . .65 F2
Peel Cres NG19 . . . . .87 D2
Peel Dr LE11. . . . . .220 C4
Peel Rd NG9. . . . . .101 E8
Peel St
Langley Mill NG16 . . . . . .143 B6
Long Eaton NG10. . . . . . .193 E8
Nottingham NG1 . . . . . . .223 D4
South Normanton DE55. .113 B6
Sutton in Ashfield NG17 .101 A3
Peets Dr NG23 . . . . .110 F2
Pegswood Dr
Arnold NG5 . . . . .147 F2
Woodborough NG5 . . . . .148 A2
Pelham Ave
Ilkeston DE7 . . . . .157 C1
Nottingham NG5 . . . . . . .173 B8
Pelham Cl NG24 . . . . .139 F8
Pelham Cres
Beeston NG9 . . . . .184 B7
Nottingham NG7 . . . . . . .222 B2
Pelham Ct 4 NG5 . . . . . .173 B8
Pelham Gdns NG24 . . . . .139 F8
Pelham Rd
Kirkby-in-Ashfield
NG17. . . . . .115 A6
Nottingham NG5 . . . . . . .173 B8
Retford DN22. . . . . .39 D7
Pelham St
Mansfield NG18. . . . . . . .102 C7
Newark-on-Trent NG24 . .139 F8
Nottingham NG1 . . . . . . .223 E2
Sutton in Ashfield NG17 .100 D2
Worksop S80 . . . . .36 A1
Pelham Way NG19 . . . . . . .89 D3
Pella Cross NG15 . . . . . . .130 D7
Pemberley Chase
NG17. . . . . .114 D8

Pennhome Ave 8
NG5. . . . . .161 C2
Penniment La NG19. . . . . .87 B2
Pennine Cl
Huthwaite NG17 . . . . .99 E8
Long Eaton, Breaston
NG10 . . . . .182 A1
Long Eaton, New Sawley
NG10 . . . . .193 D4
Mansfield Woodhouse
NG19 . . . . .88 C4
Newton DE55. . . . . .99 A3
Nottingham NG5 . . . . . . .147 B1
Pennine Dr
Kirkby-in-Ashfield
NG17. . . . . .114 D4
Selston NG16. . . . . .128 F7
Pennington Way NG15 . .145 E3
Pennington Wlk DN22 . . .40 A6
Penn La LE14. . . . . .202 F4
Penn Moor Cl NG10 . . . . .193 A6
Penn St NG17. . . . . .100 F3
Penny Emma Way
Kirkby-in-Ashfield
NG17. . . . . .115 A8
Sutton in Ashfield NG17 .114 F8
Pennyfields Bvd NG10 . .193 A7
Pennyfoot St NG1. . . . . . .173 E4
Penny Gdns NG9. . . . . . . .183 A8
Penny Gn S80. . . . . .45 A5
Pennyroyal Way NG17. . .115 A4
Penny Way NG18 . . . . . . .102 D1
Penrhyn Cl NG3 . . . . .223 F4
Penrhyn Cres NG9 . . . . . .183 B4
Penrith Ave NG12. . . . . . .176 A4
Penrith Cres NG8 . . . . . . .160 C2
Penrith Pl NG19 . . . . .101 D8
Penrose Ct NG16 . . . . . . .129 A7
Penrose Rise NG5 . . . . . .161 B4
Penryn Cl DE55 . . . . .113 C6
Penshore Cl NG11 . . . . . .184 D1
Pensom St NG22. . . . . .77 B3
Penson Gdns NG13 . . . . .177 D6
Penswick Gr NG24. . . . . .125 F2
Pentland Ct NG19. . . . . . .101 D5
Pentland Dr
Carlton in Lindrick S81 . . .25 E7
Nottingham NG5 . . . . . . .147 B2
Pentland Gdns NG10 . . . .182 A1
Pentrich Rd NG16. . . . . . .158 C7
Pentrich Wlk NG18 . . . . .103 B5
Pentwood Ave NG5. . . . . .147 F2
Penzance Pl NG18 . . . . . .103 B7
Peppercorn Gdns NG8 . .172 C5
Pepperly Hill Cl DN22. . . .50 A3
Pepperly Rise DN22. . . . . .50 A4
Pepper Rd NG14 . . . . .148 E8
Peppers Dr DE74 . . . . . . .203 B2
Pepper St
Nottingham NG1 . . . . . . .223 E2
Sutton in Ashfield NG17 .101 A2
Percival Cl NG17. . . . . . . .100 E3
Percival Cres NG17 . . . . .100 E3
Percival Rd NG5 . . . . .161 C2
Percival St S81 . . . . .35 E5
Percy St
Eastwood NG16. . . . . . . .144 A2
Nottingham NG6 . . . . . . .160 D3
Sutton in Ashfield NG17 .100 D2
Peregrine Ct NG7. . . . . . .222 A2
Peregrine Ct S81. . . . . . . .35 C7
Peregrine Gdns NG21. . . .89 F5
Peregrine Rd NG15. . . . . .131 D1
Perivale Cl NG16. . . . . . . .159 C5
Perkins La
Calverton NG5 . . . . .148 E7
Grimston LE14 . . . . .218 F2
Perkin's La LE14. . . . . . . .219 A1
Perkins Way NG9 . . . . . . .183 D3
PERLETHORPE. 62 F3
Perlethorpe Ave
Carlton NG4 . . . . .162 E2
Mansfield NG19. . . . . .88 A1
18 Nottingham NG3. . . .173 E4
Perlethorpe Cl
5 Carlton NG4 . . . . . . .162 E2
Edwinstowe NG21. . . . . . .75 D3
Perlethorpe Cres 6
NG4 . . . . .162 E2
Perlethorpe Dr
Carlton NG4 . . . . .162 E2
Hucknall NG15 . . . . .145 E4
Perlethorpe Rd DN22. . . .63 D7
Perlthorpe Ave NG20 . . . .74 D8
Perry Gdns
Brinsley NG16 . . . . .143 D7
Nottingham NG5 . . . . . . .161 B3
Perry Gr
Bingham NG13. . . . . .177 F4
Loughborough LE11. . . . .220 C1
Perry Rd NG5. . . . . .161 B3
Pershore Dr DN11 . . . . . . .9 B5
Perth Cl NG19 . . . . .88 E5
Perth Dr NG9 . . . . .170 F1
Perth St NG1 . . . . .223 E3
Petanque Way NG21. . . . .104 A1
Peterborough Rd NG23 . .98 B1
Peters Cl
Arnold NG5 . . . . .162 C6
Eastwood NG16. . . . . . . .144 C2
Petersfield Cl
Mansfield NG19. . . . . . . .101 C6
Nottingham NG5 . . . . . . .160 F7
Petersgate NG10 . . . . . . .182 A1
Petersgate Cl NG10. . . . .182 A1
Petersham Mews NG7 . . .222 B1
Petersham Rd NG10 . . . . .182 A1
Petersmith Cres NG22. . . .77 C6
Petersmiths Cl NG22 . . . . .77 C6
Petersmiths Dr NG22 . . . .77 C6
Petticoat La NG25 . . . . . .121 D1

Petworth Ave NG9 . . . . . .182 F3
Petworth Dr NG5. . . . . . . .160 F4
Peverel Dr NG18. . . . . . . .102 E4
Peveril Cres NG10 . . . . . .193 A5
Peveril Dr
Ilkeston DE7 . . . . .157 D2
Nottingham NG7 . . . . . . .223 D1
Sutton in Ashfield NG17 .100 C2
West Bridgford NG2 . . . .185 C5
Peveril Mews NG7 . . . . . .222 C2
Peveril Rd NG9 . . . . .184 A7
Peveril St
Hucknall NG15 . . . . .146 A8
Nottingham NG7 . . . . . . .222 B4
Pharaoh Ct NG8 . . . . .159 D2
Pheasant Hill NG19 . . . . . .88 A1
Pheonix Rd NG16 . . . . . . .144 B4
Philip Ave
Eastwood NG16. . . . . . . .144 A1
Kirkby-in-Ashfield NG17 .115 B2
Nuthall NG16 . . . . .159 C6
Philip Cl NG21 . . . . .118 C8
Philip Gr NG4. . . . . .162 E2
Philip Rd NG24 . . . . .139 E5
Phillipott Cl NG24. . . . . . .140 D8
Phoenix Ave NG4 . . . . . . .162 E2
Phoenix Cl
Mansfield NG18. . . . . . . .102 E1
Nottingham NG2 . . . . . . .173 B2
Phoenix Ct
Eastwood NG16. . . . . . . .144 A1
Gainsborough DN21 . . . . .24 F7
Nottingham NG7 . . . . . . .184 F8
Phoenix Ctr NG6. . . . . . . .160 A4
Phoenix Inf Sch 1
NG4 . . . . .162 E1
Phoenix La
Fernwood NG24 . . . . .140 F3
Fernwood NG24. . . . . . . .141 A3
Newark-on-Trent NG24 . .140 F2
Phoenix Pl NG5. . . . . .160 B4
Phoenix Rise NG19 . . . . . .86 F5
Phoenix St NG17 . . . . . . .101 B4
Phyllis Cl NG15 . . . . .130 F1
Phyllis Gr NG10 . . . . .193 F7
Piccadilly NG6. . . . . .160 D6
Piccadilly Ct NG19 . . . . . .88 C6
Pickard St NG18. . . . . . . .102 E7
Pickering Ave NG16. . . . .143 F2
Pieris Dr NG11. . . . . .184 C1
Pierpoint Pl NG17 . . . . . .114 F6
Pierrepont Ave NG4 . . . .162 E1
Pierrepont Gamston Prim
Sch NG2 . . . . .186 B6
Pierrepont Rd NG2 . . . . . .174 A1
Pierson St NG2 . . . . .139 E5
Piggott Ave NG5. . . . . . . .162 E3
Pike Ave NG17 . . . . .197 D2
Pilcher Gate NG1 . . . . . . .223 E2
Pilgrim Cl
Ranby DN22. . . . . .38 E6
Ravenshead NG15 . . . . . .116 F2
Pilgrim Ct S81. . . . . .34 F7
Pilgrim Rise DN10 . . . . . . .3 C1
Pilgrims App DN21. . . . . . .24 F6
Pilgrims Way DN21. . . . . . .24 F6
Pilgrim Way S80. . . . . .35 F2
Pilkington Rd NG3. . . . . . .162 A1
Pilkington St 8 NG6. . . . .160 B7
Pillared House La DN21 . .24 D7
Pilot Dr NG15. . . . . .145 E4
Pimlico Ave NG9 . . . . .171 B3
Pimlico Cl NG12 . . . . .176 E3
Pinder St NG1 . . . . .223 F2
Pine Ave
Langley Mill NG16 . . . . . .143 A3
New Ollerton NG22 . . . . . .77 D4
Pine Cl
East Leake LE12 . . . . . . .214 D8
Everton DN10. . . . . .11 C3
Kirkby-in-Ashfield NG17 .114 F6
Mansfield NG21. . . . . . . .103 F1
Mansfield Woodhouse
NG19 . . . . .88 C5
Newark-on-Trent NG24 . .125 B4
Newark-on-Trent NG24 . .140 F1
Shirebrook NG20 . . . . . . .72 E6
Pine Hill Cl NG5 . . . . .146 F1
Pinehurst Ave NG15 . . . .145 C5
Pines Cl NG16 . . . . .128 F8
Pines The
Beeston NG9 . . . . .183 C8
Gainsborough DN21 . . . . .24 F6
Worksop S80 . . . . .35 F2
Pines Way NG18 . . . . .116 D7
Pine Tree Cl S80. . . . . .35 E1
Pine Tree Wlk NG16 . . . . .143 E2
Pineview Cl NG18. . . . . . .102 F2
Pinewood Ave
Arnold NG5 . . . . .148 B1
Edwinstowe NG21. . . . . . .91 C8
Pinewood Cl
Kirkby-in-Ashfield
NG17. . . . . .115 C6
Southwell NG25. . . . . . . .121 D1
Pinewood Dr NG18 . . . . . .102 F2
Pinewood Gdns NG11. . . .195 D8
Pinewood Inf Sch NG5 . .148 B1
Pinfold NG13 . . . . .177 F4
Pinfold Cl
Bottesford NG13 . . . . . . .181 A3
Collingham NG23 . . . . . . .98 A1
Cotgrave NG12 . . . . .187 F4
East Markham NG22 . . . . .65 F7
Kinoulton NG12 . . . . .199 F2
Lound DN22. . . . . .20 C1
Skegby NG17 . . . . .100 F6
Woodborough NG14 . . . .149 C4
Pinfold Cres NG14 . . . . . .149 C4
Pinfold Dr S81. . . . . .25 F7
Pinfold Gate LE11. . . . . . .220 B4

Pinfold Gdns 5 LE11. . . .220 B4
Pinfold Jetty LE11. . . . . . .220 C4
Pinfold La
Averham NG23. . . . . .123 C4
Balderton NG24. . . . . . . .140 D3
Bottesford NG13 . . . . . . .181 A3
Clarborough NG23. . . . . . .40 B8
Elston NG23. . . . . .153 D5
Harby LE14 . . . . .202 C3
Kinoulton NG12 . . . . .199 F2
Misterton DN10. . . . . .6 E2
Nottingham NG11 . . . . . .185 B6
Plumtree NG12 . . . . .197 F2
Shelford NG12 . . . . .164 C1
Stapleford NG9 . . . . .182 E7
Styrrup DN11. . . . . .8 D2
Pinfold Pl LE14. . . . . .202 C3
Pinfold Rd NG16 . . . . .144 C1
Pinfold The DN10. . . . . . . .4 B2
Pingle Cl
Gainsborough DN21 . . . . .24 E8
Worksop S81 . . . . .34 E7
Pingle Cres NG5 . . . . .160 F8
Pingle La
Ossington NG23. . . . . . . .95 F7
Ossington NG23. . . . . . . .96 A7
Pingle The NG10. . . . . . . .193 D8
Pingley Cl NG23 . . . . .138 C8
Pingley La NG23 . . . . .138 C8
Pings Cl NG23 . . . . .97 E6
Pintail Cl NG4 . . . . .175 B5
Pintail Meadow S80 . . . . .35 B5
Pinter La DN21 . . . . .24 E5
PINXTON 113 C2
Pinxton Ct NG18. . . . . . . .103 B5
Pinxton La
Kirkby in A, Fulwood
NG17. . . . . .114 A7
Kirkby in A, Tichfield Park
NG17. . . . . .114 C4
South Normanton DE55. .113 C5
Pinxton Rd NG17. . . . . . .114 D3
Piper Cl
Hucknall NG15 . . . . .131 B1
Long Whatton LE12 . . . . .212 C2
Mansfield NG19 . . . . .88 B2
Piper Dr LE12. . . . . .212 C2
Piper Gr NG22 . . . . .72 D2
Piper La S80. . . . . .61 D7
Piper St NG20 . . . . .72 D2
Pipistrelle Cl LE12 . . . . . .214 B3
Pipit Gr NG11. . . . . .196 B6
Pippin Cl
Newark-on-Trent NG24 . .125 B2
Nottingham NG3 . . . . . . .173 F7
Selston NG16. . . . . .129 A7
Pippistrelle Cl DN22 . . . . .42 D8
Pitcairn Cl NG2 . . . . .173 C1
Pitch Cl
Giltbrook NG16 . . . . .158 C8
Nottingham NG4 . . . . . . .175 C8
Pit Hill NG21. . . . . .59 A1
Pithouse La LE12 . . . . . . .204 E1
Pit La
Mansfield NG19. . . . . .87 A3
Pleasley NG19 . . . . .86 F5
Shipley DE75 . . . . .157 B6
Stapleford NG9 . . . . .170 D2
Pitomy Dr NG23 . . . . .97 F1
Pitt Hill NG20. . . . . .58 F2
Pitt La DN10 . . . . .12 F3
Plackett Cl NG9. . . . . .182 F8
Plains Farm Cl NG3 . . . . .162 C5
Plains Gr NG3 . . . . .162 A4
Plainspot Rd NG16. . . . . .128 C2
Plains Rd NG3 . . . . .162 B4
Plane Cl NG6 . . . . .159 F7
Plane Rd 7 NG22. . . . . . .186 A2
Plantagenet Ct NG3. . . . .223 F4
Plantagenet St
Nottingham NG14 . . . . . .173 D5
Nottingham NG3 . . . . . . .223 F3
Plantation Ave NG22. . . . .66 A7
Plantation Cl NG5 . . . . . .147 A1
Plantation Dr DN10 . . . . .11 A1
Plantation Hill S81. . . . . . .36 B4
Plantation La S81. . . . . . . .27 B8
Plantation Rd
East Markham NG22. . . . .66 A6
Keyworth NG12 . . . . .197 D3
Nottingham NG8 . . . . . . .171 C4
Plantation Side NG7 . . . .172 E7
Plantations The 7
NG10 . . . . .193 C6
Plantin Rd NG5. . . . . .161 B1
Plant La NG10 . . . . .193 A4
Plants Yd S80 . . . . .35 E2
Platt La NG12. . . . . .198 A5
Platt St NG16 . . . . .113 D2
Platts The NG24 . . . . .139 E5
Plaxton Cl NG16 . . . . .144 B2
Player St NG7. . . . . .222 B4
Playworld * NG4 . . . . . . .162 F8
Plaza Gdns NG6 . . . . .160 E4
Pleasant Cl 2 LE11 . . . . .220 A4
Pleasant Pl DE74 . . . . . . .203 D2
Pleasant Row NG7 . . . . . .172 F7
PLEASLEY. 87 B6
PLEASLEYHILL. 87 C4
Pleasleyhill Way NG19 . . .87 C1
Pleasley Hill Way
NG19. . . . . .101 C1
Pleasley Prings NG19 . . .87 B5
Pleasley Rd
Fackley NG17. . . . . .100 B7
Skegby NG17 . . . . .100 F6

Pleasley Rd *continued*
Sutton in Ashfield NG17 .**101** A6
Teversal NG17 . . . .**86** C1
Pleasley Vale Nature
Reserve ★ NG19 . . . . . .**87** D7
Plot La NG23 . . . .**98** E4
Plough Dr S81 . . . .**25** F7
Plough Hill DN22 . . . . . .**42** D7
Plough La
Lowdham NG14 . . . .**150** D1
Nottingham NG2 . . . . . .**173** E4
Ploughman Ave NG14 . .**149** D4
Ploughmans Gr NG17 . .**100** A1
Ploughman Wood Nature
Reserve ★ NG14 . . . . . .**149** D2
Plover Dene S81 . . . .**35** C7
Plover Wharf ⟨3⟩ NG2. .**173** A2
Plowman Ct NG9 . . . . . .**182** D6
Plowright Ct ⟨5⟩ NG3. .**173** D7
Plowright St ⟨4⟩ NG3. .**173** D7
Plumb Rd NG15. . . . . . .**145** F7
Plummer La DE74. . . . . .**203** C2
Plumptre NG16. . . . . . .**143** B5
Plumptre Almshouses
NG1. . . . .**223** F1
Plumptre Cl NG16 . . . . .**143** F1
Plumptre Gdns ⟨1⟩
NG16. . . . .**143** F2
Plumptre Pl NG1 . . . . . .**223** F2
Plumptre Sq NG1 . . . . . .**223** F2
Plumptre St NG1. . . . . . .**223** F2
Plumptre Way NG16 . . .**143** F1
PLUMTREE **197** E6
Plum Tree DN22 . . . .**32** D1
Plum Tree Ave NG16 . . . .**89** B1
Plum Tree Cl DN22. . . . . .**30** D4
Plum Tree Ct DN22 . . . . .**32** D1
Plumtree Gdns NG14. . .**148** F7
Plumtree La
Bradmore NG11. . . . . . .**196** F3
Bradmore NG12. . . . . . .**197** A3
Plumtree Rd
Bircotes DN11 . . . .**9** C6
Cotgrave NG12 . . . .**187** E3
Plumtree Sch NG12 . . . .**197** E6
Plum Way NG24 . . . .**140** E2
PLUNGAR. **202** F8
Plungar Cl NG8. . . . .**172** B6
Plungar La
Barkestone-le-Vale
NG13. . . . .**192** A1
Barkestone-le-Vale
NG13. . . . .**192** B2
Plungar Rd
Granby NG13 . . . .**191** C5
Granby NG13 . . . .**191** D3
Plymouth Ave NG16. . . .**113** E2
Plymouth Cl DN21 . . . . . .**24** F6
Poachers Ct LN1. . . . . . .**57** A3
Pochard Cl ⟨5⟩ NG9. . . . .**88** F2
Pocklington Cres
NG24. . . . .**125** D6
Pocklington Rd NG23. . . .**98** B1
Podder La NG3 . . . .**162** C6
Poets Cl NG15 . . . .**145** E4
Point The NG3. . . . .**173** D8
Pollard Cl ⟨1⟩ NG24. . . .**140** A7
Pollard Dr NG18 . . . . . .**102** C7
Pollards La
Southwell NG25. . . . . . .**136** F5
Southwell NG25. . . . . . .**137** A5
Pollard's La NG25. . . . . .**136** F7
Polly Leys NG17 . . . . . .**101** B3
Polly Taylor's Rd
NG23. . . . .**67** E1
Polperro Way NG15. . . .**145** D5
Pompeia Cl NG15 . . . . . .**146** D8
Pond Cl NG24. . . . .**140** F2
Pond Cl NG24. . . . .**140** F2
Pond Hills La
Arnold NG5 . . . .**147** F1
Arnold NG5 . . . .**161** F8
Pond St NG17 . . . .**115** B5
Pond Way NG9 . . . .**171** E5
Pool Cl NG16 . . . .**113** D2
Poole Ave NG5 . . . .**162** E4
Poole Mdw NG12 . . . . . .**174** F4
Pooles Yard NG23 . . . . . .**81** E7
Popham Ct NG1 . . . .**223** F1
Poplar Ave
East Leake LE12 . . . . . .**214** D8
Kirkby-in-Ashfield NG17 . .**115** C5
Nottingham NG5 . . . . . .**161** A1
Sandiacre NG10. . . . . . .**182** A7
Poplar Cl
Bingham NG13. . . . .**178** A4
Carlton NG3. . . . .**174** D6
Cotgrave NG12 . . . .**188** C5
Sutton on Trent NG23 . . . .**96** F8
Worksop S80 . . . .**35** D1
Poplar Cres NG16. . . . . .**159** B6
Poplar Dr
Glapwell S44 . . . .**86** B8
Pleasleyhill NG19. . . . . . .**87** B4
Poplar Gr
Church Warsop NG20 . . . .**74** A6
Lidgett NG21 . . . .**91** C8
Mansfield Woodhouse
NG19 . . . .**89** C1
Poplar Rd DE55. . . . . . .**113** B7
Poplars Ave NG14. . . . . .**164** A5
Poplars Cl NG12 . . . . . .**197** F4
Poplars Ct NG8 . . . .**172** F2
Poplar St
Mansfield Woodhouse
NG19 . . . .**88** C3
New Ollerton NG22 . . . . . .**77** D4
Nottingham NG1 . . . . . .**173** E4
Retford DN22. . . . .**39** F6

Poplars The
Beeston NG9 . . . .**183** F7
Nottingham NG7 . . . . . .**172** E8
Ranskill DN22 . . . .**19** A4
Sutton in Ashfield NG17 .**101** A3
West Bridgford NG2 . . . .**185** F7
Whitwell S80 . . . .**45** A5
Poplars Way NG18 . . . .**116** E7
Poppy Cl
Shirebrook NG20. . . . . . .**72** D3
West Bridgford NG2 . . . .**185** D7
Poppyfields The NG23 . .**112** B8
Poppy Field Way
Carlton in Lindrick S81 . . . .**25** F7
Carlton in Lindrick S81 . . . .**26** A7
Poppy Gdn DE55. . . . . . .**99** B7
Poppy Mews NG15. . . . .**146** D4
Poppy Pl NG24. . . . .**125** D1
PORCHESTER **162** B2
Porchester Cl NG15. . . .**146** C7
Porchester Jun Sch
NG4 . . . .**162** A1
Porchester Rd
Bingham NG13. . . . .**177** D4
Nottingham NG3 . . . . . .**162** A1
Porlock Cl ⟨2⟩ NG10 . .**193** A8
Porritt Cl ⟨8⟩ LE12 . . . .**205** E3
Portage Cl NG12. . . . . . .**175** E2
Port Arthur Rd NG2. . . .**174** A4
Porter Cl NG11 . . . .**195** C8
Porters Wk NG3 . . . .**174** A7
Portinscale Cl NG2 . . . .**186** C5
Portland Coll NG18 . . . .**116** E6
Portland Cres
Mansfield Woodhouse
NG19 . . . .**88** D3
Meden Vale NG20 . . . . . .**60** E1
Stapleford NG9 . . . .**182** E6
Portland Ct NG5 . . . . . .**161** B5
Portland Ct Mews NG19. .**88** C4
Portland Dr
Shirebrook NG20. . . . . . .**72** F3
Shirebrook NG20. . . . . . .**73** A4
Portland Gdns NG15 . . .**145** F7
Portland Grange NG15 . .**145** E7
Portland Hill NG7. . . . . .**172** C1
Portland Hts NG15 . . . . . .**99** E4
Portland Ind Est NG17. .**115** A4
Portland L Ctr NG2. . . . .**173** D1
Portland Mdws DN22 . . . .**29** A6
Portland Pk
Kirkby-in-Ashfield NG17 . .**114** F3
Nuncargate NG17 . . . . . .**115** A3
Portland Pk Cl NG15 . . .**145** F7
Portland Pk Nature
Reserve ★ NG17 . . . . . .**114** F3
Portland Pl
Sutton DN22 . . . .**29** A6
Worksop S80 . . . .**35** F4
Portland Prim Sch
NG8 . . . .**171** C5
Portland Rd
Beeston NG9 . . . .**182** F1
Carlton NG4. . . . .**162** C2
Eastwood NG16. . . . . . .**158** B8
Hucknall NG15. . . . .**146** B6
Ilkeston DE7 . . . .**157** F3
Long Eaton NG10. . . . . .**193** B4
Nottingham NG7 . . . . . .**222** C3
Retford DN22. . . . .**39** D5
Selston NG16. . . . .**129** A7
Shirebrook NG20. . . . . . .**72** F4
Shirebrook NG20. . . . . . .**73** A4
West Bridgford NG2 . . . .**185** F6
Whaley Thorns NG20 . . . .**59** A2
Portland Ret Pk NG18. .**102** A5
Portland Row NG17. . . . .**91** C8
Portland Sq NG17. . . . . .**100** F2
Portland St
Arnold NG5 . . . .**161** E6
Beeston NG9 . . . .**184** A7
Mansfield NG18. . . . . . .**102** B6
Mansfield Woodhouse
NG19 . . . .**88** C3
Market Warsop NG20 . . . .**74** B4
Newark-on-Trent NG24 . .**139** F8
New Houghton NG19. . . . .**87** A7
Sutton in Ashfield NG17 .**100** F2
Worksop S80 . . . .**35** E3
Portland Terr
Gainsborough DN21 . . . . .**24** D7
Whaley Thorns NG20 . . . .**59** A2
Portland Way
Clipstone NG21 . . . .**89** F4
Clipstone NG21 . . . .**90** A4
Portman Ct DN10 . . . .**9** F7
Portree Dr NG5. . . . . . .**146** F1
Portside St NG14 . . . . . .**173** F2
Postern St NG1 . . . .**223** D2
Posthill Cl S80. . . . .**45** A6
Post Office La
Plungar NG13 . . . .**202** F8
Redmile NG13 . . . .**192** F3
Post Office Lane NG23 . . .**98** D5
Post Office Rd NG17 . . . .**115** B5
Post Office Yd NG14 . . . .**151** D2
Posts The NG12. . . . . . .**189** A6
Potmakers Gr NG17. . . .**101** A4
Potter La NG22 . . . .**92** D8
Potters Cl NG5 . . . .**161** A7
Potters Corner NG9 . . . .**103** A8
Potters Cl NG9. . . . .**171** D1
Potter's Hill View ⟨2⟩
DE75 . . . .**143** A1
Potters Hollow NG6. . . .**160** C5
Potters La LE12. . . . . . .**214** F8
Potters Nook S81. . . . . . .**34** F7
Potter St
Sutton in Ashfield
NG17 . . . .**101** A4

Potter St *continued*
Worksop S80 . . . .**35** F2
Potters Way DE7. . . . . .**170** A8
Pottery Ct NG6 . . . .**160** A7
Pottery Way NG6 . . . . . .**160** A7
Potwell Cl NG25 . . . . . .**136** F8
Pot Yd The NG22 . . . . . .**119** F6
Poulter Cl NG7 . . . .**172** D7
Poulter Rise DN22 . . . . . .**50** A5
Poulter St
Langwith NG20 . . . .**59** A1
Whaley Thorns NG20. . . . .**58** F1
Poulter View DN22. . . . . .**39** F5
Poulton Dr NG2. . . . . . .**173** E2
Poultry NG1. . . . .**223** E2
Powell Ct NG22 . . . .**119** F5
Powell Gdns ⟨1⟩ S81. . . . .**35** D8
Powtrell Pl DE7. . . . . . .**170** B6
Poynton St NG1 . . . .**223** D3
Poyser Cl ⟨7⟩ NG21 . . . .**161** A1
Pratt Cl ⟨4⟩ NG19 . . . . . .**87** D1
Prebble Cl NG24 . . . . . .**139** E5
Prebends Cl NG14 . . . . .**138** F4
Precinct Rd NG17. . . . . .**115** B5
Precinct The NG17. . . . .**187** F3
Premier Rd NG7. . . . . . .**173** A8
Prendwick Gdns NG5 . .**161** B8
President Pl DN11 . . . .**9** A6
Prest Ave NG20 . . . .**74** E8
Preston Rd
Balderton NG24. . . . . . .**140** E8
Rainworth NG21 . . . . . .**118** A8
Prestwick Cl NG8. . . . . .**159** D2
Prestwold Ave
Mansfield NG19. . . . . . .**103** B8
Mansfield Woodhouse
NG19 . . . .**89** B1
Prestwold La LE12 . . . . .**215** C1
Prestwood Dr NG8. . . . .**172** B7
Previn Gdns NG3 . . . . . .**173** F6
Priestgate NG22. . . . . . .**65** E6
Priestsic Prim Sch
NG17 . . . .**100** F3
Priestsic Rd NG17. . . . . .**100** E3
Primrose Ave
Farndon NG24 . . . .**139** A6
Newark-on-Trent NG24 . .**125** B4
Selston NG16. . . . .**128** F2
Primrose Bank NG13. . .**177** D4
Primrose Cl
East Leake LE12 . . . . . .**206** A1
⟨7⟩ Kirkby-in-Ashfield
NG17 . . . .**114** F7
Nottingham NG3 . . . . . .**173** D7
South Normanton DE55. .**113** B7
Primrose Cres NG4 . . . .**174** F7
Primrose Ct
Mansfield Woodhouse
NG19 . . . .**88** F4
Sutton in Ashfield NG17 .**100** F2
Primrose Gdns NG15. . .**146** D4
Primrose La NG22 . . . . . .**78** C5
Primrose Rise NG16 . . .**158** A8
Primrose St
Carlton NG4. . . . .**174** F7
Gainsborough DN21 . . . . .**24** D7
Ilkeston DE7 . . . .**157** E3
Primrose Way
Clipstone NG21 . . . .**89** F4
Shirebrook NG20. . . . . . .**72** F6
Sutton in Ashfield NG17 .**100** E1
Worksop S81 . . . .**36** A6
Prim Sch of St Mary & St
Martin The S81. . . . . . .**18** B2
Primula Cl
Nottingham NG11 . . . . .**184** C2
Shirebrook NG20. . . . . . .**72** D3
Primula Gr ⟨10⟩ NG17. . .**115** A3
Prince Charles Rd S81 . . .**35** D6
Prince Edward Cres
NG12. . . . .**175** E2
Prince of Wales St
DN22. . . . .**39** E6
Princes Rd LE14 . . . . . .**219** B6
Princess Anne Rd S81 . . .**35** E6
Princess Ave
Beeston NG9 . . . .**184** A6
Mansfield NG19. . . . . . .**103** A8
Market Warsop NG20 . . . .**74** C4
South Normanton DE55. .**113** A5
Princess Cl
Carlton NG4. . . . .**162** E2
⟨4⟩ Edwalton NG12. . . . .**185** F2
Princess Diana Ct DN21 . .**15** C3
Princess Dr NG10. . . . . .**182** B4
Princess St
Eastwood NG16. . . . . . .**143** F3
Kirkby-in-Ashfield NG17 .**114** D3
Long Eaton NG10. . . . . .**193** D8
⟨7⟩ Loughborough LE11. .**220** B3
Princes St NG18 . . . .**102** A5
Prince's St NG24. . . . . .**139** F7
Princes Wlk DN21 . . . . . .**15** F1
Prince St
Ilkeston DE7 . . . .**157** E4
Long Eaton NG10. . . . . .**193** D8
Prince William Rd
LE11. . . . .**220** A6
Prince William Way
LE11. . . . .**220** A6
Prioridge NG12. . . . . . .**188** A2
Prior Cl NG17. . . . .**101** B4
Prior Rd NG5 . . . .**161** D6
Priors Cl NG21. . . . .**178** A5
Priors Cl NG13. . . . .**178** A5
Priors The NG14 . . . . . .**150** D2
Priorswell Rd S80 . . . . . .**35** F2
Priory Ave
Annesley Woodhouse
NG17 . . . .**115** B1

Priory Ave *continued*
Annesley Woodhouse
NG17 . . . .**130** B8
Ravenshead NG15 . . . . .**117** B1
Tollerton NG12. . . . . . .**186** C1
Priory Belvoir Acad The
NG13 . . . .**181** A1
Priory Cir NG12. . . . . . .**186** C1
Priory Cl
Balderton NG24. . . . . . .**140** D3
Blyth S81 . . . .**18** A3
Gainsborough DN21 . . . . .**24** F8
Mattersey DN10 . . . .**20** A6
Priory Cres NG4 . . . . . .**162** F1
Priory Ct NG4. . . . .**162** F1
Priory Ctr The S80 . . . . . .**35** E4
Priory CV Acad The
NG16 . . . .**144** B1
Priory Farm Mws
NG14. . . . .**151** D7
Priory Gdns NG14. . . . . .**151** C7
Priory Gr NG17 . . . .**115** D5
Priory Jun Sch ⟨1⟩ NG4 .**162** F1
Priory La NG14 . . . .**151** C7
Priory Mews NG7 . . . . .**172** E2
Priory Mws S80. . . . .**35** E2
Priory Nottingham Hospl
The (Private) NG3 . . . .**173** E8
Priory Pk NG14 . . . .**151** D7
Priory Rd
Blidworth NG21 . . . . . .**118** A5
Carlton NG4. . . . .**162** F1
Eastwood NG16. . . . . . .**143** F1
Hucknall NG15. . . . .**145** E7
Mansfield Woodhouse
NG19 . . . .**88** B3
West Bridgford NG2 . . . .**186** A8
Priory Sq NG19 . . . .**88** B3
Priory St NG7. . . . .**172** E2
Priory Way DE55. . . . . . .**99** A3
Pritchard Dr
Kegworth DE74 . . . .**203** B3
Stapleford NG9 . . . .**182** E6
Private Dr NG25 . . . .**121** D2
Private Rd
Hucknall NG15. . . . .**145** E7
Nottingham NG5, NG3 . .**161** D2
Southwell NG25. . . . . . .**121** E1
Woodborough NG14 . . . .**149** B5
Private St NG24 . . . .**140** B8
Privet Ave NG17 . . . . . .**115** A6
Privet Cl NG21. . . . .**89** E3
Prize Cl NG11. . . . .**184** C1
Procters Dr NG23. . . . . . .**82** E1
Promenade NG3. . . . . . .**223** F3
Promenade The NG17. . .**115** D6
Prospect Cl NG17 . . . . . .**115** B7
Prospect Ct NG17. . . . . . .**99** E1
Prospect Dr
Shirebrook NG20. . . . . . .**72** E3
Worksop S80 . . . .**35** F6
Prospect Hill Inf Sch
S81. . . . .**36** A6
Prospect Hill Jun Sch
S81. . . . .**36** A7
Prospect Mws DN10 . . . . . .**6** F2
Prospect Pl
Nottingham NG7 . . . . . .**222** B1
Sutton in Ashfield NG17 .**100** E1
Prospect Prec S81. . . . . . .**36** A6
Prospect Rd
Carlton NG4. . . . .**162** B1
Heanor DE75 . . . .**157** A8
Prospect St
Mansfield NG18. . . . . . .**102** D6
Nottingham NG7 . . . . . .**222** A4
Prospect Terr
Gainsborough DN21 . . . . .**24** D7
Nottingham NG7 . . . . . .**222** A4
Providence Pl ⟨5⟩ DE7 .**157** E1
Providence Rd NG16. . . .**128** A4
Prudhoe Ct ⟨5⟩ NG2. . . .**173** D1
Pudding La LE14. . . . . . .**210** C5
Puggy La S81. . . . .**36** D6
Pulborough Cl NG5. . . . .**160** F4
Pulford Cl ⟨1⟩ NG24. . . .**140** A8
Pullman Rd ⟨4⟩ NG2. . . .**173** F4
Pump Hollow La NG18 . .**103** A7
Pump Hollow Rd NG19 .**103** A8
Pump La
Fenton NG23 . . . .**142** E2
Walesby NG22 . . . .**64** A2
Pump Works Cl ⟨8⟩
NG5. . . . .**161** C3
Purbeck Cl
Long Eaton NG10. . . . . .**193** A8
Mansfield Woodhouse
NG19 . . . .**88** C6
Purbeck Dr NG2. . . . . . .**185** C5
Purdy Mdw NG10. . . . . .**193** A5
Pureland Japanese Gdn
and Meditation Ctr★
NG23 . . . .**68** C5
Pyatt St NG2. . . . .**173** D1
Pye Ave NG19 . . . .**101** D7
PYE BRIDGE **128** A7
Pye Hill Rd NG16. . . . . .**128** A4
Pygall Ave NG11 . . . . . .**195** A1
Pym St NG3 . . . .**173** F6
Pym Wlk NG3 . . . .**173** F6
Pythonhill Rd NG21 . . . .**118** B8
Python Hill Rd NG21 . . .**104** B1

Q

Quadrangle The
Blidworth NG21. . . . . . .**118** A5
Newstead NG15. . . . . . .**130** D6
Quakefield Rd
NG22 . . . .**66** B6

Quaker La
Farnsfield NG22. . . . . . .**119** F5
⟨11⟩ Mansfield NG18 . . . .**102** B7
Quaker Way NG18 . . . . .**102** B7
Quantock Cl NG5 . . . . . .**147** B2
Quantock Gr NG13. . . . .**177** C4
Quantock Rd NG10. . . . .**182** A1
Quantum Bsns Pk DN22 . .**42** E8
Quarries Way NG17 . . . .**114** E4
Quarry Ave NG6 . . . . . .**160** B6
Quarry Bank NG18 . . . . .**102** D4
Quarry Cl NG15. . . . . . .**132** B8
Quarry Dale NG15 . . . . .**130** F1
Quarrydale Acad NG17 .**100** E5
Quarrydale Ave NG17. . .**100** E5
Quarrydale Dr NG17 . . . .**100** E5
Quarrydale Rd NG17. . . .**100** F4
Quarry Dale Vw NG18 . .**102** E5
Quarry Dr NG17. . . . . . .**115** B3
Quarry Gr S81 . . . .**35** C7
Quarry Hill NG10. . . . . .**182** A8
Quarry La
Linby NG15. . . . .**131** B4
Mansfield NG18. . . . . . .**101** F4
Mansfield NG18. . . . . . .**102** A5
Quarry Rd NG15 . . . . . .**132** B8
Quarry Yd NG17 . . . .**100** E2
Quartz Ave NG18 . . . . . .**102** E4
Quayside Cl NG2. . . . . . .**173** E1
Queen Elizabeth Acad
NG19 . . . .**88** A1
Queen Elizabeth Cres
S80 . . . .**35** A4
Queen Elizabeth Rd
NG9 . . . .**183** A3
Queen Elizabeth's High Sch
DN21 . . . .**15** C3
Queen Mary's Ct NG2 . .**176** D2
Queens Ave DE7 . . . . . .**170** A5
Queen's Ave NG4 . . . . . .**162** E2
Queens Bower Rd NG5 .**161** C8
Queensberry St ⟨5⟩
NG6. . . . .**160** E4
Queen's Bridge Rd
NG2. . . . .**223** E1
Queensbury Ave NG2 . .**185** C3
Queens Cl
East Markham NG22 . . . .**66** A4
Hodthorpe S80 . . . .**45** C5
Queen's Cres DN10 . . . . .**10** A7
Queen's Ct
Bingham NG13. . . . .**177** D5
Clipstone NG19 . . . .**89** D3
Newark-on-Trent NG24 . .**125** A1
Queens Dr
Beeston NG9 . . . .**184** A6
Brinsley NG16 . . . .**143** E7
Nottingham NG11 . . . . .**185** A8
Nottingham NG7 . . . . . .**184** F7
Sandiacre NG10. . . . . . .**182** B4
Queen's Dr NG16 . . . . . .**159** C6
Queens Dr Ind Est
NG2 . . . .**173** A1
Queens Farm Gdns
NG24 . . . .**140** E2
Queensfield DN21 . . . . . .**15** B3
Queens Gr NG2 . . . .**223** E1
Queen's Head Ct NG24 .**139** F8
Queen's Medical Ctr (Univ
Hospl) NG7 . . . .**172** D2
Queens Rd
Beeston NG9 . . . .**184** A6
Carlton in Lindrick S81 . . . .**25** F7
Hodthorpe S80 . . . .**45** C6
Kegworth DE74 . . . .**203** D2
Queen's Rd
Loughborough LE11. . . . .**220** C4
Newark-on-Trent NG24 . .**125** A1
Nottingham NG2 . . . . . .**223** F1
Radcliffe on Trent NG12 .**176** A4
Queens Rd E NG9 . . . . . .**184** B7
Queens Rd N N16. . . . . .**143** F2
Queens Rd S NG16 . . . . .**143** F1
Queens Rd W NG9 . . . . .**183** E4
Queen's Rd
Loughborough LE11. . . . .**220** C4
Newark-on-Trent NG24 . .**125** A1
Nottingham NG2 . . . . . .**223** F1
Radcliffe on Trent NG12 .**176** A4
Queens Sq NG16 . . . . . .**143** F2
Queen St
Arnold NG5 . . . .**148** A1
Balderton NG24. . . . . . .**140** E3
Balderton NG24. . . . . . .**140** E4
Bottesford NG13 . . . . . .**181** A2
Collingham NG23. . . . . . .**98** A1
Gainsborough DN21 . . . . .**24** D7
Hucknall NG15. . . . .**145** F8
Kirkby-in-Ashfield NG17 .**115** A4
Langley Mill NG16 . . . . .**143** C3
Long Eaton NG10. . . . . .**193** E7
⟨3⟩ Loughborough LE11. .**220** C3
⟨10⟩ Mansfield NG18. . . . .**102** B7
Market Warsop NG20 . . . .**74** A3
Newark-on-Trent NG24 . .**139** F7
Nottingham NG1 . . . . . .**223** E3
Pinxton NG16. . . . .**113** C3
Retford DN22. . . . .**39** D6
South Normanton DE55. .**113** A5
Southwell NG25. . . . . . .**121** D1
Southwell NG25. . . . . . .**136** E8
Sutton in Ashfield NG17 .**100** F4
Worksop S80 . . . .**35** F2
Queensway
Gainsborough DN21 . . . . .**24** F8
Kirkby-in-Ashfield NG17 .**115** B2
Mansfield Woodhouse
NG19 . . . .**89** A1
Nether Broughton LE14. .**219** C6
Saxilby LN1 . . . .**57** B3
Skellingthorpe LN6 . . . . .**71** F3
Worksop S81 . . . .**35** F4

Queensway Sutton in Ashfield NG17. . . . .**57** B3
Queens Wlk ⟨14⟩ NG18. .**102** B7
Queen's Wlk
Nether Langwith NG20 . . . .**59** A1
Nottingham NG2 . . . . . .**173** B1
Querneby Ave NG3. . . . .**161** E2
Querneby Rd NG3 . . . . . .**161** E2
Quibell Rd NG24 . . . . . .**140** A5
Quibell's La NG24. . . . . .**125** A3
Quince Cl LE12 . . . .**214** C8
Quines Hill Rd NG19 . . . .**89** A2
Quinton Cl NG11. . . . . . .**185** A5
Quorn Cl
Beeston NG9 . . . .**183** E3
Loughborough LE11. . . . .**220** C2
Quorndon Cres NG10 . . .**193** D5
Quorn Gr NG5 . . . .**161** A3
Quorn Rd NG5 . . . .**161** A3

R

Rabbithill La NG23 . . . . . .**83** B6
Racecourse Rd
Brinkley NG25 . . . .**137** C7
Mansfield NG18. . . . . . .**102** C5
Nottingham NG2 . . . . . .**174** A4
Nottingham NG4 . . . . . .**174** B3
Southwell NG25. . . . . . .**122** A1
Rachel Cl DN21 . . . .**15** C3
Rackhills Cl NG19. . . . . . .**88** E1
Radbourne Rd ⟨9⟩ NG2 .**173** F3
Radbourne St NG19. . . . . .**88** E4
Radburn Ct NG9 . . . .**170** E1
Radcliffe Gdns NG4. . . . .**174** D8
Radcliffe Mount NG2 . . .**173** F1
RADCLIFFE ON
TRENT. **175** E3
Radcliffe-on-Trent Inf Sch
NG12 . . . .**176** A3
Radcliffe on Trent Jun Sch
NG12 . . . .**175** F2
Radcliffe Rd
Carlton NG12. . . . .**175** B1
Cropwell Butler NG12 . . .**188** F7
Cropwell Butler NG12 . . .**189** A7
West Bridgford NG2 . . . .**186** A8
West Bridgford NG2 . . . .**186** D8
Radcliffe St NG2. . . . . . .**173** D1
Radcliffe Sta NG12 . . . . .**175** F3
Raddle Way NG24. . . . . .**140** A4
RADFORD. **222** A3
Radford Bridge Rd
NG8. . . . .**172** C5
Radford Bvd NG7. . . . . .**222** C4
Radford Cres NG4 . . . . . .**162** E2
Radford Ct NG7. . . . .**222** B3
Radford Gr La NG7. . . . . .**222** A4
Radford Prim Sch NG7 .**222** A3
Radford Rd
Nottingham NG7 . . . . . .**172** F7
Nottingham NG7 . . . . . .**222** B4
Radford St
⟨1⟩ Mansfield NG18 . . . .**102** B6
Worksop S80 . . . .**36** B1
Radley Rd NG22 . . . .**135** C7
Radleys La
Perlethorpe NG22 . . . . . .**62** F3
Perlwthorpe NG22 . . . . . .**63** A3
Radley Sq NG6. . . . .**160** D5
Radley Terr NG22 . . . . . .**135** D8
RADMANTHWAITE **87** D3
Radmanthwaite La
NG19 . . . .**87** B3
Radmanthwaite Rd
NG19 . . . .**87** D3
Radmarsh Rd NG7 . . . . .**222** A4
Rad Mdws NG10 . . . .**193** C6
Radmoor Rd ⟨7⟩ LE11. . .**220** A4
Radnor Gr NG13 . . . .**177** C4
Radnor Pl NG19 . . . .**87** C4
Radstock Rd NG3 . . . . . .**174** A7
Radway Dr NG11. . . . . . .**185** A5
Raeburn Dr NG9 . . . .**182** E2
Ragdale Rd NG6. . . . . . .**160** B8
Raglan Cl NG3. . . . .**173** D7
Raglan Ct
Beeston NG9 . . . .**172** A1
Newark-on-Trent NG24 . .**140** A7
Raglan Dr NG4 . . . .**163** B1
Raglan Gdns NG24. . . . .**140** A7
Raglan Rd DN22 . . . .**40** A7
Raglan St NG16 . . . .**144** A1
RAGNALL **68** A8
Raibank Gdns NG5. . . . .**161** E5
Railway Ave S80 . . . .**58** C6
Railway Cl NG15. . . . . . .**146** A5
Railway Cotts NG16. . . . .**158** F6
Railway Ct LN1 . . . .**57** A3
Railway Terr LE11. . . . . .**220** C5
Raines Ave S81 . . . .**35** E6
Raines Pk Rd S81 . . . .**35** E7
Rainham Gdns NG11. . . .**196** C6
RAINWORTH. **104** A1
Rainworth Heath Nature
Reserve ★ NG21 . . . . . .**104** A3
Rainworth L Ctr NG21. . .**117** F8
Rainworth Water Rd
NG18. . . . .**117** F8
Rainworth Wr Rd
NG21. . . . .**103** A3
Raithby Cl NG5 . . . .**161** A6
Raleigh Cl
Ilkeston DE7 . . . .**157** F3
Nottingham NG11 . . . . .**184** C1
Raleigh Rd NG19. . . . . . .**101** C3
Raleigh St NG7 . . . .**222** C3
Raleigh Villas NG9. . . . .**183** C5
Ralf Cl NG2. . . . .**185** E4
Ralph Way NG5. . . . .**161** C5
Ramblers Cl NG4 . . . . . .**174** E5

Ramper La LN1 . . . 55 D6
Ramper Rd
Letwell S81 . . . 16 A3
Saundby DN22 . . . 23 D7
RAMPTON . . . 42 F1
Rampton Gn Rd DN22 . . . 42 F1
Rampton Hospl DN22 . . . 53 B8
Rampton La DN22 . . . 42 D5
Rampton Prim Sch
DN22 . . . 42 D1
Rampton Rd
Laneham DN22 . . . 54 A6
Rampton DN22 . . . 42 E3
Ramsdale Ave NG14 . . . 148 D8
Ramsdale Cres NG5 . . . 161 D2
Ramsdale Rd NG4 . . . 162 E1
Ramsden Ave S81 . . . 16 F2
Ramsden Cres S81 . . . 25 F7
Ramsden Croft
Mansfield NG21 . . . 103 F1
Rainworth NG21 . . . 104 A1
Ramsden Prim Sch
Carlton in Lindrick S81 . . . 25 F5
Carlton in Lindrick S81 . . . 26 A5
Ramsey Cl
Mansfield Woodhouse
NG19 . . . 89 A2
Stapleford NG9 . . . 170 E2
Ramsey Ct 5 NG5 . . . 161 B1
Ramsey Dr NG5 . . . 162 C6
RANBY . . . 38 A6
Ranby CE Prim Sch
DN22 . . . 38 A7
Ranby Wlk NG3 . . . 173 F6
Rancliffe Ave NG12 . . . 197 D4
Rancliffe Farm Mews
NG11 . . . 196 E3
Rancliffe St NG11 . . . 223 F1
Randal Gdns 4 NG7 . . . 172 F7
Randall Cl NG24 . . . 140 D8
Randall Pk Way DN22 . . . 29 C2
Randall Way DN22 . . . 29 C1
Randal St 3 NG7 . . . 172 F7
Randol Cl NG18 . . . 101 D4
Ranelagh Gr NG8 . . . 172 B5
Rani Dr NG6 . . . 160 F4
Rani Dr NG6 . . . 160 F4
Ranmere Rd NG8 . . . 172 A2
Ranmoor Rd NG4 . . . 162 F1
Ranmore Cl NG9 . . . 171 B2
Rannerdale Cl NG2 . . . 186 C6
Rannoch Dr NG19 . . . 101 E5
Rannoch Rise NG5 . . . 147 F1
Rannock Gdns NG12 . . . 197 F3
RANSKILL . . . 19 B4
Ranskill Gdns NG5 . . . 161 A8
Ranskill Prim Sch DN22 . . . 19 B5
Ranskill Rd DN22 . . . 19 E6
Ransom Dr NG3 . . . 161 E1
Ransome Cl NG24 . . . 140 D8
Ransom Rd
Mansfield NG21 . . . 103 D3
Nottingham NG3 . . . 173 E8
Ransom Wood Bsns Pk
NG21 . . . 103 D4
Ranson Rd NG9 . . . 183 C2
Ratcher Hill NG18 . . . 103 C3
Ratcher Way NG19 . . . 103 B8
Ratcliffe Gate NG18 . . . 102 C6
Ratcliffe La
Darfoulds S80 . . . 45 E2
Ratcliffe on Soar DE74 . . . 203 C7
RATCLIFFE ON SOAR . . . 203 F6
Ratcliffe Rd LE11 . . . 220 C5
Ratcliffe St NG16 . . . 143 F2
Rathgar Cl NG8 . . . 171 D4
Rathmines Cl NG7 . . . 222 A1
Rathvale Ct NG9 . . . 183 A4
Raven Ave NG5 . . . 161 B4
Ravencroft La DN10 . . . 14 B1
Ravendale Rd DN21 . . . 24 E7
Ravenhill Cl NG9 . . . 183 B4
Ravenscourt S81 . . . 36 A6
Ravens Ct NG5 . . . 161 B6
Ravensdale Ave
Long Eaton NG10 . . . 182 B2
Mansfield NG18 . . . 102 D8
Ravensdale Dr NG8 . . . 171 C3
Ravensdale Rd NG18 . . . 102 E8
Ravensdene Ct 2 NG3 . . . 173 D8
Ravensfleet Rd DN21 . . . 7 F3
RAVENSHEAD . . . 117 B1
Ravenshead CE Prim Sch
NG15 . . . 117 A2
Ravenshill Cl DN22 . . . 19 B4
Ravensmore Rd NG5 . . . 161 B2
Ravenstone Cl NG15 . . . 145 D3
Ravenswood Rd NG5 . . . 162 A8
Ravensworth Rd NG6 . . . 160 B8
Rawson St
Nottingham NG7 . . . 160 F1
Selston NG16 . . . 129 A6
Raylaw St NG18 . . . 103 A6
Raymede Cl NG5 . . . 160 F6
Raymede Dr NG5 . . . 160 E6
Raymond Cl NG17 . . . 114 E7
Raymond Dr NG13 . . . 178 A4
Raymond Way NG10 . . . 88 C1
Raymoth La S81 . . . 35 E7
Rayneham Rd DE7 . . . 157 C4
Rayner Ct NG7 . . . 222 B3
Raynford Ave NG9 . . . 183 C4
Raysmith Ave NG25 . . . 121 E2
Rayton Ct DN11 . . . 9 A4
Rayton Farm La S80 . . . 36 F2
Rayton La
Worksop S81 . . . 36 C3
Worksop S81 . . . 36 F4
Rayton Spur S81 . . . 36 B3
Read Ave NG9 . . . 184 A6
Read Cl NG24 . . . 140 E2

Readman Rd NG9 . . . 183 A3
Read Robinson Ave LN1 . . . 57 A5
Readwald Dr NG21 . . . 104 B1
Rearsby Cl NG8 . . . 171 D5
Rebecca Adlington
Swimming Centre
NG19 . . . 88 B1
Recreation Dr NG20 . . . 72 F2
Recreation Rd
Annesley NG15 . . . 130 C8
New Houghton NG19 . . . 86 F7
Sandiacre NG10 . . . 182 B6
Shirebrook NG20 . . . 72 E6
Recreation St
Long Eaton NG10 . . . 193 F8
Mansfield NG18 . . . 102 C7
Selston NG16 . . . 129 B6
Recreation Terr NG9 . . . 182 D6
Recreation View NG20 . . . 72 E6
Rectors Gate DN22 . . . 39 E8
Rectory Ave
Gainsborough DN21 . . . 15 D1
Nottingham NG8 . . . 171 E4
Rectory Cl LE12 . . . 213 B7
Rectory Dr NG11 . . . 185 B8
Rectory Dr The NG4 . . . 162 F2
Rectory Gdns
Beckingham DN10 . . . 14 B1
Kirton NG22 . . . 78 B6
Nottingham NG8 . . . 171 F4
Rectory La
Bottesford NG13 . . . 181 B3
Claypole NG23 . . . 156 E7
Gamston DN22 . . . 50 F5
Gamston DN22 . . . 51 A5
Kirkby-in-Ashfield NG17 . . . 114 E4
Lea DN21 . . . 24 F2
Rectory Mws NG9 . . . 184 D2
Rectory Pl
Barton in Fabis NG11 . . . 194 E6
2 Loughborough LE11 . . . 220 B4
Wymeswold LE12 . . . 216 C3
Rectory Rd
Carlton NG4 . . . 174 E5
Church Warsop NG20 . . . 74 C7
Cotgrave NG12 . . . 187 E3
Loughborough LE11 . . . 220 B5
Retford DN22 . . . 39 E7
Shirebrook NG20 . . . 72 D7
Treswell DN22 . . . 42 B3
West Bridgford NG2 . . . 185 F7
Rectory St LN5 . . . 142 D8
Red Admiral Rd NG5 . . . 25 C1
Red Barn Cl DE55 . . . 99 B3
Redbarn La DE55 . . . 99 B3
Redbarn Way NG17 . . . 100 C1
Redbourne Dr NG8 . . . 172 C6
Redbridge Cl
2 Ilkeston DE7 . . . 170 A4
Shirebrook NG20 . . . 72 F2
Redbridge Dr NG16 . . . 159 D3
Redcar Cl
Carlton NG4 . . . 162 E2
Mansfield NG18 . . . 102 E5
Redcliffe Gdns NG3 . . . 173 C8
Redcliffe Rd
Mansfield NG18 . . . 102 D6
Nottingham NG3 . . . 173 C8
Redcliffe St
2 New Cross NG17 . . . 100 F4
Sutton in Ashfield NG17 . . . 101 A4
Redcroft Cl NG21 . . . 75 F2
Redfield Rd NG7 . . . 184 B8
Redfield Way NG7 . . . 184 B8
Red Flats La DN22 . . . 30 F4
Red Fox La NG17 . . . 100 C5
Redgate Cl NG19 . . . 101 E8
Redgate Pl LE12 . . . 205 E3
Redgate Sch NG19 . . . 101 E7
Redgates Ct NG14 . . . 148 D7
Redgate St
Mansfield NG19 . . . 101 E8
Pinxton NG16 . . . 113 D2
Redhill Acad NG5 . . . 147 E1
Redhill La
Bothamsall DN22 . . . 63 B8
Ompton NG22 . . . 93 D5
Sturton le Steeple DN22 . . . 32 A6
Red Hill La NG22 . . . 92 E4
Redhill L Ctr NG21 . . . 147 E1
Redhill Lodge Dr NG5 . . . 147 D1
Redhill Rd NG5 . . . 147 E1
Redholme Cl S81 . . . 25 F7
Red Kite Cl
Hucknall NG15 . . . 146 D8
6 Worksop S81 . . . 35 C7
Red La
Brinsley NG16 . . . 128 E1
Carlton in Lindrick S81 . . . 26 A2
Lowdham NG14 . . . 150 D1
Redland Ave NG4 . . . 174 F8
Redland Cl
Beeston NG9 . . . 183 C4
Ilkeston DE7 . . . 157 F2
Redland Dr NG9 . . . 183 C4
Redland Gr NG4 . . . 174 E8
Redland Rd NG16 . . . 101 E8
Redlands Prim Sch
S80 . . . 35 D4
Red Lodge La NG13 . . . 166 B7
Redman Cl DN21 . . . 15 E2
Redmays Dr NG14 . . . 164 B8
REDMILE . . . 192 F3
Redmile CE Prim Sch
NG13 . . . 192 F3
Redmile Cl NG15 . . . 145 F8

Redmile La
Barkestone-le-Vale
NG13 . . . 192 D3
Elton-on-the-Hill NG13 . . . 192 A8
Sutton NG13 . . . 179 D1
Sutton NG13 . . . 191 F8
Redmile Rd NG8 . . . 160 C2
Red Oaks Ct NG20 . . . 74 A4
Redoubt St NG7 . . . 222 A3
Redruth Cl NG8 . . . 171 C6
Redruth Dr NG18 . . . 103 B2
Redthorn Way NG23 . . . 156 E6
Redwing Cl
East Leake LE12 . . . 205 F2
Worksop S81 . . . 35 C6
Redwood NG2 . . . 185 C6
Redwood Ave NG8 . . . 171 D3
Redwood Cres NG9 . . . 184 A5
Redwood Ct
Hucknall NG15 . . . 145 F8
Mansfield NG18 . . . 102 D4
Reed Cl NG24 . . . 140 A4
Reeders Croft NG17 . . . 100 F2
Reedham Wlk 2 NG5 . . . 161 B8
Reedman Rd NG10 . . . 193 B4
Reeds Cl NG14 . . . 149 C6
Reef Cl NG20 . . . 74 A5
Rees Gdns NG5 . . . 147 A1
Rees Row DN22 . . . 42 B1
Reform St
Annesley Woodhouse
NG17 . . . 129 F8
Sutton in Ashfield NG17 . . . 100 F2
Regal Arts Ctr★ S80 . . . 35 F8
Regal Pl NG18 . . . 102 C3
Regan Way NG9 . . . 183 B2
Regatta Way NG2 . . . 186 C8
Regency Ct NG9 . . . 184 A7
Regeneration Way
NG9 . . . 184 A4
Regent Circle NG1 . . . 55 B8
Regents NG23 . . . 112 B8
Regents Pk Cl NG2 . . . 185 C5
Regents Pl NG12 . . . 185 B6
Regent St
Beeston NG9 . . . 184 A4
Kimberley NG16 . . . 158 F6
Kirkby-in-Ashfield NG17 . . . 114 F4
Langley Mill NG16 . . . 143 B3
Long Eaton NG10 . . . 193 D8
Loughborough LE11 . . . 220 A4
Mansfield NG18 . . . 102 B7
Nottingham, New Basford
NG7 . . . 161 A1
Nottingham, Standard Hill
NG1 . . . 223 D2
Stapleford NG10 . . . 182 C5
Sutton in Ashfield NG17 . . . 100 D2
Regent Wharf Pl 2
LE11 . . . 220 A5
Regina Cl NG12 . . . 175 E2
Regina Cres NG15 . . . 116 F1
Reg Taylor's Swan &
Waterfowl Sanctuary★
NG25 . . . 121 F2
Reid Gdns NG16 . . . 159 B7
Reigate Cl NG9 . . . 183 E2
Reigate Dr NG9 . . . 183 E2
Reigate Rd NG7 . . . 160 F2
Reindeer St NG18 . . . 102 E6
Remembrance Way
Barton in Fabis NG11 . . . 195 B7
Kegworth DE74 . . . 203 C5
Long Eaton NG11 . . . 194 D3
Nottingham NG9 . . . 184 F5
Ratcliffe on Soar NG11 . . . 204 A8
REMPSTONE . . . 215 D5
Rempstone Dr NG6 . . . 160 D5
Rempstone La NG22 . . . 207 A1
Rempstone Rd
East Leake LE12 . . . 214 E7
East Leake, Stanford Hills
LE12 . . . 214 A6
Hoton LE12 . . . 215 C2
Sutton Bonington LE12 . . . 213 B8
Wymeswold LE12 . . . 216 A4
Renals Way LE12 . . . 148 F1
Rendell Prim Sch LE11 . . . 220 B5
Renfrew Ct NG19 . . . 101 E4
Renfrew Dr NG8 . . . 171 E4
Rennie Hogg Rd
Nottingham NG12 . . . 185 A8
Nottingham NG14 . . . 173 A1
Nottingham NG8 . . . 172 F1
Renshaw Dr 5 NG4 . . . 162 E3
Repton Cl NG19 . . . 88 E4
Repton Dr DE7 . . . 170 B7
Repton Rd
Nottingham NG6 . . . 160 D6
West Bridgford NG2 . . . 185 E5
RETFORD . . . 39 E8
Retford Education Centre
DN22 . . . 39 C6
Retford Gate DN22 . . . 41 C7
Retford Hospl DN22 . . . 39 D8
Retford La DN22 . . . 41 F1
Retford L Ctr DN22 . . . 39 C4
Retford Little Theatre★
DN22 . . . 39 E6
Retford Oaks Acad
DN22 . . . 39 C6
Retford Rd
Askham DN22 . . . 52 E3
Barnby Moor DN22 . . . 28 B6
Blyth S81 . . . 18 B2
Boughton DN22 . . . 77 F7
East Drayton DN22 . . . 53 A3
Eaton DN22 . . . 40 B1
Gamston DN22 . . . 51 C7
Headon cum Upton DN22 . . . 52 A6
Mattersey DN10 . . . 20 C6

Retford Rd continued
North Leverton with
Habblesthorpe DN22 . . . 41 F8
North Wheatley DN22 . . . 31 C7
North Wheatley DN22 . . . 31 C8
Nottingham NG5 . . . 161 A3
Rampton DN22 . . . 42 D1
Ranby S81 . . . 37 C4
South Leverton DN22 . . . 42 A8
Torworth S81 . . . 27 F8
Walesby NG22 . . . 64 A1
West Markham DN22 . . . 65 D5
Woodbeck DN22 . . . 52 E7
Woodbeck DN22 . . . 53 A7
Worksop S80 . . . 36 C2
Retford Sta DN22 . . . 39 E5
Retford Town FC DN22 . . . 39 D6
Revell Cl
Claypole NG23 . . . 156 D7
Ilkeston DE7 . . . 157 C2
Revill Cres NG9 . . . 182 F8
Revill Ct 18 NG17 . . . 114 E7
Reydon Dr NG8 . . . 160 D1
Reynolds Dr NG8 . . . 171 F5
RHODESIA . . . 35 A4
Rhodes Way NG6 . . . 147 B6
Rhodes Wlk NG18 . . . 101 E6
Rhyl Cres NG4 . . . 162 E2
Ribblesdale S81 . . . 36 A8
Ribblesdale Ct NG9 . . . 183 A4
Ribblesdale Rd
Long Eaton NG10 . . . 193 A5
Nottingham NG5 . . . 161 C5
Ribbon Pond Dr NG24 . . . 140 A4
Riber Cl
Annesley Woodhouse
NG17 . . . 115 A1
Long Eaton NG10 . . . 193 D5
Riber Cres NG5 . . . 160 F5
Rice Hill NG22 . . . 78 C7
Richard Bonington Prim
Sch NG5 . . . 147 F1
Richard Herrod Ctr
NG4 . . . 174 D8
Richards Cl NG12 . . . 189 A3
Richards Gr NG17 . . . 114 E5
Richardson Cl NG11 . . . 184 C1
Richardson Gdns
NG12 . . . 185 D7
Richardson Rise DN21 . . . 24 F7
Richards Rd NG12 . . . 198 A3
Richard St DN22 . . . 40 A5
Richborough Pl NG8 . . . 171 C2
Richey Cl NG5 . . . 162 B7
Richmond Ave
Breaston DE72 . . . 193 A8
Calverton NG14 . . . 149 A8
Eastwood NG16 . . . 144 B2
Ilkeston DE7 . . . 157 F4
Nottingham NG3 . . . 173 F7
Sandiacre NG10 . . . 182 B4
Richmond Ct NG24 . . . 140 B4
Richmond Dr
Beeston NG9 . . . 183 E5
Mansfield Woodhouse
NG19 . . . 88 D2
Nottingham NG3 . . . 161 D2
Radcliffe on Trent NG12 . . . 175 F4
Richmond Gdns NG5 . . . 147 E1
Richmond La DN10 . . . 9 F6
Richmond Rd
Carlton in Lindrick S81 . . . 25 E6
Gainsborough DN21 . . . 24 F8
Kirkby-in-Ashfield NG17 . . . 115 D5
Retford DN22 . . . 30 A1
West Bridgford NG2 . . . 173 F1
Worksop S80 . . . 36 A1
Richmond St NG18 . . . 102 F5
Richmond Terr NG12 . . . 175 F3
Ricket La
Blidworth NG21 . . . 117 C5
Ravenshead NG15 . . . 116 F4
Ricklow Ct 1 NG5 . . . 161 A8
Rick St NG1 . . . 223 F3
Riddell Ave S81 . . . 16 E3
Ridding La DN10 . . . 3 A4
Ridding Terr NG3 . . . 223 E4
Ridge Cl NG17 . . . 100 D3
Ridge Hill NG14 . . . 150 D2
Ridge La NG12 . . . 176 A5
Ridgeway
Nottingham NG5 . . . 161 A8
Shirebrook NG20 . . . 72 F5
Southwell NG25 . . . 121 D2
Worksop S80 . . . 36 B6
Ridgeway Cl NG22 . . . 119 F6
Ridgeway La NG20 . . . 74 B3
Ridgeway St NG3 . . . 173 E6
Ridgeway Terr NG20 . . . 74 B4
Ridgeway The NG22 . . . 120 A6
Ridgeway Wlk 17 NG5 . . . 161 A8
Ridgewood Dr NG9 . . . 183 C4
Ridgewood Gr NG15 . . . 117 A2
Ridgmont Wlk NG11 . . . 195 D8
Ridgway Cl NG2 . . . 186 C5
Riding Hill Av NG20 . . . 72 D3
Riding La DN10 . . . 3 A4
Ridings The
Bulcote NG14 . . . 164 B5
Keyworth NG12 . . . 198 A3
Mansfield Woodhouse
NG19 . . . 88 D1
Ridsdale Rd NG5 . . . 161 C5
Rifle St NG7 . . . 222 A3
Rigg La
Arnold NG5 . . . 132 E3
Blidworth NG21 . . . 132 E7

Rigg La continued
Hucknall NG15 . . . 132 E5
Rigley Ave 10 DE7 . . . 157 F1
Rigley Dr NG5 . . . 160 E7
Riley Ave NG17 . . . 100 C3
Riley Cl NG17 . . . 100 C3
Ringer La S80 . . . 58 A8
Ring Leas NG12 . . . 188 A2
Ringlet Dr LE12 . . . 214 E8
Ringrose Cl NG24 . . . 140 D8
Ringstead Cl NG2 . . . 185 C5
Ringstead Wlk NG5 . . . 161 B8
Ringwood S81 . . . 36 A6
Ringwood Ave NG18 . . . 102 C4
Ringwood Cres NG8 . . . 172 C5
Ringwood Rd NG13 . . . 177 C4
Rio Dr NG23 . . . 98 A2
Ripon Rd NG3 . . . 174 A5
Riseborough Wlk NG6 . . . 146 C1
Risegate NG12 . . . 187 F3
Riseholme Ave NG8 . . . 171 C3
Riseholme Rd DN21 . . . 24 F7
Rise Park Prim Sch
NG5 . . . 146 F1
Rise Pk Rd NG5 . . . 146 F1
Rise The
Nottingham NG5 . . . 161 D3
Southwell NG25 . . . 136 D7
Risley Ct DE7 . . . 157 F3
Risley Dr NG2 . . . 173 B2
Riste's Pl NG2 . . . 223 F2
Ritchie Cl NG12 . . . 188 A2
Ritson Cl NG3 . . . 223 F4
Rivendell Acad NG4 . . . 175 C7
Riveraine Cl NG7 . . . 101 B2
River Cl DN22 . . . 29 F1
Riverdale Rd
Beeston NG9 . . . 183 C2
New Ollerton NG22 . . . 77 C6
Rivergreen Cl NG9 . . . 171 C2
Rivergreen Cres NG9 . . . 171 C2
River La
Misson DN10 . . . 4 C2
Misson DN10 . . . 5 A2
Retford DN22 . . . 39 E7
Riverlands Cl NG23 . . . 165 A5
Rivermead
Cotgrave NG12 . . . 188 A3
Newark-on-Trent NG24 . . . 139 E6
River Rd NG4 . . . 174 E4
Riverside
Southwell NG25 . . . 121 F1
Whatton NG13 . . . 179 B4
Riverside App DN21 . . . 15 B1
Riverside Cl
Bottesford NG13 . . . 181 A3
Cuckney NG20 . . . 60 A3
Riverside Ct LN1 . . . 57 C2
Riverside Mws LN1 . . . 57 B3
Riverside Rd
Beeston NG9 . . . 184 A3
Newark-on-Trent NG24 . . . 139 D5
Riverside Ret Pk NG11 . . . 185 A8
Riverside View NG20 . . . 74 B5
Riverside Way
Mansfield Woodhouse
NG19 . . . 88 D5
Nottingham NG2 . . . 173 B1
Riverside Wlk NG13 . . . 181 A3
River View
Laneham DN22 . . . 54 C7
Long Eaton NG10 . . . 193 A3
Market Warsop NG20 . . . 74 B5
Nottingham NG2 . . . 173 D1
Pye Bridge DE55 . . . 128 A6
Retford DN22 . . . 39 E3
Riverview Cotts DN10 . . . 4 C2
Riverway Gdns NG23 . . . 173 D2
Rivington Rd NG9 . . . 182 E2
Road No 1
Carlton NG4 . . . 174 F6
Carlton NG4 . . . 175 A5
Road No 2
Carlton NG4 . . . 174 F6
Carlton NG4 . . . 175 A5
Road No 3 NG4 . . . 175 A5
Road No 4 NG4 . . . 175 A5
Road No 5 NG4 . . . 175 B5
Road No 7 NG4 . . . 174 F6
Road No 8 NG4 . . . 174 F5
Roadwood La NG23 . . . 69 F8
Robbie Burns Rd NG5 . . . 161 C8
Robert Ave NG18 . . . 101 F5
Robert Dukeson Ave
NG24 . . . 125 B4
Robert Mellors Prim Sch
NG5 . . . 162 A8
Arnold NG5 . . . 161 F8
Robert Miles Jun Sch
NG13 . . . 177 F4
Roberts Cl
Dunham-on-Trent NG22 . . . 54 A1
Kegworth DE74 . . . 203 D1
Ragnall NG22 . . . 68 A3
Robert Shaw Prim Sch
NG8 . . . 172 B6
Robert's La NG15 . . . 145 E7
Robertson Gr S80 . . . 35 B5
Roberts St
Ilkeston DE7 . . . 170 A6
Nottingham NG3 . . . 173 E4
Roberts Yd NG9 . . . 184 A7
Robey Cl
Hucknall NG15 . . . 131 A1
Mansfield Woodhouse
NG19 . . . 89 B1
Robey Dr NG16 . . . 143 F3

Robey Vale S81 . . . 34 E3
Robina Dr NG16 . . . 158 C8
Robin Bailey Way
NG15 . . . 146 C6
Robin Cl
Ollerton NG22 . . . 77 C2
Sutton Forest Side NG17 . . . 101 B3
Robin Down Cl NG18 . . . 102 D2
Robin Down Ct
7 Kirkby-in-Ashfield
NG17 . . . 115 A3
Mansfield NG18 . . . 102 C2
Robin Down La NG18 . . . 102 C2
Robinet Rd NG9 . . . 183 F5
Robinettes La
Cossall NG16 . . . 158 D1
Cossall NG16 . . . 158 E2
Strelley NG16 . . . 159 A1
Robin Gdns NG12 . . . 186 A2
Robin Gr NG15 . . . 117 A1
Robin Hood Ave
Edwinstowe NG21 . . . 91 C8
Market Warsop NG20 . . . 74 C2
Robin Hood Cl NG16 . . . 143 F1
Robin Hood Dr NG15 . . . 145 E6
Robin Hood Ind Est 2
NG3 . . . 173 E5
Robin Hood Jun & Inf Sch
NG5 . . . 161 A6
Robin Hood Prim Sch
NG19 . . . 88 B4
Robin Hood Rd
Annesley Woodhouse
NG17 . . . 130 B8
Arnold NG5 . . . 147 B1
Blidworth NG21 . . . 118 B5
Robin Hood's Cave★
NG22 . . . 63 C2
Robin Hood St NG3 . . . 173 E5
Robin Hood Terr
Nottingham NG3 . . . 223 F3
Ravenshead NG15 . . . 117 B3
Robin Hood Way
Blidworth NG21 . . . 117 C6
Harlow Wood NG21 . . . 117 A6
Nottingham NG2 . . . 173 C2
Robinia Ct NG2 . . . 186 A5
Robin Mews LE11 . . . 220 A3
Robins Ct NG24 . . . 140 A8
Robinson Cl
Edwalton NG12 . . . 185 F3
Newark-on-Trent NG24 . . . 140 A4
Robinson Cres 6 LE11 . . . 220 C3
Robinson Gdns NG11 . . . 184 C1
Robinson Rd NG3 . . . 162 A2
Robinson Dr S80 . . . 35 E1
Robin's Wood Rd NG8 . . . 172 B7
Robin Way S81 . . . 35 B7
Rob La NG22 . . . 119 B3
Rob Roy Ave NG7 . . . 222 B1
Rochdale Ct NG18 . . . 103 A5
Roche Cl NG5 . . . 162 C7
Rochester Ave NG4 . . . 175 A7
Rochester Cl
Long Eaton NG10 . . . 193 A7
Worksop S81 . . . 36 A7
Rochester Ct NG6 . . . 159 F6
Rochester Rd NG21 . . . 118 A8
Rochester Wlk NG7 . . . 184 F1
Rochford Ct NG12 . . . 186 C3
Rockcliffe Grange
NG18 . . . 102 C2
Rock Ct
Mansfield NG18 . . . 102 C7
Nottingham NG6 . . . 160 D3
Rock Dr NG7 . . . 222 C1
Rocket Cl NG16 . . . 159 A7
Rockford Ct NG9 . . . 170 E1
Rockford Rd NG5 . . . 160 F3
Rock Hill NG18 . . . 102 D6
Rock Hl Gd NG18 . . . 102 D6
Rockingham Gr NG13 . . . 177 C4
Rockings View NG21 . . . 118 A5
Rocklands The NG20 . . . 72 E4
ROCKLEY . . . 51 A2
Rockley Ave
Eastwood NG16 . . . 144 A1
Radcliffe on Trent NG12 . . . 175 F4
Rockley Cl
Clipstone NG21 . . . 89 C5
Clipstone NG21 . . . 90 A4
Hucknall NG15 . . . 145 C6
Rockleys View
Lowdham NG14 . . . 150 A1
Lowdham NG14 . . . 150 A2
Rockley Way NG20 . . . 72 E4
Rock St
Mansfield NG18 . . . 102 D6
Nottingham NG6 . . . 160 D3
Rockstone Way 2 NG19 . . . 88 B2
Rock Valley NG18 . . . 102 C7
Rockwood Cl NG21 . . . 118 A5
Rockwood Wlk NG15 . . . 145 E6
Rodel Ct NG3 . . . 223 F4
Roden House Bsns Ctr
NG3 . . . 173 D5
Roden St NG3 . . . 173 E5
Roderick Ave NG17 . . . 115 B1
Roderick St NG6 . . . 160 D4
Rodery The NG18 . . . 102 E5
Rodney Rd NG2 . . . 186 A6
Rodney Way DE7 . . . 157 F3
Rodwell Cl NG8 . . . 172 C6
Roebuck Cl NG5 . . . 161 B8
Roebuck Dr NG18 . . . 102 B3
Roebuck Way S80 . . . 48 C8
Roecliffe NG2 . . . 185 E4

Roe Gdns NG11......196 B7
Roehampton Dr NG9...170 D2
Roe Hill NG14.........149 C5
Roe La NG14............149 C4
Roes La NG14..........149 A7
Roewood Cl NG17....114 F7
Roewood La NG22....107 F2
Roger Cl NG17.........100 F5
Roker Cl NG8...........160 A1
Rolaine Cl NG19.......88 C4
Roland Ave
  Nottingham NG11......185 B7
  Nuthall NG16..........159 E4
ROLLESTON...........138 A5
Rolleston Cl NG15......145 D5
Rolleston Cres NG16...144 F1
Rolleston Dr
  Arnold NG5............162 A7
  Eastwood NG16........158 B8
  Nottingham NG7.......222 B1
Rolleston Sta NG25....137 F6
Roman Bank NG19......88 D3
Roman Bank La DN10...18 E6
Roman Cres NG15......146 D8
Roman Dr NG6..........160 E4
Roman Rd S81..........35 D7
Romans Ct NG6.........160 E2
Romilay Cl NG9.........172 A1
Romney Ave NG8.......171 D2
Romsey Pl NG19........101 D6
Rona Cl NG19...........101 E5
Rona Ct NG6............160 C5
Ronald St NG7.........222 B3
Ronchin Gdns NG17....115 A4
Roods Cl NG17.........114 D8
Rook Cl LN1.............56 F4
Rookery Farm NG12....189 B6
Rookery Gdns NG5......161 F8
Rookery La NG17.......114 A8
Rookery The
  Collingham NG23......98 A1
  [1] Hucknall NG18.....102 A7
Rook's La DN10........6 E2
Rookwood Cl NG9......183 E6
Rookwood Cres NG15...145 D6
Rooley Ave NG17.......100 C3
Rooley Dr NG17........100 C3
Roosa Cl NG6...........159 F5
Roosevelt Ave NG10...193 C5
Roosevelt Rd NG17....101 B4
Rooth St NG18.........102 B6
Ropery Rd DN21.......15 B2
Ropewalk DE74.........203 C2
Ropewalk Ind Ctr DE7..158 A1
Ropewalk The
  Ilkeston DE7..........158 A1
  Newark-on-Trent NG24..140 B8
  Nottingham NG1.......223 D2
  Southwell NG25.......121 E1
Ropeway The NG17....114 E5
Rope Wlk LE12.........205 D1
Ropsley Cres NG2.....186 A8
Rosa Ct NG4...........163 A1
Roscoe Ave NG5.......147 E2
Roseacre NG9..........184 A5
Rose Ash La NG5.......161 B8
Rose Ave
  Ilkeston DE7..........157 C2
  Retford DN22.........40 A4
Rosebank Dr NG5......148 E1
Rosebay Av NG7.......172 D8
Rosebay Gdns NG21...89 F4
Roseberry Ave NG2...173 E1
Roseberry Gdns NG15..146 C6
Roseberry St NG17....115 C4
Rosebery Cl S80.......35 E3
Rosebery Hill NG18...102 C6
Rosebery St NG6......160 E3
Rosebowl Gdns DN22..39 E4
Rose Cl NG3...........173 D7
Rosecliffe Spencer Acad
  NG12................185 F2
Rose Cottage Dr NG17..99 F2
Rose Cotts NG14......163 E5
Rosecroft Dr NG5.....161 C6
Rose Ct NG10.........182 B1
Rosedale S81..........36 A8
Rosedale Cl NG16.....193 B6
Rosedale Dr NG8.....171 B4
Rosedale Gdns
  Mansfield NG19.......102 D5
  Sutton in Ashfield NG17...114 D8
Rosedale La NG15.....116 F3
Rosedale Rd NG3.....174 C6
Rosedale Way NG19...88 F2
Rose Farm Dr NG23...96 F8
Rosefield Cl NG24.....140 F2
Rosefields DN21.......15 E1
Rosefinch Wy NG19...88 F2
Rose Flower Gr NG15..146 C4
Rosegarth Wlk NG6...160 D4
Rose Gdns
  Newark-on-Trent NG24..139 F4
  Newark-on-Trent NG24..140 A4
  RETFORD DN22........39 D8
Rose Gr
  Beeston NG9..........184 B5
  Keyworth NG12.......197 F4
Rosegrove Ave NG5...147 F1
Rose Hill NG12........197 E3
Rosehill Cl LN1.......57 A4
Rosehill Sch NG3.....173 E6
Rose La NG19..........88 C4
Roseland Bsns Ctr
  NG23................181 E8
Roseland Bsns Pk
  NG23................169 F1
Roseland Way NG23...69 F2

Rose Lea DN22........39 D4
Roseleigh Ave NG3....162 B2
Rosemary Ave NG18...102 A8
Rosemary Cl [1] NG8...159 E1
Rosemary St NG18....102 A7
Rose Mdws DN22......28 D5
Rosemont Cl NG17....100 F6
Roseneath Ave NG5...146 E1
Rose Tree Pl [6] S81...35 A7
Rosetta Rd NG7.......160 F1
Rosewall Ct NG5......162 B7
Roseway DN21.........15 C1
Rose Way
  Edwalton NG12.......185 F2
  Edwalton NG12.......186 A2
  Edwalton NG12.......186 A3
Rosewood Cl
  Carlton in Lindrick S81...25 D1
  Newark-on-Trent NG24...125 D1
  South Normanton DE55...113 B7
  Worksop S81...........25 D1
Rosewood Cres DE75...143 B2
Rosewood Ct DN22....39 C5
Rosewood Dr NG17....115 C6
Rosewood Gdns
  Nottingham NG6......159 F7
  West Bridgford NG2...185 C3
Rosings Ct NG17......100 E1
Roslyn Ave NG4.......162 E2
Ross Cl
  Coddington NG24.....126 B2
  Lowdham NG14.......150 E1
Rossell Dr NG9.......182 E5
Rossendale DE7......157 E4
Rossett Ct NG2.......186 D6
Rossetti Gdns S81.....36 C3
Rossington Bsns Pk
  DN22................39 E5
Rossington Rd NG2...173 F5
Ross La NG4...........163 C7
Rosslyn Dr
  Hucknall NG15.......146 C8
  Nottingham NG8......160 A2
Rosslyn Park Primary Sch
  NG16................160 A3
Rosthwaite Cl NG2...186 C5
Roston Cl NG18.......103 B5
Rothbury Ave NG9....170 D2
Rothbury Gr NG13....177 C5
Rothbury Gr NG13....177 C5
Rotherham Baulk S81..25 C7
Rotherham Rd NG19...86 F8
Rothesay Ave NG7....222 B2
Rothley Ave NG3.....173 F5
Rothwell Cl
  Gainsborough DN21....24 E8
  Nottingham NG11.....185 A4
Rotunda The DN10....23 C8
Roughs Wood La
  NG9................183 F7
Roulstone Cres LE12..205 E3
Roundhill Cl NG17....101 C1
Round Hill Prim Sch
  NG9................183 F7
Roundhouse Cres S81..35 D7
Roundwood Rd NG15..161 C7
Rowan Ave
  Hathern LE12.........213 A2
  Ravensshead NG15....117 A1
  Saxilby LN1...........57 A5
  Stapleford NG9.......170 E2
Rowan Cl
  Calverton NG14......148 D7
  Cotgrave NG12.......188 A5
  Kirkby-in-Ashfield NG17..114 F6
  Mansfield NG18......88 D1
Rowan Cres S80.......35 E1
Rowan Croft NG17....99 F4
Rowan Ct
  HUCKNALL NG15......146 C8
  Nuthall NG16........159 B6
Rowan Dr
  Keyworth NG12.......198 A2
  Kirkby-in-Ashfield NG17..114 F6
  Nottingham NG11.....185 A4
  Selston NG16.........128 D6
  Shirebrook NG20......72 D5
Rowan Gdns NG6.....159 F7
Rowans Cres NG6.....160 B4
Rowans The
  [2] Gainsborough DN21..15 F1
  Saxilby LN1...........56 F4
Rowan Way NG24....140 B5
Rowan Wlk NG3......174 A8
Rowe Gdns NG6......160 D6
Rowland Ave NG3....162 A2
Rowland Mews NG3..173 E7
Rowley Cl NG5.......161 A2
Rowley Dr NG5.......161 A2
Rowley Sq NG7......172 C8
Rowston Cl DN21....15 C2
Row The NG13.......179 F6
Rowthorne La S44...86 B7
Roxburgh Cl
  Arnold NG5...........162 C8
  Woodborough NG14...148 C1
Roxton Ct NG16......158 F7
Royal Ave NG10......182 D1
Royal Cres S81........35 E6
Royal Ctr (Theatre Royal &
  Royal Concert Hall)*
  NG1................223 E3
Royal Mews NG9.....183 C3
Royal Oak Ct NG21....76 B2
Royal Oak Dr NG16...129 B7
Royal Way LE11......220 A6
Roy Ave NG9.........184 B4
Royce Ave NG15.....145 E4
Royds Cres S80........35 A5
Royland Rd LE11......220 A3

Royston Cl NG2.......173 B1
Ruby Cl NG5..........136 F8
Ruby Gdns NG17.....115 D4
Ruby Paddocks NG16..158 F5
Rubys Way NG24......140 E2
Ruby Wy NG18........102 C5
RUDDINGTON.........196 D6
Ruddington Ct [4]
  NG18...............103 A2
Ruddington Fields Bsns Pk
  NG11...............196 D4
Ruddington Framework
  Knitters Mus* NG11..196 C6
Ruddington Gdns
  NG12...............185 B3
Ruddington La
  Nottingham NG11.....185 B5
  West Bridgford NG2...185 B4
Ruddington Rd NG18..103 A2
Ruddington Village Mus*
  NG11...............196 C5
Ruddy Rd NG4........175 C7
Rudge Cl NG8........171 D4
Rue de L'Yonne NG23..98 A2
Ruffles Ave NG5......162 B5
Rufford Abbey* NG22..91 F6
Rufford Ave
  Beeston NG9.........183 A8
  Carlton NG4..........162 D2
  Mansfield NG18......102 C7
  Meden Vale NG20.....74 F8
  Newark-on-Trent NG24..139 F7
  New Ollerton NG22....77 C4
  Rainworth NG21......104 C1
  Retford DN22.........39 D3
Rufford Cl
  Bilsthorpe NG22......106 A4
  Clipstone NG21.......89 F2
  East Markham NG22...65 F7
  Hucknall NG15.......146 A5
  Sutton in Ashfield NG17..100 F5
Rufford Colliery La
  NG21...............104 A4
Rufford Craft Ctr*
  NG22...............91 F6
Rufford Ctry Pk* NG22..91 F6
Rufford Dr NG19......88 E3
Rufford Gr NG13.....177 C4
Rufford La
  Edwinstowe NG22....91 F8
  Wellow NG22.........92 B8
Rufford Primary Sch
  NG6................160 A7
Rufford Rd
  Edwinstowe NG21....91 C8
  Long Eaton NG10....193 B4
  Nottingham NG5......161 C3
  Ruddington NG11.....196 D7
Rufford St S80.........47 B8
Rufford View NG22...77 C2
Rufford Way NG2....186 B6
Rufford Wlk
  [1] Nottingham NG6..160 B7
  Ruddington NG11.....196 D7
Ruffs Dr NG15.......145 E5
Rugby Pk View NG20..73 E4
Rugby Rd
  Rainworth NG21......118 A8
  West Bridgford NG2...185 C5
Rugby Terr NG7......172 F7
Rugeley Ave NG10....194 A7
Ruislip Cl NG16......158 E7
Runcie Cl NG12.......187 F2
Runnymede Ct NG7...222 C3
Runswick Dr
  Arnold NG5...........161 F8
  Nottingham NG8......172 B5
Runton Dr NG6.......160 F4
Rupert Cres NG24....139 F7
Rupert Rd NG13......177 D4
Rupert St DE7.........158 A1
Rushcliffe Arena*
  NG2................185 D6
Rushcliffe Ave
  Carlton NG4..........174 D8
  Radcliffe on Trent NG12..175 F3
Rushcliffe Comp Sch
  NG2................185 D6
Rushcliffe Ct NG6....160 D6
Rushcliffe Ctry Pk*
  NG11...............196 C5
Rushcliffe Gr L Ctr NG2..205 E4
Rushcliffe L Ctr NG2...185 F4
Rushcliffe Rd NG15...145 E5
Rushcliffe Rise NG5...161 D5
Rushes NG16.........184 A6
Rushes Sh Ctr The
  LE12...............220 A4
Rushes The
  Gotham NG11........195 B1
  [8] Loughborough LE12..220 B4
  Mansfield Woodhouse
  NG19...............88 D5
Rushey Cl S80.........36 B2
Rushford Dr NG8.....171 D4
Rushland Fields LE14..211 D3
Rushley Manor NG18..102 C1
Rush Leys NG10......193 D5
Rushley View NG17...100 C5
Rushmere Wlk NG5...161 F5
Rushton Cl NG19.....88 F2
Rushton Gdns NG3....173 E7
Rushworth Ave NG2..185 E8
Rushworth Cl NG3....173 E7
Rushy Cl NG8........171 D5
Ruskin Ave NG10....193 B5
Ruskin Cl NG5.......161 D7
Ruskin Rd NG19......87 D1

Ruskin St DN21.......24 D6
Russell Ave
  Harworth DN11.......8 F4
  New Balderton NG24...140 B4
  [5] Nottingham NG8...172 A5
Russell Cres [6] NG8..172 A5
Russell Dr
  Nottingham NG8......171 F5
  Nottingham NG8......172 A4
Russell Farm Cl NG12..186 D1
Russell Gdns [5] NG9..183 C2
Russell Pl NG1........223 D3
Russell Rd NG7.......172 F8
Russell St
  Long Eaton NG10....182 D1
  Loughborough LE11...220 C4
  Nottingham NG7......222 C3
  Sutton in Ashfield NG17..100 F3
Russet Ave NG4......174 F7
Russet Gr NG10.......10 A7
Russet Way [4] NG8...172 B7
Russey Cl NG14......150 E1
Russley Rd NG9......183 A8
Ruth Dr NG5.........148 A1
Rutherford Ave NG18..102 E4
Rutherglen Pk 9 LN1...57 A5
Ruthwell Gdns NG5...147 A2
Rutland Ave
  Beeston NG9.........183 A2
  Newark-on-Trent NG24..140 A6
Rutland Cl
  Market Warsop NG20..74 A4
  Nottingham NG14.....173 B2
  Shelton NG23.........168 C6
Rutland Cres DN11....8 F5
Rutland Ct DE7.......157 D1
Rutland Dr
  Harworth DN11.......8 F5
  Harworth DN11.......9 A5
Rutland Gr NG10.....182 C5
Rutland La NG13.....181 B2
Rutland Rd
  Bingham NG13........177 F5
  Carlton NG4..........162 D3
  Retford DN22.........40 B4
  West Bridgford NG2...186 A8
  Westwood NG16......128 C4
Rutland St
  Ilkeston DE7..........157 F2
  [1] Loughborough LE11..220 C3
  Mansfield NG18......102 C5
  Nottingham NG1......223 D2
Rutlands The NG23...124 A4
Rutland Terr DE7.....157 F2
Ryan Way NG2........184 A3
Rydal Ave NG10.....182 B2
Rydal Dr
  Beeston NG9.........183 D8
  Hucknall NG15.......145 F8
  Worksop S81.........35 B8
Rydale Gdns DN10....3 A1
Rydale Rd NG5.......161 C5
Rydal Gdns NG2......186 A5
Rydal Gr NG6........160 E3
Ryder St NG6.........160 D4
Rye Croft DN11.......8 A8
Ryecroft St NG9......182 F8
Ryedale Ave
  Mansfield NG18......102 F5
  Mansfield NG18......103 A5
Ryehill Cl NG2.......173 D2
Ryehill St NG2.......173 D2
Ryeholme Cl LE12....205 F3
Ryeland Gdns NG2...173 C2
Ryemere Cl NG16....143 E2
Rye St NG7..........160 F1
Rykneld Rd
  Hucknall NG15.......146 C8
  Papplewick NG15.....131 D1
Rylands Cl NG9......184 B4
Ryton Cl S81..........18 B2
Ryton Ct [7] NG2.....173 D1
Ryton Fields S81......18 B2
Ryton Pl S80..........35 F3
Ryton Sq NG8........160 B1
Ryton St S80..........35 F3

S

Sabina Rd
  HUCKNALL NG15.....146 C8
  Hucknall NG15.......146 D8
Sabre Ind Pk NG4....175 C3
Sacheverall Ave NG16..113 D3
Sacred Heart RC Prim Sch
  NG4................174 D7
Sacred Heart Roman
  Catholic Prim Sch
  LE11...............220 A1
Saddlers Cl NG19.....88 F1
Saddlers Courtyard
  NG10...............10 A6
Saddlers Yd NG12....197 E7
Saddleworth Ct NG3..223 E4
Sadler St NG19.......101 F8
Saffron Gdns NG2....173 B2
Saffron St
  Forest Town NG19....89 A1
  [5] Mansfield Woodhouse
  NG19...............88 F1
St Agnes Cl NG8......171 D8
St Aidan's Ct [2] NG6..160 E4
St Albans Cl NG10....193 E5
St Albans Mews NG6..160 D6
St Albans Rd
  Arnold NG5...........161 E7
  Bestwood Village NG6..146 D8
  Nottingham NG6......160 D7
St Albans St NG5.....161 C3

St Andrew Cl NG11....195 B1
St Andrew's CE Prim Sch
  NG17...............100 F6
St Andrews Cl NG6...160 C7
St Andrew's Cl NG15..146 A8
St Andrews Cres NG17..100 F6
St Andrews Dr LN1....56 F4
St Andrew's Rd NG3..173 B7
St Andrew's Rise DE74..203 C1
St Andrews St
  Kirkby-in-Ashfield
  NG17...............115 B6
  Sutton in Ashfield NG17..100 E6
St Andrew St NG18...102 C5
St Andrews Way DN22..39 E3
St Anne's CE Prim Sch
  S80................35 D2
St Annes Cl S80......35 C3
St Annes Dr S80......35 C2
St Anne's La LE12....213 B6
St Annes Mews S80...35 C2
St Annes View S80....35 C3
St Annes Way S80....35 C3
ST ANN'S.............173 D6
St Ann's Gdns NG3...173 E7
St Ann's Hill NG3....173 C7
St Ann's Hill Rd NG3..173 C7
St Ann's Hospital Sch
  NG4................174 A8
St Ann's St NG1......223 E3
St Ann's Valley NG3...173 E7
St Ann's Way
  Nottingham NG3......223 E4
St Ann's Well Inf Sch
  NG3................173 E7
St Ann's Well Rd NG3..173 E6
St Anthony Ct NG7...172 E2
St Augustines Cl [3]
  NG7................161 A1
St Augustine's RC Prim Sch
  NG3................173 C8
St Augustine's Sch S81..36 B4
St Austell Dr NG11...185 B6
St Austins Ct NG4....174 F8
St Austins Dr NG4....174 F8
St Bartholomews Ct
  NG3................29 A6
St Bartholomew's Rd
  NG3................173 F7
St Botolphs Cl LN1....57 B5
St Botolphs Gate LN1..57 A5
St Catherines Cl NG24..139 E7
St Catherines St NG12..175 E2
St Catherine St NG18..102 C5
St Cecilia Gdns NG3..223 F4
St Chad's Cl NG18....102 C3
St Chad's Rd NG3....173 E6
St Christophers Rd
  NG18...............101 F5
St Christopher St [9]
  NG2................173 F4
St Cl NG12...........198 A3
St Clare's Gate NG24..140 A6
St Cuthbert's Rd [11]
  NG3................173 E5
St Cuthbert St NG3...35 F1
St David's Cl S81......36 A6
St Edmund Campion
  Catholic Prim Sch
  NG2................186 A6
St Edmund's Ave NG19..88 C3
St Edmund's CE Prim Sch
  NG19...............88 C3
St Edwin's Dr NG21...76 A2
St Emmanuel View
  NG5................147 B1
St Ervan Rd NG11....185 B6
St Francis Hospl NG5..161 B5
St Francis Way NG5...161 B5
St George's CE Com Prim
  Sch DN21...........24 F6
St Georges Cl DN21...24 E7
St George's Ct NG15..146 A8
St Georges Dr
  Beeston NG9.........182 F2
  Beeston NG9.........183 A2
St George's Dr NG2...173 B2
St George's Ms LN1...56 F4
St Georges Priory NG2..173 C2
St Giles Cl DN22......39 C8
St Giles School DN22..39 C7
St Giles' Way NG12...189 A4
St Giles' Way NG24...140 E4
St Helens Ave NG16...113 C3
St Helens Cres
  Burton Joyce NG14...163 F4
  Trowell NG9.........170 C4
St Helen's Dr NG16...128 D7
St Helen's Gr NG14...163 E3
St Helen's La NG12...120 F2
St Helen's Rd
  Retford DN22.........40 B4
  West Bridgford NG2...185 F6
St Helen's St NG7....222 C3
St James Ave DE7....170 A7
St James Ct NG10....182 B3
St James' Dr NG16....143 D8
St James Gdns NG19..88 E6
St James's Ct NG15...146 A8
St James's St
  Nottingham NG1......223 D2
  Stapleford NG9......182 D6
St James's Terr NG9..182 D6
St Jame's Terr NG9...223 D2
St John's Ave NG17...115 B4
St John's CE Prim Sch
  Stapleford NG9......182 E7
  Worksop S81.........35 E7
St John's Cl NG16....128 D1
St John's Cres NG15..146 C5

St Johns Ct S80......35 E3
St Johns Ctr* NG18...102 A7
St John's Dr NG9.....30 D4
St John's Pl [9] NG18..102 A7
St Johns Rd [4] DE7...170 A7
St John's Rd
  Ilkeston DE7.........170 A7
  Ruddington NG11.....196 C7
  Sutton in Ashfield NG17..193 D7
St John St
  Mansfield NG18......102 B7
  Retford DN22.........39 F7
St John's Terr DN21...24 D7
St Johns View NG18..102 A7
St John the Baptist CE Prim
  Sch NG4............174 E6
St Joseph's RC Prim Sch
  Boughton/Ollerton NG22..77 E5
  Retford DN22.........39 D7
  Shirebrook NG20......72 F5
St Joseph's Sch NG1..223 D3
St Jude's Ave NG3....161 E2
St Judes Way NG21...104 A1
St Laurence CE Prim Sch
  NG10...............193 E6
St Laurence Ct NG10..193 E6
St Lawrence Bvd NG12..175 E2
St Leonard's DN11....8 A7
St Leonard's Ct NG24..124 F1
St Leonard's Dr NG8..171 F4
St Leonards Way NG19..103 B8
St Leven Cl NG8......171 D8
St Luke's CE Prim Sch
  S81................34 F8
St Luke's Cl NG2.....186 B5
St Luke's St [6] NG3..173 E5
St Lukes Way NG14...53 A8
St Luke's Way NG11...175 E4
St Margaret Clitherow RC
  Prim Sch NG5......161 C8
St Margarets Ave NG8..172 C8
St Margaret'S Cl NG22..106 A5
St Margaret St NG18..102 C5
St Mark's Cl S81......35 D8
St Marks Ct NG17....114 B8
St Mark's La NG24....139 F8
St Mark's Pl NG24....139 F8
St Marks Rd NG3.....223 F3
St Marrys Cl DN21....14 A5
St Mark's St NG10....9 F7
St Martins Cl
  Blyth S81...........18 B2
  North Leverton with
  Habblesthorpe NG22..42 C8
St Martin's Cl
  Firbeck S81.........16 A6
  Nottingham NG8......171 E8
St Martins Rd DN22...42 C8
St Martin's Rd NG8...171 E8
St Martin's Wlk S80...45 C6
St Mary Magdalene CE
  Prim Sch NG17.....100 C3
St Mary's Ave NG4...162 E2
St Mary's Catholic
  Voluntary Acad NG7..172 E8
St Mary's CE Prim Sch
  NG21...............76 A3
St Mary's Church*
  NG1................223 F2
St Marys Cl NG9.....183 D1
St Mary's Cl
  Arnold NG5..........147 F1
  Bottesford NG13.....181 B3
  [5] Loughborough LE11..220 A4
  Lowdham NG14......150 D2
St Mary's Cres
  East Leake LE12......205 F3
  Ruddington NG11.....196 C7
  Tickhill DN11........8 A7
St Mary's Ct NG17...100 C3
St Mary's Dr NG21...76 A2
St Mary's Gate
  Nottingham NG1......223 F2
  Tickhill DN11........8 A7
St Mary's Gdns NG24..139 F5
St Mary's La NG13....181 B2
St Mary's Mews DN11..8 A7
St Mary's Pl NG1.....223 F2
St Mary's RC Prim Sch [13]
  LE11...............220 A4
St Marys Rd NG13....177 F5
St Mary's Rd
  Sutton in Ashfield
  NG17...............100 D3
  Tickhill DN11........8 A7
St Mary's Way NG15..146 A8
St Mary's Wlk NG16..128 B3
St Matthew's CE Prim Sch
  NG23...............81 E7
St Matthias Rd NG3..173 E6
St Mawes Ave NG11..185 B6
St Mellion Way [3]
  NG17...............114 F7
St Michaels Ave NG8..171 D8
St Michael's Ave NG4..162 E2
St Michaels Cl LE12...213 A8
St Michael's Cl NG22..120 F1
St Michael's Dr DE55..113 A7
St Michael's Gn DN22..39 D8
St Michael's Sq NG9..183 B8
St Michael's St NG17..101 B4
St Michaels View
  Farnsfield NG22......119 C3
  Selston NG16.........129 A5
St Michael's View
  NG15...............131 B1
St Nicholas Cl NG5...161 E7
St Nicholas St NG1...223 E2
St Nicholas Way
  DN10...............10 A6
St Oswalds NG22.....54 C2

St Patrick's RC Prim Sch
Clifton NG11 . . . . **185** B8
Mansfield NG18 . . . . **103** A5
St Patrick's Rd
Hucknall NG15 . . . . **145** F7
Nuthall NG16 . . . . **159** C6
St Paul's Ave NG7 . . . . **172** F7
St Paul's Rd
Gainsborough DN21 . . . . . **15** B3
Worksop S80 . . . . **36** A2
St Paul's St [1] NG8 . **172** D5
St Paul's Terr NG7 . . . **172** F7
St Peters Ave LE12 . . . . **213** A1
St Peter's Ave NG20 . . . **74** B6
St Peter's CE Jun Sch
East Bridgford NG13 . . . . . **165** C3
Ruddington NG11 . . . . **196** D8
St Peters CE Prim Sch
DN10 . . . . **12** E2
St Peter's CE Prim Sch
Farndon NG24 . . . . **139** A5
Mansfield NG18 . . . . **103** A2
St Peter's Church Walk
NG1 . . . . **223** E2
St Peters Cl
East Stockwith DN21 . . . . . **7** E2
Farndon NG24 . . . . **138** F4
New Ollerton NG22 . . . . . . **77** B4
St Peter's Cres NG11 . . **196** C7
St Peters Ct LN1 . . . . . . **55** A1
St Peters Dr NG21 . . . . **104** A1
St Peter's Gate NG1 . . . **223** E2
St Peter's La DN22 . . . . **21** D5
St Peter's Ret Pk NG18 . **102** B6
St Peter's Sq NG1 . . . . **223** E2
St Peter's St NG7 . . . . **222** A3
St Peter's Way NG18 . . **102** C6
St Philip Neri with St Bede
Roman Catholic Voluntary
Acad NG19 . . . . **102** A8
St Saviour's Cl DN22 . . . **40** A8
St Saviour's Gdns NG2 . **173** D2
St Stephen's Ave [7]
NG2 . . . . **173** F4
St Stephens Rd DE55 . . . **77** D3
St Stephen's Rd
Nottingham NG2 . . . . **173** F4
Retford DN22 . . . . **40** B4
St Swithun's CE Prim Sch
[1] DN22 . . . . **39** F7
St Swithuns Gn [2] DN22 . **39** F7
St Teresa's RC Prim Sch
NG8 . . . . **172** A8
St Thomas' Ave NG17 . . **115** B4
St Thomas Dr NG13 . . . **179** A5
St Thomas More Cl
NG9 . . . . **171** D3
St Vincent Cl NG10 . . . . **193** E6
St Wilfreds Cl NG23 . . . **110** F2
St Wilfreds Pk NG17 . . . **114** C4
St Wilfrid's CE Prim Sch
NG14 . . . . **148** E7
St Wilfrids Church Dr
NG2 . . . . **185** B8
St Wilfrids Dr NG17 . . . **114** D5
St Wilfrid's Sq NG14 . . . **148** F7
St Winifreds Cl NG11 . . **203** F4
Salamander Cl NG4 . . . . **162** D2
Salcey Dr NG9 . . . . **170** D2
Salcombe Cir NG5 . . . . **147** D1
Salcombe Cl NG16 . . . . **144** C1
Salcombe Cres NG11 . . **196** D8
Salcombe Dr NG5 . . . . **147** D1
Salcombe Gr DN10 . . . . . **9** F8
Salcombe Rd NG5 . . . . **160** F3
Salestune Mws NG16 . . **128** F6
Salford Gdns NG3 . . . . **223** F3
Salisbury Ave LE12 . . . . **205** F1
Salisbury Rd
Mansfield Woodhouse
NG19 . . . . **88** D4
Morton DN21 . . . . **15** B5
Saxilby LN1 . . . . **57** A4
Worksop S80 . . . . **35** E4
Salisbury Rd
Mansfield NG19 . . . . **101** E8
Newark-on-Trent NG24 . . . **139** F6
Salisbury Sq NG7 . . . . **222** A2
Salisbury St
Beeston NG9 . . . . **184** B7
Gainsborough DN21 . . . . . **15** C2
Long Eaton NG10 . . . . **193** E7
Loughborough LE11 . . . . **220** C4
Nottingham NG7 . . . . **222** A2
Sallie Bank La LN1 . . . . **55** B4
Salmon Cl NG6 . . . . . . **159** F7
Salmon La NG17 . . . . . . **129** D7
Salop St NG5 . . . . **161** D7
Saltburn Rd NG8 . . . . . **172** A6
Saltby Gn NG2 . . . . **185** B3
Salterford Ave NG14 . . **148** E8
Salterford House Sch
NG25 . . . . **134** B3
Calverton NG14 . . . . **133** D5
Salterford La NG14 . . . . **133** D5
Salterford Rd NG15 . . . . **145** E5
Saltford Cl NG4 . . . . . . **162** F2
Salt Hill S81 . . . . **16** B5
Salthouse Ct NG9 . . . . **184** A7
Salthouse La NG9 . . . . **184** A8
Saltney Way NG11 . . . . **185** A3
Salvin Cl NG12 . . . . . . **189** A4
Sam Derry Cl [6] NG24 . **140** B8
Samian Cl S81 . . . . **35** E7
Sampson's La NG19 . . . . **87** B3
Sampson St NG17 . . . . **130** A8
Samson Ct NG11 . . . . . **196** B6
Samuel Barlow Prim Sch
NG21 . . . . **90** A3
Samuel Brunts Way
NG18 . . . . **102** C8

Samuel Cl NG19 . . . . . . **101** F8
Samuel Unwin Ct
NG17 . . . . **101** B3
Samworth Church Acad
NG18 . . . . **102** F7
Sandale Cl NG2 . . . . . . **186** C6
Sandalwood Cl NG18 . . . **103** B4
Sandalwood Dr NG17 . . **115** C6
Sandays Cl NG21 . . . . . **173** C1
Sandbeck Ct DN10 . . . . . **10** A8
Sandby Ct NG9 . . . . . . **183** C5
Sanderling Wy NG18 . . . **88** E2
Sanders Ave NG18 . . . . **102** E8
Sanders Cl
Besthorpe NG23 . . . . **97** F7
Ilkeston DE7 . . . . **157** C2
Sanderson Dr NG3 . . . . **162** D6
Sandersons Bank DN9 . . . **1** F4
Sanderson's Bank DN9 . . **2** B3
Sandfield Ave NG15 . . . **132** B8
Sandfield Cl NG18 . . . . **103** B4
Sandfield La NG22 . . . . **78** B6
Sandfield Rd
Annesley Woodhouse
NG17 . . . . **129** F8
Arnold NG5 . . . . **161** F5
Beeston NG9 . . . . **182** E2
Nottingham NG7 . . . . **222** B2
Sandfield Way NG24 . . . **139** D5
Sandford Ave NG10 . . . **193** E7
Sandford Rd NG3 . . . . **162** A3
Sandgate NG9 . . . . **171** D1
Sandgate Ave NG19 . . . . **88** D4
Sandgate Rd NG19 . . . . . **88** D4
Sandhill La DN22 . . . . . **32** D6
Sandhill Rd
Farndon NG24 . . . . **139** A5
Selston NG16 . . . . **129** B3
Sandhills Cl NG24 . . . . **124** E1
Sandhill Sconce NG24 . . **139** D8
Sandhills Pk NG24 . . . . **124** E1
Sandhill St S80 . . . . **35** E3
Sandholes NG22 . . . . . . **119** E6
Sandhurst Ave NG18 . . . **102** C4
Sandhurst Dr
Beeston NG9 . . . . **183** C2
Ruddington NG11 . . . . **196** B6
Sandhurst Rd NG6 . . . . **146** C1
SANDIACRE **182** A6
Sandiacre Rd NG9 . . . . **182** C6
Sand La
Besthorpe NG23 . . . . **97** F7
Broadholme NG23 . . . . **70** E8
Spalford NG23 . . . . **83** A7
Torksey LN1 . . . . **44** C2
Sand Martin Cl LE12 . . **205** F3
Sandmartins Ave NG18 . **185** E8
Sandmartins Cl NG18 . . **102** C5
Sandon St NG7 . . . . **161** A1
Sandown Rd
Beeston NG9 . . . . **182** F2
Mansfield NG18 . . . . **103** B4
Sutton in Ashfield NG17 . . **101** B3
Sandpiper Cl NG13 . . . . **177** F3
Sandpiper Pl NG20 . . . . . **73** E5
Sandpiper Way NG7 . . . **222** A2
Sand Pit La LE12 . . . . . **211** C3
Sandringham Ave NG18 **185** E8
Sandringham Cres
Nottingham NG8 . . . . **171** C5
Worksop S81 . . . . **35** E6
Sandringham Ct
Harworth DN11 . . . . **9** A5
Mansfield Woodhouse
NG19 . . . . **88** B4
Sandringham Dr
Beeston NG9 . . . . **171** C1
Mansfield Woodhouse
NG19 . . . . **88** B4
Sandringham Pl NG15 . **146** B8
Sandringham Rd
Mansfield Woodhouse
NG19 . . . . **88** B4
[2] Nottingham NG2 . . . **173** F4
Retford DN22 . . . . **29** D1
Sandiacre NG10 . . . . **182** B3
Sandrock Rd DN11 . . . . . **8** F5
Sands Cl NG4 . . . . **174** E5
Sandside NG12 . . . . . . **187** F2
Sands The
Bottesford NG13 . . . . **181** B1
Long Clawson LE14 . . . . . **211** D3
Sandstone Ct [2] NG6 . **160** A8
Sandstone Mws NG14 . . **173** B1
Sandstone Pl NG18 . . . **102** E5
Sandwell Cl NG10 . . . . **193** A6
Sandwich Cl [5] NG17 . **114** C7
Sandwood Cl DE55 . . . . **99** A3
Sandycliffe Cl NG19 . . . . **88** F1
Sandyford Cl NG6 . . . . **160** C3
Sandy Gr NG18 . . . . . . **102** D7
Sandy La
Bawtry DN10 . . . . **10** A7
Carlton NG12 . . . . **175** B2
Edwinstowe NG21 . . . . **91** B8
Gamston DN22 . . . . **50** F4
Hucknall NG15 . . . . **146** A7
Mansfield NG18 . . . . **102** D7
Market Warsop NG20 . . . . . **74** B5
Oxton NG25 . . . . **134** C3
Ravenshead NG15 . . . . . . **117** B3
Worksop S80 . . . . **35** D4
Sandy La Ind Est S80 . . **35** D4
Sandymount DN11 . . . . . **9** A5
Sandymount E DN11 . . . . **9** A5
Sandymount W DN11 . . . **9** A4
Sanger Cl NG11 . . . . . . **195** C8
Sanger Gdns NG11 . . . . **195** C8
Sankey Dr NG6 . . . . . . **160** A7

Santon Cl NG19 . . . . **89** A2
Santon Rd NG19 . . . . **89** A2
Sapele Cl NG4 . . . . **163** A2
Sapling Cl NG24 . . . . . . **140** C5
Sapphire Cl NG21 . . . . **104** C1
Sapphire Dr NG17 . . . . **115** C4
Sapphire St NG18 . . . . **102** C5
Saracen Cl DN21 . . . . . . **24** C1
Saracen La DN10 . . . . . . **9** F2
Saracen's Head Yd
NG24 . . . . **139** F8
Saracens La DN10 . . . . . **10** A2
Sarah Ave NG5 . . . . **161** A2
Sarah Dr NG12 . . . . . . **185** F3
Sargent Gdns [1] NG3 . **173** F6
Sartfield Rd NG19 . . . . . **89** B2
Saskatoon Cl NG12 . . . . **175** E2
Saturn Rd NG18 . . . . . **102** E2
Saturn Way [3] NG18 . **102** E1
Saucemere Dr NG24 . . . **139** F6
Saucers The NG13 . . . . **178** E7
Saunby Cl NG5 . . . . **162** B7
SAUNDBY **23** C6
Saundby Ave NG19 . . . . **87** D1
Saundby Rd DN22 . . . . . **23** D4
School View NG13 . . . . **181** A2
School St
Kirkby-in-Ashfield
NG17 . . . . **115** B5
Loughborough LE11 . . . . **220** B4
Selston NG16 . . . . **129** A7
School Wlk
Bawtry DN10 . . . . **10** A7
Bestwood Village NG6 . . . **146** E4
School Woods Cl DE75 . **157** B6
Schrimshire's Rd
North Leverton with
Habblesthorpe DN22 . . . . **32** A1
North Leverton with
Habblesthorpe DN22 . . . . **42** A8
Schrog Hill DN22 . . . . . **41** B8
Science Rd NG7 . . . . . . **172** D1
Scofton Cl S81 . . . . **35** C8
Scolars Way NG10 . . . . **102** D5
Scollins Ct [4] DE7 . . . **157** E2
Scotholme Ave [7] NG7 . **172** F8
Scotholme Prim Sch
NG7 . . . . **172** F8
Scot La DN10 . . . . **10** A7
Scotland Bank NG12 . . **187** F3
Scotland Rd NG5 . . . . . **160** F3
Scotswood Rd NG19 . . . . **88** B6
Scott Ave NG9 . . . . **184** A5
Scott Cl
Claypole NG23 . . . . **156** D7
Nottingham NG6 . . . . **159** F5
Worksop S81 . . . . **36** C4
Scotton Sq DN22 . . . . . . **29** D1
Scott St DN21 . . . . **15** C1
Scott Way NG17 . . . . . **115** B1
Scratta La S80 . . . . **34** C2
SCREVETON **166** E4
Screveton Rd
Car Colston NG13 . . . . . . **166** C3
Hawksworth NG13 . . . . . . **167** B3
Scrimshire La NG12 . . . **187** E3
Script Dr NG6 . . . . **160** E4
Scrivelsby Gdns NG9 . . **183** D4
SCROOBY **10** A2
Scrooby Cl DN11 . . . . . . **9** A4
Scrooby Rd
Bircotes DN11 . . . . **9** C4
Harworth DN11 . . . . **8** F3
Seaburn Rd NG9 . . . . . **182** E2
Seacroft NG24 . . . . **140** E8
Seaford Ave NG8 . . . . . **172** B5
Seaforth Sq NG19 . . . . **101** D5
Seagrave Ave NG15 . . . **115** B1
Seagrave Prim Sch
NG8 . . . . **159** D2
Seagrave Rd NG8 . . . . **159** D1
Seamer Rd NG16 . . . . . **158** F7
Sean Upton Cl NG9 . . . **183** D3
Searby Rd NG17 . . . . . **101** C1
Searwood Ave NG17 . . **114** C4
Seatallen Cl NG2 . . . . . **186** C6
Seathwaite Cl NG2 . . . **186** D4
Seatoller Cl NG2 . . . . . **186** C5
Seaton Cres NG8 . . . . . **160** A1
Seaton Way NG5 . . . . . **162** D5
Second Ave
Beeston NG9 . . . . **184** C6
Carlton, Gedling NG4 . . . . **162** F1
Carlton, Thorneywood
NG4 . . . . **174** C8
Clipstone NG21 . . . . **90** A3
Edwinstowe NG21 . . . . **76** A2
Mansfield NG21 . . . . **103** F2
Mansfield Woodhouse
NG19 . . . . **89** A1
Nottingham NG6 . . . . **160** B7
Sedbergh Cl NG13 . . . . **177** B8
Sedgebrook Cl NG6 . . . **160** C3
Sedgebrook St NG19 . . **88** E3
Sedgeley Rd NG12 . . . . **186** D1
Sedgeley Ave NG2 . . . . **173** F5
Sedgmere DN22 . . . . **39** D4
Sedgwick Cl NG16 . . . . **113** D2
Sedgwick St
Langley Mill NG16 . . . . . **143** B3
Westwood NG16 . . . . **128** B3
Sedley Ave NG16 . . . . . **159** C6
Seely Ave NG14 . . . . . . **148** E8
Seely Jun Sch NG5 . . . . **161** C3
Seely Prim Sch NG5 . . . **161** C3
Seely Rd NG7 . . . . **222** C3
Sefton Ave NG9 . . . . . . **183** C4
Sefton Dr NG3 . . . . **161** D2
Selassie Ct NG9 . . . . . **159** D2
Selborne Gdns NG14 . . **173** E6
Selbourne Ct [4] LE11 . **220** C4
Selbourne St LE11 . . . . **220** C4
Selby Cl NG9 . . . . **182** E3
Selby La NG12 . . . . **197** F2
Selby Rd
Styrrup DN11 . . . . **8** E2
Selby Rd continued
East Stoke NG23 . . . . **153** D4

Farndon NG24 . . . . **139** A4
Halam NG22 . . . . **121** A3
Harby LE14 . . . . **202** A3
Kirklington NG22 . . . . **120** F7
Kneesall NG22 . . . . **93** F5
Long Clawson LE14 . . . . . **211** C3
Mansfield Woodhouse
NG19 . . . . **88** C3
North Scarle LN6 . . . . **83** D2
Norwell NG23 . . . . **110** A8
Ollerton NG22 . . . . **77** B3
Rempstone LE12 . . . . **215** D5
Saxilby LN1 . . . . **57** A1
Saxilby LN1 . . . . **70** F8
South Normanton DE55 . . **113** B4
Whatton NG13 . . . . **179** B3
School Rd
Langold S81 . . . . **16** E3
Selston NG16 . . . . **129** A7
Selby Rd continued
West Bridgford NG2 . . . . . **185** F5
Selhurst St NG7 . . . . . **172** F7
Selhurst St [5] NG7 . . . **172** F7
Selkirk Way [13] NG5 . . **161** B1
Sellars Ave NG11 . . . . . **196** C6
Seller's Wood Dr NG6 . . **160** A7
Seller's Wood Dr W
NG6 . . . . **159** F8
Sellers Wood Nature
Reserve * NG6 . . . . . . **159** E7
Selsey Cl NG16 . . . . . . **159** C2
Selsey Ct DN22 . . . . . . **29** E1
Selside Ct NG9 . . . . . . **183** A4
SELSTON **128** E7
Selston CE Inf Sch
NG16 . . . . **128** E6
Selston Cl DN11 . . . . . . **9** B5
Selston Dr NG8 . . . . . . **172** C3
Selston High Sch NG16 . **128** E7
Selston La Cntr NG16 . . **128** E7
Selston Rd NG16 . . . . . **128** B5
Selwyn Cl NG6 . . . . . . **160** E5
Selwyn St NG18 . . . . . **102** E5
Senator Cl NG15 . . . . . **146** C8
Sennen Ct DN22 . . . . . . **29** E1
Sentinel Dr
Annesley Woodhouse
NG15 . . . . **130** A6
Annesley Woodhouse
NG16 . . . . **129** F5
Serif Cl NG5 . . . . **161** B1
Serina Ct NG9 . . . . **184** B7
Serlby Pk DN10 . . . . . . **18** D8
Serlby Pk Acad
Bircotes DN11 . . . . **8** B4
Bircotes DN11 . . . . **9** C5
Serlby Rd DN11 . . . . . . **9** C4
Serlby Rd
Eastwood NG16 . . . . **144** A3
Styrrup DN11 . . . . **9** A2
Serlby Rise NG3 . . . . . **173** F6
Serotine Cl NG12 . . . . . **176** D2
Serpentine Cl NG12 . . . **176** D2
Service Rd NG16 . . . . . **143** F3
Seven Hills NG24 . . . . . **125** A3
Seven Oaks Cres NG9 . . **171** C1
Seven Oaks Rd DE7 . . . **170** A1
Seventh Ave
Beeston NG9 . . . . **184** C5
Clipstone NG21 . . . . **89** E2
Mansfield NG19 . . . . **103** A8
Severals NG9 . . . . **182** F7
Severn St NG6 . . . . **160** B7
Seward St [2] LE11 . . . **220** A3
Seymour Rd
Eastwood NG16 . . . . **143** F1
Hucknall NG15 . . . . **145** E5
West Bridgford NG2 . . . . . **186** B4
Seymour St NG3 . . . . . **173** F5
SGCS Bsns Pk NG11 . . . **184** E5
Shackleton Cl NG8 . . . . **159** D2
Shacklock Cl NG5 . . . . **147** A2
Shadwell Gr NG12 . . . . **175** F3
Shady La NG9 . . . . **183** D2
Shaftesbury Ave
Burton Joyce NG14 . . . . **164** A5
Long Eaton NG10 . . . . **193** B4
Mansfield NG19 . . . . **87** E2
Radcliffe on Trent NG12 . . **176** E3
Sandiacre NG10 . . . . **182** A5
Shaftesbury St [4] NG7 . **161** A1
Shaftesbury Way NG23 . . **98** A1
Shakespeare Ave NG19 . **88** B4
Shakespeare Cl NG4 . . . **174** E5
Shakespeare Rd NG16 . . **158** C5
Shakespeare St
Gainsborough DN21 . . . . . **24** D6
Long Eaton NG10 . . . . **182** D1
Loughborough LE11 . . . . **220** B4
New Balderton NG24 . . . . **140** B6
Nottingham NG1 . . . . **223** E3
Worksop S81 . . . . **36** A4
Shakespeare Villas
NG1 . . . . **223** E3
Shaldon Cl
Arnold NG5 . . . . **162** D5
Nottingham NG5 . . . . **146** F4
Shale La NG14 . . . . **152** A8
Shandwick Cl NG5 . . . . **148** B1
Shanklin Dr NG9 . . . . . **182** D7
Shanwell Cl NG8 . . . . . **159** D2
Shardlow Way NG18 . . . **103** B4
Sharnford Way NG9 . . . **171** B3
Sharp Cl NG10 . . . . . . **193** C6
Sharpes Wy NG6 . . . . . **147** B5
Sharphill Rd NG12 . . . . **186** B4
Sharpley Dr LE12 . . . . **205** F3
Sharrard Cl NG16 . . . . **129** A2
Sharrat Ct [12] NG18 . . **103** A2
Shaw Cres NG15 . . . . . **145** E4
Shaw Croft NG17 . . . . . **100** F5
Shaw Gdns NG4 . . . . . **175** B8
Shaw Rd
Beeston NG9 . . . . **183** B2
Gringley on the Hill DN10 . . **13** C7
Gringley on the Hill DN10 . . **12** F4
Shaw St E DE7 . . . . **170** A6
Shaw St W DE7 . . . . . . **170** A6
Shaws Orch NG22 . . . . . **120** F1
Shaw St
Mansfield NG18 . . . . **102** E7
Ruddington NG11 . . . . **196** C6
Worksop S80 . . . . **35** E3
Sheaf Pl S81 . . . . **35** E7
Shearing Cl NG4 . . . . . **163** A1
Shearing Hill
Carlton NG4 . . . . **163** A1
Carlton NG4 . . . . **175** A7
Shearsby Dr NG19 . . . . . **88** F2

Sheepbridge La NG18 . **101** F5
Sheepfold La NG11 . . . . **196** C6
Sheepwalk La
Ravenshead NG15 . . . . . . **116** F2
Ravenshead NG15 . . . . . . **116** F3
Sheepwash La
Sutton in Ashfield NG17 . . **101** B2
Tickhill DN11 . . . . **8** E8
Sheepwash Way LE12 . . **214** E6
Sheerness Cl NG16 . . . . **158** B7
Sheet Stores Ind Est
NG10 . . . . **193** D5
SHEFFIELD **255**
Blyth S81 . . . . **17** F3
Blyth S81 . . . . **18** A3
Kettlethorpe LN1 . . . . **55** F1
Kettlethorpe LN1 . . . . **56** B1
Shelby Cl NG7 . . . . **222** A2
Sheldon Cl
Long Eaton NG10 . . . . **182** B3
New Cross NG17 . . . . **100** E4
Sheldrake Rd NG4 . . . . **140** D8
SHELFORD **164** C1
Shelford Ave NG17 . . . **114** D6
Shelford Cl
Beeston NG9 . . . . **183** D4
Radcliffe on Trent NG12 . . **176** A4
Shelford Cres NG14 . . . **164** A5
Shelford Dr NG13 . . . . **177** D4
Shelford Hill
Mansfield NG19 . . . . **101** E6
Radcliffe on Trent NG12 . . **176** C7
Shelford Rd
Carlton NG4 . . . . **162** D3
Newton NG13 . . . . **165** A1
Newton NG13 . . . . **177** A8
Radcliffe on Trent NG12 . . **176** A5
Shelford NG13 . . . . **164** F1
Shelford Rise NG3 . . . . **174** A5
Shellburne Cl NG5 . . . . **160** E8
Shelley Ave
Mansfield Woodhouse
NG19 . . . . **88** B4
Nottingham NG11 . . . . . . **184** E3
Shelley Cl
Balderton NG24 . . . . **140** D3
Hucknall NG15 . . . . **145** D6
Kirkby-in-Ashfield NG17 . . **115** C7
Nuthall NG16 . . . . **159** B6
Shelley Rd NG5 . . . . . . **161** D7
Shelley St S80 . . . . **36** A3
Shelthorpe Ave LE11 . . **220** B1
Shelthorpe Com Sch
LE11 . . . . **220** C1
Shelthorpe Rd LE11 . . . **220** B1
SHELTON **168** C6
Shelton Ave
Hucknall NG15 . . . . **146** D4
Newark-on-Trent NG24 . . . **139** E5
Shelton Cl NG19 . . . . . . **87** E1
Shelton Gdns
Cropwell Bishop NG12 . . . **189** B5
Ruddington NG11 . . . . **196** B6
Shelton La NG13 . . . . . **168** C4
Shelton Rd
Mansfield NG18 . . . . **103** A2
Thoroton NG23 . . . . **167** F3
Shelton St NG3 . . . . . . **223** F4
Shenfield Gdns NG5 . . . **146** D1
Shepard Cl NG6 . . . . . . **159** F6
Shepherds Ave S81 . . . . **35** F5
Shepherds Cl NG8 . . . . **172** A4
Shepherd's Cl LE12 . . . **213** C5
Shepherds Oak NG17 . . **100** F6
Shepherd St NG6 . . . . . **145** E2
Shepherds Way NG17 . . **101** B2
Shepherds Wood Dr
NG8 . . . . **172** C7
Shepherd Wlk DE74 . . . **203** C1
Sheppards Ct NG13 . . . . **181** A2
Shepshed Rd LE12 . . . . **212** F1
Shepton Cl DE7 . . . . . . **157** D2
Shepton Cres NG8 . . . . **160** B1
Sheraton Dr NG8 . . . . . **171** E3
Sherborne Rd
Nottingham NG8 . . . . **160** A1
West Bridgford NG2 . . . . . **185** F5
Sherbrooke Ave NG5 . . **161** D6
Sherbrooke Rd NG5 . . . **161** B1
Sherbrook Rd NG5 . . . . **161** B1
Sherbrook Terr NG5 . . . **161** D6
Sheridan Cl NG24 . . . . **140** D5
Sheridan Ct NG9 . . . . . **170** F1
Sheridan Wy
Hucknall NG15 . . . . **146** A5
Nottingham NG5 . . . . **161** A3
Sheriff's Lodge The *
NG1 . . . . **223** F1
Sheriffs Way NG2 . . . . **173** C2
Sheringham Cl NG5 . . . **161** F6
Sheringham Dr NG18 . . **102** C3
Sherman Dr NG9 . . . . . **183** C2
Sherrington Cl NG11 . . **195** C8
Sherview Ave NG18 . . . **103** A7
Sherwin Cl NG3 . . . . . **223** E4
Sherwin Gr NG7 . . . . . **222** A1
Sherwin Rd
Nottingham NG7 . . . . **222** A1
Stapleford NG9 . . . . **170** C1
Stapleford NG9 . . . . **182** E8
Sherwin Wlk NG3 . . . . **223** E4
SHERWOOD **161** G2
Sherwood Ave
Blidworth NG21 . . . . **118** C5
Calverton NG14 . . . . **148** D8

Sherwood Ave continued
Edwinstowe NG21......76 A2
Mansfield NG18.......103 B3
Newark-on-Trent NG24..140 A6
5 Nottingham NG5....161 D3
Pinxton NG16........113 D3
Shirebrook NG20......72 E4
Sherwood Bsns Pk
NG15.............129 F6
Sherwood Ct NG18....102 E7
Sherwood Cres S81....18 A2
Sherwood Ct
Beeston NG9........183 C3
Long Whatton LE12...212 A4
Sherwood Dene 8
NG17............114 E1
Sherwood Dr
New Ollerton NG22....77 C4
Shirebrook NG20......72 E3
Worksop S80.........47 F8
Worksop S80.........48 A8
Sherwood Energy Village★
NG22............77 C3
Sherwood Forest Art & Craft Ctr★ NG21...76 A3
Sherwood Forest Ctry Pk★
NG22............76 A4
Sherwood Forest Farm Pk★ NG20.........89 F7
Sherwood Forest Fun Pk★
NG22............76 B4
Sherwood Forest Railway★
NG21............89 F7
Sherwood Gr
Bingham NG13.......177 D4
Calverton NG14......148 F8
Sherwood Hall Gdns
NG18............102 F8
Sherwood Hall Rd
NG18............102 E7
Sherwood Heath Nature Reserve★ NG22....76 F4
Sherwood Jun Sch
NG20............74 B3
Sherwood Lodge Dr
NG5.............132 C2
Sherwood Oaks Bsns Pk
NG18............103 B3
Sherwood Oaks Cl
NG18............103 B3
Sherwood Pines Forest Pk★ NG21.........90 E3
Sherwood Pl
Annesley Woodhouse
NG17............115 A1
Clipstone NG21......90 B4
Sherwood Rd
Harworth DN11........8 F5
Rainworth NG21.....104 B1
Retford DN22........39 E3
Sutton in Ashfield NG17..100 E1
Worksop S80.........35 F4
Sherwood Rise
Annesley Woodhouse
NG17............115 A1
Eastwood NG16......143 F1
Mansfield Woodhouse
NG19............88 A2
Nottingham NG7.....173 B8
Sherwood St
Annesley Woodhouse
NG17............130 A8
Hucknall NG15......146 C6
Huthwaite NG17......99 F3
Kirkby-in-Ashfield NG17..115 B5
10 Mansfield NG18...102 B6
Mansfield Woodhouse
NG19............88 B2
Market Warsop NG20...74 B3
Newton DE55.........99 B4
Sherwood Vale NG5...161 E3
Sherwood Way NG16..129 B7
Sherwood Way S NG17..101 E2
Sherwood Way South
NG18............102 B1
Sherwood Wlk NG15..131 A2
Shetland Cl
Mansfield Woodhouse
NG19............88 F1
Shirebrook NG20......72 D2
Shet Land Cl 3 NG18..88 F1
Shetlands The
Retford DN22........29 F1
Retford DN22........30 A1
Shilling Rd NG18....102 D1
Shilling Way NG10...193 A4
Shilo Way NG16......158 B4
Shiners Way DE55...113 A6
Shining Cliff Ct DN10...9 F8
SHIPLEY..........157 B6
Shipley Cl NG5.....162 C8
Shipley Ct DE7......157 C5
Shipley Ctry Pk★ DE75 157 A4
Shipley Rd NG8.....159 F2
Shipley Rise NG4...174 E7
Shipstone St
Ilkeston DE7........170 B6
3 Nottingham NG7...172 F8
Shipstones Yard NG6..160 C8
Shipstones Yd NG6..160 C8
Shirburn Ave NG18..102 C8
SHIREBROOK.......72 F3
Shirebrook Bsns Pk
NG20............72 F2
Shirebrook Cl DE7...157 F6
Shirebrooke Cl NG6..160 C3
Shirebrook Sta NG20..73 A4

Shire Cl S81........26 A7
Shire La NG23, NG24..156 B7
SHIREOAKS........34 E6
Shireoaks Comm
Shireoaks S81.......34 F7
Shireoaks S81.......35 A7
Shireoaks Ct 2 NG18..103 A2
Shireoaks Rd S80....35 B5
Shireoaks Row S81...34 E7
Shireoaks Sta S81...34 E7
Shireoak Triangle Bsns Pk
S81.............35 A7
Shires The
Mansfield Woodhouse
NG19............88 F1
Sutton in Ashfield NG17..100 D1
Shires Way NG23.....96 F7
Shirland Cl DE7.....157 F5
Shirland Dr NG18...103 B4
Shirley Dr NG5......162 B7
Shirley Rd NG3......173 C8
Shirley St NG10.....193 A4
Shoreswood Cl 1 NG5 161 B8
Shortcross Ave NG3..161 F4
Short Hill NG1......223 E2
Shortleys Rd DN22...54 D8
Short St
Market Warsop NG20...74 B4
Sutton in Ashfield NG17..101 A3
Short Wheatley La
NG23............112 B5
Shortwood Ave NG15..145 F5
Shortwood Cl NG1...223 F1
Shortwood La NG22...93 C8
Shorwell Rd NG3....174 C7
Shotton Dr NG5.....148 A2
Shoulder of Mutton Hill
NG17............115 B1
Shrewsbury Rd
Bircotes DN11........9 B4
Nottingham NG2.....174 A4
Worksop S80.........36 B2
Shrewsbury View DN22..29 C1
Shrimpton Ct NG11..196 D6
Shropshire Ave NG16..128 C4
Sibcy La NG24......140 D3
Sibson Dr DE74.....203 B2
Sibson Wlk NG5.....147 F2
SIBTHORPE........167 E7
Sibthorpe Hill DN22...65 C7
Sibthorpe Rd NG13..167 D5
Sibthorpe St NG18..102 A5
Sidbury Cl NG5.....162 E5
Siddalls Dr NG17...100 B3
Side La NG22.......106 E8
Side Ley DE74......203 C3
Side Row NG24......140 B8
Sidings La NG18....171 A3
Sidings Rd NG17....115 C7
Sidings The
Aslockton NG13......179 A4
Kimberley NG16......159 A6
Lowdham NG14......164 E8
Mansfield Woodhouse
NG19............88 A3
5 Newark-on-Trent
NG24............140 B8
Saxilby LN1.........57 A3
Sidlaw Rise NG5....147 B2
Sidmouth Cl NG12...197 E4
Sidney Rd NG9......183 E7
Sidney St
Kimberley NG16......158 F6
Long Eaton NG10....193 D6
Sidsaph Hill
Walkeringham DN10...13 F5
Walkeringham DN10...14 A5
Siena Gdn NG19......89 A2
Signal Rd LE14.....219 A5
Signal Way NG19.....88 B3
Sikorski Cl NG24....124 F1
Silbury Cl NG11....195 D7
Silken Holme DE55..113 B4
Silk St NG17.......100 E1
Silver Birch Cl NG6..160 B4
Silverdale NG9.....182 E5
Silverdale Ave NG19..88 B4
Silverdale Cl DN22...29 C1
Silverdale Rd NG7...160 F2
Silver Hill Cl NG8..159 D2
Silverhill Cotts NG17..100 A8
Silverhill La NG17...99 F8
Silverhow Cl NG16..186 C6
Silver St
Gainsborough DN21...24 C8
Grassthorpe NG23....81 F4
North Clifton NG23....68 E5
Retford DN22........39 D5
Silverwood Ave NG15..117 A1
Silverwood Rd
Beeston NG9........183 E6
Bottesford NG13....181 A2
Silvey Ave NG25....121 D2
Sime St S80........35 E4
Simkin Ave
Nottingham NG3.....162 A4
Porchester NG5.....162 A1
Simon Cl DN22......42 B1
Simone Gdns NG7....184 E1
Simons Ct NG9......171 D1
Simpson Cl NG24....140 E3
Simpson Dr NG21...189 B4
Simpson Rd NG19...101 D7
Simpson Wlk 4 DN11...8 F5
Singleton Ave NG18..102 E8
Sir Donald Bailey Academy The
Newark-on-Trent NG24..139 F5
Newark-on-Trent NG24..140 A5
Sir Edmund Hillary Prim Sch S81.......36 A4

Sir John Robinson Wy
NG5.............161 E6
Sir John Sherbrooke Jun Sch NG14......148 E8
Sir Thomas Ave DN21...24 E6
Siskin Cl NG9......183 C6
Siskin Ct S81.......35 C7
Siskin Dr LE12.....206 A3
Sisley Ave NG15....182 E6
Sitwell Cl S81.......36 B4
Sitwell Rd S81......36 C4
Six Hills La LE14...219 A2
Six Hills Rd LE14...219 E3
Sixth Ave
Beeston NG9........184 D6
Clipstone NG21......89 E3
Edwinstowe NG21.....75 F1
Edwinstowe NG21.....76 A1
Mansfield NG19......103 A8
Skeavington's La DE7..157 E5
SKEGBY...........100 E6
Skegby Hall Gdns
NG17............100 F6
Skegby Jun Acad
NG17............100 D7
Skegby La NG17, NG19..101 C6
Skegby Mount NG19..101 C5
Skegby Rd
Annesley Woodhouse
NG17............129 F8
Huthwaite NG17.....100 A3
Normanton on T NG23..81 C7
Sutton in Ashfield NG17..101 A4
SKELLINGTHORPE....71 F3
Skellingthorpe Rd
Saxilby LN1.........57 D2
Saxilby LN6.........71 E8
Skelwith Cl NG2....186 C5
Skerry Hill NG18....102 E7
Skerry La NG13.....181 F1
Sketchley Ct 2 NG6..160 A4
Sketchley St NG3...173 F6
Skiddaw Cl NG2.....186 D5
Skipper Cl LE12....214 E8
Skipton Cir NG3....174 A5
Skipton Cl DE7.....157 D3
Skirbeck Dr LN1.....57 A3
Skithorne Rise NG14..164 C8
Skylark Cl
Arnold NG15........132 A8
Bingham NG13......177 F3
Skylark Dr NG6.....160 D4
Skylark Hill NG12..188 E2
Skylark Ri NG9.....170 E2
Skylarks Nature Reserve★
NG12............175 A3
Skylark Way NG21....89 F4
Sky Wlk NG18......102 E1
Slack Rd DE7.......157 A3
Slack's La
Flintham NG23......152 E1
Flintham NG23......166 D8
Kneeton NG13.......152 B2
Slack Wlk S80......35 E1
Slade Cl DE55......113 B4
Slade Rd NG9......183 B5
Slaidburn Ave NG11..185 A5
Slake La NG24......124 E6
Slalom Run NG5.....162 C1
Slant La NG19......88 B4
Slater St NG17.....100 F4
Slaters Way 1 NG5..160 F5
Slaughter House La
NG24............124 F1
Slaynes La DN10.....11 A8
Sleaford Rd
Beckingham LN5.....142 E8
Beckingham NG24....127 B1
Coddington NG24....126 D2
Newark-on-Trent NG24..125 A1
Winthorpe NG24.....125 F4
Sleath Dr NG23.....110 B2
Sleights La NG16....113 C2
Slim Dr NG4.......162 D4
Slingsby Gdns NG13..177 B8
Sloan Dr NG9......171 B3
Sloane Ct NG11.....185 C3
Sloswicke Dr DN22...29 C2
Slowthorne Gdns 2
NG5.............161 D8
Smalley Cl NG16....129 A1
Small Farm Centre★
NG13............202 E7
Small Gate NG16.....88 E6
Small's Croft NG14..149 C4
Smeath La DN22.....30 C4
Smeath Rd
Normanton DN22......30 A3
Selston NG16.......129 A2
Smedley Ave DE7....170 A7
Smedley Cl NG8.....160 B2
Smedley's Ave NG10..182 B5
Smeeton St DE75....143 B1
Smew Rd NG4.......175 C7
Smite Cl NG13......179 A4
Smite La NG13......179 E7
Smith Dr NG16......143 A3
Smithfield Ave NG9..170 D4
Smiths Cl NG12.....189 A4
Smithson Cl NG24...140 C4
Smithson Dr NG8....171 E4
Smith Sq DN11.......8 F7
Smith St
Mansfield NG18.....102 E6
Newark-on-Trent NG24..140 A8
Smithurst Rd NG16..158 B7
Smithy Cres NG5....161 F8
Smithy La LE12.....212 A2

Smithy Row
Nottingham NG1.....223 E2
Sutton in Ashfield NG17..100 D2
Smithy View
Calverton NG14.....148 E7
Killarney Park NG6..147 B5
Smython Green LN6...71 C1
Snaefell Ave NG19...89 A2
Snape La
Ranskill DN22.......19 A6
Scrooby DN10.......18 E7
Styrrup DN11........9 A2
Snape Nook Ct NG6..159 F7
Snape Wood Prim Sch
NG6.............160 A7
Snape Wood Rd NG6..159 F7
Snead Ct NG5......147 A1
Sneath Cl NG5......147 A1
SNEINTON........173 E4
Sneinton Bvd NG2...174 A4
Sneinton Dale NG2..174 A5
Sneinton Hermitage
Nottingham NG2.....173 E3
Nottingham NG7.....222 F1
Sneinton Hollows NG2..173 F4
Sneinton Rd NG2....173 E4
Sneinton St Stephen's CE Prim Sch NG2.....173 F5
Snell Cl NG23.......81 E1
Snipe Pk Rd DN11.....9 B4
Snowden Dr DN22.....40 A3
Snowden Cl 2 NG5...147 B1
Snowdon Rd NG3....112 A8
Snowdrop Ave NG24..125 E1
Snowdrop Cl NG15...146 D4
Snowdrop Dr NG19...88 F4
Snowdrop Gdns S81...25 F7
Soarbank Cl NG16...158 E7
Soar La
Normanton on S LE12..213 D3
Ratcliffe on Soar NG11..203 F7
Sutton Bonington LE12..212 F8
Sobers Gdns NG5....162 B6
Softwood Cl NG6....159 F7
Softwood Mws NG8...172 A6
Soloman Pk NG16....158 B2
Soloman Rd NG16....158 B2
Solway Cl NG9......183 E5
Somerby Ct NG9....171 B3
Somerby Rd DN21.....15 F1
Somerleyton Dr DE7..170 A4
Somersall St NG19..101 E8
Somersby Rd NG5...103 B5
Somersby Rd NG5...162 A5
Somerset Cl NG10...194 A8
Somerton Ave NG11..185 A4
Somerton Rd NG5....35 C8
Songthrush Ave NG6..160 D4
Sookholme Cl NG20...72 F3
Sookholme Dr NG20...74 A3
Sookholme La NG20...73 E3
Sookholme Rd
Market Warsop NG20...73 E1
Shirebrook NG20......72 F3
Sophie Rd NG7......222 B4
Sorrel Dr
Bingham NG13......177 C4
Sorrell Sq NG21......89 F4
Soss La DN10........7 B2
Sotheby Ave NG17...101 C1
Soudan Dr NG2......173 B1
Sough Rd DE55.....113 B7
Southampton St NG3..173 E6
South Ave
Bawtry DN10........10 A8
Radcliffe on Trent NG12..176 B3
Rainworth NG21.....104 A1
Shirebrook NG20......72 F3
Worksop S80.........36 B1
Southbreck Rise S80...36 B1
Southchurch Dr NG7..184 E2
Southcliffe Rd NG4..174 D7
SOUTH CLIFTON.....68 E1
South Cres
Bottesford NG13....181 A1
Clipstone NG21......90 A3
South Croft NG22....51 F2
Southdale Dr NG4...174 D7
Southdale Rd NG4...174 D7
Southdene S81.......36 A6
South Devon Ave NG3..162 B7
South Dr NG22......105 F7
South End NG23.....111 F7
Southend Ave NG24..139 F7
Southern Wood S80...46 E8
Southey St NG7.....222 C4
Southfall Cl DN22...19 B5
Southfield NG24....140 E3
Southfield Dr DE55..113 C5
Southfield Gr NG13..177 C4
Southfield Ind Est S80..45 A4
Southfield La
Beckingham DN10....23 C8
Whitwell S80........45 A4
Southfield Rd NG8...172 D6
Southfields NG10...193 C7
Southfields Ave NG16..113 D4
Southfields Cl NG17..114 E1
Southfields Rise DN22..42 C8
Southgate NG24......39 E3
Southgate Rd NG20...74 C5
Southglade Food Pk
NG5.............160 E6
Southglade L Ctr NG5..160 F7
Southglade Prim Sch
NG5.............161 A7
Southglade Rd NG5..160 E6
Southgore La DN22...42 D8
Southgreen Cl NG18..102 E2

Southgreen Hill NG18..102 E2
South La NG23.......81 E5
Southlands NG17....100 E4
Southlands Ave NG21...15 B4
Southlands Dr DN21...15 B4
Southlands Gdns DN21...15 B4
Southlea Rd NG4....174 D7
SOUTH LEVERTON....42 C6
Southmoor Rd
Newton on Trent LN1...55 C1
Newton on Trent LN1...69 A8
Worksop S80.........36 B1
South Moor Rd DN10...13 F6
SOUTH MUSKHAM...124 D7
SOUTH NORMANTON..113 A7
South Nottingham Coll
Nottingham NG1.....223 E1
Nottingham NG4.....223 F1
South Nottinghamshire Acad NG12.......176 A3
Southolme DN21.....24 D8
South Par
Bawtry DN10........10 A6
Gainsborough DN21...24 F7
Nottingham NG1.....223 E2
Saxilby LN1.........57 A4
Worksop S81.........36 A4
Southpark Ave NG15..113 C5
Southport Terr 4 NG7 172 E7
South Rd
Beeston NG9........184 B4
Nottingham NG5.....161 B6
NG7.............172 D2
Nottingham, Dunkirk
NG7.............172 D2
Nottingham, The Park
NG7.............222 A1
West Bridgford NG2..185 E6
West Burton DN22....32 E7
South Ridge Dr NG18..102 D3
SOUTH SCARLE.....98 C5
Southscarle La LN6...83 E2
South Scarle La
North Scarle LN6.....83 D1
South Scarle LN6.....98 F5
South Scarle Rd NG23..98 B2
South Sherwood St
NG1.............223 E3
Southside NG5......162 C7
South Snape Cl NG6..159 F7
South St
Bole DN22.........23 E2
Eastwood, Bailey Grove
NG16............143 E2
Eastwood, Giltbrook
NG16............158 C8
Hucknall NG15......146 A2
Long Eaton NG10....193 E7
Loughborough LE11..220 B3
Morton DN21........15 B4
Normanton on T NG23..81 E6
Retford DN22........39 F6
South Normanton DE55..113 B6
South View
Austerfield DN10.....3 C1
Whitwell S80........45 A5
Worksop S80.........35 F5
South View Dr DN22...30 D3
Southview Gdns NG15..117 A2
South View Rd 4 NG4..162 D1
Southwark Prim Sch
NG6.............160 E4
Southwark St NG6...160 E3
SOUTHWELL.......121 C1
Southwell Cl
East Leake LE12.....205 E1
Kirkby-in-Ashfield NG17..115 A6
Worksop S80.........36 A2
Southwell Gdns NG18..103 A4
Southwell La NG17...114 F6
Southwell La Ind Est
NG17............115 A7
Southwell L Ctr NG25..136 E7
Southwell Minster★
NG25............136 E8
Southwell Rd
Farnsfield NG21.....120 A5
Halloughton NG25...135 F3
Halloughton NG25...136 B3
Kirklington NG22....120 F7
Kirklington NG25....121 A5
Lowdham NG14......150 F2
Nottingham NG1.....223 F2
Oxton NG25........134 D4
Thurgarton NG14....151 D8
Upton NG25........122 B1
Southwell Rd E
Mansfield NG21.....103 E2
Rainworth NG21.....118 B8
Southwell Rd W NG18..102 E5
Southwell Rise
Eastwood NG16......158 B7
Giltbrook NG16.....158 C8
SOUTH WHEATLEY...31 E7
South Wilford Endowed CE VA Prim Sch NG11..185 B7
Southwold Dr NG8...172 C5
Southwold Prim Sch & Early Years Centre
NG8.............172 D5
South Wolds Com Sch
NG12............209 E3
Southwood Ave NG17..100 D4
South Yorkshire Aviation Mus★ S81.......16 B7
Sovereign Gr NG10..193 B7
Sovereign Gdns NG16..193 E7
Sovereign Way
Mansfield NG18.....103 B4
Worksop S80.........25 D1
Sowter Ave NG17....100 E4

Spa Cl NG17.......114 F8
Spa Common 2 DN22...39 F6
Spafford Cl DN21....44 D8
Spa La
Mansfield Woodhouse
NG19............88 F3
Orston NG13........180 B7
Spalding Rd NG3....173 F5
SPALFORD.........83 B7
Spalford Dr LN6.....83 D4
Spalford La LN6.....83 D4
Spalford Rd LN6.....83 E5
Spalford Warren Nature Reserve★ LN6......83 A5
Spaniel Row
Nottingham NG1.....223 E2
Nottingham NG14....173 C4
Spa Ponds Nature Reserve★ NG19.....89 C4
Spa Rd DN22........39 F6
Sparken Cl S80......46 E8
Sparken Dale S80....46 E8
Sparken Hill Acad S80..46 F8
Sparrow Cl DE7.....170 A4
Sparrow Gr S81......35 B7
Sparrow Hill 6 LE11..220 B4
Sparrow La NG23.....68 B1
Spartans Cl NG17....114 E7
Spean Ct 4 NG8.....172 A5
Spean Dr NG8......172 B7
Speeds Pingle 1 LE11 220 A4
Speedwell Cl
Bingham NG13......177 C4
Newark-on-Trent NG24..125 E1
Speedwell La NG16..158 E6
Speedwell Pl S80....35 E4
Speight Cl NG24....125 C6
Spencer Ave
Arnold NG3.........162 C5
Sandiacre NG10....182 B6
Spencer Cl
Ruddington NG11....196 B7
Saxilby LN1.........57 C3
Spencer Cres NG9...182 F8
Spencer Dr NG16....159 C6
Spencer St NG18....102 A6
Sperry Cl NG16......128 F6
Spey Cl NG15......145 D3
Spicer Cl NG9......183 C2
Spicers Ct DN22.....39 F6
Spindle Ct NG18....101 E5
Spindle Gdns NG6...160 A7
Spindle View NG14..148 F6
Spinella Rd S80.....35 C4
Spinners Cl
Mansfield NG15......88 E6
South Normanton DE55..113 C6
Spinners Way NG24..140 A4
Spinney Cl
Cotgrave NG12.....187 F2
Kirkby-in-Ashfield NG17..114 C6
Mansfield Woodhouse
NG19............88 E6
Newark-on-Trent NG24..139 E6
West Bridgford NG2..186 C4
Spinney Cres NG9...182 F3
Spinney Dr NG10....182 C2
Spinneymead DN22...19 B5
Spinney Rd
Bingham NG13......177 D4
Keyworth NG12.....197 E3
Long Eaton NG10....182 C2
Spinney Rise NG9...182 F3
Spinney The
Arnold NG5.........161 E4
Bestwood Village NG6..146 E5
Bulcote NG14.......164 B5
Elston NG23.......153 D5
Farnsfield NG22....119 E6
14 Gainsborough DN21...15 F2
Mansfield NG18.....116 D7
Shirebrook NG20......72 D3
Winthorpe NG24....125 C5
Spinney Way NG11..185 A4
Spinningdale NG5...162 B8
Spinning Dr NG5....161 C5
Spion Pk Mws NG20...73 F2
Spire Cl NG17......129 E8
Spire Gdns NG24....125 B3
Spire Nottingham Hospl (Private) NG12.....186 F5
Spire View
Bottesford NG13....181 B3
Long Eaton NG10....193 B4
Spitalfields S81.....18 B2
Spital Hill
Gainsborough DN21...15 C1
Gainsborough DN21...15 E1
Retford DN22........39 F7
Spital Rd S81.......18 B1
Spital Terr DN21.....15 D1
Spitfire Way NG15..145 D3
Spondon St NG5.....161 C2
Sporton Cl DE55....113 A7
Sporton La
South Normanton DE55..113 A7
South Normanton DE55..113 B7
Spotlight Gall (Town Hall)★
NG24............139 F2
Spray Cl NG4.......174 E5
Spridgeon Cl NG10..182 B2
Springbank Prim Sch
NG16............143 E2
Spring Cl
Kimberley NG16.....159 A2
1 Kirkby-in-Ashfield
NG17............115 A4
West Bridgford NG12..185 D5
Spring Ct NG23.....112 A8
Spring Dale Gdns NG9..170 D3
Springdale La NG13..165 E2

Spring Dr NG24 . . . . 140 F2
Springfield DE74 . . . . . . 203 B1
Springfield Ave
  Eastwood NG16 . . . . . . 144 A2
  Long Eaton NG10 . . . . . 193 F8
  Sandiacre NG10 . . . . . . 182 B3
  Shirebrook NG20 . . . . . . 72 E5
Springfield Cl
  Cropwell Bishop NG12 . .189 B4
  Gainsborough DN21 . . . . 24 E8
  Mansfield NG18 . . . . . . 103 A5
Springfield Ct NG6 . . . . 159 F6
Springfield Dr NG6 . . . . 159 F6
Springfield Gdn DE7 . . .157 F2
Springfield Pastures
  NG14 . . . . 173 D8
Springfield Prim Sch
  NG6 . . . . 146 C1
Springfield Rd
  Arnold NG5 . . . . 147 E1
  Hucknall NG15 . . . . 145 D6
  Retford DN22 . . . . 39 F8
  Retford DN22 . . . . 40 A8
  Southwell NG25 . . . . . . 121 D2
Springfield Ret Pk
  NG6 . . . . 160 C8
Springfields NG2 . . . . . 185 D6
Springfield St NG7 . . . . 160 F1
Springfield Way NG17 . .115 D6
Spring Gdns
  Bawtry DN10 . . . . 10 A8
  Gainsborough DN21 . . . . 24 D8
  Newark-on-Trent NG24 . .139 E7
  Nottingham NG6 . . . . . . 171 C2
Spring Gdn Terr DE7 . . .157 F2
Spring Gn NG11 . . . . . . 195 E2
Springhead Ct NG6 . . . . 160 A6
Spring Hill
  Kimberley NG16 . . . . . . 158 F5
  Mansfield Woodhouse
  NG19 . . . . 88 B3
  Southwell NG25 . . . . . . 136 F7
  Southwell NG25 . . . . . . 137 A7
  Whitwell S80 . . . . 45 A6
Springhill Cl NG6 . . . . . 146 B1
Spring La
  Arnold NG3 . . . . 162 E6
  East Bridgford NG13 . . . 166 B2
  Elmton NG20 . . . . 58 A7
  Farnsfield NG22 . . . . . . 119 E7
  Flintham NG13 . . . . 166 F7
  Lambley NG4 . . . . 163 B6
  Long Whatton LE12 . . . . 212 C2
  Rhodesia S80 . . . . 35 A3
  Shireoaks S80 . . . . 34 F5
  Sturton le Steeple DN22 . . 32 D4
  Warsop Vale NG20 . . . . . 73 C6
  Warsop Vale NG20 . . . . . 73 D3
  Wiseton DN10 . . . . 21 B8
Springland Farm Cotts
  NG16 . . . . 159 D6
Spring Mdw
  Cotgrave NG12 . . . . 188 A3
  Kirkby-in-Ashfield NG17 .114 C3
  Tibshelf DE55 . . . . 99 B7
Spring Moor NG2 . . . . . 174 D5
Spring Rd
  Nottingham NG6 . . . . . . 160 C7
  Sutton in Ashfield NG17 .100 E2
Springs Rd DN10 . . . . 4 D6
Spring St
  Hucknall NG15 . . . . 146 A7
  Whitwell S80 . . . . 45 A6
Spring Terr NG16 . . . . . 159 D5
Spring The NG10 . . . . . . 193 B6
Springthorpe Rd DN21 . . 24 F8
Springvale Rd DN22 . . . . 64 E6
Springwell St
  Huthwaite NG17 . . . . 99 F2
  Huthwaite NG17 . . . . . . 100 A2
Spring Wlk NG16 . . . . . . 35 E1
Springwood Dr NG19 . . . 88 C2
Springwood Gdns NG5 . 161 F3
Springwood View Cl
  NG17 . . . . 100 C3
Spruce Ave NG16 . . . . . 128 D6
Spruce Ct S80 . . . . 35 B2
Spruce Gdns NG6 . . . . . 160 A7
Spruce Gr
  Hucknall NG15 . . . . 146 B4
  Kirkby-in-Ashfield NG17 .115 C6
Sprydon Wlk NG11 . . . . 195 F7
Spur Cres
  Worksop S80 . . . . 36 B1
  Worksop S80 . . . . 47 B8
Squares Dr NG6 . . . . . . 147 B5
Square The
  Beeston NG9 . . . . 183 F6
  Bestwood Village NG6 . . .146 E4
  Bottesford NG13 . . . . . . 181 A3
  Costock LE12 . . . . 206 C1
  Elmton S80 . . . . 58 A7
  Gotham NG11 . . . . 195 B1
  Keyworth NG12 . . . . 197 E2
  Nottingham NG8 . . . . . . 171 E4
  Rainworth NG21 . . . . . . 104 B1
  Retford DN22 . . . . 39 E7
Squires Ave NG6 . . . . . 160 B8
Squires Cl NG12 . . . . . . 189 B4
Squires Croft NG21 . . . . 90 C5
Squires Gr NG13 . . . . . . 177 C6
Squires La NG21 . . . . 90 B6
Squires Way NG2 . . . . . 185 C6
Squirrel Side Rd S81 . . . .35 B7
Squirrel Way 3 LE11 . . .220 A2
Sta App DN21 . . . . 24 D8
Stable Cl
  East Bridgford NG13 . . . 165 D3
  Worksop S81 . . . . 36 A7
Stable Yard LN1 . . . . 57 A3
Stacey Ave NG5 . . . . . . 160 F8

Stacey Rd NG19 . . . . 87 D2
Stadium Ave NG24 . . . . 140 A5
Stadium Cl S81 . . . . 35 C6
Stadium Ind Pk NG10 . . 193 F8
Stafford Ave
  New Balderton NG24 . . . 140 C4
  Nottingham NG6 . . . . . . 160 B6
Stafford Ct NG6 . . . . . . 159 F5
Staffords Acre DE74 . . . 203 C2
Stafford St
  Long Eaton NG10 . . . . . 193 F8
  Mansfield NG19 . . . . . . 101 F8
Stagsden Cres NG8 . . . . 171 C5
Staindale Dr NG8 . . . . . 160 D1
Stainforth St NG19 . . . . . 88 C2
Stainmore Gr NG13 . . . . 177 C4
Stainsborough Rd
  NG15 . . . . 145 C6
Stainsbury Mill ★ S44 . . . 85 D7
STAINSBY 85 B7
Stainsby Dr NG18 . . . . . 103 A3
Stainsby Gr NG17 . . . . . . 99 F2
Stakeford Ct NG15 . . . . 147 F2
Stamford Cl NG10 . . . . . 193 E4
Stamford Ct 4 NG5 . . . . 161 B8
Stamford Rd NG2 . . . . . 186 A6
Stamford St
  Awsworth NG16 . . . . . . 158 C4
  Eastwood NG16 . . . . . . 144 C1
  2 Ilkeston DE7 . . . . 157 E1
Stamper Cres NG17 . . . . 100 F6
Stanage Ct NG18 . . . . . 103 B5
Stancliffe Ave NG6 . . . . 160 C7
Standard Hill NG1 . . . . . 223 D2
Standhill Ave NG4 . . . . 174 B8
Standhill Inf Sch NG4 . . 174 B7
Standhill Rd NG4 . . . . . 174 B8
Stanesby Rise NG7 . . . . 184 E1
Stanford Gdns NG12 . . . 175 F4
Stanford Hill 1 LE11 . . . 220 B6
Stanford La LE12 . . . . . 220 D1
Stanford St NG1 . . . . . . 223 E2
Stanhome Dr NG2 . . . . . 185 D4
Stanhome Sq NG2 . . . . . 185 D4
Stanhope Ave
  Newark-on-Trent NG24 . .125 C3
  Nottingham NG5 . . . . . . 161 B1
Stanhope Cl
  Newthorpe NG16 . . . . . 144 B2
  Walesby NG22 . . . . 64 A2
Stanhope Cres
  Arnold NG5 . . . . 161 E8
  Stoke Bardolph NG14 . . .175 F4
Stanhope Prim Sch
  NG4 . . . . 162 D3
Stanhope Rd
  Arnold NG5 . . . . 161 E8
  Carlton NG4 . . . . 162 D3
Stanhope St
  Ilkeston DE7 . . . . 170 A6
  Long Eaton NG10 . . . . . 193 D8
  Nottingham NG1 . . . . . . 223 F2
Stanhope Way NG13 . . . 177 E4
Stanier Dr NG12 . . . . . . 186 A3
Staniland Cl 3 NG9 . . . .183 C2
STANLEY 85 D1
Stanley Ave 5 NG7 . . . . 173 A8
Stanley Cl NG15 . . . . . . 117 A3
Stanley Dr NG9 . . . . 171 A1
Stanley La NG17 . . . . 85 D2
Stanley Mws NG16 . . . . 158 D7
Stanley Pl NG1 . . . . 223 D3
Stanley Rd
  Mansfield NG18 . . . . . . 102 B4
  Mansfield Woodhouse
  NG19 . . . . 89 B1
  Nottingham, Hyson Green
  NG7 . . . . 173 A8
  Nottingham, Portchester
  NG3 . . . . 162 A1
  West Bridgford NG2 . . . 185 F6
Stanley St
  Gainsborough DN21 . . . . 24 D6
  Long Eaton NG10 . . . . . 193 E7
  Loughborough LE11 . . . . 220 B2
  Newark-on-Trent NG24 . .125 B1
  Retford DN22 . . . . 39 F4
  Retford DN22 . . . . 40 A4
  Worksop S81 . . . . 35 E5
Stanley Terr NG24 . . . . 140 B8
Stanmore Cl NG8 . . . . . 159 E3
Stanmore Gdns NG5 . . . 161 F6
Stannier Wy NG16 . . . . . 159 A7
Stansfield St
  Nottingham NG7 . . . . . . 222 A3
  Nottingham NG8 . . . . . . 172 A4
Stanstead Ave
  Nottingham NG5 . . . . . . 146 D1
  Tollerton NG12 . . . . 186 D1
Stanstead Prim Sch
  NG5 . . . . 160 E8
Stanthorne Cl NG11 . . . 185 A4
STANTON-BY-DALE . . . 170 A1
Stanton Cres NG17 . . . . 100 D3
Stanton Gate DE7 . . . . . 170 C1
STANTON HILL 100 C5
Stanton La NG12 . . . . . . 198 B2
STANTON-ON-THE-
  WOLDS 198 C1
Stanton Pl
  Mansfield NG18 . . . . . . 102 A7
  New Houghton NG19 . . . . 86 F7
Stanton Rd
  Sandiacre NG10 . . . . . . 182 A7
  Stapleford NG10 . . . . . . 182 B7
Stanton St NG19 . . . . 86 F7
Stanton Vale Sch
  NG10 . . . . 193 C7
Stanway Cl NG3 . . . . . . 174 C6

Stanwick Cl NG8 . . . . . . 171 E8
STAPLEFORD 182 E7
  Lincs 127 E8
  Notts 182 E7
Stapleford Bypass
  Stapleford NG9 . . . . 182 D4
  Stapleford NG9 . . . . 183 A8
Stapleford La
  Beeston NG9 . . . . 182 F3
  Brough NG23 . . . . 112 A1
  Coddington NG24 . . . . . 126 D3
Stapleford Rd
  Stapleford NG9 . . . . 170 D3
  Trowell NG9 . . . . 170 D3
Staplehurst Dr NG5 . . . 161 A4
Staple La NG24 . . . . 140 C2
Staples St NG3 . . . . 161 E2
Stapleton Rd DE7 . . . . . 157 E4
Starch Cl LE12 . . . . 205 E1
Starch La NG10 . . . . 182 C7
Starling Cl NG12 . . . . . . 185 C6
Starnhill Wy NG13 . . . . 177 E3
Starr Ave NG17 . . . . 100 D3
Starth Wood Rd NG15 . . 145 D4
Star Wlk 3 NG1 . . . . . . 102 E2
Statham St S81 . . . . 36 B5
STATHERN 202 F3
Stathern La LE14 . . . . . 202 B2
Stathern Rd LE14 . . . . . 202 C3
Stathern Wlk NG5 . . . . . 161 B7
Station App LN1 . . . . 57 A3
Station Ave
  Carlton NG4 . . . . 163 A1
  Ranskill DN22 . . . . 19 B5
Station Bvd LE11 . . . . . 220 C6
Station Cl NG23 . . . . . . 112 B7
Station Ct 3 DE7 . . . . . . 157 E1
Station Hill NG19 . . . . . . 88 B3
Station La
  Edwinstowe NG21 . . . . . 76 B1
  Farnsfield NG22 . . . . . . 119 E7
  Fiskerton NG25 . . . . . . 137 D4
  Ironville NG16 . . . . 128 A3
Station Rd
  Awsworth NG16 . . . . . . 158 C4
  Barnby Moor DN22 . . . . . 28 E5
  Bawtry DN10 . . . . 10 A7
  Beckingham DN10 . . . . . 23 C8
  Beeston NG9 . . . . 184 A5
  Bleasby NG14 . . . . 151 F8
  Bottesford NG13 . . . . . . 181 C3
  Burton Joyce NG14 . . . . 163 F3
  Carlton NG4 . . . . 174 F7
  Clipstone NG21 . . . . 89 E2
  Collingham NG23 . . . . . 112 A8
  Cotham NG23 . . . . 154 F1
  Cotham NG23 . . . . 155 A1
  East Leake LE12 . . . . . . 205 D1
  Edingley NG22 . . . . 120 E5
  Elton NG13 . . . . 179 F3
  Fiskerton NG25, NG23 . .137 E4
  Gainsborough DN21 . . . . 15 D1
  Gainsborough DN21 . . . . 24 D8
  Harby NG23 . . . . 70 E3
  Heanor NG16 . . . . 143 A2
  Hucknall NG15 . . . . 146 B7
  Ilkeston DE7 . . . . 157 F1
  Kegworth DE74 . . . . . . 203 F2
  Keyworth NG12 . . . . 197 E6
  Kimberley NG16 . . . . . . 158 F6
  Kingston on Soar LE12 . .204 A3
  Kirklington NG25 . . . . . 121 A5
  Kirton NG22 . . . . 78 B5
  Langley Mill NG16 . . . . 143 B2
  Long Eaton NG10 . . . . . 193 F8
  Lowdham NG14 . . . . 150 E1
  Misson DN10 . . . . 4 B3
  Newstead NG15 . . . . . . 130 E6
  Nottingham NG6 . . . . . . 160 C6
  Old Dalby LE14 . . . . 218 F4
  Ollerton NG22 . . . . 77 A3
  Orston NG13 . . . . 180 A5
  Rainworth NG21 . . . . . . 118 A8
  Ranskill DN22 . . . . 19 B4
  Retford DN22 . . . . 39 E5
  Rolleston NG23 . . . . 138 A6
  Sandiacre NG10 . . . . . . 182 C5
  Scarcliffe NG20 . . . . 72 A6
  Scrooby DN10 . . . . 10 A2
  Selston NG16 . . . . 113 E1
  Selston NG16 . . . . 128 E8
  Shirebrook NG20 . . . . . . 72 E6
  South Leverton DN22 . . . 42 A8
  Southwell NG25 . . . . . . 121 D1
  Sturton le Steeple DN22 . . 32 C6
  Sutton in Ashfield NG17 .101 B1
  Sutton on Trent NG23 . . . 96 F8
  Thurgarton NG14 . . . . . 151 D6
  Torksey LN1 . . . . 44 B3
  Upper Broughton LE14 . .218 C8
  Walkeringham DN10 . . . . 14 A5
  Whitwell S80 . . . . 45 A5
  Widmerpool NG12 . . . . . 208 E6
  Widmerpool NG12 . . . . . 209 A7
  Willoughby-on-the-Wolds
  LE14 . . . . 217 F7
Station St
  Bingham NG13 . . . . 177 F5
  Cossall DE7 . . . . 158 A2
  Kirkby-in-Ashfield NG17 .115 B5
  Long Eaton NG10 . . . . . 193 E7
  6 Mansfield NG18 . . . . . 102 B6
  Mansfield Woodhouse
  NG19 . . . . 88 B3
  Misterton DN10 . . . . 7 A2
  Nottingham NG2 . . . . . . 223 F1
  Sutton in Ashfield NG17 .100 F7
Station Terr
  Hucknall NG15 . . . . 146 B7
  Kingston on Soar DE74 . .203 F2

Station Terr continued
  Kingston on Soar NG12 . .204 A2
Radcliffe on Trent NG12 . 175 F3
Station View NG20 . . . . . 72 E2
Station Villas NG9 . . . . 184 A5
Station Yd NG17 . . . . . . 100 F7
Staunton Rd NG5 . . . . . 161 C4
Staunton Hall ★ NG13 . 169 B3
STAUNTON IN THE
  VALE 169 B4
Staunton Rd
  Cotham NG23 . . . . 155 A1
  Long Bennington NG13 . .169 F5
  Newark-on-Trent NG24 . .139 F5
  Staunton in the Vale
  NG13 . . . . 169 A6
Staveley Ct
  Farndon NG24 . . . . 139 A4
  1 Loughborough LE11 . .220 B5
Stavely Wy NG2 . . . . . . 186 C7
Staverton Rd NG8 . . . . . 171 E7
STAYTHORPE 138 D8
Staythorpe Rd
  Averham NG23 . . . . 123 E1
  Rolleston NG23 . . . . 138 C7
Steadfold Cl NG6 . . . . . 160 B6
Steadings The LN6. . . . . . 83 E3
Steads Cl NG4 . . . . 174 F7
Steedman Ave NG3 . . . . 162 A4
Steeles Dr NG24 . . . . . . 140 E3
Steeles Way NG4 . . . . . 163 B7
Steeple Row 3 LE11 . . . 220 B4
Steeples The NG17 . . . . 129 E8
Steetley La
  Rhodesia S80 . . . . 35 A4
  Whitwell S80 . . . . 34 E4
Steinbeck Rd NG4 . . . . . 174 C7
Stella Ave NG12 . . . . . . 197 D8
Stella Gr NG12 . . . . 197 D8
Stella St NG18 . . . . 102 B5
Stenton Cl NG25 . . . . . . 121 E2
Stephenson Rd 1 DE7 . .157 F8
Stephenson Way NG24 . 125 C3
Stepnall Hts NG22 . . . . . 77 E6
Stepney Ct NG8 . . . . . . 159 F1
Sterling Cl S81 . . . . 35 E8
Sterling Dr NG24 . . . . . 125 E1
Sterndale Rd NG10 . . . . 193 B6
Sternthorpe Cl NG23 . . . 81 E1
Steven Cl NG9 . . . . 182 F4
Stevenholme Cres
  NG5 . . . . 161 A6
Stevens Cres NG17 . . . . 100 E2
Stevens Gdns NG11 . . . 196 D6
Stevenson Rd S81 . . . . . 36 B4
Stevens Rd NG10 . . . . . 182 A5
Stewart Cl S81 . . . . 25 E6
Stewarton Cl NG5 . . . . . 148 B1
Stewart Rd S81 . . . . 25 D6
Stewart Way NG5 . . . . . 130 D7
Stiles Rd NG5 . . . . 162 C6
Stillwell Gdns 5 S81 . . . 35 D8
Stinsford Cl 6 NG5 . . . . 161 C8
Stinting La
  Mansfield Woodhouse
  NG19 . . . . 88 E2
  Shirebrook NG20 . . . . . . 72 D3
Stirling Ave
  Bawtry DN10 . . . . 10 A8
  Mansfield NG19 . . . . . . 101 E5
Stirling Cl DN21 . . . . 15 E2
Stirling Dr
  Carlton in Lindrick S81 . . 25 E6
  Newark-on-Trent NG24 . .125 E2
Stirling Gdns NG9 . . . . . 183 B2
Stirling Gr
  Kimberley NG16 . . . . . . 158 E7
  Nottingham NG11 . . . . . 195 F8
Stirling Rd NG22 . . . . . . 39 D5
Stirling Way LN6. . . . . . . 71 F4
Stockdale Cl NG5 . . . . . 147 A2
Stockgill Cl NG2 . . . . . . 186 C6
Stockhill Cir NG8 . . . . . 160 C2
Stockhill La NG6. . . . . . . 160 C3
Stocking La
  Askham DN22 . . . . 51 E3
  East Leake LE12 . . . . . . 205 D4
Stocks Fold
  East Markham NG22 . . . . 65 F7
  Tuxford NG22 . . . . 66 F7
Stocks Rd NG16 . . . . . . 158 E7
Stockton St 4 NG6 . . . . 160 B7
Stock Well NG6 . . . . 160 B6
Stockwell Gate 8
  NG18 . . . . 102 B7
Stockwell La NG12 . . . . 189 B4
Stockwell The LE12 . . . . 216 C3
Stockwith Rd DN10 . . . . 14 B8
Stodman Mews NG24 . . 139 F8
Stodman St NG24 . . . . . 139 F8
Stoke Ave NG24 . . . . . . 139 E4
STOKE BARDOLPH 175 F7
Stoke Ferry La NG14 . . . 164 A1
Stokeham Rd
  Laneham DN22 . . . . 53 F5
  Laneham DN22 . . . . 54 A5
Stoke La NG14 . . . . 163 F2
Stokes Ind Est NG18 . . . 101 E4
Stolle Cl NG5 . . . . 162 C7
Stoneacre NG5 . . . . 161 B8
Stone Ave DE75 . . . . . . 143 A1
Stone Bank NG18 . . . . . 102 D4
Stonebridge City Farm ★
Stonebridge Ct Ind Est 9
  NG3 . . . . 173 E5
Stonebridge La LE12 . . 205 F2
Stonebridge La NG20 . . . 74 A4
Stone Bridge Rd NG3 . . 173 E5

Stonebridge Way
  NG14 . . . . 148 C8
Stonechurch View
  NG15 . . . . 130 B8
Stone Cres NG19 . . . . . 101 D7
Stonecroft S80 . . . . 45 C6
Stone Cross La NG18 . . 102 B8
Stone Gr NG20 . . . . 59 A1
Stonehaven Cl NG5 . . . 148 A2
Stonehill Cl DN22 . . . . . . 19 B5
Stonehills DE74 . . . . . . 203 C2
Stonehills Way NG17 . . 101 B4
Stonehurst La LE12 . . . 213 D3
Stone La DN22 . . . . 31 D8
Stoneleigh Cl NG9 . . . . 183 C5
Stoneleigh Cl NG18 . . . 102 E5
Stoneleigh St NG7 . . . . 222 C3
Stonemasons Mews
  NG17 . . . . 115 B5
Stone Mdws NG10 . . . . 193 E5
Stonepit Cl NG3 . . . . . . 161 F1
Stonepit Wood Access
  Gotham NG11 . . . . 194 E1
  Gotham NG11 . . . . 204 E8
Stone Rd End NG23 . . . . 80 E7
Stonesby Vale NG2 . . . . 185 B3
Stones Cl 3 NG16 . . . . . 144 A2
Stonesdale Cl NG5 . . . . 161 C5
Stoney Bank NG14 . . . . 150 D2
Stoneycroft Rd NG6 . . . 160 E5
Stoneyford Rd NG17 . . . 100 E4
Stoney Houghton Gdns
  NG6 . . . . 159 F8
Stoney La
  Brinsley NG16 . . . . 143 D6
  Selston NG16 . . . . 128 E7
  Trowell NG9 . . . . 170 B5
Stoney St
  Beeston NG9 . . . . 183 F7
  Nottingham NG1 . . . . . . 223 F2
  Sutton in Ashfield NG17 .101 A3
Stoney View NG16 . . . . 143 A5
Stonish Hill NG22 . . . . . 92 C1
Stony Field La NG22 . . . 106 A6
Stoppard Cl DE7 . . . . . . 157 D2
Storcroft Rd DN22 . . . . . 40 A5
Storey Ave 7 NG4 . . . . . 162 E2
Stormont Cl DE55 . . . . . 113 B4
Stornoway Cl NG9 . . . . 184 B5
Storth Ave NG15 . . . . . . 146 A6
Storthfield Way DE55 . . 113 B4
Storth La DE55 . . . . 113 B4
Stort Sq NG19 . . . . 88 D2
Story Gdns NG15 . . . . . 146 C5
Stotfield Rd NG8 . . . . . . 171 B5
Stourdale Cl NG10 . . . . 193 A6
Stow Ct NG19 . . . . 88 E3
Stowe Ave NG2 . . . . . . 185 D5
Stow Pk Rd DN21 . . . . . 44 D8
Strafford St DN21 . . . . . . 24 D6
Stragglethorpe Rd
  Cotgrave NG12 . . . . 187 D3
  Cotgrave NG12 . . . . 188 B6
Straggle Thorpe Rd
  NG4 . . . . 175 C1
Straight Mile DN22 . . . . 38 D6
Strand The NG9 . . . . . . 183 D1
Stranraer Cl NG19 . . . . . 88 C6
Stratford Cl NG4 . . . . . . 174 F5
Stratford Cres DN22 . . . . 39 D6
Stratford Rd NG2 . . . . . 185 F7
Stratford St DE7 . . . . . . 157 F4
Strathavon Rd S81 . . . . . 25 F6
Strathglen Cl NG16 . . . . 158 E7
Strathmore Cl NG15 . . . 145 E3
Strathmore Cl NG11 . . . . 9 A5
Strathmore Dr S81 . . . . . 25 F6
Strathmore Rd NG5 . . . 148 B1
Strawberry Bank NG17 . . 99 E4
Strawberry Fields NG23 . 96 F8
Strawberry Hall La
  NG24 . . . . 125 B2
Strawberry Rd DN22 . . . 40 A6
Strawberry Way NG19 . . 103 B8
Straws Croft NG13 . . . . 165 D3
Straw's La NG13 . . . . . . 165 D3
Street La Rd DN22 . . . . . 42 E8
STRELLEY 171 B8
Strelley Cl NG15 . . . . . . 130 F2
Strelley La NG8 . . . . 171 B7
Strelley Rd NG8 . . . . . . 159 E1
Strelley St NG6 . . . . 160 B7
Striding Edge Cl NG10 . 182 B2
Stringer Cl DE7 . . . . 157 E2
Stripe Rd
  Tickhill DN11 . . . . 8 E7
  Tickhill DN11 . . . . 8 E8
Stripes View NG14 . . . . 148 F6
Strome Cl 8 NG2 . . . . . 173 B2
Strome Ct 1 NG2 . . . . . 173 C2
Stroud Cl NG13 . . . . 181 B3
Stroud Cl NG13 . . . . 181 B3
Stroud's Cl LE14 . . . . . . 211 F8
Strutt Cl 5 DE55 . . . . 99 A3
Stuart Ave
  Mansfield NG18 . . . . . . 102 F8
  New Ollerton NG22 . . . . 77 D6
Stuart Cl NG5 . . . . 162 B8
Stuart St
  Mansfield NG18 . . . . . . 102 E7
  Sutton in Ashfield NG17 .100 E1
Stubbing La S80 . . . . 35 D3
Stubbins La NG25 . . . . . 136 C5
Stubbins Wood NG20 . . . 72 E6
Stubbins Wood La NG20 . 72 E5
Stubbin Wood Sch
  NG20 . . . . 72 E6
Stubbin Wood Sch (Main
  Site) NG20 . . . . 72 D6
Stubton Rd NG23 . . . . . 156 F6
Studland Cl NG19 . . . . . . 88 D6

Studland Way NG2 . . . . 185 C5
Stukeley Ct NG24 . . . . . 125 D4
Sturgate Wlk DN21 . . . . . 24 F7
Sturgeon Ave NG11 . . . 184 E4
Sturmer Way 6 NG8 . . . 172 B7
Sturton CE Prim Sch
  DN22 . . . . 32 D4
STURTON LE STEEPLE . 32 D5
Sturton Rd
  Bole DN22 . . . . 23 D2
  North Leverton with
  Habblesthorpe DN22 . . . . 32 D1
  Saxilby LN1 . . . . 57 A7
  South Wheatley DN22 . . . 31 E7
  Sturton le Steeple DN22 . . 32 A8
Sturton St NG7 . . . . 173 A8
St.Werburghs View 4
  DE55 . . . . 99 A3
Styring St NG9 . . . . 183 F6
STYRRUP 8 D1
Styrrup Cl DN11 . . . . 8 D1
Styrrup La DN11 . . . . 8 B1
Styrrup Rd DN11 . . . . 8 E3
Sudbury Ave
  Ilkeston DE7 . . . . 170 A7
  Sandiacre NG10 . . . . . . 182 B6
Sudbury Ct NG18 . . . . . 103 B5
Sudbury Dr NG17 . . . . . . 99 F2
Sudbury Mews NG16 . . 143 E1
Suez St NG7 . . . . 160 F1
Suff La NG16 . . . . 113 C3
Suffolk Ave
  Beeston NG9 . . . . 184 C1
  Bircotes DN11 . . . . 9 D4
  Hucknall NG15 . . . . 145 C5
Suffolk Gr DN11 . . . . 9 C4
Suffolk Rd DN11 . . . . 9 C4
Sulby Cl NG19 . . . . 89 B2
Sulis Gdns S81 . . . . 35 E8
Sullivan Cl NG3 . . . . . . 174 A6
Sulney Cl LE14 . . . . 209 F1
Sumburgh Rd NG11 . . . 185 A1
Summercourt Dr NG15 . 116 F3
Summer Cres NG9 . . . . 184 B7
Summerdowns NG19 . . . 89 A1
Summer Dr NG12 . . . . . 185 D5
Summerfield Cl NG23 . . 156 E2
Summerfield Rd 11
  NG17 . . . . 114 E7
Summerfields Way
  DE7 . . . . 157 D3
Summerfields Way S
  DE7 . . . . 157 D2
Summergangs La DN21 . 24 D5
Summer Hill DN21 . . . . . 15 E1
Summer Leys La NG2 . . 223 F1
Summer's Rd NG24 . . . 125 A2
Summer Way NG12 . . . . 175 E4
Summerwood La NG11 . 195 E7
Summit Cl NG17 . . . . . . 115 A6
Summit Dr NG20 . . . . . . 72 E4
Sunbeam St NG13 . . . . . 179 B4
Sunbourne Ct NG7. . . . . 222 C4
Sunbury Gdns NG5 . . . . 148 A1
Sunderland Farm Cl
  DN11 . . . . 8 C7
Sunderland Gr
  Nottingham NG8 . . . . . . 159 D2
  Tickhill DN11 . . . . 8 C7
Sunderland Pl DN11 . . . . 8 B7
Sunderland St DN11 . . . . 8 B7
Sundown Adventureland ★
  DN22 . . . . 42 E3
Sundown Dr NG12 . . . . 188 A5
Sundridge Pk Cl NG2 . . 185 C5
Sunfield Ave S81 . . . . . . 36 A4
Sunflower Cl NG20 . . . . . 72 D3
Sunflower Dr NG12 . . . . 186 A2
Sunlea Cres NG9 . . . . . 182 F5
Sunningdale Dr NG14 . . 149 C5
Sunningdale Rd NG6. . . . 160 E6
Sunningdale Way DN21 . 15 E2
Sunninghill Dr NG11 . . . 184 E3
Sunninghill Rise NG5 . . 148 A1
Sunny Bank
  Mansfield NG18 . . . . . . 102 C3
  Newton DE55 . . . . 99 A5
  Worksop DE55 . . . . 36 A4
Sunny Bank Gdns DN10 . 12 F3
Sunnydale Rd NG3. . . . . 174 B6
Sunnymede S81 . . . . 36 A6
Sunny Row NG15 . . . . . 171 E5
Sunnyside
  Farnsfield NG22 . . . . . . 119 F5
  Whitwell S80 . . . . 45 A6
  Worksop S81 . . . . 35 F6
Sunnyside Rd NG9 . . . . 183 C6
Sunnyside Spencer Acad
  NG9 . . . . 183 B6
Sunray Gr NG15 . . . . . . 145 E8
Sunridge Ct NG3 . . . . . 173 C8
Sunrise Ave NG5 . . . . . 160 F5
Sunrise Hill Nature
  Reserve ★ NG5 . . . . . . 161 A6
Sunset Ave NG14 . . . . . 149 C6
Sunshine Cl NG16 . . . . . 113 D4
Sunstone Gr NG17 . . . . 114 D8
Superbowl 2000 ★
  NG18 . . . . 102 F2
Surbiton Sq NG8 . . . . . 160 B3
Surfleet Cl NG8 . . . . . . 171 C3
Surgery La NG21 . . . . . 118 A4
Surgey's La NG5 . . . . . . 148 A2
Surrey Dr NG19 . . . . . . 101 F8

Susan Cl NG15..........131 B1
Susan Dr NG6............160 D4
Sussex Cl NG16..........158 A8
Sussex Way NG10......182 B5
Sutherland Cl S81...... 25 F8
Sutherland Dr NG2......186 A4
Sutherland Rd NG2....174 B7
Suthers Rd DE74........203 C2
Suthers Sch The NG24...140 E1
Sutton Ave NG24.........139 E5
Sutton Back La NG15...116 B4
SUTTON BONINGTON...213 A7
Sutton Bonington Prim Sch
  LE12................213 B6
Sutton Bonington Spinney
  & Mdws Nature Reserve *
  LE12................213 A7
Sutton Cl
  Bottesford NG13........181 B3
  Sutton Bonington LE12..213 C5
  Sutton in Ashfield NG17..101 A6
Sutton Com Acad
  NG17................100 F2
Sutton Ct NG16..........143 F2
SUTTON CUM LOUND... 28 F6
Sutton Cum Lound CE Prim
  Sch DN22.............. 29 A6
SUTTON FOREST
  SIDE................101 B3
Sutton Gdns NG11......196 C6
SUTTON IN ASHFIELD..100 D5
Sutton La
  Elton NG13............179 F1
  Granby NG13...........191 D6
  Retford DN22.......... 29 A1
  Sutton NG13...........191 E8
Sutton L Ctr NG17......100 F2
Sutton Mid La NG17....114 F6
SUTTON ON TRENT.... 96 E7
Sutton-on-Trent Prim Sch
  NG23................ 97 A8
Sutton Parkway Sta
  NG17................115 B8
Sutton Passeys Cres
  NG8.................172 B3
Sutton Pool Complex
  NG17................100 E2
Sutton Rd
  Arnold NG5............147 F2
  Beckingham LN5........142 E6
  Huthwaite NG17........ 99 F3
  Kegworth DE74........203 C1
  Kirkby-in-Ashfield NG17 .114 E6
  Mansfield NG18........101 E5
  Redmile NG13.........192 C5
  Sutton in Ashfield NG17 .100 A3
Sutton Road Prim Sch
  NG18................101 F6
Swab's La
  Cropwell Bishop NG12...188 F1
  Owthorpe NG12.........199 F8
Swain's Ave NG3........174 A6
Swale Cl NG6...........160 D7
Swaledale S81.......... 36 A7
Swaledale Cl NG8......160 C1
Swale Dr **5** DN21....... 15 F2
Swale Gr NG13..........177 D3
Swales Cl DN22........ 39 C8
Swallow Cl
  Mansfield NG18........103 B4
  Nottingham NG6........160 D3
Swallow Cres NG15....132 A8
Swallow Ct DN10....... 7 A2
Swallow Dr
  Bingham NG13.........177 F3
  Claypole NG23.........156 D7
Swallow Gate LN1..... 57 A5
Swallow Gdns NG4.....162 B1
Swallow Gr S81........ 35 D7
Swallows Dr LE14......202 F3
Swallow Wlk LE12......213 A1
Swan NG21.............118 B6
Swan Ct
  12 Gainsborough DN21... 15 F1
  Sutton Bonington LE12 ..213 B6
  Worksop S81.......... 35 C7
Swan La
  Mansfield Woodhouse
    NG19.............. 88 B3
  New Ollerton NG22..... 77 C6
Swan Mdw NG4.........174 F4
Swann Yd NG17........ 99 F3
Swansdowne Dr NG7..184 F2
Swanson Ave NG17.... 99 F3
Swans Quay DN22..... 39 F5
Swan St
  Bawtry DN10........... 10 A6
  Loughborough LE11....220 B4
Swanton Cl DN22...... 29 C2
Swanwick Ave NG20... 72 F3
Swanwick Rd DE7......157 F5
Sweeney Ct **3** NG5....161 A8
Sweet Leys Dr LE12...205 E3
Sweet Leys Rd **7** NG2..173 C1
Swenson Ave NG7......222 A1
Sweyn La **6** DN21.... 15 F2
Swift Cl NG6...........143 F2
Swift Dr NG24..........140 A4
Swift's Cl LE12.........216 C3
Swifts Vw NG17........114 F1
Swigert Cl NG6.........159 F5
Swildon Wlk NG5.......160 F8
Swinburne Cl NG24....140 D5
Swinburne S **3** NG3..173 F6
Swinburne Way NG5...161 F7
Swindale Cl NG12......186 B7
Swindell Cl NG3.......162 B5

Swinderby Cl
  Gateford S81.......... 35 C8
  Newark-on-Trent NG24..125 D1
Swinderby Rd
  Collingham NG23.......112 B8
  Eagle LN6............. 84 A1
  Eagle LN6............. 84 D1
  North Scarle LN6....... 83 E2
Swindon Cl NG16.......158 B7
Swindon Rd NG9.......183 A2
Swiney Way NG9.......183 A2
Swinfen Broun NG18...102 C3
Swingate NG16.........159 A5
Swinnow Rd DN11...... 9 C4
Swinscoe Gdns NG5...160 F8
Swinstead Cl NG8.....171 F6
Swinton Copse NG22... 77 E6
Swinton Rise NG15....117 A2
Swish La NG22.........105 F8
Swithland Dr NG2.....185 E4
Swynford Cl LN1....... 55 B4
Sycamore Acad NG3...223 F4
Sycamore Ave
  Glapwell S44.......... 86 B8
  Kirkby-in-Ashfield NG17 .114 E6
  Torksey Lock LN1...... 44 C1
Sycamore Cl
  Bingham NG13.........178 A4
  Hucknall NG15.........145 E5
  Newark-on-Trent NG24..139 D3
  Pinxton NG16..........113 D3
  Radcliffe on Trent NG12 .175 F2
  Rainworth NG21.......104 B1
  Retford DN22.......... 40 A5
  Ruddington NG11......196 D7
  Selston NG16..........128 D7
  Worksop S80.......... 35 E1
Sycamore Cres
  Bawtry DN10........... 9 F7
  Sandiacre NG10.......182 A7
Sycamore Ct
  Beeston NG9...........184 A7
  Retford DN22.......... 39 E4
Sycamore Dr
  Gainsborough DN21.... 15 E2
  Ilkeston DE7...........170 B7
Sycamore La NG14.....152 B7
Sycamore Pl **2** NG3..173 C8
Sycamore Rd
  Awsworth NG16........158 C5
  Carlton in Lindrick S81 ... 25 E7
  East Leake LE12.......214 D8
  Long Eaton NG10......193 C5
  Mansfield Woodhouse
    NG19.............. 88 C3
  New Ollerton NG22..... 77 D4
Sycamore Rise NG6...160 C4
Sycamores The NG20.. 74 A6
Sycamores The
  Eastwood NG16........143 E1
  South Normanton DE55 ..113 A6
  Stanton Hill NG17......100 D5
Sycamore Works **1**
  NG6.................160 C8
Sydenham Ct **6** NG7..172 E2
Syderstone Wlk NG5...161 F6
Sydney Cl NG19........ 88 C6
Sydney Gdns **2** NG24..140 E2
Sydney Gr NG12........175 E3
Sydney St NG24........125 A1
Sydney Terr **3** NG24...140 E4
SYERSTON.............153 B4
Syerston Hall Pk
  Syerston NG23.........153 A4
  Syerston NG25.........152 F4
Syerston Rd NG18.....103 A2
Syerston Wy NG24.....125 D1
Syke Rd NG8...........160 F8
Sykes La
  Balderton NG24........140 D3
  Saxilby LN1........... 56 E5
  Saxilby LN1........... 56 F4
Sykes Mws LN1........ 57 A3
Sylvan Ave NG17.......115 A3
Sylvan Cres NG17......101 A5
Sylvan Way
  Fernwood NG23........156 A4
  Fernwood NG24........155 F7
Sylvester Ct NG21...... 76 D3
Sylvester St NG18......101 F6
Symmetry Dr S81...... 18 A6
Symmetry Way S81.... 18 A6
Synge Cl NG11.........195 C8
Sywell Cl NG17.........100 F5

T

Taft Ave NG10.........182 B6
Taft Leys Rd LE12.....205 F2
Taiga Pl S80........... 35 B5
Talbot Cl NG12........175 E3
Talbot Dr NG9.........170 D2
Talbot Rd
  Bircotes DN11......... 9 A4
  Worksop S80.......... 36 A2
Talbot St
  Mansfield NG18........102 B4
  Nottingham NG1.......223 D3
  Pinxton NG16..........113 C2
Tales of Robin Hood The *
  NG1.................223 B2
Tall Gables LE12....... 54 C1
Tamarix Cl NG4........163 A2
Tambling Cl NG5.......162 B6
Tame Cl NG11..........184 E4
Tamworth Gr NG7......184 F2
Tamworth Rd
  Long Eaton NG10......193 B4
  Long Eaton NG10......193 C5

Tangmere Cres NG8...159 E5
Tanner's La LE12.......213 A1
Tannery Rd NG16.......158 C7
Tannery Wharf NG24..139 E8
Tannin Cres NG16......160 C5
Tansley Heath NG18...103 C5
Tansy Wy NG13........177 C3
Tanwood Rd NG9......183 B1
Tanyard NG7.......... 79 E6
Tapestry Cl NG5.......161 E2
Tapton Pk **3** NG18....103 B7
Tarbert Cl NG2.........173 B2
Target St NG7..........222 A3
Tarmac Way NG20..... 73 D8
Tarn Cl NG16..........143 B4
Tarrat St **2** DE7.......157 E2
Tasmania Cl NG14.....173 C1
Tatham's La DE7.......157 E2
Tathams Orchard
  NG25................121 D1
Tatmarsh LE11.........220 B5
Tattersall Cl NG21..... 76 B2
Tattersall Wlk NG19... 88 E4
Tattershall Dr
  Beeston NG9...........184 B7
  Nottingham NG7.......222 C2
  Nottingham NG7.......222 D2
Taunton Rd NG2.......185 F6
Taunton Way DN22.... 39 E4
Taupo Dr NG15.........145 D5
Taurus Cl NG18........102 E1
Tavern Ave NG6........160 C2
Tavistock Ave NG3.....161 C1
Tavistock Cl NG15.....145 D5
Tavistock Dr NG3.......161 C1
Tavistock Rd NG2......185 F6
Taylor Cres
  Stapleford NG9........182 E8
  Sutton in Ashfield NG17 .100 F1
Taylor Pl NG14.........173 E8
Taylor's Cl NG18.......102 E8
Taylors Croft NG14....149 C4
Taylor St DE7..........157 F1
Teague Pl S80......... 35 D3
Teak Cl NG3...........173 D7
Teal Ave NG18.........103 B4
Tealby Cl NG6..........159 F7
Tealby Wlk NG19...... 88 E4
Teal Cl
  Carlton NG4...........175 B6
  Shirebrook NG20...... 72 D3
Teal Ct S81........... 35 D7
Teal Wharf **4** NG2....173 A2
Teasels The NG13.....177 D3
Technology Dr NG6....184 A5
Ted Baker Way LN1.... 57 C3
Tedburn Dr NG3........103 A2
Teesbrook Dr NG8.....171 B4
Tees Ct NG13..........177 D3
Teesdale Ct NG9.......183 A4
Teesdale Rd
  Long Eaton NG10......193 A6
  Nottingham NG5.......161 B2
Teign Bank
  East Leake LE12.......205 E3
  Mansfield Woodhouse
    NG19.............. 88 F4
Teignmouth Ave
  Mansfield NG18........102 F6
  Mansfield NG18........103 A6
Telford Dr
  Eastwood NG16........144 B3
  Newark-on-Trent NG24..125 C3
Temperance La
  Collingham NG23.......111 F8
  Collingham NG23.......112 A7
Templar Rd NG9........184 B6
Templars St NG7.......222 A4
Temple Cres NG16.....159 D4
Temple Dr NG16.......159 E4
Templemans Way
  NG25................136 F8
Templemen Cl NG15...196 B7
Templeoak Dr NG8.....171 D3
Tenantshall Cl NG8....172 A1
Tenbury Cres NG16....160 C1
Tenby Gr S80.......... 36 A2
Tene Cl NG5...........147 F2
Tenman La NG13.......166 A2
Tennis Ct Ind Est NG2..174 A3
Tennis Dr NG7.........222 C2
Tennis Mews NG7......222 C2
Tennyson Ave
  Carlton NG4...........162 F1
  Carlton NG4...........163 A1
  Mansfield Woodhouse
    NG19.............. 88 C2
Tennyson Ct NG15.....145 D6
Tennyson Dr
  Beeston NG9...........183 D2
  Worksop S81.......... 36 C4
Tennyson Rd
  Arnold NG5............161 E4
  Balderton NG24........140 D4
Tennyson Sq NG16....158 C4
Tennyson St
  Gainsborough DN21.... 15 D1
  Ilkeston DE7...........157 E3
  Kirkby-in-Ashfield NG17 .115 B4
  10 Mansfield NG18....102 B7
  Nottingham NG7.......222 C2
Tenter Cl
  Long Eaton NG10......193 D5
  Nottingham NG5.......160 F8
  Sutton Forest Side NG17 .101 A3
Tenter La NG18........102 A5
Tenters La NG22....... 92 E1
Tenzing Wlk NG24.....140 E4
Terrace La NG19....... 86 F5
Terrace Rd NG18......102 C8
Terrace St **1** NG7.....172 F7
Terrian Cres NG2.......185 F2
Terry Ave NG24........125 B3

Terton Rd NG5.........160 F8
Tetford Wlk NG19..... 88 E4
Tethering La DN10..... 12 A4
Tetney Wlk NG8........172 A6
Tettenbury Rd NG5....160 F3
TEVERSAL.............100 C8
Teversal Ave
  Nottingham NG7.......222 B2
  Pleasleyhill NG19......101 A8
Teversal Pastures Nature
  Reserve * NG17.......100 E8
Teversal Visitor Ctr *
  NG17................100 B7
Tevery Cl NG9..........182 E8
Teviot Rd NG5.........160 F5
Tewkesbury Ave NG19 .. 88 D4
Tewkesbury Cl NG2....186 A6
Tewkesbury Dr
  Kimberley NG16.......158 E7
  Nottingham NG6.......160 E4
Tewkesbury Rd NG10..193 E4
Thackeray Cl S81...... 36 B4
Thackeray's La NG5...161 E5
Thackerey St NG7......222 B4
Thales Dr NG5.........162 C7
Thames St NG6........160 B7
Thane Rd
  Beeston NG9...........184 C5
  Nottingham NG9.......184 E6
Thatcham Cl NG8......172 D7
Thatch Carr Bank DN9 .. 2 A8
Thatchmarsh Cl DE7...157 F6
Thaxted Cl NG8........171 D6
Theaker Ave NG21.... 15 F1
Theaker La DN10...... 10 D5
Theatre Sq NG1........223 D3
Thelda Ave NG12......197 E3
Theresa Ct NG24......140 D4
Thetford Cl NG5........162 A6
Thickley Bank NG20... 72 F4
Thievesdale Ave S81... 35 F7
Thievesdale Cl S81.... 36 A7
Thievesdale La S81.... 37 A8
Thieves Wood La
  NG15................116 C8
Third Ave
  Beeston NG9...........184 C6
  Carlton, Gedling NG4... 162 F1
  Carlton, Thorneywood
    NG4...............174 B8
  Clipstone NG21........ 89 F3
  Edwinstowe NG21...... 76 A1
  Mansfield NG21........103 F2
  Mansfield Woodhouse
    NG19.............. 89 A1
  Nottingham NG6.......160 D7
Thirlbeck NG12........188 A1
Thirlmere Cl NG2......186 D5
Thirlmere Cl
  Long Eaton NG10......182 B2
  Nottingham NG3.......173 F7
Thirlmere Rd NG10....182 B2
Thirston Cl NG6........159 F7
Thistle Bank
  East Leake LE12.......205 E3
  Mansfield Woodhouse
    NG19.............. 88 F4
Thistle Cl NG16........158 B8
Thistledown Rd NG11..195 E7
Thistle Gn Cl DE75....143 B1
Thistle Rd DE7.........170 A4
Thomas Ave NG12.....176 C3
Thomas Cl NG3.........223 F4
Thomas Cook Pl LE11 .. 220 C5
Thomas Parkyn Cl
  NG11................206 E7
Thomas Pl NG23.......110 F1
Thomas Rd
  Kegworth DE74........203 C1
  Newark-on-Trent NG24 ..140 F2
Thomas St DN22...... 39 F5
Thompson Ave DN11... 8 F4
Thompson Cl
  Beeston NG9...........183 C3
  Coddington NG24......125 E2
  East Leake LE12.......205 E2
  Nether Broughton LE14 .219 C8
Thompson Cres NG17..100 F1
Thompson Gdns NG5..147 A1
Thompson St NG16....143 B3
Thonock Ave DN21.... 15 E3
Thonock Dr LN1....... 56 F4
Thonock Rd DN10..... 15 E5
Thoresby Ave
  Carlton NG4...........162 D2
  Edwinstowe NG21...... 76 A2
  Kirkby-in-Ashfield NG17 .115 D4
  Newark-on-Trent NG24..140 A6
  Nottingham NG2.......173 F3
Thoresby Cl
  Harworth DN11........ 9 B5
  Meden Vale NG20...... 74 D8
  Radcliffe on Trent NG12 .176 A4
Thoresby Cres NG17...100 C6
Thoresby Ct NG3.......173 D8
Thoresby Dale NG15...146 B7
Thoresby Gall (Pierrepont
  Art Gall) * NG22...... 62 D2
Thoresby Glade NG22..106 A5
Thoresby Pk NG22..... 62 F3
Thoresby Rd
  Beeston NG9...........171 C2
  Bingham NG13.........177 C4
  Clumber and Hardwick
    S80................ 47 F3
  Long Eaton NG10......193 C6
  Mansfield NG18........103 F1
  Mansfield Woodhouse
    NG19.............. 88 A3

Thoresby St
  3 Mansfield NG18....102 A7
  10 Nottingham NG2...173 A4
  Sutton in Ashfield NG17 .101 A4
Thoresby Way DN22... 39 E3
Thoresby Wood NG22.. 65 F7
Thor Gdns NG5........146 F2
Thorn Ave NG19....... 87 F1
Thorn Bank DN9....... 2 C8
Thornbury Dr NG15....160 F7
Thornbury Hill La S81.. 16 D8
Thornbury Way NG5...160 F7
Thorncliffe Rd NG3....173 C8
Thorncliffe Rise NG3...173 C8
Thorndale Rd
  Calverton NG14.......148 F7
  Nottingham NG6.......160 C2
Thorndike Cl NG9......184 B4
Thorndike Way NG21.. 24 E7
Thorn Dr NG16.........158 B8
Thorner Cl NG6........160 E5
Thorne Rd
  Bawtry DN10.......... 10 B8
  Harworth DN11........ 8 D4
THORNEY............. 69 F7
Thorney Abbey Rd
  NG21................118 B5
Thorney Ct **8** NG18...103 A2
Thorney Hill NG3.......173 F7
Thorney Rd
  Wigsley LN1........... 69 F1
  Wigsley NG23......... 70 A2
THORNEYWOOD.......174 B8
Thorneywood Ave
  NG17................129 E8
Thorneywood Mount
  NG3.................173 F7
Thorneywood Rd NG10 .193 F8
Thornfield Ind Est NG3 .173 F5
Thornfield Way NG3...178 F5
Thorn Gr NG15.........146 B4
Thornham Cres NG17..129 F8
Thornhill Cl NG9.......171 B2
Thornhill Dr
  Boughton NG22........ 77 E5
  South Normanton DE55 ..113 B6
Thornhill La DN22..... 33 C2
Thornhill Rd DN11..... 8 E4
Thornley St **7** NG7...172 E7
Thornthwaite Cl NG2..186 C6
Thornton Ave NG5.....147 D1
Thornton Cl
  Bilsthorpe NG22.......106 A5
  Mansfield NG18........103 B5
  Nottingham NG8.......171 E4
Thornton Dale S81..... 36 B7
Thornton Mws NG3....177 D6
Thorntons Cl NG12....188 A2
Thornton St
  Gainsborough DN21.... 24 D7
  Sutton in Ashfield NG17 .100 F1
Thorn Tree Gdns NG16 .143 F4
Thorold Ct NG7........184 C2
THOROTON............167 E2
Thoroton Ave NG24....140 D3
Thoroton Rd
  Hawksworth NG23.....167 D2
  Thoroton NG13........179 D8
  Thoroton NG13........167 E1
Thoroton St NG7.......222 C3
Thoroughfare La NG23 .125 D7
THORPE..............138 F1
Thorpe Cl
  Coddington NG24......126 B2
  Newark-on-Trent NG24 ..139 E4
  18 Nottingham NG5....161 A8
  Stapleford NG9........182 D7
Thorpe Cres NG3......162 A1
Thorpe Farm Cl DN22.. 52 C6
Thorpe La
  Eagle LN6............. 84 E2
  Farndon NG24.........139 A3
  Shireoaks S80......... 34 C6
Thorpelands Ave NG19 .. 88 E1
Thorpe Lea NG14......165 A5
Thorpe Leys NG10.....193 D5
Thorpe Rd
  Eastwood NG16........143 F4
  Mansfield NG18........103 A2
  Mattersey DN10....... 20 B8
THORPE SALVIN...... 34 A6
Thorpe St
  Askham DN22.......... 52 C7
  Ilkeston DE7...........157 E3
Thrapston Ave NG5....147 F2
Threadneedle Way
  NG24................140 A4
Three Leys La DN22... 32 D3
Three Tuns Rd NG16...144 A2
Threlkeld Cl NG12.....186 C6
THRUMPTON...........194 C3
Thrumpton Ave NG10..194 A7
Thrumpton Cl DN22... 39 F4
Thrumpton Dr NG2....173 B1
Thrumpton Hall *
  NG11................194 B3
Thrumpton La DN22... 39 F5
Thrumpton Prim Sch
  DN22................ 39 F4
Thurcaton Way DE55.. 99 A3
THURGARTON..........151 D7
Thurgarton Ave **8**
  NG2.................173 F4
Thurgarton La
  Thurgarton NG14......151 D5
  Thurgarton NG14......151 E3
Thurgarton Sta NG14..151 D6

Thurland St NG1.......223 E2
Thurlby Cl NG12.......189 A4
Thurlby Ct NG19...... 88 E4
Thurlby La
  Stanton-on-the-Wolds
    NG12.............198 C1
  Widmerpool NG12.....208 D8
Thurlby Rd DN21...... 24 F8
Thurlestone Dr NG3...162 C6
Thurley Wlk NG18.....103 B4
Thurloe Ct NG11.......185 C3
Thurman Dr NG12.....187 F3
Thurman St
  Ilkeston DE7...........170 A6
  Nottingham NG7.......222 B4
Thursby Rd NG11......184 E3
Thymus Wlk NG11.....184 C1
Thyra Ct NG3..........161 E1
Thyra Gr
  Beeston NG9...........184 A6
  Nottingham NG3.......161 D1
Tiberius Gdns NG15...146 C8
TIBSHELF.............. 99 C6
Tibshelf Bsns Pk DE55 .. 99 C5
Tibshelf Inf Sch DE55 .. 99 A7
Tibshelf Rd NG17......100 A7
TICKHILL.............. 8 B8
Tickhill Castle * DN11 .. 8 A8
TICKHILL.............. 8 B8
Tickhill Rd
  Bawtry DN10.......... 9 F7
  Harworth DN11........ 8 E5
Tickhill St Mary's CE Prim
  Sch DN11............. 8 A7
Tideswell Cl NG15.....117 A3
Tideswell Ct NG18.....102 D7
Tidworth Cl NG8.......171 D5
Tilberthwaite Cl NG2..186 C6
Tilbury Rise NG8......160 B3
Tilford Gdns NG9......182 E6
Till Bridge La DN21.... 44 F7
Tiln Ct DN22.......... 29 F1
Tiln La DN22.......... 29 F3
Tilstock Ct NG16......159 A8
Tim La NG14..........163 F4
Timothy Rd NG22..... 79 C3
Tindale Bank Rd DN10 .. 6 C7
Tindall Cl NG9.........183 B2
Tinker La DN22........ 27 F6
Tinkers La NG23....... 82 F1
Tinker's La NG23...... 97 F8
Tinkers Way NG7......223 D1
Tinsley Cl NG23.......156 E6
Tinsley Rd NG16.......143 D1
Tintagel Gn NG7.......184 E1
Tintagel Green NG11..195 E8
Tintagel Way **9** NG19 .. 87 D1
Tintern Cl NG17.......115 C5
Tintern Dr NG8........160 E2
Tippett Ct NG3........173 F6
Tippings La NG22......119 F5
Tip Tree Cl NG16......158 F7
Tiree Cl NG9...........170 D2
Tishbite St **7** NG6....160 B7
Tissington Ave
  Beeston NG9...........183 C1
  3 Nottingham NG7...173 A8
Tissington Rd NG7.....173 A8
Titchfield Ave
  Mansfield Woodhouse
    NG19.............. 88 D3
  Sutton in Ashfield NG17 .100 E2
Titchfield St
  Hucknall NG15.........146 A7
  Mansfield NG18........102 A8
  Market Warsop NG20... 74 B3
Titchfield Terr NG15...146 B7
TITHBY...............189 E6
Tithby Ct **10** NG18....103 A2
Tithby Dr NG5.........161 C6
Tithby Rd
  Bingham NG13.........177 F2
  Cropwell Butler NG12..189 C6
Tithe Barn Ct NG24...125 A1
Tithe Gdns **2** NG5....147 A1
Tithe La NG14.........148 F7
Tithes La DN11........ 8 A7
Tiverton Cl
  Hucknall NG15.........145 D5
  Nottingham NG8.......160 B2
Toad La
  Elston NG23..........153 E4
  Epperstone NG14......150 A5
  Laxton NG22.......... 79 B2
Tobias Cl NG5.........160 F8
Todd Cl NG11.........195 C8
Todd Ct NG11.........195 C8
Toft Cl NG12..........187 E2
Toft Rd NG9...........183 A3
Tokenhouse Yd NG1...223 E2
Toll Bar Ave NG13.....181 A3
TOLLERTON............186 D1
Tollerton Gn NG6......160 D5
Tollerton La NG12.....186 E5
Tollerton Sch NG12....186 E1
Tollhouse Hill NG1.....223 D3
Tolney La
  Newark-on-Trent NG24 ..139 D2
  Newark-on-Trent NG24 ..139 E2
Tom Blower Cl NG8....172 A6
Tomlinson Ave NG11...195 A4
Tomlinson Cl DE55.... 99 A3
Tom Otter's La NG23.. 70 E8
Tom Stimpson Wy
  NG17................101 B3
Tom Wass Rd NG17...114 E8
Tonbridge Mount NG8 .171 D2
Tongue Way NG11.....196 A3
Ton La NG14..........150 D2
Tooley St DN21....... 24 D7
Toothill Cl NG14......148 C8

Toothill La NG18 . . . . **102** C7
Toothill Rd
Loughborough LE11 . . . . . . **220** B5
7 Mansfield NG18 . . . . **102** B7
Toot Hill Sch NG13 . . . . **177** E4
Topaz Cres NG17 . . . . **114** D8
Topaz Gr NG18 . . . . **102** C5
Top Cart Gaps NG22 . . . . **66** A7
Top La
Egmanton NG22 . . . . **79** D7
Mansfield NG19 . . . . **87** A1
Topliff Rd NG9 . . . . **183** C2
Top Pasture La
North Wheatley DN22 . . . . **31** E8
South Wheatley DN22 . . . . **32** A8
Top Rd
Blidworth NG21 . . . . **117** F2
Blidworth NG21 . . . . **118** A2
Misson DN10 . . . . **4** D3
Ruddington NG11 . . . . . . **196** C6
Thorney NG23 . . . . **69** F5
Top Row
Mansfield NG19 . . . . **87** F6
Newark-on-Trent NG24 . . **140** C8
Westwood NG16 . . . . . . **128** A5
Top Sandy La NG20 . . . . **74** C3
Top St
Askham NG22 . . . . **51** F2
Askham NG22 . . . . **52** A2
Bawtry DN10 . . . . **10** A7
East Drayton DN22 . . . . . **53** B3
Elston NG23 . . . . **153** D4
North Wheatley DN22 . . . . **31** D8
Rainworth NG21 . . . . . . **104** B1
Top Valley Dr NG5 . . . . **160** E8
Top Valley Way NG5 . . . **160** E8
Topyard La DN22 . . . . . . **30** D6
Torbay Cres NG5 . . . . . . **161** B5
Torkard Ct NG15 . . . . . . **146** A5
Torkard Dr NG5 . . . . . . **160** F8
Torkard Way NG15 . . . . . **146** B7
TORKSEY **44** B2
Torksey Ave
Saxilby LN1 . . . . **56** F4
Saxilby LN1 . . . . **57** A4
Torksey Ferry Rd DN22 . . **43** C2
Torksey Mews DN22 . . . . **39** D2
Torksey St DN22 . . . . . . **43** A2
Torksey Wlk NG19 . . . . . . **88** E8
Tor La NG22 . . . . **77** A3
Torr St DN21 . . . . **24** D8
Torvill Dr
Nottingham NG8 . . . . **171** E5
Nottingham NG9 . . . . **171** E5
Torvill Heights NG8 . . . . **171** E5
TORWORTH **19** B2
Toseland Gdns NG15 . . . **145** F4
Toston Dr NG8 . . . . **172** C4
Totland Dr NG8 . . . . **160** D2
Totland Rd NG9 . . . . **171** C2
Totley Cl NG6 . . . . **146** C2
Totnes Cl NG15 . . . . **145** D6
Totnes Rd NG3 . . . . **174** B5
TOTON **182** E2
Toton Bispham Drive Jun
Sch NG9 . . . . **182** E3
Toton Cl NG6 . . . . **160** D5
Toton La NG9 . . . . **182** E6
Tottle Gdns 2 NG7 . . . . . **172** D6
Tottle Rd NG11 . . . . **185** A8
Tow Ct NG24 . . . . **139** A4
Tower Cres NG16 . . . . . . **159** A4
Tower St DN21 . . . . **15** D1
Towe's Mount NG4 . . . . . **174** E7
Towle St NG10 . . . . **193** A4
Towlsons Croft NG6 . . . . **160** D3
Town Cres NG16 . . . . . . **113** D4
Town End NG22 . . . . **79** B3
Town End La NG23 . . . . . **167** B8
Towngate DN10 . . . . **10** A7
Townhill Sq 3 NG24 . . . **140** F2
Town La DE55 . . . . **99** B3
Town Mill Cl NG25 . . . . **121** E2
Townroe Dr NG19 . . . . . **101** D7
Townsend Ct NG5 . . . . . . **147** A1
Townside Cl NG10 . . . . . **193** B4
Townside La DN22 . . . . . **42** D3
Townside Rd DN22 . . . . . **32** D1
Town St
Askham NG22 . . . . **52** A3
Beeston NG9 . . . . **183** B8
Clayworth DN22 . . . . **21** D5
Cottam DN22 . . . . **43** D5
Grassthorpe NG23 . . . . . . **81** F4
Hawksworth NG13 . . . . . **167** C3
Lound DN22 . . . . **20** C1
Pinxton NG16 . . . . **113** E3
Sandiacre NG10 . . . . **182** B6
South Leverton DN22 . . . . **42** C7
Sutton DN22 . . . . **28** F6
Treswell DN22 . . . . **42** B3
Town View NG16 . . . . . . **158** F7
Tow Path Cl LE11 . . . . . . **220** C5
Towpath Gdns S80 . . . . . . **36** B3
Towson Ave NG16 . . . . . **143** C2
Towson Field LE12 . . . . **205** E2
Towyn St 3 NG5 . . . . . . **161** A7
Tracy Cl NG9 . . . . **171** D1
Trafalgar Ct NG7 . . . . . . **222** B4
Trafalgar Ct DN21 . . . . . **24** E4
Trafalgar Rd
Beeston NG9 . . . . **184** A4
Long Eaton NG10 . . . . . . **193** D6
Trafalgar Sq
Long Eaton NG10 . . . . . . **193** E7
Sutton on Trent NG23 . . . . **97** A8
Trafalgar Way NG19 . . . . **88** C6
Traffic St NG2 . . . . **223** E2
Trafford Gdns 1 NG8 . . . **172** D7
Tranby Gdns NG8 . . . . . . **171** F4
Tranker La S81 . . . . **35** A6
Travell's Hill LE12 . . . . . **214** A7
Travers Rd NG10 . . . . . . **182** A6
Treegarth Sq NG5 . . . . . **147** B1
Tree View NG5 . . . . **147** C1
Trefan Gdns NG5 . . . . . . **161** A7
Trefoil Cl NG13 . . . . **177** D3
Trelawn Cl 1 NG5 . . . . . **161** D2
Tremayne Rd NG8 . . . . . . **171** C6
Trenchard Cl NG13 . . . . . **177** C8
Trenchham Gdns
NG14 . . . . **163** D3
Trent Approach DN21 . . . **44** B8
Trent Ave NG11 . . . . **196** C8
Trent Bank NG23 . . . . **68** D1
Trent Bridge
(Nottinghamshire Cty CC)
NG2 . . . . **173** E1
Trent Bridge Rd
DN22 . . . . **39** E4
Trent Bsns Ctr NG10 . . . **182** C1
Trent Bvd NG2 . . . . **174** A1
Trent Cl NG23 . . . . **110** F2
Trent Coll NG10 . . . . **193** C8
Trent Cotts NG10 . . . . . . **193** F5
Trent Cres NG9 . . . . **183** E3
Trent Dr NG15 . . . . **145** D3
Trent Gdns
2 Burton Joyce NG14 . . **163** F4
Burton Joyce NG14 . . . . . **164** A4
Trent Gr DN21 . . . . **14** A5
Trentham Dr NG8 . . . . . . **172** C7
Trentham Gdns NG8 . . . . **172** C7
Trent La
Besthorpe NG23 . . . . **97** E6
1 Burton Joyce NG14 . . **163** F4
Burton Joyce NG14 . . . . . **164** A4
East Bridgford NG13 . . . . **165** B4
East Stoke NG23 . . . . . . **153** A8
East Stoke NG24 . . . . . . **138** A1
East Stoke NG24 . . . . . . **138** B1
Fiskerton NG25 . . . . **137** F2
Girton NG23 . . . . **82** E2
Gunthorpe NG14 . . . . **165** A4
Kelham NG23 . . . . **124** B5
Long Eaton NG10 . . . . . . **193** F5
Newark-on-Trent NG24 . . **125** A2
Newark-on-Trent NG24 . . **125** A3
Newton on Trent NG22 . . . **54** F1
North Clifton NG23 . . . . . . **68** C5
Nottingham NG2 . . . . **174** A3
South Clifton NG23 . . . . . . **68** D1
Trenton Cl NG9 . . . . **171** A1
Trenton Dr NG10 . . . . . . **194** A8
Trent Port Rd DN21 . . . . . **44** B8
Trent Rd
Beeston NG9 . . . . **184** B4
Kirton NG22 . . . . **77** F4
Nottingham NG2 . . . . **173** F4
Wellow NG22 . . . . **78** A4
Trentside NG14 . . . . **165** A4
Trent Side NG11 . . . . **194** D6
Trentside N NG2 . . . . **173** E1
Trent St
Gainsborough DN21 . . . . . **24** D7
Long Eaton NG10 . . . . . . **193** E8
Nottingham NG1 . . . . **223** E1
Retford DN22 . . . . **40** A6
Worksop S80 . . . . **35** E4
Trentvale Ave 4 DN21 . . . **15** F2
Trent Vale Inf Sch NG9 . . **184** B4
Trent Vale Rd NG9 . . . . . **184** A4
Trent Valley Rd NG4 . . . . **163** C4
Trent Valley View NG3 . . **162** A1
Trent View DN21 . . . . **44** C8
Trentview Ct NG2 . . . . . . **173** F2
Trent View Gdns NG12 . . **176** A5
Trent Way NG24 . . . . . . **125** B2
Trent Wlk NG19 . . . . **88** E4
Tressall Cl DE7 . . . . **170** A8
TRESWELL **42** C3
Treswell Ct 5 NG18 . . . **103** A2
Treswell Rd
Rampton DN22 . . . . **42** F2
South Leverton DN22 . . . . **42** C5
Treswell Wood Nature
Reserve DN22 . . . . . . **41** E4
Trevelyan Rd NG2 . . . . . **173** F1
Trevino Gdns 10 NG5 . . . **147** A1
Trevone Ave NG9 . . . . . . **182** E6
Trevor Rd
Beeston NG9 . . . . **183** F5
West Bridgford NG2 . . . . **186** A6
Trevose Gdns NG5 . . . . . **161** D3
Treyford Cl NG11 . . . . . . **185** A4
Triangle The
Ilkeston DE7 . . . . **170** A6
Nottingham NG2 . . . . **173** A1
Nottingham NG8 . . . . **172** F1
Tricornia Dr NG6 . . . . . . **160** B4
Tring Vale NG5 . . . . **161** A4
Trinity Ave NG7 . . . . . . **222** B1
Trinity Catholic Sch
The NG8 . . . . **172** A8
Trinity Cl DE7 . . . . **157** E3
Trinity Cres
East Markham NG22 . . . . . **66** B7
Lambley NG4 . . . . **163** C7
Wymeswold LE12 . . . . . . **216** B3
Trinity Cres N NG22 . . . . **66** B7
Trinity Cres S NG22 . . . . **66** B8
Trinity Fields Rd DN22 . . **29** B1
Trinity Rd
Edwinstowe NG22 . . . . . . **75** F2
Newark-on-Trent NG24 . . **140** A4
Retford DN22 . . . . **29** D1
RETFORD DN22 . . . . **39** D8
Southwell NG25 . . . . . . **136** C8
Trinity Sq NG1 . . . . **223** E3
Trinity St
Gainsborough DN21 . . . . . **24** D7
Loughborough LE11 . . . . **220** C3
Trinity View 1 DN21 . . . . **15** D1
Trinity Wlk NG1 . . . . . . **223** E3
Trinstead Way NG5 . . . . . **161** C7
Triumph Cl NG22 . . . . . . **106** F8
Triumph Rd
Eakring NG22 . . . . **106** A8
Nottingham NG7 . . . . **172** D4
Nottingham NG7 . . . . **222** A1
Trivett Sq NG1 . . . . **223** F2
Troon Cl NG16 . . . . **158** E7
Troon Ct DN22 . . . . **39** E2
Trough La NG16 . . . . **158** F8
Trough Rd NG16 . . . . . . **159** A8
Troutbeck NG12 . . . . **188** A3
Troutbeck Cres NG9 . . . **183** C8
TROWELL **170** C5
Trowell Ave
Ilkeston DE7 . . . . **170** A5
Nottingham NG8 . . . . **171** B5
Trowell CE Prim Sch
NG9 . . . . **170** D4
Trowell Ct 7 NG18 . . . . **103** A2
Trowell Gr
Long Eaton NG10 . . . . . . **182** C1
Stapleford NG9 . . . . **170** E3
Trowell La LE12 . . . . . . **213** E7
Trowell Pk Dr NG9 . . . . . **170** D2
Trowell Rd
Nottingham NG8 . . . . **171** D5
Stapleford NG9 . . . . **170** D2
True Lovers Wlk 1
LE11 . . . . **220** A3
Trueman Ct S81 . . . . **36** B5
Trueman Gdns NG5 . . . . **162** B6
Trueman St DE7 . . . . . . **157** F4
Truman Cl
Costock LE12 . . . . **206** D1
Nottingham NG3 . . . . . . **223** F4
Truman Dr NG15 . . . . . . **146** A4
Truman's Rd NG22 . . . . . **173** D1
Truman St
Cossall NG16 . . . . **158** A1
Kimberley NG16 . . . . **158** F4
Truro Cl LE12 . . . . **205** E1
Truro Cres NG7 . . . . **172** E7
Trusley Wlk NG19 . . . . . . **88** E4
Tryst The NG24 . . . . **125** A2
Tuckers Cl LE11 . . . . . . **220** C2
Tuckers La
Mansfield NG18 . . . . . . **102** A4
Mansfield NG18 . . . . . . **101** F8
Tuckwood Ct NG12 . . . . **207** D3
Tudor Ave NG18 . . . . . . **102** F8
Tudor Cl
Carlton NG4 . . . . **174** E5
Long Eaton NG10 . . . . . . **182** F1
Newark-on-Trent NG24 . . **140** B8
Tudor Cres NG21 . . . . . . **118** A8
Tudor Ct
Arnold NG5 . . . . **162** B5
Hucknall NG15 . . . . **145** C5
Tudor Dr
Mansfield NG18 . . . . . . **102** C4
Morton DN21 . . . . **15** B4
Tudor Gr NG1 . . . . **223** D4
Tudor Oaks NG23 . . . . . **153** D5
Tudor Rd NG2 . . . . **185** F7
Tudor Sq NG2 . . . . **185** F7
Tudor St NG17 . . . . **100** E1
Tudsbury Terr NG17 . . . **101** A3
Tudwal Cl NG5 . . . . **161** A7
Tudwal Wlk 2 NG5 . . . . . **161** A7
Tulip Ave NG3 . . . . **173** D7
Tulip Cl NG12 . . . . **188** A5
Tulip Rd NG16 . . . . **158** B4
Tunnel Rd
Nottingham NG7 . . . . **222** C4
Retford DN22 . . . . **39** E5
Tunnicliffe Cl DE7 . . . . . **157** E2
Tunstall Cres NG8 . . . . . **160** A1
Tunstall Dr NG5 . . . . **160** F4
Tunstall Rd NG5 . . . . **161** F4
Turnberry S81 . . . . **36** B5
Turnberry Ave 6
NG17 . . . . **114** C7
Turnberry Cl
Beeston NG9 . . . . **183** C6
Ilkeston DE7 . . . . **157** C2
Turnberry Rd NG6 . . . . . **160** D6
Turner Ave
Langley Mill NG16 . . . . . **143** A3
Loughborough LE11 . . . . **220** A2
Turner Cl
Nottingham NG5 . . . . **161** C5
Stapleford NG9 . . . . **182** E6
Turner Dr
Eastwood NG16 . . . . **158** B7
Worksop S81 . . . . **35** F4
Turner Gr NG15 . . . . **145** E2
Turner Rd
Long Eaton NG10 . . . . . . **193** C4
Worksop S81 . . . . **35** E4
Turners Croft DN22 . . . . **42** C8
Turner St NG15 . . . . **146** A7
Turneys Ct NG2 . . . . **173** E1
Turney St NG2 . . . . **173** D1
Turnley Rd DE55 . . . . . . **113** C6
Turnoak Ave DE7 . . . . . . **157** F5
Turnpike La NG9 . . . . . . **184** A8
Turnpike The NG22 . . . . **120** F2
Turnstone Cres NG18 . . **103** C4
Turnstone Wharf 1
NG7 . . . . **172** F2
Turpin Ave NG4 . . . . **162** D3
Turpin Cl DN21 . . . . **15** F1
Turton Cl NG16 . . . . **143** A1
Turton Dr NG5 . . . . **161** E7
Turvey La LE12 . . . . **212** D2
Tutt Cl 4 NG24 . . . . **140** F2
TUXFORD **66** B2
Tuxford Acad NG22 . . . . . **66** B3
Tuxford Ave NG20 . . . . . . **74** E8
Tuxford Ct 6 NG18 . . . . **103** A2
Tuxford Prim Sch and Early
Years Centre NG22 . . . . **65** C2
Tuxford Rd
Boughton NG22 . . . . **77** D5
East Markham NG22 . . . . . **65** C5
Egmanton NG22 . . . . **79** E7
Kirton NG22 . . . . **78** D7
Normanton on T NG23 . . . **81** A6
Walesby NG22 . . . . **64** C2
Tuxford Windmill **65** E4
Tuxford Wlk NG3 . . . . . . **173** F6
Twells Cl NG3 . . . . **173** F7
Twentylands Dr LE12 . . . **205** D1
Twickenham Rd NG17 . . . **114** A4
Twin Oaks Dr NG17 . . . . **100** C2
Twinyards Cl NG17 . . . . . **100** C2
Twistlace Cl NG9 . . . . . . **183** F4
Twist Mill Cl NG15 . . . . . **146** C1
Twitchell The
Beeston NG9 . . . . **183** E4
Newark-on-Trent NG24 . . **139** E5
Sutton in Ashfield NG17 . . **100** F1
Two Acres S81 . . . . **18** B2
Twycross Rd NG5 . . . . . . **161** B7
Twyford Gdns NG11 . . . . **184** E4
Twyford La DN22 . . . . **50** C3
Tyburn Cl NG5 . . . . **147** A1
Tylden Rd S80 . . . . **35** B5
Tylden Way S80 . . . . **35** A5
Tyler Dr NG12 . . . . **197** D2
Tyne Cl NG8 . . . . **160** C2
Tynedale Cl
Long Eaton NG10 . . . . . . **193** A6
Nottingham NG8 . . . . **160** D1
Tyne Gdns NG15 . . . . . . **145** D3
Tyrian St NG16 . . . . **158** B8

U

Ulgham Cl NG5 . . . . **147** F2
Ulldale Ct NG9 . . . . **183** B4
Ullscarf Cl NG2 . . . . . . **186** C5
Ullswater Cl
Carlton NG4 . . . . **162** F2
Gamston NG12 . . . . **186** D6
Ullswater Cres NG9 . . . . **183** D8
Ullswater Dr NG15 . . . . . **145** F7
Ulster Rd DN21 . . . . **15** D2
Underwood Ave DN22 . . . **19** B3
Underwood CE Prim Sch
NG16 . . . . **128** F1
Underwood Gdns S80 . . . **35** C3
Underwood Mews
NG8 . . . . **159** C1
Union Cl NG15 . . . . **131** A2
Union Rd
Nottingham NG14 . . . . . . **173** C5
Nottingham NG3 . . . . . . **223** F3
Union St
Beeston NG9 . . . . **184** A6
Bingham NG13 . . . . **177** E4
Long Eaton NG10 . . . . . . **193** E8
Loughborough LE11 . . . . **220** A4
Mansfield NG18 . . . . . . **102** A7
Retford DN22 . . . . **39** F7
Selston NG16 . . . . **129** A7
Sutton in Ashfield NG17 . . **100** F2
Unity Cres NG3 . . . . **162** C2
Unity Prim Sch NG7 . . . . **222** C4
Unity Rd NG17 . . . . **115** B7
Unity Sq NG2 . . . . **223** E1
University Bvd NG7 . . . . **184** C8
Univ of Nottingham
Beeston, Nottingham
NG9 . . . . **184** A8
Nottingham NG7 . . . . **172** D2
Univ of Nottingham, Centre
for Dairy Science
Innovation LE12 . . . . . **204** B3
Univ of Nottingham
Innovation Pk NG7 . . . **172** D4
Univ of Nottingham
(Jubilee Campus)
NG7 . . . . **172** D4
Univ of Nottingham (King's
Meadow Campus)
NG7 . . . . **172** F1
Univ of Nottingham,
(Sutton Bonington
Campus) LE12 . . . . . . **204** B1
Univ of Nottingham (Univ
Park Campus) NG7 . . . **171** B1
Unwin Rd NG17 . . . . **101** B3
Unwin St NG17 . . . . **100** A3
Uplands Ct NG8 . . . . **171** F6
Upminster Dr
Arnold NG5 . . . . **147** F1
Nuthall NG16 . . . . **159** D3
UPPER BROUGHTON . . . **210** B2
Upper Canaan NG11 . . . . **196** D8
Upper Coll St NG1 . . . . . **223** D3
Upper Cross La NG20 . . . **74** C4
Upper Dunstead Rd
NG16 . . . . **143** B4
Upper Eldon St NG2 . . . . **173** E3
UPPER LANGWITH **72** D8
Upper Mexborough Rd
NG16 . . . . **129** A7
Upper Mill St NG17 . . . . **101** B3
Upper Orch St NG9 . . . . **182** E7
Upper Parliament St
NG1 . . . . **223** E3
Upper Row NG22 . . . . . . **54** B2

Upper Wellington St
NG10 . . . . **182** C1
Uppingham Cres NG2 . . **185** D5
Uppingham Gdns NG2 . . **173** D2
UPTON **122** F1
Upton Cl DE75 . . . . **143** A1
Upton Dr NG5 . . . . **161** D5
Upton Hill NG22 . . . . **52** A4
Upton Mount NG19 . . . . . **87** E1
Upton Rd
Askham NG22 . . . . **52** A4
Southwell NG25 . . . . . . **122** A1
Southwell NG25 . . . . . . **137** A8
Upton Wlk DN21 . . . . **24** F7
Urban Rd NG17 . . . . **115** A5
Urban Road Bsns Pk
NG17 . . . . **115** A4
Utile Gdns 3 NG6 . . . . . **160** A7

V

Vale Ave NG20 . . . . **74** A4
Valebrook Rd
Nottingham NG5 . . . . **161** B4
Nottingham NG5 . . . . **161** C5
Stathern LE14 . . . . **202** F3
Vale Cl
Aslockton NG13 . . . . **179** A4
Eastwood NG16 . . . . **144** B2
Mansfield NG18 . . . . . . **102** E4
Vale Cres N NG8 . . . . . . **172** D6
Vale Cres S NG8 . . . . . . **172** D6
Vale Dr NG20 . . . . **72** F2
Vale Gdns NG4 . . . . **174** D5
Valentine Ave NG16 . . . . **128** E7
Vale Rd
Carlton NG4 . . . . **174** E5
Mansfield Woodhouse
NG19 . . . . **88** A4
Nottingham NG4 . . . . **174** D5
Valerian Wy NG13 . . . . . **177** C3
Valeside Gdns NG4 . . . . **174** E5
Vale The DE7 . . . . **157** E3
Valetta Rd NG5 . . . . **162** B7
Vale View
Dry Doddington NG23 . . . **156** D1
Newark-on-Trent NG24 . . **139** E5
Vallance St NG19 . . . . . . **88** B6
Valley App NG22 . . . . . . **105** F7
Valley Dr NG16 . . . . **144** B1
Valley Farm Ct 16
NG5 . . . . **161** A8
Valley Gdns NG2 . . . . . . **186** C5
Valley La NG23 . . . . **169** D8
Valley Prospect NG24 . . **139** D5
Valley Rd
Beeston NG9 . . . . **183** B5
Bilsthorpe NG22 . . . . . . **105** F7
Carlton NG4 . . . . **162** B1
Kimberley NG16 . . . . **158** D7
Nottingham NG5 . . . . **161** B4
Radcliffe on Trent NG12 . . **176** A3
Shirebrook NG20 . . . . . . **72** E5
West Bridgford NG2 . . . . **186** B5
Worksop S81 . . . . **35** E6
Valley View NG24 . . . . . **126** A1
Valley Vw NG18 . . . . . . **102** E4
Valmont Ave NG18 . . . . **103** A6
Valmont Rd
Beeston NG9 . . . . **183** A7
Nottingham NG5 . . . . **161** B4
Vancouver Ave NG12 . . . **175** E2
Vanessa Dr DN21 . . . . . . **15** C3
Vanguard Rd NG10 . . . . . **193** D5
Varden Ave NG9 . . . . . . **172** A1
Varley Cl DE75 . . . . **143** A1
Varney Rd NG11 . . . . . . **184** F3
Varsity Gr NG13 . . . . **177** B7
Vasey Cl LN1 . . . . **57** C3
Vaughan Ave
Bottesford NG13 . . . . . . **181** C2
Hucknall NG15 . . . . **131** C1
Vaughan Pl NG20 . . . . . . **72** E6
Vaughan Rd NG9 . . . . . . **183** A8
Vedonis Pk NG15 . . . . . **146** A5
Velerian Gr NG15 . . . . . . **146** A8
Vellus Ct NG17 . . . . **101** B2
Ventnor Rise NG5 . . . . . **160** F4
Ventura Dr NG5 . . . . **146** C1
Venture Ave DE55 . . . . . **113** F8
Venus Cl NG6 . . . . **160** B5
Vera Cres NG21 . . . . . . **118** B8
Verbena Cl 3 NG3 . . . . . **173** D7
Verder Gr NG5 . . . . **160** E8
Vere Ave NG17 . . . . **100** E5
Vere St NG6 . . . . **160** B7
Verne Cl NG4 . . . . **174** C7
Verney St NG19 . . . . **86** F7
Verney Way NG19 . . . . . . **86** F7
Vernon Ave
Beeston NG9 . . . . **183** F6
Carlton NG4 . . . . **162** F1
Newark-on-Trent NG24 . . **140** B8
Nottingham, Old Basford
NG6 . . . . **160** E3
Nottingham, Wilford
NG11 . . . . **185** B8
Ravenshead NG15 . . . . . **116** F1
Retford DN22 . . . . **40** A4
Vernon Cres NG15 . . . . . **117** A1
Vernon Ct
Nuthall NG16 . . . . **159** F3
Shirebrook NG20 . . . . . . **73** A4
Vernon Dr NG16 . . . . . . **159** F3
Vernon Pk Dr NG6 . . . . . **160** E3
Vernon Pk Trad Est
NG5 . . . . **160** E2
Vernon Rd
Kirkby-in-Ashfield NG17 . . **114** F6
Nottingham NG6 . . . . **160** E3

Vernon St
Ilkeston DE7 . . . . **157** F4
Newark-on-Trent NG24 . . **140** B8
Nottingham NG1 . . . . **223** D3
Shirebrook NG20 . . . . . . **73** A4
Verona Ave NG4 . . . . . . **174** F6
Verona Ct NG18 . . . . . . **103** A3
Veronica Dr
Carlton NG4 . . . . **162** D1
Eastwood NG16 . . . . **158** C8
Veronica Wlk NG11 . . . . **184** C1
Veronne Dr NG17 . . . . . **101** A6
Versailles Gd NG15 . . . . **146** A5
Vesper Ct NG18 . . . . . . **102** F8
Vessey Cl NG24 . . . . . . **140** C4
Vessey Rd S81 . . . . **35** E7
Vesuvius Way S80 . . . . . . **35** C4
Vexation La NG22 . . . . . . **91** D7
Vicarage Ave DE7 . . . . . **157** D4
Vicarage Cl
Collingham NG23 . . . . . . **98** A1
Nottingham, Old Basford
NG5 . . . . **160** F3
Nottingham, St Ann's
NG3 . . . . **223** E4
Shirebrook NG20 . . . . . . **72** E3
Vicarage Ct
3 Mansfield NG18 . . . . . **87** C1
Sutton in Ashfield NG17 . . **100** E7
Vicarage Dr
Burton Joyce NG14 . . . . . **163** D4
Clarborough DN22 . . . . . **30** D5
Kirkby-in-Ashfield NG17 . . **114** F7
Vicarage Gdns NG24 . . . **140** E4
Vicarage Gn NG12 . . . . . **186** B3
Vicarage La
Beckingham DN10 . . . . . . **14** C2
Farnsfield NG22 . . . . . . **119** E6
Kneeton NG13 . . . . **151** F1
North Muskham NG23 . . . **110** D4
Radcliffe on Trent NG12 . . **175** D4
Ruddington NG11 . . . . . . **196** C7
Scrooby DN11 . . . . **9** F2
Vicarage Rd
South Clifton NG23 . . . . . **68** F1
Southwell NG25 . . . . . . **136** C8
Vicarage St
Beeston NG9 . . . . **183** E6
Ilkeston DE7 . . . . **157** D4
Vicarage Way NG17 . . . . **129** F8
Vicar La
Misson DN10 . . . . **4** C3
Tibshelf DE55 . . . . **99** A6
Vicars Ct NG21 . . . . **89** E2
Vicar's La DN22 . . . . **43** A2
Vicar's Wlk S80 . . . . **35** F2
Vicar Water NG21 . . . . . . **89** F2
Vicar Water Ctry Pk
NG21 . . . . **89** E1
Vicar Way NG18 . . . . . . **103** B7
Vickers Cl NG5 . . . . **162** E3
Vickers St
Market Warsop NG20 . . . . **74** B4
Nottingham NG3 . . . . . . **173** D8
Vickers Way NG22 . . . . . **105** F7
Vickery Way NG9 . . . . . . **183** B2
Victor Cres NG10 . . . . . . **182** C4
Victoria Ave
Lowdham NG14 . . . . **150** E4
5 Nottingham NG2 . . . . **173** E4
Victoria Bsns Pk NG4 . . . **175** C6
Victoria Cl
Arnold NG5 . . . . **147** F1
Boughton NG22 . . . . **77** E5
Gainsborough DN21 . . . . . **24** F6
Victoria Cres NG5 . . . . . **161** D2
Victoria Ct
Ilkeston DE7 . . . . **157** F4
Mansfield NG18 . . . . . . **102** A5
Victoria Emb NG2 . . . . . **185** D8
Victoria Gdns
Newark-on-Trent NG24 . . **140** A8
Watnall NG16 . . . . **145** A4
Victoria Gr NG15 . . . . . . **131** B1
Victoria L Ctr NG1 . . . . . **223** F3
Victoria Pk NG4 . . . . **175** B6
Victoria Pk L Ctr DE7 . . . **157** E2
Victoria Pk Way NG4 . . . **175** B6
Victoria Prim Sch2 NG2 . **173** B1
Victoria Rd
Bingham NG13 . . . . **178** A5
Bunny NG11 . . . . **196** E1
Carlton NG4 . . . . **175** A6
Kirkby-in-Ashfield NG17 . . **114** F5
Nottingham NG5 . . . . **161** B3
Pinxton NG16 . . . . **113** D6
Sandiacre NG10 . . . . . . **182** B5
Selston NG16 . . . . **129** A7
West Bridgford NG2 . . . . **185** E7
Worksop S80 . . . . **35** F2
Victoria Ret Pk NG4 . . . . **175** B6
Victoria Ret Pk S80 . . . . . **35** F3
Victoria St
Carlton NG4 . . . . **162** F1
Hucknall NG15 . . . . **146** A8
Ilkeston DE7 . . . . **157** F3
Kimberley NG16 . . . . **159** A6
Langley Mill NG16 . . . . . **143** C3
Long Eaton NG10 . . . . . . **193** B5
Loughborough LE11 . . . . **220** B3
Newark-on-Trent NG24 . . **139** E4
Nottingham NG1 . . . . **223** E2
Radcliffe on Trent NG12 . . **175** D4
Selston NG16 . . . . **129** A7
Shirebrook NG20 . . . . . . **72** F4
South Normanton DE55 . . **113** A6
Stanton Hill NG17 . . . . . **100** C6

Victoria St continued
Stapleford NG9 . . . .**182** D7
Sutton in Ashfield NG17 .**100** E2
Victoria Terr DE55 . . . .**99** B7
Victoria Way NG15 . . . . . .**146** C4
Victor Terr 6 NG5 . . . . . .**161** C2
Victory Cl
1 Eastwood NG16 . . . . .**144** A2
Kirkby-in-Ashfield NG17 .**115** B6
Long Eaton NG10 . . . . . .**193** D5
Mansfield Woodhouse
NG19 . . . .**89** A1
Victory Dr NG9 . . . .**88** F1
Victory Rd NG9 . . . .**184** A4
View The NG9 . . . .**183** B7
Village Cl
Farndon NG24 . . . .**139** B5
West Bridgford NG12 . . . .**186** B3
Village Farm Cl
Stanford on Soar LE12 . .**214** C1
West Leake LE12 . . . .**204** F1
Village Rd
Normanton on S LE12 . . .**213** D2
Nottingham NG11 . . . .**184** D2
Village St
Owthorpe NG12 . . . .**199** E7
West Bridgford NG12 . . . .**186** B3
Village Way NG24 . . . .**139** A5
Villa Rd
Keyworth NG12 . . . .**197** F4
Nottingham NG3 . . . .**173** C7
Villa St NG9 . . . .**183** F7
Villas The NG20 . . . .**59** A3
Villiers Rd
Arnold NG5 . . . .**161** D4
Mansfield NG18 . . . .**102** E7
West Bridgford NG2 . . . . .**186** A6
Vincent Ave NG9 . . . .**183** F5
Vincent Cl NG15 . . . .**131** C1
Vincent Gdns 8 NG7 . . .**172** E7
Vine NG13 . . . .**181** A1
Vine Cres NG10 . . . .**182** B6
Vine Farm Cl NG12 . . . . . .**187** E3
Vine Farmyard NG23 . . . .**98** A1
Vine Rd DN11 . . . .**8** C7
Vines Cross NG16 . . . .**171** E2
Vines The NG23 . . . .**96** F8
Vine Terr LE12 . . . .**215** C1
Vine Way NG24 . . . .**140** B8
Vine Wlk NG19 . . . .**88** C6
Violet Ave
Eastwood NG16 . . . .**144** A1
Giltbrook NG16 . . . .**158** B8
Violet Cl
Nottingham NG6 . . . .**160** D3
Shirebrook NG20 . . . .**72** D3
Violet Dns NG12 . . . .**186** A3
Violet Gr
HUCKNALL NG15 . . . .**146** C2
Newark-on-Trent NG24 . . .**139** F4
Violet Hill NG18 . . . .**103** A8
Violet Rd
Carlton NG4 . . . .**162** D1
West Bridgford NG2 . . . . .**186** A8
Vision Bsns Pk NG6 . . . . .**146** A1
Vision West
Nottinghamshire Coll
(Derby Road Campus)
NG18 . . . .**102** C2
Vision West Notts Coll
(Vision Apprentices)
NG1 . . . .**223** F1
Vista The NG9 . . . .**182** E5
Vivian Ave NG5 . . . .**173** B8
Vixen Cl NG24 . . . .**139** F4
Viyella Gd NG15 . . . .**146** A5
Viyella Mews NG15. . . . . .**146** A6
Voce Ct S81 . . . .**36** B6
Voce Gdns NG15 . . . .**146** C6
Vulcan Cl NG6 . . . .**160** E4
Vulcan Gdns NG13 . . . . . .**177** B6
Vulcan Pl S80 . . . .**35** F3
Vyse Dr NG10 . . . .**193** C6

W

Waddington Dr NG2 . . . . .**185** D4
Waddington La NG23 . . . . .**97** E6
Wade Ave DE7 . . . .**170** A7
Wade Cl NG18 . . . .**102** C3
Wades Ave NG7 . . . .**172** E8
Wadham Rd NG5 . . . .**161** E5
Wadhurst Gdns NG3 . . . . .**223** F4
Wadhurst Gr NG8 . . . .**171** D2
Wadnal La NG23 . . . .**80** F3
Wadsworth Fields Prim Sch
NG9 . . . .**182** E8
Wadsworth Rd NG9 . . . . . .**182** F8
Wagstaff La NG16 . . . .**128** B4
Wagtail Cl NG9 . . . .**170** E2
Wain Ct S81 . . . .**36** B7
Waingrove NG11 . . . .**185** A3
Wainwright Ave
2 Mansfield NG19 . . . . .**87** D1
Mansfield NG19. . . . .**101** D8
Wainwright Prim Acad
NG19 . . . .**101** F8
Wakefield Ave NG12 . . . . .**176** A4
Wakefield Cl NG3 . . . .**182** A5
Wakefield Croft DE7 . . . . .**157** C3
Wakeling Cl NG25 . . . .**136** E8
Walbrook Cl NG8 . . . .**160** A3
Walcote Dr NG2 . . . .**185** C4
Walcot Gn NG11 . . . .**184** D1
Waldeck Rd NG5 . . . .**161** B1
Waldemar Gr NG9 . . . .**184** A6

Waldrom Rd NG5 . . . .**162** E3
Waldron Cl 1 NG2 . . . . . .**173** D2
Walesby CE Prim Sch
NG22 . . . .**64** A2
WALESBY **64** A1
Walesby Ct 1 NG18. . . . . .**103** A3
Walesby Dr NG17 . . . .**115** D5
Walesby La NG22 . . . .**77** C5
Walford Cl NG13 . . . .**181** A2
Walgrave Wlk 12 NG5 . . .**161** A7
Walkden St NG18 . . . .**102** B7
Walker Cl
Ilkeston NG9 . . . .**170** A4
Newark-on-Trent NG24 . . .**140** A7
New Ollerton NG22 . . . . . .**77** C5
Walker Gr NG9 . . . .**182** E6
WALKERINGHAM **13** F5
Walkeringham Prim Sch
DN10 . . . .**13** F6
Walkeringham Rd
Beckingham DN10 . . . .**14** B2
Gringley on the Hill DN10 .**13** A3
WALKERITH **14** D7
Walkerith Rd
Morton DN21 . . . .**15** A5
Walkerith DN10 . . . .**14** D8
Walkers Ave NG16 . . . . . .**143** E6
Walkers Cl
Bingham NG13 . . . .**177** E4
Bottesford NG13 . . . .**181** D2
Mansfield Woodhouse
NG19 . . . .**89** B1
Walkers Ind Est NG22 . . . .**65** C3
Walker Sq NG5 . . . .**160** E3
Walker St
Eastwood NG16 . . . .**144** A3
Nottingham NG2 . . . .**173** E4
Walkers Yd NG12 . . . .**175** F3
Walk Mill Dr NG15 . . . .**131** B1
Walks of Life Heritage Ctr★
NG22 . . . .**66** A3
Walk The DN21 . . . .**24** F7
Wallace Ave NG4 . . . .**174** F7
Wallace Gdns
Beeston NG9 . . . .**182** F2
Long Eaton NG9 . . . .**182** F1
Wallace Rd LE11 . . . .**220** A2
Wallace St NG11 . . . .**195** B2
Wallan St NG7 . . . .**222** A4
Wallet St NG4 . . . .**175** A7
Wallett Ave NG9 . . . .**183** F7
Wallingbrook Rise S80. . . .**35** B3
WALLINGWELLS **25** C5
Wallingwells La
Wallingwells S81. . . . .**25** A6
Wallingwells S81. . . . .**25** C4
Wallingwells S81. . . . .**25** C5
Wallis Rd NG18 . . . .**102** C7
Wallis St NG6. . . . .**160** E4
Wallsend Cl 16 DE7 . . . . .**157** F5
Wall St DN21 . . . .**24** D7
Walnut Ave
Shireoaks S81 . . . .**34** F7
Tickhill DN11 . . . .**8** B7
Walnut Cl
Aslockton NG13 . . . .**178** F5
Ilkeston DE7 . . . .**170** A7
Weston NG23 . . . .**81** B4
Walnut Dr
Beeston NG9 . . . .**183** B8
Calverton NG14 . . . .**148** F8
Walnut Gdns LE12 . . . .**205** D1
Walnut Gr
Cotgrave NG12 . . . .**187** F3
East Bridgford NG13 . . . . .**165** C2
Radcliffe on Trent NG12 . .**175** F3
Walnut Paddock LE14 . . .**202** B3
Walnut Rd NG13 . . . .**181** A2
Walnut Tree Cres NG19 . . .**89** D2
Walnut Tree Gdns NG6. . .**159** F7
Walnut Tree La NG13 . . . .**165** C2
Walsham Rd NG9 . . . .**183** C2
Walsingham Rd NG5. . . . . .**162** B5
Walter Halls Prim Sch
NG3 . . . .**161** E2
Walter's Cl NG24 . . . .**139** A5
Walters Cres NG16. . . . . . .**128** D6
Walter St NG7 . . . .**222** C4
Waltham Cl
Balderton NG24 . . . .**140** D3
West Bridgford NG2 . . . . .**186** B6
Waltham La
Harby LE14 . . . .**202** B1
Long Clawson LE14 . . . . .**211** E2
Waltham Rd NG15 . . . .**117** A2
Walton Ave NG3 . . . .**173** F5
Walton Cres NG4 . . . .**174** F2
Walton Dr
Keyworth NG12 . . . .**197** F3
Sutton in Ashfield NG17 . .**114** D8
Walton Rd NG5 . . . .**148** A1
Walton's La NG23. . . . .**110** E3
Walton St
Long Eaton NG10 . . . .**182** D1
Sutton in Ashfield NG17 . .**101** A3
Wands Cl NG25 . . . .**136** D8
Wan Gr NG17 . . . .**114** E7
Ward Ave
Hucknall NG15 . . . .**130** F1
Mansfield NG19 . . . .**162** A3
Wardle Gr NG5 . . . .**162** A8
Wardlow Rd DE7 . . . .**157** E3

Ward Pl NG18 . . . .**101** E6
Ward Rd NG21. . . . .**89** F4
Ward's End LE11. . . . .**220** B3
Ward St 2 NG7. . . . .**172** F8
Wareham Cl
Nottingham NG8 . . . .**160** A3
West Bridgford NG2 . . . . .**185** C5
Warkton Cl NG9 . . . .**183** C5
Warnadene Rd NG17. . . . . .**114** E8
Warner Pl LE11 . . . .**220** C4
Warners La 9 LE11 . . . . . .**220** B4
Warner St NG7 . . . .**222** A3
Warrands Cl NG25 . . . .**136** C8
Warren Ave
Annesley NG15 . . . .**130** C8
Nottingham NG5 . . . .**161** A2
Stapleford NG9 . . . .**182** D7
Warren Ave Extension
NG9 . . . .**182** D7
Warren Cl
Gainsborough DN21 . . . . .**15** B2
2 Sutton in Ashfield
NG17. . . . .**100** A2
Warren Ct NG9 . . . .**182** D7
Warrender Cl NG9 . . . .**171** C1
Warren Dr S81 . . . .**36** B8
Warrener Gr NG5 . . . .**160** E8
Warrenhill Cl NG15 . . . . . .**161** C7
Warren La
Kegworth DE74 . . . .**193** B2
Long Eaton DE74 . . . .**203** B7
Warren Prim Sch NG5. . . .**147** A2
Warren Rd
Annesley Woodhouse
NG17 . . . .**115** B1
Hucknall NG15 . . . .**145** D5
Warren The NG12. . . . .**187** F2
Warren Way NG19 . . . .**103** C8
Warren Wood Specialist
Acad DN21 . . . .**24** E7
Warrington Rd NG6. . . . . . .**160** C7
Warser Gate NG1 . . . .**223** F2
Warsop Cl NG8 . . . .**159** D2
Warsop Ent Ctr NG20. . . . .**74** B5
Warsop La NG21. . . . .**117** F7
Warsop Rd NG19 . . . .**88** D3
WARSOP VALE **73** D4
Warton Ave NG3 . . . .**173** F8
Warwick Ave
Arnold NG5 . . . .**161** E5
Beeston NG9 . . . .**183** F7
Carlton in Lindrick S81 . . .**25** A6
Carlton in Lindrick S81 . . .**26** A6
Warwick Brewery (5) NG24
. . . .**A2**
Warwick Cl
Kirkby-in-Ashfield
NG17. . . . .**115** D5
Saxilby LN1 . . . .**56** F5
Saxilby LN1 . . . .**57** A4
Warwick Dr
Mansfield NG18 . . . .**102** E7
Shipley DE7 . . . .**157** C3
Warwick Gdns NG12 . . . . .**187** F1
Warwick Rd
Balderton NG24 . . . .**140** D4
Long Eaton NG10 . . . .**194** A7
Nottingham NG3 . . . .**161** D2
Wasdale Cl NG2 . . . .**186** C5
Washdyke La
Hucknall NG15 . . . .**145** E8
Hucknall NG15 . . . .**145** F8
Washington Dr
Mansfield NG18 . . . .**101** F5
Stapleford NG9 . . . .**170** F1
Washington St DN21. . . . . .**24** D6
Wash Pit La
Colston Bassett NG12 . . .**200** D8
Hickling LE14 . . . .**210** C5
Wash Tub La NG23. . . . .**98** D4
Wasnidge Cl NG3 . . . .**223** F3
Wasnidge Wlk NG3 . . . . . .**223** F4
Watchorn Cl NG23 . . . .**122** F2
Watchwood Gr NG14. . . . . .**148** F8
Watcombe Cir NG5 . . . . . .**161** B1
Watcombe Rd NG5 . . . . . .**161** C1
Watendlath Cl NG2 . . . . . .**186** C5
Waterdown Cl NG19 . . . . . .**88** D6
Waterdown Rd NG11. . . . . .**184** D1
Waterfield Ave NG20. . . . . .**74** A5
Waterfield Way
Clipstone NG21 . . . .**89** F4
Clipstone NG21 . . . .**90** A4
Mansfield NG21 . . . .**89** F4
Water Fir Dr 2 DN11 . . . . . .**8** F4
Waterford St NG6. . . . .**160** E3
Waterfront Ctry Pk★
. . . .**7** C2
Waterfront The NG24 . . . .**139** E7
Waterfurrows La NG12 . . .**164** D1
Waterhouse La NG4 . . . . . .**163** A2
Water La
Carlton in Lindrick S81 . . .**26** A6
Long Clawson LE14 . . . . .**211** E4
Mansfield NG19 . . . .**87** B3
Newark-on-Trent NG24 . . .**124** F1
Oxton NG25 . . . .**134** B3
Radcliffe on Trent NG12 . .**175** E3
Retford DN22 . . . .**39** F8
Shelford NG12 . . . .**164** D1
South Normanton DE55. . .**113** B6
Tickhill DN11 . . . .**8** A6
Waterloo Cl DE55. . . . .**113** C8
Waterloo Cres NG7 . . . . . .**222** C4
Waterloo La NG9 . . . .**170** F6
Waterloo Prom NG7 . . . . . .**222** C4
Waterloo Rd
Hucknall NG15 . . . .**131** A2
3 Mansfield NG19 . . . . .**88** B2

Waterloo Rd continued
Nottingham NG7 . . . .**222** C4
Watermark Cl 16 NG5. .**161** B1
Water Mdws S80 . . . .**35** D1
Water Mdws Swimming
Complex NG18 . . . .**102** C6
Watermeadows The
NG10. . . . .**193** B8
Water Orton Cl NG9. . . . . .**182** E3
Waters Edge 6 NG24. . . .**125** A1
Waterside Cl
2 Loughborough LE11. .**220** B5
Sandiacre NG10 . . . .**182** B3
West Bridgford NG2 . . . . .**186** C6
Waterside Gdns NG7. . . . .**172** E1
Waterside Lound Hall Est
DN22 . . . .**64** E7
Waterside Orchard DN10. .**6** E1
Waterside Way NG4 . . . . . .**174** A2
Waterslack Rd DN11. . . . . . .**9** B4
Waterson Ave NG18. . . . . .**102** F3
Waterson Cl NG18 . . . .**103** A4
Waterson Oaks NG18 . . . .**102** F4
Waterway St W NG2 . . . . .**173** C2
Waterway St 3 NG2. . . . . .**173** D2
Waterway The NG10. . . . . .**182** C4
Waterworks Dr NG21 . . . . .**90** C5
Waterworks St DN21. . . . . .**24** D6
Watford Rd NG8 . . . .**160** B2
Watkins La NG22 . . . .**32** D6
Watkin St NG3. . . . .**223** E4
WATNALL **159** A8
Watnall Cres NG19. . . . . . .**101** E7
Watnall Rd
Hucknall NG15 . . . .**145** E4
Nuthall NG16 . . . .**159** C6
Watnall Rd Aerodrome
NG15 . . . .**145** E3
Watson Ave
Mansfield NG18 . . . .**102** C7
Nottingham NG3 . . . .**174** B6
Watson Cl NG23 . . . .**68** E5
Watson Pk DN10 . . . .**23** C8
Watson Rd
Ilkeston DE7 . . . .**157** C2
Worksop S80 . . . .**35** F2
Watson's La LE14 . . . .**202** B3
Watson St NG20 . . . .**74** B4
Watts Cl NG5 . . . .**162** C8
Wavell Cl 2 S81. . . . .**35** D8
Wavell Cres
Everton DN10. . . . .**11** A1
Mattersey DN10 . . . .**20** A8
Waveney Cl NG5. . . . .**162** A6
Waverley Ave
Beeston NG9 . . . .**184** A5
Carlton NG4 . . . .**163** A1
Waverley Pl S80 . . . .**47** A8
Waverley Rd NG18 . . . .**102** B4
Waverley St
Long Eaton NG10 . . . .**193** E8
Nottingham NG7 . . . .**223** D3
Tibshelf DE55. . . . .**99** A7
Waverley Terr NG1 . . . . . .**223** D3
Waverley Way S80. . . . .**47** A8
Waverly Cl NG17. . . . .**115** D5
Waydale LE12 . . . .**216** C3
Wayford Wlk 6 NG6. . . . . .**160** B8
Wayne Cl NG7 . . . .**184** E1
Weardale Rd NG5 . . . .**161** B2
Wearmouth Gdns
5 Nottingham NG5 . . . .**147** A1
1 Nottingham NG5 . . . .**147** F1
Weave Cl NG6 . . . .**160** E4
Weaver Ave NG4 . . . .**140** A4
Weaver Cl LE11. . . . .**220** B1
Weavers Cl LE12 . . . .**205** F3
Weaver's La NG15,
NG16. . . . .**129** F3
Weavers The NG24. . . . . . .**139** C6
Weavers Way DE55 . . . . . .**113** B6
Weaverthorpe Rd NG5 . . .**162** A5
Weaving Gdns NG5. . . . . . .**161** C5
Webb Ellis Rd NG17. . . . . .**114** F7
Webb Rd NG8 . . . .**172** B7
Webb St NG15 . . . .**130** D2
Webster Ave NG16 . . . . . .**143** F1
Webster Cl NG21. . . . .**104** B1
Webster Rd LE11 . . . .**220** D3
Wedding Dr S80. . . . .**47** A3
Weedon Cl NG3 . . . .**174** A6
Weekday Cross NG1. . . . . .**223** E2
Weetman Ave NG20. . . . . . .**74** B6
Weetman Gdns 12
NG5. . . . .**161** A8
Weighbridge Rd
Mansfield NG18 . . . .**102** C6
Shirebrook NG20. . . . .**72** F2
Shirebrook NG20. . . . .**73** A1
Shirebrook NG20. . . . .**73** A3
Weightman Ave NG4. . . . . .**162** F1
Weightman Dr NG16. . . . . .**158** B7
Weirside S81. . . . .**16** F6
Welbeck Abbey★ S80. . . . .**46** A1
Welbeck Ave
Carlton NG4 . . . .**162** D2
Newark-on-Trent NG24 . . .**125** A1
Welbeck Cl
Nottingham NG3 . . . .**223** E4
Sutton in Ashfield NG17 . .**100** F5
Welbeck College La
Welbeck S80 . . . .**36** B7
Welbeck S80. . . . .**46** A1
Welbeck Dr NG21. . . . .**75** F2
Welbeck Gdns
Beeston NG9 . . . .**182** F3
Nottingham NG5 . . . .**162** A4
Welbeck Gr NG13 . . . .**177** C4
Welbeck Rd NG24 . . . .**66** A3
Welbeck Prim Sch
NG2 . . . .**173** C2

Welbeck Rd
3 Harworth DN11. . . . . .**8** F5
Harworth DN11. . . . .**9** A5
Long Eaton NG10 . . . .**182** C3
Mansfield Woodhouse
NG19 . . . .**88** C3
Radcliffe on Trent NG12 . .**176** A4
Retford DN22 . . . .**39** E4
West Bridgford NG2 . . . . .**185** E8
Welbeck Sq NG17 . . . .**100** C6
Welbeck St
Creswell S80 . . . .**58** E8
Kirkby-in-Ashfield NG17 . .**115** C5
Mansfield NG18 . . . .**102** A7
Market Warsop NG20 . . . .**74** B4
Sutton in Ashfield NG17 . .**100** F2
Whitwell S80 . . . .**45** A6
Worksop S80 . . . .**35** F4
Welbeck Wlk NG3 . . . .**223** E4
Welby Ave NG7 . . . .**222** B2
Welch Ave NG9 . . . .**182** E8
Welfare Cl NG20 . . . .**72** E3
Welfitt Gr NG20. . . . .**59** B2
Welham Cres NG5 . . . .**162** A7
Welham Gr DN22 . . . .**40** A8
Welham Rd DN22 . . . .**40** A8
Welland Cl
Newark-on-Trent NG24 . . .**125** B2
Worksop S81 . . . .**35** F7
Welland Gdns NG13. . . . . .**177** D3
Wellcroft Cl NG18 . . . .**101** F5
Wellesley Cl S81 . . . .**35** D8
Wellesley Cres NG8. . . . . .**159** D2
Well Fen La NG23. . . . .**156** D7
Well Hill Dr DN11 . . . .**9** A4
Wellin Cl NG12 . . . .**186** B3
Wellin Ct NG12 . . . .**186** B3
Wellington Ave NG13. . . . .**177** B8
Wellington Cir NG1 . . . . . .**223** D2
Wellington Cl NG20 . . . . . .**74** B3
Wellington Cres NG2 . . . . .**185** F7
Wellington Gr NG16. . . . . . .**9** F8
Wellingtonia Cres 8
NG12. . . . .**186** B2
Wellington Pl NG16 . . . . . .**143** F2
Wellington Rd
Burton Joyce NG14 . . . . .**164** A5
1 Newark-on-Trent
NG24 . . . .**140** A4
Wellington Sq
Nottingham NG7 . . . .**222** C3
Retford DN22. . . . .**39** F7
Wellington St
Eastwood NG16 . . . .**143** F4
Gainsborough DN21 . . . . .**24** D7
Long Eaton NG10 . . . .**182** C2
Loughborough LE11 . . . . .**220** C3
Nottingham NG3 . . . .**223** E4
Retford DN22. . . . .**39** F7
Stapleford NG9 . . . .**182** C6
Wellington Terr NG7. . . . . .**222** C3
Wellington Villas NG7 . . . .**222** C3
Wellin La NG12 . . . .**186** B3
Well La
Upper Broughton LE14 . .**210** A1
West Markham NG22 . . . .**65** C3
WELLOW **77** E1
Wellow Cl NG17, NG19. . . .**101** D8
Wellow Gn NG22. . . . .**77** D2
Wellow House Sch
NG22 . . . .**77** D1
Wellow Rd
Eakring NG22. . . . .**92** E2
Ollerton NG22 . . . .**77** A3
Wellow NG22 . . . .**77** C2
Wells Acad The NG3. . . . . .**161** E2
Wells Cl
Collingham NG23 . . . .**98** D4
Mansfield Woodhouse
NG19 . . . .**88** D4
North Scarle LN6 . . . .**83** E3
Wells Ct LN1 . . . .**57** C3
Wells Gdns NG3 . . . .**173** F8
Wells La DN22 . . . .**43** D5
Wellspring Dale NG9 . . . . .**182** E5
Wells Rd
Edwalton NG12 . . . .**186** A2
West Bridgford NG12 . . . .**185** F1
Wells Rd Ctr Hospl The
NG3 . . . .**161** F2
Wells Rd The NG3 . . . .**161** F1
Welshcroft Cl NG17. . . . . .**115** A6
Welstead Ave NG8 . . . . . .**160** B2
Welton Gdns NG6. . . . .**160** A8
Welwyn Ave NG19 . . . .**88** E4
Welwyn Rd NG8 . . . .**171** E5
Wembley Gdns NG9. . . . . .**171** B2
Wembley Rd
Arnold NG5 . . . .**162** B5
Langold S81. . . . .**16** F3
Wembley St DN21 . . . .**24** D8
Wemtworth Cl NG21. . . . . .**15** E2
Wemyss Gdns NG8. . . . . . .**172** D3
Wendling Gdns NG5. . . . . .**161** B8
Wendover Dr NG8 . . . .**160** B2
Wenham La NG17. . . . .**99** F4
Wenlock Cl NG16 . . . .**158** C8
Wenlock Dr
Hucknall NG15 . . . .**146** C8
West Bridgford NG2 . . . . .**185** F5
Wensleydale S81. . . . .**36** B7
Wensleydale Cl
Mansfield NG19 . . . .**88** E1
Nottingham NG8 . . . .**160** D1
Wensleydale Rd NG10. . . .**193** B6
Wensley Rd NG5. . . . .**161** E5
Wensor Ave NG9 . . . .**183** F8
Wentbridge Dr NG18. . . . . .**103** A4
Wentworth Cl NG19. . . . . . .**88** F7
Wentworth Cnr NG24. . . . .**139** E5

Wentworth Croft DE75 .**143** A3
Wentworth Ct
Bawtry DN10 . . . .**10** A6
Kimberley NG16 . . . .**158** E6
Wentworth Gn NG22 . . . . .**39** D3
Wentworth Rd
Beeston NG9 . . . .**183** C6
Kirkby-in-Ashfield NG17 . .**114** E7
Nottingham NG5 . . . .**161** B2
Wentworth St DE7 . . . .**157** E4
Wentworth Way NG12 . . . .**186** C3
Wesleyan Chapel Wlk
NG9. . . . .**182** D7
Wesley Ave NG9 . . . .**183** F6
Wesley Cl
Balderton NG24 . . . .**140** D4
Hathern LE12 . . . .**213** A1
Wesley Gr 10 NG5. . . . . . .**161** B1
Wesley Pl NG9. . . . .**182** E8
Wesley Rd DN22 . . . .**39** F7
Wesley St
Annesley Woodhouse
NG17. . . . .**130** A8
Ilkeston DE7 . . . .**157** E4
Langley Mill NG16 . . . . . .**143** C3
12 Nottingham NG5. . . .**161** B1
Wesley Way
North Scarle LN6 . . . .**83** E3
Ruddington NG11. . . . . . .**196** D6
Wessex Cl S81. . . . .**36** A6
Wessex Dr NG16 . . . .**158** A8
Wessex Rd S81 . . . .**36** A6
West Ave
Sandiacre NG10. . . . .**182** A6
Stapleford NG9 . . . .**182** E6
West Bridgford NG2 . . . . .**185** E7
West Bank LN1 . . . .**56** F2
West Bank Ave NG18. . . . .**102** B8
West Bank Lea NG19. . . . . .**88** B1
West Bank Link NG19 . . . . .**88** B1
West Bank Mews DE74 . . .**203** C2
West Bank Wynd NG18 . . .**102** B8
Westborough La NG23 .**156** F1
Westbourne Cl
Mansfield Woodhouse
NG19 . . . .**88** E4
Retford DN22. . . . .**40** A6
Sutton in Ashfield NG17 . .**100** E8
Westbourne Rd
Selston NG16 . . . .**129** A2
Sutton in Ashfield NG17 . .**100** C3
Westbourne View
NG17. . . . .**100** C3
Westbrecks La DN22. . . . . .**43** A3
WEST BRIDGFORD **186** A4
West Bridgford Inf Sch
NG2 . . . .**185** E2
West Bridgford Jun Sch
NG2 . . . .**185** D5
West Bridgford Sch The
NG2. . . . .**185** D5
Westbrook Ave NG15 . . . .**116** A3
Westbrook Dr NG21. . . . . .**104** B1
West Brook La NG23 . . . . .**112** A6
West Burton Meadow
Nature Reserve**★**
DN22 . . . .**32** D7
West Burton Medieval
Village of**★** DN22. . . . . . .**32** F7
Westbury Cl NG9 . . . .**183** C4
Westbury Rd NG5. . . . .**161** A2
Westbury St NG6. . . . .**160** F2
Westbury Sch NG8. . . . . . .**171** E8
Westby La NG16 . . . .**158** D3
West Carr Rd DN22 . . . . . .**39** D6
West Cl NG12 . . . .**197** E2
Westcliffe Ave
Carlton NG4 . . . .**162** E1
Radcliffe on Trent NG12 . .**176** A4
West Cres NG9 . . . .**184** B4
West Croft Ct DN22 . . . . . .**42** F2
Westcroft Dr LN1 . . . .**57** A5
Westcross Ave NG9. . . . . .**182** E8
West Ct DN22 . . . .**39** D7
Westdale Ave NG17. . . . . .**101** A5
Westdale Cl NG10 . . . .**193** A5
Westdale Cres NG4 . . . . . .**162** E1
Westdale Ct
1 Carlton NG4. . . . .**162** D2
Carlton NG4. . . . .**162** D2
Westdale Inf Sch NG3. . . .**162** C3
Westdale Jun Sch NG3. . . .**162** B3
Westdale La E NG4 . . . . . .**162** E1
Westdale La W NG3. . . . . .**162** A3
Westdale Rd
Mansfield NG19 . . . .**88** D1
Westwood NG16 . . . .**128** C4
West Dr NG21 . . . .**76** A2
WEST DRAYTON **51** A2
West Drayton Ave
Clumber and Hardwick
S80. . . . .**48** F1
West Drayton DN22. . . . . .**50** F2
West End
Beeston NG9 . . . .**183** F5
Beeston NG9 . . . .**183** F6
Calverton NG14. . . . .**148** C7
Farndon NG24 . . . .**138** F4
Long Clawson LE14 . . . . .**211** C3
Long Whatton LE12 . . . . .**212** A4
Pinxton NG16. . . . .**113** C4
Sutton in Ashfield NG17 . .**100** A3
West End Arc NG1 . . . .**223** D2
West End Cl NG13 . . . .**181** A2
West End St NG9 . . . .**182** C5
West End Villas 3
NG4. . . . .**175** E3
Westerdale S81 . . . .**36** A8
Westerdale Dr NG12. . . . . .**186** C4
Westerfield Way NG11. . . .**185** A5
Westerham Cl NG8 . . . . . .**171** D7

Westerham Rd NG11...196 B6
Westerhope Cl NG12...186 C4
Westerlands NG9......182 F6
Western Ave
  Bingham NG13..........177 D5
  Kirkby-in-Ashfield NG17..115 B3
  Mansfield NG18........101 F5
  Saxilby LN1.............56 F4
Western Bvd NG8.....172 D8
Western Cl NG18......101 E5
Western Fields NG11..196 B6
Western Gdns NG8....172 D8
Western Rd LE14......219 A5
Western St NG1.......223 F3
Western Terr NG7......222 C2
Western Wlk DN10......10 A8
Westfield Cl
  Mansfield NG19........101 F8
  Sutton in Ashfield NG17..100 E2
Westfield Dr
  Ilkeston DE7...........157 D2
  Mansfield NG19........101 F8
  Worksop S80............36 A5
Westfield La
  Collingham NG23........111 E8
  Mansfield NG18, NG19...101 F8
  Woodborough NG14.....149 A4
Westfield Rd
  Annesley Woodhouse
  NG17................115 B1
  Bingham NG13.........177 D4
  Retford DN22...........39 D6
Westfield Way NG24...139 A4
West Furlong
  Cotgrave NG12.........188 A2
  Retford DN22...........39 D8
Westgate
  Southwell NG25........136 D8
  Worksop S80............35 E2
West Gate
  Long Eaton NG10......193 E7
  1 Mansfield NG18.....102 B7
  Tickhill DN11............8 A6
Westgate Ms NG25....136 D8
Westgate St NG3......173 E6
Westgate View S80.....35 E2
Westglade Prim Sch
  NG5.................160 F8
West Gr Rd DN22......39 F5
WEST HALLAM.........157 A1
Westhay Ct NG8......172 C5
West Hill
  Mansfield NG18........102 A8
  Sutton in Ashfield NG17..100 D6
West Hill Ave NG18...102 B7
West Hill Pk NG19.....88 B3
West Hill Rd DN22.....39 D3
West Hill Wy NG18....102 B7
Westholme Gdns NG8..172 C6
Westhorpe Ave NG3...173 F5
Westhorpe Dr NG10....193 C8
Westhorpe Mkt Pl
  NG25................136 C8
Westhouse Rd NG15..146 E5
West La
  Edwinstowe NG21.......76 A2
  Girton NG23............82 E1
Westland Ave NG15...145 D4
Westland Dr NG16.....113 C3
West Lawns The NG25..136 C8
WEST LEAKE..........205 A1
West Leake Lane
  NG11................204 D5
West Leake Rd LE12..205 C1
Westleigh NG19........88 D6
Westleigh Rd NG16...159 E2
West Manor Pk NG14..149 F6
WEST MARKHAM........65 B6
Westminster Ave
  Kirkby-in-Ashfield
  NG17................115 C5
  Stapleford NG10......182 C5
Westminster Cl
  Morton DN21............15 B5
  Nottingham NG3.......173 E7
  Worksop S81............36 A7
Westminster Dr NG2..176 E3
Westminster Way
  NG15................146 C4
West Moor NG2........174 D4
Westmoore Cl NG3....162 A3
Westmoor La
  Kettlethorpe LN1........55 D3
  Kettlethorpe LN1........69 D8
  Newton on Trent LN1....55 C1
  Newton on Trent LN1....69 C8
West Moor Rd DN10...13 E6
Westmoreland Ct 8
  NG5.................161 B1
Westmorland Ct DN11..9 A4
Westmorland Dr.......25 F8
Westmorland Way
  NG16................128 B3
West Nottinghamshire Coll
  (18) NG18............102 B7
WESTON..............81 B4
Weston Ave NG7......173 A7
Weston Cl
  Arnold NG5...........161 E4
  Sutton in Ashfield NG17..115 C8
Weston La NG23........81 D5
Weston Rd NG22, NG23..80 A6
Weston St DE75.......157 A8
West Pk Ct NG11.....193 D7
West Pk L Ctr DE72...193 B7
West Pk Pl DN22......39 D6
Westray Cl NG9.......171 B3
West Rd
  Nottingham NG8.......172 D4
  Thorney NG23..........69 F7

West St
  Arnold NG5...........161 E7
  Harworth DN11..........9 A5
  Hucknall NG15........146 A7
  Kimberley NG16.......159 A4
  Langley Mill NG16....143 B3
  Misson DN10.............4 B2
  Morton DN21............15 B4
  Nottingham NG2.......173 E4
  Retford DN22...........39 E6
  Shelford NG13........164 C1
  Warsop Vale NG20......73 D4
  Whaley Thorns NG20....58 F3
  Whaley Thorns NG20....59 A3
  Worksop S80............35 E2
WEST STOCKWITH.......7 D2
West Stockwith
  Park DN10...............7 C1
West Terr
  Hucknall NG15........146 A7
  6 Ilkeston DE7.......157 F1
West Thorpe LE12....217 C7
West View
  Carlton in Lindrick S81...25 F8
  West Bridgford NG2...185 D5
Westview Ct NG4.....174 F8
West View Rd NG4....174 F8
Westville Dr NG15....145 E4
Westville Gdns NG3...173 D7
Westward Ave NG9....184 A5
Westway
  Cotgrave NG12........187 F2
  Worksop S81............36 A7
West Wells La DN10...12 E2
Westwick Rd
  Nottingham NG8.......171 C5
  Nottingham NG8.......171 C5
Westwick St DE7.....170 A6
West Wlk
  1 Nottingham NG1...173 E4
  Retford DN22...........39 C8
WESTWOOD............128 C3
Westwood Dr S80......35 B3
West Wood Est DN10...9 F6
Westwood Inf Sch
  NG16................128 C4
Westwood Rd
  Bircotes DN10...........9 F6
  Nottingham NG2.......173 F4
Wetherby Cl
  Kimberley NG16.......158 E7
  Nottingham NG8.......160 B1
Wetherlam Cl NG2....173 C2
Wetlands Waterfowl
  Reserve* DN22........29 D7
Wetsyke La NG24.....140 E4
Wetton La DE55........99 A6
Whaddon Ct LE11....220 C1
WHALEY..............58 D4
Whaley Bridge Cl
  NG18................103 C5
Whaley Comm S44.....58 D4
Whaley Common NG20..58 D4
Whaley Rd
  Holbeck NG20..........58 F5
  Holbeck NG20..........59 B5
  Whaley NG20...........58 B3
  Whaley Thorns NG20....58 E2
WHALEY THORNS........59 A2
Whaley Thorns Prim Sch
  NG20................59 A3
Wharfedale Gdns NG18..103 A5
Wharfedale Rd NG10..193 A6
Wharfedale
  Nottingham NG8.......171 B4
  Worksop S81............36 A7
Wharf Gdns NG13....177 C3
Wharf La NG12.......175 E3
Wharf Rd
  9 Mansfield NG18....102 B6
  Misterton DN10.........6 F1
  Nottingham NG7.......223 D1
  Pinxton NG16.........113 D2
  Retford DN22...........39 E6
  Stanton Hill NG17.....100 C6
Wharf St DN10.........10 A7
Wharf The
  Morton DN21............15 B4
  Newark-on-Trent NG24..124 E1
Wharmby Ave NG19....87 D3
Wharncliffe Rd
  7 Ilkeston DE7.......157 E1
  Loughborough LE11...220 C3
  Retford DN22...........39 E4
Wharton Cres
  Beeston NG9..........183 F4
  Beeston NG9..........184 A4
Wharton St DN22......40 A6
Whatten Gdns* LE12..212 E5
WHATTON.............179 A3
Whatton Ct 2 NG18...103 A3
Whatton Dr NG2......185 B3
Whatton Est LE12....212 D4
Whatton Rd
  Hathern LE12.........212 E2
  Kegworth DE74.......203 C1
  Kegworth DE74.......212 B8
  Whatton Rise NG5....161 B4
Wheatacre Rd NG7...184 F1
Wheat Cl NG8........171 D5
Wheat Croft S81.......36 B7
Wheatcroft Bsns Pk
Wheatcroft Dr
  5 Edwalton NG12....185 F2
  3 Edwalton NG12....186 A2
Wheatfields Cres NG19..88 E5
Wheatfields Rd NG17..100 E7

Wheatgrass Hill NG25,
  NG23................122 D4
Wheatgrass Rd NG9...183 B5
Wheatland Dr LE11...220 C2
Wheatley Ave NG17...114 F5
Wheatley Cl
  Mansfield Woodhouse
  NG19................88 F1
  Ruddington NG11.....196 C5
Wheatley Dr NG4.....174 C7
Wheatley Gr NG9.....183 F4
Wheatley La NG23....112 B4
Wheatley Rd
  Clayworth DN22........21 F3
  South Wheatley DN22...31 F7
  Sturton le Steeple DN22..32 B6
Wheatsheaf Av 3
  NG24................125 B4
Wheatsheaf Ct NG14..163 F4
Wheeldale Cl NG8....171 B4
Wheeldon Cl DE7.....157 F6
Wheeldon St DN21.....24 D7
Wheeler Ave NG16....144 B1
Wheeler Gate
  Nottingham NG1......223 E2
  Selston NG16.........129 A2
Wheelwrghts The NG21..76 B2
Wheldon Ave NG4....162 C2
Whernside Rd NG5....161 F5
Whetstone Cl NG8....159 D3
Whickham Ct 4 NG2..173 D1
Whilton Cl NG17......101 B5
Whimsey Pk NG4.....174 E6
Whinbush La NG14...133 D4
Whinfell Cl NG7......184 F2
Whinlatter Dr NG2...186 C6
Whinleys La DN22.....41 B8
Whinleys Rd DN22.....31 A2
Whinney Bank NG19...88 D4
Whinney Hill NG19....88 D4
Whinney La
  Boughton NG22........63 D1
  New Ollerton NG22.....77 D5
  New Ollerton NG22.....77 D7
Whinney La North
  NG22................77 D7
Whinney Moor Cl DN22..39 F5
Whinney Moor La DN22..39 F5
Whinney Moor Way
  DN22................39 F5
Whinny Haugh La DN11..8 A4
Whipling Cl NG13.....179 B3
Whiston Cl NG5.......161 A6
Whitaker Cl DN22......29 C1
Whitakers Farm LE14..202 C3
Whitbread St NG7....172 F8
Whitburn Rd NG9.....182 E3
Whitby Cl NG8........171 B4
Whitby Cres NG5.....162 A5
Whitby Rd
  Eastwood NG16.......144 A3
  Harworth DN11..........9 A5
Whitchurch Cl NG5...160 F8
Whitcliffe Gdns NG11..185 A4
Whitcombe Ct DN22...39 C4
Whitcombe Gdns
  11 Nottingham NG5..147 A1
  Nottingham NG5......161 A8
White Ave S81..........16 E3
Whitebeam Cl 3
  NG12................186 A1
Whitebeam Gdns NG6..159 F7
Whitechapel St NG6..160 D2
Whitedale Rd NG14...148 C8
White Furrows NG12..187 E2
Whitegate LE11......220 C5
Whitegate Prim Sch
  NG11................184 D1
Whitegates Way NG11..99 E2
Whitegate Vale NG11..184 D1
Whitehall Ct
  Retford DN22...........39 E6
  Upper Saxondale NG12..176 E3
Whitehall Gdns DN22...39 F6
Whitehall Rd DN22.....39 F6
White Hart La NG23...142 A8
White Hart St NG18..102 B6
White Hart Yd S80.....35 E1
Whitehead Cl DE7....157 D2
Whitehead Dr NG16...143 A8
Whitehead La NG17...100 F6
Whitehouse Ave LE11..220 C2
Whitehouse Ct DN11...9 C5
White House Rd DN11...9 C4
White Lady Ct NG15...117 B3
Whitelands NG12......188 A2
White Lodge Gdns
  NG8.................171 D7
Whitely Ave 13 DE7...157 F5
Whitely Cl NG9.......182 E7
Whitemoor Ave 5
  NG8.................172 D8
Whitemoor Ct NG8...172 D8
Whitemoor La NG22...112 A4
Whitemoor Prim Sch
  NG8.................172 D8
Whitemoor Rd NG6...160 D2
Whitemoss Cl NG8....172 C5
White Park Pl DN22...39 C4
Whitere St NG5.......160 E3
White Rose Ave NG19..102 D5
White's Ave NG4......174 B6
Whites Farm DN22....24 F8
Whitestone Cl NG18..103 A3
Whitestub La NG22...106 F5

White's Wood Acad 5
  DN21................24 F8
Whites Wood La DN21..24 E8
White's Wood La 5
  DN21................24 F8
Whitewater Cl NG22...77 C5
Whitewater La
  Blyth S81.............18 A5
  Walesby NG22.........63 B1
Whitfield Cl NG11....185 B6
Whitfield St NG24....140 A7
Whiting Ave NG9.....182 F2
Whitney Cl NG19......89 A1
Whittaker Rd
  Beeston NG9..........183 A3
  Rainworth NG21......118 A8
Whittier Rd NG2.....174 A3
Whittingham Ct NG3..162 A3
Whittingham Rd NG3..162 A3
Whittle Cl NG24......125 C2
Whittle Way NG24....141 A2
Whitton Cl
  4 Beeston NG9......183 C2
  3 Nottingham NG5..147 B1
  Ranskill DN22.........19 B4
WHITWELL............45 B6
Whitwell Cl
  Ilkeston DE7.........157 E6
  Nottingham NG8.....159 E1
Whitwell Prim Sch S80..45 A5
Whitwell Rd
  Nottingham NG8.....159 E1
  Thorpe Salvin S80.....34 A4
Whitwell Sta S80......45 A5
Whitworth Dr
  Carlton NG4..........162 A3
  Radcliffe on Trent NG12..175 F2
Whitworth Rise NG5..160 F8
Whomsley Ct NG24...140 D8
Whyatt Ct NG5.......161 D6
Whyburn La NG15.....145 D7
Whyburn St NG15....146 C5
Whysall Rd NG10.....193 B7
Whyston Ct NG15....145 C5
Wibberley Dr NG11...196 B7
Wichal Ct NG15......161 C5
Wichnor Cl NG11.....184 E4
Wickenby Ave NG14..133 C1
Wickens Wlk NG3....173 E6
Wicker Cl NG6.......160 E4
Wickerwood Dr NG17..114 E6
Wicket Cl
  3 Kirkby-in-Ashfield
  NG17................115 A3
  Loughborough LE11...220 A2
Wicket Gr NG7.......222 A2
Wickets The
  Bottesford NG13.....181 B1
  Market Warsop NG20...74 B3
Wickliffe Pk NG23....156 D6
Wickstead Cl NG5....161 F3
Widdington St NG15..147 F2
Widdowson Cl NG6...159 E8
Widdowson Rd NG10..193 B5
Widecombe La NG11..195 D8
Wide La
  Hathern LE12.........213 A1
  Wymeswold LE12....217 C3
Wide St LE12.........213 A1
WIDMERPOOL.........208 B5
Widmerpool La
  Keyworth NG12......208 B8
  Keyworth NG12......208 D1
  Stanton-on-the-Wolds
  NG12................198 B1
Widmerpool Pk NG12..208 B4
Widmerpool Rd
  Wysall NG12..........207 D3
  Wysall NG12..........207 D4
Widmerpool St NG16..113 C2
Widnall Dr NG13.....177 D6
Widows Row LN1......55 B5
Wighay Rd NG15.....131 A2
Wigley Cl NG3........173 E6
Wigman Rd
  Nottingham NG8.....171 E7
  Nottingham NG9.....171 D8
Wigsley Rd
  Harby NG23...........70 C2
  North Scarle LN6......83 D5
  Thorney NG23..........69 F4
  Thorney NG23..........70 A4
Wigthorpe La S81......26 A4
Wigwam Gr NG15....146 C7
Wigwam La NG15....146 C7
Wilberforce Rd
  Mansfield NG19.........87 D2
  West Bridgford NG2...185 A5
Wilcox Ave NG19......88 A5
Wilcox Dr NG16......129 A1
Wilde Cres NG16.....129 A6
Wilden Cres NG7.....184 E2
Wilders Way DE74....203 A2
Wildflower Gr NG17..100 D1
Wild Flower Rise
  NG18................102 C8
Wild Hill
  Fackley NG17.........100 A7
  Huthwaite NG17.......99 E7
Wildman St NG7......222 C4
Wildman Villas DN10...14 B1
WILFORD............185 B6
Wilford Ave NG13....177 D6
Wilford Cl NG24......140 B8
Wilford Cres NG11...196 C8
Wilford Cres E NG2...173 C1
Wilford Cres W NG2..173 C1

Wilford Gr
  Nottingham NG2......173 C1
  West Bridgford NG2...185 D8
Wilford La NG2.......185 C7
Wilford Rd
  Mansfield NG18.......103 A3
  Nottingham NG2......223 E1
  West Bridgford NG11..185 D5
Wilford Sports Complex
  NG2.................185 D6
Wilford St NG2.......223 E1
Wilfred Ave NG24....140 C4
Wilfrid Gr NG2.......185 C3
Wilhallow La NG16...128 E2
Wilkins Gdns NG11...184 C1
Wilkinson Ave NG9...183 F6
Wilkinson Cl
  Beeston NG9..........183 B2
  Pleasley NG19.........87 A5
Wilkinson St NG7.....172 E8
Willam Hall Way NG24..140 E1
Willand Ct DN22......29 E1
Willaston Cl NG6.....160 C4
Willbert Rd NG5......148 A1
Willerby Rd NG5......162 A5
Willersley Dr NG2....173 C2
Willesden Gn NG16...159 D3
Willetts Ct NG17.....100 F1
Willey La NG16.......144 A8
William Ave NG5.....143 F2
William Booth Birthplace
  Mus* NG2...........173 C4
William Booth Primary Sch
  NG2.................173 C4
William Booth Rd NG2..174 A4
William Bradford Cl
  DN10...............3 C1
William Cl NG24......175 B8
William Gdns DN22....29 E1
William Gladstone CE Prim
  Sch The NG24........139 F6
William & Henry Mews
  LN6.................84 D3
William Lilley Inf Sch
  NG9.................182 D6
William Old Ct 3 NG8..172 A5
William Rd
  Stapleford NG9......182 D7
  West Bridgford NG2...185 E8
Williams Dr NG14....133 C1
Williams La NG24....140 E2
Williamson Gdns DN11..24 E2
Williamson St NG19..101 E7
Williams Rd NG9.....183 A3
Williams St S81.........16 E3
William St
  Hucknall NG15.......146 A7
  Long Eaton NG10....182 C2
  Long Eaton NG10....193 A6
  Newark-on-Trent NG24..140 A8
  Saxilby LN1............57 A3
William Straw Gdns S80..35 F1
Willingham Rd DN21...24 F2
Willis Rd NG24.......139 F6
Willoughby Ave
  Long Eaton NG10....182 C3
  Nottingham NG7......222 B2
Willoughby Chase DN21..24 E5
Willoughby Cl NG7...184 B8
Willoughby Ct
  11 Mansfield NG18...103 A2
  Norwell NG23.........110 A8
  Nottingham NG7......222 B1
Willoughby Gdns NG12..104 B1
Willoughby La NG12..207 F3
WILLOUGHBY-ON-THE-
  WOLDS..............217 D8
Willoughby Prim Sch
  LE14................217 C7
Willoughby Rd
  West Bridgford NG2...185 F6
  Widmerpool NG12....208 C3
Willoughby St
  Beeston NG9..........184 A6
  Cossall DE7...........158 A2
  Gainsborough DN21....24 D7
  Nottingham NG7......222 B1
Willoughby Way NG22..175 B2
Willow Ave
  Carlton NG4..........175 A8
  Carlton in Lindrick S81...25 E7
  Hucknall NG15.......145 D4
  Kirkby-in-Ashfield NG17..114 C6
  Long Eaton NG10....182 C2
  Mansfield Woodhouse
  NG19................89 A1
  Misterton DN10.........6 E2
  Ranskill DN22.........19 C4
  Shirebrook NG20.......72 D5
  Stapleford NG9......182 D6
Willowbridge Cl NG19..87 D2
Willowbridge La NG17..100 D2
Willow Brook NG2....198 A2
Willowbrook Ct 6
  NG2.................173 C1
Willow Brook Prim Sch
  NG12................198 A2
Willow Cl
  Burton Joyce NG14...163 F5
  Calverton NG14......149 C6
  East Leake LE12......214 D6
  Gainsborough DN21....15 B3
  Granby NG13.........191 B5
  Nottingham NG16.....143 B1
  Radcliffe on Trent NG12..175 F2
  Saxilby LN1............57 B3
  Selston NG16.........129 B7
  South Normanton DE55..113 B5
  Worksop S80............35 E1
Willow Cres
  Carlton NG4..........163 A2

Willow Cres continued
  Lambley NG4..........163 C7
  Sutton in Ashfield NG17..100 D3
Willow Cl NG16.......129 A4
Willowdene NG12....188 A3
Willow Dr
  Annesley Woodhouse
  NG15................129 F6
  North Muskham NG23..110 E3
  1 Shireoaks S81.......35 A7
Willow Farm Prim Sch
  NG4.................163 A2
Willow Gd NG17......101 B2
Willow Gr
  3 Harworth DN11......8 F4
  Retford DN22...........40 A5
Willow Hill DN10.......11 F2
Willow Hill Cl NG6...160 A6
Willow Holt
  Lowdham NG14.......150 A5
  Retford DN22...........39 E3
  Sutton on Trent NG23...96 F8
Willow La
  Beckingham DN10......23 C8
  Carlton NG4..........163 A2
  Langar NG13..........190 C2
  Maythorne NG25.....121 D4
  Torksey Lock LN1......44 B1
Willow Mws DN10......23 C8
Willow Poole La LE12..213 C5
Willow Rd
  Bingham NG13.......178 A4
  Carlton NG4..........175 A8
  Cotgrave NG12.......188 A5
  New Balderton NG24..140 C5
  Nottingham NG7......172 E2
  West Bridgford NG2...185 E3
Willow Rise NG10.....182 B5
Willow Rundle Dr
  NG23................153 D5
Willows The
  Everton DN10..........11 C3
  Farndon NG24.........139 A4
  Nottingham NG8......172 A7
  Pleasley NG19.........87 A6
  Worksop S80............35 E2
Willows Wlk NG24....140 A4
Willow Tree Cl NG19...89 D2
Willow Wong NG14...163 F5
Will Scarlet Cl NG21..118 A4
Willwell Dr NG2......185 C3
Wilmington Ct LE11..220 C2
Wilmington Gdns
  NG5.................161 D6
Wilmore Cl NG9......183 D4
Wilmore Way NG19...101 C5
Wilmot La NG9.......183 F5
Wilmot St
  Ilkeston DE7.........157 E1
  Long Eaton NG10....193 A5
Wilmot Way S81........36 C3
Wilne Ave NG10......193 A4
Wilne Rd NG10.......193 A4
Wilsic Rd DN11........8 A8
Wilson Ave NG17.....114 F5
Wilson Cl
  Arnold NG5..........162 B5
  Mattersey DN10.......20 A8
Wilson Rd NG16......143 F1
Wilson's La NG25....137 E4
Wilson St
  Gainsborough DN21....15 B1
  Newark-on-Trent NG24..124 F1
  Pinxton NG16.........113 D3
  Radmanthwaite NG19...87 D2
Wilsthorpe Com Sch
  NG10................182 B1
Wilsthorpe Rd DE72..193 A8
Wilton Ave LE11......220 C1
Wilton Pl DE7........157 F1
Wilton Rd NG7.......222 A4
Wilton St
  5 Ilkeston DE7......157 F1
  Nottingham NG6......160 E4
Wilton Terr NG6......160 E4
Wiltshire Ave NG16..128 B4
Wilwell Farm Cutting
  Nature Reserve*
  NG11................185 B2
Wimbishthorpe Cl
  NG13................181 A3
Wimbledon Dr NG16..159 E3
Wimbledon Rd NG5...161 A3
Wimborne Cl NG12...185 C5
Wimbourne Rd NG7...222 B4
Wimpole Rd NG9.....171 D1
Winborne Cl NG19...101 D6
Winchester Ave NG9..183 E7
Winchester Cl
  East Leake LE12......205 L1
  Mansfield NG18.......103 A3
  Worksop S80............36 A7
Winchester Cres DE7..170 A8
Winchester Ct NG5...161 E3
Winchester Dr NG19...88 D4
Winchester Mws
  NG11................9 C5
Winchester St NG5...161 D2
Winchester Terr 7
  NG5.................161 C5
Winchilsea Ave NG24..140 A7
Winco Bank Way DE55..113 C7
Windemere Ave DN11...8 F4
Windermere Cl
  Carlton NG4..........162 F2
  Mansfield Woodhouse
  NG19................88 B4
  West Bridgford NG2...186 C6
  Worksop S81...........35 E8

Windermere Gdns
NG10 . . . . 182 B2
Windermere Rd
Beeston NG9 . . . . 183 D8
Hucknall NG15 . . . . 145 F7
Long Eaton NG10 . . . . . . 182 A2
Nottingham NG7 . . . . 173 A8
Windlass Cl LE11 . . . . . . 220 D3
Windles Sq NG14 . . . . . . 149 A6
Windley Dr DE7 . . . . 157 D3
Windmill Ave NG15 . . . . 146 A6
Windmill Cl
Gotham NG11 . . . . 195 B1
Kirton NG22 . . . . 78 B6
Nottingham NG3 . . . . 173 F5
Windmill Cres LE12 . . . . . 214 F8
Windmill Ct NG12 . . . . . . 197 F2
Windmill Gr NG15 . . . . . . 146 A6
Windmill Hill NG25 . . . . 134 C5
Windmill La
Mansfield NG18 . . . . 102 C8
Nottingham NG2 . . . . 173 F5
Worksop S80 . . . . 47 B7
Windmill Prim Sch
NG2 . . . . 174 A4
Windmill Rd LE11 . . . . . . 220 D3
Windmill View NG2 . . . . 174 A4
Windmill Way
Blidworth NG21 . . . . 117 F4
Kegworth DE74 . . . . 203 B2
Sutton in Ashfield NG17 . 100 A4
Windrush Cl
Beeston NG9 . . . . 171 D1
Sutton in Ashfield NG17 . 100 A4
Windsmoor Rd NG16 . . . 143 D8
Windsor Ave
Newark-on-Trent NG24 . . 139 E6
Sutton in Ashfield NG17 . 100 B3
Windsor Cl
Collingham NG23 . . . . . . 112 A8
Gringley on the Hill DN10 . 12 E2
Hucknall NG15 . . . . 146 B8
Nottingham NG8 . . . . 172 D7
Trowell NG9 . . . . 170 A5
Windsor Cres
Arnold NG5 . . . . 162 B5
Stapleford NG9 . . . . 182 E7
Windsor Ct
Bingham NG13 . . . . 177 C4
Carlton in Lindrick S81 . . . 25 F6
Harworth DN11 . . . . 9 B5
Sandiacre NG10 . . . . 182 B4
Windsor Dr NG20 . . . . . . 74 A4
Windsor Gdns
Carlton in Lindrick S81 . . . 25 E6
Mansfield NG18 . . . . 102 D5
Windsor Rd
Carlton in Lindrick S81 . . . 25 E6
Clipstone NG19 . . . . 89 D3
Mansfield NG18 . . . . 102 D5
Newark-on-Trent NG24 . . 139 F6
Retford DN22 . . . . 29 C1
Selston NG16 . . . . 129 A8
Worksop S81 . . . . 35 D7
Windsor St
Beeston NG9 . . . . 184 A6
Stapleford NG9 . . . . 182 E7
Windyridge DN10 . . . . . . 11 C3
Windy Ridge NG20 . . . . . 74 C3
Winfield's La LE12 . . . . . . 216 E2
Wing Alley NG1 . . . . 223 F2
Wingate Cl NG8 . . . . 171 F6
Wingbourne Wlk NG6 . . 146 C1
Wingfield Ave S81 . . . . . . 36 A6
Wingfield Dr
Beeston NG9 . . . . 172 A1
Ilkeston DE7 . . . . 157 D3
Wingfield Rd NG18 . . . . . 103 A4
Wings Dr NG15 . . . . 145 D3
Winifred Ct NG12 . . . . . . 185 A6
Winifred Cres NG14 . . . . 163 F4
Winifred St
Hucknall NG15 . . . . 146 B6
Rhodesia S80 . . . . 35 A4
WINKBURN 108 A1
Winkburn La
Hockerton NG22 . . . . 121 E7
Winkburn NG22 . . . . 107 F1
Winkburn NG22 . . . . 108 A1
Winkburn Rd
Mansfield NG19 . . . . 101 F7
Maplebeck NG22 . . . . . . 107 F5
Maplebeck NG22 . . . . . . 108 A6
Winnery Cl DN11 . . . . 8 A8
Winrow Gdns NG6 . . . . . 160 C3
Winscale Ave NG16 . . . . 143 D2
Winscale Gdns 15 NG5 . 161 A8
Winscombe Mount
NG11 . . . . 195 E7
Winsford Cl NG8 . . . . 160 B2
Winstanley Dr NG24 . . . 140 E8
Winster Ave
Carlton NG4 . . . . 162 A5
Ravenshead NG15 . . . . . . 117 B3
Winster Cl NG9 . . . . 171 F1
Winster Gr S81 . . . . 35 F8
Winster Way NG18 . . . . . 103 C5
Winston Cl
Arnold NG5 . . . . 162 C5
Stapleford NG9 . . . . 182 E8
Winston Ct NG24 . . . . . . 139 E5
Winston Dr NG23 . . . . . . 153 E4
Winston Gn
Mattersey DN10 . . . . 19 F8
Mattersey DN10 . . . . 20 A8
Winston Gr DN22 . . . . 30 A1
Winston Green DN10 . . . 11 A1
Winterbank Cl NG17 . . . 100 D1

Winterbeck Cl NG13 . . . 181 A3
Winterbourne Dr NG9 . . 170 E1
Winter Closes NG16 . . . . 128 F1
Winterdale Cl NG24 . . . . 125 D1
Wintern Ct DN21 . . . . 24 D6
Winterton Cl NG5 . . . . . . 161 F6
Winterton Gdns NG5 . . . 161 B7
Winterton Rise NG5 . . . . 161 B7
WINTHORPE 125 D6
Winthorpe Prim Sch
NG24 . . . . 125 D7
Winthorpe Rd
Arnold NG5 . . . . 162 A7
Gateford S81 . . . . 35 C8
Newark-on-Trent NG24 . . 125 B3
Winthorpe St NG19 . . . . 101 D6
Wintringham Cres
NG5 . . . . 162 A5
Wire La DE55 . . . . 99 B3
Wisa Terr NG5 . . . . 161 D2
Wisdom Cl 2 NG24 . . . . 140 F2
Wiseton Rd DN22 . . . . 21 C6
Wishford Ave NG7 . . . . . 222 A1
Wisley Cl NG11 . . . . 185 C3
Wisteria Dr NG12 . . . . . . 185 F2
Wisteria Rd NG4 . . . . 175 C7
Wistow Cl NG8 . . . . 172 E8
Witch La NG23 . . . . 96 F8
Witham Cl NG24 . . . . 125 B2
Withern Rd NG8 . . . . 159 F1
Withnall Cl NG4 . . . . 162 E4
Withorn Mews NG19 . . . 101 E7
Witney Cl NG5 . . . . 160 E7
Wittering Cl NG10 . . . . . 193 E5
Wiverton Rd
Bingham NG13 . . . . 177 C4
Nottingham NG7 . . . . 173 A8
Woburn Ave NG17 . . . . . 115 C5
Woburn Cl NG2 . . . . 186 C4
Woburn Croft NG10 . . . 182 A4
Woburn Gr DN22 . . . . 39 E3
Woburn La NG19 . . . . 87 C4
Woburn Pl NG7 . . . . 87 C4
Woburn Rd NG19 . . . . . . 87 C4
Woburn Rise NG5 . . . . . 162 B5
Wodehouse Ave NG11 . 195 B2
Wolds Cl LE12 . . . . 215 E5
Wolds Dr NG12 . . . . 197 F3
Wolds Farm Bsns Pk
NG12 . . . . 209 B8
Wolds La NG12 . . . . 198 B7
Wolds Rise NG12 . . . . . . 197 F3
Wolfit Ave NG24 . . . . 140 E5
Wollacombe Cl NG3 . . . 162 D5
WOLLATON 171 E4
Wollaton Ave NG4 . . . . . 162 E2
Wollaton Cl NG18 . . . . . 103 B7
Wollaton Cres NG9 . . . . 183 E8
Wollaton Ct NG6 . . . . . . 160 E6
Wollaton Hall★ NG8 . . 172 A3
Wollaton Paddocks
NG8 . . . . 171 C4
Wollaton Pk★ NG8 . . . . 171 F3
Wollaton Rd
Beeston NG9 . . . . 183 E7
Kirkby-in-Ashfield NG17 . 115 C5
Nottingham NG8 . . . . 172 D5
Wollaton Rise
Nottingham NG8 . . . . 171 E2
Retford DN22 . . . . 39 E3
Wollaton St NG1 . . . . . . 223 D3
Wollaton Vale NG8 . . . . 171 E2
Wolseley Ct NG17 . . . . . 100 F3
Wolsey Ave NG7 . . . . . . 222 B3
Wolsey Cl
Papplewick NG25 . . . . . . 136 D8
Southwell NG25 . . . . 121 D1
Wolsey Dr NG17 . . . . 115 B7
Wolsey Rd NG24 . . . . . . 125 B3
Wolsey Way 2 LE11 . . . 220 A4
Wong La DN11 . . . . 8 A8
Wood Ave
Creswell S80 . . . . 58 C8
Sandiacre NG10 . . . . 182 A5
Woodbank Cl NG22 . . . . 106 A6
Woodbank Dr NG8 . . . . . 171 D2
WOODBECK 53 A8
Woodbeck Rise
Retford DN22 . . . . 29 E1
Retford DN22 . . . . 39 E8
WOODBOROUGH 149 C3
Woodborough Rd
Mansfield NG19 . . . . 87 E1
Nottingham NG3, NG1 . . 161 E2
Woodbridge Ave NG11 . 184 E3
Woodbridge Cl DE75 . . . 143 B1
Woodchurch Rd NG5 . . 147 B1
Wood Cl
Mansfield NG18 . . . . 102 F8
Ruddington NG11 . . . . . . 196 B6
Woodcoates Rd NG22 . . . 67 B5
Woodcroft Rd LN1 . . . . . . 56 F4
Wood Dr DE74 . . . . 203 C3
Wooden Beck Hill
DN10 . . . . 13 C4
Woodend S80 . . . . 35 B5
Wood End Dr NG15 . . . . 117 A2
Woodfield Gdns S81 . . . . 35 E6
Woodfield Rd
Gainsborough DN21 . . . . 15 F1
Nottingham NG8 . . . . 159 E1
Pinxton NG16 . . . . 113 D4
Wood Gate NG1 . . . . 220 B3
Wood Gate NG4 . . . . 162 A5
Hucknall NG15 . . . . 146 B6
Woodgate Cl NG12 . . . . 187 E3
Woodgate Ct NG7 . . . . . 222 C3

Woodgate La
Beckingham LN5 . . . . 142 E8
Cotgrave NG12 . . . . 187 D3
Woodgate Rd LE12 . . . . 214 C8
Wood Gr NG14 . . . . 148 F8
Woodhall Cl
2 Kirkby-in-Ashfield
NG17 . . . . 114 E7
Mansfield NG18 . . . . 102 F8
Woodhall Cres
Saxilby LN1 . . . . 56 F4
Saxilby LN1 . . . . 57 A4
Woodhall Gdns NG18 . . 102 F8
Woodhall Gn DN22 . . . . . 39 D2
Woodhall Rd NG8 . . . . . 172 B5
Woodhead Cl NG21 . . . . . 76 B1
Woodhedge Dr NG3 . . . 174 A8
Woodhill Lk LE14 . . . . . . 218 E3
Woodhill Ave DN21 . . . . . 15 E2
Woodhill Rd NG23 . . . . . . 98 A1
Woodhorn Cl NG5 . . . . . 147 F2
Woodhouse Cl S80 . . . . . 35 B5
Woodhouse Ct NG19 . . . 88 C2
Woodhouse Gdns
NG11 . . . . 196 B8
Woodhouse La
Carlton in Lindrick S81 . . . 26 A7
Skegby NG17 . . . . 100 A7
Sutton in Ashfield NG17 . 101 A7
Woodhouse Mws NG5 . 161 A2
Woodhouse Pl NG22 . . . . 66 A2
Woodhouse Rd
Mansfield NG18 . . . . 102 B8
Norwell NG23 . . . . 109 E8
Norwell Woodhouse
NG23 . . . . 109 E8
Woodhouse St NG3 . . . . 173 F5
Woodhouse Way NG16 . 159 D3
Woodkirk Rd NG7 . . . . . 184 F2
Wood La
Barkestone-le-Vale
NG13 . . . . 192 C1
Beckingham DN10 . . . . 23 B8
Carlton NG4 . . . . 163 A2
Creswell S80 . . . . 58 D8
Drakeholes DN10 . . . . 11 F2
Egmanton NG22 . . . . 79 F5
Gotham LE12 . . . . 205 A6
Gringley on the Hill DN10 . 12 E3
Grove DN22 . . . . 41 E4
Hucknall NG15 . . . . 145 F7
Kersall NG22 . . . . 94 A1
Kingston on Soar NG11 . 204 F7
Market Warsop NG20 . . . . 73 F7
Nether Langwith NG20 . . . 59 D1
North Wheatley DN22 . . . . 22 D1
Shirebrook NG19 . . . . 72 E1
South Scarle NG23 . . . . . . 98 E6
Treswell DN22 . . . . 41 F5
West Markham NG22 . . . . 65 B4
Wiseton DN10 . . . . 12 A1
Woodland Ave
Gainsborough DN21 . . . . 15 B3
Huthwaite NG17 . . . . 99 E4
Ilkeston DE7 . . . . 157 D4
Nottingham NG6 . . . . 160 D5
Worksop S80 . . . . 36 B1
Woodland Chase DN21 . . 15 E1
Woodland Cl
Clipstone NG21 . . . . 90 B4
Cotgrave NG12 . . . . 187 F2
Farnsfield NG22 . . . . 120 A6
Hodthorpe S80 . . . . 45 C6
Radcliffe on Trent NG12 . 176 B3
Woodland Cres NG18 . . 102 F4
Woodland Ct LN1 . . . . . . 44 B1
Woodland Dr
Mansfield NG18 . . . . 102 F4
Nottingham NG3 . . . . 161 D2
Nuthall NG16 . . . . 159 F4
Southwell NG25 . . . . 121 D1
Worksop S81 . . . . 35 E6
Woodland Gr
Arnold NG5 . . . . 161 D4
Beeston NG9 . . . . 183 D5
Carlton NG4 . . . . 174 F6
Mansfield Woodhouse
NG19 . . . . 88 C4
Market Warsop NG20 . . . . 74 B4
Shirebrook NG20 . . . . 72 D2
Woodland Pk View
NG18 . . . . 101 F5
Woodland Rd
Mansfield NG18 . . . . 102 F8
West Bridgford NG2 . . . . 173 F1
Woodland Rise NG15 . . 117 A2
Woodlands NG24 . . . . . . 125 D7
Woodlands Cl
Newark-on-Trent NG24 . . 139 E6
Wymeswold LE12 . . . . . . 216 C3
Woodlands Dr LE11 . . . . 220 A2
Woodlands Farm Cl
NG15 . . . . 145 D4
Woodlands Gr NG15 . . . 145 D4
Woodland Spinney
NG23 . . . . 152 E2
Woodlands Sch NG8 . . . 172 A8
Woodlands The
Blyth S81 . . . . 18 B6
5 Mansfield NG18 . . . . . 88 B1
Newark-on-Trent NG24 . . 140 E8
4 Radcliffe on Trent
NG4 . . . . 175 E3
Woodlands Way NG17 . 100 C1
Woodlands Wlk NG20 . . 73 F1
Woodland View
Southwell NG25 . . . . 136 D8
Whaley Thorns NG20 . . . . 59 A3
Woodland Way NG16 . . 143 E2

Woodland Wlk
Collingham NG23 . . . . . . 112 B8
Kirkby-in-Ashfield NG17 . 115 D5
Woodlane Gdns NG3 . . . 173 F7
Woodlark Cl
Rainworth NG21 . . . . 118 A8
Worksop S81 . . . . 35 D6
Woodleigh NG12 . . . . . . 197 E2
Woodleigh Gdns NG5 . . 162 B2
Woodley Sq NG6 . . . . . . 146 C2
Woodley St NG11 . . . . . . 196 C7
Wood Link NG6 . . . . 159 E7
Woodlinkin Gr S81 . . . . . 16 F3
Wood Nook Cl NG16 . . . 128 F6
Woodpecker Cl
Bingham NG13 . . . . 177 F3
East Leake LE12 . . . . 205 F3
West Bridgford NG12 . . . 185 C6
Worksop S81 . . . . 25 D1
Woodpecker Dr NG21 . . 118 B8
Woodpecker Gr NG7 . . . 101 B3
Woodroffe Way LE12 . . . 205 E3
Woodrow Av NG8 . . . . . 172 A8
Woodruff La NG22 . . . . . 106 A5
Woodsend NG4 . . . . 163 F4
Woodsetts La S81 . . . . . . 25 A1
Woodsford Gr NG7 . . . . 184 E2
Wood's Foundation CE Prim
Sch NG14 . . . . 149 B4
Woods Hill NG17 . . . . . . 100 C2
Woodside
Eastwood NG16 . . . . 143 E3
Farnsfield NG22 . . . . 120 A6
Retford DN22 . . . . 39 C8
Sutton in Ashfield NG17 . 100 E7
Woodside Ave
Mansfield NG18 . . . . 102 B8
Nuthall NG16 . . . . 159 B5
Radcliffe on Trent NG12 . 176 B3
Woodside Cres
Ilkeston DE7 . . . . 157 D5
Long Eaton NG10 . . . . . . 193 B8
Woodside Dr NG5 . . . . . 161 D8
Woodside Rd
Beeston NG9 . . . . 183 F8
Beeston, Chilwell NG9 . . 183 B3
Burton Joyce NG14 . . . . . 163 D3
Radcliffe on Trent NG12 . 176 B3
Ravenshead NG15 . . . . . . 116 F3
Sandiacre NG10 . . . . 182 B5
Shirebrook NG20 . . . . 72 E5
Shireoaks S81 . . . . 34 F7
Woodside View DN11 . . . 9 B4
Woods La NG14 . . . . 148 E2
Wood's La NG23 . . . . . . 153 A1
Wood St
Arnold NG5 . . . . 161 F8
Eastwood NG16 . . . . 143 F3
Ilkeston DE7 . . . . 157 F1
Mansfield NG18 . . . . 102 A7
Market Warsop NG20 . . . . 74 B5
Newark-on-Trent NG24 . . 140 B8
Nottingham NG7 . . . . 222 C3
Woods Terr DN21 . . . . . . 15 C2
Woodstock Ave NG7 . . . 222 A4
Woodstock Cl NG24 . . . 140 C8
Woodstock Rd NG9 . . . . 182 F3
Woodstock St NG15 . . . 146 B6
Woodston Wlk NG5 . . . 148 A2
WOODTHORPE 161 E5
Woodthorpe Ave
Arnold NG5 . . . . 161 E4
Loughborough LE11 . . . . 220 B1
Woodthorpe Ct NG5 . . . 161 E3
Woodthorpe Dr NG3 . . . 161 E4
Woodthorpe Gdns
NG5 . . . . 161 F3
Woodthorpe Hospl
(Private) NG5 . . . . 161 D4
Woodthorpe Inf Sch
NG5 . . . . 161 F5
Woodthorpe Rd
Loughborough LE11 . . . . 220 B1
Nottingham NG3 . . . . 161 F3
Woodview NG12 . . . . . . 188 A2
Wood View NG12 . . . . . 186 B4
Woodview Bsns Ctr 13
NG5 . . . . 147 A1
Woodview Ct NG4 . . . . . 174 C5
Woodview Gdns NG19 . . 89 F2
Woodville Cl NG9 . . . . . . 183 C6
Woodville Dr NG5 . . . . . 161 C2
Woodville Rd 2 NG5 . . . 161 C2
Woodward Ave NG9 . . . 183 B2
Woodward Gdns NG5 . . 148 E7
Woodward St NG2 . . . . 173 D1
Woodwards The NG24 . 140 C6
Woodyard La DN22 . . . . 40 A1
Wooliscroft Way DE7 . . 157 C2
Woollaton St NG15 . . . . 146 B7
Woolmer Rd NG2 . . . . . 173 C1
Woolpack La NG1 . . . . . 223 F2
Woolpack St DN22 . . . . . 39 F7
Woolsington Cl NG8 . . . 159 D2
Woolsthorpe Cl 2
NG8 . . . . 172 A6
Wooster Cl NG12 . . . . . 186 A3
Wootton Cl
East Leake LE12 . . . . 205 E2
Nottingham NG8 . . . . 171 D7
Worcester Ave NG19 . . . 88 C6
Worcester Cl
Lowdham NG14 . . . . 150 E1
Worksop S81 . . . . 35 D6
Worcester Gdns NG5 . . 161 E5
Worcester Mews NG19 . . 88 C6
Worcester Rd NG5 . . . . 161 E5
Wordsworth Ave
Hucknall NG15 . . . . 145 D6
Mansfield Woodhouse
NG19 . . . . 88 B4

Wordsworth Ave continued
Sutton in Ashfield NG17 . 100 B3
Wordsworth Dr NG24 . . 140 D5
Wordsworth Rd
Arnold NG5 . . . . 161 D7
Awsworth NG16 . . . . 158 C4
Nottingham NG7 . . . . 222 A4
West Bridgford NG2 . . . . 185 E6
Workhouse La NG25 . . . 122 A1
Workhouse Southwell
The★ NG25 . . . . 122 A1
WORKSOP 35 C5
Worksop Coll S80 . . . . . . 47 B7
Worksop College Prep Sch
(Ranby House) 22 B7
Worksop L Ctr S81 . . . . . 35 E6
Worksop Mus★ S80 . . . . 35 F2
Worksop Post 16 Centre
S81 . . . . 35 E5
Worksop Priory CE Prim
Sch S80 . . . . 35 F1
Worksop Rd
Babworth DN22 . . . . 49 C7
Babworth S80 . . . . 48 F8
Blyth S81 . . . . 18 A2
Clumber and Hardwick
S80 . . . . 48 D8
Cuckney NG20 . . . . 60 A4
Darfoulds S80 . . . . 34 C1
Edwinstowe NG21, NG22 . 76 D5
Holbeck S80 . . . . 45 D1
Holbeck S80 . . . . 59 E7
Nottingham NG3 . . . . 173 F5
Ollerton NG22 . . . . 77 A4
Whitwell S80 . . . . 45 A7
Whitwell S80 . . . . 45 A8
Woodsetts S81 . . . . 25 A4
Worksop S80 . . . . 36 E1
Worksop S80 . . . . 47 F8
Worksop S80 . . . . 48 A8
Worksop S80 . . . . 36 F1
Worksop Sta S80 . . . . . . 35 F4
Worrall Ave
Arnold NG5 . . . . 161 F7
Long Eaton NG10 . . . . . . 182 E1
Worsborough Cl NG18 . 101 E5
Worthington Rd NG24 . . 140 E3
Worth St NG4 . . . . 174 E8
Wortley Ave NG9 . . . . . 170 D3
Wortley Cl DE7 . . . . 170 A8
Wortley Hall Cl NG7 . . . 172 C2
Worwood Dr NG2 . . . . . 185 C4
Wossock La LE12 . . . . . . 204 F3
Woulds Field NG12 . . . . 187 F1
Wragby Rd NG7 . . . . 222 A3
Wray Cl NG3 . . . . 173 E5
Wren Ct
Long Eaton NG10 . . . . . . 193 A4
Worksop S81 . . . . 35 C7
Wren Dr NG6 . . . . 146 E3
Wrenthorpe Vale
NG11 . . . . 195 E8
Wright Dr DN11 . . . . 9 C5
Wright Gdns DN21 . . . . . 14 A5
Wrightson Cl NG17 . . . . 101 B3
Wrights Orch NG12 . . . . 197 E2
Wright St
Carlton NG4 . . . . 175 A7
Newark-on-Trent NG24 . . 140 B8
Wright Wilson St DN22 . . 39 F6
Wroot Rd
Finningley DN9 . . . . 1 A5
Finningley DN9 . . . . 1 B6
Wroughton Ct NG16 . . . 144 A2
Wroxham Dr NG8 . . . . . 171 C3
Wycar Rd NG22 . . . . 106 A4
Wychwood Dr NG9 . . . . 170 D2
Wychwood Rd NG13 . . . 177 C4
Wycliffe Gr NG3 . . . . . . 161 E2
Wycliffe St NG7 . . . . 160 F1
Wycombe Cl NG11 . . . . 195 D8
Wycombe Grange 1
NG19 . . . . 88 F2
Wye Gdns NG7 . . . . 172 D6
Wyggeston Rd NG13 . . . 181 B2
Wykeham Rd NG5 . . . . . 162 A5
Wyke La NG24 . . . . 138 F5
Wykes Ave NG4 . . . . 162 F2
WYMESWOLD 216 C4
Wymeswold CE Prim Sch
LE12 . . . . 216 C3
Wymeswold Ind Est
LE12 . . . . 216 A1
Wymeswold Rd 1 LE12 . 216 B1
Wymeswold Meadows
Nature Reserve★
LE12 . . . . 216 E3
Wymeswold Rd
Hoton LE12 . . . . 215 E2
Rempstone LE12 . . . . 215 E5
Thorpe in the Glebe
LE12 . . . . 216 C8
Wysall NG12 . . . . 207 C2
Wymondham Cl NG5 . . 162 A6
Wynbreck Dr NG12 . . . . 197 F3
Wyndale Dr NG18 . . . . . 103 A5
Wyndham Ct NG9 . . . . . 183 B4
Wyndham Mews NG3 . . 173 B2
Wyndham Way NG19 . . . 87 B4
Wyndings The NG5 . . . . 161 F4
Wynhill Ct NG13 . . . . . . 177 C5
Wynlea Dr S81 . . . . 16 F6
Wynndale Dr NG5 . . . . . 161 A3
Wynndale Prim Sch
NG18 . . . . 103 A5
Wynward Cl DE7 . . . . . . 157 C3
Wynwood Cl NG9 . . . . . 183 B2
Wynwood Rd NG9 . . . . 183 B1
Wyrale Dr NG8 . . . . 159 E1
WYSALL 207 D3

Wysall La
Keyworth NG12 . . . . 197 E1
Keyworth NG12 . . . . 207 D2
Rempstone LE12 . . . . 215 F6
Widmerpool NG11 . . . . . 208 B4
Willoughby-on-the-Wolds
LE12 . . . . 217 B8
Willoughby-on-the-Wolds
NG12 . . . . 208 A1
Wymeswold LE12 . . . . . . 216 D5
Wysall NG12 . . . . 207 F2
Wysall Rd
Costock LE12 . . . . 206 E1
Keyworth NG12 . . . . 197 B1
Wysall NG12 . . . . 207 A2
Wyton Cl NG5 . . . . 161 A5
Wyvelle Cres DE74 . . . . 203 C3
Wyvern Ave NG10 . . . . . 193 D6
Wyvern Cl NG16 . . . . . . 158 A8
Wyville Cl NG7 . . . . 222 A3

Y

Yalding Dr NG8 . . . . 171 C4
Yalding Gdns NG8 . . . . . 171 C4
Yarnsworth Rd NG24 . . 140 A4
Yarrow Dr NG11 . . . . . . 196 E5
Yarwell Cl NG3 . . . . 174 C7
Yatesbury Cres NG5 . . . 171 E8
Yates Croft NG22 . . . . . 119 E7
Yates Gdns 2 NG5 . . . . 161 A8
Yellowhammer Dr S81 . . 35 D7
Yellowhammer Way
NG5 . . . . 148 D8
Yeoman Ave NG6 . . . . . 146 F4
Yeoman Cl S80 . . . . 36 A1
Yeoman Park Sch NG19 . 88 C4
Yeomans Ct NG7 . . . . . 222 C2
Yeovil Ct 3 NG18 . . . . . 103 A2
Yew Barrow Cl NG2 . . . 186 C5
Yew Cl
East Leake LE12 . . . . 214 D8
Nottingham NG5 . . . . 161 D2
Yewdale Cl
Nottingham NG11 . . . . . 195 D8
West Bridgford NG2 . . . . 186 C5
Yews Farm Ct DN11 . . . . 8 B3
Yews The S81 . . . . 16 C6
Yew Tree Ave
Gamston DN22 . . . . 51 A5
New Ollerton NG22 . . . . . 77 C5
Radcliffe on Trent NG12 . 175 D3
Yew Tree Dr
Bawtry DN10 . . . . 9 F7
Huthwaite NG17 . . . . 99 F2
Shirebrook NG20 . . . . 72 D5
Yew Tree La
Carlton NG4 . . . . 163 A2
Nottingham NG11 . . . . . 184 C2
Yew Tree Rd
Cotgrave NG12 . . . . 188 A5
Elkesley DN22 . . . . 50 B4
Hucknall NG15 . . . . 146 B4
New Ollerton NG22 . . . . . 77 C5
Upton DN22 . . . . 52 B6
Yew Tree Way NG24 . . . 125 F2
Yonge Cl NG12 . . . . 175 E2
York Ave
Beeston NG9 . . . . 183 F4
Sandiacre NG10 . . . . 182 A5
Westwood NG16 . . . . 128 B4
York Cl
Carlton NG4 . . . . 162 F2
East Leake LE12 . . . . 205 D1
York Dr NG8 . . . . 159 D2
Yorke Dr NG24 . . . . 125 B3
Yorke St
Hucknall NG15 . . . . 146 A7
Mansfield Woodhouse
NG19 . . . . 88 B2
York Gr NG7 . . . . 115 C5
York Mws NG5 . . . . 161 E8
York Paddock NG22 . . . . 65 F7
York Pl S81 . . . . 34 F7
York Rd
Harworth DN11 . . . . 9 A4
Long Eaton NG10 . . . . . . 182 D1
Loughborough LE11 . . . . 220 A3
Shirebrook NG20 . . . . 72 E3
Tickhill DN11 . . . . 8 B7
York St
Carlton NG4 . . . . 175 A7
East Markham NG22 . . . . 65 F7
Mansfield NG18 . . . . 102 A5
Nottingham NG1 . . . . 223 E4
Sutton in Ashfield NG17 . 100 E3
York Terr
Market Warsop NG20 . . . . 74 B4
Misterton DN10 . . . . 7 A2
Pinxton NG16 . . . . 113 C1
Young Cl NG6 . . . . 159 F5
Young Cres NG17 . . . . . 101 B2
Youngs Av NG24 . . . . . . 140 E2
Youngs Cl NG24 . . . . . . 125 E2
Yvonne Cres NG4 . . . . . 174 F7

Z

Zambra Ct NG12 . . . . . 186 A1
ZOUCH 213 B3
Zouch Rd LE12 . . . . 213 A3
Zulla Rd NG3 . . . . 173 C8
Zulu Rd NG7 . . . . 160 F2